THE
JEWISH
TRAVELER

THE
JEWISH
TRAVELER

Hadassah Magazine's Guide to the World's
Jewish Communities and Sights

edited by
Alan M. Tigay

JASON ARONSON INC.
Northvale, New Jersey
London

This book was set in 9 point English Times by Lind Graphics of Upper Saddle River, New Jersey, and printed by Haddon Craftsmen in Scranton, Pennslyvania.

Library of Congress Cataloging-in-Publication Data

The Jewish traveler : Hadassah magazine's guide to the world's Jewish
   communities and sights / edited by Alan M. Tigay. — [New ed.]
     p. cm.
   Includes index.
   ISBN 1-56821-078-7
   1. Jews—Social life and customs. 2. Voyages and travels—1981—
Guidebooks. I. Tigay, Alan M. II. Hadassah magazine.
DS143.J46 1994
910′.2′02—dc20   93-31386

Manufactured in the United States of America. Jason Aronson Inc. offers books and cassettes. For information and catalog write to Jason Aronson Inc., 230 Livingston Street, Northvale, New Jersey 07647.

For my father,
who gave me his sense of direction

Contents

Acknowledgments

Over the past ten years I have noticed I have a greater and greater tendency to sit through the credits at the end of a movie. Sometimes it's for a specific purpose, like to find out whether those upstate New York landscapes in *The Last of the Mohicans* were really filmed in New York (they were actually shot in North Carolina), but just as often I have simply felt compelled to sit, to pay homage to the hundreds of people whose contributions made the film possible. Now I understand why.

Every month over that same decade, as one more Jewish travel feature ran in *Hadassah Magazine,* I became indebted to more and more people who made the magazine and me look good, and in the process of turning the magazine columns into a book the number increased, it seems, exponentially. Literally hundreds have helped, and those I mention here are only those whose contributions seemed to go beyond the call of duty, friendship, or responsibility.

First I want to thank the thirty-two writers who wrote the book's chapters. Truth be told, I would have preferred to write them all myself. That other writers made many of the trips I dreamed of, or dreamed up, is a source of envy. That each of them did such a good job of turning my dream into their own is a source of great respect. I must single out Phyllis Ellen Funke, who alone accounts for twenty-eight of the book's one hundred chapters. She is as much a collaborator on the entire book—including chapters she did not write—as someone who fulfilled individual assignments.

This book would not have been possible without the support of the Hadassah family. Zelda Shluker, the magazine's senior editor, has been a constant source of ideas since the column began. Dorothy Silfen, the magazine's editorial secretary, has been a resourceful and indefatigable researcher, coordinator, and liaison with writers, photographers, and artists. Joan Michel has been the chief copy editor of the magazine column for five years, and her red pencil has improved virtually every chapter she worked on. Roselyn Bell, the magazine's former senior editor, helped make the column a success in its early years and has remained a member of the Hadassah team. Nancy Kroll Margolis, the magazine's former director of advertising and associate publisher, was one of the first to see the possibility of transforming the magazine feature into a book, and supported the idea until it became a reality. In the transformation to book form, I had valuable support from Meyer Fecher, Julie Fax, Adam Dickter, and Shani Friedman. For translating written images into illustrations, I am indebted to Karen Caldicott, whose drawings grace fifty of the chapters.

My special thanks to Edith Zamost, chairman of *Hadassah Magazine,* and Frieda Lewis and Rose Goldman, her predecessors, who have supported this project and put up with the demands it made on my time. Thanks, as well, to Deborah Kaplan and Carmela Kalmanson, the current and immediate past presidents of Hadassah, for their encouragement over the years.

The success of The Jewish Traveler is in no small measure due to the help of dozens of people in the travel industry, many of whom have gone well beyond the call of duty to help. I especially want to thank Sheryl Stein of El Al Israel Airlines, Maureen Ambrose and Nils Flo of SAS, Krzysztof Ziebinski at LOT Polish Airways, and Jeffrey Kriendler, longtime communications director of Pan American

World Airways. Among the people from various national travel organizations who have gone out of their way on more than one occasion are Erika Faisst Lieben of the Swiss National Tourist Office, Hedy Wuerz of the German National Tourist Office, Pilar Vico of the Spanish National Tourist Office, Mary Bakht of the Hong Kong Tourist Association (and formerly of the Japan National Tourist Office), and George Hern and Marion Fourestier of the French Government Tourist Office.

Every chapter in the book has benefited from people in the city covered, and in the year it took to update all the earlier chapters I have been aided not only by the original authors but by contributors from around the world. I'd particularly like to thank Roxanne Abrams and Bernard Fishman in Baltimore, Gabor T. Szántó in Budapest, Kenneth E. Collins in Glasgow, Eric Beare in Hong Kong, Suzanne Belling in Johannesburg, Douglas Davis in London, Evelynne Joffee in Melbourne, Sherry Stein in Montreal, Jeffrey H. Tigay in Philadelphia, Edita Machova in Prague, Seebert J. Goldowsky in Providence, Carla Falk in Rome, Morton Narrowe in Stockholm, and Marian Turski in Warsaw. Many people closer to home have also offered advice on the communities they know best, including Kamil Muren on Istanbul; Marvin Tokayer and Michael Schudrich on Tokyo; Alexander Smuckler on Moscow, St. Petersburg, and Vilna; and Marlene Schwartz on Rio de Janeiro and São Paulo.

Without the Jewish family there is no such thing as Jewish travel. My own family is the inspiration for everything I write. So I thank my wife, Lois, and my son, Rafi, who always put up with my absences twice — once while I travel and again while I recreate the trip on my computer.

No director ever had a better circle of family, friends, and support staff. I sit through the credits at the end of a movie because I have come to understand their importance. If this book allows me to stand tall, the names listed here belong to the people who lent me their shoulders.

Introduction

Travel guides aren't supposed to be controversial, but I'm going to go out on a limb and assert that Toronto has the best bagels in Canada.

Ask most Canadian Jews where the best bagels are found and they will unequivocally name Montreal. Even the Fodor's guidebook says the Quebec metropolis is Canada's bagel capital. Some Toronto Jews, to be sure, will stand up for their own, but if you put the question on Toronto's Bathurst Street you will find many Montreal partisans, as well as those who simply acknowledge that there is a legitimate debate. There's even a bagel place in Toronto—St. Urbain's, named after a street in Montreal's old Jewish neighborhood—that sells "Montreal bagels." Just try to find a Toronto bagel in Montreal. It's like looking for a Chevy dealer in Tokyo.

The conventional wisdom about Canadian bagels has little to do with taste, but it has quite a bit to do with the philosophy of this book. The differences are environmental. Montreal's Jews live in, and are influenced by, an atmosphere of Gallic bravado. Toronto Jews live more under the influence of British understatement (especially about their food). Being a minority in a society that is itself a minority has left Montreal Jews more in an oppositional mode. Montreal has the most predominantly Orthodox Jewish community in North America, and Toronto is more typical of the Jewish mix south of the border. The same cultural forces that produced such a difference (the monolithic religious ethos of French society versus the pluralism that increases as one moves from Britain toward the United States) also contributes to different attitudes toward bagels.

From its inception as a column in *Hadassah Magazine* in 1983, The Jewish Traveler has focused on what makes each Jewish community distinct. It takes as a given the things Jews around the world have in common and goes on to explore what each Jewish community has that no other has—how in each spot on the globe Jews have influenced, and been influenced by, the local conditions, peoples, and environment. The organization of chapters by city reflects not only the space limitations of a magazine column but also the great differences between Jewish communities in the same country.

Of all the world's peoples, Jews have been city dwellers the longest, and each city's essence is different. There are environmental and cultural reasons why Jews in New York speak quickly and Jews in Charleston speak slowly, why Jews in Antwerp are insular and Yiddish-speaking and Jews in Brussels are integrated and French-speaking, why São Paulo Jews are considered hardworking and Rio Jews considered recreation oriented. Similarly, wherever Jews have lived they have altered the landscape in different ways, from the disproportionate Jewish contribution to the movie industry in Los Angeles, to the Jewish cartographers of Majorca, from the Jewish *nouveaux philosophes* of Paris to the Jewish taipans of Hong Kong.

Back when The Jewish Traveler was in its infancy, the paradigm was set in a meeting I had with the veteran Jewish travel writer Gabriel Levenson. He was headed for Venice, a place he knew well, and gave me an institutional outline of synagogues, Jewish organizations, and philanthropy. I thought about what was missing from the picture and then asked him to find a Jewish gondolier. There have, in fact, never been Jewish gondoliers, but Levenson came back with something better—the story of Luigi

Luzzatti, who began his political career by organizing the gondoliers into a union and went on to become Italy's first Jewish prime minister.

Since then the writers of the column have always looked for those people and situations that best illustrate Jewish integration into the local scene—the stories that help travelers bridge the distance between Jewish familiarity and the different lives they would live as Jews in other corners of the world. In these pages you'll read about beautiful synagogues and talented Jewish artists, but you'll also discover Jewish tango composers in Buenos Aires, the Jewish Ski Club in Zurich, and flower arrangement classes at the Jewish Community Center in Tokyo.

That, I think, is what separates this guide from the burgeoning number of Jewish travel books that have appeared in the past decade. Most fall into one of two categories—worldwide guides that have listings of sights, synagogues, Jewish organizations and institutions with little or no description; and guides richer in detail that focus only on a single city or country. *The Jewish Traveler* is the only guidebook I know of that covers the world and also makes the effort to stress what is unique about every community.

If this approach distinguishes *The Jewish Traveler* in the 1990s, however, it is far from new. Benjamin of Tudela, the great Spanish Jewish traveler who described the known world from Iberia to China a century before Marco Polo, also put every Jewish community he visited into a bigger picture. "Benjamin's Jews exist within the context of their larger civilization," wrote Michael A. Singer in the introduction to the 1983 edition of *The Itinerary of Benjamin of Tudela*. "It is the peculiar merit of Benjamin's *Itinerary* to view Jews as part of their environments rather than in contrast to their environments."

Putting each Jewish community in its broader context requires covering more than tourist sights. Listed in every chapter are books that bring the Jewish community to life. Because fiction often illustrates more effectively than fact, there has been an attempt to find at least one novel set in each Jewish community. Where fiction is not available, and often even where it is,

memoirs, histories, and sociological studies have been noted. And with the proliferation of video stores, we have added movies that can be viewed not only for enjoyment but also as homework for an upcoming trip.

Incidentally, in addition to the books noted with each chapter there are two sources that were consulted in the preparation of every chapter. The *Encyclopaedia Judaica* is a rich source of historical information on every Jewish community in the world. The annual *Jewish Travel Guide* published by London's *Jewish Chronicle* contains the most comprehensive worldwide catalog of synagogues and Jewish institutions. On the European chapters two important sources have been *Synagogues of Europe* (MIT Press) by Carol Herselle Krinsky and the vintage *Traveler's Guide to Jewish Landmarks of Europe* (Fleet Press) by Bernard Postal and Samuel Abrahamson.

Like Benjamin of Tudela, many modern travelers have had the experience of running into a familiar situation or person in a faraway place and coming to a new appreciation of the familiar in a new context; such experiences also form bonds to the people and situations that forever influence the traveler's vision. This, too, has informed *The Jewish Traveler*, and over the years the responses to the column have made clear that the farther one is from home, or the more exotic the setting, the more memorable the experience.

While the travel column has traditionally prompted more letters than any other in the magazine, those columns that have evoked the biggest response have been the ones from the farthest corners of the Jewish experience, in places like China and India, Kenya and New Zealand.

A case in point is Kaifeng, where a community of Jews flourished for centuries, long after intermarriage and acculturation made them as Chinese as their neighbors. The fascination with the Chinese Jews is certainly out of all proportion to their importance in Jewish history. Today the number of organizations and academic programs dedicated to the study of Kaifeng's Jews probably exceeds the number of Jewish organizations in the city at the community's peak in the fifteenth century.

The Kaifeng chapter in this book is the only one that wasn't originally written according to the format that the book and magazine columns follow. Wendy Abraham, who at the time was writing her doctoral dissertation on the Kaifeng community at Columbia University, did the magazine article as a feature story on the descendants of Kaifeng's Jews still living in the city, and their awareness of their ancestry. In addition to the many letters sent to the magazine by fascinated readers, the article won for Ms. Abraham the Boris Smolar Award for Student Journalism. She was subsequently asked to write the epilogue for the 1990 reissue of *Peony*, Pearl Buck's classic novel of the Chinese Jews. As *The Jewish Traveler* was being prepared for publication, Ms. Abraham updated her original article and adapted it to the format of the travel column.

Turning a magazine column into a book is like taking a road show to Broadway. Everything has already been tried out in front of an audience. We know what works and what doesn't. Reader response — the ultimate review — has prompted corrections and additions. In the theater, corners that had to be cut because of tight road-show budgets can be squared again; good material that had to be cut from travel articles because of the limitations of magazine space has been restored here. And every one of the chapters has been updated. Readers of the book, no less than the magazine, are encouraged to send recommendations for future editions to the magazine's editorial office at 50 West 58th Street, New York, NY 10019.

Some caveats are in order. While most chapters are listed by a city name, the exceptions are the island communities of Barbados, Curaçao, Majorca, and New Zealand. While synagogues in the United States are quite accessible, security at European synagogues is generally strict. When in Europe, it's best to call a synagogue before visiting. Restaurants come and go with regularity, and kosher restaurants are no exception. While every attempt has been made to be as up-to-date as possible, it is always best to check ahead. We have tried to indicate whether restaurants are kosher or mentioned for other reasons, but, again, it is always best to check.

One would think museums are more stable institutions than restaurants, and they are. But one of the things that emerges from these pages is the explosion of Jewish cultural awareness around the world in the form of new Jewish museums. In the decade since this column debuted, dozens of Jewish museums around the world have either opened or moved to new quarters. Most of the locations and openings were confirmed as the book went to press.

One final word of caution. Adding up Jewish achievements city by city, country by country, and century by century, one might conclude that there is little in the world in which Jews have not had a role, and that is something in which Jews take pride. But after I noted in the Stockholm chapter that "Jews have won 18 percent of the Nobel Prizes," a Swedish friend objected to my choice of words — saying it sounded as if Jewish laureates were competing as Jews on a Jewish team. I should point out that Swedes score quite low on the index of ethnic pride, tending to view it as a form of ostentation.

But my friend had a point (and I changed the sentence to read that "18 percent of the Nobel Prizes have been awarded to Jews"). If we have made a disproportionate contribution to the world — and I believe we have — it is not because Jews are inherently better than others but because of the value we place on community, learning, and *tikkun olam*. Unlike a team sport, where one does better if the opponent knows less, we and the world profit by learning more from one another. If we have learned more, and contributed more, it is at least in part because we have traveled more.

Jews have always traveled, not only to escape persecution but also to trade, or simply to see. From Benjamin of Tudela to the expression "wandering Jew," the Jewish penchant for movement is enshrined in literature and language. "Our people wandered before they were driven," said Joseph Kalonymos, a character in George Eliot's proto-Zionist novel *Daniel Deronda*. Now that the Jewish homeland has welcomed the driven among us, Jews are wandering still.

But there is a fundamental difference today. In the modern world masses of Jews travel primarily for pleasure, and return to the same home. And with the proliferation of resources, Jewish travel can be more enriching now than ever before. I was once introduced to an audience as "the twentieth-century Benjamin of Tudela," but however much it did for my ego, the introduction missed the point. Benjamin wrote for Jews who would never see what he described. Today the mantle of the great Jewish traveler can be claimed not by one Jew but by all.

What follows are 100 chapters on Jewish communities and sights. Taken individually, readers have found them a welcome feature in *Hadassah Magazine*. As a whole they add up to the broad sweep of Jewish history and contributions around the world, told from the standpoint of what today's traveler can see.

But there are still gaps in the story. The Jewish Traveler is an ongoing part of *Hadassah Magazine*, and our writers are still exploring new places, investigating new theories. I have yet to quantify something I have known from childhood—that Detroit has better bagels than New York. But that's another story, one yet to be told.

—Alan M. Tigay
Montclair, New Jersey

Albuquerque and Santa Fe

For any Jew who has visited Israel, there's something familiar about New Mexico. Perhaps it's the hot, arid climate, or the endless blue sky. Or the mountains to the north, and desert to the south. Or the blending of cultures — Hispanic, Native American, and Anglo. One might even go so far as to say that Albuquerque and Santa Fe are New Mexico's Tel Aviv and Jerusalem.

Ever since the Spanish set foot on New Mexican soil in 1590, the Land of Enchantment, as the state's license plate proudly proclaims, has been a "Promised Land" for Jews. In the late sixteenth century, it was a haven for crypto-Jews — Conversos — fleeing the Inquisition. In the nineteenth century it became a sanctuary for German Jews. And today it is a refuge for Jews fleeing the demands of hectic modern life.

And no wonder. The big, beautiful sky and majestic mountains seem to have a calming effect on even the most frenetic of souls. In fact, you're probably more apt to hear Albuquerqians or Santa Feans tell you about the recent breathtaking sunset they've seen than about their latest business deal. And if not the sunset, then perhaps it's the sacred Native American pueblo dance they've witnessed, or an all-night Spanish celebration they've attended. For the Jewish traveler in search of such an escape — regardless for how long — Albuquerque and Santa Fe may be just what you're looking for.

History: It isn't clear when New Mexico's prehistoric Indians settled down to an agrarian lifestyle, and small villages began to appear. The Anasazi, or "ancient ones," built a sophisticated urban settlement replete with huge stone apartments, terraced farmlands, and an intricate road system in Chaco Canyon. This civilization reached its height during the twelfth century c.e. The Anasazi were the forebears of New Mexico's nineteen Pueblo Indian tribes who built small adobe villages throughout the state. *Pueblo* is the Spanish word for "town."

In 1540 the Spanish *conquistadores* (conquerors), led by Francisco Coronado, arrived in what is now New Mexico in search of legendary cities of gold. Unsuccessful in their quest, Coronado and his men returned to New Spain and its capital, Mexico City, leaving behind a path of pillaging and bloodshed.

It would be almost fifty years before the first group of Spanish colonizers arrived, and even then their expedition was not legally sanctioned by the Spanish throne. It is believed that the majority of these colonizers were crypto-Jews, Catholic converts practicing Judaism in secret, who had come to escape the Inquisition.

The Inquisition was relentless in its search for converts who secretly practiced Judaism, in Spain or its colonies. When the Spanish government learned about the illegal expedition to New Mexico, the entire group was forcibly returned to Mexico. Many were tried and convicted as heretics before the Inquisition.

A second group of colonizers arrived legally in 1598. At first they settled in an Indian village on the east bank of the Rio Grande about thirty miles north of what is today Santa Fe. The colony failed, however, and in 1610 a new governor led the bedraggled settlers south, establishing a new town, La Villa Real de Santa Fe de San Francisco de Asis (the Royal City of the Holy Faith of St. Francis of Assisi), better known simply as Santa Fe.

Although the precise number is un-

1

known, many of these early colonists in both Santa Fe and Albuquerque (which was founded a century later) were crypto-Jews. In fact, in 1661, the colony's governor, Don Bernardo Lopez de Mendizabal, was arrested and accused of practicing Judaism in secret. Today thousands of their descendants still live in the state.

The next wave of Jewish settlers didn't arrive in New Mexico until the 1840s. Eager to create new lives for themselves in this wild, uncharted Mexican Territory (Mexico had declared its independence from Spain in 1822), they traveled via the Santa Fe Trail, which stretched from Missouri to Santa Fe. Mostly German men, with names like Ilfeld, Seligman, Staab, Spiegelberg, Nordhaus, and Goldstine, they came not as Jews per se but as pioneers. Most became merchants. The United States Army of the West, which had an outpost in Santa Fe, was one of their best customers. This was particularly true for Solomon Jacob Spiegelberg, who was made sutler, the appointed merchant who followed the troops or camped near the fort, and sold tobacco, liquor, and other goods.

The German Jews built numerous family businesses, selling wool, hardware, dry goods, and pharmaceuticals. Over time their descendants became involved in all aspects of New Mexican life—from banking to politics. Henry Jaffa, the first mayor of Albuquerque (1885–95), and Arthur Seligman, a governor of New Mexico (1931–33), were Jewish.

One tale New Mexican Jews like to tell is the story of Simon Bibo, the Jewish Indian chief. Bibo was a German-born cantor's son who followed his older brothers to Santa Fe, where he became fluent in English, Spanish, and many of the Native American tongues of the region. In 1882, he established the first trading post in Acoma's Sky City, where he fell in love and married Juana Valle, granddaughter of a former chief, or governor, as the position was called. In 1885, Bibo became the first non-Indian to be elected governor of the tribe. He created public schools in the pueblo, which caused a storm of controversy, eventually forcing him and his family to leave Acoma.

Like Bibo, most of the early New Mexican Jews were not observant and rarely identified as a group, so Jewish life was relegated to the privacy of the home. The first Jewish institution, a B'nai B'rith Lodge, was not founded until 1883, forty years after the first German Jews arrived. The first synagogue in Albuquerque, Congregation Albert—a Reform temple— began in 1897, followed by the Conservative synagogue, B'nai Israel, in 1920. The Santa Fe Temple did not open its doors until 1953.

Community: Of Albuquerque's population of 375,000, about 8,000 are Jews. During the 1970s and 1980s when the Jewish population doubled, individuals and families arrived from all over the United States. In recent years, the city has become a magnet for retirees and "snowbirds"— winter vacationers.

In addition, Albuquerque is home to the descendants of many—perhaps thousands—of crypto-Jews. Most are strict Catholics today, but many continue to practice rituals that are clearly Jewish in origin—lighting Friday night candles, not eating pork or mixing meat and milk at the same meal, and conducting a private marriage ceremony under a tent following a church wedding. In recent years, many Converso descendants have sought out the guidance and advice of Albuquerque's rabbis, and a handful have even returned to the faith of their ancestors.

Many of Albuquerque's Jews are employed by the United States government, one of the two major industries in the state, the other being tourism. They work in the scientific laboratories at Los Alamos and Sandia Government Lab. Others are teachers at the University of New Mexico, physicians, lawyers, or artists or small business owners (furniture, sporting goods, Indian pottery, tourist attractions, art dealers).

Albuquerque has four synagogues and an active *chavurah* group. Congregation B'nai Israel has 425 families; Temple Albert has 525; the Rio Rancho Jewish Center (an independent synagogue composed of retirees) has about 30 families; the Natialat Shalom (an independent congregation) has about 25. The Havurah Hamidbar, an informal group which holds services regularly, has about 60 members.

In recent years Santa Fe has become home for just about anyone hoping to disappear quietly into the sunset. There are about 1,500 permanent Jewish residents among the city's population of 80,000. Tourism is the city's only real industry, so most people not in the travel business are freelancers—artists, writers, and crafts people. New Age healers are ubiquitous, as are retirees, opera aficionados, Yuppie dropouts, doctors, lawyers, gallery owners, and small business operators. One of the most popular Native American trading posts is Gold's Curio Shop, owned by a Jewish transplant. And representatives of the rich and famous, including Steven Spielberg and Dustin Hoffman, call Santa Fe home at least part of the year.

As the only synagogue in town, Temple Beth Shalom, formerly the Santa Fe Temple, tries to be all things to its congregation of 400 families. The Friday night service is Reform, and the Saturday morning is Conservative. An Orthodox group (with its own rabbi) called Padres Yisroel, conducts services in the building's old sanctuary and has a Hebrew day school.

Following the tradition of the nineteenth century pioneers, the majority of Albuquerque and Santa Fe Jews remain unaffiliated and are very much assimilated into New Mexico's cultural mosaic. There have never been Jewish clubs or community centers, let alone Jewish neighborhoods. In fact, it was early Jewish families who founded the state's first country clubs, which were open to all.

The interplay of New Mexico's three distinct cultures can be seen in Jewish homes and in communal programs. Many Jews are fluent in Spanish, and multicultural events, such as a Judeo-Hispanic Seder held at Temple Beth Shalom in Santa Fe, or a Native American–Jewish dialogue in Albuquerque, are common.

Albuquerque Sights: Albuquerque's main Jewish sights are its synagogues, Congregation B'nai Israel and Congregation Albert. Blending gracefully with its southwestern surroundings, B'nai Israel (4401 Indian School Road) is built in the shape of the tent of Moses, beckoning the Wandering Jew in the American desert. Under the pavilion's dome is a large amphitheater,

where the eye is drawn to a modernistic rendering of the eternal light in the shape of the Star of David. It was created by Ted Egri, a New Mexico sculptor, whose bronze works depicting the Jewish holidays also line the halls of the sanctuary.

When the Jews of Albuquerque decided to establish the first synagogue in 1897, they raised funds by auctioning the name of the congregation to the highest bidder. Alfred Grunsfeld was the winner with a high bid of $250, and he chose to honor his father, Albert. The cornerstone of the 1897 building stands at the entrance to the modern Temple Albert (3800 Louisiana Boulevard, N.E.), its biblical quote, "Seek me and live" (Amos 5:4), over the arched doorway welcoming congregants and visitors. The modern building's carefully placed arches and the desert colors of terracotta and blue seem to combine features of southwest and Middle East architecture. The centerpiece of the main sanctuary is a turquoise sculpture adorning the ark, called "Lights of the Generation," created by congregation member Hilda Volkin.

The synagogues and the Albuquerque federation offer a wide variety of events and activities of interest to residents and visitors. The federation's women's division sponsors lectures and debates, and in recent years has organized an annual tour of Jewish Santa Fe. Travelers can obtain information about activities from the Jewish Federation at (505) 821-3214.

To get a sense of what lured Jewish settlers to New Mexico in the nineteenth century, visitors should go to Albuquerque's historic Old Town area (Central Avenue and Rio Grande Boulevard), which, as the site of the original Spanish colony, maintains its flavor. Activities revolve around the central Plaza, just as they have for three centuries. At its center is a park with a Victorian band shell where at any given moment someone might give a scheduled or impromptu performance. Nearby, under the outside arcades of the restored adobe buildings, Pueblo Indians sell their jewelry and crafts. Inside, people sample restaurants specializing in New Mexican cuisine, and visit art galleries, studios, and gift shops with works by local artists and artisans.

Old Town, which extends for several

blocks beyond the Plaza, is especially beautiful during the Christmas season when *luminarias* (candles placed in paper bags filled with sand) line the streets. This Hispanic tradition is also practiced by New Mexico' s crypto-Jews, who light them on the eight days preceding Christmas. They add one for each night until there are nine burning on Christmas day, creating a life-size *menorah.*

The Albuquerque Museum (2000 Mountain Road), also located in Old Town, has a permanent exhibition tracing four hundred years of history of the Rio Grande Valley, as well as changing art, science, and history exhibits. Just across the street (1801 Mountain Road) is the Natural History Museum, with a walk-through erupting-volcano exhibit replete with enormous dinosaurs and an Ice Age cave.

While there is no kosher restaurant in town, about 150 families belong to a kosher food co-op (505-265-3222), which imports kosher goods from Chicago. Albuquerque does have a vegetarian restaurant, Adam's Table, at 3617 Copper Avenue, N.W. (505-266-4214).

Santa Fe Sights: It's difficult to walk down the streets of Santa Fe without attaching the word *charming* to every nook and cranny. But beware, this is a tourists' town, which means that while everything from hotels to restaurants to shopping to festivities is within walking distance, during the high season (June to August, and especially when the opera is in town in July) it can be wall-to-wall people.

While there are several places of Jewish historic significance, sightseers might want to begin their visit at Temple Beth Shalom (205 East Barcelona Street) — to get a sense of life among the Jews in Santa Fe today, and of old-fashioned do-it-yourself Judaism. Built in 1984, the synagogue was a true labor of love among its congregants. Ed Mazria, the architect, is a member, as are those who built the Ark doors, lectern, and reading table, and handcrafted the eternal light. A spirit of community is behind every architectural feature, including the *bimah,* which juts out into the audience, separated by only one step, and the forty-five-degree angle of the seats, enabling the congregants

to look not only at the rabbi but also at one another.

Jewish cultural activities are sponsored by Beth Shalom or the Jewish Historical Society of New Mexico. Programs at the temple are eclectic, ranging from art shows to historical exhibitions about the Holocaust. Activities often involve non-Jewish segments of the population, such as visits to the surrounding Indian pueblos. Call the temple (505-982-1376) for information about events.

The Jewish Historical Society collects and preserves archival material about New Mexican Jews. It also organizes field trips, lectures, and musical programs focused on the state's Jewish past — such as a concert of Sephardic and Ladino music. Information about the Jewish Historical Society's programs can be obtained through its director, Susan Campbell, at (505) 986-4600.

After Beth Shalom, the next logical place to visit is the heart of Santa Fe, its Plaza (Lincoln Avenue, East Palace Avenue and San Francisco Street). Once the end of the Santa Fe Trail, the Plaza has always been the center of commercial, religious, and secular activities. Although today its architecture has been restored to its early Spanish style, during the 1800s the facades were unmistakably Victorian. This was the era when the Jewish merchants, rather than today's chic boutiques, galleries, restaurants, and curio shops, occupied the Plaza's storefronts. Old nineteenth-century photographs show the Victorian establishments owned by Spiegelbergs, Ilfelds, and the Staab brothers.

On the north end of the Plaza is the Palace of the Governors, the former governors' residence, which is now a state museum with a collection of memorabilia from the region's three cultures. Under its *portal* (arcade), Native Americans sell their jewelry, pottery, blankets, and other wares.

Adjacent to the Palace of the Governors is the State Museum of Fine Arts where local artists, including the late Georgia O'Keeffe, are represented. On the other side of the Plaza is one of Santa Fe's most famous landmarks — La Fonda Hotel (100 E. San Francisco). Guidebooks explain that this five-story adobe structure was built in 1919 through a local subscription of $200,000 worth of bonds. What they don't say is that these funds were raised primarily by Jews, led by one of the Staab brothers. With its Mexican tile, leather furniture, vega-beamed ceilings, hand-painted murals and exhibition galleries with works of regional artists, La Fonda Hotel is quintessential Santa Fe. Another popular hotel in town located a few blocks from the Plaza is La Posada de Santa Fe (330 E. Palace Avenue), once the Victorian home of Abraham Staab.

Just up the road from La Fonda is St. Francis Cathedral, which has its own Jewish connection. Construction for the Romanesque Catholic church began in 1869 under the direction of Archbishop Jean Baptiste Lamy. The industrious Frenchman received large contributions from many of Santa Fe's Jewish merchants, particularly from Abraham Staab. While it has never been clear why they were so generous, in return for their help the Archbishop had the Tetragrammaton—the Hebrew letters of God's name— inscribed over the cathedral's main entrance.

Santa Fe, of course, is known for its art colony. While there are galleries and studios throughout town, the largest nucleus can be found on Canyon Road, where art lover and novice alike can view the eclectic works of New Mexican artists. The Santa Fe Opera, located seven miles north of town, is in residence in July. The Santa Fe Chamber Music Festival, with guest artists from all over the world, takes place during July and August in the auditorium of the Fine Arts Museum.

Given its penchant for attracting the New Age set, Santa Fe has several vegetarian restaurants to choose from, including the Natural Café at 1494 Cerrillos Road (505-983-1411) and Pranzo's at 540 Montezuma Road (505-984-2645).

Personalities: Among Jews prominent in New Mexico today are Representative Steve Schiff (one of the state's two congressmen), Mayor Sam Pick of Santa Fe, and Albuquerque District Attorney Bob Schwartz. In Albuquerque three of the largest and most popular stores are owned by Jewish families—American Furniture (the Blaugrunds); Western Warehouse (the David Cooper family); and Gardenschwartz Sports (the Art Gardenschwartz family). Artist Judy Chicago lives in Santa Fe.

Reading: Fiction that will put you in the mood for Jewish travels in New Mexico include Harvey Fergusson's novel, *The Conquest of Don Pedro* (University of New Mexico Press), whose hero is a nineteenth-century Jewish peddler who settles in New Mexico, and Tony Hillerman's *Skinwalkers* (HarperCollins), in which one of the characters is the daughter of a Jewish merchant and a Native American woman. John Nichols's *The Milagro Beanfield War* (Ballantine), offers a good picture of rural New Mexican life; Willa Cather's *Death Comes to the Archbishop* (Random House) is based on the life of Archbishop Lamy. A good overview of the state's Jewish experience can be found in Henry Tobias's *A History of the Jews in New Mexico* (University of New Mexico Press).

General Sights: High on the list of general sights should be a visit to any of New Mexico's nineteen Indian pueblos. All celebrate special feast days with sacred Native American dancing and song. Each of the tribes specializes in certain forms of craft-making and pottery, which are sold at the pueblos. The Indian Pueblo Cultural Center at 2401 12th Street, N.W., in Albuquerque (505-843-7270), provides information about the pueblos and their scheduled ceremonies. Owned and operated by the tribes, the center has a historical museum, an inexpensive restaurant, and a huge gift shop. Indian dance and crafts demonstrations take place on weekends, except in the winter. For the more daring and experienced traveler, nothing can compare to a visit to the Chaco Culture National Historical Park. Accessible only by a seemingly endless dirt road, Chaco is the ancient city of the Anasazi people. Over twelve hundred miles of roadways lead to the more than twenty-five hundred sites that make up the Chaco complex. The most spectacular ruin is the Pueblo Bonito, a five-story single structure with eight hundred rooms and extending across three acres. For information about Chaco, call the visitors' center at 505-988-6727.

To get a sense of New Mexico's Hispanic culture, there are numerous Spanish towns

5

with customary plazas and interior patios. Many are located north of Santa Fe along Highway 76, also known as the "High Road to Taos." Of particular interest is Chimayo, where the Ortega family has been weaving woolen blankets and rugs for eight generations.

Day Trips: Sixty-five miles of the original Santa Fe Trail takes you from Santa Fe to Las Vegas, New Mexico. Known as one of the roughest places on the frontier, Las Vegas was frequented by the likes of Billy the Kid and Doc Holliday. Here, too, is a historic Spanish Old Town with restored adobe structures. Unlike Santa Fe and Albuquerque, however, Las Vegas's Victorian past is intact, with over nine hundred buildings listed on the National Historic Register. Among them are the mercantile establishments and homes of German Jews, now occupied by present-day owners. Visitors might also plan a short stop to the Montefiore Cemetery.

Fifty-two miles west of Albuquerque just off I-40 is the Acoma Pueblo. While it consists of three separate villages, the oldest and most dominant is Sky City, perched 357 feet above on a rock mesa. Guided tours are given by tribal members. For centuries, Sky City, like Masada, protected its inhabitants against warlike tribes. Far from New Mexico's Tel Aviv and Jerusalem, the state still has parallels to the Jewish experience.

—Patricia Giniger Snyder

Amsterdam

Amid browsers at the silver Judaica for sale in a corner of Amsterdam's Portuguese Synagogue, an Israeli was overheard to remark, "Amsterdam is one of the only cities in Europe where I will wear a *Magen David outside* my shirt."

It was a fitting remark to make while standing in the large, ornate *shul* built in 1675, a giant statement by a community of Spanish and Portuguese immigrants that previously had to pray in secret.

Both the vociferous Israeli and the three hundred-year-old synagogue make their point — being Jewish is and always has been a lot easier here than in much of Europe.

Maybe it's because the Dutch believe in minding their own business; there is little interest in scandal ("We have no equivalent to Donald Trump because no one here would bother to read about him," one native remarked). In fact the climate is so liberal there are those who would say it goes overboard. Drugs are legal; so is prostitution. Street life, street art, and street performance abound. Bicycles are the most common form of transportation even for senior citizens. Amsterdam is a multilingual port city, and the Dutch are comfortable with foreigners from every continent. Few in Amsterdam will sneer at you for speaking English, or just about any other language.

History: Amsterdam has a long history as a haven for people seeking religious freedom, particularly Jews. Fleeing the Inquisition in Spain and Portugal, the first group of Jews from the Iberian Peninsula reached the city in 1598. By 1619 the Jewish population of Holland had grown to the point that the legal scholar Hugo Grotius was asked by parliament to draft rules governing the treatment of Jews in the region. The document, extremely tolerant for its time, lifted all degrading medieval restrictions. In 1657, Jews were officially declared subjects of the state.

Enjoying freedom of worship and movement, these Jews were also encouraged in their commercial ventures. They were a major force in developing the country's overseas commerce and trade routes, and pioneered in the diamond, tobacco, and silk industries, opened sugar refineries, and were involved in organizing the Dutch East and West India companies.

In its constant conflicts with Spain and Portugal over trading footholds in South America, the Dutch West India Company was often guided by Jewish shareholders in Amsterdam. Many of them had family and other contacts in Brazil and were able to take commercial advantage of their relationship. Dutch Jews also had a hand in promoting trade in the West Indies as well as in Genoa, Livorno, and the Near East. Indeed, it was Dutch Jews, expelled from the Brazilian coast, who in 1654 founded what was to become the Jewish community of New York and the United States.

Throughout the seventeenth century Amsterdam was a center of Jewish learning and intellectual ferment; it was there that rabbis were trained for Sephardic communities around the world. In 1626, Manasseh Ben Israel, a Sephardic rabbi, printer, writer, and friend of Rembrandt, founded the first Hebrew printing press in the Netherlands. Thirty years later, Manasseh Ben Israel's petition to Oliver Cromwell was a crucial factor in the ultimate reestablishment of a Jewish community in England.

But the seventeenth century saw more than progress. In 1656 the *parnassim* (leaders) of Amsterdam's Portuguese Jewish congregation excommunicated Baruch Spinoza for his radical view of theology. In 1675 the congregation consecrated its synagogue in the presence of the city's burgomasters and alderman. (In 1954, David Ben Gurion proposed that the Portuguese Synagogue revoke the excommunication ban on Spinoza; the synagogue declined.)

Fleeing the looting of the Frankfurt ghetto, German Jews first arrived in 1614; Polish Jews came soon after to escape pogroms and the Chmielnicki massacres of 1648. Their numbers quickly exceeded the Sephardic community's, and the Ashkenazim built their first synagogue in 1671.

These later arrivals were first peddlers and old-clothing dealers, and some eventually opened their own shops. They developed trade with Eastern Europe and Germany and throughout the eighteenth century were active in foreign exchange, comprising about half of all foreign-exchange brokers in the country. By the end of the 1700s several prominent Ashkenazic families were associated with the court Jews of Germany and served as agents in procuring loans from Dutch banks. Others were diamond brokers in foreign courts. But despite the affluence of a minority, the majority of Ashkenazim suffered during the economic crisis that hit the Netherlands at the end of the century and had to depend on the affluent.

The early nineteenth century under Napoleon was also when Dutch Jews — by now the largest Jewish community in Western Europe — were granted complete civil equality. The Netherlands became the first country in Europe to elect Jews to its parliament; a Jewish upper class flourished in the midst of an impoverished one. Abraham Carel Wertheim represented North Holland in parliament for twenty years. A member of the city council and the first Jew in the provincial government, he was known for his many acts of philanthropy.

In 1867 diamond workers established a strong trade union under the leadership of Henri Polak. The first such trade union in the Netherlands, it was soon dominated by Jews. As an outgrowth, socialism gained in popularity in the Jewish working class, and Polak went on to form the SDAP (Social Democratic Workers Party), forerunner of the largest modern-day socialist party in the Netherlands.

The Nazis invaded the Low Countries in May 1940. Fierce Dutch resistance — and local support of Jews — is well documented, and the Nazis had to enforce stronger anti-Jewish measures in Amsterdam than elsewhere. When Amsterdam Jews were ordered to wear yellow stars, many gentiles wore them too. In November 1940, Dutch Nazis abetted by German soldiers started violent riots in the Jewish quarter. A Jewish resistance immediately arose, supported by non-Jews from many of the neighboring quarters. A Dutch Nazi was killed in one of these fights, and a Jewish tavern owner was executed by firing squad.

To combat the violence the controversial Jewish council was established by the civil governor. It was run by Jews who thought the community (and probably they themselves) would escape the worst by cooperating with the conquerors. Their first task was to encourage resistance members to surrender weapons. Shortly afterward the Germans carried out reprisals, arresting 425 Jews and sending them to Buchenwald.

On February 25, 1941, the city's dock workers went on strike to protest the deportation of Jews. The strike spread to almost all public and many private enterprises, bringing the city to a virtual standstill for almost two days. In the end it did little. Thousands of Jews were eventually rounded up and sent to Westerbork concentration camp, and from there almost all were sent to extermination camps. In 1941 there had been 79,000 Jews in Amsterdam, 150,000 in the Netherlands. By the end of the war, 15,000 Jews remained in Amsterdam, 30,000 in the country.

Community: Despite its smaller postwar numbers, Amsterdam's Jewish community is flourishing. Synagogues, Jewish communal institutions, and Zionist organizations have been reestablished, albeit not in the same area. With the exception of the Portuguese Synagogue, to which many elderly worshipers walk over an hour each way to form a *minyan* on *Shabbat*, the old Jewish quarter exists now as a series of monuments and museums.

The houses of the old Jewish quarter

were destroyed by the Nazis, as was the Jewish working class. The diamond industry is now largely owned and run by non-Jews, though Jews are still well represented in textile manufacturing. Most of Amsterdam's younger Jewish generation now opt for the professions.

The bulk of Jewish activity has shifted to the southern suburbs (Amsterdam-Zuid), where the city's professional class had already established itself even before the war. The synagogues are here, and this is the place to see men in *kippot* chatting in Hebrew or Yiddish outside the kosher butcher's.

Like much of Europe, Amsterdam's affiliated Jewry is divided between the Orthodox Ashkenazic establishment (about 9,000 are registered) and the Liberal (Reform with some traditional elements), with about 2,000 members. Though the Sephardic Portuguese Synagogue can seat 2,000, today's congregation numbers about 700.

These different elements of Amsterdam Jewry are served by one newspaper, the *Nieuw Israelietisch Weekblad* founded in 1875. After London's *Jewish Chronicle,* it is the oldest Jewish newspaper in Europe and is known for its lively coverage of politics and culture.

Sights: Amsterdam is designed as a series of circles, and on foot it often feels confusing. A good map will help (from the tourist information center across from the central station, telephone 272-727). And one of the leisurely boat tours, also across from the central station, will give you a general idea where the major attractions are. A boat ride also reveals the charm of Amsterdam's canals and houseboats, and allows an advance look at the length of the line at the Anne Frank House at Prinsengracht 263 (telephone 264-533).

The old Jewish quarter is a short walk from the center of town. At the top of the main street, Jodenbreestraat (Jew's Street), is the Rembrandthuis at number 4–6, where Rembrandt worked and lived. The narrow corner house has been preserved as a museum and showplace for a vast collection of the artist's work (telephone 249-486). It was the Jewish painter Josef Israels (known as

Open secret: On Prinsengract visitors climb the stairs to Anne Frank's hiding place

the nineteenth-century Rembrandt) who saved the house from destruction early in this century.

Rembrandt's biblical scenes are some of his best works, and he often used Jewish models, portraying them with dignity and strength. Manasseh Ben Israel and Rembrandt's financier and physician, Ephraim Bueno, both commissioned portraits that now hang in the Rembrandthuis collection. *The Jewish Bride* (which hangs in the Rijksmuseum) is said to portray Esther preparing to meet Ahasuerus, but the model is known to have been Bueno's daughter. Among the most beautiful of the master's biblical scenes on display in his home are the four etchings he did for Manasseh Ben Israel's mystical tractate *Piedra Gloriosa* in 1655. The book—written in Spanish— describes the coming of the Messiah. Some of the master's etchings depict Nebuchadnezzar's dream, David and Goliath, Jacob's ladder, and Daniel's vision of the four beasts (the lion and lamb lying together).

A short walk from the Rembrandthuis at Jonas Daniel Meijerplein 2–4 is the new Jewish Historical Museum (telephone 269-945) in the historic German synagogue complex. Before 1987 the museum had been located in the Amsterdam Historical Museum in De Waag (old weighing house); its transformation is nothing short of a rebirth. Thought for years to be damaged beyond repair, first by the Nazis, then at the end of the war by hungry, freezing Dutch looking for firewood, the four synagogues in the museum complex have been completely restored and expanded. The design maintains the feeling of the seventeenth-century sanctuaries while adding modernizing touches such as glass enclosures over the lanes that once separated the buildings, a circular staircase, wide white exhibition halls and a kosher café–bookstore, the only place for kosher breakfasts and lunches in the area.

The four synagogues reflect the rapid growth of Amsterdam Jewry in the seventeenth and eighteenth centuries. The Great Shul, built in 1670 and consecrated in 1671, soon proved too small for its expanding community, and the Obbene (upper) Shul was created behind it in 1672, above a meat market, Following suit—again in an attempt to gain space—were the Dritt (third) and the Neie Shuls, consecrated in 1700 and 1730 respectively. In 1752 the Neie was replaced by a large new synagogue, which can be seen today. Between the Grote (Great) and the Neie Shuls is a section of what was once the *mikveh*.

The museum is most successful in giving an overview of the Jewish community and its history. Many of the exhibits are geared to the neophyte, and the traveler with some Jewish background might want to spend less time with the sections on general Jewish history and practice and more with the collection of Dutch Jewish memorabilia and the magnificent silver ritual objects from the Great Synagogue, displayed in what was once the main sanctuary. Of particular note are the works of Jewish artists, a sign that Amsterdam's Jewish cultural life is very much alive today.

Around the corner from the synagogue complex, at Plantage Middenlaan 24, is the Hollandsche Schouwberg (Dutch Playhouse). At one time a gathering spot for Jewish audiences to watch primarily Jewish actors, it later became another kind of gathering spot—a deportation point for Jews being rounded up by the Nazis. Today it is a Jewish memorial. Most of the original theater has been torn down, but some jagged stone walls that formed the stage remain. In front of the stones is a grass-covered rectangle with a simple inscription in Dutch and Hebrew: "In memory of those who were deported from here 1940–45."

Across the road, on the Mr. L. E. Visserplein, is the Portuguese Synagogue. Consecrated in 1672, it has been in continuous use except during the war, when it escaped destruction because Dutch authorities proclaimed it a national monument. This had been the first time in the history of Europe that Jews were allowed to build a synagogue larger than a house, and, finally able to worship openly, they built meaning into each architectural element. The ark is made of polished Brazilian rosewood with a gold-plated interior. Twelve mammoth carved columns, one for each of the twelve tribes, hold up the women's balcony. In keeping with Sephardic tradition, the floor is strewn with sand. Light is supplied in the sanctuary by 613 candles, one for each of the 613 *mitzvot*. According to legend the candles were extinguished one at a time during Spinoza's excommunication ceremony; in fact the synagogue was not consecrated until nineteen years after the ban was issued.

The community's library, Etz Haim, dates to 1616. Started for the congregation's rabbinical school, it contains many priceless first editions, including the early Hebrew books printed by Manasseh Ben Israel.

The Winter Synagogue, a small chapel in back of the main sanctuary of the Portuguese Synagogue, was a *yeshivah* before the war. Written on the walls are the names of each of the original synagogue members. Tours of the building can be arranged by calling Ruth and Shlomo Perez, the care-takers (telephone 245-351).

In the square behind the synagogue is the Dockworker Statue, a memorial to the national strike of 1941. People gather around it every year on February 25 to commemorate that act and to encourage continued resistance to totalitarianism.

Spinoza's actual excommunication took place in the original Portuguese Synagogue, which stood at what is now Waterlooplein 133–167. Just a few steps down the street is where the philosopher was born, in a house whose site is now occupied by the Moses and Aaron Church.

The number-14 tram directly across from the Portuguese Synagogue will deposit you a block or so from the Anne Frank House at Prinsengracht 263. Second only to the Rijksmuseum in the number who visit each year, the building where the Franks and Van Damms hid from July 1942 to August 1944 is now a museum.

Groups of about forty people from all over the world climb the narrow stairs, walk through the kitchen where so many family squabbles and celebrations took place, and stare at the movie-star memorabilia still pinned to Anne's walls. A video, simultaneously translated into six languages, gives a brief history of the Third Reich, but it is hardly more affecting than the still-visible pencil marks on the walls where the family measured their children's growth spurts.

In addition to the exhibit on the shelter's inhabitants, there are exhibition areas on such subjects as the history of anti-Semitism and racial discrimination in South Africa. The Anne Frank House serves as an educational resource for schoolchildren all over Europe, and Anne's diary is now printed in more than fifty languages. The statement of purpose of the Anne Frank Foundation is not only the preservation of the Annex, which serves as a reminder of the past, but also to continue the struggle for a better world. This is a fitting mandate on behalf of the girl who wrote: "It's really a wonder that I haven't dropped all my ideals, because in spite of everything I still believe people are really good at heart."

In a series of basement rooms at Prinsengracht 690, a short walk from the Anne Frank House, is one of the best kept secrets in Jewish Amsterdam, the Israel Gallery. It was started in the early 1960s by Sara Grumprecht-Linke, who traveled all over Europe and Israel collecting and publicizing the work of Israeli painters. In the late 1960s Grumprecht-Linke was asked by the Israeli government to go to Germany on a cultural exchange with the work of about forty of these painters. Her trip helped establish friendlier relations between two countries still caught up in intense post-Holocaust emotions.

Grumprecht-Linke died in 1991, but her partner and friend, Marta Weissing, still runs the gallery. It is a gathering place for the city's Israelis. Recent exhibits have included the work of the Spanish painter Gonzalo Torne, of Converso ancestry; Meir Salomon, an Israeli artist living in Amsterdam; and more recently the Yugoslav artist Branislav Mihajlovic. As interesting as the gallery is Weissing herself, who has strong opinions on everything from Israeli politics to German reunification. Stop by for the paintings, but also to drink some wine, or listen to Israeli music (telephone 243-562).

General Sights: The Rijksmuseum is a must. It offers a welcome chance to view the works of Rembrandt and his contemporaries in an expansive setting, and to see the largest art collection in the Netherlands.

In addition to twenty-two of Rembrandt's works, the museum's permanent collection includes *Interior of the Portuguese Synagogue* by Emmanuel DeWitte, figures by Joseph Mendes de Costa, and the works of Jozef and Isaac Israels. Also represented are Vermeer, Frans Hals, Albert Cuyp and Jan Steen. Sculpture, furniture, tapestry, silver, Delft earthenware, Saxon and Dutch porcelain are all displayed in the sculpture and handicraft section.

Side Trip: The Hague, seat of the Dutch government, is more sedate than cosmopolitan Amsterdam, although it has lost much of the aristocratic feel people ascribed to it before World War II. Though Baruch Spinoza lived in the Hague only for the last seven years of his life, the city has many monuments and landmarks noting his presence, from the portrait that hangs in the Historical Museum to the houses he lived in within and near the city to his burial site.

Spinozahuis, at Paviljoensgracht 72–74, is where the philosopher lived from 1670 to 1677, earning his living as a lens grinder. He is remembered with a stone plaque on the three-story gabled house. Just down the street is a statue of Spinoza as a student; during the wartime occupation the Dutch refused German orders to dismantle the monument.

Spinoza spent what many regard as his three most productive years in Rijnsburg (1660–63). When the house he lived in went up for sale in 1896, the Spinoza Society was founded for the purpose of buying it and transforming it into a monument. Today this typical Dutch country house is the Spinoza Museum, which includes many of his personal belongings and his library. The Spinoza Society also sponsors lectures and seminars and publishes books.

Back in the Hague, Spinoza's burial site is in the churchyard of the Nieuwe Kirk (New Church). His excommunication barred him from interment in a Jewish cemetery, but a stone bearing the Hebrew word *amcha* ("your people") stands at the site, placed there by the Israel Spinoza Society in 1956, the three hundredth anniversary of his excommunication.

The Hague's Jewish Community Center and synagogue are located at Houtmanstraat 11 (telephone 070-347-3201); there is also a Liberal synagogue at Princessegracht 26. One of the city's most popular attractions is Madurodam, a miniature city (on a 1:25 scale) in which windmills turn; cars, buses, and trains move; music plays; and lights go on at dusk. Though it is based on no particular city, the buildings are typically Dutch, including a model of the Portuguese Synagogue in Amsterdam. The city was built by the family of George Maduro, a member of one of Holland's oldest Jewish families who was a World War II military hero and who died at Dachau. All proceeds from Madurodam support charities.

Recommendations: The only kosher restaurant near the old Jewish quarter is the cafeteria of the Jewish Historical Museum, but M. Mouwes at Utrechtstraat 73 (telephone 235-053) is a kosher deli where you can get sandwiches and kosher goods for take-out. Down the street at number 126 is the vegetarian Golden Temple restaurant. Delicious for dinner but not inexpensive, it offers unusual fruit shakes, good salads, and almost anything made with tofu and tempeh.

Kosher *Shabbat* meals are available from Mrs. B. Hertzberger, Plantage Westermanlaan 9C (telephone 234-684). For kosher food, nice people, and a *heimish* environment, take a short tram ride to the "new" Jewish area of Amsterdam Zuid. At Scheldestraat 45 is Sal Meyer Sandwich shop, where you can get a great corned-beef or pastrami sandwich and a good sense of Amsterdam's observant community. Like most Jewish neighborhoods, everybody seems to know one another (this is, after all, the only game in town), and the regulars come in around 8 P.M. The same family runs a kosher butcher shop next door. Both facilities are Sabbath observant and under rabbinic supervision.

The nearby Betty's coffee shop on Rijnstraat 75 bills itself as kosher style. It offers a variety of Israeli and Eastern European specialties and an upscale atmosphere at moderate prices.

Near the kosher restaurants of southern Amsterdam is one of the better Jewish bookstores, Joachimsthal's Boekhandel at Europaplein 85. For collectors of rare Judaica and Hebraica there is De Pampiere Wereld at Keizergracht 428 and Spinoza at Prinsengracht 493.

Mozes Gans's shop, Premsela Hamburger at Rokin 120, is a firm of jewelers and silversmiths in service to the royal family for almost two centuries.

Reading: *The Diary of Anne Frank* (Washington Square) can be purchased at the Anne Frank House to benefit the foundation (which sorely needs the money). *Etty: A Diary, 1941–43* (London, Jonathan Cape) is one of the most moving books to come out of occupied Europe, and is extremely popular in the Netherlands, where Etty Hillesum is regarded as a national martyr.

Hillesum was in her twenties when the Germans marched into Amsterdam, and her diary gives an older, broader perspective on the period than Anne Frank's. A secretary for the controversial Jewish Council during the war, she was allowed greater mobility than most Jews at the time. Her descriptions give a view of the Council that she, like many, saw as trying to save Jewish lives, though in the end it sent many people to their deaths. The author writes in great detail not only about the occupation but also about her own inner life. She died in Auschwitz in 1943 at the age of twenty-nine.

The novels of the Dutch-Jewish writer Harry Mulisch are easily available in the United States. Mulisch is a product of a Jewish mother who died in a concentration camp and a father who was jailed after the war for collaborating with the Nazis. *The Assault* (Pantheon), set in postwar Amsterdam, is his most famous novel; another is *Last Call* (Viking Penguin).

Peter Van Vollenhaven, a royal son-in-law of Queen Juliana and Prince Bernhard, had "maternal and paternal Jewish ancestors," according to a story published in the Royal Netherlands Genealogical Society publication at the time of his wedding to Princess Margriet. The story did not raise many eyebrows in the Netherlands; in fact, it got little attention at all.

—*Sharon Pomerantz*

Antwerp

Carol Channing notwithstanding, diamonds are no longer a girl's best friend. Career, marriage, motherhood, or passage of an equal rights amendment are decidedly more important. But the precious stones continue to play the major role in the lives of the 18,000 Jews of Antwerp, Belgium's great port city on the river Scheldt.

Indeed, the port and the diamond industry are the very core of Antwerp's economy. The former is the third busiest and the latter is by far the biggest in all the world. Most of the city's adult Jews are involved in the cutting and polishing of diamonds, or in their purchase and sale; and the industry as a whole is still largely in Jewish hands.

History: History and geography have combined to give Jews preeminence in the field, ever since the Middle Ages, when the diamonds of India first appeared in Europe. The trade routes from West to East passed through the Indian Ocean, Asia Minor, and the Mediterranean by way of the ports and urban centers in which Jews had reestablished themselves after the destruction of the First and Second Temples and their own dispersion from ancient Israel.

Diamonds were still so new and rare a commodity in Europe that the medieval guilds had not yet gotten around to barring Jews from dealing in them. Settled in the key shipping points, from Madras to Marseilles, Jewish merchants became entrenched in diamond commerce and diamond processing, about which the established world then knew little and cared less.

When the Sephardim were expelled from Spain and Portugal at the end of the fifteenth century and found refuge in the Protestant Low Countries (modern Holland and Belgium), they carried with them to Amsterdam and Antwerp the skill of generations of traders, cutters, and polishers of diamonds. Admitted to England 150 years later, the Spanish and Portuguese Jews organized the diamond exchange in London as the terminal point for the shipment of raw stones from India, later Brazil, and more recently South Africa. From London the unprocessed items were, and still are, sent on to Amsterdam and Antwerp.

The demanding tasks of classifying, cutting, and polishing remained the monopoly of the Sephardim in these two cities, their numbers increased starting in the 1880s by the poor Ashkenazic immigrants fleeing the pogroms in Eastern Europe, who were first hired as unskilled workers, and many of whom eventually set up their own shops. As more and more refugees poured into Amsterdam and Antwerp, an Ashkenazic majority developed among both bosses and workers in the industry.

By the turn of the century, two unrelated circumstances had joined to bring unexpected prosperity to the Antwerp Jewish community. The city had become a major port of embarkation for the mass Jewish migration to America; at the same time, the discovery of diamonds in South Africa, replenishing the dwindling supply from India, and the spectacular growth of the industry seduced many of the would-be Americans into staying in Antwerp.

It was a boom period. Poor Jews who had eked out a meager living as tailors in the mud alleys of East European *shtetls*, as well as some who had been diamond merchants in the cities and towns of Poland, could now adapt their craftsmanship to cutting and polishing diamonds in a civilized city. The pay was good and would get better, as powerful diamond workers' unions were formed in both Antwerp and Amsterdam.

Diamond processing and trading became central to the community. The concentration of Jews in the industry and the enterprise they brought to it made Antwerp the diamond capital of Europe. Even the Nazi invasion of Belgium could not permanently topple that eminence. As the German troops were taking over the city, the diamond industry was leaving for London, New York, Cuba, and Palestine. Ten days after Belgium was liberated from German occupation, diamonds were back in Antwerp—factories, exchanges, and shops. Despite the war and the heavy losses the Jewish community had suffered, its dominant position in Antwerp diamonds would remain.

The Antwerp Jews who survived the German occupation did so through the efforts of the National Committee for Jewish Defense. Affiliated with the Belgian resistance movement, this group saved the lives of ten thousand adults and found refuge with Belgian Christian families for three thousand children. Almost all of them were returned to their own families after the liberation. In Belgium there were none of the tragic legal fights, as in France and other occupied countries, where Jewish parents had to sue to regain custody of their own children who had been reared in Christian homes or institutions and had been baptized.

Survival was also based on strong support from the Belgian government, the Catholic church, and the general, particularly the French-speaking, population. Unlike the French police, who methodically rounded up the foreign Jews of Paris for shipment to the concentration camps, the Belgian police refused to collaborate. In May 1942, when the Germans demanded that Jews put on the hated yellow badge, they could not find a single Belgian policeman who would help carry out their orders.

That year, Elisabeth, the queen mother, actively intervened to save Jews. Joseph Ernest Cardinal van Roey ordered his priests to denounce publicly the yellow badge decrees and alerted the Vatican (to little avail) to the "anti-Christian" implications of such racist measures.

Community: Today, on Antwerp's Pelikanstraat, the main street of the diamond district, Yiddish is the *lingua franca*. More than 80 percent of the city's Jews work and live in this area. The Yiddish shop signs are mostly gone, but bearded men hurrying along the sidewalks wear the wide-brimmed black hats and overcoats of *hasidim*, and even the blond, young, conspicuously Aryan policeman walking his beat on a Friday afternoon offers storekeepers a *gut Shabbos* greeting—with a Litvak accent.

There is no longer so concentrated and lively a Jewish presence in all of Europe, except, on a smaller scale, along the Rue des Rosiers in Paris. The Jews of Amsterdam who survived the Hitler years are dispersed on the outskirts of the city. Its diamond industry has never recovered: a few Jews remain as diamond merchants, but there is no longer a Jewish working class, once the spearhead of a powerful trade union movement that successfully struck for minimum wage laws almost a hundred years ago.

The revival on Pelikanstraat in Antwerp is in marked contrast, despite the Jewish community's massive losses during the four years of German occupation. Before World War II it numbered more than fifty-five thousand persons, 20 percent of the city's population. When Antwerp was liberated in 1944, some eight hundred Jews returned from the hiding places in which they had been supplied with food and other essentials by the Jewish underground.

They were the nucleus of a present-day community that is, for the most part, an Eastern European transplant, composed largely of refugees or their children, from the displaced persons camps of the years immediately after World War II. They cling to the Orthodoxy of the prewar *shtetl* or the ultra-Orthodoxy (half the community are *hasidim*) in which many Holocaust survivors found spiritual and psychological support. Liberal Judaism, strongly entrenched in neighboring Holland and in nearby Brussels, has few adherents in Antwerp.

The economic base of the remarkably cohesive community is the diamond industry, where almost all Jews work. Such a base permits a viable, self-contained, and self-imposed ghetto to thrive. There is no need to assimilate into an outside gentile world. Intermarriage is still a rare phenomenon. Even doctors, lawyers, and other professionals who function outside the diamond *eruv*—and there is one in fact, its boundaries recognized by municipal authorities—look inward to the community as their spiritual and social heart.

There is a tight network of institutions, including the day schools, which enroll 95 percent of the Jewish children in Antwerp (the highest proportion in the world). They start at the nursery school level and continue within the system through high school. The teachers—like the rabbis, cantors, and other religious functionaries—are paid by the state, and at the prevailing wage. Judaism is recognized as one of the four national faiths entitled to state subsidies. Secular subjects taught in Jewish schools are paid for by the government.

Flemish is the language of instruction in the day schools, but pupils are almost equally fluent in French, the country's second language, and in Hebrew, since most of the university-bound will do their studies in Israel. They are also likely to speak Yiddish, the mother tongue of their grandparents, and English, increasingly a necessity in the international diamond community, whose members fly between Antwerp, New York, Tel Aviv, and Johannesburg with the greatest of ease and frequency.

Sights: Pelikanstraat begins at the central railroad station and runs a half-dozen blocks parallel to the train tracks. A few of the more affluent have moved to the other side of the tracks—the "right bank"—but most Antwerp Jews live where they work: on Pelikanstraat itself or on the narrow side streets leading to it.

On the fifth floor of number 106 is the office of Louis Davids, editor of the *Belgisch Israelitisch Weekblad*, a weekly newspaper (circulation 8,500) that reaches every Jewish household in the country. Here one can buy the latest edition of the publication's annual travel guide, a detailed fact book on synagogues, kosher restaurants, bookshops, and other institutions in Antwerp, Brussels (the national capital), and other European Jewish communities.

If Pelikanstraat is a city within a city, then its generally inaccessible diamond center is a city within a city within a city. However, tourists can visit a reasonable facsimile—Diamondland, just around the corner from the central railroad station. Workers there perform the various processing phases, and guides tell visitors everything they ever wanted to know about the "four C's" of diamonds: color, clarity, cut, and carat (weight). Purchases can be made at a savings of 40 to 50 percent. Entrance is free, but passports must be shown. Diamondland is at Appelmanstraat 33A (telephone 234-3612).

One needs special permission to get into the closely guarded diamond exchange at the head of Pelikanstraat, or to lunch at the kosher dining rooms within that complex of bourses, offices, and workshops. But the surrounding area hosts a welcoming array of bakeries and restaurants, bookstalls, and jewelry stores, where one can breathe, eat, speak, and feel Jewish to the full extent of stomach, eye, heart, and mind.

Nearby is the Romi Goldmuntz Center, at 12 Nervierstraat (239-3911), where excellent, moderately priced lunches are served. The modern building, akin to New York's 92nd Street Y, hums with activity. This is the place to meet local people—at Israeli folk dancing, a lecture on Kafka, a concert of Bach or Ernest Bloch, a table of bridge, or a lively game of Scrabble (in Flemish).

Well worth the effort is a visit to one of the two major schools—the Tachkemoni, for example, whose orientation and curriculum might be described as modern, state-of-the-art Orthodoxy. Such a trip can be arranged through Bernard Kahan, a trustee of the school.

Jewish Antwerp is a self-contained entity. Technology, computers, and electronic security systems give its essential core—the diamond center—the content of the 1990s, but the outward look of Pelikanstraat is of a century earlier.

General Sights: Antwerp is a bustling, modern, highly mechanized seaport, and a treasure-house of medieval guildhalls, Gothic churches, Flemish building facades, and museums filled with the works of such favorite sons as Rubens, Van Dyck, and Brueghel, the younger.

Travelers should spend at least a day in leisurely exploration of Pelikanstraat and at least three more just skimming the cream off Antwerp's cultural riches. One inevitably visits the Rubens House, its elegant rooms decorated with paintings by the master and furnished with the household objects he collected in the course of a brilliant and successful career.

On everyone's sightseeing agenda are the Town Hall, a magnificent Renaissance structure, and the Plantin-Moretus Museum, the definitive exhibit hall of the art of printing. It contains, along with its centuries-old printing presses and fonts of type, a rare Gutenberg Bible and a copy of the Polyglot Bible, a monumental eight-volume work in five languages—Hebrew, Aramaic, Syriac, Greek, and Latin.

Less well-known are the zoo, right in the heart of Antwerp, next to the central railroad station, and the open-air museum at Middelheim, on the city's outskirts. Here in a landscaped park are more than three hundred great works by such nineteenth- and twentieth-century sculptors as Rodin, Maillol, Zadkine, and Henry Moore. This permanent display is unguarded. According to the season, snow may drape marble, bronze, or steel surfaces; raindrops may trickle down, or glittering sunlight be reflected. But there is never the mark of a vandal or graffiti doodler.

Behind the Town Hall is the extraordinary low-cost modern housing development built around and in harmony with the sixteenth-century Butchers' Hall. The hall, now a museum, was commissioned by the butchers' guild as the one meat market in all Antwerp, and it continued as such until the French Revolution, when the guilds were abolished. Now the Butchers' Hall exhibits the arts and crafts of the city, including a unique collection of locally produced harpsichords.

The tall museum building overlooks the docks of the river Scheldt, from which thousands of Jewish migrants embarked on the steam vessels of the Red Star Line for the final stage of their long journey from Eastern Europe to America. One more recent Jewish refugee from Russian tyranny who lives in Antwerp is Valery Panov, the dancer and choreographer, now the artistic director of the Royal Ballet.

Recommendation: Directly opposite the central railroad station is the DeKyser Hotel, a five-star establishment patronized mainly by knowledgeable visitors and diamond merchants. The other world of Pelikanstraat is just around the corner.

—*Gabriel Levinson*

Athens

Athens still likes to dream. When the full moon comes up over the Acropolis and flood lamps bathe the Parthenon in ethereal light, it is possible — almost — to waft back, through the imagination, to the glory that was Greece.

With dawn's break, and the modern city's roar to life, the illusion fades. The ancient ruins still hover majestically. But surrounded by twentieth-century realities, they are merely silent sentinels recalling a world that was but that has long since been overtaken.

Yet amid the crush of traffic jams and crowds that clog ancient byways, the heirs of Jews who once represented their people in this land, so near yet so far away from their own roots, still hang on. Individually, they are well imbedded in a society that benefits from their progressivism and cosmopolitanism; communally they are often on the fringe, if not the cringe. Nevertheless, they are always proud of their unique position. In a country that has known much conquest, among a people that has known much subjugation, they see themselves as the one unbroken human bridge between the Greece of before and the Greece that now is.

History: Like faraway stars in a historical galaxy, the Jerusalem-Athens-Rome constellation, however faint, still emits light. From this ancient triumvirate came the cornerstones of Western civilization. Obviously, the peoples of this triad touched; it is equally obvious that they were rivals. And while Athenians saw Yerushalmis as competing philosophers, Yerushalmis — as related in talmudic-midrashic literature — attempted to show their own superior wit and wisdom by beginning many stories with the phrase "An

Athenian came to Jerusalem." But, perhaps in the sense that Harvard might meet Yale on the playing field but not in the clubrooms, few from Athens made their way to Jerusalem and vice versa.

Nonetheless, relations between Athens and Palestine can possibly be traced back to the early sixth century B.C.E., when coins minted during the Persian occupation of Judea were inscribed "*Yahud*" and bore the image of an owl similar to that on the drachma of Athenian Attica. Following Alexander the Great's conquest of Palestine in the third century B.C.E., Athenian activity there probably increased. In the succeeding centuries, Athenians established relations with the Hasmonaean state, at one point — around 105 B.C.E. — resolving to honor Hyrcanus, the Jews' high priest and ruler, by bestowing upon him a crown of gold and placing a bronze likeness in their Temple of Demos and the Graces. Athens and Herod also maintained an amicable relationship.

Meanwhile, the Jewish Diaspora had started, rippling up the coast of Asia Minor. Searching for opportunity beyond Palestine, Jews settled on Aegean islands, in Anatolia, the Peloponnesus; and in Attica. There, on the mainland around Athens, they joined the descendants of slaves probably transported in biblical times, where the first Jew known by name was one "Moschos, son of Moschion the Jew," mentioned in writings around 300–250 B.C.E. in a small state between Athens and Boeotia. But though they were also noted in Delphi during the second century B.C.E., concrete information on a community in Athens exists only from the beginning of the first century C.E., when Agrippa I wrote to Caligula that there were Jews in Attica. And though Paul — born Saul, a Jew, in

Tarsus — preached to Jews in an Athens synagogue during that century, no indication yet exists that the community was significant.

With the decline of classical Greece, Athens became a generally neglected and underpopulated backwater. Jews may have remained, but when Benjamin of Tudela arrived in Greece during the twelfth century, he mentioned communities in Khalkis, Corfu, Patras, Corinth, Thebes, Salonika, and elsewhere but said nothing of Athens. When the Turks conquered Athens in 1458, they gave residents the opportunity to prohibit Jewish settlement there. But, though most coming to Ottoman lands after their expulsion from Spain in 1492 went to Salonika, Istanbul, or Izmir, a few did land in Athens. Though a French traveler in 1705 wrote of finding fifteen to twenty Jewish families there, some historians doubt even the presence of that handful. And those who were there during the period of the Greek uprising against the Turks, 1821–29, were considered, as they were elsewhere, Turkish allies and either killed or forced to flee. Prior troubles and massacres at this time ended Jewish history in many areas of Greece, particularly the Peloponnesus.

But after at least the southern part of Greece won its freedom and Athens, in 1834, was named the capital of the independent country, a Jewish community began developing in earnest. Following the lead of financier Max de Rothschild who arrived in the retinue of King Otto I of Bavaria, other German Jews followed and, with the help of Sophie Marbois, the duchess of Plaisance, who also was residing in Athens and had deep sympathy for Judaism, they acquired a site for a synagogue in 1843. Greek authorities were sufficiently sensitive to Jewish feelings in 1847 that, because the Baron de Rothschild was in Athens then, they banned a popular religious procession in which Judas Iscariot was burned in effigy. But the mob took revenge, sacking the house of David Pacifico, a British subject and honorary consul of Portugal. In response, England, in 1850, sent a fleet to Piraeus and seized Greek ships. Consequently, Athens canceled the synagogue project.

By the century's end, however, the community managed to obtain a firm toehold, with the Jewish population increasing from 60 in 1878 to about 250 in 1887. After it was officially recognized in 1889, three small synagogues were quickly established under the presidency of Charles de Rothschild. Jews from Izmir arrived, followed by a large influx after the Balkan Wars. With the northern cities of Ioannina and Salonika (and their Jewish communities) becoming part of Greece, and the economic situation in Athens improving, Jews from various parts of the country headed to the capital. By the beginning of World War II, when 77,000 Jews lived throughout Greece, the Athens community numbered 3,000.

Since many new Athenians were of Romaniote — or Greek — background and spoke Greek as their native tongue, they blended better than in places where their background was Sephardic and their language, Ladino. This orientation was to serve as excellent protection when Greece was attacked by the Axis forces — Italy, Germany, and Bulgaria. The Italians launched the first salvo October 28, 1940; the Germans entered April 6, 1941; and the entire country was occupied by June 2, 1941.

With each power initially controlling a different zone, however, the treatment of the Jews varied greatly from place to place. And since Athens and the Peloponnesus first were administered by the Italians, who disregarded the racial laws, the Jewish population swelled to about 6,000 and remained free from persecution. After the Italian surrender to the Allies, though, in September 1943, the Germans took over and began in earnest to pursue the Jews.

Athenian Jews held two aces. One was a strong rabbi, Elijah Barzilai, who, instead of heeding German demands for a list of community members, fled to a provincial village and warned other Jews to do likewise. They could, too, since, unlike Jews elsewhere, particularly in Salonika, they were considered Greeks by their neighbors and thus were trusted. While the Germans did manage to flush out and deport 1,500, some escaped by small boats to Asia Minor and then Palestine. And in good part thanks to the Archbishop Damaskinos, who instructed all monasteries and convents in Athens and surroundings to shelter

19

endangered Jews, a considerable percentage survived.

Of these, many joined Greek partisan units and participated in major sabotage activities, including 40 who participated in blowing up the bridge on the main rail link between northern and southern Greece. In Salonika and Thessaly, as well as in Athens, partisan units made up primarily or entirely of Jews under Greek or British officers also worked to provide intelligence to Allied headquarters in Cairo. In Auschwitz, 135 Greek Jews, along with some French and Hungarians, blew up two crematoriums before being killed.

When Greece was liberated in the fall of 1944, 10,000 Jews were still in the country. But the war's end brought such civil strife and economic privation that many sought to leave. Authorities made emigration difficult, especially because men were subject to the draft. But little by little, Jews did depart for Israel and elsewhere.

Despite cordial domestic relations between Greeks and Jews, however, official relations with Israel were cool from the outset, with Greece having been the only European country to vote against the 1947 United Nations partition plan. The government also took its time establishing diplomatic relations and, particularly after the Six Day War, Arab terrorists turned Athens into a base for various activities. Though somewhat contained during the days of the junta, when Pasok—Andreas Papandreou's Socialist Party—was in power, during the 1980s terrorists enjoyed a haven and anti-Semitic nuances, such as graffiti on buses and jokes in the theater about putting Jews in ovens, entered the general parlance. In recent years, however, noticeable containment efforts have been made and better relations with Israel, especially in the tourism field, have been encouraged.

Community: In a country where nationalism ranks high, Jews make a special effort to underscore the difference, however semantic, between "Israelis" and "Israelians." Though many privately maintain ties with the Jewish state just down the pike, they try not to identify with it too publicly. Thus they limit their political efforts to influence-peddling rather than overt demonstrations.

Following the wartime-high demographics, the Jews in the Greek capital of four million now number about 3,000. By and large, they have bounced back from privation to achieve wealth, or at least a comfortable living standard. Taxes on the community support their establishments. These include a school for nursery level through sixth grade; a Jewish Youth Center at 9 Vissarionis Street (visiting Jewish young people are welcome; telephone 36-37-092); and two synagogues—one Romaniote, above the Community Center at 8 Melidoni Street, which functions primarily on the High Holy Days; the other, at 5 Melidoni, practicing the Sephardic ritual at evening services Mondays, Thursdays, and Fridays, and Saturday mornings and evenings. Though Melidoni Street, in the neighborhood called Thesion, was once the heart of the community as well as of Athens, Jews have now moved to such suburbs as Patissia and, more recently, to Marosi, Ecali and Halandri.

Athenian Jews consider themselves "traditional." But, although there is a kosher butcher in Athens, various rituals are considered difficult to follow. For further information, contact the Athens Jewish Community at 32-52-875 or 32-53-229. Having felt isolated from other Jews when tourism diminished during the socialist period, community members now look forward to contact with visiting Jews.

Sights: Antiquities apart, a prime target for sightseers of all ilks is the Jewish

Antiquity amid traffic: Living in the shadow and the reflection of the Parthenon

Museum of Greece, 36 Queen Amalias Avenue, barely a ten-minute walk from Syntagma (Constitution) Square in the heart of today's city. This little gem, the creation of Nicholas Stavroulakis, is a marvel for presenting, within a small space, not only the Jewish history of an area from Anatolia to Venice, but also the region's general story.

A mere sampling of its wide assortment of artifacts includes a seventeenth-century Venetian Torah from the Patras community, with a wood and gold-leaf cover resembling a fire hydrant; a painted and embroidered nineteenth-century tablecloth from the synagogue in the northern city of Veria; a nineteenth-century ark curtain bearing a delicately appliquéed floral pattern, probably from Istanbul but found in Ioannina; *megillot*, betrothal objects, and *tallesim* from Ioannina, decorated with the silver filigree for which that city is known; Purim cookies from Salonika in shapes representing various professions (slippers for shoemakers, scissors for tailors); the sword and Silver Cross for heroism of the Athenian-born Daniel Sevillia, killed fighting for Izmir in 1921; and photos ranging from Jews in the Greek army to one shot of topless women in a *mikveh*.

Two museum highlights are the reconstructed—and reconsecrated and functional—synagogue from Patras, containing its original *bimah* and several pews; plus one room representing the interior of a Jewish home in the eastern part of Greece when it was under Turkish rule. Divided in half and painted the robin's egg blue often found in Asia Minor, the walls are decorated with various panels bearing stylized strawberry and floral patterns in red, gold, and green. Here can also be found Jewish outfits from Ottoman times—men's turbans and caftans; elaborate dresses with brocade aprons over silk tunics and full-sleeved lace blouses, topped with nunlike headgear of brocade and accentuated by thigh-length strings of coins. Also included are ritual objects indicating practices, traditions, and superstitions exotic to the world farther west. The museum is open 9 A.M.–1 P.M. daily except Saturday (telephone 32-31-577).

Among Athens's antiquities, in the agora, or marketplace, under the Acropolis, lie what many believe from the layout and stones bearing *menorah* and *lulav* carvings found nearby are the remains of a fifth-century C.E. synagogue. Though difficult to distinguish without a knowledgeable guide, they are found by going to the far end of the Temple of Efestou, near the statue of Emperor Hadrian, and positioning oneself with Lycabettus Hill on the left, and the Acropolis on the right. What can be seen are mosaic remains intermittently cut by a stone path; two stone cubes, perhaps from the altar; and a curved piece of edging.

In the Monastiraki area just outside the agora is the celebrated-in-song Athens. Suffused with Oriental music and teeming, especially on Sundays, with crowds perusing the jumble of unmatched shoes, beach chairs, old books, games of chance, and organ grinders, it is known as the Yusurum Market—after the Jewish Yusurum family from Istanbul who had a junk shop in the area around the turn of the century.

The Jewish community's administrative center on Melidoni Street is a short walk away. Its pride is the Beth Shalom Synagogue, 5 Melidoni, renovated in 1968 and boasting two impressive stained glass windows, one representing Isaiah's ascent in a chariot, and the other, the delivery of the Ten Commandments on Mount Sinai. Laid out with the *bimah* and ark together at the western end, the decor is white-themed and restrained, with a marble floor; copper, wood, and glass trim; and silver hanging lamps bearing memorial candles floating on oil. This synagogue holds 500, with women upstairs. Telephone 32-52-773 or the community center.

Khalkis: The Jewish community of Khalkis, a two-hour train ride from Athens on the island of Euboea, is said to be the oldest in Europe. Dating back more than twenty-two centuries, it was subjected to time's vagaries. But though it suffered during various periods and under various regimes, its history is thought to be uninterrupted. When the city was walled and divided, the Jewish quarter represented a fair slice.

Venizelou Street today, once the town moat, is the border between old and new Khalkis. And just a couple of blocks beyond, on Kotsou Street, stands the much-rebuilt Romaniote synagogue. A small, yellow, stucco building lying within an arbored courtyard, its interior is a square room with marble pillars, crystal chandeliers, and seating around the walls. In the surrounding neighborhood are the run-down houses of the quarter whose main street is Androutsou. Almost all homes here were once Jewish-owned, but today's community has dwindled to 150. Two minutes from the town center by taxi is the Jewish cemetery. While most graves date from the sixteenth century to the present, some are thought to be fifteen hundred years old.

Near the main bridge linking Khalkis with the mainland is Heroes' Square. Next to the statue of a priest is a commemorative bust of Colonel Mordechai Frizis, a leading member of the Khalkis Jewish community and the first Greek officer killed in World War II. The current president of the community is Marios Maisis, who can be found at his shop at 46 Kriedotou Street (telephone 27297).

Aegina: A short boat ride from Athens' port of Piraeus lies the Saronic Gulf island of Aegina. A couple of blocks from the harbor, to its left upon disembarkation, is a Temple of Apollo. And there, roped off in a grove of firs, opposite the entrance booth and before reaching the museum's cashier, is the remaining mosaic floor of a Roman-era synagogue from the second or third century. In gray, white and brick-red tones, it is a design of circles, ovals, and interlocking twists, encompassing some fragments of Greek. But no sign designates it and the bits of Greek inscriptions are not translated. Among the theories attending the synagogue's origin is one saying it was built by Jewish tanners and dyers who fled, with other Greeks, when the mainland was invaded by barbarians. Another has them escaping a devastating plague. Regardless, the floor was unearthed in 1811.

Rhodes: On Rhodes, less than an hour's flight from Athens, the Jews and the island's celebrated Colossus had a relationship, however posthumous. After the Colossus—a hundred-foot bronze statue of Apollo that bestrode the harbor and was one of the Seven Wonders of the Ancient World—toppled during an earthquake in 224 B.C.E., it apparently lay around until the Muslim conquest in the seventh century. The new Muslim ruler, according to the legend, ordered the statue cut to pieces, which were then sold to a Jew. Whether he was from Edessa or Rhodes is not clear, but he purportedly carted away ninety camel loads of statuesque pieces.

Most of today's Rhodesian Jewish community, despite a venerable and significant history, has gone the way of the Colossus. Evidence suggests a Jewish presence on Rhodes in the second century B.C.E. During the following century, Herod made several visits, including one in which, in return for proclaiming his allegiance to Rome, he was reconfirmed king of Judea. When Benjamin of Tudela arrived in the twelfth century, he found a community of 400. During the Knights of St. John's rule (1309–1522), when the Jewish quarter was next to the massive city wall near the port, the community's fate varied. When the Jews fought against the besieging Turks, they were regarded favorably. After an earthquake and plague, however, they were expelled, only to be captured at sea and brought back to the island as slaves. These captives then helped the Turks during their conquest in 1522 and subsequently Rhodes developed into a significant Sephardic center in which the Jews outnumbered Turks, producing Jewish scholarship and prosperity. When Rhodes came under Italian rule in 1912, the community numbered about 4,500 and attracted Italian Jews who established a rabbinical seminary. Following the Italian capitulation in World War II, however, the Germans occupied the island and deported to Auschwitz the 2,000 or so remaining Jews, of whom only 160 survived. Today there are about 35 Jews, members of seven families. Of these just three families were originally Rhodesian. There are significant communities of Rhodesian Jews today in, among other places, Seattle and Zimbabwe.

The small community still on the island has a headquarters within Rhodes's monumentally walled city, at 5 Polydorous Street (telephone 22364), and one of the old Jewish Quarter's four synagogues remains. At 1 Simiou Street, which runs off Dossiadou Street, the synagogue was first built in the 1600s; restored in 1731; and refurbished again more recently. Standing behind a whitewashed wall, it is a beige building upon whose brown doors painted-over *Magen Davids* are barely visible. An overgrown arbor provides a quiet entrance spot—the pavement of which is made of tiny stones in wavelike design around a zigzag pattern. The elaborate interior has a central *bimah* covered with burgundy draping; crystal chandeliers; wall paintings depicting the Ten Commandments; Oriental-carpeted floor; several impressive *menorahs*; and detailed wood carvings. Friday evening services are held at 6 during the tourist season.

Dossiadou Street opens into the Square of the Jewish Martyrs (Martyron Evreon, in some places marked "Perikleous"), a shady plaza of sidewalk cafés, punctuated by a fountain adorned with seahorses. Curving out from the square and winding down to one of the walled-city gates—Pili Milon, the gate nearest the commercial port for large passenger ships—is the Street of the Jewish Martyrs. It edges the old Jewish quarter, a warren, these days, of narrow slate sidewalks; stairways sometimes bridged by arches; and many crumbling residences. Turning left along the waterfront and continuing beyond the city walls is Mandraki Harbor, where the Colossus stood.

Crete: Apparently the biblical Caphtor and the original home of the Philistines as mentioned in Deuteronomy, Crete has through the centuries known various rulers, glories, and vicissitudes. Though it had a fairly thriving Jewish community during this century, all that remains now of twenty-five hundred years of history is one shell of a synagogue in Hania, the former capital of Crete. In the former Jewish quarter bordering Kondilaki Street, its facade has two half-moon windows; its courtyard, metal work dating from 1700 that may have been part of the community *matzah* oven. Though in sad need of repair, hope exists that it will one day house the names of Holocaust victims and a photo exhibit of old Hania. The synagogue key can be obtained from residents of 32 Kondilaki.

Elsewhere in the Aegean, note that under the Ottoman ruler Selim II (1566–1574) Don Joseph Nasi was appointed duke of Naxos and the surrounding islands. And amid the ruins of Delos lie those of a synagogue. It is thought to date from the first century B.C.E., which would make it the oldest known Jewish house of worship in the Diaspora.

Personalities: As journalists, writers, and artists, Jews have made a niche in Greece. Among these are Mario Modiano, formerly a BBC correspondent; Victor Eliezer, a radio and television journalist; Avraam Benaroya, an editor involved in founding Greece's first labor union; Jean Cohen and David Ezrati, who contribute to publications in Greece and Israel; Alberto Eskenazi, a theater and television actor; and Jack Menahem, who selects music for television films and presents a popular music program on the radio every Sunday evening at nine. Though a wartime convert to Christianity, filmmaker Nestoras Matsas retains an affinity for his Jewish roots. Karhos Koon—whose name was said to have originally been Cohen—distinguished himself as a director of classical Greek dramas in ancient Greek theaters. And the Izmir-born Rosa Askanazi was a kind of Greek Edith Piaf, becoming, in 1920s Athens, the leading exponent of *rebitika*—the underworld music of dope peddlers and pimps that ultimately gained status as urban folk music.

In scientific and technical fields, those achieving prominence have been Harry Peres, a radiologist; John David Kalefezzas, professor of nuclear physics; Daniel Alkanatis, building engineer; and Abraham Constantini, an engineer who excavated rights of way for the railroad. Dr. Emanuel Aruch also made a name as a partisan fighter.

Reading: Since the successful war of independence from Turkey in 1821, Greek writers have generally treated Jews in humanistic terms in their literature. Among outstanding writers who have written of Jews are the poet Konstantinos Cavafy, whose poem, "Of the Hebrews A.D. 50," deals with Jewish assimilation; while Nikos Kazantzakis also includes Jews in his works, including his autobiographical *Re-*

port to Greco (Simon and Schuster). The Jewish author Joseph Sciaki included a short story on Jewish life in Athens in his collection *Bitter Truths*.

Recommendations: Despite a spate of new hotels in Athens, the venerable and stately Grande Bretagne remains truly grand. Included among the Leading Hotels of the World, it is centrally located on Syntagma Square and, with its expansive lobby, high ceilings and spacious rooms— many of whose balconies face the Acrop- olis—is evocative of more elegant times. The Greek flag carrier, Olympic Airways, offers a touch of the Aegean style as it serves Athens nonstop from New York, with connections throughout Greece. While there are no kosher restaurants in Athens, there are health-food stores and a vege- tarian restaurant, the Eden, at Flessa 3.

Jewish life is not what it once was in Athens, but it flourishes nevertheless, and like Greece itself, contains the stuff of dreams.

—Phyllis Ellen Funke

Atlanta

While Atlanta is not as old as its graceful sister cities Savannah, Charleston, and New Orleans, the Georgia capital has been just as much at the crossroads of southern history during its turbulent 150 years. Atlanta rose from the ashes of General William Tecumseh Sherman's fiery torches after the War Between the States, like the mythological Phoenix on its city seal, to become a cosmopolitan metropolis of 2.8 million and a hub of commerce and transportation. Yet a bit of the old southern flavor lingers in the speech, food, culture, and gentility of this thriving center of the New South, and there is a "Shalom, y'all" quality to the Jewish community as well.

History: Jews were part of Atlanta from the start, when the town was a terminus built by the Western and Atlantic Railroad from Chattanooga, Tennessee. Several German Jews arrived in 1843, the year the town was granted a charter as Marthasville, in honor of the governor's daughter. The town was incorporated in 1845 and renamed Atlanta.

The first Jewish arrival in Marthasville was Jacob Haas, who established a dry goods store with Henry Levi. Caroline Haas was the first white female born in Atlanta. Soon after, American-born Sephardic Jews arrived from South Carolina. Most began as merchants, some going into the countryside as peddlers, others opening shops in town. During the Civil War, Jews were caught up in the slavery issue and the passions that flared with it. Those opposed to secession fled North; the small remaining community sided with the gentile majority, some enlisting in the Confederate Army, some paying substitutes to serve in their places. A few Jews became blockade runners and speculators and were often de-nounced in the press. Wartime stresses from inflation, shortages, and military setbacks made the Jews, perceived as a foreign element, convenient scapegoats.

Atlanta's first Jewish organization, the Hebrew Benevolent Society, grew by 1866 into the Hebrew Benevolent Congregation; in 1877, it built a magnificent sanctuary on Peachtree Road, called The Temple. David Marx, The Temple's rabbi from 1895 to 1948, led his flock of affluent German Jews toward Reform Judaism. Atlanta's first Orthodox congregation, Ahavath Achim, was founded in 1877 by newly arrived Eastern European Jews.

During Reconstruction, more Jews settled in the South, bringing capital and goods needed by the poverty-stricken population. The four Hungarian-born Rich brothers arrived in Atlanta from Cincinnati, opening two small retail stores. These grew, within a generation, into the second largest retail concern in Atlanta, and eventually into one of the South's finest chains. Most Atlanta Jews owned their own businesses immediately after the Civil War, many in light manufacturing or commerce. Later, Jews entered banking, real estate, education, and professional fields.

The impoverished Russian Jews who began arriving during the 1880s had modest beginnings, but they retained their Orthodox heritage and established their own institutions. A group of Sephardic Jews arrived in Atlanta in 1912, after the Italian occupation of Rhodes. A second wave of Sephardim, fleeing Turkey and Yugoslavia after World War I, also settled in Atlanta.

Early in the twentieth century, Atlanta's population soared from an influx of rural tenant farmers seeking work in mills and factories, and Jews were a target of criticism for their part in the new industrialization. In 1913, in this unstable atmosphere of social change, the disfigured body of Mary Phagan, the thirteen-year-old daughter of a dispossessed tenant farmer, was found at the Jewish-owned pencil factory where she worked. A storm of anti-Semitic hatred was unleashed and a boycott of Jewish-owned stores throughout the South was organized.

Leo Frank, the superintendent of the factory, a young Jew from New York, was convicted of the crime on circumstantial evidence and sentenced to death after a highly emotional, month-long trial at the Fulton County courthouse. The jury found the "Yankee Jew" guilty in less than four hours and a crowd of several thousand outside the courthouse screamed in jubilation over the sentence. During the wild celebration in the streets of Atlanta, terrified Jews locked their businesses and fled.

People from across the country came to Frank's defense, and his case was appealed all the way to the United States Supreme Court, to no avail. Governor John Slaton, convinced of Frank's innocence, commuted his sentence to life imprisonment in June 1915. Two months later, however, Frank was abducted from a state prison farm by a mob and hanged from a huge oak in Marietta.

Those traumatic events, during which half of Georgia's 3,000 Jews fled the state, led directly to the formation of the Anti-Defamation League of B'nai B'rith, and also to the reactivation of the Ku Klux Klan. Frank's name was cleared in 1986, when eighty-five-year-old Alonzo Mann confessed he had seen another man carrying Phagan's body. Mann, then Frank's office boy, claimed he was silent during the trial because he feared the real killer. Frank was granted a posthumous pardon by the state of Georgia shortly afterward, bringing to a close an episode sometimes referred to as the "American Dreyfus case."

Scars of the Frank case kept some Atlanta Jews from supporting the early civil rights struggle. Rabbi Jacob Rothschild of The Temple became the leader of Atlanta Jews who, ultimately, did become involved in the movement. In October 1958, The Temple was damaged by dynamite, believed the work of neo-Nazis. In contrast to the Frank era, the entire Atlanta community offered financial and moral support, and Atlanta Jews felt a new sense of acceptance.

Community: Metropolitan Atlanta's Jewish population has grown steadily from 9,630 in 1945 to 65,000 today, making it the largest Jewish community in the Deep South. Many Jewish servicemen stationed at nearby Fort Benning and Fort McPherson during World War II liked Atlanta and later moved there, and many Jewish students at Emory University and the Georgia Institute of Technology remain in Atlanta after graduating. Jewish singles from nearby towns have flocked to Atlanta's Jewish "marriage market" for decades, and northern retirees have discovered the city in more recent years. Postwar refugees, Russian Jews, and Israelis have also added to the population.

Large corporations like Georgia Pacific and IBM have hired Jewish professionals for their Sun Belt headquarters. But locally bred Jews have accepted opportunities in other locales, so native-born Atlanta Jews are not so easy to find.

Atlanta's communal organizations were formed in the early 1900s. Today Atlanta has twenty-three synagogues, a Jewish Community Center, Jewish Federation, Bureau of Jewish Education, four day schools, and Yeshiva High School, as well as a home for the aged.

Most of these impressive facilities are located in the northeast and northwest sectors, where Atlanta Jews have migrated. Synagogues can now be found in suburbs where few, if any, Jews lived until recent years — Marietta (where Leo Frank was hanged), Dunwoody, Gwinnet, Roswell, and Snellville.

The old Jewish neighborhoods in the heart of Atlanta, around North Capital Avenue and Washington Street, which once had the flavor of a European *shtetl,* no longer exist. The tempting aromas from Central and Manhattan Bakeries, Gold's and Merlin's Delis, and Gilner's Butcher Shop are gone. The Georgia State Archives Building now stands on the site of the Jewish Educational Alliance Building, forerunner of the Jewish Community Center. The Turkish bath on Butler Street, known as "the bud," and its beautiful marble *mikveh* are just memories. To experience the rich heritage of Atlanta's early Jews, one can visit the beautiful synagogues and communal buildings where later generations have lovingly continued their tradition.

Sights: You'll need a car and maps to see Atlanta's many sights, although the city's MARTA subway has a Peachtree Street loop, and some downtown hotels have shuttle buses.

The Temple, a national historic landmark, at 1589 Peachtree Road, N.W., is easily identified by its classical Ionic columns and two tablets of the Decalogue above the main entrance. The cornerstone of The Temple's first synagogue, which was Atlanta's first Jewish house of worship, is preserved at its northwest corner.

The sanctuary has pews in Colonial Williamsburg style, their simplicity contrasting with the ornate carved bas-relief friezes of Judaic symbols such as the *shofar* and lion of Judah that decorate the high-domed ceiling. The dome is similarly carved with symbols depicting the twelve tribes of Israel and their pastoral life, and is illuminated by one large antique crystal chandelier and two gold-and-red chandeliers. Gold curtains form a semicircle around the ark to suggest the tentlike shape of the ancient tabernacle. The arched windows are translucent, with diamond-shaped insets of deep red and blue. The Friendship Hall and corridors are decorated with paintings, batiks, sculptures, and Judaica. Call The Temple (404-873-1731) for information about services and events.

The Atlanta Jewish Community Center, 1745 Peachtree Road, N.E., has a newcomers club and welcomes visitors to the varied activities at its main site (and at its Zaban Branch, 5342 Tilly Mill Road in Dunwoody). The popular Center Players and Teen Theater groups present Broadway hits and other productions, and the new "Yinglish Theater" group presents productions for Yiddish speakers. There is an annual book fair, and Judaica collections are exhibited periodically.

On the lower level of the Jewish Community Center is the Atlanta Jewish Federation's Zachor Holocaust Resource Center, designed by Atlanta architect Benjamin Hirsch. This exhibit is entered through a rough wooden door like that of a railroad transport car. The exhibit recalls the Holocaust through the photographs and personal mementos of Atlanta survivors. A "Westminster Torah" from the Nazis' Museum of the Extinct Race in Prague is displayed. The resource center is open by appointment only; call Jane Leavey at the federation (404-783-1661) to arrange for a visit.

Next door, at the Atlanta Jewish Federation, 1753 Peachtree Road, N.E., there is a changing exhibit in the lobby featuring photographs, documents, and objects relating to Atlanta's Jewish families and organizations. These exhibits are prepared from the Archives of the Atlanta Jewish Community, which are maintained by the federation. For general federation information, call (404) 873-1661.

The unique synagogue of Sephardic Congregation Or VeShalom, 1681 North Druid Hills Road, N.E., is well worth a visit. Its lobby is decorated with oil paintings by Jewish artists and a three-dimensional stained-glass sculpture in orange and green tones, mounted on brass, portraying peaceful figures under the sun—in keeping with the congregation's name, "light and peace." The main sanctuary has a high ceiling of wood inset with twelve stained-glass windows of brilliant hues of red, blue, and green that depict the twelve tribes of Israel. Two fifteen-foot stained-glass windows, also in bright colors, show the Tree of Life intertwined with the Burning Bush to form the name of God at the top. The windows were designed and crafted by Sol Beton, a member of the congregation. Call (404) 633-1737 for information on prayer times and special events.

Orthodox Congregation Beth Jacob's synagogue at 1855 LaVista Road, N.E., has a service-in-the-round sanctuary. Its stained-glass windows of warm gold tones are set in graceful Mediterranean arches and feature medallions engraved with symbols of the twelve tribes. The *mehitzah* is a low wooden partition. Call (404) 633-0551 for information.

Two other synagogues important in Atlanta's Jewish history are Ahavath Achim and Shearith Israel. "AA," as it is called, began as Orthodox; today it is Conservative, and Atlanta's largest Jewish congregation. It is located at 600 Peachtree Battle Avenue, N.W. Shearith Israel, also Conservative, is located at 1180 University Drive, N.E.

Holocaust survivors living in Atlanta and their American-born children founded an organization called Hemshech and commissioned a monument to memorialize the Six Million. A memorial service is held annually at the massive stone monument in Greenwood Cemetery (telephone 404-753-2128) located at 1173 Cascade Avenue, S.W.

Downtown, there is a miniature Statue of Liberty—a gift of the Georgia B'nai B'rith—on the northwest side of the Georgia State Capitol. In the north wing, there is a bust of Governor John Slaton, who commuted Leo Frank's death sentence to life imprisonment. Several blocks from the Capitol is the site of the old Fulton County Court House, now torn down, where Frank's trial was held, just across the street from the new courthouse at Martin Luther King Boulevard and Pryor Street.

Culture and Eating: Atlanta's
Jewish calendar is filled who numerous activities—from theater and athletic events held at the Jewish Community Center to lectures and socials at the synagogues. Major speakers and musical groups such as the Israel Philharmonic Orchestra visit Atlanta often. Atlanta's weekly Jewish newspaper, the *Atlanta Jewish Times*, lists synagogue services and current activities. The paper can be found at bookstores, delis, the Atlanta JCC, and synagogues. The JASS-line (call 404-874-JASS) is a listing of Jewish singles events.

Arthur's Deli at 2166 Briarcliff Road, N.E., is under Orthodox supervision and has eat-in or take-out meals. Quality Kosher Deli is across the street at 2161 Briarcliff. The Stage Deli is at 3850 Roswell Road, N.W.

Personalities: Atlanta Jews have excelled in many fields and worked diligently for the community and Israel. Samuel Weil was elected to the Georgia legislature in 1869. Aaron Haas, nephew of Jacob Haas, became the city's first mayor *pro tempore* in 1875.

Lithuanian-born builder Ben Massell was dubbed "Atlanta's one-man boom," after he built seven miles of office towers and shops on Peachtree Street. His nephew, Sam Massell, was elected Atlanta's first Jewish mayor, in 1969, serving two terms. In the Carter White House, Stuart Eizenstat was assistant for domestic affairs and policy, while S. Stephen Selig III was head of business liaison.

Morris Abram, an Atlanta lawyer, left to practice law in New York; he has headed the American Jewish Committee, the United States Civil Rights Commission, and the Conference of Presidents of Major American Jewish Organizations. Daniel Boorstin became one of the nation's leading historians and the Librarian of Congress.

Among the honorary Jewish Atlantans who helped bring the city's trademark film to the screen are David O. Selznick, producer of *Gone with the Wind*; Max Steiner, composer of the movie's score; and the epitome of the southern gentleman (as Ashley Wilkes), the English Jewish actor Leslie Howard.

General Culture and Sights: The
Carter Presidential Center, at One Copenhill, off Highland Avenue, N.E., is a beautifully designed complex framed by a Japanese rock garden and has a wonderful view of Atlanta's ultramodern skyline. The combined museum and presidential library also houses offices of the Carter Center of Emory University, a bipartisan "think tank" that holds seminars on issues ranging from public health to arms control. Mementos of Jimmy Carter's childhood, early career, marriage, and family life are exhibited in one section.

Other sections recall the milestones of the Carter years, including a section on "peace in the Middle East." There is a large photomural of the historic signing of the Camp David Accords at the White House with the three leaders—Jimmy Carter, Menachem Begin, and Anwar Sadat—shaking hands. Through videotapes, the leaders tell why they became involved in the Middle East peace negotiations, describe their personal participation and how the negotiations developed and were finally resolved. The original records of the Camp David Accords are among the library's documents, although they are not on display.

Exquisite state gifts presented to the Carters by many countries are also displayed, including a painting on silk by the Israeli artist Menashe Kadishman.

Atlanta's art and entertainment scene has expanded in recent years, offering visitors a variety of culture and entertainment, from ballet to jazz, from Shakespeare festivals to Broadway hits. The Robert W. Woodruff Arts Center, 1280 Peachtree Street, N.E., is one of the best arts centers in the South. Its spacious High Museum of Art has an excellent sampling of Renaissance art, nineteenth- and twentieth-century graphics, Asian and African art, and changing exhibits. Its Renaissance collection includes two large companion pieces by Giovanni Battista Gaulli: *Abraham's Sacrifice of Isaac* and *Thanksgiving of Noah,* and Charles Joseph Natiore's *Jacob and Rachel Leaving the House of Laban.* The High Museum periodically mounts exhibits of Jewish interest.

Atlanta's centrality in the civil rights movement is evident in the "Sweet Auburn" section east of downtown. The Martin Luther King, Jr., Historic Site, a ten-block area maintained by the National Park Service, includes the modest Queen Anne-style home where Dr. King was born (501 Auburn Avenue), the Martin Luther King, Jr., Center for Nonviolent Social Change, which includes his gravesite and exhibits on the civil rights leader's life (449 Auburn) and the Ebenezer Baptist Church (407–413 Auburn) where he served as copastor with his father.

Atlanta's importance as a supply center during the Civil War is dramatically portrayed in The Cyclorama of the Battle of Atlanta in Grant Park at Georgia and Cherokee Avenues, S.E. This huge, three-dimensional panorama vividly re-creates the bloody conflict of July 22, 1864, through paintings, miniature soldiers, narration, and multimedia effects. The museum section displays Civil War memorabilia, including a painting of Judah P. Benjamin, the Jewish secretary of state and secretary of war of the Confederacy.

Reading: Margaret Mitchell's perennial favorite *Gone with the Wind* (Macmillan) captures the era when Jews first settled in Atlanta. Richard Kluger's *Members of the Tribe* (Doubleday) is a fictional account of the Leo Frank case, although the author moved the venue to Savannah. *The Provincials*, by Eli N. Evans (Atheneum), is a thorough yet amusing personal history of southern Jewry. *Jews of the South,* essays collected by the Southern Jewish Historical Society, is available from Mercer University Press, Macon, GA 31207; $12.95, plus $2.50 for postage. *Jews in the South,* edited by Leonard Dinnerstein and Mary Palsson (Louisiana State University Press), contains essays on southern Jewry. A helpful *Guide to Jewish Living in Atlanta*, published by the *Atlanta Jewish Times*, is on sale at local bookstores.

Recommendations: The revolving rooftop restaurant at the Regency Hyatt Hotel downtown has a breathtaking view of Atlanta. The Omni International, also downtown, is attached to a complex of shops and restaurants. The elegant suburban Ritz Carlton, near Lenox Square and Phipps Plaza shopping center, has two fine restaurants and weekend packages. The Doubletree on Seven Concourse Parkway and Ravina near Perimeter Drive are Atlanta's newest plush suburban hotels.

The spring, when azaleas and dogwoods are flowering, or the colorful autumn, are two beautiful times to visit Atlanta. In either case, in the Jewish community, there is always a friendly "Shalom y'all" to make visitors welcome.

—Helen Silver

Baltimore

F. Scott Fitzgerald and the talk show host Larry King might not have much in common, but they agreed on Baltimore. Fitzgerald dubbed it "the beautiful little city on the harbor"; King says it is America's most underrated city. The point both have made is that Baltimore is somehow overlooked, but it was not always so. It was once a bustling port, the second largest city in the United States. It also attracted weary Jewish immigrants right from the boat.

Today the city is best known for its urban renaissance—a jazzy revival for a restrained, subtly genteel city proud of its distinctive ethnic neighborhoods. Like other groups, Jews have their own enclaves, the most conspicuous referred to as the Upper Park Heights corridor, an area that reaches several blocks to each side of Park Heights Avenue in the city's northwest corner. Numerous synagogues and Jewish organizations make their homes in the area. But Baltimore's Jews can be proud of more than institutions. They have made a disproportionate contribution to the city's modernization and cultural revitalization.

History: Maryland was not one of the colonies noted for religious tolerance, and Jews avoided it for nearly a century and a half after its founding in 1634. One Jew who did wander into the colony, Jacob Lumbrozo, was arrested under a law that made denial of Christianity a capital offense; luckily, he was freed in an amnesty.

The atmosphere changed with the oncoming Revolution and the diversification of Maryland's economy. The first Jew arrived in Baltimore in 1773. Unlike many who were to follow from across the ocean, Benjamin Levy, a businessman, did not make a particularly long trip: he came from Philadelphia. Several Jewish families made Baltimore their home shortly thereafter, but some restrictions remained until 1826. That was the year Maryland passed its "Jew bill," enabling Jews to hold public office without taking a Christian oath. Solomon Etting and Jacob Cohen, two leading Baltimore Jews, were joined by the non-Jewish legislator Thomas Kennedy in pushing for the bill's passage; both were elected to public office a year after the bill's passage.

It was in the 1830s and 1840s that Baltimore attracted its first wave of Jewish immigrants to form a true community. They came from Germany and settled near the port in East Baltimore. It was there that the Lloyd Street Synagogue, the third oldest in the United States, was built in 1845 (by a congregation established fifteen years earlier). Subsequent waves of immigrants boosted the Jewish community from one thousand in 1840 to eight thousand in 1860. During this period Baltimore saw battles over Jewish religious ideology. The leaders of the camps were Rabbi David Einhorn, who took over the Reform Har Sinai Congregation in 1855; the Orthodox Rabbi Abraham Rice; and Rabbi Benjamin Szold, who arrived in 1859 and advocated both moderation and tradition.

During the Civil War, Baltimore's Jews were as divided as the rest of Maryland. Rabbi Einhorn led the Jewish antislavery group, while Rabbi Bernard Illowy defended the status quo. Leopold Blumenberg fought with the Union Army and rose to the rank of brigadier general.

The mid-nineteenth century saw the beginnings of a mercantile and business class that persists to this day among Baltimore Jews. Men who started as peddlers formed the core of the garment industry. Others took advantage of Baltimore's location as the "Gateway to the South," and the possibilities opened by the B&O Railroad to amass fortunes in industry and commerce. The first merchants, mostly German, became known as "Uptown Jews," and some of their heirs are still prominent in the community.

Eastern European Jews, particularly from Russia, began arriving in the 1880s, fleeing pogroms and repressive regimes. By the time large-scale immigration was cut off in 1924 they had transformed Baltimore Jewry into a community of sixty-five thousand. The newcomers, who became the "Downtown Jews," moved into the East Baltimore areas from which the wealthier Germans had begun to escape, many going to work in the garment sweatshops owned by German Jews.

Though American history is replete with stories about established Jews looking down on more recent arrivals, Baltimore had one particularly prominent exception. Henrietta Szold, daughter of Benjamin Szold, and a local teacher and social worker, could often be seen at Locust Point (now an industrial area) meeting the boatloads of often penniless, dazed immigrants. Many learned English at Szold's "Russian Night School," which became the prototype for night schools across the country. Henrietta Szold herself went on to greater prominence as editor of the *American Jewish Year Book*, the first woman to study at the Jewish Theological Seminary in New York, and ultimately, in 1912, the founder of Hadassah.

Baltimore welcomed a smaller stream of immigrants—refugees from Nazi Germany—in the 1930s and 1940s. Today the community continues to grow, attracting immigrants from Iran and the former Soviet Union, and young Orthodox families from other parts of the United States.

Community: Baltimore's Jewish community of 95,000 is a study in contrasts and a model of cooperation. Worship services are held in *shtiebels* and *chavurot*, in addition to every imaginable size and style of synagogue. Har Sinai is the oldest continuously operating Reform congregation in the country. Some of the older Jewish neighborhoods are quite stable, and home to three generations of a family.

Park Heights is an established neighbor-hood of two- and three-story homes built before World War II. Most of the city's Orthodox community is there, as well as the major synagogues and the main Baltimore Jewish Community Center. Along the streets it is not uncommon to hear a sprinkling of German, Yiddish, or Hebrew.

Three factors contribute to the continued vibrancy of the Upper Park Heights area. CHAI (Comprehensive Housing Assistance, Inc.) is an organization that encourages Jewish families to resist suburban flight and assists with rentals and home purchases; a neighborhood grassroots surveillance program has helped reduce crime; and the Baltimore *eruv*, encircling the neighborhood, adds to the pleasure and convenience of the Orthodox Sabbath.

Pikesville, outside the city limits, is emerging as the new center of Baltimore Jewry. Built after the war, it is a typical American suburb with ranch-style homes and shopping centers. Other neighborhoods with significant Jewish populations include Greenspring, Owings Mills, Randallstown, and Mount Washington.

The sense of tradition is fueled by Baltimore's rich and varied Jewish educational system. Some children from the Washington area—where the Jewish community is considerably larger but much weaker in roots—are bused to Baltimore Jewish day schools. The Baltimore Hebrew University is the only institution in America that awards Ph.D.'s in Jewish communal service, in addition to offering the traditional courses of Jewish studies. Programs from nursery school to the Ner Israel Rabbinical College—located on Yeshiva Lane—contribute to Baltimore's reputation as a center for Jewish learning.

Personalities: Baltimore has long been a Zionist stronghold. Funds were raised there for Palestine as early as 1847, and the only American delegate to the First Zionist Congress in 1897 was from Baltimore. In addition to Henrietta Szold, the city was home to Harry Friedenwald, a founder of the Zionist Organization of America.

In 1946, Mose Speert and Herman Seidel led Baltimore Zionists in rescuing and stocking an aging bay steamer. Renamed the *Exodus 1947*, it carried 4,500 Jewish refugees to Palestine, only to be captured by the British and returned to Germany.

The city's Jews have contributed to the general as well as Jewish welfare. Joseph Meyerhoff, a real estate developer, was behind virtually all of the city's major cultural institutions, from the Baltimore Symphony (which plays in the Joseph Meyerhoff Symphony Hall) to the Baltimore Museum of Art, the Walters Art Gallery, the Mechanic Theater, and the Center Stage. He was also the main benefactor behind the University of Maryland's Jewish Studies program. Jacob Blaustein, who made his fortune in oil, has also contributed much to Baltimore's cultural institutions.

First columns: The Lloyd Street Synagogue is a short walk from the Inner Harbor

Other Jewish names that have emerged from Baltimore include Jerold Hoffberger, onetime owner and still a director of the Baltimore Orioles; Alan Guttmacher, long-time president of the Planned Parenthood Federation; Shoshana Cardin, who chaired both the National Conference on Soviet Jewry and the Conference of Presidents of Major American Jewish Organizations; Bernard Sachs, the neurologist who first described Tay-Sachs disease; and Louis Bamberger, founder of the department store chain. The city has also produced writer Leon Uris; rock composer Jerry Leiber, who wrote many of Elvis Presley's hits; and "Mama" Cass Elliot. Of the many Jewish politicians in Maryland history, Isidor Rayner, a United States senator from 1905 to 1912, stands out for his advocacy of civil rights at a time when segregation ruled his state.

Sights: Reminders of a Jewish presence in the city's core are the Lloyd Street and B'nai Israel synagogues, which, together with the Jewish Historical Society of Maryland, at 15 Lloyd Street, comprise the Jewish Heritage Center, in the heart of Baltimore's old Jewish neighborhood.

The Lloyd Street Synagogue, at the corner of Lloyd and Watson, is a Greek Revival building with some features intact since 1845 and others faithfully reconstructed. The synagogue has an early *mikveh*, a Torah ark that is a replica of the original, and a turn-of-the-century *matzah* oven. It also has a stained-glass window believed to be the first in the United States that incorporated a Star of David as a motif.

B'nai Israel, at Lloyd and Lombard, is a Moorish-Gothic building dating to 1875. One of the synagogue's most striking features is its hand-carved wooden ark. Unlike the Lloyd Street Synagogue, B'nai Israel is a functioning synagogue and holds *Shabbat* and holiday services.

The Jewish Historical Society of Maryland's collection of more than 100,000 items includes religious objects, art, and documents. Included are the complete papers of Benjamin Szold; the paintings and papers of the artist Saul Bernstein; and ceremonial objects, furniture, papers, and possessions of prominent founders of the Maryland Jewish community. The society has a library noted for its genealogical resources and also mounts periodic exhibits, such as a recent one on immigration and early Jewish life in Baltimore. Call the society at (410) 732-6400 for details of events and exhibits or for information on its free tours of Jewish Baltimore.

Lloyd Street, by the way, runs into Lombard Street, whose unofficial, and perhaps equally known, name is "Corned Beef Row." Attman's, Lenny's and Jack's delis are still on Lombard, but they're not kosher.

The Jewish march northwest from the center of town is reflected in the eclectic architecture in buildings put up as synagogues which now, by and large, house churches. The collection includes Greek Revival, American Moorish, Romanesque, and Bauhaus designs. This architectural path leads to Park Heights, where the synagogues are less distinctive, perhaps, but seem to be more permanent. One of the Park Heights synagogues most worth seeing is the Baltimore Hebrew Congregation, at 7401 Park Heights Avenue. Founded in 1830 as Nidchei Yisrael, it is the descendant of the Lloyd Street Synagogue. Initially Orthodox, it joined the Reform movement in the 1890s. In its present home, built in the 1950s, the most striking features are sixteen stained-glass windows tracing the history of the Jewish people from the Bible to the establishment of modern Israel.

At 7310 Park Heights Avenue is Temple Oheb Shalom, another descendant of Baltimore's first Jewish congregation. Before the Baltimore Hebrew Congregation itself joined the Reform movement, some of its younger members became dissatisfied with what they regarded as rigid Orthodoxy. They left the congregation in 1853 and founded Oheb Shalom and, six years later, brought Benjamin Szold to Baltimore to be their rabbi. Today the two related synagogues are within sight of each other. Oheb Shalom's current home was designed by Walter Gropius and features a vaulted sanctuary and a peaceful landscape punctuated by tall pines.

In addition to its synagogues, Park Heights is the area for Jewish shopping and eating. The Jewish stores — groceries, bakeries, bookstores, and so on — are mostly on or near Reisterstown Road.

Culture:
The Jewish community's annual showcase is the Jewish Festival, held Labor Day weekend; in recent years it has been held in a variety of downtown locations. It features continuous entertainment and Jewish artists and craftsmen.

The Jewish Community Center, at 5700 Park Heights Avenue (telephone (410-542-4900), is a lively spot for exercise and entertainment. It offers lectures, concerts, theater, and art exhibits, all with a Jewish flavor. During Jewish Book Month, in November, it hosts a book fair with more than twenty thousand books of Jewish interest. There is another Jewish center farther out in suburban Owings Mills, at 3506 Gwynbrook Avenue (telephone 410-356-5200).

In addition to being the best place to check for Jewish events, the *Baltimore Jewish Times* is perhaps the best Jewish weekly in America. Founded in 1919 by David Alter, and still independently published by Alter's grandson, the paper is known for its probing, sometimes controversial articles.

General Sights:
Baltimore's downtown Inner Harbor, which Jews, including Joseph Meyerhoff, were prominent in planning, is a glittering tribute to the city's renewal. Once an eyesore, it is now home to boutiques, restaurants, an aquarium, and a diverse array of street performers.

The city's Bolton Hill and Eutaw Place sections will give the visitor a feel for Baltimore's Victorian era. Often compared to Boston's Beacon Hill, Bolton Hill has been called more a state of mind than a neighborhood. F. Scott Fitzgerald, Alger Hiss, and Gertrude Stein all chose to live in what is still one of the city's most attractive neighborhoods.

Not far to the north of Bolton Hill is Johns Hopkins University. After visiting the pleasant wooded campus, which had its beginnings in 1874, take a drive through nearby Roland Park, an area of large stately homes and mansions and the most chic part of town.

Day Trips:
Astride Chesapeake Bay, the nation's largest, Baltimore is a convenient base from which to explore the beauty and lush heritage of the area immortalized in James Michener's *Chesapeake*. Less than an hour to the south lies Annapolis, chartered in 1708 and named for Princess Anne, later queen of England. Its eighteenth-century waterfront and adjacent back streets and narrow alleys are exquisite examples of colonial charm. In addition to being the Maryland capital, Annapolis is home to the United States Naval Academy, established in 1845. The academy's spacious grounds and imposing architecture provide a tranquil contrast to the bustle of the nearby harbor.

The Naval Academy has buildings named for Hyman Rickover, "father" of the nuclear submarine, and Albert Abraham Michelson, an 1873 graduate and a Nobel

Prize winner for his work on measuring the speed of light.

The Jewish community of Annapolis numbers two thousand. The oldest synagogue is the Orthodox Kneseth Israel at Spa Road and Hilltop Lane. Many Jewish midshipmen worship there or in suburban Arnold at Conservative Congregation Kol Ami (517 Mystic Lane), Reform Temple Beth Sholom (1461 Old Annapolis Road), or in the new interfaith chapel of the Naval Academy.

For those interested in a longer day trip out of Baltimore along the bay, there are the many old fishing villages of Maryland's Eastern Shore. Two fine examples are Oxford and St. Michaels. Oxford, population 800, was one of Maryland's most important pre-Revolutionary ports and a haven for pirates such as "Blackbeard" Teach. A visit to Oxford must include the Robert Morris Inn, restored home of Robert Morris, whose son, Robert, was a signatory of the Declaration of Independence. Nearby St. Michaels, once a shipbuilding center, is no less picturesque. A visit there should include fresh seafood and beer at one of the town's open-air dockside restaurants.

Reading: A good place to find the flavor of Baltimore's early Jewish community is in the many biographies of Henrietta Szold. The three best are *Summoned to Jerusalem* by Joan Dash (Harper & Row); *Woman of Valor* by Irving Fineman (Simon & Schuster) and *The Szolds of Lombard Street* by Alexandra Lee Levin (Jewish Publication Society). Other books worth looking at are *The Making of an American Jewish Community* by Isaac M. Fein (Jewish Publication Society) and *The Maryland Bicentennial Jewish Book,* edited by A. D. Glushakow (Jewish Voice Publishing). For a fictional look at Jewish life in Baltimore, try Robert Kotlowitz's *Sea Changes* (North Point Press). For general Baltimore fiction there is William Manchester's *The City of Anger* (Little, Brown) or Anne Tyler's *The Accidental Tourist* (Random House).

Eating: Both elegant and casual restaurants cater to the kosher community of Baltimore and the city's *kashrut* observant visitors. Among the places to try are Chapps (Chinese, meat), Pomona Square, 1700 Reisterstown Road; Kosher Bite (meat), 6309 Reisterstown Road; Tov Pizza (dairy), 6313 Reisterstown Road; Royal Restaurant (meat), 7006 Reisterstown Road; Milk and Honey Bistro (dairy), Commercentre, Reisterstown Road at I-695; Dunkin Donuts (yes, it's kosher), 7000 Reisterstown Road; and Metro Stop, downtown at 105 East Baltimore Street.

What more could you ask for? Watch soon for a kosher concession in Oriole Park at Camden Yards. Perhaps when it opens Baltimore will be underrated no more.

—Ginni Walsh

Barbados

"The *sukkah* will be built on Sunday morning—if the hurricane doesn't hit." Such words—the foremost announcement at *Shabbat* services one recent fall evening—well reflect the relationship between today's Jewish community on Barbados and its environment. The appearance of muumuus and T-shirts in the temple; the use of turquoise-and-white beach chairs for pews; and voices tinged with the banana-boat lilt that could easily break into "Day-O" further bespeak the encroaching West Indian tropics.

On the island of Barbados, unusual in its comparative prosperity, literacy, stability, tolerance, and general sense of well-being, there stands a windmill—a symbol of the past. A suggested sightseeing destination recently restored to operating condition, the Morgan Stanley Mill recalls the days when, for this island and others like it, sugar was the economic king.

As tourist literature observes, the mill, a vital cog in the sugar-processing operation, descends from models used in Brazil when the Dutch had a foothold there. Further, historians note that such machinery came to Barbados not long after the British colonized the island 350 years ago. The mills—and, indeed, sugar itself—were brought to Barbados by the Jews.

History: The British planted their flag on this West Indian island in 1627; by the following year, a letter had been sent to James, earl of Carlisle and lord proprietor of Barbados, stating: "The island business has not yet yielded above £200, which the writer paid to Jas. Maxwell." The signatory was one Abraham Jacob.

Perhaps Jewish traders had stopped on the island earlier; more trickled in shortly thereafter. But with Oliver Cromwell opening British domains to Jewish settlement and the 1654 retaking of the Brazilian seaport of Recife by the Inquisition-inclined Portuguese, many Jews chose balmy Barbados over chilly Amsterdam.

Their arrival was documented in the 1654 "Minutes of Council of Barbados" with the notation "Ordered that the consideration of the Jews and foreigners brought from Brazele to the Island be presented at the next sitting of the Governor and Assembly." In 1655, Cromwell issued a pass for Dr. Abraham (Aaron, in some sources) de Mercado, an elder of the Recife community, and his son, David Raphael, to settle and practice medicine. Barbados's Jews were granted the right to worship publicly before the Jews in London were, and by the 1660s, the congregation, Nidhe Israel (The Scattered of Israel), had built a synagogue in Bridgetown, the capital.

As the community grew—reaching more than 300, or 5 percent of the general population, by 1680, and 800 by the mid-1700s—it attracted distinguished rabbis. Among them were, in 1678, Eliahu Lopez, a Converso from Málaga who was a disciple of the rabbi of Recife and, a century later, Raphael Hayyim Isaac Karregal of Hebron. The community also built at least one other synagogue. In Speightstown, twelve miles north of Bridgetown, it established Semach David (Offshoot of David). According to a contemporary account, the building was destroyed in 1739 during a melee that ensued when a non-Jew who had crashed a Jewish wedding was accused by the host of theft.

By that time, the Jews of Barbados were so well entrenched not only in the sugar business, but also in trading and banking—with an outreach to much of the Caribbean—that some claimed they controlled nearly all of Barbados's commerce. Though documentation is uncertain, a handful also appear to have owned plantations and slaves; some properties still bear such names as Mount Sinai and Mount Tabor. The Jews also were well respected and involved themselves so significantly in island activities that, in 1833, the newspaper *The Barbados Mercury* noted: "There is indeed no portion of our civil, political or religious institutions which they [the Jews] have not contributed [to] to improve, or benefit, and to them and their liberality there is no charitable association of the island which is not deeply indebted."

Nevertheless, the Jews remained outside the island's mainstream, both by choice and, at least during their residence, by mandate. Though not brutally discriminated against, they were officially categorized as among the island's "foreigners and strangers" and, consequently, endured certain civil and economic constraints. Initially, they were denied the full benefits of the island's judicial system. They were taxed more heavily than others and they could not sell goods retail, or trade with blacks. They were regularly expected to present the governor with a "Jew pie"—gold coins, which they had probably minted themselves, baked in a pie crust.

Full freedom came at the beginning of the nineteenth century. Indeed, Barbados was the first British possession to grant Jews full political rights. Still, the nearly concurrent emancipation of the slaves, a drop in the price of sugar, and a devastating hurricane in 1831 that destroyed much of the island's economy along with the synagogue, led to widespread emigration. Though enough Jews remained following the storm to rebuild the synagogue elaborately, by the turn of the century fewer than 20 were active. In 1929, with only one man, Edmund Baeza, still acknowledging his heritage, the synagogue was sold.

Consequently, when in January 1932 Moses Altman and Dina and Moses Mass, Polish Jews fleeing Europe, decided spontaneously to leave a Venezuela-bound ship in Barbados, they found no welcoming committee. Starting as peddlers, they plied their wares around the island. Soon they were successful enough to attract other family members, friends and friends of friends. Within two years, there was, once again, a *minyan*.

Community: The Jewish community in Barbados is eclectic. Though most members are of Polish and Romanian descent, there are a few Americans, Germans, Guatemalans, Cubans—and even Chinese. Indeed, one Jew living in Barbados married a Chinese woman who converted, and one of their sons did likewise. Estimates of the numbers of resident Jews range from 50 to 80. The post–World War II high of between 30 and 50 families has been diminished by the departure of children seeking education or Jewish spouses elsewhere.

Because the older generation has maintained a low profile; because Barbados has one of the Caribbean's better interracial records; and because the Jews are only a handful—a minority among Indians, Arabs, and other minorities within a population of 250,000—they have almost no independent identity in the eyes of most islanders.

Nevertheless, they are, as one community member discreetly put it, "reasonably comfortable," with most engaged in commerce, real estate, and manufacturing. And they reflect a disparate range of social and religious attitudes, with schisms existing between restrained elders and outspoken children, between newcomers and old-timers, and between traditional and liberal worshipers.

Although it once maintained a community center, the congregation no longer supports extracurricular activities beyond a quarterly newsletter with a shaky future. However, individual community members undertook a major historical project: restoring the old Bridgetown synagogue. During the years following its sale, and the subsequent dispersion of its adornments, signs of its origins were almost obliterated. Though Eustace Maxwell Shilstone, an Anglican solicitor with a profound interest in the Jewish cemetery on the grounds of the synagogue, had tried to buy the synagogue to preserve it as a national memorial, another solicitor outbid him. In 1934, when a Mr. Hutchinson purchased the building for offices and began destroying the cemetery for garage space, Shilstone, who would eventually write a book about the tombstones' inscriptions, warned that no good would come of his actions. Shortly thereafter, Hutchinson suffered a stroke and died. Subsequently, the synagogue harbored law offices, hardware supplies, and records of the Turf Club, which governs the island's popular horse-racing activities. Meanwhile, its interior was gutted and the thirty-seven-foot-high sanctuary was divided into two stories. Additionally, its shapely lancet windows were made rectangular.

When the Barbados government selected the site for its new Supreme Court building—which would have meant relocating some graves—Moses Altman's son and grandson went into action. Paul Altman, the grandson, found in the Barbados Museum four 1923 photographs that illustrated the synagogue's former beauty; he and his father, J. H. Altman, then launched a campaign to save the structure and to restore it to grandeur. At the urging of the Barbados National Trust, which tends to the island's old edifices, and the prime minister's office, the Parliament ultimately voted unanimously for preservation (with a philatelic first-day cover of four stamps being issued to commemorate the old synagogue). And though it was not yet finished, the synagogue was used for the first time in almost one hundred years when the Barbados Jewish community hosted a conference and an exhibit from Israel's Diaspora Museum on "Jews of the Caribbean" in 1987.

The consequence of theological conflict for Jews who worship in the restored synagogue is a Conservative-bordering-on-Orthodox service with a town-meeting flavor. From November to April services are held there at 7:30 Friday evenings and on most Saturday mornings. The rest of the year services are held at True Blue, a former residence on Rockley New Road in Christ Church, near Bridgetown. There is no rabbi; one is imported from the United States or Canada when necessary. When a *mohel* is needed for a *brit milah*, the new baby's family flies one in from Miami or Curaçao.

Sights: As one of the two oldest synagogues in the Western Hemisphere, the house of worship in Bridgetown is the prime attraction. It is located downtown, a couple of blocks north of Broad Street (Bridgetown's main shopping thoroughfare) and opposite the Central Police Station. Synagogue Lane borders it on two sides and in an encircling gray stone wall is a gate displaying three Stars of David.

Thanks to the restoration project, all the additions of the past sixty years have been removed. The exterior of the hurricane-proof (two-feet-thick) coral and mortar walls are beige with white trim. Slats cover its windows, which are now their original shape. Inside, where old photographs of the synagogue are displayed, Doric columns have been reconstructed using portions of earlier ones. The divisive flooring has been removed for the rebuilding, upstairs, of the wraparound women's gallery—enclosed by latticelike fencing that incorporates pieces said to be remnants from the original seventeenth-century structure.

Meanwhile, various adornments from the nineteenth-century building have been tracked to out-of-the-way places, such as the Bevis Marks Synagogue in London and the Dupont Winterthur Museum in Delaware, the latter now the repository for the old chandeliers. The Ten Commandment tablets which had hung over the ark surfaced closer to home, in more alien surroundings. They had been purchased by one Lady Carter, wife of a British governor of Barbados, and taken to the official residence, Ilaro Court, just outside Bridgetown on Government Hill. When, after independence, Ilaro Court became the prime minister's home and Bernard St. John moved in, the tablets were found cemented to a wall overlooking the swimming pool. St. John's daughter removed them and returned them to Paul Altman.

Other important objects—a pew bench, a brass *chanukkiyah*, an alms box and an 1817 London-made clock—are currently in the collection of the Barbados Museum (Garrison, St. Michael). However, it is still not certain which of the scattered accoutrements will be returned to the synagogue.

Adjoining the block that is the site of both synagogue and cemetery, on a small traffic island opposite the Free Library where Pinfold Street meets Coleridge, stands a nineteenth-century gift to Bridgetown from the scion of one of its Jewish families. The Montefiore Fountain, which originally stood on Beckwith Place, was erected in 1864 by John Montefiore in memory of his father to commemorate the introduction of piped water to the city. Looking like a detached, delicately filigreed church spire, the four-sided monument features red, white, and green tiled recesses on all facets, within which reside fifteen-inch-high allegorical marble figures. These sculptures represent justice, fortitude, temperance, and patience, and carry the inscriptions "Do wrong to no one," "To bear is to conquer," "Be sober minded," and "Look to the end."

Just south of Synagogue Lane and running parallel to Broad Street is a lively pedestrian avenue now called Swan Street. Today, the scene features overhead banners; umbrella-covered stands selling coconuts and pineapples, snow cones and sunglasses; and many Indian proprietors, who live in apartments over the shops. Formerly, however, this was the living arrangement for Jews who resided and worked here, on what was once Jew Street.

While there is no Jewish neighborhood today, True Blue, the square, low, chocolate-and-cream-colored house became the synagogue about twenty years ago because it was then central to many families. (Jimmy Altman, 426-5792, has the keys.) Furthermore, it was only a couple of blocks from Hart's Cap, the street upon which stands an aqua-trimmed house once called Macabi. Early in the history of today's community, this was Moses Altman's home, in which a room was set aside for services. Also in the vicinity, at Accra Beach, stands a freshly painted gray-with-white-trim structure housing Lewis' Drug Mart. Recently, workmen who were renovating the building uncovered a mosaic on the top step of the entranceway. It features a Star of David in blue, red, and black against a yellow background. Though the property's former owner was a Mason, it is unlikely that he displayed the design. No other clues exist as to its origin.

Personalities: Even before the synagogue restoration project, Paul Altman was well-known on the island. His real estate firm, Alleyne, Aguilar and Altman Ltd., manages most of the island's more desirable homes. Also locally famous are Jimmy Altman, who runs Altman's dry goods store on Broad Street; the Oran family of Oran Ltd., which manufactures aluminum products and patio furniture; and Oscar Pillersdorf, who, by bringing the first industrial sewing machine to the island for his now-defunct Reliance Shirt Factory, laid the foundation for Barbados's flourishing needle trade. He also became a developer of low-cost housing, for which he received the government's Silver Crown of Merit. Aaron Truss, one of the part-Chinese Jews, became the first Jewish member of parliament and the cabinet, and served in the mid-1980s as minister of tourism and the environment. Various prominent blacks on the island today are aware of Jewish ancestry. Among them is former Prime Minister Errol Barrow, who believes his family name is derived from Barukh.

Although the claim is disputed, descendants of Yahacob Rodrigues Marques, who died in Barbados in 1725, say that he was an ancestor of Bernard Baruch. Other members of the earlier Barbadian Jewish community had even stronger ties to the United States. Joseph Bueno da Mesquite settled in New York and purchased the land for New York's Chatham Square Cemetery, considered the oldest architectural monument in New York. An early emigrant buried in Barbados was Moses Nehemiah, one of Virginia's pioneer tobacco cultivators and the first known Jew in that state. A group from Barbados founded a short-lived Jewish community in Newport, Rhode Island, in 1677, more than eighty years before the building of the Touro Synagogue.

General Sights: With its clear aqua seas and its pristine pink-and-white coral beaches, pear-shaped Barbados, twenty-one miles long and fourteen miles wide, is a tropical island idyll. Thanks to its history, which blessed it with only one colonial ruler—who bestowed gentility upon it—and, in plantation days, a relatively calm owner–slave relationship, Barbados, one of the smallest independent countries on earth, has been fairly strife free. It is a lovely island to drive around: its boulder-strewn Bathsheba coast is spectacular; its mahogany forests, brooding; its swordlike, silver-green cane fields rustle metallically in the breeze. Barbados boasts a number of well-preserved plantation houses. And the Atlantis Submarine Company offers recreational submarine rides to coral reefs and shipwrecks.

Reading: E. M. Shilstone's *Monumental Inscriptions in the Jewish Synagogue at Bridgetown: Barbados with Historical Notes from 1630* has just been reprinted by Macmillan Caribbean and is available at Roberts Stationery, 9 High Street, Bridgetown. Other books on Barbados include *A Regency Rascal* by Lieutenant Colonel W. P. Drury, about the brigand Sam Lord, and *Caribbee* by Thomas Hoover (Doubleday).

Recommendations: The recently redone and upgraded Grand Barbados Hotel, on the beach just outside Bridgetown and about a mile's walk from True Blue, offers comfortable accommodations in welcoming surroundings. American Airlines offers connections to Barbados from virtually all over the country.

—Phyllis Ellen Funke

Barcelona and Girona

A statue of Christopher Columbus stands at Barcelona's Plaça Portal de la Pau, right where the explorer returned to Spain from his first voyage to America. This is perhaps the best place to contemplate the inconclusive stories of the voyager's Jewish ancestry. One of the most intriguing pieces of circumstantial evidence has to do with the timing of his departure from Spain. Ferdinand and Isabella had set August 2, 1492, as the deadline for all Jews to be out of the country. Somewhere between midnight and dawn on August 3, Columbus set sail, passing many ships bearing emigrating Jews. He departed not only in the year of the expulsion, but virtually at the hour.

If Columbus were returning to Barcelona today, he couldn't pick a better spot. His statue stands at the foot of the tree-lined Ramblas, one of the great strolling streets of the world—filled with cafés and shops, newspaper and book stalls, vendors selling birds and beads—into which spill people from narrow alleys and broad avenues. Two miles up the Ramblas, and a few blocks over, stands the synagogue and Jewish community center of modern Barcelona. It's a vibrant place, filled with youngsters babbling in Spanish and Hebrew. Most are from families that have come in the last two generations from former Spanish colonies in North Africa and some, undoubtedly, are descendants of the people Columbus passed off the Spanish coast as he sailed for the New World.

History: To understand Barcelona and its Jews, past and present, you have to understand the diversity of Spain's cultural and religious history. Barcelona is the capital of Catalonia, a region with its own language (Catalan) and identity. Catalonia has the highest living standard, the strongest anti-Franco tradition, and the least affection for bullfighting of any region in Spain. Although the Catholic church is probably weaker in Republican, secular Barcelona than anywhere else in the country, Catalonia has been Christian far longer. The Moors were driven out of the northeastern corner of Spain in 801 C.E. after only three generations of occupation. They stayed in Granada until 1492. Central Spain and the northeast were not united until 1479, under Ferdinand of Aragon (whose domain included Catalonia) and Isabella of Castile, so until the last few years before the expulsion, Spanish Jewry never lived under a single sovereignty.

In the mid-ninth century C.E., Amram Gaon of Sura, in Babylonia, sent a responsum to Barcelona, the first recorded reference of a Jewish community in the city. Sources from the tenth and eleventh centuries mention Jews owning land in Barcelona. The mountain on which Jews owned considerable land in that era, and placed their cemetery, is still known as Montjuic—"Jews' mountain."

From the eleventh to the middle of the fourteenth century, Barcelona was home to Jewish artisans, merchants, minters, scholars, and poets. The counts and kings employed Jews as financiers and treasurers, diplomats and advisers on Muslim affairs. Under the protection of the sovereign, the Jewish quarter was an autonomous entity located near the royal palace; the same was true in smaller towns in Catalonia, where Jews served local counts.

While it is true that Spanish Jewry fared somewhat better under Muslim rule, in fact Jews were tolerated more under Christian *and* Muslim authorities when the dominant culture was on the rise; once the power of the majority had solidified, Jewish fortunes tended to decline. The biographies of Spain's two most illustrious Jewish scholars bear this out. When the Rambam (Maimonides) left Córdoba in 1148, his family was fleeing Muslim persecution. When the Ramban (Nachmanides) left Catalonia in 1267, he was fleeing the power of the church.

Though it was more than two centuries before the expulsion, Nahmanides' trouble was a turning point for Spanish Jewry. At the suggestion of Pau Christiani, a converted Jew who had joined the Dominican order, King James I of Aragon convened a public debate on the validity of Christian and Jewish teaching. The king promised Nachmanides, the sole Jewish debater, complete freedom of speech. The Disputation of Barcelona, as it became known, took place during the last week of July 1263 in the royal palace.

Ecclesiastical authorities claimed victory, but their actions were signs of defeat. In response to Nachmanides' defense of Judaism and critique of Christian dogma, they urged that the debate be stopped, even though it was never formally concluded. Thereafter the Dominicans revamped the arguments they used in attempting to convert Jews. After Nachmanides returned to his home in Girona and issued a written account of the debate, some church authorities sought to have him tried before the Inquisition for blaspheming Jesus. A bull issued by Pope Clement IV in response to the case became the basis for prosecuting suspected Judaizers under the Inquisition. King James sought to protect Nachmanides, but pressure mounted from the church and the Ramban left Spain for *Eretz Yisrael*.

James I was the last king of Aragon to have a Jewish treasurer and mintmaster, although the community remained secure for most of the next century, when the Jews numbered about 5,000, or 10 percent of the city population. Even as persecution mounted in the fourteenth century, the Jews always had friends. The king tried to protect the community from mobs during the Black Death epidemic of 1348 and, although some Jews were killed by rioters, Barcelona was one of the few cities in Europe where fewer Jews died from the mob than from the plague.

When anti-Jewish riots swept Spain in 1391, the city fathers and artisans of Barcelona attempted to protect the Jewish community. And though Catalonians may sometimes overstate the role played by outsiders in their problems, there is evidence that the violence in Barcelona was started by a band of Castilians. King John I condemned twenty-six rioters to death, but the Jewish losses — to death and forced conversion — were much greater. The king encouraged Jewish survivors to return to Barcelona, but few did, and Jewish life there was at a virtual end by 1400.

Elsewhere in Catalonia, Jewish life continued. The community in Girona was never as big as that of Barcelona, but it was a great center of Jewish scholarship, and site of the first school of Kabbalah in Spain. Discrimination mounted in Girona during the fifteenth century. The community was ordered to close all but one synagogue in 1416; in 1431, the last treasurer converted; in 1442, the area of the Jewish quarter was reduced. Most of the remaining Jews went into exile in 1492. (The Italian name Ghirondi is derived from Jews who fled Girona).

Conversos played a prominent role in the commerce of Barcelona in the 16th century, but the ravages of the Inquisition and assimilation eventually put an end to any kind of Jewish presence.

In contrast to southern Spain, where there were strong Jewish communities up to 1492 and from which many Jews emigrated, by the time of the expulsion most of the Jews of Catalonia had converted to Christianity. This difference had two consequences. In Catalonia, there were more people with something to hide and they did much more to cover the physical traces of the Jewish past. On the other hand, more Jews blended into the general population, and today it is perhaps more usual in Barcelona than in Madrid for Catholics to wander into the synagogue wanting to find clues about their ancestry.

Community: The modern Jewish community of Barcelona is a phenomenon of this century, but it is rooted in the expulsion of 1492. Many of the Jews who fled Spain fanned out across the Mediterranean, and in this century Jews returned to

Spain from many of the same places. The first came from Morocco and Turkey, shortly after the turn of the century. The breakup of the Ottoman Empire brought Sephardim from Salonika and the Balkans. A government decree in 1924 granted Sephardim abroad the right to claim Spanish nationality. The 1920s and 1930s also saw an influx of Ashkenazim from Germany and Eastern Europe.

During the Spanish Civil War, Republican Barcelona was the base for many foreign volunteers of the International Brigade, a contingent with so many Jews (30 percent, according to some historians) that Yiddish was something of a lingua franca among troops. The American Abraham Lincoln Battalion was about 40 percent Jewish. After the fascist victory in 1939, many Jews left Spain, but refugees came in during World War II and several thousand — Sephardim and Ashkenazim — were offered protection.

In the late 1950s and early 1960s, Jews from Morocco, particularly Spanish Morocco, began arriving in large numbers. It is these families — from Tetuan and Tangier, especially — that now constitute 80 percent of Barcelona Jewry. During the 1970s there was an influx of Jews from Argentina, Chile, and Uruguay, many of whom returned to South America when tensions eased in their countries of origin.

There are about 5,000 Jews in Barcelona today, virtually the same number that lived in the city in the Middle Ages. Barcelona itself, with more than 2 million residents, is about forty times the size of the pre-Inquisition city. The Barcelona Jewish community is about equal in size to that of Madrid, and almost identical in origin, but there is a good-natured rivalry between the two that mirrors the cooler rivalry that exists between the two cities. Conditioned by Jewish history, Barcelona's Jews are sympathetic to the Catalan renaissance (most expressions of Catalan culture, including the language, were suppressed under Franco), but it is Spanish, not Catalan, that most of them speak at home.

In 1954, the Communidad Israelita Barcelona built a community center housing the first synagogue erected in Spain since 1492. Many of the city's Jews live in the vicinity of the building, in the San Gervasio and Plaça de Francesc Macia areas. The community also supports a day school in the city's beautiful Bonanova section.

The majority of the city's Jews are engaged in business or are lawyers, doctors, and professors. Jews are just beginning to enter the city's public sector.

Barcelona sights: Barcelona is Paris writ small, and one of the most charming sections of the charming city is the Gothic Quarter, just off the Ramblas. And in the heart of the Gothic Quarter, the oldest part of the city, is the Call (from the Hebrew *kahal*) as the Jewish quarter of every Catalonian town was known.

The narrow streets of the Call look as if they come from the Middle Ages, although few, if any, of the buildings in the area date from the days when Jews lived there. The street layout, however, is more or less unchanged, and there is some evidence of where various Jewish institutions and landmarks stood.

If you're coming from the Ramblas, the first part of the Jewish quarter you'll see is the Call Menor, which extends about half a block on each side of Carrer de Ferran — a commercial lane graced with wrought iron balconies — from Rauric to Avinyo. This is the newer section of the Call, which didn't become a Jewish neighborhood until 1257. The parish church of Sant Jaume, which dates to 1580, is believed to stand on the site of a former synagogue. As you wander the alleys of the Call Menor, don't be alarmed if you see a sign that says "Bar Kike." What looks like an English-language epithet is actually the diminutive form of the Spanish name Enrique.

The Call Major, where Jews lived at least as far back as the twelfth century, runs along Ferran roughly from Banys Nous to Plaça Sant Jaume, and up the side streets to the Plaça Sant Felip Neri. The buildings are mostly four-story structures, and the streets are as narrow as seven feet.

The main gate of the Call most likely stood at the corner of Carrer del Call and Sant Domingo del Call, where archeological remains of a kosher butcher shop have also been found. The Carrer del Call is a lively street of clothing stores, antique dealers, stamp and coin shops, stand-up cafés, and jewelry stores, some of which display Star of David pendants in their windows.

The side streets off the Carrer del Call are quiet and so narrow they stand in almost perpetual shadow. The main synagogue of the Call stood near 7 Sant Domingo del Call, a five-story building with wooden arched doors. Around the corner, embedded in the wall of a building on Carrer Marlet, is a stone bearing the Hebrew inscription *Hekdesh Rabbi Shmuel Hasardi*, believed to be from a thirteenth-century Talmud Torah. The stone is actually a copy of one found on the site in 1820; the original is a few blocks away in the City Historical Museum.

At the Plaça de Sant Jaume the Jewish quarter ends but other Jewish connections unfold. A left turn out of the plaza onto the twisting Carrer de Paradis will take you to the back of Barcelona's imposing cathedral. The Plaça Sant Iu, sandwiched between the Cathedral and the Frederic Mares Museum, is a pleasant spot where street musicians often perform. On the wall of the museum is the coat of arms of the Inquisition. And on the cathedral and museum walls that surround the square you can spot, here and there, building blocks with Hebrew writing, mostly ancient burial stones. (Part of the floor in the cathedral's courtyard is made of Christian tombstones). Inside, the Mares Museum has a huge collection of Christian iconography and a small collection from Barcelona's Jewish past. In room 46 is an assortment of prayer books, Torah pointers, spice boxes, and a *Megillat Esther*.

Around the corner from the Plaça Sant Iu, the dead-end Plaça del Rei is the probable site of the Disputation of Barcelona. Its buildings—the back of the Mares Museum and the Chapel of Santa Agata—rose on the site, and incorporated some of the remains, of the palace of the kings of Aragon. In this square, too, can be found building stones with Hebrew inscriptions.

The newest building on the Plaça del Rei is the City Historical Museum, which has two rooms devoted to archeological evidence of Jewish settlement in Barcelona. In addition to the original stone from the Talmud Torah on Carrer Marlet, it has a detailed diagram of the Jewish quarter and various artifacts from the city's "Arab Baths," which were operated by Jews. It

also has a collection of eleventh-century gravestones from the Jewish cemetery on Montjuic.

Montjuic itself is on almost every Barcelona itinerary. It is the city's main park and was the main site of the 1992 Olympics. Not much of the Jewish past can be seen there, although the Archeological Museum, like the City Historical Museum, has some tombstones from the Jewish necropolis. If you want to see approximately where the cemetery was, go up to the Mirador del Alcalde, which offers a spectacular view of the city and the Mediterranean. Just below the lookout point is a clay-pigeon shooting gallery. The cemetery was near the gallery entrance, and along the road that runs in front of it.

The center of modern Jewish Barcelona is located at Carrer de l'Avenir 24 (the street name is Porvenir in Spanish). Like most Jewish institutions in Europe, security measures (locked door, no sign, mounted video camera) give the stone building an impenetrable look, but the *Magen David* and menorah patterns in the grillwork around the door and the ground-floor windows make it look, if not attractive, at least integrated into the landscape. The synagogue interior, with wooden pews and a central *bimah*, is highlighted by beautiful brass and crystal chandeliers—eight hanging from under the galleries and one large one in the center of the sanctuary.

In addition to the main synagogue, which follows a Sephardic rite, the bustling center also houses a small Ashkenazic chapel (used mainly on High Holy Days), a *mikveh*, a kosher snack bar, a library, a documentation center and facilities for concerts, conferences, and lectures. The center is also the best place in Barcelona to call for information about activities and kosher food (telephone 200-8513).

Girona Sights: The hometown of Nachmanides is about sixty miles northeast of Barcelona. There is no Jewish community in Girona today, but the Jewish remains are as striking as those in Barcelona, if not more so. Much of the old Jewish quarter has been restored to its medieval appearance and even some lanes that were sealed during the fourteenth century have been reopened in the past few years. In addition, the scholars and tourist authorities of Girona and the province of Catalonia have given great attention and care to preserving and rediscovering evidence of the city's Jewish past.

The main street of Girona's Call is the Carrer de la Força, which runs roughly parallel to, and two blocks in from, the river Onyar. Not only are the streets and stairways of the sloping quarter narrow, in some places the tops of the gray stone buildings seem to converge, which gives the place the aura of another time and another world. Some of the buildings date to the fifteenth century, and in a few doorways you can still see the indentations for *mezuzot*. If you visit during the annual flower festival in May, you can see several such doorways, and more than a dozen courtyards, as homeowners in the quarter open their front gates to the public. At any other time, you can see at least one *mezuzah* indentation in a doorway in the square in front of the City Historical Museum, just off la Força.

Ancient maps of the area indicate that a synagogue stood approximately at 17 la Força, near the Valenti furniture store. A few feet away, at 8–10 la Força, is the Bonastruc ça Porta Center (which takes its name from the Catalan name of Nachmanides), home of the Catalan Museum of Sephardic Culture. The museum, a multi-floor complex, features a model of the Call, reproductions of medieval manuscripts, and a variety of photographs. There are continuous showings of a film in English, *Girona, the Mother of Israel: The Jews of Catalonia*. The center's collection is still growing, and plans call for its expansion into twelve galleries, which will include decorative arts and ritual objects, interactive videos and films, documents, and paintings. The building will also house the Nachmanides Institute for Sephardic and Kabbalistic Studies which will be, among other things, a research center on the history of Jews in Spain and, specifically, of Catalonia.

A café is located in the courtyard one flight up from the center's entrance on la Força. It is adjacent to the exit onto Carrer Sant Lorenc, more a stairway than a street. This section of the Call was the site of the last functioning synagogue in Girona. Lleo Avinay, the leader of the community, who lived at 15 Sant Lorenc, signed a document of sale for the building in 1492.

At the top of Sant Lorenc is a delightful restaurant, L'Hostelat del Call. Though not kosher, it serves a range of fish dishes, and it is the perfect place to contemplate the surroundings.

Tombstones from the cemetery on Girona's Montjuic, many of which can be easily read, are in the cloister of a former Romanesque church which is now the city's Archeological Museum. Also in the museum is an original synagogue cornerstone (a copy of which is in the Catalan Museum of Sephardic Culture).

Side Trips: There are many medieval Catalonian towns and villages that have Jewish artifacts. About fifteen years ago, in Besalú, north of Girona, a house renovation led to the discovery of an ancient *mikveh*, which is now the main sight in a town worth visiting just for its charm. There are Calls in La Bisbal, the ceramic center of Catalonia, and in Peratallada. The Jewish past is preserved in the name of Vilajuiga, which means "village of the Jews." The simple church in the village is believed to be a former synagogue.

Figueres is both the gastronomic capital of Catalonia and the home of the late Salvador Dalí. The Theatre Museu Dalí is a monument to the artist and a paradise for Dalí lovers. Among the displays is the surrealist's depiction of Sigmund Freud's *Moses and Monotheism*. The exhibit includes a series of lithographs on the Exodus, the Golden Calf, and the Tablets of the Law, and, placed under an octopus and a rhinoceros head, a copy of Michelangelo's *Moses*.

General Sights: Catalonia is an artistic wonderland of which Dalí is just one example. Architecturally, Barcelona is one of the most beautiful cities in the world. Not to be missed are the works of Antoni Gaudí — apartment buildings as well as the famous, unfinished Temple of the Sacred Family (Sagrada Familia). Other artists whose works can be seen in the area are Joan Miró, a native of Catalonia, and Pablo Picasso, who was educated in Barcelona.

Ahead of the curve: Gaudí's buildings make Barcelona a sight for more eyes

Reading: There is no shortage of scholarly works on the Jewish history of Spain in general or Barcelona and Girona in particular. The closest thing to a standard work on the subject is Yitzhak Baer's two-volume *History of the Jews in Christian Spain* (Jewish Publication Society). The easiest traveling companion is the brochure "Catalonia and the Jews, " published by the Catalonian Tourist Office and available in the United States from the Spanish National Tourist Office. To get the flavor of Barcelona, you'll do no better than Eduardo Mendoza's novel, *The City of Marvels* (Harcourt Brace Jovanovich). For an impressionistic look at Barcelona in the 1930s see Jean Genet's autobiographical *Thief's Journal* (Grove Press). For a more down-to-earth memoir, there is George Orwell's *Homage to Catalonia* (Harcourt Brace Jovanovich).

Tips: Virtually all Catalans speak Spanish, but visitors — especially those who know some Spanish — are often confused by the differences in Spanish and Catalan spelling and pronunciation: Gerona is Spanish, Girona is Catalan; Catalans always pronounce the *j* in names like Juan and Jaume. The most quintessential form of Catalan culture is the sardana, a kind of melancholy hora. You can see the dance performed on Sundays in the central square of virtually any Catalonian village, or at the Plaça de la Catalunya in Barcelona. The Spanish National Tourist Office (665 Fifth Avenue, New York, NY 10022; 212-759-8822) has brochures and details on Jewish sights across Spain. Iberia is the only arline that serves Barcelona from both the United States and Israel.

Spain has become extremely popular among Jewish travelers and, on your flight, you may think you are watching more Jews arrive than Columbus saw leaving.

—Alan M. Tigay

Basel

In Basel, residents often carry three bill-folds, since they may play tennis in Germany at lunchtime and eat dinner in France before returning to sleep in Switzerland. Indeed, situated where the three countries come together, Basel, Switzerland's second-largest city, has a special multinational flavor.

Not surprisingly, it harbors a Jewish community, small but vigorous, that reflects this crossroads location. But Basel lives in the annals of world Jewry for a more significant reason: it is where Theodor Herzl held the First Zionist Congress, leading to the establishment of the State of Israel.

History: The First Zionist Congress was not supposed to take place in Basel; it had been scheduled for Munich. Because of rabbinical protests in Germany, Herzl shifted it to a Basel concert hall, the Stadt-Casino. Held August 29–31, 1897, it concluded with the adoption of the Basel Program, which became the fundamental guideline for the Zionist movement until Israel's founding. On September 3, 1897, Herzl wrote in his diary: "To summarize the Basel Congress in one sentence—which I shall be careful not to pronounce publicly— it is this: I have founded the Jewish state in Basel."

Herzl wanted to make Basel the permanent center of the Zionist movement, with a special congress building there to be called the "House of the Jewish People." This wish was unfulfilled, but Basel did host nine more congresses, including the second, attended by Chaim Weizmann; the sixth, at which Herzl agreed to accept a British plan for settlement in Uganda; the tenth, which was conducted in Hebrew for the first time,

and the twenty-second, the last held in the *galut,* or exile, in December 1946.

Basel has known three Jewish communities. The first was established in the early thirteenth century, when Basel was a German free city and Jews could buy and sell land, as well as lend money, even to Basel's bishops. Protected by the city council, they prospered until the Black Death of 1348, when they were accused of poisoning wells.

At the instigation of the guilds—which they could never join—six hundred Jews were burned at the stake, and in 1349 the community disbanded. A church council edict in 1434, requiring compulsory attendance by Jews at conversionist sermons, helped ensure that there would not be another community in Basel for four centuries.

Thanks to its paper mills and printing presses, Basel became in the sixteenth century a center for humanism and, as such, printed Hebrew texts. Christian printers there published the Psalms, a Hebrew Bible, a censored version of the Talmud, and the works of Hebrew teachers at Basel's university. To have such works properly proofread, they obtained residency permits for Jews.

During the French Revolution, when anti-Semitism was rampant in Alsace, Basel permitted Alsatian Jews in the city temporarily, and by 1805 there were enough to form another community. While they were under severe civil and religious restrictions, and underwent at least two expulsions between then and the emancipation of Swiss Jewry in 1866, contemporary Basel Jews date their community from the start of the nineteenth century.

The Jews of Basel established a small congregation in the 1840s, consecrating their Great Synagogue in 1868, and after the granting of full civil rights in 1872 the community grew rapidly. First, Jews from southern Germany arrived; later, pogroms drove in Jews from Russia and Poland. Though constrained by Swiss immigration laws, Basel also provided a temporary refuge for some Jews escaping Hitler and after World War II became a haven for Jews from Hungary and Czechoslovakia.

Community: There are about three thousand Jews in Basel. Except for a handful of Jews of Eastern European origin who have separated themselves into an ultra-Orthodox community, complete with a synagogue at Ahornstrasse 14, most belong to the Great Synagogue at the corner of Eulerstrasse and Leimenstrasse, not far from downtown Basel.

If there is a Jewish neighborhood in Basel, it extends from the Great Synagogue to Ahornstrasse, a distance covered with a half hour's walk. The area, in the southwestern section of the city, is called the Schutzenmatt Quarter, after a main street that runs through it. In general, the Jews of Basel consider themselves completely integrated into the life of the city—the government includes a Jew along with representatives of other faiths at all official functions—and they hold positions in academia, the arts, local government, and banking. The Jewish-owned Dreyfuss Bank is one of Basel's most important private banking institutions. Many Jews own shops, including several on the Freiestrasse, Basel's main shopping street.

Sights: Built around a medieval core, Basel blends the present with the past in a manner that blurs the distinction. The city is the home of pharmaceutical giants Sandoz, Ciba-Geigy, and Hoffmann-La Roche and of several major cultural and artistic institutions. But it also harbors its share of quaint little streets, hidden courtyards, and fanciful fountains, among which the sites of Jewish interest are closely intermingled.

Right behind the towering Barfüsser (Barefoot) Church, a fourteenth-century Franciscan structure, between the bustling Steinenberg and Barfüsserplatz stands the Stadt-Casino, site of the First Zionist Congress. A concert hall now as in Herzl's time, it is not officially open for viewing. Yet, to the distress of those rehearsing, visitors always seem to find their way to the auditorium where the 208 original delegates gathered. On the wall to the right of the stage there is a bronze plaque that reads: "On Theodor Herzl's initiative and under his guidance, the first Zionist organization was established leading to the foundation of the State of Israel."

Across the old city—about a fifteen-minute walk past the marketplace in the heart of town, with its shocking salmon-and-gilt-colored town hall—is Die Drei Könige Hotel (The Three Kings Hotel) where Herzl stayed during the congress. Founded in 1026 and said to be Switzerland's oldest hostelry, this massive national landmark has been visited by Napoleon, Dickens, Voltaire, Metternich, and a Japanese shogun. The famous photograph of Herzl standing on a balcony looking across the Rhine was taken outside room 122.

State of mind: Herzl in Basel during the first Zionist Congress in 1897

From the hotel it is only a few steps into the town's old streets, lined with Gothic, Renaissance, and Baroque houses in shades of bubble-gum pink, mint green, and lemon. Number 12 on Spalenberg is a four teenth-century balcony-rimmed cabaret, the Theater Fauteuil. During the early nineteenth century, it was home to a founder of the Dreyfuss Bank.

Forking off Spalenberg is Heuberg, or Mount of Hay, so called because the butchers who once lived there grew hay on their roofs to feed their livestock. The courtyard of number 33 is adorned with stone slabs bearing Hebrew inscriptions. And on Unterer Heuberg, which curves away from Heuberg, are the sites of earlier synagogues, at number 9 and number 21. To the left of number 21 is a green door leading to a narrow alley, Guggeliallee, or Chicken Alley. Reputedly, it is so named because some of the chickens killed by the *shochet* would fly, in spasms, over the wall into the alley.

Nearby, at Kornhausgasse 8, is Basel's small but fine Jewish Museum. The only one in Switzerland, it contains memorabilia, from *chuppahs* to Torah covers, of the Jews of Alsace, Lengnau, and Endingen — the latter two places being the only other Swiss towns where Jews previously were allowed to own land. Also on display are sixteenth-century books in Hebrew that were printed in Basel, including a Hebrew grammar from 1524 and a Latin and Hebrew Bible from 1546. A montage presents photographs of delegates to the First Zionist Congress. In addition, there is a first-edition copy of Herzl's *Der Judenstaat* and a number of his letters. The museum's courtyard is adorned with fragments of Jewish tombstones found in Basel, dating as early as 1222. The museum is open Mondays and Wednesdays, 2–5 P.M., and Sundays 10–12 A.M. and 2–5 P.M. Admission is free. Call 261-9514 for information on exhibits.

The Great Synagogue, at Leimenstrasse 24, is an imposing buff-colored building, topped by two large Byzantine cupolas and decorated with yellow and orange stained-glass windows that cast a golden glow in the sanctuary. Officially, it is Orthodox, but there is a men's choir and its members embrace a broad spectrum of opinion. The structure also encompasses a second, smaller synagogue and a *mikveh* (telephone 23-98-50). Next door to the Great Synagogue is the community center and Hebrew day school, as well as a library and various social facilities.

Mostackerstrasse runs behind the synagogue, and at number 17 stands Victor Goldschmidt's bookshop of Jewish incunabula, prayer books, and articles for the Jewish home.

Two other synagogues are at Birmannsgasse 7 (telephone 24-77-16) and Rudolfstrasse 28 (24-28-45).

Culture: The community center hosts a wide range of cultural activities, including stage productions and lectures. For information, call 272-9850 or the Great Synagogue. A booklet, in German, *Wissenswertes . . . Jüdisches Leben in Basel,* lists all organizations, institutions, and activities of interest to Jews, and a guide in English is being published. Basel has three Jewish periodicals, including the weekly *Jüdische Rundschau-Maccabi.*

Personalities: Jews from Basel who made a mark beyond city limits include Tadeus Reichstein, who won the Nobel Prize for medicine in 1950; art historians Adolf Goldschmidt and Werner Weissbach; and the antique dealer George Segal, who has been the president of Switzerland's Art and Antiques Fair. The most widely known of Basel's Jewish community are the four Oscars — Academy Awards. They belong to movie producer Arthur Cohn, grandson of a chief rabbi of Basel, who won them for *The Garden of the Finzi-Continis,* among others.

General Sights: Worth a visit is the Kunstmuseum (St.-Alban-Graben 16), established in 1662 and considered the world's first public art gallery; its collection includes *The Rabbi* by Marc Chagall and *The Synagogue* by Konrad Witz. Also worth seeing are Jean Tinguely's fountain of wrought-iron objects and figures that splash, spray, and sprinkle water (in front of the Basel City Theater); and Basel's crowning structure, the red and gray sandstone cathedral, the Münster (at Münsterplatz), in which, on the east side of the transept, there is a *Magen David.* (An employee in the cathedral, recently asked about the star, explained matter-of-factly that it was a symbol of the House of David, of which Jesus was a descendant.)

Behind the Münster is a terrace called the Pfalz, which looks across the Rhine to the Vosges Mountains and the Black Forest.

Eating: The kosher restaurant Topas operates in the Jewish Community Center. Proprietor Albert Dreyfuss creates kosher dishes with a French and Swiss flavor. His menu, while including such Eastern European staples as potato kugel and kreplach, also offers entrecote, with a Café de Paris sauce, and the Swiss dishes Rösti and geschnetzeltes—finely cut veal with mushrooms and onions in a "cream" sauce. The Hilton, Euler, Drei Könige, and International hotels also offer kosher food.

For an unusual snack, visit Marcel Hess, the Kosher Sausage King, at Leimenstrasse 41. Officially, this emporium, its windows covered with paintings of sausages, is one of Basel's two kosher butcher shops, but it is also the headquarters of the "kosher" winner of two gold medals in *treife* Swiss sausage contests. Hess, who has never tasted a nonkosher sausage, relies on others to tell him if he's gotten the flavor right. Like Herzl's first efforts in Basel, Hess's obviously come to a good end.

—*Phyllis Ellen Funke*

Beersheba

In the four hundred years that the Ottoman Turks ruled what is today Israel, their crowning achievement was the construction of a regional railroad network. But while the rail lines created an important base for commerce, they also denuded the land's natural forests. The Jewish National Fund is still at work repairing the damage the railroad extravaganza wreaked on the trees of Israel.

Conquerors once made their presence felt by creating new cities, but between 1517, when they took control of Palestine, and 1900, the Turks did not build a single town. Then, with the British in Suez breathing down their necks, they decided to build a regional center in Beersheba. The town, they said, would be a civic center for the nomadic Bedouin who wandered the surrounding deserts. The problem was that the Bedouin had done fine without a civic center for hundreds of years, and convincing them that they needed Beersheba was no easy task.

The Turks put up a few beautiful buildings and deemed them Beersheba's civic center. The mosque was no more useful to the Bedouin than the city itself. Used to having their closest neighbor a two-days' walk away, Bedouin had learned to pray alone. All they needed was a small patch of earth on which to kneel.

But the Turks got one thing right in the building of Beersheba. They set up a weekly marketplace, where area residents could bring their wares. One of the drawbacks of nomadic life is the uncertainty of opportunities to sell and trade livestock and handicrafts. The market found favor among the Negev Bedouin, and brought them streaming into town every Thursday. Eventually Turkish fears proved well founded, and they lost control of Palestine to the British in 1917. But the Bedouin market, despite many changes, continues to operate. Today, locals call it the Plastic Market, because it has much in common with markets all over the country. You can buy fruits and vegetables, Bart Simpson T-shirts and plastic kitchenware, Bedouin crafts and—if you really need one—a camel.

History: Beersheba's history dates back to biblical times. Abraham settled there after the destruction of Sodom and Gomorra—a logical choice, considering that Beersheba lies at the crossroads between Egypt, Jordan and Syria. It also had a reliable water supply from underwater wells; to this day, the city's water comes from deep below the earth's surface.

After the Jews left Egypt, Beersheba was part of the land allocated to the tribes of Simeon and Judah. It marked the southern boundary of Israel, giving rise to the phrase "from Dan to Beersheba"—Israel's equivalent of "from coast to coast." During King David's reign, the city was an important point along southern trade routes. It was from Beersheba that Elijah set out on his journey to Horeb. The ruins of a fortified city at Tel Beersheba give many hints about life between the tenth and seventh centuries B.C.E.

During Roman and Byzantine periods, the area was largely neglected. When it was the focus of activity, it usually was in the role of a military or administrative center. When the Muslims arrived in the seventh century C.E., Beersheba entered a long period of dormancy—until the Turks decided it was time to reestablish the city. To the end, the Turks misled themselves with images of grandeur. In 1915, they established a monument to their defeat of the British—

two years before the British had even attacked the city. And when General Allenby actually rode into town, he handily defeated the Turks. A few years later the British dismantled the railway.

For the next thirty years the town never had more than 2,500 residents. The Jews left during Arab riots in the 1930s. The Egyptians occupied the city early in Israel's War of Independence, and the Arab residents left when the city was retaken by the Israelis in October 1948.

Community: Although it is located at the geographic center of the country, Beersheba lies beyond the limits of Israel's main population centers. But Israel accomplished what colonial powers never dreamed of. From its modest beginnings, the modern city of Beersheba has grown at a pace unrivaled in the new country.

Beersheba has played an important role in absorbing immigrants in every wave of immigration since 1948. Many of the refugees from Eastern Europe and Arab countries who flocked to Israel in the 1950s found their way to the city, pushing the population to more than 50,000 within a decade of independence. In the 1970s, many Soviet Jews settled in the city, leading to the establishment of the Beersheba Sinfonietta, one of Israel's top-class classical music institutions.

In the early 1990s, some 20,000 more immigrants from the former Soviet Union and Ethiopia settled in town. This huge influx — which brought the population to 125,000 — gave the city the momentum to sustain a major growth boom, as evidenced by the huge wave of construction that has rendered most city maps obsolete. Local boosters believe that the newcomers will catapult Beersheba to unprecedented prosperity.

Sights: Beersheba isn't a high priority on most Israeli itineraries, but it should be. Touring options run the gamut from archeological excavations that shed light on ancient history to fascinating encounters with unknown cultures, such as the Bedouin and the Jews from Cochin, India. In and around town are a variety of attractions that provide insight into many aspects of Israeli and desert reality. For information

on opening hours and new attractions that might be of interest, call 057-36001, or stop by the Municipal Tourist Information Office, located at City Hall on Hanesi'im Boulevard and open around the clock.

Start with the Yad Lebanim memorial to the Beersheba soldiers who have fallen in battle. The facility, located opposite City Hall (telephone 057-37744, open daily until 4:00 P.M.), is noteworthy for its structure and the story behind it. Beersheba's first mayor, David Tuvia, dreamed of building a giant synagogue that would unite the immigrants who had come from every corner of the Jewish world. He began to build it in the 1950s, but the project was doomed from the start — architecturally, spiritually, and religiously. The massive structure didn't have enough support beams to hold the proposed roof; most of the city's residents were happy praying in the neighborhood synagogues that adhered to the prayer style brought from the old country; and a centrally located synagogue was also too far for most citizens to walk to on *Shabbat*.

Construction was halted and the cement structure sat empty for many years. Then, in 1973, a group of parents of fallen soldiers acquired the building and set up a memorial to their children, as well as a museum of the history of Beersheba. Today, a memorial to the young men and women who died defending Israel shares the building with the historical documents, maps, photographs, and artifacts that effectively tell the city's old and new history.

The buildings the Turks erected to serve as a civic center can be seen in the Old City, where a walking tour of about two hours will give you a good feel for the area. The tourist information office can provide details of a figure-8-shaped path that will take you through Ha'atzmaut, Herzl, Hahistadrut, KK'L and surrounding streets and past all the important sights in the Old City. Blue signs mark each historic sight along the way and offer a bit of information about the role played by each place in the city's history.

At the center of the loop are several old buildings on Ha'atzmaut, including the Ottoman governor's residence, which today houses the Negev Museum. The old Turkish railway station is now a museum of visual arts. At the corner of Ha'atzmaut and Hativat Hanegev is a striking Arab-style building that was a school for Bedouin girls, was used for many years by the army, and now stands empty, awaiting funds for renovation.

The Sheikh's Residence, at the corner of Ha'atzmaut and Hahistadrut, is an impressive old building that was home to Sheikh Araf el Araf, whom the British appointed governor after taking control of Palestine. A statue of General Allenby stands in Allenby Park, on Herzl Street. At the corner of KK'L and Trumpeldor is the site of the Negev's first Jewish flour mill. Beersheba's art quarter is at the corner of Beit Eshel and Palmah Streets.

Perhaps the best way to understand the city's ancient history is to visit the excavations at Tel Beersheba National Park, on Hebron Road northeast of the center of town. The fourteen-acre site lies at the center of what archeologists believe was the administrative center of a large city between the tenth and seventh centuries B.C.E. Excavations and restorations show a well-protected walled city that includes a few houses and a public square. The huge storehouses found at the site led experts to surmise that the walled city was at the center of a larger urban settlement. An observation tower at the heart of the excavations affords a panoramic view of Beersheba and the surrounding Negev Desert. Next to the *tel* is the Man in the Desert Museum, based on Ben Gurion University's extensive research on the man–desert relationship.

Many believe that the 130-foot-deep well at the entry to this compound is the well referred to in Genesis 21 regarding the covenant between Abraham and Abimelech. Whether it is or isn't, visitors can't help closing their eyes and picturing the patriarch Abraham walking down the streets of ancient Beersheba. (Another theory holds that the stone-encased well at the corner of KK'L and Hebron Road, in the Old City, is the one dug by Abraham.)

A few miles west of town is the Israel Air Force Museum, devoted to the fighting force that has destroyed more than thirteen hundred enemy planes while losing only fifteen of its own in dogfights. The main attraction is the huge collection of planes that have served in the IAF. Aviation buffs can spend hours inspecting the Mustangs, Kfirs, Cessnas, and Boeings. An old Boeing 707 has been remodeled and is used as a theater showing films about the air force, as well as selections about flight and other relevant topics. Excellent guides regale visitors with stories from the IAF's early days, including tales about the daring acts of one young pilot named Ezer Weizman, today the president of Israel.

A few miles east of Beersheba lies Moshav Nevatim, home to several hundred Jews from Cochin, India. Ever since the community made *aliyah* together in 1954, they have been concentrated in several communities around the country, of which Nevatim is one of the most important. The *moshav*'s synagogue is misleadingly plain from the outside. The interior—with its richly colored fabrics, woods, and other traditional elements—is a close copy of one of the synagogues left behind in Cochin. In a nearby building, visitors can learn about the Cochin Jews in a museum that displays artifacts, photographs, and an ever-changing slide presentation. With advance arrangements, Cochini meals can be had.

Then there's the Bedouin Market. Try to arrange to be in Beersheba on a Thursday, when the bazaar operates from 6:00 A.M. to 1:00 P.M. on Hebron Road. Even if you don't find open-air fruit and vegetable stands charming, you're sure to be taken with scenes of young Bedouin leading their herds to market. Yes, the camels and donkeys are for sale, but the embroidery, carpets, jewelry, and other Bedouin wares are easier to fit into a suitcase.

Side Trips: As the capital of the Negev, Beersheba is a convenient starting place for most of Israel's desert attractions. South of town is Kibbutz Sde Boker, where David Ben Gurion spent his last years. Israel's first prime minister was a lone voice supporting the greening of the desert in the state's early years, when many questioned the viability of such efforts. The reply of the Old Man (as he was called): "If the Nabateans could farm here, then so can we." Ben Gurion's *kibbutz* home has been turned into a museum (telephone 057-560320, admission free), preserving the living room and study as they were when he lived there.

No visit to the Negev would be complete without seeing Masada, the mountaintop fortress where 1,000 brave Jews took their own lives rather than surrender to the conquering Romans after the fall of Jerusalem in 70 C.E. The best way to visit Masada is to time your journey to reach the top by daybreak. The sunrise over the Dead Sea—which, depending on the time of year, can be anywhere between 4:30 and 6:00 A.M.—is breathtaking. Visitors can reach the top on foot or by cable car. The three-minute cable car definitely provides the more comfortable route, but if you hike up you'll get a sense of what the Romans faced when they spent four years trying to get inside the fortress.

Atop the mountain, archeological restorations give a graphic picture of what life was like for the Jewish zealots. The bathhouse, water cisterns, and synagogue—the oldest known house of prayer in Israel—are all visible. From the mountaintop lookout, you can see remains of the Roman camps that surrounded the outpost while the conquerors built the stone and gravel ramp that ultimately won the battle.

There's much more to Bedouin culture than the Bedouin Market, and a visit to the Negev isn't complete without taking some time to learn about this ancient people. A short drive north of the city, adjacent to Kibbutz Lahav, is the Joe Alon Center, highlighted by the Museum for Bedouin Culture. The museum documents Bedouin life in the Negev and Sinai. Lifelike scenes depict traditions of the nomadic tent-dwelling community. Although most Negev Bedouin now live in houses, many aspects of their culture are preserved. For a look at the traditional Bedouin lifestyle, visit Salem's Tent, on the museum grounds. Salem will greet you, roast and grind coffee beans over an open fire, and treat you to Bedouin hospitality. As you sip your coffee or tea, he'll answer any questions you want to ask: about tent life, his two wives, the changes experienced in the move to permanent towns.

Not far from the museum is Rahat, the largest Bedouin town in Israel. With 23,000 residents, it offers proof of the changing Bedouin reality. Visit the Bedouin Heritage Center, where you'll drink more coffee and tea in a tent, see how Bedouin carpets and other crafts are made, ride a camel, and even enjoy a feast of typical Bedouin cuisine.

Beersheba is the gateway to many of Israel's natural attractions. Hiking and nature buffs will want to go through the Ramon crater, bathe in the sweet-water pools at Ein Gedi and take a dip in the buoyant Dead Sea, the lowest point on earth.

Culture: Two institutions in particular have put Beersheba on Israel's cultural map. The Sinfonietta (on Hameshachrerim Road) is a remarkably accomplished orchestra, thanks in large part to its many Russian immigrant artists. The Beersheba Municipal Theater (on Shazar Boulevard) performs locally and all over the country.

Personalities: From the time Elijah left Beersheba to the arrival of Ben Gurion, few noted personages made their home in the Negev, but that's beginning to change. Pop singer Yehudit Ravitz grew up in Beersheba. One of the most prominent Soviet scientists to settle in Israel is Herman Branover, who lives and works in the city. The late Yigael Yadin, one of Israel's foremost archeologists and a minister of education, hailed from nearby Kibbutz Hatzerim.

Recommendations: About an hour south of town, in Mizpe Ramon, the Mizpe Ramon Inn offers suites and a wide range of desert hiking activities. In Beersheba, the Desert Inn is the only four-star hotel. More hotels are on the way. Unlike earlier plans, the Israeli enterprise of building a city in the desert seems to be working.

—Carl Schrag

Berlin

The play at the Theater des Westens dealt with a familiar metaphor. Ostensibly about a young German with a Jewish girlfriend who sells his mirror image to the devil, the underlying message is that Germans will never regain their identity until there is a reconciliation with the Jews.

The elderly woman working the coat-check counter in the theater lobby looked Prussian from head to toe, except for the silver Star of David dangling from her neck. No, she told a curious foreigner, she was not Jewish, but she had been to Israel five times and loved it. Asked if she knew any Hebrew, she replied, "A few words." By way of example she then uttered *"Slihah,"* which, in the context, seemed to mean "forgive me."

While it may be understandable, it is still surprising to witness this modern German phenomenon. Nowhere is there a country with so few Jews (50,000–75,000 out of 80 million Germans) where Jewish issues are so inescapable in the national discourse. Books on Jewish subjects are best-sellers in Germany, much as they are in America, except that in Germany they are bought mainly by non-Jews. Courses and lectures at Berlin's Jewish Community Center are attended by large numbers of gentiles, and non-Jewish observers, particularly young-sters, are ever present at Berlin synagogue services. More young Germans than Americans, it seems, have worked on *kibbutzim.*

This is not to say that Germany has the ideal climate for Jews. It is no more devoid of anti-Semitism than other Western countries (although it is more carefully observed). In the 1970s, dislike for Israel was evident in some leftist circles; unable to deny the Holocaust, some took comfort in finding fault with Jews. Since Germany's reunification, anti-Semitism and general xenophobia have been recaptured by the right. Perhaps more disturbing than the political fringes is the debate among histo-rians and politicians on the nature of the Holocaust — between those who argue that it was a uniquely horrible event in human history and those who seek to "normalize" it as an inevitable, albeit terrible, out-growth of war. (The modern debate has a parallel in the 1870s, when scholars argued about the Jewish contribution to German culture; one of the today's proponents of the uniqueness of the Holocaust is Hans Mommsen, great-grandson of Theodor Mommsen, a proponent of the Jewish con-tribution in the nineteenth century.)

The debate, however, is nothing if not part of the constant presence of "the Jews" on the German scene, and it is a presence that the German government and people cope with, if not always comfortably. The leader of Germany's Jewish community, Ignatz Bubis, is a fixture in the German media, routinely consulted on matters of civil and human rights. It was cause for rejoicing back in the 1980s when Israel's President Chaim Herzog, on a state visit, said that "West Germany is Israel's best friend in the world after the United States."

And what is perhaps most fascinating is how the Jewish–German drama is played out in Berlin. When the city was still divided, adrift one hundred miles behind the world's political border, one might have expected Berliners to be more preoccupied with the Russians than with the Jews, and in many ways they were. But Berlin, like New York, can juggle a lot at once, and the nation's interest in things Jewish has always been, if anything, more pronounced in Berlin; when the American TV miniseries "Holocaust" aired on German television, for example, Berliners watched in greater proportion than other Germans.

History: Despite a history of more than 750 years, Berlin is a young city by German standards, as is its Jewish community. It was far removed from the main Jewish settlement areas in the Rhineland and the villages of Franconia and Bavaria. Only with the development of Berlin in the nineteenth century as the center of a unified Germany did the Jewish community experience the explosive growth that made it the center of German Jewry.

The first mention of Jews in Berlin is in 1295, although there was an older, and larger, community in Spandau, which is today at the city's western edge. Jews were expelled from Berlin in 1349, when the Plague swept the city; in 1446; in 1510, after a Host-desecration charge; and in 1571.

In 1671, at a time when many of Germany's territorial princes had taken on Court Jews, or *Hofjuden*, to run their financial affairs, Berlin admitted 50 Jewish families expelled from Vienna. This marked the beginning of the modern Jewish community, and a continuous Jewish presence, including the entire twelve years of the Third Reich.

During the eighteenth century, Berlin Jews worked mainly as bankers and traders in precious metals and stones. The community grew slowly from 1,000 in 1700 to nearly 2,000 in 1743. A number of Jews became wealthy as purveyors to the army and mint during the Seven Years War (1756–63) and were granted the same rights as Christian bankers. Economic advisers like Veitel Heine Ephraim and Daniel Itzig are credited by historians with saving Prussia from defeat during the war and enabling it to recover from the conflict.

Toward the end of the eighteenth century, the Jewish community began to modernize and also to contribute to German culture in more visible ways. The philosopher Moses Mendelssohn — friend of Lessing, defender of Judaism, articulator of the Enlightenment — was at the forefront of both of these movements. In 1778 he was instrumental in founding the Jüdische Freischule, designed to foster Jewish and general education. Mendelssohn's was the first of several Jewish homes to become a gathering place for the social and intellectual elite of Berlin — Jewish and non-Jewish.

A series of acts and edicts between 1809 and 1812 conferred Prussian citizenship on Berlin's Jews. Though citizens, the Jews did not achieve formal civic equality until 1860, after which they entered German public life, especially in Berlin, with increasing visibility. Jews were particularly prominent in journalism, the arts, and commerce.

The rapid advancement of German Jewry was due to the country's fragmented history. When Jews were expelled from England, France, and Spain, it was centuries before communities were reestablished in those countries. But because Germany was, prior to 1871, a collection of duchies, free cities, and bishoprics, expelled Jews had always been able to settle in the next town. When the cities — and the society — opened to them they moved in not as immigrants from faraway lands speaking foreign languages but as fully adapted Germans ready to participate immediately in the new nation's cultural and economic life.

The nineteenth century also saw the rise of Reform Judaism in Berlin. Beginning in the 1840s, the new movement was characterized by liturgical reforms, the introduction of an organ, and, for a time, Sabbath services on Sunday. Opposition grew with each change, and in 1869 Azriel Hildesheimer and his adherents broke from the main body of Berlin Jewry to start an Orthodox congregation. The Liberals would continue to be predominant in Berlin, but Liberal–Orthodox relations in the central, noncongregational organizations of the Jewish community were generally harmonious. By 1930, the city had seven Orthodox synagogues and nine Liberal or Reform.

Many of the Jewish successes of the nineteenth century had their dark counterpoints in the twentieth. Many Germans in the lower classes, to which the tolerance practiced by some of the social elite had never filtered down, accepted the argument that Jews controlled the media and the country's finances. Although Jews never constituted more than 5 percent of Berlin's population, or much more than 1 percent of Germany's, the prominence of individual

Jews or their concentration in some fields were convenient targets for extremists. There was a wave of anti-Semitic propaganda after the 1919 murder of Rosa Luxemburg, the Jewish leftist leader, in Berlin. Walter Rathenau — whose father, Emil, was the founder of A.E.G., the German "General Electric" — became foreign minister in the Weimar Republic but was assassinated in 1922 by anti-Semitic nationalists.

The persecution of Jews under the Nazi regime is one of the best documented episodes of history. What is usually not appreciated is how German Jewry — particularly in Berlin, where 170,000 Jews lived — was transformed as a community between 1933 and 1938. Increasingly cut off from the rest of the country by racial laws, boycotts, and persecution, the Jews, many of whom had had minimal ties to their coreligionists, were forced into an independent community existence. Jewish schools were set up to accommodate children barred from Aryan schools. Jewish cultural and sports organizations flourished to serve the most educated part of the German population, suddenly cut off from the rest of society. Jewish books and newspapers were published on a scale never before seen. And Jewish politics intensified, fed by those who still hoped to find a niche in Germany and those who believed Zionism was the answer. In some ways, it was the most vibrant period in the history of Berlin Jewry.

About half of Berlin's Jews emigrated between 1933 and 1938, when community life began to unravel. In the summer, the anti-Jewish violence and arrests took on massive scale. The turning point was *Kristallnacht*, the night of November 9–10, 1938, when synagogues were burned and Jewish shops looted all over Germany. Jewish organizations were closed, newspapers shut down, religious services confined to three synagogues, and Jews restricted in their movements. Emigration — for those who could find a place to go — was permitted until 1941, the year in which the remaining Jews were forced to wear yellow stars.

Mass deportations to the ghettos and death camps (mainly to Thereisenstadt and Auschwitz) were carried out between the fall of 1941 and the spring of 1943, when

Berlin was declared *Judenrein* — free of Jews. The main assembly point was a former Jewish old-age home on Grosse Hamburgerstrasse. But the Nazi regime never operated quite as efficiently, or free of opposition, as its reputation — even in Berlin. During one roundup in 1942, a group of non-Jewish women married to Jewish men staged a violent street demonstration, prompting the Gestapo to release their husbands. A group of Jewish communists attacked an anti-Semitic exhibition that year — for which they and 250 other Jews were shot. The Nazi claim notwithstanding, approximately 6,000 Jews (many of mixed parentage) survived the war in Berlin.

Community: Much as German unification in the 1860s transformed Berlin's Jewish community, the fall of the Berlin Wall in 1989 transformed it again. Not only did the Jewish communities of east and west come together, the city became a magnet to Jews from farther east, and within a year after reunification Berlin surpassed Zurich to claim a distinction it had not had since the 1930s — the largest Jewish community in the German-speaking world. The influx, mainly from the former Soviet Union, has presented Berlin's Jewish establishment with an ironic problem. In the early twentieth century German Jews complained that their eastern brethren were "too Jewish," an alien element in their midst. Nowadays Jewish leaders lament that the newcomers, cut off from their roots for so long, are not Jewish enough.

Between the fall of the wall and 1992, Berlin's Jewish community grew by 50 percent, reaching 10,000. Counting those not registered as community members, the number may be closer to 20,000. The community is supported by taxes from its registered members, direct government support, and income from real estate.

Despite the influx, however, the Berlin community is perhaps the most "German" of any in the country. Today, as much as 90 percent of German Jewry has roots in Eastern Europe, but the proportion is somewhat smaller in Berlin. Aside from the numbers, anyone who compares the various Jewish communities in Germany comes away with the sense that Berlin

Jewry in particular feels a palpable connection to its Jewish past. Indeed the very Germanness of the Berlin community has added to its eastern ranks. In Germany, where immigration is a municipal affair, the Berlin Jewish community has used its influence since the 1970s to gain admission for Russian Jews.

Central issues for the community today are vigilance against racism and anti-Semitism, absorption of immigrants, and restoration of Jewish property, especially in what was East Berlin. Before the war, poorer Jews, including most of the Eastern European immigrants, lived in and around Alexanderplatz; a slightly better-off class occupied pensions around Wittenbergplatz; upper-middle-class Jews lived along the Kurfürstendamm and through Charlottenburg; and the richest Jews lived in the Grunewald.

With the exception of Alexanderplatz, which the East Germans transformed with massive apartment blocks, Jews, albeit in smaller number, live in the same neighborhoods today. Most of western Berlin's synagogues, as well as the Jewish Community Center, are within walking distance of Kurfürstendamm. Since reunification, however, there has been something of a Jewish return, in the form of communal activity if not residence, to the area around Oranienburgerstrasse — a stone's throw from Alexanderplatz.

Sights: In addition to sights of specific Jewish interest, Berlin is loaded with symbols of Jewish contributions to German and world civilization, and to reminders of the Holocaust. Streets around town include Heinrich Heineplatz and Mendelssohnstrasse, Rathenauplatz and Gustav Mahlerplatz, Spinozastrasse and Rosa Luxemburgplatz. Berlin department stores like Wertheim and Hertie still bear the names of their Jewish founders, and newspapers like *Berliner Morgenpost* and *Berliner Zeitung* trace their roots to Leopold Ullstein, the Jewish publisher who founded them. The Renaissance and Volksbuhne theaters and the Hebbeltheatre, all still active, were founded by Jews. In front of the Wittenbergplatz subway station is a simple black and yellow sign that says, "Places of terror that we are never allowed to forget," after

which are listed the names of ten concentration camps. Unlike memorials in buildings or at the site of death camps, this one seems deliberately put in the way, so that even the most casual stroller or commuter will consider the past.

Signs of Berlin's Jewish history, recent and remote, are all over. What is emerging as the new Jewish heart of the city, however, is on Oranienburgerstrasse, in what used to be East Berlin. When the "New Synagogue" was completed in 1866, it was the largest Jewish house of worship in the world. Severely damaged on *Kristallnacht*, it suffered further damage from Allied bombs in 1943. For years after the war it stood in ruins, its great Moorish dome gone, trees growing in the hollow shell not only on the ground floor but in patches of earth that sat on the second floor. Renovation of the building began under the East German government, a year before the wall came down. The project is scheduled for completion in 1995.

The orange-and-yellow brick facade has been cleaned, and an exact replica of the original gold dome, topped by a Star of David, is now in place, as are two smaller domes on the synagogue's flanking towers. The sanctuary will not be rebuilt — there is no longer a need for a 3,400-seat synagogue in Berlin — but the reconstructed portion of the building will house a museum of Berlin Jewish history, a cultural and community center, an auditorium for films and stage performances, an education center, and an archive of German Jewry. It will also have a small synagogue. "We are going to give God an address on Oranienburgerstrasse again," says Konstantin Münz, a former East Berlin filmmaker who oversees the reconstruction for the community.

Renovation is already complete at the old East Berlin Jewish community headquarters, two doors from the synagogue at Oranienburgerstrasse 28. Some of the community offices and activities from the much larger — and space-poor — headquarters in western Berlin have already been transferred to the east. While waiting for the synagogue project's completion, the building hosts cultural programs as well as a library and administrative offices.

On the ground floor of the community building is Café Oren, a kosher fish and dairy restaurant that is always packed at night and on Sundays—mostly with non-Jews. Around the corner at Tucholsky-strasse 40 is the Oren's rival, Beth Café, another kosher restaurant, run by Adass Jisroel—a small, independent community that has reclaimed some of its prewar property, including a synagogue in the courtyard behind the café.

Berlin redux: As before the war, Jews live along the fashionable Kurfürstendamm

Head east on Oranienburgerstrasse and you'll soon hit Grosse Hamburgerstrasse, long an address of Jewish institutions. Despite its imposing name, it is a short and narrow street, and until recently little remained of its Jewish importance but monuments and a small cemetery. It was in 1778 that Moses Mendelssohn opened his Jüdische Freischule on the street, which taught both secular and Jewish subjects. Many of those educated at the Free School during its forty-eight years of existence went on to become leaders in the Reform movement of Judaism. Mendelssohn is buried in the cemetery across the street from number 26. In 1993 a new Jewish high school opened on the site of Mendelssohn's school.

In the twentieth century the street was also home to a large Jewish home for the aged, which the Gestapo took over in 1942 and used as an assembly point for Jews being deported. Some that the Nazis found useful lived in the building for long periods, and most of the 55,000 who passed through the building during the next three years knew the fate that awaited them. Most were sent to Auschwitz, but many sought passage to Thereisenstadt instead, where they knew chances of survival were better. Today, only a memorial plaque, standing in front of the cemetery, bears witness to the Jews shipped to their deaths from the site.

Evidence of a happier chapter in Berlin's Jewish story can be found nearby in the Nikolai district. The reconstructed Ephraim Palais, at the corner of Poststrasse and Mühlendamm, is still called by the name of its builder, Veitel Heine Ephraim, an eighteenth-century jeweler and, later, economic adviser to the Prussian emperor. When he was granted rights equal to those of Christian bankers, he built what came to be regarded as the most beautiful mansion in Berlin. The house, which has a riverfront restaurant on the ground floor, is a yellow stone structure with a red tile roof, and is recognizable by its golden wrought-iron balconies.

The Ephraim Palais is near Berlin's historic Rathaus, or Red City Hall. The street that runs along the northeast side of the Rathaus is Judenstrasse—named for the Jews who inhabited the area in the sixteenth century.

The fate of the Oranienburgerstrasse synagogue was in marked contrast to that of the Rykestrasse synagogue, for years the only functioning Jewish center of worship in East Berlin. A red-brick structure built in 1903, it was perhaps the best preserved synagogue in the city after the war. When, during the war, the building was transformed into a stable, the magnificent Byzantine *bimah* and ark were protected by a barrier erected, according to local legend, by a sympathetic engineer. The synagogue is in a courtyard entered through the double arches of a street-front building. A pointed arch tops the synagogue building. Inside is a sanctuary with a seventy-five-foot ceiling from which hang six chandeliers. A women's gallery surrounds the prayer hall on three sides, and a sweeping arch towers above the ark on the eastern wall.

Most services these days are in the small chapel with mahogany pews just off the main sanctuary. But if you miss the aesthetics of the larger hall, a service in the chapel is still a memorable experience. Even with as few as 15 in attendance, the synagogue has as diverse a collection of worshipers anywhere — old Germans, 1950s immigrants from Eastern Europe, new arrivals from Russia, longtime communists, former East German dissidents in old sweaters and jeans, young people (some straight looking, some dressed as punks), people who know the service well, and those who just seem to sit and meditate.

(Despite *Kristallnacht*, several Berlin temples survived the war. Courtyard synagogues were so close to other buildings that fire brigades tried to contain the damage. Visiting German synagogues, however, is not always easy. Since most community activity takes place at the community centers, synagogues tend to be open only at prayer times. Also bear in mind that synagogue security is tight.)

The main address of Berlin Jewry is still in the western part of the city. The Jewish Community Center at Fasanenstrasse 79–80 stands on the site of the great Liberal Synagogue opened in 1912 and heavily damaged on *Kristallnacht*. The modern building incorporated into its facade the domed arch that stood above the main synagogue entrance and one of the intact columns. Though some of its offices and functions have moved to Oranienburgerstrasse, this is still the seat of Berlin Jewry, and the place to call (884-2030) for information on community events, *kashrut*, or prayer times at any of the city's synagogues. The center has a theater, lecture and exhibit halls, a sixty thousand-volume library and a kosher restaurant, as well as a synagogue used mainly on the High Holy Days. There is a small permanent exhibit in the lobby featuring ritual objects and a photographic history of the Fasanenstrasse synagogue. Typical of the special exhibits was the recently mounted display of paintings based on set designs of the theater director Max Reinhardt.

The gem of synagogues in western Berlin is the Liberal congregation in the courtyard at Pestalozzistrasse 14. The red-brick neo-Romanesque building was opened in 1912, damaged on *Kristallnacht*, and restored after the war. The sanctuary is surrounded by four large alcoves and three *Magen David* stained-glass windows. With its eclectic custom and ritual, the synagogue is designated as Liberal. The sexes sit separately but almost equally — men in the central portion of the main floor and women in the side sections of the main floor as well as in the traditional upstairs gallery. The cantor sings in Sephardic Hebrew but his choir uses Ashkenazic pronunciation.

Also worth seeing is the Orthodox synagogue in the courtyard of Joachimstalerstrasse 13, which survived *Kristallnacht* because it was not yet a synagogue. Built in 1902 as a Masonic lodge, the light-gray stone building with narrow arching windows has the look of a turn-of-the-century mansion. The finely sculpted walls and ceiling are complemented by red, blue, and yellow stained-glass windows and mahogany-stained pews. A five-minute walk from the Fasanenstrasse community center, it is the only Berlin synagogue with weekday services. Its building also houses several Jewish community organizations.

The exhibits in the Oranienburgerstrasse center will complement the city's existing Jewish Museum, which is a division of the Berlin Museum. Like the Oranienburgerstrasse building, however, the Jewish Museum is in transition. The bulk of the collection is housed temporarily in the Martin Gropius Bau, a Wilhelminian style building noteworthy for its location. It is adjacent to one of the few sections of the Berlin Wall left standing, and next to an open field that is all that is left of Gestapo headquarters.

In this inauspicious locale is a cornucopia of Judaica: a Worms *machzor* from 1272; a copy of the first German translation of the Babylonian Talmud (the czar ordered several dozen copies, the king of Prussia, none); paintings of prominent Berlin Jews; and various *Kiddush* cups, menorahs and other ritual objects, many of which were found in Berlin antique shops in the 1950s. One of the most striking objects is a drawing of a Yom Kippur service of German soldiers at the siege of Metz, during the Franco-Prussian war; the worshipers are garbed in *tallesim* and pointed Prussian helmets.

This corner of Berlin was ignored during the early postwar period. Hard against the wall, it attracted mostly Turkish immigrants. Ironically, it was the opening of the Gropius building and its mostly Jewish collection in the early 1980s that focused attention on the former Gestapo site next door. The building had been the Prince Albert Hotel before being occupied by the Gestapo; heavily damaged by Allied bombings, it was razed in 1945. Plans to build on the lot were ultimately scrapped in favor of the open-air "memorial learning area" that it is today. Called Topographie des Terrors, it is a mostly bare patch of ground with some basement excavations remaining. In a corner of the lot next to the Gropius Bau is a small building sitting on top of the most extensive of the basement chambers. Inside is a photo exhibit on the Gestapo and its tactics as well as of the history of the neighborhood. On the lower level are several rooms built by inmates from the Sachsenhausen concentration camp. Though the bare brick rooms give the impression of prison cells (and some Berliners still believe they were torture chambers), they were, in fact, part of the building's kitchen.

The main building of the Berlin Museum is a few block from the Gropius building, at Lindenstrasse 14. The Lindenstrasse building also has a Judaica room which features, among other things, a model of the Fasanenstrasse synagogue and a micrographic drawing of Kaiser Wilhelm II, done after the kaiser had given money for the rebuilding of a synagogue in East Prussia. In addition to the Judaica, the Berlin Museum has many portraits by Jewish artists, such as Max Lieberman and Lesser Ury, and turn-of-the-century cityscapes by Julius Jacob.

The entire Lindenstrasse building was scheduled to close in 1993, probably for the duration of the construction of the new Jewish Museum building next door. The new museum, which will show German history through the experience of Jews, is designed to attract Jewish and non-Jewish audiences. The controversial design will feature a zigzag-shaped modern building with a black "void" running across its length. Standing for the period from 1933–45 — the pivotal years through which all German Jewish history before and since will be considered — the void will confront visitors as they walk through each exhibition room.

At Stauffenbergstrasse 13, near the Tiergarten, stands a memorial to an honorable episode of the Nazi period. The German Resistance Memorial (Gedenkstätte Deutscher Wiederstand) is located in the former Army High Command building where German officers, led by Generals Claus Graf Schenk von Stauffenberg and Ludwig Beck, plotted to kill Adolf Hitler. When the plot failed on July 20, 1944, several of the officers involved were captured in the building and executed on the spot. The building is now a museum of the entire range of German resistance. Its unusual setup includes twenty-six rooms, each dedicated to a different aspect of the Third Reich and German resistance. There are rooms documenting resistance — amid collaboration — among artists, workers, Christians, students and the military, as well as exhibits on the development of Nazism, the history of the Weimar Republic and the persecution of Jews.

Berlin has monuments to many of its prominent Jewish sons and daughters. One example is Walter Rathenau, who achieved the highest political office — foreign minister — of any Jew in German history. Rathenau was, according to the historian Gordon Craig, "like Heinrich Heine, a disturber of the peace, one whose achievements were a provocation that brought the hatred of less gifted men down upon him. Unfortunately for him, he had neither the wit nor the joy in outraging the philistines that sustained Heine, nor did he possess Heine's superb self-confidence, which enabled him to admit his Jewishness without for a moment doubting his essential Germanness." Unlike Heine, however, Rathenau resisted baptism. "I could have avoided . . . disadvantages by conversion," he wrote, "but then I would have been condoning the breach of justice committed by the ruling classes."

Three months after being appointed foreign minister, Rathenau was assassinated, riding in an open car, at the corner of Erdenerstrasse and Königsallee. A stone monument marks the spot today. There is another plaque at Rathenau's house, the yellow-stone Empire-style mansion at 65 Königsallee.

Berlin's western outskirts have the city's recreation areas—lakes and beaches, forests and villas. It was in this atmosphere that the fate of European Jewry was prescribed. At 58 Am Grossen Wansee is the site of the infamous Wansee Conference, the meeting in January 1942 at which the Nazis embarked on the Final Solution—the extermination of the Jewish people. Built as a seaside home in 1914, the Grecian-style villa was bought by the SS in 1940. Reinhard Heydrich convened the conference; Aldolf Eichmann took the minutes. Today the place where they met is a museum—the Memorial Home of the Wansee Conference—documenting the segregation, persecution, and genocide of Europe's Jews. Photos line the walls of each room—of Aryan-only park benches and of Jewish freedom fighters in the Warsaw Ghetto, of death camps and of all the conference participants who had them built. In addition to exhibits the memorial building has a multimedia library and hosts educational seminars.

Also in Berlin's western reaches is Spandau, best remembered as the longtime prison home of Rudolf Hess. The neighborhood is also the site of the Spandau Citadel, a twelfth-century fortress that is used for festivals and cultural events. In the 1960s archaeologists found sixty Jewish tombstones, dating from the fourteenth century, embedded in the citadel's wall. Though there are plans to eventually transfer the stones to the Jewish Museum, they are currently arranged in the courtyard of the citadel. Some of the Hebrew inscriptions are readable, and a large sign, in German, deciphers nineteen of them. The number of stones found indicated the importance of the Jewish community of Spandau; even Berlin Jews were buried in Spandau during this period. The cemetery from which the stones came was destroyed when Jews were blamed for spreading the Plague in 1349–50.

Culture: More often than not, at least one of the city's theaters features something of Jewish content or interest. If you don't understand German—or can't make a go of it with Yiddish—look for a show you're already familiar with, particularly a musical, and see it in a foreign language.

Specifically Jewish culture in all its forms can be found at the Jewish Community Centers on Fasanenstrasse and Oranienburgerstrasse. Two publications—the weekly *Berliner Allgemeine Jüdische Wochenzeitung* and the community's monthly *Berlin-Umschau*—list lectures, plays and exhibits at the community centers and elsewhere. Both publications also give prayer times for all of Berlin's synagogues. In addition to community-center spectacles, many of Israel's cultural companies, from Habima to the Israel Philharmonic and the Jerusalem Symphony, regularly include Berlin on their itineraries.

Personalities: Two of the leading Berlin bankers of the nineteenth century were Gerson von Bleichroder, financier of Germany's railroads and advisor to Bismarck; and Carl Furstenberg, financier of heavy industry and also noted for his wit. Leading theater figures of the twentieth century were the composer Kurt Weill, who continued his career in the United States in 1935, and Max Reinhardt. The film director Ernst Lubitsch, maker of *Ninotchka,* left Berlin for Hollywood in 1922. Walter Kerr elevated literary criticism to an art form; some of his poems were put to music by Richard Strauss. Hugo Preuss, creator of the Weimar Constitution, was a liberal post-World War I minister of interior; Otto Landsburg was a conservative minister of justice. Berlin was also the home of the poet Nelly Sachs and the philosopher and kabbalist Gershom Scholem.

Leo Blech and Otto Klemperer were both conductors of the Berlin Opera. Today the director of the German State Opera-Berlin is Daniel Barenboim. Noted postwar German Jewish writers include Edgar Hilsenrath and Stefan Heym. Among the Berlin natives who fled as children were Aryeh Neier, director of the American Civil Liberties Union, director Mike Nichols, composer-conductor André Previn, and former senator Rudy Boschwitz of Minnesota.

The best-known Jewish personality of postwar Berlin was undoubtedly Heinz Galinski, a Holocaust survivor who rebuilt the community and who used the weight of his personality and German conscience to make himself and the Jewish community a force on the national scene. Galinski died in 1991, but he established the role of Jewish community head as a major position in German life.

General Sights: Seeing the sights of Jewish interest in Berlin will take you across the general landscape, from the shops and cafés along the Kurfürstendamm to the Reichstag and the Brandenburg Gate. If you want to get away from twentieth-century concerns, visit the Charlottenburg Castle, with its apartments and household objects of the Prussian royal family and collection of antiquities. The Pergamon Museum has spectacular antiquities, including entire building facades, from ancient Rome, Greece, and Babylonia.

You can spend an entire day in the Dahlem Museum complex. The Rembrandt collection in its Picture Gallery (section E, second floor) is one of the best in Europe, and about half of the Rembrandts are on Hebrew Bible themes. The best known is *Moses Holding the Tablets of the Law.* Look also for *Jacob Wrestling with the Angel, Joseph's Dream, Joseph Accused by Potiphar's Wife, Samson and Delilah,* and *Portrait of a Young Jew.* In addition to Rembrandt's works, the museum has Willem Dorst's *Vision of Daniel,* Orazio Gentileschi's *Lot and His Daughters,* and Jacopo Amigone's *Abraham Offers Jacob.*

Reading: The great novel of 1920s Berlin is Alfred Döblin's *Berlin Alexanderplatz* (Frederick Ungar Publishing). Another view of the era can be found in Christopher Isherwood's *Berlin Stories* (New Directions), the basis for the musical *Cabaret.* Harold Nebenzal's *Café Berlin* (Overlook) is a compelling novel of a prewar cabaret owner who spends the last four years of the war hiding in a Berlin attic. The Berlin airlift, with Jewish characters, is the focus of Leon Uris's novel *Armageddon* (Doubleday). Gershon Scholem's memoir, *From Berlin to Jerusalem* (Schocken), offers some insight into the German Zionist movement that developed two decades before Hitler. *Stella*, by Peter Wyden (Simon and Schuster), is a chilling account of Jews who worked for the Gestapo and describes life in the building on Grosse Hamburgerstrasse from which Berlin's Jews were deported.

In addition to the film versions of *Berlin Alexanderplatz* and *Cabaret*, there is the 1932 classic *Grand Hotel* and the more recent Broadway adaptation, both based on the novel by Vicki Baum; and one of the funniest movies ever made, *One, Two, Three,* in which James Cagney plays the Yiddish-spouting Irish director of Coca-Cola in West Berlin.

Recommendations: The German National Tourist Office, 122 East 42nd Street, New York, NY 10168 (212-661-7200) has a wealth of information on Jewish sights and deals with Jewish inquiries on a daily basis. The Kempinski Hotel, across the street from the Jewish Community Center on Fasanenstrasse, is a luxurious inn in an ideal locale. The Berlin Hilton is convenient to the more easterly Jewish sites in and around Oranienburgerstrasse. Wherever you stay, however, you will be near some Jewish point of reference. Whether as shadows of the past or outposts of the present and future, the Jewish presence is everywhere in Berlin.

—Alan M. Tigay

Birobidjan

You had expected the place to retain some Jewish flavor. Still, after a wearying four-hour train journey across a swampy sub-Arctic landscape eerily devoid of habitation, you are thrilled upon arrival at your destination to find the name of the city emblazoned in Hebrew lettering on the side of the station.

You walk several blocks to your hotel on the town's main drag, which turns out to be called "Shalom Aleichem Street." In your room, you find a complimentary copy of the local Yiddish-language newspaper. Later, after an indifferent meal in the hotel restaurant cum dance hall, you choke up a bit when the local rock band breaks into its signature tune—a sweetly romantic ballad called "Jewish Eyes."

Where in the world are you anyway? Certainly not in Israel, despite the manifold signs of *Yiddishkeit.* No, this somewhat surreal Jewish burg plunked down literally in the middle of nowhere is Birobidjan, the down-home and *heimisch* capital of the Jewish Autonomous District (JAD), a remote and little known region in the far east of Siberia. The JAD happens to be the world's only Jewish political entity besides Israel, and at nineteen thousand square miles, it is twice the size of Israel itself.

Ironically, given Birobidjan's uniqueness in the Jewish world, relatively few western Jews are even aware of its existence, and those who do know something about the place tend to refer to it in distinctly derisive terms. Indeed, even Birobidjan's most ardent civic boosters concede that until the collapse of Soviet Communism in 1991, the JAD's negative reputation was richly deserved.

Birobidjan was, after all, the creation of the murderous Soviet dictator Joseph Stalin, who founded the place in 1934 with the hope of solving Russia's centuries-old "Jewish problem" by creating a Jewish homeland in the wilds of Siberia and encouraging as many Russian Jews as possible to emigrate there.

As it turned out, the grandiose Birobidjan project never really got off the drawing board. Only a few thousand Jewish idealists were willing to trade the relative comfort and security of their homes in European Russia and Ukraine for lives of back-breaking labor in a swamp-ridden wilderness. And whatever appeal the place might have had as a nascent Jewish polity vanished in the 1940s after Stalin closed Jewish schools and theaters in Birobidjan and elsewhere in the Soviet Union, falsely accusing Jewish writers and doctors of plotting against the Soviet leadership.

Birobidjan became a grotesque Potemkin village of Jewishness, a place Soviet propagandists pointed to as evidence of their goodwill toward the Jews. Genuine Jewish expression was virtually banned. Official anti-Semitism was so rife that many Jews in the Jewish Autonomous District reregistered their nationality as "Russian," to increase their children's educational and employment opportunities. Despite the discrimination and the climate, however, the Jewish veneer of Birobidjan survived.

Only with the easing of repression in the past few years has there been a modest renaissance of Jewish expression in the JAD. But that resurgence has been undercut by the emigration to Israel and the United States of several thousand Birobidjan Jews—including those most committed to their Jewishness.

Recently declared a free economic zone with considerable political autonomy, the

JAD is today a friendly and unpretentious place that, while admittedly short on creature comforts, has much to offer adventurous Jewish visitors interested in exploring one of the strangest anomalies of twentieth-century Jewish life.

History: The JAD was officially inaugurated in 1934. The concept of creating a Jewish region in a hitherto unpopulated part of Siberia flowed from Lenin's nationalities policy, which posited that each of the scores of ethnic groups in the far-flung Soviet Union should have its own territory where it could nurture its individual language and culture while contributing to the overall building of socialism. The commissars also viewed the Birobidjan project as a politically correct alternative to the counterrevolutionary virus of Zionism, which had received its most ardent support from Russian Jews.

Yiddish-speaking *shlichim* (emissaries) were dispatched to centers of Jewish activism around the world to recruit young idealists to come to the Soviet Union to build the new Jewish paradise in the Far East. One who answered the call was Ilya Bliecherman, a Birobidjan resident now in his late eighties, and one of the last survivors of Birobidjan's pioneering era. A Polish Jew with communist sympathies who had emigrated to Argentina in his teens, Bliecherman was immediately inspired to join the pioneering enterprise after listening to an emissary from Moscow in 1931.

"We were tremendously enthusiastic because we had been dreaming about the revolution, and now we were being offered a chance to participate in building it," he recalls. Upon arriving in the nascent Siberian Jewish enclave the following year, Bliecherman joined a rural commune of young idealists, who spent years clearing virgin forests, draining swamps, and preparing the land for farming. "The conditions were brutal," Bliecherman says. "But despite the hardships, I was doing exactly what I wanted to do." It was only in 1936, when Stalin began his murderous purges, that Bliecherman and many of the other true believers who had come from Russia and abroad had occasion for doubt. "One by one, the people began to disappear from our commune," he remembers. "At first I assumed that those arrested really were enemies of the people. But then they began arresting people who were close to me, who I knew had done nothing wrong. But no one could open his mouth. We were all deathly afraid we would be next."

Only a handful of Birobidjan's best and brightest who were arrested during the 1930s purges ever emerged from the gulag. Bliecherman, who managed to avoid their fate because he was protected by a friend in the Cheka, the precursor of the KGB, moved to Birobidjan city after the war just in time to witness the impact of Stalin's "anticosmopolitan" campaign on Jewish life here. The intelligentsia, artists, and writers were all arrested, and the Jewish schools were closed down. Many Jews sought to protect themselves by changing their family names to Russian ones.

Although Stalin thoroughly vitiated the Jewishness of the JAD, he still had a sinister plan to fill it with Jews. At the end of 1952, the Soviet press was filled with fantastic stories about Jewish doctors plotting to kill the Kremlin leadership — all part of a campaign orchestrated by Stalin, who had grown ever more anti-Semitic in his later years. The planned culmination of the hate campaign was to be the exile of the entire Soviet Jewish population to Birobidjan and other parts of Siberia. Only the dictator's death in March 1953 led to the last-minute cancellation of the planned deportation.

For more than thirty years thereafter, Birobidjan lingered as a sluggish backwater, off limits to foreign visitors — presumably to prevent Jews from the West from finding out how fraudulent was the Soviet presentation of Birobidjan as a Jewish paradise. While the Yiddish-language *Birobidjaner Shtern* managed to keep functioning, it was essentially a Jewish version of *Pravda*, utterly devoid of Jewish content, and fond of excoriating Israel as the "racist Zionist entity." Also during this period nearly all the Jews who lived on agricultural communes in the JAD abandoned the difficult life on the land, moving into the town of Birobidjan or back to Russia proper.

Jewishness began to make a limited comeback in the last years of Leonid Brezhnev's "period of stagnation." Perhaps out of concern that Jewish critics of the Soviet

Union would point out the anomaly that there was no functioning synagogue in the JAD, the Birobidjan city administration sanctioned the opening of a tiny one-room *shul*, despite the near total lack of interest in Judaism by Birobidjan Jews.

The real revival of Jewish culture in Birobidjan began in 1989. A Jewish cultural center was set up with a full complement of programming, including courses in Jewish music and dance for children, and courses in Yiddish for both children and adults. An annual festival of Jewish songs was inaugurated. *Shlichim* from Israel were allowed to visit, both to teach Hebrew and promulgate *aliyah*. A Jewish day school opened in 1992.

The *Birobidjaner Shtern*, which now publishes daily in both Yiddish and Russian (only a small percentage of the paper's readers today are conversant in Yiddish) made a 180-degree turn from its former anti-Zionist orientation and now writes in warm terms about life in Israel. The regional administration also began courting Israel, hoping to parlay the JAD's unique Jewish status into foreign economic ties.

But the Jewish revival has been sapped by the emigration to Israel of many of the region's best educated residents. The vast majority of the Jews who have stayed on have only the most minimal connection to Jewish culture and identity. "Birobidjan is the capital of the Jewish Autonomous District, and we are therefore doing everything possible to make Birobidjan a center of Jewish culture," says the town's mayor, Victor Bolotov, an ethnic Russian who is not Jewish. The next several years will tell whether there is enough *Yiddishkeit* left to make that a realizable dream.

Community: The last official census, conducted in late 1991, recorded 8,900 Jews in the JAD, only 4 percent of a total population of 220,000 that is mainly composed of ethnic Russians and Ukrainians. (Nearly all of the Jews live in the capital city of Birobidjan, which has a population of 100,000.) The Jewish population seems stable because as identifying Jews emigrate many who have long been registered as Russians are now openly proclaiming their Jewishness, and a sizable percentage of the

non-Jews acknowledge that they have some Jewish blood.

Jews and non-Jews agree that if anti-Semitism exists in Birobidjan at all, it is on a much lower level than anywhere else in the former Soviet Union. Even the vast majority of the non-Jews seem interested in nurturing ties with Israel and world Jewry in the hope of ending the region's isolation and of spurring economic development.

Community leaders say that their main concern is not so much that virtually the entire Jewish population is about to emigrate, but rather that only a small percentage of those who call themselves Jews have much Jewish identity or involvement in Jewish life. The low level of Jewish identification can be seen most dramatically at the city's only synagogue, a humble wooden house on a muddy side street on the eastern edge of town (at 3 Mayakovsky Street). Normally locked during the week, it opens on *Shabbat*, but generally to welcome a large and enthusiastic contingent of Seventh Day Adventists, led by a converted Jew named Boris Kaufman, who serves as synagogue *shamas* for both the Jews and the Adventists. The community has never had a rabbi. A few elderly Jews turn up for prayer on most Saturdays, but there are rarely enough for a *minyan*. A larger number turn up on the High Holy Days and on Passover.

Despite the absence of Jewish religious life, there has been a vigorous surge in Jewish organizational activity. The Birobidjan Council of Jewish Organizations now includes ten member groups, including a women's group, a Betar chapter, a Hebrew teachers' organization, a businessmen's cooperative, an organization dedicated to the perpetuation of Yiddish, and a Maccabi sports club.

The most ambitious of the Council's projects is the National Jewish Primary School, which recreates the last Jewish school in Birobidjan, closed by Soviet authorities in 1948. The school combines the standard Russian curriculum with instruction in Yiddish, Jewish history and culture. Less attention is being devoted to Hebrew. Community officials say that while they do not oppose *aliyah*, they are hoping the school will promote a love of Yiddish among the younger generation of Jews and help ensure the survival of a Jewish community in Birobidjan.

Sights: The best way to reach Birobidjan is to fly from Moscow to the eastern Siberian city of Khabarovsk and then take the train from there. (Khabarovsk can also be reached from Japan or from Anchorage via Alaska Airlines.) Adventurers with time on their hands can also reach Birobidjan from Moscow on the Trans-Siberian Express, a trip that takes seven days. After crossing the wide Amur River just outside Khabarovsk, the train enters the eastern JAD—a marshy, flat-as-a-pancake landscape that sometimes evokes the Everglades. Staring out the greasy window of the train at the swampy, almost featureless, landscape, one gets an appreciation of the overwhelming hardships that must have confronted the Jews who set out to drain swamps and hack their way through virgin forests.

Built on once malarial swampland, the city of Birobidjan itself retains a rural flavor. In much of the city streets are muddy and unpaved and lined with the one-storied *izbas* (colorful wooden houses with distinctively carved windows) that are so characteristic of Russian small towns. The largest factory in town produces farm machinery, and cows graze in a pasture alongside the city's modern and pretentious Philharmonic building, an example of late communist grandiloquence jarringly out of character with the humble nature of the rest of the place.

Although Birobidjan sprawls along an east-west axis, the central district, squeezed between the railway station and the sluggish Bira River, is only about four blocks wide, and all sites of Jewish and general interest, with the exception of the slightly out of the way synagogue, can be seen on foot.

A good place to start is the Historical Museum of the JAD, which is located at 25 Lenin Street. (Birobidjan has been slower than cities like Moscow and St. Petersburg in erasing visible manifestations of the communist period; hammer and sickle symbols still hang from the facades of most public buildings. Nevertheless, visitors to Birobidjan should be aware of the possibility that Lenin and other streets may have been renamed by the time they arrive.)

The Historical Museum has two main exhibitions, one focusing on the rich natural ecology of the region, and the other a stunning evocation of the JAD's history called "To Be or Not to Be: Repressed Jewish Culture in the JAD." The exhibition begins with evocative black-and-white blown-up images of purposeful pioneers who came from western Russia, as well as America, Argentina, Poland, and other countries, standing up to their knees in swamp water, as they struggle to build communes in the Siberian wilderness. The faces are smiling and full of hope, achingly similar to photographs of the founding *kibbutz* fathers and mothers at Deganya and Ein Harod.

All too soon, though, the visitor enters a hall dedicated to the Stalinist liquidation of the Jewish intelligentsia of Birobidjan, symbolized by a huge Star of David fashioned from barbed wire. Here are pictures of members of Jewish schools and theaters closed by the dictator and haunting photographs of the doomed artists and writers alongside letters they sent home from the bleak gulag camps before succumbing to sickness and cold. The exhibition ends on a more hopeful note, showing the reorganized Jewish theatrical and classical music ensembles that began springing up in the 1980s. The viewer is left to ponder whether the renaissance comes in time to resuscitate the vibrant Jewish life so ruthlessly smothered by Stalin fifty years ago.

The other must-see museum in Birobidjan is the Museum of Old Testament Painting, located in the Birobidjan House of Culture, 11 Shalom Aleichem Street. The museum is Russia's only art museum devoted to Hebrew Bible themes, with more than two hundred works by modern painters—Jews and non-Jews from Birobidjan and all around the former Soviet Union. Many are avant-garde works painted in the Stagnation period and only recently shown in public for the first time. Some mix biblical and modern political imagery, like a prophetic painting of a vainglorious but collapsing Tower of Babel looking suspiciously like the Soviet Union of the Brezhnev era, by a Novosibirsk artist named Tolpekin. There are lushly surreal Rousseau-like evocations of the Garden of Eden, and a picture of a blue-jean clad

Jacob struggling with an angel clearly meant to represent his conscience.

The House of Culture is the home of both the Birobidjan Jewish Theater and the Eva Folk Dance Collective, which perform most weekends when they are not traveling around the former Soviet Union or abroad. The Jewish theater group is known for splashy musical numbers ranging from Shalom Aleichem to the modern Jewish experience; a recent production portrayed the travails of a Russian posing as a Jew who made *aliyah* to Haifa. Eva, which sponsors both children's and adult troupes, performs Israeli and traditional *shtetl* dances, as well as Russian and Ukrainian folk dances.

The offices of the Jewish community of Birobidjan are also located at the House of Culture, and a visitor seeking to find out what is going on Jewishly in town should drop in and talk to the friendly people there. To get a glimpse of the town's most concrete manifestation of the Jewish revival, visit the new Jewish school, located in Public School Number Two on Lenin Street, next to the Historical Museum — the very site of the last Jewish school in town closed down in 1948.

After you have toured the requisite Jewish sites, visit the city's fascinating outdoor market (alongside the East Hotel on Shalom Aleichem) where you can see a colorful collection of Siberian babushkas, Central Asian merchants, and traveling gypsies selling fruits, vegetables, and combinations of roots and berries said to have medicinal value against a variety of ailments. Also worth a look is the garish Philharmonic Hall, which is part of a complex of grandiose buildings wedged between Soviet Culture Street and the Bira River.

Side Trip: If Birobidjan's Jewish story today is fully urban, it should not be forgotten that many of the early Jewish pioneers came to farm and settle the land. You can get a feel for those rural Jewish roots and a glimpse of collectivist agriculture in post-Soviet Russia by visiting the *kolkhoz* (collective farm) of Valdheim, about ten miles south of the city. There is only one Jew left in the village of about 2,000 — a seventyish widow named Faiga Faiman, but when the place was founded in the mid-1930s, virtually the entire population was Jewish. At the village's prominent World War II memorials nearly all of those honored have Jewish names. One, Vladimir Israelovitch Peller, was honored with several of the former Soviet Union's highest military honors, and received the oddly medieval-sounding title "Cavalier of Three Orders of Glory."

If Birobidjan seems slow paced and laid back, Valdheim (the name means "house in the forest" in Yiddish) is downright somnolent. Cows wander unhurriedly down the main street, and in the general store villagers and passers-by conduct the kind of leisurely, lingering discussion on the state of rural Russia that suggests that even on a workday afternoon no one is in any great hurry to get about their business.

Everyone seems to agree that despite all the promises from Moscow of imminent land privatization, nothing much has changed at Valdheim; the collectivist agriculture of the past sixty years continues essentially unaltered. Most people seem to prefer it that way; the younger ones with initiative who might have shaken things up have mostly moved to the city.

Faiman, who still heads a work brigade in the potato fields, is, like her urban counterpart Bliecherman, a true believer in the socialist ideal. She says the collapse of the Soviet Union is "not exactly a wonderful development," explaining, "We appreciated Soviet values." She lives alone in a cozy house on the main street of town that she built with her husband and appreciates visitors with whom she can reminisce over a cup of tea. Brought from Ukraine by her parents as a young child, she recalls that her primary-school education was in Yiddish and that Russian was taught as a foreign language. Three of Faiman's children now live in Birobidjan and one daughter in Israel. But she herself will never leave. "I love living and working on the land," she asserts. "I would go crazy to be cooped up in a city apartment."

The southwestern part of the JAD, a rugged land of five thousand-foot mountains, rushing rivers, and a rich wildlife including elk, bears, and wolves, is a naturalist's delight. Almost completely uninhabited and unpenetrated by roads, the area is now beginning to be developed for ecological tourism by local entrepreneurs and the JAD government. The region is said to include some world-class caves, including one that is two hundred feet deep and has an underground lake that is perpetually frozen over.

Recommendations: There is only one Birobidjan hotel even remotely close to Western standards — the Vostok (East) Hotel at 1 Shalom Aleichem Street. (To confuse matters, the hotel is popularly referred to as the "Central" Hotel, so don't be surprised if you mention the "Vostok" and no one knows what you are talking about.) The price is certainly right; unlike tourist hotels in Moscow and other major Russian cities, which demand hard currency at West European rates, the Vostok at last check still allowed foreigners to pay for their rooms in rubles (on a recent visit this still came to $6 a night). The rooms are small but clean and the furniture is plain, and the Vostok is one of the few Russian hotels with mosquito netting on the windows — a touch you will certainly appreciate if you visit in the summer.

Some restaurants in town claim to specialize in Jewish cuisine; most of them offer pork dishes among their culinary specialties. The best of an indifferent lot may be Maas. Located in the Philharmonic building, the tiny restaurant has a private entrance marked by a large Star of David. It offers an eclectic collection of Russian Jewish dishes including a beef in a tasty sweet-and-sour sauce and salted fish in a butter sauce. The clientele is interesting too; many of Birobidjan's young entrepreneurs — most of whom seem to be Jewish — get together to cut deals.

Information on eco-tourism can be obtained through the JAD regional government, or through the Eva Association, which has its office at 2 Shalom Aleichem Street, directly across from the Vostok. The Eva Association, a semiprivate concern with close ties to the regional government, is also the place to turn for Western businesspeople interested in learning about opportunities in the JAD. Birobidjan is largely undeveloped with abundant raw materials, and its free-trade-zone status, its location along the Chinese border, and — locals hope — the intangibles that come with being a "Jewish region," make the JAD a potentially more profitable candidate for development than other parts of Russia.

Western Jews who visit, whether for business or simply to see the lost Jewish enclave in the Far East, can expect a warm welcome from Birobidjaners. Anxious for contact with foreigners after decades of isolation, the residents of this remote land — Jews and Russians alike — are friendly, openhearted people with a commitment to hospitality. Like elsewhere in Russia, people are hard pressed by soaring prices and food shortages. But that won't prevent them from inviting you to their homes for memorable evenings of food, conversation, and frequent shouts of *l'chayim* over the vodka bottle. The people of Birobidjan, like the wide open spaces they inhabit, truly merit the adjective "unspoiled."

—Walter Ruby

Bombay

Bombay is to India what New York is to the United States: a brawny, bustling gateway akin to, but atypical of, the country onto which it opens.

This is India's wealthiest city—its primary port, its commercial hub, even its Hollywood. Indeed, Bombay produces more films annually than the United States; its high-rises command rents that rival New York's. Cars and people clog its streets; it teems and throbs at all hours of the day—and night.

By Indian standards, Bombay is untraditional; change touches it far faster than it does other spots, making it the country's pacesetter. Furthermore, it is cosmopolitan, attracting both foreigners and Indians from every corner of the land. Hundreds pour in each week to a metropolis that offers jobs, if not housing. The newcomers speak ten—maybe twenty—different tongues; they mingle with others of variegated background. Hindus, Muslims, Sikhs, Jains, Christians, and Parsis all participate in the whirl of Bombay. So, too, do Jews.

Community: The Jewish community in Bombay today—perhaps 5,000 in all—is actually made up of the remnants of three decidedly distinct communities. By far the largest group in the city are members of B'nai Israel, those Jews who consider themselves indigenous; who speak Marathi, the language of Bombay's state of Maharashtra; and who date their presence in the region back two thousand years. The tiniest segment—if, indeed, a mere handful can be considered that—are Cochinese, whose ancestors arrived in India at least one thousand and possibly two thousand years ago. And 150, maybe a few more, remain of those who came to India last, but made the biggest splash—Jews from Iraq called Baghdadis, who settled only in the nineteenth century, but whose numbers included members of the renowned Sassoon dynasty.

Once the Cochin Jews had a thriving community of their own on India's Malabar Coast, 600 miles south of Bombay. The Baghdadis had been primarily businessmen who spoke Arabic, hobnobbed with the British, and held themselves aloof from the other Jews. Among the many buildings they erected were two synagogues in Bombay and one, a churchlike structure, in Poona (or Pune), a hill city about one hundred miles from Bombay. The B'nai Israel themselves once numbered thirty-five thousand, had entered many walks of Indian life, and had eight synagogues in Bombay and fourteen in nearby areas.

What decimated all these groups was the birth of independent India in 1947 and of Israel in 1948. The Baghdadis, fearing reprisal for their close association with the British, headed primarily for England, Canada, and the United States, while the Cochinese and the B'nai Israel, motivated by both economics and idealism, emigrated to Israel.

Thus, even in Bombay, India's Jewish center, the remaining Jews have more or less banded together. They intermarry, share social, civic, and philanthropic events, and visit one another's synagogues. Indeed, the Baghdadis, who once scorned the B'nai Israel way of practicing the Sephardic rite, now hire B'nai Israel men to make a *minyan*. Essentially, then, the Bombay Jewish community of today is a B'nai Israel one—as it was originally.

History: The B'nai Israel of Bombay, who have lived far removed from the main stream of Judaism, tell a story that, both in length and in content, differs decidedly from most other Diaspora communities. Indeed, a key feature in this history, which, after all, is not of the Western world, is the total absence of anti-Semitism.

The start of the tale is not certain. It may have begun with Jews escaping persecution in Israel following the destruction of the First Temple, or perhaps the Second Temple. Or these Jews may have merely been traders sailing the route of King Solomon's ships to the once flourishing port, just north of Bombay, of Suparika (now Nala-Soparal)—which some today think was the biblical Ophir.

In any event, B'nai Israel tradition says that, off the Konkan Coast—which is the mainland just across the creek from the islands that have formed Bombay—there was a shipwreck, which only seven couples survived. They settled where they climbed ashore, at Navgaon, down the coast from Bombay, and became coconut-oil pressers.

Because, in a caste-conscious land, this had a low social rating, some say the Jews chose it to render their women undesirable to the local populace. Probably, though, they adopted this occupation initially because they knew it from their homeland. Later they worked in agriculture and the military, in the service of nawabs and maharajahs who appreciated their lack of allegiance to either the Hindu or the Muslim cause.

Since all had been lost in the shipwreck, the B'nai Israel had no written guidelines for practicing Judaism. Thus, as the centuries passed and they spread out along the Konkan Coast, they began adopting some of their neighbors' practices. However, they did keep those rituals they remembered— certain dietary laws, circumcision, the Sabbath (at first they were dubbed *Shanwar telis* or "Saturday oilmen" for not working that day), and the *Shema*, which became an all-purpose prayer.

Then, in the eighteenth century (although a B'nai Israel legend places it in the eleventh), a Sephardic Jew, David Rahabi, visited the B'nai Israel, decided they were indeed Jewish, and began instructing them in Judaism—which they took to Bombay.

They weren't the first Jews to set foot there, however. In the sixteenth century, when Bombay was still a group of seven fishing islands controlled by Portugal, the Portuguese leased the main one, for his services to the viceroy, to García da Orta, a noted Converso scientist and physician. A century later, though, in 1661, Portugal gave the islands to England as part of the dowry for Catherine of Braganza when she married Charles II. And shortly afterward one Benjamin Franks jumped a ship under Captain William Kidd's command there and provided the deposition that led to Kidd's London trial for piracy.

The B'nai Israel began crossing the creek to Bombay when the British started turning it into a trading area and a fort. With their military prowess, they assumed they could find government jobs. At least one distinguished himself early on. Samuel Divekar, who joined the East India Company in 1750, ultimately became a commandant and went into battle against the powerful Tipu, sultan of Mysore. Tipu was a ruthless Muslim who gave his prisoners of war a choice: conversion to Islam or death. According to legend, when Divekar was captured, brought before Tipu, and asked his religion, he stated it. The sultan's mother, who was watching, interrupted, saying that because the Koran spoke well of the Jews, Divekar should be spared.

When he returned to Bombay in 1796, in gratitude he built the first B'nai Israel synagogue. Initially it was called the Samuel Street Synagogue, because the street on which it stood had been named for Divekar; it was later renamed Shaar Harahamim, or Gate of Mercy.

At about this time the Baghdadis, driven by persecution in Iraq, began moving East, and David Sassoon, founder of the Sassoon dynasty in India, arrived in 1833. He and his eight sons and their descendants made their mark as the "Rothschilds of the East." Internationally, they developed a great trading empire—a major item was opium— and in Bombay they built hospitals, schools, and libraries, as well as two Baghdadi synagogues, Magen David, in 1861, and Keneseth Eliyahoo in 1884. Among the Sassoons who distinguished themselves individually were Albert Sassoon, who constructed the Sassoon Docks, the port's first major pier; Flora Sassoon, considered Bombay's first businesswoman; and Sir

Sassoon J. David, founder and chairman of the Bank of India and a mayor of Bombay.

Since the Baghdadis did little, however, to teach Hebrew to the B'nai Israel, Scottish and American missionaries with-thoughts of conversion filled the gap. Though they didn't achieve their goal, Hebrew and Hebrew studies became—150 years ago—a program for a degree at Bombay University.

Meanwhile, B'nai Israel Jews were producing leading military officers—in fact, 50 percent of the Indian officers of the East India Company were B'nai Israel—and later contributed at least two generals, a rear admiral, and a host of colonels to the Indian armed forces.

Bombay also had a B'nai Israel mayor, Elijah Moses; as well as actor David Abraham, popularly known as "David"; the actress Ruby Meyers; and Joseph David Penkar, who wrote the script for India's first talkie. Dr. Jerusha J. Jhirad became the country's first Indian chief medical officer, and Dr. Abraham S. Erulkar was Mahatma Gandhi's personal physician. Another Jewish doctor who made his mark in India, though not born there, was Waldemar Mordecai Haffkine. He created the first effective anticholera and antiplague vaccines and was the initial director in chief of the Haffkine Institute in Bombay, now the center of India's bacteriological research.

Two contemporary Bombay Jews noted on the international scene are Professor Nissim Ezekiel, a poet who heads the English department of Bombay University; and Abraham Sofaer, the judge who presided over the trial of Ariel Sharon versus *Time* magazine in New York. One non-Jew from Bombay whose link with the Jewish people is profound is Zubin Mehta, director of the Israel Philharmonic Orchestra and former director of the New York Philharmonic.

Jewish communal activity in Bombay today revolves around philanthropic and social work. Jews now living in the city run the gamut from the real estate speculator who owns nearly three thousand acres of downtown Bombay and lives in a first-class neighborhood on Malabar Hill to the barefoot and indigent who live in the "hutments," or shantytowns. To promote the general welfare and well-being of the entire Indian Jewish community, the Council of Indian Jewry has been formed.

India's traditional anti-Israel position never seemed to agitate Bombay's Jews. They saw it as a pragmatic stance of a country that is one-ninth Muslim and non-aligned, as well as of the inevitable viewpoint of a nation that itself opposed, and still opposes, a British partition plan. Besides, the Israeli flag always flew over the Israeli consulate in Bombay and India's Jews traveled back and forth freely. Now that full-scale diplomatic relations have been established, the consulate in Bombay, so long the sole Israeli outpost, is subordinate to the Israeli Embassy in New Dehli.

Sights: When on the trail of Indian Judaica in and around Bombay, sightseeing assumes more than the usual dimensions as Westerners are thrust into a world far removed from most hitherto experienced. Indeed, even within the city, many sights are tucked behind unprepossessing, graffiti-covered walls and gates in neighborhoods reminiscent of Kipling. Pushcarts—and pullcarts—still running on wooden wheels rumble up and down winding, twisting, unpaved streets. Naked and near-naked children play in front of peeling, often crumbling, houses and huts. Barefoot vendors hawk nuts and fruits, baubles, and old clothes; others, beturbaned, squat atop burlap bags in tiny, dark cubbyholes. The crush is claustrophobic; the din is deafening; the air is redolent of spices. And then, at the moment of greatest disorientation, from a hovel steps a man in a dhoti or a woman in a sari who offers the greeting "*Shalom.*"

Indeed, a visit to Bombay's old Jewish neighborhoods—Dongri, Mandvi, and Byculla—means leaving the beaten tourist trail completely. Even if you are armed with addresses, it is virtually essential to travel with a guide, so difficult is it to find the right path or alley, and so regularly do street names change. En route to the Jewish sites are the city's largest train terminal, the Indo-Gothic Victoria Station, and the frenetic Crawford Market. But quickly the scene becomes one of dilapidated, decaying tenements with wash flapping from balcony railings. Jews once lived in these buildings, some still adorned with delicately carved woodwork and traces of turquoise and pink paint; Jews even once owned many of them. But today they are filled primarily with Muslims.

These areas harbor several synagogues and prayer halls—some nearly derelict, others still functioning. And each has its own special flavor and treasure—be it a particularly elaborate Torah covering or an intricately woven Indian carpet on the floor. Yet, there are similarities as well. The synagogues are small, sometimes only storefront size and, in Sephardic tradition, have altars in the center of the room with women's galleries upstairs. Almost all use teak for the ark. Many are decorated with strings of tiny colored Christmas-tree-type lights. Hanging all around are large, acorn-shaped glass lamps fueled with coconut oil, which are lit when donations are made. And all synagogues are entered barefoot.

Among those B'nai Israel places of worship worth seeing are Shaar Harahamim, with its ornate ark carvings and its ten wood-encased Torahs covered in crimson, royal purple, and blue velvet (254 Samuel Street); Shaare Rason, with its cut-glass lamps, its ark outlined with red, green, orange, and yellow lights, and its Indian-rug-covered altar (90 Tantanpura Street); Tiferet Israel, with its red and green lights, its green, blue, and decal-covered oil lamps, and its carpeted altar (92 K. K. Marg, Jacob Circle); Magen Hasidim, a well-kept ocher and brown building, with two pillars framing its front entrance, a tiled outdoor pavilion, and an illuminated *Magen David* (8 Mohomed Shahid Marg, formerly Moreland Road); and Etz Hyeem Prayer Hall, upstairs in a rickety building, and sharing a floor with the office of the Friends of Indian Jews, a charitable organization helping the destitute (19 Umerkhadi, 2nd Cross Lane). Diagonally across the way from the prayer hall building is a white sign with red lettering. In Marathi and Hebrew, it says *"basar kasher,"* one of three kosher butchers in and around Bombay. (The others are in Kurla and Thane, the latter, an outlying suburb with a fair-sized Jewish community these days and an active synagogue.)

Not far from the prayer hall is Mazagaon Road, where the Sir Elly Kadoorie School Compound, with ORT India, is located. The Kadoorie School is one of two Jewish high schools in Bombay (the other is the Jacob Sassoon High School), but it now admits children of all backgrounds. In Byculla, at 36 Sussex Road, is Rodef Shalom, a Reform synagogue, which appeals to young people.

The first Baghdadi synagogue, Magen David, is located on Sir J. J. Road, sharing grounds with the Jacob Sassoon school; while Keneseth Eliyahoo, an airy, powder-blue synagogue with a marble floor, is conveniently found in the downtown Bombay Fort area, on Dr. V. B. Gandhi Marg.

Side Trip: But to understand truly the circumstances from which the B'nai Israel come, the Konkan Coast itself must be visited. This lush area, so covered with palm and mango trees that often the sunlight cannot get through the leaves, can easily be seen in a day with a car and driver.

Just a half hour beyond the bridge to the mainland is Panvel (or Penwel), a typical Konkan Coast town with dirt streets trod by cows and barefoot people transporting major loads on their heads. This is home to seventeen Jewish families—about eighty persons in all—and the Beth-El Synagogue on Mahatma Gandhi Road.

This synagogue is in a "courtyard" edged by dark shacks that use sheets for walls; on the ground outside these living quarters are spread burlap bags for drying peppers in the sun. Inside the synagogue—the paint peeling from its aqua-colored walls—are several Torahs adorned with gold and silver, and the inevitable hanging lamps.

About a half hour farther, there is another synagogue in the town of Pen. But the primary Konkan destination is Alibag, about two hours from Panvel, and its surroundings—since this is the area where the Jews first settled.

The sky-blue synagogue in Alibag is set among the palm trees (as is the turquoise, pink, and yellow one at nearby Rewdanda). It stands off a road of thatched-roof shacks once inhabited by B'nai Israel. This is a town where many women still wash their pots and pans in the streets and draw water from a common well. It is progressive, however, when compared with the villages around, where perhaps a hundred Jews still live, some in grand houses, but others in huts so deep among the palms that a trail of bread crumbs along the winding dirt paths seems in order.

About a mile and a half from Alibag is Khadala—a special site for the B'nai Israel. They venerate the prophet Elijah, almost as if he were a patron saint, keeping his picture in their homes and holding special celebrations in his honor. On a rock well off the road, overlooking a pond, is a marking that is said to have been made by his chariot and the horse's hooves as it bore the prophet to Heaven.

About ten miles from Khadala is Navgaon, the exact place where the B'nai Israel believe their ancestors landed. There is an ancient cemetery there with plain rock markers allegedly over the graves of the original survivors and those who drowned. A large white monument with a six-pointed star as its base has recently been erected in their memory.

Cochin: Six hundred miles down the coast from Bombay—an easy trip by air and an adventure by ground—is the remnant of India's Jewish community in Cochin. Jews have lived in Kerala on the Malabar Coast for perhaps two thousand years, although it wasn't until the sixteenth century that they left their home in Cranganore and sought protection from a friendly rajah in Cochin. The city was an international trade crossroads, and its people today bear the traces and mixtures of civilizations that came in every direction—not only Hindus, Muslims, Jews, and Syrian Orthodox Christians, but people of fascinating features, like brown skin with slanted blue eyes. In this diverse atmosphere, Jews always felt comfortable even though, true to their environment, they formed their own caste system based on color and origin.

The community numbered 2,500 in 1948, and most headed for Israel as soon as they heard of its independence. The remnant, fewer than 30 people, is still centered in Jewtown, a name that carries no stigma in India, located in the city's Mattancherry section (a short walk from the ferry terminal). Jews used to occupy virtually all the houses on Jewtown Road, where they sold fruits, vegetables, and spices or worked as oil pressers and carpenters; the smell of spice is still in the air of the narrow street, though most of the homes and businesses now belong to non-Jews. Only a few of the wealthier Jews—barred by Indian law from taking their fortunes with them—stayed in Cochin when the community emigrated virtually en masse.

At the end of Jewtown Road sits one of the jewels of the world's collection of synagogues. The Paradesi Synagogue, built in 1568 and reconstructed after a Portuguese bombardment in 1662, is distinguished by its tile roof and its bell tower. Under the bell tower is a clock tower featuring, on different sides, numerals in Roman, Hebrew, and Malayalam characters. The small sanctuary is noted for its hand-painted, willow-patterned, blue-and-white Chinese floor tiles, imported in the eighteenth century, and the many brass and crystal lamps that hang, densely packed, from the ceiling. In addition to *Shabbat* and holiday services, the synagogue is open to tourists Sunday through Friday between 10:00 A.M. and noon, and between 3:00 and 5:00 P.M. On most tours visitors are shown copper plates—at least one thousand years old, perhaps sixteen hundred—granting the right to Joseph Rabban to start a Jewish community.

The best person to contact about the Jewish community and the synagogue is Shabtai Samuel Koder on Princess Street in the city's Fort Cochin section (telephone 24288 or 24988).

General Sights: On Bombay's Elephanta Island, seven miles by launch from the triumphal arch known as the Gateway of India, are four rock-cut temples with large sculptures and sculptured panels dedicated to the god Shiva, which are thought to have been hewn between 450 and 750 C.E. This is a half-day trip.

Along the Bombay waterfront is Chowpatty Beach, where virtually no one swims but everyone "hangs out," doing his or her own thing. The annual Ganesh Chaturthi Festival, when clay statues of the elephant-headed god are thrown into the sea, winds through the city and culminates at Chowpatty Beach.

Atop Malabar Hill, an upscale residential

area with good views of town, are the Hanging Gardens, with hedges cut into animal shapes. Nearby are the Towers of Silence, where Parsis lay out their dead. The Parsis, incidentally, feel a strong kinship with the Jews and are very much like a Jewish minority—well educated and constituting a largely commercial class. It is probably no accident that Zubin Mehta comes from their ranks.

Among Bombay's museums are the Prince of Wales Museum, with archaeological and natural history exhibits and, within the same compound, the Jehangir Art Gallery, Bombay's leading gallery specializing in modern Indian art.

Reading: *Baumgartner's Bombay,* by the Indian author Anita Desai (Knopf), is a touching story of German Jewish refugees in India. Though set more in Calcutta, Gay Courter's novel *Flowers in the Blood* (Dutton) provides a rich portrait of India's Baghdadi Jews. *The B'nai Israel of Bombay* by Schifra Strizower (Schocken) is a good sociological study of Bombay's Jewish community.

Recommendations: The Searock Hotel, though out of the center of Bombay, is an exceptionally friendly hostelry, with a strictly vegetarian restaurant on its premises. For assistance with visiting Jewish sights in and around Bombay, good contacts are Esther Moses of the Indian Government Tourist Office (telephone 29-31-44) and the Council of Indian Jewry (27-04-61). Such contacts are particularly useful in a city where everything—from phone numbers to street names—changes with regularity. Bombay is a place to expect the unexpected. Fortunately, most of what is unexpected will enrich the journey.

—Phyllis Ellen Funke

Boston

Boston is a city on a hill, a city by the sea, and a city whose history resonates in the American memory. Grade school lessons — about Paul Revere's ride, the shot heard round the world, and literary giants like Adams, Thoreau, Emerson, and Alcott — impart a personal quality to the public history of the city. It's as though our collective national "*yichus*" begins in Boston.

In counterpoint to Boston's fine old brick buildings and cobblestone streets, New England's largest city has its fair share of steel and glass skyscrapers too. Rich in world-renowned universities, medical centers, and cultural institutions, Boston has further polished its reputation as the "Athens of America" by becoming a leader in the high-tech revolution. The "Brain Belt" of bedroom communities to the north and west of the city are home to many cutting-edge computer and biotechnology firms.

The Hub, as natives sometimes call it (that's short for hub of the universe), is a walkable city. You can get from the fashionable shops on Newbury Street by way of the blooming Boston garden with its famous "swan-boat" pond, down to popular Faneuil Hall marketplace and the harbor, all in an hour's stroll. Tourists come from all over the world to walk the Freedom Trail, visit the U.S.S. *Constitution* (*Old Ironsides*, the Navy's oldest commissioned warship), and explore the museums.

Walking through Paul Revere's neighborhood past the Old North Church, where the signal was "one if by land, two if by sea," you find yourself in the middle of one of Boston's distinctive ethnic enclaves. Snatches of animated conversation overheard on the streets and in cafés, immediately identify the North End as the first stop for many Italian immigrants. There is no trace of the vibrant Jewish community housed in these narrow brick tenements during the nineteenth century, but there are clues to the city's Jewish history scattered around the city.

History: Boston's Jewish presence is pervasive but subtle — a mixture of circumspection and pride that reflects a past of early rejection and eventual success. During its first two hundred years, there was no Jewish community in Boston. Indeed, the early history of Jewish Boston is the story of a handful of individuals. The first Jew known to arrive in the colonial port received a very chilly welcome. Solomon Franco sailed into the harbor in 1649 with cargo for one of the colonists. Within days, he was told to get out of town.

Of course, the Puritan settlers were inhospitable to anyone who disagreed with their particular religious vision. Dissenting Christians Roger Williams and Anne Hutchinson were also shown the door. But there was special irony to the Puritans' treatment of Jews, since they liked to think of themselves as a "chosen people" whose migration and search for a promised land echoed the story of the ancient Hebrews. Indeed, Hebrew was a required part of the curriculum when Harvard College opened its doors in 1636. However, Judah Monis, the only Jew to receive a Harvard degree before 1800, was only permitted to teach Hebrew at Harvard after he converted to Christianity. History records, however, that Monis insisted on keeping the Sabbath on Saturday.

With few exceptions, Jews steered clear of the Massachusetts Bay Colony, Boston, and most of New England until nearly the middle of the nineteenth century. Religious intolerance aside, the work that drew Jews to other parts of the country — trading and peddling in particular — were more than adequately filled by Yankees. In fact, New England was the last area in America to see significant Jewish settlement.

But a New England labor shortage in the 1800s coincided with the immigration of German Jews, and by 1845 Boston's first synagogue was founded. In the 1880s, Russian and Eastern European Jews arrived in large numbers so that by 1900, there was a community of some 2,000, with four hundred self-help and charitable organizations — from burial societies to baseball teams.

In the early part of this century, Boston boasted seven Yiddish newspapers. Zionism found strong support in the Jewish North End community, where some of the nation's first *Ivriyahs* — schools for teaching modern Hebrew — were established. Boston is the home of several Jewish American "firsts." The first Federation opened its doors in 1895. In 1921, the first Bureau of Jewish education was organized, one of its first acts being the opening of the first Hebrew teachers college.

Community: In its role as an educational center, Boston's importance to the national Jewish community is out of proportion to its numbers. Although it is only the sixth-largest Jewish community in the United States, countless Jews have spent important parts of their lives at one of the area's fifty-four colleges and universities as undergraduates, medical students, postdoctoral fellows, or law students. Of the 228,000 Jews in metropolitan Boston, more than 30,000 are college students. More than 80 percent of Boston's Jewish community have some college education and 29 percent hold advanced degrees.

Judah Monis's experience is a very distant footnote today. Jews are esteemed members of virtually every faculty in the city, and even Harvard's latest president is a man named Rudenstine. Jewish Studies programs flourish at Harvard, Tufts, Wellesley, and Boston University, where Nobel laureate Elie Wiesel teaches.

Brandeis University, founded in 1948 as a result of a nationwide, grassroots effort, is the youngest university in the country with a first-rank reputation for academic excellence. Its two hundred fifty-acre campus in suburban Waltham is a point of pride among Boston Jews, who attend lectures there and support its many programs in the arts. In Brookline, Hebrew College, which runs a high school as well as a degree program, continues to train Hebrew teachers, and has also become something of a community *lehrhaus*, with an extensive *Ulpan* program and many adult education courses. It is no wonder the American Jewish Studies Conference, which brings together the best and brightest, holds its annual meeting in Boston.

Jewish education in Boston is widely available to children from preschool through high school. There are eight day schools in the area, representing all three major movements in Judaism.

Boston is as religiously diverse as any Jewish community in the world. There are eighty congregations serving the area, along with many independent *minyanim* and *chavurot*, small groups that meet for religious study and observance in people's homes. The great hasidic leader Grand Rabbi Levi Yitzhak Horowitz is known around the world as the Bostoner Rebbe. Also making his home in the area is Rabbi Joseph Baer Soloveitchik, "the Rav." A talmudic scholar and leader of the modern Orthodox movement, Soloveitchik founded the Maimonides Hebrew Day School.

Boston is also the birthplace of "alternative" Judaism. Havurat Shalom, founded in 1968 as a religious community and seminary, helped give rise to what has come to be called the Jewish renewal movement. Havurat Shalom continues to function in Somerville as a center of Jewish education and worship outside the mainstream. Congregation Beth El in suburban Sudbury published the first gender-neutral *siddur*, which has gone through eight printings since it first appeared in 1980.

Boston is known as a city of ethnic neighborhoods, and during their history in the city, Jews have lived in many of them — starting in the South End, moving to the North End, Chelsea, Beacon Hill, and the West End, which was demolished in a fit of "urban renewal" in the early 1960s. The forties and fifties saw Jews in the three-family triple-deckers and elegant homes of Roxbury, Dorchester, and Mattapan, where imposing synagogue buildings now serve as churches and community buildings for the area's predominantly black population.

In the past few decades, Jews have settled in virtually every one of the eighty cities and towns that make up the metropolitan Boston area, with communities in quaint Yankee ports like Marblehead to the north, and western bedroom towns like Acton. During the 1980s, the southern suburbs in particular experienced an explosion of Jewish growth; the population of the town of Sharon is estimated to be at least 70 percent Jewish. The southern towns are served by a Jewish community center, a *mikveh*, and a day school.

Sights: Despite this dispersion, nearly one-quarter of the area's Jewish population live in the towns of Brookline and Newton. Ted Mann, the Jewish mayor of Newton for more than twenty years, once described his suburb as "the second-largest Jewish community in the northeast." (He's right if you discount Canada and relegate Philadelphia to the mid-Atlantic region.) No surprise then that Newton is home to the campus of the Leventhal Sidman Jewish Community Center, one of the largest in the country.

Still, Brookline is the commercial heart of the city. Jews from all over New England come to buy *challah*, kosher meat, and Jewish books on Harvard Street, where shop windows are papered with announcements about concerts of Jewish music and lectures on Jewish topics. Yiddish and Russian are often heard on the street.

Among the bakeries and markets is the Israel Bookstore (410 Harvard), one of the largest purveyors of Jewish and Hebrew books in the country, and also a publisher of religious texts. More books are available across the street at Kolbo (435 Harvard), which enjoys a national reputation for its selection of contemporary Judaica and fine art by American and Israeli artists.

For many years, Harvard Street was home to the city's only two kosher restaurants. However, since the mid-1980s, there has been a boom in kosher dining. In addition to Rubin's Delicatessen (500 Harvard) and the vegetarian Café Shalom (404a Harvard), kosher food is available at Victor's Pizza, Rami's (falafel and chicken

shwarma), and Ruth's Kitchen (Oriental take-out from a Korean war bride who converted to Judaism).

Nor do you have to be in Brookline to eat kosher anymore. Haim's Delicatessen is located near the Bostoner rebbe's *shul* in Brighton, and The King David serves *glatt* Middle Eastern fare in Sharon. Probably the best-known kosher eatery in town is the Milk Street Café, a vegetarian fixture located in the city's financial district (50 Milk Street) that now has thriving outposts in the Longwood Medical Area and in downtown Post Office Square.

After a meal on Harvard Street, you might want to go to 1187 Beacon Street for a look at Congregation Ohabei Shalom, Boston's oldest synagogue. Originated by ten families in 1842, Ohabei Shalom split twice during the nineteenth century, giving rise to two of the city's other leading synagogues: Temple Israel and Congregation Mishkan Tefila. Ohabei Shalom became the first Reform congregation in New England in 1871, and in 1928 moved into its current home, an impressive Byzantine-Romanesque structure. Notable for its beautiful copper dome, the sanctuary boasts a one hundred-foot ceiling, unobstructed by columns. Call (617) 277-6610 for information on services and events.

Temple Israel, whose founders parted company with Ohabei Shalom in 1854, is the largest congregation in New England. Its landmark Greek Revival meetinghouse on the Riverway in Boston (Plymouth Street and Longwood Avenue), built in 1928, houses an eleven hundred-capacity auditorium used for lectures and concerts. One of the hidden gems inside Temple Israel is the Wyner art gallery, which has a small but elegant collection of Judaica and changing displays of Jewish art.

Temple Israel serves a neighborhood that includes the Longwood Medical Area, home to seven major hospitals, one of which is Beth Israel. A nonsectarian institution since its founding in 1915, "the BI" nevertheless maintains a special relationship to the Jewish community that founded it. In 1910, Jewish women campaigned door-to-door selling miniature bricks at five cents apiece; the goal was a facility that would not only provide health care, but also function as a training facility for

Jewish students who were excluded by quotas at other teaching hospitals.

The low-lying modern structures of the Brandeis University campus nestle along wooded hills in Waltham. The most distinctive building is the Castle, a medieval-looking tower left over from a time when the land was occupied by a small medical school. The castle now functions as a dorm and student center.

Brandeis is the site of the Rose Art Gallery, the Yiddish Film Archives, and the Jewish Historical Society, which attracts scholars from around the world with seventy-five thousand volumes and nearly seven million manuscripts, photographs, newspapers, and artifacts of the American Jewish experience. The Historical Society is the repository for the papers of organizations such as the American Jewish Congress and the Jewish Welfare Board, and of individuals, such as Rabbi Stephen S. Wise and actress Molly Picon.

Culture: Boston boasts an internationally acclaimed symphony orchestra, one of the country's finest art museums, and a landmark public library. It is also rich in Jewish arts, especially music. With several albums to its credit, the Klezmer Conservatory Orchestra was one of the groups that helped revive the popular Yiddish repertory and introduce it to new generations of listeners. The Zamir Chorale, a community chorus, performs a diverse repertoire that includes everything from Israeli folk songs to major choral works by Handel. Safam, a popular local folk-rock band, specializes in original Hebrew and English songs. Performing in Ladino and using ancient instruments, Voice of the Turtle plays music of the Sephardic tradition.

Hamakor, a local Israeli folk-dance troupe, has created movement for virtually every kind of Jewish music. And the annual Boston Jewish Film Festival, held at the Museum of Fine Arts every autumn, attracts 5,000 buffs to three weeks of movies from around the world.

Information about performances, and about all communal matters, is available in the *Jewish Advocate* and the *Boston Jewish Times*.

In the visual arts, the Pucker Safrai Gallery, at 171 Newbury Street (Boston's gallery row) features some of the world's finest Jewish painters, printmakers, and sculptors, including David Sharir, David Aronson, Samuel Bak, and Marc Chagall. Kolbo, on Harvard Street in Brookline, is a national showcase for contemporary Judaica with works in porcelain, wood, paper, fabric, and stone.

Reading: Boston contains a great treasury of Jewish books: Harvard owns more than 150,000 volumes in Hebrew, Yiddish, and English; Brandeis has over 90,000. Hebrew College's library has some 85,000 volumes, and the public libraries in both Boston and Brookline boast impressive collections.

Boston plays a part in books and memoirs from several different eras. Mary Antin's classic, *The Promised Land: The Autobiography of a Russian Immigrant* (Princeton University Press), chronicles the misery of Jewish Boston in the nineteenth century. Theodore H. White's *In Search of History: A Personal Adventure* (Warner Books) includes memories of the historian's Dorchester childhood. A recent best-seller in Boston was *The Death of an American Jewish Community* (Free Press) by Hillel Levine and Lawrence Harmon; it chronicled the destruction of the city's inner-city Jewish neighborhood by banking interests.

Personalities: Countless Boston Jews have national and international reputations in science, music, letters, the law, and even sports. The Boston Celtics wouldn't be the Boston Celtics without Arnold "Red" Auerbach, who has been immortalized in bronze (cigar and all) at Faneuil Hall Marketplace. Another monument to a beloved local Jewish celebrity is to the late Arthur Fiedler, longtime conductor of the Boston Pops. A huge bust of Fiedler was constructed near the Hatch Shell on the Charles River Esplanade, where the maestro led many of the Pops' free summer concerts. Composer-conductor Leonard Bernstein was a native of the Boston area and a graduate of Harvard.

Justin Kaplan, the Pulitzer Prize–winning biographer, lives in Cambridge with his wife, novelist Anne Bernays, who also happens to be the daughter of Edward Bernays, the "father of modern public relations." Historian Oscar Handlin is a Bostonian, as

General Sights: Boston has something to delight visitors of every age and interest. During the summer, pleasure boats cruise the harbor affording the best views of the city. A few blocks from the famous Museum of Fine Arts is the less famous but more charming Isabella Stewart Gardner Museum, where extensive greenhouses provide stunning floral displays for the mansion's ethereal courtyard. The Children's Museum, Computer Museum, and Boston Tea Party display are conveniently clustered on Museum Wharf, itself only a few blocks from the New England Aquarium.

For the inveterate shopper, Filene's Basement remains a must. It just so happens that the Filene's retail business was founded by one of the city's most prominent early Jewish families, which, like so many others, entered the dry goods business by way of a lone Yiddish Yankee peddler.

Scraps of evidence about the long and varied heritage of Boston's Jews are visible if you know where to look. For example, across Boylston Street from the Boston Gardens, where the city's signature swan boats delight children of all ages, you'll see an alley called Hadassah Way, named for a rummage sale that was held there for many years. And nearby, among the elegant brick townhouses on historic Beacon Hill, there is the Vilna Shul (16 Philips Street), which was founded by Lithuanian Jews and served the large West End community until its demise in the early sixties.

All in all, Solomon Franco, the seventeenth-century Jew who was chased out of town, would be amazed by Boston today. He might well find it a comfortable place to make a Jewish home.

—Anita Diamant

Conduct becoming: Native son Bernstein made music around the world

are *New York Times* columnist Anthony Lewis, *Boston Globe* columnist Ellen Goodman, and attorney-author Alan Dershowitz. It was altogether fitting that America's Jewish-sponsored nonsectarian university should be named after Bostonian Louis Brandeis, the first Jew appointed to the United States Supreme Court.

Barbara Walters and Mike Wallace are two Bostonians who have spent time in virtually every living room in the nation. And Leonard Nimoy, of Spock fame, has even traveled to distant galaxies.

Brooklyn

You can take Manhattan if you want glitz and glitter. But to experience traditional *Yiddishkeit* in the borough with the largest Jewish community in the United States, go to Brooklyn, my friend.

Rival to New Yorkers' affection, Brooklyn has always been seen as the provincial sibling to its cosmopolitan, skyscraper-crowned elder. Its coveted space and oceanfront have been the destination of immigrants, businesses, and developers who wanted a bigger piece of the American pie at a lower price. An escape hatch for some, it was and still is for many a steppingstone to greener, more distant pastures. And Jewish Brooklynites—whether their native tongue is distinctively Brooklynese, Yiddish, Arabic, or Russian—are passionate about their borough. No matter where a native is transplanted, Brooklyn is in the bones. Brooklyn Jewish childhoods have served as colorful and often nostalgic ingredients of novels, films, and television shows.

Harvard law professor Alan Dershowitz extols lifelong friendships formed in his Brooklyn youth in his book, *Chutzpah* (Little, Brown). Bensonhurst-bred talk-show host Larry (Zeiger) King explains in *If You're From Brooklyn, Everything Else Is Tokyo* (Little, Brown), "No matter where we live or travel, there is an unbroken bond between us that forever ties us to our roots, to the borough of Brooklyn." Some people never leave the borough. Norman Mailer, who lives in Brooklyn Heights, finds Brooklyn "the most real place I've ever been in my life." If you haven't experienced Brooklyn, America's third-largest city before it became a borough in 1898, you are missing a flavorful, even exotic slice of life.

Once home to tribes of Algonquin Indians, Brooklyn today is the stomping ground of other diverse tribes—Satmar, Stolin-Karlin, Bobov, Puppa, Belz, Gor, Spinka, Vizhnitz, Tzelem, and the most widely recognized, Lubavitch. These *hasidim* and their mitnagdic, modern Orthodox, Sephardic, secular, and émigré brethren help comprise the borough's 371,000 Jews, a veritable ingathering from Eastern Europe, Asia, Africa, and the former Soviet Union. The Jewish population had peaked in the early 1950s at around a million, before the movement to Queens and Long Island. Jewish Brooklynites have enriched the borough for more than 160 years, not only religiously, but culturally, politically, and economically.

History: Although there was a Jewish presence in Brueckelen (as the Dutch named it) as far back as 1660, when Asser Levy bought property there, there was no permanent Jewish community until the 1830s; the first settlements were in Borough Hall and Williamsburg. Among immigrants from Bavaria and Alsace were a variety store owner, cart man, and auctioneer. By 1850 Jews were prominent in the feed business, tailoring, dry goods, cigar making, meat packing, and some were machinists, watchmakers, rope makers, pharmacists and junk dealers. They also opened breweries and a fireworks company. A&S department store (founded by Abraham Abraham, who was later joined by Macy's Isidore and Nathan Straus) began as a dry goods emporium in 1865.

An apocryphal story relates that the new settlers had to row across the East River to Manhattan on Friday afternoon for services and return to Brooklyn on Sunday. Public Jewish worship wasn't held until 1851, when Kahal Kodesh Beth Elohim was organized; its first, elegant, building was erected in 1876 at 274 Keap Street, and it adopted the Reform ritual. Today the building houses a hasidic girls' school. This synagogue later merged with Reform congregation Beth Israel to become Union Temple.

Brooklyn's first synagogue building, Congregation Baith Israel Anshei Emes, was dedicated in 1862 at Boerum Place and State Street. It was near a stable, and soon there were complaints that loud praying from the synagogue was disturbing the horses. In 1905 the Orthodox-turned-Conservative synagogue moved to 236 Kane Street (near Court Street), a building that originally housed a Dutch Reformed church. It is popularly known as the Kane Street Synagogue.

Many early Jews first visited Brooklyn to attend funerals, after burials were banned in Manhattan. The first Jewish cemetery in Brooklyn, Union Fields in Cypress Hills, opened in 1848. The oldest section has an 1890 monument to Jewish Civil War veterans; the graves of Supreme Court Justice Benjamin Cardozo, Emma Lazarus, Commodore Uriah P. Levy, and Rabbi Judah L. Magnes are nearby. In the newer Workman's Circle burial ground in Mount Carmel Cemetery are Sholom Aleichem; Benjamin Schlesinger, founder of the International Ladies Garment Workers Union; Abraham Cahan, editor of the Jewish Daily *Forward*; and the Yiddish poet Morris Rosenfeld.

The first Jewish settlers suffered their share of anti-Semitism. Jewish funeral processions were often attacked by thugs. But they also had friends. In 1877 in Plymouth Church, the Reverend Henry Ward Beecher — brother of Harriet Beecher Stowe, who wrote *Uncle Tom's Cabin* — defended the Jews, creating a national stir in a sermon that remains a classic of philo-Semitism. His speech was a response to a real estate promoter who didn't want Jews to patronize his lavish new Manhattan Beach resort — and spoil the neighborhood.

In 1881, after czarist pogroms, a flood of Eastern European Jews poured into Brooklyn, joining the German-Jewish immigrants. In the years after World War I, more than one-third of all foreign-born people moving to Brooklyn were Jews from Russia and Poland. In 1923 Brooklyn had 740,000 Jews and became the borough with the largest Jewish population.

Soon there were Jews living in the shorefront communities of Coney Island, Brighton Beach, Manhattan Beach, and Seagate. Coney Island — the Disney World of its time — drew the sweaty masses during the summer; part of its attraction were the shows of Samuel Gumpertz, which specialized in freaks, midgets, child acrobats, Buffalo Bill's Wild West exposition, and the magic of Harry Houdini. A still-functioning landmark on the boardwalk is the original Nathan's Famous where, beginning in 1915, proprietor Nathan Handwerker promoted the nickel (nonkosher) hot dog.

By 1900, Brownsville rivaled the Lower East Side as a mostly Jewish neighborhood (in the 1930s it was 95 percent Jewish). At its peak 400,000 lived there. Its cheap rents, available jobs, and rural environment attracted more than 15,000 sweatshop workers. The dynamic and intensely Jewish neighborhood's center was Pitkin Avenue: It was *the* place to be for its restaurants, Yiddish theaters, and shopping. Many of Brooklyn's first Jewish labor, educational, and community institutions were started there. Today none of Brownsville's two hundred synagogues remains open. The most infamous Brownsville residents were Louis "Lepke" Buchalter and partner Jacob "Gurrah" Shapiro of Murder, Inc., a killer squad of mostly Brooklyn Jewish thugs. (Buchalter was executed at Sing Sing.) Despite that infamy, most Brownsvillians were respectable citizens and achievers. Among myriad writers who lived or wrote here was Arthur Miller, whose parents' house on East Third Street became the model for Willy Loman's.

Several conduits to the outer reaches were constructed at the turn of the century: the Williamsburg Bridge in 1903 (newspapers nastily termed it "Jew's Highway" because of its easy trip from the Lower East Side), the Manhattan Bridge in 1909 (designed and built by Leon Solomon Moisseiff, a Russian-born Jew), as well as the elevated and subway lines. Williamsburg became the first stop to suburbia. That decade saw the biggest spurt in Brooklyn's Jewish population as prospering and adventurous Jews moved to Borough Park,

81

Crown Heights, Bedford-Stuyvesant, Park Slope, Brooklyn Heights, Bensonhurst, East New York, Flatbush, and Brighton Beach. In 1929 Williamsburg, I. Rokeach & Sons built a modern factory to produce kosher foods.

By the end of the building boom and at the beginning of the Great Depression, at least one critic complained of the "Harlemizing" of Brooklyn. This was an anti-Semitic, not an anti-Black, remark; he was referring to the solid rows of apartment buildings on streets like Ocean Avenue that were reminiscent of those in Harlem when that neighborhood was heavily Jewish. Among the builders was Chanin Brothers, which got its start building small houses and apartment buildings in Bensonhurst before it advanced to building the Chanin Building, the Roxy and other Times Square theaters, and apartments on Central Park West.

Community: People have been taking a closer look at Brooklyn lately. A recent *New York Times* headline read: "Are You Urbane? Not If You Don't Know Brooklyn." A new Sidney Lumet film, *A Stranger Among Us*, is notable for its complimentary view of the hasidic community. Local friction between blacks and *hasidim* was dramatically captured in *Fires in the Mirror*, Anna Deavere Smith's one-woman show at New York's Joseph Papp Public Theater (which has been filmed for public television by American Playhouse). *The New York Times Magazine* cover story in March 1992 was about "The Oracle of Crown Heights," the Lubavitcher rebbe. A *Forward* survey in New York and Washington showed that the rebbe was the most widely recognized Jewish leader. There was also a turn toward nostalgia with television's *Brooklyn Bridge*, a show about an endearing Jewish family in the 1950s — soda fountains, stoop ball, the Dodgers, the whole *shmear*. There's also a slew of "I Remember Brooklyn" books hot off the press.

Brooklyn's Jewish population — which is 16 percent of the borough's total — continues to shrink as people move to Long Island (especially West Hempstead), Monsey, and the New Jersey towns of West Orange and Teaneck and other suburban parts.

After World War II, the borough saw a renewed influx as *hasidim*, particularly *Satmar*, moved to the area called the "New Jerusalem." The Jewish neighborhood extends from the Williamsburg Bridge to Flushing and Bushwick Avenues. The once-attractive resort area had declined soon after public housing was built, and many Jews moved on. But the Satmar (from the village of Satu Mare, or St. Mary, in the Hungarian-speaking part of Rumania) have remained and multiplied. The ultra-Orthodox community remains distinct from all others.

On Bedford near the corner of Ross stand, facing each other across the street, the homes of the previous and the current Satmar *rebbes*. Most *hasidim* live on Bedford Avenue and their influence is apparent in a newly renovated apartment building on that street: the balconies are staggered to allow for the construction of *sukkot* so they can conform to *halakhah*: One must be able to see the stars through the roof.

Yiddish signs proclaim Lee Avenue as the main shopping area for the hasidic community. The gloomy exteriors contrast with the safety and vibrancy of this community. There is a hasidic-run security force called *shomrim*. While hasidic entrepreneurs work in a variety of fields, many are employed in New York's diamond district on Forty-seventh Street and at Forty-seventh Street Photo. Because the Satmar do not wish to mingle with "outsiders," they maintain their own bus system. Satmar headquarters is at Congregation Yetev Lev D'Satmar at 152 Rodney Street.

Flatbush was once site of Ebbets Field, home of the much-loved and much-maligned Dodgers. After finally winning a World Series against the Yankees in 1955, the Brooklyn Bums traitorously moved to the West Coast, for which they have never been forgiven by their most fanatical fans. Brooklyn-born comedian Richard Lewis once quipped that he traced "a lifelong depression" to the Dodgers' departure. It is said that the team catered to Jewish fans by keeping a Jewish coach, Jake Pitler, on the baselines.

Although Flatbush boasts of many Jewish centers, hasidic and mitnagdic synagogues and notable *yeshivot* — there are two and three to a block along Ocean

Parkway—home to thirty-five thousand close-knit Syrian Jews from Aleppo (including smaller representations of Damascene and Egyptian, Lebanese, and North African Jews, and recently arrived Israelis). They too started out on the Lower East Side, Williamsburg, and Bensonhurst (which still has a large Syrian congregation, Magen David) but are solidly settled in Flatbush, with families, synagogues, centers, and schools close by. Since the 1940s they've built a strong community. About 77 percent of Aleppans live in a compact community on and just off tree-lined Ocean Parkway between Avenue I and Avenue Y. Syrian Jews rarely intermarry (the rate is less than 10 percent): A 1937 rabbinical edict stipulates that any intermarried Syrian is excommunicated. Because the Syrian synagogues are more tolerant of members' personal religious behavior, neither the Conservative nor the Reform ideology have made inroads into the community. Syrian Jews have been successful in imports and exports, especially electronics and clothing. One of the more prominent Sephardim from this community is Edmond Safra, chief executive officer of Republic National Bank.

Brighton Beach has been transformed from the "Miami North of the senior set" into a revitalized "Little Odessa," with the influx since the 1970s of more than 25,000 Jews from the former Soviet Union, putting back the neighborhood's bloom. There are Russian (nonkosher) restaurants and nightclubs with vodka, caviar, kvass, dancing, and the music of "Oy Odess"; food shops where you can buy Russian specialties; bookstores; bright, well-ordered fruit stands; and an enlivened boardwalk. One innovative entrepreneur along Brighton Beach Avenue has dealt his former homeland a sardonic blow: in his laundromat-gift shop he sells such items as pins of Lenin, gold-fringed red banners with communist slogans, T-shirts that say *perestroika* and *glasnost* and undershorts with a hammer-and-sickle motif. By all signs the newcomers are acculturating well: though they continue to predominate, each year there are fewer signs in Cyrillic letters than before.

While East New York and Brownsville are no longer Jewish neighborhoods, Ca-narsie and Bensonhurst are still Jewish strongholds. But congested and drab Borough Park, where Orthodoxy predominates, is probably the most thriving and dynamic part of Jewish Brooklyn. While Borough Park has Yemenite, Israeli, and "modern" Jews, it is primarily hasidic territory with more than twenty dynasties. Though many residents are professionals or are engaged in a variety of businesses and trades, the hundreds of *shuls, yeshivahs,* and rabbinical seminaries would seem to be the main industry, to judge by their proliferation. There are 40 *yeshivah*s and 250 *shuls* in a 200-square-block radius in Borough Park. There are even two hasidic window clerks in a local post office. Take a walk along Fourteenth Avenue from Fifty-third Street to Forty-fifth Street to get the flavor of this *yeshivah-* and *shul*-rich neighborhood.

In Williamsburg, Bensonhurst, and Crown Heights, as well as in Borough Park, *shtreimels, sheitels, payes,* and *tzitzis* are alive and well and worn with pride. Outsiders who come to study and shop in these neighborhoods take home with them more than the *seforim, mezuzahs,* kosher pizza, and *shmurah matzah* they purchase. Neither is Brooklyn *Yiddishkeit* just a local brew; its influence is worldwide. Lubavitcher *hasidim* are deeply entrenched in Crown Heights. They have political clout and proprietary rights in a neighborhood once threatened with deterioration and desertion by its Jews. The rebbe, Menachem Mendel Schneerson, directs his worldwide flock of 200,000 *hasidim* from 770 Eastern Parkway; 20,000 live in the neighborhood. National Chabad headquarters is at 784–788 Eastern Parkway.

Lubavitch emissaries are everywhere—from Oklahoma to Tanzania; *mitzvah* tanks corral Jews to put on *tefilin* or make a *brocha* whether they're on the Lower East Side or on the Golan Heights. The Lubavitch publishing house is the largest distributor of Jewish books in the world; the group's telephone hotlines and newscasts operate twenty-four hours a day. Neither are they self-conscious about putting forth their message (to help bring the Messiah) in full-page advertisements in *The New York Times*.

Until his recent illness, the nonagenarian

rebbe would stand for hours on Sundays to greet visitors, pious Jews or politicians, celebrities like Bob Dylan or Israeli Knesset members, and hand each a crisp dollar bill to be dispensed as charity (which entrepreneurs promptly offer to laminate as keepsakes). His *farbrengen* (public addresses), which attract thousands, are televised on cable television and transmitted around the world.

You can also find a Jewish Yuppieville in Park Slope and Brooklyn Heights. Young professionals, writers, and artists are renovating the nineteenth-century brownstones along Carroll, Garfield, and Montgomery streets. Congregation Beth Elohim, Eighth Avenue and Garfield Place (better known as the Garfield Place Temple), founded in 1861, was Brooklyn's first Reform synagogue. Brooklyn Heights has been for over fifty years one of New York's most charming, accessible, and fashionable residential areas with some of the finest old brick and brownstone houses. It is a twenty-minute walk across the Brooklyn Bridge to Manhattan.

Sights: The subway is convenient for getting to most places—although it is not noteworthy for its esthetics. Given the dispersal of Jewish sights, however, a car can be equally convenient. The best way to start with any of the main Jewish neighborhoods is to walk to its main street—Lee Avenue in Williamsburg, for example, or Brighton Beach Avenue in "Little Odessa."

Go to Williamsburg, Borough Park, or Crown Heights on Simhat Torah or Purim or for a hasidic wedding—all spill out into the streets. On Purim night go to the Bobover *shul* for its lively Purim *shpiel*. Call Lubavitch at (718) 493-9250, 774-4000, or 778-4270 to find out where you can watch the baking of *shmurah matzah* before Pesach, or to take one of their many varied tours—to see the *mikveh*, or to watch a *shofar* being made.

There is pre-Passover baking at the Shmurah Matzah Factory at Thirty-sixth Street and Thirteenth Avenue (718-438-2006). If you want to see where the Gold family has been making horseradish for three generations, go to 895 McDonald Avenue. Wander on Kingston Avenue for the flavor of the community; that's where

people shop and eat. In Flatbush, Kings Highway is lined with Middle Eastern restaurants, appetizing and pastry shops and groceries—announced not only by their signs in Hebrew and Arabic but by the aroma of falafel and Eastern spices.

Walk down Forty-eighth Street in Borough Park to watch the people, especially the stylish young mothers pushing their baby carriages; read the signs in store windows to find out about concerts and lectures; enter the bookstores to marvel at the breadth of the collections of Judaica. This is the neighborhood that has it all: what you don't see in the store windows is sure to be sold in a basement. Just ask.

Visit the $3-million Bobover Synagogue and Holocaust Center, at Fifteenth Avenue and Forty-eighth Street, with its Moorish arches, rounded stained-glass windows, Venetian floral motifs, and floor-to-ceiling marble. Its angled ark and podium is modeled after that of the Portuguese Synagogue in Amsterdam. The building is large enough to hold several thousand; its benches, tables, and *bimah* can be moved to accommodate a variety of activities—prayer, a *rebbe*'s *tish* when the furniture is realigned as one large table, or to make room for dancing in the center. One-way mirrors, designed by architect and travel writer Oscar Israelowitz, allow women to see and enjoy the services from the balcony, but prevent the men from viewing the women. The women's entrance at Forty-seventh Street has limestone portals and arched windows.

The Sephardic Community Center, 1901 Ocean Parkway, in Flatbush, built in 1982, is a centerpiece of modern architectural beauty with a Mediterranean flavor. It is made of white, precast stone. Go when there is a presentation of traditional Middle Eastern music (telephone 718-627-4300).

Magnificent synagogues abound. The Orthodox Young Israel Beth El of Borough Park (4802 Fifteenth Avenue; telephone 718-435-9020) has 120 lights in its massive dome that form the pattern of a Star of David. Temple Beth El was organized in 1906 and was the first congregation in the neighborhood; it merged in 1988 with Young Israel to form the current congregation. The present building was constructed in 1920 and designed in the Moorish Revival style. The main sanctuary was designed to have near-perfect acoustics, and among the great cantors who served the congregation was Moshe Koussevitski.

The Reform Union Temple (17 Eastern Parkway; 718-638-7600) — the mother synagogue of Brooklyn (it represents the joining of Beth Elohim and Temple Israel) — is opposite the entrance to Prospect Park and the Brooklyn Public Library. During World War II, the congregation housed a Red Cross Blood Bank and was a designated Emergency Disaster Center. With twelve stories, it may be the world's tallest synagogue. Its auditorium has a hand-painted concrete ceiling; the sanctuary has stained-glass windows and a Saville organ. The colorful fresco depicts the history of the synagogue, beginning with the tabernacle in the wilderness. In the foyer there is a bronze plaque in memory of Colonel David (Mickey) Marcus who was killed in Israel's War of Independence.

The Orthodox Sephardic Congregation B'nai Yosef (1616 Ocean Parkway in Flatbush; 718-627-9861) makes up for its nondescript exterior with its unusual interior: It has eight thousand square feet of cinder block walls and two levels completely covered with murals. It took artist Archie Rand three years to create the iconography on thirty-seven themes. Before completion it was subjected to a rabbinical review and declared "fit" by the late Rabbi Moshe Feinstein, the leading halakhic decisor of his time.

The eclectic work is visually alive and glowing with color. Styles range from Abstract Expressionist to Color Field to quasi-Pop figuration; the colors are as varied — signaling the interlocking complexity of the Jewish faith and multifaceted themes. The panels depict stories from the Bible interwoven with images from Kabbalah. There is also a large panel representative of contemporary Jewish history. The Holocaust panel is flanked by painted ropes to symbolize the binding of Isaac. Recognizable symbols such as the *shofar, talit,* menorah, *Magen David* as well as natural objects — trees and fruit of Israel, fish and animals — emerge from seas of color.

The Orthodox Sephardic Shaare Zion Congregation, 2030 Ocean Parkway (718-376-0009), is the premier congregation of the Sephardic community in Flatbush. Built in 1958, it has an award-winning, theater-in-the-round design. The exterior is of marble, brass, and wood with a turquoise and white Star of David on its curved front windows. Magnificent ceiling-high wood-paneled doors lead into the sanctuary. A wooden ark is set against a white marble-columned background and surmounted by the Decalogue in marble. On either side, framed by wood and a wavy textured pattern in brass, are modern sculpted menorahs.

The borough's myriad *yeshivahs* may be its crowning glory. There are 217 Jewish schools in Brooklyn — 176 of them *yeshivahs* and day schools. Day schools such as the Yeshiva of Flatbush, at 919 E. Tenth Street, and *yeshivahs* and rabbinical seminaries, such as Torah Vodaath, 425 E. Ninth Street, also in Flatbush, have worldwide reputations. The founder of Torah Vodaath, Rabbi Shraga Feivel Mendelovitz, was instrumental in setting up Torah Umesorah, the National Society of Hebrew Day Schools, which promoted the growth of day schools in this country.

If you are a stargazer, you might want to visit the Erasmus High School Museum (911 Flatbush Avenue; 718-282-7803) to see yearbooks and other memorabilia of some of the school's celebrated graduates — Barbra Streisand, Oscar Brand, Beverly Sills, Eli Wallach, and Neil Diamond.

If you want an insider's look around the borough, contact Brooklyn born-and-bred Lou Singer. His tours will give you eye-opening views of the area's architecture, ethnic neighborhoods, history, and good dining. Call him at (718) 875-9084.

Culture: *The Jewish Press* and *The Jewish Week* are good sources for finding out what's happening culturally in the Jewish community. Walt Whitman Hall at Brooklyn College in Flatbush is where Yoel Sharabi, Mordechai Ben David, Shlomo Carlebach, the Miami Boys Choir, and the Piamentas concerts are usually presented.

There once were two Jewish theaters in Brownsville, when that area enjoyed its Yiddish heyday. Today the Shorefront Y in Brighton Beach (3300 Coney Island Avenue; 718-646-1444) offers a long menu of activities for the community. Because it caters to the émigré community, its program brochure is published half in Russian.

The Brooklyn Museum, Eastern Parkway and Washington Avenue (telephone 718-638-5000), has no permanent Judaica collection but does occasionally have special exhibits on Jewish subjects. Of interest, however, is a frieze of Moses, Daniel, Jeremiah, and Isaiah on the exterior of the museum. There are also busts of Brooklyn-born comedian Alan King and entertainer Danny Kaye.

The Chai Gallery (Chasidic Art Institute), 375 Kingston Avenue, is unusual in that it showcases the considerable talents of sixty hasidic artists, and an increasing number of Russian émigrés (telephone 718-774-9149).

For young folks there is the Jewish Youth Library (1461 46th Street; 718-435-4711), with a large number of books in English, Hebrew, and Yiddish.

Eichler's is one of the best-stocked book and Judaica stores with branches in Borough Park (5004 13th Avenue) and Flatbush (1429 Coney Island Avenue).

Personalities: One of the most politically prominent Jewish sons of Brooklyn is Abraham D. Beame, who became New York's first Jewish mayor in 1973. Abe Stark was the first Jew to be elected borough president of Brooklyn. Howard Golden is the most recent in a long line of Jewish borough presidents.

Many major cultural institutions in Brooklyn grew because of Jewish vision and philanthropy. Nathan Jonas played a key role in establishing Brooklyn College, which has graduated several generations of Jewish students. Joe Weinstein, an immigrant who built the Mays department store chain, was called "Mr. Brooklyn" because of his munificent endowments to a variety of organizations. Julius Bloom, once director of the Brooklyn Academy of Music, made it the borough's principal mecca for the arts.

The roll call of prominent Jews — many in the entertainment industry — with roots in Brooklyn is inordinately long. According to Larry King, "It's no surprise that many successful people . . . came off those Brooklyn streets. Brooklyn taught survival, not in a mortality sense, but in a speak-up-for-what-you-want sense. You didn't get far by being shy in that town."

To name a few heavyweight survivors: film directors Woody Allen, Mel Brooks, and Paul Mazursky; comics Henny Youngman and Buddy Hackett; publisher Ralph Ginzburg; writers Norman Mailer, Bernard Malamud, Erich Segal, Joseph Heller, Gerald Green, Norman Podhoretz, and Alfred Kazin; the late science-fiction writer and polymath Isaac Asimov; actors Elliot Gould, Zero Mostel, Alan Arkin, Eli Wallach, and Lauren Bacall; columnists Sylvia Porter and Jane Brody; opera star Beverly Sills; theatrical impresario Joseph Papp; economist Milton Friedman; Colonel David "Mickey" Marcus, a West Pointer who organized and led the Israeli Army; singer-actress-director Barbra Streisand; singer-composers Neil Sedaka, Marvin Hamlisch, and Barry Manilow; opera star Robert Merrill; composers Aaron Copland and George Gershwin; Dadaist Man Ray (Emmanuel Radnitsky) and artist Peter Max; Supreme Court Justice Ruth Bader Ginsberg and Nobel physicist Isidor Isaac Rabi. Danny Kaye and his wife, composer-writer Sylvia Fine Kaye, hailed from Brooklyn, too. The borough also produced some great athletes: Dodgers pitcher Sandy Koufax; Boston Celtics coach Red Auerbach; Sidney Franklin, the only non-Latin bullfighter in Mexico; Sid Luckman, one of the all-time greats of college and pro football; and Howard (Cohen) Cosell, the sports reporter with the staccato delivery.

Eating: You won't starve in Brooklyn — culinary *Yiddishkeit* is thriving; every neighborhood boasts kosher pizza and falafel shops, bakeries, sweet shops, supermarkets, dairy, deli, and meat restaurants and take-out places. In Borough Park, several are located along Thirteenth Avenue, including Taam Eden Dairy, 5001 13 Avenue. Elegant upscale dining is at Ossie's Table (1314 50th Street); Café Shalom (1305 53rd Street) offers cappuccino and espresso. Sephardic delicacies are found in stores along Kings Highway, including the fifth-generation Oriental Mansoura Pastry (515 Kings Highway), Kosher Korner Middle East supermarket (492 Kings Highway), Istanbul Turkish Restaurant (702

Kings Highway) and many more. Other eateries are on Avenues J, M, and Coney Island.

For kosher Chinese cuisine there is Shang-Chai, 2189 Flatbush Avenue and Yun-Kee, 1424 Elm Avenue, both in Flatbush. In Crown Heights go to Kingston Avenue—there is Hungarian at Mermelstein's (351 Kingston Avenue) and deli at Ess & Bentch (299 Kingston Avenue). In Williamsburg the eating places are Landau's Glatt Kosher Deli at 65 Lee Avenue and Itzu's at 45 Lee Avenue.

Hotels: If you are attending a *simchah* in Borough Park and all you need are sleeping accommodations, try the Park House Hotel, 1206 Forty-eighth Street. It has no dining facilities but offers kitchenettes. Five minutes from Lubavitch headquarters there is the Crown Palace Hotel (570–600 Crown Street) which offers a cafeteria, *glatt* kosher catering and even entertainment.

Reading and Viewing: *A Stranger Among Us* is the latest in Brooklyn-Jewish films. Four others are based on Chaim Potok's *The Chosen,* Neil Simon's *Brighton Beach Memoirs,* Isaac Bashevis Singer's *Enemies: A Love Story*, and William Styron's *Sophie's Choice.*

The book *Jewish Landmarks of New York* by Bernard Postal and Lionel Koppman (Fleet Press) blends history and anecdotes of early Brooklyn (out of print, it is available in libraries). The distinctive Sephardic odyssey in America is detailed in *Magic Carpet: Aleppo-in-Flatbush* by Joseph A. D. Sutton (Thayer-Jacoby). *From Suburb to Shtetl, The Jews of Boro Park* (Temple University) by Egon Mayer is a thoughtful sociological study. There is no end to newly published illustrated books. *When Brooklyn Was the World: 1920–1957* (Harmony) by Elliot Willensky is a trip down memory lane, as is *Brooklyn: People and Places, Past and Present* (Abrams) by Grace Glueck and Paul Gardner. For a close look at Jewish athletes—many from Brooklyn—read *Ellis Island to Ebbets Field: Sport and the American Jewish Experience* (Oxford University Press) by Peter Levine. *Holy Days: The World of a Hasidic Family* (Summit) by Lis Harris offers an intimate and affectionate portrait of Eastern Parkway Lubavitch culture.

In fiction (in addition to those made into films), there is *To Brooklyn with Love* by Gerald Green (Trident); *The Assistant* by Bernard Malamud (Farrar Straus & Giroux); *A Stone for Danny Fisher* by Harold Robbins; and *Before My Life Began* by Jay Neugeboren (Simon & Schuster), all of which deal with past generations growing up in Brooklyn. *Damaged Goods* by Thomas Friedman (Permanent Press) presents a contemporary look at the Orthodox Brooklyn milieu. *Leaving Brooklyn* by Lynne Sharon Schwartz (Houghton Mifflin) is a coming-of-age story set in the 1950s. *The Kingdom of Brooklyn* by Merrill Joan Gerber (Longstreet Press) describes a bittersweet childhood in Flatbush in the 1940s.

You could, in fact, spend years reading about Jewish Brooklyn, past and present. But don't do it. Brooklyn is there to be experienced.

—Zelda Shluker

Brussels

Long before Brussels was designated as the capital of a unifying Europe, the city was known for such prosaic things as waffles and cobbled streets, chocolate and lace, French fries and parks. It was never a primary center of Jewish life, but Jews have been present for much of its history, and of the things for which it is best known, at least two of the city's parks do have Jewish connections. The Botanic Garden, on the Boulevard du Jardin Botanique, was created by Abraham Leo Errera, a nineteenth-century Belgian Jewish botanist. The Bois de la Cambre, south of the center of town, in the closest thing Brussels has to Jewish suburbs, is the place where local Jews enjoy the out-of-doors.

History: Jews first reached Belgium as traders accompanying the Roman legions that conquered the area under Julius Caesar. They were also among the first merchants and artisans in Brussels after the city's seventh-century founding. By all accounts, Jews were treated well during the Roman period and the first century of Frankish rule. Jews expelled from England in 1290 and France in 1300 found haven in today's Belgium.

Though the cycle of persecution and renewal had already been through a few turns, the fourteenth century was an especially miserable time for Jews who made their home in Brussels. During the Black Death epidemic of 1348–49, Jews were accused of poisoning the wells and were massacred. The community had barely reconstituted itself when, in 1370, Jews were accused of desecrating Hosts—the consecrated wafers used in communion. Several Jews were burned at the stake and the community was expelled. After that, Jews

were largely absent from the scene for the better part of three centuries.

Some Conversos arrived from Spain in the sixteenth and seventeenth centuries, but there was no significant Jewish presence in Brussels again until Spanish rule ended under the 1713 Treaty of Utrecht. In the succeeding hundred years, during which Belgium was under Austrian and French rule and united with Holland, Jews from Germany, the Netherlands, and Alsace settled in Brussels. It was under Napoleon that the Consistoire Central Israélite, Belgium's representative Jewish body, was founded and under the Dutch that the first modern synagogues rose in Brussels. When Belgium achieved independence in 1830, religious freedom was decreed.

Immigration from Poland and Russia fed the community in the late nineteenth and early twentieth century and, after 1933, refugees from Germany arrived. In the cities Jews pioneered in the leather, textile, and clothing industries, and in the Charleroi region many became coal miners. In Antwerp the diamond business became, and remains, an overwhelmingly Jewish world.

On the eve of World War II, there were thirty thousand Jews in Brussels. Many of Belgium's Jews, perhaps a majority, fled to France or overseas in advance of the German invasion of 1940, but some were lured back by Nazi efforts to assuage Jewish fears at the beginning of the occupation. Deportations began in July 1942; Jews were sent first to an assembly camp near Mechlin and then to extermination camps in the east. Roughly half of Brussels's prewar Jewish population died in the Holocaust.

That the toll was not higher was due to several factors. The Belgian constitution never permitted mention of religion on documents of civil status, so the Germans had a harder time identifying Jews. When Jews were ordered to register and have a *J* stamped in their passports, more than a quarter simply didn't show up. Unlike neighboring Holland, where deportations were handled by the Gestapo, in Belgium it was the responsibility of the local civil administration. Also unlike Holland, which was a noncombatant in World War I, the Belgians had recent memory of a German occupation, which helped in the quick formation of a resistance movement.

The biggest reason for the relatively high survival rate of Belgian Jews was, in fact, the reaction of the Belgian people. The Belgian Resistance actively participated in Jewish rescue efforts; some of its flyers instructed the public how to hide Jewish neighbors. A Jewish resistance group, the Committee for Jewish Defense, had an extensive network for hiding Jewish children and a press that produced underground newspapers in Yiddish, French, and Flemish, and even a lending library. The Catholic church and the royal family were also notable in their defense of Jews. After the war, Queen Elisabeth became the first member of a royal family to visit Israel.

Brussels was an important transit point for postwar Jewish migrants to Israel and the United States; there was a time during the 1950s when the Jewish population approached the prewar level. By the 1960s, however, it had stabilized and today numbers 25,000.

Community:
One can hardly describe the Jewish community of Brussels without distinguishing it from that of Antwerp. No other country has two Jewish centers so nearly equal in size and so different in character. Antwerp, in the Flemish-speaking part of Belgium, has 13,000 Jews; the community is close-knit, predominantly Orthodox, Yiddish-speaking, and heavily concentrated in the diamond business. The Jews of Brussels are acculturated, French-speaking, Zionist but secular, and widely distributed professionally. They share more with the Jews of Paris than with the Jews of Antwerp. Intermarriage, comparatively rare in Antwerp, is about 50 percent in Brussels. Like America, however, Brussels

is experiencing a rise in non-Jewish spouses becoming involved in Jewish affairs and converting to Judaism. About 20 percent of the city's Jewish children attend Jewish day schools and an additional 70 percent take Jewish-Studies classes offered in the public schools.

There is nothing in the way of an old Jewish neighborhood. Jewish stores exist but are not concentrated in one area. The neighborhoods with the largest Jewish presence are Uccle, Ixelles, and Forest (near the Bois de la Cambre) and, closer to the center, St. Gilles, upper Anderlecht, and Schaerbeek.

Judaism is legally recognized along with Catholicism and Protestantism, and rabbis' salaries are paid by the state. The state also subsidizes Jewish day schools in Brussels and Antwerp, where both secular and religious subjects are taught. The Consistoire Israélite de Belgique, which represents all the country's Jews in its dealings with the government, is located at 2 Rue Joseph Dupont. In addition to its political function, it is a good place for travelers to call with questions about Jewish activities and events (telephone 512-2190).

Personalities:
Jews were prominent in all phases of Belgian life by the beginning of the twentieth century. Four-time Foreign Minister Paul Hymans became president of the League of Nations Assembly. General Louis Bernheim was one of the nation's most decorated soldiers in World War I. Between the wars General Ernest Wiener was commander of Belgium's military academy. Brussels has also produced personalities as diverse as anthropologist Claude Lévi-Strauss, Gerald Frydman, one of the chief animators for Walt Disney Studios, designer Diane Von Furstenberg, and chanteuse-hostess Régine.

Sights:
Brussels is, above all, a great city for walking, with such an endless collection of cafés that you can rest your feet and watch the city go by at almost any point. The center of the city is a maze of narrow old-world streets. The Grand Place, a market square faced by the ornate facades of old guildhouses, is one of the most charming squares in Europe. The Royal Museum and the Albert I Library (both of

which have Judaica as well as general exhibits) and the Parc de Bruxelles are all within walking distance of the Grand Place.

Square one: The Grand Place is one of the most charming plazas of Europe

Many of the city's Jewish sights are in the center of town. There are no signs left, but the stairway leading up from Rue Ravenstein to the Palais des Beaux-Arts is the approximate site of the entrance to the Jewish ghetto destroyed in the fourteenth century. A few blocks to the north is the Cathedral of St. Michel (also known as Ste. Gudule), which dates from the thirteenth century. An imposing Gothic structure, the cathedral's best-known feature is the set of stained-glass windows designed by Bernard van Orley, an early sixteenth-century artist. In the windows you can see how the fourteenth-century ritual accusation against the Jews—the "Profanation of the Host"—has been preserved in memory. One window in the Chapel of the Holy Sacrament depicts Jews desecrating the communion wafers.

The alleged incident became a recurrent theme in Belgian literature and art. There was some talk in the 1960s about removing the offending window. Instead, church leaders left it in place and put up a plaque indicating that the scene depicted is legend, not fact.

Several blocks south of the Ravenstein ghetto site is the Rue de la Régence Synagogue. The stately Romanesque building (which is usually entered at 2 Rue Joseph Dupont) was designed by the Christian architect Désiré DeKeyser and completed in 1878. The facade features a three-story, gabled central section flanked by four-story towers. A rose window dominates the third story and a stone ark containing the Tablets of the Law stands atop the central gable. The sanctuary features painted-glass windows bearing scenes from Mount Sinai and pictures of Jewish leaders. It has white stone arches and high-backed wooden pews, a carved wood *bimah* and a priest's pulpit, at the top of a curved stairway, used only on Yom Kippur.

The synagogue building also houses several Jewish organizations, including the Consistoire, representing Jews from the entire country, and the Communauté Israélite de Bruxelles. The Belgian Jewish Museum is located there as well.

Though the synagogue on Rue de la Régence is by far the most striking, Brussels has more than a dozen Jewish houses of worship. Two in particular—the Schaerbeek Synagogue at 126 Rue Rogier and the Sephardic Synagogue at 47 Rue du Pavillon—are actually closer to some of the city's main hotels.

The National Monument to the Jewish Martyrs of Belgium is in Anderlecht, at the corner of Rue Emile Carpentier and Rue Goujons. It stands in the middle of a quiet residential neighborhood, a stark square with a menorah made of chains and a wall bearing the names of the 23,838 Jews killed after deportation from Belgium during the German occupation. Behind the main square is a smaller memorial to Jews who fought in the Belgian Resistance, with dates that carry a message of their own, such as Helena Ascheim, 1928–42, and Sally Dussman, 1925–44.

Throughout Brussels are sights and monuments of more general interest with Jewish connections. The Louis Bernheim Monument in Square Marie-Louise honors the Jewish general who became a World War I hero. The headquarters of the Liberal Party at 13 Rue de Namur is called the Paul Hymans Center, for the statesman who was one of the founders of the League of Nations. Near the Military Cemetery, on the Boulevard Auguste Reyers, is the Monument aux Fusillés, honoring the 342 members of the Belgian Resistance executed by the Nazis; among the martyrs, who are buried behind the monument, were many Jews.

The David and Alice Museum, 41 Avenue Leo Errera in Uccle, houses the art collection of David van Buuren—a Dutch Jew transplanted to Brussels—and his wife Alice. The building is Art Deco, the collection includes masters as well as modernists, and it is set in a beautiful, labyrinthine garden.

Culture: Many of the Jewish organizations in Brussels sponsor cultural events on a regular basis. One of the best places is the Centre Communautaire Laic Juifs at 52 Rue Hôtel des Monnaies. The center hosts lectures and seminars that feature leading Jewish figures—who speak French. Lecturers in the past few years have included Shimon Peres, Albert Memmi, Arthur Hertzberg, Bernard Henri Lévy, Beate Klarsfeld and Simone Veil. The center also hosts concerts and art exhibits as well as a Yiddish theater troupe that performs mainly during the winter. Call 537-8216 for the latest cultural activities. Another good place for lectures is the Martin Buber Institute at 44 Avenue Jeanne (telephone 648-8154).

There are two Israeli nightclubs, and several other Israeli-owned shops, on the Rue de la Fourche in the center of the city. To find listings of community events look in the monthly magazine *Regards* (published by the Centre Communautaire Laic Juifs) and the weekly *Israël d'Aujourd'hui*.

Side Trips: Knocke and Ostend are beach resorts frequented by Belgian and British Jews. The trip to either from Brussels is little more than an hour, but it's worthwhile to stop for a day along the way in Bruges, a medieval city whose canals have earned it the title "Venice of the North." The synagogue in Knocke is at 28 Van Bunnenlaan (telephone 611-0372). The Ostend synagogue is at 3 Maastrichtplein (telephone 703-558).

Recommendations: There are many fine hotels in Brussels. The best combination of luxury and location is to be found in the Hyatt Regency on Rue Royale, next to the Botanic Garden. It is a fifteen-minute walk from the Schaerbeek and Sephardic synagogues and a half-hour walk from the Rue de la Régence. The city's only kosher restaurant is Chez Gilles at 52 rue de Suède. To find out about kosher food and prayer times at various Brussels synagogues, call the Consistoire at 512-2190. If you want one more Jewish activity before you leave Brussels, remember that the international airport has a synagogue. Though it doesn't host the largest of Jewish communities, Brussels has Jewish outposts in the center and at the gate.

—Alan M. Tigay

Budapest

They were heady days, those days of autumn, when the red stars over Budapest came down. Change was in the air; there was a special spirit among the citizenry and the Jews reflected it in microcosm.

Kol Nidre services at the huge Dohány synagogue had a festive air — hordes of people excitedly packed its pews, aisles, and tiers, noting the Israeli flag alongside the Hungarian flag on the altar. Habimah representatives arrived to arrange for the Israeli troupe's upcoming visit, the Batsheva Dance Company opened at the elegantly renovated Budapest State Opera House, and El Al threw a party.

An art-bookstore window displayed an illuminated *megillah* and advised passersby to order it for Christmas. A lovely young blonde posed with a *hasid* in an ad for kosher Hungarian wine. And people who hadn't admitted to being Jewish on Monday, Tuesday, or Wednesday came forth on Thursday.

It may not have been the old glory days when virtually a quarter of Budapest's population were Jews, credited with creating central Europe's most vibrant and arguably most beautiful city. But, after decades in which *Jew* was a dirty word and anything connected with the notion was anathema, Judaism in Hungary appeared to be staging a comeback.

History: Jews have long had a special relationship with Hungary. Perhaps because they and the dominant Magyars perceived each other as wandering people, the Jews throughout the centuries achieved some sort of symbiotic stability. Not that they were loved unconditionally; there were cyclical persecutions and expulsions, reconciliations and returns. Nevertheless, rarely has a minority acculturated to the extent that most Jews Magyarized, assimilating to a degree little known elsewhere. Many Jews — even religious ones — saw themselves as Hungarians first, locked into a special love–hate relationship with the country of their birth.

Their history in this land straddling east and west is composed of many threads, complicated by Hungary's tendency to expand and contract with regularity: Victories and defeats often changed borders, populations, and rulers. And the history of the capital city of Budapest is more knotted still. Before 1873, there was no such place, there having been three separate towns — Buda, Óbuda, and Pest.

We know through archaeological finds that there were Jews in the area when it was part of the Holy Roman Empire. Historically, restrictions directed at them tell us that Jews from Germany, Bohemia, and Bavaria had arrived toward the end of the eleventh century to settle in towns — including Buda — ruled by the bishops. During the First Crusade in 1096, King Colomon saved Hungary's Jews from the army that had devastated Jewish communities between Regensburg and Prague.

By the twelfth century, Jews had grown so important economically that more restrictions were added, followed by still others in the thirteenth. But Hungary's rulers often opposed anti-Semitic regulations, which were therefore not strictly enforced.

The first expulsion of Jews took place in 1361. They were allowed back a few years later to a much improved atmosphere, but the situation worsened again and anti-Jewish sentiment was fanned by a 1494 blood libel in the town of Trnava.

When the Hungarians were vanquished by the Ottoman Empire in 1526, many Jews left with the retreating army and, given the Turks' relatively benevolent attitude, established congregations in leading Balkan communities. And when central Hungary was incorporated by the Turks in 1541, not only former residents returned to Buda, but Sephardim from the Balkans and Asia Minor as well. At one point, a Jew became physician to the pasha. By the seventeenth century, Buda had become the seat of one of the empire's most important Jewish communities.

Jewish fortunes fell again when the Austrians conquered Buda in 1686. The Jewish quarter was ravaged and half its thousand residents were killed. Under Hapsburg rule, the situation seesawed regularly. While anti-Jewish sentiment generally increased, particularly during Maria Theresa's reign (1740–1780), there were bright spots, especially under Joseph II (1780–1790).

By 1690 the Jews of Buda had begun to reestablish themselves, and the adjacent village of Óbuda was rehabilitated in 1712. In 1784, the country's first secular Jewish school opened in Óbuda and its linen weavers, especially the Goldberger factory, gained an international reputation. Fifteenth- and sixteenth-century records indicate there were Jews in Pest at that time; they even owned houses and land. But, forbidden residence after 1686, the Jews were not able to resume settlement until Joseph II's reign. During this period, migration from Poland and Moravia increased, so by 1787 there were 81,000 Jews in Hungary. They formed the basis of the modern community.

During the nineteenth-century turmoil in Europe, minorities rebelled for nationhood and the Industrial Revolution spawned workers' concerns. Though still not equal citizens, Hungarian Jews fought with Magyars in 1848–49 for independence from Austria. This stood them in good stead in Budapest: During the first Hungarian National Assembly in July 1849, Jews were granted complete civil and political rights, "wiping out the enormous debt owed to the heroic descendants of the illustrious Maccabeans." But when Austria squelched the revolution, it again suppressed the Jews until 1867, when Hungary finally became the other half of the Austro-Hungarian Empire. They were emancipated that year

and, under comparatively liberal leaders, the situation continually improved. By 1885 intermarriage was permitted, and in 1895 Judaism was officially recognized by the state as an accepted religion.

Immigrants from Galicia and Russia joined Hungarian Jews, whose ranks fueled Hungary's drive toward the twentieth century. Since the true Magyar considered himself a man of the land, the towns were largely populated by minorities. Among these, the Jews gained prominence in commerce and the professions, holding controlling interests in industry, banking, law, medicine, and the press. They even leased and purchased land, becoming successful enough landowners to be titled aristocrats (among them were the Herzogs, Kornfields, and Hatvanys). But eventually a familiar cry rang out: "The entire wealth of the nation runs through Jewish channels." At the other end of the spectrum, however, so many were poverty-stricken that from their ranks came the majority of the leaders of the Hungarian Social Democracy Movement—dubbed "Jock" for Jew. The anti-Semitic waves of the 1880s touched Hungary, particularly the blood libel of Tisza-Eszlar in 1882. In the blood libel, Károly Eötvös, one of Hungary's leading lawyers, defended the accused Jews and won their acquittal. Nevertheless, anti-Jewish animosity was to continue, but for many years mainly as an undercurrent.

The dismemberment of the Austro-Hungarian Empire following World War I reduced Hungary to one-third its former size and upset its equilibrium. A Bolshevik regime seized power in 1919; many Jews were in the forefront, including the leader Béla Kun. Four months later this government was overthrown and a period of terror ensued. Because of their involvement with the communists, the Jews became special targets. In 1920, Admiral Miklós Horthy began a twenty-four-year reign as regent, during which on-again, off-again restrictions often limited the Jews' civil rights and earning power.

In part because Nazi-allied Hungary was the last country to be occupied by the Germans—who did not enter until March 1944—the Holocaust in Hungary was singular. Early in the war, many Jews from territories newly annexed by Hungary were deported or used for slave labor. But though even more severely restricted than before, Hungarian Jewry held its own. Though the main reason for the German occupation was Hungary's desire to negotiate a separate peace with the Allies, also on the list of reasons was Hitler's feeling that the country's leaders were dillydallying over the Final Solution.

Eichmann was in charge. Against him was time—and a glimmering awareness in the Allied world of what the Nazis were up to. On Eichmann's side was the expertise gained elsewhere. The Jews in "zones" outside Budapest were rounded up and shipped off with great dispatch; by July 7, 50,000 from Budapest—the last zone in Eichmann's scheme—were in Auschwitz. At that point, deportations were stalled by various interventions. The "trucks for lives" negotiations took place. Sensing the war's outcome, the Hungarian government maneuvered for a more favorable place in Allied eyes. And neutral countries, led by Sweden's Raoul Wallenberg, began issuing protective documents. None of these tactics stopped the Nazi death machine, but they did save some lives. In early winter 1945 the Russians "liberated" Budapest.

Community: Like most of Hungary today, the Jewish community is in flux. Most of it is concentrated in Budapest, where population figures are subject to constant revision. With virtually every Jew commenting that on Yom Kippur he saw someone else he had no idea was Jewish, estimates now range from 60,000 to 150,000.

The discrepancy results partly from the policy of Hungary's communist regime which, by confining Jewish life strictly to religious dimensions, further spurred Hungarian Jewry's deep-rooted assimilationist tendencies.

The Alliance of Hungarian Jewish Communities, located at Sip utca 12, is the representative body of the nation's Jews. It replaced the old Central Board of Hungarian Jews, which by the time of the democratic revolution had come to be regarded as an organization led by Stalinists and police informants.

Another new organization is the Jewish Cultural Federation in Hungary. Its loosely defined membership includes non-Jews as well as Jews; among other things, it has organized classes on secular Jewish themes. And in the country of Herzl's birth, Zionist organizations flourish once again.

Sip utca oversees the function of the twenty-two synagogues currently operating in Budapest plus twenty-five elsewhere in the country; it also directs Jewish schools, *Talmud Torahs*; a hospital, nursing homes, an orphanage, and a new social club for young people, The Shofar. Among the community's cultural activities are the newspapers *Uj Elet* and *Szomblat*, two adult and two children's choirs, and an international cantorial festival.

Prior to World War II, practicing Hungarian Jews fell into three categories— *Neolog* (somewhere between Reform and Conservative), Orthodox, and *Status Quo Ante,* somewhere between the two. In Budapest today, only a few hundred consider themselves Orthodox. The *Status Quo Antes* are increasingly active, while the majority are *Neologs*—of one sort or another.

Since 1877 the community has been greatly buttressed by the presence of the Rabbinical Seminary of Budapest, which, as the only such seminary in Eastern Europe during the postwar years, not only schooled its own rabbis but also those serving its neighbors.

While expressions of anti-Semitism are not uncommon in today's outspoken atmosphere, it's speculated that the apparent interest in things Jewish (many non-Jews study Hebrew and Yiddish at the Hungarian Academy of Sciences' Center for Jewish Studies) indicates a feeling throughout society that the absence of a strong Jewish presence has somehow diminished it.

Sights: A backwater until the union of the three townships in the 1870s, the glittering cosmopolitan boomtown Budapest that emerged by the end of the century has often been called a Jewish creation. Almost all its major buildings and institutions came into being toward the end of the 1800s, and Hungarians today point out that what is still impressive dates from then. In fact, Budapest was once unkindly dubbed "Judapest." Wary now of such labeling and heirs to a different tradition, contemporary Jews do not cite the ethnic origins of secular creations.

Perusal of some figures gives at least an inkling of Jewish strength once upon a time. Prior to World War I, when the 900,000 Hungarian Jews represented about 5 percent of the population, nearly 60 percent of the country's merchants were Jews; 45 percent of the contractors, 26 percent of those in the arts and literature (with 42 percent of the journalists); 45 percent of lawyers; and 49 percent of the doctors. With nearly 250,000 of those Jews then living in Budapest, it is impossible not to walk the city's streets, to pass its elaborate *Belle Epoque* buildings, its graceful bridges, its bustling cafés, without sensing their presence. Indeed, one learns that the marble-decorated New York Coffee House, a still-extant fabled watering spot for Budapest's glitterati, was in its heyday owned by a Jew. Not surprisingly, the Jews lived all over — the banking aristocracy in palaces in the hills of Buda, the bourgeoisie in the less lofty streets of Pest.

Some concentrated in Pest near the Danube on either side of the Margaret Bridge. Near the Pest end of the bridge is a new memorial plaque to the Jews shot and thrown into the Danube in 1944 by the Germans and their Hungarian Fascist allies. Many of the mansions of this still-elegant residential area became "safe houses" during the Second World War, and the vicinity came to be known as "the protected ghetto." One of the local streets has been renamed Raoul Wallenberg utca — and comes complete with a bronze bas-relief of a man in a fedora — commemorating the Swedish diplomat who saved so many Jews.

From the time Pest first began to develop, an even larger cluster of Jews began to form around the spot where the Dohány Street Synagogue was built. This currently somewhat grimy downtown area is surrounded by streets named Majakovskij, Kertész, Wesselenyi, and Rumbach and abutted by the synagogue on Dohány. During World War II, Jews from all over the city were herded into this confine, which was surrounded by a high wooden fence and turned into another, larger ghetto — the only one at war's end with enough people to be liberated.

The Dohány Street Synagogue and the complex of Jewish-related buildings surrounding it is the neighborhood's centerpiece. Consecrated in 1859, the imposing Moorish-influenced structure is the largest Jewish house of worship in Europe. With its two almost full-length tiers, it seats around four thousand; five thousand have been estimated to crowd in. Services are accompanied by organ and choir.

A Holocaust memorial stands behind the synagogue. Built in the form of a weeping willow, its drooping branches form the Tablets of the Law; leaves are inscribed with the names of wartime victims.

Adjoining the synagogue is another structure, some of whose arches open onto a courtyard of Holocaust graves, housing the Jewish Museum. The site itself is significant because Theodor Herzl was born in a flat formerly on the spot. The museum's collections are impressive. Among the ritual objects either made or used in Hungary are *rimmonim* from seventeenth-century Florence; Seder plates made by the Jewish-founded Herend china factory, Hungary's most famous china producer; a *chanukkiyah* topped by the figure of Napoleon; and micrography. A darkened room chronicles the Hungarian Holocaust with concentration-camp clothing, dresses fashioned from *tallesim*, and drumheads made from Torahs. Near the entrance to the exhibits are stone testaments to the long-time presence of Jews in this region, including the replica of one from the third century proclaiming the existence of a synagogue in that part of the Roman Empire. The original is displayed in the National Museum of Budapest, while the Museum of History has many Jewish tombstones.

For lack of heat, the Jewish Museum is open only between Pesach and Sukkot. However, there are articles of Jewish interest in other Budapest institutions as well, including Rembrandt's *The Old Rabbi* in the Museum of Fine Arts; works of Jewish artists in the National Gallery; occasional displays in the "Resistance" section of the Workers' Museum; and the Kaufman Library of illustrated manuscripts, now housed by the Academy of Science.

Around the corner from the Jewish Museum, on Wesselenyi, is a synagogue honoring World War I soldiers, and Goldmark

Hall, scene of various theatrical presentations. (Jewish theater was performed there during the war.) Turning yet another corner off Wesselenyi is Sip utca, which has informally lent its name to the community's headquarters housed at number 12. The walls of its columned, gilt-trimmed reception room on the second floor are covered with paintings of past community leaders, some so assimilated that they wore noblemen's garb.

Other Jewish establishments also stand in and around these parameters. Among the synagogues are the main Orthodox one at Kazinczy 27; an old-style one, often used in movies, at Vasvari Pal utca 5; the Polisher Shul at Majakovskij 6, used two hundred years ago, in Maria Theresa's time, by peddlers from the provinces who couldn't get home before dark. The octagonal synagogue at Rumbach utca 5–15, with its towers and elaborate facade, has recently been renovated.

Kosher food establishments include a sausage factory at Kazinczy 41; the Central Jewish Kitchen at Pava utca 9–11 which distributes food to the needy; a coffee and pastry house at Dob utca 22; and the old Hanna Restaurant at Dob utca 35. The newest and most attractive kosher establishment these days, however, is the Shalom (Salom) Restaurant, Klauzal Ter 1–2, which offers Eastern European Jewish specialties and kosher Hungarian wines and brandies (telephone 1413-396 or 1221-646, except Sundays).

The Buda hills bear witness to Jews of the more distant past. In the thirteenth century they lived on the west side of what is now Szent-György utca. A 1278 tombstone taken from the cemetery is in the "One Thousand Years of the Hungarian Capital" exhibit at the Budapest Historical Museum. In this area stands the Fehervari Gate, one of two gates to the Castle District; in a former guise, it was called Jewish Gate. On a glade just beyond this passage, at the corner of Szilágyi Erzsebet fasor and Nagyajtai utca Sarok stands a new and intriguingly designed red marble statue honoring Raoul Wallenberg.

On a major street of old houses in the Castle District itself, at Tancsics Mihály utca 26, a medieval Jewish House of Prayer has been turned into a museum. In existence well into the Turkish period, it was built at the end of the fourteenth century and features two primitive wall drawings illustrating biblical passages. It also offers a blown-up black-and-white map of the old district. In its vaulted courtyard are tombstones from the thirteenth to the seventeenth centuries.

Across the street in the garden of number 23, the ruins of another synagogue have been found. It was to this synagogue that its congregants ran when the Austrians besieged Buda in 1686. Recent excavations revealed their bones, which have been given a Jewish burial in the main cemetery. Though the site is currently covered over for lack of money, plans for development exist.

Though most structures now on the Tancsics Mihaly utca date from a later period, this thoroughfare was long known as Jewish Street. And, in a house with a balcony just a few steps from the House of Prayer, Beethoven wrote his *Eroica* Symphony.

Also on the Buda side of the Danube is an elegant old synagogue erected in 1820 by the Jews of Óbuda, now a television studio. Near the crest of the Apostal Street hill, number 13 was reportedly a Jewish-owned mansion confiscated by Eichmann for his personal residence.

Day Trips: Much of Hungary is reachable for day trips from Budapest, by car or by train.

One intriguing destination is Sopron, virtually on the Austrian border. There, a medieval synagogue dating from the turn of the 14th century has been restored. Recessed from the street line at 22–24 Uj utca, it features vaulted arches, drawings of holiday scenes in the old times and, through a courtyard door just before the entrance desk, a stone well that was the *mikveh*. A special feature of the structure is a separate but attached women's hall, one of the oldest in Europe. Female congregants could watch the main service by peering through horizontal slits into the main sanctuary. It was one of the first public buildings in Sopron, when the town was young.

Though Uj utca means "New Street," this

still-charmingly medieval thoroughfare was probably built around the time of the town's establishment and was named Zsido utca, or "Jew Street," being the customary spot where Jews could live. A second synagogue stood at number 11 (whose courtyard now contains an ice-cream parlor). Among Sopron's early Jewish families was one named Israel, which resettled in Vienna and became bankers to the Hapsburgs.

Jews were barred from Szeged in the south of Hungary until the end of the 18th century. However, by the beginning of the twentieth century they had a sufficiently solid foothold to build a large, ornate synagogue on Josika utca, which some consider the world's most beautiful. It features cupolas, minarets, buttresses, gables, and stained-glass windows and has recently been restored, thanks to an unnamed former townsman now living in Florida.

Also worth visiting is Miskoic, north of Budapest, where the synagogue (at Kazinczy utca 7) dates to 1863, and was built according to plans of Ludwig Förster, designer of the Dohány Street Synagogue. Miskolc also has a *mikveh* and a kosher restaurant in the building of the Jewish community.

Personalities: While few today will finger fellow Jews, outstanding or otherwise — loudly proclaiming that such identification bears no relevance — past rosters bespeak the community's talents. Among the literati with roots in Budapest have been Arthur Koestler, Ferenc Molnár (author of *Liliom,* on which the musical *Carousel* was based); Felix Sultan, who wrote *Bambi*; journalist Joseph Pulitzer; humorist Ephraim Kishon; and Lengyel Menyhert, who penned the story on which *Ninotchka* and later the musical *Silk Stockings* were based.

The British film industry was built largely by the trio of Korda brothers, led by Alexander. Hollywood as well was greatly influenced by Hungarian Jews such as Adolph Zukor, George Cukor, William Fox of 20th Century Fox, Joseph Pasternak, and Jan Kadar. Entertainers include Paul Lukas, Peter Lorre, Lili Darvash, the Gabors, Theodore Bikel, and Harry Houdini — who was portrayed on screen by the son of another Hungarian Jewish immigrant, Tony Curtis. Musicians include Eugene Ormandy, Antal Dorati, Sigmund Romberg, Georg Solti, George Szell, and contemporary pianist Annie Fisher. Other cultural figures include the architect Marcel Breuer and photographers Robert and Cornell Capa. Of a scientific bent were Edward Teller and Leo Szilard, who helped develop the atomic bomb; Janos (John) von Neumann, a father of the computer age; aircraft developer Karman Todor; and Sándor Ferenczi, a Freud disciple and founder of the Budapest school of psychoanalysis. Contemporary writers known throughout Hungary include György Moldova, Andras Mezei, and István Orkeny. Not to be forgotten is Hannah Senesh, executed by the Nazis in Budapest's old Military Court after parachuting into Europe to save Jews.

Reading: *Charmed Lives* (Random House), a biography of the Korda brothers by Michael Korda, and *Robert Capa* (Saber and Saber), a biography by Richard Whelan, contain some descriptions of Jewish life in prewar Budapest. If it can be found, *Bondy Jr.* by Lajos Hatvany (London, Hutchinson, 1932) is a novel depicting how Hungarian Jews moved out of rural obscurity to nobility. *Budapest 1990* (Grove Weidenfeld) by John Lukacs is a look at the city in its prime with due mention of the Jews. There is also Charles Fenyvesi's *When the World Was Whole* (Viking Penguin) and Jonathan Katz's *Out of the Ghetto* (Harvard University Press).

Recommendations: Austrian Airlines and Malev, the Hungarian airline, serve Budapest via Vienna. Malev also has two nonstop New York-to-Budapest flights per week. Hungary is now included in the Eurailpass network. Hydrofoils also ply the Danube between Vienna and Budapest. For location, comfort, courtesy and efficiency, plus splendid views of the Danube and one of the largest breakfast buffet menus ever encountered (it even includes goulash), the Atrium Hyatt is unsurpassed. And with freedom in the air, Budapest can be enjoyed like never before.

—Phyllis Ellen Funke

Buenos Aires

Enrique Pinti is a kind of multicultural Jackie Mason, a fast-talking comedian whose one-man act, "Salsa Criolla," is the longest running show in the history of the Buenos Aires stage. "We are an Italo-Spanish-Jewish society, which is a chaotic mix," says Pinti in his lampooning of Argentine culture. "From the Spanish we got envy; from the Italians deceit and the habit of talking a lot and never saying anything. And on top of all that comes the permanent lament of the Jews. Jews always complain."

Porteños — as the citizens of Buenos Aires are known — often make the same observation (minus the comedy) about the three dominant cultural influences in Argentina. From casual conversation and guidebook prose one might think the Jews number about a third of the country's 32 million people, but that isn't quite true. People of Spanish origin make up about 40 percent and Italian descendants are about another 40 percent. Jews are slightly less than one percent.

Leave Miami heading south and you will find Jews only with effort — until you hit Buenos Aires. There, from the shops along Calle Florida to the demonstrators in the Plaza de Mayo, from the cafés to the Teatro Colón, from the huge University of Buenos Aires to the Chamber of Deputies, the Jewish position in the landscape is obvious.

Though some of the Jewish history of Argentina — distant and recent — has been troubled, in the years since democracy returned, the Jewish presence seems appreciated by large segments of society.

The profile of Jews on the Argentine horizon can be gleaned from three very different stories that appeared on a relatively typical day in the English-language *Buenos Aires Herald*. One concerned an arrest for desecration of a Jewish cemetery, which seemed to attract more media attention than similar incidents in the United States. A second was a profile of Luis Isidoro Berkman, the country's oldest practicing attorney, who among other things was defense counsel for one of the junta presidents court-martialed after the restoration of democratic rule. The third story was about the first public appearance of soccer hero Diego Maradona since his arrest on drug charges; he showed up at a park and went jogging with the Argentine Hebrew Society soccer team.

History: Buenos Aires was a backwater in the Spanish colonial empire, far removed from the seat of government and the Inquisition based in Lima. That made it attractive for some Portuguese Conversos, who arrived after 1580. Throughout the seventeenth century there were accounts of crypto-Jews in Buenos Aires, and one secret Argentine Jew fell victim to an auto-da-fé in Lima in 1639. But the record gives no hint of the number of Conversos during the period or the extent of their Jewish practice. By the time Argentina won its independence in 1810, the country was essentially without Jews.

In 1812, Bernardino Rivadavia, Argentina's first president, decreed freedom of immigration and respect for human rights. A few months later the Inquisition was officially abolished. The Constitution of 1853 likewise called for religious freedom of nationals and foreign residents. But Jews did not immediately flock to the country. Unlike the United States, where both the legal and cultural climate were conducive to Jewish settlement long before large numbers came, in Argentina the official status of the Roman Catholic church (to this day, the president of the republic must be a

Catholic) stood between the abstract freedoms of the constitution and ultimate freedom of movement for Jews.

The first recorded Jewish event in Buenos Aires was a wedding in 1860. Two years later a *minyan* met for the High Holidays and eventually developed into the Congregación Israelita de la República Argentina, to this day a fixture of central Buenos Aires. Immigration surged after pogroms in Russia began in 1881. Starting in 1889 Jewish agricultural colonies were established, especially in the provinces of Entre Rios, La Pampa, and Santa Fe, and between 1906 and 1912 Jewish immigration peaked at over 13,000 per year. The first were Ashkenazim, but they were followed by Jews from Morocco and the Ottoman Empire.

There was little anti-Semitism before World War I, but the situation changed after the Russian Revolution. Jews were generally identified as "Russians," and anti-revolutionary reaction turned into overt anti-Semitism during the Semana Trágica (January 7–13, 1919) when a general strike led to a pogrom. Jews were beaten and their property looted and burned while the police stood by. The violence threatened to spread, but Jewish leaders made a public appeal, prominent liberals criticized the government for inaction, and the president received a Jewish delegation.

By 1920 there were 150,000 Jews in Argentina and more were coming every day despite increasing restrictions. Most became farmers, peddlers, artisans, or shopkeepers. The rising tide of Argentine xenophobia coexisted with a flowering of Jewish life — cultural and religious organizations sprang up, the Yiddish press and theater flourished, the first Jewish hospital opened, and debates between Zionists and communists both enlivened the community and kept it from uniting.

The immigrant generation also saw the origin of one of the more piquant, and ultimately false, pictures of Argentine Jewry. Because all the immigrant groups were predominantly male, prostitution boomed, and Jews were no exception. The Jewish community ostracized those involved, who in turn started their own mutual-aid society, Zvi Migdal, and had their own synagogue and cemetery. The pressure was kept up, however, and by 1930 virtually all Jews had been driven out of the business. The Jewish community was probably the only one that eradicated prostitution from its ranks.

But a generation passed, and Jews looking for a colorful past continued to talk about Zvi Migdal. Others wrote about it, even romanticized it. The result is that today the Jewish "contribution" to prostitution is remembered perhaps more than that of any other group's.

The rise of Juan Perón, with his fascist leanings and pro-Nazi sentiments, alarmed Jews in the 1940s, as did his return in the 1970s and the success of his party in the 1980s. But Perón seemed to bear out the idea that elected leaders, no matter how corrupt or demagogic, are better than out-and-out dictators. The generals who overthrew his widow, Isabel, in 1976 were far harder on the Jews than Perón.

Though Perón introduced Catholic religious instruction into public schools and admitted many escaped Nazis to the country (while stopping Jewish immigration), he also declared sympathy for Jewish rights and for Israel. Among the Nazis allowed to slip into Argentina was Adolf Eichmann, chief engineer of Hitler's Final Solution. In 1960 Israeli agents tracked Eichmann down in a Buenos Aires suburb, seized him, and spirited him out of the country. Anti-Semitic activity increased in Argentina after Eichmann's trial and execution in Israel.

Under the military regime of 1976 to 1983, Jews were disproportionately represented in the groups — academics, journalists, psychiatrists — targeted for kidnapping and torture. Estimates vary, but of the 16,000 *desaparecidos* (those who disappeared and were never accounted for) close to 10 percent were Jewish.

But as the military's power waned, so did its anti-Semitism. When the Jewish community expressed its patriotism during the Falklands/Malvinas war, the government responded by appointing — for the first time — Jewish military chaplains.

Jews rallied to support Raúl Alfonsín, who became Argentina's democratically elected president in 1983. Opponents tried to paint him as a Jewish candidate — dubbing his Radical Civic Union the "Radical

Synagogue"—but the tactic failed, and Alfonsín appointed many Jews to high office.

The community was alarmed once more when the 1989 election was won not only by a Peronist, but one of Arab origin, Carlos Saúl Menem. After Menem took office, however, many Argentine Jews were amazed at how unfounded their fears had been. With far fewer Jewish supporters, Menem appointed almost as many Jews as Alfonsín. He has visited Israel and offered to mediate the Arab–Israeli disputes. The morning after the cemetery desecration near Buenos Aires, the president was on the phone with David Goldberg, head of the DAIA, the political arm of Argentine Jewry, to express outrage and solidarity, and to promise results. Desecrations of Jewish cemeteries are not new in Argentina; arrests are, and one was made within a week.

But neither democracy nor a sympathetic president can offer complete protection. In April 1992 Jews in Argentina and around the world were shocked by the powerful bomb that destroyed the Israeli Embassy in Buenos Aires, killing 32 people and injuring more than 100.

Community: Argentine Jews number 250,000 today (though many argue that the figure is too high or too low), 200,000 of whom live in Buenos Aires. The city has by far the largest concentration of Jews in Latin America. They are predominantly native born (and almost as monolingual as American Jewry). About 85 percent are Ashkenazic and 15 percent Sephardic.

But the community is no longer growing. The children of most of the Jewish farmers have long since gone to the city, and in the recent decades of political turmoil and economic decline far more have emigrated than immigrated.

Buenos Aires Jewry has what appears to be a European cultural structure overlaid with an American religious framework. In the United States the mutual-aid societies that helped immigrant Jews move into the mainstream were replaced by organizations that served a native-born Jewish community. But Argentina was not a melting pot, and the original structure still serves a more self-contained and self-governing community. (Conversely, Jews have not had to change as much to assimilate, since the Spanish and Italian social structure is much closer to Jewish tradition than is the Protestant milieu into which American Jews moved. As one observer puts it, "The *Yiddishe* mama is just like the Italian and Spanish mama.")

Many Jews began moving away from Orthodoxy as soon as they got off the boat, and after World War II only Zionism held the community together. It took Marshall Meyer, a young American rabbi who arrived to take over the country's first Conservative synagogue, to create a revolution.

Meyer went on to found Communidad Bet El, today the largest Jewish congregation in Argentina, and the Seminario Rabínico Latinoamericano, which has sent rabbis all across Latin America. After twenty-six years he left a transformed community in which Conservative Judaism was the vanguard (twenty-one Conservative synagogues in Buenos Aires alone) and Reform Judaism had a foothold.

Meyer captured the imagination of young Argentine Jews with "Jewish liberation theology," a philosophy that is concerned with the world and emphasizes Judaism as a system of ethics. And what he preached he practiced. He stood up for the rights of those imprisoned—Jewish and non-Jewish—by the military regime. In a system where the government got away with murder by blaming disappearances on terrorist groups, Meyer saved lives by gathering information on prisoners and making it public. He sometimes made pastoral visits to prisons to see known detainees and then "got lost" wandering the cell blocks looking for people whose arrests had never been reported.

Alfonsín appointed Meyer to the government commission that investigated the disappearances. The rabbi returned to the United States in 1984 and is now the leader of Congregation B'nai Jeshurun in New York.

Though perhaps not as integrated as American Jews, Jews are more a part of the Argentine mainstream today than they have ever been. They are prominent in the arts—especially film, music, and journalism. On the other hand, Jews are absent from the higher ranks of the military, the foreign ministry, and the judiciary.

An example of Jewish influence on Argentina can be seen in what is reputed to be the most heavily psychoanalyzed nation in the world (the confluence of a traditional Jewish profession and the brooding Argentine character); an example of the Argentine influence on Jewish life was seen a few years ago when the state-run radio did a documentary on Jewish tango composers and performers.

When Jews first arrived they were barred from the traditional avenues to wealth such as land ownership, church administration, and government, but they were on the ground floor of a modern capitalist economy. This resulted in Jews rising quickly to the ownership of large commercial and industrial enterprises. Jews either had a hand in starting, or at one time dominated, the nation's furniture, fur, textile, chemical, electronics and auto industries. Banco Mercantil and Banco Comercial were both founded by Jews. And just as the country was becoming known around the world for its agricultural exports, Jewish farmers established the first agricultural cooperatives.

The first Jewish neighborhood in Buenos Aires was Once (pronounced "own-say"), where many Jewish institutions are still concentrated. Jews can also be found clustered in the Buenos Aires neighborhoods of Villa Crespo, Floresta, and Belgrano, and in the suburbs of Olivos, Martínez, San Isidro, and Avellaneda.

Organized Jewish life revolves around a system of initials; even some locals don't know what they stand for. The best known communal organization is the DAIA (Delegación de Asociaciones Israelitas Argentinas), set up in 1939 to protect Jewish rights and represent the community to the government. AMIA, the Ashkenazic mutual-aid society, does everything from providing aid to the Jewish poor to funding schools (more than 60 percent of Jewish children go to day schools) to staging plays by Sholem Aleichem. For information on events in the community, AMIA (at Pasteur 633; telephone 953-9777) is a good place to call, though it may take time to find someone there who speaks English. ECSA (at Larrea 674) performs many of the same services for Sephardim.

In some ways Argentine Jewry looks the way American Jewry once looked, and in other ways the resemblance is growing. Buenos Aires has one of the world's four remaining Yiddish dailies (the others are in Paris, Tel Aviv, and Birobidjan, in Siberia). One of the newest Jewish organizations in the country is the Fundación Hadassah Argentina, located at Rodriguez Pena 1385 (42-2354).

Sights: Buenos Aires has the frayed-at-the-edges feel of New York or Paris in the late 1940s. It also has the look. Subway cars and department-store floors are made of wood. Open windows in buildings, buses, and trains signal the absence of air conditioning. Movie theaters have big screens and vendors sell candy in the aisles. Elevators have operators and metal gates, people drive old cars while children sit on their laps, and most adults smoke. The ubiquitous strains of the tango are reminiscent of resort, wedding, and *bar mitzvah* music of a bygone era. Visiting the Argentine capital is like stepping into a time warp.

Believe it or not, Buenos Aires rivals New York in having the best synagogue architecture in the world. This may sound more credible when you consider the competition. In Israel synagogue design tends to be functional at best; in the United States most of the attractive prewar sanctuaries were left behind and replaced by colder, more modern structures. In much of Europe the historic synagogues were destroyed by the Nazis or shuttered by the Soviets.

But Buenos Aires has kept its treasures. Many of the synagogues built before World War II are still used by Jews who have not moved as far from their grandparents' homes as have their counterparts in the United States.

The flagship of Argentine Jewry is the Congregación Israelita de la República Argentina, at Libertad 773. Often referred to simply as "Libertad," Argentina's oldest congregation is the most centrally located in Buenos Aires and has the most imposing building. Built at the turn of the century, modeled after the Synagogue de la Victoire in Paris and dedicated in 1932, the gray structure is entered through wooden doors framed by a sweeping stone arch, which in turn is topped by the Tablets of the Law. The high-ceilinged sanctuary has low-

Dances with raves: Street tango is a popular and inexpensive form of entertainment

backed wooden pews, a red carpet down the center, and a balcony curving around the back. Downstairs in the attractive weekday chapel you can attend what may be the world's fastest *Minchah-Maariv* service.

The synagogue also houses the small Museo Judeo de Buenos Aires, which has a good collection of local Jewish memorabilia, from ritual objects to photographs of the early agricultural settlements. Unlike the synagogue, which posts prayer times at the entrance, the museum hours vary, so call in advance (45-2474).

The Libertad edifice illustrates the proximity of Jewish life in Argentina and the Jewish contribution to the larger society. It is just a block from the Teatro Colón, one of the world's great opera houses. Even *porteños* who have never set foot inside often invoke the Colón as proof of their city's high culture. Sergio Renan, the general director, and Cecilio Madanes, the artistic director, are both Jewish, as are many of the Colón's teachers. As the Libertad prepared for a recent Shavuot, the Colón opera house opened its winter season with *Nabucco,* Verdi's opera on Nebuchadnezzar's conquest of Jerusalem and the Babylonian captivity.

Once is the *porteño's* answer to the Lower East Side. Fewer Jews live today in the neighborhood where the community got its start and more and more of the businesses are owned by Koreans, but Once lingers in the popular imagination as the Jewish *barrio*. Among the synagogues of Once is Yesod Hadat, at Lavalle 2449, built in 1932 by Jews from Aleppo. The building's beige stone facade faces the busy street, but through the front door you come to an open courtyard surrounded by three stories of arched colonnades. Beyond the courtyard is the sanctuary, where a stone central *bimah* sits under a cupola with small windows depicting the twelve tribes of Israel.

Also in Once is the Sociedad Hebraica Argentina at Sarmiento 2233, the city's best-known Jewish cultural center. Akin to New York's 92nd Street Y, Hebraica has concerts, lectures, and a high school, but it is probably best known for its films — many by Jewish directors and most having Jewish themes. Its programs are listed in the Buenos Aires dailies.

Two other Jewish clubs, where the emphasis ranges from culture to sports, are Hacoaj, at Estado de Israel 4156 (884-270) and C.A.S.A. Sefardita at General San Martin 77 in Vicente López (791-8460).

There is another gem of a synagogue in San Telmo, the Bohemian district where the tango was born and still thrives. Located at Piedras 1164, the synagogue founded by Moroccan Jews has a dome-topped archway entrance set back a few feet from the street's building line. The long and narrow interior has floral-patterned stained-glass panels on the ceiling and behind the ark. A women's gallery surrounds the sanc tuary, but more women seem to sit in the front row on the main floor — equal but separate — than in the balcony.

After Once and the central districts, Belgrano has the highest concentration of Jewish sights. The upper-middle-class neighborhood has narrow tree-lined streets of villas, town houses, and apartment buildings.

Communidad Bet El, the Conservative synagogue started by Marshall Meyer, is a wonderful complex occupying most of a square block. Located at Sucre 3338, it consists of modern white stone and red brick buildings mixed with older Spanish and Italian-style villas all surrounding a courtyard-playground dotted with rubber and palm trees. There is a day school for children, so the place is always full of life, and the synagogue can get as many as eight hundred worshipers on a typical Shabbat morning.

Also in Belgrano, at José Hernandez 1750, is the Seminario Rabínico Latinoamericano. Though seminaries don't usually qualify as tourist sites, this one is an exception. In keeping with the philosophy of Argentine Conservative Judaism, the seminary is very much open to the world. In addition to the rabbinical school (which ordained its first woman in 1992), it is a center for interfaith dialogue. It also has a high school, a graduate school of Jewish studies, adult education, lectures, exhibits and a Bet Din. You are more likely to hear English (and Hebrew) spoken at the seminary than at other Jewish institutions in Argentina. Call 783-2009 for information on its activities, or if you have language difficulties getting through to other institutions.

Templo Emanuel, the first Reform synagogue in Buenos Aires, is in another corner of Belgrano at Tronador 1455. At Emanuel you can see a Jewish stereotype stood on its head. In contrast to American Reform temples and the beautiful Orthodox synagogues of Buenos Aires, Emanuel symbolizes the tenuous hold of Reform Judaism in Latin America. It is a simple, white stone building in which congregants sit on folding chairs.

Perhaps more typical of the city's fortyfive synagogues is in suburban Vicente-López. There, not far from where Israeli

agents found Adolf Eichmann in 1960, is a synagogue founded by German Jewish refugees. Congregation Lamrot Hakol ("In Spite of Everything") starts with the ubiquitous courtyard situated behind a red brick wall at Caseros 1450. The striking feature of the sanctuary is that the walls are almost completely covered with memorial plaques. The Conservative congregation, no longer exclusively German, has a lively atmosphere; like Bet El, there is a school on the premises.

Personalities: The best-known Argentine Jew is still undoubtedly Jacobo Timerman, whose newspaper, *La Opinión*, was an outspoken opponent of the military regime until it was shut down. Timerman was imprisoned and tortured; then, after an international campaign on his behalf, he was released and allowed to go to Israel. He returned to Argentina after the dictatorship fell and is still highly regarded among Jews as a journalist, but he earned the everlasting ire of the community for the highly critical book he wrote on Israel's war in Lebanon.

René Epelbaum, who lost three children to the military regime, was one of the founders of the Madres de la Plaza de Mayo, mothers of *desaparecidos* who staged weekly demonstrations in front of the Casa Rosada (Government House) demanding information on their children. Even since democracy has been restored, the mothers have continued their marches.

Other noted Argentine Jews are the pianist and conductor Daniel Barenboim and Cesar Milstein, who won the 1984 Nobel Prize in medicine. Lalo Schiffrin is a Grammy-winning composer and Tato Bores, a television comedian whose political satire show has run for twenty years. Horacio Verbitsky, who writes for the leftist daily *Pagina 12*, is known for his articles exposing government corruption. The nation's leading film directors include Leon Klimovsky, Luis Saslavsky, Juan José Jusid and Carlos Sorin. Alejandro Romay owns Buenos Aires's television channel 9. Alberto Gerchunoff, chronicler of the Jewish gauchos, was the literary critic of *La Nación*, Argentina's leading daily. Luis Rubenstein was a composer who set up a tango academy. Engraved on the tombstone of

Manuel Sucher, another composer, is a *bandoneon,* the accordionlike tango instrument.

Ernesto Sabato, perhaps Argentina's leading novelist, is not Jewish but his wife, Matilda, is, and he has long been close to the Jewish community. Equally close was the late Jorge Luís Borges, who featured Jewish themes in some of his poems and who openly wondered about possible Converso roots.

Side Trips: Argentina is larger than the United States east of the Mississippi, so unless you are going for a month, forget about seeing "the country." There are sizable Jewish communities in Córdoba and Rosario, but most travelers who have at most one or two opportunities to venture out of Buenos Aires go farther afield where the contrasts with urban life are greater. Two popular destinations are Bariloche, a ski resort in the Andes, and Iguazú Falls in the northern jungle where you can also cross into Brazil and Paraguay.

Reading: Among the explicitly Jewish Buenos Aires novels are Mario Szichman's *At 8:25 Evita Became Immortal* (Ediciones del Norte), about a Jewish family trying to assimilate in the 1950s, and Francine Prose's *Hungry Hearts* (Pantheon), a hilarious story about a Yiddish theater troupe's South American tour in the 1920s. The hero of Isaac Bashevis Singer's *Scum* (Farrar, Straus & Giroux) left Poland to live in Buenos Aires. A moving and mystical tale about Buenos Aires under the junta is Lawrence Thornton's *Imagining Argentina* (Bantam). Manuel Puig's *The Buenos Aires Affair* (Dutton) is evocative of the city and its personality.

The House on Garibaldi Street (Bantam), Isser Harel's account of Eichmann's capture, is both a riveting true story and a guidebook to Buenos Aires. Timerman's *Prisoner Without a Name, Cell Without a Number* (Random House) is a textbook of the brutality of the military regime. For a good historical and sociological overview, see "Latin American Jewry Today" by Judith Laikin Elkin, in the 1985 *American Jewish Year Book.*

Eating: Considering the amount of beef traditionally consumed by Argentines and the relative paucity of kosher homes among Buenos Aires Jews, it was until a few years ago difficult for visitors to maintain a kosher diet. Vegetarianism, however, is catching on, and there are some kosher restaurants to choose from. Among them are Kasher Center at Córdoba 2424; Sukat David at Azcuenaga 583; and Maadanim at Nazca 544.

Recommendations: You can't do better in location or atmosphere than the Sheraton Buenos Aires. The accommodations are luxurious, it's a three-minute walk from shopping on Calle Florida and about twelve minutes on foot to the Libertad Synagogue. At least twice a week something seems to happen there — a performance, an awards ceremony, the visit of a sports team — that puts it on the television news the next day.

Aerolineas Argentinas offers comfortable service from New York and Miami. You can get kosher meals on their flights, and be sure to ask for their guide for Jewish travelers in Argentina.

Argentina is not as well represented as Europe in the guidebooks. For further information there is the Argentine National Tourist Office, 12 West 56th Street, New York, NY 10019.

Americans think of Buenos Aires as having reversed seasons, which is technically true, but its southern latitude is equivalent to that of Charleston, South Carolina, in the north, so June winters are quite mild.

The main barrier for most American tourists traveling to or in Argentina is the language. Do a good job of brushing up on your Spanish and — Enrique Pinti notwithstanding — you'll have little to complain about.

—Alan M. Tigay

Cairo

Most of us first had our consciousness raised about life for Jews in Egypt when we recited *Avadim hayinu l'Pharaoh b'Mitzrayim* (We were slaves to Pharaoh in Egypt) at the Passover Seder. The biblical accounts of the sojourns of Abraham, Jacob, and Joseph in Egypt and the bondage there of the Children of Israel are indelibly imprinted on our collective memory. Succeeding Jewish experiences in the land of the Pharaohs have fluctuated between prosperity and scholarship under tolerant rulers, and persecution and decimation under fanatical sovereigns.

The Jewish community of Egypt is the second oldest in the world. There have been Hebrews in Israel since Joshua's conquest, and Hebrews have lived in Egypt since the days of the First Temple, according to literary sources.

Cairo became a must for serious Jewish travelers after 1977, when President Anwar Sadat made his historic visit to Jerusalem. Since relations between Egypt and Israel were normalized two years later, tens of thousands of Israelis have also traveled to the capital of the Arab world's largest and most influential country.

Drawing world Jewry to Cairo are not only spectacular antiquities and teeming bazaars of copper and gold. Cairo has had a Jewish population since the city was founded as Fustat more than a dozen centuries ago. Their presence and their contributions to both the city and to Judaism have linked Cairo inextricably to Jewish history.

History: Physical evidence of three thousand years of Jewish presence in Egypt is scarce. Some tourist guides will take you to a desolate spot along the Nile and show you the ostensible place where Moses was found among the bulrushes. More tangible evidence is the eight-hundred-year-old Ben Ezra Synagogue in old Cairo (the original Fustat), just behind an ancient Coptic church built over a crypt where Joseph, Mary, and the infant Jesus are said to have taken shelter when they fled to Egypt to escape Herod's wrath.

A booklet published by the Cairo Jewish community, available at the Ben Ezra Synagogue, deduces from the story of Joseph and Mary continuous Jewish residence in Egypt since biblical times. "Joseph was a Jew," the booklet says, "and the logical thing for him to do was to go to his own people for a refuge."

Jews may have lived in old Cairo since its founding in 641. By the tenth century, there were three Jewish communities in the city, as Mesopotamian Jews joined the Palestinian community and the dominant Karaites. The city became the religious and cultural center of Egyptian Jews, with many noted scholars and yeshivahs.

It was in Fustat that Maimonides lived and wrote. Arriving around 1165 after years of wandering from his native Córdoba, he spent the first eight years writing and serving as the Jewish community's religious and lay leader, supported by his brother, a gem dealer. Among other things it was the leadership of Maimonides that ended the dominance of the more numerous Karaites. It was only after his brother's death, when he began practicing medicine to support his family, that he produced his greatest works, including the *Guide to the Perplexed* and the *Mishneh Torah*.

Old Cairo's decline had begun by Maimonides's time, and Jews began moving to new Cairo. As in other Muslim cities, Jews as well as Christians were alternately persecuted and tolerated. Particularly under the Mamelukes, from 1250 to 1517, suffering intensified. In 1301 and again in 1316, Jewish and Christian houses of prayer were closed. In 1354, a mob razed all non-Muslim homes that were higher than Muslim ones. During the fifteenth century, synagogues were inspected to make sure that additions to them, which were forbidden, had not been built. Also under the Mamelukes, the economic situation of the Jews, who had been artisans and merchants, was undermined, as they were barred from trading in spices and other products.

By the seventeenth century there were three communities: Mustaravim (native, Arabic-speaking Jews), Maghrebim (from today's Morocco and Algeria), and Spanish refugees. The Spanish Jews excelled in Jewish scholarship and their halakhic decisions were universally accepted.

The Ottoman Turks followed the Mamelukes, interfering less in the affairs of the Jews than their predecessors — except when incited by Muslim fanatics. On such occasions, synagogues were again closed and burials had to be held quietly or at night to avoid Muslim attacks on the funeral procession. When the Turkish governor — who threatened to slaughter Cairo Jews unless the Jewish director of the mint handed over a huge sum of money — was murdered before he could carry out his threat, the community instituted the celebration of Purim Mitzrayim (Egyptian Purim).

Things worsened for the Jews under the Turks before they improved under an independent Egypt. Moses Montefiore and other wealthy Jews from abroad visited Cairo in 1840 and set up modern schools for Jewish children. Economic development attracted Jewish immigrants from other Mediterranean countries. By the early twentieth century the Jewish community had rebuilt itself numerically, economically, politically, and culturally. In 1882, there were 5,000 Jews in Cairo; in 1917, there were about 25,000, including one thousand Karaites and a small number of Ashkenazim.

Jews were among the founders of the fashionable residential districts of Ma'adi, Zamalek, Heliopolis, and Garden City. The community, most of whom were merchants and industrialists, supported a network of synagogues, schools, charitable institutions, and hospitals; it published newspapers in French, Arabic, and Ladino.

By the end of World War II, there were 42,000 Jews in Cairo, about two-thirds of all those in Egypt. During the war, many Palestinian Jewish soldiers of the British Army's Jewish Brigade were stationed there, including Royal Air Force pilot Ezer Weizman.

Things began to change after the war. In November 1945, a mob organized by "Young Egypt" attacked the Jewish quarter, leaving a synagogue, a Jewish hospital, and an old-age home in ashes. After the State of Israel was declared in 1948, hundreds of Jews were arrested; bombs exploded in Jewish neighborhoods; Jewish businesses were looted. Between 1948 and 1959, some twenty-five thousand Jews took the hint and left Egypt.

This scenario was repeated in 1956, during the Sinai Campaign, and again in 1967, during the Six Day War, with fewer and fewer Jews to arrest and deport. Most who left had to sign statements agreeing not to return and transferring their property to the Egyptian government.

Community: Today the Jewish community is approaching extinction. It numbers less than 100, almost all of them elderly; the last wedding was held in 1980. The Jewish community headquarters is at 13 Sebil el-Khazender Street and is open from 11 A.M. to 2 P.M. (telephone 824-613 or 824-885); the community president is Emile Rousseau. The other important Jewish address is the Israeli Embassy, at 6 Ibn Malik Street in Giza (telephone 361-0458 or 361-0528). Another good place for information is the Israeli Academic Center at 92 El-Nil Street (telephone 349-6232 or 348-8995).

Cairo was once the world center of the Karaites. Now the Karaite center is in Ramle, Israel, and the Karaite community of Cairo has been reduced to 15 elderly men and women, all of them single except for the *chakham* (religious leader).

Sights: The Ben Ezra Synagogue, located at 6 Harett il-Sitt Barbara, is known for its twelfth-century wooden doors and, inside, its Moorish design featuring many arches, hanging lamps and stone central *bimah*. Rebuilt in the nineteenth century and restored in the last few years, its history stretches back much further. Today, it looks much as it did on the historic day nearly a century ago when Professor Solomon Schechter, then of Cambridge University, carried a ladder up to the women's gallery and climbed through a trap door into the attic *genizah*. For a thousand years, this was the burial place for every book, manuscript, contract, letter, will and any other document containing the name of God. Schechter and other researchers would eventually uncover some 400,000 items—80 percent of which are now at Cambridge.

An illustrious Cairo synagogue not on any tourist itinerary is the Ben Moshe, or Rambam, Synagogue. It is located in the Mouski Quarter, not far from the Khan el-Khalili market, a section once known as Harat el-Yahud, the old Jewish quarter, where Jews no longer live. Unfortunately, the roof of the main building fell in some years ago. There has been talk of repairing it but, unlike the Ben Ezra Synagogue, no one has provided funds for the repairs.

There is one functioning synagogue in Cairo—Shaar Hashamayim, at 17 Adli Pasha Street, in the heart of the business district a few blocks from the Nile Hilton. Saturday and holiday services are often attended by Israeli embassy officials and visiting Jewish tourists. The entrance, guarded by local police, is from the alley at the side of the synagogue.

Elsewhere in the city, there are Jewish sights in various states of decline or repair. There are plans to reopen the Karaite synagogue in Abbasia; for information call the head of the Karaite community, Joseph Qodsi, at 931537. The City of the Dead—the vast cemetery located on the city's eastern fringe and populated by squatters—has a Jewish section (in Basatin) with many mausoleums; as in the rest of the necropolis, the dead in the Jewish section now share space with the living.

The Egyptian Museum houses some artifacts of Jewish history. On the first floor, in the section dedicated to Akhenaton (Amenhotep IV), are letters from Tell el-Amarna, the capital of Akhenaton's empire, to Jewish cities such as Megiddo and Akko, which were under Egyptian sovereignty. The letters form the most important surviving collection of written sources on the political history of Palestine at the end of the fourteenth century B.C.E. Across the hall from the Akhenaton exhibit is a stele (a stone with a rounded head bearing an inscription) written by Merneptah, the son of Ramses II. The inscription mentions the name Israel for the first time in an Egyptian text and places the nation somewhere in Palestine. It is regarded as evidence that the biblical exodus had already taken place, sometime during Merneptah's reign (1236–1223 B.C.E.). The stele was taken from the Great Temple of Amon in Karnak, a mile east of Luxor in Upper Egypt.

If you want to see how Jacob and Moses lived, or simply to get a glimpse at Egyptian life around 2500 B.C.E., visit the Pharaonic Village, situated (appropriately enough) on Jacob Island in the Nile. Traversed by canals, staffed by guides in period dress, and surrounded by three thousand trees to block out all traces of the modern world, the thirty-two acre village has exhibits on ancient Egyptian life, economy and religion.

Personalities: Cairo's preeminent Jews were rabbinical scholars, of whom Maimonides—the Rambam—was only the most outstanding. In addition to his scholarship and community leadership, he was also the sultan's physician. According to tradition, he wrote his codes and responsa in Hebrew and Arabic in an alcove of the Rambam Synagogue. His son Abraham and grandson David were also *negidim* (leaders) of the Egyptian Jewish community. Elderly members of the Jewish community still come to the synagogue alcove to light candles and pray.

Though the Jews of Ethiopia were isolated from mainstream Jewry for more than a millennium, there was intermittent contact with Egypt. Rabbi David Ibn Zimra, chief rabbi of Egypt in the sixteenth century, was the first to recognize the Beta Israel as Jews. Gershon ben Eliezer Soncino, the last printer of the famous Soncino family, introduced the first Hebrew printing press in Cairo in 1657. It was also the first one in the Middle East outside of Palestine.

One of Egypt's leading financiers in this century was Victor Harari, a Cairo native who served on the board of governors of Egypt's National Bank. The bank itself was established with the help of Ernest Cassel, a Jewish-born German who is also known for financing the construction of the first Aswan Dam. The Mosseris were prominent bankers and entrepreneurs from the eighteenth century to the twentieth; various members of the family were responsible for building the first Egyptian railroad, construction of the King David Hotel in Jerusalem, securing permission for Solomon Schechter to investigate the Cairo *genizah*, and founding the Egyptian Zionist movement. The Egyptian film industry was pioneered by director Toto Mizrachi, whose son Moshe is a prominent Israeli director. Joseph Cataoui was Egypt's chief revenue officer and his son, Joseph, became minister of finance in 1923; another son, Moses, was president of the Cairo Jewish community for forty years. More recent figures to emerge from Cairo include cartoonist Raanan Lurie and the Israeli poet Ada Aharoni. The Ambache sisters became the women behind two of Israel's most popular leaders—Suzy married Abba Eban and Aura married Chaim Herzog.

Side Trips: The pyramids and Sphinx are in Giza, about an hour from central Cairo. The sound-and-light show is in English on Saturdays, Mondays, and Wednesdays. Dress warmly even on hot summer days; the desert cools quickly at night. The script of the sound-and-light show has not been changed since Camp David: Islam and Christianity are mentioned as monotheistic religions, but Judaism is not.

Most of the glories of ancient Egypt are an hour's flight from Cairo in Luxor on the site of Thebes, the ancient capital of Upper Egypt, in Aswan, in Abu Simbel, and points in between. The most pleasant way to see everything without strain is to take a Nile cruise, which stops at various temples between Luxor and Aswan. The food is good and the guides are informative and helpful.

When you get to Aswan, however, you are on your own. The guides know nothing about the fascinating Jewish community that lived in Aswan even before Ezra and

Nehemiah rebuilt the Temple. On Elephantine Island, which is a two-minute ferry ride from the Aswan dock, are the ruins of an ancient Jewish temple. Early in this century, a well-preserved archive of papyri written in Aramaic was discovered there, chronicling the history of this unique Jewish outpost.

The Elephantine community was founded in 525 B.C.E. by a battalion of Jewish soldiers hired by the pharaoh to protect his frontier against Nubian invaders. The army post existed for hundreds of years, and the papyri document a fascinating exchange of correspondence between the Elephantine community and the Jewish authorities in Jerusalem. One of the customs of Elephantine Jews that differed from current *halakhah* was that both women and men could divorce their spouses.

In the Great Temple in Luxor are several inscriptions of Jewish historic interest, which guides will point out if asked. One concerns the occupation of Israel by Thutmose III, the pharaoh who conquered Megiddo, and mentions Jerusalem, Akko, and Eilat. The stele of Sesostris III shows his route to Canaan via the northern Sinai and gives the names of some of his Jewish tribute bearers; during Israel's occupation of the Sinai, many of the sites along Sesostris's route were discovered by Hebrew University archaeologists. The relief of Sheshonk I describes Israel and his pillage of the Temple Mount after King Solomon's death.

Recommendations: Most of Cairo's luxury hotels run Nile cruises between Luxor and Aswan. For more information before you leave home, contact the Egyptian Government Tourist Office, 630 Fifth Avenue, New York, NY 10022 (telephone 212-246-6960).

Reading and Viewing: To brush up on the history of Arab–Jewish relations in Egypt, read *Jews and Arabs: Their Contacts through the Ages* by S. D. Goitein (Schocken) and Jacob M. Landau's *Jews in Nineteenth-Century Egypt* (New York University Press). Laurie Devine's novel *Nile* (Simon & Schuster) portrays Arabs and Jews in Egypt since 1948. For a fictional picture of Egyptian life, with a few Jewish characters, try Lawrence Durrell's *Alexandria Quartet* (Dutton).

With the advent of video stores, you can now get in the mood for either Passover or a trip to Egypt by picking up Cecil B. DeMille's 1956 epic *The Ten Commandments*. A theatrical alternative is Andrew Lloyd Weber's *Joseph and His Amazing Technicolor Dreamcoat*. Of course, you probably don't have to go farther than your own bookshelf to find the most ubiquitous source on Jews in Egypt—the Passover *Haggadah*. History has its ironies. In 1980, the staff of the newly established Israeli Embassy looked all over Cairo for a hall in which to conduct a Seder for 150 people. They finally found a place that had the space, met the security requirements, and was willing to purchase a new set of dishes for *kashrut* purposes. It was the Pharaoh Hotel.

—Jesse Zel Lurie

Cape Town

No wonder South Africa became "the beloved country." For so many new arrivals, their first glimpse was of Cape Town. And Cape Town, the country's oldest city, just happens to be one of the world's more spectacularly situated urban areas. Bordered by the sea and wrapped around the base of three peaks — including the dramatically flat-topped Table Mountain — Cape Town, though second now in size to Johannesburg, remains the doyenne of South Africa's towns.

As the country's original gateway, it also retains its wellspring status. Not only did many eventual titans of development pass through en route to the interior, but many stayed — using Cape Town as a base for endeavors that ultimately affected the entire nation.

It was in Cape Town where, long before apartheid, Europeans, Africans, and Asians mingled to form the "Coloured," or mixed-race, population. And it was in Cape Town that the Afrikaners, as the descendants of Dutch settlers are known, began their stormy but symbiotic relationship with fellow whites from England.

In Cape Town, too, took root the South African Jewish community, whose early — and thorough — integration into the country's economy has made it one of the world's most affluent. From the first days of Cape Town and the Cape colony — that area encompassing the African continent's southern tip — the Jews either pioneered or predominated in trade, commerce, and finance. So doing, they achieved a distinction in Jewish history. In a society thus far based on racial divisions, the Jews — .05 percent of the overall population, 2.3 percent of the 4.9 million whites — are in the peculiar position of being part of the dominant minority white establishment.

History: For as long as the Western world has been aware of South Africa, the Jews have been associated with it. Portugal's Jewish scientists and cartographers contributed significantly to Vasco Da Gama's discovery of the Cape of Good Hope in 1497. And when the Dutch East India Company founded its colony in 1652, Jews were involved. Though the company accepted only members of the Reformed Christian Church, it traded with Jewish merchants in Holland, and nonprofessing Jews were among the Cape's first settlers.

Religious freedom came to the Dutch colony in 1803 and was guaranteed when the British occupied the Cape in 1806. Among the first settlers sent by England in 1820 to strengthen their eastern frontier were about 20 Jews — including the brothers Joshua and Benjamin Norden. Joshua is memorialized in the Grahamstown cathedral, perhaps the only Jew so honored in a South African church. On Kol Nidre night 1841, at Benjamin's home in Cape Town, the first South African Jewish congregation was founded.

During the nineteenth century's first half, Jews seeking fortune and adventure in this little-known land hailed primarily from England, Germany and Holland. Coinciding with the Boers' Great Trek inland away from the British, the Jews brought skills needed in the hinterlands. Jews scattered to the interior where their stores in villages and at railway sidings often became the local business and social centers. The Mosenthals, from Germany, established a chain of trading stations throughout the cape and helped stabilize the rural economy by providing long-term credit to storekeepers, who then extended it to farmers. Before a banking system developed they issued their own bank notes, accepted widely enough to finance industries. The de Pass family, arriving from Britain in the 1840s, developed shipping, fishing, and coastal trading, as well as sugar enterprises. Jews were innovators in fields as diverse as wine production and ostrich feathers, clothing and steel making.

The discovery of diamonds in 1867 and gold in 1886 began transforming a rural country into a modern industrial society. Enough Jews responded to the opportunity to swell the South African fraternity to 4,000 by 1880. Included were future mining magnates Barney Barnato who, with rival Cecil John Rhodes, founded the omnipotent diamond operation, De Beers Consolidated Mines—later controlled by Ernest Oppenheimer and his Christianized son, Harry.

Though the first Jewish tycoons had Anglo-German roots, word of successful Lithuanians filtered back to the old country and Litvaks soon came to dominate the immigrants' ranks. South Africa was particularly appealing to the Lithuanians because their preindustrial experience had equipped them well for its economic vacuum. Not wage earners (as, say, in Poland), but small independent artisans, traders and middlemen, tavern keepers, shoemakers, tailors, they became shopkeepers in Cape Town and around the mines, as well as peddlers in the hinterlands. So familiar a figure did the itinerant hawker become that the Afrikaans-speaking Boers coined a word to describe him. Possibly deriving from the Dutch word for Moses or the German for schmooze, he was called a *smous* (pronounced *smoos*). So many Jews arrived that by 1890 there were 10,000, and by 1910, 40,000. Of these perhaps 70 percent were from Lithuania, and South African Jewry was dubbed a Lithuanian colony.

While some rural fundamentalist Boers harbored stereotypical Christian prejudices about Jews—compounded perhaps by resentment of their creditors—others, devoted to the Old Testament, felt a kinship between the Bible's "Chosen People" and their own destiny in South Africa.

Though Jews fought on both sides during the Boer Wars, the arrival of English Jews bolstered the British side. In 1902–03, however, Cape Jews faced an attempt to restrict immigration to persons reading and writing the characters of European languages. Though ostensibly aimed at Asians, particularly Indians, such categorizing included those speaking Yiddish. Thanks to successful community lobbying, however, the 1906 Cape immigration law declared Yiddish a European language. And despite an influx limited by Anglo-Boer tensions, perhaps 20,000 more Jews arrived—the majority of South Africa's immigrants—peaking between 1924 and 1930.

Sentiment to restrict immigration also surfaced when the Afrikaners who had begun moving to urban areas found themselves "poor whites." In 1930, with both Afrikaner and English support, a Quota Act curtailed immigration, but because it excluded Germany from quotas, 6,000 Jews fleeing Nazism entered South Africa by 1936. Meanwhile, Nazism was influencing increasingly militant and nationalistic Afrikaners who began forming rabidly anti-Semitic organizations. Though Jews today note there was no physical violence, the hatred fanned by these organizations resulted in demonstrations against the 1936 arrival of a chartered refugee ship, the *Stuttgart*. And in 1937 another immigration law, the Aliens Act, set up an elaborate selection process that effectively closed the door on all but a trickle of Jews.

Community: Among 2.4 million other Cape Townians, the 20,000-member Jewish community—though now smaller than Johannesburg's and one-sixth of all South Africa's—fiercely maintains its independence and pride in being the country's senior center of Judaism. Insisting also that it is the most liberal and harmonious, it sees itself as the image in which all others have been created. Given this microcosmic status, it reflects South African Jewry's individuality.

Historian Gustav Saron has described this community as "a case of pouring Litvak spirit into Anglo-Jewish bottles." A blend of Western and Eastern Europe, it mixes London's United Synagogue ritual with the intellectual *mitnaged*—as opposed to hasidic—tradition. Though few descendants of the original Anglo-Jewish settlers remain, at least as Jews, their legacy prevails in the religious services to the city's seventy-four Jewish institutions.

Cape Town Jewry is 80 percent Orthodox and 20 percent Reform, but only about 5 percent are *shomer Shabbat*. The community supports twelve Orthodox and two Reform synagogues. The leading Orthodox ones are the Gardens, or the Great Shul, home to South Africa's original congregation; the Green and Sea Point Hebrew Congregation, which, with over 2,000 members, is the largest in all Africa; and the Claremont synagogue. There is also a small Lubavitch congregation and a strong Sephardic one, comprised of Jews from the island of Rhodes, via Zambia and the Congo.

Originally the Jews lived in the downtown "city bowl" of Cape Town; in the Gardens area, around the main synagogue; in Tamboers Kloof; and later in Oranjezicht. More recently they have spread across the mountains to the large homes and rolling gardens of Constantia and Bishop's Court; to such southern suburbs as Newlands, Claremont, and Rondebosch; and the Atlantic coast areas of Kenilworth, Clifton, Bantry Bay, Camps Bay, and Sea Point—where their concentration per square block is probably the greatest in South Africa.

Eighty percent of the community's children attend Jewish day schools, which run from primary grades through high school. The Jewish Board of Deputies, which represents Jewish concerns to the community at large, funds, with the Zionist Council, the monthly *Cape Jewish Chronicle,* which lists all activities of Jewish interest. (Call the Board of Deputies, 232-420, for information.) The Belmont, Cape Town's only kosher restaurant, is in Sea Point (434-0829 or 439-1155).

Though the Lithuanians joined the mainstream, one tenet of their beliefs remained unalterable—their undiluted, unswerving Zionism. Coming as they did into an already pluralistic society—with no melting-pot concept—there was no pressure to drop their identifying spiritual baggage. Consequently the Zionist Federation was the first nationwide Jewish institution and long its dominant one.

In some South African government circles Zionism was viewed favorably. Given the Afrikaners' feelings for the biblical Israelites, many were predisposed to Israel's establishment. One of the country's leading statesmen, Jan Christiaan Smuts—to whose centrist United Party many Jews flocked—was strongly pro-Zionist. In 1917, as a member of the British Imperial War Cabinet, he helped formulate the Balfour Declaration. When Smuts was defeated by Daniel Malan's National Party in 1948, some Afrikaners saw a parallel between their own sudden supremacy over the English and Israel's establishment. Consequently Malan, though the party's leader during the era of pro-Nazi tendencies, determined as prime minister to end his country's concerns about Jewish influence and even visited Israel in 1953. His mellowing toward Jews, however, was not matched by a similar attitude toward South Africa's nonwhite majority. The National Party solidified the country's tradition of racial separation with a rigid system it dubbed *apartheid.*

Though there was Afrikaner sympathy for Israel's geopolitical position, and admiration for its achievements, during the 1960s, when Israel aligned itself with other African states against apartheid, relations became so strained that South Africa suspended the right of its Jews—among Israel's largest Diaspora financial supporters—to transfer funds to the state.

The situation changed again after the Yom Kippur War when most of the African countries, under Arab pressure, broke relations with Israel. Only then did Israel upgrade its diplomatic post in Pretoria to embassy status and substantially increase trade. But this further complicated the Jews' internal conflicts, especially regarding apartheid.

Individually, South African Jews have historically helped the less privileged. Before he took his nonviolent struggle from South Africa to India, among Mohandas K. Gandhi's closest white associates between 1906 and 1914 were Henry Polak and Hermann Kallenbach. During the 1930s Jews like Gabriel Weinstock, Ben Weinbren, and Solly Sachs were among the color-blind organizers of nonwhite trade unions. And after apartheid was officialized in 1948 Jews played a prominent role in the struggle against it. Of the seventeen leaders of the African National Congress underground caught during the Rivonia arrests in 1963, all five whites were Jews. Among other well-known Jews sympathetic to or active in the ANC have been Selma Browde, Audrey and Max Coleman, Albie Sachs and Joe Slovo (also leader of the South African Communist Party), who, after twenty-seven years abroad, returned to Cape Town as part of the ANC team negotiating an end to white minority rule.

But if South African sociological studies have found the Jews less prejudiced than other groups, collectively—at least until very recently—they have often been ambivalent, if not silent. And after episodes of violence, particularly during the 1970s, many, fearing for their future as a minority within a minority, either emigrated or sent their children abroad. In Cape Town as elsewhere, figures indicate a communal erosion of 20 to 30 percent, resulting in a "missing generation" between ages twenty and forty. Some émigrés have returned, however, and the community has also been augmented by an Israeli influx.

Though the ultraconservative among South Africa's whites express anti-Semitic attitudes, they are generally considered a fringe element. Muslims, too, are becoming militant. And because South African Jews equate anti-Zionism with anti-Semitism, they worry about the stance toward Israel of many traditional anti-apartheid activists.

Sights: A graceful mixture of commercial center and resort—not to mention South Africa's legislative seat—Cape Town, with its juxtaposition of contemporary architecture and Cape colonial, is a pleasant city for perusing.

Ambling through the Gardens—so-called because they are just that—the first stop is the Great, or Gardens, Synagogue on Hatfield Street and, adjacent to it, Cape Town's first synagogue, now housing the Jewish Museum. The colonnaded "old" *shul* was built in 1849 to house South Africa's first congregation, called Tikvath Israel, or Hope of Israel—with a bow toward the Cape of Good Hope. The sanctuary, hung with photos of former rabbis, newspaper clippings and *chuppah* covers—and featuring banks of laurel-wood-and-cane pews—is still used for student services and weddings. Upstairs, in the museum proper, are ceremonial objects, some

of which belonged to early community members. Especially noteworthy are works by two nationally celebrated South African Jewish artists. Moses Kottler is represented by a bust of a former congregation leader, Rev. A. P. Bender, and Israel "Lippy" Lipshitz by a monotype called *The Tortured Jew* and a convex bronze mirror in a Burmese-teak frame carved with biblical figures. The museum is open Tuesdays and Thursdays, 2–5 P.M. and Sundays, 10 A.M.–12:30 P.M. (telephone 451-546).

The Great Synagogue, inaugurated in 1905, seats thirteen hundred in a Baroque-style building, with a large cupola over the *bimah*. Painted in shades of eggshell and dusty pink, its interior was decorated by Jewish craftsmen, some of whom subsequently became members. Services are held daily; call 451-405 for times.

Nearby is South Africa's parliament, which houses, as part of its library, the Mendelsohn Library, one of most important collections of Africana extant. Assembled and presented to the nation by turn-of-the-century diamond magnate and bibliographer Sidney Mendelsohn, an English-born Jew, it encompasses seven thousand books and three hundred paintings, sketches, and photographs. Of particular interest are books on the Boer War (which, like the others, contain Mendelsohn's own bookplate, bearing a likeness of his great friend Cecil Rhodes); and watercolors depicting the southern African scene by the eighteenth-century traveler François Le Vaillant. The collection also features Mendelsohn's diamond signet ring with his initials carved into the incredibly hard stone. Admission to the library is by special arrangement; call 403-2140 for details.

Also nearby is the National Gallery. Visitors entering through the front entrance come immediately upon the "Liberman Doors," financed and donated to the gallery by Hyman Liberman, Cape Town's first Jewish mayor. Carved by H. V. Meyerowitz, they feature iconographically depicted biblical scenes. The gallery also houses the de Pass family's art collection and works by sculptor Lippy Lipschitz, who taught at the University of Cape Town.

On Hof Street, also in the Gardens district, is the rambling, arched, and porticoed

Helmsley Hotel. Now owned by the ultra-upscale Mount Nelson Hotel, originally it was Benjamin Norden's home, where the first South African Jewish congregation held services. On Harrington Street, in an area of frilly Victorian buildings, is the oldest Jewish bookstore in South Africa.

In the historic heart of Cape Town, on Greenmarket Square, is another gift from a Jewish family to the country. In the old Town House, built between 1755 and 1761, is the Michaelis Collection of seventeenth-century Dutch and Flemish artists. The future of the building—which served as the City Hall until 1905—was in doubt until businessman Max Michaelis said he would donate the paintings in "gratitude for the many happy and prosperous years . . . spent in this beautiful country" on condition that the building be turned into an art gallery. Rembrandt and Frans Hals are included in the collection. In the modern Civic Center, also downtown, hang portraits of many Cape Town mayors, a large proportion of whom have been Jews.

Of note in Cape Town's immediate suburbs is the Kaplan Center on the University of Cape Town campus. The lobby of the center houses a collection of photographs from the South African Jewish past. Included are settlers on the road; Jewish Boer soldiers; Herman Kallenbach with Gandhi in his Cape Town days; Benjamin Norden; Barney Barnato with the directors of De Beers in 1875; and the 200 orphans brought by Isaac Ochberg to Cape Town from Russia after World War I. Also, on a back road in Rondebusch stands the Irma Stern Museum, housing works by Stern, one of South Africa's most prominent painters.

Beyond Cape Town proper, amid the striking scenery of the farmlands and the so-called Wine Route, are also numerous sights and sites from the Jewish past and present. Among the more picturesque synagogues in the region are the 1927 structure in Paarl, on Synagogue Street; and the one in Stellenbosch, on Van Ryneveld Street. Along the Wine Route are several Jewish-owned or operated vineyards, including Zandwijk Wine Farm, the country's only kosher winery.

Side Trip: One of the most entertaining forays into the Jewish past is to Oudtshoorn, once called the Jerusalem of Africa. A five-hour drive from Cape Town (or a short flight and drive) this spot in the semiarid Little Karoo is home to the once Jewish-based ostrich industry. Until World War I, ostrich feathers represented the height of chic in certain fashionable circles. And ostriches thrive around Oudtshoorn.

Afrikaners were the first to farm the wild, flightless birds, but it was Jews—primarily from Shavli and Chelm in Lithuania—who turned the feather trade into a multimillion-dollar operation while simultaneously attempting to reconstruct their erstwhile lifestyle in a strange land.

Morally supported by the religious Afrikaners—in an instance where they acculturated to Afrikaner rather than English society—the Jews, far more than their counterparts in other small communities, sought to live traditionally. Since they couldn't agree on a definition of "traditional," however, even in this tiny spot, they divided. When the first synagogue, a sturdy brick structure on Queen Street, was deemed too anglicized, the newer, less sophisticated immigrants from Chelm built their own St. John Street Synagogue.

For it, they lovingly reconstructed the elaborate, onion-domed ark from their synagogue in Chelm. Though the original ark—and synagogue—were destroyed by the Nazis, the Outdtshoorn model was, when the St. John Street Synagogue fell into disuse—exactingly transferred, along with other synagogue items, to the Jewish Gallery in Outdtshoorn's C. P. Nel Museum.

The museum also features displays on the ostrich trade, the town, and wildly fanciful houses built by feather merchants. But the best fun comes from visiting an ostrich farm—including the Safari Ostrich Farm run by the Lipschitz family, where one can stand on ostrich eggs, dine on ostrich steak, watch the big birds race, and even ride them.

Personalities: While Jews have been far more involved in politics on the municipal level than the national—the only Jewish cabinet member having been Henry Gluckman, Jan Smuts's minister of health in 1945—in 1991 South Africa sent Harry Schwartz, its first Jewish ambassador, to

Washington. Helen Suzman was for years not only the lone woman in Parliament but also the sole representative of the liberal Progressive Party. Justice Richard J. Goldstone, head of an independent commision to prevent violence during the transition to democratic rule, has won praise and respect from both sides of the racial divide for his investigations into everything from police sabotage of the ANC to armed clashes between rival African groups; *The New York Times* said that many South Africans had come to regard him as "a cross between King Solomon and the Ghostbusters."

Jews have long been prominent in Cape Town business, and business was often in the forefront of fighting apartheid. Raymond and Wendy Ackerman, founders of the Pick 'n Pay supermarket chain, put their first black store manager in the market nearest then-Prime Minister Pieter Willem Botha's Cape Town residence, where all the cabinet ministers' wives shopped.

Cape Town's performing arts scene has included Phyllis Spira, prima ballerina of the city's ballet company; opera singers Aviva Pelham, Andrea Catzel and Patricia Sandan; and Moyra Fine, theater producer and impresario.

Dr. Hannah Reeve-Saunders has headed both the Cape Town physicians' organization and Groote Schuur Hospital, where Dr. Christiaan Barnard performed the world's first heart transplants. The first two recipients, Louis Washkansky and Philip Blaiberg, were Jewish.

Among Cape Town Jews who have made names for themselves outside the country are Abba Eban and Michael Comay.

Reading: Little of Nadine Gordimer's work draws on her Jewish background, but in *A Sport of Nature* (Knopf) she deals in passing with a Jewish family. Like Gordimer, Dan Jacobson, who grew up in Kimberley, also writes primarily about society at large, but his short story, "The Zulu and the Zayde," became a Broadway show and in 1966 he wrote *The Beginners* (Macmillan) portraying the fortunes of a Jewish immigrant family. Antony Sher, a Cape Townian now living in London, has written *Middlepost* (Knopf), loosely based on the life of his immigrant Lithuanian grandfather who was a *smous* in Cape Province, as well as *The Indoor Boy* (Viking).

For general reading on Cape Town, try the novels and short stories of Richard Rive. For general reading on South Africa, there are J. M. Coetzee's *Waiting for the Barbarians* (Penguin); Gerald Gordon's *The Crooked Rain* (MacDonald); Marc de Villiers's *The White Tribe Dreaming* (Viking); Gordimer's work, especially *A Soldier's Embrace* (Jonathan Cape, London); and James Michener's *The Covenant* (Random House).

Recommendations: In addition to air service, Cape Town and Johannesburg are connected by the luxurious Blue Train. The ease of traveling in the country is in contrast to its problems, but the physical splendor of Cape Town and the hinterland make it clear why South Africa is the beloved country to all who call it home.

—Phyllis Ellen Funke

Caracas

Call it what you will: ir-, a-, un-, or de-regulated. How else to describe a place where grand villas sprawl through neighborhoods abutting ramshackle slum dwellings; where high-rise concrete monoliths jut from luxuriant tropical ground cover; where a new driver, lacking parking ability, explains that there are no driving tests; where the airport bank refuses travelers' checks signed in other than black or blue. To the first-time visitor, at least, contemporary Caracas comes across chaotically.

Dramatically set in a three thousand foot-high valley—and climbing ever further up the Avila mountain walls—the literal and figurative Caracas cacophony exists largely because of the city's rapid expansion. Since World War II, when the population of all Venezuela was 4 million, the capital city itself has swelled to that size.

Thanks to a tolerance bred of being a predominantly mestizo population, postwar outsiders of various sorts—from Spain, Portugal, and Italy, as well as elsewhere in Latin America—viewed Venezuela as a comfortable, casual, and hospitable land. Overlooking its inclination toward periodic dictatorships (perhaps because, by and large, they were more benevolent than others in the region), immigrants flocked to this oil-rich country. Among them were Jews who, joining those brethren already established, lent their energies to Venezuela's growth. Working especially in the commercial, construction, and industrial fields, they partook of the blessings of a place overtly prosperous, at least until its currency crashed in the mid-1980s.

Though some would underplay or even deny the significance of intangibles, others, including prominent gentiles, credit Venezuelan Jews with contributing more than just know-how. In a climate conducive to living off the land, and in a society so relaxed that nearly 65 percent of its births are illegitimate, the Jews are noted for their work ethic and family values. Says one non-Jewish observer cognizant of today's undercurrents of political, social, and economic uncertainty, "We need the Jews because they keep us on track."

History: Since Eldorado wasn't found in Venezuela—nor, initially, anything much else of overt commercial value—the Spaniards generally ignored this New World holding on South America's northern rim. Nor, consequently, was the Church interested. Thus rumors of Conversos did not flourish and Venezuela never knew the Inquisition.

But with friendlier colonial governments controlling properties nearby, Jews established themselves elsewhere in the vicinity. Whether they came from Iberia via England, Holland, or South America after the Inquisition crossed the Atlantic, they settled early in the Caribbean. And they influenced Venezuelan history from the Dutch-held island of Curaçao, just forty miles offshore. From there, where they attained prominence in an economy built largely on shipping and attendant trades, they often found themselves dealing with the Venezuelans. They had a common cause in containing the region's rampant piracy. And with Venezuela generally ignored by its mother country, its governors had to seek supplies elsewhere, even if that meant dealing with the Dutch competition.

In letters to Spain as early as 1710 there was mention of Jews who traded with Venezuelan Creoles and who established a small Jewish colony in coastal Tucacas.

Destroyed and rebuilt, along with Venezuela's first synagogue, it finally fell to the arrows of eighteen Indians stirred by a Spanish governor jealous that he wasn't getting taxes from Venezuelan–Dutch trade arrangements.

The Jews did not reenter the Venezuelan tapestry until the early nineteenth century, but then did so gloriously, as supporters of the Venezuelan-born liberator, Simon Bolívar. During his fight for South America's independence, when Bolívar fled the Spaniards, he escaped to Curaçao. There, among many Venezuelan patriots, Bolívar and his sister found sanctuary with an influential Jewish lawyer. As Bolívar's first foreign protector, Mordechay Ricardo spurred others to the cause. When Bolívar resumed his mainland fight, among his generals were two Jews — Benjamin Henriquez and Juan Bartolome de Sola Ricardo. The latter first roused Venezuelans as a journalist, then fought with Bolívar in Colombia, and ultimately commanded the cavalry in the decisive fight that drove the Spaniards to the sea.

With the Spanish defeat, and Curaçao's vistas shrinking, some island Jews began moving to Venezuela — by the 1830s to Coro, then Cabello, and finally to Caracas. Most were professionals (doctors, lawyers, engineers), and they found themselves in a comparatively fluid society. Unlike other Latin American countries, where a Spanish aristocracy was entrenched, impermeable, militaristic and church-oriented, Venezuela was relatively secular, more influenced by 19th-century positivism than by Catholicism. Given this flexible social structure, Jews obtained important positions, becoming university rectors, congressional presidents, national poets (David Elias Curiel and Salomon López Fonseca), and government bankers. Though most people descended from the first generation of Venezuelan Jews remain proud of their origins, virtually all — the Curiels, Henriquezes (whose ranks include a respected humanist priest), Señors, Chumaceiros, and Caprileses (whose newspaper chain includes *El Mundo* and *Ultimas Noticias*) — are now Christian.

Inspired, perhaps, by their successes, however — and surely encouraged by dreams of a new land into which they would linguistically fit — young Castilian-speaking Jews from Spanish Morocco followed the earlier Sephardim. Their first Torah, from Tetuan, arrived for the Tiferet Yisrael congregation in 1894; Jews came also from Melilla and Tangier, with smaller numbers immigrating from Egypt, Lebanon, Syria, and the Balkan peninsula. In the late 1920s, they founded Caracas's first Jewish communal organization, the Asociación Israelita de Venezuela. Almost concurrently, however, in part because of the United States's newly closed doors, enough Ashkenazim — primarily from Romania, Bessarabia, Poland, and Hungary — had arrived to form their own group, the Unión Israelita de Caracas. Nevertheless, nearly 75 percent of the city's Ashkenazim arrived only after World War II.

Between 1930 and 1960, Venezuela, like many other countries, imposed restrictions on Jewish immigration. But because the restrictions were not as stringent as elsewhere they were circumvented by the possession of false baptismal certificates. By 1950 the number of known Jews in the country had increased from the 1,000-odd counted in 1926 to 6,000; by 1960, at least 1,000 more had arrived, mostly from Egypt, Hungary, and Israel. Uncounted numbers also entered from Cuba, Argentina, Peru, and other subsequently beleaguered Latin American countries.

Beyond immigration legislation, however, Venezuelan Jews have known little anti-Semitism. In fact, Jews are considered prime marriage material by Venezuela's upper echelons (partly because they are regarded as undilutedly white). Until recently, the only noticeable anti-Jewish sentiment has been more anti-Israel than otherwise, fanned by the New Left after Israel's victory in the Six Day War. Some estimates put Venezuela's Arab population at 300,000, and rumor has it that Muammar Qaddafi is financing a mosque in a prime Caracas neighborhood. In 1992 about 50 neo-Nazis staged an unauthorized one-night demonstration. Rapid intervention by city officials led to its prompt termination. But while Jewish Caraqueños downplay the episode, some more outspoken ones, especially aware of current societal concerns, note undercurrents of insecurity.

Community: Among the world's Jewish communities, the Caraqueños, at first glance anyway, must enjoy one of the highest overall living standards. Though the recent years' recession has pushed some onto lower levels (one estimate places 20 percent in the needy category), the rest remain on middle- and upper-middle-class rungs.

Their leaders take great pains to underscore that harmony exists between Ashkenazim and Sephardim, noting that, while each group goes its own way religiously, they are united in matters political, social, cultural, and educational. In fact, the Jewish school, though created by the Ashkenazim, is attended by 70 to 90 percent of the children of both groups, and has been a decisive factor in breaking barriers among the younger generations. Though virtually all the fifteen or so synagogues in Caracas are, by United States standards, Orthodox, most Jews, regardless of background, identify with their heritage more culturally and Zionistically than ritualistically. The Sephardim may have a higher percentage of regular worshipers than the Ashkenazim, but they are also considered more flexible in their approach to religion. According to rough estimates, less than 3 percent of Caraqueño Jews keep kosher and attend services every week, while those who are genuinely *shomer Shabbat* are numbered at less than 1 percent. Ultra-orthodoxy also has its adherents, especially among the young, and the Lubavitch movement runs two facilities in Caracas.

Despite the happy, homogeneous official picture, however, disparate vibrations come through. Though neither Sephardim nor Ashkenazim currently denigrate the other, differences in mentality are still evident. Given the Sephardim's original language facility—even those who didn't speak Spanish were familiar with Ladino—plus the absence of a ghetto background, their claim to have fit more easily into the overall picture seems warranted. Meanwhile, the Ashkenazim, with their high numbers of Holocaust survivors, at least until recently clustered together. Centered in the San Bernardino area, they created their own world, with all the institutions needed within a couple of blocks. Only when the new school facility was built on the grounds

of the Hebraica sports and social club in the eastern part of the city did they begin to move in that direction, with Jews of all backgrounds now living in such areas as Sebucán, Los Chorros, Las Mercedes, El Cafetál, Los Palos Grandes, Altamira, La Florida and Los Caobos.

Protestations to the contrary, insecurities persist, most obviously demonstrated by a general unwillingness to reveal even such basic statistics as population size. A spate of explanations is offered—from fear of appearing too strong to fear of the opposite, not to mention the Holocaust survivors' inherent aversion to list making. Estimates of Jewish population figures range from 5,000 to 500,000, with reality probably around 35,000. Although some claim an equal balance between *Ashkenazim* and Sephardim, other sources note that Caracas hosts about 2,500 known Ashkenazi families to the Sephardim's 1,700. So-called mixed marriages exist in virtually all families. Today's younger generation has perhaps found a true common denominator by sharing a feeling of being Venezuelan at heart.

Sights: Despite disclaimers concerning their significance in Caracas's development, evidence of Jewish involvement in this lively but convoluted city sprouts—often unexpectedly—in numerous nooks, crannies, twists, and turns.

Emerge from the streamlined new subway at the Sabana Grande stop for the café-clogged walking street of the same name, and diagonally facing is a sign proclaiming a postcard-and-souvenir shop, Casa Cohen. Take a spin around the fountain-punctuated traffic circle of Plaza Venezuela and there, planted on its own plot of grass—is a tall, bronze, modernistic, spikey menorah—unless authorities finally caught up with the Lubavitchers who put it up for Hanukkah and then failed to remove it promptly

Across the bordering highway, on four hundred acres, stands the Central University of Venezuela. Noteworthy in its own right for integrating art and architecture and incorporating works by such as Fernand Léger, Jean Arp, and Alexander Calder, it also includes the School of Dentistry, founded in 1898 by Mortimer

Ricardo, a Jewish émigré from Curaçao. Heading into Caracas's historic downtown — an area possessing traces of the Spanish colonial past — one initially confronts the red marble plaza and towering, shimmering, copper-tinted glass structure of the Banco Unión headquarters. Its president, Enrique Benacerraf, is Jewish.

Peaceful foundation: Venezuela's colonial era was unmarred by the Inquisition

The city's old capitol building surrounds a cobbled interior courtyard studded with royal palms, and is topped by a gold-colored cupola. And in the grand salon, beneath the cupola, on the right-hand wall as you enter, is a painting, *Firma del Acta de la Independencia*. It depicts the signing of Venezuela's Declaration of Independence and prominently features, in the front, an elegant man with white hair, General Miranda. Though his provenance has not officially been documented, many note that Miranda was a Sephardic name.

Also in the old downtown area, on Avenida Lecuña, opposite the main bus station, stands the small, square Clinic David Lobo, a hospital named for a leading turn-of-the-century Jewish pediatrician; and, in the Barrilito neighborhood, off Calle Linares, near Avenida Urdaneta, rises the Red Cross building, among whose

founders, in 1895, were Mortimer, Salomon de Jongh, and David Ricardo — the last having been its first president. Their photograph once hung in the lobby, but no one now knows its whereabouts. A copy, however, exists (along with other pertinent memorabilia) in the private collection of a relative, Ricardo de Sola, who designed, built, and lived in the sprawling, Spanish-style house called *Mi Solar* (My Sun) on Avenida San Felipe, which he now rents to the Israelis for their embassy.

The Jewish presence is also prominent in and around Caracas's new cultural heart known as Parque Central. Considered a city-within-a-city for its residences, shops, restaurants, and malls, it also features a plethora of edifices devoted to the various arts. Heading right from the main entrance of the Caracas Hilton, the development's central landmark, is a free-form building of the much-favored beige concrete that is home to one of Latin America's leading contemporary art collections. Housing works by Chagall, Picasso, Miró, Braque, Matisse, Moore, and others, it was founded by a Jew and bears her name — Museo de Arte Contemporaneo de Caracas Sofie Imber — emblazoned on its outside wall in letters that look like Hebrew. Following a footpath and crossing a pedestrian bridge in front of the Hilton entrance leads to the complex of theaters called El Ateneo de Caracas (The Caracas Atheneum). Turning left off the elevator on its first floor is, as proclaimed in brass letters, the Sala de Arte y Ensayo Margot Benacerraf. This movie salon, specializing in such golden oldies as *Rear Window, Reds,* and *Raging Bull,* is named for a contemporary Jewish film producer and director. A wall on the ground floor of the Hilton itself bears a piece by the contemporary Caraqueño sculptor Harry Abend.

Beyond the Parque Central complex, but within walking distance — ironically just behind the incomplete mosque — is the Boulevard Amador Bendayan, on which stands a gray concrete building that is the Teatro Amador Bendayan. Its name spelled out in large black letters, it honors a Jewish television personality who was popular for the entertainments and fund-raising telethons he produced. Containing office space as well as an auditorium for events ranging from dance festivals to voodoo rites, it is part of a larger project conceived by Bendayan, Casa del Artista, which will also one day provide housing for artists.

Among other public sites named for Jews are the José Beracasa Sport Center, honoring a sports promoter, in the suburb of El Paraiso; and, at the end of Avenida Principal de Las Palmas, heading toward the mountains, and on the Avenida Maimonides itself, a red brick, foliage surrounded plaza and playground called Maimonides Square.

Just beyond Avenida Alegría Beracasa lies Hebraica, the sports and social club on whose grounds the high school stands. (Tourists can enter by showing passports and, preferably, membership in Jewish clubs elsewhere. For information, call 34-46-31, 2, 3, or 4.)

Among other sights directly related to the Jewish community is the main Sephardic synagogue, Tiferet Yisrael, on Avenida Mariperez in Los Caobos (781-1942). The foundation for the current building was laid in 1956 and features a central pulpit surrounded by hard wooden seats and pillars flanked by potted trees. Its walls contain tall, narrow, brightly colored stained-glass windows in various geometric, floral and arabesque patterns. Its most singular feature, however, is the cylinder that rises over the ark, reaching skyward like a modernistic steeple. This cylindrical theme is continued architecturally in the fluting flanking the auditorium itself. The adjacent Sephardic Center features a gallery of presidents, containing portraits of all deceased community leaders.

The main Ashkenazi synagogue lies on the upper floors of the Unión Israelita center, an unmarked building in San Bernardino on Avenida Marqués del Toro (telephone 51-52-53). It is modern, circular and austere, with dark woodwork and a plush white carpet leading up to the bronze ark doors. Perhaps its most noteworthy detail, however, is the cinder-block grillwork of the walls, which open directly to the outside. Minus panes of glass, fresh air circulates continuously, a tribute to Caracas's generally fine climate.

Side Trips: Margarita Island, a short flight from Caracas, has one of the world's youngest Jewish communities—and its small gem of a synagogue, Or Meir, opened in 1990 (Calle Carnevalli in Porlamar, behind the Hotel Los Pinos; contact Rabbi Moshe Emergui at 61-23-76). The community dates from the mid-1970s, when developers started turning this free port into a haven for tourists in search of warm-weather bargains. About 25 families—mostly with young children—comprise the 90 percent Sephardic community of nearly 100. Many are observant, buying kosher food in the Ratan Supermarket. *Mezuzot* can be seen on the doorposts of many shops along Santiago Merino, one of Porlamar's main business streets. There may well have been a Jewish presence on the island earlier. High on a hill overlooking the town of Asunción is a clay-colored fortress, Castillo de Santa Rosa, one of the highlights on any island sightseeing tour. To the left of the entrance, above the jail door, is a sign commemorating the imprisonment, on July 26, 1818, of the daughter of one of the island's leading families, Luisa Caseres de Arismendi. Luisa, to whom a statue also stands next to Simon Bolívar Square in Asunción, was the only woman imprisoned for resistance activity during the independence fight against Spain, and Caseres, at the time, was known as a Sephardic name.

The newly developing mainland resort area of Puerto La Cruz also has a small congregation (call Centro Israelita de Oriente, Calle Esperanza, 66-7010). And be sure to take the day cruise operated by Nelson & Nelson. But any real sense of Venezuela can be obtained primarily by traveling south into the interior. Flying past Angel Falls, the world's highest waterfall, is merely a start.

Personalities: Though long wary of the political arena, in recent years, Jews have become involved. Prominent in today's government are Ricardo Hausman, the minister of economic planning, and Paulina Gamus, secretary of culture. Lolita Andijar is a leftist member of the congress. Previously, Ruth Lerner de Almea was a minister of education; while Bernardo Kliksberg has been known as an advisor to top political figures on the international scene.

In Caracas-raised Baruj Benacerraf,

Venezuelan Jewry can boast of a Nobel Prize winner in medicine. Jacobo Garciente, a former dean of the Faculty of Engineering at Caracas's University Metropolitana, wrote a textbook on highway engineering used throughout the Spanish-speaking world and also engineered many of Venezuela's highways.

Among leading figures of Jewish descent are René de Sola, a recent president of the Supreme Court; Jose Curiel, a former minister of public works; and Hans Neuman, president of *The Daily Journal,* Caracas's English-language newspaper.

Culture: Caracas's Jewish community publishes a weekly newspaper, *Nuevo Mundo Israelita.* There is also a weekly radio program on Jewish affairs, Shalom 91.9 on Station Avila, 91.9 FM, every Sunday 3–4 P.M., hosted in Spanish by architect Menahem Belilty.

Jews have written about their experiences in the city for the Caracas stage. Among such plays are Elisa Lerner's piece involving a Jewish mother, *My Life with Mother;* and works by Johnny Gavlovsky and Isaac Chokrun, a former director of Venezuela's national theater. None has yet been translated to English, however. An unpublished translation does exist, though, of Klara Ostfeld's popular memoir, *Light and Shadow of My Life* (contact the Unión Israelita for copies).

Various Jewish organizations also hold periodic cultural events. In addition to those lectures, performances and concerts sponsored by Hebraica, the Sephardic community holds a Sephardi Week every other year, usually in June, with conferences and presentations on culture. WIZO runs an annual two-week art exhibit, between Passover and Shavuot, that has become one of most important in Venezuela.

Recommendations: American Airlines, an island of order amid the hurly-burly, has regular daily connections to Caracas from all parts of the United States. Internal flying, however, must be done on local carriers. A specialist in Venezuelan travel is Inter-Island Tours, 37 East 28th Street, New York, NY 10016 (telephone 212-686-4868). In Caracas, the strategically located Hilton, one of Latin America's most comprehensive hotels, provides a welcome oasis—and its executive floors are among the best of their kind. (The Avila caters to visitors wanting to walk to synagogue, but is considered somewhat down-at-the-heels these days.) The Hilton on Margarita Island is among those upscale properties close to town. The new and attractively low-rise Golden Rainbow Resort is a half hour from downtown Puerto La Cruz.

In Caracas, kosher food is available at such kosher stores as the Delicatesses Mini Market (72-01-74); Delicatesses La Dorée (52-78-23 or 52-95-87); Rey David (51-00-64 or 51-08-42); and La Belle Delicatesses (781-72-04). Also certain restaurants at the Hebraica are certified. Call Eduardo Lisogorsky (34-46-31 or 34-46-76) for information. Once you know where you are going to eat and sleep, the chaos of Caracas can be enjoyed.

—Phyllis Ellen Funke

Casablanca

On Africa's doorstep, in Europe's backyard, and at the Atlantic edge of the Arab alliance, Morocco is flavored by the East's exoticism and the West's progressivism. The kingdom balances between influences — teetering supremely, and to date moderately, among forces political, religious, geographic, and otherwise. Marching to its own drummer, Morocco has been fairly free to choose its own stance toward its ancient and intricately ingrained Jewish community. This posture is perhaps best described as pragmatically flexible.

Consequently, Jews have often played golf with King Hassan, cut his hair, and ministered to his medical needs. They've trained his fighter pilots and traveled as royal emissaries; served in his government and outfitted his army. Though they do not assimilate, they interact with the king's Muslim subjects on every level. And when Israeli Prime Minister Yitzhak Rabin headed home from Washington after his historic handshake with Yasser Arafat, he stopped in Morocco — where the Arab king greeted him in Hebrew.

But Moroccan Jews have also known the spectrum's less glorious end — from the ignorance and squalor of isolated mountain villages to the poverty and primitivity of mud huts in the desert. In insecurity and indigence, secretly and openly, they've flocked to Israel in such great numbers that they and their children comprise the largest ethnic group in today's Jewish state. Deep roots and faith in the future, however, have held enough behind to make theirs also the largest remaining Jewish community in the Arab world.

Pockets of Jewish residence — and historical traces — exist in numerous places. But drawn by twentieth-century urbanization, the greatest numbers now cluster in Casablanca, Morocco's commercial center and largest city. Sometimes beleaguered, sometimes beloved, Moroccan Jews defy categorization as much as the country from which they hail.

As a latter-day creation — an artificial amalgam of peoples pressed together by necessity rather than evolution — the community is a meld of types who until a generation or two ago wouldn't, and probably couldn't, have given each other the time of day.

Figures on Morocco's Jews vary, but in rough numbers there were 300,000 Jews in the country in 1950 out of a general population of 9 million. Now there are 9,000 Jews out of 30 million. Of these, Casablanca has 6,000–7,000 — about the same number it had at the turn of the century.

The city's majority hail from the south, descending from the country's earliest Jews whose arrival, some say, predates the First Temple's destruction and who, whenever they came, converted significant numbers from the indigenous Berber tribes. Subsequently the Berber Jews probably absorbed Arab Jews traveling with, or in the wake of, the conquering armies of Islam.

In time the native Jews, known as *toshavim,* were joined, and scorned, by *megorashim,* Jews expelled from Spain and Portugal who became the establishment. The newcomers were so insular that contact between even Catalonians and Aragonians was long proscribed. When the French-based schools of Alliance Israelite Universelle reached Morocco (the first was established in 1862) a middle class, espousing Western values, emerged among the newly educated.

Aliyah was the province primarily of the underprivileged *toshavim;* most *mego-*

rashim who left Morocco went to Europe and Canada.

History: By 1000 C.E., Morocco's Jews were at their spiritual and intellectual zenith; centers of learning flourished and scholars from Spain, including Maimonides, arrived. Though many left during times of often-fatal intolerance (some for Christian Spain; others like Maimonides, for Cairo) the Merinid dynasty, installed in 1269, doted on them. Not only were Jews made intimate courtiers, they also controlled the Sahara gold trade and Morocco's exchanges with Christian countries. Through these and other administrations, Morocco prospered.

The fifteenth century was tumultuous. Many Jews died or were forcibly converted in the violence that overthrew the Merinids. Yet Sultan Muhammad al-Shaykh al-Wattasi, in power when Spain and Portugal expelled their Jews, welcomed those who fled to his land. Initially the newcomers experienced difficulties. But from the sixteenth century on, the Jews resumed a vital role in Morocco's diplomacy and commerce, using their initiative and extensive foreign connections to virtually dominate the country's foreign trade.

To Jewish hands came control of entire enterprises. Conversos from Iberia were persuaded to emigrate and reconvert, some bringing a new process for extracting sugar from cane that made Morocco the leading producer of the world's best sugar for two centuries. The Jews were the sole manufacturers of beeswax, wine, and items from precious metals; they imported tea from China and textiles from England and France. Until 1912 they dominated nearly all Morocco's maritime operations, while those at court were often bankers or merchants of the sultan, passing their roles from father to son. The sultans continued to use Jews as negotiators with the Christian world. And European countries entrusted them with their Moroccan interests. In 1610 Samuel Pallache, a Jew, signed a pact of alliance between Morocco and the Netherlands, his country's first with a Christian nation.

Jews also contributed to the rise of the Alouite dynasty, the house in power today. They gave financial support to the first Alouite, Mulay al-Rashid (1660–72) and helped him win control of Fez by secreting him for a night in the *mellah,* or Jewish quarter, before he entered the city. When he died, Jewish connections relayed the news to his brother so quickly that the latter, again with Jewish monetary backing, proclaimed himself the ruler before anyone else could. This sultan was Mulay Ismail (1672–1727), one of Morocco's most outstanding monarchs.

Despite occasional horrors, during the next 150 years the Jews maintained and expanded their commercial, financial, and diplomatic roles—with almost all consular activities involving Europe coming their way. This was to prove a mixed blessing, however, since as the European powers bared colonialist fangs in the area—France conquered Algiers in 1830—the Jews acquired an image as agents of foreign powers. When in 1912 the French made most of Morocco their protectorate, the Jews, though still officially second-class citizens, flourished under France's civil administration.

Sultan Muhammad V's stance toward the Jews during World War II set the tone for Moroccan-Jewish relations—internally and internationally—ever since. Jews suffered under the Vichy government's anti-Jewish laws, but they were not dispossessed or deported, thanks in large part to the sultan's insistence that they were under his protection and that all his subjects were equal. And despite Jewish fears—fears that inspired many departures—when Morocco gained its independence in 1956 and Muhammad V returned from exile, not only were the Jews for the first time granted citizenship, some were appointed to major positions in the judicial and administrative branches of government.

Though Morocco did not recognize Israel, King Hassan II, who succeeded his father in 1961, attempted mediation on several occasions—through Moshe Dayan, who visited Morocco secretly during the 1970s, and through Shimon Peres, who visited openly as Israel's prime minister in the 1980s.

Meanwhile, Morocco's attitude toward emigration has fluctuated. Currently, Moroccan Jews quietly visit Israel—and vice versa—especially since Hassan II, apparently missing the Jews' initiative, issued an invitation for all émigrés to return.

Community: Casablanca's Jewish community is diminished but far from dead. About thirty-five synagogues — most tiny and tucked out of the way — are operational. The main synagogue, built in 1949 and seating five hundred, is Beth El, scene of all major Jewish functions. Only about one-third of Casablanca's Jews are considered observant these days, though about half are thought to keep kosher. Recently the *hasidic* Lubavitch movement has made its presence felt.

The community maintains various services, including a home for the aged and a medical facility, Centre Medical Maimonide, whose patients are Jews but whose doctors often are Muslim. Of the nine Jewish schools still operating in Morocco, six are in Casablanca. Jews also frequent two clubs, Cercle de l'Union, a social institution, and SOC, a sports club.

Though Morocco does not separate church and state, it recognizes two official religions — Islam and Judaism. Thus though Islamic law generally prevails, rabbi-judges adjudicating in the king's name administer Jewish justice in such civil matters as marriage, divorce, and inheritance. For those who peruse newsstands an intriguing item can be found under the nameplate of the newspaper *Le Matin de Sahara et du Maghreb*. There the date is given according to the Gregorian, Arabic — and Hebrew — calendars.

With the exception of occasional performances in French, Hebrew, or Arabic at SOC, there is little Western-style Jewish culture in Morocco. Rather than look for professional entertainment, one experiences Moroccan Jewish culture by watching Moroccan Jews observing their festivals and living their lives. Aspects of Arab culture have been adopted by some Moroccan Jews, from their apparel — which may include veils and *djallabahs* (large, loose-fitting garments) — to the ululations attending various ceremonies. In addition, they venerate certain Jews as saints. The tombs of such men, often in the countryside, are regarded as shrines for pilgrimage. While these places are open for prayer year round, many are the object of mass tributes at Lag B'omer. Called *hiloulas,* and frequently joined by Muslims, they are great camp-out festivals at which lambs are slaughtered, bonfires built, and candles burned in tribute and supplication.

Sights: Cinematic suggestion notwithstanding, Casablanca — which had only 20,000 inhabitants in 1900 — is an essentially twentieth-century creation. As such it does not bespeak the mystery of the East.

With prodding and palm crossing you can get a guide to take you to some hole-in-the-wall in the *medina* — or walled city — which, he will swear, was the prototype for the hangout haunted by Bogart and Bergman in the classic 1942 film. But given one such place — opposite the Imperial Cinema on Rue (not "Boulevard") Anfa, and featuring peeling walls, beat-up tables, radio-transmitted Arab music, and cat stench — be prepared for disillusion.

However, this locale virtually borders a particularly Eastern Jewish phenomenon, the *mellah*. From the Hebrew word for salt, a city's *mellah* is the section designated for Jewish residence.

On occasion the *mellah* was used like a European ghetto for punitive containment — the first instance occurring in Fez in 1438 during an attempt to force the Jews to convert. But *mellahs* were not always walled and prisonlike, and sometimes they benefited the Jews. Indeed, for special protection the *mellah* was deliberately situated against palace walls (a stratagem discernible in cities like Marrakech, where such a palace still stands). And when the *mellah* closed itself in — for example on the Sabbath — it was a kingdom unto itself, an inviolable Jewish world.

Those attuned to design subtleties note that the primary difference between the *mellah* and the rest of the *medina* was its architecture. Though in some cases time may have eradicated such distinctions, the *mellah* supposedly boasted balconies and outward-facing windows, while the Muslim buildings shut out the public.

Because it is comparatively new — Jews arrived in the area only around the mid-nineteenth century — Casablanca's *mellah* lacks certain historical features. Yet it serves well as an introduction to Eastern lore and living quarters.

Enter from Rue des Anglais and be assaulted by the smells of the East. Cardamom and cumin, mint and honey (not to mention ordure) permeate narrow alleyways clogged with veiled women carrying baskets and men in *djallabahs* pushing bicycles. Tiny stalls open to the street purvey everything from almonds and peanuts to brasswork and watches. And just inside the gate of the Bab Marrakech market is a row of Moroccan-style kosher butcher shops, with whole cow carcasses, their flanks stamped "kosher" in Hebrew, hanging out over the street.

Though the *mellah* once fetidly housed hordes of *toshavim* running from penury, most Casablanca Jews no longer live there. They are now spread through the nearby residential neighborhoods bordering the Place Verdun, along those boulevards and streets named Bordeaux, Ziraoui, Lusitania, Moulay Youssef, and Anfa.

Most synagogues and community institutions are in this area. Beth El, a beige stucco building in whose yard are two Magen David–shaped fountains, looms behind a wall on Rue Verlet Hanus. Synagogue Elias Hazan, on occasion decorated with streamers of plastic flowers, stands on one of the local streets named for a Jew, Rue Lt. Roger Farrache. Near Rue du Soldat Albert Levy—where Rue Sarah Bernhardt and Rue Rachel run into a small traffic circle—stands the Villa Chetrit, the home of a textile magnate with a charming private synagogue. (No formal visiting rules seem to exist for the synagogues. Entry is gained by ringing doorbells, appearing at prayer time, or calling the community offices at 226-952 or 222-861).

The area's contemporary focal point is the sprawling Place Muhammad V. Towering over it is the Hyatt Hotel, on land once part of the *mellah*. Between the Hyatt and the station for Rabat trains stands the whitewashed shrine of Sidi Belyout, Casablanca's patron saint. Because he defended the Jews, they honor him. But because they themselves cannot enter the shrine, they send their Muslim servants to pray for them. Among the avenues running out from Place Muhammad V is the broad palm- and lantern-lined walking street, Prince Moulay Abdallah. A fashionable promenade, virtually all its shops were Jewish owned during French days. Much of the real estate in the area is still Jewish owned, though no one trumpets it.

Off the nearby Rue Lahrizi, kosher restaurants come and go. The one perennial is Gan Eden, 10 Passage Abitbol (telephone 278-803). Of recent vintage is La Truffe Blanche, next to 57 Rue Tahar Sebti, whose sign reads Hallal 277–263.

Day Trips: Rabat, forty-five minutes by train from Casablanca, has been Morocco's capital since 1913. Surrounded by twelfth-century rose sandstone ramparts, it and the adjacent city, Salé, were once hangouts for pirates—aided and abetted at times by Jews. As befits a capital, Rabat is strewn with stately Moorish-style edifices. A particular magnet for Moroccan Jews is the monumental tomb of Muhammad V, whom they remember regularly in prayers for his World War II stance. The primary synagogue for the area's 400 Jews, a large, airy room with lace curtains above a floor-level community room, is located in downtown Rabat at 3 Rue Moulay Ismail.

A smaller but far more picturesque one, nearly two hundred years old and decorated with hanging lanterns, Moroccan carpets and brightly cushioned seats, is found in the Rabat *mellah* off Avenue Hassan II. There's a kosher restaurant at 7 Rue Patrice Lumumba.

The Salé *mellah* is a must. To approach it is to walk onto a set for *Beau Geste*. The *medina* is surrounded by crenellated red sandstone walls punctuated by soaring Moorish arches. And the best remaining gate, Sahat Bab Mrissa, leads directly into the *mellah*. Only one Jew—Youssef Bitton—still lives in this relatively tidy tangle. But along the main alleyway of low whitewashed houses can be found numbers 54 and 81, both former synagogues.

In the Salé cemetery on the Meknes road near the Lycée Plateau is the burial place—now an object of *hiloula*—of one venerated local Jew, Rabbi Raphael Encaoua. Known for his Solomon-like decisions, Encaoua died in 1934 and lies in an octagonal gazebo-type shrine decorated with arabesques and hung with colored lights. Ovens filled with the hardened tallow from melted candles surround the site, at which a caretaker peddles postcards of the rabbi.

Other saintly Jews lie within easy reach of Marrakech, a one-time capital city in an oasis of palms at the base of the high Atlas Mountains. About three hours south of Casablanca by train, less by car, Marrakech, with its walls, towers, squares, and alleys, is movie-land Maghreb.

Marrakech has had a Jewish community almost since it was settled about a thousand years ago. With 600 members, it is today Morocco's second largest. Its history is particularly pocked with expulsions and devastations. But it is in Marrakech that many Conversos settled and reconverted, ultimately gaining control not only over the native Jews but also, under the Saadian sharifs (1523–1659), of the entire government. Even when Marrakech ceased to be the capital, its Jews lived better than those elsewhere and, in the eighteenth century particularly, it was a thriving center for talmudic and kabbalistic studies.

Until 1920 the Marrakech *mellah* was Morocco's largest. Marked on some city maps, it is best entered near the Bahia Palace. But except for a few massive doorways which were used to close it off, a couple of dingy and difficult-to-locate synagogues and a Dickensian old-age home, little remains from the Jewish past. Just beyond the *mellah* lies a complex of pink-toned garden apartments in an area nicknamed, because of the heat, the Fire Garden. This was also once a Jewish quarter. The jewelry section, or *Bijouterie,* of the *souk* (market) area within the *medina* was once entirely Jewish. About a third of these shops remain.

The nearby saints lie about an hour's drive in different directions from Marrakech. One route, through the Ourika Valley—lush in spring with poppy fields and stands of apples, almond, apricot, fig and olive trees—leads, on the left, less than ten minutes beyond the Ourika Hotel, to the burial place of Rabbi Shlomo Bel Hanech. Supplicants—who can be found every day—come with petitions; should their wishes be granted, it is said, a snake appears. The sanctuary around his tomb, a walled enclosure surrounding an aqua-trimmed courtyard, was built about fifty years ago.

Past the Royal Equestrian Club and en route to Amizmiz, a turnoff to a marked trail at kilometer 35 leads to the multilevel, multicourtyard complex at the burial site of Rabbi Raphael Hacohen, a miracle worker. The spot lies just beyond a Berber village called Achboro, a cluster of square, reddish mud huts behind a mud wall. It is noteworthy because it resembles villages once occupied by Jews.

Personalities: Moroccan Jews and their descendants have had a major impact on Israel. Two examples are President Yitzhak Navon, whose ancestors left Morocco for *Eretz Ysrael* in the seventeenth century, and former Foreign Minister David Levy, who was born in Rabat and came to Israel when he was eighteen.

Moroccan Jews have had an impact on the United States as well. In 1787 Isaac Cordoza Nunes, from the sultan's court, and Isaac Pinto, an American of Moroccan birth, were largely responsible for negotiating the first treaty between the United States and a foreign country. In 1845, David Levy-Yulee, whose family had come from Morocco via the West Indies, became the first United States senator of Jewish origin.

Other prominent Jews of Moroccan origin are René Cassin, the French jurist and winner of the 1968 Nobel Peace Prize; Baruj Benacerraf, the Harvard researcher who won the 1980 Nobel Prize in medicine; Jo Amar, one of Israel's most popular singers; and Shlomo Benhamu, chief rabbi of Argentina.

Recommendations: Royal Air Maroc offers hospitable and gracious service on nonstop flights between New York and Casablanca; kosher meals are available on request. The Casablanca Hyatt Regency, standing at the *mellah's* edge and adjacent to Jewish neighborhoods, could not be better located. The Rabat Hyatt Regency, on the outskirts of town and possessed of a delightful garden, offers a posh escape from the urban hubbub. In Marrakech, the Hotel de la Mamounia within the *medina* walls is peerless. Staying in such surroundings it is possible to practice Morocco's daily exercise of keeping one foot in the East and one in the West.

—*Phyllis Ellen Funke*

Charleston

"Historic" and "charming" are the adjectives most often used to describe the beautifully preserved antebellum city of Charleston, South Carolina. Behind the sparkling white piazzas, colorful gardens, and soft Southern accents, however, is a community of sturdy survivors. Through wars, natural disasters, and depressions, Charlestonians persevered and today are proud of their traditions and thriving city. The city's recovery from Hurricane Hugo's devastating assault in September 1989 is the latest example.

History: Charleston's Jewish community of 4,500 in a metropolitan area of 500,000 has a long and rich heritage going back to the late 1600s, three centuries during which Jews made great contributions to the city's development. The Jewish immigrants who arrived at the busy seaport of Charles Towne, founded by the English in 1670, were part of successive waves of newcomers—English, Scotch-Irish, French Huguenots, Germans, and others—all seeking religious and economic freedom. Their diverse cultural backgrounds shaped a fascinating and unique city—architecturally, culturally, and religiously. Charleston's Jewish community achieved many "firsts" during those centuries.

The first reference to a Jew in the colony appeared in 1695, the year the diary of Governor John Archdale mentions a Spanish-speaking Jew as his interpreter. In 1697, four Jewish merchants arrived. They were followed by Sephardic Jews from the West Indies, chiefly Barbados, and from Spanish and Portuguese colonies where the Inquisition was in force.

Jews in South Carolina were granted more freedom than in any other British colony under the 1669 Carolina Charter. They were permitted to become merchants, traders, and landowners.

Two remarkable Jews of colonial Charleston were Moses Lindo and Francis Salvador. Lindo, an expert indigo sorter from London, helped develop the growing of indigo in South Carolina's Low Country. In 1763, he was appointed inspector general for indigo, the main crop in the colony after rice. Salvador, son of wealthy English Sephardim, came to Charleston to manage family-owned land. His intelligence and good manners helped get him elected to the first and second Provincial Congresses of South Carolina in 1775 and 1776—the first Jew elected to public office in North America. He helped draft the first state constitution and served in South Carolina's first General Assembly.

In August 1776, Salvador, who was strongly anti-British, fought in a local militia against Cherokee Indians equipped by the Tories. He was shot in an ambush and scalped, the first known Jew to die in the American Revolution.

When Charleston was occupied by the British in 1780, the entire population rose to its defense. All of the city's Jewish men enlisted in military service, with many serving in Captain Richard Lushington's company.

For a generation after the Revolution, Charleston's five hundred Jews constituted the largest, wealthiest, and most cultured Jewish community in the United States. Jews branched out into many trades and professions, including politics. A few wealthy Jews bought land and became planters. The arts flourished and Jews, who were fully integrated into Charleston's lively society, participated in this cultural flowering. Mordecai Manuel Noah and

Isaac Harby wrote plays that were produced at the Dock Street Theater (the premiere of Harby's *Alberti* was attended by President James Monroe). Jacob Cardozo edited, and later owned, *The Southern Patriot,* one of Charleston's first newspapers. A talented Charleston painter, Solomon Nuñes Carvalho, was official artist on John C. Frémont's fifth expedition to the West in 1841, afterward writing an account of his adventures on Frémont's last and most dangerous trip.

Penina Moïse, born in Charleston in 1797, wrote poetry on Jewish themes even after she became blind later in life. Many of her poems were set to music and are still sung in English-speaking Reform temples. She was the first Jew in the United States to publish a book of poetry, *Fancy's Sketch Book,* in 1833.

It was not just in culture, however, that Jews were well integrated into antebellum Charleston. There were Jewish slave owners (some of whom freed their slaves before it became illegal to do so). There was also at least one Jewish slave auctioneer, Abraham Seixas, who was—wouldn't you know it—a New Yorker.

During the Civil War, Jewish men of all ages served in Confederate ranks. Although Charleston was not burned or occupied like Atlanta, the Union's relentless daily bombardment inflicted great devastation. After the war the South was so impoverished that many Jews left Charleston to earn a living elsewhere. The war marked the end of Charleston's prominence, but the postwar poverty also helped preserve the city's architecture and ambiance.

Charleston's Jewish population increased with the arrival of Russian and Polish Jews between 1880 and 1914. Some Holocaust survivors and, more recently, Jews from the former Soviet Union have settled in Charleston. Today many young professionals return to Charleston after completing college. The city is again prospering, from the expansion of its port and the growth of industry and tourism.

Community: Charleston had enough Jews by 1749 to organize a congregation, Kahal Kadosh Beth Elohim, which built a splendid Georgian synagogue in 1794. After the synagogue was destroyed in the great Charleston fire of 1838, an impressive Greek Revival synagogue was built on the same site. At that time, the Orthodox Sephardic service was liberalized and an organ installed, making Beth Elohim the first Reform congregation in the United States. Today it is the oldest Reform congregation in the world. Its sanctuary is the second oldest in America, and the oldest in continuous use.

In 1764, Beth Elohim established its Coming Street Cemetery, America's largest colonial Jewish burial ground. The venerable gravestones with their unique stonecutting relate the saga of the congregation's rabbis and leaders, poets and matriarchs, and soldiers from the American Revolution, the War of 1812, and the Civil War.

Members of Beth Elohim organized the Hebrew Benevolent Society in 1784 and the Hebrew Orphan Society in 1801, the oldest of their kind in the nation and still active today. Beth Elohim's Sunday School, second oldest in the nation, was organized in 1838.

Orthodox Congregation Brith Sholom, founded in 1855 by German and Polish Jews, was the first Ashkenazic congregation in the South. In 1911, Congregation Beth Israel was founded by Russian Jews. The two congregations merged in 1955, becoming Brith Sholom–Beth Israel. Conservative Synagogue Emanu-El was founded in 1947.

Some Jews still live in Charleston's old city, which was once, like Jerusalem, surrounded by a wall. In the 1930s, St. Philip Street, in the historic section, was a Jewish neighborhood. Today many Jewish families live in suburban South Windermere and neighborhoods west of the Ashley River near the Jewish Community Center and the Addlestone Hebrew Academy on Raoul Wallenberg Boulevard.

Sights: At Charleston's Visitor Center (once an old train depot) at 385 Meeting Street, volunteers, exhibits, pamphlets, and a delightful multimedia presentation are available to help visitors plan their stay. You can park at the center and take DASH (Downtown Area Shuttle) trolleys along two routes that traverse the historic and business districts, including the colorful market (three blocks of crafts and shopping), the Waterfront Park with its magnificent pineapple fountains and view of the harbor, and house museums. Or don sturdy walking shoes and go exploring. Plaques identify most buildings of note. Take a stroll down King Street, from Calhoun to Broad, to see prosperous Jewish-owned stores, exactly where Jewish shops have been for centuries.

The sanctuary of Kahal Kadosh Beth Elohim, designated a national historic landmark in 1980, is at 90 Hasell (pronounced "hazel") Street, between King and Meeting streets. Built in 1840 to replace the previous sanctuary destroyed by fire, the Greek Revival temple has withstood much more than its predecessor. It was damaged by Union shells in the Civil War, by the great Charleston earthquake of 1886, and by Hurricane Hugo in 1989.

Beth Elohim's sanctuary is especially beautiful by day, when light streams through its pastel stained-glass windows accented with religious symbols. The ornate plaster ceiling is perfectly preserved; the massive ark is of carved Santo Domingo mahogany.

During the Civil War, when Charlestonians believed their city would be burned like Atlanta, all the city's religious valuables were sent to Columbia for safekeeping. As luck would have it, Sherman burned Columbia instead of Charleston. The one Torah kept in Charleston for daily services is still in Beth Elohim's ark. Of the items sent to Columbia, only one badly burned Torah and one bell from a finial were retrieved. In 1987—121 years after it was presumably looted by a Union soldier—one more item pulled from the smoke in Columbia made it back to Charleston: A silver filigree basket (originally presented to Beth Elohim by Joshua Lazarus in 1840 or 1841) was returned to the congregation by its latter-day owner.

Beth Elohim is open, with guides present, from 10 A.M. to noon, Monday through Friday. Visitors are welcome to worship on

Stage whispers: From the walls of the renovated Dock Street Theater have echoed dialogues from every era of Charleston's—and America's—development

Friday at 8:15 P.M. and Saturday at 11 A.M. (no Saturday services in midsummer).

The Beth Elohim Archives Museum at 86 Hasell Street is open 9 A.M. to 3 P.M., Monday through Friday. The archives display records, paintings, and photographs that document the congregation's history— which is the history of Charleston Jewry— and also beautiful ceremonial objects. Also on display is the silver basket that was absent from the synagogue for so long.

Orthodox Brith Sholom–Beth Israel, also in the historic district, occupies a handsome building at 182 Rutledge Avenue (telephone 803-577-6500). Stained glass windows decorated with Judaic symbols and a cast iron balcony railing and chairs from Brith Sholom's 1875 building decorate the main sanctuary.

Synagogue Emanu-El (Conservative) has a modern sanctuary at 5 Windsor Drive in suburban West Ashley (telephone 803-571-3264). The mellow wood paneling and large glass windows of the main sanctuary blend with the greenery of the outdoor biblical herb garden. The colorful ark curtain of silk velvet depicting Jacob's dream was designed by Lydie Egosi.

Several points of Jewish interest are located in the City Hall area at the corner of Broad and Meeting Streets. In Washington Park, behind City Hall, there is a plaque in memory of Francis Salvador, the only Jewish soldier of the American Revolution to be individually honored in Charleston.

On the second floor of City Hall, another plaque honors Saul Alexander, a rags-to-riches immigrant who left his fortune to local charities of all creeds. Names of several prominent Jewish women of Charleston are included on a plaque called the "Women's Hall of Fame" on the third floor.

Nearby, at 88 Broad Street, is the original building of Charleston's Hebrew Orphan Society, where Judah P. Benjamin, who would one day be secretary of state of the Confederacy, was a student as a boy. A Hebrew inscription can be seen high on the facade. The house that belonged to Benjamin's father is at 35 Broad Street.

A short walk away, at 89–91 Church Street, is a three-story house that was the model for "Catfish Row" in George Gershwin's opera, *Porgy and Bess*. Gershwin

lived in Charleston during 1934 while he composed the opera.

The Coming Street Cemetery, about two miles away at 189 Coming Street, is always locked, but arrangements can be made for a guided tour by phoning Beth Elohim at (803) 723-1090.

Grace Episcopal Church, at 98 Wentworth Street, features a beautiful stained-glass "Women's Window" with biblical and contemporary heroines. One of those pictured is Hadassah founder Henrietta Szold, shown teaching arithmetic to Jewish children in *kippot*. Call the church at (803) 723-4575 for information about visiting.

Culture: Visitors are welcome at the monthly Sunday breakfast lectures sponsored by Beth Elohim's brotherhood and at monthly breakfast *minyan* and annual scholar-in-residence lectures at Emanu-El. The Jewish Community Center, at 1645 Raoul Wallenberg Boulevard (west of the Ashley River), has lectures, Israeli entertainers, a health club, and events for singles and seniors. Call the center at (803) 571-6565 for the latest events.

In 1985, the College of Charleston began a Jewish Studies program that includes lectures and concerts open to the public. Call the College of Charleston Office of Special Events at 792-5525.

General Sights: Charleston is often called the "cultural capital of the South." Its star attraction is Spoleto U.S.A., begun in 1976, the brainchild of Gian Carlo Menotti. During this lively annual music festival in late May and early June, the city hosts concerts, operas, ballets, and plays with world-renowned performers. Free concerts are presented daily in many of Charleston's historic churches.

The Dock Street Theater at 135 Church Street, restored in 1936, appears as it did when plays of early Jewish playwrights were performed there. In addition to seeing the theater while attending a performance, it can be viewed from 10 A.M. to 6 P.M., Monday through Friday.

The Charleston Symphony performs six concert series a year. Besides the Dock Street Theater, plays are presented at the Queen Street Playhouse and the College of

Charleston. There are also two resident ballet companies.

In addition to the many historic houses open for tours, there are nine museums and art galleries, including the Charleston Museum, 360 Meeting Street; Gibbes Museum of Art, 135 Meeting Street; and the world's largest naval museum, the aircraft carrier U.S.S. *Yorktown* in Charleston harbor. The Thursday and Saturday editions of the *Post and Courier* carry details.

Charleston's lovely setting lures visitors outdoors—to the harbor, Fort Sumter, and nearby beaches and resorts. Charles Towne Landing, a state park, fifteen minutes' drive from downtown on South Carolina 171 is on the site of Charleston's first settlement. Animals and plants then indigenous to the state are seen in their natural setting. Replicas of a 17th-century trading vessel and colonial village illustrate life in the colony. Visitors can picnic, walk, rent a bike, take a tram.

Close to town along the Ashley River Road (Highway 61) is a cluster of botanic and architectural sights that includes Drayton Hall, Magnolia Plantation and Gardens, and Middleton Place. Drayton Hall, built between 1738 and 1742, was the only Ashley River plantation house not damaged by Sherman and is the only pre-Revolutionary mansion remaining today.

No visit to Charleston is complete without a trip to at least one of its gardens, which are at their peak when azaleas and dogwoods bloom in late March and early April. Magnolia Gardens, a mile from Drayton Hall, has a section of plants mentioned in the Bible arranged in the shape of a Star of David, clustered around a statue of David as a boy. The area is surrounded by larger trees and shrubs, including palm, olive, cedar of Lebanon, pomegranate, apple, and Moses' bulrushes.

Cypress Gardens, a lovely swamp garden created from what was once the freshwater reserve of a rice plantation, is twenty-four miles north of the city on Highway 52.

Personalities: Charleston Jews gained recognition in diverse fields. Dr. Leon Banov, Sr., was a pioneer in public health, responsible for Charleston's becoming the first city in the United States to require pasteurization of milk, introducing measures to eradicate malaria, and opening maternal and well-baby clinics throughout Charleston County. Franklin J. Moses was chief justice of the South Carolina Supreme Court during Reconstruction. Willard Hirsch was South Carolina's best-known sculptor, and William Halsey, of Jewish ancestry, is Charleston's best-known painter. Joshua Lazarus introduced illuminating gas to America's cities; Carrie, Anita, and Mabel Pollitzer were leading suffragettes. Leon Keyserling was chairman of the Council of Economic Advisers under President Truman. Arthur Freed, the songwriter and producer (*An American in Paris; Singin' in the Rain*), is a Charleston native.

Two of the city's most prominent Jewish citizens today are David Stahl, conductor of the Charleston Symphony, and Reuben Greenberg, the city's black police chief, whose grandfather was a Russian-Jewish immigrant.

Reading: *The Jews of South Carolina* by Barnett A. Elzas takes readers through 1905. It is available in hardback from Beth Elohim, 86 Hasell Street, Charleston, SC, 29401, for $30, including postage. *This Happy Land: The Jews of Colonial and Antebellum Charleston,* by James William Hagy, is available from the University of Alabama Press, Box 870380, Tuscaloosa, Alabama, for $49.95. *The Jews of Charleston* by Charles Reznikoff (Jewish Publication Society) is out of print but may be found in libraries. Charleston is one of the locales in Eli Evans's *Judah P. Benjamin: The Jewish Confederate* (Free Press). For a fictional look at early South Carolina Jews, read *This New Land* by Lester Goran (Signet Books). For a more general fictional look at Charleston's history, read *Charleston* by Alexandra Ripley (Doubleday).

Recommendations: Among the restaurants worth trying are Nosh with Josh, 217 Meeting Street, which serves vegetarian Middle Eastern dishes. In the same block are Hyman's Seafood and two delis, Nathan's and Aaron's. To sample Low Country specialties, try Magnolia's, 185 East Bay Street; Carolina's, 10 Exchange Street; or Colony House, 15 Prioleau Street—all near the new Waterfront Park.

The elegant Mills House Hotel, 115 Meeting Street, captures the flavor of old Charleston. King's Courtyard Inn at 198 King Street is one of the many popular small inns in the historic district. The new Omni Hotel, also on King Street, is only a few steps from Beth Elohim. Remember to reserve early for Spoleto and the peak spring season.

Charleston can be crowded in March and April, and hot in July and August but, like its troubled history, it wears its burdens well. It never loses its charm.

—Helen Silver

Chicago

When Jacob "Greasy Thumb" Guzik, Al Capone's treasurer and a leading figure in the Chicago crime syndicate, was at the height of his power, he brought many lawsuits against newspapers for portraying him as a gangster. One day in the 1930s, legend has it, Guzik stormed into the Chicago office of the Jewish Daily *Forward*, brushed past the secretary, and approached the editor, shouting, "Stop running editorials denouncing me."

The editor remained calm. "Sir," he said, "we are not afraid of you at the *Forward*, and we refuse to allow you to intimidate us. Besides, why do you care what we print?"

Guzik slammed his fist down on the editor's desk. "I care," he said, "because my mother reads it."

Jake Guzik was a powerful man, more successful at controlling politicians, judges, and trade unions than he was with Jewish journalists. But even if most of us do not want to claim him as one of our own, his life is a testament to the prominence of Jews in all aspects of Chicago life. In addition to organized crime — and much more worthy of mention — Jews have been driving forces behind the architecture, business, culture, philanthropy, sports, and media in Chicago, so much so that it is hard to separate the Jewish community from the city itself. No matter where you go in this bustling city, it is possible to find some Jewish connection.

History: Movement has always characterized the Chicago Jewish community. In the beginning, Jews came from the Germanic corridor — Prussia, Austria, Bohemia and sections of modern-day Poland — fleeing oppression to settle in Chicago as early as 1832, five years before the city's incorporation. In 1845, the first

High Holiday services were conducted above a storefront at Lake and Wells Streets, and a year later the Jewish Burial Society was organized and a one-acre plot of land purchased in what is present-day Lincoln Park. This became Chicago's first Jewish cemetery, Mount Mayriv.

By 1847, an outbreak of cholera had filled the cemetery and discouraged new immigrants from settling along the shores of Lake Michigan. That same year, Kehilat Anshe Mayriv — Congregation of the Men of the West — the first Jewish congregation in Chicago, was founded by Bavarian Jews. In June 1851, KAM built the first synagogue in Chicago at Clark and Jackson streets, a site now occupied by the Kluczynski Federal Building. It was followed by B'nai Sholom, founded by Posen Jews in 1852, and Chicago Sinai, the first Reform congregation, in 1861. The two oldest congregations later merged into KAM-Isaiah Israel.

By 1871, there were ten congregations and several thousand Jews living in Chicago. Then, on Simchat Torah of that year — October 8 — the Great Fire began that destroyed most of the city. The Standard Club, founded by German Jews in 1869 as a social and recreational center, had a clubhouse at 13th and South Michigan Avenue that was used by General Philip Sheridan as his headquarters when martial law was established following the fire.

Henry Greenebaum, one of four brothers who arrived in the midst of the cholera epidemic, rose to prominence in both the early Jewish community and the political and financial realms at this time. A close friend of Stephen A. Douglas and an ardent Unionist during the Civil War, he was elected to the Chicago City Council in 1856, representing the old Sixth Ward. After his

Greenebaum Brothers Banking House burned to the ground during the Chicago Fire, he told depositors they would receive their money as soon as the vaults cooled down. This was seen as an unusually generous gesture at a time when authorities were having difficulty securing the city from looting and rampant crime.

The expansion of the Jewish community after the Great Fire was slow but steady. The flames had destroyed Jewish residences near the downtown business district, forcing many to relocate. The more prosperous German Jews, who made up the majority, moved south along Michigan, Wabash, and Indiana Avenues, eventually settling into Washington Park, Kenwood, Hyde Park, and South Shore; the Eastern European Jews moved west of the central business district, into the Maxwell Street ghetto.

Between 1880 and 1900 anti-Semitism in Eastern Europe drove fifty-five thousand Russian and Polish Jews into the Maxwell Street market neighborhood, an area bounded by Canal, Halsted, Polk, and 15th Streets. The area soon became a large *shtetl*. Yiddish was the language of choice; dozens of Hebrew schools and Yiddish theaters were organized, and forty Orthodox *shuls* were built within walking distance of the intersection of Halsted and Maxwell, in the heart of the area.

The Maxwell Street ghetto was a tough, mean, overcrowded place, where as many as four families were packed into flimsy, wooded lean-tos lacking proper ventilation and plumbing. In addition to the open-air market, kosher butchers and bakeries, secondhand clothing stores, peddler wagons, synagogues and *cheders*, there were an abundance of gambling houses and bordellos. Thus, it came as no surprise when the area produced gangsters such as Guzik, Ike Bloom, Davey Miller, and Samuel "Nails" Morton, the last two also taking an interest in the welfare of their own people, often coming to the aid of elderly Jews who had been attacked and robbed by Irish and Polish gangs.

Jews worked in the most squalid conditions above the storefronts of the rundown wooden tenements of the area, toiling for the city's garment industry. By 1910, Jews made up almost 70 percent of all Chicago tailors, but they earned less than eight dollars a week on the average and were often required to put in twelve to eighteen hours a day. This era of growing disenchantment among the laboring classes culminated in September 1910 with a strike against Hart Schaffner and Marx and other large clothing manufacturers. Spearheaded by Sidney Hillman and Bessie Abramovitz—who were later married—and Jacob Potofsky, the strike organized Jewish workers against a powerful Jewish manufacturing concern, a phenomenon in those days when labor and capital were divided by race and religion. The efforts of these activists resulted in the formation of the Amalgamated Clothing Workers Union of America, which won important concessions on behalf of the workers. Today, a bust of Hillman stands in the reception room of the Sidney Hillman Center of the Amalgamated Clothing Workers of America on Ashland Avenue.

Around this time, the ghetto began moving outward, most notably to North Lawndale and Douglas Park, Chicago's Jewish West Side, and by the 1920s Douglas Boulevard became the Jewish Main Street. This era also saw the emergence of Jewish involvement in the political process, as the Jews of Lawndale exerted considerable influence at City Hall through Mike and Moe Rosenberg, the patron saints of the 24th Ward Democratic machine. The Rosenbergs succeeded in placing twenty-eight-year-old Jacob Arvey in the alderman's chair in the early 1920s and, a decade later, were instrumental in the election of Governor Henry Horner, the grandson of Harry Horner, one of Chicago's original Jewish settlers and a founding member of the Board of Trade.

In 1940, the Lawndale area had more than 100,000 Jews, but the number dropped by half within six years as younger Jews started "moving up" to Albany Park and Rogers Park, and the black community expanded.

Today, there are no Jews on the West Side, and even the Jewish community in West Rogers Park is in decline as Jews continue to move farther out. Many of the newest immigrants—some 15,000 Soviet

Jews who have arrived in recent years — have bypassed the city altogether and found homes in the suburbs.

Community: With more than 110 synagogues, 7 Jewish community centers, and myriad services and agencies, Chicago is an established and thriving Jewish community. Today, 260,000 Jews — representing a wide variety of religious and secular life — live in the metropolitan area. More than two-thirds live in the suburbs — especially to the north, along Lake Michigan from Evanston to Highland Park, and to the northwest from Skokie to Deerfield. There are smaller pockets on the South Side, in Hyde Park; in the southern suburbs; and, to the west, in Oak Park, a suburb famous for its concentration of Frank Lloyd Wright homes.

Chicago has long been the center of Jewish life in the Midwest. In addition to attracting foreign immigrants — most recently from the former Soviet Union — the community has also grown from the movement of young Jews, many of whom are single, into the area from smaller Midwest cities.

The largest concentration of Jews in the city is in West Rogers Park, between Kedzie, Western, Peterson and Howard streets, where a sense of a traditional Jewish community is kept alive by a cluster of kosher restaurants, food stores, bookstores, Judaica shops, synagogues, Hebrew schools and social service organizations. This is still the heart of Chicago's orthodox community, and institutions in the neighborhood are often bustling on Friday as people prepare for *Shabbat*.

West Rogers Park is far from a Jewish preserve, however. Jews coexist there with an increasing number of Indians, Pakistanis, Assyrians, Japanese, Chinese, Koreans and, most recently, Croatians. A walk down Devon Avenue, in the heart of the neighborhood, is like a visit to the United Nations.

One of the Chicago Jewish community's greatest strengths, in fact, is its generally harmonious relations with other ethnic and religious groups. Jewish leaders have taken the initiative in forming interfaith dialogues, especially with the city's huge Polish community. Among other projects, the Jewish community has sponsored missions of Polish-American journalists to Israel, jointly sponsored educational programs for the public schools with the archdiocese of Chicago, and published a statement with the Catholic community calling for the need to respect each other's views in the abortion debate.

Sights: Chicago became the architectural center of America in the late nineteenth century — thanks, in part, to the Great Fire that left lots of room for experimentation — with the development of the skyscraper and the skeleton-frame building. With much of the city left to be rebuilt, Jews stepped in and contributed more than their fair share.

Chicago's first great Jewish architect was Dankmar Adler (1844–1900), son of KAM's rabbi and partner of Louis Sullivan. Together with Sullivan, he is credited with pioneering the modern office building. The restored Auditorium Theatre, at Congress and Michigan, in the famed Adler and Sullivan Auditorium Building of 1889 (now home of Roosevelt University) attests to Adler's acoustical genius. Today, the magnificent red marble column from the entrance to the Central Music Hall, Adler's favorite commission, sits atop his grave at the Mount Mayriv cemetery, 3600 Narragansett Avenue. The Central Music Hall was demolished in 1900, the year of Adler's death, to make way for the Marshall Field State Street store.

KAM's fifth home, now the Pilgrim Baptist Church at Thirty-third and Indiana Avenue (near Michael Reese Hospital), is one of the lesser-known extant Adler and Sullivan works, and its architecture, acoustics, and Sullivan ornamentation inside make it a worthwhile place to see.

KAM's current building, 1100 East Hyde Park Boulevard, is also worth viewing, not only for its architecture but also for the Morton B. Weiss Museum of Judaica. The synagogue's Byzantine-style exterior and sanctuary, designed in 1923 by Alfred Alschuler, were based on a second-century synagogue in Tiberias. The structure is octagonal with eight perfectly round arches. Inside, the ark is made of travertine marble; the elaborate stained-glass windows depicting biblical figures and inscriptions draw many tourists to the building, which was declared a Chicago landmark in 1977.

Chicago Sinai, the other survivor from Chicago Jewry's earliest days, occupies a simpler, postwar building at 5350 South Shore Drive in Hyde Park. The most prominent bow to luxury is the marble-lined lobby; marble also surrounds the ark in the sanctuary, which seats seventeen hundred.

In sharp contrast with the classical KAM and the simplicity of Chicago Sinai are several city and suburban synagogues to the north. The largest Orthodox synagogue in the city is B'nai Ruven at 6350 N. Whipple Street in West Rogers Park. Its jutting brick and dark wood give the *shul*, designed by Chicago architect Irving Moses and completed in 1968, a rustic feeling. On top, the sanctuary spirals up into a dome, where the Torah scrolls are kept, giving the worshipers a feeling of ascension.

The older and major portion of the North Shore Congregation Israel, 1185 Sheridan Road in Glencoe, was designed by Minoru Yamasaki on the former Lady Esther estate. The structure, resembling a white pagoda in front and consisting of a series of narrow arches on its sides, is built of concrete on glass on metal. The sanctuary has a "concept of light" theme; many of the windows are not only sources of light, they also represent the synagogue's relationship with the outside world.

Another noteworthy building is the North Suburban Synagogue Beth El, at 1175 Sheridan Road in Highland Park. Architect Percival Goodman designed the modern sanctuary on the grounds of an old estate. Beth El is also home to Kol Ami, a Judaica collection with a permanent collection and special exhibits.

The University of Chicago, nestled in Hyde Park not far from KAM, has many Jewish connections in its past. When it was founded as a Baptist school more than a century ago, the university benefited from the financial support of such philanthropists from the retail business as Julius Rosenwald, the head of Sears, Roebuck and Company, and Leon Mandel. William Rainey Harper, the first president of the university, was not a Jew, but he was a world-renowned biblical scholar and Hebraist, producing, among many other works, a grammar of biblical Hebrew. Jews who have won Nobel Prizes during their tenure at the University of Chicago are Albert Michelson (physics) for his studies of light, which contributed to Einstein's theory of relativity; Saul Bellow (literature); and Milton Friedman (economics). Also at the University of Chicago, the Regenstein Library on Ellis (east of South Woodlawn) houses the twenty thousand-volume Ludwig Rosenberger Judaica Library.

Also in Hyde Park is the Museum of Science and Industry, a favorite of generations of Chicago schoolchildren, opened in 1893 as the Fine Arts Building for the Columbian Exposition. When the World's Fair closed, Julius Rosenwald, anxious that the architecture of the building be preserved for future generations, gave $3 million on the condition that his name not be used in connection with the museum.

Traveling north on the lakefront, the best view of Chicago's skyline is from the front of the Adler Planetarium, a treat that doesn't cost anything. Opened in 1930, the planetarium, endowed by Max Adler (Julius Rosenwald's brother-in-law), was the first in the Western Hemisphere and one of the few also to house a museum. There you will find one of the three finest collections of antique scientific instruments (the other two being in Oxford and Florence).

The Adler Planetarium and its lakefront neighbors—the Shedd Aquarium and Oceanarium and the Field Museum of Natural History—are on a landfill engineered by Jacob Sensibar, a Chicago Jew who earned the title "World's Greatest Earth Mover." Most of Chicago's distinctive twenty-one-mile lakefront was created by Sensibar's firm, Construction Materials Corporation, between 1914 and 1916. Some of the landfill was carried from the other side of Lake Michigan in hopper dredges that Sensibar invented. Later, he was instrumental in the reclamation of forty-four thousand acres of swampland in Israel's Huleh Valley. Nearly every Chicagoan claims that the lakefront is the city's greatest natural asset.

Another place not to be missed is the Spertus Museum of Judaica at 618 South

Michigan. Part of the Spertus College of Judaica, the museum is spread out over eight floors in a Jewish Federation-owned building. It features an outstanding permanent collection of antique Judaica, including an extensive collection of Torahs. Recent exhibits have covered the history of Sephardim, and photographs of Jerzy Kosinski, who willed his literary estate to Spertus. The museum also houses the Field Gallery of Contemporary Art; a Holocaust memorial, which relates the history of Nazi persecution through photographs, artifacts, and videos; and the Rosenbaum Artifacts Center, a hands-on museum for children that offers classes and workshops as well as puppet shows, storytelling, and singalongs.

Not to be forgotten at Spertus is the seventy thousand-volume Asher Library, the largest Judaica library between New York and Los Angeles, and the Chicago Jewish Archives, which is open to researchers.

Many sights of Jewish interest can be seen in the Loop, Chicago's business district, including a bust of Julius Rosenwald that stands in front of the Merchandise Mart in the heart of the area.

Not far away, in Herald Square on Wacker Drive, is the Haym Salomon Monument. This sculpture was the last commission of Lorado Taft, who died before its completion in 1941, and depicts George Washington flanked by Robert Morris and Salomon, a Polish-born Jew who died broke after donating his fortune to help pay the bills of the American Revolution. It is the only statue of Washington in the country where the first president is not standing alone. A Chicago lawyer, Barnet Hodes, pushed to make Salomon part of the city sculpture. While it was being created in the 1930s, however, there was a rash of anti-Semitism and Nazi Bund activity in Chicago, and Hodes thought that the sculpture was in danger of being vandalized. "I went to Lorado Taft and induced him to lock Washington's and Salomon's arms," Hodes said. "That way, any disfigurement of Salomon would also have injured Washington and would have been a national disgrace."

In 1989 the city renamed the Wabash and Wacker Bridge after Irv Kupcinet, the popular *Chicago Sun-Times* columnist who grew up in the Maxwell Street area. More recently, Plymouth Court, where the current Standard Club is now located, was rededicated to honor Judge Abraham Lincoln Marovitz, a friend of Richard Daley who swore the late mayor into office five times, and a longtime legal figure in the city.

Several sculptures by Jewish artists can be viewed by walking through the Loop. These include a steel piece by Louise Nevelson, *Dawn Shadows*, at Madison and Wells; a bronze by Milton Horn, *The Spirit of Jewish Philanthropy*, next to the Jewish Federation at Franklin and Madison; a Chagall mosaic, *Four Seasons*, at Dearborn and Monroe; and two sculptures by the Israeli artist Yaacov Agam, one at 20 N. Clark Street and one in the Harris Bank building at 111 W. Monroe Street.

At 16 S. Clark, sandwiched between two office buildings, is the Chicago Loop Synagogue, a structure known for its beauty and simplicity. Mounted on the outer wall of the Orthodox *shul* is *The Hands of Peace*, a bronze and brass work by Henri Azas. Inside, a large marble tablet with the Ten Commandments in Hebrew and English stands in the entranceway. The most spectacular feature of the synagogue is Abraham Rattner's magnificent stained-glass window, located on the sanctuary's eastern wall. Based on the text of Genesis 1:3, and titled *Let There Be Light,* the window is best viewed from the inside during daylight hours. In addition to daily services at the Loop Synagogue, Lubavitch Chabad of the Loop, at 401 S. LaSalle, holds daily and holiday prayer services as well as a lunch-and-learn program.

A sight which is not only associated with Jews, but which documents much of the early history of Jewish immigrants in the city, is Jane Addams–Hull House Museum, now owned by the University of Illinois at Chicago. Located in the Hull Mansion at 800 S. Halsted Street, just south of the old Maxwell Street area, it is a historic site and memorial to Jane Addams, her innovative and world-famous settlement house programs and associates, and the neighborhood they served. An exhibit on the surrounding neighborhood as it appeared at the turn of the century includes material on the Russian, Polish, and Lithuanian Jews who were an integral part of the area.

During the summer the Chicago Jewish Historical Society sponsors a series of day-long bus tours to parts of the city and surrounding area with sights of historic and contemporary Jewish interest. The "Chicago Jewish Roots" tour explores the history of the old immigrant neighborhoods, including Maxwell Street, Lawndale, Humboldt Park, Logan Square, Albany Park, and Rogers Park. The "Southern Suburbs" tour goes through Homewood, Olympia Fields, and Flossmoor. A "South Shore" tour to Northwest Indiana travels through Hammond, Gary, and Michigan City, stopping at local synagogues. A "Summer Safari" explores the Jewish communities in Southwest Michigan, an area that has traditionally been to Chicago Jews what the Catskills were to New York Jews. For prices and reservations for these tours, call (312) 663-5634.

Eating and Shopping: Chicago has the variety of kosher restaurants, food stores, and Judaica shops that one would expect to find in a large city. Most are located in West Rogers Park, on Devon Avenue, from Kedzie to California Avenue, a strip that has recently been renamed in memory of Golda Meir. These shops include Gitel's Kosher Bakery, at 2745 W. Devon, which specializes in fancy French pastries, catering, and made-to-order wedding and birthday cakes and sweet tables; Tel Aviv Kosher bakery, at 2944 W. Devon, which makes pareve cheesecakes, breads and special-occasion cakes; the Milk Pail, 3329 W. Devon, a complete grocery and deli, carrying everything from produce to party trays; and Rosenblum's World of Judaica, 2906 W. Devon, which carries a wide selection of Jewish books, music, and religious articles and gifts.

Jewish shops and restaurants can also be found in the suburbs, especially on Dempster Street in Skokie. Hamakor Gallery, 4150 W. Dempster, specializes in limited edition prints and sculpture by Jewish artists. Slice of Life, 4129 W. Dempster, is an eclectic vegetarian restaurant specializing in fresh fish, pizza, pasta, and desserts, especially cheesecake. In Highland Park, the Arthur M. Feldman Gallery, 1815 St. Johns Avenue, has the largest antique Judaica collection west of New York, as well as furniture, fine art, coins, and ancient and modern jewelry.

Personalities: In addition to Nobelists like Michelson, Bellow, and Friedman, Chicago has produced many Jewish figures of national and international prominence. Admiral Hyman Rickover, father of the nuclear submarine, grew up in the Maxwell Street area, as did William Paley, the founder of CBS, and Arthur Goldberg, the Chicago lawyer who became secretary of labor, a Supreme Court justice, and the United States ambassador to the United Nations. Other Jewish Chicagoans include comedian Shelly Berman, author Meyer Levin, presidential advisors Stuart Eizenstadt and Kenneth Adelman, former commerce secretary Philip Klutznik, antiwar activist Daniel Ellsberg, playwright David Mamet, actor Mandy Patinkin, playwright Ben Hecht, columnists Abigail Van Buren and Ann Landers, and Jack Benny, from nearby Waukegan.

The last stop for many Jews in Chicago—and a notable sight for its sheer size and colorful history—is Jewish Waldheim Cemetery. Located west of the city in suburban Forest Park, Waldheim is the largest consecrated Jewish burial ground in the world, consisting of a conglomerate of three hundred cemeteries and more than 175,000 graves. Waldheim has been a burial ground in one form or another for centuries, going back to the time when the Pottowatomi and Illini Indians buried their dead there; the first Jewish burial took place in 1875. In the cemetery's heyday, the Metropolitan Elevated had a funeral-car route to Waldheim. Today, the cemetery, which has a number of ghost stories associated with it, houses the graves of many prominent Chicago figures, including those of the anarchist Emma Goldman (who is buried near the five condemned Haymarket rioters in the nonsectarian section), the director Michael Todd, former Illinois

Governor Sam Shapiro, and gangster Samuel "Nails" Morton.

Culture: In addition to museums and galleries, Chicago is home to many cultural programs of Jewish interest. The seven Jewish Community Centers in the city and suburbs host a wide range of educational, cultural, social, and athletic programs aimed at people of all ages. The JCCs of Chicago also operate the National Jewish Theater out of the Mayer Kaplan JCC, 5050 Church Street, Skokie, a performing arts center dedicated to the exploration of the contemporary Jewish experience through works by Jewish playwrights. Four plays are presented each year between October and June in a subscription series that in the past has included such critically acclaimed works as *The Dybbuk*, *The Heidi Chronicles*, and *A Shayna Maidel*.

Another cultural program of note is the JCC literary series, which features celebrated Jewish authors reflecting on issues of relevance to the Jewish community. In the past, the series has featured Nora Ephron, Saul Bellow, Chaim Potok, and the late Isaac Bashevis Singer. Tickets for the programs can be purchased, along with tickets for the National Jewish Theater, by calling the Mayer Kaplan JCC.

The Jewish Film Foundation presents feature films — dramatic and documentary — of Jewish interest at conveniently located theaters throughout the city suburbs. Screenings are often followed by lectures, panel discussions, and performances. For information about screenings, call (312) 588-2763.

"A Buffet of Jewish Thought," a monthly lecture series on contemporary Jewish issues and concerns, is sponsored by the Chicago Community Kollel at the Hyatt Regency Chicago at noon on the last Tuesday of the month. The lectures are presented by Jewish leaders who are authorities in their fields; a kosher buffet follows. For reservations, call (312) 262-9400.

Reading: Most notable of the comprehensive histories of the community is H. L. Meites's *History of the Jews of Chicago,* a 1924 book recently reprinted by the Chicago Jewish Historical Society. The University of Chicago recently reprinted *The Ghetto,* sociologist Louis Wirth's 1928 study of Jewish communities, ranging from the medieval Jewish ghetto, where Jews were locked in at night, to Chicago's old West Side. *A Child of the Century* (Simon), the memoirs of Ben Hecht, includes material on Jewish Chicago. *The Dream Seekers* (William Morrow), a new novel by Grace Marks, details the lifestyles of upper- and lower-class Jews in Chicago just before the turn of the century. *I Came a Stranger: Story of a Hull House Girl,* by Hilda Satt Polacheck, is a touching memoir of the author's immigration to Chicago as a young woman at the turn of the century. Lincolnwood author Charlotte Herman writes children's books set on the old West Side, including *A Summer on Thirteenth Street, Milly Cooper 3B* and *Milly Cooper Take a Chance* (Dutton).

Saul Bellow and Meyer Levin have long been staples of Chicago's literary history. Bellow's *Humboldt's Gift* and *The Adventures of Augie March* (Viking Penguin) are autobiographical novels of a Jewish childhood on the West Side. Meyer Levin's *The Old Bunch* (Citadel Press) is about a group of Jews living in Chicago during the World's Fair in 1933. *Compulsion* (Dell) is Levin's fictionalized account of the Leopold and Loeb case that scandalized and pained American Jewry in 1924; Nathan Leopold and Richard Loeb, scions of affluent German Jewish families in Hyde Park, decided to commit "the perfect crime" and murdered fourteen-year-old Bobby Franks. Evanston writer Susan Sussman has written two novels with local settings — *The Dieter* and *Time Off for Good Behavior* (Pocket Books).

Recommendations: The Hyatt Regency Chicago, owned by the Pritzker family, has some of the best kosher cuisine in the city, as well as superb views of Lake Michigan, the Chicago River, and the skyline.

In a city where the Jewish community has been characterized by movement, it is only natural that the Jews should be spread out, and this is definitely the case in

Chicago. Renting a car is advisable; although the city has good public transportation, many of the old neighborhoods are no longer safe, while the newer areas are difficult and expensive to reach from the Loop. Having a car will also allow you to explore areas off the beaten path and to discover Chicago's Jewish roots for yourself. You can rest assured that a Jewish connection is waiting for you in all corners of this vibrant city.

—*Elizabeth Bernstein*

Cincinnati

Like Jerusalem, Cincinnati is built on hills. From the tops you can see an endless panorama, which at the start of the 19th century so beckoned to the adventurous that it made Cincinnati the biggest city in what was then the American West.

There is some dispute over who was the first Jew in Cincinnati. It is known that in 1814 Jonas Horwitz, a Pennsylvania physician, tried to set up practice in the Queen City. He advertised a smallpox vaccine and pledged to treat the poor gratis. But the would-be Jewish pioneer was treated by his professional colleagues much as the 1990 Cincinnati Reds received the visiting Oakland Athletics. Fearful of the competition, local doctors had him run out of town.

History: It was another Jonas — Joseph Jonas, a native of Plymouth, England — who became Cincinnati's first permanent Jewish resident. He had read about the young city on the north bank of the Ohio, and after greeting relatives in New York on his arrival in the New World in 1817, he pushed on to the hinterland, pledging to remember both his Jewish roots and his faith in the Almighty.

Two years later David Israel, also from Plymouth, arrived with his wife and brother, adopting the name Johnson. By the time Cincinnati had 10,000 inhabitants it also had David's son, Frederick A. Johnson, the first Jewish child born in the city.

Abraham Jonas, Joseph's brother, also arrived in 1819, but after a few years he grew restless and eventually moved to Kentucky, where he entered politics and served in the state legislature. He continued his political activity after moving to Illinois in 1838, and that same year he met another young Illinois politician, a namesake with whom he formed a lifelong friendship. As far as anyone has determined, Abraham Jonas was Abraham Lincoln's first Jewish friend.

Meanwhile, unlike many pioneers who struck out for worldly fortune, Joseph Jonas was as good as his word. He became a watchmaker and silversmith, and he also gathered together the small number of Jews gravitating to Cincinnati. By 1824, he was the leader in forming a congregation. There were about 14 Jews in the area who worshiped together on the holidays. Ten of them met in a private home and formed Bene Israel, which still exists as Rockdale Temple.

The community, which formed the first congregation west of the Alleghenies, felt it had a religious calling beyond the ordinary. Like their biblical ancestor Abraham, they believed they had been guided to a new land for a higher purpose — to keep Judaism alive in uncharted territory. In his diary Jonas laments, "If only a few of the most able and respectable would commence sincerely keeping their Sabbaths and festivals," as he was.

To the surprise and delight of the growing congregation, the bigotry they had known in Europe was almost nonexistent in Ohio. Fifty-two Christians donated twenty-five dollars apiece to help them build their first sanctuary on Broadway, between Fifth and Sixth Streets. Completed in 1835, Bene Israel was an imposing classical edifice with massive columns, a domed roof, and a richly decorated interior.

Harsh conditions in Central Europe in the 1840s brought many German Jews to Cincinnati, and they eventually became the dominant Jewish religious force in the city. Religious tolerance combined with great financial opportunity saw the Jewish population rise to 10,000, most of German

141

origin, by the eve of the Civil War, making Cincinnati's the third-largest community in the United States. At this time Joseph Jonas, along in years, became the first Jew elected to public office in Ohio, serving from 1860 to 1861 in the state legislature.

In 1840, Congregation B'nai Yeshurun was formed; two other congregations followed in 1847 and 1855. The first English-speaking lodge of B'nai B'rith and its first western unit began in Cincinnati in 1849. America's first Jewish hospital was founded in the city in 1850.

Rabbi Isaac M. Wise came from Albany in 1854 to serve as the spiritual leader of B'nai Yeshurun, then an Orthodox synagogue. During his forty-six years in Cincinnati he influenced the development of Reform Judaism from his pulpit. Dreaming of modernizing the "forms, formulas, customs, and observances" of the religion to conform with what he believed American Judaism should be, he saw the changes as a boon for Jews in Cincinnati and across the new land. Even today the estimated 56 percent adherence of Cincinnati Jews to Reform Judaism is far above the national average.

Not to be left behind, Bene Israel hired Rabbi Max Lilienthal. Together the two rabbis introduced many liturgical reforms. Services were abbreviated, head covering abolished, two-day holidays shortened, and many prayers recited in English. Wise established *The American Israelite,* the second Jewish newspaper in America (after Isaac Leeser's *Occident* in Philadelphia). It is printed to this day, proclaiming itself "The Oldest English Jewish Weekly in America."

Situated on the Ohio River, the boundary between free and slave America, Cincinnati was always in a sensitive spot in North–South relations. Though Ohio was a staunch member of the Union during the Civil War, the southern half of the state was "Copperhead" country, where economic and familial ties with the South created considerable antiwar feeling. The Jews reflected the mixed sentiments of the larger community. When the Democratic Party nominated Wise for the state senate in 1863, his board of trustees, most of whom were Republicans, forced him to decline.

Cincinnati-area congressmen played roles in the two Civil War issues that bore directly on Jews. When Congress stipulated that army chaplains must be Christian, Congressman Clement Vallandigham— leader of antiwar Democrats who was later jailed on charges of treason—was outspoken in advocating the right of rabbis to become chaplains; Congress ignored his advice and a year later President Lincoln intervened to have the law changed. When General Ulysses S. Grant issued his infamous order expelling all Jews from the military department of Tennessee, Cesar Kaskel, a Jewish businessman from Paducah, Kentucky, set out to see Lincoln. En route he stopped in Cincinnati to enlist the aid of local Jewish leaders, and he was later escorted to the White House by Congressman John A. Gurley of Cincinnati. Lincoln had the order revoked.

Jewish life flourished in Cincinnati after the Civil War. The Union of American Hebrew Congregations was founded there in 1873; Hebrew Union College began two years later and the Central Conference of American Rabbis followed in 1889. As the only rabbinical seminary in the United States at the time, Hebrew Union College attracted Jewish scholars and students from all over the country. Of the three organizations, only the HUC is still based in Cincinnati.

By 1910, with immigrants arriving from Eastern Europe, the Jewish population of the city peaked at 28,000, about 8 percent of the general population. But Cincinnati's fortunes were declining as the river became less important to the nation's economy; as the city's star faded, so did its centrality in American Jewish life.

Community: Today there are 21,000 Jews in Cincinnati out of a metropolitan population of 1.7 million. Many Cincinnati Jews began their working lives in America as peddlers. Most did not stay in the business; but in 1860, sixty-five of seventy wholesale clothing firms in Cincinnati were owned by Jews, making it the ready-made clothing capital of the West. A good number were in the dry-goods business and quite a few worked in the production of liquor and cigars. Pawnshops, movie theaters, insurance businesses, and even some banks had visible Jewish ownership.

Jews and Christians, often both of German background, mingled socially during the first fifty years of Jewish settlement, but in the late nineteenth century anti-Semitism erupted, and social clubs and exclusive schools were closed to Jews. The Jewish role in public service and philanthropy, however, was unshaken.

More than a century ago the Jewish population started moving from its traditional downtown strongholds of Mound, Clark, and Clinton Streets and the West End. After World War I many moved to Avondale and Walnut Hills, and in time to suburban Roselawn, Amberley, Golf Manor, and Wyoming. Today the majority of Jews are in the northern metro area, and most synagogues have followed them out.

Sights: Although sights of Jewish interest are scattered throughout the city, they fall generally into three areas—downtown; the Mount Adams section (take I-71 to Reading Road); and Clifton Avenue (take I-75).

Public Landing, part of a new riverfront walk, recreation, and park complex, was the spot where Joseph Jonas and the first few Jewish residents landed in the early nineteenth century.

The historic Plum Street Temple, the main sanctuary of B'nai Yeshurun (also popularly known as the Isaac M. Wise Congregation) is located downtown at Eighth and Plum streets. While the congregation maintains its headquarters, school, and small chapel at its suburban campus at 8329 Ridge Road, it opens the older sanctuary for holidays and weddings. (Call 513-793-2556 for the tour schedule.)

The Plum Street Temple opened to the public in 1866. With Gothic and Moorish influences, it has two slender minarets extending from the sides of the central core

Wise to the word: The Gothic and Moorish Plum Street Temple, dedicated in 1866, was a laboratory for the development of Reform Judaism across America

and pointed arches over each of the three front doors; above the middle door is a stained-glass rosette window. Inside, the ceiling soars above a lavishly decorated sanctuary. Two rows of pillars supporting Oriental arches flank the center aisle. The ark is framed by twin towers and an illuminated Decalogue.

One of Cincinnati's natural treasures is Eden Park, minutes from downtown and high on a hill. In it is the Krohn Conservatory, one of the country's largest gardens under glass, named for Irwin Krohn, founder of Red Cross Shoes. Also in the park is the Seasongood Pavilion, an entertainment center named for Mayor Murray Seasongood, who led a political reform movement in the 1920s.

The Robert S. Marx Playhouse on Mount Adams Drive is named for a World War I hero, later judge of the Superior Court of Ohio. He was also the first national commander of the Disabled American Veterans.

The Cincinnati Art Museum has works donated by Jewish patrons as well as paintings of Jewish interest. Included in the collection are a pair of 1818 portraits of Moses Judah and his wife by William Dunlap; a Rubens painting of Samson and Delilah; *The Finding of Moses* by Salvator Rosa; and *David and Goliath* by Bernardo Strozzi. It also has Middle Eastern antiquities donated by Nelson Glueck, who was president of Hebrew Union College.

The Hillel Jewish Student Center at 2615 Clifton Avenue, opposite the University of Cincinnati, is the only Hillel mentioned in the AAA Travel Guide. Thanks to the boundless enthusiasm of its director, Rabbi Abraham Ingber, it boasts a unique collection of architectural Judaica from across the Midwest. Ingber is often called by people who have artifacts in their garages or basements from small-town synagogues that have closed.

The Hillel lounge, which he calls the "Lion's Den," has mounted on the walls several tablets with rampant lions, which at one time graced holy arks. In the sanctuary are lecterns, stained-glass windows, and eternal lights that are incorporated into the ambiance of everyday religious observances of the students who use the center. A few

years ago Ingber rediscovered the 1860 building of Shearith Israel, now a warehouse, and long believed destroyed. He researched publications from the period and came up with a description of the synagogue, enabling him to identify many architectural features to confirm his find. In poor condition, the structure in the 600 block of Ruth Lyons Lane (downtown) is the oldest standing synagogue building west of the Alleghenies.

The University of Cincinnati's neighbor is Hebrew Union College. HUC's Skirball Museum, located in Mayerson Hall, is divided into areas devoted to different aspects of Judaism. In the gallery on the third level of Mayerson Hall the focal point is the Torah section. Via earphones visitors can hear a re-creation of the Hillel–Shammai debates and see a bronze of the two rivals by the artist Jules Butensky.

Another area of the museum is devoted to American Jewish history with the emphasis on Cincinnati. Wise's desk is displayed, and in a collection of antiquities there is a jar brought back by Glueck from the caves of Qumran. The museum also has a children's "discovery room" where groups can participate in a hands-on work and study program.

Also on the HUC campus is the Klau Library, with four hundred thousand items, and its Dalsheimer Rare Book Room. Its oldest volume is a handwritten Bible in Persian square characters from the eleventh century. Nachmanides' commentary on the Pentateuch, believed to be the first printed Hebrew book; a collection of Chinese–Hebrew texts from Kaifeng; the first printed Jewish prayer book in English; and a large, rare collection of Spinoza's works are among the library's prizes.

In 1947 Glueck inaugurated the American Jewish Archives to "gather, preserve, and make available for study documentary material that would illuminate the realities of American Jewish life." The facility is open for research and it also has a small museum. For information on any of the HUC sights, call (513) 221-1875. The college has guides and also offers a booklet for self-guided tours through the grounds and buildings.

Culture: Aside from the many secular places and events in which Jews play a part, there are a few purely ethnic happenings each year. The department of Jewish studies at the University of Cincinnati has an annual lecture series. Recent lecturers have included writers Chaim Potok, Mordecai Richler, and Saul Bellow. The Hillel center has a gallery featuring an ongoing exhibit of up-and-coming Jewish artists. HUC has a film fest, lectures, and concerts during the year. Its Exhibition Gallery in the administration building has several small displays.

The Jewish Community Center of Roselawn, 1580 Summit Road (513-761-7500), hosts an annual book fair and art exhibit, a Jewish culture series, and the Stagecrafters community theater. The center also has reciprocal membership for travelers who are members of JCCs in their hometowns.

Personalities: For a community of its size, Cincinnati can boast large numbers of prominent Jewish natives and residents during its almost two centuries. Six mayors have been Jewish, including Gerald (Jerry) Springer, who is now the television news anchor for the city's NBC affiliate. Actresses Theda Bara (born Theodosia Goodman) was a product of Cincinnati, as were artists Henry Mosler and Moses Ezekiel. More recent products are Steven Spielberg; James Levine, the musician and artistic director of New York's Metropolitan Opera; Jim Dine, the painter and sculptor; and Yippie-turned-Wall Street consultant Jerry Rubin. Lillian Wald, founder of the Henry Street Settlement, and Adolph Ochs, publisher of *The New York Times,* were Cincinnati natives who made their marks in New York. On the other coast, Joseph Strauss, who built the Golden Gate Bridge, was Cincinnati born.

The city's contributions to medicine include Henry Heimlich, developer of the Heimlich maneuver for choking victims, and Albert Sabin, who did research on his polio vaccine at the Children's Hospital. Businessmen include Charles Fleischmann, founder of the yeast company; Fred Lazarus, the department store magnate;

and Dov Behr Manischewitz, who baked his first *matzah* in Cincinnati in the 1880s.

The Cincinnati Reds were owned during the late 1920s and early 1930s by Sidney Weil. Sandy Koufax may have pitched in Brooklyn and Los Angeles but he attended the University of Cincinnati. Most leaders of Reform Judaism have called Cincinnati home at one time or another, including Leo Baeck and Judah Magnes. Louis Finkelstein, chancellor of the Jewish Theological Seminary in New York, was also a Cincinnati native.

Reading: *The Jews of Cincinnati* by Jonathan D. Sarna and Nancy H. Klein is a well-documented illustrated work that traces the development of the Jewish community from its modest origins to the realization of its early hopes for freedom and prosperity in the heartland of a new country. (The book can be ordered from the Center for the Study of American Jewish Experience, Hebrew Union College, 3101 Clifton Avenue, Cincinnati, OH 45220.)

Eating and Sleeping: Hillel provides Friday and Monday kosher dinners for those who call in advance during the school year (513-221-6728). Kosher food can also be found at Marx's Hot Bagel stores in three locations (Springdale, Roselawn, and Blue Ash). Pilder's Kosher Meats at 7601 Reading Road sells sandwiches and hot take-out dishes. Down the street at number 7648, Bilkers Food Market also has food to go. Simcha's Kosher Deli is at 1436 Section Road in Roselawn. The only hotel within easy walking distance of an Orthodox Synagogue is the Carrousel Inn Motel, about half a mile from the houses of worship in Roselawn. Rabbi Hanan Balk of the Golf Manor Synagogue is the chairman of the Orthodox Rabbinical Council and can arrange home hospitality for observant visitors (513-531-6654), as can Chabad House (513-761-2555 or 513-821-5100).

The Omni Netherlands, Hyatt Regency, and Westin hotels and the Phoenix Banquet Hall can all provide kosher meals at short notice. For a different hotel experience, there is the 1882 landmark Cincinnatian, restored to its original elegance. For cozier lodgings, try the 1850 Amos Shinkle Townhouse across the river in Covington, Kentucky.

As the facilities and Jewish prosperity indicate, today's Jewish arrivals to Cincinnati can expect a warmer reception than was accorded Jonas Horowitz, whose fate is now reserved for diamond denizens from Oakland.

—Deborah Barcan

Copenhagen

A large stone from Eilat, whose Hebrew inscription identifies it as a gift of friends of Denmark in Israel, rests in Israels Plads (Israel Square) near the city flower market in Copenhagen. Similarly, a stone from Denmark can be found in Kikar Dania (Denmark Square) in Jerusalem's Beit Hakerem neighborhood. These monuments are symbols of the reciprocal friendship that has existed between Danes and Jews for most of their shared history, particularly in the 20th century.

History: That shared history is not very long, however. It was just over three centuries ago—in 1684—that Israel David, court jeweler and unofficial banker to the king of Denmark, and his partner, Meyer Goldschmidt, were granted permission to hold religious services. Though such services were limited to the confines of their own houses—where they would conduct them for many years—and though no sermons could accompany them, the act of regal dispensation marked the beginning of organized Jewry in the Danish capital.

The next step, in 1693, was the purchase of land for a cemetery. The following year, Sephardic Jews (David, Goldschmidt, and their fellow congregants were Ashkenazim) were also allowed open worship—a "privilege" that refugees from the Spanish and Portuguese Inquisition had gained in Amsterdam as early as 1608. For the next three centuries, a rich and varied Jewish life would emerge in Denmark, notably in Copenhagen.

There was one significant interruption of that continuous presence: the exodus of all the Jews in Denmark, one jump ahead of the SS commandos dispatched to carry them off to Auschwitz. The pharaoh was Adolf Eichmann, the Red Sea was the waters of the Øresund, the narrow strait that separates Denmark from Sweden, through which the Danish Israelites made their escape. The Promised Land was Sweden, which offered the refugees not only milk and honey, but housing, education, and jobs till war's end brought a jubilant homecoming to their native country.

The safe journey of 7,000 men, women, and children was made possible by the Christian people of Denmark. On the first day of Rosh Hashanah in 1943, the Germans, who had occupied the country since 1940, planned a series of roundups of the Jews of Copenhagen, who would be conveniently assembled in the synagogue or in their homes. But these raids were thwarted by the quick action of the Danes. At risk of their own lives, they hid their Jewish fellow citizens in attics and basements, church belfries, and funeral parlors, until safe transportation to neutral Sweden could be arranged. During the ten days between Rosh Hashanah and Yom Kippur, the escape was effected.

The events of 1943 were perhaps the most heroic chapter in a history of Danish Jewry that began in 1619, when King Christian IV appointed Albert Dionis, a Sephardi who had established a prosperous import-export business in Hamburg, to operate the royal mint in the newly founded town of Gluckstadt. Dionis coined money so effectively—his gold ducats engraved with the Tetragrammaton (the four Hebrew letters of the name of God) financed Christian's successful war against Sweden—that the grateful king invited other Sephardim to settle in Gluckstadt and Copenhagen, his capital.

The king himself, who had some knowledge of Hebrew and considered it the language of God, believed the inscriptions on the coins had brought him heavenly protection in his victory over the Swedes. Indeed, he placed the same four Hebrew letters on the entrances and pulpits of some of the churches he built, where they are still in evidence.

On a more practical level, Christian IV brought Sephardic Jews from Hamburg and Amsterdam into his kingdom because he hoped that with their knowledge of languages, their mercantile experience, and their network of familial connections throughout Europe and the Middle East, they could stimulate commerce in Denmark, as they had in the great trading cities of Germany and the Netherlands. The first century of their immigration saw little more than a few scattered *minyans* throughout the country. As late as 1684, when Meyer Goldschmidt chanted his first *Kiddush*, there were only 19 Jews in Copenhagen.

Community: There are perhaps 7,500 Jews in Denmark, about 20 percent of whom come from longtime Danish families. The community has been augmented in the last generation by 1,500 exiled from Poland during the anti-Semitic purges of 1968 and 1969. Jewish institutions are supported by the community's power to tax its members. While nearly all of Denmark's Jews live in the capital, they are so dispersed among its 1.5 million inhabitants that nowhere do they form a distinctly Jewish neighborhood.

In a national population of 5 million, the Jews of Denmark have never been a large group, but their impact on the economy, culture, and national well-being has been enormous. Jewish enterprise in the 19th century was responsible for the development of brewing, distilling, shipbuilding, and tobacco processing and other important industries that are still basic to the Danish economy.

Ties with Israel have traditionally been warm. At Yad Vashem, the Holocaust memorial in Jerusalem, Denmark is the only country whose citizens are honored en masse for their rescue of Jews during World War II.

Sights: The Danes have a special way of describing their metropolis; they call it *hyggelig* ("cozy"). Indeed, the sightseer who

walks its streets (the best way to explore Copenhagen) will find that *hyggelig* is the inevitable word for this European capital.

A human scale persists in the Old City. The ramparts of the twelfth-century market town founded by Bishop Absalon live on as street names. The moats that enclosed the medieval castles are now small lakes bordering the ancient quarter; the hunting enclosures of the nobility are small parks. The streets themselves are narrow and gently curving, in defiance of the rigid geometry of nineteenth-century urban planning, as if they had been bent by the prevailing west wind. The seventeenth- and eighteenth-century houses are two and three stories high—gabled, baroque, their facades almost impish in their decorations. There is an abundance of outdoor cafés, flower markets, fruit stands, and young craftsmen displaying handmade wooden toys or jewelry on cobblestoned pavements.

The Round Tower at Købmagergade, built as an observatory in 1637–42, contains a spiraling ramp so wide that Czar Peter the Great could drive a team of horses from street level to the pinnacle; the Tetragrammaton is inscribed over the entrance. Inside the church next door, the Torahs of the Great Synagogue were hidden from the Nazis.

Danish design in furniture, jewelry, silver, porcelain, and furs is perhaps the best in the world; and everything, from class to kitsch, is available on the pedestrian street which cuts through the heart of the Old City. It's the famous Strøget (pronounced "Stroyat"), more than a little honky-tonk these days, though all the best shops, like Illums Bolighus, are still there. Try, also, some of the charming and less frequented side streets like Pistolstraede and Fiolstraede.

The Great Synagogue is just a short detour from the Strøget. A turn on Jorks Passage will take the walker past cafés and the narrow streets that surround Fredericus Sextus University. A right turn on Krystalgade will lead to the synagogue at number 12. Built in 1833, the synagogue is set behind an iron fence. The base is salmon-colored stone, topped with faded yellow brick. Though the exterior is modest, the Hebrew inscription over the entrance is more welcoming than most doorpost greetings: Welcome in the name of God. Non-Jews as well as Jews have received the welcome. When the synagogue held its 150th-anniversary service in 1983, it had the Danish royal family in attendance.

The plain exterior does not prepare the visitor for the white-and-gold elegance inside. The magnificent two-story-high sanctuary (a women's balcony rings three sides of the second story, with the ark occupying the fourth) has tall pillars and a ceiling frieze of gold and blue. Unfortunately, the synagogue and the senior citizens' home adjacent to it sustained structural damage—since repaired—from a terrorist bomb in July 1985.

The Great Synagogue holds daily, Friday evening, and Saturday morning services. In summer, there is a festive *Kiddush* after Sabbath prayers, and on Sunday mornings, Rabbi Melchior or his colleague, Rabbi Bent Lexner, conducts a study group. The language is Danish, a barrier to most visitors, but there is no difficulty handling the real Danish pastry and schnapps that wrap up the weekly colloquiums.

Since there has never been a ghetto in Copenhagen, the Jewish sights are interspersed among those of general interest. Worth seeing is the Resistance Museum (Frihedsmuseet), in Churchill Park (telephone 33-13-77-14). The museum has a dramatic exhibit of the 1943 rescue of Danish Jewry, amid photos, documents, and computerized information on anti-German sabotage throughout the wartime occupation.

The Royal Library, 8 Christians Brygge (telephone 31-15-01-11), has one of the great Judaica collections of Europe. Ask for Ulf Haxen, the curator, to make an appointment.

The Jewish Community Center, 6 Ny Kongensgade (telephone 33-12-88-68) with its administrative offices, library, *mikveh*, small museum, and gift shops is worth a trip, as are the community's Caroline School at 18 Bomhusvej (telephone 31-29-95-00) and Machsike Hadas Synagogue (Orthodox) at 12 Ole Suhrgade. And don't forget Israel Square, with its daily fruit and flowers and a weekend flea market.

Tivoli Park, in the very center of town, is even better than the hyperbolic tourist brochures would lead you to believe. Its land-scaped gardens are the best in Denmark; there are twenty-five restaurants (of as many different cuisines), a pantomime theater, bands, vaudeville, and, before closing time (which is midnight), a brilliant fireworks display on Wednesday, Friday, Saturday, and Sunday.

Personalities: In this century, Niels Bohr, one of the pioneers of atomic science and a leading figure on the Manhattan Project to develop the atomic bomb, and Victor Borge, the musical comedian, spring to mind as outstanding Danish Jews.

In the early nineteenth century, for example, there was Mendel Levin Nathanson, considered the father of Danish journalism. Under his editorship, the *Berlingske Tidende* became the country's leading newspaper, a position it still holds as the voice of conservatism, as opposed to the more radical *Politiken,* whose chief editor is Herbert Pundik. Pundik is a Danish-born Jew who made *aliyah* with his family, but still spends three weeks of each month at his office in Copenhagen.

Nathanson was also a prosperous businessman, an economist whose writings are still studied, the author of the standard work on Danish Jewish history, and the organizer of the present well-structured community. He founded the country's first and only Jewish day school, the Caroline School (named after the Danish queen of the time), which still flourishes as a model educational institution.

A later namesake, Henri Nathansen (note the *e*), was the foremost Danish playwright of his time. Born in 1868, he became the director of the Royal Theater in 1909 and wrote works that are still performed. One of them, *Indenfor Murene (Within the Walls),* is esteemed as one of the finest plays in the language. It deals, as do many of his other works, with the problems of intermarriage, and with the questions of assimilation in a free society—like the Danish—where anti-Semitism is virtually nonexistent. At seventy-five Nathansen fled to Sweden in 1943 with his fellow Jews; he could not adjust to conditions of life in a new land and committed suicide in 1944.

Another important literary figure was Georg Brandes, a friend of Henrik Ibsen and the most important Danish critic and historian of the late 19th century. During that period his brother, Edvard, led the Liberal Party and served as the Liberal Government's minister of finance. Another politician of national stature at the time was Herman Trier, the president of the parliament.

General C. I. De Meza was commander-in-chief of the Danish Army when Denmark suffered a disastrous defeat at the hands of Bismarck's Germany. Though De Meza was known to be a Jew, there was not even a ripple of anti-Semitism in the expressions of dismay that followed the loss of the war and of the important border territory of Schleswig-Holstein.

Perhaps the most famous Danish Jewish family is the Melchiors, who have given the country generations of bankers and rabbis, statesmen and musicians since the eighteenth century. Moritz Gerson Melchior was the friend and benefactor of Hans Christian Andersen. In Rolighed, the Melchior home, the world-renowned writer of fairy tales passed his declining years and died.

A lateral descendant of Morris Gerson Melchior was the late chief rabbi of Denmark, Marcus Melchior, spiritual leader of the community during its time of exile in Sweden. Marcus's older son, Bent, succeeded his father and is the current chief rabbi of Denmark; another son, Arne, has served in the national cabinet as minister of communication, transportation, and public works, and is also an active member of the Jewish community. Two grandsons of Marcus are also in the rabbinate: Michael Melchior, the sole rabbi in Norway, divides his time between Israel and Oslo, and Uri Schwartz, once the rabbi of Finland, now lives in Israel.

Eating: There is a restaurant in the Jewish Community Center which is open weekdays, 5:30–8:00 p.m., and a kosher delicatessen at Lyngbyvej 87. Kosher groceries can also be purchased at T. A. Samson, Røhrholmsgade 3.

Reading: There are no English translations of works by Danish Jewish writers. Harold Flender, an American, wrote *Rescue in Denmark* (published by the Anti-Defamation League of B'nai B'rith); Leni Yahil, an Israeli, wrote *The Rescue of Danish Jewry* (Jewish Publication Society); and Leo Goldberger, a Dane, wrote *The Rescue of the Danish Jews* (New York University Press). A good fictional account of the rescue is Elliott Arnold's *A Night of Watching* (Scribner's). The rescue of Danish Jewry is also chronicled in Kenneth Madsen's film *A Day in October*. For another cinematic look at the Danish Resistance, there are some moving Copenhagen scenes in the 1962 film *The Counterfeit Traitor,* which starred William Holden.

SAS (9 Polito Avenue, Lyndhurst, NJ 07071; 201-896-3565) offers periodic Jewish heritage tours of Denmark and will arrange Jewish tours at the request of travel agents.

A good travel companion is *Jewish Life in Denmark,* available from the Danish National Tourist Board or local travel agents. It contains a map of the Old City and a block-by-block itinerary of the important sites. The Danes have seen to it that Jewish travelers, no less than any other and perhaps more, will feel cozy in Copenhagen.

—Gabriel Levinson

Córdoba, Granada, and Seville

On the wall of a courtyard in Seville's erstwhile Jewish quarter lies a small picture-tile bearing the label *Susona*.

According to tradition Susona was the beautiful daughter of Don Diego Suson, who belonged to a family that, during the deadly anti-Jewish riots through much of Spain in 1391, had officially converted. But secretly its members and various friends still practiced Judaism. And when the Inquisition was introduced, Suson organized an underground to work against it. But his daughter, who had a Christian lover, betrayed the group and all were burned. Supposedly, Susona then retreated to a convent. When dying, though, she repented and instructed that her body be hung in front of the house she had betrayed.

Though centuries have passed, echoes of Susona's story still reverberate in her native Seville and in such places as Córdoba and Granada, where Jews once lived in this region known as Andalusia. Andalusia is that part of Spain where the clichés come from—clicking castanets, fiery flamenco dancers, fierce bullfighters, dark-eyed Gypsies (Carmen, to name one, and Don Juan). Stretching across the southern tier of the Iberian Peninsula, with coasts edging both the Atlantic and the Mediterranean and only the Strait of Gibraltar separating it from Africa, it has long served as a transitional zone between continents and cultures.

This may well be the part of Iberia where the Jews first set foot. So much a part of the area's fabric did they become that they even worked their way into local folklore—with at least one famous song that survives to this day recalling a Jewish woman whose charms drove her townsfolk to distraction. The Jews of the region knew glory days, especially during the Golden Age of Córdoba, when with Arab scholars they

worked to keep alive the ancient Greek teachings that later lit the Renaissance.

But if Andalusia was a point of entry, it was also the point of exit. The riots of 1391, which marked the beginning of the end for Spanish Jewry, started in Seville; there, too, the Inquisition was introduced. And when the end came, it also came in Andalusia—in Granada, where in their stronghold, the Alhambra, Ferdinand and Isabella signed the Edict of Expulsion.

More perhaps than many other parts of Spain, Andalusia abounds with excellent traces of the Jewish past, and distinguished efforts, especially in recent times, have been made to preserve and showcase what remains of this history. But beyond the tourist towns along the Costa del Sol, there are in Andalusia only a smattering of resident Jews. And of these, most maintain profiles ranging from low to eerily invisible.

History: Was Iberia the place of exile the Bible called Sepharad? Or was it a spot near Tarshish in Asia Minor? Among the legends attending Jewish settlement in Spain is one that places Jews in or near Seville after the First Temple's destruction and another locating some of Nebuchadnezzar's exiles in the area of Granada. Regardless, the Iberian Sepharad acquired overtones of "homeland," and some Jews who probably arrived with the Greek-speaking, Roman-oriented forces in the earliest days of this era were surely entrenched by the time of the Visigoths' fifth-century conquests.

Though initially the Jews lived untroubled, by the seventh century the Visigoths had grown sufficiently intolerant that they ordered all non-Christians in the realm to be baptized or leave. Such measures were enforced with varying degrees of zeal, but while many remained who practiced Judaism secretly, by the eighth century no communities were openly Jewish.

Consequently, when the Moors entered Spain on April 27, 711, both Jews and Muslims rejoiced in the other's presence. The once-secret Jews happily allied themselves with the Moors, whom they saw as liberators, and benefited as well from the wealth and property left by the fleeing Visigoths. From the Moors' viewpoint the Jews were useful for garrisoning their conquests — holding the fort for them, as it were — thus freeing their armies to march more easily northward.

Under the Umayyad caliphate, which established itself in 755 with Córdoba as its capital, Jews flourished in many fields including medicine, agriculture, commerce and crafts. So accepted were they that in 839 a Frank bishop converted to Judaism and married a Jewish woman. Their heyday in southern Spain, however, came in the tenth and eleventh centuries when they attained political as well as cultural prominence.

This was well symbolized by the rise in tenth-century Córdoba of Hisdai Ibn Shaprut. Shaprut, who led the Jewish community, was also court physician, chief of customs and foreign trade, a patron of such scholars as Dunash ben Labrat and Menahem ben Saruk, and the chief go-between from the caliph to the Christians. In the next century, by which time Berbers had conquered Córdoba and Andalusia had begun to fragment, Samuel Hanagid, a refugee from Córdoba, achieved similar status in the newly independent Granada. Called by the Moors *Gharnatat al-Yahud* (Granada of the Jews) because they believed the Jews had founded it, the principality had a largely Jewish population when Hanagid became vizier, commander of the army (1030–1056), and community leader. Joseph, his son, however, incurred such enmity that he was assassinated in 1066, leading to severe attacks on Granada's Jewry.

Seville, too, received Jewish refugees, first from Córdoba, then from Hanagid's Granada. Its community, which engaged in medicine and commerce, also had a virtual monopoly on the dyeing profession. In the mid-eleventh century, Isaac ben Baruch Albalia, a wealthy scholar and chief rabbi, was named court astrologer and other Jews attained power as well. But perhaps the most distinguished Jewish family from Seville, the Abravanel, established itself only in the fourteenth century.

By then the face of Iberia had changed considerably. When the Almoravid dynasty, which had conquered southern Spain in 1086, was supplanted in 1146 by the fanatic Almohads, Jewish life in Andalusia was virtually wiped out — among the refugees being the eleven-year-old Córdoba-born Moses Ben Maimon (Maimonides). While the south declined, the "reconquest" of Spain by the Christians gained force, with Córdoba falling to another Ferdinand in 1236 and Seville in 1248. At the start of the fourteenth century five separate kingdoms existed on Iberia — and only Granada remained Muslim.

Rolling stone: A statue of Maimonides now graces a square in the city he fled as a child

Moving from place to place as their fortunes changed, the Jews were political chameleons, changing color to serve their benefactors and accommodate those in power. The Christian rulers came to appreciate them as the Muslims had, and even after persecution they bounced back to positions of status. Because they were often allied directly with various monarchs who afforded them special protection, the Jews incurred the enmity of rival nobles and the middle class. Thus when the ringleaders of an anti-Jewish riot in Seville on Ash Wednesday in 1391 were ordered flogged, the general populace seized this as an excuse to move against the Jews. The massacres began in June and spread quickly. The Jewish communities in Seville and Córdoba as well as elsewhere were virtually destroyed, and thousands who were not killed hastily converted.

During the next century these converts, or Conversos, as well as Spain's remaining Jews, lived on edge. While many Jews maintained their privileged positions, the Conversos, with entrée to a variety of formerly closed avenues—among these, marriage with the aristocracy and power in the church—achieved even greater heights. Jewish leaders, especially Abraham Senior, are often credited with having brokered the marriage uniting Isabella of Castile with Ferdinand of Aragon. Isaac Abravanel became the couple's treasurer. Tomás Torquemada, believed to hail from a Converso family, became the queen's confessor. Luis Santangel is generally considered the man who—in large part from fund-raising among fellow Conversos as well as Jews—convinced Isabella to send Columbus on his way.

But the success of the Conversos, or "New Christians," rankled "Old Christians." And contemporary historians believe the Conversos felt threatened by the continued presence of practicing Jews. Many Spaniards today express the conviction that the Crown was hopelessly in debt to the Jews for financing its war against the Moors, not to mention Columbus's venture.

Coincidence or not, the events of 1492 occurred in rapid succession. Isabella and Ferdinand conquered Granada on January 2; shortly thereafter they gave Columbus the go-ahead. On March 31 they announced the edict expelling the Jews. Jewish leaders, including Senior and Abravanel, argued the Jews' case and offered large sums on their coreligionists' behalf. But, so the story goes, just as the queen was wavering Torquemada raced in brandishing a crucifix. He slammed the cross beside the pile of money on the table crying, "Here he is; now sell him." The Jews were given four months to leave the peninsula where they had lived for more than fifteen hundred years.

Community: To search out Jews in Andalusia's interior—that is, beyond the Costa del Sol—is to sense, however distantly, Inquisitional aftershocks. Though Jews individually began returning to Spain in the last half of the 19th century, and their communities were granted legal status in 1967, of the 15,000 living in Spain only a smattering reside in the Seville-Córdoba-Granada triangle.

In Seville, a city of 700,000, a small community numbering between 60 and 70 exists. But since not enough members of the current congregation are sufficiently active, services are not held regularly. When they are, they take place in a private apartment. Since its owner is about to reclaim the property, the congregation's future location is uncertain. (Contact Simon Hassan, 27-55-17 for information.)

This community was established about a century ago by Jews primarily from Spanish Morocco, and at its zenith numbered about 200. It was dealt one blow when its synagogue accidentally burned in the 1920s and another when Seville allied itself with Francisco Franco's regime in the 1930s. Though Franco often succored Jews—allegedly having had some Jewish blood himself—his policies were not considered conducive to Jewish life in Seville, which all but disappeared.

It was rejuvenated in 1967 with the reestablishment of a congregation. Because the Jews are so inconspicuous, because of national antagonisms toward nearby Morocco, and because the religious enemy is currently perceived to be Protestantism, the Jews today benefit from the attitude, as one put it, "that the enemy of my enemy is my friend." Seville's Jews belong to the city's middle class, counting agricultural engineers, doctors, ship outfitters, and farmers among their ranks. Yet because of Seville's low rung on the economic ladder and, speculates one Jew, "because it is such a

Catholic city," the community has not thrived. It meets these days merely for High Holiday services, Passover, and special occasions. And despite claims that anti-Semitism is nonexistent, one registered community member declared he was not Jewish and that there were no Jews around. Similar attitudes prevail in Granada and Córdoba, where Jews are less numerous and less visible.

The woman running the Córdoba gift shop called Sefarad—filled with tapes of Ladino songs, books on Spanish-Jewish history and Israeli-made items—though identified by several other residents as Jewish, insisted it wasn't true. The proprietor of a photo shop on a street where Israeli tourists had been wished *Shalom* said this was a subject he would not discuss.

As someone in Seville observed, "In this part of the world, Jews are in the same category with the ancient Egyptians—historical beings found in museums, not out upon the streets."

Seville Sights: If Jews themselves are still museum pieces, however, the places they inhabited are living, lively museums. In fact, Seville's El Barrio de Santa Cruz, which is actually the old *aljama,* or Juderia, or Jewish neighborhood, is one of the city's chief tourist attractions. Entering through the curve of the well-preserved medieval Arco de Juderia—often occupied by a flamenco player strumming his guitar beneath the sign proclaiming Juderia—the area is one of little squares dotted with sidewalk cafés; beautifully landscaped and open-to-view interior courtyards; and twisting, ivy-draped passageways bearing such names as "Pimienta" for the spices once sold there by Jews and "Los Levies" for those who once lived there. Though there is a street named for "Susona"—previously called "The Street of Death"—the death's-head tile appears in Plaza Doña Elvira. Almost hidden by tree branches, it is fixed under a balcony's overhang, above and just to the left of a sign, Las Cadenas, at number 10.

On a street bearing its name stands the church, Santa María la Blanca, once the quarter's best-known synagogue. A large yellowish building trimmed with red, the Convent of Madre de Diós was also once a synagogue. And on the doors of the nearby church of Santa Cruz, six-pointed stars stand out in relief.

Diagonally across from the Juderia's main entrance is the symbol of Seville, the minaret-turned-tower, Giralda, and right next to it the cathedral, which contains not only Columbus's official tomb, but also the silver tomb of Ferdinand III, who reconquered Seville from the Moors. His casket bears inscriptions in Latin, Arabic, and Hebrew in honor of the good relations he maintained with all peoples. The Jews were so happy to receive him that they gave him keys to the city. Held together by a maroon cord and engraved in now-hardly-visible Hebrew, they say, "The King of Kings will open; the King of the Land shall come," and can be seen in the treasury of the cathedral's sacristy in a showcase to the right of the entrance, against the wall.

Seville also possesses the Archives of the Indies, which houses many original documents from the New World's administrations; and the archives of Columbus. But most material is available only to scholars.

On the banks of the canal leading into the River Guadalquivir, just to the left of the Triana Bridge, stands Seville's newest monument. A beige stone conglomeration of U's, it was commissioned from one of Spain's leading contemporary sculptors, Eduardo Chillida, and is called "Tolerance" in commemoration of the quincentenary of the Jews' expulsion. "Tolerance" is not far from Seville's famed bullring, but a good walk from Carmen's tobacco factory, now a university building.

Córdoba Sights: Despite its secrecy concerning its Jewish present, Córdoba displays its Jewish past to the hilt. The Jews lived on the narrow cobbled streets that still twist and turn, in an area running from the Mezquita, the sprawling mosque-turned-cathedral, along the remnants of the city walls toward the Almodovar Gate. This Moorish arch was once called "The Jews' Gate" because it opened directly into the Juderia.

Today the Juderia's houses appear freshly whitewashed, their black wrought-iron trim and their cascades of window-box flowers adding contrast and color to the dazzle of the paint jobs. These buildings line streets and edge plazas whose name-plates—Calle de Juderia, Judios, Plaza de Juda Levi (for the 12th-century Hebrew poet who lived here)—boldly proclaim their provenance. Not to mention others, Roperiea, Curtidoria, Alcaiceria, which name the trades—clothiers, tanners, silk exchangers—of their erstwhile residents.

On the quarter's main street, Calle de Juderia, a solid wooden gate in a beige stone wall opens at scheduled times into a tiny vine-draped courtyard. This leads into a small, square, high-ceilinged chamber that is Córdoba's 14th-century Moorish-style synagogue. Like so many other synagogues in Spain, Córdoba's was turned into a church. But unlike most, its structure was not changed and still visible are the upstairs women's gallery (sometimes closed), the detailed plasterwork, and the fragments of Hebrew inscriptions on the down-to-the-bare-brick walls. There is a sound-and-light program designed to explain the synagogue's significance.

A few steps away is a statue of Maimonides erected in 1964. On a small square—Plaza de Tiberiades, or Tiberias, the Israeli city where the thinker is thought to be buried—the statue shows him with eyes downcast and book in hand. Just beyond is the Plazuela de Maimonides, near his probable birthplace (and the location as well of Córdoba's bullfighting museum). Among other spots bearing Jewish names are the Maimonides Hotel; the Juda Levi bar—facing the municipal tourist information office which provides pamphlets in Hebrew; and the Sefarad Shop.

Granada Sights: On a hill high above Granada stands the Alhambra, a fortress-city whose eight miles of encircling walls enclose a complex of gardens, pools, fountains, and palaces. The Hall of the Ambassadors, in which Ferdinand and Isabella decided both to send Columbus on his voyage and expel the Jews from the country, is virtually the first sight on the standard tour.

The Hall opens onto the Court of the Lions, a spacious, tennis court-sized plaza containing a pool in which the Hall of the Ambassadors is reflected and edged by a forest of arches supported by 124 marble columns. In this, the oldest area of the Alhambra—identified by scholars as part of the grand palace built by Joseph Hanagid—the court's centerpiece is the basin-like fountain borne by twelve water-spouting lions. The lions, only two of which are originals, are variously said to represent the Lion of Judah, the twelve oxen in similar formation in Solomon's Temple, and the twelve signs of the zodiac. They were, however, a gift from the Nagid family and, as the courtyard is entered from the Hall of the Ambassadors, the lion immediately to the left of the water channel has a special mark on its forehead. Visible on this copy is a worn triangle between the eyes; it reputedly is what remains of a *Magen David*. Because many Jews worked on the Alhambra's decoration, *Magen Davids* appear in walls and doors as well. They can be found as the central feature in the geometric pattern on the far wall of the Hall of Kings and on the decoration of the room at the far end of the Lions' Courtyard.

Also within the Alhambra stands a palace erected by Carlos V. In its room 11 in the "historic paintings" section hangs a large canvas painted in Paris in 1889 by Emilio Sala. In much dramatic detail complete with king, queen, pleading Jews, and ranting Torquemada, it depicts *The Expulsion of the Jews*. Upon leaving the Alhambra to walk down the hill to the city, the stony stairs on the left side of the road, which begin to the right of the Alhambra Palace Hotel, descend through the *aljama* that existed here in the great fortress's shadow. The quarter's central area was the marketplace on the Plaza Realejo which, surrounded by small shabby shops, still exists.

Recommendations: Iberia Airlines, which serves the United States and Israel from Spain, has regular connections to cities throughout the country. RENFE, Spain's national rail system, has a variety of train passes for a network reaching major destinations. Intercity buses provide alternative public transportation.

With Spain currently reexamining its Jewish heritage, increasing numbers of sites and sights are being spotlighted well to the advantage of the Jewish traveler.

—*Phyllis Ellen Funke*

Curaçao

Witness: A handwritten ledger open to the first day of business more than a century and a half ago; a mahogany ship's wheel attesting to far-flung interests over the seas; oil paintings of ancestors staring down. To sit in the boardroom of the Maduro Holding Company, an international conglomerate headquartered on Curaçao, surrounded by these antiquities, is to sense the presence of a taipan. And a Jewish one, at that.

Nor is this situation unusual on this balmy Caribbean island in the Netherlands Antilles. Here, forty miles off the South American coast, much of history is tied to the tales of the (relatively) numerous Jews and their many merchant princes.

Indeed, from nearly the outset, the Jews, with almost total economic power, contributed so abundantly to molding the course of this often-prosperous island that there are few other places in the world today with such a Jewish visibility. Streets, buildings, social institutions, monuments, the official calendar of events, the indigenous language, and even the drinking water all reflect the potency of a Jewish residence running nearly 350 years. Thus it is, too, that with such a longevity record, Curaçao boasts the longest established, uninterrupted Jewish community—and the oldest standing, continuously used synagogue—in the Western Hemisphere.

History: Since Curaçao was discovered in 1499 by Alonso de Ojeda, a lieutenant of Columbus, it is likely that Jews in the guise of Conversos were among the first Westerners on the island. And when, in 1634, the Spaniards were beaten off by the Dutch—who had harbored refugees from the Spanish and Portuguese Inquisitions—the conquerors' interpreter was Samuel Co-hen, a Portuguese Converso. Cohen left behind at least one other known Converso, but because that individual later left for Mexico, ongoing settlement on Curaçao by Jews began only in the 1650s.

Though authoritative sources—both on and off the island—conflict on the sequence of events, the Jews appear to have arrived during that decade in three small waves.

Because other settlers were having difficulty securing a toehold on the island, whose semiarid terrain was not hospitable to agriculture, thought was given to abandoning the spot. But in 1651, the directors of the Dutch West India Company (many of whose stockholders were Jews) wrote to Governor Peter Stuyvesant that a Jewish patron, Jan (or João) de Illan, had organized a band of his coreligionists willing to give the place a try.

These ranks increased after 1654, when the Portuguese in Brazil reconquered Recife from the Dutch. Again running from the Inquisition, some Jews en route back to Holland stopped off in the Caribbean and stayed. By the decade's end, another group of Recife refugees—among those who had made it back to Holland—decided, under the leadership of Isaac da Costa, to return to the tropics.

Initially, these Jews were settled as farmers on land just north of today's capital, Willemstad. But already in the letter to Stuyvesant the suspicion was raised that they had little intention of tilling the soil. And very soon they did, indeed, start moving into the walled town, where the splendid and easily defensible natural harbor—so strategically situated between North and South America—was becoming a focal point of trade and commerce for the region.

While Curaçao grew into a major stopover for such contemporary merchandise as Venetian pearls, pendants, thimbles, scissors, knives, bells, agricultural products and, primarily, slaves, the Jews became shop owners and ship owners, chandlers and landholders; 200 even became ships' captains. By the end of the eighteenth century — when the Jewish population peaked at about 2,000 and accounted for the majority of free individuals on the island — much of the waterfront activity and most of downtown Willemstad was in Jewish hands.

As Jewish economic power developed, so did their community. Although the year in which the initial synagogue was constituted is debatable, it apparently existed by 1654, the time now officially cited, since a letter from abroad bearing that date arrived on Curaçao addressed to "the illustrious Gentleman the Mahamad of the Holy Congregation Mikveh Israel." And in the Jodenwyk, or Joden Kwartier (Jewish Quarter), a cemetery, whose gate now reads Bet Hayim (House of Life), was consecrated in 1659.

By 1674, the community had grown sufficiently to engage a rabbi from Amsterdam and, by 1703, after using a number of converted houses, it erected a structure specifically designed as a synagogue. Less than thirty years later this too was deemed undersized, and work was begun on a building patterned after Amsterdam's Portuguese Synagogue. Curaçao's Mikve Israel was consecrated *erev* Pesach 1732.

Mikve Israel is located in the primary downtown section of Willemstad known as Punda. This area lies on the right bank of the neck of water that leads into the harbor and divides the town in two. As the sons of Mikve Israel, sent to Germany for their education, returned to Curaçao, they brought the new ideas of Reform Judaism. Finding the established congregation resistant to change, those wanting a modernized ritual broke away. They consecrated the Sephardic Reform Temple Emanuel — named in honor of the New York synagogue — in 1867. It was only a century later that they returned to the parent organization, merging into what is now officially the United Netherlands Portuguese Congregation Mikve Israel-Emanuel.

The move was a survival tactic. Just as Temple Emanuel was forming, slavery was abolished on Curaçao. With it went much of the island's economic importance. The Jews had, like others of wealth at the time, owned slaves. Though today they are generally considered not to have been significantly involved in the commerce itself, many were nevertheless sufficiently affected by its cessation to have left the island.

Curaçao's Jewish population received an infusion in the mid-1920s with the arrival of Ashkenazim, mostly from Russia, Poland, and Rumania. By 1932, about 30 of these families had formed an organization, the Club Union, and began praying together. After using several houses as synagogues, they bought two adjacent properties in town. One served the club, and the other, in 1956, was established as Congregation Shaare Tzedek. The congregation moved again in 1986 to a more residential area.

For official purposes, today there are about 450 Jews on Curaçao, though some unofficial tallies give a slightly higher estimate.

Community: Curaçao Jewry was once considered "The Mother of Communities" in the New World; it contributed substantially to the establishment of communities in such other locations as New York, Newport, and Jamaica. Today, the remaining Jewish community, about equally divided between Sephardim and Ashkenazim, is still vital.

While some people hold dual membership, worship remains separate. Shaare Tzedek, now located at Lilieweg 1A, in the upscale suburb of Mahaai, is Orthodox (services Friday at 7 P.M. and Saturdays at 6:30 A.M.). Mikve Israel (services Fridays at 6:30 P. M. and Saturdays at 10 A.M.) is liberal Reconstructionist, with special individualizing touches, such as a prayer in Portuguese for the Dutch monarch. The gap between them — largely a social one — has been rapidly closing. (The Ashkenazim had arrived poor and had worked in the refinery or as small businessmen and peddlers.)

Many who successfully established themselves merchandising to the general citizenry suffered when, some years back, the Venezuelan currency crashed. Then, not having put down sufficiently deep roots, they emigrated.

The Sephardim attribute their current tenacity, despite a decreasing birthrate, to their attachment to their *snoa* (from the Portuguese *esnoga,* or synagogue). Names that hail from the early days—Henriques, Alvares Correa, Jesurun, Gomes Casseres and Pardo—are still prevalent today. Along with such personages who contributed to Curaçao in several spheres, Daniel de Leon, born on Curaçao, became a founder of the Socialist Labor Party of the United States and editor of *The Daily People.* And Madurodam, the miniature town near The Hague in Holland, was built by the family in memory of Curaçao's George Maduro, a lieutenant in the Dutch Army who was the only Curaçaoan Jew to perish in a concentration camp, dying of disease in Dachau.

Beyond their own community, however, the Jews have made an indelible, though sometimes not-so-tangible, imprint on the community at large.

One outstanding contribution in this arena has been to the development of the island's indigenous language, Papiamento. It is a fusion of tongues, including the Hebrew that existed in the dialect of the island's earliest Jews. For example, the Papiamento for "good luck" is *beshimanto,* from *besiman tov;* and "cemetery" is *betahim,* from the Bet Hayim burial ground. In fact, the first known written document in Papiamento is a love letter composed in 1775 by a Jew.

Furthermore, the Jews founded most of the island's service clubs and charitable organizations. They once had a social group (Club Curaçao) so elite that gentiles wanted to join; and they contributed so heavily to the churches that there is a saying, "Every church on the island has Jewish stores." Today, the rabbi, Aaron Peller, gives a sermonette every Thursday at 6:57 P.M. in the time slot on local television (channel 8) called *Tempu Pa Dios,* or "Time for God." And, as the Maduros once brought fresh water into town, now, according to Paul Ackerman, the island's honorary Israeli consul, Israeli engineering has contributed to the construction of the island's desalinization plant.

Sights: Given the extent of the Jewish presence, there are few spots on the island that have not felt its touch. Though the Jews never did do much cultivating, the landscape is dotted with the *landhuis,* or plantation houses, they once owned, probably as second homes. Among these are Klein Santa Marta, now a residence for the handicapped; Habbai, once "gabbai," and now a Catholic home for elderly women; Pos Cabaai; Rooicatootje; Montana; Zeelandia; and De Hoop, or "The Hope," from *tikvah,* currently headquarters for a leading political party. One house that can be visited is the Biblioteck S.A.L. (Monqui) Madure—the Maduro Library—housing Judaica and other Antillean items, including calendars, prayer books, and multigenerational photographs (open 9 A.M. to noon or by appointment; telephone 375-5119).

Numerous other "Jewish" mansions, in styles ranging from Dutch Colonial to Victorian, can be found in Willemstad proper, especially in and around the neighborhood called Scharloo, once almost entirely peopled by the Jewish merchant princes. Some have been elegantly restored and converted to government offices. Among the most impressive are the carmine-with-white-trim Seroe Bonito, on the Pietermaai Plein; the Pachi Da Sola House, or "Kranshi," on the Waaigat, now the civil registry; on Scharlooweg itself—the area's chief thoroughfare—the jade-green-and-white "Wedding Cake" with lacelike trim housing the Central Historical Archives; and George Maduro's home, Beau Sejour, now the credit union. It has a tree-lined, tiled path leading to a pillared porch and is topped by an intricately decorated center gable. In front of another, now burned-out Maduro house, where Scharlooweg meets Plaza Hoyer, there stands a monument to Elias Solomon Levy Maduro.

Downtown Willemstad itself is a monument to the Jewish past. Among the main roads leading in to it is the four-lane Abraham Mendez Chumaceiro Bulevar, complete with a bust of this lawyer (1841–1902), a prime mover in bringing universal suffrage to Curaçao. The waterfront thoroughfare along which dock the Venezuelan produce boats of Curaçao's "Floating Market" is called I. H. (Sha) Capriles Kade, after the highly regarded individual who helped found and direct the Maduro and Curiel Bank. The largest in the

Netherlands Antilles and Aruba, its headquarters stand at the street's end and houses a public reading room stocked with newspapers and magazines from abroad. The bank fronts on J. A. ("Jojo") Correa Plaza, a shady square with benches and palm trees, named for another of the institution's founders.

Branching off the plaza in one direction is Madurostraat, a major shopping street; and in another, Heerenstraat, one of the downtown's more fashionable avenues. Some Jewish-owned shops here—the Casa Leon and Ackerman's, among others—recall the days when almost all had Jewish proprietors. But for an even better glimpse, stand with your back to Meena's and look up. There, on a fancily scalloped gable, next to one that reads 1706, is the Hebrew date 5466. (Other similar dates exist elsewhere, along with such building names as Beit Levy, but they are difficult to locate.)

Heerenstraat parallels the Amsterdam-like waterfront one block away. There, at the foot of Curaçao's famous landmark—the Queen Emma floating bridge (opened a century ago by Dr. Solomon Cohen Henriquez, deputy governor of the Antilles)—stands the stucco-decorated Penha and Sons. Now an emporium purveying designer products, it was constructed in 1708 and is officially celebrated as Willemstad's oldest building. A couple of blocks away is the expansive town circle, Wilhelmina Plein, dominated by the churchlike spire of the now-deserted, yellow-and-white Temple Emanuel.

Running off Wilhelmina Plein is Columbustraat where, at its intersection with Hanchi di Snoa (Alley of the Synagogue), stands the community's centerpiece, Mikve Israel.

A high yellow plaster wall, punctuated by massive doorways, protects the complex. Within is a black-and-white tiled courtyard edged by ancillary structures and the synagogue itself. White walled and pillared, with mahogany pews and central reader's lectern beneath a high arched ceiling and glistening brass chandeliers, it conveys spaciousness and evokes awe. Its special features include the *banca,* or dais, against one wall, for the board of directors of the synagogue; a massive old organ; and a

sand-covered floor, said to symbolize, among other things, the sand of the desert during the Exodus. But more practically, it muffles footsteps—as it once did in the secret synagogues of the Conversos. Along with key chains, blue Delft tiles, commemorative stamps honoring the Maduro operation, and a cookbook, called *Recipes from the Jewish Kitchens of Curaçao,* the gift shop within the complex carries both a pamphlet and a booklet with extensive description and color photographs of the synagogue.

Also in the complex is a museum—open 9–11:45 A.M. and 2:30–4:45 P.M.—with contents almost entirely from Curaçao. Along with various brass and silver ceremonial objects still used in the synagogue is a 1739 *ketubah,* a treasure chest that may have come from Spain, and local family memorabilia. In the entrance yard is a *mikveh* (in fact, there was once a Hanchi di Banyo or Alley of the Bath, but it is not clear where it was) and replicas of some of the tombstones from Bet Hayim Cemetery. They are elaborately carved with sculptures relating to the names of the deceased, their occupations, or the Bible. Several, for uncertain reasons, bear skulls and crossbones. The cemetery itself lies on the outskirts of Willemstad in the heart of the old Jewish quarter, now engulfed by Curaçao's mammoth oil refinery.

General sights: The Amstel Brewery boasts of producing the world's only beer made with desalinated water. The snorkeling and diving off Curaçao, though less touted than nearby Bonaire's, are good. And Curaçao has some tiny, idyllic beaches, though they are well out of town.

Recommendations: The Van der Valk Plaza is a business-style hotel in downtown Willemstad within easy walking distance of most major sights. The smaller Avila Beach Hotel, on the edge of town, has a fine reputation, and the new Lion's Dive Hotel, near the seaquarium, is airy and comfortable. There is no specifically kosher food in restaurants; it exists, frozen, in supermarkets in the suburbs. Jewish life, on the other hand, on this island with a rich Jewish past, is far from frozen.

—Phyllis Ellen Funke

Denver

If you are on your way to a music festival, to ski in Vail, or to backpack in Rocky Mountain National Park, it is likely that you will also hang your cap in Denver, about a dozen miles from the foothills of the Rockies. Once a magnet for health- and wealth-seekers, the capital of Colorado is a booming metropolis.

Despite auto pollution, the majestic mountains, from the Front Range to the Continental Divide, are still visible in the summer from the Kansas border, 150 miles east. The celebrated 125-mile skyline from Pikes Peak to Longs Peak almost every day stands out against a backdrop of clear blue to fiery red at sunset.

It was for the clear, dry air that tuberculosis sufferers would flock to Denver "chasing the cure" in the world-class, free National Jewish Hospital for Consumptives (NJHC) or the Jewish Consumptives Relief Society (JCRS).

History: In the 1859 "Pikes Peak-or-Bust" gold rush, a dozen Jewish men, mostly German immigrants, crossed the plains to the junction of Cherry Creek and the Platte River, where the first gold was found. They were exuberant, hardworking, exemplary in behavior, even elegant. These pioneers served in the city council and territorial government and started the public library and literary societies, including the Denver Club, which later excluded Jews.

The most outstanding Jew in Colorado's early history was Otto Mears, known as "the Hebrew pathfinder" and "the pathfinder of the San Juan," for his network of toll roads and railroads over almost impassable terrain, especially in the San Juan Mountains. His control over the eleven counties he helped to create gave the balance of power in the state to the Republicans. Colorado was admitted to statehood in 1876, and Mears was chosen as the first presidential elector to go to Washington and cast the decisive vote for Rutherford B. Hayes — hence another nickname, "the President-maker." Mears was a treaty mediator who spoke the Ute language with a Yiddish accent. The imaginative creator of gold and silver filigree railroad passes, which are prized by museums, he also proposed covering the state capitol dome with 24-karat gold leaf when he was chairman of the board of capitol managers. His memorials include a stained-glass portrait in the window outside the state senate chamber, the naming of Mears Junction, near the site of his first toll road, and Mount Mears in the San Juan Mountains.

Along with the gold seekers to Colorado came the health seekers. Frances Wisebart Jacobs, wife of Abraham Jacobs, a city councilman and civic leader, was the "mother" or "queen of the charities" and a founder of what is today the United Way. The NJHC — today the National Jewish Center for Immunology and Respiratory Medicine — was originally named for Mrs. Jacobs. Her stained-glass portrait is in the dome of the new state capitol, the only woman so honored.

Czarist persecution in the 1880s brought a large wave of Russian Jews. Among them was Dr. Charles Spivak, a leader in the early JCRS. National Jewish leaders, troubled by the heavy settlement of Jews on the East Coast, devised plans to distribute them throughout the country. Best known among the agricultural colonies that were set up to absorb Jewish immigrants was Cotopaxi. A pious group that was duped into settling there, in the barren mountains near the Arkansas River, was rescued by

Denver Jews. The Galveston plan—one of the schemes to distribute Jewish immigrants west of the Mississippi—and Denver's growing reputation as a "kosher" city drew people to the communities along the foothills.

After World War II, many young veterans who had been stationed in Denver returned, but it was not until the energy boom of the 1970s and the discovery of powdered snow by the international jet set that the population exploded. In addition, aerospace industries, government agencies, and high technology have created almost unmanageable growth.

Community: During the pioneer period there was great cooperation among all groups, but the 1920s saw a rise in anti-Semitism as the city and state governments were taken over by the Ku Klux Klan (members included the governor and other officials). After the scandals that brought down the Klan, there was a significant decrease in anti-Semitic activity. In 1984, however, Alan Berg, a Jewish radio show host, was assassinated by a right-wing group in Denver, although only one of his attackers was from the city.

The natives, Jewish and non-Jewish alike, are not entirely happy with the influx of newcomers. Denver is not equipped—because of the shortage of water and the delicate atmosphere—to be a big city. However, the community of 45,000 Jews does offer a full Jewish life.

The city has a broad spectrum of congregations, including Lubavitch and Reconstructionist, chapters of most major organizations, and five Jewish schools, two of them boarding schools. Judaic Studies are taught at the University of Denver. Yet two out of three Jewish children receive no Jewish education, and Denver's intermarriage rate—72 percent, according to a recent survey—is the nation's highest. At one time, rabbis from the various ideologies who were members of the Rabbinical Council conducted joint conversion instruction groups. This unique venture disintegrated in 1984 when the Orthodox, reaffirming their own standards in accepting only converts who would observe *Shabbat* or *kashrut*, withdrew.

The early Jewish settlers were scattered, the wealthier living east of Cherry Creek, today's downtown. They continued to move east and south. The less affluent lived between the creek and the Platte River. The only early Jewish neighborhood was West Colfax, west of the river to the city limits. Most of the Yiddish-speaking Jews settled there. The largest congregation in West Colfax, the Hebrew Educational Alliance (Orthodox), at 1555 Stuart Street, attracts members from every part of the area. Also located there is a large hasidic community and the two Jewish boarding schools.

A guide to community events, news, and institutions is the *Intermountain Jewish News,* which is available at newsstands throughout the area (telephone 303-861-2234). To find out about kosher food, contact Rabbi Moshe Heisler at 303-595-9349.

Sights: Not far from where Denver's first Jewish residents lived are the city's prime Jewish sights. On the campus of the Auraria Higher Education Center, which incudes the University of Colorado at Denver and two smaller colleges, more than 34,000 students pass two precious edifices of the Jewish past on their way to classes.

One is the Emmanuel Gallery. Orthodox Jews had joined in forming Congregation Shearith Israel in 1899 (which the city directory listed as "Chariot of Israel"). In 1903 the congregation purchased the building, until then an Episcopalian church, which would remain its home for more than half a century. Perhaps the oldest church building in continuous use in Denver, it was the oldest synagogue in use when it became an art gallery. Its sturdy stone walls, topped with a golden *Magen David*, are in striking contrast to the skyscrapers behind it.

Also on the campus, Golda Meir's home is located on Historic Ninth Street, now a park dominated by a dozen restored modest houses, including a Jewish-owned corner grocery store. The small brick double terrace has been restored to the way it looked when the future prime minister of Israel left her home in Milwaukee so she could attend high school. She moved in with her sister, who was in Denver because of tuberculosis. The little house was moved several times from its original location in West Colfax. It was burned and vandalized; it was finally settled on the campus in 1988. In the basement is the Golda Meir Center for Political Leadership.

Jewish homeland: Golda Meir's Denver house moved almost as often as she did

If you stay in a downtown hotel, you can walk or use public transportation to the most interesting sights around the civic center. The state capitol, with the stained-glass windows of Otto Mears and Frances Wisebart Jacobs, are east of the center. A few blocks from there you can catch a shuttle bus to the restored Larimer Square, once synonymous with Jewish merchandising. A few miles east are the Botanic Gardens at Tenth and York, site of the first Jewish cemetery. The garden has an outdoor exhibit of biblical plants.

Although they didn't intend it, when the architects of Babi Yar Park finished laying out the paths, they found that they had formed a *Magen David*, visible from the air. The park, on the eastern edge of Denver at South Havana and Yale avenues, memorializes the 100,000 Jews massacred by the Germans in a ravine near Kiev. On twenty-seven acres, partially landscaped with austere monuments that evoke the tragedies of the Holocaust, part of the grounds is left to weeds and grass to suggest the place where the murders occurred. Among the impressive sculptures is a simulation of a boxcar crossing a ravine, two huge blocks of polished granite, the People Place and the Grove of Remembrance. The park is easy to miss, but well worth the trouble of a careful search.

Restorations abound in Denver. The oldest is the Four-Mile House Historic Park at 715 South Forest Street. Although its only Jewish connection is that it was on Abraham Jacobs's stage route until the railroad came in 1870, the house and farm are a living museum of life from 1859 and 1883, when the two sections of the house were built.

Impressive in its simplicity is the memorial chapel at Temple Emanuel, located at 51 Grape Street. In the monochromatic, rosy beige, sunlit room are the delicately carved furnishings — ark, Torah, Torah stand, rabbi's chairs and candelabra — from the pre-war synagogue in Kolin, Czechoslovakia. Other furnishing are from the temple's earlier home on Pearl Street. Call ahead (303-388-4013) to make sure the chapel is open.

BMH, as everyone calls Beth Hamedrash Hagodol, at 560 South Monaco Parkway, houses the Mizel Museum of Judaica, which stages four exhibits a year, rotating visiting shows with the museum's permanent collection. The annual Judaic Art Show is one of many exhibits that keep the walls of the Jewish Community Center covered. The JCC is located at 4800 Alameda Avenue; call (303) 399-2660 for information on events and programs.

Personalities: Aside from Otto Mears, the most distinguished of the politically active Jews in Colorado history was United States Senator Simon Guggenheim, who endowed almost every college in the state with a building. He was particularly generous to the Colorado School of Mines. It was in Leadville that the Guggenheim fortune was dug out of the A. Y. and Minnie mines.

Tuberculosis brought more than Golda Meir's sister to Denver. At the JCRS, H. Leivick and David Edelstadt wrote Yiddish poetry, and the poet Yehoash (Solomon Bloomgarden) collaborated with Dr. Spivak in translating the Bible into Yiddish and compiling a Yiddish dictionary.

Nationally known business figures were Jesse Shwayder of Samsonite Luggage and David May of the May Company department stores. The writer Joanne Greenberg lives in Golden, outside Denver, and teaches at the Colorado School of Mines.

Day Trips: Jews lived and conducted religious services in practically every Colorado town and mining camp. A trip to Central City, the "richest square mile on earth," can start along West Colfax. On the way, at 1600 Pierce Street, is the site of the former Jewish Consumptives Relief Society, now the AMC Cancer Research Center. The hospital campus, on the National Historic Register, embodies a century of medical progress, reflected in the variety of buildings, which include one of the original patient "tents" and a synagogue-museum. To tour the museum, call (303) 239-3409.

Continue west to I-70, turning off at the Black Hawk–Central City exit. The picturesque town is still the site of the Central City Opera, and the appearance is still of the nineteenth century. Unfortunately, gambling is winning over all other attractions.

You can return through Colorado State Park, stopping for spectacular views and nature walks. From the park through Golden Gate Canyon, after about a dozen miles, you will enter the Park of the Red Rocks, with its magnificent natural amphitheater.

The Air Force Academy along I-25 has tours that include the Jewish chapel with its unusual sanctuary. Of special importance are the nine paintings by Israeli artist Shlomo Katz, on the themes of brotherhood, justice, and flight. Among the local touches in the chapel are the Torah covers designed by the Colorado artist Arielle Z. Miller.

After Vail and Aspen, the most popular Colorado destination is Mesa Verde National Park, a worthwhile visit if you want to take a longer trip. In this area are the San Juan Mountains, where Mears built the spectacular Million Dollar Highway from Ouray to Silverton. A marker (not always there) indicates his achievement. A four-wheel-drive vehicle can be taken into the rugged and historic terrain where Mears lived and worked. The area includes Telluride, today the home of a film festival and ski resort.

Reading: *Golda: The Romantic Years* by Ralph G. Martin (Scribner's) contains chapters on Golda Meir's Denver days. The University of Denver publishes Phil Goodstein's *Exploring Jewish Colorado*. Out of print but available in many libraries are *A Centennial History of the Jews of Colorado* by Allen Breck; *Pioneers, Peddlers and Tsadikim: The Story of the Jews in Colorado* by Ida Uchill (Sage Books); John Dunning's novel *Denver* (Times) about the Ku Klux Klan and a Jewish family in West Colfax; and *Talked to Death: The Life and Murder of Alan Berg* by Stephen Singular (William Morrow).

But do as much reading as you can before you travel. Once in Colorado, there's a lot more to occupy your eyes.

—Ida Libert Uchill

Dublin

Mothers in Kelly-green tams . . . daughters with copper curls and peaches-and-cream complexions . . . men in tall silk black hats . . . matrons upon whose tightly permanented hair saucer-shaped bonnets tilt to parallel the patrician slant of their noses. . . .

But then . . . but then . . . one drops the book she is holding and when she retrieves it, kisses it. It is, after all, her *siddur*. And this is, after all, a *Shabbat* service. It just happens that it is taking place at Dublin's Adelaide Road Synagogue, virtually in the heart of Catholic Ireland.

But, again . . . "Who ever heard of an Irish Jew?"

Initially, the query may seem oxymoronic — so much so, in fact, that it has become the title of a short story collection on the subject. But with a bit of contemplation, some logic lights the matter. Never mind that ancient Gaelic legends connect the Irish and the Israelites — tales that link various fairy folk and other island inhabitants with the Ten Lost Tribes; tales that have both Jacob's pillow and his ladder to heaven coming to rest in Ireland.

More to the point are the parallels between two peoples of long historical memory — the persecutions they've suffered; the wanderings they've endured; the deep faiths they've sustained; the family values they've nurtured; and, to some at least, the similar senses of black, ironic humor they've developed to brighten darker days. Not to mention a mutual gift of gab — and guilt. From this perspective then, the surprise is, perhaps, not that there are Irish Jews to begin with, but that there are so few.

History: Legends notwithstanding, the first actual report of Jews in Erin can be found in the eleventh-century *The Annals of Inishfallen*. This record of Irish glories notes that in 1079 "five Jews came over the sea." Though they brought gifts for the high king, the annals say they were sent back again. The Jews did apparently make some impact, though — as forerunners of the Israel Government Tourist Office. Not long after their visit, the king went on a trip to the Holy Land.

At least a smattering of Jews, probably merchants and financiers, appear to have lived in Ireland during the Middle Ages because the Exchequer of the Jews at Westminster had an Irish branch. But these probably left in 1290 with the Jewish expulsion from England. The Inquisition and expulsion from Iberia seem to have sent some northward, however, in the fifteenth and sixteenth centuries. A man with a Converso-sounding name, (William) Annyas, shows up as the lord mayor of Youghal in Cork in 1555. By the last decade of the 1500s, when Trinity College was founded in Dublin, it offered Hebrew Studies. And in 1608, Zebulon Bericke was made an honorary citizen of Waterford for his contributions to that city.

By 1660 or so, a Sephardic synagogue had been established in Crane Lane off downtown Dame Street, very possibly by former Conversos from Holland in the export trade. Their numbers increased after England's "Glorious Revolution" of 1688, especially since, two years later, a London Sephardi, Isaac Pereira, was appointed commissary general to William III's expeditionary force and employed others who later based themselves in Dublin. The London Sephardic community helped by lending Torah scrolls and contributing to the purchase, in 1718, of the Ballybough Cemetery on Fairview Strand.

Some Jews scattered beyond the city as well—to Waterford, Cork, and Belfast in particular. But by the end of the 18th century, in part due to assimilation and conversion (one Abraham Jacobs became a priest who translated the Anglican Book of Common Prayer into Hebrew in 1717), the Sephardic community was in such disarray that the synagogue closed. And though about forty Ashkenazi families of jewelers and pencilmakers had arrived from Germany, Holland, Poland, Bohemia, France and England, government bills making Jewish naturalization difficult or impossible were upheld. By the time the liberalizing influences of the continent's Napoleonic era reached Ireland in 1816, when the last exclusionary act was repealed, only three Jewish families remained in Dublin.

But word of the new situation traveled fast enough that by 1822, enough Jews had gathered from Germany, Poland, and England to reestablish the community, founding a synagogue on Stafford (now Wolfe Tone) Street. Many made their way into Protestant society through involvement with Freemasonry. During the potato famine of the mid-19th century, Baron Lionel Rothschild of London negotiated an 8-million-pound loan to help alleviate the situation. By 1881, 450 Jews lived in Ireland.

But the majority had yet to come. They arrived during the next twenty years, as the great emigration from Eastern Europe began. Many were from the Russian Pale, primarily Lithuania, and a fair portion had run out of money at the last stop before the Atlantic crossing. By 1901, they numbered 3,769 and had established congregations in Cork, Limerick, Waterford, and Londonderry in addition to several synagogues and prayer halls in Dublin. They clustered, in the Irish capital, primarily south of the River Liffey, in areas known as Dolphin's Barn and Portobello. But they called their world "Little Jerusalem." Initially, they were petty traders and moneylenders, but later entered the manufacturing, furniture, clothing and jewelry businesses.

For the most part, they lived in peace. Limerick experienced some anti-Jewish rioting in 1884, and Cork in 1894. But their primary problem came ten years later in Limerick when a priest, recently back from a France embroiled in the Dreyfus affair, attacked the Jews as usurers and called, from his pulpit, for an economic boycott (which lasted two years). The community of 200 dwindled—and the priest assumed a money-lending role himself. But by World War I the congregation had reestablished itself.

When the ongoing Irish struggle for independence from England flared again—signaled by the Easter Rebellion of 1916—the Jewish community officially maintained neutrality. But Jewish homes, particularly in Dublin, served as shelters for many revolutionaries, and various individuals publicly associated themselves with the freedom fighters. Among these were the Dublin-born solicitor Michael Noyk, who was a friend of the patriot Michael Collins and defender of many Sinn Fein nationalists; Ireland's first chief rabbi, Isaac Herzog, a friend of Ireland's first president, Eamon de Valera; and Robert Briscoe, a member of the Irish Republican Army (IRA), which sent him to the United States in 1917 to raise funds from Irish Americans. Some later said Briscoe taught Vladimir Jabotinsky guerrilla tactics for fighting the British in Palestine that he had learned fighting them in Ireland. Be that as it may, he was the first Jew elected to the Irish Parliament and the first Jew elected lord mayor of Dublin—a post he held twice, 1956–57 and 1961–62.

When the southern part of Ireland gained independence in 1921, the Jews in the new state also became free of England—though, to the dismay of many in the south, those in Belfast remained loyal to London's chief rabbi. Severe restrictions on immigration prior to World War II, combined with official Irish neutrality during the war, clouded matters for the Irish Republic's Jews. But the country's 1937 constitution recognized Judaism as a minority faith and guaranteed freedom of religion, a stance that has been upheld till today.

Ireland's relatively weak economic situation, plus the creation of Israel—not to mention "The Troubles" in Northern Ireland, which added psychological distance to the one hundred-odd-mile span between Dublin and Belfast—spurred a postwar decline in its Jewish community. Nor has the community been bolstered by the official

Irish attitude toward the Jewish homeland. Though Ireland gave Israel de facto recognition on February 12, 1949 (and presumably supported the state privately for its fight against the British), it held up de jure recognition until the mid-1970s because of Vatican pressure. Economic ties to Arab countries plus Syria and Libya's penchant for training the IRA (in its contemporary incarnation) have further complicated matters.

But not all is so gray-green. Irish volunteers annually walk for charity from Tiberias to Jerusalem, traveling to what they still doggedly call "The Holy Land" on charters flown by El Al—which has recently appointed a representative in Dublin to promote travel to Israel (Alan Benson of Easy Travel; telephone 772-057). Reciprocally, New York's Loyal League of Yiddish Sons of Erin marches in the annual St. Patrick's Day parade.

Community: Where Irish Jewry is concerned, depending on the speaker, the glass is either half full or half empty. On the pessimistic side are negative demographics, which have, in a population of 3.25 million, seen a decline from a post–World War II high of nearly 5,000, to 3,300 in 1961; 2,100 in 1981; and about 1,400 today. More than 70 percent are over forty. On the optimistic side are the community's vigor and vibrancy, which support its institutions and have an impact on all society far beyond bounds suggested by its size. Indeed, it points with pride to having, within the 166-person Dail, or parliament, three elected representatives to the 150,000-strong Protestant community's mere one.

Having acquired the friendliness for which the Irish are celebrated—no one is long a stranger in their midst—it is a comfortably situated community. Comprised primarily of lawyers, accountants, and other professionals, most now live in such south Dublin suburbs as Rathgar, Rathmines and Terenure. In addition to the Adelaide Road Synagogue of the Dublin Hebrew Congregation, 36-37 Adelaide Road (telephone 761-734, 766-745, or 694-044), which is "traditional"—or Orthodox—and under the chief rabbinate, other active synagogues under community auspices include the Terenure Hebrew Congregation, between 32 and 34 Rathfarnham Road (908-037, 905-555, or 908-544); Machzikei Hadass at 77 Terenure Road North (908-413, 906-130); and the synagogue within the Jewish old age home, "Denmark Hill," on Leinster Road West (972-004).

Among other Jewish institutions, communal and otherwise, are the Edmondstown Golf Club, Edmondstown, Rathfarnham, about half of whose membership is non-Jewish; a Maccabi Sports Club on Kimmage Road; a *kashrut* commission; and a comprehensive day school, located in the community headquarters at 1 Zion Road. Established largely because education in Ireland has been traditionally church-based, with nondenominational schools only just beginning to make inroads, the Jewish school is attended by 80 to 90 percent of Dublin's Jewish children. Close to half the students in the school are non-Jewish, however, with Jewish students separated for specifically Jewish studies and nuns from the favorably disposed Sisters of Zion coming to tutor Catholics.

Noteworthy although it exists beyond Jewish officialdom—with its own synagogue, cemetery, and Hebrew school—is the Progressive, or Conservative, congregation at 7 Leicester Avenue, Rathgar (telephone 973-955), which lists about seventy-five families on its roll. Founded in 1946, it holds, from the viewpoint of its leaders, the hope for Irish Jewry's future. This is due in part to its more liberal membership qualifications, which have allowed it, unlike the overall community, to increase its numbers, perhaps 10 percent since its inception. Its best-attended services are Friday nights.

Ireland's chief rabbi—who sometimes serves as *mohel* for the son of an American woman in Kilkenny or for the four sons of a Yemenite Israeli married to an Irishman in the prime horse country of County Kildare—is accorded the same status as leaders of Ireland's four other recognized religions. Like the Catholic cardinal and the Protestant primate—each of whom gets ten minutes on prime-time national Irish television twice a year, before Christmas and Easter—the rabbi has his time after the 6 P.M. Sunday news before Rosh Hashanah and Passover. Moreover, he is called to consult on such public and political issues as Anglo-Irish relations; divorce; and abortion.

Conversely, at times, the man-in-the-street Irishman seems disproportionately preoccupied with the "Jewish Question." Not only do certain cities and towns throughout the country go out of their way to preserve and memorialize their Jewish connections, but also, individuals frequently appear in print on the subject. Two cases in point: recent editorial discussions on the roots of the 1904 Limerick troubles, and columns upon columns in *The Irish Times* on the anti-Semitism, or lack thereof, of such patriot-writers as the late Arthur Griffith and Oliver St. John Gogarty.

Sights: Given the city, and country, in question, sightseeing, not surprisingly, can take on mythic proportions—especially when the matter of James Joyce, his *Ulysses*, and the Jews comes into play. But first, the more prosaic—if there is such a thing in Ireland.

Beyond the "Little Jerusalem" area, Dublin boasts numerous spots with Jewish associations. Just off Grafton Street, Dublin's fashionable pedestrian thoroughfare, lies Powerscourt, Townhouse Centre, a Georgian mansion-turned-mall. And on the second level, overlooking a courtyard filled with greenery and live piano music, sits Chompys–The Deli (telephone 679-4552), where the leading item on the menu is "The Great Jewish Chicken Soup," subtitled "a world-famous institution." And following it are such dishes as "Chomp-a-Bagel," "Bagelmania," and "Lox Stock and Bagel—Choice of New York Bagel, lox (smoked salmon), bacon, and cream cheese." The menu also has corned beef and pastrami sandwiches. Opened in June 1991, it is the creation of Frank Zimner, who was driving a taxi in Scottsdale, Arizona, when he got into an argument with a passenger, Susan Hamilton, a London Jew, over where the best bagels in the world were baked. The two quickly became a couple and decided to settle the dispute by trying to produce them in Dublin.

At the foot of Grafton Street lies Trinity College, home not only to the world-famous illuminated manuscript, the *Book of Kells*, but also to the Weingreen Biblical

Antiquities Museum. On the fifth floor of the New Arts Block—the building through which the college's Nassau Street entrance passes—in room 5036 is a collection of Middle Eastern artifacts. It includes items from digs at Lachish, Jericho, and Jerusalem, and was assembled by Jacob Weingreen, who, before his retirement, taught Hebrew and Semitic Studies at Trinity and authored what is arguably the world's most used classical Hebrew grammar text. Professor Weingreen worked with the noted archaeologist Kathleen Kenyon during her 1933 Holy Land expedition, and the glass-enclosed showroom bearing his name contains pieces from that and other excavations. One of its more striking items is an oval clay coffin lid, with Humpty-Dumpty-like features upon it, circa 1200 B.C.E., found at Lachish. Because opening hours are irregular, appointments should be made by calling assistant curator Heather Rice at 702-2229.

Crossing to the Liffey's north side—where the main thoroughfare is O'Connell Street, home to the General Post Office, the primary scene of the Easter Rebellion—a right turn on Abbey Street leads to the renowned Abbey Theatre, which, during the early part of this century, staged productions not only of O'Casey, Synge, and Wilde, but also of Dublin's Yiddish theater troupe.

A ten-minute walk west of O'Connell Street along the Liffey stand Dublin's Four Courts, the Irish houses of justice. And atop the main entrance rises a statue of Moses. (Don't be surprised to find other Hebrew Bible and Jewish motifs elsewhere in Dublin, either. Hebrew words have been spotted in such churches as the three hundred-year-old one on Mary's Street, and the current church sculptor, Imogene Stuart, has asked the chief rabbinate for details concerning Jewish ritual objects so they may be included in works designed for new churches.)

Heading back to O'Connell Street, a stop might be made, just off the Liffey, at the Davis Gallery, 11 Capel Street (telephone 726-969). This showplace is owned by Gerald Davis, a well-exhibited Irish-Jewish painter who, though he now claims to be bored talking about it, has made for himself a perhaps even bigger name by impersonating the character who is, however fictional, probably Dublin's most famous Jew—Leopold Bloom, the hero of James Joyce's *Ulysses.*

Which leads inevitably and inexorably back to "Little Jerusalem"—and its contemporary centerpiece, the Irish Jewish Museum. Here, fact and fiction intermingle. Though in some places, particularly along sections of Clanbrassil, street widening and other urban renewal projects have altered various cityscapes, this general area, with its small, almost miniature, red or gray-beige brick row houses—often grimy but with brightly-painted doors of lemon, turquoise, scarlet and, of course, forty shades of green—still strongly suggests an earlier Dublin era. Overt reminders exist, too, of the once-omnipresent Jewish life here.

A most imposing one is the red brick-with-beige-trim Victorian-Edwardian structure housing the Dublin Hebrew Congregation, the Adelaide Road Synagogue, 36–37 Adelaide Road. Founded in 1892, it has a long, narrow interior with dark wooden ceiling beams; carpeted but creaky stairs; and plush burgundy cushions on straight, narrow pews, which make it seem more like an old mansion than a house of worship. In Lithuanian style, it has a central *bimah* adorned with two mammoth brass candlesticks facing the ark, whose surrounding wall is painted a robin's egg color (which some Jews disapprovingly describe as "Madonna Blue").

At the corner of Lennox Street and Richmond is a kosher bakery, The Bretzel. Though now operated by non-Jews, its *kashrut* certificate hangs prominently among ads for yoga lessons, moving vans, and guitar courses. And on Sunday mornings, it is an ethnically mixed madhouse where bagels and raisin bread sell out quickly.

At 228 South Circular Road stands what was formerly the Grecian-styled Greenville Hall Synagogue. Though almost sold for a mosque (many members of Dublin's Arab community live in the old Jewish neighborhood), it was bought some years ago by an engineering firm that has preserved its apse and the facade, which bears, though not in the best condition, six stained-glass windows featuring *Magen Davids.*

At 33 Bloomfield Avenue stands the two-story red brick house, marked with a plaque, where Chief Rabbi Isaac Herzog lived before moving on to become Israel's first chief Ashkenazi rabbi; and on the same street is Bloomfield House, formerly the Jewish Day School. There were prayer halls on neighboring streets such as Oakfield Place, Heytesbury Street, and St. Kevins Parade. And along Lower Clanbrassil Street almost every shop was formerly owned by Jews. At least two holdouts remain—the kosher butcher-cum-grocery, Suissa's Continental Centre, at number 31, and B. Erlich's, at number 35.

At number 52, a brick row house with a bright brass knocker, hangs a plaque that reads, "Here, in James Joyce's imagination, was born Leopold Bloom, citizen, husband, father, worker, the reincarnation of Ulysses." (The door to 7 Eccles Street, where he supposedly lived with Molly, is preserved in The Bailey, a pub on Duke Street, off Grafton.) But much more of Bloom and his surroundings is presented in the museum—which also has a story of its own to tell.

At 3 and 4 Walworth Road, off Victoria Street, the Irish Jewish Museum is on the premises of two small houses that once formed a synagogue. Founded in 1916, though generally known as the Walworth Road Synagogue, it was nicknamed "The Rebels' Synagogue"—an appellation that may have referred to its congregants as much as to the 1916 uprising against the British. The synagogue itself is preserved on the second floor of the museum, opened June 20, 1985, by Israel's president, Chaim Herzog, the Belfast-born, Dublin-raised son of Rabbi Isaac. Downstairs, and in storage for want of display room, is memorabilia spanning 150 years (not to mention for-sale souvenirs including Kelly-green satin *yarmulkes*).

In this secular area—the reception hall of the former synagogue—the history of Ireland's Jews is traced and their involvement in various commercial, business, and professional activities is presented. Among the items displayed are photos of former rabbis; the trowel used for beginning the foundation of the Bloomfield Avenue Jewish Day School; a Jewish midwife's register from the early twentieth century; the documents appointing Maurice E. Solomons, stockbroker, the consul general in Dublin of the Austro-Hungarian Empire; a *mohel*'s bag with its paraphernalia; works by the late artist Harry Kernoff, a member of the Royal Hibernian Academy, known for his creation of a particularly demonic leprechaun; labels from kosher foods produced in Dublin, plus a can of kosher flea powder for pots and pans; and a label from one of Ireland's best-known international exports, written in Hebrew for Israelis — Guinness ale.

But perhaps the most sight-specific exhibit is the one on Joyce and the Jews. Together with a booklet, "Educational Jewish Aspects of James Joyce's *Ulysses*," published in 1992 by the museum, it presents some aspects of the relationship between the seminal writer and the Jews. Noting that Joyce not only was well acquainted with Jews and their customs from his days in exile, but also that he identified with them, since he, too, felt outcast from his native land, it attempts to give life to certain aspects of *Ulysses*. One display identifies (and on a map in the booklet, even locates) such real-life characters named in *Ulysses* as M. Shulomowitz, Joseph Goldwater, M. Moisel, J. Citron, and Minnie Watchman. Meanwhile, another presents such ceremonial items mentioned in the book as the *shofar, tallit,* and *Haggadah.* Note is also made of the annual celebration of "Bloomsday" — June 16, 1904 — when portions of *Ulysses* are read and Bloom's steps retraced.

The museum, which serves green bagels on St. Patrick's Day and which hopes to expand to 5, 6, and 7 Walworth Road when funds permit, is open May to September, Tuesdays, Thursdays and Sundays, 11 A.M.–3:30 P.M.; and October to April, Sundays only, 10:30 A.M.–2:30 P.M.; or by appointment with its curator, Raphael Siev (telephone 760-737). Siev, Ireland's chief negotiator for the Common Market, also conducts hour-long walking tours through "Little Jerusalem" for groups at 3 P.M. Sundays during July and August, and by prior arrangement.

Side Trips: A "Passover Bridge" in Ireland? Try Cork. Ireland's third largest city, the port of Cork lies two-and-a-half hours south of Dublin by express train. Though Cork's Jewish congregation was originally formed around 1725 by shipowning importers and exporters of wines and preserved meats, it dwindled by century's end, only to be revived in the late 1800s by Jews primarily from Russian lands. Cork city and other ports in this area were the last provisioning stop for immigrant ships headed for the United States. And Cork garnered its quota of refugees without the funds to go further.

Others came, particularly from Lithuania, to join established family members and, being the farthest-flung community in the British Isles, the Jewish community developed a fiercely independent spirit and a flavor it believes is decidedly different from Dublin's. This attitude persists, though only twenty Jews remain. With just five adult men for services, they bring in *minyan*-makers for the High Holy Days and continue to maintain their synagogue. At 10 South Terrace, it is a dignified, two-story, gray-blue building, fronted by three arches over pine doors and a *Magen David* at the apex of its facade. Its interior is designed in the Lithuanian style, with a central *bimah* facing the ark. Carpet strips of Israeli blue cover its dark wooden aisles. (Community president Fred Rosehill will open it; call him at work, 274-280, or at home, 275-820.) A few steps away, at the end of South Terrace, leading across a water channel off Union Quay, is a footbridge officially known as Trinity Bridge. But since it was opened in 1977 by the then lord mayor, Gerald Goldberg — to which a plaque attests — it is often referred to as "The Goldberg Bridge." Or, with the Corkmen's penchant for jokes, by the double pun, "The Passover Bridge."

The old Jewish area — still affectionately called "Jewtown" by both gentiles and Jews — lies in the southern part of Cork, off Albert Road. About a half a square mile, it now consists of small red-brick row houses. Allowing light and air into the Hibernian Buildings housing block is a sizable swath of wall-enclosed green, crisscrossed by paths, studded with benches, and known, via a sign in Gaelic, as "Pairc Shalom." Edged by East Ville and Monerea Terrace and inaugurated in April 1989 by Ireland's Minister of Energy, it exists because of the pleasant childhood memories of an Irish non-Jew, Pat Dineen, chairman of Cork's gas company. When, some years ago, the gas company erected a new building in the neighborhood, it had some land left over. Since Dineen happily remembered the days when his father had lived in the vicinity, he suggested to the municipal authorities that he present this land to the city and associate it, in some way, with the area's erstwhile residents. Especially recognized by a plaque on a bench to the left on one entrance is the Elyan family, direct descendants of the Vilna Gaon.

Is Limerick still atoning for persecuting its Jews in 1904? Some say yes; others see the gesture as simply a natural interest in preserving a bit of the past. In any case, on the Dublin Road, three-and-a-half miles east of the city, across from Horler's Petrol Station, the city and county of Limerick have united to help restore and maintain Limerick's Jewish cemetery. The gate, bearing a *Magen David,* is always open to the two-tennis-court-sized area, where a plaque on the wall of the caretaker's house notes that the reopening of the site in 1991 was attended by a rather unusual trio—the Catholic and Protestant bishops of Limerick, plus Ireland's chief rabbi. The restoration was inspired by the Liverpool-born Stuart Clien, now a businessman in Limerick, and Louis Fine, the last known Jew born in Limerick to have remained there. Fine is now retired from the family business, a jewelry store, N. Fine (for his father, Nathaniel). Run by his son, a Catholic, it is a well-known shop in Limerick's heart, on O'Connell Street, corner of Cecil. The small, slight Fine, who has held, among other positions, the chairmanship of the Limerick Trustee Bank and the presidency of Limerick's Chamber of Commerce and golf club, points to his almost century-old shop as proof that not all Limerick's Jews left after 1904. The remaining community continued to worship for many years in its Wolfe Tone Street synagogue, now a private house.

Among other spots of Jewish interest in Ireland is the startlingly modern, polished-steel Israeli sculpture, presented by Chaim Herzog in memory of Cearghall O'Dailaig, fifth president of Ireland, to the picturesque village of Sneem in County Kerry.

While the Jewish community of scenically splendid Northern Ireland, with its center in Belfast, numbers 250, it falls under English rather than Irish rabbinical jurisdiction and, depending on the political situation, is more or less removed from the Republic of Ireland. Its synagogue and community center stand at 49 Somerton Road.

Personalities: Paradoxically, contemporary Irish Jews point out, as their numbers shrink, their public involvement seems to grow. Apart from Robert Briscoe and Gerald Green, other Jewish lord mayors have been Sir Otto Yaffe in Belfast (elected in 1899) and Ben Briscoe, Robert's son, in Dublin (elected in 1988). Along with Mervyn Taylor and Alan Shatter, the younger Briscoe is part of the Jewish membership of the Irish Parliament. Also known for their public service are Henry Barron, a judge of the High Court; the recently retired Hubert Wein, a district court judge; and Herman Good, also formerly a district justice.

Other well-known Irish Jews, past and present, include the Elliman family, which owned a chain of movie houses and theaters; the actor Gerry Alexander; Maurice Abrahamson, the only Jew on the board of a major Irish bank, Allied Irish Banks; and the industrialist Martin Simmons. The long reach of the Irish Jewish family permitted the Irish-born Madeleine Epstein to become Sean O'Casey's physician in England, and gives Irish ties to writers Geoffrey Wigoder, Leslie Hazleton, and Joyce biographer Richard Ellmann.

Reading: Though Joyce's works (not to mention Sean O'Casey's autobiography) are necessary reading for a sense of early 20th-century Dublin, somewhat more contemporary—and accessible—are the works of David Marcus. In addition to his collection of short stories, *Whoever Heard of an Irish Jew?*, he has written two novels—*A Land Not Theirs* and its sequel, *A Land in Flames* (Bantam)—focusing on Cork's Jewish community of the 1920s. *Kaddish in Dublin* by John Brady (St. Martin's) is a recent mystery. There are also Robert Briscoe's story, *For the Life of Me,* written with Alden Hatch (Little, Brown) and, for general history, Louis Hyman's *The Jews of Ireland, from Earliest Times to the Year 1910* (Irish University Press).

Recommendations: No more welcoming oasis exists so near yet so far from the center of a major European capital than Dublin's Conrad Hotel. Modern but not sterile, cheerful but not suffocating, it lies within a few minutes' walk of both Dublin's downtown and the Adelaide Road Synagogue—not to mention the erstwhile Little Jerusalem. Aer Lingus, with Ireland's traditional friendliness and warmth, flies the green to Shannon and Dublin from New York and Boston.

While no kosher restaurants operate in Dublin on a regular basis, the Maccabi Sports Centre Restaurant serves lunch on Sundays; establishments such as the Conrad will, with a couple of days' notice, provide kosher meals; and the Jewish community and Bord Faílte (Irish Tourist Board) have lists of kosher caterers as well as vegetarian restaurants. Though most independent tourists to Ireland rent cars, Irish trains and the country's bus system, Bus Eireann, provide unparalleled glimpses into snippets of local life. The Irish Tourist Board, 757 Third Avenue, New York, N.Y. 10017; (telephone 212-418-0800), offers a detailed information sheet on the land which, Joyce writes in *Ulysses*, "they say has the honour of being the only country which never persecuted the Jews."

—Phyllis Ellen Funke

Eilat

Generally taxi drivers expect passengers to identify their destination with a street address. Eilat's cabbies often don't recognize streets; instead they work by names and landmarks. If you're going to visit a friend in another hotel, you give the hotel's name. Fair enough — that could happen anywhere. But if you're going to visit, say, a local rabbi, the situation is the same: "The numbers aren't logical," one driver explained as he asked for the family name.

"Ah, what business do you have with the rabbi?" the driver asked. "Are you getting married?" When told the meeting was not about a wedding, he frowned and asked, "A divorce?"

Why such interest? "He married me and my wife," the youngish driver explained. "He was good to us. He let us have the ceremony in the desert a few miles north of town, right on the border. We wanted to do it in Sinai, because that's where we met, but he helped us do it as close as possible."

This story sheds a lot of light on Eilat. Behind the glitz of the hotels, restaurants, and discotheques that cater to tourists from around the world, Eilat retains a small-town intimacy. Visitors who jet in for a few days may not notice, but the locals still pride themselves on knowing all their neighbors.

Eilat's development has been closely related to Israel's relationship with the Sinai Peninsula. Prior to 1967, when Egypt held Sinai, Eilat was Israel's most exotic escape from the pressure-cooker reality of daily life. During the 1970s, when the Sinai coast and desert beckoned, Eilat seemed more like a transit station en route to Sharm el Sheikh or the interior than a destination in and of itself.

Eilat's fortunes started to change when Egypt's late President Anwar el-Sadat made his historic journey to Jerusalem in November 1977. That trip set in motion the process that culminated in Israel's withdrawal from the last strip of Sinai beach, at Taba, in 1989.

The peace process thrust Eilat into the spotlight in Israel and around the world. It also made it the last stop for Israelis and tourists seeking to get away from it all. Although Sinai still has an allure for many Israelis, most go no farther than Eilat.

The city rose to the challenge, and in the past decade its somewhat tawdry image has given way to that of a first-rate international resort city. Its hotels have the highest occupancy rates of any in the country, and thousands of Europeans flock there each week during the winter season. When bookings drop, as they did during the Persian Gulf crisis, local boosters have learned to stay confident that the storm will pass. And when business sags, the hotels offer the best deals.

Eilat's rapid turnaround was facilitated by a 1985 government decision to grant it tax-free status. The label is more enticement than reality. Eilat's 25,000 residents still pay most of the same taxes that burden their compatriots to the north. The biggest change, as far as residents and visitors are concerned, is the abolition of value-added tax, which adds 16 percent to the cost of everything in Israel.

History: Israelis laugh when you ask them about Eilat's history. In the country of Jerusalem and Safed, Masada and Caeserea, what's so interesting about the history of a beach resort? Still, Eilat's past stretches back to biblical times.

During the Bronze Age (3150–1200 B.C.E.) the area around Timna, just north of Eilat, was a world center of copper mining — the ancient Egyptians mined the area between the fourteenth and twelfth centuries B.C.E.

The earliest mention of Eilat itself is in Deuteronomy, in the account of the Israelites' wanderings in the desert after the Exodus from Egypt.

According to 1 Kings 9, King Solomon built a navy at Etzion Geber, beside Eilat, to protect his kingdom and to establish maritime trade on the Red Sea. Between the sixth and fourth centuries the Nabateans increased Eilat's importance as a trade route, as evidenced by Nabatean rock drawings of caravans and boats that have been found as far north as the site of Kibbutz Yotvata and the Uvda Valley.

During this period the city was located a few miles east of its present location, where the Jordanian port of Akaba lies today, and it was called Aila. It remained an important trade and military point for the Romans, Greeks, Byzantines, Christians, Arabs, Mamelukes, and other nations and peoples that ruled the land over the centuries. It had a Jewish presence for much of the time, augmented in the seventh century C.E. by Jews expelled from the Arabian peninsula by Muhammad. Some time between the middle of the tenth century and the Crusader period, Jewish settlement in the area came to an end.

In 1842 the Ottoman Turks took control, although the final border separating the Turkish colony from British-controlled Sinai was not determined until 1906. The border dispute between the colonial powers set the scene for the lengthy squabble that Egypt and Israel waged over Taba. The international arbitration panel that awarded the sliver of land to Egypt in 1988 relied heavily on records of the 1906 dispute.

Although the British gave the site of contemporary Akaba to Jordan in 1922, the tip of the remaining Palestine Mandate that bordered the Gulf of Akaba was awarded to Israel by the United Nations partition plan of 1947. Israel's founding fathers realized the site could be developed, so great military preparations went into securing it. After the War of Independence began, the Jordanians got to the site first; the Israelis did not take the territory until March 12, 1949 (without firing a shot).

The first civilians settled there late that year. The city immediately began to absorb thousands of new immigrants who flooded into the country in 1949 and the 1950s. But until 1956, the Egyptians blocked the Strait of Tiran to Israel, so Eilat's port wasn't even built until nearly a decade after the city was established.

Transport and tourism have long been the city's main industries, although the salt and copper mines located north of town have at certain times employed many residents.

Community: Compared to Jerusalem or Haifa, which have substantial non-Jewish minorities, Eilat's citizens are virtually all Jewish. The paradox is that this most Jewish city in the Jewish state lacks a distinctly Jewish feeling or character. While many American Jewish visitors feel the country's Israeli character is a reasonable stand-in for the religious character of other Jewish communities around the world, Eilatis joke that they are barely a part of the State of Israel. Indeed, Israelis call Eilat "the closest thing to moving abroad without paying the travel tax."

Despite these jokes, Eilat is clearly an Israeli creation. During most of the year, Hebrew is the main language heard around town (between November and March, German, Swedish, French, Finnish, and English give Hebrew a good bit of competition along the beaches and in the night spots). Its residents study in Israeli schools and celebrate the Jewish holidays, and many of its young people dream of life in Tel Aviv after their army service is completed.

Most Eilat residents are secular, but the city has nine synagogues. All but one are small neighborhood *shtiebels* that draw worshipers of a particular ethnic background (Ashkenazic, Moroccan, and so on). The Central Synagogue has a *mikveh* and serves as the hub of religious life.

Sights: Eilat's greatest draw is its beach and water sports. When Israel controlled the Sinai Peninsula with its long Red Sea coastline, locals tended to scoff at Eilat's value as a diving center. Every tourist who had ever visited Eilat, they complained, had taken a piece of coral home as a souvenir, leaving nothing in the city's waters.

Today Sinai is Egyptian, and a psycho-

King Solomon's beach: The farthest Israelis can go without moving abroad

logical barrier prevents many people from crossing the border, so Eilat's coral looks better than it used to. A couple of miles south of the main tourist area and a few hundred yards from the Egyptian border checkpoint at Taba lies Coral World, an underwater observatory complex alongside the Coral Reserve, which provides one of the city's best areas for snorkeling and diving. Eilat's blue-green waters are filled with many multicolored surprises. From Coral World you can also take the four-hour cruise to Coral Island.

Sun worship beats all other seaside activities in Eilat by a wide margin, although waterskiing, parasailing, and windsurfing are all popular sports. At Dolphin Reef on the South Beach you can get an up-close view of marine mammals. Divers can swim alongside dolphins and sea lions under the watchful eye of marine-life specialists. Facilities also include a bathing beach and videos about marine life. For details call 059-75921 or 73417. General tourist information is available from the Israel Government Tourist Office (telephone 059-172-268).

Among the city's other attractions are Har Tzefakhot, a mountain west of Coral Beach that offers great views of Eilat and the surrounding water and mountains; the Eilat Express Minitrain, which boards near the Galei Eilat and Lagoona Hotels; and Minigolf-The Promised Land, which combines miniature golf with a miniature Israel tour.

The Israel Palace Museum, near the Caesar Hotel, portrays Jewish history through dioramas. The Wadi Art Gallery, in Wadi Shlomo, has a permanent exhibit of paintings, lithographs, ceramics, and sculpture by Israeli artists.

Most of the modern repertoire of the Eilat Dance Company addresses themes related to desert life and the cultures of the nomadic tribes that have roamed the Arava and the Sinai. The troupe also draws on biblical and hasidic themes. Between November and April the company performs every Tuesday evening at the Phillip Murray Center, located near City Hall. It travels in the summer—to Eilat's sister city of Los Angeles and other points abroad.

The city's mainstream culture consists of entertainment in the hotels and the innumerable discotheques open until the wee hours of the morning. The most spectacular discotheque, Sheba's, located in the King Solomon Hotel, doesn't even open for business until 11 P.M. each night.

If the desert to the east is Egyptian, the desert to the north is still Israeli. An easy side trip, about eighteen miles from Eilat, are Timna Park and King Solomon's Pillars, a set of desert-colored sandstone formations. A few miles closer to Eilat are the Timna Copper Mines, close to where King Solomon is believed to have mined three thousand years ago.

Eating: Eilat's international character shines brightly in an assortment of Italian, French, American, fish, and Chinese restaurants. The Chinese eateries usually have Asian waiters; everywhere else you're likely to stumble across vacationing Swedes who are working to earn pocket money. If you need a culinary reminder that you are indeed in Israel, stop for hummus or falafel at take-out stands. Every hotel in town has a kosher restaurant, but many of the city's other eateries do not have rabbinic supervision. Asking to see the restaurant's *kashrut* certificate is the best assurance of kosher food.

Personalities: Israel's top entertainers play Eilat, and many artists, singers, and politicians got their start in the city. Pop singers Chava Alberstein and Gidi Gov studied in Eilat and made their debuts before local audiences. Knesset member and detective novelist Michael Bar-Zohar has had a home in Eilat since the 1960s. (Unfortunately, none of his books, or those of any other Israeli writer, for that matter, are set in Eilat.) The city's feisty young mayor, Rafi Hochman, made international headlines with his stubborn determination—ultimately unsuccessful—to keep Taba within his municipal boundaries.

Recommendations: Eilat is served by El Al and its domestic subsidiary, Arkia. The city's premiere hotels are the Neptune and the King Solomon Palace. Other four- and five-star facilities include the Moriah, Lagoon, and Sport. Neot Hakikar is a travel agency with years of experience running desert tours and forays into Egypt.

As with any resort, much of Eilat's social life and entertainment takes place in the various hotels, so you may find yourself visiting several during your stay. This explains the orientation of the taxi drivers. But even if you venture into residential Eilat with a driver who doesn't know all the street names, you are unlikely to get lost. The town is small, and chances are the driver knows the people you are visiting.

—*Carl Schrag*

Florence

A tourist enters a little jewelry store near the Church of Santa Croce in Florence. There is a puzzled look on her face. Why, she wants to know, is there, at the apex of the facade of one of Italy's grandest Gothic churches, a design that looks suspiciously like a Star of David?

The clerk is stumped, as she is every time someone inquires about the six-pointed star adorning this outstanding Franciscan landmark. But she is not alone. There is no mention of it in leading guidebooks. Nor does Florence's official tourist office have a clue.

Sights and History: The saga of the star on Santa Croce, however, reposes with the Jewish community in Florence, a community of 1,000 that traces its existence to the fourteenth century. It is one of a host of indications of the ongoing Jewish involvement in the fabric of the quintessential Renaissance city of Tuscany. According to Yohanna-Miriam Pick Margolies, a local Jewish leader and niece of Samuel Hirsh Margulies, chief rabbi of Florence from 1890 to 1922, the star was mandated by the architect—who just happened to be a Jew from Ancona.

Niccolò Matas, Margolies relates, was one of several architects competing for the commission to design the facade in the late 1850s, when it was decided that the plain brick front of the vast fourteenth-century church should be replaced with the more imposing black-and-white marble. Matas's design won, with no questions asked about the star, because it is regarded as a symbol of Jesus. What is more, a star formed by two superimposed triangles is a mystical sign—the upward-pointing triangle representing man trying to raise himself by praying to God; the one pointing down

representing the grace of God descending on man.

Matas's background was not revealed until contract-signing time. Then his origins became clear because, as a presumably observant Jew, he requested Saturdays off. And he had another request. Since Santa Croce is Florence's pantheon, containing the tombs of Machiavelli, Michelangelo, and Galileo, among others, and since all architects who worked on the church were supposed to be buried there as well, Matas wanted his place among the renowned.

But the Franciscan brothers were opposed to burying a Jew on such hallowed ground. And the Jewish community itself was aghast at the thought of a Jew lying in Santa Croce. So Matas was buried under the top steps of the church's entrance, right in front of its massive, sculptured main center door. The burial slab remains today, a white, cracked-marble rectangle.

While the Santa Croce star is perhaps the most dramatic and obvious demonstration of the Jewish presence in Florence—indeed, Santa Croce, on the Piazza di Santa Croce, is a sightseeing "must" on all tourist itineraries—a hint of far deeper Jewish involvement may be found by sharply discerning eyes in a fresco on the wall of the Benozzo Gozzoli chapel in the Palazzo Medici Riccardi (Via Cavour 1, up the stairs, immediately to the right of the entrance). Though called *The Journey of the Magi,* this work is said to represent the trip to Florence in the fifteenth century of the potentates of Byzantium. On one side is the entourage from Constantinople. On the other is a portrait of the entire Medici family with court. And among the sages of that court is Elijah Delmedigo, a Jew.

Delmedigo was one of several Jewish men of letters held in esteem by the scholars and humanists of the Renaissance, and it was from him that the thinker Pico della Mirandola learned the Hebrew language, literature, and philosophy—disciplines considered important by the well educated of that day. Beyond representing the Medicis' appreciation of Jewish thinking, Delmedigo's presence in court also speaks of the position of the Jews in Florence at that time.

Most of them had come from Pitigliano, on the edge of Tuscany, which had been established by descendants of Jews brought to Italy as slaves after the fall of Jerusalem in 70 C.E. (The Italian surname Servi, meaning slave, belongs only to Jews.) Though Jews appeared in Florence in the fourteenth century, the first official invitation to them—a group of about a hundred moneylenders—went out in 1430. Bankers themselves, the Medicis appreciated these Jews. Since many records lie unplumbed in the city archives, however, one can only speculate on their help in financing works of the Renaissance.

There were, of course, segments of Florentine society that despised the Jews. A demonstration of this antipathy exists in the fourteenth-century church of Or San Michele, on Via de' Calzaiuoli (Street of Hosiers). On the right, upon entering this sanctuary, stands a statue of St. Anne and child. On the statue is a Latin inscription phonetically rendered in Hebrew letters. It translates to "I am the light of the world" and is believed to have been engraved there to convey to the Jews the power of Jesus, after a young Jewish boy, in the sixteenth century, allegedly committed a sacrilege against the church, for which he was executed.

When the Medicis were in power—a situation that seesawed—the Jews were treated well. In fact, the Jewish tenure in Florence was generally fairly comfortable even when they were ghettoized by Cosimo I in 1570. He did so in return for receiving from the pope the right to absolute rule of Tuscany as its grand duke.

But Cosimo acted reluctantly, and he did not segregate everyone. He chose some families to live near him in the shadow of the Pitti Palace, presumably so he could have moneylenders nearby. Those ten families—enough to form a *minyan*—lived on a

narrow street that, until the Fascists changed its name during World War II, was Via de' Giudei (Street of the Jews). Today, the street is Via dei Ramaglianti, off Via dello Sprone, and a rough area along the wall is thought to be the remnant of a synagogue.

The ghetto itself, because it could contain no churches, was built in the worst part of town—in the red-light district. Nothing remains today of the ghetto, for the area, known as the Old City, has been completely rebuilt. However, it stood between what are now the bustling Via Roma, Via Brunelleschi, Via de' Pecori and Piazza della Republica.

After several false alarms, the ghetto was permanently opened in 1848; some Jews moved across the street to Via dell' Oche, where they built at least two synagogues. Today, near an archway leading to number 5 on that narrow, cobbled road, a wall plaque commemorates one such site, as well as the liberation of Florence's Jews by the Allies in 1944.

The Jewish community that left the ghetto was not as purely Italian as that which first entered. By the 1600s, encouraged by Cosimo I, Jewish refugees from Spain and Portugal had begun arriving in droves. They were rich, aristocratic, cultured, and, unlike the Italian Jews who practiced a religious ritual that derived directly from the Temple in Jerusalem, they followed the Sephardic rite. They established their own synagogue in the ghetto, and by the time of emancipation it was the dominant one.

Of top priority to the liberated Jews was the building of a synagogue "worthy of Florence." On land purchased at what was then the city's edge, the Jewish community erected a structure inspired by the Byzantine church in Constantinople, Hagia Sophia.

The onion-domed, arabesque-decorated structure, which opened in 1882, stands at Via Luigi Carlo Farini 4 (telephone 245-252) and is a national monument. Though Florence's Jews now live all around the city, a century ago most clustered within walking distance of the synagogue—the poorer Jews, to its right; the wealthier ones including, reportedly, the Uzzielli family, to the left, in palaces, some of which bordered the exclusive park, Piazza d'Azeglio (Azalea Square).

By the eve of World War II, there were about 3,000 Jews in Florence. But many who perceived the threat began emigrating. When racial laws were promulgated in Italy by Mussolini, Florentines tried to protect their Jews. Nevertheless, 248 were rounded up by the Nazis and sent to their deaths, including the rabbi, Nathan Cassuto.

Personalities: Rabbi Margulies (1858–1922), a Polish Jew who immersed himself in the Italian and Sephardic rites, was Florence's chief rabbi from 1890 until he died. In 1899 he founded the Collegio Rabbinico Italiano, reviving Jewish life in Italy; his work erased some of his community's insularity by establishing contacts between Italian and European Jews, and lifted Florence to the center of Italian Jewry. Umberto Cassuto (1882–1951) followed in Rabbi Margulies's footsteps. An Italian historian and biblical and Semitic scholar, he was rabbi of Florence and director of the rabbinical seminary. He wrote the history of Florence's Jews in the Renaissance and, in 1939, became a professor of Bible studies at the Hebrew University in Jerusalem.

Another distinguished scholar and ardent Zionist who taught Jewish history, Bible, and Hebrew language at the seminary was Rabbi Hirsch Perez Chajes (1876–1927). He, too, helped propel Florence to the focus of Jewish culture in Italy, before he moved on to become the chief rabbi of Vienna.

Contemporary Jewish personalities in Florence include the painter Dorothée Heyman; Liliana Treves Alcalay, a singer and ethnomusicologist; and Amnon Barzel, director of the Center for Contemporary Art.

Also associated with the city is Amadeo Modigliani, the painter and sculptor. He was born in nearby Livorno (Leghorn), studied in Florence, and later became known as the foremost portraitist among the "Montparnasse Circle" of Jewish artists, who were drawn to Paris at the turn of the twentieth century. (Two other Jewish families that originated in Livorno were those of Moses Montefiore and Benjamin Disraeli.)

But perhaps the personality most associated with Florence is a Jew who never set foot in the city—King David. Davids by Michelangelo can be found in The Accademia, in front of the Piazza della Signoria, and in Piazzale Michelangelo (where there is also a good view of the city and synagogue). Donatello's *David* is in the Uffizi Gallery.

Sights and Community: Today's Jewish community of 1,000 supports the massive, Byzantine-style synagogue and museum, an elementary school, an old-age home, *mikveh*, and an ad hoc theater group.

The community is well integrated into Florentine society. Unlike Milanese Jews, who are mostly businessmen and industrialists, or Roman Jews, who are primarily merchants and shopkeepers, Florentine Jews can be found in a variety of other occupations as well, ranging from medicine to photography, sculpting (the works of Dario Viterbo are known internationally) to Etruscology (the study of ancient Etruria, today's Tuscany).

Most are well educated; few are needy. But like other Florentines, they tend to be somewhat closed, even to Jews from other cities in Italy. What is more, few among them speak languages other than Italian— though an amateur theatrical group was formed some years ago to perform, on occasion, a comedy, *La Gnora Luna* ("Madame, the Moon"), in the Judeo-Florentine dialect that disappeared about two hundred years ago.

Only a handful of Florentines are Orthodox; not many more are observant. And, though the Great Synagogue is officially Orthodox, following an Italo-Sephardic ritual, it permits deviations. Since the war, for example, women have been permitted to join male members of their family downstairs, in the rear, for certain prayers. The synagogue is also distinctive because it reflects the influences of Catholicism—in its pulpit, which is at the top of a winding staircase, and in its use of the organ on some holidays. Though damaged during the war and the Arno flood in 1966, the thousand-seat sanctuary, which sits behind a great wrought-iron gate, in a well-landscaped garden, still has elaborately frescoed walls, *Magen Davids* inlaid in its marble floors, and an ark with doors of gold.

Upstairs, there is a small museum that contains photographs of the ghetto and brocaded Torah covers in carmines, greens, and yellows; old *megillahs*; and the key to the chapel of an association that used to ransom Jews captured by the Barbary pirates. There is also a blowup of Elijah Delmedigo as seen in the Medici court fresco. Call the synagogue number for hours.

Also situated on these communal grounds is the Nathan Cassuto Hebrew School and *mikveh*. The Home for the Aged is at Via Carducci 11.

At Via Ricasoli 26 is La Giuntina, a Jewish publishing house with a store selling Jewish books as well as Sephardic and Italian-Jewish music. David Vogelmann, the owner, is also the Italian translator of Elie Wiesel.

Side Trips: Jewish travelers visiting the Leaning Tower will be surprised by the Jewish art, history, and life in colorful Pisa, a fifty-five-minute train ride from Florence. On both sides of the main hall of the city's train station are murals, completed in 1992, by the leader of the Italian neo-futurismo movement, the Pisan Jewish artist Daniel Schinasi. Schinasi's self-portrait — with a *tallit* over his head — can be found in the lower right foreground of the mural depicting the *Battle of Mallorca*. In the second mural, *Homage to Galileo,* you'll see not only the heroic scientist and the villainous Queen Isabella and Pope Urban VIII but also several members of Schinasi's family, including the artist, again in a *tallit*. Schinasi has also woven into the landscape two shadowy, almost diaphanous figures, representing survivors of a more recent aggression against the Jews, the Holocaust.

The Leaning Tower is not the only sight on the Field of Miracles. The piazza also has a massive cathedral, a no less imposing baptistry, and a small Jewish cemetery, visible through a set of iron gates. What a modern Jewish consecrated ground is doing among all these venerated sites of Christendom is baffling. According to Marco Schinasi (the artist's brother and also president of the Pisa community; tele-

phone 542-134), the cemetery's caretaker was cleaning around his father's grave one day and stumbled across the top of an old tombstone, which turned out to be but one of more than one hundred from the sixteenth century.

Pisa's 150-year-old synagogue (Via Palestro 24, telephone 27-269) provides religious services for the city's forty Jews and also houses the Circolo Pardo-Roques, named for a benevolent Pisan Jew whose story is told in Silvano Arieti's book *The Parnass* (Basic Books).

Seventy minutes by train from Florence is Bologna, which has not one but two leaning towers, plus a refreshing network of arcaded streets and the oldest university in Europe. Bologna's synagogue, entered through Via Gombruti 9, was built in 1954 on the ruins of the synagogue destroyed during World War II. To see the facade of the synagogue, which serves the city's seventy Jews, go around the block to Via Mario Finzi. To get inside call Rabbi Alberto Someck (227-931) for an appointment. Bologna's old ghetto is found along the Via dell'Inferno, near which you can still see a street sign for the ancient Via dei Giudei (Street of the Jews).

Siena, an hour away from Florence, is one of Italy's most beautiful cities. Its synagogue is located near an archway at Vicolo delle Scotte 14, just in from Via del Porrione. A plaque there commemorates those Jews from Siena deported during World War II.

Eating: The popular Italian kosher restaurant Il Cuscussu closed in 1993, but its location next to the synagogue (Via Farini 2a) and the large number of Jewish tourists make it a fair bet that another kosher establishment will follow. In the meantime, there are a few vegetarian restaurants to choose from. Gaugin, on Via dei Pilastri, specializes in Greek-Jewish and Sephardic dishes; its owner, Jean-Michel Carasso, was born to Greek-Jewish parents in the Belgian Congo. Two other vegetarian restaurants are the one called, simply, Vegetarian, on the Via delle Ruote; and Club, in Scandicci, close to Florence.

Reading: Though Il Cuscussu is gone, some of its recipes survive in *The Classic*

Cuisine of the Italian Jews, by Edda Servi Machlin (Everest House, Dodd, Mead). Others were contributed by one of Il Cuscussu's owners, Jennie Bassani Liscia, who is the sister of Giorgio Bassani, author of *The Garden of the Finzi-Continis* (Atheneum), a novel about a Jewish family in Ferrara. Machlin's book, by the way, is more than a cookbook; it is a history of Pitigliano, the Italian *shtetl* to which many Florence Jews trace their roots.

Another, perhaps better known, literary tie-in exists in the hills overlooking Florence. There is the Villa I Tatti, once the home of Bernard Berenson, the American art historian and connoisseur who lived most of his life in Italy. This villa, now the property of Harvard University, is said to have been the model for the home of Aaron Jastrow of Herman Wouk's *The Winds of War* (Little, Brown). With its history, style, and understated Jewish connection, the villa is a microcosm of Florence.

—*Phyllis Ellen Funke*

Frankfurt

The position of Frankfurt's Jewish community is perhaps best illustrated by an extraordinary event that took place a few years ago. Thirty Jewish protesters marched on stage of the Kammerspiel Theater to prevent the premiere of a contemporary play by Rainer Werner Fassbinder that they regarded as anti-Semitic. Instead of booing the demonstrators off the stage, the audience engaged them in an emotional three-hour discussion on anti-Semitism and freedom of expression. "I do not feel myself offended by this play," said Daniel Cohn-Bendit, the Jewish radical who led the 1968 student uprising in Paris and who was sitting in the audience, "but I welcome your protests. You are in the tradition of 1968. This will be the first demonstration in the history of Frankfurt that will not be broken up by the police."

It was an evening of real-life theater. Cohn-Bendit was right; the police didn't intervene. Indeed, the city's mayor and political establishment agreed with the demonstrators. The play was never performed. The Jewish community—sensitive but bold, and widely respected—won its point.

But what happened that night turned out to be only the first round of vindication. What had most incensed the Jewish community about Fassbinder's play was a character, simply called "The Rich Jew," supposedly based on local real-estate developer Ignatz Bubis. Eight years later, Fassbinder was dead and Germany's radical left was in ruins. Bubis, meanwhile, had been elected head of the German Jewish community, and won such widespread respect for his defense of human rights during the attacks on foreigners in 1992 that he was touted as a candidate for president of Germany. It had been a long time since a Jew from the banks of the Rhine had had such an impact on the country.

The Jewish community of every German city today is a shadow of what it was before World War II. But one thing has remained constant: Frankfurt-am-Main is, and always has been, the most Jewish city in the country. Though Berlin has had more Jews for most of the last century, Frankfurt has always had at least twice as many on a proportional basis. For influence and depth of history, Frankfurt Jewry cannot be matched. When the Nazis came to power, in fact, Frankfurt was the only major German city with a Jewish mayor. Ludwig Landmann was forced to resign in March 1933, six weeks after Hitler became chancellor.

History: Frankfurt had a flourishing Jewish community, led by merchants, in the twelfth century and possibly earlier. Between the thirteenth and seventeenth centuries, however, the community lived through repeating cycles of well-being and persecution. There were massacres and expulsions in 1241, 1349, and 1614, but the community always restored itself within a few years.

It was in 1462 that Jews were first required to live in the walled Judengasse (Jews' Street). Although the ghettoization represented both physical and social hardship, once inside the Jewish community developed more intensely. Never permitted to expand the ghetto beyond its original boundaries, the Jews subdivided houses and added stories. The population within the walls grew from 100 at the time of the ghetto's establishment to 3,000 in 1610.

By the end of the sixteenth century the community inside the walls was not only prosperous but also a center of Jewish learning. And although pressure from the city's guilds and petty traders led to the plundering of the ghetto in 1614, after which the Jews were expelled from the city, they were almost immediately allowed back and the leaders of the pogrom were put to death. The riots had been led by Vincent Fettmilch, and ever since the Frankfurt community has observed Adar 20 as Purim Winz (Purim of Vincent), with their own personal Haman.

The eighteenth century saw the rise of Mayer Amschel Rothschild, whose family got its name from the red shield that hung in front of its house in the ghetto. Scion of an old but undistinguished mercantile family, Rothschild turned his coin, antique, and money-changing business into one of Europe's leading banking empires. The family became a symbol to Jews of communal achievement and responsibility, and to anti-Semites a symbol of the power of Jewish money.

In the early nineteenth century, Frankfurt established itself as a center of Reform Judaism. By the 1840s, Reform Jews dominated the community, accounting for the large majority of Frankfurt Jewry. The rise of Reform Judaism paralleled the French Revolution, the Napoleonic occupation of Frankfurt, and the German revolution of 1848, all of which contributed to Jewish emancipation. Emancipation, in turn, weakened the authority of the Reform-dominated community board; in 1851 a group of Orthodox rabbis, led by Samson Raphael Hirsch and backed by the Rothschilds, capitalized on the loosening control and established their own religious association, and eventually their own *kehillah*. Thereafter, Orthodoxy and Reform coexisted as separate communities in Frankfurt.

From 1900 until 1933 — when the community numbered about 30,000 — Frankfurt's Jews were at the peak of their influence. In 1900, Jewish Frankfurters paid 427 marks per capita in taxes while non-Jews paid 103 marks. Shortly before Hitler's rise, it was estimated that Jews were responsible for 35 percent of the economic activity in Frankfurt, although they were only 7 percent of the population.

Despite the community's history, the fate of Frankfurt Jewry in the Nazi era was no different than that of the rest of Germany's Jews. After *Kristallnacht*, the night in November 1938 when the nation's synagogues were burned, hundreds of Jewish men were sent to the Dachau and Buchenwald concentration camps. More than half of Frankfurt's Jews emigrated before the war broke out. In 1941, those remaining were deported, first to ghettoes in Poland and Russia and later directly to concentration camps.

Community: There are 7,000 Jews in the Frankfurt area today, and the community is characterized by aging, prosperity, and irony. Today's community has only the most tenuous link with prewar Frankfurt Jewry. German Jews who survived the war did not, by and large, return to Germany. Today's community is made up overwhelmingly of postwar refugees from Eastern Europe. The once great Reform Jewish tradition is gone. The one Frankfurt synagogue that survived *Kristallnacht* — the Liberal Westend Synagogue — is today Orthodox.

The West End has the greatest concentration of Jews, as was the case before World War II, but the area can no longer be called a Jewish neighborhood. There are also Jews in the East End, where the other synagogues are located. While all the city's synagogues are Orthodox, they vary in ritual from Frankfurter to Mainzer to Polish.

The largest number of Frankfurt's Jews are self-employed, particularly as shopkeepers and real estate brokers. There are no more Jewish bankers. Despite Germany's recent history, and despite the Kammerspiel protest, Frankfurt's Jews feel they are little different from the rest of Western Jewry; their main problem, they say, is assimilation, not anti-Semitism.

Many Frankfurt émigrés maintain ties to the city. Every few years the city of Frankfurt brings over dozens of former Jewish citizens. Visitors are treated to receptions in the fifteenth-century City Hall (the Römer), memorial meetings, and sightseeing. Though many people accept the city's invitations, there are also many who refuse to accept German largesse.

Sights: Frankfurt's ghetto, the Judengasse, was gone long before Hitler came to power. The gates were opened by Napoleon's troops and by the end of the nineteenth century the area was no longer predominantly Jewish. But you can still stand on the spot. From the Zeil—the pedestrian mall that runs through the center of the city—turn south on Fahrgasse and make a quick left to An der Staufenmauer. You'll pass through an arch of what was the city wall in the twelfth century and became the ghetto wall in the fifteenth.

You'll be on Börnestrasse, a narrow, dead-end street of apartments and offices. This is where, for over four hundred years, Jews became victims and millionaires. The configuration of the street changed after the Allied bombings of World War II. The Börnestrasse synagogue was on the same site as the ghetto house of worship until it was destroyed on *Kristallnacht*; a plaque on the building that houses a city statistical office identifies the site. Just past the synagogue plaque the street now curves in the opposite direction from the old Judengasse. The Rothschild home probably stood on a site that is now one block over, near the Canon copier store on Kurt-Schumacher-Strasse.

The Westend Synagogue, at Freiherr-vom-Stein-Strasse 30, is the only one in the city with any history. The large gray-stone building is typical of early twentieth-century temple architecture, and certainly a rarity in Germany. The main sanctuary features vaulting stone arches on four sides under a massive cupola and Star-of-David stained-glass windows in blue and white. Other Frankfurt synagogues can be found at Baumweg 5–7 (an attractive gabled, gray-stone building that was a Jewish school before World War II) and at Röderbergweg 29.

If you go the Westend Synagogue it is worthwhile to walk through the West End itself, a hybrid neighborhood of functional postwar apartment buildings and of stately prewar homes that survived Allied bombings. Since 1986 it has been home to the new Jewish Community Center, probably the most impressive Jewish structure built in postwar Germany. It is the community's nerve center, with concerts, lectures, a youth center, and the offices of the community administration and rabbinate. Though the regular entrance is at Westend-

strasse 43, the more striking side is on Savignystrasse. Huge iron menorah shapes sit high above the entrance, and rising from the ground to several feet above the roof is a single blank tablet of the Law, with cracks to symbolize the break between the German and Jewish peoples. Call the center (740-721) for information on community events, *kashrut*, and services at city synagogues, or look in the weekly *Frankfurter Jüdisches Gemeindeblatt*.

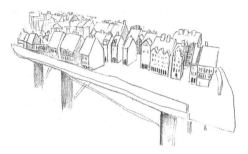

Over the wall: A Jewish Museum model takes visitors into the old Frankfurt ghetto

If the community center represents building anew, then the Jewish Museum, (which opened in 1988 at Untermainkai 14–15) stands for retrieving a bit of the past. Located in a house that once belonged to the Rothschild family, the museum covers the history of Jews in Frankfurt from the twelfth century and offers exhibits on Jewish rituals, life, and festivals. Ninety percent of the visitors are non-Jews. Well combined with the museum's high-tech resources—like computerized, viewer-selected film displays—are several rooms in the classicist building, erected in 1821, that have been restored to their nineteenth-century decor.

By far the most striking feature of the museum is the model of the old Frankfurt ghetto. The Judengasse burned in 1711, and the plans from its reconstruction, which still exist, were used in building the museum exhibit. A map of the 1:50-scale wooden model identifies 194 buildings, including the ghetto synagogue and the Rothschilds' home. On most days the model sits in one piece and visitors walk around it, much in the way Christians viewed the actual ghetto only from the outside; on Tuesdays, however, it is open in the middle and visitors can stroll down a walkway between the two sides of the street.

Other items in the museum include a silk Seder banner with complete Passover instructions in text and pictures, Moritz Oppenheim's portrait of Lessing and Mendelssohn, and a circular device that converts dates from the Jewish calendar into the secular calendar. In addition to an exhibit on Frankfurt Jewry during the Nazi era, the historical exhibit portrays in startling detail the coexistence, in the late nineteenth century, of Jewish achievement and anti-Semitism. The museum is open from 10 A.M. to 5 P.M. Tuesday, Thursday, Friday, Saturday and Sunday, and to 8 P.M. Wednesday; it is closed Monday.

Paulskirche (just opposite the Römer, the fifteenth-century city hall) is where the Frankfurt National Assembly met in 1848–49. A product of the liberal revolution—whose failure, among other things, produced a wave of Jewish emigrants to the United States—the assembly made an abortive attempt to unify Germany. Several Jewish delegates attended, and two of the primary doctrines adopted by the assembly were those of human rights and emancipation. Perhaps there is an ironic connection between the assembly's failure to produce a nation and the Holocaust memorial that stands outside Paulskirche today.

Side Trips: Mainz, Worms and Speyer lie along a fifty-mile stretch of the Rhine west and south of Frankfurt. Jewish settlement in Mainz may date to the Roman period, and there is documentary evidence of Jewish communities in all three cities by the tenth century. By the twelfth century the three towns were the leading Jewish centers of Germany and were collectively referred to in Hebrew sources by the acronym *Shum*. The *Takkanot Shum*, resolutions passed at the synodal assemblies of the communities, had an impact on Jewish autonomy and self-help all over Germany, and the customs and rituals of Mainz in particular had a great impact on the *Shulchan Arukh*.

Of the three cities of Shum, only Mainz has a Jewish community today, numbering 130. The attractive synagogue in the modern Jewish Community Center, at Forsterstrasse 2, has arched windows, black iron chandeliers, and an ark holding three Mainz Torahs that survived *Kristallnacht*. The center hosts lectures and other community events. Call 613-990 for information on activities and hours of religious services.

Saint Stephen's Church in Mainz has Germany's only Chagall windows. Like the stained-glass windows the artist did for churches in France and Switzerland, most of the images at St. Stephen's are from the Hebrew Bible. There are organized tours of the church as well as regular lectures emphasizing the Jewish origins of Christianity. Call 231-640 for information.

In Worms, where Martin Luther faced the Imperial Diet in 1521, the Judengasse looks much as it did in the Middle Ages. The curving, cobbled street—which runs parallel to the remnants of the city's north wall—is lined with pastel-colored houses, mostly of three stories. The most important sites are just off the Judengasse at Synagogenplatz. Many times damaged and restored, the Rashi Synagogue of today is a faithful reconstruction of the house of worship built on the site in 1034. Though the great talmudist spent only five years studying in Worms, in the 1060s, his name has been linked with the city. Partly because there are no tangible places associated with him in his home town—Troyes, France—Rashi disciples flock to Worms. The synagogue's high-vaulted stone interior requires little adornment. Candelabra hang from the ceiling and there is a stone ark topped with three crowns. The "Rashi chapel," added in 1642, has a chair that may have been used by the scholar. A large room to the left of the *bimah* was a separate women's synagogue built in the thirteenth century; it now stands empty except for a memorial marker for the 500 Worms Jews who died in the Holocaust.

Adjacent to the synagogue is Raschi-Haus, a building housing a Judaica museum as well as the city archive. Opened in 1982, it stands on the site of structures that served, over the centuries, as a *yeshivah*, a Jewish community hall, a hospital, an old-age home and, in 1941–42, as the assembly point for deportation of Jews to death camps. The Judaica collection features a copy of the 1272 Worms *machzor* (the original is in Jerusalem) and other ritual objects, from Torah crowns to wimples. It traces the history of Jews in Worms and even has a map of the Judengasse identifying the families that occupied the homes in the Middle Ages.

Just beyond the southwest corner of the city wall is the densely packed Worms' Jewish Cemetery, the oldest in Europe. The two thousand tombstones have stood up well since the first one was put in place in 1076. Many great scholars are buried in Worms, and a section of the cemetery, designated the "valley of the rabbis," has directional signs in modern Hebrew to guide the many visitors.

The great Worms Cathedral is one of three in Germany (the others are in Bamberg and Trier) with statues of the female forms of Ecclesia and Synagoga and the only one where the statues are still in their original places, outside the main portal. Though the statues were meant to signify Ecclesia (the church) triumphant and Synagoga defeated, time and design have reversed fate. In all three cathedrals, the swooning blindfolded figure of Synagoga has remained intact; and in all three, the arms of triumphant Ecclesia have broken.

The most important Jewish sight in Speyer is the *mikveh*, on Judenbadgasse. Built in Romanesque style in 1084, it is the best preserved medieval Jewish ritual bath in Europe. It operated until 1534. Descending a long staircase, the visitor passes indentations for lanterns and benches where husbands waited for wives. The bath, fed by the Rhine, is in a garden that used to belong to an adjacent synagogue. On the right, at the entrance to the *mikveh* grounds, is a remnant wall of the synagogue built in 1100; an indentation can still be seen where the ark stood. From May to October, the *mikveh* is open 10 A.M. to noon and 2 to 4 P.M. At other times it is necessary to go with a tour guide. Judenbadgasse is an appendage of Speyer's Judengasse, a cobbled street of white, gray, and salmon houses with tiled roofs. Opposite the houses, beginning at about number 9, much of the eleventh-century ghetto wall still stands.

Eighty minutes into Bavaria from Frankfurt is Würzburg, a beautiful city noted for the Residenz, the eighteenth-century Ba-

roque palace of its prince-bishops; the cathedral of St. Kilian, a restored Romanesque church built on the site of a former synagogue; and, facing town from across the Main, Marienberg Castle. The Residenz and the cathedral, and other buildings in the town, are adorned with the brilliant sculpture of Tilman Riemenschneider. About 100 Jews live in Würzburg (compared to 2,000 before the war). A plaque marks the spot of the Dormerschulestrasse Synagogue, destroyed on *Kristallnacht*. Jewish community life today is centered at the postwar synagogue and the adjacent home for the aged. The complex at 11 Valentin-Beckerstrasse—particularly the synagogue interior, reminiscent of prewar German sanctuaries—is worth a visit. In 1982, Würzburg gave its annual culture prize to a native son, the Israeli poet Yehuda Amichai.

Personalities: Jews have contributed richly to Frankfurt's intellectual life. Among those born in the city or who worked there in the 1920s and 1930s were the social scientists Herbert Marcuse and Teodor Adorno and the theologians Martin Buber and Franz Rosenzweig. Two pioneers of modern psychology, Erik Erikson and Erich Fromm were Frankfurt natives, as is the more recently prominent Ruth Westheimer. Also associated with Frankfurt were Nahum Goldmann, the Zionist leader; Moritz Oppenheim, the artist; and Leopold Sonnemann, founder of *Frankfurter Zeitung,* ancestor of the *Frankfurter Allgemeine.* The paper is now one of the leading dailies of Germany.

General Sights: Goethe's house is a faithful reconstruction of the poet's eighteenth-century world. In cobbled Römerberg Square, in front of the City Hall, there is still a medieval feeling, enhanced by new construction of period buildings. The Palmengarten, with its palm trees and rose and alpine gardens, is a pleasant place for a walk.

Across the Main from the center of town is Sachsenhausen which, though it became part of Frankfurt six hundred years ago, maintains an identity of its own. Alt-Sachsenhausen is a part-honky-tonk, part-Middle Ages maze of restaurants and taverns where patrons drink beer and the local brew of apple wine. Also in Sachsenhausen is the Städel, one of Germany's leading art museums.

Reading: For a good fictional look at Jewish life in Frankfurt between 1900 and World War II, read *Yesterday's Streets* by Silvia Tennenbaum (Random House). *12 Kaiserhofstrasse* (some editions bear the title *The Invisible Jew*) by Valentin Senger (Dutton) is the true story of a Jewish family that managed to live through the war in Frankfurt without being captured. For a four-century biography of Frankfurt's most famous Jewish family, read *The Rothschilds* by Frederic Morton (Atheneum). For a contemporary picture there is *Strangers in Their Own Land: Young Jews in Germany and Austria Today* by Peter Sichrovsky (Basic Books). For an answer to the perennial question of how Jews can live in post-Nazi Germany, Sichrovsky's book is a good place to start.

Recommendations: The German National Tourist Office (122 East 42nd Street, New York, NY 10168; 212-661-7200) has brochures, pamphlets and fact sheets on Jewish as well as general travel in the Frankfurt area. If you're looking for a hotel that combines modern amenities with old-world charm, the Frankfurter Hof is perfect. It is centrally located and also favored by those who attend the periodic reunions of former Frankfurt Jews. Intercity rail service in Germany is convenient and efficient. Public transportation in Frankfurt works well but can be confusing if you don't know German. If you do get confused or lost, keep asking directions. As was proved at the Kammerspiel Theater, you don't need to worry about speaking up.
—*Alan M. Tigay*

Geneva

Among international cities, Geneva, on the Alps-bordered lake that bears its name, is arguably the queen. Historically a crossroads in the heart of Europe, its selection as headquarters for the League of Nations enhanced its magnetism for various globe-spanning operations—including those for, of, and concerning the Jews. Thus, this French-speaking city, which was long an independent entity before joining the Swiss Confederation, has served as the European seat for such organizations as the Jewish Agency, the American Jewish Joint Distribution Committee, ORT, and the World Jewish Congress—which was founded there.

Lending Geneva additional significance for world Jewry is its Swiss-conferred neutrality, which has fostered upon its stages such dramas as the initial receipt of information concerning the Final Solution and the exchange of Israeli and Arab prisoners.

Yet Geneva's internationality exists almost as a superstructure above the foundations of a chic little city whose personal concerns are as hometown as they are cosmopolitan. In this context exists the resident community of Jewish Genevese, working, with discretion but determination, to maintain its place—and peace—on the tightrope between the local and the global, the mundane and the cosmopolitan.

History: Prior to the nineteenth century, the Jewish presence in Geneva appears to have been scant. Jews may initially have settled in this city-state after 1182, following their expulsion from France by Philip Augustus. They are first mentioned in an official document at the end of the thirteenth century and were primarily moneylenders and moneychangers. Permitted to live only outside Geneva's city limits, however, they paid a tax each time they entered for business (pregnant women paid double). During the Black Death in 1348, they were accused—in Geneva as elsewhere—of having poisoned the wells, and many were executed. In the next century, relations with the Christians grew difficult and, after 1428, Jews were confined to a specified quarter in what is now Geneva's Old Town. Their situation continued to deteriorate, and in 1488 Jewish physicians were forbidden to practice. Two years later, all of Geneva's Jews were expelled, and they were absent for three hundred years.

Nor was their return initially triumphant. In 1783, when Geneva was under the jurisdiction of the dukes of Savoy, some Jews from Alsace-Lorraine and Germany were permitted residence in Carouge, a Geneva suburb. Following the French Revolution, when Geneva was annexed by France, they were granted equal citizenship. But when in 1815 Geneva joined the Swiss Confederation, Jewish rights were curtailed again, until midcentury when Jews were granted civic liberties and the freedom to worship. The community was officially recognized in 1853 and established its synagogue in 1859.

While it took on the conservative coloration of the Swiss, the community—or at least its young members—was stirred up, at century's turn, by conflicting political winds. To Geneva, the city of such thinkers as John Calvin and Jean-Jacques Rousseau, came intellectual refugees from Russia, Poland, and other points east. Unfurling their particular banners were, among others, Lenin and Trotsky on one front, and Chaim Weizmann, who lectured at the University of Geneva from 1900 to 1904, on another. Also in town at the time was Albert Einstein, who in 1909 received the first honorary degree awarded—on its

350th anniversary—by the University of Geneva.

The years before and during World War II strained the community, as it strove to aid endangered coreligionists elsewhere. Though some anti-Semitism was evident, Genevese Jews were never physically threatened.

Following the Sinai campaign in 1956, Geneva, which previously had absorbed only a handful of Sephardim, experienced an influx of Jews from Arab countries— Egypt, Lebanon, Syria, Iraq, Sudan and Morocco. These newcomers have made a significant mark not only on the Jewish community, but also on the city itself.

Community:
Is it a house divided or a house united? Today, Geneva's Jewish "community" is composed mainly of members of the largest of its three Ashkenazic synagogues and its Sephardic one. They share not only a community center, but also a chief rabbi.

The community center, Maison Juive, at 10 rue Saint-Leger (telephone 20-46-86), offers various joint facilities, including a kindergarten, Hebrew school, and thirty thousand-volume library (which has a large collection of eighteenth- and nineteenth-century Judaica). Chief Rabbi David Messes, of Moroccan origin, shuttles regularly between the older, nominally Orthodox, Geneva Synagogue and the Sephardic Hekhal Haness—performing the *bar mitzvahs*, weddings, and services at both. This duality acknowledges the ascending importance of the Sephardim. There are 5,000 or more Jews living in Geneva; 3,000 are community members. Outside the official community, 600 belong to a young, Liberal congregation, and 200 to an ultra-Orthodox one. Ethnically the community is 48 percent Ashkenazim and 52 percent Sephardim.

In fact, the latter have made a substantial impact on the former. Prior to 1956, the primarily Ashkenazic community had done its best to assume a low profile, choosing to blend as much as possible with the Swiss. From the old-timers' viewpoint, the Sephardim have brought an entirely different mentality and style, preferring, especially when in real estate and construction, to make public their accomplishments. Hence,

the fashionable Noga Hilton, on the lakefront, is an anagram of its owner's name, Nessim Gaon, a Sudanese Jew who is also president of the World Sephardic Confederation. Similarly, it is generally known that the glitzy new urban mall, Confederation Center, in the heart of downtown Geneva's most elegant shopping area, is owned by Gabriel Tamman, Gaon's brother-in-law.

Actually, Jews owned most of Geneva's leading stores until about twenty years ago. Carryovers from that time include Le Bon Genie, a chain of luxury boutiques belonging to the Brunschwig family, and the La Placette department store chain, headed by the Nordmann and Maus families. Today, however, Jews tend more toward banking, business and the professions— law, medicine, teaching, engineering. The community, which contributes to such civic projects as the restoration of the Cathedral of Saint-Pierre, is essentially middle- and upper-middle-class.

Its Swiss sense of discretion is sometimes sorely tested, however, because of its unique position vis-à-vis international relations. Since most world problems—and the personalities concerned with them—alight in Geneva, the Jews must determine how to respond. Yesterday the question was whether to communicate with Gorbachev, when he came to town, about refuseniks in the former Soviet Union, or how to react to Arafat. Tomorrow it may be something else. While they have indeed demonstrated publicly on occasion, they usually choose to work behind the scenes. Thus, while appreciative of their unusual situation, they prefer public relations to bombast.

Sights:
To some, the stylistic difference between the two main synagogues says it all. In downtown Geneva, not far from the Old City, The Geneva Synagogue, on Place de la Synagogue at the end of Rue de la Synagogue, is a great Moorish-style structure. Simply decorated with blue-and-white trim and gold-toned stained-glass windows, its encircling arches bespeak solidity.

Hekhal Haness, the Sephardic synagogue, is further from the town center, at 54 ter Route de Malagnou, up an unmarked, almost hidden driveway (to the right of number 56). Consecrated in 1972, it is, with its rose-marble floors; turquoise ark and pulpit coverings; and massive, irregularly tubed glass chandelier, typical of what might be called an American-modern design. Unlike the older synagogue, which is open only for services and by special appointment, Hekhal Haness is always open (telephone 736-96-32).

The Liberal Synagogue, Beit Gil, is at 12 Quai du Seujet, in a contemporary commercial complex (telephone 732-32-45); the Orthodox Machsike Hadass is in rented quarters, at 2 Place des Eaux Vives (telephone 735-22-98).

The buff-colored residential buildings in the upscale nearby neighborhoods of Malagnou, Florissant, and Champel house much of Geneva's Jewish community. In this area are a Jewish bookstore, Librairie Menorah, at 9 Rue de Contamines; and Rue Ernest Bloch, named for the composer.

In the same general direction, just outside Geneva, is the town of Carouge, which, in the 1700s, when it was under the Savoy family, hoped to rival Geneva. Of Italian design, with a shady esplanade for a main street, it was here that the Jews first found residence when they began returning to the region. And east of Carouge lies the village of Veyrier, virtually on the border with France. This is of particular Jewish significance because it is the site of Geneva's current Jewish cemetery—just over the border. When, in the early 1920s, land for a new cemetery was needed, Geneva's laws prohibited the establishment of religious burial grounds within city limits. So the Jews purchased Swiss land for the chapel—which boasts striking stained-glass windows by the Swiss Jew Ruth Heim—and adjoining French land for the gravesites. This situation served some Jewish refugees well during World War II, since they hid in the nearby Haut Savoie mountains of France and slipped through the cemetery to Switzerland at night.

Eclecticism governs Geneva's other sights and sites of appeal to Jews. At the foot of the Old Town, on 2 Terrasse Saint-Victor, stands an 1860s columned, Second Empire-style mansion that has been converted into Geneva's only private modern-art museum. Called Petit Palais, it and the collection it contains are owned by rubber magnate Oscar Ghez de Castelnuovo, a Sudanese Jew whose mother was the daughter of Baron Giscomo di Castelnuovo, physician to King Victor Emmanuel II of Italy. The collection, parts of which often travel, covers most major modern periods, while keeping a spotlight on leading Jewish painters of the times. Mané-Katz is represented by, among others works, *Rabbi with Red Beard and Torah*. Along with Cézannes, Gaugins, and Picassos are works by Chaim Soutine and Jules Pascin, as well as Chagall's *Wandering Jew* and *The Rabbi,* and the largest collection extant of Moise Kislings.

In the hilly, cobblestoned Old Town itself runs a narrow street of four- and five-story French-style, cream-colored houses that are now some of Geneva's most fashionable addresses. This is the Rue des Granges, and where it meets Place Grand Mezel is the site of the old ghetto. (In the window of a shop for old manuscripts on the parallel Grand Rue was recently found the envelope of a letter to one Pawel Pokryzywa of Wrocław, Poland, from Menachem Begin.) On the nearby Rue du Soleil Levant stands a sculpture of the prophet Jeremiah by Auguste de Niederhausen, a student of Rodin. In the heart of the Old Town rises the Cathedral of Saint-Pierre, with an attachment on its south side called the Chapel of the Maccabees. Built by and for a Catholic cardinal and dedicated to an early Protestant martyr, it was nevertheless named for the Maccabees after relics, purportedly of the family, were placed there in the fifteenth century.

Not far away, on Rue de Candolle, stands a modern restaurant, Café Landolt, on the site of the turn-of-the-century brasserie formerly frequented by the likes of Lenin, Trotsky, Ferenc Molnár, and Chaim Weizmann. In the park edged by the Rue de Candolle stands a statue, considered one of Geneva's finest sculptures—*David Defeating Goliath*—by the Genevese Jean Chaponniere.

Seen best from the water—on a sightseeing lake cruise that passes famous residences—is the spired, red-brick mansion that is the official residence of Edmond de Rothschild. It is partially visible from the road as well, in the suburb called Pregny-Chambery. En route is the International

Museum of the Red Cross, among whose exhibits is one on the Holocaust. The museum's courtyard is dominated by both a cross and a crescent. In light of the organization's refusal to approve Israel's Magen David Adom as one of its symbols, it is ironic that Henri Dunant, who inspired the organization of the International Committee of the Red Cross in 1863 and the First Geneva Convention in 1864, worked actively for a Jewish homeland.

General Sights: Because it is situated on a lake and two rivers—the Rhone and the Arve—Geneva boasts numerous waterfront views. In nice weather, a promenade from left bank to right (or vice versa), across the Pont du Mont-Blanc, is delightful, as is a water-bound sightseeing excursion. Since Geneva calls itself the "watch capital of the world," a visit to its Clock and Watch Museum is in order. And, since there is no gainsaying Geneva's place on the international political scene, visitors should at least glance at the Palais des Nations, erstwhile home of the League of Nations, now seat of many United Nations offices in Europe.

Culture: The Jewish community sponsors a choir, Choral de la Communauté Israelite de Genève, as well as lectures. It also publishes a monthly newsletter-type brochure. For news, however, it relies on two bilingual publications produced in German-speaking Switzerland—the *Israelitisches Wochenblatt,* a weekly from Zurich; and *Jüdische Rundschau,* from Basel.

Personalities: Apart from those Jews who have stopped in transit, among those Geneva residents—past and present—who have distinguished themselves are Ernest Bloch, the musician; Albert Cohen, some of whose novels in French touched on the Jewish experience (his best-known include *Belle du Seigneur* and *Mangeclous,* from which a film was made); François Brunschwig, first Jewish president of the Geneva Bar Association; Pierre Toledo, owner of the Pharmacie Principale chain; Bruce Rapoport, head of the Inter-Maritime Bank; Jean Halperin, longtime chief of the UN language division in Geneva; Jean Starobinski, a leading literary critic; George Steiner, the critic and writer who teaches comparative literature at the University of Geneva; Jeanne Hersch, the university's first female professor of philosophy; Edmund Safra, of Republic National Bank of New York and Safra Bank; Edmond de Rothschild; and, to much embarrassment, Bernie Cornfeld.

Eating: The Shalom Restaurant on the main shopping street, upstairs at 78 rue du Rhone (telephone 728-90-93) offers ample generic kosher meals, served by waiters worthy of New York's Lower East Side. There's also a pizzeria at 50 Route de Malagnou; and a kosher dairy snack bar operates between noon and 2 P.M. in the community center.

Recommendations: In addition to the Noga Hilton, other Jewish-owned hotels are the Cournavin and the President. Swissair, which flies to Geneva from New York, Boston, Chicago, and Atlanta, remains one of the most pleasant, efficient, reliable and easy-to-deal-with airlines around. Like Geneva itself, it has international-class service with a small-town feeling.

—*Phyllis Ellen Funke*

Gibraltar

Since Gibraltar, the imposing British bastion on the strait connecting the Atlantic and the Mediterranean, is linked to Spain by an isthmus, it is not really an island. But it might as well be.

Given its location (at the southern European extremity, not nine miles from Africa), its status (a Crown Colony, however autonomous, appended to London), its population (a melange of 30,000 mostly Mediterranean peoples), its size (barely two square miles, not all of which is habitable), and its appeal (to Spain, which for fifteen years tried to cow it by sealing its only border), Gibraltar has — and little wonder — developed its own modus vivendi.

It had the advantage of starting from scratch since, after 1704, when England wrested the fortress from Spain, nearly all the Spanish inhabitants left. Apart from the Royal Navy and other garrison members, those repopulating the promontory — forming a city at the "Rock's" base — included Maltese, Genoese, and Jews. They built a society permeated by Mediterranean warmth but regulated by British discipline.

Faced with the periodically besieging Spanish on one side and the seas that inhibited expansion on the other, Gibraltar's new residents learned, for the sake of survival, to accommodate and tolerate. What is more, with no agriculture, and few resources beyond its harbor, Gibraltar became a largely mercantile community in which Jews, present from nearly the beginning, played such an integral part that at one time almost half the shops on Main Street were Jewish owned.

The Jewish presence is pervasive, a situation best illustrated by noting that in the 1970s and 1980s Gibraltar's two highest officials, Chief Minister Sir Joshua Hassan and Mayor Abraham William Serfaty, were Jews. Outside Israel, there is probably no national or colonial entity in the world with such a distinction.

History: Those Jews who headed for the Rock after 1704 were not the first to set foot on Gibraltar. Historians mention some living there in the fourteenth century who issued an appeal for help in ransoming Jews captured by Barbary pirates, and others reportedly used it as a way station in their flight from the Inquisition. But those who came with British rule were Sephardim living, since the Inquisition, in North Africa, Italy, the Netherlands, and England.

At first they confronted a serious obstacle. According to the 1713 Treaty of Utrecht, in which Spain confirmed Britain's possession of the Rock, neither Moors nor Jews could live in Gibraltar under any circumstances. Jews quickly made themselves useful to the British, however, by negotiating with Morocco for goods whenever Spain threatened to, or actually did, cut supply lines. By 1717, there were probably 300 Jews on the Rock, but they lived under the threat of expulsion, and after several token attempts by the British to enforce the treaty's terms, the Jews were, during a moment of British-Spanish détente, evicted.

Had Spain and Britain remained friendly, the Jews would probably have remained barred. But when the Spanish embargoed Gibraltar again and Britain needed help from Morocco, the Moroccan king — who had at least one Jewish confidante — intervened. Morocco, he said, would supply Gibraltar only if it were open to all his subjects, both Moors and Jews. Britain continued trying to dance at two weddings, but by the siege of 1727, during

Solid as the rock: Gibraltar's Jewish presence is old, pervasive, and widely appreciated by residents of the British colony astride the Mediterranean's gate

which the Jews stood fast, it was clear they were in Gibraltar to stay.

They began obtaining property grants, including one for the first officially sanctioned synagogue, Shaar Hashamayim. By 1739, all the family names still prevalent today were present — Hassan, Benady, Serfaty, and Benyunes. By 1753 there were 600 Jews in the enclave, making up one-third of the civilian population. The community included not only the wealthy merchants who dealt with Morocco, but also small traders, shopkeepers, laborers, boatmen, tailors, shoemakers, peddlers, and porters. The largest property owner on Gibraltar also came from their ranks. Isaac Aboab was referred to as "the king of the Jews," both affectionately and otherwise.

Indeed, occasionally, the fine houses of Gibraltar's Jews were targets of resentment, and once, in 1780, they were subjected to a mild pogrom during which doors and windows were broken and the Jewish cemetery desecrated. But, comparatively speaking, Gibraltar's Jews encountered few internal difficulties.

Though the Great Siege of 1779–83 drove some Jews to London, others stayed on, working as privateers or in other defense-related positions. Abraham Hassan so distinguished himself in the army that he was granted land. Later, during the Napoleonic Wars, Aaron Nuñez Cardozo, who enjoyed the friendship of Lord Nelson, discovered a conspiracy that threatened the fortress. He too was granted land in the heart of town, on which he built a grand house that is now the City Hall.

Midway through the nineteenth century, when the Rock was at the pinnacle of its strategic importance, most retail trade was being handled by the 2,000 Jews then living in Gibraltar. They were attending new synagogues formed to handle the overflow, publishing a paper in Ladino, *Cronica Israelita*, and patronizing the theater in numbers sufficient to darken the stage on Friday nights.

Their presence in Gibraltar continued with little interruption until World War II when all civilian residents were evacuated to Madeira, Tangier, and England. After the war, some did not return.

During the war, Gibraltar became a conduit for some refugees escaping from Hitler; later, with the establishment of Israel, it became a staging ground of Moroccan Jews bound for the new state. There has been no great *aliyah* among Gibraltarians, however, and the size of the Jewish community today is about 600.

Community: The Jews of Gibraltar, says James Levy, president of the community, are "integrated but not assimilated." By this he means they live happily and comfortably among other Gibraltarians, work and play with them, yet maintain a decidedly—and overtly—Jewish way of life.

Indeed, the Gibraltar community, almost entirely Sephardic and assertively proud of it, is known for its religious conservatism and cohesiveness. While estimates vary, and range widely, from 20 to 90 percent, a large number of Jewish Gibraltarians are *shomrei mitzvot*. No Jewish shops open on Saturdays or Jewish holidays. Almost every Jew observes *kashrut*, at least at home (using meat imported from the Netherlands and Britain). Many attend daily services. Children wear *kippot* in the streets, and more women than fifty years ago are covering their hair according to strict Orthodox observance. In addition, despite the community's appreciation of new blood, its conversion rules are so strict that it recognizes only those performed in Gibraltar or the United Kingdom, and decidedly not those of Morocco.

Not surprisingly, though, there are chinks in this apparently solid front. With time, there have been intermarriages— enough so that one community member comments, "There are Cohens on Main Street who haven't been Jews for a hundred and fifty years." Meanwhile, another Jewish observer notes that if the Jews do not "cheat" on their diet in Gibraltar, probably a good third do when they get to Spain, not to mention those who ride on Saturdays.

Nevertheless, according to retired Chief Minister Hassan, in Gibraltar each religious group expects others to practice their tradition, which makes it relatively easy to be observant. Jewish officials, for example, are usually asked before official functions what they can eat; such events are carefully set with an eye to religious calendars.

Besides crediting Gibraltar's scant size and deep Jewish roots for this tolerance,

one Jewish businessman thinks that such détente exists because, while the Jews form a minuscule minority, and the Roman Catholics the overwhelming majority, they unite since neither is part of the small Protestant Establishment. From another viewpoint, Gibraltar's Jews can mix yet maintain their Jewishness, because the Sephardim, more than the once-ghettoized Ashkenazim, are used to adapting themselves to their environment.

Gibraltar's little community supports four synagogues, all of which operate on *Shabbat* and holidays, but only one of which is used—on a quarterly rotation basis—for daily services. The leading synagogue, from which the entire community is addressed, is Shaar Hashamayim. A small synagogue for children has also been established in Gibraltar's Jewish school, with services conducted by the students. And, in all, "God Save the Queen" is sung, in Hebrew, on holidays.

The community also maintains a club, an old-age home, and various social service operations, taking pride in its ability to look after its own.

While it has no spectacularly rich members, the community is reasonably prosperous, with about 20 percent of Main Street's establishments still in its hands. This represents a recent decline, since some shopkeepers have sold to incoming Indians, and more in the current generation are pursuing professional careers instead. Gibraltarian Jews, though, are involved in all fields— from police work to surveying. And they live all over Gibraltar, if for no other reason than that housing is so scarce.

For all its remoteness, insularity, and inbreeding—it seems as if everyone is related to everyone else—and for all the pettiness this engenders, James Levy asserts that the community is healthy. Furthermore, though the community has been static for some years, Levy now sees renewed growth, as young couples have larger families and expatriates return.

The return stems largely from the opening of the Spanish border. Once cause for concern—lest young people spend their weekends "over there" and undesirable elements (that is, terrorists) enter—the revived freedom of movement is now viewed as a positive factor that could lead to contact with other communities. In fact, the primary worry of Gibraltarian Jews today seems to be the loss of status they may suffer now that Sir Joshua is no longer in office and the problems the public wearing of *kippot* could cause—since this, in some eyes, underscores their difference from the rest of the population.

Personalities: The most outstanding Jew in Gibraltar is still Sir Joshua, who was first elected mayor in 1945 and went on to win reelections in all but one term until his recent retirement. In 1964, he was chosen chief minister and, as such, pleaded Gibraltar's case for remaining British before the United Nations. The late Abraham Serfaty followed him to the mayoralty in 1979. Solomon Seruya, a Main Street proprietor, divides his time these days between Gibraltar and Jerusalem, where he is vice president of the Sephardic Council and where, in 1976, he was appointed Israel's ambassador to the Philippines. Samuel Benady is the head of the Gibraltar Bar.

Sights: Though Gibraltar may be a ministate—with no one of its attractions more than minutes from the other—it has managed to cram a fair number of sights into a small area. Its four synagogues, in fact, exist on the very fringes of the bustling Main Street area.

Of prime interest is Shaar Hashamayim, behind an unprepossessing wall at 47–49 Engineer Lane. As Gibraltar's principal Jewish place of worship, the synagogue is known both as the Esnoga Grande (Great Synagogue) and the Cathedral Synagogue. The congregation generally dates its founding to 1724 and claims to be the oldest such Sephardi institution in Europe after the Portuguese Synagogue in Amsterdam and Bevis Marks in London.

Originally, the synagogue property was entered from a road that juts off Engineer Lane at a right angle, running past the red-and-white wall of Macs Corner, a restaurant. Once called Synagogue Lane, this curving way is now Serfaty's Passage, one of several streets named for Jews. (Among others are Benzimra's Alley, Serruya Ramp, Abecasis's Passage and Benoliel's

Passage—where the houses of the namesakes once stood.)

When a storm destroyed the first Shaar Hashamayim in 1766, adjacent land was purchased for the construction of a larger, more elegant edifice. The synagogue, entered today from Engineer Lane through an elaborately decorated tiled courtyard, is quietly dignified, with its marble pillars, its traditional central pulpit, and its mahogany trim for the walls, the ark, and the gracefully carved pews—all accentuated by an impressive collection of silver lanterns.

Gibraltar's largest synagogue, however—and its only free-standing one—is Nefusot Yehuda, a three-hundred-seat structure towering above a beige stucco wall on a corner plot at 65 Line Wall Road. Built for a congregation established around the start of the nineteenth century, Nefusot Yehuda exhibits a Moorish influence, its galleries and walls covered with intricate arabesques. It also boasts ornate chandeliers and Torah crowns.

Discreetly located behind a brown door in a gray wall, next to a Barclays Bank and opposite the police station, is the little second-floor synagogue Etz Hayim, at 91 Irish Town. Opened for prayers in 1759, it is Gibraltar's oldest extant Jewish worship hall; even before then, though, it was a *yeshivah*.

Gibraltar's newest—and smallest—synagogue is Abudarham, its name in gold letters on a black door on the alley-like Parliament Lane at Number 20. The red-carpeted, wood-paneled sanctuary is illuminated by numerous chandeliers and oil lamps suspended from the ceiling.

Etz Hayim and Abudarham can be entered only during services. Arrangements can be made to view the two larger synagogues in off hours, however, by contacting Mrs. Esther Benady, secretary of the Jewish Community, mornings at 72606 (fax 40487). The phone rings in the Jewish Community offices at 10 Bomb House Lane, the address, as well, for the Jewish school and *mikveh*. Across the street, at 7 Bomb House Lane, is the Jewish Club, with rooms for cardplaying and a kosher restaurant which tourists can use.

The kosher bakery, a pink stucco building with "Chalah" written in blue letters above "Croissants," stands near Nefusot Yehuda on Line Wall Road, while the kosher butcher is located just off John Mackintosh Square, next to the Bacchus Restaurant, in the heart of town.

The square is bordered on one side by the massive white City Hall, once Aaron Cardozo's home. And, opposite, at the Main Street side of the square, stands the House of Assembly. In its central passageway — called here the lobby — is a sculptured wall plaque honoring Gibraltar's World War I dead. Its list of names is headed by a medallion of a Jewish soldier, "Lieut. S. Benzecry," and a notation calling him "The Hero of Bourlon Wood."

Away from the town center, where Line Wall Road elbows around to the city walls, is the Jewish old-age home. The eight-room institution, named for the benefactor who provided homes for all faiths, is called the Mackintosh Jewish Home.

Much farther out of town, halfway up the Rock, is the area known as Jews' Gate, in honor of the gate that once stood there leading to the old — and still extant — Jewish cemetery.

General Sights: Though Jews' Gate can be reached from the midstation of the cable car up the 1,398-foot Rock, it is, perhaps, better visited by car, on a tour that includes the stalactites and stalagmites of St. Michael's caves, the tunnels of the gun emplacements, and of course the entrancingly playful Barbary apes of the Rock. (With luck, from there one will see a plane land on Gibraltar's east-west runway, which completely crosses the isthmus and extends into the sea, running right over the main road into town.)

But for most, the chief attraction of Gibraltar is Main Street's shopping, where, though it no longer enjoys free-port status, bargains still can be found. Among the prominent Jewish-owned shops here are Cohen & Massia's (jewelry, watches), S. M. Seruya Ltd. (jewelry, perfumes), Bena-

mor's (luggage), Princess Silks (fabrics), Janine (boutique), Teo (clothing), Attias (toys), and Benzaquen (antiques).

Day Trips: With the Spanish frontier now open, the entire Costa del Sol and even Granada are within a day's reach of Gibraltar. Here and there along the coast are signs of a renewed Jewish presence in Spain, primarily exhibited in shop names, occasionally accompanied by a *Magen David*. In Marbella, Torremolinos, and Málaga, there are synagogues. In addition, in the garden of Alcazaba Castle in the heart of Málaga, stands — his head bowed in contemplation, his cloak pocked by the weather — a statue of Ibn Gabirol, the poet-philosopher born there in 1021.

Recommendation: The Rock Hotel, just beyond town, defines "luxury" in rather Spartan terms, but offers acceptable accommodation, and vegetarian or fish diets if desired.

Reading: Among the fiction set in Gibraltar are Paul Gallico's *Scruffy* (Doubleday), about one of Gibraltar's apes; John Masters's historical novel *The Rock* (Putnam); John D. Stewart's *Gibraltar: The Keystone* (Murray); and Warren Tute's *The Rock* (Ballantine). For factual works on Gibraltar's history, look for the books of local author George Palao and *Gibraltar: The History of a Fortress* (Harcourt Brace Jovanovich) by E. Bradford. The Gibraltar Bookshop, at 300 Main Street, managed by Anita Benady, stocks many of these volumes. Her brother, Mesod "Tito" Benady, wrote the pamphlet, "The Settlement of Jews in Gibraltar, 1704–1783," as well as the popular *Guide-book to Gibraltar*. When it comes to getting around the rock, it's one of the local Jews who wrote the book.

—Phyllis Ellen Funke

Glasgow

Glasgow's is surely the only Jewish community in which young men were encouraged to wear skirts. Until recently the plaid minikilts—which predated the similar American fashion—were part of the traditional regalia worn by members of the city's Jewish Lads and Girls Brigade, complete with bagpipes and drums. One of the numbers in the brigade's repertoire was a rather tinny version of *Hatikvah*; Israel's national anthem is written in a minor key, which bagpipes cannot produce.

The bagpipe band is a thing of the past (though the Jewish Lads and Girls Brigade still exists) but it signifies something that is still true. Glasgow's Jews—who comprise the majority of Scotland's Jewish community—are well-integrated and accepted in their city.

Although the port city of Dundee once had a thriving community of a few hundred, the number has dwindled. Only a few Jews live in Aberdeen and in smaller communities in the Highlands. Edinburgh's Jewry has become consolidated into one synagogue, accommodating about 600 members. And while it still has well-attended *Shabbat* services and a popular Jewish literary society, the bulk of Scotland's Jewish life is concentrated an hour's drive to the west—in Glasgow.

Glasgow is a big, brawny city of over 1 million, currently experiencing the transition from industrial town to twenty-first-century metropolis. With many of its industries overwhelmed by Asian competitors, the city has suffered in recent years from high unemployment, crime, ugly slums, and vast jerry-built housing projects.

But Glasgow is determined to overcome these problems and has begun making noble efforts to do so. Visitors are immediately struck by a cheery bustle of activity as Glaswegians enjoy their downtown pedestrian shopping malls, the most extensive park system of any city in Great Britain, and an enviable cultural life that includes several orchestras and theaters, a half-dozen intriguing museums, two growing universities, the annual Mayfest arts festival, and an annual garden festival that attracts international participation.

At the same time, the city has begun assiduously steam cleaning its many monumental Victorian public buildings and houses, putting a bright face on numerous architectural treasures from a richer, more confident era. In addition, the worst of the high-rise housing projects erected in the 1960s have been recognized for the aesthetic and social errors they were, and are being torn down. To support these metropolitan improvements, the city is making a vigorous push to establish new, science-based industries.

In short, evidence abounds of a renewal of the fierce Scottish doggedness, pride, and ingenuity that 150 years ago turned this small fishing port on the Clyde River into one of the richest centers of the industrial revolution. And Glasgow's Jewish community is very much involved in every aspect of the city's renaissance.

History: The history of Scottish Jewry is surprisingly brief—and, in the main, surprisingly happy. Prior to 1800, few Jews were known to have ever crossed beyond Hadrian's Wall, the ancient barrier between England and Scotland erected by the Romans to keep out warrior clans from the north. There are records of applications from individual Jews for trading and residence permits in Scotland from as far back as 1680, but the first community wasn't formed until 1816, in Edinburgh. Glasgow's Jewish community got its start seven years later and quickly overtook Edinburgh's in size.

The community grew slowly during the nineteenth century and Glasgow had about 60 Jewish families in 1858. By the time the Garnethill Synagogue was built in 1879, the city's Jewish population had grown to 700. It was two years after the opening of the Garnethill Synagogue that the pogroms began in Russia and Eastern Europe that would drive so many Jews west. Though most headed for America, several thousand settled in Great Britain. Some wandered up to Scotland from England, while others were transported directly to Glasgow, Dundee, or Aberdeen.

Many immigrants viewed Scotland as merely a transit point on their journeys to North America; others, according to legend, were told by ship captains that these English-speaking ports of call were in fact New York, and advised to disembark before the ship turned back to the Baltic or the Black Sea.

Whatever the reasons for their arrival, a number of hardy individuals found Scotland's northern climate and landscape pleasantly reminiscent of Lithuania or Estonia — and they found the population congenial. The Scots were usually serious, businesslike, and ambitious and, like the Jewish settlers, had a long tradition of valuing education. Most of all, they were fairminded and unprejudiced. While there was a history of Protestant–Catholic conflict, the Scots harbored no ill feelings toward Jews.

The newcomers found this environment appealing. Some headed for the Highlands as *trebblers* (travelers, or peddlers, in the quaint Scots-Yiddish dialect that soon developed). Because the rural areas were poor and thinly populated, however, the majority moved to the cities. There they were delighted to find a booming British Empire economy and numerous opportunities — including education at the universities — open to all.

Many Jewish immigrants initially labored as tailors, cobblers, or small merchants, largely clustered in the notorious Glasgow slum known as the Gorbals. But Scottish Jewry was generally quicker to escape poverty than the Jews who settled on New York's Lower East Side. By the 1920s, Jews were well represented in Scotland's professional, academic, and business communities (including the Scotch whisky industry). Jews became especially prominent in faculties of medicine. Indeed, many Jews denied entrance to medical schools in the United States because of quotas were soon finding places in the renowned medical schools in Glasgow and Edinburgh.

Personalities: Diverse Jewish personalities have risen to national prominence in Scotland. Sir Ian Bloch was a leading distiller and philanthropist; though best known as a pioneering chemist, Sir Ian Morris Heilbron was the first director of research for Britain's brewing industry; Sir Isaac Wolfson was a retail magnate whose philanthropy made his name a household word in Israel. Also from Glasgow are labor leader and parliamentarian Sir Emanuel Shinwell (who died in 1986 at the age of 101), writer Chaim Bermant and sculptor Benno Schotz. From nearby Edinburgh came Jeremy Isaacs, founding director of Britain's Independent Television and now head of London's Royal Opera Society; Malcolm Rifkind, who has served as Margaret Thatcher's secretary for Scotland and John Major's defense secretary; and literary critic David Daiches. Also living in Scotland, in the village of Trossachs, is the American-born writer Israel Shenker. Scotland has two Jewish sheriffs (as lower court judges are known) — Gerald Gordon in Glasgow and Hazel Cosgrove in Edinburgh. It was two Jews who probably did more than anyone to put Scotland in the modern American consciousness. A good many travelers to Scotland are, on some level or another, searching for the *Brigadoon* created by Alan Jay Lerner and Frederick Loewe.

Community: Glasgow Jewry numbers around 7,000; the figure is uncertain because the community is shrinking owing to intermarriage and migration to England (mainly to Manchester and London), Israel, or the United States. Nevertheless, those who remain in Glasgow do their best to promote a lively Jewish life.

Glasgow's oldest and most handsome synagogue stands atop Garnet Street near the city center. The Garnethill Synagogue was built in 1879 to serve congregants who were mostly from comfortable German and Polish backgrounds. Among the waves of later — and much poorer — immigrants from Lithuania and elsewhere in Eastern Europe, it was known as the *Anglische Schul,* or the English synagogue, reflecting the congregation's prosperous, well-established, and British character (top hats, no doubt, were common there).

Today, with the bulk of Glasgow's Jewish community living in the suburbs, the midtown Garnethill functions largely as a museum. This was acknowledged recently when the community's archives were set up as a permanent exhibit in the synagogue. Yet Garnethill still serves as a major gathering point on holidays and for many of the community's social and cultural events.

Most of the religious and community life has shifted several miles to the south, since the Jewish population today is found almost entirely across the Clyde River, in such neighborhoods as Clarkston, Giffnock, and Newton Mearns. South of the river there is one Reform congregation — the New Synagogue, at 147 Ayr Road. The half-dozen Orthodox synagogues in the area range widely in their degree of Orthodoxy, with most comparable to American Conservative congregations, except for the separation of men and women during services. The largest of these congregations is the Giffnock and Newlands Synagogue, on Maryville Avenue.

The Glasgow Jewish Representative Council building, which houses the community and social center and Jewish Welfare Board office, is at 49 Coplaw Street (telephone 423-8917). The Glasgow edition of the Manchester-based *Jewish Telegraph* has offices at 43 Queen Square; look in the paper or call the office (423-9200) for information about synagogue services or community events.

Glasgow also boasts a Jewish golf and country club, Bonnyton, which was founded in 1920. Anti-Semitism, rare as it was, did have a foothold in certain bastions of Scotland's national sport. Ironically, the Jewish club became so desirable that non-Jews sought to join it, and today the membership is roughly half Jewish.

Eating: Freed's Kosher Restaurant is located in the Jewish Welfare Centre (in the same building as the Glasgow Jewish Representative Council) at 49 Coplaw Street (open Sunday to Thursday). There is a kosher dairy restaurant at the Glasgow Maccabi Centre at May Terrace in Giffnock. Kosher food products can also be found at delicatessens in the Jewish neighborhoods, and the city has numerous natural food and vegetarian Indian restaurants. Most Glaswegians agree that the finest vegetarian dining spot in Scotland is Hendersons, at 94 Hanover Street in Edinburgh (telephone 225-4991). Jewish favorites among the region's Indian vegetarian restaurants are Ashoka Vegetarian in Glasgow and Kalpna in Edinburgh.

Sights: Because Glasgow's Jewish history is so brief, and with the Gorbals slum having been completely erased, there is really no Jewish landmark other than the Garnethill Synagogue — an imposing three-story red-brick building at 125–127 Hill Street. The interior features polished woodwork, a wood-paneled arched ceiling, elaborate brass light fixtures, traditional stained-glass windows and a carved wood ark with the oriental or Ottoman dome motif so popular in European synagogues built in the latter half of the nineteenth century.

More contemporary contributions to Glasgow's Jewish aesthetics are the stained-glass windows of the Queens Park Synagogue, on Falloch Road. Completed in 1990 by the Scottish stained-glass artist John Clark, the twenty-two windows depict a variety of Jewish themes. The windows on the north and south walls of the building show the festivals of the Jewish calendar; the large west wall window features *Shabbat;* the window above the ark on the east wall symbolizes the Creation and the giving of the Torah.

The work of Benno Schotz, who is generally acknowledged as Scotland's greatest sculptor, is displayed at major museums such as the Glasgow Art Gallery and Museum, the University of Glasgow and the Glasgow Art College, where Schotz headed the sculpture department from 1938 to 1960. His public works include stone figures for the central Bank of Scotland building on Sauchiehall Street, and friezes for the churches of St. Matthew, St. Cerfs, and St. Charles. The latter features a sixty-figure depiction of the Stations of the Cross, one of the largest of Schotz's many commissions for the Roman Catholic Church. The best-known of Schotz's work on Jewish subjects (portraits of David Ben Gurion and Theodor Herzl and his Holocaust memorial called *Unto the Hills,* among others*)* are in Jerusalem.

Many of Glasgow's Jews have contributed culturally as board members of such institutions as the Scottish National Orchestra, the Scottish Chamber Orchestra, the Citizens Theatre, and the ballet and opera societies.

General Sights: The most notable art museums are the Kelvingrove, the Hunterian, and the new Burrel Collection, which is set in a large, wooded park. Two other delightful institutions are the People's Palace, which is a museum of everyday Glaswegian life over the past one hundred years, and the Botanical Gardens, adorned with remarkable Victorian glass houses.

Day Trips: Edinburgh is an hour east of Glasgow (even less by train). The famous Edinburgh International Arts Festival takes place during the last three weeks of August. The Edinburgh Hebrew Congregation (4 Salisbury Road) is a more modest building than the Garnethill Synagogue, and it is considerably less ornate, both within and without. Yet the synagogue is large enough to accommodate several hundred people in an open forum configuration in which congregants sit in ranked seating on three sides of the *bimah*. Although the synagogue is nominally Orthodox, there is no upper gallery for women, as there is at Garnethill; men and women sit across from each other,

on opposite sides of the ark. The sanctuary, which is on the building's second floor, features blond wooden paneling and modern carpeting. A separate social hall downstairs is used for lectures and banquets, and can accommodate three hundred to four hundred people.

Scotland is reputed to have more castles per square mile than any other country in Europe; the fortress at Stirling, which is an hour's drive north of Glasgow, is one of the finest. Loch Lomond is a beautiful lake about a half-hour's drive from Glasgow. Two hours away, reachable by car and ferry, lies Dunoon, a picturesque seaside summer resort that in its heyday was to Glasgow's Jews what the Catskills are to New York's.

Reading: Chaim Bermant has set several novels, including *The Patriarch* (Ace), in Glasgow. Ralph Glasser's *Growing up in the Gorbals* (Chatto and Windus, London) is an especially harsh account of Glasgow slum life. Evelyn Cowan presents a more pleasant view in her memoir *Spring Remembered—A Scottish Jewish Childhood* and in her novel *A Portrait of Alice,* both published by Taplinger. Jack Ronder's fictional family saga, *The Lost Tribe* (W. H. Allen, London), tells the story of Jews in Dundee and Edinburgh. *Second City Jewry,* by Kenneth Collins (Scottish Jewish Archives), tells the story of the Jews of Glasgow from 1790 to 1919. Collins's previous book, *Aspects of Scottish Jewry,* is out of print but available in some libraries.

Glasgow has no Jewish bookstore, but Levingstone's bookshop at 55 Sinclair Drive carries a small stock of Jewish books. Some are sure to give you greater insight into the contemporary Jewish community—and the history of the boys in kilts.

—*Lev Bearfield*

Haifa

Haifa residents will joke that the best thing about their city is the road to Tel Aviv—but don't think for one moment that they believe it. Haifaites are exceptionally proud of their home, and believe wholeheartedly that they live in Israel's most beautiful city. White and busy on the slopes of the Carmel, encircling a purple saucer of Mediterranean, Haifa has been compared with Naples and San Francisco, but—in the eyes of the faithful—it easily surpasses them both.

A heterogeneous community of 280,000 people, Haifa is Israel's third-largest city, its primary port, and the administrative and commercial center of the country's northern region. It is a town of tree-lined streets, shady parks, flower-decked gardens, beaches, hills, museums, theaters and concert halls, which nevertheless supports Israel's heaviest industries, its best engineering institutes and its most sophisticated high-technology plants.

Its staunch, sturdy architecture, its factories, oil refineries, foundries and blast furnaces impose themselves on the incomparable views of Haifa's bay and suburbs, giving the town a solid-as-a-rock atmosphere—and capturing the spirit of a hardworking community imbued with rock-solid values.

History: In 1898, when Theodor Herzl sailed past Haifa Bay, today's huge port area was still a tangled marsh, with Bedouins encamped on nearby sand dunes, grazing their flocks on the Carmel hills above. Herzl, however, saw Haifa with the eyes of the future. In *Altneuland* he described with uncanny accuracy the city he envisioned, in which "huge liners rode at anchor [in the bay]. . . . At the top of the mountain there were thousands of white homes and the mountain itself was crowned with imposing villas. . . . A beautiful city had been built close to the deep blue sea [and] a serpentine road [led up] Mount Carmel."

Although Haifa began its meteoric growth only in this century, its history is far older. King Solomon and the prophet Isaiah sang the praises of the Carmel. It was in Haifa that Elijah defeated the 450 priests of Baal under Ahab and his wife Jezebel (1 Kings 18:19–40). Modern Haifa can be traced to a small Phoenician port founded on the bay in the 14th century B.C.E., when a Jewish village clung to the northwest peak of Mount Carmel.

Postbiblical Jewish sources are filled with trivia about Haifa. The city is referred to as a fishing village whose people, among other things, could not distinguish between the pronunciation of the guttural letters het and ayin. According to the Talmud, it was off the coast of Haifa that the murex, the shellfish that produced the purple dye used for the *tallit*, was caught.

In the eleventh century C.E., Haifa was a flourishing Jewish center. Although it was well fortified, the city was sacked during the First Crusade (in 1100), with its Jewish majority and its Egyptian garrison slaughtered. Then, overshadowed by the Crusader towns of Acre to the north and Caesarea to the south, the city slept for nearly eight hundred years.

In 1905, the Turks built the Haifa-Damascus railway, and the city acquired its first real prominence. Its development was spurred by the arrival of East European Zionist idealists around the turn of the century, and confirmed by the British, who took up where the Turks left off. They modernized the port, building an oil pipeline terminus and turning the city into today's center of commerce, shipping, and communications.

Israel's independence in 1948 gave a further boost to Haifa's rapid industrial and residential expansion. Cheap housing was built on the outskirts of the city to accommodate mass immigration. Kiryat Motzkin, the large, bustling suburb on Haifa Bay, built in 1934 and extended in the 1950s, is one example. Haifa's European-born mayor, Abba Khoushy, was anxious to attract Western immigrants to his city, and to this day more than 75 percent of Haifaites are of Western descent.

Community: Although most Haifa residents today are Israeli born, a sense of Europe continues to pervade the city. You hear almost as much German, Russian, and English—British English, not American English, residents hasten to point out—as Hebrew. Haifa drivers are more likely than their bigger-city counterparts to yield to pedestrians and to other cars. In a country of inveterate litterers, Haifa is clean. It is said that Abba Khoushy used to get up at 5 A.M. to check that the street cleaners were doing their job.

The quality of life in Haifa is high, and its orientation is toward work and family. Pleasures are healthy and high-minded; summers are for surfing, the beach, and hiking in the Carmel; winters are for concerts and plays. When the United States Sixth Fleet anchors in Haifa Bay, local prostitutes can't handle the extra trade, and their Tel Aviv colleagues come up to help out. "We're ten years behind Tel Aviv," say Haifaites, and they are proud of it.

Two fundamental attitudes imbue the city: tolerance and the work ethic. The gleaming golden dome of Haifa's Baha'i temple, symbol of unity and brotherhood, announces the city's tolerance. Haifa is also a model of Jewish-Arab coexistence in Israel and of amicable secular-Orthodox relations.

Compromise is the keynote. Jews and Arabs live in the same neighborhoods, and even the same apartment blocks. There are Haifa streets named for Arabs. Haifa's Beit Hagefen is a rare, mixed Arab–Jewish community center whose Arab–Jewish dance troupe performs countrywide. And when an intifada-inspired bomb was thrown in a Haifa mall in August 1988, Haifa's Jews and Arabs hurried to reassure one another that coexistence would prevail.

Religious-secular tension, too, is remarkably absent from the city. Haifa is the only town in the country where there is *Shabbat* bus service, with the buses running undisturbed by the city's ultra-Orthodox residents, who simply close their neighborhoods to traffic. Almost as remarkable for Israel, Haifa has had, unopposed, a school of Reform ideology for more than fifty years: the Leo Baeck school serving more than one thousand pupils.

The work ethic is Haifa's other identifying feature. "In Jerusalem you pray, in Tel Aviv you play, but in Haifa you work," went the old taunt, and with good reason. This workingman's city headquarters the Israel Navy, Zim Shipping Line, Israel Shipyards, Israel Railways, the Israel Electric Company, the giant Solel Boneh contracting company, Haifa Oil Refineries, Haifa Chemicals, and Israel Petrochemicals—but it has had the last laugh on those who sneeringly dubbed it "a bourgeois workers' village." "Red Haifa," the workers' stronghold of the 1950s, has become Israel's "high-tech city" of the 1990s. Elscint medical diagnostics, Elbit computer systems and Fibronics fiber optics are three Haifa high-technology firms with international reputations. The Technion Institute of Science and Technology and the University of Haifa sustained the evolution of Haifa from the city of the stolid laborer to Israel's version of the Silicon Valley.

Sights: Haifa is a triple-decker sandwich. On the first layer, around the bay, are the port and naval base. On the second, halfway up in the mountain, is the commercial center. And on the third, atop Mount Carmel, is the residential and luxury hotel area.

The port drones with industry. Ships load and unload at the 10,000-ton floating dock and the container terminal. The Dagan Grain Discharge Silo, for many years the tallest industrial building in Israel, unloads 480 tons an hour. Oil is pumped ashore, flowing north to the spidery steel webs of the oil refineries.

The strip of land on which the warehouses, port offices, railway lines, and nearby streets stand was reclaimed from the sea. It is now among the seediest areas in Israel, but still worth a visit. Boat tours of the harbor leave from here. The Dagan grain silo has a museum (located in Palmer Square) showing how mankind's oldest industry developed — from the cultivation and handling of grain to its storage and distribution. And the Carmelit, a toylike funicular, will carry you the mile from the port to the top of the Carmel quickly and efficiently. Israel's only subway, the Carmelit, opened in October 1959, with its port area stop named Paris Station to honor its French builders.

Another fast way up the mountain is Haifa's aerial cable car, whose sea-level station is in Bat Galim, further south along the bay. It covers the distance up to the Stella Maris lighthouse in two minutes.

The heart of Haifa is on the middle layer of the sandwich, Hadar Hacarmel — the glory of the Carmel. Here are the shops, restaurants, and hotels, the malls, offices, and business section. The old Technion was the first building here, put up in 1912 and now tucked away behind the main artery, Herzl Street. An Oriental-style edifice, it was built by Germans planning to train Jewish engineers to work for the Turks. But fierce controversy broke out over whether the language of instruction should be Hebrew or German, and the school did not open until 1925. In the intervening years, it became, in turn, a delousing station, a slaughterhouse, and a hospital. It was finally renovated, enlarged to cover eight acres and used as an engineering school, but it rapidly outgrew its premises and was replaced by Technion City on the outskirts of Haifa.

Zionist Avenue (known as United Nations Boulevard until the infamous 1976 United Nations vote equating Zionism with racism) is the scenic route past the Baha'i shrine up to the Haifa sandwich's third layer, the top of the Carmel. A magnificent panorama of Haifa unfolds as the road climbs, with Acre beyond, jutting into the sea, and the white cliffs of Rosh Hanikra visible across the bay. At night, thousands of lights sparkle across the city and on ships at anchor in the harbor.

In the sunlight, the dome of the Baha'i temple glitters with twelve thousand fish-

Bay window: The Baha'i temple sits on Mount Carmel looking over the city and shore

scale tiles, each glazed with gold leaf. The shrine is the burial place of the faith's herald, Mirza Ali Mohammed, called el Bab, who was executed in Persia in 1850 at age 31. His mausoleum, the temple, and its splendid gardens are open to visitors.

Sharing the summit of the Carmel with the Baha'is are a number of five-star hotels (the Dan Carmel and the Dan Panorama are two of the most popular); the Israel navy, which is headquartered at Stella Maris; and a sect of Carmelite monks, whose patron is the prophet Elijah. Their monastery, on the southern Carmel, served as a hospital to Napoleon's army when he besieged Turkish Acre in 1799. Soldiers who died there are buried in front of its entrance, under a monument surmounted by an iron cross. At the foot of the mountain on which the monastery stands, at Cape Carmel, is Elijah's Grotto, where the prophet may have found shelter when he fled the wrath of Ahab.

Faith and science lie at opposite ends in Haifa. On the northern end of the mountain is Haifa University, with its controversial tower rising high against the skyline. Designed by the architect Oscar Niemeyer, it opened in 1963 and houses the Reuben and Edith Hecht Archeological Museum.

Nearby is the modern three hundred-acre Technion City campus, opened in 1954. Designed on the principle of garden development, it has more than fifty buildings, including split-level student dormitories, hydraulic models, and supersonic wind tunnels. Guided tours of the campus are available.

Culture: For a small city, Haifa leads a rich cultural life. Atop the mountain, it has its own symphony orchestra and a Sports Hall for national and international basketball, soccer, and gymnastics, as well as a Municipal Theater at 50 Pevsner Street in Hadar Hacarmel.

Down the street from the theater, the old Technion houses Technoda, the National Museum of Science and Technology, which displays basic scientific and technological principles, as put to use by Israeli industry.

South of Technoda, Herzl Street becomes Shabtai Levi Street and at number 26 it reaches Haifa's new Museum Center. The Center comprises collections of ancient and modern art, ethnology, Jewish folk art, costume, and religious artifacts of Jews from Islamic countries.

At the foot of the Carmel, on Allenby Street, two museums testify to the city's seafaring spirit. The Clandestine Immigration and Naval Museum at number 204, opposite Elijah's Grotto, is a monument to Jewish immigrants trying to run the British blockade. One of their ships, the *Af Al Pi* ("Nevertheless"), stands on the road outside the museum. The other museum is the National Maritime Museum at number 198. Conceived by former naval officer Ben Elie, whose hobby was model ships, the museum explores ancient navigation and the history of harbor towns in the Holy Land.

Personalities: Chava Alberstein, perhaps Israel's most popular singer in the post-1967 generation, grew up in Haifa. Novelist A. B. Yehoshua lives — and has set some of his books — in the city. Throughout history Haifa has also been known for its visitors and temporary residents. Rabbi Nahman of Bratslav spent Rosh Hashanah in 1798 in Haifa. A century later Theodor Herzl arrived at the port for his first visit to Palestine. In the 1930s a young Raoul Wallenberg worked at the Haifa branch of his family's bank.

Reading: Herzl's novel *Altneuland* (Old-New Land, Herzl Press) is rich in Haifa descriptions, actual and fanciful. Shulamith Hareven brings modern Haifa into literature in her *City of Many Days,* and Yehudit Handel locates her *Street of Many Steps* in the city, as well. A. B. Yehoshua's *The Lover* (Doubleday) is set in Haifa at the time of the Yom Kippur War.

General Sights: Haifa is a convenient and pleasant base from which to see all of northern Israel — from the Mediterranean Coast across to the Golan and the Galilee. Closer by are a number of sights that are well worth the half-day trip. The walled Crusader town of Acre, with its eighteenth-century fortress and citadel, fifteen miles north of Haifa along the bay, is evocative and picturesque. Part of the prison has been turned into a museum honoring the underground heroes who were jailed there under the British before independence.

North of Acre on the Nahariya road is Kibbutz Lohamei Hagettaot, home of the Ghetto Fighters Museum of the Holocaust and Jewish resistance.

Beit Shearim, thirteen miles southeast toward Nazareth, was the second-century seat of the Sanhedrin and the necropolis of Jews from all over the world in the third and fourth centuries. Two Druze villages, Daliyat el-Carmel and Isfiya, served by the number 92 bus from Haifa, welcome visitors. Ein Hod, an artists' village fourteen miles south of Haifa, has a gallery, a restaurant, and occasional concerts and plays.

Haifa isn't served by international air carriers. You can fly, drive, or take the train from Tel Aviv. Looking a bit toward the past, the only way to make Haifa your first stop in Israel is by ship. Like the values and tangibles the city has achieved, you have to work a bit to get there.

— Wendy Elliman

Helsinki

They tell several versions of the same story. One goes as follows: During World War II, Finland, having just lost 10 percent of its territory to Russia in the Winter War, became an ally of Germany. Although Germany did not occupy Finland and its troops did not officially operate side by side, German units were stationed in the northern part of the country where they sometimes required aid from the Finns.

And so it came to pass that troops under the command of Finnish army captain Solomon Klass were called to the rescue of some Germans. After they had successfully completed their mission, the German commander came to extend his thanks. The Finnish officer responded in German. "How come you speak German?" wondered the Reich's representative. "Because," said Klass, "I am Jewish and my mother spoke Yiddish."

With that the German grew pale, clicked his heels, gave the Heil Hitler salute and left. Klass received the Iron Cross for his efforts but never wore it.

This tale well illustrates both the anomalous position of Finland's Jews and the anomalous position of Finland itself.

Although the national roots of this Nordic country extend back for centuries, Finland, having been a possession first of Sweden and then of Russia, gained its independence only in 1917. And still feeling in a precarious position, especially vis-à-vis the "Great Bear" on its border, this extremely homogeneous society, despite its apparent alignment with the West, assiduously maintained political neutrality.

It is only in the last few years that the thousand-odd Jews of Finland, today well integrated into this prosperous modern society, feel that they, like many other Finns, are no longer "living on the edge." With the end of communism in the former Soviet Union the edge has changed. But it is still the edge.

History: Since Finland was for so long a part of Sweden, which had restricted Jewish settlement, Jews have lived in Finland officially for only about 150 years. They did come, even during Swedish domination in the eighteenth century, as traders, interpreters and Finland's first foreign-language teachers. But if they chose to stay they had to convert — an event warmly celebrated by the Lutheran church. From the names, some believe that a number of leading Finns are descended from these Jews; one was Zacharias Topelius, a nine-teenth-century writer known as "the Hans Christian Andersen of Finland." But since they were and remain unaware of their ancestry, these early connections have been lost.

It took the Russian conquest in 1809 to give Finland its first recorded Jewish citizens. They came as cantonists, Jewish children conscripted into the czar's army, to serve in the far reaches of empire. Boys from the Pale of Settlement were taken from their families at age twelve — though many were younger — and educated harshly in cantonments until they were of army age. They were then expected to serve twenty-five years, during which authorities hoped they would be alienated from family and faith.

Those sent to Finland were garrisoned in Helsinki, which the Russians made the capital in 1812; in Turku, the capital under the Swedes; and in Vyborg, now in Russia. In the Turku castle and in the fortress of Suomenlinna, which guards Helsinki harbor, rooms were designated for use by the Jewish soldiers, probably for prayer. The first *minyan* in Finland is believed to have been formed around 1830.

In 1858, the czar proclaimed that cantonists finishing their service could remain where they were with their wives and children. Most Russians went home; most Jews stayed.

At first, the Jews were not welcomed by the Finns, though over the next fifty years the positions of the Russian and Finnish authorities would be roughly reversed. Finnish authorities imposed a variety of restrictions limiting the Jews' place of residence and freedom of movement and occupation. Virtually the only work Jews could do was deal in old clothes. From this *shmatah* business grew contemporary Finland's textile industry.

Despite government constraints the Jews managed to establish themselves. Unlike Jewish settlers in other Nordic countries (most of whom had more cultured backgrounds), many Jews in Finland landed there because they had been their families' least promising son. But they managed — bringing in relatives, friends, and mail-order brides; starting businesses when they could get municipal clerks to look the other way.

By the 1870s, proponents of Jewish civil rights could be found in the Finnish Parliament, the intelligentsia, and the upper class, with the strongest opposition coming from the clergy, farmers, and trade unions.

Russian Zionists decided to hold their 1906 convention in Helsinki because restrictions on meetings and free speech were much tighter in Russia proper. The Finnish Parliament finally voted by an overwhelming majority to abolish restrictions against Jews in 1909. But Russia never ratified the law and Jews did not get full civil rights until Finland won independence eight years later.

Polish refugees from World War I and Russians escaping the Bolshevik revolution swelled Finnish Jewish ranks to 1,600 by the 1920s. Given the new freedoms, Jews — often adopting Finnishized Hebrew surnames — fully integrated and entered many walks of life: medicine, law, industry, and academia. Then in November 1939 came the 100-day war with Russia followed by World War II.

Finns emphasize that their military involvement with Germany was pragmatic and that further Russian victories would have been disastrous for them. Finnish Jews did not oppose this position. About 110 served in the Winter War and 200 more served later, a few as officers. Given all that is known today, however, they are ambivalent about their wartime situation.

Under German pressure to deport Jews — Himmler himself reportedly brought a list of 2,000 names — Finnish authorities at one point turned over 50 of the several hundred Austrian and Baltic refugees they were harboring. But when it was learned that the first 8 deportees had landed in a concentration camp, the Finns refused further cooperation.

Responsibility for the deportation was never officially determined, but Field Marshal Carl Gustav Mannerheim, who was in charge, attended Jewish community memorial services during the war. Meanwhile, Sabbath services — conducted by Isak Smolar in what came to be called "Schulka's Schul," were held at the Finnish front lines.

Three years after the end of World War II, 29 Finnish Jews left to fight for Israel's independence. They were followed by nearly 300 others who made *aliyah* during the 1950s and 1960s.

Because of Soviet politics, official Finnish enthusiasm for Israel cooled following the 1967 war — particularly since the Finns represented the Soviet Union's interests in Israel. Helsinki subsequently hosted the first talks on restoring Russian-Israeli relations and became an important transit point for Soviet Jews emigrating to Israel.

Fanned by its affinity for another small country bordered by enemies, Finnish popular support for Israel never flagged. So many Finns have served as volunteers at Kibbutz Kiryat Anavim, outside Jerusalem, that residents sometimes refer to the place as Kiryat Finland. Support for Israel has always been abetted by Finland's religious Christian fundamentalists, including about 1,000 believers who observe *kashrut* and *Shabbat*. Finland's Israel Friendship Committee, composed of Jewish and Christian groups that look to Israel for inspiration, works for the Jewish state's well-being. It is not unusual to see the Finnish flag — white with a blue Nordic cross — juxtaposed with the exactly color-matched Israeli one.

Community: Living in a world where the sun sometimes barely sets and sometimes barely rises immediately confers a certain distinction on Finland's Jewish community, since special consideration must be given to determining *Shabbat* and holiday observances. With both of Finland's synagogues—in Helsinki and Turku—below the Arctic Circle where there is always some difference between day and night, *Shabbat* can begin any time before sundown. Candle lighting is arbitrarily set for 8:45 P.M. in summer, with *Havdalah* at 1:05 A.M. Sunday in early July. The real problem comes in winter, when Friday night services start around 3 P.M. Above the Arctic Circle, with periods of unending day and night, the issue remains moot. While visitors are advised to follow local custom, the few Jews living in "midnight sun" areas are not observant.

Theoretically it's possible to be a fully observant Jew in Finland today. Unlike in Sweden and Norway, *shechitah* (ritual slaughter) is permitted. In the absence of a *shochet* today's kosher meat comes from Denmark, but Helsinki has a kosher butcher. With a week's notice you can order kosher meals through the community. For all community-related inquiries, call 692-1297 or 694-1302.

And though Finland has no rabbi now, there is a *minyan* every morning in Helsinki—and with notice one can be arranged in Turku. But of the 850 Jews in Helsinki, 150 in Turku, and about 100 scattered elsewhere (with a handful in Tampere, to which all Vyborg's Jews evacuated when Russia took the city during the war), no more than 10 percent observe more than the major holidays.

Nevertheless most of these middle-class Jews pay the 1.5 percent community tax that supports religiously affiliated activity. The community maintains a headquarters in Helsinki, an old-age home, and a day school (through grade nine) attended by most of Helsinki's Jewish children, including virtually all children with at least one Jewish parent.

In addition there are various cultural, service, and athletic organizations including a Hebrew Club, a Tradition Circle, and a Judaica Club, which presents visiting lecturers on Jewish subjects about once a month, usually in English. An information bulletin, *Hakehilah,* is published six times a year. A choir, Hazamir, which performs Hebrew and Yiddish songs regularly at festivals and interfaith gatherings, has recorded *Folk Songs in Yiddish* ("Jiddishinkielisia Kansanlauluja"), available in larger record stores in Finland.

Finland's Maccabi, formed in 1906, is said to be the oldest sports club in Europe. Its winter camp is held in the same place as that of Finland's Islamic community's, whose largely Turkish membership—also a tiny minority with a similar local history—is compatible with the Jews. In fact, the Jewish and Islamic football teams play an annual friendship match.

Finland's tight immigration law is one factor that keeps its Jewish community small. Consequently, many Jews intermarry—though often with spouses converting to Judaism. Some who made *aliyah* have returned, while about 100 Israelis and some Russians have entered the country through marriage. Finnish Jews have been especially active in nurturing Jewish life among their more numerous fellows in Estonia, and this role, some community leaders feel, has given the Finnish community a renewed sense of purpose.

Sights: Because it was designed by Carl Ludvig Engel, who also planned St. Petersburg, Helsinki—at least until recently—has been a stand-in for Russia in such films as *Reds, White Nights,* and *Gorky Park.* (As has the rest of Finland: remember the birches and snow fields of *Dr. Zhivago?*) Hard bound by the Baltic, it has been called a "city of light" more for its fair coloration and open, airy layout than its winter frostiness.

One of the warm-weather joys is a stroll down the broad, shaded Esplanade to the lively open marketplace and the big, bustling harbor. Boats leave regularly, running past a few skerries, to the sprawling island fortress of Suomenlinna, where Helsinki's first Jews were garrisoned. Jews once peddled their rags at various spots on and near the harbor, most notably on waterfront land now occupied by the President's Palace, and on the site of the massive Bank of Finland building on Snellmaninkatu. Nearby, at Senate Square, rises the Lutheran cathedral, with the Hebrew name for God chiseled over the western entrance and on the eastern wall.

In a neighborhood known for its diplomatic residences stands the Slavonic Library of Helsinki University. Located at Neitsytpolku 1b, it boasts a unique collection of Jewish publications. Because a law decreed that everything published in Russia be sent to Finland, it houses nineteenth- and early twentieth-century Jewish publications, including encyclopedias, magazines, almanacs and music—in Russian.

On the wall of the head office of the Post Bank on Kaivokatu, opposite Helsinki's central railroad station, is a modernistic mural featuring blues, oranges, and horizontal and vertical lines. It was painted by the noted Finnish Jewish artist Sam Vanni.

In the Forum shopping center and other locations are branches of the leading department store chain, Pukeva. Owned by the Jaari family, it is the largest Jewish firm in Finland. Fashionable Jewish-owned fur shops are at Unioninkatu 27, Eerikinkatu 4 and Mikonkatu 3.

In a waterfront area near the Hakaniemi Market, where the Strand Intercontinental Hotel (not to be confused with the "plain" Intercontinental) now stands, is the site of Helsinki's first synagogue. It existed until the early 1900s, when plans were drawn up for the current synagogue near the city's commercial center.

The city of Helsinki donated the land for the new structure at Malminkatu 26. The synagogue, designed by the Finnish architect Jac Ahrenberg and built in 1906, is a white fenced-in structure topped by a Byzantine-like cupola. Three two-story arched windows are flanked by rows of circular windows. The interior, decorated with an old Hebrew-lettered clock, a multilevel chandelier, and elaborate lions of Judah holding the Ten Commandments over the ark enclosure, seats six hundred in wooden, straight-backed pews around a central *bimah.*

Attached is the community center built in 1967, with classrooms, club rooms, and old-age facilities. Here you can see the wreath presented to the community in 1944 by Field Marshal Mannerheim, as well as the architect's drawings for the synagogue and other community memorabilia. A sculpture by Harri Kivijarvi and Sam Vanni commemorates World War II's martyrs.

While there are no Jewish neighborhoods in Helsinki today, some small cottages where Jews once lived and worked are located in the area of the bus station at the nearby intersection of Annankatu and Simonkatu.

Side Trip: Turku, Finland's oldest city, is two hours by train west of Helsinki. Though ravaged by fire in 1827, as a port with a lengthy tradition it boasts the charm of continuity. It was a priest working among the troops in the worthy old Turku castle who wrote that the Jewish soldiers had the right to use two rooms for services, suggesting the presence of women. The first Jew native to Turku, Abraham Jankel Klimscheffski, was born in the fortress in 1859.

Another impressive medieval structure is the cathedral where Jews arriving in Swedish times were converted. Just behind the cathedral, also in the heart of old Turku, are two libraries of interest to Jews. A yellow building at the Faculty of Theology of the Swedish Academy houses a Judaica Library of religious books. And opposite is a white structure, built before the fire, containing the Donner Institution's library of Jewish philosophy and history.

During the 1880s and 1890s, 95 percent of Turku's Jews clustered in ghetto-like fashion along Lantinen Pitkakatu—Western Long Street—using an area at road's end (where it now curves at Aninkaisten silta) as a marketplace. A rented room served as a synagogue until, in 1912, a proper one opened nearby at Brahenkatu 17, on land donated by the city. The two-story, domed, gold-with-ivory-trim structure effectively mixes Byzantine and Art Nouveau styles. The main prayer hall upstairs, now white with blue accents, has Art Nouveau–decorated pillars and pews. Exhibited downstairs are a rare Talmud printed in Vilna in 1885; photos of the committee that built the synagogue and early Finnish Zionists; a scroll listing the twenty-three Finnish Jews killed in World War I; and an award from Mannerheim to mothers who lost sons. Old-timers recall well-attended wartime services conducted as German troops marched by without disturbing them. An adjacent community house was built in 1956. (Visits are by appointment; call 312-557.)

Within easy walking distance along Kritinankatu in a more commercial area are a number of well-frequented dry goods stores owned by Jews. And at Linnankatu 17 is Dennis's Pizzeria owned by Dennis Rafkin, whose pizzas, now in Finnish supermarkets, have a reputation as the best readymade pies in the country.

Among Turku's general sights are the Sibelius Museum, the Handicrafts Museum — in a few wooden houses that withstood the fire — and the quaint nearby town of Naantali, reached both by land and boat through a bit of Finland's archipelago.

Personalities: The best-known Finnish-born Jews are Max Jakobson, Finland's ambassador to United Nations from 1965 to 1972 (a one-time candidate for secretary-general whose bid was allegedly blocked by the Soviets); and Max Dimont, author of *Jews, God and History*. On Finland's political scene is Ben Zyskowicz, who in 1979 (at the age of twenty-four) became the first Jewish member of the Finnish Parliament; he chaired the legal committee dealing with constitutional revision.

Jewish artists include painter Sam Vanni, a member of the Finnish Academy; and Rafael Wardi, a recent "painter of the year" who contributed graphics for a Finnish *Haggadah*. Among popular performers — some of whom have made their mark performing songs in Yiddish for general audiences — are Marion Rung, Hillel Tokazier, Jhonny (Eljon Liebkind), Roni Kamras, and Seela Sella, an actress who sings Polish and Ukrainian ghetto partisan songs as well as Yiddish ones, and has recorded *It Burns — "S'Brent"* in Yiddish or *"Se Palaa"* in Finnish. Her husband, Elis, is Helsinki's chief secretary of cultural affairs. Classical musicians include the late Simon Pergament, a composer and conductor, and the upcoming violinist Sharon Jaari. Herbert Katz is a well-known jazz musician.

Arjeh Scheinin, a dentist and former headmaster at the University of Turku, is celebrated as the chief of the research group that developed xylitol, a made-from-wood sugar substitute that is used in brand-name chewing gums. Karmela Belinki is a journalist and producer for the Finnish Broadcasting Company. And the late impresario Mauritz Stiller — brother of Abraham Stiller, who played a major role in saving Finland's Jews from the Holocaust — went to Sweden where he discovered Greta Garbo.

Reading: However small, there's a literature reflecting the Jewish experience in Finland; certain works have been generally popular. Little has been translated into English. A historical work in English is *Finland and the Holocaust — The Rescue of Finland's Jews* by Hannu Rautkallio (Holocaust Library). In addition, Max Jakobson has written *Finland and Reality* and *Finland Survived — An Account of the Finnish-Soviet Winter War, 1939-1940* (both Otava Publishing). For the special flavor of Finland, look for works by Jubani Aho, F. E. Sillanpaa, Eeva Kilpi, Minna Canth, and playwright Hella Wuolijoki. Try Stockmann's Academic Bookstore across the street from the Stockmann department store's main building.

Recommendations: Finnair, one of the most accommodating and civilized airlines flying the Atlantic, offers daily nonstop flights from New York to Helsinki and twice-weekly flights from Los Angeles and Toronto. In the heart of Helsinki, the homey Hotel Klaus Kurki provides charm and intimacy. The Hotel Hamburger Bors in Turku is comfortable and conveniently located opposite the main outdoor market where Jews once peddled. Finland may be on the Western and Jewish edges, but it has the comforts of home.

—Phyllis Ellen Funke

Hong Kong

Jackie Mason claims the Chinese are anti-Semitic. "For five thousdnd years Jews have been eating in Chinese restaurants," he says, "but have you ever seen one Chinese eating in a delicatessen?"

What Mason needs is a visit to the Beverly Hills Deli, which has branches on Hong Kong Island and in Kowloon. He'll see lots of Chinese munching on corned beef or kreplach. What he won't see are Jews. Not only is the deli noteworthy more for its existence than for its quality, not only is it *treif*—this is, after all, Hong Kong—but Jews, resident and visitor alike, are eating Chinese. Sometimes it seems the Beverly Hills Deli exists mainly to contradict Jackie Mason.

Hong Kong has never been a major center of Jewish life, and as a community Jews have had little impact on the place. One could perhaps spend years there without ever noticing an obvious Jewish connection. But consider the following:

In Kowloon you can stroll along what is probably the premier shopping street of Asia, which was built by a Jewish engineer and named for him after he became the colony's governor. At the foot of Nathan Road, where it meets Hong Kong's busy harbor, you can stay in one of the world's great hotels, the Peninsula, which has been Jewish owned for more than sixty years. You can then cross the harbor to Hong Kong Island either through the Harbour Tunnel or on the Star Ferry, both of which have Jews among their primary owners. On the Hong Kong side you can easily find a *minyan* in the financial district. If you are touring, you can get to the top of Victoria Peak via the Jewish-owned Peak Tramway.

History: Perhaps Jews have done well in Hong Kong because the Chinese balance between modernity and tradition so mirrors the Jewish experience. This is a place where business executives carry cellular telephones but where no skyscraper can be built without accounting for *fung shui,* the Chinese science of determining the proper balance of natural elements. *Fung shui* can be applied not only to the bank towers of Hong Kong Central but also to Ohel Leah Synagogue, which escaped a wrecking ball a few years ago—despite the wishes of many in the Jewish community—and still sits gracefully on Robinson Road.

The first Jews arrived in Hong Kong in 1842, the year it was founded as a British colony. For years the British had been shipping opium to China, using it to trade for the tea, silk, porcelain, and spices it sent back to Europe. When the Chinese banned the importation of "foreign mud," the British attacked, won the right to trade in treaty ports along the China coast, and were ceded Hong Kong Island. The Kowloon peninsula was added in 1860, and in 1898 Great Britain signed a ninety-nine-year lease on the adjacent New Territories. Under the 1984 treaty with China, Britain will return the entire colony to China when the lease on the New Territories expires in 1997.

The first Jews in Hong Kong were from the Sassoon family, whose mercantile empire spread from their original home in Baghdad, through Bombay to China. The Sassoons' clerks and managers were all Baghdad Jews. One of the young clerks brought out was Elly Kadoorie, who arrived in 1880, ultimately started his own business and became a true Jewish taipan, as Hong Kong has long called its most successful businessmen. Elly's children and grandchildren remain business leaders and Jewish community leaders to this day.

The community was organized in 1857 and its synagogue, Ohel Leah, was opened in the Hong Kong Midlevels in 1901. Reflecting the rough balance that existed in the community for many years, the synagogue was built by the Sassoons and the adjacent Jewish Club by the Kadoories.

By the turn of the century the predominantly Baghdadi community numbered more than 100. Though far from the mainstream of Jewish life, in one sense Hong Kong's Jewish community fit a Jewish pattern going back centuries. Most in the community were involved in trade and relied heavily on contacts with Jewish traders in other ports around the world. This is almost as true in the 1990s as it was in the 1840s. Despite the similarity of activity, however, Hong Kong differs from the classic Jewish model in two respects. Unlike the ports of Europe, the Jews have never been a dominant commercial force. And they have never been resented or persecuted.

Because it was the only Jewish address for thousands of miles, the Hong Kong community, like other remote outposts, was always hospitable to wandering Jews. Descendants of the Jews of Kaifeng have from time to time shown up on Ohel Leah's doorstep, looking for a way to their past. In 1924 a Russian circus (by some accounts, all Jewish) came to town and one of the performers requested that his newborn daughter be named in the synagogue. On the day of the ceremony the entire circus, from acrobats to tigers, showed up at the synagogue.

Until 1949, Hong Kong had always been part of the China route for traders and émigrés. After the Russian Revolution, several thousand Jews fled east to Harbin, in Manchuria, and some eventually sought opportunities in Shanghai and Hong Kong. German Jews made the same journey in the 1930s, and a trickle of Austrian and Polish Jews came out as well.

World War II brought Jewish life in Hong Kong to a standstill. Those who did not exit before the Japanese seized Hong Kong in December 1941 were interned at the Stanley Barracks. The Japanese looted and damaged the Jewish Club, which was torn down after the war and rebuilt in 1949; the synagogue was used as a warehouse but survived.

But if the Japanese invasion stunted Jewish life in Hong Kong, the 1949 communist victory in China revitalized it. Hong Kong had been a backwater compared with Shanghai, where the Jewish population, swollen by waves of refugees, reached 15,000 on the eve of World War II. With Mao Tse-tung's victory most Jews headed for the United States, Israel or Britain. But those with an affinity for China chose Hong Kong. Many who had Shanghai-based businesses with Hong Kong branches shifted their headquarters to the British colony.

Community: There are about 1,500 Jews in Hong Kong today (out of a total population of 6 million) and by most accounts the community is growing; about 1,000 are affiliated with the community.

Only about one-third are long-term or permanent residents. A 1989 survey found that by nationality Hong Kong's Jews are 39 percent American, 27 percent British (which includes Hong Kong British and the descendants of the community's Baghdadi founders), and 17 percent Israeli. For both the long-term and short-term residents in the Jewish community, trade is still the leading occupation.

Though there is only one synagogue in town, there are four distinct religious groups. The ritual at Ohel Leah's main sanctuary can be described as mainstream Sephardi Orthodox (although Ashkenzim make up more than three quarters of the congregation). A separate *minyan* of Lebanese Jews has its own services in the synagogue. Lubavitch hosts *Shabbat* services at the Hong Kong Hilton. The United Jewish Congregation, affiliated with the Reform movement, holds High Holiday services at the China Fleet Club and *Shabbat* services at other clubs or in members' apartment.

In most respects Hong Kong's Jews are much like the other non-Chinese who make up perhaps one percent of the colony's population. This is certainly true with respect to the main topic of conversation — 1997.

Hong Kong has been nervous about the

Chinese takeover ever since the 1984 agreement to transfer power was announced, despite Chinese agreement not to interfere with its economy. After the Tienanmen Square massacre in 1989 the mood was depressed. But Hong Kong—true to its capitalist origins—has always been built on confidence, and the current mood is decidedly upbeat. As one long-term Jewish resident puts it, "China isn't taking over Hong Kong in '97; Hong Kong is taking over China." His view, far from unique, is that the Chinese government will realize that it is in everyone's interest to keep Hong Kong as it is, and to let it be the economic engine that will drive China forward.

Sights: The center of Jewish spiritual life in Hong Kong is at Ohel Leah, whose Victorian birth, white Gothic exterior and Oriental (as in Middle-Eastern) interior all belie a quaint simplicity—and the intense battle, recently settled, over its future. Located at 70 Robinson Road in the Midlevels (about halfway up Victoria Peak), Ohel Leah is approached along a winding street of high rises that overlook the harbor. Currently the principal entrance to the grounds is behind the building, and it leads through a lush garden noted for its banyan trees and its *mikveh*.

Cane-backed chairs sit on a plain stone floor in the sanctuary. Simple arched stained-glass windows surround the interior, filtering color past the narrow women's gallery and onto the wooden central *bimah*. Two marble stones adorn the entry—one explaining that the synagogue is named for Elias David Sassoon's mother, Leah; the other dedicated to Jews who died in the defense of Hong Kong during World War II. In addition to *Shabbat* services, *Shacharit* services are held in the synagogue every morning; *Minchah-Maariv* services are held at the Jewish Club in Hong Kong Central.

Fourteen Torahs sit in Ohel Leah's ark. Five of them were found in Cat Street (Hong Kong's fabled thieves' market) in 1974 and are believed to have originated in the synagogue of Kaifeng. Ohel Leah did have one Torah that was certifiably from Kaifeng, but it was shipped to the Hebrew

University in 1925 and, as far as anyone can tell, lost en route.

The serenity of Ohel Leah's setting is marred for the moment by construction going on just a few feet from the front door. Back in the mid-1980s, the community came up with a plan to solve a chronic financial pinch and provide modern facilities. Given the astronomical growth in land prices since the synagogue was completed in 1902, the community would tear down the synagogue, allow a developer to put up a high-rise apartment building that would include a new synagogue and recreation club, and earn enough from the transaction to endow Jewish life for many years to come.

But the plan didn't come to pass, perhaps because of Ohel Leah's *fung shui*. The debate over whether to tear down the synagogue pitted two camps of the Jewish community against one another and eventually involved Hong Kong preservationists and an appeal to the chief rabbi of England, and Queen Elizabeth II.

The Solomonic solution was that the synagogue would be spared. The high-rise is going up just a few feet away, on the former site of the Jewish Recreation Club; when completed the new building will include forty apartments owned by the community and, according to the original plan, a new Jewish Club.

When the old club building was torn down, the Jewish Recreation Club relocated to temporary quarters in Central Hong Kong. The move has been so unexpectedly positive—attracting unaffiliated Jews because of its location and its facilities—that there is some talk of its staying in Central even after the high-rise is completed.

The club is located at 4/F Melbourne House, 33 Queen's Road, Central (telephone 801-5440). A sampan superimposed on a Star of David greets visitors as they enter the elegant wood-paneled quarters. The club has social and holiday events, a health center, lectures, two kosher restaurants, a library, a small shop selling food and books on Hong Kong Jewry, and the daily *Minchah-Maariv* service. Visitors can take out temporary memberships. When visiting the club be sure to pick up a copy of the "Jewish Club News." For information on services or events of the United Jewish Congregation, call 802-0012.

The land that has been in the Jewish community the longest is the cemetery in Happy Valley, just a few blocks from Hong Kong's main racecourse. (The popularity of horse racing in Hong Kong is roughly equivalent to the combined popularity of baseball and football in America.) Located at 13 Shan Kang Road, the cemetery is a patchwork pattern of above-ground and underground tombs surrounded by apartment towers. The grounds themselves are not unusual, but this is surely the only Jewish cemetery in the world entered by walking under an arched bridge that connects a Buddhist high school to an adjacent temple. As you walk the narrow pathway to the cemetery, the yellow stone temple with an orange pagoda roof is to the right and the Pokuk School is to the left.

Many Hong Kong visitors stay on the Kowloon side of the harbor, where more of the colony's nightlife is located, and cross the harbor on the Star Ferry, by taxi through the Harbour Tunnel, or by subway. Of the three ways to cross over, only the subway is without a Jewish connection. The tunnel and the ferry are among the holdings of the Kadoorie family.

If you think Times Square is the neon capital of the world, you haven't seen Nathan Road and the narrow streets and lanes that radiate from it. Much of the shopping and entertainment in Kowloon is found along Nathan Road. Some streets are veritable neon tunnels, with signs for restaurants, shops, and nightclubs hanging over the traffic without giving a hint of whether they are attached to the buildings on the right or the left side.

There wasn't much commerce in Kowloon when Matthew Nathan, a major in the Royal Engineers, transformed a meandering buggy path lined with banyan trees into the wide road that he envisioned as a major commercial center. So unlikely did development seem that the road was dubbed "Nathan's Folly." Today it is one of the busiest thoroughfares in Asia. Nathan himself was eventually knighted. He became governor of Hong Kong in 1904, the only Jew ever to hold the post.

Some of the masterpieces of the Ka-

Nathan's famous: A shock of neon tangle off Kowloon's busiest thoroughfare

doorie hotel empire sit at the foot of Nathan Road, looking across the harbor at the Hong Kong skyline. The grande dame of Asian hostelries is the Peninsula, with its luxurious, old-world charm. The family acquired the hotel in 1928. It was used by the Japanese general staff during the war, and when Lawrence Kadoorie returned to Hong Kong in 1945 he had to ask permission of the British command to stay in his own hotel, but he got it back, and restored its reputation. The Peninsula is owned by the Hong Kong and Shanghai Hotel Corporation, founded by the Kadoories; though now a public company, the Kadoories are still the majority shareholders. If you prefer the sleek and modern, the Peninsula Group also owns the Kowloon Hotel, across the street from the Peninsula. (In addition to the hotels and its substantial interest in the ferry and tunnel, the hotel corporation owns the Peak Tram.)

No trip to Hong Kong is complete without a visit to the New Territories, the largely rural hinterland of the colony. The Kadoories have made their mark there as well. Many of the refugees who poured into Hong Kong after 1949 were farmers; the Kadoories offered interest-free loans, built dams, wells, orchards and fish ponds, subsidized grants of livestock and farm buildings, and helped more than 300,000 people adapt to new lives. At the Kadoorie Experimental and Extension Farm, high-elevation farming techniques and animal husbandry innovations have made the Jewish taipans known in agricultural circles across Asia. From research done at the farm, the traditional swayback of the Hong Kong pig was eliminated, prompting Lord Kadoorie's observation, "We Kadoories know everything about pigs but the taste."

In addition to their philanthropy in Hong Kong, the Kadoories have made major educational contributions to Nepal and Israel. One of the graduates of the Kadoorie Agricultural School in Israel is Prime Minister Yitzhak Rabin.

The Kadoorie farm, located off Paak Ngau Shek in the Lam Tsuen Valley, is also a favorite spot for picnics. The manicured gardens make it seem more a park than an agricultural laboratory. A trip to the farm can be combined with a visit to the Kat Hing Wai village of Kam Tin. Built in the seventeenth century, the village is surrounded by a wall featuring guardhouses and arrow slits to fend off attackers. Inside the walls the narrow lanes have old and modern buildings and images side by side.

The closest you can get to the atmosphere felt by the Jews of Kaifeng is at the Sung Dynasty Village at Lai Chi Kok in Kowloon. There are no explicit Jewish references in the village, but it was during the Sung Dynasty (960–1279 C.E.) that the Jewish community of Kaifeng was at its peak, and Kaifeng itself was China's capital. The design of the village was inspired by the painting *Upriver Parade in Ching Ming*, which depicts life in Kaifeng. A wooden bridge takes visitors over a lazy stream. People in period dress walk among shops selling tea, fans, silk, and handicrafts. There is also a temple, a restaurant, a "rich man's house," and regular performances of acrobatics and wedding processions. Inside the walls one feels far from ultramodern Hong Kong.

Back on Hong Kong Island is another Chinese historical village. The Middle Kingdom, looking over Aberdeen Harbor on the island's south side, has seven open-air exhibits devoted to different periods of Chinese history from the time of Confucius up to the twentieth century. Craftsmen and artists work and perform in full-size replicas of public squares and pagodas. A theater offers Chinese opera, folk dancing, and kung fu.

General Sights: Before trains, planes, and automobiles, waterways were the world's main transportation routes; early nineteenth-century illustrations show the Hudson River was as gridlocked as the late twentieth-century San Diego Freeway. One of the few places where the water is still as crowded, and as fascinating, is Hong Kong. Its harbor is packed with sampans and hydrofoils, ferries and yachts, tugs and naval vessels, cargo ships and cabin cruisers, barges and passenger liners. A ride in the harbor is a must.

The best view of the harbor, and of Hong Kong, is from Victoria Peak. A popular pastime on the far side of the island is a ride through the boat city of Aberdeen or a meal on one of its floating restaurants. In Kowloon, the night market on Temple Street and the surrounding area is not only a unique shopping experience but also one of the best places to hear popular Chinese music, which all the market's tape vendors broadcast to the throngs.

The best way to escape the big-city pace of Hong Kong is to visit the outlying islands. Sparsely settled Lantau has fishing villages reminiscent of old China and the Po Lin Buddhist Temple and Monastery where, among other things, you can have an excellent vegetarian lunch. Boats to the outlying islands leave from the dock next to the Star Ferry terminal in Kowloon.

Reading: Hong Kong is rich in literature. If you want a Hong Kong Jewish novel there is *East Wind* by Julie Ellis (Arbor House); it's a romantic tale of a Jewish mixed marriage—he's from Kaifeng, she's from New York—and it covers all the bases, from the Jewish commercial enterprises of the early 20th century to Ohel Leah Synagogue. The classic novel of the Kaifeng Jews is Pearl Buck's *Peony* (Bloch/

Biblio). Two other novels with Chinese-Jewish plots are *Mandarin* by Robert Elegant (Simon and Schuster) and *Deliverance in Shanghai* by Jerome Agel and Eugene Boe (Dembner Books).

General Hong Kong novels include *Tai-Pan* and *Noble House* by James Clavell and *The World of Suzie Wong* by Richard Mason. (If you prefer to do your homework by video, *Suzie Wong* is good; *Tai-Pan* is a bomb.)

Eating and Recommendations:

The Hong Kong Tourist Association has brochures and fact sheets on every aspect that could interest a traveler, including details on the sights of Jewish interest and on vegetarian restaurants. Write to the HKTA at 508 Fifth Avenue, New York, NY 10036 (telephone 212-869-5008). They also have offices in Chicago (312-782-3872) and Los Angeles (310-208-4582).

The only kosher restaurants in Hong Kong are the ones in the Jewish Recreation Club. There are, however, many good vegetarian restaurants serving Chinese and Indian food — among them Bodhi Vegetarian Restaurant (four locations in Kowloon, one in Causeway Bay on Hong Kong Island), which serves Cantonese food, and Woodlands (8 Minden Avenue in Kowloon), which is Indian.

If you must have a pastrami sandwich, there are not only the two Beverly Hills Delis but also a Lindy's in Kowloon. It won't be like the fare on the Lower East Side, but at least you'll have something to tell Jackie Mason.

—Alan M. Tigay

Houston

"Houston is *the* city of the second half of the twentieth century," Ada Louise Huxtable wrote in *The New York Times*, when the Texas metropolis was in the heyday of its tremendous oil-fueled growth, sprouting gleaming skyscrapers and comfortable suburbs at a dizzying pace. By the final decade of the century, however, Houston's growth had slowed and it had come to resemble other major American urban areas in its varied economic base, cosmopolitan cultural offerings reflecting a diverse ethnic makeup, and a big-city fear of crime.

Like the Jews, of Texans it has been said that they are just like everybody else, only more so. Houston's Jewish community is in a way a microcosm of American Jewry in its diversity of origins, its religious and organizational patterns, and its once-concentrated but now dispersed neighborhoods. But any discussion of the Lone Star State's largest Jewish community will surely include a few claims for the "more so."

History: While most American-Jewish history lessons begin with the arrival of Sephardic Jews from Recife in New Amsterdam in 1654, Texans claim that the first Jew to set foot in what is now the United States was a Portuguese Converso, Gaspar Castano de Sosa, who crossed the Rio Grande in 1590. Castano was looking for the Pecos River and silver and had the rank of lieutenant governor of the large province of Nuevo León, which ran from the Gulf of Mexico to Mexico's Pacific coast. He had received his appointment from the province's governor, Luís de Carvajal. Several members of Carvajal's family (including a nephew with the same name), were accused of practicing Judaism in secret, and though the governor himself was a devout Catholic, for a time suspicion fell on him as well.

It is likely that Castano's desire to explore the wilds of West Texas was motivated by the wish to escape the Inquisition.

The difference between Converso adventurers and their kinsmen in New Amsterdam a half-century later was that the former, running from the Inquisition's long arm, did everything in their power to conceal their Judaism, and so left no Jewish traces, let alone permanent settlements. The sinking of Jewish roots came much later, in the nineteenth century, with the arrival of English-speaking settlers from the United States.

A Jew by the name of Samuel Isaacs was among the "Old Three Hundred" who came with Stephen F. Austin to Texas in 1821, when the territory was under Mexican rule. Before independence fifteen years later, there were Jews living in Velasco, Nacogdoches, San Antonio, and Bolivar. Jews fought with Houston at San Jacinto, with Colonel William J. Fannin at Goliad, and two Jews died at the Alamo. During the nine years that Texas was an independent nation, Henry de Castro, a French Jew from a Converso family, brought 5,000 people from Alsace-Lorraine to Medina County and had the town of Castroville and Castro County named in his honor.

Houston was founded four months after independence and the French-born Eugene Chimene, who had fought at San Jacinto, was the city's first Jewish resident; by 1837, there were enough Jews for a *minyan*. In the early days, Jacob de Cordova, a Sephardic Jew from Jamaica, was a city alderman; he also helped lay out the plan for the town of Waco and introduced the Order of Odd Fellows to Texas. A member of Houston's first Chamber of Commerce, Cordova also wrote books about Texas and, in 1858, toured England and the East

Coast of the United States to recruit settlers. Two early Jewish entrepreneurs were Morris A. Levy, who helped organize the Houston Ship Channel Company, which made Houston a port for oceangoing vessels, and Henry S. Fox, one of the founders of the Houston Cotton Exchange.

Despite the prominence of some of its members, the Jewish community of Houston grew slowly at first, from 17 adults in 1850 to 68 (plus 40 children) a decade later. A plot of land was purchased for a cemetery in 1844. In 1854 a home was converted to a synagogue—the first in Texas—and the Orthodox Beth Israel Congregation was formed. Zacharias Emmich was its first spiritual leader, acting as rabbi, cantor, and *shochet*.

Although Houston had the first Jewish cemetery and synagogue in Texas, Galveston, fifty miles southeast on the Gulf of Mexico, had a larger Jewish community until 1880. Galveston was the cultural capital of Texas for much of the 19th century; while people were still shooting each other in gunfights elsewhere in the state, the citizens of Galveston were going to the opera. It remained one of Texas's major cities until it was devastated by a hurricane in 1900. German Jews rose to great prominence in Galveston. In 1866, 21 out of 26 Galveston merchants were Jewish. While New York didn't have a Jewish mayor until 1975, by 1915 Galveston had had three.

After 1880, Eastern European Jews began following their German coreligionists to Texas and to civic prominence. One Russian Jew became a director of the Houston Gaslight Company and another was president of the Houston Light and Power Company. The new wave of immigrants founded two Orthodox synagogues, the largely Galician Dorshe Tov and the Russian-Polish Adath Yeshurun, which merged into Congregation Adath Yeshurun in 1891. Adath Yeshurun later merged with Conservative Beth El, which was founded in 1924, to form Congregation Beth Yeshurun. In 1991 Beth Yeshurun celebrated its one hundredth anniversary, claiming to be "the oldest continually active synagogue of its kind in Texas, and the largest."

The influx of Eastern European Jews was greatly swelled, after 1907, by the Galveston Plan, the brainchild of philanthropist Jacob H. Schiff and writer Israel Zangwill, to divert the masses of Eastern European Jewish immigrants from New York and the East Coast to the sparsely settled areas between the Mississippi and the Rockies. Galveston, already a minor port of entry, was chosen because there was a Bremen-to-Galveston passenger line, run by the North German–Lloyd Shipping Company, and because of the presence in the city of a dynamic circuit-riding rabbi, Henry Cohen, who could provide community leadership and support for the plan.

Houston was one of many cities that benefited from the program, which settled 10,000 Jews before it ended on the eve of World War I. Though statistically the Galveston Plan was a failure—thousands and thousands of Jews continued to pour into the East—the program may have had a subtler success. Scholars point out that it did more than anything else to create a Jewish presence throughout the country, a situation that undoubtedly contributed to the ultimate acceptance of Judaism as one of America's three major religions.

The Eastern Europeans who settled in Houston, unlike their counterparts in the East, accommodated themselves to and were absorbed into the culture of the German Jews. Not crowded into tenements, they found opportunities to prosper quickly, mixed with non-Jews socially and in business, and adopted the courtesy and friendliness of the southern milieu. The newcomers did add their own institutions, however, founding, among other things, a Zionist organization in 1903 and a Workmen's Circle in 1915. *The Jewish Herald-Voice,* the community's only newspaper, began publishing in 1908.

Beth El, Houston's first Conservative synagogue, was founded in 1924, and in 1925 took over the building formerly occupied by Beth Israel. Meanwhile, Beth Israel, long since liberalized, had become a classic Reform temple. The leading figure in the community during the early decades of the twentieth century was Rabbi Henry Barnston, who occupied the Beth Israel pulpit from 1900 to 1943 and helped found the Houston Symphony and the Museum of Fine Arts. Jewish participation in civic and political life was less visible between the wars, however, because Ku Klux Klan activity made Jews wary.

Many German refugees arrived in the 1930s, to be followed by more Eastern European refugees after World War II. In 1943, as the call for a Jewish state grew, anti-Zionist sentiment grew in Houston, led by the American Council for Judaism. Temple Beth Israel adopted a set of "basic principles" excluding from membership anyone who professed a belief in Israel as the homeland of all Jews. "We consider ourselves no longer a nation," the principles stated. "We are a religious community, and neither pray for nor anticipate a return to Palestine." A minority of dissenters from the principles withdrew to form another Reform congregation, Emanu-El. (Today, of course, it is perfectly kosher to be a Zionist at Beth Israel.)

Community: The Jewish community of greater Houston now numbers about 42,000, which makes it medium-sized among American Jewish communities, close in Jewish population to, say, Pittsburgh. Those numbers represent a large proportion of newcomers, as the Jewish population has tripled since 1955. Houston Jews come from all parts of the United States as well as from Russia, Mexico, South America, and Israel. Fast as it has been, the Jewish growth has not been as great as the phenomenal burgeoning of the city as a whole. While Houston surpassed Philadelphia as the fourth-largest American city in the 1980s, metropolitan Philadelphia has some 290,000 Jews; Houston has less than one-fifth that number. Jews make up about 2.5 percent of Houston's population, a smaller proportion than in most metropolitan areas. This explains why the Houston Jewish community combines the close-knit feeling of a middle-sized town with big-city sophistication and large-scale institutions.

In its early days, Houston was, of course, much more *shtetl*-like than it is today. Initially, most Jews settled in First and Second Wards, later moving on to Third Ward, near the first site of Congregation Beth Israel, a frame building on LaBranch Street. The Eastern European immigrants at the end of the nineteenth century tended to move into Fifth Ward, around Franklin and Navigation, or Sixth Ward, around Houston and Washington streets — areas now without Jews.

The second area of settlement, beginning in the 1920s, was in Washington Terrace and then Riverside Terrace, along North and South MacGregor. This area, more spread out than the first area of settlement, was home for most of the synagogues and the Jewish Community Center through the end of the 1950s.

Then the Jewish population shifted to the southwest, first to the subdivisions along North and South Braeswood Boulevard and later to Meyerland. The congregations and the Jewish Community Center rapidly followed the people in their southwestward movement. In the seventies this move continued into Fondren Southwest and the Memorial–Spring Branch area. Today Jews can be found sprinkled in suburbs that surround the city — with synagogues opening in Kingwood and the Woodlands to the north and in Clear Lake, next to the NASA Space Center on the way to Galveston. Nowadays Houston has not one area of Jewish settlement but many; the southwest is still the Jewish core of town, if not exactly an ethnic stronghold.

As in many middle-sized Jewish communities, Houston's Jews affiliate in sizable proportions with their many Jewish institutions, both religious and secular. Religiously, Houston follows the national pattern of Reform and Conservative predominance, with the largest synagogues being Congregation Beth Yeshurun (Conservative) and Temples Beth Israel and Emanu-El (Reform). Emanu-El recently began holding a daily *minyan*, an unusual feature in a Reform congregation. Orthodoxy remains numerically small but varied, with a Sephardic congregation and a Chabad Lubavitch Center in addition to the regular Orthodox congregations. Young Israel, which recently moved into a new building in the Fondren area, is in the process of securing an *eruv* around its neighborhood. Altogether there are more than twenty synagogues in Houston and the surrounding area.

There are Jewish day schools on the

elementary level from all the major Jewish religious movements: the Irvin M. Shlenker School at Beth Israel (Reform), the William S. Malev School at Beth Yeshurun (Conservative), the Hebrew Academy (independent, but with Orthodox leanings) going up to high school, and the Torah Day School, sponsored by Lubavitch. In addition, the I. Weiner Secondary School, a community-based junior high school, takes a centrist philosophy.

Economically, Houston Jews are predominantly professional, with a strong concentration in business, including direct retail and businesses supporting retail. Given the importance of the oil industry to Houston's economy, Jews have had to overcome some discrimination in hiring from companies that do business with Arab countries. This economic anti-Semitism is not limited to the oil companies but also affects construction and engineering firms that have Arab clients.

To counteract this subtle anti-Israel bias, and to promote better understanding between the Jewish and African-American communities, Houston has had, since 1980, one of the most successful programs for developing a positive image of Israel among black youth. Founded by Mickey Leland, an African-American congressman who was a staunch supporter of Israel, the Youth Kibbutz Internship annually sends ten minority youth to Israel for a summer and encourages them to speak about their experiences on return. Leland died in a plane crash while on a humanitarian mission to Ethiopia in 1989, but the program that bears his name lives on.

Sights: The major Jewish institutions in Houston—the synagogues, Jewish Community Center, and the Seven Acres Jewish Geriatric Center—are built Texas-style: big, spread-out, commodious, and pleasant to look at. Temple Beth Israel, at 5600 North Braeswood, for instance, is an ultramodern structure that was expanded to house a day school after the temple was built. In its lobby are twelve needlepoints based on the Chagall windows at the Hadassah–Hebrew University Medical Center in Jerusalem.

Temple Emanu-El, at 1500 Sunset Boulevard, across from Rice University, has in its lobby a three-figure bronze statue called *The Bar Mitzvah*. A museum named for the synagogue's first rabbi, the Robert I. Kahn Gallery, includes a Leonardo Nierman tapestry called *Genesis* and a bronze sculpture by Alexander Liberman called *Sacred Precincts*.

Congregation Beth Yeshurun, at 4525 Beechnut, features as the focus of its large sanctuary a twenty-six-foot-high ark with stained-glass background in a Burning-Bush motif. The foyer contains a large memorial to the Six Million, and its Louis and Mollie Kaplan Museum of Judaica houses an eclectic collection of books and ritual objects. The walls of the social hall are decorated with needlepoint recreations of a series of biblical lithographs by Israeli artist Reuven Rubin.

The United Orthodox Synagogues of Houston, at Greenwillow and South Braeswood, has a Holocaust memorial glass sculpture by Herman Perlman.

The Jewish Community Center at 5601 South Braeswood Boulevard brings together all elements of the community for cultural, educational, and recreational events. It offers extensive sports facilities—two swimming pools, a health club and fitness center, a gymnasium devoted exclusively to gymnastics, tennis and racquetball courts, and ball fields. Its Kaplan Theater is used for artistic and educational events, and its halls, classrooms, and library serve everybody from preschoolers to senior citizens. Call the center at (713) 729-3200 for information about programs and events. The JCC has a West Houston branch in the Memorial area (at 783 Country Place) and recently opened the Bertha Alyce Early Childhood Center in the Fondren area.

Next door to the JCC, at 5603 South Braeswood, are the offices of the Jewish Federation of Greater Houston, the Bureau of Jewish Education, and the Community Relations Committee. If you can't find the information you want about community events in the *Jewish Herald-Voice* (713-630-0404), try the federation (713-729-7000).

The Holocaust Education Center and Memorial Museum of Houston opened in 1993 at Calumet and Caroline streets. It has permanent and temporary exhibits, an archive, library, and classrooms. It is also involved in Holocaust education for the Jewish and general communities. For information call (713) 789-9898.

Seven Acres, the Jewish Home for the Aged, is worth seeing for its Texas scale. The 290-bed facility at 6200 North Braeswood provides nursing, convalescent, and social service care for its residents, and reaches out to the community with its health maintenance, cultural and recreational activities to elderly outpatients in need of supervision, "meals-on-wheels," large-type library, and eye clinic.

General Sights: After you've seen the Astrodome, Astroworld, and the Transco Waterfall, step back and look for the contributions Jewish Houstonians have made to the institutions of their city. Near the University of St. Thomas is the Rothko Chapel, the last major work of Jewish abstract artist Mark Rothko. The chapel displays fourteen expressionist paintings by Rothko, and in front, facing a reflecting pool, there is a twenty-foot steel obelisk dedicated to the memory of Dr. Martin Luther King, Jr. At the Texas Medical Center, a five-hundred-acre, twenty-nine-institution complex, is the twelve-story Jewish Institute for Medical Research, an affiliate of Baylor College of Medicine.

Worth the hour's drive out of the city is a visit to the Lyndon B. Johnson Space Center, where you can see displays of spacecraft, moon rocks, a lunar roving vehicle, and a lunar module.

After visiting the NASA space center, continue on to Galveston to look at the beautiful Victorian homes along Broadway, which look much the way they did when German Jews played a leading role in what was then a major city. The city is still home to about 700 Jews, as well as a Conservative synagogue, Beth Jacob, on Avenue K and a Reform temple, B'nai Israel, on Avenue O.

If you make Galveston a day trip, visit the Texas Seaport Museum at Pier 21 of Galveston Island to see *Elissa*, Texas's tall ship, as well as exhibits on Galveston history and an interactive computer with records of more than 110,000 immigrants who entered through its port. You may find relatives who arrived here instead of Ellis Island. Then stay for dinner at one of the fine fish restaurants along the pier.

Culture: Major metropolis that it is, Houston boasts a rich variety of cultural attractions: a noteworthy ballet company, a fine arts museum, and the Houston Symphony, whose past conductors have included Leopold Stokowski, André Previn, and Sergiu Comissiona, who is Jewish. The De Menil Museum houses one of the last great private art collections. And the Houston International Film Festival, held annually, is the world's largest in number of films submitted.

Jewish culture, too, is rich if sporadic. The high point of the year is the November Jewish Book Fair, sponsored by the JCC, and one of the best of its kind in the country. Speakers in recent years have included Saul Bellow, Alan Dershowitz, Elie Wiesel, Camelia Sadat, Yael Dayan, and Chaim Potok. In addition to the speakers, the array of some fifteen thousand books is truly impressive. Jewish Education Week, in February, sponsored by the Bureau of Jewish Education and the Federation, has brought noted Jewish scholars such as Eli Grad and Isadore Twersky to Houston.

Elijah's Cup, a gallery at 5550 North Braeswood, carries original Judaica by known and soon-to-be-discovered artists.

Personalities: Houston's Jews have excelled in many fields. In education, Norman Hackerman retired in 1985 after serving as president first of the University of Texas and then of Rice University. Joseph Melnick, a leading virologist, became dean of graduate research at the Baylor College of Medicine. Aaron Farfel was chairman of the Board of Regents of the University of Houston from 1971 to 1979, and Alfred R. Neumann was the founding chancellor of the University of Houston–Clear Lake.

In politics, Billy Goldberg was chairman of the state Democratic Party. In music, Fredell Lack is an acclaimed violinist. In space, Jeffrey Hoffman, the first Jewish astronaut, took four *mezuzahs* with him on the space shuttle *Discovery*. Judith Resnik, who died on the space shuttle *Challenger* in 1986, also made her home in the area.

On the literary scene, both Max Apple, author of *Free Agents* (Harper & Row), and Rosellen Brown, author of *Tender Mercies* and *Civil Wars* (Knopf), write and teach at Houston universities. Julia Wolf Mazow has anthologized Jewish women's fiction in *The Woman Who Lost Her Names* (Harper & Row). Charles Hoffman, a Houston native, went on *aliyah* and became an acclaimed reporter for *The Jerusalem Post* and, more recently, an author and expert on Eastern European Jewry after the fall of communism.

A folk singer who blends his Jewish and Texas heritages in unique ways is Kinky Friedman ("the first Texas-Jewish country-music star") who had the audacity to name his group "The Texas Jewboys." In recent years Friedman has taken to writing mystery novels (good ones, too), but they are set in New York.

Eating: It is a sign of Houston's coming of age that there is now more than one kosher restaurant in town. Simon's Gourmet Kosher Foods, a meat restaurant and kosher supermarket, is located at 5411 South Braeswood. Just across the bayou from it, on North Braeswood and Chimney Rock, is Nosher, a dairy restaurant and appetizing store. In addition, there is Wonderful, a strictly vegetarian Chinese restaurant at 7549 Westheimer. For those who seek "kosher style" but not kosher, Alfred's, at 9123 Stella Link Road, serves both blintzes and pastrami. Several bakeries and bagel shops, including the excellent Three Brothers bakery on South Braes

wood, are under rabbinical supervision, and many top hotels offer kosher catering. For *kashrut* information, contact the Houston Kashrut Association at (713) 723-3850.

Getting Around: Houstonians don't believe in walking, except around shopping malls and through the tunnels that link many of Houston's downtown office buildings. The best way to get around is by car on the extensive but often congested freeways. Houston drivers are generally courteous, obeying the signs that admonish them to "Drive Friendly."

Reading: Two books that explore Texas Jewish history in depth are *Deep in the Heart of Texas* by Ruth Weingarten and Cathy Schechter (Texas Jewish Historical Society) and *Pioneer Jewish Texans* by Natalie Ornish (Texas Heritage Press). For an informative portrait of Houston Jewry, read Elaine H. Maas's chapter on Jews in *The Ethnic Groups of Houston,* edited by Fred R. von der Mehden (Rice University Studies). For a sketch of suburban life in the most Jewish of Houston suburbs, read Max Apple's vignette, "This Land Is Meyerland," published in the literary magazine *Antaeus.* The history of the Galveston Plan is detailed in Bernard Marinbach's *Galveston: The Ellis Island of the West* (SUNY Press). The film *West of Hester Street,* produced by Allen and Cynthia Mondell, also tells this fascinating story. And after that, listen to Kinky Friedman's album, *Sold American,* to get the full flavor of Jewish Texana.

—Roselyn Bell

Istanbul

East may be east and west, west, but who says the twain never meet? In Turkey, that land bridge connecting Europe and Asia, and especially in Istanbul, which straddles both continents, the two certainly seem to come together. Or at least try to.

Not that the relationship is easy. While a young Turkish student on an airport bus fervently asks an American, "Why don't you see us as Western when we are Western?" a recent rise in the number of covered heads on Istanbul's streets bespeaks Turkey's underpinnings in the Eastern—and Muslim—world.

As Turkey strings its tightrope between Western alliances and mores and Eastern geopolitical realities, its Jews—as actually do all its peoples—work on their own balancing act. For the moment their footing appears firm. With the occasionally overt, more often subtle, support of the government, they are currently waving the Turkish flag diligently. They do so, they say, in thanks to the land that gave many of their ancestors a long, healthy, and happy refuge.

In fact, five hundred years ago as Spain's Queen Isabella and King Ferdinand were expelling their Jews, Sultan Bayazid II, who ruled the Ottoman Empire from 1481 to 1512, was taking them in. Needing loyal subjects to populate a broadly expanding realm, he reportedly declared, "You call Ferdinand a wise king, he who has made his country poor and enriched ours!"

But as one thoughtful Istanbul Jew recently explained, the Jews have been treated well because "We have been 'good boys.'" Left hanging—though Turkish Jews would vehemently deny it—is what happens if or when they are "bad."

History: *Bereishit*—in the beginning . . . there was Turkey. If the Garden of Eden ever existed, it is generally thought to have been situated in the area of the Tigris and Euphrates Rivers—whose headwaters rise in eastern Turkey. Noah's Ark presumably came to rest on Mount Ararat, also in eastern Turkey. And from Haran, in southern Turkey, Abraham and his family began their journey to Canaan (Genesis 12:4). Thus it could be argued that the ancestors of the Jews have been in this area since the beginning of at least biblical time.

Drifting westward from Central Asia, the Ottoman Turks by the mid-14th century had conquered the Byzantine strongholds in Asia Minor and in 1354 crossed the Hellespont, or Dardanelles, to gain their first European toehold at Gallipoli. This people actively propagandized to establish loyal populations and supposedly Sultan Mehmed II (1451–1481), aware of the difficulties created for Jews by Christians, issued a proclamation to all Jews saying, in part, "Let him dwell in the best of the land, each beneath his vine and beneath his fig tree, with silver and with gold, with wealth and with cattle. Let him dwell in the land, trade in it, and take possession of it." Also at this time, Rabbi Isaac Sarfati of Adrianople stimulated an influx of Ashkenazim from Germany, Austria, and Hungary by writing to them about the favorable conditions in Ottoman lands. When the Ottomans took Constantinople in 1453, changing its name to Istanbul, Jews probably participated in the conquest.

From this time, their fate would be so closely bound to the Turks' that often they must have appeared as synchronous shadows. When the Ottomans were in ascendancy, so were the Jews; when the former declined, so did the Jews. On the upswing in 1492, the empire was further boosted by the Sephardic Jews' arrival, which heralded a two-century-long Golden Age for both

221

peoples. The Jews brought the printing press, their knowledge of firearms (which helped defeat the Mamelukes in the Holy Land in 1515), and their scientific acumen. So many were fine physicians that they became court doctors. The most influential of these were members of the Hamon family who for three generations during the 16th century dominated both the Jewish community and the court. The most notable of these, Moshe (1490–1567), administered to Suleiman the Magnificent.

In addition, he served as a diplomatic agent and arranged to transfer into Istanbul much of the wealth of the Portuguese Converso bankers Doña Gracia Mendes and her nephew, Don Joseph Nasi, the most prominent of the Sephardic financiers.

Jews so flourished in business that they monopolized the Ottoman mint and customs houses. And with their international networking they virtually controlled the empire's financial and economic system. In 1551, Niccolo Nicolia, a French diplomat visiting Istanbul, scene of the most important Jewish concentration, observed: "They increase daily through the commerce, money changing, and peddling which they carry on almost everywhere on land and on water; so that it may be said truly that the greater part of the commerce of the whole Orient is in their hands. In Constantinople, they have the largest bazaars and stores, with the best and most expensive wares of all kinds." By the mid-sixteenth century, the 200,000 Jews in Ottoman lands—in contrast with the 75,000 in Eastern Europe—comprised the largest and most prosperous community in the world of the time.

Rather than integrating into Ottoman society, however, they, like most other minorities, lived in their own closed communities and communities within communities, based on area of origin. Virtually all Ottoman subjects were classified as to position—and often made to wear clothing and observe other restrictions that denoted their place. The Jews were excoriated as well more than once, and under the pain of death, for public displays of wealth.

Turkish Jewry was weakened from within by the divisiveness caused in the mid-seventeenth century by the advent of Shabbetai Tzvi. Born in Izmir, he preached he was the messiah, sought to depose the sultan, and ultimately converted to Islam. Those who followed him originated the sect of "Jewish Muslims" called the Donmeh ("the turned")—which still exists.

Early in the nineteenth century when the Ottomans began modernizing—declaring general equality and permitting the use of secular courts and schools—Jews began to progress again. Modernizers from the outside—the French Alliance Israelite Universelle in 1860, then competitive British and German organizations—arrived with westernizing ideas. With educational barriers broken, Jews, in the last half of the century, were studying in technical and medical schools and the University of Istanbul.

The nineteenth century's nationalistic sparks inflamed the empire's other minorities, with the Greeks and Armenians often in violent revolt, and other peoples gaining independence. Such activity left the Jews, who appeared untouched by such influence, as the only trusted minority, thus enhancing their already favored status. Their numbers were increased as the last sultans invited Jewish refugees from Germany, Austria-Hungary, France, and Russia, and by the twentieth century, Istanbul's Jewish population swelled to 100,000.

By 1908, Turkish patriots were sufficiently disgusted with the empire's disintegration that the Young Turks, abetted somewhat by Jewish intellectuals (including Moise Kohen, or Munis Tekinalp, a theoretician), and supported generally by the Jews who had also suffered from European meddling, revolted against the reactionary sultan. This move set off a chain reaction leading to several internecine conflicts and wars, including World War I, and the Ottoman Empire's ultimate breakup. Throughout, the Jews supported the Ottoman efforts and prospered, particularly since they no longer faced competition from other now neutral or disloyal minorities. But they were destined to be jarred when, in 1923, Mustafa Kemal—or Ataturk—created the Republic of Turkey.

So determined was Ataturk to yank Turkey into a Western version of the twentieth century that he secularized everything, separating church and state so completely that Turkish was mandated as the language of prayer even in mosques, and clergymen were prohibited from wearing clerical garb in public. To foster a national spirit, he also banned all organizations with international ties. Though he loudly proclaimed his appreciation for the Jews as the "one people . . . who have proven their loyalty to this nation and land," they no longer received favored treatment. No longer able to teach religion easily or associate officially with such foreign organizations as the World Zionist Organization and even B'nai B'rith, they found themselves scrambling with everyone else. Hindered by ignorance of the Turkish language and prior existence within closed circles, as Turkish nationalism intensified the Jews found themselves, for at least a generation, regarded as outsiders.

During World War II Turkey proved itself a safe haven and Turkish citizenship an effective passport out of hot spots. Several anti-Semitic incidents did occur, and in 1942, the badly strapped Turkish government levied a tax on property that, though ostensibly on all, hit non-Muslims hardest. The financial ruin of many, plus various postwar political upheavals, created a climate conducive for Jewish emigration. Between 1948 and the 1980s, about a quarter of Turkey's Jews left for the United States, France, and Canada, while half — mostly the poorer ones — headed for Israel.

Throughout the Ottoman presence in Asia Minor, its attitude toward the land of the Jews' origin had been ambivalent. As a part of its empire, the Ottomans supported Jewish population there and, given Istanbul's proximity, the city became a major center in the support network for the holy Jewish cities. But as nationalistic ideas spread, the Ottomans began fearing Jewish nationalism as well. And when Theodor Herzl proposed buying the land, the sultan, supported by Turkish Jews who perhaps saw political Zionism as another European-stimulated curse, refused. The pro-British activities of Palestinian Jews during World War I were viewed as anti-Turkish and exacerbated the situation. But when World War II broke out, Turkey granted Jews crossing its borders safe passage and, in 1940, accepted the presence in Istanbul of 15 *Aliyah* and Jewish Agency agents, including Teddy Kollek and Moshe Sharret. Turkey voted in the United Nations for Israel's establishment, but given its geo-graphic situation — and its need for Arab money — the relationship between the two countries seesaws. Though it is lately on an upswing, during the repeal of the UN resolution equating Zionism with racism, Turkey abstained.

Community: When Arab terrorists attacked the Neve Shalom Synagogue on September 6, 1986, killing 22, the Istanbul Jewish community — and, by proxy, all others in Turkey — changed significantly. Given the outpouring of horror, indignation, and sympathy from all elements of Turkish society, plus the world's sudden attention, this hitherto retiring, self-effacing, and comparatively closed group now was exposed to the limelight. Not only was the episode seen as the most outrageous anti-Jewish action in Turkish history, it was also seen as an assault on Turkish sovereignty.

The high profile taken by Turkey's Jews during the celebration of the five hundredth anniversary of the arrival of Sephardim from Spain would have been hard to imagine before the Neve Shalom attack. Many Jews still assert that the attack has nothing to do with their new public position. Some attribute their current openness to Turkey's change from military government to democracy. Others don't recognize differences at all. And such an acknowledged unawareness provides one insight into the chameleon character of this old and enigmatic community.

The current Turkish-Jewish population is about 27,000, of which 24,000 live in Istanbul. After the period of intense secularization, when all roots were denied, they, like other Turks, are taking another look at their heritage. Though this has not yet meant a significant increase in religiosity — Istanbul's Jews are nominally Orthodox but in practice Conservative or Reform — the community operates sixteen synagogues (including three reserved just for summer use), plus an old-age home, a hospital, and schools. The focus of Jewish social life is the social club — seven at last count.

As today's Jews come out of their shell, they are integrating their housing as well. On the Asian side, they live in the areas of Yeldegirmen, Kadikly, Kuzguncuk, Haydarpassa and Suadiye; on the European side, Harbiye, Gayretepe, Nisantas, Sisli, Esentepe, Etiler, and Bebek (the last two, extremely upscale). They have also moved as close to the Black Sea as the pleasant, countrylike Buyukdere. More central neighborhoods bear reminders from previous residences — areas near and along the Golden Horn such as Galata, Balat, Haskoy, Kagithane, Pera, Ortakoy and Uskudar.

Though a Jew, Salamon Adato, helped found Turkey's Democratic Party, there has not been a Jewish elected government official in about twenty-five years. Nor are Jews particularly engaged in the general culture (a realm in which the Donmehs distinguish themselves). Primarily they are in business and, in recent years, have contributed mightily to making Turkey one of the world leaders in the leather clothing industry.

Sights: From the ancient to the ultra-contemporary, from the secular and cosmopolitan to the religious and parochial, Istanbul is excellently endowed with destinations related to the Jewish past and present — yet since much remains uncatalogued, much still must remain uncounted.

The third floor of the Archaeological Museum, for example, has not, at least until recently, been widely touted. Though the antiquities displayed on the lower floors may be more artistically impressive, the collection from the area labeled "Syria-Palestine" is mind-boggling in its own right. The remnants and shards date back to the thirteenth century B.C.E., several containing inscriptions in Aramaic and Hebrew. There's a terra cotta censer of the type found in the seventh layer of Meggido and a tenth-century B.C.E. limestone calendar in Hebrew from Gezer, which gives, in poetic language, the agricultural phases of the year. There's pottery from Samaria and an inscription apparently from the Second Temple area threatening death to intruders who enter the courtyard. But perhaps most surprising is the inscribed tablet in midroom, from the southern end of Hezekiah's Water Tunnel in Jerusalem, which tells the story of its construction.

At the other end of the time line is the newly created walking street, the Istiklal Caddesi, once the "Grande Rue de Pera"

through the heart of the city's then most fashionable neighborhood. In the mid-nineteenth century, this area, from the Galata Tower to Taksim Square, became the city's economic and social center, filled with fine mansions and elegant shops. In fact, this was the location of Wagon Lits' offices at the eastern end of the Orient Express. And here was built the still-standing Pera Palace Hotel, where Agatha Christie stayed — and from which she once mysteriously disappeared. Yet much had decayed until the last couple of years when the flagship store of the Vakko chain — Turkey's more compact but extremely chic answer to Paris' Galeries Lafayette — established itself on Istiklal Caddesi, with the paving of the long and now-bustling pedestrian area largely paid for by its Jewish owner, Vitali Hakko.

Also unspecified are the many gems in the Topkapi Palace that must have been cut by Jews — since they were the gem cutters in the sultans' days. (Regardless, see the Topkapi dagger, immortalized by the movie.) Not to mention the gold and silver services in the Dolmabahce Palace, which at least one guide acknowledges were, indeed, made by Jewish goldsmiths and silversmiths. Or the six-pointed star worked into the great chandelier in the monumental cathedral-turned-mosque, and now a museum, Hagia Sophia — inspiration, it is said, for such synagogues as Florence's and San Francisco's Temple Emanuel.

Istiklal Caddesi boasts a new tramway running from Taksim Square to Tunel Square from which a downhill walk leads into the Galata area, defined by the Galata Tower, which was, from the 1500s until recently, a noted Jewish neighborhood. In the narrow, crowded, steep streets of the district are still clustered some of Istanbul's best-known synagogues, including the Neve Shalom (Buyuk Hendek Caddesi 67); Ashkenazi (Yuksek Kaldirim 37), and Italian (Sair Ziya Pasa Sokagi at Laleli Cesme Sokagi) synagogues — plus the unprepossessing offices of the chief rabbinate (Abdullatif Yeminici Sokagi 23), and Zulfaris Synagogue, facing Karakoy Square, dating from 1671 and now converted into a Jewish museum.

Formidable security now encases all such spots, and the first thing seen now inside

Transcendental Edification: The Hagia Sophia—once a cathedral, then a mosque, now a museum—has been the inspiration for synagogues as far away as San Francisco

the refurbished Neve Shalom is the list of persons killed in the terrorist attack and the lobby's grandfather clock, its hands stopped eternally at the moment of the assault. The paint job now is beige and café-au-lait, with beige-orange marbleized walls, and a great gilt chandelier bearing *Magen David* motifs. To the pulpit's left, however, an outlined, blackened area remains in memory of the attack. Because few Jews live in the area today, Neve Shalom remains primarily ceremonial, used essentially just for weddings and funerals.

The long and narrow Ashkenazi Synagogue, whose facade boasts three Oriental arches and octagonal rosette windows, has an interior surmounted by a soaring blue dome and highlighted by an elaborately carved ebony ark. Though Ashkenazim predated Sephardim in Istanbul, this synagogue was built at the beginning of the twentieth century to cater to the influx of refugees from Kishinev.

The Italian Synagogue dates from the 1880s, when factional disputes among the Jews led some to seek protection from the Italian ambassador. This synagogue, approached through a black-and-white-tiled, vine-covered courtyard, boasts a Gothic-like facade, crystal chandeliers, velvet draperies, and worn Turkish carpets on the floor.

The Balat area, however, across the Golden Horn, had had a Jewish community from Byzantine times and until the first decades of this century, remained the Jews' spiritual center. Of the nineteen synagogues that once existed here, only two remain— including Istanbul's most outstanding, and oldest, one, the Ahrida (Kurkcu Cesme Sokagi 9), probably named for Ochrid in Macedonia from which its original worshipers may have come.

The Ahrida's foundation may precede the fifteenth century; the present building may date from the late fifteenth century. But the current, carefully planned restoration, which has turned the interior into a cream-shaded sanctuary, utilized seventeenth-century plans. The detail notwithstanding, the Ahrida's most noteworthy feature is its central *bimah*, designed as the prow of a ship. Some say this represents Noah's Ark; others, the ships bringing the Sephardim from Spain.

On the street perpendicular to Ahrida's entrance—a working-class thoroughfare crisscrossed by vines and laundry lines and echoing with Eastern music—stands the Yanbol, or Yambol, Synagogue (Duriye Sokagi 16). It is also named for a Macedonian city, perhaps the one represented in the painting on the ceiling. With Turkish carpets and cushioned seats around a central, also forward-leaning *bimah*, the Yanbol has a cozy, living-room-like feel.

Among other Istanbul synagogues is Etz Haim (Mullim Naci Caddesi 38), up the Bosphorus in Ortakoy, on a specially designated site for synagogues that once held three. Two were Sephardic, one Ashkenazic. The major Sephardic one burned accidentally in 1941 but its marble ark, dated 5666, remains embedded in the courtyard wall. The Sephardic prayer hall, however, has been refurbished, and the Ashkenazic one remains as well.

Across the nearby Bosphorus Bridge, on the Asian side, in suburban Kuzguncuk are two synagogues. Though officially called the Merkez Synagogue (Icadiye Caddesi 9) and Virane (Yakup Sokagi 8), they are popularly known in local Jewish parlance as "Kal de Abaso" and "Kal de Arivel," referring to their respective positions on a major street down a hill and hidden away up a hill. Though primarily used on holidays and special occasions, the Merkez has walls painted with trompe l'oeil panels and a dome covered with paintings of Israeli scenes, while the Virane, whose floors are covered with a riot of Oriental rugs, is homey and used in cold weather, since it is more easily heated. Also on Istanbul's Asian side, in the Haydarpasa area—site of the Selimiye Barracks where Florence Nightingale worked—is the Hemdat Israel Synagogue (Izzettin Sokagi at Sungertasi Sokagi). When the synagogue was being constructed in the late nineteenth century, Greek Orthodox factions tried to stop it by sending a military unit. The sultan—Abdulhamit II—stopped this action. Hence, the synagogue's name, "Hemdat" ("who is compassionate"), a play on Hamid, meaning "compassionate." The synagogue's arabesque paintings have recently been restored.

Though not of historic importance, the center of Istanbul's current Jewish life— with services every day—is Sisli Beth Israel (Efe Sokagi 4), in the Sisli area a couple of miles north of Taksim Square. In addition to such community-maintained operations as the Jewish Home for the Aged (Haskoy Mektebi Sokagi 10) and the Or Hayim Jewish Hospital (Demirhisar Caddesi), in a garden setting on the shores of the Golden Horn, is the impressive memorial in the Ashkenazi Jewish Cemetery (Zincirlikuyu Caddesi) to the victims of the Neve Shalom attack. The memorial features a three-dimensional menorah and a wall of tiles

forming different configurations of green, blue and dusty-rose flowers, interspersed with yellow *Magen Davids*. One large agglomerate centers around a large star, dramatically splattered in blood red.

Religiously beyond the pale—of the established Jewish community, at any rate— are two groups with roots deep in Judaism. The Karaites, who have lived in Istanbul since Byzantine times (and who gave their name to the Karakoy area), are so removed that, should they wish to join mainstream Judaism, they must be converted—and must go to Israel to do so. About 100 remain, however, and maintain, however perfunctorily, a synagogue in Haskoy, at Mahlul Sokagi 2. Built on a hill, it is noteworthy because, in Karaite fashion, it is underground. Consequently, when it is not open, only a bit of its door, at most, four feet of it, descending to less because of the slant, can be seen. It stands in a ramshackle neighborhood of picturesque wooden houses. The crumbling one facing it is said to have been the rabbi's.

On the Asian side, in the Bulbul Dere and Uskudar areas, are mosques and a cemetery of the Donmehs. The Donmehs, called by some "Jewish Muslims," are descendants of Shabbetai Tzvi's followers who converted to Islam when he did. Until recently a closed group, they follow certain Jewish practices—such as Sabbath candle lighting and no-smoking rules—in secret. Many of Istanbul's hailed originally from Thessaloniki and constitute a wealthy and cultural elite—a position attributed by many to their "Jewish genes."

Many secular Jewish sights in Istanbul result from the nineteenth-century ascendancy of Abraham de Camondo who, because of his great wealth and banking ability, was dubbed "the Turkish Rothschild." His mansion, a monumental white palace-like edifice right on the Golden Horn waterfront in the Haskoy area, is now regional headquarters for the Turkish navy and not open to the public. On a hill overlooking the Cevreyolu (Istanbul Bypass Expressway) stands the Camondo Mausoleum, visible from the highway. But Camondo's loveliest architectural legacy is the one in Galata—the gracefully curved double flight of stairs, called the Camondo Staircase, and connecting the lower end of Camekan Sokagi to Bankalar Caddesi—the Bank Street—also called Voyvoda Caddesi.

The Grand Bazaar, a monumental maze in the old part of town, once hosted numerous Jewish shopkeepers. But few remain, even in the bazaar's immediate surroundings. (One exception, on Nuruosmaniye Caddesi 84, the main street leading into the covered bazaar, is Kismet, Inc., where Isaac Savariego and Silvyo Benbasat sell Oriental carpets and kilims.) The new International Press Center, in the restored Sepetciler Summer Palace, on the waterfront bordering Kennedy Caddesi, is also thought to have a connection, however tenuous, to the Jews. This particular structure, filled with Byzantine arches, was built in 1643 and was used by the sultans to send off and welcome back their navies. But it is said that from this spot, earlier sultans, most notably Beyazit, watched the arrival of the ships bearing the Sephardic Jews.

Izmir (Smyrna): Few ruins of the ancient world tell it like it was the way two archaeological sites within easy reach of Izmir do. Ephesus is considered by many to be antiquity's best-preserved city. And to tread the huge blocks that paved its streets, to see its marketplace, its public sanitary facilities, its twenty-four thousand-seat amphitheater, is to have some genuine sense of stepping back through time. Yet only one tenth has been excavated so far, and the heavy money says that when it is, a synagogue will be unearthed.

That there were Jews here is almost unquestionable, since the apostle Paul preached in Ephesus and his first targets were the Jewish congregations. Concrete evidence exists in a form not yet officially explained. On the main street of Ephesus stand the remains of the library of a second-century C.E. governor-general of a large portion of Asia Minor. At the library's entry stand eight columns. And on the top step, the seventh up from the absolute bottom of the flight, near the base of the third column from the left, facing inside, is a clearly defined scratching in the stone of a menorah.

The other site is far larger and grander, though it does not bear any symbol so defining as the menorah. This is the second-century Roman synagogue of Sardis, once the capital of the Kingdom of Lydia, ruled between 560 and 546 B.C.E. by the wealthy King Croesus, the first monarch to mint coins. The synagogue, not much shorter in length than a football field, features numerous remaining mosaic floor patterns; a line-up of six columns along each side; and two altar areas, topped by inverted V's, obviously influenced by Greek architecture. Just outside the synagogue, along one wall, was Sardis's business center, with many Jewish proprietors manning the "shops" now separated by crumbling stone partitions.

In Izmir itself, a short flight or an eight-hour drive from Istanbul, several traces remain of a community that, when the town began its seventeenth-century development as a center for Mediterranean commerce, had been one of the most important Jewish settlements in the Ottoman Empire. Of the 15,000 who lived in this pleasant seaside city before 1948, only about 2,000 remain.

Though they now reside primarily in the prestigious Alsancak area, where they have built a new synagogue, Shaar HaShamayim, the primary sights are concentrated in and around the bazaar, once the community's heart. In the rundown area edging the bazaar entrance near the municipal parking lot and opposite Emlak Bankasi, Shabbetai Tzvi was born. In the bazaar is a street now known simply by its number, "927." But not long ago, this was called Havra Street, for the nine synagogues and many Jewish shops that once dotted the way.

Now only two synagogues are easily seen. One is the Senora Synagogue, at number 77. An airy sanctuary, whose dominant color is white, though trimmed with muted turquoise and gold, it boasts a piece of Ottoman art—a work featuring flowers in a vase on its left wall— as well as framed prayers around the walls in the tradition of Ottoman mosques. Its four central pillars are topped by arches; its Torah covers are silk velvet, embroidered with real gold thread; and its Eternal Light always burns pure olive oil. The Shalom Synagogue, at 38C, off a passageway filled with shoes, heels, and shoe trees, is wildly colorful.

Almost everything, from the walls to the benches, is bright turquoise. Cushions covered with a bright floral pattern pad the benches edging the walls and running perpendicular to the ark. The floor is covered with Turkish carpets, some of which display minaret motifs. But most striking is the ceiling painted, as the ceilings of wealthy Ottoman homes were, with geometric kilim designs and colors meant to look like carpets.

A narrow walkway with merchandise samples hanging overhead, "927" runs into the larger Anafartalar Caddesi and, at number 331, the Metin Sasson Jewelry Shop, one of about one hundred shops in the bazaar, is still owned by Jews.

Driving south along the waterfront to the erstwhile Jewish neighborhood of Karatas leads not only to the Beth Israel Synagogue, Mithat Pasa Bulvari 245, but also to the "Asansor" or elevator, the first in Izmir, constructed in 1907 by Nissim Levy. Levy made his fortune by charging for the ride from one street to another one on a higher level, one hundred feet up a cliff side. Though the old water-run contraption has been replaced and the freestanding building recently refurbished (there's an excellent view of the waterfront from the top), a sign above the entrance still proclaims the structure's provenance—in French and Judeo-Spanish, written in Hebrew characters, with the Arabic "Marshallah" ("With God's Blessing") above in calligraphy. Contact David Palombo (telephone 25-63-53), who speaks French, Hebrew, and Judeo-Spanish; or Ahmet Dundar Ozar, an exceptionally knowledgeable guide (telephone 59-57-39).

Edirne (Adrianople):

Like an aging beauty queen, the synagogue of Edirne, 155 miles from Istanbul, evokes great pity because the shadow of erstwhile glory remains. In a strategically located border city whose fate has risen and fallen with its frequent changes of ruler, the Jewish population—which dates from before the fall of the Second Temple and which, in this century, once embraced 28,000—now comprises just 4 families.

Though this soaring synagogue structure, modeled after Vienna's, is now a sham-

bles—with its roof caving in and shrubbery growing from interior dirt—it is still possible to appreciate its pillared sanctuary; lofty arches; and remains of gold, blue, and red-toned frescoes adorning walls and the three-sided women's gallery. A yellowish building, its facade features three arched windows, decorated with ironwork and topped by a *Magen David*. Unlike most other Turkish synagogues, this one towers above its surroundings—which still contains some of the former community's weather-beaten, wooden houses. The building is freely and easily entered, though a Bulgarian refugee family now lives rent free on the premises. The building is located on a street called Maarif Caddesi, but it is best to tell your taxi driver that it's near the Greek consulate.

Bursa:

The Ottoman capital in the fourteenth century, Bursa was the center of the empire's international silk trade—from which the many Jews engaged in the business sent their ships to Venice, the Persian Gulf, India, and beyond. When the Sephardim arrived in this city (160 miles from Istanbul), they joined, and ultimately engulfed, the Romaniote (Byzantine) Jews already living in a special quarter that today is kept, though without fanfare, as what this country would deem a "historic district." Turning from a main street, Altiparmak, up a hill, Otel Sokagi, the second street on the left, Sakarya, is blocked to traffic and its old buildings preserved. Dotted with old-style globe-bulbed street lamps, it is lined with gray, beige, and ochre-tinted three- and four-story houses. Some are built in reverse steps, with the second floor jutting out beyond the first and the third overhanging the second. On the wall at number 24 is a fountain. The accompanying plaque, which begins in Turkish, "Burada Araba Yikamak Yasaktir Saul Markos," declares that this memorializes Shaul Marcus, a wealthy, philanthropic twentieth-century Jew.

From this century's pre–World War I high of 3,500, Bursa's Jewish community has shrunk to 33 families, or 133 persons. Its oldest synagogue, Etz Chayim, burned; another, Mayor, somewhat beyond the fountain (and to the right of an orange-red sign for the Piccolo Bar), is chained closed. The active one, however, Gerush, at number 59, operates behind a freshly painted white-and-brownish-rose wall with a newly varnished door to its courtyard.

Though dating from the Sephardic influx, it appears richly renovated, with pinkish walls, marble floors, and plushly cushioned, burgundy-toned seats. The layout is literally a circle in a square, with eight pillars and a ring of seats surrounding the central pulpit topped by a central dome whose interior is covered by a floral design painted to look like draperies. A special feature is an upstairs lectern, used by the *chazan* on the High Holy Days. Friday evening, Saturday morning, and Monday and Thursday services are held. Contact Uriel Areza at 36-86-36; he speaks Hebrew and Judeo-Spanish.

Canakkale: Hard by the Dardanelles—the Hellespont of antiquity—and not far from Troy, Canakkale, 220 miles from Istanbul, could not be more strategically situated. According to legend, the castles guarding the narrow watery passage between the Aegean and the Marmara Sea were built, even before the 1453 Ottoman conquest of Constantinople, by Gypsies and Jews. Though over a thousand Jews lived in Canakkale earlier in this century, only 23 remain. But among them is Sami Kumru, part-owner and general manager of the Dardanelles Plant, Turkey's largest frozen food factory and one of the country's top industries. The plant is located about three miles south of the city, on the right side of the Izmir road; however, its trucks can be seen throughout the country.

Canakkale's century-old Mekor Hayim synagogue, opened with a mammoth key and only for festivals when there's a hard-to-get *minyan*—feels as empty as it looks. It stands behind a wall in an older section of town, once the community's heart, near streets named for the community. The easiest to find is Yeni (New) Havra Street paralleling the synagogue. Sami Kumru can be reached by calling 196-153-53; Kursad Akkarpat, general manager of the Akol Hotel, 194-56, can make the contact for opening the synagogue.

Personalities: The best-known Jews in Turkey are probably industrialists, often those involved in multifaceted endeavors. Jak Kamhi holds the Sony franchise and heads Profilo, which makes and sells home appliances. Other leading lights include journalist Sami Kohen of the Istanbul daily *Milliyet*; painters Bubi (Davit Hayon) and Habib Gerez; photographers Izzet Keribar and Yusuf Tuvi; advertising leaders Eli Aciman and Izidor and Yakup Barouh; and writers Mario Levi and Jak Delcon. Beyond Istanbul, native son Meshulam Riklis has achieved prominence as an American financier; and in Israel, Mordecai Gazit has had a successful political career, while his brother, Shlomo, was formerly director of military intelligence.

The rail link that made Istanbul the terminus of the Orient Express—thus firming Turkey's foothold in Europe—was built by Baron Maurice de Hirsch, the German Jewish financier and philanthropist.

Culture: Members of the community—primarily women volunteers—publish *Salom,* a newspaper in Turkish, with one page in Judeo-Spanish (Ladino), every week. The paper also has a cultural center and organizes presentations at its art gallery. Call *Salom* for information on community events at 147-30-82 or 140-41-44.

Deeply concerned with preserving Turkey's Judeo-Spanish heritage—as well as Jewish-Turkish music—is the quartet Los Pasaros Sefaradis. In addition to international performances, they give concerts and minilectures regularly in Turkey. They've also made four tapes, and one of their songs, "The Romance of Rika Kuriel," about a Salonikan girl and her doomed fiancé, has been a hit in Europe. For information, call Karen Gerson at 146-95-60.

Reading: Novels set in Istanbul include Eric Ambler's *The Light of Day* (Knopf) and Elia Kazan's *America, America.* Shabbetai Tzvi has been a subject of much scholarship; the best-known treatment is Gershon Scholem's *Sabbatai Sevi: The Mystical Messiah* (Princeton). Mahmut Makal's *Portrait of a Turkish Family* gives a good look at life during the Republican period.

Recommendations: Though a variety of Western-style luxury hotels now exist in Istanbul, the doyenne of these, the Istanbul Hilton, gloriously situated overlooking the Bosphorus, maintains a rare warmth and charm. The new Izmir Hilton promises to become a landmark in its own right. Turkish Airlines operates the only nonstop service between the United States and Istanbul. Among several agencies with Jewish-related itineraries is Foundation Tours, sponsored by the Quincentennial Foundation (telephone 800-742-6782).

While understanding Turkish may be daunting, pronouncing it is not, since it is phonetically written in the Latin alphabet introduced as part of Ataturk's westernizing reforms — another aspect of the sometimes confusing, always intriguing, East-West split in Turkey's personality.

—Phyllis Ellen Funke

Jerusalem

Jerusalem is a modern city suffused with its past. It is, above all, a city of contrasts — between ancient, old and new, between a polyglot of living and dead cultures, and between traditional and secular ways of life. It lies at the crossroads of East and West and at the juncture of three continents. Capital of an industrialized and technologically sophisticated nation, it is steeped in spirituality and trapped in its turbulent history.

Jerusalem is a place where the melting pot never took hold. It remains today, as always, a mosaic of peoples, faiths and ideas — inwardly troubled, outwardly serene, and unexpectedly resilient.

History: Just over three thousand years ago, an obscure warrior-king named David captured a small settlement, high up in the Judean Hills. Its name was Jeru-Salem, meaning the "foundations of wholeness" or "peace." David kept both the settlement and its ancient name. Bringing the Ark of the Covenant to Jerusalem, he turned his mountain conquest into the national and religious capital of Israel — an act that was to echo through the centuries.

David's city was no larger than two football fields laid side by side. His son Solomon extended the city northward, launching a massive building program that included the Holy Temple. He turned the "city of David" into a center of international renown, which has attracted conquerors from his day to ours.

Jerusalem has been conquered thirty-six times, besieged more than fifty times, and destroyed ten times. Egyptians, Assyrians, Babylonians, Persians, Greeks, Romans, Muslim caliphs, Crusaders, Mamelukes, Ottoman Turks, and finally, the British all fought for the city, ruled over it, and met defeat in their turn. Each of them contributed to Jerusalem. They built palaces, temples, churches, mosques, water channels, and thick defensive walls; administrative, commercial and legal systems — layer upon layer, through culture and time.

Early Jerusalem is well chronicled in the Hebrew Bible, but the two thousand years that followed the destruction of the Second Temple by the Romans in 70 C.E. is also rich in Jewish history. Jews were always present, during the Byzantine, Crusader, Mameluke, and Ottoman periods. When the city was under siege during the First Crusade, in 1099, Jews defended it alongside Muslims and were massacred with their neighbors when the city fell. An idea of the constant cycle of exile and return can be gained by the experience of those who survived the First Crusade; sold into slavery, many were redeemed by Jewish communities in Europe and planted embryonic seeds of Zionism in the communities in which they found refuge. When Jews were able to return to Jerusalem, Jewish communities in Europe and the Middle East could always be counted on for support.

Much of what can be seen in the Old City of Jerusalem today dates from the period after the Ottoman conquest in 1517. Suleiman the Magnificent had the city wall rebuilt between 1537 and 1541. Under Suleiman the city also began to re-emerge as a center of Jewish scholarship, though for a time its scholars lived in the shadow of Safed.

It was not until the 1860s that Jerusalem overflowed the confining protection of the Old City walls. Sir Moses Montefiore built Mishkenot She'ananim west of the Jaffa Gate (to which Yemin Moshe was added a generation later) and this started an ethnic trend. Driven by overcrowding and filth,

Jewish neighborhoods began to rise westward along Jaffa Road toward the Mediterranean coast. The city's Christian Arabs built southeast toward Bethlehem, and its Muslim Arabs north in the direction of Damascus. It was at the time that the city spilled beyond its walls that Jerusalem regained its Jewish majority.

When Israel fought its War of Independence in 1948, the cease-fire line sliced through the city. Jewish Jerusalem, now perched on Israel's eastern frontier, became capital of the recreated state, and Arab Jerusalem was annexed by the Hashemite kingdom of Jordan. A wall divided the two halves of the city for the next nineteen years.

Despite the wall and despite international refusal to recognize the city as Israel's capital, Jerusalem rapidly became the center of Jewish national life. Reunified during the Six Day War of 1967, it began a meteoric growth, more than doubling its population to over half a million people during the next twenty-five years.

Community:
Since King David stormed Jerusalem, there have always been Jews in the city. Through starvation and disease, persecution, war, and devastation, the city's Jewish population has dwindled but never ceased to exist.

Today it numbers 392,000 — 72 percent of Jerusalem's 545,000 residents. They come from all 101 nations of the exile — merchants from Iraq, craftsmen from Yemen, farmers from Ethiopia, scientists from the former Soviet Union, and professors from the universities of Europe. They come from the great cities of North America, the steppes of Russia, the remote reaches of Kurdistan, and isolated villages high in the Atlas Mountains.

In the time-honored tradition of "two Jews, three opinions," Jerusalem's Jewish community contains almost every shade of Jewish affiliation and nonaffiliation. Dozens of hasidic dynasties have followers in Jerusalem, from the golden-garbed descendants of those who came in the seventeenth century when the movement was born, to the black-coated *hasidim* who escaped the flames of Nazi Europe.

Jerusalem's Orthodox Jews also embrace a variety of traditions — molded in Germany, the Netherlands, Morocco, India, Iran, Ethiopia, North America. Their hats and knitted, embroidered, or cloth head coverings identify their ideologies. Conservative, Reform and Reconstructionist Jews from the West are growing in number in Jerusalem, earnestly pursuing an elusive dialogue.

And there are the Jerusalem Jews who claim no religious affiliation. They regard their observant coreligionists with detachment, bewilderment and, increasingly, with hostility.

The cultural and ethnic boundaries between Jerusalem's Jews remain in place, but somehow the intricate mosaic usually works. The community is unself-conscious and cosmopolitan, displaying — more often than not, until now — a sympathetic curiosity in the customs and practices of their fellow citizens.

Sights:
Jerusalem grew by neighborhoods. Each preserves its own special flavor and tradition, and to see only one or two is to miss what the city is about.

There are Jerusalem-lovers, scholars, and tour guides who maintain that a lifetime is insufficient for seeing the city. But to dip into a panorama of neighborhoods is to glimpse beneath Jerusalem's grand exterior and into its complex inner life.

The Old City is chronologically and emotionally the first of Jerusalem's neighborhoods, boasting Mount Zion and the Jewish Quarter, with its Western Wall. Entering Jaffa Gate will bring you directly to the Citadel (often called, erroneously, the Tower of David), where a Museum of the History of Jerusalem opened in 1989. Through a pleasing variety of displays, films, and exhibits, the Museum takes you on a three thousand-year journey through the city's thickly layered, multifaceted past. The star feature of the museum, however, is the building complex itself, parts of which date from the Maccabbean, Herodian, Crusader, Mameluke, and Ottoman periods. That the museum was able to mold its story into the contours of the old stones is a crowning achievement.

The Dung Gate is nearest to the Western Wall and the Temple Mount. From there you can go to the rebuilt Jewish Quarter by crossing the plaza and climbing the steps at the side farthest from the Wall. They will take you into an area of rebuilt streets and courtyards, apartments, *yeshivahs*, and synagogues, their architecture synthesizing thousands of years. The Jewish Quarter was in ruins when Israel returned to the Old City during the Six Day War, but the postwar architects did more than recapture what had been left behind in 1948. They created a neighborhood whose narrow lanes and small apartments are part of a splendor and serenity one normally associates with wider spaces.

The stairways from the Jewish Quarter lead down to the holiest site in Judaism, the Western Wall. The wall, part of the perimeter of the Second Temple, was all that was left of the complex after Titus sacked Jerusalem in 70 C.E. As a symbol of lost Jewish sovereignty, it was dubbed the "Wailing Wall," and it remained a place of lamentation from afar after it was cut off from Israel during the War of Independence in 1948. With Jerusalem's reunification in 1967, a large, open plaza was built in front, and the confidence of the new Israel was reflected in the preference for the term "Western Wall." More than thirty feet of the wall are now below ground. Of the part that shows, the large limestone blocks are Herodian; smaller stones were added later by Byzantines, Arabs, and Turks.

The wall is noted not only for its stones but for what is between them. It is common for worshipers to write prayers on pieces of paper and tuck them into the cracks between the large blocks. The wall is a busy place where you can find a *minyan* most times of day or night. As you face the wall, the men's section is to the left, the women's to the right. *Bar mitzvahs* are common, and in the open plaza there is always a crowd.

Museums in the Jewish Quarter dip into its history. The Old Yishuv Court Museum at 6 Ohr HaHayim Street includes Ashkenazic and Sephardic synagogues and guest rooms showing how Jews lived and worshiped in Jerusalem in the nineteenth and early twentieth centuries; the building is also believed to be the birthplace of the Ari, Rabbi Yitzhak ben Shlomo Luria, in 1534.

The Burnt House (Tiferet Street), charred when the Second Temple burned, and the magnificently restored Herodian House (Hakaraim Street) provide tantalizing glimpses of the daily routine of two thousand years ago. And the rebuilt Cardo allows you to shop along the same street that once catered to the matrons of Roman Judea.

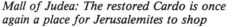

Mall of Judea: The restored Cardo is once again a place for Jerusalemites to shop

The first neighborhoods outside the Old City walls mark the beginning of the modern city. These include Yemin Moshe between King David Street and Mount Zion, financed by Sir Moses Montefiore in 1868, now restored as an artists' quarter.

Mahane Yehuda, behind Jaffa Road, was built in 1887 and is now a bustling open-air market. Mea Shearim, an ultra-Orthodox quarter, is entered through Rabbi Avraham Mislonim Street. Mea Shearim's maze of lanes, arches, courtyards, and houses with outdoor cisterns make its charm greater for visitors than for residents. The Bukharan Quarter, founded in 1891 by wealthy Jews from Russia, was the first to be built with Jerusalem stone. On occasion, some residents still don the national costume of their ancestors.

In the 1920s and 1930s, Jerusalem began expanding both east and west. Mount Scopus, from where would-be conquerors from Alexander the Great to Jordan's Arab Legion looked down on Jerusalem, became a hill of science. The Hebrew University opened there in 1925, followed by the Hadassah Medical Center in 1939. Both have been rebuilt since Jerusalem was reunified in 1967.

The early decades of the century also saw the Jewish Agency compound built on King George Street, the King David Hotel on King David Street, and the Rehavia neighborhood in central Jerusalem. The city also moved west. New garden suburbs rose in Kiryat Moshe, Bet Hakerem, and later in Bayit Vegan. The Holyland Hotel in Bayit Vegan has a 1:50 scale model of Jerusalem in Second Temple times showing the Temple, the hippodrome, streets, and houses. So meticulously accurate is the fascinating model that it is changed according to new archaeological discoveries.

The showpiece buildings of western Jerusalem were built during the first nineteen years of statehood. The Hebrew University and Hadassah Hospital, banished from Mount Scopus, built themselves new facilities at Givat Ram and Ein Karem. The Medical Center includes a synagogue with the twelve luminous windows—one for each of the tribes of Israel—designed by Marc Chagall. The beautiful windows—from the yellows of Naphtali, Levi and Joseph to the reds of Zebulun and Judah—have come to reflect the fortunes of the state. They were hit by shrapnel during the Six Day War and surrounded with sandbags during the Gulf War; in between they have attracted thousands of tourists to the hospital and provided a unique atmosphere for patient-worshipers.

The Knesset moved into its modern home on Rehov Eliezer Kaplan in 1966. The giant seven-branched menorah outside the striking square building was sculpted by Benno Elkan; inside, the giant tapestries in the reception hall are by Chagall.

The Knesset is in the middle of a complex of public and government buildings that also includes the Israel Museum and the new Bible Lands Museum. The Israel Museum, set in low-lying modern buildings that seem to hug the hills they occupy, is the country's largest, and it includes the world's foremost Judaica collection. It displays classical art and sculpture, gems of Jewish history (including the complete interiors of synagogues from seventeenth-century Italy and nineteenth-century Germany), Jewish art and folklore. It also has the Billy Rose Sculpture Garden and a popular, hands-on youth wing. In a separate building known as the Shrine of the Book—a white dome shaped like the lid of the pot in which its contents were found—the museum houses some of the Dead Sea Scrolls. The scrolls inside are all at least two thousand years old. The oldest—more than a thousand years older than any other known complete biblical manuscript—is the Book of Isaiah.

Two neighboring hilltops on the western edge of the city were set aside as memorials in 1953: Mount Herzl to the visionary Theodor Herzl and Jewish and Zionist leaders who came after him; and the Hill of Remembrance to the six million Jewish victims of the Holocaust. Their memory is preserved at Yad Vashem, the museum and documentation center devoted to the Holocaust. Actually a series of monuments and museums, Yad Vashem is spread out across the Mount of Remembrance. Its Hall of Remembrance has a mosaic floor inscribed with the names of the largest death camps; on the grounds are also art and photo exhibits and sculptures, one of the most striking of which is dedicated to Yanusz Korchak, who gave up an offer of freedom and went to Treblinka with the orphans in his care. But perhaps the most remarked upon feature of Yad Vashem is the Avenue of the Righteous, the lanes of trees planted in honor and memory of gentiles who risked—and sometimes gave—their lives to rescue Jews. Trees are being planted all the time as stories emerge; the largest number are from Poland; but there are disproportionate numbers from Italy and the Netherlands. One tree honors an entire nation—Denmark—while another honors Raoul Wallenberg. Hundreds of others represent the Holocaust's lesser-known but equally deserving heroes.

Following the Six Day War of 1967, Jerusalem strove to sew up the seam between its reunited halves. Residential neighborhoods were built across the old border in Ramat Eshkol and French Hill. The bitter battle for the city is commemorated at Ammunition Hill, now a park and museum on Sderot Eshkol; the hill was a

Jordanian stronghold whose fall paved the way for the liberation of the Old City.

Jerusalem's population rocketed after reunification, and huge satellite suburbs were built to accommodate the influx — first at Gilo, Ramot, East Talpiot, and Neve Yaakov, and later at Givat Zev, Pisgat Zev and Maalei Adumim. Jobs were needed for the new Jerusalemites without destroying the city's unique fabric and history. So high-tech parks have been developed, notably on Mount Scopus and in Ramot, where research and assembly plants create space-age medical, communications, and solar technologies.

Culture: Jerusalem has more than two hundred parks and gardens, four world-class museums, two orchestras, an international book fair, a music festival, movie festival and a thriving cinema center.

The Friday *Jerusalem Post* lists events for the week ahead (shorter event listings appear in the *Post* every day). Jerusalem's musical tastes stretch from the Jerusalem Symphony Orchestra and chamber music at the Targ Center in Ein Karem to Western pop and rugby songs in downtown bars and cafés, hasidic songfests, Christian hymnals, and Sephardi and Arab-style music making.

The city's half-dozen theaters and theater clubs enthusiastically produce everything from Shakespeare in Hebrew, to Broadway hits, to the works of local poets and playwrights — often with simultaneous translation into English.

Samples of a recent representative week include Mozart's *Marriage of Figaro*; a jazz jam session; readings focusing on peace in art, prose poetry and literature; a lecture on aspects of impending drug disaster in Israel; children's dance troupes from Spain and Israel; and a Persian music concert played on Persian instruments.

Lectures — academic, religious, and political — and study groups are offered all over the city most evenings of the week. There is usually folk dancing, to watch or to join, at the International Cultural Center for Youth (12 Emek Refaim), the Khan Theater, the Hebrew University or one of the hotels. Local arts and crafts are made and sold in the House of Quality and at Hutzot Ha-

yotzer — both just outside the Old City walls.

In 1993, Jerusalem joined the world's big-time mall club with the opening of what *Time* magazine called "the largest shopping center in the Middle East." Built by David Azrieli (who coined the Hebrew *kanion* for shopping mall), it comprises shops, restaurants, and supervised play areas for children on a scale that brings Jerusalem sharply from the spiritual and academic spheres into the commercial. The mall is on Eliyahu Golomb Street, across the road from the city's new soccer field, known — affectionately and officially — as Teddy's Stadium.

One of the greatest joys of Jerusalem is sitting in its cafés, imbibing the atmosphere. Three especially good spots are the terrace café/restaurant of the Cinematheque, the film center on Hebron Road overlooking the Valley of Hinnom and the Old City; the shaded garden of the Ticho House (Beit Ticho, 7 Rabbi Kook Street), the former home of artist Anna Ticho and her ophthalmologist husband, now a museum behind the busy Jaffa Road; and the colorful Ben Yehuda pedestrian mall in the center of the new city.

If you have the chance, try to attend one of the many outdoor concerts — which range from opera and classical music to folk music and Israeli pop — in Sultan's Pool, a valley below the Old City walls that is one of the world's best open-air theaters. Once part of Jerusalem's ancient water-conservation system, the pool was rebuilt by Suleiman the Magnificent. Now it is part of the nation's culture network.

Food culture reflects the two thousand years of Diaspora — kosher and nonkosher versions of Hungarian, French, Russian, Chinese, Japanese, Indian, Ethiopian, Moroccan, Iranian, and plain *heimish* cooking.

Reading: Books about Jerusalem fill libraries. A ruthlessly selective list for the visitor includes Kathleen Kenyon's *Digging Up Jerusalem* (Praeger), among the most enjoyable and readable archaeological studies of the city. Martin Gilbert's *Jerusalem History Atlas* (Macmillan) is a digestible and painless way of following the city's serpentine history since 70 C.E. *0 Jerusalem* by Larry Collins and Dominique Lapierre (Pocket Books) is a lengthy but fast-moving street-by-street saga of the city during the siege and battles of 1948. *Footloose In Jerusalem* by Sarah Fox Kaminker (Crown) may offer the best guide to seeing Jerusalem on your own. *Jerusalemwalks* by Nitza Rosovsky (Holt, Rinehart & Winston) can also help you find your way to the must-see sites of the city.

From the mass of novels based in Jerusalem, a recent one that gives real insight into the city during the past two hundred years is A. B. Yehoshua's *Mr. Mani* (Doubleday). Other recent Jerusalem novels include Anne Roiphe's *Lovingkindness* (Summit), which explores the life of *baalei teshuvah* among the city's *hasidim*, and *Crimes of the City* (Simon and Schuster), Robert Rosenberg's introduction of police detective Avram Cohen. Also worth reading are Elie Wiesel's *A Beggar in Jerusalem* (Random House) and S. Y. Agnon's *Shira* (Schocken).

Personalities: Jerusalem has been home to or destination of the molders of Jewish history and destiny. King David made it his capital and King Solomon ruled it. Herod built it up and Jesus led his followers there. The giants of contemporary Israel, people like David Ben Gurion and Golda Meir, fought for and lived in Jerusalem. It was in Jerusalem that Eliezer Ben-Yehuda revived the Hebrew language.

One name stands out today among Jerusalem's myriad sons and daughters of fame: the city's mayor of nearly three decades, Teddy Kollek. Every place in the city – old and new, Arab and Jewish, center and suburb, parkland and industrial area – bears his touch. The son of an assimilated Viennese family, Teddy is the first and only mayor of reunified Jerusalem. Under a now-legendary gruff – and often plain rude – exterior, it is his dynamism, tolerance, sensitivity, and supreme pragmatism that normalized life in the capital and won not only the support of the city's Jewish and non-Jewish residents but global acclaim as well.

A sampling of the people who have made their home in Jerusalem includes the writer Aharon Appelfeld, Soviet Jewry leader Natan Sharansky, and the talmudic scholar Adin Steinsaltz.

Day Trips: On King David Street, roughly at the traffic lights past the King David Hotel, lies part of the watershed that Jerusalem straddles. Rain falling west of it finds its way to the Mediterranean; rain on the east trickles into underground springs that feed the Dead Sea.

Even with all there is to see in Jerusalem, it is worth fitting in at least two out-of-town trips – one east and one west – to understand what the watershed means to Jerusalem and its history.

Twenty minutes westward, toward Tel Aviv, are the well-watered slopes and woods of the Judean Hills. By road or by the slow but scenic railway, there are kibbutzim with guest houses and public swimming pools: Maalei Hahamisha, Kiryat Anavim, and Shoresh. Stop at the ruined Crusader convent of Ein Hemed (also called Aqua Bella, both names meaning "beautiful waters") and climb up to the Castel. The Martyrs' Forest, with its monumental *Scrolls of Fire* sculpture, and the Stalagmite Cave (Ma'arat Hanetifim), near Bet Shemesh, should also be seen.

Eastward from the city, the picture changes dramatically. Jerusalem lies on the edge of the Judean Wilderness, an austere moonscape whose sparse winter rains produce delicate desert flowers and deadly flash floods. This is where prophets, hermits, and fugitives roamed throughout millennia. Here in the dusty heat lies the Dead Sea at the lowest point on the surface of the earth; the flower-filled oasis town of Jericho – perhaps the oldest urban settlement in the world – with blocks from its massive walls still lying where they came tumbling down; and the oases of Ein Gedi and Nahal Arugot, their springs and waterfalls coursing through steep rocky gorges into pools where hyena and desert ibex drink.

Recommendations: The hotel with perhaps the best combination of location, comfort, and beauty is the Laromme, next to Liberty Bell Park. For history and style, the King David Hotel is still in a class by itself. For contemporary luxury try the Jerusalem Hilton or the Regency Hyatt on Mount Scopus. El Al, which lands forty-five minutes away at Ben Gurion Airport, is the closest thing to Jerusalem in the air.

Trivia: The living Bible is the theme of two parks—one in Jerusalem and one outside the city. The Biblical Zoo, recently rehoused in a new commercial and leisure complex at Manhat in west Jerusalem, has collected almost all the mammals, birds, and reptiles mentioned in the Bible. It displays them, wherever it can, in biblical tableaux—though it has not yet encouraged a lion to lie down peaceably with a lamb.

A half-hour drive west of Jerusalem, toward Ben Gurion Airport, is Neot Kedumim, a park where the Bible's landscapes are recreated with all the biblical trees, flowers, herbs, and spices that its dedicated botanists can identify. Though the city has been conquered thirty-six times, some things in and around Jerusalem haven't changed.

—Wendy Elliman

Johannesburg

As metropolises go, Johannesburg is a Johnny-come-lately. Though legends had abounded of an African area glimmering with gold, it was not until 1886 that a prospector in the South African province known as the Transvaal literally tripped over an outcropping of what just happened to be the richest gold reef yet discovered. Then, to this bleak and windswept stretch of land known as the Witwatersrand (ridge of white waters), thousands flocked, seeking their fortunes and in the process creating sub-Saharan Africa's largest city. Among these numbers—and in substantial and significant fashion—were Jews.

They were already well established in this land. With roots going back to the earliest settlement of Cape Town, plus mining experience developed over two decades of working in and around the diamond digs at Kimberley, veteran South African Jews, primarily of German and British extraction, quickly formed a large part of the nucleus of gold-mine operators popularly known as "the randlords." But since the discovery of gold under what became Johannesburg coincided with the start of the great Jewish migrations from Eastern Europe, many Jewish immigrants also found their way to the new city, albeit in areas peripheral or secondary to mining.

Hence, Jews of varied backgrounds were involved almost from day one with the founding of South Africa's commercial, industrial, and financial hub, which also became the focal point of their life in the country. And today, as South Africa's largest Jewish community and one of the world's wealthiest (in the center of the world's most important gold-producing operation), the Jews of Johannesburg are generally on the upper economic, civic, cultural, and social rungs of South Africa's primary city.

History: When in the 1830s the Boers began their Great Trek into South Africa's hinterland, some Jews also began to move away from their original base of settlement on the southern coast. But while the Boers were primarily escaping British domination and seeking agricultural opportunity, the Jews moved to provide the prospective farmers with goods and commercial know-how.

In fact, from South Africa's earliest days providing know-how had been a Jewish forte—from the Jewish mapmakers who had helped lead Vasco da Gama to the Cape of Good Hope in 1497 to those involved with the Dutch East India Company, which established Cape Town in 1652. Among those whose activities pointed the way from Cape Town to Johannesburg were members of the Mosenthal family, who built trading stations in villages and at railway sidings, and created credit operations that benefited farmers. When the event occurred that would precipitously turn South Africa from an agricultural area into an industrial one, Jews were on the spot. They were in Kimberley, near the Transvaal border, in 1867 when diamonds were first discovered. And thanks to the centuries-old relationship between the European market in precious stones and the Jews, those in South Africa were readily able to perform trading transactions. The first diamond found was taken to a store owned by the Lilienfeld family, who disposed of it through their cousins, the Mosenthals', well-developed trade network—the same connections that would in 1869 handle the disposition of the 83.5-carat "Star of Africa."

In addition to the old-timers, among the newcomers attracted by the promise of great and instant wealth were such future mining magnates as Lionel Phillips, David Harris,

238

Alfred Beit, George Albu, Solly Joel, and two who would become legendary—Barney Barnato and Sammy Marks.

The English-born Barnato—Barnett Isaacs until his music hall appearances led him to adopt a stage name—was a colorful character given to acting in Shakespeare and sporting fancy waistcoats. He was Cecil J. Rhodes's prime rival for control of the diamond fields and ultimately joined with Rhodes's company to form the omnipotent De Beers Consolidated Mines. In addition he acquired large holdings in the Johannesburg goldfields where his operation became one of the major mining units and his influence and acumen in 1895 saved the Rand from a serious slump. Two years later, however, for reasons unknown, while sailing back to England he disappeared overboard.

Marks went to Kimberley as a general merchandiser. He switched to diamond trading and then mining, amassed a fortune, and went on to the Witwatersrand gold fields. But he made his most important contribution to South Africa's development as the Transvaal's first significant industrialist—exploiting the area's coal potential; planting fruit farms and forests; manufacturing bricks, glass, and leather goods; pioneering the steel industry; and establishing what has become the South African Breweries. Along the Vaal River, which forms one of the Transvaal's borders, he founded the town of Vereeniging.

Unlike many contemporaries, Marks identified openly with Judaism. Since he had chosen to settle in the Boer-based, ultra-Calvinist Transvaal Republic he, like all other non-Protestants, suffered several civic disabilities. A close friend and confidant of Paul Kruger, president of the republic, Marks pushed to have the restrictions mitigated. But Kruger failed to convince other politicians in time to prevent the turn-of-the-century outbreak of the Boer–British Wars, fueled partly by the grievances of foreigners who had flooded the area when gold was discovered. During the Boer–British hostilities—in which Jews fought on both sides—Marks helped mediate between the two factions. With the Boers defeated, a union of the four British South African colonies was formed in 1910. The Jews gained equal status with other whites, and Marks served as a senator in the first Parliament.

Though he had come to South Africa from England, Marks, unlike other Jewish tycoons of his day, had begun life in Lithuania. When word of his success—and the success of the few other Eastern European immigrants in South Africa—trickled, then tumbled, back to the *shtetl*, so many were inspired to follow that 6,000 arrived during the 1880–90 decade; another 30,000 by unification in 1910 and 20,000 more by 1930. Most settled in the Johannesburg area, and because about 70 percent were Lithuanian, South African Jewry was dubbed a Lithuanian colony.

The city's first congregation, the Witwatersrand Old Hebrew Congregation, was formed in 1887 and opened its first synagogue in 1888. Four years later South African President Paul Kruger dedicated the Park Synagogue of the Johannesburg Hebrew Congregation. Factionalization developed between old-timers and newcomers, but when the Great Synagogue—more commonly known as the Wolmarans Street Synagogue—was consecrated in 1914 it proved a unifying force.

Most Jews of the generation succeeding the mining boom turned from precious stones and metals to other endeavors. Flourishing in a country that was calling for rapid industrialization, they became pioneers in such fields as food processing; clothing, textile, and furniture manufacture; insurance; hotel keeping; advertising; mass entertainment; fashion; and the establishment of supermarket, department store, and discount store chains.

Jewish contributions to the general prosperity of South Africa notwithstanding, however, there was a period when, fueled in part by resentment of their success, newly urbanized Afrikaners—until then often sympathetic to the Jews for their biblical roots and the perceived similarities of their history—joined with the British to curtail immigration. But because the Quota Act of 1930 was aimed at eastern and southern European countries, up to 6,000 German Jewish refugees entered South Africa by 1936. Because of growing anti-Semitic sentiment among more militant and nationalistic Afrikaners, however, demonstrations were held against the arrival of the refugee ship the *Stuttgart*. And the Aliens Act of 1937 essentially stopped the influx of Jews.

In the uncertainty of post–World War II

South Africa, many Jews emigrated—so many during the racial troubles of the last two decades that much of the current twenty-to-forty-year-old age bracket has been considered lost. But the arrival of uncounted numbers of Israelis is believed to be keeping population figures in balance. The landmark 1992 referendum in which white voters supported the dismantling of apartheid staved off another exodus.

Community: Like much of the rest of South Africa, the Johannesburg Jewish community of nearly 70,000 has been living on tenterhooks. In a country where, as a Jewish Johannesburg-based journalist put it, "just living and breathing the air these days is political," many Jews, in the unusual position of being an integral part of the establishment, felt their entire existence was on the line prior to President F. W. de Klerk's referendum.

From the days when Gandhi began his campaign of nonviolent resistance to oppression in South Africa, Jews had involved themselves in the fight for equality—on an individual basis. In the years of apartheid's deepest entrenchment, the lone antiapartheid member of Parliament was Helen Suzman, reelected for more than two decades from a predominantly Jewish suburb of Johannesburg; her Progressive Party eventually grew from a fringe group to the official opposition and her dream of a truly democratic South Africa became the policy of the ruling National Party in 1990. Of the seventeen leaders of the African National Congress underground caught during the Rivonia Arrests in 1963, all five whites were Jews. The highest-ranking white ANC official, also the former leader of the South African Communist Party, was Joe Slovo.

As a community, however, the Jews have until very recent times been politically silent. Burned by its opposition to the National Party in 1948—which after the elections began instituting apartheid—the South African Jewish Board of Deputies adopted the view that the Jewish community as such should take no collective political stance, and the board made few public comments on apartheid until the 1980s, when it condemned the policy. In 1990, it came out in favor of de Klerk's negotiations

for multiracial government. Meanwhile, to allay Jewish fears of sporadic anti-Semitic outbursts both from the white right wing and an increasingly vocal Muslim population—some of whom supported Saddam Hussein during the Gulf War—de Klerk, in addressing the Board of Deputies, assured the Jews of their future in the "New South Africa."

But it is not up to de Klerk alone to decide where the Jews will fit under the new order. Since Nelson Mandela's release from prison in 1990, Jews have wondered if they have a friend in the leader with the largest following in the country. Shortly after Mandela gained his freedom, Israeli-born Rabbi Ady Assabi of the Progressive Imanu-Shalom Congregation invited him to speak in his synagogue. This was a time when many Jews, in and out of South Africa, were worrying about Mandela's apparent embrace of Yasser Arafat.

In fact, white South Africa's attitude toward Israel has generally been more positive than that of most countries, with one of its early leading statesmen, Jan Christiaan Smuts, having played a leading role in passing the Balfour Declaration. Except during the 1960s, when Israel aligned itself with African countries against apartheid, the majority of Afrikaners have historically been sympathetic because they saw parallels between the Jews' dream of a homeland and their own, and more recently because of both countries' international isolation. This has well suited South African Jewry, which unequivocally equates Judaism with Zionism. For his part Mandela has sought to reassure the Jews, assuring them of his support for Israel's right to exist.

While Judaism is not a religion of choice among black South Africans, the black township of Soweto has in recent years had a congregation that called itself Jewish. Once as large as 2,000, subsequently reduced to 200, it was under the leadership of V. J. Msitshana, who uses the title of rabbi. While a political prisoner on Robben Island—with Nelson Mandela—he insisted upon being served kosher food. The one known South African black formally embracing Judaism is entrepreneur Geoffrey Ramokgadi of the Tswana tribe, who underwent a halakhic conversion in Swaziland.

Sights: Johannesburg sprawls. While its downtown reflects a bit of the old but mostly the new, much life that passes for the city's takes place off the tangle of highways streaming into the suburbs — where the Jews, following the "tenement trail" to the northeast, have moved into Berea, Yeoville, Houghton, Sydenham, Glenhazel, Highlands North, Sandton City, and Morningside. Consequently, sightseeing is not tidily accomplished.

For instant insight into the city, however, and an overview, a glimpse from the fiftieth-floor observation deck of the Carlton Centre reveals not only the contemporary landscape but also the mine dumps that were Johannesburg's raison d'être. On Commissioner Street, the Carlton Centre itself, a current landmark, is home to the Carlton Hotel, founded by Isaac Schlesinger, a prominent Jew in the insurance field who also contributed significantly to developing show business in South Africa.

For another "overview," albeit on the ground and under, visit Gold Reef City, four miles south of downtown Johannesburg on the spot where gold was first discovered. Gold Reef City is a cross between Colonial Williamsburg and Disneyland, with the vital exception that the chief attraction is real. In addition to the reconstructed Wild West-type streets of old Johannesburg, with a Barney's Pub serving Barney's Draft Beer beneath a photograph of the Jewish "randlord" Barney Barnato, Gold Reef City also offers the opportunity to go, hard hat on head and lantern in hand, 689 feet down a shaft of a genuine gold mine, the Crown Mines, which operated from 1916 to 1977. Along with an exhibition and demonstration on gold and gold smelting, the excursion provides a convenient peephole into this business so vital to South Africa and once so dominated by Jews.

Also in downtown Johannesburg, between Market and Pritchard Streets runs Diagonal Street, South Africa's answer to Wall Street. It features a mix of two-story, old-time buildings edging sidewalks lined with flower and spice vendors, and towering, glass-and-steel high rises. The latter house several of South Africa's most prominent mining houses, now conglomerates — many currently or previously led by Jews — as well as the country's stock exchange.

Other secular sights with Jewish associations are the Alexander Theatre, started by Muriel Alexander; and the Africana Museum in the Johannesburg Public Library on Market Street, which possesses — though undelineated and therefore difficult to search out — photographs of various Jewish Johannesburg pioneers.

Other displays featuring Johannesburg's Jewish past plus further relevant memorabilia are presented by Johannesburg's Jewish Museum at the corner of Main and Kruis Streets. On the fourth floor of Sheffield House, home to various Jewish organizations including the Jewish Board of Deputies and a Jewish library, the museum collection is eclectic. Of specifically African-Jewish interest are an African-sculpted stone *mezuzah* case; two Torahs from Maputo (formerly Lourenço Marques), in the former Portuguese colony of Mozambique; cornerstones of defunct South African congregations; a letter to Paul Kruger in Hebrew and Dutch from Jewish schoolchildren; and an eighteen-inch-high silver cup presented in 1857 by Jewish residents of the Colony of the Cape of Good Hope to Benjamin Norden, founder of South Africa's Jewish community. A copper tray, about two feet in diameter with a six-pointed star in the center surrounded by pomegranates, a coffee jug, and fish, has an unusual provenance. It was given to the museum by the wife of an Afrikaner army officer, Major Martin Liebbrandt, deputy military attaché in Vienna in the mid-1970s. He reportedly bought it for his wife in a Viennese antique store whose owner said it had belonged to the Jewish community in Eizenstadt and that it was stained with blood. When the stains proved impossible to remove, the major's wife, remembering the Bible said that the spoils of war should return to the House of Judah, gave it to the museum.

On Wolmarans Street, Johannesburg's Great Synagogue, topped by a dome, still stands and is generally open to the public on weekdays. Patterned after Istanbul's Hagia Sophia mosque, its interior conveys a sense of the circular as it spreads beneath a Wedgwood-blue cupola. A special feature behind the women's gallery is a chorus-line-like woman's dressing room with a great stretch of mirrors and cushy couches.

In the nearby suburb of Yeoville, at the corner of Grafton Road and Raleigh Street, stands the elaborately carved building of the Johannesburg Beit Din. On Barnato Street in another nearby suburb, Berea, stands the Etz Chayim Synagogue, which houses the Yad Vashem Memorial. Created around a centerpiece that is a tree trunk cut off at the top as if struck at the height of growth, nine wood panels designed by the late South African artist Ernest Ullman depict the Jews' tragic history through the centuries, as well as their courage and spirit. (Ring bell for entry.)

Perhaps the premier sight of specifically Jewish interest, however, is Johannesburg Jewry's memorial to the Holocaust. About five miles northwest of the city proper at the entrance to the Westpark Cemetery, this sculpture, created by the South African artist Herman Wald, features three pairs of facing hands, each holding a huge *shofar.* The three pairs of *shofars* curve inward, forming an incomplete arch that projects a depth apparently stretching to infinity above a symbolic Eternal Light.

Side Trip: An hour's drive north of Johannesburg is Pretoria, South Africa's jacaranda-trimmed capital. In addition to the statue of Paul Kruger in the town center, Church Square, which Sammy Marks paid for, there are in front of Kruger's erstwhile home at 60 Church Street two benevolent-looking marble lions, presented to Kruger in 1896 by Barney Barnato. They are popularly known as "The Barnato Lions." Inside the Kruger house is a letter written in High Dutch from the Johannesburg Hebrew Congregation thanking him for granting sites on which to build a synagogue and a school. About eight miles from Pretoria on its eastern outskirts, Exit 115 along the N-4 reads "Sammy Marks" and leads to the newly created museum that was the tycoon's home. A well-preserved Victorian structure set amid glorious gardens, it is special because Marks did not allow anything to be removed. Hence all is original — from the completely set dining room table to the huge billiard room surmounted by a photo of Sammy and his father, to the Bible in Hebrew. The Sheba Gold Mine, which he owned, is still operating in Barberton in the eastern Transvaal, about three hours' drive away. A bit farther afield, but worth at least an overnight, is Kruger National Park, Africa's largest, which features the continent's greatest variety of wildlife in one designated area.

Personalities: Among various internationally known show-business luminaries from Johannesburg and environs are actress-director Janet Suzman (a niece of Helen Suzman); the late actor Laurence Harvey; and the late John Cranko, seminal director and choreographer of the Stuttgart Ballet. A branch of Broadway's Shubert family resides in South Africa, retaining the original Lithuanian name, Shubitz. John Berks is a popular talk show host and disc jockey. Barney Simon, a playwright, has been the artistic director of the Market Theater, which has presented black and experimental plays as well as Athol Fugard's.

Leading journalists include Arnold Benjamin, satirical columnist for *The Star,* Johannesburg's leading English daily; Johnny Johnson, editor of *The Citizen,* the government newspaper; and political photographer David Goldblatt. Among prominent Jews working in governmental capacities are Parliament members Lester Fuchs and Tony Leon; and Harry Schwarz, a former opposition politician who became South Africa's ambassador to the United States in 1989. Steelmaker Mendel Kaplan is one of South Africa's leading industrialists and chairman of the board of governors of the Jewish Agency. Beginning with the case of Steve Biko in 1977, Dr. Jonathan Gluckman, a Johannesburg pathologist, has received both accolades and death threats for his accusations that the South African police had tortured and killed many suspects in custody.

Reading: While the Nobel Prize-winning writer Nadine Gordimer has somewhat tenuous ties to her Jewish background, passages in *Something Out There, The Conservationist* and *My Son's Story* (Viking) touch tangentially on Jewish life, while *The Lying Days* deals with Johannesburg in the late 1940s. Among works set against the Johannesburg Jewish scene are *Market Street: A Novel of South Africa* by Arthur Markowitz (Fieldhill Publishing House, Johannesburg); *Johannesburg Friday,* about life in a Jewish family on one Friday in the 1950s, by Albert Segal; Rose Zwi's family saga–style trilogy from immigrant grandparents to 1980s Johannesburg: *The Inverted Pyramid, Exiles,* and *Another Year in Africa*; Kimberley-born Dan Jacobson's *The Beginners* (Macmillan), set in the 1960s; and Jillian Becker's trilogy about a wealthy Jewish family, *The Virgins, The Keep,* and *The Union.* For history past and contemporary see *Running to Maputo* (HarperCollins) by Albie Sachs, an ANC executive; *The Randlords*, about the mining magnates, by Geoffrey Wheatcroft; *A South African Journey* by Adam Hochschild (Viking); and *Fighting Years* by Steven Mufson (Beacon Press). Barney Barnato was recently the subject of a South African Television series.

Recommendations: With many visitors to the Johannesburg area electing to stay outside the city center, the Sandton Sun in the heart of the Jewish-built Sandton City shopping center is a good option, offering kosher meals on request. The Courtleigh, in Berea, has recently become a kosher hotel. The suburb of Yeoville currently abounds with kosher pizzerias and Tel Aviv-type cafés; among its better known kosher restaurants are the King Solomon, serving meat; the King David, its dairy cousin; and Maxine's. On Thursday nights various catering establishments (among these, the Terrace) and the Carlton Hotel serve kosher buffets to South African residents and the tourists whom many look forward to greeting in the new South Africa.

—Phyllis Ellen Funke

Kaifeng

A glimmer of nostalgia can be detected in the eyes of Shi Zhongyu (pronounced Sh'r Jongyu) as he recalls Passover rituals in Kaifeng of 1928. Then a seven-year-old boy, Shi watched the substitution for the traditional rooster's blood—colored paint mixed with water—dabbed over the doorpost of his home with a Chinese writing brush. This festival, he recalls, was combined with features of the Chinese New Year. Another custom, celebrated separately, would take place in May, when Shi's mother would cook cakes containing no yeast.

"When the Hans [ethnic Chinese] celebrate New Year's, they have some Buddhist idols that they worship," Shi explains. "We didn't have those statues in our family. We only had the memorial tablets for our ancestors, in front of which we would place food offerings of mutton rather than the pork used by other Chinese, to show our respect for our Jewish ancestry."

The story of China's Jews is supposed to have ended. But there are still people in Kaifeng who claim Jewish ancestry and recall Jewish holidays and rituals—over a century after the synagogue near South Teaching Scripture Lane was destroyed for the last time. Over 150 years after the last Chinese rabbi in Kaifeng conducted services, taking with him at his death the last real knowledge of Hebrew and Bible, Jewish memory persists.

If you ask Chinese Jews how many of their ranks remain, estimates range from 100 to 300, although it is not clear if they mean individuals or only male heads of households, since Chinese Jews trace their descent patrilineally, as is the Chinese custom. This, of course, raises problems for other Jews who define Jewishness matrilineally, according to *halakhah* (Jewish law); by this criterion Chinese Jews haven't been Jewish for hundreds of years.

In fact, the Reform and Reconstructionist movements, in adopting patrilineal descent in the 1980s, legitimated a practice that Chinese Jews trace back at least as far as the Ming dynasty (1368-1644). A Ming emperor conferred upon the Jews seven surnames by which they are identifiable to this day: Ai, Gao, Jin, Li, Shi, Zhang and Zhao. Although other Chinese may have one of these surnames, Chinese Jews and their descendants will have *only* one of these seven names. Two names of particular interest, Shi and Jin—meaning Stone and Gold, respectively—echo common surnames today among Western Jews.

A Jewish community as such no longer exists in Kaifeng. Indeed, most of those of Jewish descent do not even know each other. "In Kaifeng, we Jews have virtually no contact with each other," one reports. "Only if someone says, 'My name is Li. I've heard my grandfather say I'm also a Jewish descendant,' do we know there are some links between us." But among individuals a strong sense of ethnic identity remains, and they are eager to share this and learn from foreign Jews who travel to Kaifeng.

History: Chinese Jews boast one of the most amazing stories in the annals of the Diaspora. Archeological evidence points to a Jewish presence in China as early as the eighth century, the Jews having arrived, most likely, from Persia along the Silk Road.

Arab and European travelers, including Marco Polo in the thirteenth century, spoke of meeting Jews or hearing about them during their travels in the Middle Kingdom, as China was then called. Polo records that Kublai Khan himself celebrated the festivals of Muslims, Christians, and Jews alike, bespeaking the existence of Jews in sufficient numbers in China to warrant attention by its rulers.

But it was not until the Jesuit missionary Matteo Ricci met Ai Tian, a Kaifeng Jew, in 1605, that the existence of this exotic community came to the attention of the West. Ai had heard that there were Westerners in China who steadfastly maintained their belief in one God, but who were not Muslims. What else could they be, thought Ai — having never heard of Christianity — but Jews?

The Jesuits who visited Kaifeng during the eighteenth century were intent on befriending Chinese Jews and studying their holy writings. They were motivated by a prevailing belief in Europe that the rabbis of the talmudic era had excised certain passages from the Torah that spoke in specific terms of the coming of Jesus. If only they could find the Torah of the Chinese Jews, who knew nothing of Christianity, they reasoned, they would be able to locate the deleted passages. They hoped to bring back an unexpurgated Torah — proving to Western Jews that their rabbis had deceived them — and they envisioned mass conversion to Christianity as a result.

Needless to say, the Jesuits did not find what they were looking for. They did, however, write letters to Beijing and to Rome, which have become a part of the Vatican archives. In these letters, they described the daily life and religious observances of the Chinese Jews, noting the great pride and care with which they maintained their synagogue. Jean Domenge, a Jesuit who visited Kaifeng in 1722, drew sketches of the interior and exterior of the synagogue, illustrating the degree of assimilation that had occurred among Chinese Jews by this time.

Set in a typical Chinese courtyard structure, with many pavilions dedicated to ancestors and illustrious figures from Jewish history, the synagogue (called the Temple of Purity and Truth, a name common to mosques as well) had a separate hall for the ritual slaughter of animals. Inside on a front table were incense sticks burned in honor of the patriarchs Abraham, Isaac, and Jacob.

On the Sabbath, the Jews read from the Torah, only after it was placed on a special "chair of Moses." Above this chair loomed a great tablet with gold Chinese letters proclaiming, "Long live the great Qing [dynasty] Emperor" a requirement for Muslim, Confucian, Buddhist, and Taoist temples as well until the establishment of the Republic of China in 1911. The Chinese Jews, however, put the *Shema* in Hebrew, which the non-Jews could not understand, above the proclamation, as a sign that God was the highest of all.

The Jesuits sent back rubbings of the two steles, or stone monuments, that had been erected in the courtyard of the synagogue compound. The earliest inscription on one of the steles, dating to 1489, tells of the history and religious beliefs of the Jews. It points to the year 1421, when the emperor conferred upon An Cheng, a Jewish physician, the surname Zhao, as the turning point for the acceptance of the Jews into Chinese society. From that time on, Chinese Jews would prove able to pass the civil service exam and thus be accepted into the mainstream Confucian society far out of proportion to their small numbers. Local gazetteers from the sixteenth through the twentieth centuries attest to this.

The 1489 inscription also notes that the first synagogue was erected in 1163, after the Jews were ordered by the emperor to "keep and follow the customs of your forefathers and settle at Bianliang [Kaifeng]." The stele itself was erected to commemorate the reconstruction of the synagogue after a devastating flood in 1461 — one of several that would destroy the synagogue and kill many Kaifeng inhabitants over the next few centuries.

An inscription on the back of the 1489 stone, dated 1512, suggests the existence of established Jewish communities in other parts of China. It records for posterity the donation of a Torah scroll by a Mr. Gold (Jin) of Hangzhou to the Kaifeng *kehillah*. This inscription also attempts to draw parallels between the basic tenets of Confucianism and Judaism, a simple enough effort since both emphasize the moral basis for conducting one's daily affairs. The notion of *tzedakah*, common to Confucianism and Judaism, is duly noted.

With a ban on proselytizing and the banishment of missionaries by the Yong

Zheng Emperor in 1724, contact between Westerners and Chinese Jews came to a halt and would not resume for over a hundred years. During the intervening century, assimilation took its toll, as a letter from a Kaifeng Jew to the West, written in the mid-nineteenth century, attests: "Morning and night, with tears in our eyes and with offerings of incense, do we implore that our religion may again flourish. We have everywhere sought about, but could find none who understood the letter of the Great Country [Hebrew], and this has occasioned us deep sorrow."

Lack of a rabbi and the dilapidated state of the synagogue undermined the Jewish community's confidence in its future. Although circumcision and observance of the dietary laws were still reported, the poverty rampant among the Jews—like that of their Chinese neighbors—led some to attempt to sell parts of the synagogue building and even some of the manuscripts. Scrolls of the Law and other Hebrew manuscripts were in the end sold to Protestant missionaries during the nineteenth century. Many are now in the Klau Library of the Hebrew Union College in Cincinnati. One Kaifeng Torah is at the Jewish Theological Seminary of America and another at the American Bible Society, both in New York.

Some time between 1850 and 1866, the synagogue was destroyed for the last time. But not until 1900, with the establishment of the Shanghai Society for the Rescue of the Chinese Jews, was a concerted effort made by Western Jews to help their brethren in Kaifeng. By then it was practically too late. Two Kaifeng Jews, a father and son of the Li clan, went to Shanghai at the behest of the Shanghai Society. They were joined in a later visit by six other members of the Kaifeng community, who all expressed eagerness for financial support to rebuild the synagogue.

But shortly after the turn of the century, pogroms in Russia and the resulting Jewish emigration diverted funds and attention away from Kaifeng, and a synagogue for the Kaifeng Jews was no longer considered a priority for the Shanghai Jewish community, faced as it was with life-and-death Jewish crises elsewhere.

The elder Li remained in Shanghai until his death in 1903 and was buried in the

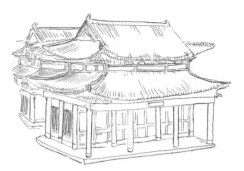

Before the flood: The Kaifeng Synagogue as it looked on South Teaching Scripture Lane

Jewish cemetery there. His son—given the name Shmuel when he was circumcised—was raised by the family of D. E. J. Abraham. Shmuel lived in Shanghai for nearly fifty years, returning after World War II to Kaifeng, where he died. His son, who also grew up in Shanghai, was sent to Kaifeng after the communists came to power in 1949.

People and Sights: Shmuel's son, Li Rongxin (pronounced Rungsheen), lives in Kaifeng today. Past eighty, he is healthy and full of stories of Jewish life in Shanghai—of the synagogue on Museum Road near where the Li family lived, and of the foreign Jews, mostly from England, with whom he had contact—and of Jewish practice in Kaifeng.

The small room Li calls home is filled with correspondence from Western Jews he has met over the years since Kaifeng was opened to tourists. He has accumulated something of a Judaica library, as they have given him copies of *Haggadahs* and Hebrew primers. Nevertheless, his knowledge of Jewish law and custom seems tinged with *bubbe meisehs* passed down among Chinese Jews—such as the "fact" that Jews observe the Sabbath in part by fasting. (Interestingly, the 1489 stele does state that Jews are to fast four times a month.)

When the American Jewish Congress started sending Jewish tour groups to Kaifeng in the early 1980s, the Chinese government would send Jewish spokespersons to meet with them. Shi Zhongyu, Shi Yulian, and Zhao Pingyu were the only Jews brought before tour groups, and the controlled meetings were brief. However eloquent, the Chinese Jews inevitably left visitors disappointed, as the Westerners struggled to understand the strong ties that somehow bound them together, as well as the differences which seemed at times insurmountable. Indeed, many on those early tours left feeling that the Chinese Jews were frauds who didn't observe Jewish holidays and traditions and had no knowledge of Hebrew or Jewish life. And to top it off, they gave the politically correct line of the Chinese government about Israeli aggression. Since the establishment of diplomatic relations between China and Israel in 1992, however, this is no longer the case.

How close *do* these Chinese Jews feel to Jews around the world? Many feel a special bond of common ancestry and heritage, but the political world in which they lived before the diplomatic breakthrough precluded a deeper understanding of Jewish ties to the Land of Israel. Nevertheless, pride in their past is very real, as can be seen by their listing their children as "Youtai" (Jewish) on all certificates of registry, next to the space allotted for nationality, where they once might have written "Han" (ethnic Chinese).

Zhao Pingyu, a retired tax collector and a member of the Planning Committee of the Tourist Bureau of Kaifeng, shows his family's nationality certificates to visitors to his home at 21 South Teaching Scripture Lane. The enterprising Zhao is preparing a minimuseum which will recount the many contributions and scholarly successes attained over the centuries by his ancestors. To this end, he has built a model of the old synagogue as his father and grandfather told him it looked. It is along the lines of the model of the Kaifeng synagogue in Beit Hatefutzot (the Diaspora Museum) in Tel Aviv, only Zhao has added two stone lions in the front, which stood there throughout the centuries.

"In the course of researching the history of the Zhao clan, one must also understand things which pertain to the original synagogue," says Zhao. "At least this will enable me to pass this knowledge on to my own descendants so that they will understand their history. During my research of the synagogue, I discovered that the last restoration was undertaken by my family."

Given that Judaism has been traced patrilineally in Kaifeng for centuries, Zhao finds himself in a peculiar position: He is one of the few Chinese Jewish descendants with an extensive knowledge of his people's history and has only daughters—five of them—to whom it will be passed on. Like Tevye, Zhao has had to accommodate to changing times. He has decreed that any children his daughters have should be registered as "Youtai," even if their fathers are not of Jewish descent. And they have all agreed. In fact, one has joined her father in a small-scale enterprise of making Chinese *kippot* to be sold to Jewish tourists—which they hope will bring in much-needed funds for the museum project.

Although he has amassed a formidable Judaica collection from Jewish tourists over the years, Zhao cannot read the English or Hebrew books. However, he does appreciate having them and hopes that one of his daughters, whom he would like to send to the United States or Israel to study Judaism, will someday return to Kaifeng and explain them to her father.

South Teaching Scripture Lane is a narrow, poorly paved road lined with traditional Chinese houses on both sides. The site of the synagogue is adjacent to the Zhaos' home, and local tour guides can point it out. Adjacent to the Zhaos' home is the hospital, which stands on the site of the synagogue that gave the street its name. "[The synagogue] was destroyed in the flood of the Yellow River," says Zhao. "After the flood [in the mid-nineteenth century], many Jews fled to other parts of the country. They went north, south, east, and west, scattered in all directions. After they left, they managed to make a living where they were and never bothered to return. So some of them [now] don't even know they are Jewish. At that time we also left, without any choice. But we couldn't make a living, so we came back. After this, we had no house, no way to make a living, so we just set up a house next to the original synagogue temporarily and slowly made our lives again. That's how we came to remain on this street."

Few Kaifeng Jewish descendants display

the knowledge of their ancestry that Zhao Pingyu possesses. When shown a Star of David, for example, Ai Dianyuan did not recognize it as a Jewish symbol. Nevertheless, Ai displays an attitude typical of most Jewish descendants in Kaifeng today: they know they are of Jewish descent only because they were told by their fathers, and they have a strong desire to pass this one bit of information on to their children.

There are indications that the Jews once had hopes of being recognized as a national minority. In 1952 Ai Fengmian was picked by his neighborhood committee to go to Beijing to represent Chinese Jews as one of the national minorities in a ceremony held by the then three-year-old government of the People's Republic. Ai met and shook hands with Mao Tse-tung, Chou En-lai, and Deng Xiaoping. China has fifty-five national minorities recognized on the basis of common language, traditions, customs, and geographic area. The Muslims constitute the second largest minority in China, after the Zhuang, and they are able to retain their study of Arabic and religious observance in mosques. The Jews, however, long ago lost knowledge of Hebrew and, with the destruction of the synagogue, a communal meeting place for worship.

Many Jews were, in fact, swallowed up by Islam over the years, since it was the religion whose customs and practices were most like those of Judaism. One such person is Jin Xiaojing, a sociologist at the National Minorities Research Institute of the Chinese Academy of Social Sciences in Beijing, who discovered her Jewish roots in 1980. Jin Xiaojing's daughter, Qu Yinan, a former Beijing journalist, studied at the University of Judaism in Los Angeles. Since the mid-1980s increasing numbers of Chinese scholars of non-Jewish descent have pursued Judaic studies in Israel and the United States with Chinese government support.

Shi Zhongyu is typical of those who exhibit a deep desire to recover their heritage. His childhood memories of celebrating Passover and seeing brass Stars of David wrapped in red silk hidden in a medicine chest are still vivid. "The yarmulkes I saw in my family were not made up of four sections [like the one given him by a tourist], but rather were composed of six pieces," he recalls. "They were dark blue with black trim, and there was Hebrew writing embroidered on it. They used yellow thread to embroider it with. . . . These belonged to the previous generation. It was always kept in the closet. . . . As I remember now, the number of the edges probably has something to do with the Sabbath. The story goes that on the first day God created such and such, the second day God created such and such, and so on, finishing creation on the sixth day. So because of this, the yarmulke has six or seven parts. I heard this from my mother. It's really regrettable we no longer have these things."

Shi is working with Wang Yisha, former curator of the Kaifeng Municipal Museum, who probably knows more contemporary Chinese-Jewish descendants than anyone else, to reconstruct the genealogies of the Kaifeng Jews, in particular of the Shi clan. The Hebrew Union College in Cincinnati donated two microfiches of the Chinese-Jewish Memorial Book of the Dead to aid their research — one to the museum and one to Wang Yisha himself.

The Kaifeng Municipal Museum now houses the two extant steles from the synagogue, but visitors are advised to request access to them through the China International Travel Service (CITS) in Beijing or before departing from home. Since almost all other Sino-Judaic relics are outside of China, efforts are being made by several organizations, most prominently the California-based Sino-Judaic Institute, to have replicas of such items as the jade chime that called the Jews to worship and the cylindrical Torah case made and donated to the museum.

The CITS, the official Chinese travel agency, has been attempting to establish greater tourist contact between Western Jews and Kaifeng. In the past, tourists have been discouraged by the many inconveniences of traveling to Kaifeng (still a long way from the amenities afforded by Shanghai and Beijing) and the paucity of actual things to see relating to the history of the Chinese Jews: Often the two steles may be seen only with considerable haggling on the part of tour leaders with CITS officials. However, tacit approval has been given for a plaque at the site of the synagogue and, perhaps less realistically, there has even been talk of reconstructing the Jewish house of worship itself.

Still, it is not that long since a journey to Kaifeng was liable to include interrogation by the security police on suspicion of gathering secret information or attempting to proselytize the Chinese Jews who—so I was told at my own grilling—don't even exist anymore; speaking to people in their homes was supposedly illegal, and those on tourist visas were expected to visit pagodas, not talk privately with individuals. Such occurrences have been reported much more recently in Kaifeng than in Beijing and Shanghai, where contacts between foreigners and Chinese are the norm.

In the past few years access to the Jewish descendants by Western tourists has alternated between open and severely restricted. Since the establishment of Sino-Israeli diplomatic relations, it appears to be as relaxed as it has ever been.

Reading and Resources: If visiting Chinese Jews has its difficulties, doing homework is relatively easy. The classic novel of the Jews of Kaifeng is Pearl Buck's *Peony* (Charles Bloch/Biblio Press). Scholarly and popular nonfiction works include Donald Daniel Leslie's *The Survival of the Chinese Jews* (E. J. Brill), Michael Pollak's *Mandarins, Jews and Missionaries* (Jewish Publication Society), Sidney Shapiro's *Jews in Old China: Studies by Chinese Scholars* (Hippocrene) and William Charles White's *Chinese Jews* (Paragon).

Several organizations in China and the United States are engaged in research on Chinese Jews and in fostering ties between the West and China's remnant community.

A good source of information is the Sino-Judaic Institute, 232 Lexington Drive, Menlo Park, CA 94205 (telephone 415-725-3436). It's difficult to keep track of which tour operations are offering Kaifeng itineraries at any given moment, but Al Dien, president of the institute, is likely to be more up-to-date on tours than anyone else. The institute also publishes a newsletter, *Points East*.

Wang Yisha is president of the Chinese Judaic Study Society of Kaifeng, 404 Gongyuan Lu, Building 63, Unit 4, Kaifeng, Henan Province (telephone 552-374; fax 552-320). The Jewish Historical Society of Hong Kong, 4/F, Melbourne Plaza, 33 Queen's Road Central, Hong Kong, has sponsored lectures and published articles on the Kaifeng community. There are Jewish studies associations in Shanghai and at Nanjing University.

Some tourists have left Kaifeng wondering whether the Chinese Jews aren't a hoax to get visitors and their money into the city. Having spoken to many of the Jewish descendants in the privacy of their homes, having heard their stories and even discussed Middle East politics, I cannot agree. There are precious memories of Jewish life in Kaifeng that are worth recording for future generations of Chinese Jews and for Jews around the world. I saw in the Chinese Jews a mixture of two of the greatest civilizations—certainly the oldest—the world has known. What I ask myself is not why Judaism and Jews as a community no longer live on in Kaifeng but, rather, how they could have survived in that far corner of the world with a Jewish identity for so long.

—*Wendy Abraham*

Kiev

Babi Yar is a symbol of Jewish suffering, but it also stands for how dictatorships can lose control. For years Soviet authorities refused to acknowledge that most of the people killed by the Germans at the ravine on the edge of Kiev had been Jews. A monument put up in 1959 referred only to "fascist occupiers" and "citizens of Kiev."

Precisely because of the Soviet resolve to suppress the Jewish dimension of the tragedy there, Babi Yar became a rallying point. The Russian poet Yevgeny Yevtushenko wrote his best-known poem about Babi Yar, lamenting the absence of a monument; both poem and poet were among the first chinks in the great monolith of Soviet information control. When the government tried in the early 1960s to erase the memory by erecting a housing project on the site, non-Jews joined Jews in the protests that had the project stopped. After 1967, young Jews in Kiev would hold rallies at Babi Yar on the anniversary of the massacre, just as Moscow Jews would rally at the Choral Synagogue on Simchat Torah. Thus did a place where Jews were murdered become a monument to Jewish survival and endurance. When Jewish leaders from Kiev dedicated an explicitly Jewish monument at the site on September 28, 1991 — the fiftieth anniversary of the first killings — they were joined not only by Jews from Israel and the United States, but also by representatives of the Ukrainian and Soviet governments. Given that the Soviet Union itself would pass into history two months later, sanctioning the memorial it had so long prevented was one of its last official acts.

The victory was, nevertheless, built on Jewish ashes — an apt metaphor for the sudden freedom in one of the world's most important Jewish communities.

History: Kiev was at the commercial crossroads of Western Europe and Central Asia, a distinction that attracted Jews virtually from the city's founding in the eighth century. Though the first Jews were transient merchants, by the tenth century there was a settled community, when visitors from the Jewish kingdom of Khazaria tried to persuade Kiev's Prince Vladimir to convert to Judaism. In the eleventh century the city's abbot, Theodosius the Blessed, was in the habit of visiting Jewish homes to conduct disputations on the merits of Judaism and Christianity. By the fifteenth century, when the Jewish community had achieved a measure of prosperity and become a center of scholarship, it had some internal disputations — between Rabbanite Jews and Karaites.

The cyclical pattern of persecution, expulsion, and return — so familiar in European Jewish history — began in Kiev in 1495. At times Jews were allowed to reside in the city; at times only Jewish merchants could enter alone for up to a day; at times no Jewish presence was allowed at all. The low point came in 1648-49, when Bogdan Chmielnicki's troops killed 200,000 Jews in their effort to free Ukraine from Poland's yoke. The ban on Jewish settlement was renewed with Kiev's annexation to Russia in 1667.

No Jewish community would form in Kiev again until the second partition of Poland, in 1793, added thousands of Jews to the Russian realm. By 1815 the city had 1,500 Jews and two synagogues. Christian authorities objected as strenuously as ever to a Jewish presence, and in 1835 the Jews were expelled one more time. They continued to enter the city as tradesmen, and at the city's annual trade fair more than half the participants were Jews. Finally in 1861 two sections of the city—Podol and Lyebed—were assigned for Jews who could manage to get residency permits. With the exception of the years under German occupation, Podol has been a center of Jewish life ever since.

In the last quarter of the nineteenth century and the first quarter of the twentieth, Kiev provided a textbook example of how Jewish life can grow and flourish amid raging anti-Semitism. There were pogroms in 1881 (supported and encouraged by local authorities) and 1905 (during which the police stood by). Large-scale pogroms threatened to break out in 1911 after a Jew assassinated Prime Minister Peter Arkadyevich Stolypin in Kiev, but this time the authorities intervened. Throughout the period the police made regular raids looking for Jews without residence permits.

It was an event in Kiev that, perhaps more than anything else, brought Russian anti-Semitism to the attention of the world. On March 20, 1911, the mutilated body of a twelve-year-old Christian boy was found in a cave outside the city. Although the police traced the murder to a gang of thieves, the anti-Semitic Union of Russian People (the Black Hundreds) and the minister of justice concocted a blood libel out of the case. They charged that Mendel Beilis, superintendent of a Kiev brick kiln, had killed the child so that Jews could use his blood for ritual purposes. Beilis was imprisoned for two years, during which protests were heard from scientists, politicians, clergymen, and writers from around the world. At his trial, the main "expert" witness on Jewish blood rituals was a priest with a criminal record. The chief rabbi of Moscow, joined by Russian academics, refuted the charges. A jury composed of Russian peasants delivered a unanimous not-guilty verdict; fearful of revenge from the Black Hundreds, Beilis and his family fled, settling first in Palestine and ultimately in the United States.

But such incidents hardly kept Kiev's Jewish population from growing; it increased from 14,000 in 1872 (a little more than 10 percent of the total) to 81,000 on the eve of World War I. Jewish merchants flourished; the community supported hospitals and schools and built beautiful synagogues. Jewish writers (including Sholom Aleichem) made their home in Kiev, and Kiev University had the largest concentration of Jewish students of any Russian university.

The last restrictions on Jewish residence in Kiev were lifted during World War I and after the Russian Revolution, and more Jews poured into the city. By 1939 the community numbered 175,000—20 percent of the population. In the early years of communism Kiev was a major center of Jewish culture—with schools, Yiddish newspapers, a Jewish state theater—but beginning in the 1930s Jewish culture was systematically destroyed. And on September 21, 1941, when it must have seemed that nothing worse could happen to Kiev Jewry, the Germans captured the city.

Some Jews managed to escape to the east in advance of the German occupation, but the majority were trapped in the city. On September 28 the German authorities ordered the city's Jews to report the next day, with documents, money, and warm clothes, to the corner of Melnikova and Dukhtorovsky streets or face execution; the Germans themselves had spread rumors that the Jews would be relocated to ghettos or labor camps. Instead, they were marched to the nearby ravine, Babi Yar, executed, and buried in mass graves. More than 33,000 were murdered in the first two days, and by the time the killings were over 200,000 had died at Babi Yar.

Many Jews returned to Kiev after the war, and despite the continued suppression of Jewish life the Jewish population is believed to have reached 200,000 by 1960. There were cracks in official anti-Semitism when plaques were put up on the home of Sholom Aleichem and at Babi Yar in 1959, but for every step forward there was at least a half-step back. The Sholom Aleichem plaque, which acknowledged the writer's Jewishness, was replaced a year later with one that omitted his origins; the Babi Yar monument never mentioned Jews. Only in the 1970s did the Soviet authorities finally allow one form of Jewish expression—emigration. The tap was turned on and off during the seventies and eighties, and then the power that controlled the flow disappeared.

Community: Estimates of the number of Jews in Kiev today vary widely. Many have emigrated but some from smaller Ukrainian towns have moved in and many people officially registered as Russian or Ukrainian in recent years have been dusting off Jewish pasts. The middle figure in the range puts the community at 90,000. In all of Ukraine there are about half a million Jews.

Given the history of Ukrainian anti-Semitism (Ukrainian guards were willing participants in the German-led massacres at Babi Yar), relations between Jews and the new Ukrainian regime are remarkably good. There are anti-Semitic graffiti and some acts of anti-Jewish vandalism, but the Ukrainian nationalist movement, Rukh, has been outspokenly supportive of a Jewish role in the new Ukraine. President Leonid Kravchuk has explicitly denounced anti-Semitism; he is also a member of the Babi Yar Committee, which has plans to expand the new monument at the massacre site into a memorial complex.

Podol is still the center of Jewish life in Kiev, though Jews can now be found all over the city. Those closer to the center of town are more likely to speak Russian at home. Those farther out, because they came from the hinterland or because of the neighborhoods they live in, are more likely to speak Ukrainian. Jews are disproportionately represented among the city's doctors, engineers, and musicians, among teachers (especially languages and mathematics), and in the film industry.

Jewish organizations are proliferating, and currently number about thirty. There is a Jewish day school, a *yeshivah*, self-help organizations, and a proliferation of Hebrew classes. A Jewish theater company performs Sholom Aleichem within blocks of where the great Yiddish writer lived; gentiles as well as Jews come to see the performances in Yiddish and Russian. Much of the community's efforts are focused on raising money to sustain Jewish life and on retrieving property that was lost to the communist regime, especially the old Great Synagogue in the center of town. About the only complaint one hears about the atmosphere in the city—other than over the economic situation, which affects everyone—is that the property of the Russian Orthodox church was returned more quickly; but no one in the Jewish community seems to doubt that everything they are claiming will ultimately be given back.

The changes for Jews in Kiev were more abrupt than for Jews in Moscow, where years of intense foreign scrutiny served as a temporal buffer between the darkest days of totalitarian rule and the transition to freedom. "It happened here so suddenly that some people are afraid things will return to the way they were in the past," says Dmitry Levin, president of Kiev's one functioning synagogue. "Suddenly the government began to like Jews."

Sights: It happens to many Jews when they first set foot on the streets of Kiev. There is a sense that you have been here before. Most of the Jews who emigrated before the Russian Revolution never saw the distant metropolises of Moscow and St. Petersburg, but virtually every Jew from the Pale of Settlement trod the streets and alleys of Kiev at some point. The Kiev of the 1990s looks much as grandparents described the Kiev of the first decade of the century. Close to 90 percent of Warsaw was destroyed in World War II but less than 20 percent of Kiev. If other European cities offer a Jewish view, Kiev offers a strong sense of Jewish *déjà vu*.

Like much of Kiev, Podol looks as if it hasn't changed since before the Revolution. The neighborhood lies just north of the city center, along the Dniepr. Balconies protrude from the two- and three-story buildings, most from the mid-nineteenth century, that line the straight streets. Paint peels faster than charm from many of the yellow, green, and orange structures.

In the middle of this time warp, at 29 Shchekovitskaya Street, is Kiev's synagogue, which despite years of wear and sorrow looks in some ways as regal as it did when it opened in 1894. It has been in continuous use, except during World War II when the German occupiers used it as a stable. Because it is the nerve center of a large Jewish population, it bustles, with communal workers and students in *kippot* congregating in the building, in the courtyard to the side and on the street in front.

The two-story stone building is painted orange with white trim. Graceful Byzantine arches adorn its front door and second-floor windows. The sanctuary features two

World of Sholom Aleichem: Kiev's synagogue once again hums with activity

the second-floor level. The building is scheduled to be returned to the Jewish community shortly. There are already plans to convert it into a Jewish community complex, including a museum devoted to Jewish life in the Ukraine, a stage for the still-homeless Jewish theater, and a school.

Shota Rustaveli Street—a busy commercial thoroughfare clogged with people, streetcars, and automobiles—was once home to the city's wealthiest Jews. A few doors from the former Great Synagogue is the Kinopanorama. Now one of Kiev's largest theaters, it was originally the home of Joseph Brodsky, scion of the family of industrialists and philanthropists that at one time produced one-quarter of the sugar in Russia and built many of the country's Jewish institutions (including the Great Synagogue down the street and Kiev's first Jewish hospital). You can attend cultural events and exhibits at the theater, but few of the interior details remain from Brodsky's time. Some design details remain in Brodsky's private synagogue—now the theater director's office—but that part of the building is not open to the public.

At the beginning of the century Sholom Aleichem lived in the apartment building at Krasnayarmeski 5. Though she said her earliest memory was the 1905 pogrom in Kiev, Golda Meir also remembered seeing the great writer as she played in the building's courtyard. The three-story yellow brick structure, built in the 1880s, was gutted in 1992 and is undergoing reconstruction. When it opens—in 1995, according to the plan—it will include a Sholom Aleichem museum.

The juxtaposition of Jewish dreams and Jewish suffering, and the permanent tension built into the Ukrainian-Jewish relationship, can be seen in the proximity of Sholom Aleichem's house and Bogdan Chmielnicki Square, just five blocks away along Vladimirskaya Street. In the square sits the seventeenth-century Cossack leader and Ukrainian national hero. There are signs that the new Ukrainian leadership is learning that the hero's popularity doesn't travel as well as the statue on horseback would suggest. Poles hate Chmielnicki as much as Jews, and Ukrainian officials were embarrassed recently by the chilly reaction of visiting Polish dignitaries who were

bimahs, one in the center and one in front of the ark. Signs of its elegant beginnings and later hard times are the marble pillars supporting the women's gallery and the worn linoleum floor. Surrounding the sanctuary on the baby-blue face of the balcony are symbols that stand for the zodiac and the months of the Hebrew calendar. On the wall above the ark (also on a baby-blue background) are the Ten Commandments and the words of the priestly blessing, *Mah Tovu* and *Etz Chayim Hi.*

The rambling building also houses community offices and a day school, a *mikveh* and a *matzah* factory. *Shechitah* takes place on the grounds as well. There are daily services. *Shabbat* services attract an average of fifty to sixty people. Call 416-13-83 for information on services or community activities.

Kiev Jews and visitors from abroad used to look mournfully at the Puppet Theater on the corner of Shota Rustaveli and Rognyedinsky Streets. The blue-and-white building dating from 1902 was once Kiev's Great Synagogue, and many of its original features are still evident. There are arches over the front doors and arched windows at given what the local authorities considered an honor—medals bearing the Cossack's likeness.

Babi Yar lies northwest of the city center, along Melnikova Street. The original monument is south of the street, on the site of a wartime German prison camp and several hundred yards from where the Jews were killed. Amid fields of grass and dandelions, surrounded by dirt paths lined with flowering trees, is Lysenko Borodai's stone sculpture—a jumble of victims, some defiant, some simply dying—dedicated to those who perished at Babi Yar. The only hint that the vast majority of the victims were Jews is that one of the memorial plaques to the "citizens of Kiev" is in Yiddish.

It was the Soviet government's refusal to acknowledge the Jews killed at the ravine that prompted the Russian poet Yevgeny Yevtushenko to publish his famous poem in 1961. "Today, I am a Jew," he wrote, "Now I go wandering, an Egyptian slave . . . / And now I perish, splayed upon the cross/ The marks of nails are still upon my flesh/ I am Dreyfus whom the gentry hound . . . / I am that little boy in Bialystok/ Whose blood flows, spreading darkly on the floor . . . / Let the glad "Internationale" blare forth/ When earth's last anti-Semite lies in earth/ No drop of Jewish blood flows in my veins/ But anti-Semites with a dull, gnarled hate/ Detest me like a Jew/ O know me truly Russian through their hate." Yevtushenko was attacked by the regime's literary apologists, but his point stuck.

When the green light was finally given for a memorial explicitly recognizing the Jewish victims of Babi Yar it was decided to place it closer to the actual site of the killings. The new monument is across Melnikova, at the end of a stone path that runs between the high-rise tower of Ukrainian television on the right and a hockey school on the left. The first part of the monument, a stone *menorah* sitting on a stepped pedestal, was sculpted by Yuri Paskevich. The Babi Yar Committee, headed by a prominent Kiev film director, Alexander Schlaen, is raising money to build a memorial complex on the site, which will include a museum and archive dedicated to all the Ukrainian Jews killed during World War II. The committee is also at work on a complete list of the people killed at Babi Yar.

Reading: The writer who best captured the Ukrainian Jewish experience was Sholom Aleichem, although you need a scorecard to know which places he is writing about. Kiev is always referred to as Yahupets. Anatevka, the village in the Tevye stories from which *Fiddler on the Roof* is derived, was a real place, too, the village of Boyarka, about fifteen miles from Kiev. One of Sholom Aleichem's novels set mostly in Kiev is *In the Storm* (Putnam), which centers around three Jewish families in a Kiev apartment building amid the pogroms, revolutionary activities, and assimilationist tendencies of the early 20th century.

The Fixer (Farrar, Straus & Giroux), by Bernard Malamud, is a Pulitzer Prize-winning fictional account of the Beilis blood libel and trial, which brought both Kiev and Russian anti-Semitism to worldwide attention in 1911. The 1968 movie version (with Alan Bates as the Beilis character) is one of the better screen adaptations of good literature. The definitive history of the trial is Maurice Samuel's *Blood Accusation: The Strange History of the Beilis Case* (Knopf). Matt Cohen's novel, *The Spanish Doctor* (Viking Press), focuses on a Jew who leaves Spain in the midst of the 14th-century pogroms and ends up in Kiev.

Babi Yar has been treated in many media. The classic Russian novel about the massacres of Kiev Jews is *Babi Yar* by Anatoly Kuznetsov (Dell). Dmitri Shostakovich set Yevtushenko's poem to music in his Thirteenth Symphony.

Side Trips: All of Ukraine is a side trip from Kiev, and the direction Jewish travelers take these days usually depends on where their parents or grandparents came from. With places like Berdichev, Vinnitsa, and Chernovtsy to the west; Uman, Nikolaev, and Odessa to the south, Kiev is the center of the Jewish genealogical route; and unlike Poland, most of the smaller cities and towns in Ukraine still have Jews. For information on Jewish genealogical tours contact Miriam Weiner, 136 Sandpiper Key, Secaucus, NJ 07094. For general Jewish tours to Kiev and the former Soviet

Union, contact Alexander Smuckler at All Ways International, 5 Penn Plaza, Suite 102, New York, NY 10001 (telephone 212-947-0505).

Recommendations: Kiev isn't the French Riviera, but neither is getting there or staying there a Spartan experience. Several airlines now have direct flights from European gateways, and the night train from Moscow is an option reminiscent of rail travel in America decades ago. The Rus 1 and Rus 2 hotels are comfortable if not sumptuous.

The story used to be told that Party Secretary Brezhnev told a crowd, "By the year 2000 every Russian will have his own airplane." A heckler by the name of Goldberg interrupted, asking, "What do we need airplanes for?" Brezhnev, visibly irritated, replied, "Idiot! Suppose you are in Moscow and you hear that in Kiev they have potatoes." Nowadays, the Brezhnevs are gone; Moscow seems to have more fuel for cars and airplanes, but Kiev seems to have more bread and potatoes; and the Goldbergs can ask any questions they like.

—*Alan M. Tigay*

Lisbon

The Portuguese once spent a great deal of time exploring the shores of North America. If you're among those who believe that turnabout — however belated — is fair play, you're sure to find plenty worth discovering in Lisbon.

Set on a series of hills above the Tagus River, Portugal's capital city combines the sights of Old World Europe with the smells of the sea. The influence of the Tagus and the nearby Atlantic are felt in the city's weather, warm but breezy, and its cuisine, abundant in fish — especially *bacalhau*, dried salt cod that is prepared in dozens of different ways. Even Fado, the traditional music of Lisbon, is a mix of flamenco-style guitars and Italian-opera dramatics with origins in the emotional outpourings of women whose husbands and lovers abandoned them for the sea.

Portugal's history as a country of explorers and navigators has lent its capital an air of worldliness. Once the center of the transatlantic push to the New World, Lisbon is an open-minded city. And yet because of its relative isolation on the western part of the Iberian peninsula, its late admittance into the European Community, and its status as Western Europe's poorest country, it is less cosmopolitan than most other European capitals.

The city has retained a unique appearance as well; chief among the visual hallmarks that set Lisbon apart from its more homogeneous European neighbors are the tiled facades of many of the city's older houses and stores. The building fronts provide not only color but protection from the ravages of time, low maintenance budgets and salt air; the edifices covered with blue, green, and white hand-painted ceramic squares have fared far better than those whose mint-green, yellow, and pink paint has been allowed to chip and weather. The mixture of the two types of buildings characterizes the city as much as its parks, public squares, and outdoor sardine grillers. And one needn't look up at the buildings to witness the Lisbon finesse with mosaic work; even the sidewalks are made of small tiles — white and black granite stones, actually — arranged in swirls, pictures, and Greek-key designs along Avenida da Liberdade, the city's main pedestrian boulevard, and on many of the side streets.

Lisbon's smaller streets are charming and friendly (just be sure to wear flat shoes). Meandering through the alleyways of the older neighborhoods — the Bairro Alto and the Alfama — is a good way to get acquainted with the city's flavor and history. Unfortunately, less of that history than one might expect is visible to the twentieth-century visitor; an earthquake in 1755 leveled much of the city, killing 30,000 people and tumbling nine thousand buildings. Much of the city's history perished too, including the signs of its Jewish past.

History: Jews have been living in Lisbon for almost one thousand years and were well established by the time of the twelfth-century Christian conquest and the subsequent establishment of the kingdom of Portugal by King Afonso I in 1147. After Afonso took the throne, Jews were installed as royal treasurers, physicians, astronomers, and tax collectors. In 1248 the city became the seat of the *arraby mor,* as the country's chief rabbi was designated.

The tide turned toward the end of the fourteenth century. In 1373 Lisbon's Jewish quarter was attacked and many Jews killed. Jews were removed from positions of power. Nevertheless, the Portuguese rulers prevented the widespread pogroms that swept Spain in 1391 from spilling over their borders.

But as in Spain, pressures increased in the fifteenth century. In 1455, the Cortes (local assembly) of Lisbon demanded restrictions on Jewish life and activity. Though Jews fleeing the Spanish Inquisition were given grudging refuge in 1492, the Portuguese soon caught the anti-Semitic fever. In 1497 Jews were herded into Lisbon and forcibly converted to Catholicism. Those who left settled mainly in the Ottoman Empire, especially Smyrna and Salonika; Lisbon's remaining "New Christians," or Conversos, were scorned and discriminated against, and many were thrown into dungeons.

During the sixteenth century many Conversos remained Jewish in secret, and the Inquisition was active in tracking them down; Lisbon's first auto-da-fé took place in 1540.

There were still Jews in dungeons when the earthquake struck in 1755. The upheaval allowed prisoners to escape, and refugees to flee the oppressive atmosphere of Lisbon and emigrate to England.

The reconstruction of Lisbon was undertaken by the Marques de Pombal, a powerful royal minister. In 1773 he abolished all legal distinctions between "Old" and "New" Christians, further assimilating those Jews who remained and diminishing what had once been a large and vital Converso community. Small numbers of Conversos, particularly in northern Portugal, continued to practice Judaism in secret.

Not long after Conversos made their way to London in the eighteenth century (where they became a force in the English Jewish community), the trade route inevitably brought new Jews to Lisbon, where they were now allowed to practice Judaism under British protection. Most were from Gibraltar, though there were some from North Africa and a few from England itself. The community received recognition as a "colony" (not a community) in 1868. The first synagogue, built in 1902, had to be hidden behind unmarked gates, but by 1910 full equality was decreed.

After World War I, the largely Sephardic community—most of whom maintained British citizenship—began receiving Ashkenazic immigrants. In the 1940s the trickle became a flood, as 45,000 refugees from Nazi-occupied Europe sought haven there and were allowed to live in peace and safety. After the war years, though, many emigrated to the United States, Canada, Brazil, or Israel, and today only 300 Jews remain in Portugal, with most of them living in Lisbon. Once home to Jewish scholars, astronomers, and sages, Lisbon is today only a remnant of a Jewish community.

In northern Portugal, in and around the town of Belmonte, descendants of Conversos continued to practice Jewish rituals into the present. In the past decade some have come into the open, and a number have formally converted back to the faith of their Jewish ancestors.

Community: Today there are fewer Jews in Portugal than in some large New York apartment buildings. With fewer than 10 percent of these observant, it is difficult for either of the city's two synagogues to get a *minyan*. Though nominally Ashkenazic and Sephardic, each attracts a mixture of Jews from both traditions, prompting the question of why two synagogues exist within one mile of each other, each attracting fewer than ten men on many Saturday mornings. The key to this puzzle lies in an old Jewish joke: No longer separated by Occidental and Oriental Jewish traditions, the two *shuls* today provide each local Jew with "the synagogue I go to and the one I wouldn't go to if you paid me."

Those who call the Sephardic synagogue Shaare Tikva "the one I go to" pray with the city's only rabbi, Avraham Assor. Born and educated in Tangier, Assor has been the spiritual leader in Lisbon for more than forty years. His son, Isaac, serves as *chazan* at Shaare Tikva; given the exquisite beauty of his voice, it is even more surprising that the *shul* cannot attract a quorum. During the 1980s the number of worshipers dwindled, and the Jewish hospital (and the *mikveh* it housed) were closed.

Several of Lisbon's young Jews work for the local office of El Al, and the city boasts an Israel-Portugal Chamber of Commerce. The annual Yom Haatzma'ut celebration is well attended, as are special events, like the recent visit of the Israeli handball team, which came to play against a group of Portuguese Jewish athletes. Many of these events take place at the Jewish Community Center at 10 Rua Rosa Araujo (telephone 572-041). Functioning as a social club, the building is locked when not in use, and tourists should arrange in advance to visit.

Though Lisbon is one of the few places where the Lubavitcher rebbe Menachem Mendel Schneerson hasn't sent a *minyan*, a small group of observant Jews has started an organization called Friends of Chabad (though they aren't *hasidim*) and are trying to keep religious practice alive. The group maintains a small storeroom of kosher products and frozen meats imported from Israel, since there is no kosher butcher in Portugal (once a month the rabbi slaughters meat for himself and some community members) and has begun renovating the Ashkenazic synagogue. For information about it as well as access to the food shop, call Solomon Marquez at 534-928. Call Assor at 530-396 to arrange for kosher meals or with prayer-time inquiries.

Sights: Perhaps the restored facilities of the Ashkenazic Synagoga Ohel Jacob, in an apartment one flight up at 110 Rua Elias Garcia, will render it worthy of a special visit. In the meantime, it is a jumble of folding chairs and construction gear. Like the social club, the *shul* is locked when not in use.

The Sephardic synagogue at 59 Rua Alexandre Herculano is also locked when not in use, but the caretaker is around most of the time, and her son, who is fluent in English, is gracious about answering tourists' questions. The synagogue was built in the first decade of the twentieth century, when the newly recognized community was growing and it was decided the time had come to unite the various *minyanim* existing in apartment buildings around the city. In 1948 termite damage made a full overhaul necessary; at the time the Jewish community was so large and active that a second tier was added to the women's balcony as part of the rebuilding.

Both tiers look down on a traditional Sephardic sanctuary: The *bimah* is in the center with pews facing it from behind and both sides, and a red carpet leads up to the

ark. Adornments include silver Torah finials and a *tzedakah* box on the *bimah*. The most acute reminder that this synagogue is in Portugal is the traditional inscription above the ark reminding worshipers to *da lifnei mi atah omed* (know before Whom you stand); the message is rendered not in paint nor gold leaf as in many other sanctuaries, but in a mosaic made of the glazed tiles that are the country's trademark. On the staircase leading up to the women's gallery is a tapestry depicting the encounter between Saul and Samuel after the fight against Amalek.

In the nineteenth century Jews were buried in a pocket park off the British cemetery near Rua da Estrela. They bought the land from the British because the Portuguese government forbade the burial of Jews on nationally owned land. They used it until it was full and the government was persuaded to let them have their own cemetery, located on Avenida Afonso III on the eastern end of town.

The tombstones in both cemeteries are simple, and time has worn many of the names away. In the newer cemetery the stones are clearer, and one can see memorials to many Berliners who fled to Lisbon during World War II and to the Jewish soldiers who died in the war in Angola, a Portuguese colony that won its independence in 1975. In that decade, as today, Jews were integrated into Lisbon's society and culture.

Indeed, even when Jews were separate they were not ghettoized; there is a street in the Alfama, Lisbon's oldest district, called Rua da Judiaria. Only a few hundred yards long, the street never housed many Jews; that the Jews clustered there was no more unusual than the existence of Jewish neighborhoods in twentieth-century America. To search out Rua da Judiaria, walk downhill from Largo San Rafael off Rua de San Miguel, which is marked on a well-detailed map. The Alfama is worth at least a half-day of wandering. The streets offer bird's-eye glimpses of the river, and—even more important—a good glimpse into Portuguese working-class life today.

Start at the top, at the Largo das Portas do Sol, and head down the winding streets and staircases. You'll pass children playing, housewives hanging laundry out to dry, and more than a few merchants hawking dried salt cod; this is Lisbon's street life. The friendliness will serve you well when you (inevitably) get lost and need direction back to a street big enough to be listed on your map.

If you continue east after a walk around the Alfama you'll see Castelo São Jorge up on a hill. Follow your eyes and enter the park that surrounds the castle for terrific views of the city while you burn off the thousands of calories you can easily ingest in the cloyingly sweet Portuguese desserts. You'll climb literally hundreds of stairs before you reach the castle's top vantage point, but if the day is clear the trek is worth it; from above, the dirt and decay that detract from Lisbon's beauty at street level are invisible and all that remains is the charm.

Personalities: Among Lisbon's more notable Jewish residents were Isaac Abrabanel, the philosopher and biblical scholar who served as treasurer to Portugal's King Afonso V and later to Spain's King Ferdinand. His son, Judah Abrabanel, was a poet and Renaissance philosopher. Both fled the Inquisition and died in Italy.

Pedro Nuñez was the chief cosmographer of Portugal and, for his treatise on the sphere, became regarded as the father of modern cartography. Among the descendants of Portuguese Jews who made a mark on the world were Baruch Spinoza and Manasseh Ben Israel, the Amsterdam scholar who played a role in convincing Oliver Cromwell to formally readmit Jews to England. And it was descendants of Portuguese Jews who in 1654 founded what was to become the world's greatest Jewish community, in New York.

Though Jews and Conversos kept low profiles for several centuries, the freedom of the last one hundred years provided an opportunity for Moses Bensabat Amzalak to rise to prominence in the government of Antonio de Oliveira Salazar, the dictator who ruled Portugal from 1932 to 1968. Amzalak was an economist and author, well respected for both his wisdom and his commitment to the Jewish community. He served for many years as the community's president.

Portugal produced a righteous gentile, Aristedes de Sousa Mendes, who as a consul in Bordeaux disobeyed orders and issued papers to many Jews fleeing the Nazis.

General Sights: The second-best view of Lisbon awaits you on the other end of the riverfront atop the Torre de Belém. Yes, more stairs. Lots of them. But again, the climb culminates in a great view, this time of the river itself and of the Ponte 25 Abril, the longest bridge in Europe and one of the city's many commemorations of Portugal's independence. Connected to the riverbank by a wooden gangplank, the tower was built in 1512 by Francisco de Arruda to defend the harbor. That harbor lies below you as you look around from the tower's peak, and on a clear day you can see well across the river as well as up to Lisbon's hills.

The Museu de Arte Popular (folk art museum) on Avenida Brasilia is a short walk from the Torre of Belém and shows great artistic diversity. In addition to housing the various pottery styles that characterize Portugal's different regions, the museum showcases handmade kitchen utensils, saddles for cart-drawing donkeys, and decorations made of finely cut paper.

The collection of the Museu Nacional de Arte Antiga features Renaissance art and, among its Christian contents, portraits of some Hebrew Bible figures including King David and the Prophet Isaiah, both Spanish-school paintings from the fifteenth century. Newer art — indeed Portugal's newest — is housed at the Centro de Arte Moderna Calouste Gulbenkian at 45 Avenida de Berna.

A visit to a Fado house (a small restaurant where music is performed) is a must — most of the Casas de Fado clustered in the Bairro Alto attract fewer locals than the Statue of Liberty on a weekday. But don't let their touristy atmosphere put you off. Though you don't have to eat or drink, there's a minimum charge, and the haunting music is unlike any you've heard before.

Reading: The Alhambra Decree (Carmi House), David Raphael's novel of the expulsion from Spain, is notable in its inclusion of Portugal in its landscape. As a neutral capital in World War II, Lisbon was a scene of much intrigue. Novels that capture the flavor of the time include *To Catch a King* (Stein and Day) by Harry Patterson and *The Judas Code* (Stein and Day) by Derek Lambert.

Recommendations: TAP/Air Portugal has flights to Lisbon from several American cities, and they've moved many of their New York–area flights from Kennedy to Newark.

If you'd like to check out Lisbon's consumer culture, visit the Amoreiras shopping center. Its postmodern skyscraping buildings so sharply contrasting with Lisbon's low-lying tile-covered houses caused an up-roar when construction began, and there are still plenty of natives who believe the complex — which also houses offices — augurs the death of Lisbon as a civilized city. The remainder of the city's residents, though, spend their time in the mall's somewhat confusing corridors buying clothes, housewares, and movie tickets. Like American malls, Lisbon's has a food court; lest you forgot where you are though, the snack shops have names like "Bacalhau King." Even if Lisbon's architecture is gradually (very gradually) becoming similar to the rest of the world's, its food remains distinct and so does the city itself. And therein lies its charm.

—Susan Kleinman

London

They say it about life, but it's true of London: The best things are free. The National Gallery, the National Portrait Gallery, and the British Museum, all world leaders and all containing important items of Jewish interest, are prime examples. But London is synonymous with theater, and the finest — pomp and ceremony included — can be seen free from the Strangers' Gallery in the ancient British Parliament, where Jewish politicians often star in dazzling debates. Street theater at its best is available at Speakers' Corner (Hyde Park) on Sunday afternoons or outside the queen's London residence at Buckingham Palace when they change the guard each morning.

History: There were individual Jews in England in Roman and Anglo-Saxon times, but it was William the Conqueror — shortly after his arrival in 1066 — who opened the gates for what was to become an organized community by encouraging Jewish merchants and artisans from northern France to cross the channel. In London these refugees from anti-Semitism and seekers of economic opportunity settled first in the area now known as Old Jewry. While the Jews of England in medieval times continued to suffer the slings and arrows of anti-Semitic caricature, blood libels, wholesale massacres such as the one at York in 1190, and the Crusades undertaken by Richard the Lion-Hearted, their presence — because they contributed to the "outrageous fortune" of the ruling classes — was nevertheless tolerated. But on Tisha B'av in 1290, Edward I, who perceived them as no longer economically necessary to the Crown, unceremoniously expelled the country's 16,000 Jews. It would be 350 years before England again had an organized Jewish community.

Henry VIII and, in turn, Elizabeth I tolerated small numbers of Spanish and Portuguese Conversos who worshiped secretly as Jews in London and Bristol. Dr. Hector Nuñes became a hero by being the first to warn that the Spanish Armada had sailed in 1588. On the other hand, Dr. Roderigo López, Elizabeth's personal physician, was hanged after a false charge of treason.

It was not a king or queen who opened the gates again but Oliver Cromwell, spurred by the petition of Amsterdam's Rabbi Menasseh Ben Israel (known to us mainly from Rembrandt's portrait). That Shakespeare found it artistically necessary to dramatize the story of a Jewish moneylender named Shylock for an English society that was virtually devoid of Jews may be one of the curiosities of literary history, though some say the character was based on the luckless Dr. López. It is possibly due to the atmosphere portrayed in *The Merchant of Venice* that the readmission of Jews was never formalized. Repeated petitions for Jewish admittance failed, but in 1656 Cromwell's oral guarantee and the approval of the Council of State allowed those already in the country to proclaim their faith openly and permitted others to enter from Holland. Spanish and Portuguese Jews came first, opening their first synagogue in 1657. German Jews followed, opening a synagogue in 1690. Together, Sephardim and Ashkenazim would build one of the most highly organized Jewish communities the Western world has ever seen.

Jews were not the only people attracted to England by its tolerance. The German-born composer George Frideric Handel, who lived most of his adult life in England, spoke fondly of his new home as "a country where no man suffers any molestation or inconvenience because of his religious principles." Handel had grown up in a philo-Semitic atmosphere, and though he is best known for his *Messiah*, he composed no fewer than fourteen oratorios on Hebrew Bible themes, including *Judas Maccabeus* and *Esther*. Unlike Shakespeare, the composer had actually visited Venice—in 1710—and it is possible that the Purim dramas that drew many Venetians to the ghetto also contributed to Handel's *Esther*, which debuted at London's Crown and Anchor Tavern in 1732. Handel's works undoubtedly contributed to greater acceptance of Jews in England, and to their treatment in literature.

Limitations placed on Jewish activity in England were never as strict as on the Continent, but spurred by the emancipation in France and the Catholic emancipation in Britain in 1829, Jews agitated for their own official equality. The first emancipation bill passed the House of Commons in 1833, but it was consistently defeated in the House of Lords. In 1847, the city of London elected Lionel de Rothschild its parliamentary representative, but continued opposition in the House of Lords blocked the legislation that would have allowed him to take the required oath on a Hebrew Bible. Repeatedly elected by his constituency, Rothschild was finally able to take his seat in Parliament in 1858, when a compromise allowed each house to set its own form of oath.

Since then, Parliament has never been without Jewish members, and in recent times the Jewish delegation has consistently exceeded 40. A Hebrew Bible, used whenever a Jewish member of Parliament takes an oath, sits in the House of Commons' Treasury Box. One of Lionel de Rothschild's most ardent supporters in Parliament was Benjamin Disraeli; although baptized, the future prime minister never hid his Jewish origin and, in fact, took pride in it. "Yes, I am a Jew," Disraeli once said in response to an anti-Semitic slur from another MP, "and when the ancestors of the right honorable gentleman were brutal savages in an unknown island, mine were priests in the temple of Solomon." Twenty-seven years after Lionel de Rothschild was sworn into the House of Commons, his son

Nathaniel joined the ranks of Lords—the first professing Jew raised to the peerage.

In 1863, Rothschild and Isaac Goldsmit, the most prominent member of the Ashkenazic community, joined with Sir Moses Montefiore, the recognized head of the Serphardim, to solidify the Board of Deputies of British Jews. To be sure, the Sephardim still had their *chakham* (leading rabbinical authority) and *mahamad* (communal council) firmly entrenched in Bevis Marks Synagogue. These were eclipsed by the Board of Deputies and by the vision of Rabbi Nathan Marcus Adler, who united all Ashkenazic congregations in the London metropolitan area into a United Synagogue and created the chief rabbinate of England, on the model of the Anglican Church, with its archbishop of Canterbury.

The modern history of the Jews of London is a story of stability and volatility. During a period when the great masses of Jews were distinguished by their ability to avoid calling attention to themselves and were simply living out their lives in a comfortable environment, many individual Jews with ambition were able to rise meteorically.

Sir David Salomons became the first Jewish lord mayor of London in 1855; Disraeli, of course, was one of the great Victorian prime ministers. In addition to Montefiore and the Rothschilds, there were the nouveaux riches of later waves of immigration, like Sir Isaac Wolfson and Lord Israel Sieff, who learned the lessons of noblesse oblige from their predecessors and used their fortunes to support the Jewish communities of both England and Israel. Wolfson, by the way, is the only man besides Jesus to have a college in both Oxford and Cambridge named after him.

As Handel's oratorios were to the eighteenth century, so was George Eliot's novel *Daniel Deronda* to the nineteenth—explaining to the world the Jews' longing for a homeland in Palestine. It was England's Lord Balfour who issued the 1917 declaration that recognized these aspirations officially. And it was England that gave the new state its first president, Chaim Weizmann.

Other Jews born in or associated with London include the pioneering economist

David Ricardo; Harold Abrahams, the Olympic runner whose story is told in the film *Chariots of Fire*; David Mendoza, considered the father of modern boxing; Harry Marks, founder and first editor of the *Financial Times*; Brian Epstein, manager of the Beatles; anthropologist Ashley Montagu; playwright Harold Pinter; hairstylist Vidal Sassoon; and comic actors Marty Feldman and Peter Sellers. Herbert Samuel was the first professing Jew to serve in a British cabinet (in 1909) and in 1920 became high commissioner for Palestine—in effect, the first Jew to rule in Eretz Israel in 2,000 years. Joseph Julius Kanne, decorated twenty-one times in the Crimean War, was Queen Victoria's courier and arranged all her European travels. Arthur Sullivan, Gilbert's partner, had Jewish ancestors on his mother's side. American Jews native to England include Abe Beame, New York's first Jewish mayor; labor leader Samuel Gompers; Harlem Globetrotters founder Abe Saperstein; and comedian Henny Youngman.

Community: About two-thirds of Great Britain's 350,000 Jews live in London. The Board of Deputies of British Jews, which dates from 1760, comprises representatives from all Jewish denominations and is the community's united voice in dealing with the government and other secular authorities; it puts Israel's case to political leaders and to British society, monitors anti-Semitic activity, and works with other groups—such as Indians and West Indians—to safeguard minority rights.

Numerically, the Eastern European Jews who began arriving after 1880 have long since overwhelmed their Sephardic and German predecessors. Nominally, the community is predominantly Orthodox: about three-quarters who marry under religious auspices do so in an Orthodox synagogue. But most Orthodox English Jews would be more accurately described as traditional.

Until World War II, Jewish London was almost exclusively confined to the Cockney East End. The former Jewish homes and stores are intact, some with the original signs, but the curries of recent immigrants from Bangladesh have now replaced the gefilte fish of Eastern Europe, while the

Jews have relocated en masse to the solid, self-confident suburbs of north London.

If affluence is the engine that has propelled British Jews to the peaks of power, the chief stoker was Margaret Thatcher, whose "enterprise culture" of the eighties was perfectly in sync with the up-by-your-bootstraps philosophy that the community exemplified. Not only did many Jewish entrepreneurs prosper beyond their wildest dreams, but also Jewish politicians were promoted in unprecedented numbers to the most senior government posts. Even the chief rabbi benefited from Thatcher's affinity. In 1987, he was elevated to the peerage and now, in happy retirement, Immanuel Jakobovits glories in the title "Lord."

Sights and Neighborhoods: To see Jewish London, head north from the city center through St. John's Wood (genteel/establishment) and on to Hampstead (intellectual/arty), Golders Green (professional/religious), and Hendon (serious/scholastic). Just beyond the metropolitan boundary you will find full-blown British suburbia in Edgware, Stanmore, and Ilford, the last of which boasts the largest Jewish concentration in Europe. Stamford Hill, a curious appendage, is the haunt of hasidic groups and also home to Jews from India, Iran, Yemen, and North Africa.

Hampstead is the place for trendy Jews to see and be seen. Home to many of the city's artists, writers, and actors, it occupies the highest point in London and offers magnificent views of the city. It is also the natural habitat of the casually elegant classes who had a sufficiently well-developed sense of self-preservation to survive the sixties. Having made it, they felt confident enough in 1992 to elect Oscar-winning actress Glenda Jackson (on a socialist ticket) as their parliamentary representative.

The most elegant commentary on Hampstead and its lifestyle can be found at 20 Maresfield Gardens, tucked behind the overpriced coffee shops, boutiques, and galleries. This gracious home provided a refuge for Sigmund Freud in his last year. Two days after the Germans marched into Vienna in 1938 the father of psychoanalysis told his disciples, "After the destruction of

Jerusalem by Titus, Rabbi Jochanan ben Zakkai asked permission to open a school at Yavne for the study of Torah. We are going to do the same." Freud's Yavne is open to the public and contains the good doctor's personal effects, including his archaeological collection and that famous couch. The house has not acquired the fossilized texture of a museum, perhaps because it remained the home of his daughter Anna until 1982.

A brisk walk across Hampstead Heath takes you past two famous pubs, the Old Bull and Bus and the Hare and Hounds. Farther on you are likely to pass the homes of such diverse personalities as Erich Segal, author of *Love Story* and now professor of classics at Oxford University, and the deposed King Constantine of Greece, before you enter into Golders Green, the heart of Jewish London.

Here, knitted *kippot* and black hats proliferate on sidewalks sprinkled with kosher restaurants, bakeries, butcheries, and kosher-only supermarkets. Down Golders Green Road are Jewish bookstores, gift shops, and purveyors of "religious requisites." Most residents are not observant, but enough are to justify cutthroat competition. In and around the road are dozens of synagogues, temples, and *shtiebels*. The best known, Munk's (the popular designation of the Golders Green Beth Hamidrash, on Golders Green Road near Boardwalk Lane), is a thirty-second dash from Bloom's Restaurant. Opposite Munk's is Ohel David, a synagogue of Baghdadi Jews from India.

Hendon begins where Golders Green runs out, separated only by the busy North Circular Highway, which was intended to carry traffic swiftly around the periphery of London but which is itself often choked to capacity. While Golders Green has the heavily Orthodox Menorah boys' school, Hendon is the educational powerhouse of the community with the more relaxed Hasmonean and Independent schools, as well as its own generous serving of synagogues representing all denominations.

Three institutions are particularly noteworthy in Hendon and the adjacent suburb of Finchley. First is the modest, modern campus of Jews' College on Albert Road (telephone 081-203-6427), an affiliate of London University and training ground of the community's future rabbis. It also offers a range of adult-education courses on Jewish themes. Yakar, in Egerton Gardens (081-202-5551), not only runs religious services but is also known for its lecture series. Recent guests have ranged from the Likud's Ehud Olmert to Bethlehem's Palestinian Mayor Elias Freij to Nobel Laureate Archbishop Desmond Tutu.

Finchley is home to the Sternberg Centre, located in an old Georgian manor house on East End Road (081-346-2288). The largest Jewish community center in Europe, it offers Reform religious services and a range of imaginative adult-education activities, from art classes and literary seminars to Jewish walking tours. The jewel in its crown is the London Museum of Jewish Life, which reflects community life in Britain since 1656 through documents, photographs, and objects. The center also has a biblical garden and a Holocaust memorial. Reform rabbis are trained at the Leo Baeck College, an affiliate of the center.

The best-kept secret in London is the stately home of Kenwood (081-348-1286), on the edge of Hampstead Heath. The house contains a small but exquisite collection of Rembrandts, Vermeers, and Van Dycks, as well as English masters Gainsborough and Turner. It was left to the nation by the Iveagh family on condition that the public be allowed free access, which makes it a popular *Shabbat* diversion for observant Jews who live a comfortable thirty-minute walk away in Golders Green. An additional attraction is the huge lawn where music lovers spread out informally on long summer evenings to enjoy open-air concerts that invariably end with a spectacular fireworks display. There is also a regular program of indoor chamber music and poetry readings on weekday evenings.

Adjoining Kenwood is the quaint suburb of Highgate, where the local cemetery in Swains Lane has attracted generations of Russian and Chinese pilgrims to the grave of the erstwhile Jew Karl Marx who, like Freud, shaped the twentieth century. Ironically, this is one of the few private cemeteries in London. Marx, grandson of a rabbi in Trier, Germany, was baptized at the age of six; he formalized his philosophy and wrote *Das Kapital* in the Reading Room of the British Museum, which has barely changed since the revolutionary philosopher graced its hallowed portals. You can see the house where Marx lived from 1851 to 1856 at 28 Dean Street in seedy Soho, near the theaters and London's old red-light district.

There are many places and sights of Jewish interest in central London. The Board of Jewish Deputies, headquarters of British Jewry, is located in Woburn House on Tavistock Square (near Euston Station, 071-388-4525). Also in the building is the Jewish Museum, founded in 1932, which houses a collection of ceremonial Jewish art, including an elaborately carved sixteenth-century Italian ark, illuminated marriage contracts, a small eighth-century Byzantine gold plaque embossed with Jewish emblems and the earliest dated Purim *Megillah* (1647). Among the paintings featured is the richly detailed *Simchat Torah* by Solomon Hart, the nineteenth-century English artist known for his Jewish themes. Adjoining Woburn House is Adler House, seat of the chief rabbi and the London *Bet Din*.

At 21 Dean Street (just down the street from the house where Karl Marx lived) is the West End Great Synagogue, which houses the Ben Uri Gallery, one of the largest collections of Jewish art. The synagogue is on the tourist path and thoughtfully offers visitors precooked frozen meals.

The Central Synagogue on Great Portland Street, consecrated in 1954, is a modern, cantilevered structure with twenty-six stained-glass windows representing the Jewish festivals. It stands on the site of a synagogue destroyed during the blitz in 1941.

The Marble Arch Synagogue, 32 Great Cumberland Place (near Speakers' Corner in Hyde Park), is the successor to London's first Ashkenazic congregation, founded in 1690. The congregation's last building in the East End was destroyed during a German bombardment in 1941, and the postwar decision to rebuild in the West End was in recognition of the migration of the city's Jewish population. Unlike most synagogues, Marble Arch is not a freestanding structure but part of a semicircular row of buildings. Located near many major hotels, it is particularly convenient for tourists.

West London Synagogue, 34 Upper Berkeley Street, is the oldest Reform congregation in London; the current building (also convenient to West End hotels) dates from 1870. The Gothic-like facade features a high, semicircular arch under a pointed gable. On the east wall of the stunning Byzantine sanctuary, a dome sits atop the arched ark.

The heart of London is the square mile called "The City," where traces of the Jewish past nestle up against sites associated with the literature and folklore of the English-speaking world. There is still a street called Old Jewry, dating from before the expulsion in 1290. There were synagogues in Old Jewry as well as on Gresham and Coleman streets. A synagogue also stood on the site of the present National Westminster Bank, at 52 Threadneedle Street.

At the corner of Threadneedle and Cornhill is the Royal Exchange, with its murals by Solomon J. Solomon, once president of the British Royal Society of Artists. Among the Solomon works in the exchange is a portrait of Nathan Mayer Rothschild, founder of the London house of the family banking firm. The southeast corner of the exchange was once known as "Jews' Walk."

Nearby is Bevis Marks, on St. Mary Axe, the splendid but simple Spanish and Portuguese synagogue completed in 1701. The oldest synagogue in the British Commonwealth, tradition says it was paid for by a Quaker, Joseph Avis, who forbade work on *Shabbat* and Jewish holidays. Queen Anne is said to have provided an oak beam from a warship for use as a roof girder. The seven massive hanging candelabra represent the days of the week, and the twelve pillars that support the women's gallery represent the tribes of Israel. These days, the synagogue is lit by electricity, but when candles are used on *Shabbat* it takes ninety minutes to light them. Modeled on the Portuguese Synagogue in Amsterdam, Bevis Marks still serves the Spanish and Portuguese community; it is best to call before visiting (071-626-1274) to make sure the synagogue will be open. St. Mary Axe, by the way (pronounced "Simmery Axe") was also the home of *The Sorcerer* of Gilbert and Sullivan.

Splendid but simple: The entry to Bevis Marks synagogue on St. Mary Axe

Close to Bevis Marks is the site of the 1657 synagogue—the first after Cromwell's admission of Jews to England. A plaque on the rear of the Cunard Building on Creechurch Lane commemorates the "site of the First Synagogue After the Resettlement, 1657–1701." This was the synagogue referred to by Samuel Pepys in his *Diaries*.

Most of the Jewish residents and institutions have left the East End, although many businesses there are still Jewish owned. Cemeteries and former synagogues remain, as do the open-air markets, staffed by new generations of immigrants. The heart of the area depicted in Israel Zangwill's *Children of the Ghetto* was along Petticoat Lane and Hessel Street. The former synagogue at 19 Princelet Street is being converted into a museum of immigrant history in collabora-

tion with the London Museum of Jewish Life. You can take a trip into recent history with one of the daily Jewish East End walking tours run by the East End Tourism Trust (071-377-8795).

London's great museums and galleries are rich in works by Jewish artists and of Jewish subjects. The British Museum, on Great Russell Street, contains a wealth of material from ancient Israel and Judea. The Ancient Palestine Room is the repository for much of it. There are ornately illustrated Hebrew manuscripts, including the *Mishneh Torah* (in Maimonides's own handwriting), a fourteenth-century Pentateuch, a Torah from Kaifeng, and the Golden *Haggadah*, which dates from about 1320. Also in the museum's possession are Rembrandt's etchings of Jewish types and biblical scenes. The department of manuscripts has the original Balfour Declaration—a typewritten letter from Foreign Secretary Balfour to Lord Rothschild. And in the Magna Carta room is the original of the 1215 document so famous as a declaration of rights—with its tenth section restricting the claims of Jewish creditors against the estates of landowners who have died in their debt. The section was deleted from subsequent editions of the document.

The National Gallery has several of Rembrandt's paintings of Jewish characters. The National Portrait Gallery houses the images of eminent English Jews, from Moses Montefiore to Israel Zangwill and including generations of Rothschilds and Disraelis. The Tate Gallery has Jacob Epstein's bust of Albert Einstein. The Victoria and Albert Museum has in its collection *menorahs* dating from the 12th century as well as spice boxes, an array of Italian Jewish wedding rings and synagogue adornments from Italy and Holland. And near the Tomb of the Unknown Soldier in Westminster Abbey is a pair of six-foot bronze candelabra by the German-Jewish refugee sculptor Benno Elkan—one with figures from the life of Jesus, the other with thirty-two figures from the Hebrew Bible.

The weekly *Jewish Chronicle* provides a sampling of the Jewish community's concerns and listings of Jewish events. The alternative monthly *New Moon* has more extensive listings. Up-to-date information on a wide range of Jewish subjects, from kosher restaurants and hotels to your nearest synagogue or Hadassah or B'nai B'rith outlet is available from a telephone hotline (071-387-4044) run by the Board of Deputies. The service is designed for locals who need information on communal matters, but it welcomes inquiries from Jewish visitors, too. It operates Monday through Thursday from 10:00 A.M. to 5:00 P.M. and on Friday from 10:00 A.M. to 1:00 P.M.

Eating: Golders Green is kosher country. You will find a branch of Bloom's restaurant at 130 Golders Green Road, still serving its old-style *lokshen* but now challenged by two brash Israeli newcomers, Dizengoff (number 118) and Solly's (number 148), which appeal to more exotic tastes. Two excellent kosher bakeries, Carmelli's and Cousins', are on the same block. Around the corner, on Finchley Road, are two kosher Chinese restaurants, the high-class Zizzi's (number 1023) and, down the road, takeout Marcus's (Halleswell Parade). A few doors away is Uncle Ian's Diner (Monkville Parade). Not kosher but "Jewish style," Uncle Ian's offers no frills but is always packed. Reuben's (20 Baker Street) and Curzon Plaza (56 Curzon Street) are the only kosher restaurants in the West End, while the East End is home to the original Bloom's (90 Whitechapel High Street) and the upstart Kosher Luncheon Club (13 Greatorex Street), a fish and dairy restaurant that was lauded by *The Times* as "simply excellent."

Eating kosher can be exceedingly expensive but need not be ruinous. Packaged foods in stores may be kosher, even if not so labeled. A comprehensive guide to kosher food is contained in a 166-page pocket book entitled *The Really Jewish Food Guide,* available from the London *Bet Din,* Woburn House, Tavistock Square, London WClH OEZ. A "Kashrut Hot Line" (071-383-2468) provides regular updates.

Side Trips: Given its size, much of England can be covered in day trips from London, and many spots have sights of Jewish interest. Two in particular, however, represent the height of Jewish achievement and the depth of Jewish suffering in England.

Ramsgate, where the Strait of Dover abuts the North Sea, is the site of the Montefiore Estate. Sir Moses Montefiore, who lived to be 101, was knighted by Queen Victoria for his philanthropy and his efforts on behalf of persecuted Jews in Eastern Europe and the Middle East. In 1833, he built on his estate a private synagogue modeled on the one in his native Livorno. The building, in the shape of an irregular octagon, has a simple neoclassical exterior and interior walls of white and brown marble. In his mansion are portraits of Sir Moses and Lady Judith and many testimonials to Montefiore's beneficence. The Montefiores are buried on the estate grounds. To visit the estate contact A. G. G. Da Costa, 33 Lutton Avenue, Broadstairs (0843-62507), or call the Spanish and Portuguese synagogue in London at 071-289-2573.

Farther afield—closer, in fact, to England's second- and third-largest Jewish communities in Manchester and Leeds—is York. Clifford's Tower, once part of a castle but now a stone ruin, was the site of the massacre of York's Jews in 1190. The entire community had taken refuge there when mobs attacked the Jewish quarter, and there is a memorial stone on the site. In 1990, in commemoration of the eight hundredth anniversary of the massacre, England's Union of Jewish Students organized a conference on racism at York University.

Reading: For a quick historical perspective, read Jonathan Romain's *The Jews of England* (Jewish Chronicle Publications) and for an enlightening account of the contemporary Jewish community and its quirks read Stephen Brook's *The Club* (Constable). Barbara Tuchman's *Bible and Sword* (New York University Press) is a fascinating account of Britain's complicated love affair with the Jews and the Holy Land. A classical work is Cecil Roth's *History of the Jews of England* (Clarendon).

Sir Walter Scott's *Ivanhoe* provides a picture of England's Jews in medieval times, including the York massacre; the movie version of the novel starred a London-born actress who would later convert to Judaism—Elizabeth Taylor. André Schwarz-Bart's *The Last of the Just*

(Atheneum) also begins with York. Shakespeare has a romance with a Jewish woman in Faye Kellerman's *The Quality of Mercy* (Morrow). The late 19th century is covered by Israel Zangwill's *King of the Schnorrers* (Adama), a delightful story on the transition between Sephardic and Ashkenazic dominance of the community, and *Children of the Ghetto* (Macmillan), the defin-

itive East End novel. Novels set in the 20th century include C. P. Snow's *The Conscience of the Rich* (Scribner's) and Chaim Bermant's *The Last Supper* (Dutton). There are, no doubt, toddlers in the north London suburbs, living today the experiences of twenty-first-century British-Jewish literature.

—Joseph Lowin

Los Angeles

The Messiah has not yet arrived in Southern California, but when he does, Los Angeles Jews will be ready. "Los Angeles is today the bellwether of American style and taste and culture," the *Guide to Jewish Los Angeles* declares with becoming modesty. "Los Angeles Jewry is today the bellwether of American Jewish life. . . . After all, Los Angeles Jews are God's people, and they live in the City of the Angels."

Hyperbole aside, Los Angeles is home to the third-largest Jewish community in the world, trailing only New York and Tel Aviv and ahead of Jerusalem. Jewish Angelenos have played major roles in fashion, finance, politics, academia, commerce, and of course the entertainment industry.

Like Southern California's semidesert terrain, made green by water from the distant Sierra Nevada mountains and the Colorado River, Jewish life in Los Angeles has been nourished by streams of immigrants from other states and countries. National leaders and influential centers of culture and learning have sprouted where once it was difficult to drum up a *minyan*.

Still, the community lacks the rootedness and cohesiveness of more established habitats. From the gold rush days on, many Jews, like their diverse neighbors, came to the city to start anew and sever their ties with the past. It is easy to disappear in Los Angeles. Less than half the city's Jews maintain even the most minimal ties with a Jewish institution, and only one in four belongs to a synagogue. In Los Angeles innovation is more revered than tradition, informality more than convention, and new forms of religious, social, and sexual practice—some rational, others off-the-wall—flourish unhindered.

History: Los Angeles's sonorous birth name, El Pueblo de Nuestra Señora la Reina de Los Angeles de Porciuncula (the Village of Our Lady, the Queen of the Angels of the Porciuncula [River]), bespeaks the city's Spanish roots. Founded in 1781 as one of a string of Spanish settlements along the California coast, the village was nearly sixty years old when Jacob Frankfort, a tailor, arrived as apparently the first Jewish resident.

In 1850 Los Angeles had fewer than 2,000 residents and only 8 Jews. All 8 were bachelors, 6 were from Germany, and all but Frankfort were merchants. They lived next door to each other in four adjacent downtown dwellings at Aliso and Los Angeles streets—the city's first Jewish neighborhood.

The first charitable organization in Los Angeles was the Hebrew Benevolent Society, founded in 1854 to establish a Jewish cemetery for those "belonging to the Hebrew Church," which is now the site of Dodger Stadium. Congregation B'nai B'rith, founded in 1862, has evolved into Wilshire Boulevard Temple, a thriving Reform congregation.

By the turn of the century, Jews numbered about 2,500 of the city's 100,000 citizens. Fueled by an influx of Eastern European Jews, including many tuberculosis victims escaping East Coast sweatshops, Jewish social services began to develop.

The Kaspare Cohn Hospital, founded in 1902, ultimately evolved into the massive Cedars-Sinai Medical Center. The Duarte Sanitarium, established in 1914 by the Jewish Consumptive Relief Association, became the City of Hope respiratory center. The Federation of Jewish Charities, founded in 1911, was the forerunner of today's Jewish Federation Council, which serves some five hundred affiliated agencies and organizations.

In the five years following World War I, the Jewish population rose from 19,000 to 45,000. Boyle Heights, in the eastern part of the city across the Los Angeles River, became the predominant Jewish enclave, supporting twenty-seven synagogues and *shtiebels*; Brooklyn Street was lined with stores advertising their wares in Yiddish.

Many pillars of the community made a modest living as junk dealers. After Pearl Harbor, when scrap metal suddenly became worth its weight in gold, the owners found themselves millionaires practically overnight and soon thereafter moved from B.H. to B.H. (Boyle Heights to Beverly Hills).

Following World War II, when the number of Jews in Los Angeles tripled again, both newcomers and old Boyle Heights residents moved west and north to the Fairfax district, Beverly Hills, West Los Angeles, and the San Fernando Valley. These areas remain the main Jewish population centers.

Community: Give or take a few 10,000, there are about 650,000 Jews among the nearly 9 million people of Los Angeles County, and another 90,000 in neighboring Orange County. Despite a high intermarriage rate and low birthrate, Los Angeles Jewry keeps growing through an influx of newcomers from older American cities and abroad. Prominent immigrant communities, with their own neighborhoods, newspapers, and social centers, are from the former Soviet Union (40,000–60,000, centered in West Hollywood); Iran (35,000, primarily in West Los Angeles and Beverly Hills); and Israel (especially in the Fairfax area and the San Fernando Valley). Estimates on the number of Israelis range from 40,000 to up to 200,000, with Jewish Federation demographers using a working figure of some 100,000. Other Jews have arrived from South Africa, England, and Latin America.

While one or two generations ago, enterprising Jews sought business and entrepreneurial careers, today they are turning increasingly to medicine, law, accounting, teaching, and social work. They hold prominent places in these fields, as well as in real estate development, construction, and high-tech industries, and have become highly visible in the politics of the country's largest state. Scholars, scientists, and administrators are numerous and influential at the University of California, Los Angeles, California Institute of Technology and the once WASPish University of Southern California. Jews founded the Columbia, Universal, Warner Bros., Paramount, 20th Century Fox and MGM movie studios.

Though these once-proud film fiefdoms are now owned by large foreign and domestic corporations, most of the key executives are still Jewish and the screenwriters' guild is practically a Semitic closed shop. Jewish producers also play key roles in the television, recording, and popular music industries. Jews in the entertainment fields have even founded four, often feuding, congregations, each of which holds services once a month and on High Holy Days.

Where once Jews stayed out of the political limelight, in recent years they have taken center stage. Despite growing competition from Hispanic and Asian-American candidates, six out of fifteen City Council members are Jewish, as are four of the area's representatives in Congress, almost half the members of the public school board, and the Los Angeles County sheriff.

Relations between the Jewish community and the main ethnic minorities — African-Americans and the rapidly growing Latino and Asian populations — have been strained by increasing competition for political and economic power and estranged by the distances between the Jewish population centers and the minority neighborhoods. The riots of April 1992 were a traumatic shock for all Angelenos and resulted in a concerted Jewish effort to aid the homeless and hungry in the black districts. Relations with the Japanese-American and Korean-American communities, which would like to emulate what they perceive as Jewish cohesion and clout, have grown closer since the civil disturbances.

Totaling close to 150 congregations, Los Angeles synagogues include tiny storefront *shtiebels*; huge "temple-plexes" with thousands of members; conventional Orthodox, Conservative, Reform, and Reconstructionist congregations; and a temple established by gay Jews. Alternative Judaism is expressed through secular services conducted by the Society for Humanistic Judaism, and by *havurah*-type *minyans*, such as at Temple Beth Am on La Cienega Boulevard, at Adat Ari El and Valley Beth Shalom in the San Fernando Valley, and a peripatetic Moveable *Minyan*, which meets at private homes. For additional information, phone the Southern California Board of Rabbis at (213) 852-7710.

News of Jewish interest is covered by the *B'nai B'rith Messenger, Heritage*, and *Jewish Journal*, all published on Fridays. There are also two Hebrew-language weeklies, *Hadashot LA* and *Israel Shelanu*. UCLA students put out *Ha'Am*, the largest and one of the oldest Jewish campus papers in the country.

The thirteen-story Jewish Community Building, known affectionately or otherwise as the "Jewish Pentagon," is located at 6505 Wilshire Boulevard, near San Vicente Boulevard. The building houses the Jewish Federation Council and many of the major national Jewish organizations with offices in Los Angeles. The central phone number is (213) 852-1234. The JFC is divided into five geographical regions, each with its own office. The Bernard Milken Jewish Community Campus in West Hills serves the 250,000 Los Angeles Jews residing in the San Fernando Valley. The federation participates in the annual Jewish Festival in late May and organizes the biennial Exodus Festival in the San Fernando Valley.

Sights: Fairfax is the traditional center of Jewish life, inhabited by a mixture of retirees, *hasidim,* and Russian and Israeli immigrants. Fairfax Avenue, between Third Street and Melrose Avenue, is lined with Jewish bookstores, gift shops, kosher markets, multinational restaurants and "kosher-style" delis; the landmark Canter's at 419 N. Fairfax Avenue is open around the clock, except for Rosh Hashanah and Yom Kippur. A wall mural facing Canter's parking lot depicts the history of Los Angeles Jewry from 1850 to the present.

Contrary to common assumption, "the golden ghetto" of Beverly Hills is not the heartland of Los Angeles Jewry. The independent city, surrounded on all sides by the city of Los Angeles, has only 35,000 permanent residents, of whom about half are Jewish.

During the past decade, other Jewish neighborhood clusters have developed. Pico Boulevard, just east and west of the Robertson Boulevard intersection, has become a center of modern orthodoxy. The blocks are lined with kosher markets and a dozen *glatt* kosher restaurants, ranging from Italian, Mexican, and Chinese to Israeli and Persian, as well as fast-food and fried-chicken establishments. The Milky Way, serving dairy dishes, is owned by Leah Adler, mother of producer-director Steven Spielberg. It is likely the only kosher restaurant anywhere with stuffed figures of E. T. and Howard the Duck sitting at the bar. For guidance on kosher restaurants and markets, phone the Kashrut Hot Line at (818) 762-3197.

Plummer Park in West Hollywood is the favorite meeting spot for Russian-Jewish immigrants. Santa Monica and Venice are seeing a resurgence of Jewish life focused on two beachfront synagogues, Mishkon Tephilo (Conservative) and Pacific Jewish Center (Orthodox), both led by dynamic young rabbis. The upscale Hancock Park, once a blueblood enclave, has seen an influx of *hasidim* and other Orthodox Jews.

With a quarter million Jewish residents, the San Fernando Valley by itself would rank among the top ten Jewish communities in the world. The "Fairfax" of The Valley, as Angelenos generally call it, is in North Hollywood. A cluster of kosher restaurants, bakeries, meat markets, and falafel dispensers is located at the intersection of Burbank Boulevard and Whitsett Avenue. The upscale Valley communities of Encino and Sherman Oaks have a high proportion of Jewish residents.

Several current and former synagogue buildings are architecturally noteworthy. Wilshire Boulevard Temple, the descendent of Los Angeles's first congregation and still among the city's largest, is an example of the "synagogue as cathedral" mode, once favored by Reform congregations. Located at 3663 Wilshire Boulevard, the building features a mosaic-inlaid dome, a large rose window, Byzantine columns in black marble, and a permanent exhibit on Los Angeles Jewry.

The Sephardic Temple Tifereth Israel at

10500 Wilshire Boulevard in Westwood is a beautiful white stone structure that would be at home in Jerusalem. The temple features a traditional Sephardic interior and an outdoor Spanish garden.

Congregation Talmud Torah, more familiarly known as the Breed Street Shul, is among the few living legacies of the once-vibrant Jewish community in Boyle Heights. A large brick structure with polished wood interior fixtures, the shul was featured in the original 1927 talkie *The Jazz Singer,* with Al Jolson, and the 1980 remake with Neil Diamond. Located at 247 N. Breed Street, the congregation, whose first president was movie mogul Louis B. Mayer, still holds services three mornings a week and on major holidays.

Two former buildings erected by Sinai Temple, the city's oldest Conservative congregation, are under new management but retain the religious symbols and Hebrew inscriptions of their former worshipers. The original Sinai Temple building at Twelfth and Valencia streets is now the Welsh Presbyterian Church, and the inscription on the ornate second Sinai home at Fourth and New Hampshire Streets now reads The Korean Philadelphia Presbyterian Church.

For history buffs, the Jewish Historical Society of Southern California conducts guided bus tours. The tour includes historic synagogues as well as the one-time "official" Jewish bordello at First Street and Boyle Avenue in Boyle Heights. For information about the tours, phone the society at (213) 653-7740.

There are two statues and one monument of Jewish interest in the Fairfax area. A statue of American Revolution financier Haym Solomon—erected by the Jewish War Veterans—stands in the West Wilshire Recreation Center at Third and Gardner streets. In the adjoining Pan Pacific Park is the Los Angeles Holocaust Monument, consisting of six twenty-four-foot high columns of black granite, symbolizing both the 6 million victims and crematoria smokestacks. Nearby at Fairfax Avenue and Beverly Boulevard, in front of Great Western Bank, stands the statue of Raoul Wallenberg, honoring the Swedish diplomat credited with saving 90,000 Hungarian Jews.

The Jewish Community Centers Association serves the far-flung Jewish neighborhoods through seven centers, a senior center on the Venice boardwalk, outreach programs for immigrants, kosher food banks, a singles' connection, and the annual Jewish Festival. A recent addition at the Westside JCC (5870 W. Olympic Boulevard) is My Jewish Discovery Place, a hands-on children's museum. It is open to the general public. For information about events and activities at any of the centers, call (213) 938-2531.

Los Angeles is home to several museums and galleries featuring Judaica and Jewish art. The Skirball Museum at Hebrew Union College (3077 University Avenue, adjoining USC) offers outstanding exhibitions of Judaica, art, and antiquities. Permanent exhibits include Project Americana Sampler, dealing with the American-Jewish experience; Torah ornaments and traditions; the anatomy of an archaeological dig; and Jewish celebrations. By the end of 1994, the museum will become part of HUC's Skirball Cultural Center, a $60 million complex, designed by the Israeli architect Moshe Safdie, on a fifteen-acre Santa Monica mountain site. The new center will offer programs in the arts, lectures and conferences, and hopes to give visitors a wide range of experiences and insights into how Jews have influenced and been influenced by American society.

Together with the University of Judaism and Stephen S. Wise Temple, both just across the San Diego Freeway, the Skirball Center will form a new cultural-educational-religious focus of Jewish life. Nearby, the Getty Center, a $360 million museum and art education complex, is scheduled to open in 1996. Both the Jewish Community Building and the University of Judaism (15600 Mulholland Drive) mount frequent art exhibits.

The Martyrs Memorial at the Jewish Community Building and the Simon Wiesenthal Center (9760 W. Pico Boulevard) house museums and offer educational programs devoted to the Holocaust. The Wiesenthal Center's Beit Hashoah/Museum of Tolerance is a hands-on family and multimedia learning center in such areas as personal prejudice, group intolerance, civil rights, 20th-century genocides, and the Holocaust.

The Michael Hittleman Gallery (8797 Beverly Boulevard) showcases exclusively Israeli art and the work of Marc Chagall. Gallery Judaica (1312 Westwood Boulevard) carries fine arts and ritual objects, sculptures, and a selection of 85 different *ketubot*. The Jewish Quarter (365 N. Beverly Drive) features gifts, art works, antiques, and *ketubot*.

J. Roth Bookseller (9020 W. Olympic Boulevard) offers "everything Jewish under one roof," including some 15,000 books ranging from leftist to rightist, secular to hasidic, as well as Jewish detective stories, children's books, Jewish and Israeli newspapers and magazines, and ceremonial objects. Veteran proprietor Jack Roth and his son Laurence provide personalized service and encourage browsing. Eric Chaim Kline Bookseller (1343 Third Street Promenade in Santa Monica) offers used and antiquarian books in Judaica, Hebraica, and general fields.

Culture: The three major branches of Judaism are represented in Los Angeles by institutions of higher learning. The LA campus of Reform Judaism's Hebrew Union College, which offers joint study and degree programs with adjacent USC, trains rabbis, Jewish educators, and communal workers. On the crest of the Santa Monica Mountains, the Conservative movement's University of Judaism has established a liberal arts undergraduate college, three professional schools, two think tanks, and an extensive adult-education program on its handsome campus. Yeshiva of Los Angeles, an affiliate of the Rabbi Isaac Elchanon Theological Seminary, shares quarters with the Simon Wiesenthal Center on Pico Boulevard. There is an active network of Lubavitch *shuls*, schools, and counseling centers throughout the city. In Simi Valley, just beyond the San Fernando Valley, Brandeis-Bardin Institute runs a "laboratory for living Judaism" that offers lectures, weekend programs, and summer sessions for children, college students, and adults. Many public and secular universities offer Jewish study and Hebrew classes, and UCLA confers an undergraduate degree in Jewish studies.

It's not easy to keep track of the full menu of Jewish events in Los Angeles, but a good start is to read the local Jewish newspapers, check posters in Jewish neighborhoods, or call the Community Calendar at the Jewish Community Building (213-852-1234).

Jewish news and entertainment programs can also be found on television and radio. The Jewish Television Network is on the air five evenings a week on different cable channels with news, interviews, and reports from the community and Israel. For listings, phone JTN at (310) 273-6841.

Personalities: Jewish Angelenos, reflecting the demographic tilt from the East Coast to the West Coast, are increasingly extending their influence to the national scene. Two former presidents of the Jewish Federation, Republican Albert Spiegel and Democrat Edward Sanders, have both served as White House advisers for Jewish affairs and remain influential in their respective parties. So does attorney Mickey Kantor, who served as national chairman of the Clinton-Gore campaign and is now the United States Trade Representative. Four rabbis—Harvey Fields and Isaiah Zeldin (both Reform), Harold Schulweis (Conservative) and Abner Weiss (Orthodox)—are recognized leaders within the Jewish and general communities and as West Coast spokesmen within their national denominations.

Hollywood as the world's dream factory was largely created through a combination of drive and *chutzpah* by such immigrant and East Coast pioneers as Louis B. Mayer, Samuel Goldwyn (Goldfish), Harry Cohn, Adolph Zukor, William Fox (Fuchs), and the four Warner brothers. The autocrats of old are gone, and though their studios are now subservient to large Japanese, Australian, and United States corporations, most of the studio heads and top decision makers remain Jewish, including Michael Eisner and Jeffrey Katzenberg at Disney, Mike Medavoy at Tri Star, Peter Guber at Sony Pictures, Marvin Davis and Sherry Lansing at Paramount, and Lew Wasserman and Sidney Sheinberg at MCA/Universal. By dint of his influence in the entertainment industry and the Democratic Party, Wasserman was until recently considered the single most powerful Jew in Los Angeles. The title is now shared by Michael Ovitz,

Hollywood's super deal maker, and David Geffen, entertainment entrepreneur and White House friend.

Marquee names who clearly identify themselves as Jews include Barbra Streisand; Richard Dreyfuss, an active spokesman for the Peace Now movement in Israel; Dustin Hoffman; Ed Asner; Leonard Nimoy; Kirk and Michael Douglas; and Elizabeth Taylor. Filmmakers of note are Steven Spielberg, Barry Levinson, and Paul Mazursky. And would you believe, as progeny of mixed marriages, Robert DeNiro, Harrison Ford, and Paul Newman?

On the political scene, considerable clout is wielded by the "Berman-Waxman machine," named for Congressmen Howard Berman and Henry Waxman, whose power base is the liberal and affluent Jewish communities in West Los Angeles and the lower San Fernando Valley. City Councilman Zev Yaroslavsky, who got his start as an activist for Soviet Jews, is highly visible and expected to move up the political ladder.

Even from jail, junk-bond king Michael Milken continued through his family foundations as arguably the city's foremost philanthropist, especially in the areas of Jewish and general education.

More Jewish writers prefer the bracing climate of New York, but Los Angeles is home to mystery writers Jonathan and Faye Kellerman, film critic and author Michael Medved, and poets Robert Mezey and Deena Metzger. Dennis Prager is a popular local writer and radio-show host.

General Sights: The kids of all ages will probably insist on taking in Disneyland, Universal Studios, and the dubious glamour of Hollywood Boulevard, touristy though they may be. An alternate for movie buffs is the Burbank Studios two-hour VIP walking tour showing the inner workings of the Warner Bros. studio (though no actual film productions). Cost is $25 and reservations should be made a week in advance by phoning (818) 954-1744.

Visitors justifiably complain how difficult it is to get a real feel for an amorphous and sprawling city like Los Angeles, once unkindly described as fifty suburbs in search of a city. A good way to explore a cross-section of L.A. is to drive the length of Sunset Boulevard, starting downtown at Olvera Street, the founding site of the city and a bit of old Mexico. From there, head west through a barrio, past the television studios of Hollywood, the independent city of West Hollywood, the handsome homes of Beverly Hills; skirt the UCLA campus, then follow the winding road through Pacific Palisades to the beaches of the Pacific Ocean. From there you may want to head south, stopping at the Santa Monica pier with its echoes of Coney Island and Atlantic City, to the Venice beach and boardwalk, where everything you've heard about weird Los Angeles and its kooky inhabitants comes alive. Breakneck roller bladers and bicyclists whiz past strolling musicians, undiscovered artists, T-shirt peddlers, street-corner preachers, iron-pumping muscle persons, pizza and taco vendors, and just about every other form of exhibitionism under the warm Southern California sun. Among those watching the passing parade are Orthodox worshipers after services at the Pacific Jewish Center and bench regulars from the Israel Levin Senior Citizens Center.

Widespread slander to the contrary, L.A. does have a downtown. A walk or minibus ride along First Street, starting at Hope Street and heading east, passes the attractive Music Center, with its playful fountains and the Jacques Lipchitz sculpture *Peace on Earth,* City Hall and the Civic Center, the Los Angeles Times building, and the restaurants and shops of Little Tokyo.

Among the city's less-publicized attractions are two museums, both with hands-on exhibits for youngsters and their parents. The Children's Museum is downtown at 310 N. Main Street, and the Natural History Museum's Discovery Center at 900 Exposition Boulevard. The most complete listing of entertainment and cultural events is in the Sunday Calendar section of the *Los Angeles Times.*

Day Trips: The picturesque seaside community of Santa Barbara is 90 miles up the Pacific Coast Highway, and 40 miles farther on is Solvang, a transplanted Danish village. In the opposite direction,

San Diego and the Mexican border town of Tijuana are 120 miles south of Los Angeles. For a seagoing adventure, try a day trip to Catalina Island, with its rugged coastline, sailing boats, buffalo herds, and flying fish. The Catalina Express runs frequent daily round trips (telephone 310-519-1212).

Reading: Two standard reference works are *Jewish Life in Los Angeles: A Window to Tomorrow* by Neil Sandberg (University Press of America) and *History of the Jews of Los Angeles* by Max Vorspan and Lloyd Gartner (Huntington Library). An excellent book on the founders of the movie industry is Neal Gabler's *An Empire of Their Own: How the Jews Invented Hollywood* (Crown Publishers), whose fictional complement would be Budd Schulberg's classic *What Makes Sammy Run?* (Random House). Faye Kellerman uses the mystery genre to explore the Orthodox community of Los Angeles in *The Ritual Bath* (Arbor House), while her husband, Jonathan Kellerman, sets loose psychologist-sleuth Alex Delaware on the mean streets of the city in *Silent Partner* and *Time Bomb* (Bantam). Many of Tillie Olsen's short stories touch on local Jewish life.

The dusty stacks of your local library may hold a copy of *Rabbi Burns* (Covici Friede), a 1931 novel by Aben Kandel that presents a somewhat unflattering portrait of Los Angeles Jewry, centering on a character supposedly based on Edgar F. Magnin, the legendary "Rabbi to the Stars" for six decades.

Available from the Jewish Historical Society (telephone 213-653-7740) are the 1982 *Jewish Los Angeles — A Guide* and copies of its highly readable Legacy series on the Fairfax district, Hollywood, the local garment industry, and the role of Jewish women. Upcoming volumes will deal with Boyle Heights and the Sephardic community.

Recommendation: Many leading hotels offer kosher meals on request, but the only totally kosher facility is the Beverly Grand at 7257 Beverly Boulevard in the Fairfax area, which caters to observant Jewish travelers (telephone 213-939-1653). Jewish travelers seeking community information or in need of assistance can call the Jewish Community Building at (213) 852-1234.

Trivia: The Teichman Mikvah at 12800 Chandler Boulevard in North Hollywood is the first solar-heated ritual bath in America.

The first Jew buried in the first communal cemetery in 1855 was one Harris Caspar, who operated a small store in the gold rush country north of Los Angeles. According to a contemporary account, the unfortunate merchant was fatally shot by a miner from Greenhorn Gulch, "because he (Caspar) refused to sell a pair of pants on credit."

Hard by the Los Angeles International Airport, gleaming like a white beacon to the incoming jets, stands a tall six-columned monument, surrounded by a cupola that shades an oversized sarcophagus containing the mortal remains of Al Jolson. Inside the dome, a painting of Moses, holding the Tablets of the Law and surrounded by fluffy clouds, looks on approvingly. A circular inscription praises "The Sweet Singer of Israel — The Man Raised Up High." Adjoining, the sculpted jazz singer rests on one knee, arms outstretched and mouth open, as if eternally serenading his "Mammy" to the planes above and to the cars whizzing by on the freeway below. Beneath the elevated monument, a broad waterfall cascades down the mosaic tile steps to the entrance of the Hillside Memorial Park and Mausoleum.

At the Sinai Memorial Park, high in the Hollywood Hills, a large mural depicts the history of the American Jewish community. In the same location stands the Warsaw Ghetto Memorial by Bernard Baruch Zakheim.

A phenomenon in other communities is that the Jews start as outsiders but become insiders as newer, equally exotic immigrants arrive. But in Los Angeles, Jews had an earlier start. The first City Council met on July 3, 1850, with Morris L. Goodman as one of its seven members. Goodman, one of the town's eight Jewish residents, was the only American citizen on the council. Minutes of the meeting were written in Spanish. Did he know he was a bellwether?
—*Tom Tugend*

Luxembourg

If a once-upon-a-time land still exists in Western Europe, Luxembourg is it. A grand duchy a third smaller than Rhode Island, squeezed to near invisibility by Germany, France, and Belgium, it is a land where castles rise on lofty hilltops, rivers burble though lush forests, and the countryside unfolds green and serene. To complete the idyll, the crown prince and princess look like a couple from Central Casting.

Luxembourg's fairy-tale aura extends to its contemporary situation. With a population of only 365,000, it is one of Europe's more sparsely settled states. Thanks to its iron and steel industries, its agricultural resources, the great outreach of Radio Luxembourg, the presence of various Common Market operations and the 120-odd banks situated there because of them, it boasts one of the Continent's highest living standards. Because it continues in its historical role as a crossroads—the Burgundians, French, Spanish, and Germans being among its erstwhile occupiers—it is highly cosmopolitan but maintains a dignified individuality.

Little wonder that the people of this prosperous land are said to be connoisseurs of the good life, one that supports hosts of fine boutiques, significant artistic displays, and more Michelin-starred restaurants per capita than any other country. Little wonder then, too, that Luxembourg's 1,000 Jews are comfortably ensconced alongside their fellow countrymen, enjoying, fostering, and perpetuating the pervading sense of well-being.

History: Jews have been relatively comfortable in Luxembourg. While they have felt waves of anti-Semitism, there were no ghettos, no pogroms. Even early on, Jews could own land. And when the Holocaust came, many Jews who thought to save themselves could and did.

The area's first Jews probably arrived around the start of the Common Era, as peddlers following the Roman army that established Trier, now in Germany. Jews were noted there at various times during the Middle Ages: in Luxembourg City in 1276; as immigrants from Trier in the early fourteenth century; as massacre victims during the Black Death in 1349. Against the wishes of the emperor, Charles IV, survivors were expelled. And, apparently, the outlook was good enough to encourage their return by 1367, since mention was made then of a "Jews' Gate" in the town of Echternach. The Ping-Pong game of expulsion and return would be played at least twice more during the two centuries that followed, until the expulsion decree of 1530 was fully implemented.

With Napoleon's rise to power, and the reestablishment of Luxembourg's territorial integrity, the Jews returned. A trickle began from Alsace-Lorraine, and by 1808 there were 75 families. They built their first synagogue in 1823, and by 1838 had broken away from Trier's sway to form their own consistory. In 1843 they appointed Samuel Hirsch, a pioneer of Germany's Reform movement, as their first chief rabbi. Before emigrating to the United States in 1866, Hirsch set the community on a Liberal course.

The 1870 loss of Alsace-Lorraine by France to Germany spurred a new influx of refugees. They came as farmers, traders, and cattle dealers (and virtually monopolized that field until World War II). They pioneered the country's leather and textile industries and worked for Luxembourg's fledgling steel operation.

Small Jewish pockets formed all over the map. Some communities built their own little synagogues; others, on the Sure River facing Germany, preferred to cross to Trier to worship. In 1894, a new synagogue rose in Luxembourg City. At the century's end, the community in industrial Esch-sur-Alzette, Luxembourg's second city, built its own temple.

The Jewish population peaked between the two world wars. Impoverished immigrants from Eastern Europe, primarily from Poland and Romania, arrived, bringing an Orthodox outlook that necessitated the establishment of a second synagogue in Luxembourg City. Austrian and German Jews also came, some wading across the Sure. When Germany invaded Luxembourg on May 10, 1940, the country harbored from 3,500 to 4,000 Jews.

About 1,000 fled immediately to France, many during the night of the invasion. With annexation in August 1940, the racial regulations of the Reich went into effect, and the Germans, who at that point seemed merely to want to be rid of the Jews, threatened deportation unless there was "voluntary" emigration. Thus, by May 1941, about 700 managed to leave on quasi-valid visas. The Jewish consistory organized about 1,000 more into small groups and, equipped with German permits, sent them mainly by bus into France. A hundred or so more left in January 1942. The remaining 750 were deported to Thereisenstadt, from where they were dispersed; fewer than 35 survived. Just one full Jew — Charles Judah — managed to hide in the countryside.

During the war, however, the groundwork was laid for strong ties between Luxembourg and the future Jewish state. Luxembourg's Grand Duke Jean became a colonel-in-chief in the Irish Guards and served in the same regiment as Chaim Herzog. Today, the two are reportedly on a first-name basis and have, within the last couple of years, paid each other visits. Apart from supporting the establishment of Israel and its application for Common Market membership, Luxembourg was the sight of the 1952 agreement between Konrad Adenauer and Moshe Sharett in which German reparations were awarded to Israel.

Community: Not so long ago, when the geography of the Middle East was not quite what it is today, a joke rippled through Luxembourg's Jewish community. What, it was queried, was the difference between the Suez Canal and the Grand Rue (the main shopping street of Luxembourg City)? The answer: at the canal, the Jews were only on one side, while on the Grand Rue, they were on both.

Although this may slightly exaggerate Luxembourg's Jewish presence today, the mere existence of such joking speaks strongly of the Jewish entrenchment.

At the war's end, about 1,500 Jews returned to Luxembourg City, Esch-sur-Alzette, and other spots. Most were merchants. Previously, their merchandising skills had been so prevalent that the four corners of a prime Grand Rue intersection were in their hands. But while some went into the professions, enough reestablished themselves as leading tradesmen to reinforce as household words such shop names as Maison Moderne, A la Bourse, and Rosentiel, a top department store.

The community also rebuilt its institutions. Despite its size, it developed all the communal, charitable, and Zionist organizations supported by larger communities. It is culturally active, with events sponsored regularly between October and May in both Luxembourg City and Esch. The Jewish community is scattered, living throughout the city and country. Since Luxembourg doesn't separate church and state, Judaism is a state religion. Consequently, the government subsidized the replacement of the destroyed synagogues in Luxembourg City and Esch-sur-Alzette, contributed to the erection of monuments to war victims, and recently underwrote the renovation of the primary synagogue. Additionally, it pays the salaries and housing costs of the cantor and rabbi, and the latter is invited to all official events. (Since the current rabbi holds a French passport, he is probably the only civil servant in the country today who is not a Luxembourg citizen.) Reciprocally, the synagogue holds services honoring national holidays, which are attended by government officials. On such occasions, there are often more non-Jews than Jews present, and even the grand duke has been known to make an appearance.

The tenor of the services is currently undergoing change. From a liberal, Ashkenazic ritual that included a mixed choir and organ, services have become more traditional and Sephardic, thanks to an influx of Jews following the decolonization of North Africa in the 1960s. The current cantor was born in Algeria and, although he leads the Ashkenazic ritual, he does so with a Sephardic lilt.

Despite the North Africans' arrival, however, and some individuals coming to work for the European Community, many believe the demographics are against Luxembourg's Jews. There are only one or two births a year versus six or eight funerals. Because Luxembourg does not have a full-scale university, many young people leave to study—and do not return.

Sights: Because Luxembourg is tiny, and because it has good roads and public transportation, no two destinations are more than a couple of hours apart. The obvious starting point is Luxembourg City, some ramparts still intact, perched with apparent invincibility above the deep green valleys of the Petrusse and Alzette Rivers.

The new synagogue, dedicated in 1953, rises in a fashionable neighborhood at 45 Avenue Monterey, across from the headquarters of Radio Luxembourg, at the edge of the city's parkland (call 44-25-69, 2–6 P.M.). An edifice of ultrasimplicity, outside and in, it seats about 400 in dusty-rose surroundings brightened by the light from predominantly red and blue stained-glass windows. While the main sanctuary is open Saturday morning, Friday night services usually take place in a community room downstairs. Along with Sunday-school classrooms, the downstairs also contains photos of the old synagogue. An elaborate, Moorish-style building destroyed virtually stone by stone over a period of several weeks in 1941–42, it stood in the heart of the business district, where Rue Aldringen runs into Rue Notre Dame (and across from the place where, in July 1886, Franz Liszt gave his last piano recital). After the war, the Jewish community gave the property to the state, which erected upon it the administrative building for the Coal and Steel Union, the first institution of the Common Market.

A stroll through the nearby pedestrian area, bordering and including the Grand Rue, passes various Jewish-owned shops. The prestigious corner where Rue Fosse and Côte d'Eich meet the Grand Rue was once entirely in Jewish hands, the Bank of China building having been a fur shop that, in 1944, became Allied Command headquarters. Part of the Avenue Emile Reuter, which feeds into the Grand Rue, was once called the Juddegaas, or Rue des Juifs. On the Rue de la Senois, dramatically overlooking the Petrusse Valley, the Fondation Roehr-Katz, popularly known as the Maison Israelite, pleasantly accommodates 30 senior citizens (telephone 44-25-31).

Though nearby, Esch-sur-Alzette seems to its residents like another world. The Jewish community of about 60 is close-knit and provides a disproportionate number of leaders to the community at large. Here, too, many shops along the main thoroughfare, Rue de l'Alzette—Kirsch, Karina, Toma, Brust—have Jewish proprietors. The synagogue stands at the juncture of Rue du Canal and Rue Dieks, its stained-glass panels intercepted dramatically by vertical concrete beams. Though it has no rabbi, the beautiful synagogue has regular services—using Torahs from the old synagogue that were saved during the war years. Like the synagogue in Luxembourg City, Esch's also displays photos from the past.

Further commemorating the past is the Resistance Museum in Esch, which features a section devoted to the Jews. Among the displays are photos of the deportation; specimens of the deportees' clothing; copies of the discriminatory regulations issued by the Germans; letters from concentration camp inmates; and photos of Jewish life in Luxembourg before the war. Esch has also marked the war years by creating a small, weeping willow-draped park on the spot, off Rue de l'Eau, where the previous synagogue stood. Renamed Place de la Synagogue, it bears a bronze, geranium-surrounded plaque decrying the destruction.

Elsewhere, among other memorials to the Holocaust is a gated one, off the main thoroughfare of Medernach, where squawking geese crossing the road still attest to the farming community of which the Jews once were members. The three somber, gray-marble tablets were designed by the Luxembourg sculptor Vercollier and erected outside the monastery of Cinquefontaines, near the northern town of Troisvierges, from which the Jews were deported — along the bypassing tracks of the line to Liege.

Synagogues in various states of disuse still exist in several other towns. In the spa-and-casino enclave of Mondorf-les-Bains, where a state-of-the-art health resort has just opened, the synagogue stands on Rue des Moulins. The local government has begun structural repairs and plans exist to restore its Jewish character. It may include a small museum and will be used for cultural activities. In Ettelbruck, a centrally located town of patrician houses on the edge of the Ardennes — near which a statue of General George Patton looks toward the spot where he turned the Battle of the Bulge for the Allies — the synagogue stands at 20 Rue de Warken, on Rue de la Synagogue. Currently it is a carpet shop, Orient-Galerie, rented from the Jewish community by an Iranian. Though its interior is covered with Persian carpets, and the exterior Hebrew lettering is covered with the store's sign, it is still possible to see traces of its provenance, including a stained-glass window in the shape of the Ten Commandments. In Grevenmacher, a delightful town in the heart of the wine-growing area on the Moselle River and home of the Bernard Masson wine cellars, the synagogue can be found at 28 Rue de Luxembourg, about one hundred yards beyond the Shell station.

Side Trips:
Some destinations easily visited from Luxembourg City are outside the country. A twenty-minute train trip takes the visitor to Arlon, in the Belgian province of Luxembourg, where, a five-minute walk from the station, along Rue de la Synagogue, stands a brownish building built in 1863 and said to be the oldest synagogue in Belgium. Though the town still has a rabbi, only about 30 Jews live here. Contact with the community can be made through André Grumbach (telephone 321-6330) or Rabbi Jean-Claude Jacob (217-985 or 226-671).

Also less than an hour from Luxembourg City is Trier, Germany, where the Judengasse, just off the city's main market through the Kleine Judenpforte, contains remnants of the old ghetto. The contemporary synagogue, which serves a community of 70, is at the corner of Kaiserstrasse and Hindedburgstrasse. Trier is the birthplace of Karl Marx, and the family house on Brückenstrasse has been rebuilt as a museum.

General Sights:
In Luxembourg City, the Grand Duke's Palace is an impressive structure combining three styles — Renaissance, French, and Moorish. President Chaim Herzog of Israel was the first foreign visitor to be housed here, and the edifice flew the Israeli flag. The American military cemetery, just outside the city, is the burial place of General Patton. Deikirch boasts a fine museum to the Battle of the Bulge. Although there are only a handful of Jews now in Echternach, this picture-book town once had a thriving community and is renowned for its "Dancing Procession," which attracts thousands of pilgrims on Whit-Tuesday.

Personalities:
Several contemporary Jewish Luxembourgers have made marks in fields beyond merchandising. Paul Cerf, a former journalist and senior officer of the European Community, has written two books in French on the war years: *Longtemps J'aurai Memoirs* ("Long Shall I Have the Memory") and *L'Etoile Jaune au Luxembourg* ("The Yellow Star in Luxembourg"). Edmond Israel is currently chairman of the board of CEDEL, one of the world's leading bank-clearing institutions, and general manager of Banque Internationale du Luxembourg, the country's largest bank. Alex Bonn, a leading lawyer, has served as president of the State Council, which acts like a supreme court, passing judgment on the constitutionality of laws. And Henry J. Leir, a pioneer in the import and export of nonferrous metals, is probably Luxembourg's leading philanthropist, giving to both Jewish and non-Jewish causes. One of his projects has been the restoration of Bourscheid Castle, thought to encompass ruins from seven different periods.

Among the noteworthy of bygone generations are Guido Oppenheim, a landscape painter who died in Thereisenstadt; the Reinhart family, which pioneered the glove-making industry; Marcel Cahen, a cigarette manufacturer who became a member of Parliament and assistant mayor in Luxembourg City; and Gabriel Lippmann, a physicist and the only Nobel Prize winner ever born in Luxembourg.

Reading: There are no English translations of works on Jewish subjects by Luxembourgers. However, Henry Miller describes Luxembourg in *Quiet Days in Clichy* (Grove Press). Among earlier authors who have written about the Grand Duchy are Victor Hugo, who lived in exile in Vianden, and Johann Wolfgang von Goethe, who visited the country as a war correspondent.

Recommendations: Le Royal, the only centrally located five-star hotel in Luxembourg City, is intimate, courteous, elegant, and less than a ten-minute walk from the synagogue. While Luxembourg has no kosher restaurants, Le Royal, which handles many Jewish functions, will make special catering arrangements if given advance notice. Luxembourg has no airline. Icelandair, which has substantially upgraded its service and image to become a sleek operation, is the only transatlantic carrier flying directly from the United States to Luxembourg. To get to one small, storybook land, it's the only way to go.

—Phyllis Ellen Funke

Madrid and Toledo

The man at the airport's government tourist office insists on telling a Jewish visitor about all his Jewish friends. The hotel concierge proudly reveals he knows the synagogue's address by heart. And the shopkeeper reports, in detail, about a television program he saw on Ladino music. Thus Madrid — in the name of Spain — informs Jews that, five hundred years after their having been expelled, they are welcome back.

Not just welcome, but wanted. The many programs, seminars and exchanges that marked the 500th anniversary of the Jews' expulsion were simply the continuation of a trend that began with the return of democracy in the 1970s. There were similar flurries of activity or festivity marking the establishment of diplomatic relations with Israel in 1986 and, two years earlier, marking the nationwide observance of the 850th anniversary of the birth of Maimonides. Throughout these periods of commemoration, newspaper articles and media presentations have celebrated the Sephardic contribution to Spain, while Spaniards, aware that multitudes descended from Conversos have Jewish blood, hurried to check out their roots.

This is not all that is hurrying Madrid these days, of course. After years of isolation from mainstream Europe, Madrileños rush to catch up with the late 20th century. Hence, their city — a stylishly contemporary one of broad boulevards and grand plazas, of fashionable new neighborhoods and atmospheric old ones — hums, at almost all hours, with action.

Madrid's 3,000 Jews are also caught up in this. While too new to have a definite place yet in the scene, they go with the flow, happy to participate and happy, once again, to be Spanish.

History: Madrid did not become Spain's capital until after the Jews' expulsion, but even as an eleventh-century Moorish stronghold the city did have a small Jewish community. There was also a town nearby called Alludén — from the Arabic *al-Yahudiyin* ("the Jews"). The Madrid community flourished in the 13th century, until the imposition of restrictions on usury rates, real estate dealings, and relations with Christians.

But in the days when Spanish Jewry knew glory, Toledo — forty-five miles south of Madrid, about an hour by today's transport — was Spain's capital and a leading Jewish center. By the twelfth century, 12,000 Jews lived there; in 1391, it had Spain's largest Jewish population.

Under Muslim rule, Toledo grandly contributed to the Golden Age, becoming a headquarters for both religious and secular scholarship, a place where Jews, as intermediaries between Muslims and Christians, translated Arabic works on mathematics, astronomy, and Greek philosophy into the vernacular and Latin — works that would reappear with the Renaissance. After the Christian reconquest, Jews remained undisturbed for a while and rose to such high state positions as diplomat, financier, interpreter, adviser, even royal scribe; in addition, they owned land, vineyards, and slaves.

According to tradition, Toledo's Jewish community was the oldest on the Iberian Peninsula, having descended from exiles from the tribes of Judah and Benjamin who fled the destruction of the First Temple. More likely, however, they arrived with the Visigoths during the fourth or fifth century and were discriminated against until the Muslim invasion of Spain in 711 under

Tarik (who, some say, may have been a Jew).

Among the outstanding Jews from Toledo during the Middle Ages were Meir Ibn Megas, who established a talmudic academy there; Abraham Ibn Ezra, a witty, peripatetic translator, grammarian, and biblical expert whose commentaries accompany most scholarly Hebrew Bibles today; Joseph Ferruziel (Cidellus), a member of the Royal Court, from a family that considered itself of the House of David—and behaved accordingly; and Judah Halevi, physician, philosopher, and poet, whose religious poems have become part of the High Holy Day prayer book, and whose passion for Zion is best represented by the poem that begins, "I am in the West but my heart is in the East."

One Spanish Jew who was not universally revered in Toledo was Maimonides. The city was a center for challenging the writings of the Rambam (a native of Córdoba) on the grounds that they were undermining the faith.

From the twelfth until the mid-fourteenth century, the Jews of Toledo were occasionally attacked or harassed and, on one occasion, imprisoned in their synagogues until they paid a special tax. The real trouble began in 1366, when a vicious, three-year civil war began between Pedro the Cruel and his bastard brother Henry. Perhaps because Pedro had used Jews to execute his tyrannical policies—they were, particularly, his tax gatherers—they were turned upon with a vengeance and, as the city changed hands several times, the Jews not only were forced to raise 1 million gold coins, but also suffered the death of 8,000 of their community.

Next, the Jews were forced to wear identifying badges and give up their Spanish names. In 1391 riots against the Jews of Seville spread throughout the country. In Toledo almost all the synagogues were burned and the Jewish quarter ravaged. Many abandoned Judaism for Christianity—becoming Conversos.

Until then, Jewish converts had been eagerly welcomed. But suddenly there were far too many to be easily absorbed. They began marrying into the Spanish aristocracy and occupying the country's best positions. Some even turned against other Jews;

Pablo de Santa María, né Solomon Levi, did a brilliant job of forcing Jews to convert. But many grew jealous of the roles now played by the Conversos and in Toledo, as elsewhere, Conversos were persecuted—and often slaughtered. Churchmen began to question the purity of their faith and, in 1480, established the Inquisition to root out heretics. One of the instigators of the Inquisition was the infamous Tomás de Torquemada, said to have descended from Jews himself.

There remained only one further step for Spain to take to rid itself of its Jews. On March 31, 1492, King Ferdinand (also said to have had Jewish blood) and Queen Isabella, gave the Jews four months to leave Spain, under pain of death.

After Philip II made Madrid the Spanish capital in 1561, it became the scene of numerous autos-da-fé—including some for Portuguese Conversos who had made the city the principal center for their activities. During the seventeenth century, when Portuguese Conversos were influential in the royal court, the possibility of readmitting Jews was raised, but rejected because of opposition from Inquisition authorities.

Only after 1869, when Spain received a new constitution, could Jews begin to return to the city in safety. By then the Conversos who had stayed in Spain had, for the most part, dropped their secret practices and had become Christian in memory as well as in practice. Madrid did attract Jews from North Africa in the 19th century and, during World War I, gave refuge to Jews from Eastern Europe, among them the Zionist leader Max Nordau. There was little community organization until the passage of a law, in 1924, granting citizenship to individuals of Spanish descent. During the Spanish Civil War the community dispersed.

In Francisco Franco (another said to have Jewish blood) the Jews found great ambivalence. Franco outwardly decried what he called the universal "Anglo-Judeo-Masonic conspiracy" and allied himself with Arab causes (particularly after Israel and other democracies denied his bid for United Nations membership because of his fascism). However, as leader of a country not overrun by Germany in World War II, he gave asylum to some Eastern

European refugees; in 1967 he provided passports for Egyptian Jews on the run.

Community: The Spanish Jewish community of today began forming after World War II and now numbers about 15,000. In 1967, along with other non-Catholic groups, it was given legal status, allowing it to create associations and own property. In 1980, Spain abolished the concept of a state religion. And with the establishment of diplomatic relations with Israel, some see the closing of a circle that began with the expulsion of 1492.

After 500 years, Jews named Salama, Castile, and Toledano are back in the Spanish capital. And some young, idealistic members of the community dream of a presence as rich and significant as the one in Maimonides' time. Meanwhile, the primary thrust in Madrid is to keep its small community of 3,000 united.

Madrid's Jews hail from three backgrounds. The first—a fairly small contingent—came from Eastern Europe during or immediately following World War II. In the 1950s and 1960s, as Morocco gained its independence and incorporated Tangier, Jews, primarily from the northern cities, arrived and now constitute about 70 percent of the community. Also during the 1960s, Madrid saw an influx of Latin American Jews, fleeing that region's upheavals. Together with a handful from Israel, England, Hungary, and the United States, they comprise the community's remainder.

Jewish Madrileños work in fields ranging from high-tech electronics to commerce, with many professionals among the younger generation.

Culturally, the community considers itself Sephardic—and makes a decided distinction between its heritage and that of Jews who truly intermingled in the Diaspora with Arabs. Religiously, though, it is reluctant to define itself—lest it alienate even one precious member. It has sought a common denominator, described by one cautious leader as "mildly Orthodox." Samuel Toledano, secretary-general of Spain's Federation of Jewish Communities, says of the Madrid contingent, "Since everyone disagrees, we think we are on the right course."

Beth Yaacov Synagogue, to which 525 families belong, opened in 1968. The Jewish community, which has its headquarters in the synagogue building, supports a variety of institutions, including a day school in the fashionable Madrid suburb of Moraleja (where many Jews live) attended by 160—or 25 percent—of the children in grades one through ten, a youth camp about twenty miles from Madrid, two kosher butchers, a cemetery, and a country club.

Spanish Jews say they are free to socialize as they choose; in fact, these days—perhaps because they are still novelties—they even find themselves lionized.

Jewish heights: Toledo was where Sephardim made—and left—their greatest marks

Madrid Sights: Beth Yaacov, Madrid's first synagogue since 1492, is down a little street that looks like an alley. It's at Calle Balmes 3, near Plaza de Sorolla, in Madrid's downtown area.

The discreet building—guarded by a police car day and night—also houses a small chapel, two social halls, a Talmud Torah room for Sunday classes, a *mikveh*, a library, and facilities for kosher catering. (In fact, a section of one hall can be blocked off as a kosher restaurant, if tourists call in advance.)

The synagogue itself boasts marble floors covered with Oriental-style runners, and in its one wall open to the light are modernistic red, white, and blue stained-glass windows. As part of a university course in the humanities, Spain's Queen Sophia studied Judaism and attended services here in May 1976. The office numbers are 445-9843 and 445-9835. Be prepared for a security check on entering.

At Calle del Duque de Medinaceli 4, near the American Express office, is the Arias Montano Institute for Jewish Studies, a government-sponsored center, founded in 1941 for research in Hebrew, Sephardic, and Near East studies. It is known for its library of more than sixteen thousand volumes and rare manuscripts and publishes a semiannual journal called *Sefarad*. Bear in mind that nonresearchers and tourists without credentials are dissuaded from visiting. The same applies for the Jewish Studies department at the University of Madrid.

Visitors are more than welcome, however, at Sefarad, the one Jewish-owned shop on the Gran Vía, Madrid's primary shopping street. Located at number 54, it features, along with other Spanish gift items, antique Mediterranean menorahs, contemporary Jewish-themed tiles, and a porcelain rabbi originally made exclusively for the store by Lladró.

In areas not far from the Gran Vía once existed Madrid's Jewish neighborhoods. One *judería* is believed to have stood where fashionable homes and apartment buildings now rise near the Royal Palace. It was bordered by the Calle de Bailén, the Plaza de Isabel II, the Calle Mayor, and the Calle Santiago, and included the Plaza de Oriente which was, until the nineteenth century, a maze of alleys. Another *judería* may have been on the Calle de la Fé, now a dark, narrow street in the old town, not far from the Atocha Railroad Station; a synagogue situated next to the Church of San Lorenzo was destroyed in the riots of 1391.

General Sights: The Prado, with its matchless collections of masterpieces by Velázquez, Ribera, Murillo, Goya, El Greco, Rubens, Titian, Raphael, Correggio, Tintoretto, and others, is one of the world's great art repositories. What is more, a number of its works have a particular attraction for Jews. Some are of interest not because of the theme but because of the faces, which often seem decidedly ethnic. Others present relevant — if not necessarily pleasant — subjects, such as money-changers and autos-da-fé. And still more — often by the masters — are on Hebrew Bible themes. Among those to look for are Veronese's *Moses Rescued from the Nile*; Ribera's *Jacob's Dream* and *Isaac and Jacob*; Poussin's *The Triumph of David*; Caravaggio's *David Victorious Over Goliath*; Bassano's *Entrance of the Animals to the Ark;* Murillo's *Rebecca and Eliezar*; Tintoretto's *Moses, Esther Before Ahasuerus* and *The Queen of Sheba's Visit to Solomon*; Durer's *Adam and Eve*; Berruguete's *Auto-da-Fé Presided Over by St. Dominic de Guzmán*; and Reymerswaele's *The Money-Changer and His Wife*.

In the heart of the old town, surrounded by a network of narrow streets, is the expansive, portico-encircled Plaza Mayor, scene of countless autos-da-fé. Also in the center of town is the Puerta del Sol, near which may have been another *judería*. The Archaeological Museum, at Calle de Serrano 13, has a collection of Jewish artifacts from Toledo — worth visiting, but hardly a substitute for a visit to Madrid's older neighbor.

Toledo Sights: Toledo is one of those places in Spain where the reminders of the country's Jewish past still stand. Built of golden-hued limestone, the walled city, set high on a cliff, has — for its situation and for its erstwhile tripartite spirituality — been compared with Jerusalem. Its streets are narrow, steep, cobbled, and laid out like a Minotaur maze. But though its many blind alleys make it easy to get lost, recently placed directional signs — with *Magen Davids* on a red background — clearly point the way to the most significant Jewish landmarks.

Though Jews lived in areas throughout the city, the primary *judería* was in the city's southwest quarter, a good view of which may be had from Paseo de San Cristóbal, also known as Montichel. The main neighborhood stretches as far north as the Cambrón gate, formerly named "Gate of the Jews," documented in 1254. It is bisected by Calle del Ángel, once Calle de la Judería (now the name of a small branch street), where the remains of what some believe were *mikvehs* have been uncovered. Even before the Middle Ages, the quarter was walled and had its own fortress—which made it something of an independent town.

Here, legend and speculation combine with today's tangibles. While records indicate the existence, at one time or another, of ten synagogues and five chapels, only two major synagogues still stand (though the church, Posada de la Hermandad, is said to have been a Jewish chapel).

On the Calle de los Reyes Católicos, near the city's wall, in the heart of the old *judería*, is the oldest of Toledo's Jewish monuments, the synagogue-turned-church, Santa María la Blanca, built in 1203. It stands off the street in a garden where, even in winter, birds chirp in the tall trees.

Built in the *mudéjar* style—developed by Moors living in Christian lands—the interior is a chorus of columns topped by the swirls of arches which, from different perspectives, form a variety of overlaying patterns with each other. The capitals are delicately molded in pine-cone motifs and some old tile work remains on the floor. In addition to having been a church, this structure, newly—and dramatically—well lit, knew incarnations as a dance hall, a barracks, a carpenter's workshop, and a refuge for reformed prostitutes. Recent excavations, begun to discover the sources of dampness seeping into the structure, have revealed not only its foundations but also traces of previous buildings on the site. Just what, if anything, was of Jewish origin, however, has yet to be determined.

On the north side of Santa María is a narrow street called Callejón de los Jacintos (hyacinths), the setting of a sad legend. According to the story, a beautiful Jewish woman named Salome lived here, behind a window edged with hyacinths. Though it was forbidden, a Christian nobleman, Don Diego de Sandoval, loved her passionately. One day, he picked the flowers, left them within Salome's reach and, as she watched, drew his dagger and committed suicide.

Nearly next door to Santa María, in the vicinity of the street now called Calle de San Juan de los Reyes, stood the kosher slaughterhouse, the butchers, and the Jewish castle. Nearly next door, but on Santa María's other side, is the square

today known as Plaza de Barrio Nuevo, formerly the center of the *judería* and its commercial hub. Nearby is the Calle de San Juan de Diós and off it runs the current Calle de la Judería. At number 4 is a structure popularly known as the Jew's House. Possessed of a patio, tall lobed windows, and fancy lacelike stonework, it is not certain if this was once a synagogue or a rich Jew's home.

No question exists about the *judería's* most prominent structure, the synagogue-cum-museum called El Tránsito. Its entrance is on Calle de Samuel Levi, named for Samuel Levi Abulafia, who lived next door in a palace. Later the mansion was rebuilt as Casa del Greco, the painter's home.

Abulafia, a shrewd politician, allied himself with Pedro the Cruel and was his treasurer until enemies denounced him as a traitor and had him tortured to death. Earlier, though, thanks to Abulafia's position, he was, despite a ban on such structures, given permission to build a synagogue for his private use. El Tránsito was completed in 1357, four years before he died. Designed by Rabbi Meyer Abdeli from Granada, the most renowned architect of the time, El Tránsito, restored in 1990, is reminiscent of the Alhambra. The interior is rectangular with a seemingly soaring forty-foot-high ceiling elaborately carved from cedars of Lebanon. The walls have been freshly cleaned to reveal in all its intricacy the filigree work covering them—delicate designs representing grape leaves, palmettos, and lilies of the valley. Circling them is a band of Hebrew lettering with quotations from the Bible and the Psalms—a motif included in Madrid's Beth Yaacov. One Tránsito wall is dominated by a recessed window panel in front of which stand three foliated arches casting lacy shadows on the opposite wall. On another wall windows alternate with closed-in arches. Overlooking the room is the women's gallery.

The synagogue is the focal point of Toledo's expanded and upgraded Sefardi Museum, whose showcases stand in areas adjoining the sanctuary. Its permanent collection is designed to show the history of the Jews from their arrival in Spain, through the Golden Age and the Expulsion, to their resettlement in other lands. In addition to original objects from Spain, antiquities from Israel have been sought to illustrate pre-Spanish habitation; outfits and amulets from Turkey, Morocco, and elsewhere illustrate postexpulsion life. Among the highlights are an eleventh-century tombstone from Toledo; a thirteenth-century illuminated Hebrew-Arabic Bible page; seals of the Inquisition; and a fifth-century ritual wash basin, about eighteen inches square and found in Tarragona, carved with a primitive menorah, schematic *shofar*, Tree of Life, and peacocks. Additional tombstones lie in the adjoining courtyard. Museum officials hope to find additional space to display paintings on Jewish subjects — such as a nineteenth-century watercolor of Segovia's synagogue — which the museum possesses. Its catalogue currently is in Spanish only.

In Toledo's Cathedral — near which is a small Jewish enclave, the merchant district's Alcana, once thrived, and through which a Calle de la Sinagoga still runs — darker aspects of the Spanish-Jewish past have left their marks. High on a wall down a long corridor to the right of the tourist's entrance exists a plaque celebrating the Jews' expulsion. And over the entrance is a mural depicting the kidnapping by Jews from the sanctuary of a blond boy who is later shown crucified so that the Jews might cut out his heart for ritual use. Reportedly, the cathedral also has documents of property sales involving Jews and Christians, a Hebrew Bible, and a charity box with a Hebrew inscription, but these are not on display. Hebrew inscriptions show up elsewhere near the city's center — on a lintel at Calle de la Plata 9, at the Tower of San Justo, on tombstones from the Jewish cemetery turned into building blocks. At a site now the Plaza de Zocodover, several autos-da-fé were held.

More details, plus maps, are found in *A Guide to Jewish Toledo,* published in 1990 by Codex and available at most bookstores in the city.

Day Trips: In Segovia, the Castilian city of moats and castles, the Church of Corpus Christi was originally the main synagogue. Built in the thirteenth century in the *mudéjar* style, it resembles Toledo's Santa María la Blanca. It was converted into a church in 1420, after Jews were accused of desecrating the Host and, in 1572, it became the property of Franciscan nuns. The *judería* was originally situated around the Calle de la Judería and, later, around the Barrio Nuevo or Judería Nueva, where the church of La Merced, probably once a synagogue, stands today.

The medieval walled city of Ávila was the birthplace in 1515 of the religious educator Santa Teresa. The descendant of a Converso silk merchant from Toledo, she attempted, with San Juan de la Cruz, probably of similar background, to reform the Carmelite order. The town's Church of Todos Los Santos and the Chapel of Mosen Rubi (Calle de López Núñez) are thought to have originally been synagogues. Torquemada is buried in the Sacristy of Ávila's Convent of Santo Tomás.

El Escorial is the site of the monastery of San Lorenzo and the summer palace of King Philip II, completed in 1584. Effigies of the six kings of Judah are sculpted on the walls of the palace's Patio of Kings, while the monastery contains a superb collection of medieval Hebrew Bibles and illuminated manuscripts. These were assembled. in the sixteenth century by a Converso, Benito Arias Montano. He traveled through Europe to save Bibles banned by the Church and offered them to Philip as the foundation for a royal library, of which Arias Montano became the director. The library is open to visitors, but few, if any, Bibles are on display and may generally be seen only by researchers.

Personalities: Since Madrid's Jewish community is young, there has not been much time for luminaries to emerge. However, on the national board of the Socialist Party is Enrique Mujica Herzog, who is half-Jewish and openly identifies with his origins. He was a strong advocate of the establishment of relations with Israel. Jacob Hassan is a professor of Sephardic Culture at Madrid University and Elena Benarroch is developing an international reputation as a fur designer. Another international reputation is that of Lita Milan Trujillo, the widow of Rafael Trujillo, the dictator who admitted many Jewish refugees to the Dominican Republic during World War II. Mrs. Trujillo is a Hungarian Jew from Jaffa.

Reading: For contemporary history, see Haim Avni's *Spain, Franco and the Jews* (Jewish Publication Society). For the past, the JPS has published Yitzhak Baer's *History of the Jews in Christian Spain* and E. Ashtor's *History of the Jews in Moslem Spain*. For the atmosphere of pre-Expulsion Jewish life in fiction there is Matt Cohen's *The Spanish Doctor* (Viking Penguin) and David Raphael's *The Alhambra Decree* (Carmi House). For an overview of Spain in general, Spanish Jews and non-Jews suggest James Michener's *Iberia* (Random House). To recommend Hemingway is to state the obvious.

Recommendations: The Spanish National Tourist Office (665 Fifth Avenue, New York, NY 10022; 212-759-8822) has made Spain's Jewish heritage one of its specialties, and offers a wealth of information for travelers. In Madrid, the Villa Magna is an ultraelegant, ultrafashionable hotel conveniently located just beyond the city's commercial heart on the broad, north-south boulevard, Paseo de la Castellana. The travel agency Viajes Transit, Fernando el Católico 12 and Vallehermoso 40 (telephone 447-7916), handles kosher requests. Not everyone in Spain's travel industry knows synagogue addresses by heart, but in the country's desire to welcome Jewish visitors and explore its own Jewish past, you may be left with that impression.

—Phyllis Ellen Funke

Majorca

There was pride in the tour guide's face as he led a visitor down the main shopping street in the old section of Palma de Majorca. "This shop is owned by Jews," he said, "and that one over there. The one across the lane was Jewish owned until a few years ago, and the next two after that are still Jewish."

What was unusual was that he was talking about people who are not Jewish by any routine standard, people whose families haven't been Jewish, in fact, for more than 500 years. Nevertheless, these shopkeepers are regarded as Jews by many Majorcans.

Most people go to Majorca for the climate, but the island has a unique place in Jewish history. Stories of Conversos, people forced to convert who continued to practice Judaism in secret, are well known. But only in Majorca, situated in the Mediterranean 130 miles south of Barcelona, is there a large group of people descended from Jews who still form a community. All over Europe there are churches built on the sites of former synagogues, but only in Palma are the people who worship in a church descended from the people who worshiped in a synagogue on the same site. Only in Majorca are there people living on the same streets with the same occupations as their Jewish ancestors of five hundred years ago; only in Majorca is there a Catholic community with a high incidence of a Jewish genetic disease.

History: The Balearic Islands, of which Majorca is the largest, were at the crossroads of the trade routes between Spain, France, Italy, and North Africa, and Jews settled the area as early as the fifth century. The earliest evidence is of a community on Minorca, Majorca's neighbor to the east, but little information has come down from that time. There is more substantial evidence of permanent communities in the twelfth century, by which time Majorca was the major center.

Many Jews came to Majorca in the twelfth century when it was still under Muslim rule. This was after the Almohads (the same fundamentalist Muslim rulers who prompted the family of Maimonides to flee Córdoba) attacked southern Spain.

When the Christian King James I of Aragon conquered the island in 1229, there were Jews in his retinue. Under his benign rule, Jews were given property rights, and the community grew with infusions from southern France and North Africa.

Jews lived all over the island and contributed greatly to Majorca's prosperity in the thirteenth and fourteenth centuries. They were involved in agriculture and trade, as gold- and silversmiths, shoemakers, and moneylenders. Jewish cartographers from Majorca were the leading mapmakers of their day. Abraham Cresques is believed to be the creator of the famed Catalan Atlas, which is in the Bibliothèque Nationale in Paris; even as Jewish fortunes in Majorca declined at the end of the fourteenth century, he was granted royal protection and was also asked to appoint the Jewish community's ritual slaughterer. Abraham's son, Judah Cresques, was employed by Henry the Navigator, the Portuguese explorer who fathered of the age of exploration.

Though they had originally lived in the Almudaina, the fortress in the middle of Palma (once referred to as "the fortress of the Jews"), the Jews soon moved into the surrounding streets. Toward the end of the thirteenth century, the Jewish section was between Temple and Calatrava streets. Many of the descendants of the Jews from that period live on the same streets today.

Jewish fortunes usually depended on the

willingness of the reigning monarch to oppose the church. There was a time in the early fourteenth century when Christian clergy were forbidden to enter the Jewish quarter. Difficulties often arose when Muslim slaves wished to convert to Judaism. In 1314, the Jewish community made the strategic error of accepting two German Christians as converts and the king joined the local bishop in levying a fine on the Jews and converting the synagogue into a church (though they were allowed to build another synagogue).

Perhaps the biggest turning point came with the Black Death of 1349. The anti-Jewish riots that broke out after the plague became a periodic feature of life in Majorca until 1391, when pogroms swept across Spain. In that year, many of Majorca's Jews were killed or forced to convert. Within a few years, Jews who had managed to keep their lives and their faith and immigrant Portuguese Jews settled in next to the Conversos (reversion to Judaism was illegal), and Jewish life continued under siege. The next four decades saw more forced conversions, legal restrictions, and a blood libel until, in 1435, the last 200 Jews on the island either converted or fled to North Africa. More than a half century before the expulsion from mainland Spain, Majorca's Jewish community officially ceased to exist.

But in some ways little changed. Many Majorcans who were ostensibly Catholic practiced Judaism in secret, and though the Inquisition was active in the late fifteenth and early sixteenth centuries, it later grew dormant.

It reasserted itself in the 1670s. In 1678 more than 100 Conversos were arrested; their seized property constituted the largest confiscation of the Spanish Inquisition. In 1688 a large group of Conversos attempted to flee the island but were captured; 86 were arrested and, after a three-year trial, 37 were burned at the stake.

That might have been the end of things, but in 1693 Majorca's chief inquisitor decided that the penitential robes worn by the defendants at the autos-da-fé should be exhibited in Palma's Dominican church, along with the names of those who had worn them. The fifteen posted surnames were associated with the Inquisition for the next 127 years. Though there had been many more Converso surnames in the seventeenth century, it was the families with these particular names that became the Chuetas. The word—which, according to different theories, is either "little Jew" or a variation on the word for "pork"—is regarded as derogatory by most of the community, but among the small minority who today feel a positive attachment to their Jewish roots it seems to be used with pride.

By the time the robes and names were burned in 1820, by a mob protesting the Inquisition, most Chuetas were Catholic inwardly as well as outwardly. What kept them together was not a secret faith but public prejudice. Despite laws against discrimination, the Chuetas remained social outcasts, locked out of the university, professions, and marriage with non-Chuetas. The extent to which they married only within the community can be seen in the findings of a Majorcan epidemiologist who discovered that some Chuetas suffer from Familial Mediterranean Fever, a genetic disease common among Sephardim in Israel.

It was only with the postwar tourist boom, with the mass invasion of outsiders, that the Chuetas began to look like insiders and discrimination began to dissipate. Palma's mayor, Ramon Aguilo, is a Chueta (there are about 15,000 on the city, in a general population of 300,000), but not everyone loves him. During one election campaign a message scrawled on a wall across the street from city hall read, "Aguilo is a Jew."

Community: Jews are among the foreigners who have invaded Majorca, as tourists and as permanent residents. About 160 are members of the official Jewish community, the largest number from England, followed by France, the United States, and a group of German Jews from Chile. Community members say there are at least several hundred more Jews on the island who are unaffiliated.

Until a generation ago, most Chuetas thought of their Jewish ancestry as something to hide. The majority were faithful Catholics and their "Jewishness" was seen as burdensome. In the 1960s, however, a small group began meeting to talk about and study Jewish subjects. Though few wanted to go through formal conversion, they expressed a Jewish identity and took an intense interest in Israel. Several today are active in a Balearic-Israel friendship society. Only one Chueta, Nicolas Aguilo, has converted; he now lives in Israel, where he has taken the name Nissan Ben-Avraham.

Ben-Avraham is something of a folk hero to the foreign Jewish colony of Palma, some of whom remember him as a curious boy who attended their services in the early 1970s. Recently on a rare visit home, he showed up unexpectedly on a Friday night and was asked to lead the service. The difference between the foreign Jews and the descendant of Majorca's fourteenth-century community was easily apparent; the expatriate Jews of Majorca are a clean-shaven lot who follow a Liberal ritual; the bearded Ben-Avraham is decidedly Ortho-dox. He was not the only Chueta present. Community members say that at a typical *Shabbat* service three or four are in atten-dance.

Sights: Palma's synagogue is on Calle Monseñor Palmer, half a block from the sea. Located on the ground floor of a modern apartment building, the white walls and arched doorways nevertheless evoke an Old World feeling. For information on Friday night and holiday services, call Dr. Arnold Spicer, the community president, at 23-86-86, or Joe Segal at 22-36-55.

The modern synagogue, however, is by no means the only place in Palma of Jewish interest. Most of the places associated with the medieval Jewish community and the Chuetas are in the heart of the city's old section.

It is along the Calle de la Platería—the street where the Chueta guide pointed out all the "Jewish" shops—that the least has changed since the fourteenth century. The Plateria is located in what was once the Call Menor, or little quarter; the "Call" comes not from the Spanish word for street but from the Hebrew *kahal*, or community.

The narrow street, actually a pedestrian mall, is lined with jewelry stores inter-spersed with grocery and clothing shops. Many of the stores are owned by Chuetas in the same trades as their Jewish ancestors. Twenty years ago, virtually all the shops on the street were Chueta-owned; most of the

jewelry stores still are. Star-of-David pen-dants are displayed in the windows, per-haps more an indication of the clientele than of the ownership. Chuetas also own shops and apartments on Calle de Jaume II, two blocks over from the Platería.

The Platería is in the shadow of Santa Eulalia, a church with a large proportion of Chueta worshipers. At the end of the Placa Santa Eulalia opposite the church, turn left into Fortuny, a street that winds into the Calle del Call, the residential heart of the old Jewish quarter. After a few yards, the Calle del Call branches into the Calle del Sol and Calle Montesión, the two main streets of the quarter.

On Montesión—Mount Zion—a street graced with elegant bay windows and court-yard gardens, the main landmark is the Montesión Church, which stands on the site where Palma's great synagogue stood in the fourteenth century. Like Santa Eulalia, many of those who worship at Montesión are Chuetas.

The ironically named Calle del Sol is a quieter street, so narrow that the sun rarely peeks in. The yellow-, orange-, and salmon-colored buildings are adorned with wrought-iron railings and green shutters.

The Plateria and the Calle del Call are both a short walk from two of Majorca's most popular attractions, the Almudaina and the Palma Cathedral. Both have Jewish connections.

The Palacio de la Almudaina was the fortress built by the Moors when they ruled the islands, and where many of the Jews who arrived with King Jaume I lived after he conquered the island. Today it is noted for its museum of arts and armor, its garden, and its view of the Palma harbor.

Across the Plaza Almoina from the for-tress is the Mediterranean-Gothic Cathe-dral. In the small museum are displayed two six-foot Sicilian *rimmonim* from the fifteenth century. The main stained-glass window over the transept has a Star-of-David design, something even the most knowledgeable guides seem unable to ex-plain.

Personalities: There is a question al-ways on the periphery of Jewish travels on the Spanish mainland that hits the visitor square in the eyes on Majorca: was

Christopher Columbus a Jew? It is a matter of faith among some in Palma that he was both Majorcan and Jewish. A skeptic who reads the official record and listens to all he hears in Palma is likely to come away half-convinced.

Officially, Columbus was a Catholic from Genoa, but the historical record strongly suggests that he was not an Italian by culture. Most of his written records were in Spanish, and when he wrote in Latin his mistakes were typically those committed by Spanish, not Italian, speakers. He is said to have felt comfortable in the company of Conversos, and the interpreter he took on his first voyage, Luís de Torres, was baptized just before they sailed—on the very day in 1492 that Ferdinand and Isabel had set for all Jews to be out of Spain. In Palma, there was a Genoese community living next to, and engaged in many of the same trades as, Jews. Columbus is said to have been cryptic when speaking of his background, and a Genoese identity would have been an easy cover for a Majorcan who wanted to obscure his Jewish ancestry.

But evidence also suggests that Columbus was, if not a faithful Catholic, at least a discretionary one. And since the Jews of Palma had all converted by 1435, the more likely explanation is that the explorer had some Jewish ancestors, was possibly from a Majorcan family, but was not necessarily Jewish or Converso.

Side Trips: Palma is located on a flat, fertile plain on the southern side of Majorca, but a trip to the island isn't complete without a look at the mountains. One worthwhile detour is the eleven-mile trip along narrow, winding mountain roads to Valldemosa. It was in the guest house of the monastery there that the composer Frederic Chopin spent the winter of 1838–39 with his lover, the French novelist Aurore Dude-vant, better known by her pen name of George Sand. One of the things she noticed was the local attitudes toward Chuetas. She wrote, "When one observes the relentless hatred by which the unhappy Jews are still pursued in Majorca, even after twelve to fifteen generations of conversion to Christianity, it is hard to believe that the spirit of the Inquisition has died out so entirely." The monastery is now a museum, several rooms of which are devoted to the famous lovers.

Another popular day trip is the journey by narrow-gauge railway and tram through the mountains to the beach at Puerto de Soller.

Reading: There is a lot written about the Chuetas in Spanish, little in English. One of the best accounts is a chapter in *Acts of Faith: A Journey to the Fringes of Jewish Identity* by Dan Ross (St. Martin's Press). George Sand's account of her stay is in her memoir, *A Winter in Majorca*. There are quite a few general novels set on the island, including Gail Godwin's *The Perfectionists* (Harper and Row); most of the works of the English mystery writer Roderic Jeffries are set in Majorca.

Recommendations: Majorca may seem as though it is drowned in hotels, but they are not enough to handle the (literally) millions of tourists who visit the island annually. It is best to have a reservation well in advance, especially in the summer.

Among the local hosts who know Palma's Jewish history, one favorite is Juan Aguilo, a Chueta merchant and part-time guide (telephone 71-16-31). He conducts tours in Spanish and French, and will be happy to tell visitors, with pride in his eyes, which stores on the Platería are Jewish.
—*Alan M. Tigay*

Melbourne

If it's Monday in New York, it's Tuesday in Melbourne. That's the time differential between these two cities at opposite ends of our globe. As one Melbourne rabbi put it: "On that great day, when the Messiah comes to lead all the Jews out of exile and back to Jerusalem, we Australians — with a twenty-four-hour head start — will already be settled in."

Meanwhile, pending the Messiah's arrival, the 95,000 Jews of the island continent are making do. If cosmopolitan Sydney is their Tel Aviv (to offer neat, simplistic analogies), the more conservative Melbourne is their "Down Under" Jerusalem.

History and Comparison: Sydney's founding fathers were convicts, sent to remote Australia from the slums of London for such crimes as stealing bread. In their initial landing at Botany Bay in 1788, there were at least 6 Jews. Sydney's Jewish population of 32,000 is largely derived from Central European forebears: Germans, who managed to escape their homeland just before World War II, when Australia allowed 7,000 to enter; Hungarians, fresh from the displaced persons camps or, a decade later, refugees from the Russian invasion of their country in 1956. Their religious commitment tends to be less zealous than that of the Melbourne Jews, the schism between Orthodoxy and Liberal (Reform) Judaism less marked. Melbourne's 40,000 Jews are of largely Eastern European origin.

Modern Sydney, with a romantic nod toward its scarlet past, is rather laid-back, free-swinging, open-minded (it is reported to have the largest homosexual population in the world, after San Francisco's). Perhaps the key adjective for Sydney is *secular*. By that token, the word for Melbourne would be *religious*. Named for the Whig prime minister at the time of Queen Victoria's coronation in 1837, the city has retained, until now at least, a certain nineteenth-century formality. The early settlers were respectable yeomen and merchants, adherents of the Anglican, Catholic, and Presbyterian churches. Among the group of 145 good citizens who established Melbourne in 1835, there were two Jews — no less orthodox than their fellow pioneers and as obedient to the authority of the chief rabbi of Great Britain as the Christians were to that of the archbishop of Canterbury or the pope.

Most of Melbourne's early Jews came from England, Germany, and Austria and settled near their shops and business in the heart of the city on Collins, Bourke, and Elizabeth streets. The city's first synagogue, the Melbourne Hebrew Congregation, was founded in this area in 1847. To the genteel Judaism of these early immigrants, however, much larger numbers of East European immigrants brought the assertive *Yiddishkeit* of the *shtetls*. They came to Melbourne in two successive waves — the smaller, in the 1890s, fleeing the pogroms of czarist Russia; the larger, after the Holocaust, composed of the homeless remnants who chose Australia because of its relatively open immigration policies, or perhaps simply to put the greatest distance between themselves and the horrors they had experienced in Europe. In addition to being fed from abroad, Melbourne attracted the children of immigrants who had settled as peddlers or gold prospectors in the smaller towns of Victoria.

From the beginning Melbourne Jews have been upwardly mobile. The early arrivals from Poland and Russia were itinerant peddlers or workers. The peddlers settled down and became merchant princes. The watchmakers opened jewelry factories. The tailors became the clothing manufacturers. The carpenters and the cabinetmakers turned to the mass production of furniture.

Their children and grandchildren, enacting a scenario parallel to the American one, are "overrepresented," they proudly assert, in the arts and the professions. Melbourne Jews have held every political post, from city councilman—including a number of lord mayors—to cabinet minister and governor-general.

Community: The Jews of Melbourne today are 20 percent liberal and 80 percent traditional, though many from both groups are, in practice, what Americans would think of as Conservative Jews. Lubavitch is also a large and growing presence in the community. Despite the divisions among the three groups, however, they offer a variety and intensity of Jewish life unequaled on the continent.

Since World War II, the Melbourne community has more than doubled its numbers. It supports some two hundred organizations, among which are twenty-eight Orthodox and three Liberal synagogues, two homes and a sheltered workshop for the aged, nine day schools, eighteen part-time schools, ten kindergartens, two museums, art galleries, libraries, a publishing house, a weekly newspaper, a monthly literary magazine in English and Yiddish, a Yiddish theater and choir, sixteen Zionist groups, seventeen youth clubs, sixteen sports organizations, twenty-one *landsmanshaften*, and six hours per week of radio programming. With so broad a range of structures and activities, it is no wonder that Australian Jews look to Melbourne as their spiritual center, their Jerusalem, the very core of continuing identity.

The same mobility that has characterized the economic life of Australian Jewry applies to its living space, but the direction in Melbourne is not so much upward as southward. The impoverished immigrants settled initially in the working-class districts, such as Carlton and Brunswick, then moved to Balaclava and St. Kilda, south of the Yarra River, which bisects the city. With prosperity, their descendants have moved to such

elegant suburbs as Caulfield and Toorak—easily the equivalents of Beverly Hills and Scarsdale.

One indication of Melbourne's central role among Australian Jewry is the attendance in full-time religious day schools. Eighty percent of Jewish children go to one or another of the kindergarten-through-high-school institutions. Mount Scopus, the first in the country, founded in 1948, has 25,000 students and is said to be the largest in the world. A leading Melbourne businessman and Jewish community leader ascribes this extraordinary enrollment to what he calls "the tyranny of distance." So far removed from the Jewish mainstreams in the United States and Israel, he says, Australian Jews feel more keenly the need to give their children an unassailable identity in a land where Jews make up only 0.5 percent of the total population—and which, moreover, tempts them with the assimilationist seductions of an open, egalitarian society, virtually free of anti-Semitism.

Sights and Neighborhoods: In a city of 3.2 million, the Jews of Melbourne are hardly visible, but a real and *heimish* presence lingers in the concentration of kosher restaurants, butchers, and groceries on Carlisle or Acland Street in the city's St. Kilda district.

The key sight of Jewish Melbourne is the Melbourne Hebrew Congregation, the oldest and largest in the city, at Toorak and St. Kilda Roads, South Yarra. Founded in 1841, the Orthodox congregation moved to its white Victorian structure, topped by a Byzantine-style copper dome, in 1930. Inside, the beautiful wood-paneled sanctuary also features an Italianate eternal light and vividly colored abstract stained-glass windows.

The Jewish Museum of Australia, originally housed in the Melbourne Hebrew Congregation, was scheduled to move to its own building at 26 Alma Road, St. Kilda, late in 1993. The museum's permanent collection includes ritual objects from home and synagogue, paintings and sculpture by Jewish artists, personal and Holocaust memorabilia, photographs, oral-history tapes, costumes and documents, and Australian Judaica. It also features a slide-

and-sound show, *Arrival and Survival,* about the 150-year history of Jews in Melbourne.

Temple Beth Israel, headquarters of Liberal Judaism, is at 76–82 Alma Road in St. Kilda. The largest religious building in Melbourne, it seats well over two thousand people. Other area synagogues worth visiting are the St. Kilda Hebrew Congregation in Charnwood Grove, St. Kilda, which is full of old-world charm, and the Kew Synagogue, 53 Walpole Street in the eastern suburb of Kew, one of the more tastefully designed modernist temples.

The Kadimah Cultural Centre, 7 Selwyn Street, Elsternwick, shows Yiddish plays and films and has a large library of works in Yiddish and English. Melbourne's B'nai B'rith office also offers a range of activities, most notably its Thursday lecture and kosher lunch (99 Hotham Street, East St. Kilda; telephone 527-4491). Gilgul is a popular Jewish theater company which stages traditional and avant-garde productions in English and Yiddish. Melbourne's first Jewish Festival of the Arts was held in 1993. The city's ethnic radio station, 3EA, features daily programs in English, Hebrew, and Yiddish.

For information on Jewish events in Melbourne, write or call the Jewish Community Council of Victoria, 219 Balaclava Road, Suite 6, in Caulfield (telephone 523-5566). The council's annual directory is also useful as a guidebook.

Personalities: Sir Isaac Isaacs, born in Melbourne in 1855 to a Polish immigrant family, became the nation's chief justice and the first native to serve as governor general. Like James Madison in the American constitutional struggles, Isaacs was the major figure in the development of an Australian constitution that would assert the sovereignty of a federal government over its component states. He was a practicing Jew, but he rejected Judaism's national, cultural, and political aspects. A staunch Anglophile and anti-Zionist, he strongly defended Britain's role in Palestine. At the age of ninety, Isaacs was still appearing in public, eloquently supporting the policies of Ernest Bevin, the british foreign secretary who fought Jewish immigration to *Eretz Yisrael* and deported "ille-gals" to the detention camps in Cyprus. (Isaacs was also a creature of his time; Zionism did not take over the mainstream of Australian Jewish thought until the 1930s.)

Sir Zelman Cowen, a leading jurist and educator, followed very much in Isaacs's footsteps. Cowen wrote a biography of Isaacs in 1967, and in 1977 he became Australia's second Jewish governor-general. Unlike the subject of his biography, however, Cowen has long been active in Zionist affairs.

Sir John Monash, one of the most revered figures in Australian history, is best known as the commander in chief of the combined Australian–New Zealand Armed Forces, the Anzacs, in World War I. Lloyd George, Great Britain's wartime prime minister, called him the finest military leader in the British Empire. A religious Jew all his life, Monash became the president of the Zionist Federation of Australia in 1930. Shortly before his death, he was named a full general. Named in his honor, Monash University in Melbourne is one of Australia's leading educational institutions.

The most prominent person in Australian Jewish communal life is Isi Leibler, a co-chairman of the World Jewish Congress. Melbourne's Jewish mayors have ranged from Sir Benjamin Benjamin, who served from 1887 to 1889, to the most recent, Irvin Rockman. Other Melbourne Jews widely known to the Australian public are filmmakers Bob Weis and Ben Lewin and the playwright Ron Elisha, whose *In Duty Bound* and *Einstein* have satirized Jewish identity and values. Sam Lipski, who rose to prominence as a television newsman, edits the weekly *Jewish News.*

The achievement of an Isaacs or a Monash is not unique among Australian Jews. They have always enjoyed a climate of acceptance and a freedom from anti-Semitism — except for a time in the hallowed precincts of some of Melbourne's private clubs, where the Judeophobia of the British upper classes once prevailed.

Eating and Shopping: The center of Jewish life in Melbourne is still in Balaclava and St. Kilda, where you can find an abundance of kosher restaurants, butchers, bakers, and Jewish stores. The fare at Singer's, on the corner of Balaclava and Hawthorn Roads, is tasty and relatively inexpensive. Shimon's on Balaclava Road is an Israeli-style steak house offering table and carry-out service. You can eat the best *latkes* in the Southern Hemisphere in Scheherazade's at 99 Acland Street.

General Sights: Melbourne is a lovely European-style city of stately architecture and magnificent gardens. The Botanical Gardens, in the city's center, are especially worth visiting. You can get around town by a tram network reminiscent of Judy Garland's St. Louis. Stop at the municipal zoo and see such unique "Down Under" creatures as kangaroos, koala bears, and duck-billed platypuses.

Only God could make these animals, but the city affords such spectacular man-made wonders as the Collins Place complex, designed by I. M. Pei. The tallest structure in Australia, it encompasses a glass-covered acre of shops, boutiques, and restaurants. One of its fifty-story towers houses the five-star Regent Hotel, with 377 rooms built around an atrium, a hollow interior core fifteen stories high. Each room faces outward, offering views as superb as the hotel's food and services.

Reading: There are many good works of fiction by Melbourne Jews about the Jewish experience in their city, although they are generally available only in Australia. Look for On *Firmer Shores* (Globe Press) by Serge Liberman, a prize-winning collection of short stories about growing up Jewish in a poor, gentile neighborhood. Judah Waten's *Love and Rebellion* (Macmillan) is another volume of short stories dealing with immigrant adjustments to the country. Morris Lurie (a kind of Australian Philip Roth) is the author of *Running Nicely* (Thomas Nelson), frenetic short stories about a variety of restless protagonists — who are really variations of Lurie himself. Harry Marks's *Unicorn Among the Wattles* (Hyland House) is a novel about a Jewish soldier's painful readjustment to civilian life in Melbourne. Nancy Keesing's John *Lang and the Forger's Wife* (John Ferguson) is a study of Lang, a Jew and the first native-born Australian novelist.

Good histories include the two-volume *Jews of Australia: A Thematic History* (Heinemann) by Hilary L. Rubenstein and W. D. Rubenstein, Hilary L. Rubenstein's *The Jews of Victoria, 1835–1985* (Allen & Church), and Suzanne Rutland's *Edge of the Diaspora* (Collins).

Melbourne's Jewish literature, like its history, is rich. In the most Victorian Jewish community in the world, the past and present coexist very nicely.

—Gabriel Levenson

Mexico City

Mexico City is the ultimate urban experience. It has bustle worthy of New York, sprawl worthy of Los Angeles, crowding worthy of Tokyo, squalor worthy of Bombay, and a friendly demeanor worthy of Rome. With 18 million people, it is fast on its way to becoming the world's largest city—and in terms of people within the city limits, it probably already has that distinction. Amid such numbers, the city's Jews are a mere speck, but a speck that flourishes like no other in the Diaspora.

Though Mexico has an identity all its own, there is one area, particularly evident to tourists, in which it is similar to Israel. That is in the national interest in archaeology. And just as Israel sometimes focuses on its biblical history at the expense of the two-thousand-year Diaspora, so Mexico has a tendency to focus on its Indian heritage at the expense of its Spanish colonial past.

History: There were New Christians (nominal Catholics of Jewish birth) with Hernán Cortés, who conquered the Aztecs in 1521, and Conversos made up a large portion of the Spanish settlers in the sixteenth century—in spite of regulations closing the country to all but those who could show Catholic ancestry for at least four generations. By 1550 there were probably more crypto-Jews in Mexico City than Spanish Catholics, and the Judaism of Mexico's Conversos—with circumcision commonly practiced and *kashrut* observed at least in approximation—is believed to have been closer to normative Jewish practice than that of Conversos in Spain.

Conversos prospered in early Mexico and the development of the country's trade and commerce was largely due to their efforts. They were not immune to the Inquisition, however, even though it was imposed less harshly than in Spain. Mexican Conversos were burned at the stake as early as 1528, when the conquistador Hernando Alonso was among the victims. Things got worse after the Inquisition established an office in Mexico City in 1571. When Spain annexed Portugal in 1580, a new wave of Portuguese Conversos made its way to Mexico. The knowledge that the Portuguese included many secret Jews in their midst and their success in business made them favorite targets of the Inquisition.

Between 1596 and 1659, virtually every public auto-da-fé in Mexico City had at least one Jew among the accused. The autos-da-fé and public executions were public events, often attended by thousands. The most intense period of persecution was between 1642 and 1649. The auto-da-fé of April 11, 1649, included 109 victims. Thirteen who refused to renounce Judaism were burned at the stake; many who did renounce their faith were executed less painfully. Among those burned was Tomás Treviño de Sobremonte, a leader of the Jewish community and prominent merchant who had had his fortune confiscated by the Inquisition. According to the record, as the flames reached his body he shouted, "Throw on more wood—after all, I'm paying for it." Throughout the colonial period, about 1,500 people were convicted of following Jewish practice, of whom about 100 were executed.

The Conversos had assimilated by the nineteenth century, although many prominent Mexicans have claimed Jewish descent, including Presidents Porfirio Díaz, Francisco Madero, and José López Portillo, and the great muralist Diego Rivera. "My Jewishness is the dominant element in my life," Rivera wrote in 1935. "From this has come my sympathy with the downtrodden masses which motivates all my work."

Modern Jewish settlement began in the 1820s, when a small number of German Jews arrived in Mexico City. Mexico secured its first international loan from the Jewish banking firm of Goldschmidt in London. It wasn't until the 1860s, however, that the beginnings of Jewish communal activity were seen. Emperor Maximilian, who ruled from 1864 to 1867, brought with him from Europe many Belgian, French, and Austrian Jews, including his personal physician, Samuel Basch. Though some from his entourage may have feared retaliation when Maximilian was overthrown, the new president, Benito Juárez, was a staunch advocate of religious freedom and left the Jews alone. By 1885 Mexico City had its first Jewish congregation.

Jews from Russia and Galicia arrived in the late nineteenth century. Syrian Jews began arriving in the 1890s and were followed by Jews from other parts of the Ottoman Empire. More Eastern European immigrants came after World War I, particularly after the United States closed its doors to large-scale immigration in 1924.

Jewish merchants in the early twentieth century had an impact similar to that of their Converso brothers of the sixteenth. They introduced to Mexico the system of buying on credit, which raised the living standard of the lower classes. A campaign against immigrant merchants, many of them Jewish, in Mexico City's Lagunilla Market in the 1920s, had the effect of improving the Jewish economic condition. Jewish stall owners responded by opening private stores, most of which prospered. Banco Mercantil, founded by Jews in 1929, financed many Jewish business ventures and paved the way to Mexican-Jewish prosperity.

Though he never belonged to the Jewish community, the most famous Jew ever to live in Mexico was Leon Trotsky. Having fled from country to country after Stalin chased him out of the Soviet Union, Trotsky arrived in Mexico City—through the intervention of Diego Rivera—in 1937. It was while living there that he admitted to a reporter from the Jewish Daily *Forward* that German and Soviet anti-Semitism had convinced him of the need for a Jewish territorial base (though he did not see Palestine as the answer). Trotsky was assassinated in Mexico City in 1940.

Community: There are about 40,000 Jews in Mexico City—making up about 80 percent of the Jews in the country. The main areas of Jewish settlement are in Condesa, an older neighborhood southeast of Chapultepec Park; Polanco, a newer section north of the park; the suburb of Tecamachalco; and Lomas de Chapultepec. There are still many Jews in commerce, particularly the garment trade, but more and more Jews are entering the liberal professions.

Mexico City Jewry is a study in contrasts—close-knit yet diverse, a part of the Mexican fabric and yet a community apart. Unlike the usual pattern, the community's great wealth does not seem to be a prelude to assimilation. Intermarriage is low (estimates are in the 5 to 10 percent range) and Jewish families are large (though not as large as a generation ago), perhaps because fewer Jewish women than in the United States work outside the home. Seventy-five percent of Jewish children attend one of the city's eight Jewish day schools.

Historically, the community has been fragmented, and its various parts—Polish, German, Hungarian, Syrian (with separate communities from Damascus and Aleppo), American—have their separate synagogues. Zionism, acculturation, and Mexican xenophobia have helped unify the communities, but perhaps the biggest unifying factor is the Centro Deportivo Israelita, or Jewish Sports and Cultural Center. A combination country club and community center, it is the one organization to which virtually every Jew in Mexico City belongs. The sports center is to Mexican Jewry what the army is to Israel—the place where all the communities meet. On any given Sunday, a visitor can be forgiven for thinking that every Jew in Mexico City is at the center's sprawling complex on Avenue Avila Camacho.

Formally, all Mexico City Jews are represented by the Comité Central Israelita (Central Jewish Committee), the political arm of Mexican Jewry, located at Cofre de Perote 115 in Lomas Barrilaco (telephone

540-7376 or 520-9393). Located in the same building is Tribuna Israelita, the human relations arm of the community, which promotes closer ties with Mexican society as a whole. The largest constituent of the Comité Central is Nidhei Israel, the Ashkenazi central body. La Union Sefardi represents Sephardic Jews, although Syrian Jews are represented by Alianza Monte Sinai (Damascus) and Comunidad Maguén David (Aleppo). Intermarriage among Jewish groups has led to the demise of separate German and Hungarian communities. Two newer groups, Beth El and Beth Israel, are ethnically mixed, more liberal religiously, and tend to have Mexican-born Jews as members. Each group has its own synagogue and institutions.

In addition to the Ashkenazi and Sephardi communities, there are two groups of indigenous Mexicans practicing Judaism. In the city's Vallejo section is a group of mestizos—people of mixed Spanish and Indian descent—who claim Converso ancestry. In the village of Venta Prieta, about sixty miles north of Mexico City, another mestizo group practices Judaism. Although the Jewish origins of the Venta Prieta group seem less clear, visitors have noted that their commitment to Jewish life and to Israel is firm. Beth Israel's rabbi, Semuel Lerer, has been especially involved in reaching out to the Mexican population in general and to the groups who claim Converso ancestry in particular.

Mexico is not a melting pot like the United States, and there is a certain xenophobia directed against all immigrant groups, Jews included. Until recently, according to Judith Laikin Elkin, a scholar specializing in Latin American Jewry, Mexico City's community hardly functioned within a Mexican national context. She reported one synagogue leader saying that Mexican society would not look favorably on the Jews observing Mexican Independence Day. With the growth of a native-born Jewish community, this is changing, but the insularity of Jews is still easy to see. The way it is reflected in the general culture is perhaps epitomized in Carlos Fuentes's novel *The Hydra Head,* in which most Mexican Jews are depicted as Israeli agents.

Mexico had a hard time shaking an anti-Israel label after the country's 1975 vote in the United Nations for the infamous "Zionism-is-racism" resolution. A Jewish boycott of travel to Mexico had a tremendous impact on the country and, coincidentally, hurt a good number of Mexican Jews in the travel industry. The government apologized for its vote, and it is worth noting that all of the recent Mexican presidents, with the exception of Luis Echevería, who was in office at the time of the UN vote, have had good relations with the Jewish community. A few years ago, when a senator gave an anti-Semitic speech in the Mexican national assembly, he was kicked out of the ruling party. When the UN repealed the condemnation of Zionism in 1991 Mexico not only voted for repeal but was one of its leading promoters.

Sights: You can spend a month wandering through this fascinating city without stumbling across a Jewish sight, but they are there nevertheless. Some spots in central Mexico City have Jewish associations that are far from apparent. The Plaza Santo Domingo, at the corner of Brazil and Venezuela streets, is today a picturesque square filled with sidewalk secretaries; known as *evangelistas* (gospel writers) and working on ancient typewriters, they cater to those who can't type and those who can't write. Three hundred years ago, however, this lively square was the site of autos-da-fé, the trials of the Inquisition, at which many Conversos were condemned.

Alameda Park, adjacent to the beautiful Palace of Fine Arts (Bellas Artes), is one of

Agony and ecstasy: Beautiful Alameda Park, on the former site of Inquisition executions

the city's loveliest spots, with fountains, gardens, sidewalk musicians, and all the life of the central plaza in the world's largest Spanish-speaking city. The Spanish colonial rulers considered it a place for entertainment as well, but in those days the biggest public spectacles were the executions of the Inquisition, including the burnings of those convicted at an auto-da-fé.

Three blocks south of the Plaza Santo Domingo, and about five blocks east of Alameda Park, is the Zócalo, the huge open plaza that is the city's heart. A visitor can spend an entire day seeing sights within five minutes of the Zócalo. At the top of any list would be the Rivera murals in the National Palace (Palacio Nacional), the seat of Mexico's government, on the east side of the plaza.

The most ambitious of the Rivera murals is on the wall of the palace's main staircase. A panoramic portrayal of Mexico's history, it begins with the founding of Tenochtitlán as the Aztec capital in 1325 and goes up to the Mexican Revolution of 1910. Portrayed are epic events and heroes of the nation. A bit to the left of the mural's center is a scene from the Inquisition—two figures with bowed heads in conic hats standing in front of a priest holding an open Bible.

Also worth seeing in the area of the Zócalo—one block north of the National Palace—is El Templo Mayor. It was long considered a relatively unimportant Indian ruin, until in 1978 electrical workers stumbled across evidence that revealed it to be the site of the main Aztec temple of Tenochtitlán; it is now the city's most important archaeological site.

Perhaps the best feature of the Zócalo area, however, is its ambiance, with street vendors and street life to the north and east of the plaza and shops to the west. The best view of the area is from the rooftop restaurant of the Hotel Majestic, where Madero Street meets the Zócalo.

Of more specific Jewish interest is Nidhei Israel, the Ashkenazic community center at 70 Acapulco Street. It houses two kosher restaurants, an attractive synagogue, a library, and a Holocaust museum (open Monday–Thursday, 9:00 A.M. to 6:00 P.M., and Friday, 9:00 A.M. to 1:00 P.M.). The center is also the headquarters of several Jewish organizations. Along with the Comité Central, it is a good place to call for information on Jewish events or sights in the city (211-0501).

The most Jewish atmosphere is to be found in Polanco, a neighborhood of elegant Spanish-style homes mixed with middle-class high-rise apartment buildings. Stroll along shady Horacio Boulevard on a Saturday and you'll see families walking to and from the synagogues that dot the area, as well as newsboys with distinctly Indian features delivering Yiddish papers.

The synagogue of Bet-El is located at Horacio 1722. The first Mexican synagogue to align itself with Conservative Judaism, it attracted many native-born Mexican Jews looking to move beyond the ethnic-based synagogues of the immigrant generation. Its services, always with a good proportion of children in attendance, are among the liveliest to be found in North America.

Beth Israel, at Virreyes 1140, is another multiethnic congregation. Also aligned with the Conservative movement, in practice it seems closer to Reform, and its lingua franca is English.

The Sports Center, or Centro Deportivo, is worth a visit, not only because it is the "in" place among Mexico City's Jews, but because of its cultural attractions. It houses a theater, which usually runs plays on Jewish themes during the summer; an excellent photo gallery; and a small art gallery. Foreign visitors are welcome. The Sports Center's huge grounds were used as a storage and staging area for relief supplies after the earthquake that devastated parts of Mexico City in 1985. For information on Sports Center events, call 557-30-00.

The Jewish cultural event of the year is the annual music festival, usually held in October and November, at which world-class Jewish artists perform in the Palace of Fine Arts (Bellas Artes). Even if you are not visiting at the time of the festival, the Palace, next to Alameda Park, is a must on any itinerary. Its Art Nouveau exterior and what has been dubbed Aztec Art Deco interior (with lots of dark and reddish Mexican marble) are delights to the senses. A combination exhibition hall and theater, the Palace is home to, among others, the popular Ballet Folklórico.

For those interested in archaeology and ethnohistory there are two more important places: the National Museum of Anthropology in Chapultepec Park, which Mayor Teddy Kollek of Jerusalem has praised as "probably the greatest museum created in our generation," and the pyramids at Teotihuacán, about forty-five minutes north of the city. The seventh-century pre-Aztec structures are spectacular, but for all that is known of the area's ethnic history, little is known of the civilization that built what may be the Western Hemisphere's most impressive ancient buildings.

Personalities: Perhaps the best known Jewish name in Mexico is Zabludovsky. Jacobo Zabludovsky is a television anchorman, often referred to as the Walter Cronkite of Mexico. Other noted members of the clan are Jaime, Mexico's top negotiator for the North American Free Trade Agreement (who sits opposite Mickey Kantor on the American side); and Abraham, a prominent architect. Sergio Nudelstejer is one of the Spanish-speaking world's leading biographers. The late Leon Dulzin went on *aliyah* and headed the Jewish Agency. Enrique Krauze is a leading expert on the Mexican Revolution. Prominent Mexican writers include Sabina Berman, Miriam Moscona, Angelina Muñiz and Esther Seligson.

Brooklyn-born Sidney Franklin went to Mexico City in the 1920s to study Mayan history. While there he developed such an intense interest in bullfighting that he decided to make it his life's work. After making a success of himself in Mexico he went on to Spain, where he became a friend of Ernest Hemingway's. "Franklin . . . is one of the most skillful, graceful, and slow manipulators of a cape fighting today," Hemingway wrote in *Death in the Afternoon*. "He is a better, more scientific, more intelligent, and more finished matador than all but about six of the full matadors in Spain today. . . ." Franklin's autobiography, *Bullfighter from Brooklyn*, was published in 1952, and after his retirement he became a broadcaster of televised bullfights in Mexico City.

Reading: A good companion to take on the plane is *Aztec* by Gary Jennings (Avon), the great Mexico City novel. Not only does it give details (gory and otherwise) of Aztec culture, it provides a fascinating picture of the attitudes and practices of those in charge of the Inquisition. Tales of Israeli agents notwithstanding, few writers capture modern Mexico City better than Carlos Fuentes. Two of his books especially evocative of the city and its characters are *Burnt Water* (Farrar, Straus & Giroux) and *Where the Air is Clear* (Obolensky). For a more sweeping, nonfictional, look at the city, there is Jonathan Kandell's *La Capital: The Biography of Mexico City* (Random House).

Recommendations: Mexico City's seven-thousand-foot elevation makes it an ideal vacation spot in any season. It can be combined with a trip to one of the country's coastal resorts or be a trip in itself. If you want elegance, modernity, and a Jewish neighborhood to stay in, the best place is the Hotel Presidente Chapultepec, on the edge of Chapultepec Park in Polanco. Mexico City's subway is one of the world's bargains, and Line 7 runs through Polanco. Taxis are plentiful and relatively cheap. Be sure the driver uses the meter, called a taxímetro. Barring that, instead of giving the name of your hotel, tell the driver the intersection at which it is located; the fare will be considerably less.

If you are interested in local culture but put off by the language barrier, don't give up so easily. Mexico City's theater life is good and lively and often features Spanish versions of Broadway shows; if you see one with which you are already familiar, it can be quite enjoyable. Recent runs of *Fiddler on the Roof* and *Joseph and His Amazing Technicolor Dreamcoat* have been especially popular. Like the sights in the center of the city, all you have to do to find the Jewish angles is look beneath the surface.

—Alan M. Tigay

Miami to Palm Beach

If it hadn't been for Israel, Florida might have embodied the Zionist dream. It has good weather, the feel if not the reality of a Jewish majority and, perhaps most important, no enemies. At least no human enemies. But as Hurricane Andrew bore down on the Florida coast in August 1992 it had in its sights more Jews than any natural disaster in history; headed straight for Miami Beach, at the last minute it veered southwest, bypassing the most heavily Jewish sections of the region. With the storm behind it, south Florida began to recover, some parts quickly, some parts slowly, but Andrew left lessons and images in its wake. On the negative side, Andrew showed that dreams of paradise, no less than dreams of Zion, have their down side. On the bright side, a Jewish communal structure set up to defend against human enemies proved adept at helping everyone in south Florida cope with a natural one; the Greater Miami Jewish Federation was lauded by state officials for its disaster relief work, and Jewish organizations from around the country sent aid as well.

History: Although southeast Florida, from Miami to Palm Beach, has the large majority of Florida's Jews, it is also the region with the shortest Jewish history. Jews had made their mark on the state long before anyone dreamed that Miami would amount to more than an isolated trading post. There may have been Conversos with Ponce de Leon when he landed in Florida in 1513 looking for the Fountain of Youth. The evidence suggests that the territory's third Spanish governor, Pedro Menéndez Marqués, was a Converso. Later in the Spanish period Jews settled in Pensacola and St. Augustine, though their freedom from persecution wasn't secured until

Florida was annexed to the United States in 1820.

Moses Levy, a Caribbean lumber magnate of Moroccan descent, moved to Florida the following year. He planted sugar cane and fruit trees, continued to prosper, and became one of the state's leading citizens. His son, David Levy Yulee, was instrumental in attaining statehood for Florida in 1836 and became its first United States Senator. But there were differences between father and son. Moses wanted to start a Jewish colony on his plantation, and he advocated the abolition of slavery. David was estranged from Jewish life (though contrary to many accounts there is no evidence that he was ever baptized) and a defender of slavery who served in the Confederate Congress.

The Levy family wasn't unique. Colonel Abraham Myers, after whom the city of Fort Myers is named, was one of at least half a dozen Jewish officers who served in the Florida Indian Wars of the 1830s and 1840s. Throughout most of the nineteenth century the small Jewish community (fewer than 100 when Florida became a state in 1845) lived free of apparent anti-Semitism. The only prejudice David Levy Yulee encountered in his public life was in Washington, not in Florida.

But if the Jews got to north Florida ahead of anti-Semitism, it was prejudice that got to south Florida first. In 1896, after a freeze had killed citrus and sugar cane crops as far south as Palm Beach, the railroad and resort builder Henry Flagler decided to extend his tracks to Miami. Flagler wanted no Jews in his hotels and he attached restrictive covenants to his land sales. A generation later Carl Fisher, the pioneer in developing Miami Beach and Fort Lauderdale, adopted the same attitude. A genteel anti-Semite, Fisher told his hotel staffs that most Jews could be identified by their names and there was no need for signs that said "No Jews Allowed"; some Jews who were rich enough were even qualified to be his friends.

The first Jew in Miami was Samuel Singer, who arrived from Palm Beach in 1895, a year ahead of Flagler's trains. But most of the Jews who arrived in Miami before the turn of the century were moving north from Key West, which had imposed a discriminatory tax on itinerant peddlers. There had been a sizable Jewish community in Key West from the 1880s, started by Joseph Wolfson, who was shipwrecked there in 1884; he was soon followed by friends and family from Iasi and Husi, Rumania. Key West was the home of the American cigar industry, and Jews were involved in every aspect of it—as workers, employers, and even tobacco growers. The industry was also the first meeting ground for Jews and Cubans. The friendship between Louis Fine and Theodore Perez led to Jewish support for the Cuban independence movement. The affinity developed around cigars remains a feature of Florida life today.

The first ad hoc congregation in Miami was organized for the High Holidays in 1896, but the community was off to a false start. A yellow fever epidemic broke out in 1899, and many of those who didn't fall victim to the disease left. It wasn't until 1912 that the first permanent congregation, B'nai Zion, was founded. Its successor, Beth David, sits regally today on S.W. Third Avenue—a far cry from the first services held in a vacant room over Henry Seitlin's store.

The Florida land boom of the 1920s brought more Jews to the area, but again optimism about Jewish life was premature. Like Miami's Jews, the first fledgling congregation in Fort Lauderdale held Yom Kippur services above a member's restaurant in 1926. The next night, a devastating hurricane—the standard by which all hurricanes until Andrew were judged—brought communal life to a halt. What the hurricane didn't destroy, the coming real estate bust did. As late as 1940 the Jewish population of Florida was only 20,000.

Two things caused the revolution that changed Florida from a Jewish backwater to a Jewish headquarters—World War II and air conditioning. With the war came not only Jewish soldiers. When restricted hotels were requisitioned by the army or the government, they began admitting Jews. As more Jews saw Florida, more wanted to stay, and the development of temperature control convinced many winter visitors to sever all ties to the north and move to the state permanently.

Community: What is the most Jewish place in America? It was New York from 1800 to 1980, but today it's the megalopolis that stretches from Miami to Palm Beach. The 515,000 Jews who live in the area account for 13 percent of the region's 4 million people. Metropolitan New York's 2 million Jews lag almost 2 percentage points behind.

Long before the demographic honors shifted, many places in south Florida were famous for their Jewish ambiance. Amid the Yiddish banter on Miami Beach's Collins Avenue and the condos of Fort Lauderdale, the tropical architecture that looks vaguely like Tel Aviv's and the synagogues that dot the landscape, it is gentiles who feel like a minority—unless they are Hispanic.

Contrary to popular belief, south Florida Jewry is not overwhelmingly a community of retired people, as its extensive Jewish school network, from elementary school to university, testifies. It is a lively collection of people of all ages that has produced one of the most richly diverse Jewish communities in history.

Miami was the first American Jewish community in which most of the people came not from Europe but from elsewhere in the United States. Instead of *landsmanshaften* from Bialystok and Berdichev, it has associations of Jews from Chicago and Cleveland. New York high schools have been known to hold their reunions in Miami Beach. A Jew from Europe cut his ties with the old country, but a settler in Miami Beach, especially one who didn't stay twelve months a year, generally did not. Jewish fund-raisers in Florida never heard "I gave at the office"; instead, until a few years ago, they heard "I gave in Philadelphia." This began to change as the community became more of a year-round phenomenon. Today a Jewish organization that doesn't have a fund-raising arm in Palm Beach County cannot consider itself big league.

Though the community generally traces its roots to the cities of the North, a unique feature of south Florida Jewry is its Latin element. There are about 5,000 Cuban Jews and about an equal number from a variety of Latin American nations—Chile, Peru, Argentina, Nicaragua. Though relatively small in number, they form a bridge between two of the area's largest cultural groups.

For more than a decade the trend has been for the Jewish population to head north from Dade County (Miami and Miami Beach) toward Broward and Palm Beach Counties. Hurricane Andrew concentrated its fury on Dade, and if it had a lasting impact on the Jewish community, it was to accelerate the trend. Many who lost homes or businesses and were covered by insurance decided to do their rebuilding in the counties to the north. But if it isn't quite as Jewish as it once was, Miami Beach is still the most predominantly Jewish part of the metropolitan area. Across Biscayne Bay there are Jewish concentrations in south-

west Miami, Kendall (the only Jewish neighborhood to suffer extensive damage from Andrew), Coral Gables, North Miami, and North Miami Beach. In Broward County Jews can be found in large number in Hollywood, Hallandale, western Fort Lauderdale, Plantation, Coral Springs, and Tamarack. The heaviest concentrations in Palm Beach County are in Boca Raton and West Palm Beach.

Jewish community life in southeast Florida is overseen by no fewer than five federations. Aside from questions about *kashrut* or cultural events, the federations are usually the best places to start with inquires about local Jewish life. Moving south to north, the places to call are the Greater Miami Jewish Federation (305-576-4000), the Jewish Federation of South Broward in Hollywood (305-921-8810), the Jewish Federation of Greater Fort Lauderdale (305-748-8400), the South County Jewish Federation in Boca Raton (407-368-2737), and the Jewish Federation of Palm Beach County (407-832-2120).

Sights: Miami Beach is Florida's Lower East and Upper West Sides combined, the place where Jews first settled en masse and

Lower, lower East Side: Migration down the Atlantic shore ended at Miami Beach, still the heart of South Florida's half-a-million-strong Jewish community

to which many of the well-heeled still aspire to homes on the Intracoastal Waterway. Threatened a decade ago by crime and middle-class flight, South Beach — known for its collection of Art Deco buildings — was saved within a few years by a gentrification program that would have taken a few generations anywhere else.

Washington Avenue has been referred to as the Orchard Street of Miami Beach; it's an exaggeration, but the atmosphere is distinctly Jewish. The atmosphere actually extends most of the length of Miami Beach, from the small Art Deco hotels in the south to the imposing high-rises in the north. Most of the commercial strips along Collins Avenue have Jewish stores and restaurants. Miami Beach also has more than its share of attractive and unusual synagogues and Jewish landmarks.

One of the synagogues remaining in South Beach is Beth Jacob at 311 Washington. The cream-colored Art Deco building with a copper Moorish dome was built in 1936 and shows its age. It has a checkered past and a promising future. Once known as the "gangster *shul*" because Meyer Lansky and friends worshiped there, it is the future home of the Jewish Museum of Florida. The nucleus of the museum is Mosaic, an exhibit assembled in 1991 and scheduled to tour the state and the country before settling in a renovated Beth Jacob in 1995. The collection is composed mainly of photographs and artifacts and paints a fascinating portrait of the state's Jewish history and residents. There are photos of Jewish cigar makers and photos of Jews with alligators (mostly stuffed, one live). There is a pocket watch with Hebrew numbers on the face and Moses and the Ten Commandments engraved on the back; a miniature *tefillin* and Torah; a grapefruit brand label in Yiddish; and a mah-jongg set typical of the many used by vacationers and retirees. One of the most poignant photos in the exhibit is that of eleven-year-old Herbert Kaliner, posing with his family on the ill-fated *St. Louis* in 1939. Packed with German-Jewish refugees bound for Cuba, the ship was forced to return to Europe. After it was turned away at Havana, the ship had cruised off the Florida coast waiting for the State Department to answer an appeal for asylum. Kaliner saw the palm trees and hotels on the shore, and vowed that he would some day live in Florida. The only one of his family to survive the Holocaust, he made good on his promise in 1954.

If Herbert Kaliner represents the Jews who made it through World War II, the Holocaust Memorial at Dade Boulevard and Meridian Avenue stands for those whose dreams did not come true. Designed by the sculptor Kenneth Triester and set amid sun and palms, the memorial — more of an open-air museum — uses contrasting elements to convey a sense of horror amid peace. Jerusalem stone vies with black granite, a lovely pool studded with lilies surrounds an island with sculpted victims. At the center of the island is a huge hand, covered with climbing figures, reaching for help. The island is reached by a sloping stone corridor, designed to simulate the path to the death camps, in which you hear the voices of a children's choir singing *Ani Maamin*. Many familiar Holocaust photos appear in a stunningly different medium — printed on the granite wall reminiscent of the Vietnam Veterans Memorial. If you see only one Jewish sight in Miami Beach, make it this one.

Near the Holocaust Memorial is Miami Beach's largest and most imposing synagogue, Temple Emanu-El, at 1701 Washington Avenue, across from the Jackie Gleason Theater of the Performing Arts. The synagogue is a white stone structure with red marble columns over wooden doors. The Ten Commandments, also in red marble, sit atop the entrance. The high-domed octagonal sanctuary is dominated by mahogany and red upholstery. In addition to being a pleasant place to pray, Emanu-El is also known for its lecture series. Call (305) 538-2503 for information on services and events.

One of the more distinctive synagogues in history and design is Beth Sholom, at 4144 Chase Avenue. It started as a soldier's congregation in World War II, and in the 1950s its members commissioned the architect Percival Goodman to design a sanctuary. Goodman came up with an enveloping brown dome, which critics and admirers alike have compared with the architecture of the Flintstones. The dome's arched windows are in the form of multicolored Stars of David. Beth Sholom is known not only for its architecture but also for its culture and entertainment program—which became so successful that it eventually outgrew the relatively small sanctuary and moved out into the community. Over the years the likes of Vladimir Horowitz, Yo Yo Ma, Yitzhak Perlman, Luciano Pavarotti, Beverly Sills, Leontyne Price, and Zubin Mehta with the Israel Philharmonic have performed there. Beth Sholom also has a biblical garden and a small museum. For information on services, and on the lectures and cultural events still held in the synagogue, call (305) 538-7231.

Two other places worth a visit in Miami Beach are the Cuban synagogues. The Cuban Hebrew Congregation (Ashkenazi, primarily Lithuanian) is at 1700 Michigan Avenue, but be sure to take a look at the new wing, entered from Lenox Avenue, with its uneven facade and windows that look as though they were inspired by Antonio Gaudí. Temple Moses, the Cuban Sephardic synagogue (the members are primarily of Turkish origin), is at 1200 Normandy Drive; though the building is more conventional, the welcome is warm.

Miami itself is the anchor of south Florida, and although the state's capital is 350 miles north in Tallahassee, Miami remains the capital of the tropics, an international city that serves as a magnet for travelers, businesses, and refugees of various kinds from as near as Cuba and Haiti and as far as Montreal and Buenos Aires. It is a place where Jews are an integral part, where many Jewish organizations have their offices, and where despite its mostly undistinguished architecture some Jewish landmarks can be found. Among other spots, fans of the Israeli artist Yacov Agam will want to see the rainbow-colored facade he created on the Villa Regina, a high-rise condominium at 1581 Brickell Avenue.

Beth David, south Florida's oldest congregation, has its tropical/classical home at 2625 S.W. Third Avenue. The sandstone edifice built in 1949 occupies an entire palm-lined block; the main entrance is under a half-dome supported by six columns. The massive white-walled sanctuary features a *bimah* of Brazilian mahogany

and a series of narrow pointed arches that wrap from the walls onto the ceiling. Right off the sanctuary is a cavernous chandeliered ballroom.

But perhaps Beth David's most striking feature is its Beck Museum of Judaica, located in the lobby between the main entrance (used only on *Shabbat*) and the sanctuary. Among the rare items on display are a tiered Austrian Seder plate, a Hungarian prayer schedule with moveable clock faces, a seventeenth-century Persian Torah box in velvet, a miniature traveling Torah from Bavaria, and pop-up New Year cards from prewar England and Germany. The collection also includes Torahs, menorahs, *ketubot*, and other ritual objects from Europe, North Africa, and Asia. Two sculpted wood reliefs—one depicting the Holocaust, the other modern Israel—are like bookends at the front and back of the museum. On the ceiling are painted windows showing holiday scenes—which are reflected in the polished granite floor. For information about services and events at Beth David, call (305) 854-3911.

Beth David began as an Orthodox congregation and is today Conservative. Its Reform offshoot is Temple Israel, at 137 N.E. l9th Street. The neighborhood is now predominantly African-American, and Temple Israel has been kept in its home, dedicated in 1928, by the willingness of its 650 members to commute and a realization that wherever they might rebuild, no one builds synagogues the way they used to. The temple's Oriental face with a Persian-style arch over the entrance gives only a hint of the splendor inside. In the main sanctuary fourteen arches surround the pastel walls of blue and beige. Prominent interior features are the gently arching blue ceiling, the mahogany ark, and the series of arched stained-glass windows showing Jewish and American symbols. The feeling of the place is one of calm, almost simple, elegance.

The juxtaposition couldn't be more stark, therefore, in the adjoining Gumenick Chapel, dedicated forty years, and an entire world, later. The gray stone interior has blue and red rococo windows and wrought-iron railings and menorahs on the *bimah*. The chapel was designed by Kenneth

Triester, who also did the Holocaust Memorial in Miami Beach. Here again Triester used contrasts, but where the contrasts at the Holocaust Memorial added up to understatement, at Temple Israel they add up to overstatement. For information about Temple Israel events and services call (305) 573-5900.

If the Jewish center of gravity in south Florida is now in Broward County, the strongest magnet affecting the balance is Palm Beach County. Places that were once synonymous with anti-Semitic exclusion are now downright *heimish*. On Worth Avenue, in the cafés on Royal Poinciana Way, even at the Breakers Hotel, Henry Flagler couldn't say "cheers" without a *"l'chayim"* coming back.

Figuratively the Jewish flag flies today right on North County Road, Palm Beach's main street, in the form of Temple Emanu-El. If it is comfortable, however, it looks like it comes from another place. Emanu-El gleams North-African white amid the Spanish-mission-style beige walls and red tile roofs of nearby churches, stores and the landmark Palm Beach Post Office. The Conservative synagogue's stone building (190 North County Road; telephone 407-832-0804) features four graceful Mediterranean arches and an entrance reached from street level by two curving stairways. The rectilinear sanctuary has arched stained-glass windows, an open *bimah* and an ark door in the same shape as the windows. The recent history of Emanu-El is a microcosm of the history of south Florida Jewry. The temple was built in the 1960s when the community was mostly elderly and the members never dreamed they would need a big school. By the eighties the community had not only grown, it had also gotten younger. The lot size was too small, and Palm Beach too densely packed, to allow for much of an addition. Emanu-El did a moderate expansion and redesigned some space; the result is a mazelike building that often seems to be choking with activity, with meetings and classes going on in every corner. To members it's confining; to the visitor it seems packed with vitality.

There is more room across the Intracoastal Waterway in West Palm Beach, where the in-your-eye Jewish presence is most visible in the synagogues on waterfront Flagler Drive. One gem is Temple Beth El, the Conservative synagogue at 2815 North Flagler. Though its asphalt-shingled dome is barely visible from outside, inside it is an integral part of a magnificent sanctuary. The laminated acacia ceiling is in the shape of an ascending spiral that simulates the folds of a tent and culminates—where the high end of the slope meets the low end—in a "great window" that floods the *bimah* with light. The pews, which seat nine hundred, are upholstered in bright orange and all face the *bimah* at a 45-degree angle. Call (407) 833-0339 for details of events and services.

A few blocks to the south is the Reform Temple Israel, at 1901 North Flagler, a simple and elegant white tropical complex arranged around a courtyard. The small single-aisle sanctuary evokes Jacob's tents with its pointed white ceiling. The glass-encased ark has a door with a *menorah/tree-branch* pattern through which the Torahs are visible. The sanctuary, as well as the synagogue's school and offices, is entered from a bamboo-fringed courtyard. Entry to the various wings is through tile-framed doorways under covered walkways. Call (407) 833-8421 for information on services and special events.

Culture: The Jewish communal campus has reached a state of high art in Palm Beach County. The West Palm Beach campus at 3151 North Military Trail is a sprawling, aqua and salmon complex housing the Kaplan Jewish Community Center with its theater, museum, and gallery; a kosher restaurant; the Palm Beach federation offices; schools; and a variety of other organizations. The JCC Art Gallery hosts one major exhibit a year and has smaller shows between main events; artists exhibited since the center opened in 1991 have included Yacov Agam, Yankel Ginzburg, and Jack Fox. Among the plays staged by the resident Odyssey Theatre Company have been *The Loman Family Picnic* by David Margulies and Thornton Wilder's *The Skin of Our Teeth*. For information on center events and activities, call (407) 689-7700.

The Jewish Community Campus of

south Palm Beach County is at 9801 Donna Klein Boulevard in Boca Raton. It houses the same array of communal institutions in a very different architectural setting—gray brick with bright red iron pillars holding canvas canopies over the lanes that run between the various buildings. (In an intriguing donor-recognition innovation, the lanes are named for the center's various benefactors.) The Levis JCC is the cultural centerpiece of the Boca Raton campus. Its theater has featured Joel Grey singing Broadway melodies, Nehemiah Persoff in a one-man show as Sholom Aleichem, musicals and dramas. Its concerts range from classical to jazz to *klezmer*.

Jewish cultural programs can also be found—in slightly less luxurious surroundings—at the JCCs in Dade and Broward Counties. The JCC in Fort Lauderdale is at 6501 West Sunrise Boulevard (305-792-6700) and the one in Hollywood is at 2838 Hollywood Boulevard (305-921-6511). The South Dade JCC in Miami is at 11155 S.W. 112th Avenue (305-271-9000). The North Dade branch is at 18900 N.E. 25th Avenue in North Miami Beach (305-932-4200). The Miami Beach JCC is at 4221 Pine Tree Drive (305-534-3206).

There is also a fair amount of Jewish-oriented culture at the area's various secular institutions, from the Kravis Center for the Performing Arts in West Palm Beach to the Broward Center of Performing Arts in Fort Lauderdale, from the Metro-Dade and Gusman Centers in Miami to the Jackie Gleason Theater in Miami Beach. In Miami Beach there is popular Jewish entertainment all over, especially in the hotels that line Collins Avenue. There are comedians, cabarets and theaters and, often as not, the performances are on Jewish themes. The entertainment—like the hotels and condos—tends to be fancier above Forty-First Street, where most of the street movement is in cars. But the atmosphere is more intimate below Forty-First, where much of the traffic is on foot.

Information about Jewish and general cultural events can be found in the Miami, Fort Lauderdale, and Palm Beach dailies, and in the Jewish weeklies (the *Jewish Tribune* and the *Jewish Journal*), each of which publishes separate editions for the three counties in the region.

Personalities: Jews have played a major role in the industries for which south Florida is best known—tourism and real estate. There was a time when the vast majority of the Miami Beach's hotels were Jewish-owned, although they are now increasingly controlled by national chains and outside syndicates. Later generations of Florida Jews have become civic leaders, like the nineteenth-century Levys. Alfred Stone, son of one of Miami's first Jewish residents, gained friends and enemies when he hosted an African-American Baptist Convention at his Blackstone Hotel in Miami Beach in 1954; his family's lives were threatened, and after rabbis around the state gave sermons on civil rights, synagogues in Miami and Jacksonville were bombed. Stone remained active; his son, Richard, became Florida's first Jewish senator since David Levy Yulee. Other Jews prominent in state life have been Abe Aronowitz, who became Miami's first Jewish mayor in 1953, and Hank Meyer, perhaps the only public-relations man in the Florida State Hall of Fame, who got there largely through his successful efforts to make Miami Beach world famous. North Florida has produced two Jewish codebreakers— Admiral Ellis Zacharias of Jacksonville, who helped break Japanese codes during World War II, and Orlando's Marshall Warren Nirenberg, who won the 1968 Nobel Prize in Medicine for breaking the genetic code.

Eating: *Kashrut* observers won't starve in Florida. For general *kashrut* information try the Rabbinical Association of Miami (305-576-4000) or call Dr. Jerry Berman at (305) 651-3531. Because of their larger Orthodox concentrations, Miami Beach, North Miami, and North Miami Beach have the largest number of kosher restaurants. Those mentioned often by locals include Embassy 41, Embassy Peking, Giuseppe Goldberg's, King David Delicatessen, Royal Hungarian, Yosi Peking, and Zelig's, all in Miami Beach. North Miami Beach has Hamifgash, the Famous Pita Hut, Matilda's, Shalom Restaurant, and Wing Wan. Broward County has Eastside Kosher and Shalom Kosher in Margate; Famous Levy's and Jerusalem of Gold in Sunrise; Jerusalem II of Brooklyn in Hollywood and Mayer's Embassy Steak House in Hallandale. The only kosher restaurants in Palm Beach County are the West Palm Kosher Restaurant in Drexel Plaza (West Palm Beach) and Café Tamar in the Kaplan JCC. Sara's Kosher Pizza has branches all over the area. Popular Jewish-style but nonkosher restaurants include Acme Smoked Fish in Fort Lauderdale and Too-Jay's, which has seven branches in Palm Beach County.

Reading: *The Shawl* by Cynthia Ozick (Knopf) is the story of a Holocaust survivor living in Miami Beach. Wartime Florida is evoked in *No Enemy But Time* by Evelyn Mayerson (Doubleday). *The Last Resorts* by Cleveland Amory (Grosset and Dunlap) gives a flavor of the anti-Semitism that was once the norm in south Florida. There is also *Sadie Shapiro in Miami* by Robert Kimmel Smith (Simon & Schuster).

General Sights: The attraction of beaches is obvious, but there are things to see and do in the Miami area that escape the attention of many. The Cuban quarter, Calle Ocho (S.W. Eighth Street in Miami) is well worth a visit, as is the Villa Vizcaya, Miami's Italian Renaissance palace. Italianate style is also evident along Worth Avenue in Palm Beach, still one of the world's great shopping streets. Boat rides on the Intracoastal Waterway offer pleasures not experienced in the Atlantic or in Biscayne Bay. And the Everglades is an easy day trip.

Recommendations: South Florida has hotels for every budget, taste, and level of *kashrut* observance. Among the kosher hotels in Miami Beach are the Caribbean, the Crown, the Cadillac, the Royal Palm, and the Sans Souci.

Two of the area's leading hotels perhaps sum up the Jewish presence in southeast Florida — the elegant, traditional Breakers in Palm Beach, and the massive, modern Fontainbleau in Miami Beach. The Fontainbleau (today part of the Hilton chain) was Jewish from the beginning; it is still a favorite of Jewish tourists and Jewish organizations looking for convention and catering facilities. Built in 1954 by Ben Novak and designed by Morris Lapidus, it is best known to locals for Richard Haas's thirteen-thousand-square-foot mural that makes drivers on Collins Avenue think they are headed straight for the hotel's swimming pool. Star of the Flagler empire, and still owned by Henry Flagler's heirs, The Breakers in Palm Beach once barred Jews; today it caters kosher dinners for Hadassah, Israel Bonds, the Anti-Defamation League, and a host of other Jewish groups. Its clientele, in fact, is almost indistinguishable from that of the Fontainbleau.

Most travelers avoid Florida in the summer, when the weather is sultry and hurricanes hover offshore. But the old saw that "Miami is dead after Pesach" is no longer true. The Jewish presence is a permanent, year-round proposition. If it isn't Zion, more than a half-million Jews have voted with their feet to designate it as America's promised land.

—Alan M. Tigay

Milan

Mention Milan to most people, and chances are they'll think of La Scala and fashion. But there is more to this emblem of the new industrial Italy than opera and shopping.

With its soaring office buildings, bustling piazzas, and seemingly nonstop procession of pedestrians, trams, and cars at all hours, Milan scarcely reflects typical Italian *la dolce vita*. Rather, it is a model of surprising efficiency and industry, in which its nearly 10,000 Jews play an active, if low-key, part. Its 1.5 million inhabitants are involved in international banking and finance, fashion, retailing, and industry. Although Milan rarely finds itself on the itinerary of travelers (other than fashion editors and opera buffs), its growing reputation as a cultural and gastronomic center should change that. With Malpensa Airport a less chaotic alternative to Rome's Da Vinci, and its proximity to such northern Italian attractions as Florence, Venice, the Lake district, and Bologna, Milan is certainly worth considering for those contemplating a trip to Italy.

Milan has Italy's second largest Jewish population, after Rome's. Yet most of the Milanese Jews are so well integrated into the city's life that locating visible signs of Jewish life in this metropolis can be an elusive task. But the sights and people are there to be found, and worth finding.

History: One reason for the lack of a readily identifiable Jewish quarter or community goes back to Milan Jewry's origins. Three Jewish inscriptions from the Roman period and evidence of a synagogue destroyed in 388 C.E. indicate the presence of an earlier community. But unlike other Italian cities, today's Jewish presence is a relatively recent phenomenon. It was only about 150 years ago that Jews were allowed to live in the city, after a medieval banishment.

During most of the Middle Ages, Jews had been tolerated by the rulers of Milan. There were isolated incidents of anti-Semitism, notably in 1475, when there were accusations of ritual murder against Jews in Trent. But in 1597 there was a general expulsion of nearly a thousand Jews who had settled in the surrounding smaller towns; by that time, Milan itself had no resident Jews. From then until 1840 Jews were permitted in Milan only during working hours.

Consequently, the Jewish community that reestablished itself in the mid-nineteenth century was an offshoot of the nearby Mantua community, which was in continuous existence since before the Middle Ages. There, the Jews were artisans, merchants, bankers, musicians and, of course, court physicians to the ruling dukes.

In 1600, there were 6,000 Jews in Mantua, representing nearly 8 percent of the population. As inhabitants of Mantua under the protection of the Gonzaga family, the Jews enjoyed relative tranquility and prosperity—punctuated by periods of repression, characterized by a 1612 edict that they must live in a ghetto and wear a distinctive mark on their clothing. In 1708, when the duchy came under Austrian control, conditions for the Jews eased somewhat.

Once Milan reopened to Jews as a place of residence, the community's growth paralleled the rise of Milan itself, to which the Jews contributed their enterprise and talents. In 1840, there were 200 Jews; by 1890, there were close to 2,000. Milan emerged as an industrial and business center, and as the city thrived, so too did the city's Jews flourish in a climate of tolerance. In 1859,

Milan became part of the new Italian kingdom, and the Jews were granted full rights.

It was early in the twentieth century that Milanese Jews reached an apotheosis of Jewish identity and activity. It was during the 1920s that most of the Jewish cultural institutions grew. By the 1930s, the Jewish population reached 8,000, as refugees from Germany and Central Europe began to cross the Alps into northern Italy. During World War II, 800 Milanese Jews were deported to the death camps; only 50 returned. At the end of the war, Milan became a center of clandestine emigration to Palestine.

Community: Today, Milan's Jewish community is a thriving, if segmented, group, not unlike the rest of Italian Jewry. Since World War II the community has grown, primarily through the immigration of Egyptian, Libyan, and Iranian Jews. It is divided between highly assimilated, culturally Jewish Italians who are descendants of either the Mantovanese community or immigrants from other Italian cities and relatively recent arrivals from the Middle East.

There is no old Jewish quarter. West of the city center, however, there is a modern Jewish community in the Lorenteggio section, which has sprung up around the school and the new Iranian Jewish Center. Since the school and the center are a 30-minute ride from downtown Milan (bus 54), many of the city's younger Jewish families have moved there to make it easier for their children to receive a Jewish education.

The community's headquarters is at Via Sally Mayer 4–6 and the administration is next door at number 2. This is the best place to call with questions about community events (4830-4684). Another complex of organizations is at Via Eupili 8. The community supports a variety of local and international Jewish institutions. The city has two synagogues using the Italian rite; four Sephardic, two Persian, and one Ashkenazic. Kosher meals are available, by prior arrangement, from the New Home for the Aged, Via Leone XIII 1 (telephone 481-6048), and there are five kosher butchers.

Most of the Jewish immigrants have integrated into the community. Many among the Egyptians, not to mention the earlier wave of prewar refugees from Germany and Austria, married Italian Jews. The Iranians, however, maintain a tightly knit community and are more traditionally observant than the other groups.

The majority of Milan's Jews are in business and industry. While the Iranians tend to be shopkeepers, primarily of antiques, rugs, and jewelry, other Jews are prominent in journalism, academia, medicine and law. And most of them are financially secure, if not wealthy.

During the 1970s there was a substantial *aliyah* by young Milanese Jews (in response to the victory of the Six Day War), but today's youth are just as likely to remain in Milan or, if they emigrate, to go to the United States. Nevertheless, a phenomenon in recent years has been the renewed interest of young Milanese Jews in their Jewish heritage, as has been the case throughout Italy.

Sights: Milan is more business oriented than the other large cities of Italy, but as a music and fashion capital it has much to offer the traveler. From La Scala to the Duomo (Italy's only Gothic cathedral), from the Galleria to Parco Sempione, you will feel the pulse of a well-dressed, cosmopolitan city with the work habits of northern Europe and the recreational resources of the Mediterranean.

Many Jewish sights are in the center of the city. The Central Synagogue at Via Guastalla 19 should be the first stop. The building sums up the community's past and present. Completed in 1892, it was virtually destroyed by Allied bombings in 1943 and rebuilt after the war. The original facade still stands, with oriental mosaic around the door and, at the top, a large Decalogue enclosed in its own ark; extravagantly ornate, its antique marble, its columns and cut-out archways are striking to the eye. The interior, in sharp contrast, is emphatically modern and nonrepresentational. The sky-lit sanctuary is rectilinear, as opposed to the Oriental curves of the prewar period. There is fine mosaic-and-gold work surrounding the ark, as well as lavish use of reddish-pink marble throughout. The synagogue is also home to a contemporary conference room that is used by the community's organizations. In addition to the Italian-rite services in the main sanctuary, the synagogue houses a small Sephardic chapel. The ark in this chapel comes from an ancient synagogue in Pesaro.

The townhouse at Eupili 8 includes a synagogue and various community organizations. It also houses one of the more unusual institutions in Italy—the Contemporary Jewish Documentation Center (Cdec), a library and archive (telephone 316-092 or 316-338). Many non-Jewish Italians—scholars and journalists, especially—regularly make pilgrimages to this modest site because it has the only complete records of Italian-Jewish history, specifically during the era prior to and including World War II. The archive also has an extensive collection of documents and oral histories on anti-Semitism in Italy during the past twenty-five years. The staff is dedicated and friendly; though their English may be sketchy, they are accommodating to visitors. The library is open weekdays from 9 A.M. to 12:30 P.M.—but, as with many other Italian institutions, it is best to telephone ahead.

The nerve center of the Jewish community is at Via Sally Mayer 4–6. Here you will find two synagogues, a day school and rabbinical school, the community's social service arm, and various communal agencies. The street, by the way, is named for a noted Jewish industrialist and philanthropist. The little synagogue, completed in 1987, is contemporary in design. Interestingly, it was built by the same architect—Eugenio Gentile Tedeschi—who rebuilt the Central Synagogue on Via Guastalla after the war. The day school has 650 students, drawn from both the observant and nonobservant groups in the community.

If you have time, visit the Iranian synagogue and cultural center at Via Montecucolli 27 (telephone 415-1660 or 412-0480) for a sense of the vitality of Milan's Jewish community. The synagogue reflects the cultural background of its congregants: It has a sky-blue tile exterior, punctuated by gold flecks (to resemble the heavens), which is heavily Middle Eastern in flavor and design. The interior, however, is modern, letting in light and air.

Milan doesn't have the plethora of Renaissance Hebrew Bible figures found in Rome and Florence, but it does have a noteworthy Moses. Like Michelangelo's controversial *Moses* in Rome, the statue of Moses in the Palazzo Arcivescovile also has horns. The large and imposing work by Antonio Tantardini is another example of the misreading of the biblical word *keren* as horn rather than as a ray of light.

Side Trip: For a feeling of what Jewish life in Lombardy was like when Jews lived in an ancient ghetto, it's worth a trip to Mantua, to find the roots of the Milanese Jewish community. Since train connections are difficult and unreliable, it's best to rent a car for the one-and-a-half-hour trip.

Mantua in its heyday had several synagogues, three in the Italian rite and three Ashkenazic. Today you can see the remains of the ghetto, as well as the ancient cemetery and one of the synagogues that still stands at Via Govi 11 (0376-321-490). Its past glory reflects the kind of detailed Italian artistry that would be associated with a Giovanni Bellini. What remains is a national monument. The interior of the synagogue contains ornate stonework, with elaborate marble curlicues and columns around the Ark, and the ornamentation that is still visible on the walls and ceilings gives the visitor some inkling of its former grandeur.

General Sights: No one goes to Milan without trying to see La Scala, which is the ultimate opera experience. If you are unable to get tickets to a performance (which takes place in a red velvet, jewel-box-like, intimate setting), you can still go to the museum, next door, and see pictures of past divas and performances.

Nearby is the impressive Galleria Vittorio Emanuele, a nineteenth-century shopping arcade, which is the social center of the city. With its cafés, restaurants, book shops and other stores, it is thronged with Milanese strollers at nearly all hours of the day and night. Directly across is the Duomo, the third largest church in the world and the largest Gothic structure in Italy.

Behind La Scala is a neighborhood known as La Brera (for its proximity to the Pinoteca di Brera, an art gallery with masterpieces by El Greco, Raphael, Piero della

Francesca, and others). Its galleries, small antique shops, and other stores are a welcome change from the rest of Milan's bustling commercial districts. Few travelers leave Milan without shopping, whether at the Rinascente department store (one of a chain) across from the cathedral or along the shopping streets of Corso Buenos Aires. For pricey but enjoyable window-shopping, don't neglect Via Spiga, Via Montenapoleone, Via Sant'Andrea, and Via Manzoni, where top Italian designers — from Ferré to Valentino — have boutiques. The Sant'Ambreus is a good place to grab a cappuccino and dessert for refueling.

Personalities: Milanese Jews have successfully blended into the fabric of the city, and many professions and institutions have had Jews in prominent positions. Among the best known names are Guido Arto (textiles), Guido Roberto Vitale (finance), Guido Jarach (manufacturing), and past Jewish community president Giorgio Sacerdoti (law). Noted journalists include Ugo Stille, former editor of the Milan daily *Corriere della Sera;* and Annie Sacerdoti, editor of the Jewish community bulletin and author of *Guida all'Italia Ebraica,* an Italian-language guide to Jewish Italy.

Milanese Jews also count among their number journalist Stefano Jesurun, who wrote *Essere Ebrei in Italia (To Be Jewish in Italy).* Jews active in theater and music in Milan include Leo Wächter, Sergio Israel, and Fabio Treves.

Jewish personalities of the past associated with Milan include the Resistance hero Angelo Finzi, executed by the Germans outside the city in 1945, and Claudio Treves and Filippo Turati, founders of the Italian socialist movement, who are buried in Milan. Milan was also one of the places Albert Einstein called home; he lived in the city from 1894 to 1900.

Culture: Though Milan's Jews are part of the larger cultural picture, they produce a wide range of specifically Jewish cultural events — music and dance, plays and lectures — at the synagogues and cultural centers. The best place to call for information on community events and activities is the secretariat of the community center, at 4830-4684. The first thought conjured up by Milan might be fashion or La Scala, but the city has much to offer the Jewish traveler as well.

—*E. Merri Rosenberg*

Minneapolis–St. Paul

Why was Mary Richards always so cheerful despite the cold Minnesota winters? Why did she stay in Minneapolis and endure those dateless Saturday nights, not to mention Lou Grant's grumpiness?

Probably for the same reasons so many real people love the Twin Cities. With more theaters and museums and less crime than other metropolitan areas, with an abundance of lakes within the city limits, and a can-do attitude about long winters, Minneapolis and St. Paul are rated among the most livable of American cities.

Lou Grant was one of television's vaguely Jewish characters, though off camera there is nothing vague about Ed Asner's Jewishness. Mary's friend Rhoda Morgenstern was explicitly Jewish, though she was played by the non-Jewish Valerie Harper. And Mary herself? In real life, a few years after the show's last episode she married a Jewish doctor and began studying Judaism (though contrary to rumor she has not converted).

In a way the Jewish angles of the Twin Cities are much like those of the "Mary Tyler Moore Show." They are mostly beneath the surface and they are not necessarily the most significant features, but the end product would be very different without them. Perhaps most important, the Jewish angles intersect gracefully with all the others.

Residents of Minneapolis and St. Paul are quick to point out that their twinship is fraternal, not identical. Saint Paul, the state capital, is older and more staid; its traditional architecture and quieter nightlife contrast sharply with the glass and steel skyscrapers in Minneapolis, a city whose youthful atmosphere is fueled by a larger college population and a bigger culture scene, with performing and visual artists who've fled from more expensive, dangerous cities.

History: For the most part the Jewish communities of Minneapolis and St. Paul have always been separated by differing histories and by the eastern side of Minneapolis in which few Jews have lived, creating a sort of no-(Jewish)-man's-land between the two communities.

There was a time when Jews felt more welcome in St. Paul than in Minneapolis. Jews arrived in St. Paul shortly after it was founded in 1849 and in a sense were in on the ground floor; by the time the first Jews arrived in Minneapolis just after the Civil War, the social order was already set. For a long time the St. Paul community was predominantly American born, which kept it closer to the mainstream; in a much shorter time, the American-born Jewish pioneers of Minneapolis were numerically overwhelmed by Eastern European immigrants. And for several generations, the atmosphere of St. Paul, with its Irish Catholic influence, was simply more tolerant than that of its heavily Scandinavian twin.

It is in the sense of openness that the twins have grown more similar as the entire area has grown more diverse. Not only are Jews well integrated throughout the Twin Cities, so tolerant is the area's reputation that it has long been regarded as a haven for interracial families. To give an idea of how quickly things changed in Minneapolis, in the 1930s journalist and social critic Carey McWilliams dubbed the city the "anti-Semitism capital of the United States"; by 1961 Minneapolis elected its first Jewish mayor, Arthur Naftalin, fully twelve years before Abraham Beame became the first Jewish mayor of New York.

St. Paul's first Jews were of German origin. The early settlers, many of whom had already achieved some business success in New York or the Southeast, established themselves quickly. The St. Paulites accepted their new Jewish neighbors and helped support their retail stores — and their social ascent.

St. Paul's first synagogue, Mount Zion, was established in 1856 and ultimately aligned itself with the Reform movement; in 1872, Orthodox Jews founded Sons of Jacob. Beginning in 1882, Eastern European Jews arrived, encouraged by the promise of business opportunity — and a firm shove westward by New York Jewish philanthropists who preferred to love their unwashed Russian-immigrant brethren from afar. Although St. Paul's Americanized Jews were no less embarrassed by their greenhorn coreligionists than the New York Jews were, they rallied to the immigrants' aid. To help acclimate their neighbors, local Jews established the Industrial School (whose name was soon changed to Neighborhood House). Similar to New York's Educational Alliance, the school offered classes in Americanization as well as specific skills-training programs.

As the number of Jews in St. Paul grew, so did the range of synagogues and associations that sprang up to serve them. The Conservative Temple of Aaron was established in 1912, and a Hebrew school soon followed, along with a Jewish Community Center, a convalescent home, and a home for the aged, one of the few programs started in partnership with the Minneapolis Jewish community.

The first synagogue in Minneapolis, Shaarai Tov, was founded downtown in 1878. When Eastern European Jews began arriving, the Russians moved to North Minneapolis and the Romanians to the South Side. By the 1930s, when Minneapolis Jews outnumbered St. Paul Jews almost two to one, there were close to 100 Jewish organizations in Minneapolis alone.

The story of the Twin Cities' Jews in the past fifty years echoes in many ways that of other midsize American Jewish communities. As the prospering Jews moved to the suburbs, the synagogues on Minneapolis's North Side were deserted and sold to churches that served an incoming black population. But in some respects the story of Minneapolis and its Jews is different. The cities have not lost everything to the suburbs; graceful synagogues — and Jews to fill them — are still to be found in South Minneapolis and in St. Paul.

Community: Today there are 22,000 Jews in Minneapolis and its suburbs and 7,700 in the St. Paul area. Though small, the collective Jewish community is perhaps the most active in the United States. More than 80 percent of local families are affiliated with a synagogue or Jewish organization. Each of the Twin Cities has Orthodox, Conservative and Reform synagogues, a Jewish Community Center, and a Jewish school. Kosher food is readily available and philanthropy is active.

West of downtown Minneapolis, St. Louis Park (often referred to as "St. Jewish Park") is the most densely Jewish suburb of the metropolis, with the Minneapolis JCC, the Minneapolis Jewish Day School, synagogues, and a kosher butcher. Recently, an *eruv* was erected to allow St. Louis Park's growing number of young Orthodox families to push strollers and carry on *Shabbat*. Other areas with substantial Jewish concentrations include South Minneapolis, Golden Valley, Minnetonka, and New Hope. On the St. Paul side, the main areas of Jewish residence are Highland in the city, and suburban Mendota Heights.

Sights: The most important Jewish sights in the Twin Cities are the synagogues. Though the area has its share of utilitarian *shuls* it also has a surprising number noteworthy for their architecture or for what they represent historically. It also has one in arguably the best setting for a synagogue in America.

Founded as Congregation Shaarai Tov, the congregation now known as Temple Israel dedicated its first building in September 1880. Fifty years, two fires, and one move later, the congregation built its current home at the corner of Twenty-fourth and Emerson Avenues South.

The congregation hired the architectural firm of Liebenberg and Kaplan, noted for its design of Art Deco movie theaters. A booklet available at the synagogue explains the symbolism of many features of the gray stone edifice. The pillar-fronted facade represents the influence of Greek culture on Judaism.

The original portion of the synagogue was built during the Depression, and the lobby that lies beyond these imposing pillars is much less grand than synagogue foyers built in more prosperous eras. Indeed, it's just a few feet from the main entrance to the five inner doors that lead to the sanctuary—each of whose portals is crowned by a name of one of the Five Books of Moses. The twelve columns in the sanctuary signify the twelve tribes of Israel. The organ grille is decorated with the Egyptian acanthus motif, a reminder of slavery, and the six windows in the sanctuary recall the six great periods of Jewish history—the Creation, the Patriarchs, the Exodus, the Temple Period, the Prophets, and the post-biblical era.

In 1983, as part of a general expansion, Temple Israel completed a second entrance in which fiberglass-reinforced, precast concrete pillars echo in more modern fashion the 1930 structure and unify the old and new wings. With a membership of nearly 2,000 families, the synagogue's huge sanctuary is filled on holidays and when the St. Paul Chamber Orchestra performs there six times a year.

In North Minneapolis another synagogue has aged in a very different way. Unlike Temple Israel, which has evolved with its community, the former home of Mikro Kodesh on the corner of Oak Park and North Oliver Avenues now serves as headquarters for Pastor Paul's Mission, a soup kitchen that serves the area's needy residents. When the pastor bought the structure from the Jewish community, it lay in disuse and disrepair, and he is working to remodel the building to serve his project's needs. Those who wish to see this fine example of turn-of-the-century synagogue architecture should do so quickly; though the Stars of David that adorned the original roof and the sculpted Ten Commandments and synagogue name that were installed atop the *bimah* are still intact, they have been joined by a plethora of crosses and a paint job in a color that ought to be against anybody's religion. Mikro Kodesh itself merged with other congregations to form B'nai Emet, located today at Ottawa Avenue South and Highway 7 in St. Louis Park.

Adath Jeshurun, a Conservative synagogue at 3400 Du Pont Avenue South, captures an atmosphere that is fast disappearing elsewhere. Located in South Minneapolis, it is an integral feature of one of the most stable urban neighborhoods (though never predominantly Jewish) in the country. The building is a large, comfortable place which, though built in 1927, seems to evoke American Jewry of the 1950s in its first flush of postwar self-confidence.

At the other end of the spectrum, but also among the best of its genre, is Beth El, the modern, vaulting Conservative synagogue—built in the shape of a *shofar*—at 5224 West 26 Street in St. Louis Park. The airy sanctuary, which has light entering from all sides, features stained-glass windows depicting the nation-shall-not-lift-up-sword-against-nation theme from Isaiah.

For perhaps the best synagogue setting in America you have to cross the Mississippi into St. Paul. There on a high bluff above the river sits the Temple of Aaron (616 South Mississippi River Boulevard). The synagogue, designed by Percival Goodman, is noteworthy for its wood-dominated sanctuary in which massive sweeping beams meet at a star in the middle of the ceiling. The ten earth-toned stained-glass windows that surround the sanctuary depict the stages of a Jewish lifetime. Temple of Aaron takes on earthly as well as spiritual concerns. During the hotly contested 1987 baseball season it featured a large sign on its lawn saying, in Hebrew, "Win Twins!" That was the year the Minnesota Twins won the World Series.

The Twin Cities are well served by two Jewish Community Centers. In St. Paul, the JCC is at 1375 St. Paul Avenue (telephone 612-698-0751); the Minneapolis JCC is at 4300 South Cedar Lake Road in St. Louis Park (612-377-8330). Both these modern buildings are filled with cultural, sports, and community-welfare activities. *The American Jewish World,* the community paper, has listings of upcoming events; read it to find out about speakers, performers, and cultural programs.

General Sights: One spot often missed by tourists in the Twin Cities is Fort Snelling. A military outpost since 1825, part of the fort has been restored by the Minnesota Historical Society (612-296-6126) as a living history museum of the United States Army. Visitors can watch "soldiers" performing infantry drills, visit barracks, and interact with the costumed residents—including "soldiers' wives," craftspeople working in the blacksmith and carpentry shops, and the hospital assistant, all of whom are trained to answer in character any question about their lives on the fort. The Roundtower, which once overlooked the endless prairies, today offers a clear view of downtown Minneapolis. If you'd like a more unusual way to practice your Hebrew than worshiping in one of the Twin Cities' many synagogues, you can pick up a copy of Fort Snelling's brochure in Hebrew (it's available in two Chinese dialects, too).

There are plenty of educational tourist activities closer to the downtown areas. At the edge of the Mississippi River in downtown Minneapolis, the St. Anthony Falls Lock and Dam offers insight into the river transportation that has helped support the Twin Cities since they were first settled. Though many of the Twin Cities' shopping areas now live in the shadow of the huge Mall of America in Bloomington, the riverfront is also the site of the charming St. Anthony Main, an enclosed, renovated mall.

Even the most sincere efforts to make outdoor strolling pleasant are virtually useless during the winter, when Minnesota temperatures drop below zero and often stay there for weeks at a time. The cruel winds and the thinking of a few enterprising minds led to the urban development with which Minneapolis is most frequently associated: its skyway system. The elevated walkways, temperature controlled to offer relief from the wind in the winter and the humidity in the summer, connect most of the downtown office buildings and many of its shopping complexes. It's common for people to spend an entire day working,

shopping, and running errands in town without stepping outside once.

But if you hide from the elements in Minneapolis you'll miss out on the natural beauty and recreational activities that help keep Minnesotans happy even when the weather's miserable. There are twenty-two lakes within the borders of Minneapolis and St. Paul, many of them open for ice skating in the winter, canoeing in the summer, and a variety of other activities. Equipment for these favorite Twin Cities pastimes can be rented from several companies around town, as can cross-country skis and bikes, rollerskates, and rollerblades.

Many of the mansions along St. Paul's Summit Avenue have been restored to their original grandeur after interim incarnations as rooming houses. Noted residents of this dramatic boulevard included F. Scott Fitzgerald, who had several addresses on this street; each time his father couldn't make the rent they moved up the block. South of Summit Avenue, the Highland section (where the Temple of Aaron is located) is home to many Jews today. Grand Avenue, one block south of Summit, is lined with trendy shops and cafés, catering to the 1990s counterparts of those who built homes on Summit Avenue in the nineteenth century.

For art in a formal setting, the Twin Cities offer several fine museums: The Walker, at 725 Vineland Place in Minneapolis, is one of the nation's finest with a wide array of exhibits and a recently completed outdoor sculpture garden whose centerpiece is a giant cherry on an even bigger spoon, by pop artist Claes Oldenburg. Across the river in St. Paul, the Minnesota Museum of Art offers a wide range of American artists. The museum occupies two sites: one, in the Landmark Center, Fifth Street at Market, is home not only to the gallery but also to several musical groups, some of which give free concerts in the building's center court.

Eating: To replenish the calories you've burned with a day of city sports, the Twin Cities have lots of good, inexpensive restaurants. Vegetarian eateries, including New Riverside Cafe at 1810 Riverside Avenue (612-333-4814), appeal both to the local starving artists and to anyone else who appreciates good food at good prices. The many Vietnamese restaurants that dot the area have lots of vegetarian offerings, too. For strictly kosher Middle Eastern food—and hole-in-the-wall ambience—try the Old City Cafe, 1571 Grand Avenue in St. Paul. The Hillel at the University of Minnesota serves meals (612-379-4016), and Knollwood Place, an upscale retirement facility, has a dining room open to outsiders who make reservations. For information on times call 612-933-1833.

One Jewish institution known to almost everyone in Minneapolis is the Lincoln Del, a traditional (but nonkosher) delicatessen. It has two locations, one in St. Louis Park and one in Bloomington.

Personalities: You don't have to look to the "Mary Tyler Moore Show" to find Jewish personalities—real or ersatz—connected with the Twin Cities. The 1990 Minnesota election for the United States Senate was, in fact, an all-Jewish affair, with Democrat Paul Wellstone defeating the incumbent Republican Rudy Boschwitz. Shortly after Arthur Naftalin completed eight years as mayor of Minneapolis, Larry Cohen was elected mayor of St. Paul, serving from 1972 to 1976. Jews prominent in the local arts scene include Evan Maurer, director of the Minneapolis Art Institute, and one of his predecessors, Samuel Sachs; and Martin Friedman, recently retired director of the Walker Arts Center. Those who have achieved renown after leaving the Twin Cities are the screenwriter Max Shulman, social critic and writer Midge Decter, comedians Al Franken and Pinky Lee, former Du Pont chairman Irving Shapiro, and the late film producer Mike Todd.

Burton Joseph, a grain trader who became chairman of the Anti-Defamation League of B'nai B'rith, and his wife, Geri, who was United States ambassador to the Netherlands, live in Minneapolis, and Miriam Freund-Rosenthal, a former Hadassah national president, was a longtime resident of St. Paul.

Though Hibbing is a bit out of the Twin Cities' metropolitan range, it produced Minnesota's best-known Jewish son—Bob Dylan. Dylan is as far from the "Mary Tyler Moore Show" as you can get in American culture, but as Minnesota demonstrates, it can produce a wide range of products with Jewish angles.

—Susan Kleinman

Mother of Waters: The Mississippi connects and divides the Twin Cities and its people, and provides perhaps the most picturesque setting for any synagogue in America

Montevideo

In Montevideo—capital and heart of that city-state-like country called Uruguay—they tell a visitor immediately how different Uruguayans are from their neighbors across the Rio de la Plata, the Argentinians.

Uruguayans tell you that they are quieter and more reserved; less arrogant and militaristic; freer of caste and aristocracy; more egalitarian and far more secular. Proudly they note the extent to which Uruguay has separated church and state—a distinction made with such determination that Christmas Week is called Family Week; Holy Week, Tourism Week; and once there was a time when newspapers could not spell the word God with a capital *G*.

But then, on a large and potentially mighty continent, Uruguay, in more ways than just these, is an anomaly.

It is a comparative midget—barely larger than North Dakota—set between the Argentine and Brazilian giants. Artificially formed, it served as much as a buffer between South American and European power players as a palliative for local nationalistic hungers. Thanks to its atypical and relatively recent antecedents—with liberal British and continental thought influencing this 19th-century creation—it has enjoyed a tolerance, heterogeneity, and pluralism rarely found in South America. And this stance has yielded, occasional lapses notwithstanding, a stability and prosperity so peculiar to the region that the country has sometimes been dubbed "South America's Switzerland."

Given, as well, its primarily immigrant society; the highest rate of literacy in Latin America; a fine health-care standard and other social benefits, it is difficult to imagine a more promising climate for Jewish, or any other, refugees.

History: With a past that knew insinuations of the Inquisition but no big trials, Uruguay may well have a significant Converso legacy. Conversos were known to have been in the Rio de la Plata area by the sixteenth century, first as refugees from Spain, later from Holland. There is also a mention of Conversos in an early chronicle of Colonia del Sacramento, founded in the eighteenth century by the Portuguese.

Some traces can still be found. Uruguay's president, Luis Alberto Lacalle de Herrera, says that, at least according to his great-grandmother, his family may have had Jewish origins. He reportedly says "shalom" frequently and calls the Sephardic synagogue "home." Furthermore, it is related that his mother always went to the market on Friday evenings—a market where an old Spanish woman covered her head with her hands and lit candles because, she claimed, it was an ancient tradition.

Nonetheless, documentation of today's Jewish community dates only from 1880. From that point, the immigration pattern is, with one noteworthy deviation, roughly similar to that of other Latin lands. First came the Sephardim, whose familiarity with the language and lack of a ghetto mentality permitted them to integrate quickly. Some were aiming for Buenos Aires, the New World's Spanish-speaking metropolis; others were leaving there in search of more favorable vistas. They hailed from Ladino-speaking communities in Syria, Cyprus, Morocco, Egypt, Greece, Turkey, and the Balkans, as well as France. Some had money; some did not. Those with padded pockets settled in downtown Montevideo; those with empty wallets alit in and around the port, particularly in an area called Goes, which, to those from Izmir, resembled home. By 1905, the Jews' arrival had been duly noted; not until 1912, though, in a private house in Goes, was the first *minyan* formed.

By 1916, enough Ashkenazim — primarily from Poland, Russia, and Lithuania — had arrived to form Montevideo's first *Chevrah Kadisha* and, by 1917, the city's first synagogue. The majority came, though, during the 1920s and early 1930s, propelled southward by the new United States immigration restrictions. They were tailors, shoemakers, meatpackers, and peddlers, and many had no idea where they were going. Large numbers headed to Goes, which became a Latin American Lower East Side. Distinguishing this group of immigrants from those to other lands, however, was the relatively high proportion of secular leftists who would go on to create a community of their own.

Though not entirely immune to fascist influence, in the years immediately preceding World War II Uruguay kept its doors open to Jews longer than did most other countries. Hence, by the end of the 1930s, it had a community of German Jews, whose numbers rose after the war when they were joined by relatives who had survived the Holocaust. While there was, following the establishment of Israel, a considerable *aliyah* — augmented later to 18,000 with the arrival of political dissidents — there was also an influx to Uruguay of Jews from, among other places, Algeria, Egypt, and Rhodes.

As second- and third-generation Uruguayan Jews succeeded their parents, their social standing rose. The majority earned university degrees and entered the professions. They moved from Goes out along the eastern waterfront to the more upscale highrise neighborhood of Pocitos, and by the 1960s they were sufficiently well integrated that assimilation became a communal concern.

Nevertheless, they remained a vulnerable group and, by the mid-1960s, when Uruguay began experiencing economic difficulties, the Jews felt it not only in their wallets but also in the political arena. Neo-Nazi groups emerged in the heretofore quiescent military, and though their influence was negligible, they were part of the kind of political polarization in which Jews traditionally feel ill at ease. Nevertheless before and during the military government that ruled Uruguay from 1973 to 1985, Jews could be found at both ends of the spectrum. Jews served as ministers of economics prior to and during the dictatorship. Meanwhile Mauricio Rozencoff, a writer and children's dramatist, spent twelve years in prison for having been second in command of the leftist urban guerrillas, the Tupamaros, whose activities, at least in part, provoked the coup that brought the military to power.

During these years, dissidents and economic casualties emigrated, many to Israel, for which Uruguay has long maintained a particular affinity. In fact, it expressed its support for Jewish aspirations in Palestine and the Balfour Declaration as early as the San Remo Conference in 1920. When UNSCOP (United Nations Special Committee on Partition) was formed following World War II, Uruguay was among the twelve member countries. Its representative, Enrique Rodriguez Fabregat, cast one of the deciding votes for Israel's establishment. And Uruguay was the first Latin American country to recognize the new state. Relations have generally been cordial ever since, with extensive trade, agricultural and educational exchanges. During the Persian Gulf crisis, Uruguay was in the lead condemning the Scud attacks. Reciprocally, a forest in the Judean hills honors Uruguay's national hero, José Gervasio Artigas.

Community: Like their other countrymen, Montevideo's 30,000 or so Jews, while maintaining their identity through Zionist and cultural activities, are primarily secular. Nevertheless, about fifteen synagogues exist in Montevideo, and the Jews have a central umbrella organization, the Comité Central Israelita, under which exist four distinct religious communities. These include the Ashkenazic, which represents about 60 percent of Montevidean Jewry and whose synagogues are the largest and most numerous; the Sephardic, comprising 30 percent, with two synagogues; the German, with 10 percent; and the Hungarian, with 100 to 200 members. All are organized in the so-called traditional manner, with one exception. The German synagogue, Nueva Congregación Israelita (at Rio

Branco 1168), recently hired its second Conservative rabbi. Thanks to his ministration, which invites active participation in Jewish life through *onegs*, youth groups, and other United States–inspired concepts, this synagogue now attracts about 150 persons on Friday nights. It's the largest congregation in the city.

Beyond the central committee's purview are two additional groupings. During the last decade, Lubavitch has established a 100-member congregation and small school in Pocitos. And also to be accounted for, though not community members, are leftist Jews, including Jewish communists. This group, perhaps numbering between 3,000 and 4,000, is heir to the Marxist ideals of immigrant mothers and fathers and maintains a separate communal structure with its own cultural activities and newsletters, and even its own cemetery.

The primary community maintains three schools with curricula taught in Spanish and Hebrew. Each has its own orientation, from secular to religious to Zionist. About one-third of the city's Jewish children, numbering 2,100, attend these schools. The community sees itself as consisting of a small upper-middle class; a large middle class that is diminishing during currently troubled times; and about a 10 percent lower-class population. The current generation of Uruguayan Jews demonstrates a low level of interest in conducting community affairs.

In many ways, though, it reflects its society in general, with which it maintains close contact through various interfaith activities, including Seders for 300, attended primarily by Catholics and Protestants. While feeling isolated from the Jewish scene beyond Uruguay's borders—including the bustle of nearby Buenos Aires—Uruguay's Jews also consider themselves freer than other nearby communities. Again, using Buenos Aires as a reference point, they say they have escaped the microscope often turned on their Argentinian compatriots.

Sights: Uruguay has been called "The Purple Land," the way Kentucky is "The Bluegrass State." If the landscape of gently rolling hills is viewed at just the right season, in just the right light, it bears a purplish hue, thanks to the wildflowers that cover it. But beyond the *estancias*, or ranches, of the countryside, and the coastline, the primary sightseeing target is Montevideo, a pleasant waterfront city of European cast, today somewhat genteelly down-at-the-heels, thanks to the sluggish economy.

Its avenues, parks, boulevards, and back streets bear, if not with abundance, then with singularity, various signs and signals of the Jewish presence. In the area of the broad Plaza Independencia, which unofficially marks the division between colonial Montevideo and the more modern city, stands a mausoleum of Uruguayan granite and marble. A tribute to José Artigas, one of the architects of Uruguayan independence, it was designed by the Jewish architect Alejandro Morón. Half a block from the plaza is the Téatro Solis, an acoustically fine opera house and the center of Uruguay's musical activity. An area behind it has been renamed Golda Meir Square.

Running eastward from the Plaza Independencia is one of Montevideo's main thoroughfares, Avenida 18 de Julio, which opens into the Parque José Batlle y Ordóñez. Here stands the seventy-five thousand-seat Centenario Stadium, which hosted the first World Soccer Cup in 1930. Erected to celebrate the nation's one hundredth anniversary, it was built primarily by Jewish workers. And farther east, closer to the waterfront, stands the Parque Hotel Casino and, opposite it, Parque Rodo. Along with a statue to José Enrique Rodo, a major Latin American literary figure, it also boasts another celebrity donated by the Jewish community. Just off the seaside at Ramírez Beach, near the junction of Avenida Antonio Rodríguez and Dr. Pablo de María, opposite the casino, stands a statue of Albert Einstein.

Throughout Montevideo's shopping districts, in the new area and more obviously in the narrow streets of the old town, are reminders that Jews once, and still today, own many stores. Calle Rincón was once filled with Jewish-owned fabric and textile stores and even now, La Opera and Sassoon's arc important shops. One of Montevideo's oldest importing emporiums, that of Isaac Trompunski, stands at Calle Soriano 800—in an area where most of the clothing stores are Jewish-owned as well. In this vicinity also stand banks—such as Bank Hapoalim at the corner of Calle Soriano and Florida—signaling both Uruguay's role as a banking haven and traditional Jewish involvement in this business, especially through old credit union connections.

Heading inland from the waterfront, north and northwest, off the Avenida Libertador, lies the old Jewish neighborhood of Goes. Now a shabby residential area, its streets are lined with two-story houses of faded blues, beiges, roses, and greens. But with their wrought-iron work and balconied facades, they suggest an architectural grace that might one day prove ripe for gentrification. Traces of the Jewish past abound—places like Jaime Schnapp's funeral home at Domingo Aramburú 1679, the only such parlor still extant in Montevideo; or the big, white building at the corner of Calle Blandengues and Porongos, which was the first Jewish school. Urchins in this neighborhood occasionally still use Yiddish words, picked up from their parents who were contemporaries of Jews who have now moved on.

Calle Alvear, a street of typical construction for the neighborhood, was the chicken-flickers' street, where Jewish families came to buy kosher chickens. In the Barrio Reus, punctuated by Calle Emilio Reus, virtually all homes during the 1930s and 1940s belonged to Jews, and many, though they now live elsewhere, still maintain businesses there. The shops along the tree-shaded Calle Arenal Grande also still are primarily Jewish owned.

Where Calle Arenal Grande runs into another street to form a V-shaped plaza was the spot where Jews used to gather to debate the relative merits of Zionism and communism. Still operating in the neighborhood is the Bar Leon, named for its former Jewish owner, where locals met to play chess. Behind a beige stucco wall and bright green doors, at Democracia 2370, is the still-functioning "Polisher Shul," its walls covered with murals ranging from red drapes painted against blue skies to the symbolically portrayed reception of the Ten Commandments on Mount Sinai. (For information regarding services here and at other Ashkenazi synagogues, call Ashke-

nazi community headquarters, Canelones 1084, at 987-172, 980-337, or 915-478.)

Bespeaking more contemporary Jewish concerns are photos possessed by the Jewish community from annual exhibitions begun in 1989 on Jewish life in Uruguay. Displayed in the community headquarters at Rio Negro 1308, among the more striking is one of a home in downtown Montevideo—address unknown—marked with the Hebrew letter tsadi. This was a message from one tradesperson to another that the resident did not pay his bills. (For information on the photos' current disposition, call the Comité Central Israelita at 916-1057.)

The Sephardi synagogue, Comunidad Israelita Sefaradi, at Buenos Aires 234 (telephone 86021), is also worth a look. It is an elegant building, inaugurated in 1956, whose facade features four pillars edging three bronze doors with panels featuring menorahs and *Magen Davids*. Beyond its muted marble lobby in red, black, and beige tones, its sanctuary, modeled after the Portuguese synagogue in Amsterdam, is filled with light-colored, carved wooden pews with six-pointed stars at each end. Its most impressive feature is the great arch rising over the *bimah* which uses stone grillwork to encase stained-glass squares of royal blue, turquoise, orange, and brown. The hall is lit by a chandelier featuring a great six-pointed yellow star within a circle of bulb-lit, clustered menorahs.

Side Trips: About an hour's drive from Montevideo along Uruguay's coast is Periapolis, an Old Worldly spa town heavily frequented since the 1920s by Jews, especially wealthy Argentinians. The town's showcase, along with its beachfront promenade, is the Hotel Argentina, a massive 535-room structure that nowadays caters to those who believe in spa cures and to crowds seeking bargain weekends.

Periapolis's Miami-like heyday has passed, however, in favor of the ultra chic Punta del Este, eighty-five miles from Montevideo, farther along the coast. To Uruguayans, this jet-set resort, with its expensive hotels, gourmet restaurants, modish boutiques, trendy nightclubs, and fine beaches, is, as one put it, "another country, not ours." Or, as a recent headline in *The New York Times* proclaimed, "For Argentines, There's No Place Like Uruguay." Developed during the 1960s— thanks, among others, to Mauricio Littman—its clientele is roughly 50 percent Argentinian and Brazilian-Jewish, though Uruguayan Jews who can afford it have bought there too. Both the downtown and the suburbs reveal the Jewish presence, from centrally located Israeli bank branches to suburban villas bearing names like Sucati, Miklati, Halomi, Pinati, and Galiziau.

Culture: The community has established annual photo competitions held during June or July on Jewish life in Uruguay, and hopes, eventually, to exhibit the contributions on an ongoing basis. Since 1957, every afternoon from 12:30 to 2:30, CX 46 Radio America has presented the Voice of Zion, a talk-and-interview program on Jewish subjects conducted by José Jerozolimski, who also edits *Semanario Hebreo*, a weekly for the Jewish community. The Jewish club, Hebraica-Maccabi, at Camacua 623 (telephone 961-246), has a schedule of cultural events, such as concerts by the Israel Philharmonic. Visitors can obtain a special ticket to use its five gyms, pool, restaurant, and other facilities.

Personalities: While many of Uruguay's leading Jewish lights have emigrated, some have stayed to make an impact, especially in the academic, artistic, and professional worlds. Well known in the first category, especially for his frequent appearances in various media, is Nathan Pilosoff, professor of philosophy at the University of Uruguay. Teresa Porzecanski is a leading social anthropologist and au-

thor as well as director of Montevideo's social service school. Samuel Lichtenstejn directs Montevideo's public university. Prominent in cultural life are theater director Jaime Yavitz; art critic Alicia Haber; Angel Kalenberg, director of the Museum of Modern Art; and artists Raoul Pavlotzky, Zoma Baitler, and José Arditti. Political figures past and present include Senator José Rorzeniak; deputies Leon Lev and Alberto Couriel; Nahum Bernstein, vice minister of education in the previous government; Dr. Jaime Schneider, vice minister of public health before the military government; and Eduardo Blair, a leading leftist.

Recommendations: Hogar de Padres, the senior citizens' residence of the Nueva Congregación Israelita, welcomes tourists to its kosher dining room; the facility is at Camino Castro 635 (telephone 39-01-16 or 38-01-20). The vegetarian Restaurante Vegetariano is on Avenida 18 de Julio. In Pocitos, at Ellauri 681, Mac Rico serves kosher traditional Uruguayan food mixed with a bit of Israeli and Arab cooking; one hybrid is *falafelitos*, the proprietor's own tasty falafel concoction.

Reading: Though most of the book is set in New York and Buenos Aires, the climactic chapter of Francine Prose's hilarious novel *Hungry Hearts* (Pantheon) has a Yiddish theater troupe wandering the streets of Montevideo looking for a certain rabbi who can exorcise a dybbuk. The contrast with the two larger Jewish centers illustrates the point Montevideans often make—their city, and their Jewish community, are different.

—Phyllis Ellen Funke

Montreal

The theater troupe at the Saidye Bronfman Centre decided to practice a bit of outreach to the city's French Canadian majority by staging a play by the Québécois dramatist Michel Tremblay. It wouldn't have attracted much attention for Montreal's leading Jewish cultural institution to produce Tremblay in English and, after all, French Canadians regard the English language as an instrument of cultural domination. So instead the players at the Bronfman Centre staged *Les Belles-Soeurs* in Yiddish. In a corner of North America that has yet to shake off the vestiges of anti-Semitism, the play was one of the most positive ways the Jewish community had ever thrust itself into the French Canadian spotlight.

Both the existence of a first-class Yiddish theater company and the production of *Les Belles-Soeurs* are indicators of how Montreal's Jewish community differs from others in Canada and the United States. It is closer to its roots, and unlike their counterparts elsewhere on the continent, Jewish Montrealers constantly ask themselves whether they are welcome in their home. The question posed by the production of Tremblay's play is whether attempts by Jews and French Canadians to understand each other can stem the tide of Jewish migration to points west and south.

History: Neither Jews nor Protestants were permitted to live in Quebec under French rule. The first Jews arrived in Montreal in 1760 as civilians attached to the British Army, which had conquered Quebec the previous year; ever since, Anglophone and Francophone Montrealers alike have regarded the Jews as a segment of the English-speaking community.

The first Jewish residents were engaged mostly in trade, especially in furs. Typical of the pioneers was Ezekiel Solomon, a Berlin-born merchant who came to Canada as an army purveyor and went into the fur trade; with Montreal as home and (winter) base, every spring he would travel the river route to Fort Mackinac (in today's Michigan) and trade for furs from the Indians and *voyageurs* who brought in their goods from deeper in the hinterlands.

Solomon was a leader of Montreal's first Jewish congregation, Shearith Israel, founded in 1768. Some of the founders, of Spanish and Portuguese origin, had belonged to the synagogue of the same name in New York, and though it had a good representation of Ashkenazim it adopted the Sephardic *minhag*. In 1768 the congregation erected its first building at the corner of Rue Notre Dame and Rue St-Jean in what is today Vieux Montréal (Old Montreal).

It wasn't until 1831, however, that the congregation, along with Jewish communities in Quebec City and Trois Rivières, received legal recognition from the Legislative Assembly of Quebec. Thereafter, the Jewish community played an increasingly active role in the affairs of the city. Abraham de Sola, who became *chakham* of Shearith Israel in 1847, was also a professor of Hebrew and Oriental literature at McGill University and a longtime president of the Natural History Society of Montreal. In 1858 German and Polish Jews were numerous enough to break from Shearith Israel and form an Ashkenazic synagogue, Shaar Hashomayim.

The Jewish community grew slowly, however, and numbered only 7,600 in 1901. Rapid growth began only after the turn of the century when large-scale immigration from Eastern Europe began—spurred by

Czarist pogroms, persecution in Romania, and, finally, the imposition of restrictive immigration quotas in the United States—bringing the Jewish population to 80,000 on the eve of World War II; postwar refugee immigration brought the numbers to a peak of 120,000 around 1970.

The good old days, as many Montreal Jews remember them, stretched from the 1920s to the 1950s when Boulevard St-Laurent was like a Jewish city—Canada's answer to the Lower East Side. Jewish-owned stores were everywhere, there were street-corner synagogues and *yeshivahs*, and the neighborhood's language was Yiddish. Since Quebec had no public nondenominational schools, Jews filled the area's Protestant schools. They weren't fully accepted by either English- or French-speaking Montrealers, but they flourished.

Community: The decade from 1975 to 1985 saw an outflow of both capital and English speakers from Montreal, mostly in the direction of Toronto. According to legend, some apartment buildings in the Jewish sections of Toronto shake when, during a televised hockey game, the Montreal Canadiens score a goal. Today Montreal's community numbers about 90,000, and the city is unique for the relationship between its Jews and its majority culture. Quebec has a history of anti-Semitism, although it is not always easy to distinguish animosity toward Jews as Jews from resentment toward Jews as merely one of the more successful elements of the Anglophone population. Even the nonbigoted often view Jews as Anglophones first. *La Presse,* one of Montreal's French dailies, ran a feature article not long ago on the overwhelmingly Jewish suburb of Côte St-Luc. The article never mentioned Jews; it referred to the community simply as an English-speaking enclave.

Many Jews are ambivalent about the cause of their French Canadian neighbors. Jews tend to be more sympathetic than other English speakers to the French Canadians' effort to protect their cultural heritage, and of all the segments of the Anglophone community the Jews have the highest proportion of bilingualism. But the Jewish community took offense at Quebec's language legislation, such as the law requiring that all commercial signs be in French only (though there has been ongoing debate about permitting bilingual signs). While most Jews insist that the exodus that began in the 1970s was not a result of the separatist Parti Québécois's rise to power, they agree that the economic conditions brought on by a separatist provincial government pushed a lot of people out. After the return to power of the Liberal Party in 1985, and especially after a nationwide recession made the rest of Canada less of a draw, the exodus abated and some departed Montreal Jews even returned. With the renewal of independence fever surrounding the constitutional referendum of 1992, however, the uncertainty that fueled the exodus continued.

The Jewish community of the 1990s is still vibrant, but it doesn't have the same face as the community of the 1950s. The arrival of French-speaking Jews from North Africa transformed Montreal Jewry from an entirely Anglophone group to one that has roots on both sides of Montreal's linguistic track. Francophone Jews now make up about 20 percent of the community.

Despite Quebec's cultural tensions, there is no denying that the Jewish community has been influenced by the dominant ethos. Montreal's is the most predominantly Orthodox of North America's Jewish communities, a reflection of the French Catholic view of religion's place in society. Unlike the rest of Canada and the United States, public schools are something new to Quebec, and even today the churches play a prominent role in public education. Though Jews used to attend the Protestant (and English-speaking) schools, today 40 percent of Montreal's school-age Jewish population attends Jewish day schools—by far the highest percentage anywhere in North America. And because Montreal didn't have, until recently, its own public library system, an extensive Jewish Public Library, with its own branches, grew to serve both the Jewish and general community.

The main concentrations of Jews are in the suburbs of Côte St-Luc, Westmount, Hampstead, and Outremont, and in the

Snowdon–Côte des Neiges area inside the Montreal city limits. There is a growing community farther out in Dollard-des-Ormeaux and a shrinking one in Chomedey.

Jews have always exerted an influence beyond their own neighborhoods in Montreal. They have traditionally been highly visible in commerce, particularly in the garment industry, and they show up frequently in French Canadian literature, such as in the novels of Gabrielle Roy. Canada's former prime minister, Pierre Elliott Trudeau, grew up among Jews in Montreal, and there are those who claim he has a good understanding of Yiddish. At one time in the 1970s, Montreal's three major sports teams—the Canadiens of hockey, the Expos of baseball, and the Concordes of football—were all Jewish owned.

Sights: The tour of Jewish Montreal starts with the place that became the community's heart in the early twentieth century. The area called "The Main" stretches along Boulevard St-Laurent (the dividing line between the city's east and west sides) from downtown north to Boulevard St-Joseph, and from St. Louis Square on the east to Outremont on the west. Although it is now more Greek and Portuguese than Jewish, the neighborhood is still studded with Jewish stores and landmarks.

The Main looms larger in Canadian Jewish mythology than does the Lower East Side for Jews south of the border. Its Jewish heyday was more recent, fed by a later generation of immigrants; the neighborhood remains accessible and, certainly compared with United States standards, safe. Along the commercial St-Laurent, along St-Urbain with its row houses and long staircases that give second-floor apartments access to the ground, it is not at all hard to conjure up images of the world of Canada's Jewish fathers and mothers. Some of them are still there. St. Louis Square was a Jewish gathering point in the 1940s; today it is frequented by Haitian and Vietnamese immigrants. St. Viateur Park, farther to the west, still turns into a hasidic center on summer weekends.

The landmarks of The Main begin just north of the Avenue des Pins with the

Jewish gastronomic outposts—Warshaw's Supermarket (3863 St-Laurent), Moishe's Steak House (3961 St-Laurent) and the perennial favorite, Schwartz's Hebrew Delicatessen (3895 St-Laurent). Schwartz's is also a landmark of sorts to Quebec's language laws. The obligatory French sign outside says "Charcuterie Hébraïque"; the smoked meat tastes the same in any language. (While the atmosphere is unmistakably Jewish, neither Moishe's nor Schwartz's is kosher.)

Beth Shlomo, 3919 Rue Clark, is a corner synagogue in a red-brick row house, one of the last of its kind. A few blocks to the north, the former Beit Hamidrash Hagodol, at 4170 St-Urbain, is now home to the Portuguese Association of Canada, though the former name in Hebrew is still visible above the double-arched entrance. One block farther north, at 4251 St-Urbain, is the former Baron Byng High School. The Protestant school, known for its high-achieving Jewish students, closed down when Jews left the neighborhood; today the building is a youth center. In Mordecai Richler's novel *The Apprenticeship of Duddy Kravitz*, Baron Byng was referred to as Fletcher Field High.

Perhaps the most charming of the old synagogues in the neighborhood is the recently closed Yavneh Shul at 4690 Hutchinson, also located in a red-brick building, at the corner of Rue Villeneuve. Several buildings belonging to the Collège Français on Fairmont had Jewish origins and their signs are still visible. The B'nai Jacob Synagogue stood at number 172, and an arch above the modern addition still says in Hebrew, "This is the gate of God." The building at number 155 was the Yiddish Folkshul.

Fairmount is also home to the neighborhood's two best known landmarks. The Fairmount Bagel Bakery, at number 74, attracts Jews and non-Jews from the city, and former Montreal Jews—having spread the reputation as they settled all over the continent—make pilgrimages there when they visit home. You can visit anytime; the place is open, according to one youngster behind the counter, "24 hours a day, 366 days a year." Both the Fairmount Bagel Bakery and Wilensky's, a few steps away at number 34, were used in filming the movie

The Apprenticeship of Duddy Kravitz. Wilensky's is an old-fashioned lunch counter, featuring hard, round seats at a counter and its own library. Richler himself lived in the 5700 block of St-Urbain.

Jews started moving to Westmount, a suburb entirely surrounded by Montreal, in the 1920s and that is where Shaar Hashomayim, the Ashkenazic congregation founded in 1858, is located today. Once the largest congregation in Canada and (with 1,600 member families) still the largest in Montreal, it occupies most of a square block at 450 Kensington, off Sherbrooke. Though affiliated with the Conservative movement, the synagogue has separate seating for men and women. In addition to the services, cultural events, and school classes that go on in the building, there is also a small museum.

Though Shaar Hashomayim was built in stages from the 1920s to the 1960s, the exteriors of the older and more modern wings are unified by arched windows all around. The entrance to the main sanctuary consists of three stone arches with mahogany doors. But the feature for which the synagogue is known across Canada is the sanctuary's rich mahogany interior. Two-thousand people can fit in the straight rows of wooden pews. The ark is topped with three arched alcoves incorporating Star of David windows; arched windows also adorn the side walls. The red carpeted aisle is so long that, according to an old congregation joke, wedding couples are sometimes ready for divorce by the time they reach the *bimah.*

A few blocks away is Canada's oldest Reform congregation, Temple Emanuel-Beth Sholom, founded in 1882. The temple has been at its current site, at 4100 Sherbrooke, since 1911, but it was destroyed by fire in 1957 and today's yellow brick building with Mediterranean arched windows was rededicated three years later. The ceiling of the temple's modern sanctuary looks like the folds of a tent top; at the angles formed by the folds, high above the wooden pews, are windows that flood the room with light The temple also has a museum, and memorial plaques dedicated to members who died in World War I and World War II.

If The Main is the community's old heart, the current center of Jewish life is in the Snowdon–Côte des Neiges area. The main drags are Côte Ste-Catherine and Victoria. On these streets, and some of the streets that radiate from them, can be found the city's highest concentration of Jewish institutions, bookstores, butchers, cafés, and restaurants.

If there is a nerve center to the Jewish community, it would have to be the 5100 block of Côte Ste-Catherine. On the south side of the street (5170 Côte Ste-Catherine) is the Saidye Bronfman Centre, the place to find art exhibits, theater, concerts, and lectures. Like New York's 92nd Street Y, it is a Jewish cultural institution that reaches well beyond the boundaries of the Jewish community, as the production of Tremblay's play suggested.

On the ground floor of the Bronfman Centre is an art gallery that exhibits works by Canadian artists, Jewish and non-Jewish. The Yiddish Theatre of the Saidye Bronfman Centre, under the direction of Dora Wasserman, is the foremost company of its kind in North America. Recent works produced in Yiddish have included *Fiddler on the Roof,* Sholom Aleichem's *Adventures of Menachem-Mendl,* and I. L. Peretz's *The Innkeeper.* Productions in English have included *Driving Miss Daisy* and *The Heidi Chronicles.*

The Bronfman Centre is also known for its children's programs (art and acting classes, a puppet festival and workshop) and for concerts, lectures, and adult education. Call the center at (514) 739-2301 for information on programs and events.

Across the street from the Saidye Bronfman Center, at 5151 Côte Ste-Catherine, is the building housing the Federation CJA (Jewish Montreal's umbrella organization), the Holocaust Memorial Centre, the Jewish Public Library, and a variety of Jewish welfare organizations. The best place to call with questions about Jewish services, sights, or events are the federation (514-345-2624) and the Jewish Information and Referral Service (514-737-2221). Questions about *kashrut* are best put to the Jewish Community Council (514-739-6363).

The Holocaust Memorial Centre on the building's lower level is noteworthy not only for its chronicle of how Jews were killed but also for its exhibit on how European Jewish life looked before it was destroyed. Many of the artifacts in the exhibit were given by survivors who settled in Montreal after World War II. Among the items in the display are prewar ritual objects, ghetto newspapers, and a Yiddish typewriter from turn-of-the-century Poland.

Canada's oldest congregation, Shearith Israel—the Spanish and Portuguese Synagogue—is a few blocks away at 4894 Rue St-Kevin. Though the building of yellow and orange brick is for the most part utilitarian, it makes up in human atmosphere what it lacks in aesthetics. The congregation had long since attained an Ashkenazic majority (while maintaining the original Spanish and Portuguese *minhag*) until the 1960s when many Sephardim arrived in Montreal. The largest group in the congregation is now of Moroccan origin, but there are Iraqi and Lebanese Jews as well, not to mention the many Ashkenazim who still belong. School classes in the building and the Herzliah Talmud Torah next door give the place a lively air, and members always go out of their way—on *Shabbat* or at the weekday services—to show hospitality to visitors.

The highest concentration of Jews in the Montreal area is in the suburb of Côte St-Luc. This neighborhood of one- and two-story homes and apartment buildings is where you will find not only Jewish stores but places like Rambam Park, Maimonides Hospital, and streets with names like Einstein and Ashkelon. The shopping center most frequented by Montreal Jews is Côte St-Luc's Cavendish Mall.

One of the synagogues worth visiting in Côte St-Luc is Beit Rambam, a two-story red brick building with slit windows at 5780 Westminster. The predominantly Moroccan congregation has a receptive atmosphere and may be one of the best places in Montreal to practice French (utter a few words and no one will let you lapse back into English). Beth Israel–Beth Aaron, the Orthodox congregation at 6800 Mackle Road, has been adding to its home since it moved to Côte St-Luc in 1966. The most striking feature of the modern complex is the main sanctuary, completed in 1986, which has no straight walls. The brick-and-wood interior is lit by skylights and narrow windows along the walls that jut out and meet at various angles.

One of the few areas of growth for Montreal Jewry in the past generation has been in Dollard-des-Ormeaux, on the other side of Dorval Airport from Côte St-Luc. A middle-class neighborhood of ranch homes and neat lawns, it began attracting young Jewish families in the 1960s. Beth Tikvah, founded with support from Yeshiva University in New York, has grown up with the neighborhood and now has 800 member families. Its complex at 136 Westpark Boulevard is a modern brick structure in which the stepped-brick patterns (in the roof and window designs) are reminiscent of the Second Temple. The skylit, semicircular sanctuary is decorated with stained-glass windows in brown and desert tones. Like many other Montreal synagogues, the community activities and school on the premises keep the place busy seven days a week.

A good companion to seeing Jewish sights in Montreal is *Rendez-vous à Montreal: A Guide to Jewish Montreal* put out by the Federation's Jewish Information and Referral Service (514-737-2221). Another good companion would be Allan Raymond, who gives tours of Jewish Montreal; call him at (514) 489-8741 or write to him in advance at 139 Finchley Road, Hampstead, Quebec H3X 3A3. The best places to find listings of other Jewish cultural events are the *Canadian Jewish News* (Montreal edition) and *The Suburban,* both weeklies. Some events, especially those at the Saidye Bronfman Centre, are also in the regular listings of Montreal's French or English dailies.

Personalities: Montreal has produced more than its share of Jewish talent and personalities. First and foremost is Richler, whose books have put The Main on the world's literary map—and, like many writers who tell all, earned him the enmity of many in the community he came from. Poets from The Main include Leonard Cohen and A. M. Klein. Also from Montreal are comedian Mort Sahl; actor William Shatner; journalist Elie Abel; David Lewis, the late head of Canada's New Democratic Party; and Eric Berne, the psychologist who founded transactional analysis. When Robert Bourassa defeated the separatists and was elected Quebec's premier in 1985 he appointed Herbert Marx as his justice minister; Marx subsequently resigned over Bourassa's failure to rescind the restrictive language legislation the Parti Québécois had enacted. Montreal-born Louis Rasminsky was governor of the Bank of Canada and an architect of the International Monetary Fund; Victor Goldbloom was the first Quebec Jew appointed to the Canadian Senate.

One of the best-known Jews among French Canadians is Sonia Ben Ezra, a talk show host on French-language radio. Sheila Finestone is a member of Parliament from Montreal, and Gerry Weiner is the province's minister of multi-culturalism. Irwin Cotler is one of the country's most prominent lawyers (and sometimes referred to as Canada's Alan Dershowitz).

Perhaps the best known Montreal Jewish family is the Bronfmans. They are known in many circles as owners of Seagrams, Ltd., as founders of the Canadian Jewish Congress, and as philanthropists. Edgar Bronfman is president of the World Jewish Congress and has been, over the years, one of the leading crusaders for Jewish rights around the globe. Phyllis Lambert, also of the Bronfman family, is a prominent architect.

Eating: There are many Jewish eateries around the city, but some of the most popular (like the Brown Derby, a popular breakfast spot, and the Ben Ash chain, not to mention Schwartz's) are not kosher. Most of the city's half-dozen kosher restaurants are Moroccan owned, which means a kosher meal in Montreal is more likely to include couscous than *cholent*. The consensus among locals is that the best of the kosher restaurants is El Morocco, at 3450 Drummond Street. New additions to the scene include Kotel (1422 Stanley), convenient to many downtown hotels; and Ernie and Ellie's at 6900 Boulevard Décarie. A popular neighborhood spot is Mitchell's, the kosher restaurant in the Snowdon YM-YWHA at 5500 Westbury.

Reading: There is a wealth of literature with Montreal's Jewish community at the center. Saul Bellow's *Herzog* (Avon) has a Montreal setting. Those of Richler's novels most evocative of The Main are *St. Urbain's Horseman* and *The Apprenticeship of Duddy Kravitz* (Bantam); there is also *The Street,* a collection of Richler's short stories. One of the most widely read works during the campaign surrounding Canada's Constitutional referendum in 1992 was Richler's *O Canada! O Quebec!*, a sometimes strident and often on-target critique of Quebec's politics, with due notice to the role of Jews in the province. Peter Newman's *Bronfman Diary* (McClelland & Stewart) focuses on the famous family.

General Sights: Many a tour starts with Vieux Montréal, the old city where some buildings date back to the eighteenth century. Today it's a colorful area of churches, markets, and squares, street musicians, restaurants, and cafés. There's no trace of the first synagogue building of Shearith Israel, which stood at the corner of Notre Dame and St-Jean. Nineteenth-century buildings now line the streets in this corner of the city, but a stroll past the site is a reminder that the Jewish presence in Montreal is old indeed. Other worthwhile pursuits are a walk or calèche ride up to Mount Royal Park for its spectacular view, shopping in the extensive underground city, theaters, and museums. What many travelers miss is the Latin Quarter, along Boulevard St-Denis, an area of cafés, bistros, and restaurants where little English is heard. Prince Albert Street between St-Denis and St-Laurent is a charming pedestrian mall of restaurants in restored row houses.

Side Trip: Quebec City is a three-hour drive up Route 20, and it is as different from Montreal as New York is from Nieuw Amsterdam. Like Jerusalem, the town's old city is surrounded by a wall; inside there are narrow, winding streets that seem little changed from the eighteenth century. Below the walled city, on the bank of the St. Lawrence, the restored buildings date back to the seventeenth century.

Quebec City's Jewish community was never large. Two Jews settled there in 1767, and in 1790 John Franks was appointed the first chief of the Quebec Fire Brigade. In the nineteenth century, Jews served in city government and were prominent merchants. Sigismund Mohr, an electrical engineer from Germany, was the pioneer of hydroelectric development in Canada; his work not only lit Quebec City but also put the province on the road to becoming, literally, a North American power broker.

The Jewish community, which peaked at about 500 in 1961, today numbers fewer than 100, mostly university professors, provincial government workers, merchants, and people in real estate. The city's one synagogue, Beth Israel-Ohev Shalom, is at 1251 Place de Mérici, about a 25-minute walk from the old city (telephone 418-688-3277).

Recommendations: Montreal has no shortage of hotels for all tastes and budgets, but particularly noteworthy are Le Meridien, atop the Complexe Desjardins and convenient to the underground malls, and the more moderately priced Château Versailles, an old-world hostelry located in four converted mansions on Rue Sher-brooke. The trip to Quebec City is worth it if only to stay at the Château Frontenac, a huge Victorian hotel that dominates the cityscape and has no peer. Much of Montreal, from the centrally located tourist attractions to the Jewish neighborhoods in the west, is easily accessible by Métro, the city's subway system; Côte St-Luc is accessible by bus, but a trip to Dollard-des-Ormeaux requires a car. The best way to see Quebec City is on foot.

While it may seem obvious that summer is the only season in which to visit a Canadian city, in fact, Montreal and Quebec City deal admirably with the coldest of temperatures. Quebec City has a winter festival that is one of the year's biggest draws, and Montreal's extensive underground transport and shopping network make it possible to cover much of the city in winter without stepping into the cold. Outdoor strolling is certainly easier from April to October, but the fascinating dynamics of the French-Jewish-English encounter take place—on stage or in signs, in the culture and on the street—twelve months a year.

—Alan M. Tigay

Moscow

A genre of humor posits that there are more Jewish organizations than there are Jews. The way things are going in Russia, however, it is no joke. More than 400,000 Jews have left the former Soviet Union since 1989, but as the Jewish population falls the number of Jewish organizations soars. If, as sociologists would say, present trends continue, the old jokes would become reality.

Both the emigration and the madcap organization are, of course, products of freedom, undeniably the greatest level of freedom Jews have ever enjoyed in Russia or the former Soviet Union. The dark side is the freedom of anti-Semites to express themselves as well. On balance, are the changes of the past few years good for the Jews? There are signs to fit every theory.

At an exhibit of Jewish artists in Moscow's Central Artists' House two non-Jews—one a Russian, one with an Armenian accent—are overheard trying to best one another by citing cultural contributions Jews have made to the world.

Where the statues of Communist founders once stood, one now sees empty pedestals. Only at the pedestal where Yakov Sverdlov, the leading Jewish Bolshevik, once stood, have Russian nationalists erected a cross.

On the Moscow metro people read Jewish books openly, often prompting a "*Chag Same'ach*" or "*Shabbat Shalom*" from fellow travelers. In 1991, the first Hanukkah celebration was held in the Kremlin.

Meanwhile Pamyat, the anti-Semitic nationalist organization, holds demonstrations and competes openly for the hearts and minds of the Russian people.

Perhaps the most important change with respect to the Jews is the transfer of anti-Semitism from the public to the private sector. This leaves the Jews and their friends the freedom to fight back when necessary.

History: Despite the deep Jewish roots in Russia, Moscow's Jewish community got a late start. It wasn't until the end of the eighteenth century—more than a century after Jews first settled in New York—that Jews were given permission to reside even temporarily in the Russian capital.

There had been individual Jews in the city before then, not to mention apostate Jews. Unlike Spain, Russia did not hold converted Jews in suspicion and some became nobles. One noble family went by the name of Yevreinov (Israelov). Any Jew who ever read *Anna Karenina* must have been struck by the novel's most admirable figure, the nobleman Constantin Dmitrovich Levin, said to represent Tolstoy himself.

Ivan the Terrible invited a Jewish physician from Venice to practice in his capital, and had him thrown into the Moscow River when one of his royal patients died. Peter the Great had at least one Jewish adviser. But it was the partition of Poland, and with it the absorption of masses of Jews into the Russian empire, that led to a real Jewish presence in Moscow. Jewish merchants began visiting the city with greater regularity until, in 1790, local merchants tried to have the Jewish competition eliminated. Local industrialists supported the right of Jews to live in Moscow, and a compromise was worked out in 1791. Jewish merchants were forbidden to settle in the inner districts of Russia, but they could reside temporarily in Moscow; most stayed at the Glebovskoye Podvorye (later they were required to stay there), an inn in the heart of the city's market quarter.

In 1855, Czar Alexander II allowed Jews to live, still temporarily, in any part of Moscow. A few years later he permitted permanent settlement for Jewish military veterans. The categories of Jews allowed to live in the city were further expanded so that their number in Moscow grew from fewer than 500 in 1858 to 35,000 in 1890. The first synagogues were built, and Jewish entrepreneurs such as the Polyakovs (railroads and banking) and K. Z. Wissotzky (tea) became household names. Even after the ascent of the reactionary Alexander III and the onset of pogroms in 1881, Moscow's liberal governor, Prince Dolgorukov, brother of the more liberal Alexander II, protected the Jewish position.

Things changed when Dolgorukov was replaced by Grand Prince Sergei Alexandrovich. As the story goes, one day the prince walked past the Choral Synagogue on Arkhipova Street and, mistaking it for a church, crossed himself. When his error was pointed out he ordered the building's cupola removed and shortly thereafter decided to rid Moscow of Jews completely. The expulsion order was issued on the eve of Passover 1891, and when it was over more than 30,000 Jews had been forced to leave; it was only after the end of Sergei's term in 1905 that the Jewish community began to recover.

The two decades surrounding the 1917 Russian Revolution marked a time of great Jewish activity, growth, and dislocation in Moscow. In this period the Jewish population grew from 10,000 to 130,000. Jewish schools were opened; Yiddish and Hebrew newspapers sprang up; Habima, the Hebrew theater, and the State Jewish Theater were born. Jews held important positions in the city's cultural life, and figures like Trotsky and Sverdlov (neither of whom had much use for a Jewish identity) were leading political lights.

Emigration virtually ended with World War I, but Moscow wasn't a place from which to emigrate in any case. Migrants came from *shtetls*, and Moscow was for some as much a magnet as New York. Jewish life had its own revolutions, however. Jewish workers denounced Jewish industrialists, and as the 1920s progressed Zionist activity was stamped out. Habima, which had premiered S. An-ski's *The Dybbuk* in 1922, was one of the last Zionist survivors. In 1926 the company emigrated to Tel Aviv. Sverdlov had died prematurely and Trotsky was forced into exile. The flowering of Jewish culture and leadership was short-lived.

But as Jewish cultural activity came to a halt, Jews continued flocking to Moscow, numbering perhaps 400,000 at the beginning of World War II. The Germans were stopped in 1941 within ten miles of Moscow (you can see the spot on the trip into the city from Sheremetyevo Airport). As Jewish refugees entered the city, Jewish soldiers headed for the front; half a million Jews served in the Red Army during the war, and 200,000 died.

During the war the government set up the Jewish Anti-Fascist Committee, led by the great theater director and actor Solomon Mikhoels, to help mobilize world Jewish opinion to aid in the war effort. Mikhoels attempted to continue the committee's activities, on behalf of Holocaust survivors, after the war, but Stalin suppressed the organization in 1948 and had its leaders arrested and executed. In 1952 Stalin also concocted the Doctors' Plot, in which he accused nine doctors (six of them Jews) of planning to murder Communist leaders. The public execution of the accused and the coinciding mass expulsion of Jews from Moscow were canceled by Stalin's timely death.

After the war Jewish life and identity were underground phenomena, but they occasionally burst forth for the world to notice. When Golda Meir, Israel's first ambassador to the Soviet Union, showed up at the Choral Synagogue for Rosh Hashanah in 1948, a spontaneous mass demonstration broke out. By the late 1950s, thousands of young Jews began gathering in front of the synagogue on Simchat Torah to dance and sing Yiddish and Hebrew songs.

Elie Wiesel watched the festivities outside the synagogue on Simchat Torah in 1965 and helped galvanize American support for Soviet Jewish rights with his description of the event in *The Jews of Silence*. Then Soviet Jewry itself was electrified by the Israeli victory in the Six Day War.

The activism of Soviet Jews after 1967

through highs and lows of emigration is one of the great chapters of Jewish history. The Jewish movement was one of the first cracks that led eventually to the democratization and the breakup of the Soviet empire. Figures like Anatoly Shcharansky (now Natan Sharansky) and Yuri Orlov campaigned for human rights as well as Jewish rights, and the Jews undoubtedly inspired many non-Jews who wanted to shake Russia to its foundations.

Community: Though Jews are recognized as a nationality distinct from Russians, the cultural and behavioral marks Russian and Jewish cultures have made on one another are indelible. From the popular Russian music with a lilt that sounds positively Israeli, to the ubiquitous Russian sentences that start with "Nu?" it is often difficult to sort the trappings of one culture from another.

Classic Russian literature is filled with Jewish characters. Among the Russian writers with favorable attitudes toward Jews were Leo Tolstoy, Vladimir Korolenko, and Maksim Gorky. The discussions that go on today among the intelligentsia and the Russian Orthodox church on whether the Jews are good or bad for Russia mirror discussions that were cut off in 1917 (or continued in a communist context). The current Russian Orthodox patriarch, Aleksey II, is regarded as a friend of the Jews (he addressed a gathering of rabbis in the United States), which has prompted attacks from factions within the church.

Indeed, one gets the sense that the entire former Soviet Union has turned the clock back to 1917 and is trying to pick up from there. Religious institutions, banks, and stock exchanges are reemerging — sometimes in the same buildings that were taken from them after the Revolution. Cities and streets have returned to their pre-Revolution names. Old political parties and newspapers are being reborn. And Jews are a part of it all.

Community leaders put Moscow's Jewish population between 200,000 and 250,000 — and holding. Most Jewish Muscovites trace their origins to Ukraine or White Russia, although there is a sizable minority from the Caucasus Mountains. Moscow Jews are more Russified than their small-town com-

patriots and therefore less likely to emigrate. On the other hand, it seems that every time a Jew leaves, someone else reclaims a Jewish identity cast off by parents or grandparents.

There are no neighborhoods where Jews predominate, although more live near the center of Moscow than in the outlying sections. (Two exceptions are Malakhovka and Saltuykovka, suburbs which have long had a sizable Jewish presence; each has a synagogue and a Jewish cemetery.)

In a city of 10 million, Jews still make up a noticeable proportion of the middle class. As in the United States, they are especially prominent in law, medicine, science, film, and theater, and to a somewhat lesser degree as journalists and economists.

Ask a Russian Jew to describe the difference between today's free Jewish life and the suppression experienced just a few years ago and you are likely to be told, "The difference cannot be described. It had to be seen and felt." In a remarkably short time, Moscow Jewry's organizational structure has come to resemble that of a typical Western Jewish community — synagogues, schools, *yeshivot*, cultural organizations, historical societies, community centers, self-help and Zionist groups and camps.

Though all three Moscow synagogues are Orthodox, there is a Reform group, Hineni, which will ultimately have its own building as well. Various forms of religious, economic, and cultural support are flowing into the community from the West and from Israel. In addition, the government is in the process of returning communal property seized after the Revolution.

The umbrella organization representing the Jews of the Commonwealth of Independent States is the Va'ad, which is dedicated to supporting and rebuilding Jewish life and fighting anti-Semitism. Located at Varshavskoye Shosse 71, the Va'ad is a good place to call with questions about Jewish activities in Moscow (telephone 110-4853). The Shalom Theater is located in the same building.

Of the 150 other Moscow-based Jewish organizations, two are of special importance for Jewish visitors. The Jewish Cultural Association sponsors exhibits, holiday events, concerts and seminars. It lobbies for human rights and runs seminars on how to teach about the Holocaust. Among its many activities, it organized the first contingent of Russian Jewish youth to go on the March of the Living in Poland. For information on the association's events and activities, call 290-1286.

Tchiya—the Center for the Study of Jewish Religion and Culture—whose services often overlap with those of the Jewish Cultural Association, is more akin to a Jewish community center. It sponsors plays, concerts, and lectures; hosts sporting events; runs an *ulpan*; has a job bank; keeps synagogue schedules; and conducts Jewish history tours of Moscow (in English and Hebrew as well as Russian). For information about Tchiya's activities call 952-1317 or 236-8579.

Sights: Hidden behind the facade of the Communist architecture that appeared on Soviet postcards is the extremely attractive face of the Russian capital. Much of the nineteenth-century city survives, and individual buildings dating from the fifteenth century, many of them churches, are common.

Most Moscow tours begin with the Kremlin, the church complex and fortress from which the city grew, and the adjacent Red Square. The square almost became a site of explicit Jewish interest, but the honor was avoided by Stalin's death.

Toward the south end of the square near St. Basil's Cathedral is a circular stone platform. This was once a stage for public announcements—of war, of peace, of new laws—and until the eighteenth century it was the site of public executions as well. It was here that Stalin planned to execute the Jews accused in the Doctors' Plot and, in preparation for the deportation of the city's Jewish population, drum up an anti-Semitic demonstration.

There is a cluster of Jewish sights in the city's Kitay-Gorod section just east of Red Square. The six thousand-room Hotel Rossiya on the north bank of the Moscow River occupies a substantial chunk of the neighborhood that hosted the city's first Jewish community. The area was called Zaryadye, and in the seventeenth century it was a collection of curving, narrow streets where nobles and merchants lived in mansions

and hotels. Parts of the neighborhood stood until the hotel was built in 1967.

Nothing remains of the Glebovskoye Podvorye, the inn where Moscow's first Jewish residents—merchants and demobilized soldiers—lived, but the spot where it once stood is behind the Rossiya. A long section of the old Kitay-Gorod wall still runs along the east side of Kitayski Proyest. Directly across the street from Kitayski 7 is a driveway through the wall; the inn stood on the left side of the driveway entrance. The Hotel Rossiya, like the Glebovskoye Podvorye before it, is especially convenient for Jewish visitors since it is the closest of the major hotels to Moscow's main synagogue.

The Choral Synagogue is located at Arkhipova 8, but before entering it is worth making a stop down the street at the corner of Arkhipova and Solyanka. The three-story yellow stone building there—whose ground floor is now occupied by a produce store—was the city's first "Great Synagogue." When it was completed in 1870, during the reign of Alexander II, many city dignitaries were in attendance. It was here that Tolstoy studied Hebrew so he could read the Bible in the original. The building next door housed the Imperial Jewish Alexandrian Professional School.

But the community outgrew the building quickly and Eliezer Polyakov bought land farther up the street for the Choral Synagogue, which opened in 1891—on the eve of the expulsion of the Jews from the city.

It was in the narrow street in front of the Choral Synagogue that much of the drama of Soviet Jewry's freedom struggle was played out from the 1950s to the 1980s. This was where Jews gathered to sing, dance, exchange information, or merely to express their identity.

Visitors enter the synagogue through the columns of its neoclassic facade. Inside the eclectic main sanctuary (designed by the same architect who built the Pushkin Museum) is a high arched ceiling and a series of chandeliered arches over the women's gallery. Above the marble *bimah* are floral wall decorations of grape vines and three small, modern stained-glass windows. The synagogue has daily and *Shabbat* services (call 924-2424 for information).

In addition to being a religious center the

synagogue is also a nerve center. Classes for children and adults are in session all the time and *shochets* slaughter sheep and chickens in the courtyard. There is always a crowd in front on Arkhipova Street. For those who have forgotten what it is like to live in a country where not all Jews are comfortably middle class, a warren of beggars is always at the front door.

One of the most attractive streets in Kitay-Gorod is Nikolskaya, a graceful and bustling thoroughfare of shops and former hotels that looks unchanged from the nineteenth century. This was the birthplace of Israel's leading theater company, Habima. Though it never had a permanent site, much of Habima's life in Moscow was lived on Nikolskaya. Many performances were given in the green stone building at number 17, next to the Byzantine Gothic edifice that houses the Institute of History.

Perhaps nowhere in Moscow is Russian society's new face so evident as at Pushkinskaya Square at the corner of Tverskaya Street and Tverskoy Boulevard. Here sits *Izvestia*, once the newspaper of the Supreme Soviet. Across the street is one of the few places that still has long lines in Moscow: McDonald's. Next door is a place where the prices keep any lines from forming—the city's first Cadillac dealership.

Down fashionable Tverskoy Boulevard is another cluster of Jewish sights. The two-story building at number 15 was the home of Eliezer Polyakov. In addition to financing much of Jewish communal life in the late nineteenth century, the family of bankers and railroad builders supported the czar's army in wars against Turkey, founded a school for railroad technicians and contributed to the building of the Pushkin Museum. All three brothers received titles of nobility. Eliezer was also the model for Bolgarinov, the Jewish railroad magnate in *Anna Karenina*. Next door to the Polyakov residence, the two buildings flanking the garden entrance behind an iron fence at number 13 were Polyakov's Land Bank.

Around the corner at Malaya Bronnaya 2 is the building that housed the Jewish State Theater under the direction of Solomon Mikhoels. The yellow stone building is still used as a theater and a plaque on the facade identifies its Jewish past. Mikhoels was one of the leading theater figures of his time, and the Jewish State Theater (known as GOSET, from its Russian initials) performed everything from Sholom Aleichem to Shakespeare. One of the great theatrical events of the 1930s was seeing Mikhoels as King Lear. When Stalin liquidated the Jewish Anti-Fascist Committee he personally ordered Mikhoels's execution.

Just around the next corner on Bolshoye Bronnaya Street is the Polyakov Synagogue, a lime-colored stone building that the family erected as its own *shul*. Shut down in 1939, it was returned to Jewish auspices in 1990. Shortly after that a man came by with the original ark, which he had kept in his apartment for more than forty years. The Polyakov Synagogue was an object of struggle between Chabad, which now runs it, and Hineni, which plans to open a synagogue in a former Jewish school on Malaya Bronnaya. For information on Reform services and activities in the meantime, call 161-2998.

Just off Tverskaya, at Stankievicha 12, is an apartment building that was home to Moscow's leading Jewish artists in the 1920s and 1930s. You can peer in through the glass on the front door and see the Star of David pattern in the floor tiles. It was here that Marc Chagall painted scenery for the Jewish State Theater. Isaac Babel and Peretz Markish were frequent guests. The only private apartment in the building belonged to Mikhoels.

A bit off the beaten path but well worth the trip is the wooden Marina Roshcha Synagogue. Marina Roshcha ("Mary's Forest") was on Moscow's fringe in the 1890s, when thousands of Jews were expelled from the city. It was a poor neighborhood, which the police were loath to enter, with more than its share of beggars, thieves, and prostitutes. Given the times, Jews often found it easier to strike deals with the underworld than with the czarist authorities and many found refuge here.

It's a bit tricky to find, but the synagogue is off Obraztzova Street, at Vycheslavchev Pereulok 5-A. The big yard is strewn with large menorahs and broken-down cars. A big sign outside the building says in Rus-

Into the woods: The Marina Roshcha Synagogue, built by refugees from central Moscow

sian, "Prepare for the coming of the Messiah." The interior furnishings are nondescript but the groups of *hasidim*, young and old, studying around tables in the sanctuary look as if they come from a Roman Vishniac photograph of prewar Poland.

On a twist of the street before reaching the synagogue you'll see one of the wooden houses with ornate window decoration that was typical of Moscow until the nineteenth century.

Moscow has dozens of museums, but if there is time for only one it should be the Pushkin Museum of Fine Arts on Volkhonka Street. Its Egyptian, Greek, and Roman antiquities (some originals, some copies) and its array of French Impressionists are spectacular. Included in the collection are Picasso's *Old Jew with a Boy,* Louis Boulagré's *Trial of Solomon,* copies of Michelangelo's *Moses* and Donatello's *David*, as well as works by Chagall and Pissaro.

One sight not on many Moscow itineraries is Three-Stations Square surrounded by the St. Petersburg, Yaroslavl (Trans-Siberian), and Kazan railway stations. In an architecturally rich city, the stations are among the greatest gems, but they are also worth seeing for their exhibit of Russian life. In a nation with few restaurants, and where transit passengers don't bother with hotels, life is lived on station platforms.

If you recall the railroad-station scenes from the film of *Doctor Zhivago*, what you see in the stations of Moscow will look familiar.

Speaking of trains, one of the few lasting successes of communist enterprise is the Moscow metro. Several stations in the center of the system feature marble walls, mosaics and chandeliers. The man responsible for its construction was the only Jew in the Politburo who survived Stalin — Lazar Kaganovich. The subway system used to bear Kaganovich's name, but it was renamed in Lenin's honor. One suspects that like many streets and public institutions in Moscow, it will be renamed again.

Personalities: An expression of the 1920s summed up what people saw as the impact of Jews on their nation: "Tea of Wissotzky, sugar of Brodsky, Russia of Trotsky." The names referred to the Moscow importer, the Kiev sugar dealer, and the revolutionary leader chased out of Russia by Stalin.

Wissotsky not only sold tea, he also supported Zionism. The writer Ahad Ha'am was once manager of his company's London branch and his estate helped establish the Haifa Technion. Many other Moscow Jews have made their marks on Russia or on Russian-Jewish history. The writers Boris Pasternak, Ilya Ehrenburg, and Isaac Babel, the poets Osip Mandelstam and Peretz Markish, made their homes in Moscow. More recent literary figures include Anatoly Rybakov and Mark Razovsky. The leading Russian comedian is Arkady Raikin. Anatoly Shcharansky lived in Moscow (and was interrogated at KGB headquarters in Lubyanka Square), as did Yuli Kosharovsky, who was an underground Hebrew teacher for seventeen years and later led the Russian political party in Israel.

Two of Moscow's leading newspapers have Jewish editors. Igor Golembievski is editor of *Izvestia*, which, unlike *Pravda*, made a successful transition from Communist establishment to Western-style journalism. Vitaly Tretiakov is an editor of *Nezavisimaya*, one of the most prestigious papers born in the post-Communist era.

Perhaps the biggest fear among Russian

Jews today is the specter of Russian nationalism, and most Jews were shocked when Vice President Alexander Rutskoy, the leading nationalist in Boris Yeltsin's inner circle—and subsequently his arch rival—revealed that his mother was Jewish. Rutskoy is a former air force pilot who escaped from an Afghan prison camp and led the defense of Yeltsin's headquarters during the August 1991 coup. He said he felt a sense of Jewish awakening during a diplomatic mission to Israel.

Ilya Krichevsky was one of the three students killed during the coup. As surprised as Jews were to hear of Rutskoy's roots, they were perhaps more surprised when Krichevsky's funeral, with a rabbi saying *Kaddish*, was broadcast on Russian television.

Reading: The great Moscow Jewish novel has not yet been written, but there is a good deal of Moscow literature flavored with Jewish characters or written by Jewish authors. For a taste of the Jewish experience at its darkest under communism there is *The Testament* (Summit) by Elie Wiesel. Novels evocative of Moscow include Mikhail Bulgakov's *The Master and Margarita* (Fontana) and Anatoly Rybakov's *Children of the Arbat* (Little, Brown). General novels to put you in a Moscow frame of mind include Alexander Solzhenitsyn's *The First Circle* (Harper & Row), Martin Cruz Smith's *Gorky Park* and *Red Square* (Random House) and Boris Pasternak's *Doctor Zhivago* (Knopf).

Eating: Near the Kazan railway station is Gamburger, Moscow's first kosher restaurant, but one restaurant does not make a kosher paradise. For advice on finding a kosher meal call the Choral Synagogue.

Recommendations: The discomfort of traveling in Russia is overstated (unless you are on a special diet, you don't have to take your own food), but guides are essential for first timers. Learning Russian before your trip is a tall order, but a more feasible goal is learning the Cyrillic alphabet. Since most of the directional and commercial signs in Russia consist of simple words (a bakery sign is more likely to say "Bread" than "Try Our Fresh Rolls Daily") it's surprising how far you can go on a little knowledge.

For Jewish itineraries to the former Soviet Union, contact Alexander Smuckler (who once conducted Jewish tours in Moscow), at All Ways International, 5 Penn Plaza, Suite 102, New York, NY 10001. Even Smuckler's general information on travel in Russia seems more up-to-date than that of Intourist. Airline routes into and out of Moscow are changing as much as Russia itself. For reliable service that also ensures Western comfort until the last second, SAS is a solid bet. With planes taking so many Jews on one-way trips out of Russia, one wonders what they are carrying when they fly in. Perhaps Jewish organizations.

—Alan M. Tigay

Munich

Munich is a city blessed and cursed. For the city as a whole, the blessings seem to outweigh the curses. For the Jews of Munich, past and present, the opposite may be the case. But the Bavarian capital proves nothing if not the idea that Jews live and flourish even in the places of their worst memories.

While all of Germany's major cities were rebuilt and have prospered after World War II, only Munich was able to recapture, on a grand scale, the cultural and architectural grace of the pre-Nazi period. As an industrial center the city is, if anything, more important in modern Germany than it was before World War II. Though smaller than Berlin and Hamburg, it has become the most popular city in Germany for foreign visitors, and its world-class status was recognized when it was chosen as the site for the 1972 Olympics.

And therein lies the other side of the image. For Munich, aided by its environs, remains a symbol of much that has gone wrong in the world—the postwar world as well as Hitler's. It is the place where the Nazi movement got its start and it remains a linguistic symbol, thanks as much to Neville Chamberlain as to Adolf Hitler, of selling out the innocent. Since the war, it has been the locus of the worst reminders of Jewish vulnerability. At the 1972 Olympics Arab terrorists murdered eleven Israeli athletes. A few miles from the center of town is Dachau, the first Nazi concentration camp.

Though always few in number, Munich's Jews have been an integral part of the city and its history. To cite just one example, the quintessential Munich brand name is Löwenbräu; shortly after World War I, the Schüleins, longtime Jewish brewers, gained controlling interest of Löwenbräu and remained in charge until forced out by the Nazis in 1934. (When the first Schülein came to America, he founded Rheingold Brewery.) And today's Jewish community parallels the city's experience in one important respect. Though smaller than the prewar community it is, demographically, more important.

History: Jews first came to Bavaria in the tenth century, but for most of the last millennium they have lived in small, scattered communities of which Munich was, only recently, the most important. The first Jews came to settle along the trade routes to northeastern Germany, Hungary, and Russia, engaging in moneylending and the gold and silver trade.

The first reference to Jews in Munich is in the thirteenth century. For the next two hundred years the Jewish experience there followed a familiar European pattern. Jews were burned at the stake in Munich following a blood libel in 1285; were slaughtered during the Black Death in 1348–49; and suffered after a Host-desecration charge in 1413. In between these dates the community continually reconstituted itself and was granted varying degrees of privilege.

From the mid-fifteenth until the early eighteenth century Munich was, for the most part, without Jews. By the late 1600s, many of Germany's territorial princes were hiring court Jews, or *Hofjuden,* to run their financial affairs, and Wolf Wertheimer was the first court Jew brought to Munich. By 1750, there were 20 court Jews, and they formed a community.

By the nineteenth century, Jews were particularly prominent in the Bavarian livestock trade, and the Napoleonic era brought the first steps toward emancipation. But periodic anti-Jewish outbreaks and the 1848 revolution produced a disproportionate number of Bavarian Jewish émigrés; Levi Strauss and Adam Gimbel were two of many who made their fortunes in the New World.

Munich typifies the advantage German disunity held for Jews. When Jews were expelled from Spain, France, or England, they were banished from an entire country; when allowed to return after centuries they came as foreigners. When Jews were expelled from one of Germany's many independent cities, duchies, and bishoprics, however, they typically settled in a nearby town. If conditions changed, they could return easily. When tolerance spread in the eighteenth and nineteenth centuries, Jews left the villages and returned to the cities; because they had remained in Germany, they were prepared to participate immediately in German culture.

It was in 1872, the year after the birth of the German Reich, that full emancipation was achieved, but in the intervening years Munich's Jewish community grew gradually as restrictions were eased, and Jews from the villages moved to the city. From 450 in 1814, the community grew to 4,100 in 1880 and 9,000 in 1933.

In the late nineteenth and early twentieth centuries Jews were prominent in the arts, politics, and business. They were more equally represented in Bavarian politics than in other German states—after World War I, when Bavaria had a Soviet-style revolutionary government, it had a Jewish prime minister, Kurt Eisner. Munich was the home of Lion Feuchtwanger the historical novelist, and Katja Pringsheim, who married the writer Thomas Mann.

But Jewish prominence was short-lived. Eisner was assassinated in 1919 (his killer was of Jewish origin). Munich became the center of Nazi activity, the city where Hitler staged his *putsch* in 1923. Though the coup failed and Hitler went to prison, that same year most of the Eastern European Jews in Bavaria were expelled. In 1931, two years before Hitler came to power, Jewish ritual slaughter was banned in the state.

After the Nazis took power in 1933, the fate of Munich's Jews was much the same as that of the other Jews of Germany—harassment, arrests, discrimination, and boycotts. Nevertheless, the Jewish community itself experienced something of a religious and cultural resurgence amid the persecution. The main Munich synagogue was destroyed in June 1938, on Hitler's order, five months before *Kristallnacht*, the night on which synagogues were burned all over Germany. Still, the proportion of Jews who left Munich between 1933 and 1938—about 35 percent—was somewhat lower than in other cities, perhaps because other cities had larger proportions of foreign-born Jews who were either expelled or had weaker ties to Germany in the first place. During the war, 4,500 Munich Jews were deported to death camps, of whom about 300 survived. About 160 survived the war in Munich.

Community: If Munich's prewar Jewish community was more German than that of other German cities, its postwar community is less so. Most of the Eastern European Holocaust survivors who did not opt for Israel wanted to go to the United States, so they went to displaced persons camps in the American zone of occupation, the largest city of which was Munich. Some 120,000 Jews passed through Munich in the first years after the war and, inevitably, some stayed, leaving the city with the third largest Jewish community in the country, after Berlin and Frankfurt.

Most of those in today's community of 6,000 trace their roots to prewar Poland, Hungary, and Rumania. The bulk of the community are professionals—doctors, lawyers, professors—and there is a strong contingent of shopkeepers. Aside from a few who live in the vicinity of the Reichenbachstrasse synagogue, most of the city's Jews live in Nymphenburg, to the west; Schwabing, around the university; and Bogenhausen, east of the River Isar.

Sights: Munich has no predominantly Jewish neighborhood and no concentration of Jewish places of interest. Like the Jewish role in the city's history, the Jewish sights are interspersed, but it seems you can hardly find a major sight without its Jewish corner or connection.

The center of Munich is the Marienplatz, a mall marked by the gabled Old Town Hall and the Gothic New Town Hall, which also boasts the largest glockenspiel in Germany. Roughly where the parking lot of the Marienplatz stands (just north of the square) is where the Gruftgasse synagogue, built in the thirteenth century, once stood. No one is certain of the exact site of the synagogue, which was converted to a church after Jews were expelled in the fifteenth century. Nevertheless, for most of its history, Munich's Jewish life was concentrated within walking distance of the place.

A few blocks along Kaufingerstrasse, the pedestrian mall that extends west from Marienplatz, turn right on Herzog-Max Strasse and walk one block. At the corner of Maxburgstrasse, in a small park, is a stone monument, with a large menorah, marking the spot where Munich's main synagogue stood until June 1938. The monument bears an inscription from Psalm 74: "Remember this, how the enemy hath reproached the Lord."

Practically around the corner from the synagogue monument, in the courtyard at Lenbachplatz, is Joseph Henselmann's fountain-statue of Moses in the desert. Commissioned by the Munich city council, the sculpture presents an austere, bronze Moses holding a rod from which water pours forth into a pool below.

A few blocks south of the Marienplatz, in the yellow Radspielerhaus at Hackenstrasse 7, is where the German-Jewish poet Heinrich Heine lived in 1827–28. In Munich he worked as an editor and waited for a professorship that never came. A plaque marks his former home today.

The main center of Jewish activity in modern Munich is still no more than a ten-minute walk from the Marienplatz. At Reichenbachstrasse 27 is a building housing the Jewish Community Center, Munich's main synagogue, its community kosher restaurant and several Jewish organizations. The building was the site of the only Munich synagogue not completely destroyed on *Kristallnacht*; it was saved because of its proximity to the Gärtnerplatz Theater.

The outside of the building is nearly unidentifiable, partly for security reasons and partly because of a post-Nazi scourge. In 1970, a fire raged through the building, damaging not only the synagogue but also an old-age home on the premises; seven people died in the fire, which was caused by arson.

Past the reconstructed, modern exterior,

there is still an Old World feeling in the synagogue sanctuary, with its wooden benches, polished stone, and chandeliers with *Magen David* bases. Upstairs, the community center has periodic cultural events and lectures on topics of Jewish interest. (Some lectures are also held at Munich's Jewish book store, Literatur Handlung, at Fürstenstrasse 17.)

For information on prayer times and activities at the community center, call 201-4960. Munich's other functioning synagogues are at Georgenstrasse 71, in Schwabing; Possartstrasse 15, in Mittersendling; and Schulstrasse 30, in Neuhausen.

One of the essentials of any Munich tour is the Alte Pinakothek, one of the great art museums of Europe. The huge Venetian Renaissance building was erected for the art collection of the Wittelsbachs, the house that reigned in Bavaria from the twelfth to the early twentieth century. In the collection are several works on themes from the Hebrew Bible. Among those to look for are Rembrandt's *Sacrifice of Isaac,* Aert de Gelders' *Esther Before Going to Ahasuerus* and Simon Vouet's *Judith.*

Another stop on most itineraries is Nymphenburg Castle and Garden, the lavish summer home of the Wittelsbachs, built in the seventeenth and eighteenth centuries. In the south wing of the castle is the Gallery of Beauties, a collection of portraits, commissioned by King Ludwig I (1789–1868), of Bavaria's most beautiful women. Though the most famous in the collection is the dancer Lola Montez (who cost Ludwig his throne), it also contains one Jewish portrait, of Nanette Kaula, daughter of a family of court Jews, who married a cousin of Heinrich Heine.

Signs of more recent history can be seen in Schwabing, the area surrounding Ludwig-Maxmilian University. It was at Munich's university that one of the few anti-Nazi movements to surface during the war was based. Led by Hans and Sophie Scholl, and aided by Professor Kurt Huber, the White Rose movement included university and high school students. In 1942 and 1943 they distributed anti-Nazi leaflets, giving details of the Final Solution and reports on German battlefront reverses. The Scholls were caught placing leaflets in the university's main hall; they, Huber, and four others were beheaded.

Today, the main square of the university is named Professor-Huber-Platz on the east side and Geschwister-Scholl-Platz on the west side. In the southwest corner of the university's main lobby is a memorial plaque to the White Rose martyrs. In 1985, an opera based on the Scholls' activities was staged in the lobby; that same year, when President Ronald Reagan visited the German military cemetery at Bitburg, Franz Joseph Müller, a White Rose survivor (and now a retired judge), organized a counterdemonstration at the Scholls' graves. He later set up, with the American Jewish Congress, a White Rose Foundation to foster understanding between Germans and American Jews and to teach people about German resistance to Hitler.

A few miles from Schwabing is Munich's Olympiapark which was, in 1972, the scene of the greatest Jewish triumph and the worst Jewish tragedy in the history of sport. Within hours after Mark Spitz, the American Jewish swimmer, won his seventh gold medal, Arab terrorists invaded the Israeli Olympic apartment. They killed two Israeli athletes on the spot and nine later during a shoot-out with German police at a military airport.

Though most of the apartments in the Olympiapark became private condominiums after the games, the Israeli complex became a guest house of the Max Planck Institute for Scientific Research. A memorial to the eleven Israeli athletes stands in front of the apartment at Connollystrasse 31, and the small stones placed in remembrance on top of the memorial offer quiet testimony to the many visitors to the site.

Dachau:
No one should visit Munich without going to Dachau, fourteen miles to the northwest. Dachau was the first Nazi concentration camp, opened less than two months after Hitler came to power in 1933. It was a camp for all the groups Hitler regarded as undesirable—Jews, Gypsies, political opponents, and anti-Nazi clergy. Though it was not designed as an extermination camp—those would come later— arbitrary killings and mass executions, medical experiments, illness, and hunger resulted in what the museum's brochure describes as "continual extermination."

The camp's former laundry and supply rooms today house a museum that documents what happened at Dachau, the rise of Nazism, and the implementation of the plan to exterminate the Jews. Relying on photographs and camp artifacts, the exhibit is a chilling chronicle of the worst chapter in both Jewish and German history. Though the barracks were dismantled after the war, two have been reconstructed as they were when Dachau was in operation. In the back of the camp grounds are the buildings which housed the crematoria, the gallows, the gas chambers (built near the end of the war and never used) and a necropolis, marked by *Magen Davids* and crosses, dedicated simply "to thousands" who died in the camp.

Also in the back of the campgrounds are three chapels: Catholic, Protestant, and Jewish. The Jewish chapel is built below ground to symbolize the underground life of Jews under Nazi rule. Though it is visible through a gate even when closed, it seems to keep irregular hours.

Be warned on visiting Dachau that even the most dispassionate observers, people long familiar with the evidence of the Holocaust, are affected by the place. Though the Germans who work and lead tours there are, by definition, those most involved in bearing witness, there is a fascinating dynamic, filled with tension, that develops between Jewish visitors and the Germans they encounter there.

Side Trips:
If Munich has been the center of Jewish life in Bavaria for the past 150 years, an older concentration of Jewish communities was one hundred miles to the north, in Franconia (which became part of Bavaria in the early nineteenth century). Along the Romantic Road lies Rothenburg-ob-der-Tauber, a walled town—virtually unchanged since the sixteenth century—of Gothic, Renaissance, and half-timbered houses on narrow streets. The town was an important center of Jewish learning during the Middle Ages. The community's most renowned scholar was Rabbi Meir ben Baruch of Rothenburg, who in the thirteenth century attracted students from all over

Bearing witness: Dachau's museum and reconstructed barracks present a chilling chronicle of the worst chapter in both Jewish and German history

Europe; more of his responsa survive today than those of any other medieval authority.

Kapellenplatz, one block east of Rothenburg's town hall, was the site of a ghetto until 1390. The synagogue stood in what is now the plaza's parking area, about halfway between the fountain and the end of the square. Kapellenplatz, which means Chapel Square, takes its name from the Chapel of St. Mary, which replaced the synagogue and was itself torn down in 1804; it was the tradition for churches that replaced synagogues to be named for the mother of Jesus because of her recognized Jewishness. The building at Kapellenplatz 10 was a Talmud Torah and the green postwar building on the square is on the site of the town's first Jewish Dance House, as the JCCs of medieval Germany were sometimes known.

The White Tower around the corner from Kapellenplatz was part of the city's twelfth-century fortifications. Attached to the tower is a salmon-colored half-timbered building. This was the Jewish Dance House (Judentanzhaus) from 1390 to 1520. Destroyed during World War II, it was faithfully reconstructed in 1953. A low stone wall around the garden in front of the dance house has imbedded in it Jewish tombstones dating from the thirteenth century. In front of the garden wall is the beginning of the Judengasse. Most of the buildings on the narrow street date from the thirteenth and fourteenth centuries, making it perhaps the best preserved Jewish ghetto in Germany.

The Reichsstadt Muscum at Klosterhof 5 has a small Judaica collection, mostly from the nineteenth and twentieth centuries, as well as more than two dozen Jewish tombstones from the thirteenth and fourteenth centuries and a stone monument commemorating a pogrom in 1298.

Schopfloch is also on the Romantic Road, but it attracts fewer tourists than Rothenburg. If it lacks medieval charm, it is nonetheless rich in Jewish connections. Schopfloch was one of the towns that always welcomed Jews when they were expelled from other places. It had a Jewish mayor in the eighteenth century. Homes built by Jews are easily identified by the extra notch that juts down from the apex of the typical Franconian roof. Facing each other on the village's main street (just around the turn from the Town Hall) are an eighteenth-century Jewish school building and the site of the synagogue destroyed in 1938; both are marked with memorial plaques.

But the most important Jewish connection in Schopfloch is not visual but audial. A dialect peculiar to the village is peppered with words of Hebrew origin introduced by Jews, who at one time constituted half the population. Though there hasn't been a Jewish resident in fifty years, and the height of Jewish settlement was long before that, some older Schopflochers still refer to water as *mayemm,* to a home as a *bayes,* to bread as *laechemm,* and to their hometown as their *medine.* These are just a few of the dozens of words in the language locals call Lachoudish, a contraction of *lashon kodesh.* Though Lachoudish is known mostly by the village's oldest residents, Mayor Hans-Rainer Hofmann heads a movement to keep it alive. About seventy groups a year—mainly from Israel—come to see, and hear, the village.

Though it lacks Schopfloch's linguistic connections, Fürth is in some ways a larger version of the village—a city that took in Jews when other cities kicked them out. It admitted most of the Jews from neighboring Nuremberg when they were expelled in 1499, and by the eighteenth century the community had privileges virtually unique in a German city: they could build as many synagogues as they wanted, they could admit Jews from outside without asking permission, and they had representatives on the city council. Jews founded the city's first hospital in 1653 and the first Jewish orphanage in the country in 1763. In the nineteenth century some of the city's churches and synagogues exchanged choirs on Jewish and Christian festivals.

The community began to decline in the early nineteenth century when Franconia was incorporated into Bavaria, which placed more restrictions on Jews. Many then emigrated to America, though some headed for Berlin. One native of Fürth was Julius Ochs, whose son, Adolph, became owner and publisher of *The New York Times.* Another native was Leopold Ullstein, whose position in Berlin publishing paralleled that of Ochs. The city's most famous twentieth-century son is Henry Kissinger.

Fürth's contemporary Jewish community numbers fewer than 100, mostly elderly. The restored synagogue at Hallemannstrasse 2 is the same stone building that was the Jewish orphanage in the eighteenth century. Up the street at Blumenstrasse 31 is the Jewish Community Center (telephone 770-879). Nearby, at Mathildenstrasse 24, is where Kissinger lived as a child. Across the street from Kissinger's house (on Theaterstrasse) is an apartment house in which many elderly Jews live; the building is the former Jewish hospital, which functioned until 1942.

Geleitsgasse was a Jewish activity center before World War II, with four synagogues. In Geleitsgasse square, just off Königstrasse, is a modern memorial to the prewar Jewish community. Under the building at Königstrasse 89, which was home to generations of the same Jewish family from 1600 to 1880, archeologists have found a *mikveh.* The city plans to turn it into a museum of Jewish life and history in Middle Franconia. There is also a four-hundred-year-old Jewish cemetery on Schlehenstrasse.

Closer to Munich, thirty-five miles west, is the old Roman city of Augsburg, renowned for its cathedral, complete with stained-glass windows depicting biblical prophets and kings in the headgear imposed on Jews by the popes. The domed synagogue, destroyed on *Kristallnacht,* was rededicated in 1985, after a $2-million renovation. The Oriental and Art Nouveau building was reconstructed to look the way it did when it opened in 1917. The synagogue contains an exhibit of Jewish ritual objects from the Bavarian State Museum in Munich. The synagogue and community center are at Halderstrasse 8 (telephone 51-79-85).

Reading: Two of Lion Feuchtwanger's novels capture parts of Bavaria's history most relevant to Jews. *Jew Suss* (Carroll and Gras) is a novel based on the life of an eighteenth-century court Jew; the Nazis appropriated the story and turned it into an anti-Semitic propaganda film in 1939. *Success* (Viking) is set in 1920s Munich. Two recent books on the White Rose are *Shattering the German Night* by Annette

E. Dumbach and Jud Newborn (Little, Brown) and *A Noble Treason* by Richard Hanser (Putnam).

Recommendations: The German National Tourist Office (122 East 42nd Street, New York, NY 10168; 212-661-7200) is well versed in the Jewish as well as the general sights of Bavaria and offers detailed brochures as well as handling telephone inquiries. The Grand Hotel Continental offers luxury and charm in the heart of Munich and is in walking distance from many of the Jewish sights, including the Reichenbachstrasse synagogue. In a series of walks you can see evidence of all Munich's Jewish history—the curses and the blessings.

—Alan M. Tigay

Nairobi

Trivia: Where can you find the world's most beautiful synagogue garden? What country did Theodor Herzl consider as a Jewish homeland besides Palestine? Where was Yitzhak Shamir imprisoned by the British? The answer to all three questions is Kenya.

History: It almost was the Jewish homeland. Though most people picture wildlife and safaris when they think of Kenya, in 1903, fourteen years before the Balfour Declaration, the British Foreign Office offered to the Zionist movement a vast tract of fertile East African highlands to populate as an autonomous Jewish colony. Herzl warmed to the suggestion of Kenya as the new Zion and, expecting the World Zionist Congress to follow suit, a dozen Russian Jews who had made their way to South Africa decided to trek the additional distance north — to the rich Uasin Gishu Plateau in what then belonged to the Uganda Protectorate but now is part of Kenya. They had intended to move in as Canaan's founding settlers, only to discover on their arrival that Colonial Secretary Joseph Chamberlain's gift had in fact been declined.

The British may have been motivated by the desire to help Jews during a period of pogroms in Russia, but they were also interested in attracting settlers to develop a colonial outpost with great potential; in short — to echo a canard that would be heard generations later — they wanted to use Jews as tools of imperialism. Herzl's plan was tactical; he saw Kenya as a step to a Jewish home in Palestine, not a replacement. He wanted to provide quick assistance to masses of Jews on the verge of leaving Russia, prevent them from dispersing to dozens of countries, and establish political ties with the British which could be of use later on. But he misjudged the Russians in the Zionist movement, who adamantly opposed even a tactical deviation from the plan to funnel all efforts into *Eretz Israel.*

Most of the pioneering spirits who went to Kenya thinking the plan would be approved returned to South Africa. Abraham Block, however, stayed on — farming, trading, cattle ranching, speculating where and when he could. (Block would one day become Kenya's Conrad Hilton, owning nine hotels, including the classic Norfolk Hotel in Nairobi and the Mawingo Hotel in Nanyuki, which William Holden later purchased and renamed the Mount Kenya Safari Club.) Eventually Block brought his family over from Lithuania, and a wife from Palestine. Along with other Jewish colonists who, hoping to find their fortune in Africa, had drifted in over the years, he "begat" Nairobi's Jewish community.

Timberwork is all that remains of the first synagogue, built by 19 Jewish families in 1913 when Nairobi was an infant town of red dust and papyrus swampland. Although South Africa and Zimbabwe would attract sizable Jewish populations, Kenya's community would always be small by comparison.

Still, it was influential. Lawyers, doctors, architects, hoteliers, traders, and businessmen have always been counted among its Jewish inhabitants and, in the late 1950s, when the Jewish community was at its peak of 1,000, the president of the Board of Kenya Jewry, Israel Somen, was elected Nairobi's mayor.

The greatest influx of Jews into Kenya arrived immediately after World War II. Mostly Holocaust survivors, these Central European Jews moved to the Great Rift

Valley (where Louis Leakey discovered most of his finds of early man), settling around the town of Nakuru where, as coffee and crop farmers, they worked the luxuriant land. The Nakuru synagogue no longer exists, but in the Nakuru cemetery a Holocaust memorial plaque still stands.

A less permanent group of Jews who spent time in Kenya were the members of the Irgun Zva'i Leumi and Lohamei Herut Israel, including future Prime Minister Yitzhak Shamir. Captured by the British, they were sent by train to Kenya in March 1947, and imprisoned in the town of Gilgil. Though several escaped, most remained behind bars until Israel's independence. Today the detention camp at the foot of the Knayamwe Hills serves as an army barracks and can only be visited with government permission.

In 1963, when the sun set on Britain's East African empire, colonial administrators — Jews among them — returned to London, and some whose families had come to Kenya as refugees headed for Israel. But others have come in, including Jews working for the UN or other international organizations and Israelis working on government contracts.

Prior to the 1973 Yom Kippur War, Israel and Kenya had especially strong political and economic ties. Although in 1973 Kenya, like most African countries, severed diplomatic relations with Israel, trade ties continued, and diplomatic ties were eventually restored. Israel helped establish Kenya's School for Social Workers in Machakos, and numerous Israeli agricultural and irrigation experts assisted in various development projects.

Two Israeli construction companies, Solel Boneh and H and Zed, have between them built much of modern Kenya — highways, water supply projects, pipelines, airstrips, housing and office buildings, government ministries — and continue to do so. Kenya has also been one of the prime locations of Hadassah's medical work in Africa, including one of the most extraordinary surgical stories of the era. In April 1990 a team of ophthalmologists from Hadassah Hospital in Jerusalem set up a field hospital near Nakuru and, over the course of three days, performed four hundred operations on blind people (mostly for cataracts and glaucoma) of all ages from the towns and villages of Kenya's Rift Valley; when it was over, 98 percent of the patients could see.

Community: Though Israeli–Kenyan diplomacy has fluctuated with the political barometer, the government of President Daniel arap Moi maintained unofficial links with Israel even during the time of Israel's greatest isolation and today has among the closest ties to Israel of any African regime. Many Kenyans study in Israel, participating in programs in labor, cooperatives, soil management, and the like, while a transient community of several hundred Israelis, most of whom work for Israeli companies, small-scale industries, or in private enterprise, lives in Nairobi. These Israelis make up a large portion of Kenya's Jewish population of 600.

Sights: Originally built as the British Protectorate headquarters, an "irreputable place in the sun for shady people" (at least for the immigrant population) in the 1920s and 1930s, Nairobi is a bustling urban center today with nearly a million people and all the problems of most third-world capitals.

Slum communities lie adjacent to neighborhoods with elegant villas, modern architectural wonders tower above sprawling poverty. One of the world's poorer nations, Kenya is also one of the most prosperous in Africa. Full of contradictions, Nairobi is always interesting, and its languid pace should be enjoyed.

Members of the Jewish community uphold the Jewish traditions, and services are held Friday evenings and *Shabbat* mornings in the Nairobi Hebrew Congregation, built in 1955. The white brick synagogue, in the center of Nairobi at the corner of University Way and Uhuru Highway, features the Tablets of the Law at the apex of its tentlike roof. It also has stained-glass windows and pieces of wood from the old temple decorating the entranceway.

The Nairobi synagogue also claims distinction as the synagogue with the most beautiful garden in the world. Sharing the landscape of jacaranda and flame trees, hibiscus, and other flowering bushes and plants is the synagogue's Vermont Memo-

Hibiscus and jacaranda: Far from the major centers of Jewish life, Nairobi lays claim to the world's most beautiful synagogue garden

rial Hall, a community center where religious classes, social events, and Israeli celebrations are held.

The pace of a bygone era is in evidence at the elegant stone-built Norfolk Hotel which, since opening its doors in 1904, has served as home for romantics and adventurers. It is also a landmark to the Jewish presence in Kenya, a fact that has not been lost on Israel's enemies. Abraham Block, who by the 1920s had been involved in nearly every sort of adventure—including a spell in jail for having sold a cow improperly—purchased the Norfolk in 1924, and it remained in his family for more than sixty years.

Block and, later, his sons Jack and Tubby played host to the wild happenings and mischief of royalty, heads of state, visiting dignitaries, authors (Hemingway stayed there during his Kilimanjaro days), celebrities, and notorieties alike. Over the years, the family expanded its holdings into a hotel empire, purchasing the New Stanley Hotel in the center of Nairobi; the world-renowned forest lodge, Treetops, in the

reserve at Nyeri; and the Nyali Beach Hotel at the coastal resort town of Mombasa. His holdings also included Samburu Game Lodge, in the most northerly of the popular parks, and the Keekorok Lodge, in what is considered Kenya's finest park, the Masai Mara Game Reserve, where elephants, lions, rhinoceros, buffalo, and leopards all abound.

On New Year's Eve 1981, Arab terrorists blew up the dining wing of the Norfolk, killing sixteen people and injuring more than a hundred. Since restored to its grandeur, the Norfolk, with its covered verandas and garden cottages, reigns as the grande dame of Nairobi. A few years later, the Block family, which had already divested its other hotels, sold the Norfolk to the Lonrho chain.

Most visitors to Kenya, whether heading for Nairobi or straight to one of its thirty-seven protected wildlife areas, begin their safari at Nairobi's Jomo Kenyatta International Airport. The airport stands as a symbol of Kenya's cooperation with Israel even when there were no official diplomatic ties. While there are no telltale signs, it was here that the Israeli rescue mission stopped to refuel on its way home from Entebbe on July 4, 1976.

Two other Nairobi landmarks—the Kenyatta International Conference Center and the beautiful University of Nairobi—have a place in recent Jewish history. In 1985, the last in a decade-long series of UN-sponsored conferences on the status of women took place in Nairobi. Though most of the conferences had been characterized by resolutions attacking Israel and equating Zionism with racism, the Nairobi conference marked a turning point. Third-world delegations, led by Kenya's, resisted Arab pressure to focus on Israel and chose to discuss real women's issues, even when the discussions included Israelis. Government delegations met at the Kenyatta center while nongovernment organizations met at the university.

General Sights: Hunting is banned in Kenya's wildlife areas, but countless exotic species can be captured with the camera lens. It is only a short hike from the center of town to Nairobi National Park—a fine introduction to the wildlife and game runs to come. At the front of the park is the Animal Orphanage, where stray animals are brought and sick ones cared for. Safaris to the game parks in and around Nairobi, and to anywhere in the country, can be easily arranged in advance of your trip or after you arrive.

The Nairobi National Museum has the finest collection of fossils from Leakey's anthropological finds, as well as many original artifacts from Kenya's more than fifty tribes. Nearby is Snake Park, and every afternoon, traditional dances can be seen at Bomas of Kenya, one kilometer from the park off Langatta Road.

For those who prefer more down-to-earth entertainment, Sunday is racing day at the Nairobi Horse Club, with what must be the loveliest track in the world. Nairobi's casino is noted for more than gambling; inside the antique wood-paneled "den," beneath its whirling paddle fans, a bit of the British Empire somehow endures.

Reading: A good read that captures the transition years between colonialism and independence is Barbara Wood's novel *Green City in the Sun* (Doubleday). *The Lunatic Express* by Charles Miller (Macmillan) tells the story of the building of the six-hundred-mile railway across Queen Victoria's Africa and includes a section on the British plan to establish the Jewish nation in Kenya. More difficult to locate is *The Jews of Nairobi* by Julius Carlebach. Had Kenya become the Jewish homeland, such a book might have been in greater demand.

Recommendations: Kosher restaurants are not to be found in Nairobi, but all of the hotels offer salad bars, and many of the city's Indian restaurants have vegetarian menus. Among popular Indian restaurants favored by Nairobi Jews are those of the Minar chain (which has branches in the YaYa Centre and the Sarit Centre). The Tamarind on Harambee Avenue is good for fish. For traditional African cuisine try the Tuesday or Friday lunch at the Fairview Hotel.

The Fairview is now Nairobi's only Jewish-owned hotel. Owned and operated by Charles Szlapak, the synagogue's former *rosh kehillah* (only President Moi is permitted to use the title president), it is also a bargain compared with the hotels of the great international chains. Less than a mile from the city center, off Bishops Road, the hotel and its five acres of gardens offer the atmosphere of a residential country inn. Eliana Szlapak, Charles's mother, reputedly makes the best borscht as well as the best homemade cream cheese in all of East Africa. It's not the Jewish homeland, but it feels like a Jewish home.

—*Debra Weiner*

New Orleans

New Orleans is really two cities. On the one hand, it's a world-class tourist spot with Creole and Cajun culture, Mardi Gras and the French Quarter, Antoine's and pralines; a city of quaint street names, Dixieland jazz, and legends of decadence and pleasure. But New Orleans is also a major mercantile and maritime center, where an affluent and generous citizenry has filled its streets with art and architecture, schools and museums, libraries and parks. Though they are few, New Orleans Jews have lavished money, energy, and ingenuity on their city. For over 150 years, Jews have helped make New Orleans not only a good place to visit, but also a good place to live.

History: New Orleans was established by the French in 1718 and seesawed between French and Spanish rule until France sold Louisiana to the United States in 1803. In the 1750s, Jews began to arrive from the Caribbean, the first recorded Jew in the city being Isaac Rodríguez Monsanto. Monsanto's presence was technically illegal under the Code Noire, which barred Jews from the French colonies; when Louisiana was under a more restrictive Spanish regime from 1776 to 1800, there is no evidence of a Jewish presence at all.

Newport-born Judah Touro arrived in the sweltering bayous shortly before the Louisiana Purchase. He did what any enterprising Yankee might have done. He went into the ice business — and many other commodities as well. His beneficence to all is legendary. Besides a hospital and gifts to Jewish and non-Jewish congregations, he willed the city money to beautify Canal Street, which, in the 1850s, was briefly renamed Touro Street. Another early arrival was Ezekiel Salomon, son of the American Revolutionary patriot Haym Sa-

lomon, who was governor of the United States Bank in New Orleans from 1816 to 1821.

Touro was wounded in the Battle of New Orleans in the War of 1812, the same battle and war that elevated pirate Jean Laffite to patriot. Scholars are undecided whether to believe a purported memoir by Laffite, published belatedly in the 1950s, claiming he was reared by his Converso grandmother. He also claimed never to have been a pirate. In any case, he is New Orleans's greatest folk hero. Another legend is Adah Isaacs Menken, born in a suburb of New Orleans in the 1830s. She was one of the leading American actresses of the nineteenth century, as well as a poet. An attractive woman who was a practicing Jew, she now and then scandalized her public. Her relationships with Swinburne and Dumas père were well-known.

The first Jewish congregation, Gates of Mercy (Shaarei Hesed), was founded in 1828 and later merged with another to become the present Touro Synagogue. Of today's eight congregations, five were founded before 1900 and one in 1904. It was also in 1828 that Judah P. Benjamin arrived to begin a career that led to the United States Senate and, eventually, to his appointment as secretary of state for the Confederacy. During the occupation of New Orleans, feisty Eugenia Levy Phillips was imprisoned for laughing during a funeral procession for a Union soldier and Rabbi James K. Gutheim chose to leave New Orleans rather than sign the oath of allegiance to the Union.

Yellow fever decimated the local population at frequent intervals. In 1853, 137 Jews succumbed. As a direct result, New Orleans Jewry founded one of the first Jewish orphanages in the United States. The Touro

Infirmary, today a leading medical teaching and research center and a constituent agency of the New Orleans Federation, dates from the same period. In 1881 New Orleans Jews settled more than 150 newly arrived Russian immigrants in Sicily Island, Louisiana — the first in a series of American Jewish agricultural experiments. These poor victims of the czar now found themselves in mosquito-ridden isolation, replete with rattlesnakes and disease, with little drinking water and with former slave quarters for housing. When the Mississippi flooded a few months later, the experiment was over. Despite that effort (or perhaps because of it), New Orleans was largely bypassed by the most of the mass Eastern European Jewish immigration, which made the Jewish community by the early twentieth century predominantly native born, of German origin, and Reform.

A historic moment occurred in December 1949 when Rabbi Julian Feibelman of Temple Sinai opened the doors of his synagogue to the first integrated audience in New Orleans. Two thousand blacks and whites sat down together to hear Ralph Bunche of the United Nations, who had been denied a public hall for the meeting.

Community: There are about 12,000 Jews among approximately 1 million New Orleanians. The Jewish population is slowly increasing. Slightly more than half of New Orleans Jews live within the city limits, mainly in the Uptown area that lies between the Garden District and Tulane University; there is a smaller enclave in the Lakefront area. However, there's a growing movement to suburban Metairie, where the young, upwardly mobile families are heading. Metairie is also the locale of a Conservative congregation (Tikvat Shalom, at 3737 West Esplanade Avenue), the Orthodox Young Israel congregation (4141 West Esplanade Avenue), and the Reform Gates of Prayer (4000 West Esplanade Avenue).

New Orleans Jews have always gotten along quite well with their non-Jewish neighbors. Today, the only time there's a problem is at Mardi Gras. Jews (and many others) are excluded from the three or four most socially prominent "krewes," the clubs that sponsor balls and parades. Not that the carnival is so important, but the dining clubs associated with those krewes are also closed to Jews, and that's where important business transactions occur. It doesn't matter that these clubs, the Boston and the Pickwick, had Jewish members in the nineteenth century — or that the first king of Mardi Gras was a Jew. That was in 1872, when Louis J. Salomon, great-grandson of Haym Salomon, became the first carnival Rex. Apart from this, Mardi Gras today is enjoyed by all. The biggest extravaganza is the Bacchus parade which does have large Jewish participation.

New Orleans has provided an example of cooperation between African-Americans and American Jews, with predominantly black Dillard University serving as a forum for dialogue. The sense of common ground intensified during the 1992 gubernatorial campaign of former Ku Klux Klan leader David Duke.

Sights: The two best ways to see New Orleans as a tourist are to walk through the French Quarter and to ride one of the St. Charles streetcars. Places of Jewish interest in the French Quarter include the Hermann-Grima House, 820 St. Louis Street, built in 1831 by Samuel Hermann, a Jewish commission merchant of substantial importance. Open to the public and on the National Register of Historic Places, Hermann-Grima has fine antiques, an inner courtyard, and a separate kitchen house — all restored.

At 900–910 Royal Street, the Miltenberger Mansions were built by a wealthy Jewish widow in 1838 for her three sons. Their descendants became Catholic, but one married Michael Heine, who remained a Jew and who was a cousin of poet Heinrich Heine. Michael's daughter Alice, raised a Catholic, became the first American Princess of Monaco, when she married Prince Albert.

The Historic New Orleans Collection at 533 Royal has within its private collection several items of Jewish interest. Enter the interior courtyard and you will find a plaque, in English and Hebrew, commemorating Judah Touro's gift of a vacated church to a Jewish congregation in 1850. In the library, ask to see two rare books on the history of Jews of New Orleans that date from 1903 and 1905.

Nearby, at 540 Royal, is Nahan Galleries which features, among its general display, several Jewish artists including Théo Tobiasse, Leonardo Neirman, Yaacov Agam, Marc Chagall, and Shalom of Safed. The gallery has also cosponsored numerous exhibits with local and out-of-town Jewish organizations.

On Chartres Street, facing Jackson Square, you will find the Louisiana State Museum, where the New Orleans Tourist Office is now located. The museum includes both the Cabildo at 701 Chartres and the Presbytère at 713 Chartres, where there are galleries devoted to the history of the area, including artifacts pertaining to Judah P. Benjamin and Judah Touro. Both extremely important historically, the Cabildo and Presbytère date from 1795. The Cabildo housed the Spanish municipal government and later was the site of the signing of the Louisiana Purchase agreement. The Presbytère, originally built as a rectory, became instead a city courthouse.

The St. Charles streetcars will take you from the French Quarter through the Garden District and uptown to the campus of Tulane. The streetcars, now a National Historic Landmark, run around the clock. (It is, by the way, the only remaining streetcar line in the city; the streetcar named Desire is now a bus.) On the St. Charles route you will pass many of the homes and institutions, past and present, of New Orleans Jews. Before you reach the Garden District, at Lee Circle, you will catch a close view of the Crescent City Connection Bridge, the only bridge spanning the river from within the city limits. The bridge was opened in 1958 thanks to the efforts of Captain Neville Levy, a Jewish shipbuilder who became chairman of the Mississippi River Bridge Commission.

Touro Synagogue, the Byzantine structure that houses the sixth-oldest Jewish congregation in the United States (and the oldest outside the thirteen original colonies) is at 4338 St. Charles Avenue. The building, designed by a leading Jewish architect, Emile Weil, opened in 1909, and houses items from the congregation's earlier homes, including an ark given by Judah

Touro in the 1840s. In addition to its Greek-appointed sanctuary, Touro is also noted for its formal garden.

At 5120 St. Charles, the Milton H. Latter Public Library honors a Jewish World War II hero killed on Okinawa and is a gift to the city by his family. The beautiful mansion was built in 1907 by Marks Isaacs, a Jew who owned a department store — and one of the city's first autos. Two blocks farther uptown is the Jewish Community Center, at 5342 St. Charles. This full-service center, built in the 1950s, is on the site of the former Jewish orphanage. When you visit the JCC, cross the street and walk two blocks toward the lake on Jefferson to the Newman School. Founded in 1903 by Isidore Newman as a manual training school for children of the Jewish orphanage, Newman today is regarded by many as the best college preparatory school in the south.

Continuing toward Tulane, just off St. Charles at 1630 Arabella, is a private home, dating from the 1840s, that once belonged to Judah P. Benjamin and was used by the Union Army as a hospital during the Civil War.

At 6227 St. Charles is Temple Sinai, New Orleans's first Reform congregation. Like the Touro Synagogue, Sinai is a domed Byzantine structure, and its building was completed in 1927. Outside, the building features a frieze of the Ten Commandments and three sets of bronze double doors decorated with biblical themes. The sanctuary has stained-glass windows on three sides — with biblical and ritual symbols on the side walls and the twelve tribes of Israel behind the main balcony. The Julian Feibelman Chapel includes a tapestry sculpture made by the women in the congregation and two stained-glass windows made from windows salvaged from a former Sinai building.

Temple Sinai is also known for its Barbara Weintraub Collection of Art, which has works by Marc Chagall, Shlomo Katz, Chaim Gross, Jakob Steinhardt, and Louise Nevelson. The collection, which goes beyond Jewish themes, also includes prints by Picasso and Miró. The collection is open during Friday evening and Saturday morning services and from 9:00 A.M. to 5:00

P.M. Monday through Friday. Call the synagogue at (504) 861-3693 for further details.

Tulane University begins at 6400 St. Charles. At St. Charles and Audubon Place stands the president's mansion, a magnificent example of classical revival architecture. This was the home of Samuel Zemurray who gave this and many other gifts to Tulane. The third-floor ballroom with its Aeolian organ was the locale for parties attended by Jewish teens in bygone days. Doris Hall at Newcomb College (part of Tulane) was provided by Zemurray in honor of his daughter. Zemurray arrived in this country penniless. Soon after, when he noticed large quantities of bananas rotting in port, he went into the banana business and eventually became the head of United Fruit.

Walk down Audubon Place from St. Charles and at the corner of Freret is the Howard Tilton Memorial Library. The archives of the Southern Jewish Historical Society are there as well as records of the New Orleans Port of Entry. For information about the archives and about the Judaic Studies program on campus, contact Professor Alan Avery-Peck of the Jewish Studies department (504-865-5349).

Personalities: One of the nineteenth century's leading concert pianists and composers was a Jewish native of New Orleans, Louis Moreau Gottschalk. Jews associated with New Orleans in this century include Martin Behrman, mayor of the city from 1904 to 1920; Allan Jaffe, founder of Preservation Hall, the great Jazz Center in the French Quarter; and Joe Cahn, who heads the New Orleans School of Cooking in the city's remodeled Jackson Brewery. Two Jewish daughters of New Orleans who made their marks elsewhere are Lillian Hellman and Kitty Carlisle.

Culture: One hundred twenty miles north of New Orleans in the little town of Utica, Mississippi, is the Museum of the Southern Jewish Experience, a unique outpost that is to dying small-town Southern Jewish culture as the *genizah* was to synagogues of old. The museum is situated amid fields of soybeans and cotton on the grounds of the Henry S. Jacobs Camp, which draws kids from Reform congregations between New Orleans and Memphis. Its collection ranges from small ritual objects and photographs, to Torahs and stained-glass windows, to a fully functioning sanctuary made up of pieces from synagogues in Vicksburg and Greenwood, Mississippi. Also under the museum's direction is the one hundred-year-old Greek Byzantine synagogue in Port Gibson, Mississippi, and it hopes to purchase and restore the former home of Judah P. Benjamin in New Orleans. Far off the beaten path, the museum doesn't keep regular hours. Write to director Marcy Cohen at PO Box 16528, Jackson, MS 39236-6042, or call (601) 362-6357 to schedule a visit.

Back in New Orleans, adult education lectures and series are offered by the synagogues, the JCC, and the Tulane Jewish Studies program. There are weekend seminars for adults at the Jacobs Camp in Utica, sponsored by the Union of American Hebrew Congregations.

The Klezmania Jewish Music Orchestra performs for public and private events, as does a local folk dance troupe offering Israeli dance concerts. For details of events, call the JCC, at (504) 897-0143, or look at the biweekly *Jewish Voice*, available at the JCC or New Orleans Federation office at 1539 Jackson Avenue (504-525-0673).

General Sights: The New Orleans Museum of Art was founded seventy-five years ago and was known until recently as the Isaac Delgado Museum of Art, named for its original benefactor, a Jewish sugar merchant. The museum is open Tuesday through Sunday at Lelong Avenue in City Park (504-488-2631).

Longue Vue House and Gardens is the eight-acre estate of the late philanthropists Edgar B. Stern, a cotton broker, and his wife, Edith Rosenwald Stern, daughter of Sears, Roebuck founder Julius Rosenwald—both renowned for their philanthropy. A silver *mezuzah* adorns the estate's front doorway though, as many visitors note, it is on the wrong side. Other than family portraits, there is nothing else specifically Jewish inside, but if you enjoy seeing estates and gardens, or want to see how a prominent New Orleans Jewish family lived, by all means visit this nationally recognized showcase. The architecture is classical revival and the yellow garden is especially striking. Longue Vue is open daily except Mondays at 7 Bamboo Road in Metairie (telephone 504-488-5488).

A treat that won't cost much is breakfast of beignets and coffee at the Café du Monde in the French Quarter. An outing that doesn't cost anything is the Algiers Ferry at the foot of Poydras Street; take your car with you across the Mississippi.

Lagniappe (New Orleanese for an extra treat): No visit to New Orleans can be complete without considering food. Unfortunately, there is no formal New Orleans-style kosher restaurant. But you are in luck if you can find a copy of Mildred L. Covert and Sylvia P. Gerson's *Kosher Creole Cookbook* (Pelican). There are recipes for Oysters Mock-a-Feller (made with gefilte fish), Cuzzin Caledonia's Chicken-Fried Steak, and Baleboosteh's Bouillabaisse, plus other marvelous delicacies. For kosher home hospitality, or information on *kashrut* in New Orleans, call Dr. and Mrs. Saul Kahn at (504) 831-2230 (or write them in advance at 4000 Clifford Drive, Metairie, LA 70002).

The Kosher Cajun Deli and Grocery at 3520 North Hullen Street in Metairie is the only kosher sit-down restaurant in the area. Metairie also has the Bagel Factory at 3113 North Causeway. Serio's Kosher Delicatessen, 133 St. Charles, just outside the French Quarter, is not kosher, but kosher-style. For newcomers, there's a Shalom New Orleans kit available from the Federation.

Reading: Bertram Wallace Korn's *The Early Jews of New Orleans* (American Jewish Historical Society) remains the definitive history but only takes the reader to around 1840. *Judah P. Benjamin: The Jewish Confederate* (Free Press) is Eli Evans's biography of the Jewish Louisiana senator who became the Confederacy's secretary of state. David Max Eichhorn's *Joys of Jewish Folklore* (Jonathan David) includes wonderful tales about New Orleans Jewry, part history and part legend. A popular novel of New Orleans Jewry is Belva Plain's *Crescent City* (Delacorte). A general, and hilarious, novel set in the city is the Pulitzer Prize–winning *A Confederacy of Dunces* by John Kennedy Toole (Louisiana State University Press). Among the many New Orleans guidebooks, probably the most enjoyable and unusual is the delightful and informative *Frenchmen, Desire, Good Children and Other Streets of New Orleans,* by John Churchill Chase (Collier/Macmillan). Like everything else from New Orleans, from jazz to Jews, the city's literature is a bit offbeat, and the richer for it.

—*Rachel Heimovics*

Newport and Providence

Funny . . . Newport doesn't look Jewish. Its harbors clogged with sailboats and its streets with the boats' preppy owners, this seaside town is a page more likely torn from a J. Crew catalog than from a Jewish history book. But with a three hundred-year-old Jewish community founded by Sephardic sea merchants, Newport is a reminder that Jewish America did not begin on the Lower East Side and does not end in Lincolnwood, Illinois, or Long Island.

An hour's drive away, Providence offers an entirely different experience. Urban — and increasingly urbane — Rhode Island's capital shares the Jewish story of many other eastern cities. And while Providence has fewer Jewish sights than Newport does, it has more Jews — and more services to meet their needs.

Together, Providence and Newport offer a combination of Jewish America's yesterdays and todays, a wide variety of vacation diversions, and a warm welcome to visitors. A ubiquitous symbol in Rhode Island is the pineapple, an old seafarer's sign of hospitality: Captains returning from the Caribbean would bring the fruits back and perch them on the doorsteps of their homes to announce to one and all that the trip had been successful and that the family was receiving visitors. Providence and Newport still have the pineapple out — figuratively, at least — and each year the area welcomes millions of tourists.

History: Newport was established in 1636, three years after Roger Williams left the Massachusetts Bay Colony in search of religious freedom and founded Rhode Island. The local freedom-of-religion policy made the settlement a logical choice for Jews arriving in the New World; in 1658, descendants of fifteen families who had fled to the Caribbean from Spain and Portugal made their way up to Newport and established a congregation, which originally met in members' homes. Their right to trade was formally recognized by 1685, but this first community disbanded within a few years.

The community was revived in the 1740s, when Newport's growing prosperity attracted Jews from New York. By the mid-1750s, Congregation Nefutse Israel (Exiles of Israel) had been established. Many of the Jews who went to Newport were, like their non-Jewish counterparts, in the shipping trade and they prospered mightily. So secure did the Jews become that they soon changed their congregation's name to Yeshuat Israel (Salvation of Our People).

By 1759, with financial help from Congregation Shearith Israel in New York and communities in Curaçao and Jamaica, Yeshuat Israel had raised enough money to start building a synagogue (it would be more than a century before the name of its benefactor, Abraham Touro, was formally attached to the building).

This was the Golden Age of Newport Jewry — and of Newport itself. The shipping magnate Aaron Lopez was the city's biggest taxpayer. His fortune was built on livestock, lumber, whale oil, candles, groceries, rum, clothing — and slaves.

Newport had more than 200 Jews by 1770, but it was strangled by the American Revolution, after which much of its business and many of its Jews drifted down the coast to New York. Lopez, who supported the Revolution, fled to Massachusetts during the British occupation. The war over, he headed back to Newport but died

353

en route, never having reclaimed his financial empire.

After the Revolution, Newport's remaining Jews—who had thrived under British rule—were skittish. What if the new government persecuted them or denied their right to practice Judaism? But in 1790, on the occasion of a visit to Newport and the Touro Synagogue, President George Washington sent the congregation a reassuring letter promising that the new country would give "to bigotry no sanction . . . to persecution no assistance." The letter, considered a forerunner of the First Amendment (adopted as part of the Bill of Rights the following year) is now affixed to the sanctuary's rear wall.

But if Judaism's future in America was secure, the same could not be said for Newport. The community continued to decline, and by 1822 the last Jew had left and the Torah scrolls of the Touro Synagogue were sent to the parent congregation, Shearith Israel, in New York.

Just as it has been reborn in the 1740s, however, Newport's Jewish community was revived again in the 1880s. Though it was again a Sephardi, Abraham Pereira Mendes, who reconsecrated the Touro Synagogue in 1883, most newcomers who arrived in subsequent years were Ashkenazim.

The story of Jewish Providence has a more familiar beginning. Western European Jews—mostly German—founded the first synagogue in 1854, and bigger waves of Eastern European Jews started arriving in the 1880s. Most of the early arrivals were shopkeepers or factory workers. As in other industrial cities, these immigrants organized several local unions and social-service organizations. Fueled by the American dream, the storekeepers' and factory-workers' children became accountants and teachers; their grandchildren are doctors, lawyers—and *yeshivah bochers,* a small but growing segment of the population that like many across the country is seeing a resurgence of religious study and Orthodox observance.

Community: There are approximately 700 Jews in and around Newport today, none descendants of the original settlers. The local naval academy counts several Jews among its students and faculty, but many of them find it difficult to sink roots in a community they expect to be leaving. Jewish civilians, though, are well rooted and for the most part affiliated in some way with the community.

Because of its history, the Touro Synagogue has been a magnet for dignitaries, historians, and authors. The community's intellect is further fed by a small but ongoing adult education program run by Rabbi Chaim Shapiro, Touro's spiritual leader. Services reflect both the Eastern European background of its contemporary membership and the synagogue's Sephardic past, and include some traditions from each.

The Jewish Community Center, across the street from the synagogue, hosts secular as well as Jewish functions and is known for its celebrations at Hanukkah, Simchat Torah, and Purim. The center has an archive room with documents spanning the three hundred years of Jewish history in Newport; several members of the community are spearheading a campaign to turn the room into a historic museum of Jewish heritage.

The Conservative Temple Shalom at 221 Valley Road in nearby Middletown offers, in addition to *Shabbat* and holiday services, educational and cultural programs for its members and those of the surrounding community (telephone 401-846-9002).

The Providence area, home to 14,000 Jews, has a full range of Jewish services—Orthodox, Conservative and Reform synagogues, kosher butchers, a bakery and delicatessen, two *mikva'ot* and several after-school programs and all-day *yeshivot.* In the city proper the bulk of Jews live on the East Side, across the river from downtown and just past Brown University. Cranston, Warwick, and Pawtucket are home to the many Jewish families that left Providence's North End and South Side over the past few decades as they became more affluent.

The Jewish Community Center at 401 Elmgrove Avenue (401-861-8800), near the Brown Stadium, offers a wide range of educational and recreational services, from nursery school to adult education, from swimming to singles events and lectures. The center also houses a Holocaust memorial museum and a memorial garden outside that is used for Yom Hashoah services and personal reflection and visiting.

In addition to synagogue and JCC programs, Providence Jewry also benefits from the presence of the Hillel House at Brown University (where Jewish enrollment is estimated at 25 percent), which offers lectures and discussion groups.

Newport Sights: Dedicated in 1763 after four years of construction, and located near the center of town, Touro Synagogue is the oldest synagogue building in North America; centuries of Jewish history—American and European—live within its walls.

Designed by Peter Harrison, the building is a smaller replica of the Portuguese Synagogue in Amsterdam; Isaac Touro described the Dutch building to Harrison, who knew little about Judaism and had never seen a synagogue. Laid out like most Sephardic houses of worship, it has a central *bimah* and a women's gallery. The sanctuary's twelve columns, each made of a single tree trunk, represent the twelve tribes of Israel, and the trapdoor on the *bimah* serves as a reminder of the days in Spain and Portugal when Jews often had to hide in the basements of their synagogues. At the front of the sanctuary a glass case holds the Torah given to the congregation by the Amsterdam synagogue in 1763, when the scroll was probably two hundred years old. Written on deerskin, it stands open to the portion that recounts the Jews' thankfulness on having crossed the Red Sea—possibly chosen because Newport's first Jews felt the same sense of safety and freedom when they arrived in the colony.

Among the more unusual accoutrements in the synagogue is the central chandelier, which one legend claims was smuggled out of a Converso monastery in Portugal. Brought over from Europe by Jacob Polak, a member of the early congregation, it is a rare object indeed to find in a synagogue because of the four men's heads with long, curled mustaches and pointed turbans that surround the central stem.

Dominating the northern wall is a decoratively paneled president's seat, where George Washington sat when he visited the synagogue. It is designated for the congregation's president, who sits there during services. It is also traditional for the president to invite visiting dignitaries to join him, and the seat has been occupied by Abba Eban, Elie Wiesel, and Portuguese President Mario Soares, who came a few years ago shortly after issuing an apology for his country's treatment of Jews during the Inquisition.

Declared a landmark in 1946, the Touro Synagogue is governed by strict rules about alterations. Except for some new chairs and a carpet laid over the original, unfinished, wide-board floor (which may have been covered with dirt, as was the Sephardic custom), the synagogue looks just as it did two hundred years ago.

"The History of Touro Synagogue" by Rabbi Theodore Lewis (Newport Historical Society Bulletin No. 159) is full of details about the congregation and its building and gives a more in-depth background than that offered by the guides who lead synagogue tours. The booklet and other Touro memorabilia are available at the synagogue gift shop adjacent to the main building. For information about the synagogue and tours, call (401) 847-4794.

A short way down the road, at 82 Touro Street, the Newport Historical Society (401-846-0813) stores artifacts and documents spanning the town's history. Its archive rooms have plenty of details about Jewish history, too, in a full collection of the journal *American Jewish History* and *Rhode Island Jewish Historical Notes*.

Established by Newport's first Jewish community in 1677, the Colonial Jewish Cemetery of New England (a short walk away at 2 Bellevue Avenue) predates Touro by almost a century. It was a visit to the cemetery in 1852, when the congregation appeared to be dying out, that inspired Henry Wadsworth Longfellow to write a poem predicting the end of the Jewish people. Its last stanza reads: "But ah! what once has been shall be no more!/The groaning heart in travail and pain/Brings forth its races, but does not restore/And the dead nations never rise again." Almost 150 years later the poet stands corrected.

In addition to its points of Jewish interest, Newport's general tourist attractions draw visitors from around the world. To accommodate these thronging vacationers, Rhode Island recently built the $8 million

Gateway Visitor's Center which, in addition to information on seasonal programs, offers assistance with hotel bookings; it will also send the "Newport Travel Planner" free of charge. The Gateway is at 23 America's Cup Avenue in Newport (800-326-6030).

The Cliff Walk, restored in 1988, offers a lovely view of both the ocean front and the back lawns of the mansions for which Newport is famous. At the end of the walk you can cut inland and stroll back to town along the main streets, stopping in Bellevue Avenue's shops and visiting its museums. The Newport Art Museum at number 76 showcases local artists and holds open-air concerts in the summer. And in the old Newport Casino, at number 194, the International Tennis Hall of Fame displays tokens of America's favorite court sport.

Farther up Bellevue Avenue sit some of America's most famous mansions. The Historical Society runs tours of six of them (some of which are on other streets) and multiple-house discount tickets are available. Among the most visited of the homes maintained by the Newport Preservation Society are The Breakers and Marble House.

As awe-inspiring as these and some others are, by far the most interesting residences are two not included in the Society's tours: The Astors' Beechwood at 580 Bellevue Avenue (401-846-3772) and Hammersmith Farm on Ocean Drive (401-846-7346). Though the Astors' "cottage" is visually similar to the Vanderbilts', the tour is far livelier, for it is conducted by actors portraying members of the Astor family and their staff, who will show you around "their home" as if you had just stopped by for a visit around 1890.

Back in the center of town, don't forget to visit some of the smaller houses, many of which are still standing as they did three hundred years ago. Clustered on the streets in the historic district, they were saved a few years ago from the wrecking ball by a grassroots organization called Operation Clapboard. This dedication to preservation is part of what has kept Newport so attractive, and part of what makes it not only a pleasant place to live but also a popular place to visit.

That popularity is also partly due to the local sailing culture; indeed, you haven't truly seen Newport if you haven't sailed in her harbor. If you have the skill—and the cash—to charter your own boat, half a dozen companies offer rentals. Several other outfits offer guided group cruises; *The Spirit of Newport*'s tours depart from a central point on the wharf (401-849-3575).

Providence Sights: Rhode Island's capital is quintessential New England. Take a walk down Benefit Street, a life-size architectural history lesson, where many of the homes are open to the public; stop in at the Providence Preservation Society (24 Meeting Street; 401-831-7440) for up-to-date information. Also on Benefit Street, the Rhode Island School of Design's Museum of Art showcases a small but special international collection of paintings and sculpture, as well as an impressive array of American crafts and furniture.

The museum, of course, is just for looking, but favorite spots for browsing and buying include The Arcade (65 Weybosset Street), the oldest indoor mall in the country, and the Davol Square Marketplace, where developers have fashioned a colony of shops, galleries, and restaurants out of a renovated mill.

Temple Emanu-El, at the corner of Taft and Sessions Streets (on the opposite end of Brown Stadium from the JCC), is in many ways typical of its era. Designed in 1927 by Brown, Krokyn, and Rosenstein, it has stained-glass windows lining the slightly curved walls of the sanctuary. Although it is a Conservative synagogue, there is an upstairs gallery—not just for women but for anyone who prefers a mezzanine view. Newer additions, built in the 1940s and 1950s, are filled with artistic treasures that belie their plain exterior. The synagogue's hallways and meeting rooms are covered with paintings and lithographs; the auditorium boasts a series of painted panels by Providence artist Walter Feldman depicting stories from the Bible and Prophets along one wall and Jewish holidays on the other.

Temple Emanu-El's museum houses one of the best synagogue collections in the East—four hundred pieces of Judaica and hanging art—and offers rotating exhibits in the foyer of the main sanctuary. The collection includes circumcision knives from eighteenth-century Poland, *ketubot* from nineteenth-century Amsterdam, and a Purim *Megillah* painted on leather in Persia circa 1900. More modern items include a menorah by Robert Lipnick, a hand-painted *mezuzah* by Irene Puski and Shirley Kagan, a Steuben crystal *Kiddush* cup, and a unique art carpet by Chaim Gross entitled *Stained Glass Windows*. The collection includes one nonritual item: the wedding gown worn by Rebecca Rosenberg, in 1875 the first Jewish graduate of New York's Hunter College. The synagogue is open daily, but the museum is open by appointment only (401-331-1616).

Temple Beth-El, founded in the 1850s, moved to its home at 70 Orchard Avenue in 1954. Designed by Percival Goodman, the Reform synagogue features a 1,600-seat sanctuary and a comprehensive history gallery. Another distinguishing feature is the biblical garden on its back patio. Call the synagogue office (401-331-6070) for information about services and special events.

In all, the Providence area has sixteen synagogues. Temple Beth Sholom at 275 Camp Street (401-331-9393) is the largest of the Orthodox congregations.

Personalities: After the Lopezes, Riveras, Harts, Seixases, Levys and Polaks helped build Newport into a major port in the eighteenth century it was more than 150 years before local and individual Jews became well known across the state and nation. In politics there are Governors Bruce Sundlun and Frank Licht and State Attorney General Richard Israel. Other Jewish Rhode Islanders are broadcast journalists Fred Friendly and Irving R. Levine; Alan Hassenfeld, owner of Hasbro Toys; author S. J. Perelman; and scholar and prolific author Jacob Neusner. One of the state's most famous characters, Claus von Bulow, had his liberty saved and his life portrayed in the book and movie *Reversal of Fortune* by Alan Dershowitz from neighboring Massachusetts.

Recommendations: In Providence, Café Delight on Hope Street serves kosher vegetarian Middle Eastern dishes; Davis' Dairy—not a dairy at all but a kosher appetizer and deli market—is farther down the street.

There are plenty of large hotels and small bed-and-breakfast inns in Rhode Island. If you want some of the convenience of the former and the charm of the latter, consider staying at the Greenhouse Inn at Newport's Easton Beach. This small hotel offers well-kept rooms and ample parking, and owner Brian Gillson will be happy to answer questions about the local Jewish community (telephone 800-786-0310).

Anita Rafael of Newport on Foot (401-846-5391) gives guided tours for individuals and small groups and will tailor an itinerary to personal interests. On a guided tour or by yourself, you'll discover all the Jewish angles to a place that doesn't look Jewish.
—*Susan Kleinman*

New York

Ed Koch, New York's former mayor, was once asked by a television interviewer why, when he was criticized by political opponents, he didn't just turn the other cheek. Koch faced into the camera and, with a gleam in his eye, responded, "I'm not a Christian." His comment, though tongue in cheek, crystallized the Jewish role in New York's ethos. Not only are Jews in the Big Apple not expected to pretend allegiance to Christian values, this is a city where, to a great extent, gentiles assimilate into Jewish culture.

Lenny Bruce's observation that in New York everybody was Jewish may have been an exaggeration, but so much in this wonderful town—the national and international capital of business, culture, and the media—owes its inspiration and existence to Jews that the remark has its own logic. The community's 350-year-old synergistic love affair with New York has given the city the distinction of having the largest population of Jews—ever. If the Jewish heart is in Jerusalem, its body and soul are well settled in Manhattan Island.

In New York you don't have to be Jewish to eat bagels, blintzes, and knishes; to be a maven on the best delicatessen; to use Moishe's, Sabra's or Shleppers moving companies. Where else in the world can you find a *frum* female trader on the floor of the Stock Exchange? Yet the culinary and colloquial influences are only coincidental; major contributions are strikingly apparent in the cosmopolitan skyline, on Broadway, in the fashion industry, on Wall Street, in publishing, and in government.

History: Today's relaxed acceptance—even celebration—of Jews did not come with the early territory. When the first 23 mostly Sephardic refugees from Portuguese-controlled Brazil arrived in the port city of New Amsterdam in 1654, Peter Stuyvesant did his best to get rid of them. The governor's efforts were stymied by the Dutch West India Company (and its Jewish shareholders), which bade him to accept them "provided the poor . . . shall not become a burden to the company or to the community." Thus emerged the community's signature: Asser Levy went from penury to land ownership, along the way winning for Jews and other minorities civil rights. There were only about 100 Jews in this trading outpost until the mid-eighteenth century (though they were already spilling over into adjacent boroughs and counties).

When the British took over in 1664, Jews gained wider religious and economic rights. Only with the adoption of the state's first constitution in 1777, however, were they granted full citizenship and equality. In 1730 the first synagogue was erected by Congregation Shearith Israel, also known as the Spanish and Portuguese Synagogue, the oldest existing congregation in North America. During the Revolutionary War, the patriotic Gershom Mendes Seixas led his flock out of the state rather than live under British rule. By 1800 Jews were merchants and brokers, shipowners, coppersmiths, harness makers, carpenters, tobacconists, and accountants. Several were among the founders of the guild that later became the New York Stock Exchange.

In 1825 Ashkenazim split from Shearith Israel to form Congregation B'nai Jeshurun. In 1845 wealthy German Jews founded the Reform Emanu-El. Driven by oppression, poverty, and revolution, a sizable influx of Jews arrived from Poland and Bavaria between 1820 and 1850; after 1848 another wave came from Germany, Austria, Bohemia, and Hungary. There was

358

multiplication by division, as one pundit put it, and by the time of the Civil War there were twenty-seven synagogues serving 50,000 Jews.

Jewish social and cultural life flourished. Young men's clubs stressing social, literary, or communal interest were formed. Various Jewish organizations held elaborate balls, particularly at Purim, which were highlights of the Jewish social season. The Purim balls became a vehicle for raising funds to aid the sick and wounded during the Civil War. One of the chief northern fund-raisers was Joseph Seligman, whose New York firm sold $200 million in war bonds. Jewish soldiers predominated in Company D of the 8th New York National Guard. During the war, Samuel and Myer Isaacs led the successful effort to install Jewish chaplains in the service.

In 1880 the tidal movement of Russian and Romanian Jews began, swelling the community to 200,000 by 1890, 600,000 by 1900, and well over a million by 1910. The established Jews from Sephardic and German-speaking backgrounds (who lost their numerical primacy after 1871) tried, unsuccessfully for the most part, to encourage the newcomers not to stop in New York but to move on to the country's interior.

Later immigrants included Sephardic refugees of the Balkan War from Greece, Syria, and Turkey between 1908 and 1914; those fleeing Hitler between 1933–45; hasidic concentration camp survivors; as well as immigrants from the Hungarian Revolution of 1956, anti-Semitism in the Middle East, and revolution in Cuba; and more recently Jews from the former Soviet Union.

The acculturated Reform Jews were embarrassed by their poor, uncouth Yiddish-speaking coreligionists; they worried that their presence might fuel anti-Semitic wrath. So they set about socializing and Americanizing the newcomers (and wiping out the thriving prostitution business on Allen Street on the Lower East Side). Yet after Congress restricted immigration in 1924, it was philanthropist Jacob H. Schiff and attorney Louis Marshall who vigorously argued for unrestricted immigration. Another uptowner who tried to join the two communities' concerns in the *kehillah* experiment was Rabbi Judah L. Magnes. For

their part, the East Europeans brought with them New York's first *landsmanshaften*, self-help societies based on local origin.

Their journey from steerage to processing (at Castle Garden and later at Ellis Island) to settlement on the teeming Lower East Side is well documented. As the immigrants prospered, and subways were built, they moved uptown, especially to Harlem, and "out of town," to Brooklyn and the Bronx. Indeed New York's Jewish story is the family history of 100 million people in the United States today. The newcomers found lodging in overcrowded dumbbell tenements and became pushcart peddlers or worked in dismal sweatshops. On March 25, 1911, a fire at the Triangle Shirtwaist Company (the building still stands at Washington Place and Green Street in Greenwich Village) took the lives of 143 young women, most of them Jews; the fire led directly to the formation of the International Ladies Garment Workers Union and was a watershed in American labor relations.

Eventually, New York's huddled masses became insurance brokers; built movie palaces and radio, newspaper, and even cosmetic empires; built some of the city's grandest buildings; and prospered in the *shmatah*, or garment, industry. They also became doctors, dentists, druggists, lawyers, and teachers. They and their children made lasting contributions to high and low culture — in theater, music, literature, art, and journalism.

Community: Perhaps most symbolic of how comfortable contemporary Jews are with their dual identities is the recent appearance on Broadway of a plethora of shows by and about Jews that unabashedly air their flawed humanity. Nowadays even Jackie Mason's blatantly stereotypical ethnic humor makes New York Jews laugh rather than cringe, as it once did. And a couple of years ago when a prominent Jew was convicted for insider trading, the community's distress was noted on "Saturday Night Live" as a *shanda far di goyim*. Ari Goldman, an observant Jew and for many years a staff reporter with *The New York Times* (which once insisted that writer A. M. Rosenthal use his initials rather than his very Jewish name, Abraham), has written about his striving to reconcile his two loves, journalism and Judaism, something that was antithetical in the past. Could Russian forefathers—once abused by anti-Semitic authorities—have imagined a Shomrim Society of Orthodox Jewish police?

In contrast with Brooklyn, Queens, and the Bronx, which are losing Jewish residents, the number in Manhattan has grown over the last decade (as has Staten Island's). The diverse population of mostly secularized Jews, which includes lots of students and singles, has grown to 308,000 (of the total of 1,100,000 in the five boroughs and 2,000,000 in the metropolitan area) and is 20 percent of Manhattan's population.

There are heavily Jewish neighborhoods on both sides of Central Park, to the nineties on the East Side, and up to Morningside Heights on the West. Today's Lower East Side Jews live in cooperatives on East Broadway and Grand Street and yuppies are cleaning up the East Village and the historic Yiddish Theater district on Second Avenue. The one-time sweatshops and warehouses in SoHo (south of Houston) are being transformed into residential lofts. Washington Heights remains home to an Orthodox German-Jewish community a stone's throw from Yeshiva University.

Just as earlier Jews built the Woolworth and Chrysler buildings and the Waldorf-Astoria Hotel, builders like William Zeckendorf and the Tishman brothers still glorify the skyline. If few Jews today toil in the garment factories, they still own most of the fashion industry that dominates the area between Thirty-sixth and Fortieth Streets from Sixth to Ninth Avenues (though it is shrinking because of foreign competition) and retain leadership of the unions their parents struggled to found. The department stores (Macy's, Abraham & Straus, Bloomingdales, Lord & Taylor) and investment firms (Kuhn Loeb, Lehman Brothers, and Bache) founded by German Jews and the bearded Orthodox jewelry dealers in the diamond district (Forty-seventh Street between Fifth and Sixth Avenues) are also part of Manhattan's landscape.

The Jewish influence in print remains distinguished. In fact, in the early 1990s the old canard about Jewish control of the media finally became a fact in New York, as all three of the city's major dailies were under Jewish ownership for the first time. *The New York Times* is still the domain of the Sulzberger family; the Episcopalian-bred son of a non-Jewish mother, Arthur Ochs Sulzberger, Jr., the paper's current publisher, has quipped: "Who would believe that a Sulzberger is not Jewish?" *The Daily News*, once the property of Robert Maxwell, is now owned by Mortimer Zuckerman. The *New York Post* was owned by Peter Kalikow. Other Jewish-owned institutions are *The New Yorker* magazine and, in book publishing, Random House, Alfred E. Knopf, and Simon & Schuster.

In addition to the city's many Jewish book publishers, there has been an upsurge in general publishers printing books of Jewish interest. Random House, for example, is publishing *The Talmud: The Steinsaltz Edition*. A great deal of New York's theater world bears the imprint of the late Joseph Papp (the Shakespeare Festival and the theater that bears his name are but two examples). The Jewish influence is abundant in every aspect of culture, from stand-up comedy (can you imagine André's Kosher Komedy Klub—"the food is *glatt*, the comedy's not"—performing aboard the *Glatt Yacht*?) to the musical heritage of Leonard Bernstein and the operatic institutions introduced by Jews. Broadway, a Jewish creation, has *heimish* representation in every dimension—as writers, producers, director, actors as well as in the audience. Even before Jewish playwrights were writing intensely Jewish plays, other Jews (Rodgers and Hammerstein, Lerner and Loewe, Stephen Sondheim) were creating much of America's musical theater culture.

Jews are highly visible in politics—as they have been since the days of Asser Levy and Mordecai Manuel Noah, the nineteenth-century sheriff, surveyor, judge, playwright, and editor who was an advocate of Jewish causes. Although the state had a Jewish governor (Herbert Lehman) in 1932, New York City didn't get its first Jewish mayor until Abraham Beame was elected in 1973; the outspokenly Jewish and pro-Israel Edward I. Koch served as mayor for three terms. (Some argue that Yiddish-speaking Fiorello LaGuardia, elected mayor in 1933, was the first Jewish mayor; his mother was Jewish, but he regarded himself as Protestant. LaGuardia was a cousin of Luigi Luzzatti, Italy's first Jewish prime minister.)

New York is the home base to most national Jewish organizations—from the Orthodox, Conservative, and Reform movements, to the American Jewish Committee and American Jewish Congress, to Hadassah (at 50 West 58th Street) and many others. It is also the site of major Jewish educational institutions. All of this adds to the rich cross-fertilization of Jewish ideas and produces a cornucopia of cultural events. Even public colleges—City College was once called the Jewish Harvard in the days when the Ivy League schools had restrictive quotas—which still have large Jewish student bodies, offer curricula and community programs rich in Jewish content.

Sights: Though you can get around New York by car, the subways are faster (buses are good but slower). Battery Park is a good place to begin. There you can walk through the fortlike Castle Clinton (called Castle Garden when used for processing immigrants), take the ferry to the Statue of Liberty (where you can read Emma Lazarus's poem "The New Colossus") and Ellis Island (212-269-5755), which celebrated its hundredth anniversary in 1992. Of the millions of Jews who disembarked between 1850 and 1948, the bulk came through the "isle of tears," as S. Y. Agnon described it. The handsome red brick and limestone Main Arrivals Building has been restored as a museum. Although modernized—some think, beyond recognition—there is enough atmosphere in the Great Hall and the re-

created Board of Special Inquiry room and the fine exhibits to remind you of the immigrants' traumatic passage.

The earliest Jewish cemetery still extant is in Chinatown on St. James Place near Chatham Square. Consecrated in 1682, it was the site of skirmishes and hiding out during the American Revolution. Among the 18 Revolutionary soldiers and patriots buried here is Gershom Mendes Seixas.

Although the Lower East Side is but a shadow of its legendary Jewish past—in 1910 there were 600,000 Jews; today there are about 25,000—and although increasingly Spanish and Chinese intermingle with English and Yiddish, it is still possible to conjure up visions of yesterday. On any Sunday except a Jewish holiday, walk along Hester, Essex, and Orchard Streets; the *Khazermark* and pushcarts may be gone, but fierce bargaining still goes on. Clothing, linen, appliances, silver, Judaica, ritual items (there is an obligatory pre-*bar mitzvah* trip here to purchase *tallit* and *tefillin*)—and food stores—still bring in the crowds along Essex, Canal, Grand, and Eldridge Streets. Don't forget Guss's Pickles (35 Essex), Russ & Daughters Appetizers (179 East Houston), Yonah Schimmel Knishes Bakery (137 East Houston), Miller's Cheese (13 Essex), Kossar's Bialystoker Kuchen Bakery (367 Grand), Gertels Bake Shoppe & Luncheonette (53 Hester), Schapiro's House of Kosher & Sacramental Wines (126 Rivington) or Streit Matzoth Company (150 Rivington). The Essex Street Market (104 Essex), built to get the pushcarts off the street, is no longer a Jewish showcase—other accents prevail. To see *hondling* in action go to

Stuyvesant's loss: Ellis Island was the doorstep of America and the gateway to the formation of the largest Jewish community the world has ever seen

Essex Street before Sukkot when shoppers haggle over the best and cheapest *lulav* and *etrog*.

The Lower East Side Tenement Museum (97 Orchard; telephone 212-431-0233) is a living testament to how the other half once lived. Housed in an 1863 structure, the museum offers dramatic performances, multimedia presentations, educational programs, and exhibitions. Among the things to see inside are a dollhouse-size model of a tenement with all the working parts; an exhibit, "Meddling With Peddling: The Pushcart Wars"; lectures and several walking tours, including "Peddler's Pack: A Jewish Heritage Tour." And if your family ever lived at 97 Orchard, the museum wants to hear from you.

Among Lower East Side landmarks are the Educational Alliance (197 East Broadway), where many Jews learned English and the ways of their new home; the Henry Street Settlement (263–267 Henry), founded by Lillian Wald, which ministered to the social and educational needs of immigrants; and the Jewish Daily *Forward* (175 East Broadway). All three contributed to the greenhorns' integration into the *goldene medinah*. Today the Alliance and the Settlement serve Jews, Hispanics, African-Americans, and Chinese; the landmark Forward building is occupied by Chinese businesses and offices. Under editor Abraham Cahan, the *Forward* was the heartbeat of the community with its popular "Bintel Brief" and literary columns, its espousal of socialist views, and support of the Jewish labor movement.

Aside from the thriving press (New York had five Yiddish dailies in 1915) the area's other centerpiece was the Yiddish theater. The Jewish Rialto meandered along Second Avenue from Houston to Fourteenth Street. Jacob Adler and Boris Thomashevsky helped build the theater world that flourished from the 1920s to the 1940s. Contiguous with the theater-rich strip were the cafés and restaurants where people congregated before and after the shows. The Second Avenue Deli (156 Second Avenue)—with a sign that says "The French have Cassoulet, we have Cholent"—remains in the heart of the district.

At one time the Lower East Side had three hundred *shuls* and East Broadway is still lined with storefront *shtiebels* between Jefferson and Montgomery streets. The Mesifta Tifereth Jerusalem, the *yeshivah* once headed by the renowned halakhic decisor Rabbi Moshe Feinstein, remains at 145 East Broadway. But since many Jews have moved away, synagogues have been converted to churches or public buildings or have been vandalized. But many beautiful landmark congregations remain.

Congregation Anshe Slonim, built in 1849 and located at 172 Norfolk Street, is the oldest synagogue structure in New York. Abandoned in 1975, it was purchased recently by Al and Angel Orensanz, two Spanish-Jewish brothers. Angel, an artist, uses the lofty space in this Gothic Revival building as a studio and gallery and is looking forward to a reborn congregation. He has organized an exhibit of local history there and occasionally hosts weddings.

The magnificent Gothic, Romanesque, and Moorish-style Eldridge Street Synagogue (14 Eldridge), built in 1886, is the object of a $3-million restoration project. The national historic landmark was the first Orthodox synagogue in the area built specifically to house a Jewish congregation. The huge main sanctuary has elaborate brass chandeliers with Victorian glass shades hanging in the barrel-vaulted space. The ark is made of Italian walnut. The building will eventually function as a synagogue and museum. Call to find out about its "Ellis to Eldridge" tour and slide show (212-219-0888).

When the Jewish presence was at its peak, churches were transformed into synagogues. Today many of them, all designated landmarks, are still in use. The Beth Hamedrash Hagadol (60 Norfolk), constructed in 1852, houses the Orthodox congregation that bought the Gothic Revival building in 1885. The fieldstone Bialystoker Synagogue (7–13 Willet Street), an 1826 structure, is the oldest in the city to house a synagogue. Recently restored, the building features a lavish ark with gold leaf; ceiling and wall murals depict the signs of the zodiac and scenes of Jerusalem.

Shaarey Shomayim, the First American Roumanian Congregation (89 Rivington), was built in the Romanesque Revival style in 1888. The 2,000-capacity synagogue was famous for its cantorial singing, featuring *chazanim* such as Yossele Rosenblatt, Moishe Koussevitsky, Moishe Oysher, and brothers-in-law Jan Peerce and Richard Tucker.

Synagogues on the Upper East Side have more elegant surroundings. Temple Emanu-El (1 East 65th Street; 212-744-1400), a Romanesque-Byzantine structure seating 2,500, is the largest Reform temple in the world. The rose window located above the main entrance is Gothic, the twelve petals symbolic of the tribes of Israel. An exquisite small chapel is in the Byzantine motif. It has two domes supported by six columns of pink granite, with side walls resting on arches springing from columns of Oriental marble. The Tiffany stained-glass windows above the bronze ark depict the Holy Land. Call well in advance to arrange for a tour.

The landmark Central Synagogue (123 East 55th Street; 212-838-5122) was built in 1872 (the cornerstone was laid in 1870 by Rabbi Isaac Mayer Wise). A Moorish Revival structure with bulbous domes rising to one hundred twenty-two feet, it was inspired by the Great Dohány Synagogue in Budapest and built by Henry Fernbach, the first Jew to practice architecture in the city. The oldest synagogue building in continuous use by one congregation in the city, it houses the Folksbeine Playhouse (call ahead for tours).

The Park East Synagogue (163 East 67th Street; 212-737-6900), built in Moorish Revival style in 1890, moved to center stage in the 1970s because of its proximity to the Soviet (now Russian) Mission to the United Nations across the street. It was the scene of countless demonstrations on behalf of Soviet Jewry; a large plaque on the exterior is inscribed, "Hear the Cry of the Oppressed—the Jewish Community in the Soviet Union." The colorful building has bulbous cupolas set at different levels and surmounted by a slender shaft supporting a Star of David. The facade of the main structure rises from behind an elaborately arched portico. At each wing there is a decorative square tower, one higher than the other, each richly carved, arched, and star crowned.

Congregation Shearith Israel (8 West 70th Street; 212-873-0300) is both the rem-

nant and living presence of Sephardic New York. Also designed by Fernbach, the 1897 synagogue incorporates a wealth of artifacts from earlier structures, such as 1730 floorboards under the *bimah*. Other riches include eighteenth-century scroll decorations by silversmith Myer Myers and a three-century-old beaten brass menorah. A charming smaller chapel known as the Little Synagogue is a composite of the earlier periods, particularly Colonial. Included are a reader's desk with exquisite spindles holding four candlesticks, which on close inspection are seen to be *havdalah* sets. Made of Spanish brass, the candlesticks are thought to date from the fifteenth century, when Conversos may have designed them as hidden ritual objects. There is an 1817 *Ner Tamid* and 1834 *bancas* (benches) as well as 1896 Tiffany stained-glass windows. Ashkenazic visitors find Shabbat and holiday services at the Orthodox synagogue fascinating because of the different rituals and traditions. Call in advance for tours.

Lincoln Square Synagogue (200 Amsterdam Avenue; 212-874-6100), also known as the singles' shul, was designed as a theater in the round with an unusual see-through *mechitzah*. The exterior of the contemporary Orthodox synagogue is in the shape of a Star of David. Several *minyanim* cater to members and guests of varying Jewish backgrounds. Call for *Shabbat* hospitality.

Congregation B'nai Jeshurun, New York's first Ashkenazic synagogue, moved to its current home in 1918 (257 West 88th Street; 212-787-7600). The Moorish Revival building has been described as "an architectural masterpiece embodying the spirit of ancient Semitic art." Its facade features a tall Romanesque portal; the interior is decorated with intricate polychrome ornament. The congregation had dwindled to under a dozen and the building was crumbling when Rabbi Marshall Meyer, who had almost single-handedly built the Conservative movement in Argentina, returned to the United States in 1985 looking for a challenge. Today it is a flourishing, socially conscious congregation, predominated by young families; the baroque interior is undergoing renovation.

Once a Jewish neighborhood, Harlem

still has one Jewish outpost. The Ethiopian Hebrew Congregation (1 West 123rd Street; 212-543-1058) is a friendly attraction in a part of town many people avoid. The black congregants, who follow Orthodox ritual, claim to be descendants of Solomon and Sheba.

For a knowledgeable and enthusiastic guide around Jewish New York, call Jane Marx (212-535-7798).

Culture: At the southernmost tip of Battery Park City overlooking the Statue of Liberty and Ellis Island is the site of the planned Museum of Jewish Heritage, a Living Memorial to the Holocaust. It will house permanent and changing exhibitions, a theater, archive, and learning center. When reflected at night in the harbor the sixty-foot-high structure of stone and translucent glass will glow like an eternal flame.

Two outstanding resources for documentation are the Leo Baeck Institute (129 East 73rd Street; 212-744-6400), which houses collections of historic documents, books and photographs about Jewish life and history in Germany and other German-speaking areas in Europe and the YIVO Institute for Jewish Research (1048 Fifth Avenue; 212-535-6700), the world center for Yiddish research. YIVO has the most complete record of Jewish life in Eastern Europe—3 million photographs, letters, and documents. Founded in Vilna in 1925, it was relocated to New York in 1940 to escape the Nazis. Both offer special exhibitions.

The Jewish Theological Seminary of America, where Conservative rabbis are trained, is just north of Columbia University at 122nd Street and Broadway (telephone 212-678-8081). It is the repository for some of the rarest Jewish books in the world. The seminary's library, open to the public, has 260,000 volumes, including special finds from the Cairo *genizah.*

Also under the auspices of the JTS is The Jewish Museum (170 Central Park West; 212-399-3357), which recently reopened with twice its former exhibit space. The distinctive style of the 1908 landmark Warburg mansion, which housed the museum, inspired the design of the new wing, creating a unified appearance. The museum, founded in 1904, has more than 24,000 works of art and artifacts of Jewish history and a fine-arts collection with items by Rembrandt, Chagall, and George Segal, among others. Its ceremonial art collection is the most comprehensive in the United States and one of the largest in the world. Among major exhibits in recent years that extend beyond the parochial have been *The Dreyfus Affair: Art, Truth and Justice,* which focused on how the Dreyfus case was depicted in newspapers, paintings, photos, cartoons, and even early films; *The Circle of Montparnasse: Jewish Artists in Paris, 1905–1945,* which featured works by Chagall, Modigliani, Mané-Katz and others; and *Bridges and Boundaries: African Americans and American Jews,* which paralleled the 20th-century experience of both groups.

Yeshiva University Museum (2540 Amsterdam Avenue; 212-960-5390) uses photographs, paintings, folk art and religious articles to depict the Jewish historical experience. There are ten scale models of the world's most famous synagogues. With *The Sephardic Journey: 1492–1992,* it mounted one of the most extensive exhibits to commemorate the five-hundredth anniversary of the expulsion of Jews from Spain; it featured more than 1,000 items, from costumes to art and ceremonial objects.

The 92nd Street Y (1395 Lexington Avenue; 212-996-1100), the largest and oldest Jewish community center in continuous existence in the United states, has a singular position in the city's cultural world with notable film, concert, and literary programs and speakers (from Elie Wiesel to Dick Cavett). Events at the Y are normally listed not only in the Jewish weeklies but in the major daily papers.

One of the best places to hear Jewish ideas is at Rabbi William Berkowitz's nationally known Dialogue Forum Series. Over the past forty years he has held public dialogues with such diverse figures as the late humorist Sam Levenson, Henry Kissinger, and Rabbi Adin Steinsaltz. For information on dialogues and locations write to Berkowitz at 250 West 57th Street, Suite 1527, New York, NY 10017, or call (212) 245-7507.

New York is a city that never sleeps— Jewishly. Exhibits of art, artifacts, Judaica, photographs, and manuscripts abound, as do radio and television programs, films, and on- and Off-Broadway drama, comedy, and musicals. Israeli folk dancing is offered at several places all year round. Many are listed in the regular newspapers, but check *The Jewish Week*. Other papers that serve the city are *The Jewish Press* (Orthodox) and *The Long Island Jewish World*. There are also weekly editions in English and Yiddish of the *Forward*. The Folksbeine Theater (123 East 55th Street; 212-755-2231), the seventy-four-year-old keeper of the Yiddish theater tradition, produces dramas and musicals. The Jewish Repertory Theater (in conjunction with the 92nd Street Y) has moved to the three hundred-seat Playhouse 91 (316 East 91st Street; 212-996-1100). The American Jewish Theater (306 W. 26th Street; 212-633-9797), features new works and classics.

New York always has extracurricular Jewish events that coincide with specific dates. The annual Purim ball in March is a recent revival of the Civil War–era practice. There are celebratory Israel programs in June, including the Salute to Israel Parade, the Israel Folk Dance Festival, and Festival of the Arts. The Hebrew Arts Center's Merkin Concert Hall presents a heritage series of Jewish music; at Hanukkah you can join its annual *Judas Macabaeus* open sing (129 West 67th Street; 212-362-8060).

General Sights: The New York Public Library's Jewish Division (42nd Street and Fifth Avenue; 212-930-0601) has more than 140,000 volumes and one of the largest collections of Jewish periodicals in the country.

The site and scene of Jewish hope and anti-Israel sentiment, the United Nations headquarters (First Avenue and East 43rd Street) has stained-glass windows by Chagall. The Isaiah Wall across the street is a massive granite monument. The stairway ascending to the nearby Tudor City apartment complex was renamed Sharansky Steps in honor of former Prisoner of Zion Natan Sharansky. The portion of First Avenue that passes the steps is designated the Raoul Wallenberg Walk.

There's a permanent display of Jewish interest in the Asian Peoples section in the American Museum of Natural History (Central Park West and 79th Street). It features artifacts and history of Jewish communities in Turkey, India, Yemen, Iraq, and Iran.

Reading and Viewing: Movies that have immortalized the old Jewish neighborhoods are *Hester Street, Crossing Delancey,* and *Enemies: A Love Story.* Woody Allen movies, which cast a loving eye on the city, are also characteristically Jewish and quintessentially New York. Nonfiction classics that tell the tales of New York Jews include *World of Our Fathers* by Irving Howe (Harcourt Brace Jovanovich); *The Promised City* (Harvard) by Moses Rischin; *The Rise of David Levinsky* by Abraham Cahan (Harper and Row); and *The Spirit of the Ghetto* (Belknap Press) by Hutchins Hapgood, a non-Jew with a keen sense of understanding. The best visual chronicle of the day is photographer-reformer Jacob Riis's *How the Other Half Lives* (Dover). More recently there is Ronald Sanders's *The Lower East Side: A Guide to Its Jewish Past in 99 New Photographs* (Dover) and several books on Ellis Island, including the beautiful *Ellis Island: An Illustrated History of the Immigrant Experience* (Macmillan) by Ivan Chermayeff, Fred Wasserman, and Mary J. Shapiro. For the best detailed informal history read the books of Bernard Postal and Lionel Koppman; they are out of print but can be found in the library. Oscar Israelowitz is a prolific publisher of guidebooks to Jewish New York. His *Synagogues of the United States* is an excellent photographic and architectural survey, and Nancy Frazier's *Jewish Museums of North America* (Wiley) is also a helpful guide.

The early immigrant years are depicted in the *Bread Givers* by Anzia Yezierska (Braziller); and Henry Roth's *Call It Sleep* (Avon), as well as the novels and short stories of Herman Wouk, Bernard Malamud, Philip Roth, Saul Bellow, and Isaac Bashevis Singer. Romantic sagas of the era are by Gloria Goldreich, Belva Plain, and Fred Mustard Stewart. *Enchantment* (Harcourt Brace Jovanovich) by Daphne Merkin is set in a German-Jewish milieu; *My Life With Goya* (Arbor House) by Andrew Potok in the Hungarian-Jewish atmosphere. *John and Anzia: An American Romance* (Dutton) by Norma Rosen brings to life Yezierska's romance with John Dewey.

Personalities: To name those with connections to Manhattan is to be a name dropper. Among those who studied or taught at the Educational Alliance are David Sarnoff, dance teacher Arthur Murray, sculptor Jo Davidson and artists Chaim Gross, Ben Shahn, Leonard Baskin, Moses Soyer, Louise Nevelson, Barnett Newman, and Mark Rothko.

Other locals who made good were songwriter Irving Berlin; entertainers George Burns, Eddie Cantor, and George Jessel; actor Paul Muni; vaudevillian Menashe Skulnik; comedian Fanny Brice; playwrights Clifford Odets and Jerome Weidman; writers Yezierska, Henry Roth, Harry Golden and, in their later years, Sholom Aleichem and Nobelist Isaac Bashevis Singer. There were also the powerful union builders David Dubinsky and Sidney Hillman. Sex therapist Dr. Ruth Westheimer still lives among the German Jews of Washington Heights.

Alumni of the City College form a "Who's Who" of their own. They include financial and presidential advisor Bernard Baruch, polio vaccine developer Jonas Salk, Nobel Prize winner Arthur Kornberg, Supreme Court Justice Felix Frankfurter, and philosopher Morris Raphael Cohen.

Eating: East Side, West Side, all around the town — there are kosher eating places galore. East European dairy? Down-town there's the long-established Ratner's (138 Delancey Street) and the newer, funky Ludlow's 85 (85 Ludlow Street) where you can get herring, egg creams (with a pretzel on the side), cheesecake, and blintzes. Traditional meat dishes are at Lou G. Siegel's (209 West 38th Street). Vegetarian Chinese? Try Vegetarian Heaven (304 West 58th Street), possibly the best bargain in town. Roman Jewish? There's charming ambiance and authentic dishes at the not inexpensive Tevere "84" (155 East 84th Street). Delicious Moroccan is at La Kasbah (70 West 71st Street); gourmet French is at Levana's (141 West 69th Street).

The culinary mecca of the largely secular but intensely Jewish Upper West Side is Zabar's, a food emporium that occupies the west side of Broadway between Eighty-first and Eighty-second streets. Though not kosher, it probably caters more Seders and Yom Kippur break-the-fast dinners than any other place in New York.

Or maybe you just want to grab a falafel at the corner of Forty-seventh Street and Avenue of the Americas. Moshe's food stand comes equipped with a faucet and cup for the ritual hand washing, and the appropriate *brocha* is posted. However whimsical, this image should not surprise. It is just another sign of the Jewish presence on the landscape of a very Jewish city.

—Zelda Shluker

New Zealand

If there is one talent that has gotten the Jewish people into more trouble than any other, it is the talent of being where the action is. From Russia to South Africa, from Iran to Ethiopia—not to mention Israel—wherever there is revolution, repression, or siege, a Jewish community seems to be in the way.

If there is one place where Jews seem to have lost this talent, it is New Zealand.

The Jews of New Zealand are the most isolated in the world, separated from their nearest brethren in Australia by twelve hundred miles of Tasman Sea and from each other by distance and by the Cook Strait, which divides the country in two. As a minuscule minority of 5,000 in a nation of 3.3 million, most Jews live on the North Island around the capital of Wellington and the cosmopolitan business center of Auckland, four hundred miles north. Fewer than 500 Jews live in the South Island enclaves of Christchurch and Dunedin, the latter hosting the southernmost Jewish congregation in the world. The isolation, however, can be rewarding for visitors, as many community members extend a distinctively Kiwi and *heimish* hospitality to Jewish travelers.

History: The Tasman Sea brought the first Jews from Australia in 1829, when the Sydney firm of Cooper and Levy sent a Captain Wiseman to the South Island as trade representative, establishing Port Levy and Port Cooper (today's town of Lyttleton).

Joel Samuel Polack, who came from England in 1831, is believed to be the first Jewish resident of North Island. He and several other Jewish storekeepers and traders moved to Auckland in 1840. David Nathan, who helped found the country's first synagogue in his home that same year, married Rosetta Arons in its first Jewish wedding in 1841; their daughter, Sarah, was New Zealand's first native-born Jewish child. The bushy-bearded Nathan presided over the Auckland Hebrew Congregation four times, and he and his two sons, grandson, great-grandson and other assorted Nathans held the congregation's presidency for all but twenty-seven years between 1851 and 1977. Nathan's business legacy is equally impressive: His store, begun in a tent in 1841, grew into L. D. Nathan and Company, a conglomerate including department stores, a food division, franchises of Coca-Cola and Woolworths, breweries, investment and banking, and manufacturing.

Abraham Hort, Jr., and Solomon and Benjamin Levy were among the 700 who sailed over on the British fleet in 1839 to open the city of Wellington. In 1842, Abraham Hort, Sr., brought the rest of the *minyan*—a wife, five daughters and son-in-law, and the versatile David Isaacs, who served as *mohel, chazan,* and *shochet,* bringing *kashrut* to the distant land. The town of Levin, north of Wellington, was named after Hort's grandson, William Hort Levin.

Just as California's 1848 gold strike attracted Jews, so did a gold discovery bring Jews to South Island in the 1860s. In 1881, Dunedin's 200 Jews built a Greek Revival synagogue with 500 seats and a double balcony. Gold ran out by the early twentieth century, however, and the Jewish population declined.

In Christchurch, merchant Louis Edward Nathan founded the Canterbury Hebrew Congregation (a name designed, apparently, to avoid references to the "Christchurch Synagogue") in his home, and in

1863 crown monies and land enabled the congregation to build a small wooden synagogue. Many Jews left for "golder" pastures during the rush, traveling across the magnificent Southern Alps and building a synagogue in Hokitika. The boom turned to bust and the returning Jews built Christchurch's 500-seat Gloucester Street Synagogue in 1881.

In the 1860s, some of the country's indigenous Maori tribesmen expressed the belief that they were descended from one of Israel's lost tribes and tried unsuccessfully to set up the state of New Canaan, with the highest title of honor being the Maori word *Tiu,* meaning "Jew."

There had been some intermarriage between Jews and Maoris in the nineteenth century, and today Maoris with the names Solomon, Isaacs, and Nathan are common. Maori descendants of Asher Asher, one of the country's first Jewish citizens, are known to have a deep appreciation for their Jewish heritage. There is also a Maori settlement of Jerusalem, between Wellington and Auckland.

Joel Samuel Polack's two books, *New Zealand* (1838) and *Manners and Customs of New Zealanders* (1840) were among the first to document the history of the land, and his presentation of evidence before a select committee of the House of Lords in 1838 helped influence England's annexation. Spurred on by the gold rush, poor Russian and Polish Jews who had first emigrated to England came to New Zealand with other British Jews. In 1891, New Zealand's Parliament protested to Czar Alexander III about the persecution of Russian Jewry, yet the country accepted few immigrants, some of whom took strange new jobs as wool pressers and share milkers.

Like most of the world, New Zealand was unresponsive to the Jewish plight in Europe in the 1930s and restricted immigration. Between 1931 and 1941, only about 1,100 Jewish refugees arrived, mainly skilled workers and manufacturers with capital. After the war, Holocaust survivors and more British Jews came, followed by Hungarian Jews after the 1956 uprising. Since the 1970s, some Russian Jews—a mixture of engineers, professors, shoemakers, and others—have arrived, as well as a handful of South Africans.

Community: New Zealand still restricts immigration mainly to British-born citizens, so few Jews qualify. As some younger Jews seek job opportunities and Jewish mates abroad and the overall Jewish population grows older, there is some concern for the future of the community.

Jews have been an integral part of New Zealand society, but their isolation from other Jewish communities and their limited number prompted many organizations to form the New Zealand Jewish Council in 1981, to speak out against anti-Semitism while trying "to increase Jewish consciousness and identity."

A Jewish identity is relatively easy to maintain in Auckland, home to 1,600 Jews, and Wellington, where about 1,200 live. Each has Orthodox and Liberal (Reform) synagogues holding regular services, along with many Jewish activities and organizations. In Christchurch and Dunedin, it is more difficult.

Some of Auckland's Jews still live in the older Ponsonby section on the city's hilly northern slopes, but since the 1930s the move has been to the eastern suburbs of Mission Bay, Kohimarama, Orakei, Saint Heliers, and Glendowie.

While there has never been a Jewish neighborhood in Wellington, many families live near the central city; in the western and northwestern hill suburbs of Karori, Khandallah, and Kelburn; in the southern suburb of Brooklyn; and ten miles away in Upper and Lower Hutt.

Only about 30 Jews remain in Dunedin, the closest Jewish community in the world to Antarctica. In 1966, they sold their classic synagogue and replaced it with today's modern, 100-seat building with polished wood doors at 806 George Street. Services are held once a month. Trying to stay alive, a few years ago the community actively solicited young, Russian Jewish families with children—and were, somewhat, rewarded with a confirmed bachelor and a woman doctor.

Christchurch, the country's most English-looking city, is home to 300 Jews. The proud Gloucester Street Synagogue was built of the same stone as the nearby Gothic cathedral, but with an unmistakable Star of David incorporated in its ornate facade. Now the facade is all that remains; the building was razed in 1988 and the facade incorporated into a new synagogue on Durham Street.

Though New Zealand's Jewish community accounts for less than two-tenths of a percent of the population, it has produced leaders in the garment, hotel, and brewing industries and has been well represented in politics, education, medicine, journalism, and law, starting with Ethel Benjamin, a women's rights advocate who became the country's first female lawyer in 1897.

Personalities: Look at New Zealand's political history, and you'll see a Jewish influence. Start at the top with Dunedin's Sir Julius Vogel, "The Disraeli of New Zealand," who was twice prime minister, organized postal service to San Francisco and cable service to London, introduced government life insurance, brought in the railroad and cofounded *The Otago Daily Times,* the nation's first daily newspaper.

Sir Michael Myers was the nation's chief justice from 1929 to 1946, and Jews served continuously in the Parliament from 1863 to 1953. Eddie Isbey, the most recent Jewish member of Parliament, retired a few years ago after serving eighteen years. Auckland's first two mayors—Philip Philips and Henry Isaacs—were Jewish, as have been five subsequent mayors. Ian Lawrence served as mayor of Wellington. Christchurch and several smaller towns have been led by Jews as well.

Mark Cohen earned distinction as editor of *The Star* of Dunedin. Charles Brasch, a poet and founder of the literary quarterly *Landfall,* was a national figure, as was poet Karl Wolfskehl, who came from Germany in 1938. Frances Alda was a lyric soprano who performed at New York's Metropolitan Opera House. Poet, playwright, and novelist Benjamin Farjeon was also a part owner of Vogel's newspaper. Peter Gluckman recently became Auckland Medical School's youngest, and first Jewish, dean.

Auckland Sights: Walk into a Nathan Department Store or one of the Hallenstein Brothers, Ltd., anywhere in New Zealand and you'll see the Jewish influence in the land. You can see the colored fountain on Mission Bay's Beach Front, which was donated to the city by Eliot Davis in memory of his son Trevor, or take a respite from your travels in downtown Myers Park, given to the city by the former chief justice. Sir Ernest Davis presented the University of Auckland's medical school with the Marion Davis Medical Library in 1960 and subsequently set up an endowment to maintain the library in perpetuity.

Just a ten-minute walk up the hill from Myers Park is the throbbing heart of the Jewish community, embodied in the modern concrete and red-brick Auckland Hebrew Congregation and Communal Centre complex on Greys Avenue (telephone 373-2908), designed by local architect and congregation member John Goldwater. The airy, 750-seat synagogue is entered from a sunny courtyard and features a three-dimensional Star of David light hovering over the *bimah,* suspended from the Superdome-like ceiling just above the women's gallery.

Upstairs on the Greys Avenue side, the Alexander Astor Hall, named for the rabbi who served there for nearly forty years, is used for weddings, *bar mitzvahs* and community gatherings. In the shadows of an Orthodox setting, the kindergarten and day school's fine reputation draws many students, but with diminished growth and an older Jewish population, 80 percent of the students are non-Jewish.

Visitors can get a tour of the synagogue and center (including tea) by calling in advance. Information on communal events can be found in the congregation's monthly newsletter, *Kesher.*

The Auckland Hebrew Congregation's former home at 19A Princess Street was saved from the wrecking ball a few years ago. A bank now occupies the stately Victorian edifice, in which the synagogue was located from 1858 to 1968. Sitting opposite the Hyatt Auckland Hotel, the building sits on a hill with a magnificent view of the city's harbor. A plaque with a Star of David in the center identifies the site as "the spiritual heart for the Jewish people of Auckland."

Like the current home of the Auckland Hebrew Congregation, the Liberal Temple Shalom is also a modern structure (though much smaller), in the tradition of many suburban American synagogues. It has a

369

double arklike roof and heavy incorporation of glass in the walls. The congregation, at 180 Manukau Road, has about 100 members (telephone 544-139).

If you'd like a tour of Auckland that includes places of Jewish historic interest, contact David Levin at Shalom Auckland Tours, 36 Allenby Road, Papatoetoe, Auckland (telephone 278-7756). The tour includes a kosher lunch.

Wellington Sights: Wellington's Jewish Community Centre at 80 Webb Street was completed in 1977 and sits on the same block as the Beth El Synagogue and the Wellington Jewish Social Club. Within the gray, functional complex of buildings — the focal point for Jewish clubs and societies — are the seven hundred-seat main sanctuary and a ninety-seat junior synagogue; a hall for sports events and plays; a day school, a Hebrew school, and a nursery school.

Today, 145 years after David Isaacs brought *kashrut* to the land, Sid Braham, the former bantamweight boxing champion of Auckland, assists his son-in-law in the country's only kosher butcher shop, located in the centre.

If it weren't for the unobtrusive *Magen David* by the door, you might walk by Wellington's Liberal Temple Sinai at 147 Ghuznee Street (848-179). It looks like a neighborhood house, but you'll be warmly greeted inside this eighty-five-seat synagogue, where an estimated one-third of the members have converted to Judaism.

Julius Vogel's name has been given to two buildings. Vogel House, in Lower Hutt, is the current prime minister's residence. The Vogel Building houses the Ministry of Works and Development.

Side Trip: If you travel to Dunedin on South Island, don't miss Olveston, a magnificent Edwardian mansion that was the home of David Theomin, one of the city's most prominent Jewish citizens and president of its Jewish community. Completed in 1906 and willed to the city in 1966 by Theomin's daughter, the house at 42 Royal Terrace is both an architectural masterpiece and the repository of the family's extensive art collection.

Culture and Eating: In both Auckland and Wellington, the community centers are the prime purveyors of culture. Each contains a library with a Judaica collection, and throughout the year the centers offer musical entertainment, lectures, and special events. With many of New Zealand's Jews either refugees from central Europe or their descendants, the annual Holocaust program is a prominent event.

There are no kosher restaurants in New Zealand. Shelly's Catering Service in Auckland can provide kosher meals (telephone 630-3299). The Auckland Hebrew Congregation (373-2908) has a popular fish lunch on Thursdays. The shop in the communal center, open 10 A.M. to 2 P.M. weekdays, sells kosher meat and wine, books, and Judaica. The center also publishes a directory of kosher food products available in the country. If notified in advance, the congregation can arrange home hospitality for visitors.

In Wellington, visitors can order a kosher meal or arrange for home hospitality by contacting the Jewish Community Centre (484-5081).

General Sights: Auckland's hills descend to two magnificent harbors, where local Jewish yachtsmen sail and travelers can take a harbor cruise from the Ferry Building on Quay Street downtown, close to Queen Street's excellent shopping. To get a feel of the country, take a day tour to Rotorua, including the thermal reserve, the Maori Arts and Crafts Institute, and the Agrodome, where nineteen breeds of sheep put on a Las Vegas-like show on stage.

Wellington is an easy city to get about in by bus with a "day-tripper" ticket. You will have an excellent, panoramic view of the city from Mount Victoria Lookout or on a cable car ride from Lambert Quay up to Kelburn.

Reading: Maurice Shadbolt's *Season of the Jew* (W. W. Norton), set in New Zealand in the mid-nineteenth century, is an intense, fictionalized account of a Maori uprising led by a mission-educated would-be Moses who rejected the New Testament and declared himself and his followers to be the new Israelites.

Jewish themes have been expressed in the

poetry of Brasch and Wolfskehl, and others can be found in the book *Jewish Writings from Down Under: An Anthology of Australian and New Zealand Literature* (Micah Publications).

For historical background, there are Odeda Rosenthal's *Not Strictly Kosher: Pioneer Jews in New Zealand* (Starchand Press), Lionel Albert's *Some of the Jewish Men and Women Who Contributed to the History of Auckland, 1840–1981*, and M. L. Goldman's *The History of Jews in New Zealand* (Reed).

The monthly Zionist Federation newspaper *Jewish Chronicle* informs the community about activity in New Zealand and Israel.

But don't dwell on history too long; what's important is the living community. The Jews of New Zealand have maintained their identity and gained acceptance by their fellow citizens. They may have done it all away from the world's centers of action, but the Jewish "Kiwis" and their country are definitely worth a visit.

—*Harvey Gotliffe*

Nice

There are many good reasons to go to Nice, capital of the French Riviera—the sun, the beaches, luxurious casinos, carnivals, festivals, jazz concerts, museums, colorful markets, and a quaint old quarter. Nestled among the sights, neither obscured by the surroundings nor standing out as much as it might elsewhere, is Nice's Jewish community of 25,000.

History: References have been found to Jews in Nice in the fourth century, though little is known of a community life before 1342, when an edict compelled the town's Jews to wear distinguishing badges. When the Count of Savoy took control of Nice in 1430, he offered Jews protection from baptism, yet instituted various prohibitions and restricted them to a separate quarter, the Giudaria. Over the years, ghetto living was alternately abolished and reinstituted.

Though the community has had its ups and downs, the Jewish presence has been continuous. The first known synagogue was built in 1428. Augmenting the community of French and Italian-speaking Jews were immigrants from Rhodes, expelled by the Turks in 1499. Conversos came by way of Italy and Holland in the mid-seventeenth century. Prefiguring a massive influx that would take place three centuries later, Jews from Algeria began arriving in 1669. Over the years the diverse groups became a single community and even developed their own tongue, Judéo-Niçois, a mixture of the local dialect and Hebrew.

French Republican troops tore down the gates of the ghetto in 1792 and emancipation was proclaimed, but during a twenty-year period of Sardinian rule (1828–48) the community was ordered back behind the walls. Only when Nice became permanently French did the ghetto disappear.

The advantages of a free port with trading access to the Mediterranean and a geographical location near the crossroads of France, Italy, and Spain were not lost on homeless Jews looking for a place to settle. Add the comfortable climate and the easygoing nature of Nice denizens, and one wonders that the community did not grow faster. Even as late as the early 1900s there were only 500 Jews in Nice.

At the beginning of World War II, Nice was under Italian occupation, and many Jews from the German-occupied portions of France found refuge there. When the Germans invaded the Italian zone in September 1943, they immediately began rounding up Jews for shipment to death camps. The work of the French Resistance and Jewish youth groups, coupled with the sympathy of the local population and clergy, helped save many lives, though more than 5,000 Jews from the former Vichy zone were sent to their deaths.

Community: Several hundred Jews—natives of Nice and refugees—reestablished the community after the war, and they were shortly overwhelmed by a wave that would increase the Jewish presence more than tenfold in just a few years. The newcomers came, mostly in the early 1960s, as refugees from the French territories in North Africa. Today, more than 80 percent of Nice's Jews trace their origins to that immigration.

Nice's Jews are scattered but well organized. Though North African Sephardic culture has come to dominate the community culturally, the newcomers moved into the existing French-Jewish structure. The Consistoire, the community's representative organization, is in the Centre Michelet, a modern, elegant facility at 22 rue Michelet (telephone 9351-8980). The building is also a community and cultural center that can cater a Riviera wedding or *bar mitzvah*; it even has a *mikveh* on the premises. Another Community Center–Synagogue complex is the Centre Chalom at 23 avenue Emile-Ripert.

There is no Jewish quarter nowadays, mostly owing to the variety of occupations in which Jews engage. But many are connected through one of the numerous Jewish groups. The newest Jewish presence in the city is Hadassah; there are four B'nai B'rith lodges, a central fund that disperses aid to Jewish schools, youth groups, rest homes, and social causes, not to mention support for Israeli causes. Nice is a twin city of Netanya, and one of the most active clubs is the Netanya Club. Nice has a Jewish day school, two *yeshivot*, and a Jewish bookstore (Librairie Tanya, 25 rue Pertinax). Thirty miles out of town there is a Jewish sports center open all year long, combining camping, sports, and religious courses.

L'Arche, a monthly published in Paris, has a special Nice edition six times a year. A fortnightly, *Nitzan,* covers the activities of the community and has articles of general interest. The newsletter, *L'Atis,* serves the traditional Sephardi community. *Shalom Nitzan* is a weekly half-hour radio program dedicated to Jewish topics.

Sights: There are few signs of the Giudaria, as Nice's ghetto was called, but it was situated in the heart of today's old city, amid the elegant houses of the rue Benoît-Bunico. The house at Benoît-Bunico 18 is believed to be an ancient synagogue.

Nice has never had more synagogues than it does today, but the most prominent is the oldest, the Sephardic synagogue at rue Gustave Deloye 7 (telephone 9392-1138). Dedicated in 1886, with a splendid walk-in ark that contains twelve Torahs, it is the spiritual center of the North African community. Even during the summer it boasts a full house on *Shabbat.* Not far away, at rue Blacas 1, is the smaller Ashkenazi synagogue, lately enjoying the support of the Lubavitcher rebbe (telephone 9388-5732). Most synagogues are open only two hours daily for services. Bear in mind also that there is heavy security at all French synagogues.

Perhaps the premier Jewish sight in Nice is the Musée National Message Biblique, Marc Chagall—the most important permanent collection of Chagall's works. Located in the poshest part of Nice, on the corner of Avenue Docteur Ménard and Boulevard Cimiez, on land supplied by the government in a building erected by the government, it houses a collection donated by the artist to France, where Chagall "was born a second time." Some eighty thousand people visit every year. It was one of only two museums in France dedicated to an artist while he was still living (the other honored Picasso), and since Chagall's death in 1985 it has assumed added importance.

Message in paint: Chagall made Nice his home and the city made a home for his art

It was of Chagall that Picasso once remarked, "He must have had an angel in his head somewhere." That angelic touch is in the twelve spectacular paintings of scenes from Genesis and Exodus, the preparatory sketches (forty-five oils, ninety-one pastels), gouaches, lithographs, sculptures, and tapestries. Particularly breathtaking are the stained-glass mosaics and painted glasses. The light of the French Riviera, Chagall's home for many years, illuminates the stone-and-glass complex. Less well-known is a unique library located in the museum, dedicated to the history of religions. For information, call 9381-7575.

There are two testimonials of the Nazi scourge in Nice's old Jewish cemetery, located at Le Château, one of four denominational burial grounds atop the main hill on which the city is built. The two monuments near the cemetery's entrance are dedicated to the "Heroes of the Resistance" and the "Martyrs of the Persecution"; the first contains an urn of ashes, the other a receptacle full of soap, the remains of the many deported Nice Jews. Higher up on the hill is the Château, now a military school, and every day at 1 P.M. a naval gun is fired, as if in homage to the dead.

The cemetery, which is located in a spectacular, panoramic spot, dates from the sixteenth century, and there are vaults of old Italian Jewish families, reminiscent of non-Jewish tombs in Florence and Genoa. On the four-century-old sepulchral vault of the Landau family, an Italian architect by the name of Romanelli left not only his name but also his address in Florence, for prospective clients.

Restaurants: Not far from the main synagogue, there are several kosher restaurants, including Au Roi David (rue Clément Roassal 9) and Chez David Guez (avenue Pertinax 26). Others include La Tikvah at rue de Suisse 2 and La Colline at route de Ste-Antoine 181. Questions about events or *kashrut* that can't be answered by the Consistoire can be put to the office of Mordecai Bensoussan, the regional chief rabbi (telephone 9392-1138).

General Sights: From the Chagall museum, walk farther up the hill, on Bou-levard Cimiez. It is the central artery of a hill in the aristocratic quarter of town and has some of the most opulent private residences of the Riviera. There you will find the Matisse museum, which offers insight into the creative process of this renowned painter.

The obligatory visit, without which no one can really claim to have seen Nice, is a walk down the Promenade des Anglais, the wide seashore avenue that has been the traditional parade ground of the rich and famous of Europe for over a century. Although the traffic is heavy, the scene is still impressive and stimulating on a summer afternoon. And sipping coffee at the Negresco, probably the finest and best-known hotel on the Riviera, is no less a tradition. If you have no budget limitations, stay there and enjoy the treatment reserved for kings and magnates.

Side Trips: Saint-Paul-de-Vence is a medieval hill town about a half hour from Nice. Not only is it worth the trip to walk the twisting, narrow streets, but it is also an important artists' colony. For the last twenty years of his life Chagall lived in the secluded wood behind the Fondation Maeght, a museum of contemporary art which is itself set in a lovely pine grove. Matisse had a home in Saint-Paul-de-Vence as well. A contemporary Jewish artist who lives in the town is Théo Tobiasse.

Nice may get the largest number of tourists, but it has neither the largest nor the oldest Jewish community in the South of France. Marseille experienced the same kind of explosive growth as Nice in the 1960s and is today home to a predominantly Sephardic Jewish community of 70,000. There were Jews in Marseille during Roman times, though the oldest Jewish traces extant date only from the nineteenth century. The main synagogue, built in Romanesque style and dedicated in 1865, is at rue Breteuil 117; damaged extensively by the Nazis, it was renovated after the war. The Marseille Consistoire is located in the same building (telephone 9137-7184). The main Jewish community center is the Centre Edmond Fleg at impasse Drago 4 (telephone 9137-4201).

The best look at Provence's Jewish past is to be found outside the coastal cities. When

Louis XI expelled the Jews from France in 1394, only the Pontifical States, which included the towns of Avignon, Carpentras, and Cavaillon, were exempted. (Nice was, at the time, outside the French realm.) Jews in these three towns, together with those of L'Isle-sur-Sorgue, formed the "four holy communities" of the Comtat Venaissin and developed their own dialect, culture, food and liturgy—Comtadin—which was close to the Portuguese rite.

Avignon, once a center of Jewish scholarship, has remains from two ghettos. The older one, Carrière des Juifs, is in the middle of the narrow streets and alleys below the Palace of the Popes. Little remains of the Jews who lived in the area a thousand years ago, though some of the streets, such as the rue de Vieille-Juiverie, still bear their ancient names. The new ghetto, in the center of town, dates from the thirteenth century and has more evidence of its Jewish past, including street names like rue Jacob and chemin de la Synagogue. The modern synagogue, at place Jerusalem 2, stands on the site of the medieval house of worship destroyed by a fire in 1844. The Avignon community had dwindled to a few hundred just before World War II. The North African immigration helped boost it to 2,500.

The synagogue in Carpentras, on the northeast corner of the town square (place de la Mairie) is a national monument. It was built in 1367 and underwent major reconstructions in the eighteenth and nineteenth centuries. Around the synagogue was the carrière, an area smaller than a football field in which 160 Jewish families lived; as in Venice, when the community grew it had to build up, so that the seven- and eight-story buildings, seen from afar, looked like the most imposing part of the city.

The synagogue is unimposing from the outside but, as Carol Herselle Krinsky notes in *Synagogues of Europe,* the synagogues of Carpentras and Cavaillon "have wood paneling with classical and rococo motifs that would have been at home in Parisian salons a generation before the styles were absorbed in these provincial towns." Among the outstanding features of the Carpentras synagogue are the many hanging candelabra and the gallery-level

bimah reached by two circular staircases and surrounded by three menorahs that seem to float in the air. In the courtyard of the synagogue is the entrance to a vaulted cellar where *matzah* was baked, probably from the 17th century; the cellar has two ovens set deep into its wall and a marble slab that, according to tradition, was given by a pope for the preparation of unleavened bread. In the building's subcellar is a *mikveh* fed by a natural spring. The synagogue has *Shabbat* services and is also open daily (telephone 9063-3997).

The Carpentras community peaked at 1,000 at the time of the French Revolution, when it constituted 10 percent of the town's population. The last descendants of the medieval community died in the 1970s, and today's community of 500 is predominantly North African. In addition to the synagogue, the Cathedral of St-Siffrein is also of Jewish interest. It has a Porte Juive, on the left side, through which Jews once entered for compulsory sermons on Christianity.

If the menorahs in Carpentras seem to float, some visitors to Cavaillon think the entire synagogue there seems suspended in air. The building, at rue Hébraïque 14, rests on an archway above the street. The arch was probably the entrance to the medieval carrière. Smaller than its sister in Carpentras, the Cavaillon synagogue shares many characteristics and is also a national landmark. The crowned *bimah* is on a balcony atop fluted Corinthian columns and enclosed by a wrought-iron railing. The *matzah* bakery attached to the Cavaillon synagogue now houses the Jewish Museum of the Comtat Venaissin, which exhibits relics and documents of the Comtat's Jewish communities. Fewer than 100 Jews live in Cavaillon today. The synagogue and museum hours are irregular; if there is no one on the premises contact Mr. Mathon at rue Chabran 23, or call the Cavaillon Office of Tourism (rue Saunerie 79) at 9071-3201.

Reading: Paula Hyman's *From Dreyfus to Vichy* (Columbia University Press), which embraces the entire twentieth-century history of the Jews in France, has a considerable chapter dedicated to Nice. Saint-Paul-de-Vence's best known fictional artist is Chaim Potok's Asher Lev. In the two novels with Lev in the center—*My Name is Asher Lev* and *The Gift of Asher Lev* (Knopf)—Potok manages to evoke Saint-Paul-de-Vence and Nice and to connect them both with Brooklyn. The books make good reading while sitting in a café on the Promenade des Anglais or on the beach.

—Edna Fainaru

Oslo

And so it came to pass one recent year in Norway, where the government distributes equal amounts of financial support per capita to its various religious denominations, that the person receiving the Jewish community's portion was sent ten times the usual amount for the dozen or so Jews in one small city. Astonished, he told the authorities they had made a mistake. "No, not at all," was the response. Since the construction of two new churches in the area had required an increase in aid to those congregants, a spokesman explained, "We gave the same to the Jews as we did to the Christians."

Such sagas of official evenhandedness go far toward explaining why members of the world's northernmost Jewish community are so enthralled with their unlikely residence. Their numbers are small; the majority live in Oslo. Their roots are short, about a century at most; due to wartime decimation, forty years is more the norm. And like other Norwegians, they feel their isolation at the top of Europe.

But the Jews of the midnight sun—reflecting these days a particular vitality—also revel in the splendors of a long and lovely land, a country molded by mountains, fluted with fjords, and populated by a people who, after centuries as political handmaidens to either Denmark or Sweden, well appreciate their liberty. They now make extra efforts to extend that liberty to those few non-Vikings in their midst.

History: Given the homogeneity of Norwegian society—which produced a skittishness toward foreigners in general—it took other peoples a comparatively long time to gain the right to reside in the country. Leading the way, the Jews won access in 1851.

A few had visited earlier, but only for business. During the seventeenth and eighteenth centuries, when Norway was united with Denmark, Danish rules applied. This meant that except for the so-called Portuguese Jews, who had free access, a letter of safe-conduct was required, without which a visitor risked arrest, fines, and deportation. The regulations were followed so inconsistently, however, that in 1734 three "Portuguese" Jews from Holland, nabbed on arrival, spent two months in prison. On the other hand, Jews like Manuel Texeira of Hamburg, a co-owner of Norwegian mines, did come to trade.

In the wake of the Napoleonic Wars, Denmark lost Norway to Sweden and a new Norwegian constitution was written. But despite its liberal cast, it made Lutheranism the state religion in which all children must be raised, effectively excluding Jews. This law was so strictly enforced that in 1817 when a Jewish sailor was shipwrecked on Norwegian shores he was thrown in jail and then deported.

The 1830s brought some relaxation in attitude and the occasional issuance of safe-conduct letters. Among the recipients was Solomon Heine, Heinrich Heine's uncle, who proved instrumental in securing a loan to Norway from the Copenhagen banking house of Hambro and Son. But the real drive to repeal the ban on Jewish settlement came in the next decade and was spearheaded by Henrik Arnold Wergeland, one of Norway's greatest poets.

Wergeland, who had befriended Moroccan Jews in Paris, began submitting proposals on the Jews' behalf to the Norwegian Parliament in 1839. He also crusaded in print. Among other works on the subject, he wrote an essay, *"Indlaeg I Jodensagen"* ("In Contribution to the Jewish

Cause") in 1841, in which he posited moral, religious and financial arguments for the Jews' admission; and two volumes of poems, *The Jew* and *The Jewess*. His pamphleteering led to the creation of a parliamentary commission to study the question, which in 1842 proposed free immigration. But though the motion for free access won a simple majority three times between 1845 and 1848 — and the Ministry of Justice confirmed the rights of Portuguese Jews — the required two-thirds majority was not attained until 1851, six years after Wergeland's death.

A few Jews trickled in from Denmark and Schleswig-Holstein in the early 1850s, but even by the 1870s there were no more than 50 — of whom only about 25 were permanent residents. With the oppression of the 1880s in Eastern Europe, however, more arrived. Refugees from Russia, Poland, and Lithuania came, usually en route to England or the United States. But those without means to go farther remained in Norway — 214 by 1890; 642 by 1900.

They worked first as peddlers, then as shopkeepers, later as factory owners in an essentially peaceful, accepting, and even supportive land. Among outstanding Norwegians who celebrated their cause were Bjornstjerne Bjornson — Norway's leading national writer, a contemporary of Edvard Grieg's who fought for Alfred Dreyfus — and Fridtjof Nansen, the Arctic explorer.

With Norway bordering Russia, Russian Jews were viewed somewhat suspiciously whenever "The Bear" reared — as during the Russo-Japanese War of 1905, or World War I and the attendant Russian Revolution. In addition, the occasional churchman rippled the waters, proselytizing or enunciating stereotypes to worshipers reared in complete ignorance of Jews. But for each Norwegian who spoke ill of Jews, more spoke favorably. As a contemporary community member explains, "In Eastern Europe, the Jews were cursed for killing Jesus. In this country, they thank the Jews for giving them Jesus."

So low was the anti-Semitism quotient in Norway, even during the 1930s, that in 1936 the vote for the pro-Nazi Nasjonal Samling (National Unity) Party of the infamous Vidkun Quisling dropped from 2.23 percent of the total to 1.83 percent. And after *Kristallnacht* the Norwegian government and other indigenous organizations intensified efforts to help Jews out of Germany and Czechoslovakia. By 1940 between 1,700 and 1,800 Jews were in Norway, including nearly 300 refugees.

Given this climate, the war — which hit Norway early — hit particularly hard. On April 8, 1940, well before Norwegians had prepared themselves, the Germans invaded. Confusion reigned initially as Norwegians, inclined to resist, tried to determine the friend-foe equation. Trouble began for the Jews almost immediately, with certain professions closing them out by October. But though they felt some persecution throughout 1941, it was 1942 before the full horror began.

Beginning in March 1942, a racial department was established and passport and identity cards were marked "Jew," with forced registration starting in June. The already-in-progress roundup gained impetus after October 23 when a Quisling frontier guard fell to assassins, two of whom were Jews. Not only was all Jewish property confiscated, but all Jewish males over sixteen were subject to arrest; when heads of households couldn't be found, women and children were taken. In November one boatload of Jews departed for Poland — and Auschwitz; shortly thereafter, a second.

Especially in the beginning, Norwegians fought the anti-Jewish legislation. The bishops of the Norwegian church issued strong protests. But to no avail. On December 1, 1942, Quisling became chief of state and within a week abolished the constitution and made himself dictator.

Precise figures on the fate of Norway's Jews vary. Roughly 900 escaped arrest, with many fleeing to Sweden. The Norwegian Resistance, in which Jews served, helped considerably. About 60 Jews, including those married to non-Jews, were interned in Norway or managed to hide. A few were killed through acts of war. The remainder, up to 800, were sent to concentration camps. Fewer than 25 survived.

So keenly had the Norwegians themselves suffered — with 50,000 arrested, 9,000 sent to concentration camps, and scores of others tortured or executed — that by war's end they felt more closely bound to the

Jews. In 1946 Norway offered asylum to unaccompanied children from the Displaced Persons (DP) camps, but the offer was turned down in favor of Palestine. In 1947 the king and government invited 1,000 displaced Jews with skills useful to the country; about 400 accepted, but many of them stayed only a brief time before leaving for North America or Israel. In the 1950s when the DP camps were closed, Norway — knowing it might have to care for such persons all their lives — accepted 100 hardcore invalid cases no one else wanted. The refugees were sent to mountain hospitals where most recovered. Among them was Imre Hercz, who became a leading physician.

Norway pushed hard for the establishment of Israel. Among the staunchest supporters was Trygve Lie, the first secretary-general of the United Nations, who devoted much diplomatic energy to the resolution for Jewish statehood. Another highly respected Norwegian with an impact on Israel was General Odd Bull, chief of the UN truce supervision organization from 1963 to 1970.

Relations between the two countries have extended beyond the diplomatic to cultural, scientific, economic, and humanitarian spheres. Because of the political and ideological compatibility between Norway's Labor Party and Israel's, the two developed joint projects, including a housing complex in Israel paid for by the Norwegian version of the Histadrut. In addition, in 1949 the Norwegian Relief Organization brought 200 North African children destined for Youth Aliyah to Norway for eight months of rehabilitation. When 28 of 29 in a second group from Tunisia died in a plane crash approaching Oslo, the Norwegian public, in addition to dedicating a forest near the crash site in their memory, contributed the money to establish Yanuv in Israel for North African immigrants.

The camaraderie soured somewhat in July 1973 after Israel committed a major operational blunder in Norway. While pursuing the Black September leader who had planned the Munich massacre of Israeli Olympic athletes, Mossad agents mistakenly killed a Moroccan waiter living in Lillehammer. Thanks to Norwegian sympathy, the arrested Israelis spent only twenty-two months in prison. And one, South Africa-born Sylvia Raphael, married her Norwegian lawyer. But for Israeli intelligence, the Lillehammer affair was so distressing it is referred to with a Hebrew pun — *Leyl Hamar* (the Night of Bitterness). Twenty years later bitterness turned to hope, as Norway hosted the secret talks that led to mutual recognition between Israel and the Palestine Liberation Organization.

Norway also did battle on behalf of Soviet Jewry. Church leaders and government officials were outspoken during the days when Brezhnev ruled in Moscow. When a concert to benefit refuseniks was supported by the Norwegian Parliament and attended by many top government officials, a diplomatic crisis with Russia was only narrowly avoided. In recent years there have been episodes of swastika smearing near the Oslo synagogue and elsewhere, plus agitation from the country's 50,000-member Muslim population. But Norway's Jews, mindful that their country is among the few places that has invited Jews to settle, continue to consider it unequivocally one of Europe's friendliest lands.

Community: Before World War II professed Jews were scattered as far north as Honningsvag, the last town before North Cape, the "Land's End" of Europe. And still today, an Israeli married to a non-Jew is believed to live in this jumping-off point to the Arctic. But though Jewish names are found here and there along the route north — and there's speculation about the scene in Murmansk, just across the Norwegian border in Russia — Eda and Abel Fischer of Narvik are currently the only known practicing Jews above the Arctic Circle. In Trondheim, just below the circle, stands the world's northernmost synagogue, with a membership of 130, and there are pockets of Jews elsewhere. But all bow to Oslo, where the community today is 1,000, give or take 100.

Originally called "The Mosaic Congregation," Oslo's community was founded in 1892 and consecrated its synagogue in 1920. For a time the community was divided, with an "Israelite" congregation attracting the more religious to a synagogue dedicated the following year. The groups united, however, after World War II. Since tradition keeping is considered the only road to survival, today's congregation functions as Orthodox (with winter services beginning at 3:00 P.M., in summer at 8:25 P.M.). But most members' style of observance is closer to Conservative and Reform.

Completely integrated into the community at large, the children's native tongue is Norwegian and they attend Norwegian public schools. Jews are now found on every socioeconomic level, from house painter and shoemaker to doctor, dentist, and lawyer. In part because so many are refugees, in part because Norwegian society eschews ostentation, most—particularly the wealthy—keep a low profile.

Though they view themselves as being on Judaism's outskirts, Oslo's Jews call themselves a microcommunity, since despite their diminutive numbers they provide all necessary Jewish services. The city boasts in miniature everything found elsewhere—from a community center to an old-age home to a once-a-week religious school attended by children between ages seven and eighteen. It even has a kosher butcher shop run by an Israeli Arab across the street from the Riks Hospital. Since *shechitah* is banned in Norway, he imports kosher meat—as well as kosher pickles and cheese and gefilte fish—for use by the old-age home, the community center, and the 50 or so families that observe *kashrut*.

Though still predominantly an older community—with 60 percent of its members over sixty—Oslo Jewry has recently been revitalized. During the last few years about 45 women and 5 men have converted in. In addition Norwegians visiting Israel have often returned with Israeli spouses. The current zest is attributed to the influence of its hand-picked, specially groomed and much-admired rabbi, Michael Melchior.

A scion of the Melchior family of Danish chief rabbis, Michael was spotted by the Norwegian community when he was twenty-one. Having been without a rabbi from 1958 to 1978 and fearing for its disintegration, the community offered to provide for Melchior's education with the understanding that upon its completion he would minister to it. He has done this with innovative gusto. To involve young families in community life he persuaded a different couple every week to host the *Kiddush*. He instituted a kindergarten, a children's choir, and regular family seminars. To educate non-Jewish Norwegians about Judaism he began a program whereby public school classes regularly visit the synagogue for instruction and discussion. He often speaks on radio and television and has become a confidant of politicians. Since going on *aliyah* in 1986 he has commuted between Israel and Norway, spending sixteen to eighteen weeks in the north, being there to celebrate the High Holy Days and Purim.

Sights: Set on a fjord sprinkled with little islands and backed by mountains harboring an Olympic ski jump, Oslo is a scenically well-placed city. Though in recent years it has grown greatly, its compact heart continues to exude the steadfastness of the north.

The synagogue, at 13 Bjergstien, stands in a residential neighborhood in Oslo's north-central area on land donated by erstwhile members. Influenced by Lithuanian concepts, it boasts a high-arched ceiling bordered by a *tallit*-like design bearing the inscription "How goodly are thy tents, O Jacob, thy dwelling places O Israel." The *bimah* stands within the arch, and the floor is padded with Oriental rugs. Its stained-glass windows are ringed by *Magen Davids*, which on bright days reflect on the walls. For unknown reasons, except for removing a *Magen David* the Nazis left the synagogue and its contents untouched. The late King Olav V, then crown prince, attended its postwar reconsecration, the first time a member of the royal family had entered a Norwegian synagogue. The Jewish community center, built in 1960, stands next door. Oslo's second synagogue, destroyed during the war, was located at Karl Meiergate 16.

Among the trees of the Var Frilser's Cemetery, in western Oslo not far from the Aker Church, stands a monument erected in 1849 by the Jews of Denmark and Sweden to Wergeland honoring his support for the Jewish cause. Because Jews were not yet permitted to reside in Norway when the monument was commissioned, it had to be unveiled in Sweden. Enclosed in an olive-green-with-white-trim structure topped by a frilly Gothic-style spire, the monument consists of a stone pedestal topped by a bust of Wergeland and bears two inscriptions. On one side it reads: "To the indefatigable fighter for freedom and the rights of man and citizen." And on the other it says: "Grateful Jews outside the frontiers of Norway erected this monument to him." Every May 17, Norway's Independence Day, the monument becomes the focus of pilgrimage for Jewish youth groups who lay flowers and listen to speeches. Wergeland is also honored with a life-size statue on Karl Johansgate, Oslo's grand walking street.

A couple of blocks away overlooking the city's harbor stands its massive red-brick City Hall. In addition to a frieze of the politician Carl Joachim Hambro, this Nordic building contains large frescoes depicting wartime Norway. While they don't specifically present the Jewish scene, their visions of bombs dropping, ships sinking, and the Gestapo invading private homes reflect a powerful sensibility—not surprising since much was done by artist Alf Rolfsen, himself an Auschwitz survivor.

On the waterfront stands the formidable Akerhus Castle. Within one section of this venerable fortress, running several flights underground, is Norway's Resistance Museum, operated primarily by wives and widows of Resistance leaders. The exhibits document all aspects of the war in Norway such as the German invasion, the imprisonment of Norwegians, and the Resistance's activities, including the sabotage of Norway's heavy-water plant (dramatized in the movie *The Heroes of Telemark* starring Kirk Douglas). A special section is devoted to the fate of Norwegian Jews, including anti-Jewish signs; forms for registering as Jews; and deportation instructions. Adjacent to the museum are the execution grounds where Norwegians were shot during the war—and where Quisling was executed at its conclusion.

Miscellany in Oslo's heart includes Valerengen Church, whose stained-glass windows offer biblical scenes and in which God's name appears in Hebrew letters; the two Jewish-owned Oslo Sweater Shops—one in the SAS Scandinavia Hotel, the other in the Royal Christiana Hotel—considered among the best in town; and the Karl Johansgate, the walking street itself

which once boasted Jewish-owned shops, including the sumptuous Vollmann's department store.

On the city's periphery stand Grini Prison, once used as a concentration camp; Vigeland Park, filled with massive granite and bronze sculptures of the stages of man (in a style some feel evokes the Holocaust's hell); Vigeland Museum, whose exterior employs a six-pointed-star motif; and the museum devoted to artist Edvard Munch, supported by Jews in his early days, whose works some say foreshadowed the coming agony of the Nazi period. About fifty miles outside Oslo near Storsand is Hurum, a memorial park dedicated to the North African Jewish children killed in the 1949 plane crash.

Among other displays of general interest in and around Oslo are explorer Thor Heyerdahl's *Kon-Tiki* and *Ra II*; the polar vessel *Fram*; three Viking ships from one thousand years ago and the Norwegian Folk Museum with centuries-old structures.

Side Trip: In Norway's former royal seat, Trondheim—reachable by plane, coastal steamer, or train—stands the world's northernmost synagogue. Three degrees below the Arctic Circle at 1 Arkitekt Christiesgate, close to the large Nidaros Cathedral, the building was once a railroad station on the line from Oslo. Though heavily damaged during the war by military billeted there who threw pews out the windows and used chandeliers for target practice, it still holds *Shabbat* services at 5:30 P.M. to avoid sunset-time confusions. The community, dating back to the 1860s, now has 130 members—including many postwar arrivals from elsewhere on Norway's west coast. Initially Trondheim's Jews came on peddling trips from Sweden. Later they owned shops, especially on the street called Brattorgate. The Plaza Isak Mendelson is named for a Jew who helped build the city's exhibition hall. The Ringve Museum of Musical Instruments contains a *shofar* and an Israeli drum.

Culture: The community publishes *Jodisk Menighetsblad* (The Jewish Congregation Magazine) three or four times a year, which circulates to interested non-Jews as well. Events such as lectures and folklore presentations are organized annually, and whenever someone of interest—Benjamin Netanyahu or Chaim Potok, to cite to recent examples—is passing through on other business, he is engaged. The community also hosts and celebrates Jewish Nobel Peace Prize winners, such as Elie Wiesel, Menachem Begin, and Henry Kissinger, when they come to Oslo to receive their awards. With Melchior engaged in issues beyond the community, the Jews involve themselves deeply in activities of broader concern, such as the "Anatomy of Hate" conference organized in 1990 by Elie Wiesel and attended by, among others, President Jimmy Carter, China's Chai Ling of the Foundation for Human Rights and Democracy, and Presidents Vaclav Havel of Czechoslovakia and Vytautas Landsbergis of Lithuania.

Personalities: In a country where the highest government rank after king is president of Parliament—to whom the king bows—probably the best-known Jew in Norway today is the Parliament president, Jo Benkow.

Among other outstanding Jews are Supreme Court Justice Charles Philipson; Robert Levine, pianist and first director of Oslo's Music Academy; Oskar Mendelsohn, recipient of a king's honor for writing his two-volume history of the Jews in Norway; journalists Eva Sobert and Peter Beck; Bente Kahan of the National Theater; Leo Eitinger, professor of psychiatry at Oslo University, a refugee from Czechoslovakia via Auschwitz noted for his work on the post–concentration camp syndrome; and sexologist Dr. Bertold Gruenfeld, Norway's Dr. Ruth.

The late Carl Joachim Hambro, the speaker of Parliament when the Germans invaded—noted for helping get the royal family out of Norway quickly—was part Jewish. One of Norway's most influential theologians in the last century, Carl Paul Caspari, had a Jewish background.

Reading: Wergeland's poems *The Jew* and *The Jewess* have been translated into English but are difficult to find. Benkow's autobiography, *From the Synagogue to Parliament Hill,* though as yet untranslated, has been a best-seller. Herman Kahan, the Jewish community's current president, has coauthored his autobiography *Ilden Og Lyset (The Fire and the Light)* in Norwegian; his childhood friend Wiesel talks in *One Generation After* (Bibliophile Library) about meeting Kahan—originally named Chaim Hersh—after the war. The works of the Norwegian Knut Hamsun, despite his alleged Fascist leanings, well convey the not-too-long-ago Norwegian scene. *Night and Fog* (Norton) by Arne Brun Lie is one man's story of life in the Norwegian Resistance.

Recommendations: Oslo's only member of the prestigious Leading Hotels of the World group, the family-run Hotel Continental (opposite the National Theater and convenient to everywhere), is an elegant yet intimate hostelry that pays great attention to detail. SAS runs Scandinavian-sleek flight service to Oslo from various American gateways. When Jewish groups visit Oslo, the community offers *Shabbat* meals that may be attended by independent tourists. For further information on this and other Jewish community matters, contact Herman Kahan at 603-190. He'll get you started on exploring a land that has reciprocated Jewish appreciation.

—Phyllis Ellen Funke

Oxford and Cambridge

For centuries, the only universities in England were Oxford and Cambridge, founded in the Middle Ages and situated in the cities for which they are named. Of the two cites (both, coincidentally, fifty-seven miles from London), Cambridge is the more bucolic, with lush, manicured lawns and punting on the River Cam, and a beehive of architecturally and academically outstanding colleges. Oxford, older and more integrated into a bustling urban setting, also awes with its imposing quadrangles and venerable traditions.

Prime ministers, poets, and just about anyone intent upon rising in the British hierarchy have passed through "Oxbridge," as the pair of universities is called. (Nowadays, you can add American presidents to the list.) By the quirks and turns of history, Jews played a role in the origins of both places and then for centuries were mostly absent from the scene, only to reappear with increasing prominence after their readmittance to England in the seventeenth century. During the past century, increasing numbers of Jews have availed themselves of the intellectual and social benefits that Oxbridge attendance confers.

History: Although the city of Oxford can trace its roots back to the Saxon era, Cambridge's history reaches to pre-Roman times. It was in the 13th century that they became forever joined in the minds of men as twin citadels of learning.

In 1249, University College, the first of the schools that comprise Oxford University, was formed, probably by exiles from Paris. However, a century earlier, in 1141, a Jewish population was first recorded when they were caught in the political infighting of warring claimants to the throne.

A synagogue was established in Oxford in 1227 by descendants of those who are thought to have come over with William the Conqueror. Most local Jews at the time earned their living as either moneylenders or university landlords, positions that played a role in the student riots against them in 1244. In the period before the expulsion of all England's Jews in 1290, Oxford was one of the country's chief Jewish communities with at least 150 members.

Jewish scholars reappeared in Oxfordshire during the Cromwell era. James Levita, a believing Jew, was permitted to study in the Bodleian Library in the early 1600s. Although most Jews in Oxford in that era had converted to Christianity, Isaac Abendana, who stayed true to his faith, taught at Magdalen College in 1691. He was editor of the *Oxford Almanack and Jewish Calendar* during the last eight years of the century. Jacob, a Jew known only by his first name, is reputed to have opened the town's first coffeehouse in 1650. A plaque at 85 High Street notes this event. Cecil Roth, the Anglo-Jewish historian, believed that Jacob was the first to introduce coffee into England.

The modern Jewish community of Oxford was organized in 1842. For many years, the numbers of both permanent residents and students remained small. Then, as Hitler rose to power and World War II began, the population of fewer than 100 swelled with immigrants from abroad and those escaping the bombings of England's larger cities. Most of these people left when the war was over, but the growth of high-technology industry, research firms and the greater number of Jewish students have brought hundreds, especially during the school term.

Cambridge's history is somewhat similar

to and often intertwined with Oxford's. After several scholars were hanged in Oxford in the mid-thirteenth century, a group decamped and set up shop in the obscure market town on the Cam. However, as in Oxford, Jews, originally from Rouen, France, had put down roots in the heart of Cambridge earlier, in 1085. Before 1224 they had established a synagogue. One of the most respected scholars of his time, Benjamin of Cambridge, was one of fifty Jewish householders. Families clustered around the House of Worship, which was located at Market Square, but later in the century they spread out in a triangular pattern to an area that is now opposite St. John's College. In 1275, Queen Eleanor deported Cambridge's Jews to nearby Norwich, but some still remained in the neighborhood until the general expulsion.

Thanks to the intercession of Manasseh ben Israel, the Amsterdam scholar who petitioned Cromwell to formally readmit Jews to the country, more Jews trickled in to the British Isles after 1657. In the previous 350 years, only converts to Christianity, who came from abroad on various medical and diplomatic missions, and a handful of others who managed to evade exile had remained. In Cambridge, several converted Jews became readers in Hebrew at the university and taught the language to divinity students. In 1579, Isaac de Cardenas, a professing Sephardic Jew from Geneva, matriculated at Pembroke College.

By 1847, the modern community organized a congregation in Petty Cury in the town center where many Jews had shops. The original sanctuary was razed, and in 1940 a new synagogue was dedicated to serve a diverse population of students and permanent residents. Since 1899, the governing of the synagogue has been solely in the hands of undergraduates, as a result of various disagreements between university and townspeople.

Community: The Jewish communities of Oxford and Cambridge have much in common. Unlike most places in Britain, the two towns have an air of transience. During the school terms, the Jewish population greatly swells with students from all over the world. The resident Jewish population of Cambridge is estimated at 250, while Oxford has about 700. However, figures given by residents of both cities differ widely. Guesses as to the true size of Jewish enrollment varies from 400 to 1,000 at each university. Those involved in the Jewish communities are aware that there are large numbers of unaffiliated Jews.

Tensions between town and gown in the two Jewish communities are largely a thing of the past. The largest segment of Jewish residents in both cities is connected with the schools in some capacity. Many also work in medicine, business, and in the computer and research firms that have opened in the intellectually fertile climate. Given the proximity of London, a fair number are commuters; and a handful are retired people attracted by the abundant cultural opportunities.

All-nighters: A college town that owes its coffee houses to a medieval Jew

Oxford Sights: Because of the strong Christian influences in both places, those in search of Jewish sights may have to do some hunting. The most obvious site of Jewish interest in Oxford is the synagogue. Located at 21 Richmond Road (telephone 53042), a short walk from the center of the city, it is the second building on its site. In the 1880s, the congregation purchased a former Methodist chapel. In the 1970s, when the congregation needed more space, alumni of the university, now scattered around the world, contributed funds to replace the old building and erect a new, unified center, which houses in unique fashion all branches of Judaism under one roof. It is a modern, single-story building, constructed to blend in unobtrusively with the residential neighborhood in which it is situated. From the picture window of the synagogue's large all-purpose room there is a view of the small garden with the remains of an old stone wall. This was part of the original building. The Victorian-era *Aron Kodesh,* magnificently carved in oak, is still used, while a new ark is situated in the main sanctuary.

There are Orthodox services at the synagogue every Friday night and Saturday morning of the year, not to mention services for all the holidays and festivals. The synagogue also hosts Reform services, generally held the second and fourth *Shabbat* morning of each month. The two congregations-within-a-congregation work together to accommodate each other's needs.

A walk around Oxford takes the visitor past many reminders of the city's Jewish past. In the Middle Ages, the community lived along what is still one of the main streets, St. Aldate's, then called either Fish Street or Great Jewry. Three of their houses, now incorporated into the university and very difficult to identify, Moyse's, Lombard's, and Jacob's Hall, are thought to have been Jewish residences. Drop in at New College, founded in 1379, and look at the Sir Jacob Epstein sculpture of Lazarus at the chapel entrance. The Botanical Garden opposite Magdalen College is commemorated with a plaque as the ancient site of the Jewish cemetery.

The Bodleian Library has 3,000 Hebrew manuscripts and 30,000 volumes in Hebrew. The oldest item dates from the fifth century B.C.E. and is from Upper Egypt. Sir Thomas Bodley, namesake of the library, was a Christian student of Hebrew and owned 150 volumes in the language. The collection of Rabbi David Oppenheimer of Prague, acquired in 1827, is also here. These priceless pages are not on public display but are available to researchers on request. The library displays the bronze Bodleian Bowl, which belonged to Rabbi Yehiel of Paris in the thirteenth century. It is thought to be an alms bowl used to collect money for the needy.

Tucked away in the Draper Gallery on the upper floor of Oxford's Ashmolean Museum on Beaumont Street is a collection of antiquities excavated in Jerusalem. There is a set of six weights marked with *shekel* signs, which date back to the final stages of the Jewish monarchy. From the caves of Qumran comes one of fifty urn fragments such as the Dead Sea scrolls were found in.

Cambridge Sights:

A walk down Thompson's Lane near the center of Cambridge will bring you to Ellis Court, the unnumbered location of the synagogue. Built in 1940, and recently renovated and expanded to meet the increasing demands placed on it, it is a simple, one-story brick building. Like the synagogue at Oxford, it is without a rabbi. Services are run during the academic year by students, who also supervise the kosher kitchen. In the late 1970s the congregation split into three distinct parts and, surprisingly, this has helped rather than hurt Jewish life.

The original group—still claiming the largest number of adherents—is the Cambridge Jewish Residents Association (CJRA, telephone 354-320). They have trod the middle of the road, and it is their service you are likely to encounter if you visit when school is in session. A more Orthodox body of families constitutes the Cambridge Traditional Jewish Congregation (CTJC, telephone 68346); they, too, use the synagogue when school is out. A very active Reform group, established in 1981, founded Beth Shalom Reform Synagogue (telephone 242-953). About 100 members meet every other week in temporary quarters.

Out in the town, Peterhouse, one of the oldest colleges, stands on land once owned by a Jew. The college has the medieval deed of transfer of property in its archives. The ancient Jewish community had two centers. One was contained within a triangle made up of St. John's Street, All Souls Passage, and Bridge Street and includes the land on which the Divinity School now stands. The other center was in the market place. The

Guild Hall is the site of this long-gone cluster of dwellings. Until 1939 when new construction took place, parts of the house of Benjamin of Cambridge were still visible.

Rich in Judaica, the Cambridge University Library (telephone 333-000) has myriad Hebrew books, including the Schechter-Taylor Geniza Collection, which itself numbers tens of thousands of items. Stefan Reif, head of the Oriental department at the library and teacher of Hebrew and Judaic Studies, has been deeply immersed in researching this trove from Cairo brought in the nineteenth century by Solomon Schechter. There are group tours of the Research Institute.

The university also has the seventeenth-century collection of the Italian Rabbi Isaac Faraji. Trinity College has the Aldis-Wright collection of Hebraica. Girton College has a Mary Frere Hebrew Library. Unfortunately, unless by chance there is an exhibition of some of this material, it is available only to scholars who write in advance. The synagogue, however, has a good, small Judaica selection with many hard-to-find volumes on British Jewry.

Personalities: Oxford has a roster of luminaries with a strong Jewish connection. Herbert Louis Samuel, the first Viscount Samuel, was at Balliol College during the last years of the nineteenth century. He later became the first high commissioner of Palestine after World War I and a Liberal member of Parliament. Claude Montefiore preceded him at Balliol by a dozen years. He studied with Solomon Schechter, the biblical scholar. He was a great-grand-nephew of Sir Moses Montefiore and a great-grandson of Mayer Amschel Rothschild, who founded the Rothschild dynasty. Cecil Roth, the Jewish historian and editor-in-chief of the *Encyclopaedia Judaica,* taught Jewish studies at Merton College from 1939 to 1964. Walter Eytan, the Israeli diplomat and writer, studied and then taught at Oxford from 1934 to 1946.

Peter Oppenheimer, broadcaster and economist at Christ Church College, and Sir Isaiah Berlin, first president of Wolfson College, studied at Oxford and are members of the Oxford Congregation. Sir Zelman Cowen, former governor-general of Australia, later served as provost of Oriel College. The late Lord Segal of Wytham, a Labor peer, was a member and benefactor of the synagogue.

Even before 1871, when Jews were granted permission to matriculate as full students at Cambridge, members of the Rothschild family studied there. Sir Lionel, second Baron Rothschild of Tring, enrolled at Magdalene College in 1889. Later, Nathaniel Rothschild, a noted biologist, was a fellow of Trinity College from 1935 to 1939 and also assistant director of its zoology research department. Abba Eban, Israel's former foreign minister, spent time in Queens' College. When he left in 1934, he had garnered the rare honor of a "Triple First" in classical and Oriental languages. Several heads of colleges are Jewish.

Culture: Although Oxford's synagogue has various celebrations and programs throughout the year, many of the events of Jewish importance are held at the Oxford Centre for Postgraduate Jewish Studies. The centre offers weekly lectures, seminars, and courses in Hebrew and Yiddish at several locations. Their rich selections include a month-long summer program in Yiddish language and literature during August. Write to the attention of the executive secretary, at Yarnton Manor, Yarnton, Oxford OX5 IPY (telephone 77946).

The Oxford Menorah Society publishes a monthly magazine, the *Oxford Menorah.* In it you will find information about local Zionist and synagogue organizations and tidbits of Jewish interest. The editor can be reached at 257 Woodstock Road, Oxford OX2 7AE.

The Cambridge synagogue has a study course two nights a week. On Tuesday evenings at 8:30 P.M., Stefan Reif gives a two-hour course in Talmud at his home. At Beth Shalom before most Shabbat morning services there is a Torah study group. The congregation's newsletter, *Kol Shalom,* lists a variety of activities.

Reading: There are many books on the Oxbridge experience, but few contain Jewish themes. For a general view of life in these two universities, try C. P. Snow's *The Light and the Dark* and *The Masters*

(Scribner) or Frederic Raphael's *The Glittering Prizes* (St. Martin's Press). For the story of Oxford's first Jewish community, complete with a map showing where all the Jews lived on Great Jewry, see Cecil Roth's *Jews of Medieval Oxford*. Two more recent publications available from the Oxford Jewish Congregation are *The Jews of Oxford* by David M. Lewis and *Then and Now: A Collection of Recollections* by Freda Silver Jackson. A good depiction of the Jewish experience at post–World War I Cambridge is in the 1981 film *Chariots of Fire*, which tells of track star Harold Abraham's student days at Caius College.

Recommendations: In Cambridge, if you want to join in the kosher meal program offering weekday lunches and Friday night meals during school terms, call 68346. There are two good vegetarian restaurants in town. Nettles, which is excellent and cheap, is at 6 St. Edward's Passage, off King's Parade. It is closed on Sundays. The Kings Pantry is at 9 King's Parade. Both are centrally located.

For information about the Oxford synagogue's meal program, call the synagogue at 53042; like the Cambridge program, it operates only during school terms. The Hotel Randolph in Oxford is within walking distance of the synagogue and considered the city's premier hostelry. Your stay in either of the premier university towns may be temporary, but it will be more enjoyable for the Jewish presence that is permanent.

—*Deborah Barcan*

Paris

The Folies Bergère isn't quite the way it was. A victim of France's changing cultural tastes, it has closed and reopened in the past few years and faces an uncertain future. But if a modern Manet could no longer be sure of finding suitable subjects in the renowned cabaret, there are others on the rue de Richer that might be worthy of his attention—like the patrons of François Cachère, King Solomon's Pizza or Nathan de Tunis. In fact, the way things are going it wouldn't be surprising if some future tenant in the home of the cancan is a kosher night club.

From the shadows of the Eiffel Tower to the crevices of Notre Dame, from the narrow lanes around the Place des Vosges to the elegant mansions around the Elysée Palace, from the steep stairways of Montmartre to the broad corridors of the Louvre, Paris is as charming as ever, and in every single one of these corners there is evidence of the historic and still vibrant Jewish presence.

History: There were Jews in France during Roman times, and documentary evidence of a community in the alleys of the Left Bank (behind the present boulevard Saint-Michel) dates from the sixth century. Before Notre Dame rose on the Ile de la Cité, a synagogue stood on the island, on the site of today's flower market. Part of the rue de la Cité, in fact, was called rue des Juifs. In the early days Jews appear to have been respected and prosperous. When a local Jew was murdered in the seventh century, his death was avenged by a Christian mob. By the twelfth century Jews are believed to have owned half the land in Paris.

The cycle of expulsion and readmission so familiar across Europe began in Paris in 1182. It was the first readmission to Paris, in 1198, that brought Jews to the Marais, which is the principal Jewish neighborhood today. In the next two centuries Talmud burnings and accusations of well poisoning went hand in hand with general prosperity from commerce and moneylending and the admission—despite prohibitions to the contrary—of Jews expelled from England. The definitive expulsion of Jews from France took place in 1394.

The modern French community came from the corners of contemporary France that were missed by the expulsion—Alsace-Lorraine, the Papal area around Avignon, and Bordeaux, to which Spanish and Portuguese Conversos began to make their way in the seventeenth century. In the eighteenth century Jews from each of these French fringes came to Paris, with the wealthier Sephardim settling in the Left Bank and the Alsatians on the Right. The first kosher inn opened in Paris in 1721 and the first acknowledged synagogue in 1788. At the time of the Revolution the city had about 500 Jews, out of 40,000 in France.

Their status had begun to change even before the storming of the Bastille. Montesquieu was writing of tolerance in the 1720s, and Abbé Gregoire began his campaign for Jewish emancipation in 1785. Progress was rapid after the Revolution, with the "Portuguese" Jews becoming citizens in 1790 and the "German" Jews achieving full rights in 1791.

Napoleon Bonaparte wanted to create a Jewish communal structure sanctioned by and loyal to the state. In his typical ego-based fashion, he ordered the convening of a Grand Sanhedrin—composed of rabbis and Jewish laymen—which led ultimately to the creation of the consistories, as the national and local Jewish religious bodies are known.

As Paris became the center of a modern state it also attracted Jews from the provinces, and by the mid-nineteenth century Jews began to make an impact on the wider society. The actress Rachel captivated audiences at the Comédie Française as Racine's Phèdre and Esther; her attachment to her faith and her various affairs were well known to her public. Four years after Rachel's death from tuberculosis at the age of thirty-seven, Sarah Bernhardt made her debut at the Comédie Française, eventually going on to international renown, the direction of her own theater, and the title "Divine Sarah" bestowed by Victor Hugo.

Jews began to enter political life as well, with Achille Fould and Isaac Crémieux entering the Chamber of Deputies. Jacques Halévy was a leading composer and the Rothschild and Péreire families—at odds with one another—were at the head of French finance.

But in the search for scapegoats after the defeat in the Franco-Prussian war, some demagogues found the Jews—many of whom had origins in the provinces lost to Germany—a convenient target. In 1886 Edouard Drumont's *La France Juive* became a best-seller. He founded his anti-Semitic paper, *La Libre Parole,* in 1892, just in time to take advantage of the Dreyfus Affair.

It was twelve years from the conviction of Captain Alfred Dreyfus on charges of treason to his eventual exoneration and rehabilitation. After it was over neither French nor Jewish life would be the same. When Emile Zola wrote his famous *J'Accuse* in the daily *L'Aurore* in 1898—accusing the government and army of conspiring to keep an innocent man in jail—he had to flee to England to avoid prosecution. Seven years later, the Dreyfusards were in power.

The affair led to the conversion to Zionism of Theodor Herzl and the ultimate separation of church and state in France. It also revealed a French fault line—still in evidence today—between justice and generosity on the one hand, and order and respect for established institutions on the other. According to Dreyfus historian Jean-Denis Bredin, the struggle is not always between two French camps but something that runs within each Frenchman, producing an inner conflict that offers some explanation of France's modern history.

Jews were well represented among the artists who congregated in Montparnasse after the turn of the century. Modigliani and Chagall were the best known, but there were also Chaim Soutine and Jacques Lipschitz, Jules Pascin and Mané-Katz, Moise Kisling and Max Weber. The Paris School, to which many Jews contributed, eventually came to be seen as more indicative of French art than the French School, the native movement that grew in opposition to foreign influence.

Paris Jewry had numbered 30,000 in 1870, but the following decades brought waves of Jewish immigrants, first from Eastern Europe and then from North Africa, Turkey, and the Balkans. By 1939, the city had 150,000 Jews. The Germans occupied Paris in 1940.

Some Jews fled to England or to Vichy France. Many were hidden in villages and on farms, and despite some stories of betrayal, few were denounced. French police assisted in the deportation of foreign Jews, which began in 1941. But the Gestapo didn't trust French officials to deport their fellow citizens and handled the roundups of French Jewish nationals itself. Those deportations began in 1942. Many were assembled at the Vélodrome d'Hiver, a cycling stadium near the Eiffel Tower. From there they were sent to a camp in the suburb of Drancy and then to Auschwitz. In all, 40,000 Jews from Paris and 85,000 from France were sent to the death camps. When the war ended, many thought French Jewry would have the same fate as the other Jewish communities of Europe, never recovering its former vitality or size.

Community: Postwar refugees reached Paris from Eastern Europe, but what really revitalized French Jewry was the decline of an empire. The Jews of Algeria had been French citizens since the 1870s, and when the French left North Africa, the Jews went with them. In the 1950s and 1960s, hundreds of thousands of

North African Jews—mainly from Algeria and Tunisia but also from Morocco and Egypt—entered the country. Unlike other immigrants, most of these Sephardic Jews were already culturally French and needed little or no adjustment to participate fully in French society.

About 600,000 Jews live in France today, including 375,000 in Paris. Sixty percent are Sephardic. Jews are fairly well spread across the city, with the largest concentrations in the Marais and Faubourg-Montmartre. There is also a strong Jewish presence in such suburbs as Sarcelle, Créteil and La Varenne.

Jews may play a disproportionate role in the intellectual life of many western nations, but nowhere is this truer than in France. The reasons for this become clear by comparing France to the United States. French Jewry is more concentrated in Paris than American Jewry is in New York; Paris is far more central to French culture than any single city is in multicentric America; and intellectuals play a more visible role in shaping the French national agenda. As a result, social philosophers like Emanuel Lévinas, Alain Finkelkraut and Bernard-Henri Lévy are household names throughout France.

Jews are prominent in the nation's political life as well, and have been highly visible in the cabinets of François Mitterand. After a much publicized cemetery desecration in 1990, Mitterand led a mass rally protesting racism and anti-Semitism. The rise of the right-wing National Front of Jean-Marie Le Pen has been a cause of concern, although xenophobia has probably helped keep relations between Jews and North African Muslims proper, if not intimate.

Relations with the Catholic Church have never been better. Cardinal Jean-Marie Lustiger speaks proudly of his Jewish roots and there are those who brag of Parisian pluralism by noting that the city has a Sephardi chief rabbi and an Ashkenazi archbishop.

As in most Catholic countries, French Jewry is predominantly Orthodox. There is a small Liberal movement, but those who reject Orthodoxy are more likely to be unaffiliated than to join a non-Orthodox synagogue. Because of this arrangement, however, there tends to be more diversity within the French Orthodox camp than in the American.

The Consistoire Central Israélite de France is the supreme Jewish religious body, although there are synagogues (notably the Liberal and hasidic) that fall outside its jurisdiction. The Consistoire is the best place for visitors to call (4526-0256) with questions about *kashrut* or prayer times. Politically, the community is represented by CRIF (Conseil Représentatif des Institutions Juive de France) and the primary social welfare agency is the Fonds Social Juif Unifié. Much of the community's resources are devoted to education; prosperity and proximity allow many to send their children to summer camps in Israel, which explains in part why so many French Jews speak Hebrew.

Sights: Paris is one of those cities in which Jewish sights alone can fill an itinerary. It has spectacular synagogues, the contributions of individual Jews to the culture and the landscape are numerous, and the places of interest are spread widely enough that the traveler will see most of the city's major sights just traveling from one Jewish landmark to another.

The Jewish heart of Paris is the Pletzel, the same part of the Marais that was a Jewish quarter in the thirteenth century. The center of the quarter is made up of the streets that converge around the rue des Rosiers. Charm and history seep from the seventeenth- and eighteenth-century buildings that line the narrow lanes, and from the street names themselves. There are the rue des Mauvais Garçons (Bad Boys Street) and the rue Vielle du Temple (which Jewish children used to think was named for the temple in Jerusalem but in fact was named for an old Parisian crusader temple). In the rue des Ecouffes is an echo of medieval anti-Semitism; this was the street for Jewish moneylenders, which took its name from the kite, a predatory bird.

In the middle of the Pletzel, at rue des Rosiers 7, is Jo Goldenberg's delicatessen, one of the city's best-known Jewish landmarks. Goldenberg's is not kosher, which gives it a certain distinction in a jumble of streets packed with kosher establishments—fancy restaurants and holes in the wall, groceries and bakeries, not to mention synagogues, *shtiebels*, and Jewish bookstores. Even in winter the streets are an extension of the sidewalks, as people spill out of places with names like Diasporama and Café des Psaumes (Café of Psalms).

One of the oldest spots in the neighborhood is at rue Ferdinand Duval 20, in a building that abuts Jo Goldenberg's. The sixteenth-century building in the courtyard was once called the Hôtel des Juifs, and was one of the first places occupied by Jews from Alsace-Lorraine and Germany, who turned the area back into a Jewish neighborhood in the eighteenth century. Still an apartment building in a cobbled courtyard, it is distinguished from the neighborhood's more recent buildings by its sloped-tile roof and third-floor dormers. The gate leading to the courtyard is usually locked these days, but it's worth waiting a few minutes for a resident willing to let you in.

One of the most striking buildings in the neighborhood is the Art Nouveau synagogue at rue Pavée 10 (telephone 4887-2154), designed by Hector Guimard, best known as the creator of Paris's Métro entrances. Completed in 1913 for a congregation of Russian and Rumanian immigrants, the synagogue is set back a few feet from its eighteenth-century neighbors, and the undulating, bowed shape of its four-story facade gives the illusion of being squeezed by the buildings on each side. Narrow arched windows dot the front and a sculpted Decalogue sits on the building's gently curving top. The sanctuary has a gently arched green plaster ceiling above two tiers of balconies. The backs of the wooden pews have a wave pattern consistent with the building's design.

A three-minute walk from rue des Rosiers will take you to the Musée Carnavalet (rue de Sévigné 23), the former home and salon of Madame de Sévigné, whose letters provide a rich picture of seventeenth-century Parisian life. Her home is now the core of the museum of the city of Paris, noted for its exhibit on the Revolution. Also in the museum are rooms devoted to two of the Jewish personalities most prominent in the city's history. Rooms 124 and 125, in the ground-floor section devoted to Romanticism, have personal effects of Rachel, including a serpent necklace and a silver purse, as well as a bust of the actress.

Room 147 on the second floor has the furnishings and personal belongings of Marcel Proust—desk, bed, chaise lounge, cane, notebook and pens, and a portrait of his father.

From the Musée Carnavalet, a two-minute walk along the rue des Francs-Bourgeois will bring you to the Place des Vosges, a square rich in Parisian and Jewish history. The city's oldest square, it was laid out in the early seventeenth century, and the harmony between its colonnaded buildings and greenery became the model for city squares across France.

The apartment house at number 9 (in the square's southwest corner) was where Rachel lived in the nineteenth century and it is today home to one of France's leading Jewish political figures, Jack Lang, who served as François Mitterrand's minister of Culture and Education. Victor Hugo lived at number 6, and number 14 houses a modest second-floor synagogue.

One block west (with its back to the Place des Vosges) is the magnificent rue des Tournelles synagogue (at number 21, telephone 4274-3280). Completed in 1870, it is typical of nineteenth-century consistory synagogues. Its large stone facade is made more imposing by its position on a narrow street. A rose window sits in a sweeping gable above three stories of arched windows and doors. The sanctuary has wood pews on a wood floor under a curved ceiling with six skylights. A single arch frames the first balcony on each side, and a triple arch frames each side of the second tier. Though originally Ashkenazic, the synagogue now has a North African membership and ritual.

Across the rue de Rivoli from the heart of the Pletzel is the Memorial to the Unknown Jewish Martyr (rue Geoffroy l'Asnier 17), dedicated to Jewish victims of Nazism. The memorial is a four-story modern building set back from the street behind an iron fence and a paved courtyard. In the center of the courtyard is a large bronze cylinder inscribed with the names of death camps. A stone wall along one side of the plaza has sculpted Holocaust scenes by the artist Arbit Blatas. Inside the building are art and photo exhibits (one striking work is *Rachel Crying for Her Children*, a replica of a mosaic from a fourteenth-century fresco in Yugoslavia), a Holocaust documentation center and library. Below ground level is a crypt containing a symbolic black marble tomb in the shape of a Star of David.

Paris's second Jewish area around the rue de Faubourg-Montmartre is less cloistered than the Pletzel, its Jewish landmarks and hangouts integrated into a broader cityscape. In the blocks around where Faubourg-Montmartre crosses rue de Richer there is a plethora of synagogues large and small, kosher places (mostly North African), and the offices of various Jewish organizations. Near the center of this tangle of streets are the recently reopened doors of the Folies Bergère.

Close to the neighborhood's center is the synagogue at rue Buffault 28–30 (telephone 4526-8087), another of the classic consistorial synagogues and the first to become Sephardic, adopting a Portuguese ritual in 1906. Opened in 1877, it has three arched entryways at ground level, topped by a rose window, a roof rising to a point and, at the very top, the traditional Decalogue. Inside, wooden pews and red carpeting surround a central *bimah*; chandeliers hang from the arches over the balconies. Attached to the building next to the synagogue is a memorial plaque to the 12,000 Jewish children of Paris deported to Auschwitz. It notes that the youngsters were "arrested in schools, foyers, and streets."

The prototype of the great consistorial synagogues — and still the grandest — is a few blocks west of rue Buffault. Best known as the Victory Synagogue (rue de la Victoire 44), it is also called the Rothschild Synagogue. Designed to face the more bustling rue St-Georges (where the entrance to the adjoining Consistory building is located at number 17), the synagogue was reoriented when the empress's confessor objected to a Jewish building facing such a busy street.

The facade of the Romanesque-style building, which opened in 1874, features a central section and two side bays, each with a series of arched portals. At the top, over the central section, is the large, curved gable, rose window in the center, that became a feature of later consistorial synagogues. Inside, it is immediately clear why yet another name for the building is the Cathedral Synagogue. The eighty-five-foot ceiling caps a galleried basilica that, on sunny days, is bathed in light filtered through the circular blue, red, and yellow stained-glass windows surrounding the sanctuary. The *bimah*, up a short staircase, has special seats for the chief rabbis of Paris and of France. The ark is up a second flight of stairs and both *bimah* and ark rest under a magnificent vaulted dome. Though the inscription on the building's facade is in Hebrew, inside the words are in French — "You shall love the Lord thy God with all thy heart" above the ark and "Love thy neighbor as thyself" on the opposite wall.

The Jewish landmarks are in the lowlands of Montmartre, and at the top of the hill is Sacré Coeur, Paris's great neo-Romanesque and Byzantine basilica. At the turn of the century Montmartre still had the trappings of a village and the low rents attracted poor artists, like Picasso and Braque. They and other artists and writers (including Modigliani, Max Ernst, and the poet Max Jacob) lived at one time or another in the Bateau-Lavoir, or Boat Wash House, at place Emile-Goudeau, a cobbled square on the climb up to Sacré-Coeur.

One of the steepest streets in Montmartre is rue des Saules, and it is at number 42 that you will find the Museum of Jewish Art (telephone 4257-8415). If you can ignore the extremely modest building (which is to the Louvre as a walkup flat in the Marais is to Versailles) you'll see some real treasures, and you may even appreciate the barely controlled chaos represented by walls packed from ceiling to floor with paintings, posters, and photos (with some pieces actually sitting on the floor). There are lithographs by Chagall, sketches by Mané-Katz, and paintings by Alphonse Lévy. There are tombstones and *ketubot*, Torah covers and spice boxes, original synagogue features and reproductions.

Among the more unusual items are the collection of synagogue models, mostly from Poland and Lithuania (in wood) and France (in plaster); a diorama in metal of Solomon's Jerusalem, complete with gas street lamps; a seventeenth-century Italian Torah ark with green and gold wooden doors; a reproduction of a mosaic floor from the sixth-century Beit Alfa synagogue; and a reproduction of a fresco from the third-century Dura-Europas synagogue in Mesopotamia. The museum, open afternoons from 3:00 to 6:00, is on the fourth floor of a building that also houses a community center and a small synagogue.

Closer in mood to a Jewish Versailles is the rue de Faubourg St-Honoré, perhaps the city's most fashionable street. Just west of the Place de la Concorde are stores bearing high-fashion names — St. Laurent and Lanvin, Guy La Roche and Givenchy. But boutiques soon give way to seventeenth- and eighteenth-century mansions with grand entries leading to courtyards. Once owned by Rothschilds and Péreires, many of them are now embassies and ambassadors' residences.

Number 33, now a diplomatic club with a well-preserved eighteenth-century salon, was home to Baron Henri de Rothschild and Baron Nathaniel de Rothschild. Number 35, now the British embassy, was the home of the Rothschild rivals, the railroad builders Emile and Isaac Péreire. Number 41, now the residence of the American ambassador, was once the home of Baron Edmond de Rothschild, whose business headquarters was in the antique store now at number 45. Number 49, today the Colombian Embassy, was another home of Emile Péreire. One block west of number 49 is the Elysée Palace, the French presidential residence.

A few blocks from the Arc de Triomphe is the rue Copernic Synagogue (at number 24, telephone 4704-3727). The largest Liberal congregation in a predominantly Orthodox Jewish community, it is a favored spot for visiting American Jews looking for the French equivalent of Conservative or Reform Judaism. The synagogue is well known for a more tragic reason as well. In 1980 it was the target of the worst of a series of anti-Semitic attacks when a bomb exploded in front of its door, killing four people. Completed in 1906, it is less imposing than the consistorial synagogues, with a square stone exterior and rectangular windows and a white stone sanctuary. In the entryway are memorial plaques to members who died in World War I and to victims of the German occupation; a memorial to those killed in the 1980 bombing is on the building facade.

Closer to the Seine are several sites asso-ciated with the city's Jewish theatrical heritage. The Théâtre de la Ville de Paris, at Place du Châtelet, was once the Théâtre Sarah Bernhardt. The eldest of three illegitimate daughters born to a Dutch-Jewish music teacher, Bernhardt made her debut at the Comédie Française in 1862. Renowned for her impatience with directors, she took over the theater at Place du Châtelet in 1899 and directed it until her death twenty-four years later. The theater was recently modernized, but the second-floor Loge Sarah Bernhardt still has a nineteenth-century feel. The room displays belongings and memorabilia of the great actress, from the cane she used in *La Tosca* to a poster showing her as Joan of Arc. The corner restaurant that is part of the building is the Sarah Bernhardt Café, and has photos and posters from her performances on its walls.

If the Divine Sarah abandoned the Comédie Française, the classic theater at the Place de la Théâtre Française, the theater itself never abandoned Rachel. Born Eliza Rachel Felix in 1821, she made her debut in 1838 and made her fame in the French classics. Rachel in the role of Phèdre is the model for the statue of Tragedy in the theater's Grand Staircase (though unlike the male playwrights she is not identified). Her image — including her portrayal of Esther — is on many items in the theater's gift shop.

Just a block from the Comédie Française is the Louvre. Amid the great works of art and antiquities are many items of Jewish interest. In the Sully Wing is the Mesha Stele, bearing a thirty-four-line Moabite-language description from 824 B.C.E., recording a Moabite victory over Israel. Also in the Sully Wing are doors from the Tomb of the Kings in Jerusalem, carvings from the Tomb of the Judges, and the sarcophagus of Queen Helena of Adiabene.

Many Renaissance works on Hebrew Bible themes are in the corridors leading to the Mona Lisa. Look for Rembrandt's *Sacrifice of Abraham, The Archangel Raphael Leaves Tobias' Family,* and *Bathsheba at the Bath*; and Van Dyck's *Abraham Banishing Hagar and Ishmael.* The Louvre also has furniture and jewelry collections from Baron Adolphe de Rothschild and Count Moïse de Camondo.

The Orangerie, in the corner of the Tuileries by the Place de la Concorde, is devoted to early twentieth-century art. The first exhibit encountered, at the top of the staircase from the entrance, is of twenty-two paintings by the Expressionist Chaim Soutine. His country scenes and still lifes — from shaking houses to plucked chickens — show violence and cataclysmic movement; even his portraits look like they were painted during earthquakes. Though painted mostly in the 1920s, the works foretold Soutine's future; after hiding for two years during the Nazi occupation, his ulcers forced him to check into a Paris hospital, where he died at the age of fifty. Soutine was a roommate of Amadeo Modigliani, who is also represented in the Orangerie, along with Renoir, Matisse, and Picasso.

In the eighteenth century some of the Ashkenazim moving into Paris settled around Les Halles, the city's central market. The Forum des Halles is now a huge underground and outdoor shopping mall and in the adjacent Jardin des Halles is Place René Cassin, named for the French-Jewish human-rights activist who won the 1968 Nobel Peace Prize.

One of the most dramatic events of French and Jewish history took place in the courtyard of the Ecole Militaire, the military academy, on the Left Bank. It was there, on January 5, 1895, that Captain Alfred Dreyfus was stripped of his rank and insignia amid taunts of "Judas" from fellow officers. One of the reporters covering it from the inside was Theodor Herzl, correspondent of Vienna's *Neue Freie Presse*. Like most observers Herzl had initially believed Dreyfus guilty of espionage, but by the time he reached the Ecole Militaire that day he had his doubts. There, in the shadow of the six-year-old Eiffel Tower, a journalist and playwright enamored of French civilization was stunned by the spectacle of the degradation ceremony and shocked by the crowds at the gate of the courtyard shouting, "Death to the Jews." The experience crystallized Herzl's thinking on anti-Semitism and led him to the idea of a Jewish state.

The neo-classical buildings of the Ecole Militaire still sit regally on Avenue de Lowendal. Remove the cars parked on the cobbled lanes inside the compound and it would look much as it did a century ago. Though closed to the public, the broad courtyards are easily visible through the blue and gold fence, and tourists with French guides have been known to gain admission. The Ecole Militaire was also the site of more salutary episodes. It was in one of the smaller courtyards off the main field that Dreyfus had his rehabilitation ceremony in 1906. Amid the many French Jewish officers who have trained there since Dreyfus's time have been those, like Moshe Dayan and Chaim Bar-Lev, with a debt to a journalist who stood there on a January morning in 1895.

Herzl was living at the time at the Hotel Castille, on the Right Bank, and from his window he could hear crowds shouting anti-Semitic epithets in the nearby Place de la Concorde. It was in his room in the hotel at rue Cambon 37 that he wrote *The Jewish State*, his first Zionist tract.

Also in the shadow of the Eiffel Tower is one of the gems among Parisian synagogues, at rue Chasseloup-Laubat 14 (telephone 4273-3629). The yellow-stone structure, completed in 1913, faces a small courtyard off the street. The main portion of the building, with rose windows facing the courtyard and the street, is behind a smaller entry pavilion. The outstanding feature of the sanctuary is wood — ceiling, balconies, railings. The congregation is eclectic, with French Ashkenazim and North Africans, Russians and Germans, and is especially welcoming.

Even if you want to see only Jewish sights, you have to go to Notre Dame. There are many Jewish images at the great cathedral, and they begin directly over the main entrance. The central portal is flanked by Ecclesia and Sinagoga, two female figures — representing the church triumphant and the synagogue defeated — often found on cathedrals. Ecclesia, on the left, wears a crown she has taken from Sinagoga. Sinagoga is blinded by a serpent around her eyes, and is in a slouching position with the tablets of the law slipping from her right hand. Her staff is shattered and her crown lies at her feet. Also on the west facade, above the three front arches, is a line of twenty-eight figures representing the kings of Judaea.

Inside, the north rose window is devoted

Tour de force: A magnificent city in which Jewish sights alone can fill an itinerary

entirely to figures from the Hebrew Bible. In the inner circle are images of the prophets, in the middle are the kings of Israel, and on the outer ring are the patriarchs and high priests.

Behind Notre Dame, at the point of the Ile de la Cité, is the Memorial to the Deported, dedicated to French victims of Nazism, including Jews, Resistance fighters and dissidents, Gypsies, homosexuals, and others. Starting at an open plaza inscribed with the words "N'oubliez Pas" (Never forget), the memorial is reached by walking down a stairway and through passages that become increasingly narrow, symbolizing repression. A long tunnel leads to the tomb of the unknown martyr; the walls alongside the tomb are studded with two hundred thousand pearls, symbolizing all those sent to their deaths during the occupation.

The Latin Quarter, across the Seine from Notre Dame, has its Jewish connections. Jews had lived on the Left Bank as early as the sixth century. One of the liveliest lanes today, with some of the best street music, is rue St-André des Arts, where Sephardim

from Bordeaux and Avignon settled in the eighteenth century. The Musée de Cluny, built on the site of Roman baths, is best known for its tapestry collection. It has a collection of Jewish ritual objects, though they are not always on display and some have been transferred to the Museum of Jewish Art. Attached to the building's walls are several thirteenth-century Jewish tombstones.

Culture: Paris has a dynamic Jewish cultural life. Among the most active community centers are the Centre Rachi, near the Luxembourg Gardens (boulevard de Port-Royal 30, telephone 4331-9820), which has films, lectures, seminars, a kosher cafeteria, and a synagogue; and the Centre Communautaire–Maison des Jeunes in Montmartre (boulevard Poissonière; telephone 4233-6496), which caters to the under-35 set and has movies, dances, kosher lunches, and a bookstore.

In addition to the Louvre and the Museum of Jewish Art, many other Paris museums have items of explicit or tangential Jewish interest. The Bibliothèque Nationale has Dead Sea Scroll fragments and illuminated Hebrew manuscripts; the Pompidou Center (near the Pletzel) has works by Chagall, Modigliani, and Soutine; the Musée d'Orsay has, among its great Impressionist collection, works by Modigliani and Pisarro.

Jewish periodicals like *Information Juive* and *L'Arche* have information on community events and can be found in Jewish community buildings as well as shops in the Marais and Faubourg-Montmartre.

The French popular-culture scene is much like that in other countries, with the big names appearing more often in sports stadiums than in more intimate settings. The Olympia is the last of the smaller midcentury auditoriums. One little place, discovered by tourists but still exuding charm, is Au Lapin Agile in Montmartre (rue des Saules 22); once a hangout of Toulouse-Lautrec and, before that, of Heinrich Heine, it is a dimly lit cabaret featuring French songs from the fifteenth to the early twentieth century.

Personalities: Among the best-known French Jews today are Simone Veil, former president of the European Parliament, and the filmmaker Claude Lanzmann, who made the word *Shoah* part of the French language. Other French Jews active in politics include Jacques Attali, head of the European Bank for Reconstruction and Development, and his twin brother, Bernard, president of Air France. Top officials in the cabinet of François Mitterand have included Justice Minister Robert Badinter and Industry Minister Dominique Strauss-Kahn. Leading French journalists include Jean Daniel, editor of *Le Nouvel Observateur*, Anne Sinclair (TV), Ivan Levai (radio) and the late Raymond Aron. Writers include Marek Halter, Patrick Modiano, and the late Romain Gary.

Among popular French singers are Enrico Macias, Patrick Bruel, and Michel Berger. Actors include Roger Hanim (a brother-in-law of François Mitterand), Anouk Aimée (of *A Man and a Woman* fame), Gérard Darnon, and the late Simone Signoret. Also well-known is the great mime Marcel Marceau. André Citroën founded the auto company that still bears his name; one of Peugeot's recent presidents was Pierre Dreyfus.

At the highest levels, France has been led by Léon Blum (who served as premier before and after his wartime internment in Nazi camps) and Pierre Mendès-France (prime minister in the 1950s). Laurent Fabius, who served as prime minister in the 1980s, has Jewish origins and a Jewish wife.

Side Trip:
The TGV, France's high-speed train, has made much of the country an easy day trip from Paris. Two hours to the south is Lyon, a city with Gallo-Roman roots and a reputation as a culinary capital. Lyon was a silk and fabric center, and cloth was protected from the elements by the city's *traboules*, passageways that cut under the tightly packed buildings, connecting one to another. These labyrinthine lanes made the city a good place for Resistance fighters to hide during World War II, which led Klaus Barbie, the "Butcher of Lyon," to set up his operations there as well.

Medieval legends tell of Jews in Lyon before the fall of the Second Temple. On the eve of World War II there were about 5,000 Jews in the city, and the North African influx after the war boosted the Jewish community to its present 20,000. The Grand Synagogue is at quai Tilsitt 14, on the Saône (telephone 7837-1343 or 7842-4986). Built in 1864, it consists of an administrative building that faces the street and, through an arched entry and past a courtyard, the magnificent Romanesque sanctuary. Across the Saône is Old Lyon, and right by the funicular railway that takes you up the Fourvière, the hill against which the original city was built, is rue Juiverie, named for the area's medieval residents. Off the short street of four- and five-story buildings are courtyards and *traboules*. In the courtyard at number 8 you can see a fine example of fourteenth-century architecture.

There are twenty alternatives to the Grand Synagogue in Lyon. One place worth a visit is Neve Shalom, the beautiful Sephardi synagogue and community center at rue Duguesclin 317 (telephone 7858-1874). Lyon has several kosher restaurants, and *kashrut* updates can be had by calling any of the synagogues.

Reading and Viewing:
Among the novels evocative of Parisian Jewry are Cynthia Ozick's *The Cannibal Galaxy* (Knopf, Dutton) which opens in the Marais, and André Schwartz-Bart's *The Last of the Just* (Atheneum), which closes there. Romain Gary's *The Life Before Us* (on which the film *Madame Rosa* was based), is set in the old Jewish neighborhood in Belleville. In addition to *Madame Rosa*, which starred Simone Signoret and won the Oscar for best foreign film, movies showing French Jewish life include Louis Malle's *Au Revoir Les Enfants* and Gérard Oury's hilarious *Mad Adventures of Rabbi Jacob*.

Ernest Hemingway's *A Moveable Feast* (Scribner's) provides a good look at the bohemian life of prewar Paris, while Larry Collins and Dominique Lapierre's *Is Paris Burning?* (Simon & Schuster) provides a good look at the city's experience under German occupation. For a historical perspective there is Arthur Hertzberg's *The French Enlightenment and the Jews* (Columbia/JPS). For a good community profile look at the reports in the annual *American Jewish Year Book*. Two excellent sources on the Dreyfus Affair are *The Affair* by Jean-Denis Bredin (George Braziller), which covers the impact on France, and *Dreyfus: A Family Affair* by Michael Burns (HarperCollins), which follows the family from the French Revolution to World War II.

Recommendations: Paris has hotels of every level of charm and price. The expensive ones are listed in all the guidebooks; some of the lesser known hostelries are the Vieux Marais (rue de Plâtre 8) and the Place des Vosges (rue de Birague 12), both near the Pletzel; the Montana-Tuileries (rue St-Roch 12), near the Louvre; and the kosher Hotel Lebron (rue Lamartine 4) in the Faubourg-Montmartre section.

The French Government Tourist Office (610 Fifth Avenue, New York, NY 10020) is an excellent source of information on general and Jewish travel. It has branch offices in Los Angeles, Chicago, Dallas, and Toronto.

The best way to get to most places in Paris is by Métro, and the rail links to Orly and Charles De Gaulle Airports are excellent. Better than taking the trains is going on foot. One of the most delightful pastimes is browsing in the stalls selling old books and prints along both banks of the Seine. And wandering the streets offers constant discoveries, from a lively street market to a charming old building to kosher restaurants within earshot of the cancan.

—Alan M. Tigay

Philadelphia

"Philadelphia—Get to Know Us" is both the City of Brotherly Love's latest slogan and a good motto for its Jewish community. With its treasure of historic sights and myriad other attractions, America's fourth-largest Jewish community, and fifth-largest city, are worth getting to know.

Unlike the very visible communities of New York or Los Angeles, Jewish Philadelphia does not wear its ethnicity on its collective sleeve. But with a history reaching back to colonial times, Jews are inseparably linked to the city. And Philadelphia Jewry has been powerful in national Jewish affairs, both past and present.

History: Jews visited Philadelphia as early as 1706, but permanent Jewish settlement dates to 1737, when Nathan and Isaac Levy arrived from New York. Jewish communal activity began in the 1740s, when Nathan Levy secured land for Jewish burial and informal religious services were held. While the first Jewish congregation can be traced to this period, there is no record of the congregation's name, Mikveh Israel, prior to 1773.

The early Jewish residents, of Ashkenazic and Sephardic background, flourished under the liberal influence of the dominant Quakers and played important roles in colonial Philadelphia life. In 1748 Jews were among the founders of the Dancing Assembly, an exclusive social club that still exists.

In August 1752, what was to become the symbol of freedom known as the Liberty Bell arrived from England aboard the ship *Myrtilla,* owned by Nathan Levy and his partner David Frank, provisioner for the British army during the French and Indian Wars. The bell was cast to commemorate the fiftieth anniversary of William Penn's Charter of Liberties of Pennsylvania. The inscription on the bell, which stands in front of Independence Hall, is a quotation from the Hebrew Bible: "Proclaim liberty throughout the land, unto all the inhabitants thereof" (Leviticus 25:10).

Jewish patriots, merchants, and financiers were among the leading supporters of the coming Revolution. At least nine Jewish merchants signed the Non-Importation Resolutions against British goods in 1765, designed to protest the Stamp Act. Among the signatories were such community leaders as Mathias Bush and Bernard and Michael Gratz. The Gratzes were of the same family that later produced Rebecca Gratz, the beautiful philanthropist who founded schools and orphanages and is thought to be the model for Rebecca in Walter Scott's *Ivanhoe.*

The majority of Philadelphia's Jews supported the Revolution, although a few were Tories and at least one was expelled by the Continental authorities. Mikveh Israel's first rabbi, Gershom Mendes Seixas, was a leading revolutionary patriot. The merchant and banker Haym Salomon helped finance the Revolution, lending money without interest to members of the Continental Congress; what is surprising, however, is that he is less remembered for the spying he did on behalf of the American cause. After the Revolution Salomon worked for Jewish political rights, arguing against the New Testament oath required of all public officials in Pennsylvania; he died in 1785 but the cause was taken up by Jonas Phillips, who in 1790 succeeded in having the law changed. Salomon, along with Levy, the Gratz family, and twenty-one revolutionary soldiers, is buried in the Mikveh Israel cemetery at Eighth and Spruce streets.

In 1802, German Jews who had broken away from Mikveh Israel established congregation Rodeph Shalom, making Philadelphia the first city in the Western Hemisphere to house Sephardi and Ashkenazi synagogues. By 1830, the two-*minhag* community numbered between 500 and 1,000.

From 1846 to the eve of the Civil War, the city's Jewish community grew from 1,500 to 8,000. As the community leadership passed from descendants of the original colonists, the mostly German new arrivals found themselves as welcome as their predecessors had been.

Jews mixed well with non-Jews in the Pennsylvania regiments recruited during the Civil War—particularly in units where both the Jews and non-Jews were of German background. In 1861, when regiments were still electing their own officers, the 65th Regiment of the Fifth Pennsylvania Cavalry picked Michael Allen, a protégé of Rabbi Isaac Leeser's, as its regimental chaplain, to lead nondenominational services and minister to the needs of all faiths. Allen was forced to resign after two months because of a new law requiring chaplains to be ordained (which he was not) and a Christian. After Jewish lobbying, a new law in 1862 permitted Jews to become chaplains, and three more served the Union Army, including Rabbi Jacob Frankel, who served the six Philadelphia military hospitals.

By 1880, the preponderance of German Jews made Philadelphia's Jewish community a fairly homogeneous one of 12,000. Though smaller than New York's, it was in many ways the center of American Jewish intellectual life.

Well integrated into community life, the German Jews viewed later Jewish arrivals as embarrassingly backward. But in great waves the Russians came after 1881, bringing the city's Jewish population to 75,000 by 1900 and 200,000 by the early 1920s. The immigrants flocked to the garment sweatshops and the cigar factories, and turned a large part of South Philadelphia into the city's answer to the Lower East Side. Yiddish newspapers flourished, alongside the *Jewish Exponent,* founded by the still dominant, English-speaking German Jewish establishment.

Community: Metropolitan Philadelphia has a Jewish population of about 290,000. Despite all the changes this city has gone through since the days when Jews numbered a few hundred, the tone of Philadelphia Jewry's relations with the general community remains what it was in the 18th century when Benjamin Franklin organized three lotteries to raise money for the construction of Christ Church. Members of Mikveh Israel were among those who purchased tickets. During the Revolution, Jewish refugees came to Philadelphia from areas of the country occupied by the British and, in 1782, Mikveh Israel dedicated its first real synagogue building to serve the swollen community. When the refugees returned to New York, Charleston, and elsewhere after the Revolution, the small Philadelphia community was left with a big mortgage. Franklin and other Christ Church parishioners participated in the Mikveh Israel lottery to raise the not inconsequential sum of eight hundred pounds.

Aside from social barriers, the pattern of generally smooth relations was seriously disturbed only once, in the 1930s, by the anti-Semitic Father Charles Coughlin, whose Sunday radio broadcasts attracted a small following in the Irish community, and by the strong presence of the German-American Bund. Responding to these threats, city Jews established the Philadelphia Anti-Defamation Council, which evolved into the present-day Jewish Community Relations Council.

Philadelphia Jews have occupied virtually every public office in the city and state, including governor (Milton Shapp), United States senator (Arlen Spector), mayor (Ed Rendell), congressman, judge, city council member, and district attorney. Jewish prominence in the business world has continued unabated through the centuries as well. The seven sons of Adam Gimbel, a Bavarian immigrant who settled in Philadelphia, founded the renowned department store dynasty in 1894. More recently, Albert M. Greenfield was the real estate and banking magnate known for the restoration of Society Hill and other downtown projects.

Philadelphia has had a disproportionate impact on American Jewish life. Local Jews were instrumental in founding the American Jewish Committee and B'nai B'rith. The Jewish Theological Seminary, in New York, was founded by Sabato Morais, an Italian-born Philadelphia *chazan*.

Notables include Isaac Leeser, appointed as leader of Mikveh Israel in 1829, who sought to reconcile tradition with American ways, thus establishing a kind of proto-Conservative Judaism. Through Leeser's translations of traditional texts, he introduced English into Jewish ritual; in 1843 he founded the *Occident and American Jewish Advocate,* the country's first successful Jewish newspaper. The influence of Leeser and others who devoted their energies in the nineteenth century to reconciling Jewish tradition with American life is still felt. While Orthodox, Reconstructionist, and Reform Judaism can certainly be found in Philadelphia, it is today perhaps the most predominantly Conservative of America's major Jewish communities.

In 1867, a group of Philadelphia Jews set in motion a Jewish Studies program that would eventually work its way into the city's premier institution of higher learning. They established Maimonides College, the first rabbinical seminary in the United States. Maimonides closed after six years, but one of the founders, Moses Dropsie, later endowed Dropsie College, the first nonsectarian institute for graduate study in Judaica and related fields. In 1986 Dropsie was reconfigured as the Annenberg Research Institute, a postdoctoral center for advanced study of Judaism and related fields. And in 1992 the institute became part of the University of Pennsylvania.

Rebecca Gratz's brother Hyman endowed what became, in 1897, Gratz College, the first Hebrew teacher training school in America; the college remains at the center of Jewish educational life in Philadelphia a century later.

Dropsie's second president, Cyrus Adler, also served as president of the American Jewish Historical Society and as librarian of the Smithsonian Institution. In addition, he served as president of Mikveh Israel and

the Jewish Theological Seminary and was a founder of both the American Jewish Committee and the Jewish Publication Society of America. Founded in Philadelphia in 1888, the JPS is the oldest — and leading — publisher of Judaica in the English-speaking world.

Sights: As it has aged, Philadelphia has suffered the fate of many older American cities, but in recent decades much of its colonial real estate has been lovingly restored by community groups and the National Park Service. Mikveh Israel returned to the area after following various Jewish population shifts and now shares quarters at one end of Independence Mall with the National Museum of American Jewish History, built during America's Bicentennial.

The synagogue and museum building, on Commerce Street between Fourth and Fifth, is just a short walk from Independence Hall and the Liberty Bell. The museum (entrance at 55 North Fifth Street) is the only institution of its kind dedicated to telling the story of Jewish participation in the growth and development of North and South America. It houses many personal and religious items that belonged to colonial Jews and also hosts traveling exhibits. Its permanent exhibit, The American Jewish Experience, consists of a time-line, artifacts and a video program, and covers the full span of American Jewish life, from the first arrivals to the twentieth century. Call (215) 923-3811 for information on exhibits and events.

Mikveh Israel (entrance at 44 North Fourth Street) is the direct descendant of the synagogue founded in 1748. Call 922-5446 for information on services and events.

Nearby, between Front and Second Streets, is Elfreth's Alley, the oldest colonial street in the city and among the oldest continuously occupied residential streets in the country. Jews have lived on the street throughout its history. Moses Mordecai, a merchant who signed the Non-Importation Resolutions in 1765, lived at number 118. His widow married Jacob I. Cohen, an Indian trader, peddler, and revolutionary leader, who lived at number 124. Cohen is thought to be the hero of Stephen Vincent Benet's story "Jacob and the Indians." Cohen's holdings in Kentucky were surveyed by Daniel Boone. German Jews lived on the street close to the city's second synagogue, Rodeph Shalom, in the mid-nineteenth century. With the influx of Eastern European Jews in the 1880s, the street became something of a sweatshop district for the nascent garment industry.

The Walnut Street Theater, at Ninth and Walnut Streets, was built in 1809 and is the oldest surviving theater in the United States. In the early twentieth century, after the Arch Street Theater was razed, Yiddish theater impresario Maurice Schwartz transferred his Yiddish Art Repertory Theater to the facility.

There is a sizable Jewish presence in Society Hill, an area of restored colonial town houses near Center City. Some of the synagogues themselves are in restored buildings and are convenient for visitors staying at downtown hotels. In addition to Mikveh Israel, neighborhood synagogues include the Society Hill Synagogue (Conservative) at 418 Spruce Street and B'nai Abraham (Orthodox) at 527 Lombard Street.

On Benjamin Franklin Parkway at Sixteenth Street is the Martyr's Monument to the Jewish victims of the Holocaust. The eighteen-foot bronze sculpture was created by Nathan Rapoport, who designed the monument to the Warsaw Ghetto fighters in Poland, as well as many other memorials in Israel, Europe, and the United States. Dedicated in 1964, the Philadelphia monument was the first in America commemorating the Holocaust.

Outside the colonial area, at 2010 Delancey Place, is the Rosenbach Museum, established by bookseller A. S. Wolf Rosenbach, a president of Gratz College, and his brother Philip. They established a foundation to maintain their nineteenth-century town house as a museum, which houses an eclectic collection of rare manuscripts, fifteenth-century Judaica, art, and books. The museum houses a copy of the Bay Psalm Book of 1640, the first use of Hebrew type in the Western Hemisphere, and the original manuscript of James Joyce's *Ulysses.*

Other museums devoted to Jewish life or art are the Philadelphia Museum of Judaica at Congregation Rodeph Shalom (615 North Broad Street; telephone

215-627-6747), which specializes in Jewish art and history; the Holocaust Awareness Museum at Gratz College (Old York Road and Melrose Avenue in Melrose Park; 635-6480), which has exhibits and a documentation center devoted to the issues of bigotry in general and the Holocaust in particular; the Borowsky Gallery of the Jewish Community Centers of Greater Philadelphia (401 South Broad Street; 545-4400); and the Temple Judea Museum of Keneseth Israel (Old York and Township Line Roads in Elkins Park; 887-8700).

South Philadelphia, now home to many of the city's Italians and location of the colorful outdoor Italian market, was a port of entry for Eastern Europeans. It featured a thriving Yiddish-speaking Bohemian community and was home at one time to Naphtali Herz Imber, a colorful but alcoholic poet who received two bottles of wine as payment for composing *Hatikvah.* The Jews of South Philadelphia today are predominantly elderly, though the neighborhood still supports two synagogues and a branch of the Jewish Community Center.

Today Jews are spread throughout the city and suburbs. About a third of Philadelphia's Jews live in "the Great Northeast," a sprawling series of neighborhoods that spreads roughly from Oxford Circle to the Bucks County line. The area includes some of the most identifiably Jewish neighborhoods in the city, especially in the shopping district around Castor and Cottman Avenues, with its kosher butchers, restaurants, and other shops.

Jews first moved to the Northeast section in the nineteenth century when they settled a section of Port Richmond that became known, alternately, as "Jewtown" and "Jerusalem." Within two generations, however, they moved to row-house developments such as Oxford Circle, Mayfair, and Bustleton. The spread ultimately extended beyond the city limits into Elkins Park, Cheltenham, Abington, and other suburbs. Jewish institutional life followed, as synagogues once closer to downtown relocated.

Undoubtedly the prominent synagogue in the area is Beth Sholom, at Old York and Foxcroft roads in Elkins Park (telephone 215-887-1342). It is the only synagogue designed by Frank Lloyd Wright, and it was completed in 1959, the year the leg-

Wright stuff: Modern materials blend with traditional ideas at the landmark Beth Sholom

endary architect died. Both a landmark and watershed in synagogue design, it symbolizes the blending of modern materials and design with traditional ideas of Judaism. Built in the shape of a pointed polygon angling toward the sky, Beth Sholom suggests Mount Sinai cupped in the hands of God. According to the architectural historian Carol Herselle Krinsky, "The plan is based on the Star of David and everywhere are symbolic colors, numbers, and references." In addition to its traditional name, Beth Sholom is also known, at Wright's request, as "The American Synagogue."

Northwest Philadelphia, particularly the Mount Airy and Germantown sections, is home to much of the city's Jewish counterculture. The area contains some of the city's most integrated neighborhoods, which are characterized by a high degree of community participation. Jewish life is anchored by the Germantown Jewish Center (Lincoln Drive and Ellet Street; 215-844-1507). A Conservative synagogue, the center is also home to several *chavurah*-style *minyans*, which meet in various classrooms and chapels, a day-care and a senior center. The area is also home to P'nai Or (718 Germantown Avenue; 215-242-4074), a fellowship that meets for prayer and study under the guidance of Zalman Schachter-Shalomi, a charismatic rabbi and mystic.

The Merion-Wynnefield area straddling Philadelphia and neighboring Lower Merion Township is home to many Jewish families, as well as a black middle class. Many elderly Jews live in Wynnefield, which, along with Overbrook Park, is also

home to a thriving Orthodox community. Farther west, the Main Line communities of Bala Cynwyd, Wynnewood, and Wayne are home to affluent Jewish families in single-family homes. There are also significant numbers of Jews to the southwest, in Delaware County communities such as Havertown, Media, Springfield, and Broomall. On the New Jersey side of the Delaware River, the heaviest Jewish concentration is in Cherry Hill.

The Jewish Information and Referral hotline at (215) 893-5821 can provide answers to travelers' questions. The Jewish Federation of Greater Philadelphia (226 South 16th Street, Philadelphia, PA 19102) puts out the *Guide to Jewish Philadelphia,* which has detailed listings of virtually every Jewish institution in the region.

Eating: Philadelphia has several kosher restaurants, and some hotels can provide kosher TV dinners with advance notice. The European Dairy Restaurant is at Twentieth and Sansom streets in Center City. Two other popular spots are Jonathan's (1330 South 11th Street) and Maccabeam (128 South 12th Street). Northeast Philadelphia is home to Cafeteria Tiberias (8010 Castor Avenue) and Dragon Inn (kosher Chinese, 7628 Castor). There are also kosher cafeterias on the campuses of the University of Pennsylvania, Temple University, and Gratz College. A popular vegetarian restaurant in Philadelphia's Chinatown is The Harmony (135 North Ninth Street).

Culture: Jewish cultural activities — concerts, films, plays, lectures — are often sponsored by the Jewish Community Centers of Greater Philadelphia, located throughout the city. The most versatile JCCs are the Center City branch, at Broad and Pine (telephone 215-545-4400), especially known for its Jewish Film Festival; the Klein branch at Red Lion Road and Jamison Avenue (215-698-7300), popular for Israeli folk dancing, art shows, and discussion groups; and the Kaiserman branch at City Line and Haverford Avenue (215-896-7770), known for films, lectures, and cultural programs.

The Reconstructionist Rabbinical College, located in a former estate at Greenwood Avenue and Church Road in Wycote, sponsors frequent lectures, seminars, and exhibits, as do many of the larger synagogues. Gratz College, located on the Mandell Education Campus at Old York and West Avenues in Melrose Park, also sponsors programs of public interest, including the Gratz Community Chorus, which performs throughout the Jewish community. There are also programs of interest at the city's two Jewish day schools, Akiba Hebrew Academy, in Merion, and Solomon Schechter, with facilities in Bala Cynwyd and on the Mandell Campus.

The best source of information on Jewish Philadelphia is the *Jewish Exponent*, the century-old weekly now published by the federation. Providing in-depth coverage of Israeli and American Jewish issues and a variety of features, the *Exponent* is among the best Jewish newspapers in the country and a worthy successor to Isaac Leeser's *Occident*.

There is a variety of Jewish programming on Philadelphia radio and on cable TV. Many programs appear on WIBF (103.9 FM), including "The Barry Reisman Show," featuring Jewish music and topical discussions (daily between 3:30 and 5:30 P.M., Sundays from 9 A.M. to 1 P.M.); Sabbath services from Keneseth Israel (Saturday, 11:00 A.M. to noon); and a Russian-language program on Sunday evenings. WKDU (91.7 FM, from Drexel University) broadcasts "Sounds of Jerusalem" on Friday mornings, with news in Hebrew and English and Israeli music.

Theatre Ariel (15th and Locust Streets, 735-9481) has stage productions, readings, workshops, and speakers dedicated to the Jewish theatrical experience.

Personalities: Philadelphia is not solely populated by the ghosts of important Jewish figures from centuries past. The twentieth century has also produced its share of prominent Jewish Philadelaphians in the arts, business, and politics. William Paley, whose creative and business genius produced the CBS television network, is the son of Philadelphia cigar maker Sam Paley. Former ambassador to the United Kingdom Walter Annenberg, philanthropist, friend of presidents, publisher of *TV Guide,* and former owner of *The Philadelphia In-quirer,* is also involved in the Jewish life of the city. Siegmund Lubin, who was a rival of Thomas Edison in producing the first motion pictures, was based in the city; a more recent Philadelphia-born filmmaker is Sidney Lumet.

The liberal politics of playwright Clifford Odets and journalist I. F. Stone were the product of Philadelphia upbringings—not to mention the often beyond-the-pale politics of linguist and philosopher Noam Chomsky. Two who still make their home in the city are Ted Mann—who has served as chairman of the Conference of Presidents of Major American Jewish Organizations and headed both the American Jewish Congress and the National Conference on Soviet Jewry—and the author Chaim Potok. David Brenner, the comedian, peppers his material with references to his Philadelphia childhood. Two native Philadelphians who made their marks in music are singer Eddie Fisher and jazz artist Stan Getz.

The Pennsylvania Ballet was founded by Barbara Weisberger, and the longtime conductor of the Philadelphia Orchestra was Eugene Ormandy, who had Jewish roots. Three of the city's four major sports teams—the football Eagles, the hockey Flyers, and the basketball 76ers—are Jewish-owned. In the 1970s, the University of Pennsylvania and Temple University were both headed by Jews.

General Sights: Throughout the city there are reminders of Jewish contributions to the community at large. The beautiful building housing the Free Library of Philadelphia, located on Benjamin Franklin Parkway at Nineteenth and Vine streets, was dedicated in 1827 while Simon Gratz was the library's president. Cyrus Adler served as the facility's librarian and later as president.

The Rodin Museum, on the parkway at Twenty-second Street, was endowed in the 1920s by Jules E. Mastbaum, a theater owner who became one of the city's most prominent and generous Jewish citizens.

Also on the parkway, whose sights are easily worth an entire day, is the Academy of Natural Sciences. Located at Nineteenth Street, the academy was founded in 1812 and is the oldest scientific institution of its kind in the country.

The Franklin Institute, on Twentieth Street, is a popular museum dedicated to the mechanical and applied sciences. Its Fels Planetarium was endowed by Samuel S. Fels, a Philadelphia soap manufacturer and philanthropist.

At the top of the parkway, at Twenty-sixth Street, is the Philadelphia Museum of Art, an imposing templelike structure that houses one of the finest collections in the country. It periodically mounts exhibits of Jewish interest, such as the huge 1985 show of Marc Chagall's work that included several pieces from the museum's own collection.

Fairmount Park, one of the largest urban parks in the world, is dotted with mansions that were the homes of Philadelphia's elite as far back as colonial times. A day spent touring the mansions can be a refreshing respite from the city's bustle. Information on docent-led tours is available at local tour agencies or from the city's tourist center at 1425 John F. Kennedy Boulevard. The tourist center is a good stop for information on other city attractions as well.

Fairmount Park is also home to the Philadelphia Zoo, the nation's oldest, and a child's paradise.

Day Trips: Philadelphia is a perfect jumping-off point for a grand variety of day trips in all directions. It is two hours from the Jersey shore, which includes the casinos of Atlantic City and the quaint atmosphere and restored Victorian houses of Cape May. Along the way, travelers can stop in some of the former Jewish agricultural colonies of South Jersey such as Rosenhayn or Roosevelt.

To the west, in Lancaster County, is Pennsylvania Dutch country, home of the Amish. Upstate from the city are the Pocono Mountains, with colorful scenery in any season and a large array of resort hotels, not to mention Jewish summer camps.

It is said that when one hundred cannon were fired at the beginning of the third day of the battle of Gettysburg, the noise could be heard in Philadelphia, 120 miles to the east. At least 19 Jews—13 Union and six Confederate—died at Gettysburg. Rabbi Ferdinand Sarner, regimental chaplain of the predominantly Jewish 54th New York Volunteer Infantry, was wounded there. The historian Mel Young has speculated—based on their positions on the first day of the battle—that the several hundred Jews of the 82nd Illinois and the more than a dozen Jews of the 12th Alabama may have fired on each other.

Reading: *Jewish Life in Philadelphia, 1830–1940* (Institute for the Study of Human Issues), an anthology edited by Murray Friedman, is a fascinating collection of essays that describe the growth of Philadelphia Jewry. His sequel volume, which begins in 1940, was recently published. In articles covering such diverse topics as Jewish women and philanthropy, Irish-Jewish relations, national Jewish leaders born locally, and conflicts between German and Russian Jews, the books weave a detailed portrait.

There is little in fiction that captures the Jewish experience in Philadelphia. General fictional portraits from several periods include Howard Fast's *Citizen Tom Paine* (Duell), Theodore Dreiser's *The Bulwark* (Doubleday), and Evelyn Mayerson's *If Birds Are Free* (Lippincott). *The Sun in Mid-Career* by Christopher Davis (Harper & Row) is a biographical novel based on the life of Marc Blitzstein, librettist, composer, and creator of such works as *The Cradle Will Rock*. The Davis book is as good a place as any to start getting to know Philadelphia.

—Neil Reisner

Phoenix

Just like the other pioneers, they came in covered wagons and on the backs of mules. The sparsely populated expanse of semiarid land was acquired from Mexico in 1848 and 1853. Though the territory was at first appended to New Mexico, President Lincoln signed a proclamation in 1863 that created a separate Arizona Territory. Hearty Jews, many of them recently arrived from Germany and Eastern Europe, set out for the last frontier. Although their total count probably never reached above 2,000 during the nineteenth century, their influence went far beyond their small numbers. They became peddlers, merchants, freighters, ranchers, bankers, gamblers, miners, liquor sellers, cattlemen, and politicians.

History: Herman Bendell was the first recorded Jew in Phoenix, arriving in 1871 (the year after the town was laid out) to serve as commissioner of Indian affairs. Jews had been in Arizona for some time by then, but there is disagreement about who was the first to arrive in the future state. Some say Mike Wormser reached Phoenix prior to 1860 and later was a partner in buying and shipping grain with Michael Goldwater, Barry's grandfather. It could have been Nathan Appel who arrived in 1856 in Tucson, stood toe-to-toe with Apaches when they wouldn't let him and his mules drink water near Stein's Pass, and lived to serve in 1864 in the first territorial legislature. Because the pioneers were constantly moving in and out, perhaps no one will ever pinpoint the first modern Jewish resident.

In truth, none of these sturdy settlers could claim to be absolutely the earliest. That honor goes to unknown Conversos from Spain seeking relief from the Inquisition. When the Inquisition opened an office in Mexico City in 1571, some secret Jews headed for the far reaches of New Spain, which meant the future Arizona and New Mexico. In recent years some descendants of Conversos have come out of the closet (in some cases literally, since that's where Jewish rituals were often enacted).

Regardless of who was first, the stories of the early Jewish pioneers read as adventurously as any account of Western settlement. Big Mike Goldwater from Poland, having failed at business three times in California, set out in 1860 for La Paz, Arizona, with a wagon full of goods to sell at the town's mining camp. By 1872, still seeking their first success, the family opened a store in Phoenix, also doomed to failure. Finally, in 1878, he moved to the then-territorial capital of Prescott, where fortune smiled. Various Goldwaters, brothers and sons, went on to found a string of stores stretching from Tombstone throughout the state. "Don Miguel," as the Mexicans called him, was elected mayor of Prescott in 1885. Like many of the earliest Jewish families of the forty-eighth state, future generations—like Barry Goldwater, the United States Senator and 1964 Republican presidential candidate—would not belong to the Jewish community.

The nineteenth-century Jew in Arizona lived a life of hardship. Dodging bullets, traveling solo through Indian territory, learning English, Spanish, and Indian languages at the same time, many still sought to cleave to their faith. The September 27, 1879, edition of *The Arizona Miner* informed its readers that on the tenth of the Hebrew month of Tishrei, "Yom Kipoor . . . our Jewish friends will close their places of business and devote themselves to atoning for their sins." High Holiday services were held over Melczer's saloon and liquor store on West Adams in Phoenix, at Wolf Lukin's grocery in nearby Tempe, or at Harry Friedman's saddlery. With no rabbi for hundreds of miles, leading the services was left in the hands of the most knowledgeable.

Although the Jewish community was small, a disproportionate number of Jews rose to positions of prominence. Philip Drachman, who had been a shipmate of the Goldwater brothers en route to America, went into business with another pioneer, Isaac Goldberg. Sam Drachman, although not a rabbi, was a strong Jewish influence in the territory, traveling its length and breadth to help his isolated coreligionists maintain their faith. He presided at the 1894 wedding in Phoenix of Hugo Zeckendorf and Rebecca Goldberg. The Zeckendorf family, led by William, had a store in Tucson. Grandfather of the New York real estate mogul who bore his name, William became a miner, rancher, and legislator. Both Drachman brothers were elected to the territorial government.

Aaron Goldberg, Isaac's brother, was a member of the territorial legislature and authored the bill that moved the capital from Prescott to Phoenix. Aaron also bought the now locally famous Rosson House, a restored Victorian home in Heritage Square in the revitalized downtown. His daughter was married to Joe Melczer on February 12, 1912, the day Arizona was admitted to the Union. Three-year-old Barry Goldwater was a ring bearer.

Still one more interconnected extended family was the Solomon-Freudenthal-Lesinsky clan. Isadore and Anna Solomon had left Poland for America shortly after the Civil War. In 1876 Anna's brothers, Phoebus and Morris Freudenthal, encouraged them to journey west to join them in running a string of general stores. Traveling first by rail, then six days by stage coach with three young children, they stopped in New Mexico for four months, living in a small house with mud floors and walls. Noting in her diary "sad and dark times," Anna and her husband then put down roots in Pueblo Viejo, Arizona, and engaged in supplying charcoal for mines. As the town grew, Isadore was elected Graham County Treasurer. They ran the Solomon Commercial Company as well as a hotel next door.

In 1893 the couple had the town's first brick building erected to house their new store. They included a bank to supply credit for local farmers and ranchers. Because they were the only owners of a secure safe in the territory, it was natural over time that their bank grew. It became the Valley National, largest in the state.

Among other early pioneers were many colorful characters. David Abraham, copper miner and road builder, carried a complete set of Shakespeare along with him in his wanderings. Solomon Barth, eventually a state legislator, was said to have once owned land that included the Grand Canyon. In 1874, Barth, who won several thousand dollars and as many sheep in a card game, founded the town of St. Johns. Jake Marks, an Indian fighter, lived in Prescott, two doors from Henry Goldwater on exclusive Nob Hill (called Snob Hill by many envious citizens). He was chosen by President Grover Cleveland to be receiver of the United States Land Office there. He also served on the city council.

As the twentieth century dawned, the makeup of the Jewish community began to change. With the seal of statehood and the closing of the frontier, people seeking relief from respiratory diseases began to trickle in. In the 1920s, anti-Semitism, hitherto unknown, began to surface. Many of the most famous resorts, like the Camelback Inn, barred Jews as guests. After World War II the state's Jewish population doubled and redoubled. It shot to 20,000 in 1960, 32,000 in 1977, and has now reached approximately 80,000 statewide. Nowadays, *bar-* and *bat-mitzvah* receptions are held in the once-restricted elegant resorts.

Community: From a pre–World War II population of fewer than 3,000, the Phoenix Jewish community has grown to more than 50,000, in a metropolitan area of 2.2 million. (Despite its predominance today, however, Prescott, the first capital, and Tucson have older communities.) There is no specifically Jewish neighborhood in Phoenix, except for the streets immediately around Orthodox synagogues.

According to a recent demographic survey by the Jewish Federation of Greater Phoenix, 45 percent of the area's Jews live within the Phoenix city limits; 32 percent live in exclusive Scottsdale; 19 percent in the contiguous suburbs of Tempe, Mesa, and Chandler; and four percent in the Sun City retirement village. Not surprisingly, the community has a large number of retired people, and a large number who have lived in the state less than five years. Between one-third and half have some formal tie to the Jewish community.

The first Phoenix congregation, Emanuel, was short-lived, but in 1921 the Phoenix Hebrew Center (today's Temple Beth Israel) acquired its first synagogue building. It has since acquired a lot of company; in all, Phoenix has seven Conservative, three Orthodox, and eight Reform synagogues, as well as one humanistic, one traditional, and one *chavurah*. For full information on the Jewish Community, send for a free copy of the yearly magazine *Jewish Living,* published by the *Greater Phoenix Jewish News,* 7220 North 16th St., Suite G, Phoenix, AZ 85020.

Sights: As the oldest congregation in Phoenix, Beth Israel can claim descent from the ad hoc group that first held High Holiday services above Melczer's saloon. Its former home at 122 East Culver — the first synagogue structure in the city — is now a church. Its present home at 3310 North 10th Avenue was completed in 1949. The square-block facility, with walls enclosing several buildings, gleams white in the hot southwest sun; tropical plants add dashes of color. The complex is arranged around a central plaza used for weddings and celebrations of Sukkot, Simchat Torah, and other holidays. Inside, the wood-paneled main sanctuary is capped by a Sephardic-style copper dome. Around the dome are twelve stained-glass windows featuring, in a dominant, deep-blue tone, the tribes of Israel.

Beth Israel is also home to the premier Jewish museum of the southwest, the Plotkin Judaica Museum (named for the synagogue's longtime rabbi, Albert Plotkin, and directed since its inception by his wife, Sylvia Plotkin). In addition to hosting traveling exhibits, the museum has two permanent displays. The Life Cycle and Holiday Judaica exhibit has a wide variety of artifacts, from a fifteenth-century Egyptian Torah written on leather to seven-teenth-century German Torah breastplates, to a mismatched set of candlesticks typical of those brought to the United States by immigrants. Other items include an early twentieth-century Elijah's chair from Damascus in wooden marquetry; a *brit milah* plate, believed to be from Iran or Iraq, with spaces for eighteen candles; and menorahs from all over the world.

But the Plotkin Museum's most outstanding exhibit is a recreated Tunisian synagogue, featuring many items brought from Tunisia by Steve Orlikoff, a temple member. Most of the items in the synagogue — Torah casings, *Ner Tamid,* memorial lights, prayer books, *tzedakah* box, and the dozens of amulets above the ark — are from a synagogue in Tunis. The design of the sanctuary — based on that of a synagogue on the Isle of Djerba — features intricately tiled walls and bench bases and turquoise columns topped by three graceful turquoise-and-white arches. A tape of a Tunisian Jewish family at prayer adds to the atmosphere. Museum hours are Tuesday through Thursday, 10 A.M. to 3 P.M., and Sunday, Noon to 3 P.M.

Two other synagogues in the Phoenix area are especially worth visiting. In Sun City, former engineer Max Gimpel designed much of Temple Beth Emet, at 13702 West Meeker Boulevard. Many tourists make the trip to see the stained-glass windows which — like those at Beth Israel — represent the twelve tribes. Temple Chai, at 645 East Maryland in Phoenix, is noteworthy in that the congregants built much of the synagogue with their own hands.

Just as Jews pioneered in early Arizona, so are they involved today in marrying modern technology to the state's unique resources. Paolo Soleri, an Italian-born Jew, has created the new field of arcology, an integration of architecture and ecology. Arcosanti, his concept of the energy-efficient town of the future, is one hour north of Phoenix via I-17 to Cordes Junction. Students and workers have begun to make his concept a reality. Since 1970 people have visited his geometric adobelike buildings and attended seminars and workshops on his urban planning ideas. Tours of Arcosanti are conducted on the hour from 10 to 4, seven days a week.

Closer to the city, at 6433 Doubletree

Road in Scottsdale, is the Cosanti Foundation, where Soleri has his workshop and headquarters. If you can't make the trek to Cordes Junction, a scale model of Arcosanti is there for visitors. Also on view are his windbells and sculptures. Scottsdale is also home to the Fleischer Museum of American modern art, endowed by Mort Fleischer, and to Taliesin West, Frank Lloyd Wright's desert home and architecture school.

Among the historic houses of Phoenix is the Victorian Rosson House—which might just as easily be called the Goldberg House. Dr. Rosson, its first owner, stayed only two years. Sold to the Aaron Goldberg family in 1896, it was the site of one of Phoenix's most stylish weddings when his daughter, Hazel, married Joe Melczer there on Statehood Day, February 12, 1912. Furnishings are not original, but they do reflect how the family might have lived. The Goldberg Brothers emporium later became Hanny's clothing store.

Side Trips: You only have to be in Prescott for fifteen minutes for someone to tell you proudly that it is a four-season city. Two hours north of Phoenix and the same distance south of the Grand Canyon, its elevation brings it some winter snow and changing fall foliage. It was in 1863 that Prescott's first settlers arrived; still standing are numerous Victorian homes and stores, which give the place a distinctly eastern appearance. The nineteenth-century population included many Jewish families. Two Goldwater residences, 217 East Union and 240 South Cortez, remain, the latter now a funeral home. Cattle rancher, liquor dealer, and adventurer, Jake Marks resided in what is now a charming bed-and-breakfast inn at 203 East Union, the steep street known as Nob Hill. The Blumberg house at 143 N. Mount Vernon belonged to Russian immigrant and merchant A. J. Blumberg. At 112 South Montezuma, the Levy building along the village green is a brick commercial establishment. Across the street, the Roughriders Statue in the Courthouse Park has inscribed the names of about a dozen Jewish soldiers, including two hometown men, who rode with Teddy Roosevelt.

Tombstone calls itself "The Town Too Tough to Die." The slogan is a reminder of the days when to live there was to count your life in months, not years. Although now mainly a tourist attraction, it has kept its Wild West look and wooden sidewalks. In its first days a handful of Jewish residents made up a contingent of the rough mining town.

Tombstone Jews were a diverse group. In 1880 silver miner Abraham Hyman Emanuel, who would serve as mayor from 1896 to 1900, was superintendent of the Vizina Mine. A woman who wrote her name in big letters in the colorful days of the West was teenage runaway and showgirl Josephine Sarah Marcus. At age eighteen she wooed and won gunfighter Wyatt Earp, becoming his third wife; they are buried together in a Jewish cemetery outside San Francisco.

Long forgotten was the Jewish cemetery adjacent to notorious Boothill Graveyard, eternal home to less colorful denizens than the likes of Boothill's Clantons, Billy Grounds, three-fingered Jack Dunlap, China Mary, Red River Tom, and Dutch Annie. Almost a century passed before a chance visit brought the dead a fitting memorial. A local resident showed the site to Jewish visitors and their friend, Judge C. Lawrence Huerta. Huerta, a Yaqui Indian, was deeply moved when Israel Rubin recited *Kaddish*, and he obtained the approval of the Tombstone City Council to restore the cemetery. The Jewish Friendship Club of nearby Green Valley aided in the effort, and a nonprofit corporation carried out the work. The ground was cleared and a wrought-iron fence placed atop the remains of the cemetery's adobe brick wall. The monument they erected within the walls was made of local rock. On two sides, east and west, there is the Star of David. The south side has an Indian sun symbol; the stylized flame of a menorah spells "Shalom." The memorial contains within it both Native American and Jewish ritual items to symbolize, according to Huerta, "the harmony between the Jewish pioneers and the Indians."

Culture: The Arizona Jewish Historical Society's Greater Phoenix Chapter at 4143 N. 12th Street, Suite 1000 (telephone

602-241-7870) welcomes contacts from visitors. Though its main feature is its library, the society's collection of artifacts is growing, and its walls are covered with photos of Jewish residents and pictures of early Jewish establishments. Members mount exhibits and collect and preserve memorabilia of their pioneering antecedents.

The Jewish Community Center at 1718 W. Maryland Avenue (602-249-1832) offers a wide range of educational and cultural programs. You can write to them for their brochure listing events. The newer Scottsdale JCC, 7480 E. Butherus Road (602-998-9145), has film and lecture series.

Arizona State University, 1012 S. Mill Avenue in Tempe, has periodic lectures and conferences of Jewish interest open to all. For information on upcoming events contact Joel Gereboff (602-965-7145) or Gordon Weiner (965-5778).

The Arizona Jewish Theater Company, which performs at the Sagebrush Theater in Scottsdale and the Herberger Theater Center in Phoenix, produces a variety of Jewish plays. Among recent productions have been *Crossing Delancey, Milk and Honey,* and *The World of Sholom Aleichem.*

Personalities: Florence Eckstein is unusual in Phoenix, a lifelong resident. With fewer than 3,000 Jews in 1948, she says, "It is the exception to have been born here." Therefore, many who have made their mark in the world were either not natives or spent only a small part of their lives here. Steven Spielberg passed his high school years here. Steve Stone, who pitched for the San Francisco Giants and Chicago Cubs, moved to Phoenix after retiring from baseball.

Sam Steiger served five terms in the United States Congress. Bert Kruglick chaired the state's Republican party, and Charles Bernstein was elected a justice of the state Supreme Court. Emil Ganz, a Confederate veteran who settled in Phoenix, established the National Bank of Arizona, now the First Interstate Bank, and was mayor of the city from 1896 to 1900. His granddaughter, Joan Ganz Cooney, is the creator of *Sesame Street.*

Many of the city's department stores were founded by Jews. Diamond's is now Dillards, Korrick's became Broadway, and Goldwater's is today's Robinson's. Selling another product were the Grouskays; noted cattlemen, the family arrived in 1917 when Eli came to cure his wife's asthma. Their son, Aubrey, and the rest of the family are still active in the Jewish community.

The "Father of the University of Arizona," Jacob Mansfield, moved the state's educational system forward by promoting Tucson as the site for the institution. Tom Volgy is the current mayor of Tucson.

Reading: It is hard to separate the saga of Jewish settlement in Arizona from that of the rest of the west. The pre–World War I Arizonans were a restless group who moved and traveled throughout vast spaces. Quite a few books have been written about the Jewish western experience. *Pioneer Jews* by Harriet and Fred Rochlin (Houghton Mifflin) and *We Lived There Too* (St. Martin's) by Kenneth Libo and Irving Howe are easily obtainable. The bibliography at the end of the Rochlins' book offers a wealth of potential reading for those who want to delve more deeply. *Roots and Boots* by Floyd S. Fierman (Ktav) has several fascinating chapters on early families, such as the Goldbergs and the Solomons.

Pioneer Jews of Arizona is a half-hour video record of the state's first Jews. Obtainable from the Plotkin Judaica Museum (see above), it costs $24.95 (plus $2.00 postage if mailed).

Eating: Segal's New Place, 4818 North 7th Street, and Taster's Yogurt Café, 3407 North 7th Street, are strictly kosher. "Kosher-style" eateries abound. Boman's (3731 North Scottsdale Road), Diamond's Deli (7720 East Gelding Drive), and Hollywood Deli (2650 East Camelback Road) are all in Scottsdale. Tradition Restaurant and Deli is at 13637 North Tatum Boulevard in Phoenix. Miracle Mile Deli has one branch in Scottsdale and two in Phoenix. Kosher and nonkosher, they all offer a lot more than the first Arizona Jews brought in their covered wagons.

—Deborah Barcan

Prague

One of the first acts of the new Czech government after the Velvet Revolution of 1989 was the decision to turn the Kinsky Palace, where Franz Kafka went to school, over to the newly formed Franz Kafka Society. But more than two years after approval was given, the Society had not yet moved in. "We keep walking around it, but we can't enter," said Vladimir Zelezny, who engineered the government's approval, evoking K., the character who never reached his goal in Kafka's *The Castle*. One of the society's members is President Vaclav Havel, but the nearly empty building was still being administered by the Czechoslovak National Gallery, staffed by officials bred under a communism that suppressed the works of Prague's most famous literary son. No one doubted that the building would eventually be turned over, but the impasse demonstrated how things in Prague can turn, without irony, Kafkaesque.

A few old-style bureaucrats notwithstanding, Prague is a happening. Unleashed by the Velvet Revolution, this stunning old city is experiencing a renaissance. Or more accurately, a reincarnation. Abuzz with long-suppressed energy, alight with flaming ideas, on the banks of the Vltava (Moldau) all is in flux and ferment.

Trying to make up for lost time by dashing nonstop from A to Z, Prague teeters between liberty and license in its rush to resurrect, even reinvent, itself. Aiming to be a pulse of Mitteleuropa, this is perhaps even more an intellectual and spiritual quest than a political and economic one. If the city failed to define its terms before, it is doing so now. In part, this means envisioning itself as the once and future crossroads for cultures Czech, German, and Jewish. One ingredient creating

this productive intermingling of Central European gentiles and Jews is the inclination of the populace to embrace all that the Communists damned—hence Jews, Judaism, and Israel.

The result is a heady moment. So much so that at this time and in this place more than one thinking Prague Jew dares declare of the situation in his city, "Jewishness is in."

History: Jews have been "in" before during their millennium-long sojourn in Prague; so, too, have they been "out." Among the oldest of Europe's Jewish communities, Prague's has at times been the largest, wealthiest, and most culturally influential. It has also, however, ridden the downward seesaw with regularity.

Tradition in Bohemia—of which Prague is the capital—tells that the Jews were there before the area's recorded history; documentation first places them in the city about 970, whether as settlers or just traders is not clear. They appear to have arrived from both East and West at the same time and established two separate districts, one near the now destroyed Vysehrad Castle, the other around the still standing Prague Castle. Definitive evidence of the first Prague Jewish community dates from 1091. Initially conditions were favorable, but the First Crusade in 1096 led to looting, forced conversion, and even murder—thus completing a cycle that would be repeated frequently.

Among the good periods for Prague Jews were the eleventh to thirteenth centuries, when Jewish culture flourished; the time of Charles IV, 1346–78, when the king protected the Jews; and the early sixteenth century. Then, thanks to the support of the king and his nobility their economic situation improved, their numbers doubled to 1,200, and they founded the first Hebrew printing establishment north of the Alps. A bit later, during the reigns of Rudolf II and his successor (1576–1619), they created their "Golden Era" when some, like Marcus Mordechai Maisel and Jacob Bassevi von Treuenberg, became extremely wealthy — the latter as banker to the emperor and the first Czech Jewish nobleman.

This span also produced celebrated scholars like the astronomer David Gans, an associate of Johannes Kepler; and important rabbis, the best known of whom was Judah Loew ben Bezalel, known as the Maharal, a scientist as well as talmudist. After his death he was credited with having fashioned a living monster. This creature, the Golem, was subsequently viewed as the inspiration for Frankenstein. Furthermore, the Golem became a subject of Jewish literature and folklore (the most famous being *Der Golem*, the Yiddish play by H. Leivick), wherein the mission of this supernatural being was to protect the Jews from danger.

After the decline of Jewish status and despite outbreaks of animosity — including one surrounding the revolutionary period of 1848, which triggered a westward emigration — the Jews by the mid-1800s could pay equitable rather than exceptionally high taxes, own land, and live outside the ghetto. In 1867 they were completely legally emancipated, and in 1896 most of the old ghetto — already united as the Josefov district with the other parts of the city — was, for hygienic reasons, pulled down. By the turn of the century more than 75 percent of Prague's 27,000 Jews lived outside the area.

With emancipation came secularization and assimilation. As Jews scattered throughout Prague and the rest of Bohemia they so lost their sense of Jewishness that by the time the Nazis came, some were genuinely stunned to be singled out.

As others began to treat Jews and Jewish motifs as integral parts of the Prague landscape, the Jews — by now engaged in trade, commerce, industry, handicrafts, and the professions — became active in both the German and Czech cultural camps. Politically, they spread across the spectrum: as founders of the German Liberal Party; as leading members of the German Social Democratic Party; as supporters of Tomáš Masaryk's Czech-speaking Realists and the Czech Social Democrats.

Culturally, they made marks in theater, music, science, and perhaps most significantly in literature. As writers, Jews created in both Czech and German, and often, as translators, served as intermediaries between the language groups. But their most widely hailed work was done by the German Jewish authors known internationally as the Prague Circle. Among these were Max Brod, Franz Werfel, Egon Erwin Kisch, and the existentialist Franz Kafka.

Following World War I, when Czechoslovakia was formed from Slovakia, Carpatho-Russia, Bohemia, Moravia, and other bits of the Austro-Hungarian Empire, the new country became host to about 350,000 Jews. These comprised what has been called "perhaps the happiest and most contented Jewish community of Central and Eastern Europe." But the Holocaust ended the honeymoon.

With the Sudetenland annexed by Germany and Slovakia a Nazi client-state, the Germans, when they invaded the remains of Czechoslovakia on March 15, 1939, declared Bohemia and Moravia a protectorate of the Reich.

The first deportations to Poland occurred in October 1939. Then in the fall of 1941 the town of Terezin (Theresienstadt) was established as a central ghetto for Jews of the protectorate and a model camp for privileged Reich Jews. But it was primarily a transit stop en route to the death camps. For good measure, it had its own crematoria.

About 118,000 Jews lived in Bohemia and Moravia when war rumbles began in the mid-1930s. While thousands fled — many of whom subsequently joined Czech fighting units elsewhere — others arrived from Germany, Austria, and the Sudetenland. Thus when the Germans invaded, about 90,000 Jews were living in Bohemia-Moravia, of whom 56,000 lived in Prague. Perhaps 10 percent survived.

Decimated as they were, those Jews who did not immediately leave Czechoslovakia began re-creating communities and reviving Jewish life immediately after the war. But in 1948, just when these efforts were beginning to root, the Communists took power.

And shortly thereafter the State of Israel was proclaimed. Combined, the two events triggered a wave of emigration. With the Communist suppression Jewish life was significantly shaken.

Still, individual Jews had considerable impact, since significant numbers of the initial Communist regime's top leadership were Jews. The highest was Rudolf Slánský, the party's secretary-general. In the early 1950s when the Czech Communists exorcised "traitors" following the anti-Semitic Russian pattern, Slánský and thirteen associates were brought to trial. Of these, eleven were Jews, eight of whom, including Slánský, were executed.

The Slánský trial not only signaled the Jews that they were politically unwelcome, it also warned them to lay low in general. Nevertheless, by the 1960s, individuals were again active, particularly in the cultural arena. Through their work in theater, movies, journalism, academia, and the Writers' Union they helped create the liberal climate that produced the Prague Spring. Though few reentered politics, Ota Šik became the chief architect of economic reform under Alexander Dubček. And František Krieger, chairman of the National Front, incurred the wrath of the Soviets and the admiration of the Czechs by being the only member of the Czechoslovak delegation, following the 1968 Soviet invasion, who refused to sign the agreement legalizing this action. With the crushing of the Prague Spring 3,400 Jews joined the ensuing emigration.

But enough Jewish dissidents remained or returned to contribute impetus for the promulgation of Charter 77, the manifesto calling for a more liberal society. Helena Klimova was one of the three spokespersons for Charter 77, and from the ranks of signers came the dissidents who later formed the Civic Forum, spearhead of the Velvet Revolution.

With the Velvet Revolution, relations between Israel and Czechoslovakia were restored, reuniting the Jewish state with one of its oldest and most valuable allies. As early as 1927 Tomáš Masaryk, Czechoslovakia's first president, visited Palestine and expressed support for Jewish settlement there, a stance rewarded by the creation in Israel of the Masaryk Forest and Kfar Masaryk. In 1948, Czechoslovakia voted enthusiastically for the state's establishment and thanks to the influence of Slánský and others, quickly became the struggling nation's chief arms supplier.

After the Slánský trial, however, Israel was treated as a pariah and even trade relations disappeared after the Sinai Campaign. Following the Soviet lead, Czechoslovakia broke relations completely in 1967. Vaclav Havel announced in his first presidential speech on New Year's Day 1990 his desire to normalize the situation. When he visited Jerusalem three months later he was officially thanked for his country's early aid, without which, he was told, there would have been no Israel.

Community: At first glance, few Jewish communities would seem as vibrant as Prague's. Come lunchtime everyone with any connection to Judaism seems to flock to the kosher restaurant to rendezvous, talk, and just eat. The proceedings are an affirmation of solidarity and a perpetual celebration of the new openness. Yet the community's life is tenuous.

About 6,000 Jews are thought to reside in the Czech Republic, which includes Bohemia and Moravia, but the six federated communities in this jurisdiction have only 3,000 registered members, of which just 1,400 reside in Prague. Including Slovakia, the Jewish population of former Czechoslovakia numbers perhaps 20,000.

About 75 percent of the republic's Jews are over sixty-five and, thanks to the post-1968 emigration, the middle generation has been reduced to only 20 families.

A recent major change altered conditions for community membership to permit all who consider themselves Jewish, rather than just those halakhically acceptable, to participate. However, certain "disabilities" apply to those from mixed marriages and for those whose last Jewish relatives were their grandparents. And not everyone in such circumstances is thrilled. Hence tension exists as younger, would-be Jews seek alternative paths to their heritage.

Meanwhile, community plans and projects abound. The Federation of Jewish Communities in the Czech Republic at Maiselova 18 (telephone 231-8559 or 231-0840) is increasingly active and has begun publishing books of Jewish interest. Its guide to the Jewish past and present in Bohemia and Moravia is in four languages, including English. In addition to twice-weekly adult programs, the community also publishes a monthly newsletter, *Roš Chodeš*. The Jewish Welcome Service offers general and Jewish tours of Prague and throughout Bohemia and Moravia (call the Federation for information). A teen group of 100, built around a nucleus of children who have spent summers in Israel, meets twice a month.

Currently the community is negotiating with the government to retrieve confiscated Jewish property. Since the new restitution laws go back only to the Communist take-over in 1948, much is irretrievable. But the community is claiming, and expects to take back, the Jewish Museum. (Like the Kafka Society, the community has agreement in principle on the return of 106 properties, including synagogues and cemeteries as well as the State Jewish Museum, but it too has been frustrated in its efforts to transform agreement into action.)

Another thing Prague Jews have been looking forward to is the ordination of its next rabbi, Karol Sidon. Sidon, whose existential fiction has led to his acclamation as one of the Czech Republic's best contemporary writers, was a signer of Charter 77 and active in the synagogue until his dissidence forced him to leave. In exile, he studied Judaism in Heidelberg, for which he was given academic credits from a Jerusalem *yeshivah*. So charismatic has he proved that from a Charter-77 coterie of young people that formed around him, about ten have become so involved with Judaism they have converted.

Given the propensity of Prague toward intellectual pursuits and the Jews' almost automatic inclusion in the intelligentsia, it is not surprising to find secular, nonsectarian organizations crossing communal lines.

The Society for Jewish Culture was established in 1990 for Jews from mixed marriages who relate to their heritage in a secular way. But it already has nearly a thousand members, of whom only about a quarter are Jewish. The society's aim is education with a focus on Judaism's non-religious aspects. It can also be reached through the federation.

Metamorphosis: Prague has undergone changes Kafka would appreciate

The Franz Kafka Society also embraces Jews and gentiles and in its first two years acquired 800 members around the world. Aiming to revive the Central European atmosphere in Prague, which means celebrating the Czech, German and Jewish cultures, it plans to build a Kafka center and museum once it occupies the pink-and-white rococo Kinsky Palace on the Old Town Square. (In addition to attending school in the building, Kafka's father had a dry goods store on the ground floor and the family lived nearby.) Among its first projects is publishing the Talmud in Czech. The society is currently located at Staromestske Namesti 22 (telephone 26-08-48).

On the lighter side, there's Mispachah, a choir originally from one family that has expanded to about twenty members. Though once under police scrutiny for having stepped beyond strictly religious bounds, since the Velvet Revolution it has been giving public performances of Yiddish, Ladino, and Russian songs. Notices

413

of performances can be found wherever local cultural activities are listed.

The blurring of the line between Czech and Jewish culture is nothing new. Another cultural sharing is the similarity between *Hatikvah* and the "Vltava" section of Czech composer Bedřich Smetana's tone poem, *My Country*. Both pieces are believed to have derived from the same folk melody.

Sights: Prague is probably one of the few places in the world where the primary general sights include those of Jewish interest. Even under the communists, busloads of tourists unpiled every morning near the Parizska Street approach to the collection of structures once at the heart of the self-contained ghetto and now comprising the Jewish Museum.

Within the purview of the museum lie the historically valuable objects gathered by the Nazis from 153 Jewish communities to stock the Central Museum of the Defunct Jewish Race. Though only a small portion of this treasure is currently displayed, what is viewable represents one of the richest collections of Judaica in the world.

The most immediately noticeable building in the ghetto area is the sixteenth-century, two-tone pink, rococo Jewish Town Hall. It is particularly striking because its tower features a clock with Hebrew letter-numbers and hands running counterclockwise. The building, at Maiselova 18, also houses the Jewish community offices.

Opposite the clock-face side of the Town Hall on Cervena Street, an alleylike walkway off Parizska Street, stands the Old-New (Alt-Neu) Synagogue, the oldest preserved — and functioning — synagogue in Europe. Its first parts date from the beginning of the thirteenth century; it was completed in 1270. Built in Early Gothic style with a five-ribbed vaulted ceiling, it is among the oldest extant Gothic monuments in all Prague. The soaring arches rise above a central *bimah* surrounded by a fifteenth-century wrought-iron grille. The Golem is said to live in the attic of the Old-New Synagogue, whose name's origin is subject to ongoing debate. Despite the view that *Altneuschul* means simply "Old-New Synagogue," it may actually take its name from the Hebrew *al tnai* — "on condition"; the synagogue was built on condition that when the messianic age arrives it would be torn down and rebuilt, brick by brick, in Eretz Yisrael.

Beyond the Old-New Synagogue stands the *Chevrah Kadisha* building, now housing artworks created in Terezin. Other significant old buildings in the ghetto area are the nearby Klausen Synagogue, presenting examples of early Hebrew printing in Prague, including a facsimile of the oldest Hebrew book, printed in 1514; the Maisel Synagogue around the corner on Maiselova Street which, behind an elaborate wrought-iron fence, houses majestic silver objects, including a large Torah crown that looks as if it were designed for royalty; and the High Synagogue, currently containing carpets and Torah curtains. At one time the walls of the now closed Pinkas Synagogue bore the names of the 77,297 Jews from Bohemia and Moravia who died during the Holocaust, painted surreptitiously to avoid Communist scrutiny. When discovered they were removed, but plans call for restoring them and reopening the building.

Arguably the most visited site in the ghetto area is the Old Jewish Cemetery, entered just beyond the Old-New Synagogue. There on a small, irregularly shaped piece of land, 12,000 crowded-together tombstones mark layers upon layers of burial plots dating from 1439 to 1787. Visitors have covered Rabbi Loew's grave with notes and Paris Metro tickets. The graves of Mordechai Maisel and Jacob Bassevi are also here, along with others bearing reliefs signifying the deceased's name or profession. One section contains the graves of fetuses and stillborn babies; a plot apart from the rest contains the carcass of a dog. During a riot, it seems the mob repeatedly threw the dog over the cemetery walls as an act of desecration. After removing it several times, the Jews finally decided to bury it to end the vicious cycle.

Within easy walking distance of the ghetto area stands the Spanish Synagogue at the curve in Dusni Street opposite number 9. Though closed now, this ornate structure of Moorish arches and Arabesque-covered stonework once served Sephardic Jews. Despite its somewhat crumbling appearance, the Ten Commandments on its exterior are clearly delineated in gilt-colored Roman numerals surrounded by a pattern of *Magen Davids*. A Reform synagogue in the last century, its first organist and music director was František J. Skroup, composer of the Czech national anthem. The building's future has not yet been decided, but it may become a Jewish home for the aged.

In addition to the Old-New Synagogue, Prague's other functioning Jewish prayer hall, used by more liberal worshipers, is the Jerusalem Synagogue at Jerusalemska 7, at the corner of U Pujcovny. Also a Moorish structure built in 1906, its facade, decorated in red and yellow, features a great inset *Magen David*.

One building already returned to the Jewish community is the Smichovska Synagogue across the river at U Andela 5. There, in what had been since the war a warehouse for streetcars, the community hopes to build a modern exhibition hall. It is slated to hold, among other rarities, part of the collection of seventeenth- and eighteenth-century ark curtains now in the Spanish Synagogue.

An overview of the Jewish quarter, which extended to the Vltava, can be had from a model of Old Prague at the turn of the nineteenth century that stands, with all its minute detail, in the Prague Municipal Museum.

Beyond the ghetto area, Prague features other reminders of the Jewish presence. Among the statues dotting the famed Charles Bridge is one bearing Hebrew words. A crucifix, it is the third statue on the right going toward the castle, and the three top points of the cross each say *Kadosh*. Once in gold, they are thought to have been paid for by the community as punishment for a 1609 blasphemy against the church by one of its members. Along the river still stands the Café Slavia, one of the coffeehouses frequented by writers of the Prague Circle. Across the river in the castle area is the Golden Lane, once the home of Franz Kafka. In the area of Prague's exhibition grounds, near the Park Hotel along Dukelskych Hrdinu Street, the first transports to Terezin departed. A relief commemorating the event, by Terezin survivor Helga Hoskova-Weisova, was recently unveiled.

Back in the heart of Old Prague, in the Old Town Hall is a darkly paneled, Late Gothic and Renaissance room—the Old Council Chamber. Draped from its deeply

jutting ceiling beams are several pieces of extremely heavy chain used to close the independent towns that once comprised Prague. Among these are the chains that locked the ghetto. (The Old Town Hall is a favorite meeting place on the hour because of the figures that parade around its facade when the clock strikes.)

Nearby, outside the New Town Hall at Marianske Namesti 2, stands, to the right of the entrance, a tall, gray stone statue of a figure in flowing robes with a hand upraised as if in benediction. Placed there in 1912 by town fathers cognizant of the Jewish past, it represents Rabbi Loew.

Throughout the city there is a ubiquitous use of the Golem motif and a plethora of reminders of Kafka. Among the latter is a bronze relief of his tortured face which marks his birthplace. The sculpture stands out from a pink, curving corner wall abutting U Radnice 5, right next to a Panasonic sign near the St. Nicholas Church. Kafka's grave in the new Jewish cemetery in Olsany is a place for pilgrimage as well. This cemetery is also noteworthy for its striking Holocaust sculpture in swirling stone, representing the spirits of the Jews traveling in the smoke of the crematoria to the cosmos.

The Rudolfinum, Prague's concert hall, recently reopened after renovation. One of its leading adornments is still in place on the roof. According to an oft-told tale, workmen ordered by the Nazis to remove the statue of Felix Mendelssohn removed Richard Wagner's instead. Mendelssohn's still stands.

Side Trips: Terezin lies about forty miles from Prague. A sprawling complex, the section that held the Jews is not the small fortress usually shown, but the garrison area beyond. The barracks there still stand, some as they did when this ghetto-cum-concentration camp was dolled up for inspection by the Red Cross. Beyond the housing lie the tracks that ran to Auschwitz. And beyond them—with carts that still run inside—the crematoria, specially designed with low chimneys and burning techniques that kept their secret from the surrounding populace. In addition to the paintings that survived Terezin and Josef Bor's work, *The Terezin Requiem*, films have been made about the place and concerts performed by former inmates. *I Never*

Saw Another Butterfly was based on the writings of Terezin's children, and sections of Herman Wouk's *War and Remembrance* are set there. The Czech Philharmonic has given memorial performances at Terezin, and a "Museum of the Ghetto" is scheduled to open in the near future. Sylvie Wittmann (telephone 25-12-35 in Prague) runs tours to Terezin.

En route to Terezin is the site of Lidice, the village that was destroyed June 10, 1942, in retaliation for the assassination of Reinhard Heydrich. A museum, with cubes of earth from concentration camps, stands in the silence; a plaza overlooks the valley containing the mass grave in which all the men of Lidice were buried. They were interred by Jews from Terezin who were then executed themselves to be silenced.

Personalities: Among the outstanding names associated with Prague's past are the Bohemian-born Gustav Mahler, who conducted in the city for a while; Albert Einstein, who taught there in 1911–12; pianist Artur Schnabel; and authors Karel Polaček and Vojtech Rakous, who wrote in Czech, the latter about Jewish life in the countryside.

Prior to the Prague Spring's denouement, liberalizing Jews—and subsequent émigrés—included Eduard Goldstuecker, vice rector of Prague University and president of the Writers' Union; and filmmakers Jan Kadar and Milos Forman. Another émigré, Pavel Tigrid, became the leading publisher abroad of forbidden Czech writers, whose works were then infiltrated back into the country.

Many Jews were involved with Vaclav Havel's Civic Forum and served in the first democratic government. Vladimir Zelezny was the Forum's spokesman and a personal advisor to Havel and spokesman for the government. Jan Dobrovsky was Havel's minister of defense; Rita Klimova was ambassador to the United States; and Rudolf Slánský, son of the executed Rudolf, was ambassador to the Soviet Union.

Reading: Two generally acclaimed books by Czech Jewish authors have recently been published in the United States. They are the late Jiri Well's *Mendelssohn Is*

on the Roof (Farrar, Straus & Giroux) and *Love and Garbage* (Knopf) by Ivan Klima, who founded the Czech PEN Club in 1989. *The House on Prague Street* by Hanna Demetz is an autobiographical novel set in wartime Czechoslovakia. *When Memory Comes* (Farrar, Straus & Giroux) by Saul Friedlander provides a look at Jewish life in prewar Prague. Artur London, who survived the Slánský trials and was rehabilitated, had his account of his experiences turned into a film, *Confession*, by Costa-Gavras.

The classic work on Prague's best-known Jewish legend is *Golem* by Gustav Meyerink (Dover). The latest twist on the theme is *He, She and It* by Marge Piercy (Knopf), an intensely Jewish science fiction tale that shifts back and forth between sixteenth-century Prague and twenty-first-century America. For a timeless trip into the Czech mentality, Jaroslav Hašek's *The Good Soldier Schweik* (Viking) is a classic.

Recommendations: Swissair offers regular connections to Prague, operating them with the airline's customary gentility, efficiency, and aplomb. The only kosher restaurant in Prague is run like a mess hall in the lobby of community headquarters at Maiselova 18. Coming from the same kitchen is the food served at the kosher snack bar labeled Kosher Snacks, fronting on the walkway running past the Old-New Synagogue. Other restaurants—such as U Golema at Maiselova 8 and U Stare Synagogue ("restaurant of the old synagogue") at the entrance to the Jewish quarter—employ suggestive names but are not kosher.

Unlike Jews in other former Eastern bloc communities, those in Prague evince little fear of anti-Semitism. Because Jews have not been involved with repressive regimes since the Slánský days, they are not concerned about backlash on that count. Because ignorance of Judaism is so widespread, it is viewed almost as if it had been a forbidden underground movement. And because of the permissive atmosphere, the Jews of Prague now—despite the occasional Kafkaesque experience—present themselves with an openness bordering on abandon.

—*Phyllis Ellen Funke*

Richmond

For three centuries, the history of Richmond, proud capital of Virginia, has been characterized by frequent, sometimes traumatic, change. Originally an outpost against Indians along the falls of the James River, Richmond was founded as a city in 1737. After the Virginia capital was moved from Williamsburg in 1779, Richmond became the leading city of the South and a lively center of the state's elegant plantation society.

This era ended abruptly when Richmond was in the vortex as capital of the Confederacy. During other critical periods like Reconstruction and the Depression, Richmond's economy was saved by its main commodity—tobacco. In recent decades, Richmond has grown into a metropolitan area of 870,000 and expanded as a commercial and transportation center.

Richmond's Jews played an important part in the city's development; they adapted to the city's changes while adjusting to transitions in their own religious, social, and business lives. Today, Richmond's Jewish community of 8,000 is larger, more cosmopolitan, congenial, and "Jewish" than at any other time in its long history.

History: Isaiah Isaacs, a silversmith and trader of German origin, was the first Jew to settle in Richmond, arriving around 1769. He was also the first Jew elected to public office in Richmond, joining Richmond's Common Hall, later named the City Council, in 1788.

Isaacs' business partner, Jacob I. Cohen, became a Revolutionary War hero. Cohen and Isaacs owned the Bird-in-Hand, believed to be Richmond's first tavern, located at the foot of Church Hill near where the old Hebrew cemetery stands today.

They also had a mercantile firm, and one of their land surveyors was Daniel Boone.

In the first national census taken in 1790, there were 100 Jews in Richmond. They were almost all affluent Ashkenazim, and they regarded themselves as a cultural and religious aristocracy. They mixed with the gentile elite, and this led to a good deal of assimilation and intermarriage.

By 1820, the Jewish population had doubled to about 200, and the "First Jewish families of Richmond"—the Mordecais, the Marxes, the Hayses, and the Meyers—were all interrelated and regarded as clannish. During the 1830s, substantial emigration of German Jews began, particularly from Bavaria, and shortly before the Civil War the first Polish Jews arrived. The 1880s brought the arrival of Russian Jews. Each of these groups established new synagogues.

Many of the businesses founded by immigrant Jews are now over 100 years old, like the Thalhimer Brothers Department Store, founded by William Thalhimer, an immigrant *shochet* and part-time *chazan* from Baden, Germany. Thalhimer was later instrumental in persuading Franklin Roosevelt to make charitable contributions tax deductible.

Before the Civil War (1861–1865), most of Richmond's Jews were slave owners, like their non-Jewish neighbors, and a few were slave dealers. But some, like Isaiah Isaacs, came to regard slavery as immoral and freed their slaves.

Richmond was named capital of the Confederacy after Virginia seceded from the Union in April 1861. When the war turned against the South, anti-Semitism, not previously prevalent in the region, flared in the press, on the floor of the Confederate Congress, and in the streets of Richmond.

Jews were unjustly accused of profiteering in scarce goods and of failure to enlist. Judah P. Benjamin, who successively held the posts of attorney general, secretary of war, and secretary of state of the Confederacy, was accused of allowing too many Jewish refugees into Richmond. The Jewish quartermaster-general, A. C. Meyers, was accused of not providing adequate supplies for the army. In the autumn of 1863 there was some looting of Jewish businesses.

After an anti-Semitic article appeared in the *Richmond Examiner,* Adolphus Adler, a colonel in the Confederate Army, challenged the editor to a duel; the editor apologized. The *Richmond Sentinel*, on the other hand, appealed for tolerance, saying, "We consider it a duty to hail every good citizen as a brother. We ask him not where he was born or what his faith."

More than 100 Richmond Jews fought in Confederate ranks, particularly in two local companies, the Richmond Grays and the Richmond Light Infantry Blues. Rabbi Maxmilian J. Michelbacher of Congregation Beth Ahabah composed a prayer that was distributed to all Jewish Confederate soldiers. Many of Richmond's Jewish women were volunteer nurses in hospitals or at home.

Jewish merchants and bankers played a large role in the postwar recovery. Philip Whitlock helped establish Richmond as a tobacco center and his firm was eventually absorbed by the American Tobacco Company. Leading bankers were Gustavus Adolphus Myers, Edward Cohen (Merchants and Savings Bank), and Charles Hutzler and William Schwartzschild (Central National Bank).

Twentieth-century arrivals in Richmond included refugees from Hitler's Europe in the 1930s and Holocaust survivors in the 1940s; former Jewish soldiers who served at nearby Fort Lee; and young professionals from all over the United States, particularly the North. Today, less than a fourth of Richmond's Jews are native born.

Community: There were enough Jews in Richmond by 1789 to found a synagogue, Kahal Kadosh Beth Shalome, which is the nation's sixth-oldest congregation. Beth Shalome, which originally used the Sephardic ritual, was one of the colonial congregations to send George Washington a congratulatory letter upon his inauguration and to receive a reply. The synagogue dedicated its first building on Mayo Street on the eve of Rosh Hashanah 1822. The brick structure — since demolished — was the first synagogue building in Virginia.

Orthodox German Jews founded Beth Ahabah Congregation in 1841, but the congregation gradually grew more liberal and ultimately became a leader in the Reform movement. Beth Ahabah also has a place in history as the site of the first public school classes conducted in Richmond. The congregation's rabbi from 1891 to 1946, Edward N. Calisch, was a dynamic community leader, but preached anti-Zionist ideology to his flock.

The Orthodox Keneseth Israel was organized in 1856 by Polish Jews. In 1891, Russian Jews organized the Sir Moses Montefiore Congregation, affectionately called "Sir Moses."

In 1898, Beth Shalome merged with Beth Ahabah. Early in this century, Keneseth Israel, "Sir Moses," and the Aitz Chaim Congregation united as Orthodox Keneseth Beth Israel. The influence of these pioneer congregations is reflected in Jewish Richmond today, which has a Lubavitch center, two Orthodox, two Conservative, and two Reform congregations.

During the civil rights era of the 1960s, many Richmond Jews supported the NAACP and the Urban League. Local Jews were involved in efforts to help blacks gain access to public facilities, and were at the forefront of protest when the Richmond Community Chest asked the Urban League to withdraw itself as a beneficiary of that fund.

Richmond's early Jewish residents lived in the East End, an area destroyed in the fire that engulfed much of the city at the end of the Civil War. New neighborhoods formed around Grove and Monument Avenues and Boulevard. In the 1950s, many congregations and Jewish families moved to suburban West End. Today some Jewish families live on the South Side, across the James River.

Sights: Most of Richmond's Jewish institutions and neighborhoods are suburban, so you'll need a car and a city map. Richmond's oldest congregation, Reform Congregation Beth Ahabah, 1117 West Franklin Street, celebrated its bicentennial in 1988, based on its link with Beth Shalome. Among the synagogue's outstanding features are its stained-glass windows featuring biblical scenes, including the Garden of Eden and the burning bush. One panel of the brilliantly colored glass was created by Tiffany.

Beth Ahabah's Museum and Archives Trust, 1109 West Franklin Street, has an excellent Judaica collection, which includes books; personal, business and religious records of Richmond Jews; and restored historic photographs. George Washington's famous letter on religious toleration sent to Beth Shalome is exhibited. The museum also mounts changing exhibits, such as the recent *Jewish Silversmiths: Three Centuries of Brilliance* and *A Family Tapestry: The Hutzlers and Richmond,* which traced several generations of a prominent Jewish family. Other objects on display in the museum include scales for weighing gold brought by a German immigrant, a silver *Kiddush* cup made by a congregant, and a nineteenth-century Masonic apron. The museum is open Sunday through Thursday (telephone 804-353-2668).

Keneseth Beth Israel, Richmond's oldest Orthodox congregation, is located at 6300 Patterson Avenue. Its foyer and sanctuary are decorated with multicolored stained-glass panels and windows dedicated to congregation leaders. The sanctuary has a beautiful hanging wall sculpture of metal made by a local artist in memory of Holocaust victims, and large antique brass candelabra. The marble tile wall around the ark is carved with the Ten Commandments. A large showcase of congregation memorabilia is in the library.

Temple Beth El, established in 1931 and Richmond's largest Conservative congregation, is located at 3300 Grove Avenue. The lovely stained-glass windows in the main sanctuary, created by the late A. Raymond Katz, are on the theme of the prophets.

Richmond's second Orthodox congregation, Kol Emes, is at 4811 Patterson Avenue. The city's newest synagogues are Reform Or Ami and Conservative Or Atid. Or Ami recently moved into a new sanctuary on Richmond's South Side, 9400 Huguenot Road. The ark doors are decorated with a "Tree of Life" sculpture by New Mexican artist Cynthia Barber. Its wooden trunk of brown bark serves as a base for stylized leaves of various inlaid metals. Or Atid, 501 Parham Road, holds services-in-the-round in its circular building with a pyramid roof.

Beth Ahabah's Hebrew Cemetery, at Fifth and Hospital Streets, has a section for Jews who died serving the Confederacy. The section is surrounded by an ironwork fence, a handsome example of that period, designed by Jewish artist William B. Myers. The railings are crossed sabers; the posts are furled flags and stacked muskets topped with flat Confederate caps.

The Franklin Street Burying Ground, East Franklin Street near Twenty-First Street, is the oldest Jewish cemetery in Virginia. In the Emek Sholom section of Forest Lawn Cemetery, 4000 Alma Avenue, a Holocaust monument was erected in 1955.

The Virginia Historical Society, Boulevard at Grove Avenue, displays portraits of two of Richmond's prominent Jewish citizens: Gustavus Adolphus Myers in a portrait by Thomas Sully and noted sculptor Sir Moses Ezekiel. Also exhibited are the account books of Judah Hayes, showing his commercial dealings with Richmond merchants, and a prenuptial agreement between Boston merchant Michael Moses Hayes and his daughter Judith and merchant Samuel Myers of Virginia.

The Valentine Museum, which highlights the history of Richmond, exhibits portraits of Joseph Marx, a Richmond merchant, and his wife, Richea; and Samuel Mordecai, chronicler-historian of Richmond Jewry.

Culture: Richmond's Jewish Community Center, located at 5403 Monument Avenue (804-288-6091), is one of Virginia's leading cultural institutions. Its Sara D. November Gallery presents monthly art shows, and its music series has received citywide acclaim for recitals, chamber music, jazz, and folk concerts. Performing artists at the center have included pianist Navah Perlman (Yitzhak Perlman's daughter), The Heritage Trio, and Russian pianist Alexander Peskanov. The JCC houses the

Milton Joel Judaic Library and a Judaic art studio. The Bottom Line Gallery exhibits serious children's art and the work of talented young artists.

The Reflector, published weekly by the JCC, lists community happenings; *The Jewish News,* a regional weekly, publishes news of Jewish communities worldwide. Copies of both are available at the JCC. The sisterhoods, men's clubs, and chapters of national Jewish organizations frequently sponsor cultural programs and welcome visitors. Check with the various synagogues or the JCC.

General Sights: Monument Avenue is the embodiment of Richmond pride. The street is lined with immense bronze statues of Robert E. Lee astride his famed horse Traveler, Thomas J. "Stonewall" Jackson, J. E. B. "Jeb" Stuart, Commander Matthew Fontaine Maury, and Confederate President Jefferson Davis. A ride or stroll down Monument Avenue is a must. Start at the corner of Monument and Lombardy and head west.

There are almost thirty points of historic interest located between Monument Avenue and the state capitol, which dominates a hill in the center of town. The impressive capitol, at Ninth and Grace Streets, was designed by Thomas Jefferson in 1785 after the Maison Carée at Nîmes, France. Houdon's stately white marble sculpture of George Washington stands in the rotunda.

In the "Court End" district near the capitol are the Valentine Museum; the John Marshall House, designed and built by future Chief Justice John M. Marshall in 1788–91 at Ninth and Marshall Streets; and the Museum and White House of the Confederacy, 1201 East Clay Street, the handsome home of Jefferson Davis and of Civil War exhibits and artifacts. A combination ticket admits visitors to all three.

The Virginia Museum of Fine Arts (Boulevard and Grove Avenues) has the finest collection of paintings and art objects in the Southeast. Its new West Wing houses two outstanding collections contributed by a local Jewish couple, Sidney and Frances Lewis—a group of contemporary paintings and sculpture, and a unique collection of Art Deco furniture and Art Nouveau decorative objects. The Mellon collection of English, French, and American eighteenth- and nineteenth-century drawings, paintings, and sculpture is also outstanding.

Personalities: Supreme Court Justice Benjamin Cardozo was the great-great-grandson of one of Richmond's Sephardim, Aaron Cardozo. Admiral Lewis L. Strauss, also a native son, was chairman of the Atomic Energy Commission and President Eisenhower's secretary of commerce. Rabbi Myron Berman, author and current religious leader at Temple Beth El, was the first rabbi to serve as president of the Richmond Area Clergy Association, and was awarded the City of Richmond's Medallion for his civil rights activities. Local historian Saul Viener was the founding president of the Southern Jewish Historical Society.

Side Trip: A visit to Williamsburg is a delightful step back in time to an eighteenth-century English village. There was a small Jewish presence in Williamsburg, with records indicating that the Philadelphia merchants Bernard and Michael Gratz had business dealings in the colonial Virginia capital. Dr. John de Sequeyra, born in England of Portuguese-Jewish descent, settled in Williamsburg in 1745. He was the first visiting physician at the Public Hospital (the first hospital in the colonies for treatment of the mentally ill). He also opened an apothecary and practiced medicine in Williamsburg until his death in 1795.

There are several items of Jewish interest at the DeWitt Wallace Decorative Arts Gallery, housed in the renovated Public Hospital. A huge iron stove called a "warming machine," manufactured in England by Abraham Buzgalo, a Moroccan Jew, to heat the Williamsburg capitol, is on display. A pewter "strawberry dish," with the owner's name inscribed in Hebrew, is displayed in the metals section. At the Abby Aldrich Rockefeller Collection of American Folk Art, a number of paintings on biblical themes are exhibited.

Williamsburg's modern Jewish community consists of about 80 families. Conservative congregation Beth-El, 600 Jamestown Road, is a small brick colonial house that was once a gift shop. Inside are a handsome *bimah*, wooden paneling, and tapestries decorated with Judaic holiday designs. Call (804) 229-2247 for information on services and events.

Reading: Eli Evans' *Judah P. Benjamin: The Jewish Confederate* (Macmillan) includes a chapter on Richmond during the Civil War. *The History of the Jews of Richmond* by H. T. Ezekiel and G. Lichtenstein, published in 1917, chronicles the years 1769–1917 and can be found in some libraries. Rabbi Myron Berman's *Richmond's Jewry 1769–1976, Shabbat in Shockoe* (University of Virginia) updates Richmond Jewish history—with its long and rich past—to the present.

—*Helen Silver*

Riga

"Shalom, dear visitors to Riga. . . . " begins the pamphlet.

No joke. Riga may not have regular heat or hot water, readily available toilet paper, or proper policing capabilities. But the Latvian Society of Jewish Culture, within weeks after independence in 1991, managed to put out *The Jews in Riga: A Guide,* a surprisingly well-done, if puzzlingly omissive, thirty-two-page booklet, with fold-out map, numerous details, and the subtitle, "Fragments of the Jewish History of Riga."

That such a work exists, and came into being as early as it did, is emblematic of the generally scattershot way things are working in this Baltic capital. A people from here, a trend from there, rulers seemingly from most points of the compass, the city—and even more, the country of which it is now the pulse—appears over the days, years, and centuries to have been stitched together more by some arcane patchwork process than by any logical evolution, fusion, or progression.

As patriots are now learning, nationhood is not so simple. Having once had a flag does not a state, never mind a democracy, make. As other bits and fragments of the former Soviet empire are ruefully discovering, a far thicker glue is necessary.

Will Latvia find it, this land that—though it knew independence for scarcely two decades—was formerly one of the region's more prosperous snippets? A fast look at its apparently once-lovely portcapital is positive. A fast look at its politics is confounding. And a fast look at its Jews suggests that they may, for the time being at least, hold a significant card.

History: To simplify the history of Latvian, and, therefore, Rigan, Jewry would be to say that it virtually ended with World War II. For the roots of what exists today, the stories of Russia, Belarus, Ukraine, and other former Soviet republics must be examined instead. The truth is that few Jews with prewar Latvian birthrights remain. But to leave the tale there would do injustice to those who did go before and perhaps, too, those who would be heirs to a past thickly convoluted by the numerous power plays of Germany, Poland, Sweden, and Russia.

Today's Latvia, with its twenty-five thousand square miles, scarcely larger than West Virginia, consists of several regions, each with its distinct history. The primary dividing line is the River Duena, or Western Dvina—or today, Daugava (most Latvian places have had at least three names). Historically, Jews in the area lived mostly in the Latgale part of Livonia, north of the river, and in Courland (or Kurland) to the south.

The area first entered Western European geopolitics in the early thirteenth century, when the Germanic Knights of Livonia marched into the Baltic and subjugated the resident Finnic tribes in the name of Christianity. They founded the port city of Riga, brought it into the sphere of the economically powerful Hanseatic League, and gave the territory a predominantly German cultural cast. Even after the knights' dissolution in 1561, when Poland, Russia, and Sweden began fighting in earnest, the German aristocracy retained its position in much of the land, the indigenous population in servitude. Jews who had settled in the vicinity incurred different fates—depending on the section in which they lived and the varying attitudes of the varying rulers.

The statutes of the Livonian Knights prohibited Jews in their territories, but fourteenth-century Jewish tombstones indicate that they made exceptions for individuals. Jewish fortunes subsequently depended on whether their homes fell under the jurisdiction of Danes, Poles, or the Church of Courland. In the seventeenth century Jewish numbers increased; though local merchants and craftsmen considered them hostile rivals — which sometimes led to expulsion orders — the nobility was more tolerant. It used the Jews as tax farmers and import-export intermediaries to such an extent that it was said that every nobleman had his Jew. Those Jews who were peddlers also spread news, carrying with their packs word of distant wars and revolutions.

In 1795, control of Courland passed to Russia. Though initially the Jews were given residency and other rights, since the duchy, except for a brief period, fell outside the Pale of Settlement, their situation fluctuated. By 1897, they numbered about 51,000 — 7.6 percent of the population — and by the eve of World War I, 68,000. Having developed their own brand of Judaism, which mixed Eastern European practices with German Romantic influences, they developed a "Courland Yiddish" and evolved into a specific type known as "the Courland Jew."

After the Livonian Knights' dissolution in 1561, Livonia — with Riga — underwent somewhat different experiences. First ruled directly by Poland, it was conquered by Sweden in 1629, then by Russia in 1721. Both Poland and Sweden restricted Jewish residency and since, with Russia's takeover, it landed outside the Pale, these continued. But though officially only Jews already in the area could remain, in actuality exceptions were made. In fact, the first documentary evidence of Jews in Riga is a sales record to one "Jacob," dated 1536. And though they had to stay in designated places, by 1645 Riga had a special inn for Jewish merchants. When the Russian Empress Elizabeth, daughter of Peter the Great, expelled the Jews in 1742, top Rigan authorities asked that an exception be made for commercial reasons. She responded that economic interests were not a good argument for allowing in "the enemies of Jesus Christ." Only under Catherine II were Jewish merchants allowed back to Riga —

though again, the length and place of their stay was restricted, and again, exceptions were made.

In 1785, Jews were given permission to settle in the nearby town of Sloka (in German, Shlock), where they opened a prayer room in 1792. Gradually, too, they began "infiltrating" Riga, and during the first decades of the nineteenth century their rights were expanded. In 1840, Sloka Jews opened a school in Riga, under one Max Lilienthal, a German, and it represented one of Russia's most modern institutions to date.

The following year, they were officially permitted residence in Riga; the year after that, they organized officially as a community; and additional rights followed. By the mid-nineteenth century, 9,000 Jews lived in Livonia, with 5,000 counted in Riga, Russia's most important Baltic port after St. Petersburg; the city's Jewish population grew to 22,000 (8 percent of the population) by 1897 and to 33,000 (6.5 percent) in 1913. Jews were extremely important commercially, owning timber mills, tanneries, and clothing factories; exporting grain, timber, and flax. Apart from their involvement in banking, industry, and crafts, before World War I the majority of dentists and 20 percent of Riga's doctors were Jews. When the Jews of Courland were blamed for early Russian war defeats and 40,000 of them were deported, Rigan Jews gave refuge to many. Others returned, creating a varied, fairly cosmopolitan cultural mix. Then, following the nineteenth-century swell of Lettish (Latvian) nationalism, three districts of Vitebsk joined Courland and Livonia, and for the first time a state called Latvia came into existence.

It had high hopes and progressive aspirations, but they were short-lived. Nationalistic factions, influenced by fascism, grew bolder and, on May 15, 1934, a coup d'état turned Latvia into a totalitarian state. It had inclinations toward Nazi Germany, but as the decade ended, the Soviet Union made military demands, and in July 1940 Latvia was proclaimed a Soviet republic. Germany occupied it during the first weeks of the German–Soviet war in July 1941 — catching the Jews, not surprisingly, in the middle.

Having already established an important niche as well as an extensive internal infrastructure before the state's creation, Latvia's Jews continued after World War I to contribute significantly to building the new country. Concentrated in cosmopolitan Riga—where the languages on the street were German, Russian, and Yiddish—Jewish businessmen resumed their timber and linen export operations and imported oil, coal, and textiles. But the increasing urbanization of the formerly peasant Lett populace fueled considerable economic resentment to the point where the Jews began being squeezed out. While culturally they were inclined to look to Germany as well, many saw the Russians as saviors—to the fury of the Latvians. When the Germans inspired Latvians to begin exterminating their Jews, they responded with relish, beginning with the burning of synagogues and their human contents on July 4, 1941. Then the Nazis began importing Jews from Germany, Austria, Czechoslovakia, and elsewhere. Such "cargoes" did not need special extermination plants; with Latvian cooperation, all that was needed was a large ditch in a park or woods right in, or on the mere edges of, the city. The Kaiserwald concentration camp operated within the area of metropolitan Riga. By war's end, few Latvian Jews had survived. And among those who had, few chose to return, preferring to make new lives elsewhere. Thus it fell to a few stragglers, a few former Soviet-Jewish soldiers, and the arriving newcomers to pick up the pieces.

They responded fairly quickly. Though some Jews claim to have had little party influence, especially after the 1953 Stalin-motivated purges, others today challenge such statements. Meanwhile, a rebellious, Zionistically inclined youth turned out for appearances by Israeli performers and sports teams, while others braved condemnation and worse to bake and distribute underground *matzah*. In 1970, when several Riga activists bent on *aliyah* were charged in Leningrad with attempting to commandeer a plane and fly to Sweden, there was no doubt. Riga was officially cited as a "hotbed of Zionism."

Community: On the surface, at least, Riga has one of the liveliest Jewish communities in the former Soviet Union. Formed in July 1988, during *glasnost* and *perestroika*, the Latvian Society for Jewish Culture (LOEK), despite various divisive movements, has managed to unite most splinter groups and establish itself officially. In May 1992 it gave itself a new label—the Riga Jewish Community.

Proudly, its spokesmen point out that it is responsible for several "firsts" among Jews of the former Soviet Union. Not only was it the first community to regain, in 1990, erstwhile Jewish property for use as a community center. It also established the first Jewish school, attended now by 500-plus students learning Hebrew and Yiddish. And in September 1992 it resumed management of the hitherto state-run Bikur Holim Medical Society hospital, at 122–128 Maskavas Street. The community runs a children's theater, which performs in Yiddish and Hebrew (open to the public once a month); a senior citizens' Yiddish theater; Kinor, a children's choir; weekly solo musicales; and monthly music salons, a recent one featuring the debut of a newly formed chamber trio, "Negina." It also hopes to organize regular art shows. And, annually, on the last Sunday in November, it commemorates the Riga ghetto killings. Though it grants space to the 100-odd members of the newly evolving Reform congregation, it has little involvement with Judaism's religious aspects. The handful of Orthodox attend the Peitavas Street Synagogue, which is ministered by Lubavitch emissaries.

The vigor of the official Jewish community is generally attributed to two factors. One is that Soviet communism came to Latvia a generation after it arrived in most other republics, thus cowing people less and leaving room for memories of the vast infrastructure and intense Jewish activity that had been. In addition, the Jews aligned themselves well. One of their number, the politician Mavriks Vulfsons, was among the first to openly describe Latvia in the late 1980s as "Soviet occupied." And as early as March 1989, Jews marched, with the anti-communist, prodemocratic forces, as an entity—openly bearing a white flag with a blue *Magen David*.

Despite its seeming strength, however, the community organization faces threats, from within and without. Though it is generally agreed that there are about 18,000 Jews in Latvia—with most in Riga—the number affiliated with the community is relatively low. Estimates on the number actively involved range from 3,500 to 7,000. The low membership level points to another difficulty—many, Jews and non-Jews, for various reasons that are not anti-Semitic, distrust the community organization.

Latvia itself is in a tenuous position. Given a population less than 50 percent Latvian—which makes it, ethnically, the weakest of the Baltic states—it could submit to a rising nationalist tide. And with shadows of the 1930s playing all about, it could, one way or another, disenfranchise many of its residents—including the large percentage of its Jews who arrived after World War II. Faced with this possibility, plus an uncertain outlook generally, Jewish parents are sending their children out of the country in droves.

Sights: In microcosm, Riga reflects the many historical and cultural crosscurrents that have so buffeted Latvia. With its cramped, cobbled old Hansa town; its newer boulevards and spacious parks; its conglomeration of the Romanesque, Gothic, Renaissance and Baroque; and its hints of the Germanic, Nordic, and Slavic, Riga gives hints that with imaginative management it could well evolve into an intriguingly multidimensional place. Despite the various devastations, this is true for the Jewish eye as well.

For starters, Riga's only surviving synagogue, the Peitavas Street Synagogue, stands in the heart of the Old City—a testament to the Jews' ultimate penetration of, and acceptance in, this town. Thanks to its location, it was not destroyed; the Germans feared that fire would burn beyond control. Built in 1905, it was Riga's second most impressive Jewish house of worship (after the Choral Synagogue). Though neighboring buildings are peeling, the synagogue, at Peitavas 6–8, boasts a fairly recent coat of buff paint, trimmed with blue. Though the Germans used the building as a storehouse, the interior was not harmed. The ark was so carefully boarded up that it, and its Torahs, survived. The large hall, which seats 600 and

crowds in 2,000, is punctuated by a central *bimah* lit from above by a circular chandelier. The decor is spare—wooden floors covered by runners, stucco work in squares and rectangles—the main color, blue, with white and gold trim. The primary contemporary touches are the pictures of the Lubavitcher *rebbe* on the walls, with signs proclaiming "The Moshiach is on the way. Be part of it."

There are those who claim that much of the prime downtown real estate beyond the Old City once belonged to Jews. One case in point is the building housing the Latvian Sports Museum. The leading labeled example, though, is the massive structure housing the Jewish community headquarters, at Skolas 6. A large, vaguely dusty-rose mansion, with a columned entrance and two levels of exterior balconies, its facade is topped by gracefully scalloped roofing. Originally built in 1913–14 as a private Jewish residence, it was renovated in 1926 to house a Jewish Club and the Riga Jewish Theater, situated on the third floor. During the Soviet regime, it was home to the Communist Party's Institute for Culture and History. It has a cavernous feel, with offices and salons at many turnings, up steep, monumental flights of stairs. So large is it that it also now houses the first three grades of the Jewish school. In its lobby is a list, in Cyrillic, of the local Christians who helped Jews during the Holocaust. The community headquarters is the best place to call (289-580) with questions about Jewish sights and activities.

On the edge of the downtown area, at Lacplesa 141, stands the building that housed the first Jewish secular school, founded in 1840, which became a model of enlightened German teaching throughout Russia. The school moved to this structure, a stolid, beige Renaissance building with brown trim and separate entrances for boys and girls, in 1887. Later the building acquired a different role: during World War II it was Judenrat headquarters.

What many consider one of Riga's most magnificent twentieth-century structures, the Latvian Academy of Fine Art at Valdemara 10-A, also has Jewish connections. The gabled, turreted, chimneyed, steepled gingerbread structure of red brick, set on its own plot of greenery, boasts two *Magen*

Davids. Set high on the facade, they are so prominent that they show up on postcards from Soviet times. Reportedly, those involved with the building's construction, probably prewar Germans, ran out of money, so they appealed to the Jews. Whoever donated the funds gave them only on the condition that the stars be placed as they are.

Beyond these edifices, most of Riga's Jewish sites are just that—sites—spots on the map. They are locations of significant buildings that have since either been converted or destroyed, or of plots, fields, and forests bearing merely trees, grass, a few stones, and an occasional monument. These places attest in detail to past triumphs and tragedies, but finding them requires the help of *The Jews in Riga: A Guide,* prepared by Marger Vesterman, director of the community's Museum and Documentation Center, and available from the community for $1.50. And appreciating them requires imaginations capable of recreating ultimate horrors.

Among the book's numerous inclusions is mention of the vicinity near the crossing of Maskavas and Lacplesa Streets. Though now indistinguishably incorporated into the city at large, here stood the first seventeenth-century inn to which Jewish visitors to Riga were confined. The second one stood in the vicinity of Maskavas and Dzirnavu Streets. The neighborhood around these inns—then Riga's eastern outskirts—was once called Moscow Vorstadt, a poor, ethnically mixed area where Riga's Jews settled before they began to move toward downtown and into the "establishment." The area also contains the plot, surrounded by Liksnas, Ebreju, Virsaisu, and Lomonosov Streets, which encompassed the walled-in Old Jewish Cemetery, the Jews' first real estate in Riga. Now an open park of lawns, trees, and mud paths—named in Soviet times The Park of Communist Brigades—the only trace of the past is one flat, moss-covered stone.

Nearby, at 25 Gogola Street, stood the community's pride, The Big Choral synagogue—popularly called the Gogol Shul—a large, primarily Renaissance structure, so famous for its choir and such cantors as Baruch Leib Rosowsky and Herman Yadlovker Mandel that non-Jews also came on holidays to listen. If a time can be pinpointed, the Latvian Holocaust began here when, on July 4, 1941, 300 Lithuanian refugees already in the synagogue basement and all Jews caught on the street were driven into the synagogue, which was then burned. Excavations are currently being carried out on the large plot, and on July 4, 1989, a monument was erected. Plans call for another memorial—a "Wall of Sorrow"—made up of local stones plus one from Israel. Not surprisingly, the surrounding area comprised the Riga ghetto—the original boundaries of which were Maskavas, Vitebskas, Ebreju, Lauvas, Liela Kalna, Lazdonas, Kijevas, Jekabpils, and Lacplesa Streets. This shrank at the end of 1941 to "the little ghetto" with a Daugavpils Street border.

Not far away is the piece of greenery called the Rumbula, where grassy mounds, tended initially in the 1960s by rebelliously outspoken Jewish youths, denote mass graves. Thirty thousand Jews were massacred here alone, their demise marked as a Jewish—as opposed to anonymous—mass grave in 1989. With knowledgeable help, other similar spots can be found, in wooded areas farther outside town. Among these are Mezaparks, where, between the railway tracks and Viestura Avenue, the Kaiserwald Concentration Camp was located; Bikernieku Park; and New Jewish Cemetery, near the Smerlis area, where the funeral home—a gray building with a yellow star in a circle over a red door—still stands. To its right is a monument erected in 1990 to Zanis and Johanna Lipke, non-Jewish Latvians who, with friends, saved more than 50 Jews. The house through which they funneled them, at Maza Balasta Dami 8-1, stands well back from the road, amid a cluttered garden, and is currently occupied by their son, who himself played host in the 1960s and 1970s to rebellious young Zionists and refuseniks.

Personalities: Among the Rigan Jews best known today on the international scene are Moshe Arens, Israel's former Defense Minister, and violinist Gidon Kremer. Among other Latvian musicians past and present are Inese Gallant, Tovi Lifshitz, Eleonora Testlotz, Oleg Kagan and Michael Tal. Between 1937 and 1941, Leon Blech, chief conductor of the Berlin

Philharmonic, took refuge in Riga and was chief conductor of the Latvian National Opera. Directors such as Julius Adler once worked in the Riga Jewish Theater and today's producing director of the Russian Drama Theater is Eduard Cehovak. The great Yiddish actor and director Solomon Mikhoels was Latvian born.

Before World War II, among those Jews known in public life were Rafail Abramovitch, who became a Menshevik leader in Russia; Alexander Lipshutz, a leading physician-anthropologist and Bolshevik who emigrated to Chile; Paul Mintz, the only Jew in the government of the Latvian Republic, 1919-1921; and the lawyer, O. Grusenberg, who made a name for himself defending Maxim Gorky and Mendel Beilis and who practiced in Riga between 1926 and 1932.

Among the activists who made Riga a center of underground Zionist activity in the 1960s and 1970s were Ruth Alexandrovich, Eduard Kuznetsov, Yosef Mendelevich, and Silva Zalmanson; all but Kuznetsov, who lives in Paris, are now in Israel. One of the great Jewish artists of the postwar era was Yosef Kuzkovsky, who died shortly after emigrating to Israel in 1969.

Recommendations: Finnair remains a paragon of airborne civility as it makes regular connections from New York, via Helsinki, to Riga. Western hotel operations are taking root in Riga, but generally accommodations are inadequate, overpriced, and difficult to come by. Nor has an infrastructure yet evolved for meting out private accommodation—though, if connections can be made, individuals are often more than willing. Entry and exit are sometimes painless; on occasion, visa fees are completely waived. However, regulations have been known to change—and on the spot. Hard currency will buy acceptable food; Latvian rubles will buy a decent meal in the ground-floor cafeteria of the Jewish community house, as well as other similar establishments best known to natives.

Amid all the changes, the newest chapter in Latvia's Jewish history is being written. The last words in the chronicle of historian Simon Dubnow, who died in Riga's Holocaust, are said to have been, "Write, Jews, write. . . . " Consequently, chronicles of today's changing scene also must be kept.

—Phyllis Ellen Funke

Rio de Janeiro

Imagine a cosmopolitan city filled with Parisian-style buildings and avant-garde fashion, plunked down on a ribbon of endless beaches with mountains rising up behind them. Add to that samba music and the warm and easygoing spirit of the Cariocas — as the city's residents are called — and you have Rio de Janeiro. No wonder Jews have lived in the city since the sixteenth century and thrived there.

Rio is known for its hospitality and integration of races and nationalities that might clash anywhere else. In fact, it's one of the only cities in the world where Arab and Jewish storeowners have formed an organization to promote their businesses. Its name? S.A.A.R.A. — pronounced like the desert.

History: When Pedro Alvares Cabral, a Portuguese explorer, landed in Brazil in 1500, he was accompanied by his personal secretary who also commanded the provisions ship — Gaspar da Gama, the first Jew in Brazil. Two years later, a group of Conversos — known as *Cristãos Novos,* or New Christians — arrived to start the export of brazil, a dyewood: hence, the country's name. Another Converso, Diego Días Fernando, was one of the first owners of a sugar mill and plantation; others planted the first cotton, rice, and tobacco fields in the country. Gradually, some of the Conversos drifted to Rio de Janeiro and assimilated into the city's population. What is surprising is that today, several descendants of these original Converso families have discovered their hidden Jewish roots and have converted back to Judaism.

In 1654, the Dutch, who had taken over part of Brazil, were defeated, and the Portuguese demanded that the Jews leave the country. One group of twenty-three Jews fled from the northern port city of Recife to the Dutch colony of New Amsterdam to found what would eventually become the largest Jewish community in the world.

The first great wave of Jews to arrive again in Brazil did not occur until the 1820s, when religious liberty was established in the country. These Jews came from Morocco and Turkey and settled in the city of Manaus, on the Amazon River, where they traded in rubber. Some left the jungle for the growing city of Rio and started the first Jewish community center in 1846. Known as União Israelita Shel Gemilut Hasadim, this Sephardic synagogue still thrives today, now located at Rua Rodrigo de Brito 37. Another wave of Sephardic Jews would come from Egypt a century later, after the 1956 Sinai War with Israel.

French and other Western European Jews trickled in after the Sephardic congregation was established, and by 1900 the community numbered 200 and had two synagogues. The great wave of Jewish immigration to Rio began during World War I, and it was then that most of the community's institutions — schools and libraries, self-help and Zionist organizations, newspapers and cultural societies, not to mention more synagogues — began to grow.

Jews from Eastern Europe began to arrive in Brazil toward the end of the nineteenth century. Encouraged by Jewish agricultural projects, they settled in farms in the south. Others headed straight for Rio and gathered in the center of the city, around a plaza called Praça XI. By the start of World War II, over 30,000 Eastern European Jews had arrived. Some went into typical Jewish retail businesses such as clothing and jewelry. Others started furniture stores; some guess that the Jews must

428

have felt secure enough in Brazil to think about home furnishing. Jews are still active in these industries.

Community: The Jewish population of Rio today is about 50,000. The other large concentration of Brazilian Jewry is in São Paulo (70,000), and Jewish communities are also found in Recife, Pôrto Alegre, and Belo Horizonte.

In Rio, the Jews are evenly divided among Sephardim and Ashkenazim. And, while there may be Sephardi-Ashkenazi tensions in Israel, none exist in Rio, reflecting the city's melting-pot ethic. Jews, like all other Cariocas, are more fun-loving than their Jewish countrymen in São Paulo. Jewish life in Rio, therefore, tends to be more recreational and beach-oriented and less religiously observant. The Lubavitch hasidic community tried twice to open a Habad house in Rio and failed — while their Habad house in São Paulo does well. As one Carioca Jew observed, "The Jews in Rio are like those in Tel Aviv: on *Shabbat*, they go to the beach." Even among the more Jewishly connected, the beach has its influence on Jewish practice; Friday-night services tend to be better attended than services on sunny *Shabbat* mornings.

Like other Cariocas as well, social life for Jews centers around their clubs. These non-exclusive clubs offer meeting places and facilities for their Jewish members. The largest Jewish club in Rio, Hebraica (Rua das Laranjeilas 346), has pools, a soccer field, a restaurant (albeit nonkosher), and sponsors Jewish cultural events — including concerts, dances, films, and lectures — throughout the year.

Sights: Integration into the community was hardly a problem for Rio's Jews, who quickly dispersed throughout the city. The old Jewish neighborhood around Praça XI is gone, but the city's first Ashkenazi synagogue, Beit Yaakov, still stands at Tua Tenente Possolo 8. It is an imposing white building with a colorful, tiled mosaic of Mt. Sinai and the Ten Commandments on the outside front wall. Now called the Grande Templo Israelita, it was renovated in 1986.

For a look at what the old Jewish neighborhood might have been like, visitors should go to the area around Rua Alfándega in downtown Rio. Here is the heart of S.A.A.R.A., the Arab–Jewish retail organization founded in 1958, linking stores selling everything from rich coffee to sequined and feathered carnival costumes. S.A.A.R.A. members often meet in Restaurant du Nil on Rua Alfándega to eat *hummus* and pita and discuss business — not politics.

The largest active synagogue in the city is Associação Religiosa Israelita (ARI) at Rua General Severiano 170 in the city's Botafogo district. Known as German Liberal, this congregation also has its share of Carioca idiosyncrasies: men wear *kippot* and sit separately from women, but there is a mixed choir and an organ.

The small Orthodox Ashkenazi community in Rio is centered around the Bar Ilan school in — where else? — Copacabana. Bar Ilan, which encompasses both a synagogue and a 500-student school, has a kosher restaurant that serves daily lunches and Sunday brunches featuring gefilte fish and other traditional Jewish fare. Bar Ilan is also the only facility in Rio to bake and sell hallah and provide kosher catering; it can provide kosher meals to tourists in hotels as well. The phone number is 257-4299, and it is located at Rua Pompeu Loureiro 48. The hospitable school administration can also provide information about Rio's kosher butcher services and *mikveh*. (The Associação Religiosa Israelita uses an outdoor *mikveh* — the ocean.) Also in Copacabana is the Sephardic Congregação Religiosa Beth-El, at Rua Barata Ribeiro 489 (telephone 235-5545).

General Sights: No visitor to Rio can afford to miss the spectacular panorama from the top of Corcovado, the highest hill in the city. This hilltop, home to a statue of Jesus with his arms outstretched, is the best known topographical feature of Rio, appearing in many posters and photographs. Another view is from the top of Pão de Açúcar (Sugarloaf), which can be reached by cable car and overlooks the beaches of Copacabana, Botafogo, and the Guanabara Bay.

For those who prefer to see the natural beauties of Rio from the ground, there's Tijuca Forest, with innumerable waterfalls

Point of view: Corcovado offers perhaps the world's greatest city and sea panorama

and lush greenery. Plant lovers should also tour through the Jardim Botánico, which contains tropical flowers and an abundance of plants and palms.

The former palace of Brazilian Emperor Dom Pedro I is now the Museu Nacional which displays jewels, coins, and uncut stones dating to the early sixteenth century. More up-to-date art can be found in the Museu de Arte Moderna, whose trustees include Samuel Malamud, a Rio lawyer and the first representative of Israel in Brazil.

The beaches of Copacabana and Ipanema should also be part of a tourist's circuit for a plunge into real Carioca life. Be prepared for the hot sun and the itsy-bitsy, teeny-weeny bikinis. Afterward you can sit at one of the cafés along Copacabana Beach.

Culture and Eating: In addition to the cultural offerings at Club Hebraica and at the various synagogues, the Biblioteca Bialik, at Rua Fernando Osorio 16 (telephone 245-5272), sponsors a Sunday-morning lecture series in Yiddish on literature and other topics. There is a Jewish Museum in the building of the Federação Israelita do Estado do Rio de Janeiro at Rua Mexico 90. The Federation (telephone 240-6278) is also the best place to call with questions about community events. The restaurant at Bar Ilan is the only kosher establishment of its kind, but ARI and Beth El welcome foreigners to their Seders on the second night of Passover. Hebraica's Sunday brunches are sumptuous, but not kosher.

Personalities: Turn on Brazilian television, buy a magazine or a book, and chances are you'll bc tuning into the multimedia company Manchete, owned by Adolpho Bloch, who some say is Brazil's Jewish Hearst. Jews are also prominent in acting and music: Teresa Racquel, a leading lady, has her own theater in Rio; Flora Purim is internationally known as a singer and musician. Walter Burle Marx was the founder and long-time conductor of the Rio de Janeiro Philharmonic. Isaac Karabitchevsky is a world-renowned landscape artist whose works have been exhibited at New York's Metropolitan Museum of Art.

The mayor of Rio in the mid-seventies was Israel Klabin, who is still active in Brazilian politics and Jewish affairs. And one descendant of the Moroccan rabbinic Azulay family — founding members of Rio's first Sephardic synagogue, Gemilut Hasadim — is Daniel Azulay, seen every day on Brazilian television in a children's program. Rio was also the final home of Stefan Zweig, one of the most prominent playwrights in prewar Europe, who left Austria in 1935 and, in his depression over the war, committed suicide outside Rio in 1942.

Rio is also the home of Hans Stern, whose jewelry stores are known around the world. Stern hosts visitors at the H. Stern world headquarters in Ipanema and receives Jewish groups in his Ipanema penthouse.

Day Trips: In the mountains an hour from Rio is Petropolis, site of Dom Pedro I's summer palace, now a museum of art objects and furniture. (Visitors are given slippers to wear so that they won't scratch the floors.) During January and February, Brazil's summer season, Petropolis has a sizable Jewish weekend population. The city has one synagogue — Sinagoga Israelita Brasileira, at Rua Aureliano Coutinho 48 — and the Machane Israel Yeshiva.

If one day trip is by land, another is by sea. You can book passage on a boat that leaves from Rio and tours the tropical islands off the coast of the city. These tours can be arranged at your hotel.

Recommendations: One of the grand dames of Rio hotels is the Copacabana Palace, right on the beach. Another deluxe Copacabana option is the Rio Palace, which often caters to Jewish groups. The Caesar Park, located on Ipanema Beach, is near the trendy clothing stores along Rua Visconde de Pirajá. Less expensive in the same neighborhood is the Sol Ipanema. South American Tours of U.S.A. is a largely Jewish-run firm that can put together Jewish itineraries. They are located at 330 West 58 Street, Suite 403, New York, NY 10019 (telephone 212-489-7790).

Carnival time, usually in late February or early March, is when all of Brazil goes wild: its New Orleans-style Mardi gras runs non-stop for three days, culminating Brazil's summer and marking the start of Lent. If you want to travel to Rio then, book your trip well in advance. If you prefer to go during a calmer time, you can still catch the carnival spirit at clubs like Asa Branca, Rua Mem de Sá (telephone 252-4428), which features samba bands and famous Brazilian musicians. You can also attend rehearsals of samba schools, such as Unidos da Tijuca (Rua São Miguel 430). They exhibit the dances to be performed at carnival parades throughout the year. You can dance all night in Rio, as the saying goes, and many Cariocas actually do.

—Diana Katcher Bletter

Rome

They have seen republics and empires rise and fall, Caesars and popes come and go, but throughout the turbulent centuries, Rome's Jews have maintained their persistent presence along the banks of the Tiber, almost as eternal as the Eternal City itself. Of the approximately 32,000 Jews who live in Italy, 12,000 live in the capital.

Today, after a two-thousand-year presence, the Jews of Rome are well integrated into the city's irreverent and bustling atmosphere. In the contemporary environment, which casually absorbs ancient ruins and priceless monuments amid snack shops and newsstands, Roman Jews are nonetheless conscious of their special history.

In the shadow of St. Peter's, under the always pervasive, sometimes oppressive, and lately fraternal force of the Vatican, the Jews of Rome have carved out a place for themselves in the life of the city. The descendants of the original Judeo-Italian stock, who later mixed with Sephardic and Ashkenazic immigrants, have always been an adaptive community.

History: The Jews of Rome constitute the oldest Jewish community in Europe and one of the oldest continuous Jewish settlements in the world. Jews first arrived in Rome in 139 B.C.E. as the Maccabees' emissaries to the Senate. The early ambassadors were followed by enterprising merchants who saw rewarding trading opportunities between Rome and the Middle East. More permanent residents came as Jewish slaves who had been taken prisoner during the military campaigns of Pompey and Vespasian; it was they who established a community in the Trastevere section. The community spilled over the short bridges spanning the Tiber in the Middle Ages into the section that became the Roman ghetto and remains a Jewish neighborhood to this day. The early Jewish ranks were swelled by refugees who came to Rome after the fall of Jerusalem in 70 C.E. (Indeed, Roman Jews pride themselves on the historical purity of the Italian liturgy, which predates the Sephardic influences of the Middle Ages and may date from the days of the Second Temple.)

At the height of Roman power, the Jewish community was not simply another Diaspora outpost. If a transmillenial parallel can be drawn, it had similarities to the American-Jewish community of today. The empire may have had as many as 5 million Jews, although the city of Rome probably never had more than 40,000. They were influential enough to obtain guarantees of personal and religious freedom from Julius Caesar and the Emperor Augustus and prosperous enough to buy the freedom of Jewish slaves brought from Judea. Roman Jews are noted in the literature and public discourse of the Empire. When Cicero defended Flaccus (accused of stealing gold that Jews had contributed to the Temple in Jerusalem) in 59 B.C.E., the great orator complained that the number of Jews packing the court was so great that it intimidated the jury. A century later, the Sabbath practices of Jews were mentioned in Juvenal's *Satires* and in Tacitus's *Histories*. Though their exact sites are not known, the names of the Roman synagogues that have come down to the present time — Synagogue of the Augustei, honoring Augustus; Synagogue of the Agrippense, dedicated to Marcus Agrippa; Synagogue of the Erodii, probably dedicated to Herod — indicate the Jews' integration into Roman life and their ties to Israel.

The Jewish condition began to deteriorate when the emperors adopted Christianity in the fourth century. There was pressure to convert, and periodic anti-Jewish violence. The fortunes of the Jews declined further with the decline of the Empire. After the fall of Rome in 476, the Jewish fortune was largely a reflection of papal policy. Though many popes issued anti-Jewish edicts, there was a tendency for such pronouncements to be enforced less strictly in Rome itself than by zealous ecclesiastics abroad. In the twelfth century there was a "Jewish" pope, Anacletus II, a member of a Jewish family that had adopted Christianity in 1030. There has been speculation that Popes Gregory VI and Gregory VII also had Jewish origins or ancestors.

After the expulsion of the Jews from Spain in 1492, many exiles came to Rome, where they added their customs to those of the existing Italian community. During the following centuries, Jews also arrived from North Africa, the Middle East, and, after the Holocaust, from Poland and Germany, each group assimilating into the Roman community while maintaining its individuality.

However much a sanctuary Rome may have appeared to Jews fleeing persecution, the history of the Jews in Rome has hardly been characterized by security or serenity. Protected by Julius Caesar and tolerated to various degrees by the emperors who followed, Roman Jews were subjected to the caprices of the later Christian emperors and suffered considerably during the papal period. From the Middle Ages on, various papal bulls restricted the Jews to the trades of moneylending or dealing in old clothes. They were made to wear distinguishing signs on their garments, suffer the deprivation of the study of the Torah (small wonder that the Vatican has one of the world's largest collections of Judaica), and listen to conversion sermons in Christian churches.

During the centuries after their arrival in Rome, Jews had been at liberty to live in the Trastevere or any other section of the city they chose. In 1556, however, Pope Paul IV confined the Jews to the ghetto. Ten years later Pope Pius V ordered all but one synagogue closed, although the Jewish community worked out a compromise whereby five synagogues were allowed to function under one roof. In that narrow scramble of close, crowded streets — remnants of which can be seen today — extending barely four blocks in either direction, the Jews built "skyscrapers" of seven or eight stories on top of ramshackle buildings to house their families. The ghetto edict remained in force through 1847, and the Cinque Scole, the building housing the five synagogues, stood until 1910.

Though Italy (and some of its Jews) embraced fascism under Mussolini, it never made the leap, so common in other Axis countries, to willful extermination. "While most Italians could accept claims that Zionists were disloyal," writes Susan Zuccotti in *The Italians and the Holocaust*, "that Jewish refugees caused price increases and crowded facilities, or that [French premier] Léon Blum was a natural enemy of Mussolini's, they could not accept the persecution of the family next door." Eighty-five percent of the country's Jews survived World War II for two primary reasons — the German occupation was relatively brief, beginning in 1943, and the Italian character common to the country's Catholics and Jews. It seems never to have occurred to most Italian Jews to obey orders to report for internment, nor to their neighbors to obey orders to turn them in. Of Rome's 10,000 prewar Jews, 2,000 *were* captured and sent to their deaths at Auschwitz; an additional 73 were among the 355 prisoners executed at the Fosse Ardeatine outside Rome in retaliation for Italian partisan attacks on the German occupiers. But when the war ended, the Jews who came out of hiding were able to pick up the pieces not only of their individual lives, but of their community.

Community: After the ghetto was abolished, many of Rome's Jews continued to live nearby. Between 300 and 400 Jews live in the ghetto area today. The main addition to the community's native Italian Jews in recent years has been a sizable immigration from Libya. Some of the stores on Rome's Via del Corso are owned by Libyan Jews.

Despite centuries of deprivation and isolation, many of Italy's Jews have achieved prominence. Outstanding Jews include Bruno Zevi, a leading Italian architect;

Giorgio Bassani, from Ferrara, author of *The Garden of the Finzi-Continis;* and Alberto Moravia, whose novels include *Two Women,* the film version of which won an Academy Award for Sophia Loren. Other Jews have made their mark in business: the Stock liquor company is owned by a Jewish family, and Olivetti, the office equipment firm, was founded by Jews. And of course there is a steady stream of Jewish doctors, lawyers, and academics who hold prestigious positions in Roman society. Not surprisingly, perhaps, the Vatican has always had five or six Jewish doctors on call, even during the worst anti-Jewish persecutions.

Other distinguished Roman Jews have been Ernesto Nathan, the first Jewish mayor of Rome (1907–13), and Emanuele Conegliano, who wrote the librettos for three of Mozart's operas. In the early part of this century Luigi Luzzatti became Italy's only Jewish prime minister, though his contemporary, Sidney Sonnino, who served two terms as prime minister, had a Jewish father.

Sights: Roman Jewish life today is played out against a background of historic sites. Like the rest of Rome, where Renaissance palaces bump up against ancient ruins at almost every turn, Jewish Rome is omnipresent but sometimes invisible to the untrained eye. In the Roman Forum, the ruins of the temple of Divo Giulio—erected on the spot where the body of Julius Caesar was cremated—stand at the site of a Jewish tribute. So appreciative were Rome's Jews for the support of the assassinated Caesar that they held a vigil for several nights at his funeral pyre, and even fifty years later there were regular community visits to the site. Next to the Forum is the Coliseum, one of the more popular and certainly one of the most visible tourist attractions in Rome; historians believe that it was constructed by Jewish slaves, much as were the Egyptian pyramids.

Just as Renaissance sculptors made Florence the city of David, Rome is the city of Moses in stone. The best known sculpture is Michelangelo's, in the Church of San Pietro in Vincoli (Piazza San Pietro in Vincoli), showing the seated Moses between Leah and Rachel. The statue, which is the source of the misconception that Jews have horns,

is based on the artist's misreading of a description of Moses descending from Mount Sinai in the book of Exodus. The Hebrew text says, "Moses's face sent forth beams," but the word for "beams" can, in other contexts, mean "horns."

Off the beam: Michelangelo's Moses *bred beauty and misconception*

Bresciano's Moses, a more determined, standing figure, graces the fountain in Piazza San Bernardo. This Moses is flanked by reliefs of Joshua and Aaron. Moses as a baby, being rescued by Pharaoh's daughter, is in the Borghese Gardens (one of Rome's more tranquil and lovely spots), in the center of the fountain near Piazzale del Pincio. At the same spot are statues of Isaiah, Ezekiel, and David and a bas-relief of Joseph's dream. Also in the Borghese Gardens, note the walkway named in honor of a Polish Jewish refugee, David Lubin, a businessman and philanthropist who contributed much to Roman life.

Nor is Rome devoid of Davids. Bernini's David is in the Borghese Gallery, as is Caravaggio's David and Goliath. Other Jewish treasures in Rome's museums include Van Dyk's *Sacrifice of Isaac* in the Doria Pamphili Gallery and Roesler Franz's nineteenth-century watercolors of Rome's ghetto in the Museum of Rome.

Although much of the Judaica collection in the Vatican cannot be seen, the ceiling and walls of the Sistine Chapel feature frescoes of Hebrew Bible stories. Michelangelo's depiction of the creation, Adam and Eve, and the flood are breathtaking. A less glorious depiction is on the Arch of Titus, which commemorates the capture of Jerusalem and displays bas-reliefs of Jewish captives carrying the spoils of the Temple, including a *menorah* and silver trumpets.

The easiest place to discover today's and yesterday's Jewish Rome is in the ancient ghetto. A ten-minute walk from the Roman Forum, the ghetto lies opposite Tiber Isle (once site of the Jewish Hospital), just behind the main synagogue. The Via Portico d'Ottavia marks the major boundary of the ghetto and is still the principal shopping street of the Jewish quarter.

At one corner of this street, where one of the seven ghetto gates stood, is a plaque commemorating the 2,000 Roman Jews who perished in the Holocaust. A more substantial monument is the Fosse Ardeatine, just outside Rome on Via Ardeatine. The monument memorializes 335 Romans (including 73 Jews) massacred by the Germans on the site in 1944.

The synagogue itself, Tempio Israelitico, at Lungotevere Cenci 9, is an imposing structure that is one of Rome's distinctive landmarks, designed by Christian architects and completed in 1904. The main design mixes Roman and Greek elements and includes decorative touches of Egyptian and Assyro-Babylonian influence. The exterior features three tiers of columns topped by a four-sided cupola. It was here that Pope John Paul II made his historic visit in April 1986, entering the richly ornate sanctuary, embracing Rome's Chief Rabbi Elio Toaff and declaring to the Jewish community, "You are our dearly beloved brothers and, in a certain way, it could be said that you are our elder brothers." The synagogue has Shabbat as well as daily morning and evening services. (There are also Ashkenazic and Italian rite services in the Synagogue at Via Balbo 33.)

Inside the Tempio Israelitico is the Jewish Museum of Rome, which traces Roman Jewish history. The exhibits are divided into three sections—texts, pictures, and drawings; ritual and ceremonial objects (from hand-washing basins to Torah ornaments); and fabrics (including Torah and ark covers). Most of the objects are from the Cinque Scole, the five synagogues that stood under one roof in the Roman ghetto, and many of them are periodically taken out of their display cases and used in the synagogue. The museum is known for its knowledgeable, enthusiastic guides. (Although visiting hours are Monday through Friday, 9:30 A.M. to 2 P.M. and Sunday 9:30 A.M. to noon, as with all things Italian, the schedules are subject to sudden change. Phone ahead—687-5051—to avoid disappointment.)

Before you leave the synagogue, which can be viewed on request, walk around to the back. There you can see the bullet holes from the devastating Arab terrorist attack on Shemini Atzeret, October 1982. The event has left scars on this sensitive community; visitors to the synagogue and museum are given a careful security screening. Don't be put off by the security. Once inside, everything is easy and everyone shows a combination of Italian charm and Jewish hospitality.

Diagonally across from the synagogue is a curious church, with Hebrew and Latin inscriptions above the door lintel. Little remains of the building of the Church of St. Gregory (San Gregorio della Divina Pietá) except its puzzling exterior, but it is infamous in Roman Jewish history as one of the churches where the Jews were subjected to weekly conversion sermons during the

Middle Ages and after. The Hebrew inscription is from Isaiah: "I have spread out my hands all the day to a rebellious people which walketh in a way that was not good after their own thoughts." Another church where Jews were forced to listen to Christian sermons was San Angelo in Pescheria, also near the synagogue; the artist J. Hess depicted Jews in San Angelo's plugging their ears with wax so as not to hear the preacher's words.

The Quattro Capi (four heads) bridge crosses the Tiber Isle and links Rome's two banks. In medieval times it connected Jews who lived in the neighborhood that spilled across the river and it took its name from the Arba'a Rashim Synagogue. Though Trastevere has not been the heart of Jewish Rome since before the days of the ghetto, the house at 13–14 Vicolo dell'Atleta is believed to have been a synagogue, most likely built by Natan ben Yechiel Anav, an eleventh century talmudic scholar.

The ghetto, by the way, is not frequented only by Jews. Many Romans shop there, especially for clothing and wedding gifts. And the Italian Jewish delicacies of Limentani Settimio, a bakery at Via Portico d'Ottavia 1, are popular throughout the city.

Most visitors to Rome wouldn't dream of missing the catacombs. But instead of exploring the Christian catacombs just outside the city gates, consider a trip to the Jewish burial sites located along the Appian Way. Formerly under the jurisdiction of the Vatican, as were all the Christian catacombs, since 1984 they have been under the authority of the Italian Government. The main tunnels of the Via Appia Randanini catacomb have burial crypts, stacked three and four high like railroad berths, along both walls. Off the main corridors are family crypts, rooms in which the more prosperous among Rome's Jews reserved space. Some of the family chambers have elaborate decoration—menorahs, palm trees—along with inscriptions in Greek, the lingua franca of early Roman Jewry; they also have more recent graffiti. (A second Jewish catacomb complex in the northeast of the city is sealed, but the community eventually hopes to open it.) Check with the synagogue office about tour arrangements, or call the Jewish community offices at 580-3667.

After your excursions, relax in the Piazza Navona, a five-minute stroll from the Pantheon, and enjoy the special ice cream dish, concocted by the Le Tre Scalini café, known as *tartufo*—bittersweet chunks of chocolate nestled inside creamy chocolate ice cream.

Side Trip: For a special day trip, make time for a visit to Ostia Antica, near Leonardo da Vinci International Airport. This ancient port city is about an hour's drive (or forty-minute ride on the Rome subway) from the city and is the site of the oldest known synagogue, built between the first and third centuries. The ruins, discovered in 1961, mark the presence of what was once a prosperous and thriving Mediterranean merchant community of 500 Jews in a port city that had 100,000 inhabitants at the peak of Rome's power. Identified among the ruins are the synagogue's prayer hall, study hall, *mikveh*, *Bet Din*, and an oven for baking *matzah*. The synagogue remains are in the extreme southern corner of the excavations. The adjacent town, Lido di Ostia, is Rome's beach and also has, in virtually every coffee bar in town, Italy's best cappuccino.

Culture: For information about cultural events, such as lectures, concerts, or plays, check with the Jewish Cultural Center at Via Arco de Tolomei 2 (telephone 589-7589), or read about local happenings in *Shalom*, a monthly newspaper.

Restaurants and Hotels: Popular restaurants among Roman Jews are da Lisa (kosher, Israeli) at Via Foscolo 16–18, Margutta Vegetariano at Via Margutta 119, and Antico Bottaro at Passegiata di Ripetta 15. A kosher hotel is Pensione Carmel at Via Gioffredo Mameli 11 (telephone 580-9921). There are also several kosher butchers, bakeries, and food stores, mostly in the old ghetto area. For information on *kashrut*, call the community offices at 689-5051.

Reading: To learn more about Rome and its Jews, an ambitious place to start is the classic *The Jewish War* (Viking) by Flavius Josephus. For a more condensed, yet still comprehensive, treatment, read *Jewish Rome* by Ruth Liliana Geller, published in Italy by Viella and available at the synagogue museum. *Popes from the Ghetto* by Joachim Prinz (Schocken) tells the story of the popes with Jewish ancestry and is also quite evocative of Rome, Christian and Jewish, in the Middle Ages. Susan Zuccotti's *The Italians and the Holocaust* (Basic Books) is the definitive work on the subject. For a look at Jewish contributions to Italian literature there is *Prisoners of Hope: The Silver Age of the Italian Jews, 1924-1974* by H. Stuart Hughes (Harvard University Press).

Most Italian Jewish literature is set outside Rome. Insight into Italian Jewry can be gained by reading the novels of Giorgio Bassani, whose work, though Jewish, is set mostly in his native Ferrara. Alberto Moravia's works—like his *Roman Tales*—are set in the city, but there is nothing Jewish about them. One intriguing picture of Roman Jewish life is a scene in Morris West's *The Shoes of the Fisherman,* in which a Russian pope wanders off on his own in the city and stumbles upon a dying Jew—and then recites Hebrew prayers he learned from a rabbi while in a Soviet prison. Like everyone else in the Eternal City, the story shows that the words *Roman* and *Jewish* are hard to separate.

—E. Merri Rosenberg

Safed

Safed is sometimes called the poor man's Jerusalem, and it's easy to see why. Like Jerusalem, it clings to a mountain peak. Like Jerusalem, its heart is a maze of cobbled courtyards and alleys winding between the whitewashed walls, painted shutters, and overhanging balconies of low, oddly angled houses. Like Jerusalem, it has been garrisoned by armies for at least two thousand years, fought over by Romans, Mamelukes, Saracens, Turks, Britons, Arabs, and Israelis. And like Jerusalem, it's a place soaked in legend, a place where miracles happen, where a Divine presence seems to hover in the sweet, clear air.

But as much as it resembles any other place, Safed is unique. Hanging high in northern Israel's mountains, gazing out across the Sea of Galilee, Safed seems to belong to the higher spheres. In the words of one of its medieval poets, "In [Safed in] the morning, there's a mystery of awakening; in the evening, there's a lullaby of eternity."

History: In this place where fact and fable are so closely interwoven, history, of course, begins with legend. It is told that after the Flood, Shem and Ever, son and grandson of Noah, came to a cave south of where Safed now lies. Here they passed on the secrets of the Torah to the patriarch Jacob, who in turn transmitted them to his son Joseph. Muslim tradition also links Jacob with the holy cave: It was here, they say, that Jacob was shown the bloodied coat of many colors, and here he mourned his son.

Safed's documented history dates from the days of the Second Temple, when the doomed Jews of Galilee fortified the mountaintop that was to become Safed against the Roman legions. The Jews met defeat but some remained, and Safed joins Jerusalem, Tiberias, and Hebron as one of the four sacred cities of Israel where Jews have lived continuously for two thousand years. The city is also mentioned in the Jerusalem Talmud as one of the mountaintop points from which signal fires were set to announce the new moon and festivals during the Second Temple period.

The tactical advantage of Safed's location next drew the Crusaders over a thousand years later. On the remnant of the Jewish citadel, they built one in their chain of massive castles which dominated the Galilee. The ruins of that fortress are today the focal point of Safed's most popular park — Givat Metzuda, or Citadel Hill.

Following the armies of Rome, Judea, Islam, and Christian Europe came the thirteenth-century Mamelukes and sixteenth-century Ottomans, each of whom made Safed their northern capital. Their choice was dictated by sound strategy, but in its gentle way Safed defied their intentions. There was too much beauty there for the town to remain solely a fortress.

Its luminescence and panoramic views surely contributed to Safed's Golden Age, which dawned late in the fifteenth century and lasted for 200 years. The medieval scholars and mystics who filled the town in those years blurred the separation between heaven and earth. They inspired a generation, and their thought and creativity have infused Jewish life ever since.

In 1481 there were about 1,500 Jews in Safed and the surrounding villages, and they lived well under the protection of their Mameluke governors. But things were about to change. After the Expulsion from Spain, refugees poured in, and a second wave arrived after the Ottoman conquest of *Eretz Ysrael* in 1516. Jews — Sephardim from Spain, Italy, and North Africa and Ashkenazim from Central and Eastern Europe—traded in spices, vegetables, fruits, cheese and oil; later they established looms, whose products competed with those of Venice, and traded in honey and silk. But business was secondary to Safed's prominence. The city became best known as the center of mysticism and for its great rabbis. By the end of the sixteenth century the city had eight synagogues and the first printing press in the Middle East.

Some 30,000 people lived in Safed by the seventeenth century, but its era of greatness was coming to an end. In 1747 the town was struck by plague, and in 1759 by earthquake. A second earthquake buried 2,000 people and damaged every building. The population began to recover in the late eighteenth century, with an influx of *hasidim* and their rivals, followers of the Vilna Gaon, and by the 1830s the city had recovered its position as the commercial center of Galilee, but a more devastating earthquake in 1837 killed 5,000 (4,000 of them Jews), and Safed went back to sleep for most of the nineteenth century.

During World War I, 3,000 Safed residents died of hunger and typhoid, and in 1929 an Arab pogrom drove 3,000 Jews from the town. The year 1948 marked an upturn in Safed's fortunes and the first of the town's modern-day miracles. Then home to 2,000 mostly elderly Jews, the town was under assault for six months by 15,000 Arabs (including detachments from the Iraqi and Lebanese armies) when a Palmach force of 140, armed with homemade heavy weapons, attacked the superior Arab forces and won the town for the State of Israel.

Community: For all its history and beauty, Safed is a rugged, no-frills type of town—a combination that has attracted a diverse population.

Its first modern settlers were pious Russian Jews who, drawn by Safed's mystic history, arrived in the late nineteenth century. They were joined after the birth of the state by 13,000 disoriented immigrants from Morocco and Tunisia and exhausted Holocaust survivors from Poland, Hungary, and Romania who were settled there by the new government.

This less-than-promising mix was swelled by two hasidic communities, Chabad (Lubavitch) and Breslau, who came to Safed in the footsteps of the mystics and built their own separate neighborhoods. Their secular counterparts, Safed's artists and sculptors, also chose to live apart in their own quarter, some staying a few years, others for a lifetime.

Safed's diversified population has long fluctuated, many coming and many leaving, driven away by a chronic job shortage. Thousands of Ethiopian Jews, warmly welcomed to Safed since the mid-1980s, have since left for the greater employment opportunities of central Israel—but more than 1,000 of them have chosen to stay. They have been joined by around 3,000 Russian newcomers, maintaining Safed's reputation for one of the largest immigrant populations in the country. The latest influx has pushed Safed's population past the 20,000 mark for the first time since the eighteenth century.

The most stable ingredient of the Safed polyglot are the North American and European Jews who have settled there in the last decade. Bringing with them their traditions of civic awareness and community activism, they are beginning to have an impact on Safed life. "The people who stay in Safed have one thing in common," says longtime resident Yehoshua Sivan, formerly of London. "Whether they're Ethiopians, Americans, *chasidim*, or artists, they're pragmatic people who want to live amid beauty."

Sights: Start with two sights with two different overviews of Safed. First, the physical: Citadel Hill, the ancient fortress of Jews, Crusaders, and Mamelukes. Today it rises from the center of a cool park, slowly recovering its beauty after the heavy snows of winter 1991–92 (which, unlike previous snowfalls, affected the entire country and not just Safed). From the ruins on its 2,750-foot summit, Safed's highest point, you see the whole town, the green Galilee hills and Lake Kinneret far below.

Next, for a historical overview, go to Safed's two thousand-year-old cemetery west of the city on a steep slope facing Mount Meron. Here lie the great medieval mystics who believed the purity of Safed's air was such that the souls of those who died there flew at once to the Garden of Eden to bask in the splendor of the Almighty. In the adjoining section, fighters from Safed's 1948 War of Liberation are buried, along with the Safed children murdered by terrorists in a Ma'alot schoolhouse in May 1974.

A steep hill rises in the center of the cemetery; climb it and you'll quickly tire — a sure sign, they say, that you're walking on holy ground containing hidden graves. According to tradition, the prophet Hosea and Hannah and her seven martyred sons all found their final resting places under this hill.

The overview completed, it's time to look at the intimate one-room houses of prayer, Safed's ancient synagogues, west of Meginim Square. The Caro Synagogue, off Rehov Beit Yosef, with its stark white walls trimmed in blue, is where the renowned sixteenth-century scholar, Rabbi Joseph Caro, is said to have worked and written, drawing up his *Shulchan Arukh,* or Code of Jewish Law, which guides Orthodox Jews to this day. It is told that in the small domed room beneath the synagogue, an angel appeared to Caro and inspired him to write his mystical *Maggid Mesharim* (Preacher of Righteousness).

Nearby is the Bana'a Synagogue, believed to have been the home of the sixteenth-century Rabbi Yossi Bana'i, who is buried within its walls. One of the most attractive of the old synagogues — with a stone floor, wooden ceiling and benches — it has a beguiling legend to match: A cruel Arab governor once ordered all Safed's Jews to bring him white chickens on pain of expulsion from the town. The Jews prayed at Bana'i's grave, and overnight, all Safed's chickens turned white.

The Abuhav Synagogue also has its legend. Named for the fifteenth-century scholar and kabbalist Rabbi Isaac Abuhav, it contains a Torah scroll penned by the rabbi himself. In the earthquake of 1837, the only part of the synagogue to escape damage was the southern wall facing Jerusalem, where the scroll rested in the holy ark — a miracle attributed to the sacredness of the scroll.

Most famous of all Safed's ancient synagogues is the Sephardic Ari Synagogue at the foot of the old city, close to the cemetery. Built during the lifetime of Rabbi Isaac Luria, who was known as the Ari (an acronym for *Amar Rabbi Yitzchak* — "Rabbi Yitzchak said"), it is exquisitely crafted, with low arched ceilings, finely carved wooden doors, and a surrounding wall that was to make it an important stronghold for Jewish forces during the War of Independence. The synagogue contains a small niche, where the Ari studied and prayed — and it is said that on one memorable occasion he summoned Abraham, Isaac, Jacob, Joseph, Moses, Aaron, and David to read from the Torah.

The second Ari Synagogue, the Ashkenazic, stands outside the sixteenth-century boundaries of Safed, on Najara Street at the edge of town. It was here, according to tradition, that the Ari and his followers gathered to welcome the Sabbath bride.

The rival of Safed's synagogues in the eyes of modern tourists is the city's Artists' Quarter. Below Jerusalem Street is a cluster of quaint stone houses built around a former mosque. After the War of Independence, Safed's municipality offered these then-empty houses to artists as studios, and thus was born the Quarter, which displays and sells original work.

Safed's mystical quality has attracted some of Israel's best artists, as well as others who deal strictly in kitsch — fast-selling canvases of the Western Wall, dancing rabbis, and venerable Jews with wrinkled faces. Today, around fifty painters, potters, and sculptors work in Safed in oil, charcoal, lithograph, batik, watercolor, ceramic, and stone. Most of them reflect Safed's changing hues — its early-morning and just-dusk light bathing the city and its hills in blues, purples, and yellows — and its stones, steps and alleyways, its *chasidim*, children, and cloaked figures.

Culture: Safed has a handful of small but worthwhile museums. It its old city are the Meiri Museum of the History of Safed and, housed in a former mosque, a permanent exhibition of the work of Safed artists. The Museum of the Art of Printing, which displays the first Hebrew printing press, is located downtown in the Artists' Quarter; Safed was the first place in Eretz Israel to encourage the art of printing, and the museum traces the history of the craft. And on the northern rim of Citidel Hill, the Bible Museum displays the works of the artist Phillip Ratner.

The special quality of Safed combined with the energy and dedication of a young American couple, Aharon and Miriam Botzer, has created one of Israel's most successful work-and-study programs for Diaspora youngsters. Started in 1980, it is called Livnot Ulehibanot, "to build and to be rebuilt," and brings groups of young men and women from English-speaking countries to Safed for three months.

The "building" part of the program is physical restoration of Safed's old city, and occupies half of each day. "Being rebuilt" is the study of Jewish heritage through history, faith, and thought. Of the more than 900 youngsters who have passed through the program so far, one-third have returned to live in Israel. "Whether you decide to make aliya or to build your life outside Israel, the program is a healing experience for us all," says one recent graduate.

Reading: Safed has inspired authors as well as artists. Its legends are told by Ze'ev Vilnay, the late doyen of Israeli guides, and by Dov Silverman, both in books titled *Legends Of Safed*. Silverman, who has lived in Safed since 1972, is also working on a historical novel set in the town, and Israeli novelist Yehoshua Bar-Yosef locates a number of his stories in Safed as well.

The story of Safed's medieval mystics is lyrically told by James Michener in *The Source* (Fawcett, Random House), and Leon Uris's *Exodus* (Doubleday) devotes a dramatic chapter to Safed's 1948 battle and its "atomic weapon," the Davidka.

Personalities: Safed's greatest sons are surely its medieval scholars, the two most influential of whom are Joseph Caro and Isaac Luria. Caro, born in Spain, left with the Expulsion in 1492. He came to Safed, whose countryside may have reminded him of the stark Spanish landscape, and lived out his eighty-seven years here. It was in Safed that he compiled the *Shulchan*

Arukh. His text is plain and even abrupt. But charged with the authority of total grasp, Caro's handbook has something in it of Safed's stark and stony hills, its rugged landscape and crystal air.

Isaac Luria, most famous of all Jewish mystics, was born in Jerusalem, raised in Egypt, and lived in Safed for only eighteen months. His only published writing is a short early commentary. His predictions, cures, divine revelations, and acts of levitation were all recorded by followers, who believed his insights into Torah were divinely inspired. Some said he was the Messiah, and others believed he spoke with the angels.

Little that is tangible remains of the Ari. There are legends and fables. There are tales of him dancing into the Safed hills at sunset to greet the Sabbath bride. And there is a vast spiritual infusion into Judaism that lasts to this day.

In modern Israel Safed's best known personalities are its artists. The most famous is Israel's Grandma Moses, the late Shalom of Safed.

Day Trips: Safed is perched amid some of the most beautiful countryside in Israel. The Huleh Valley Nature Reserve lies thirteen miles north of the town. Most of this once-desolate swamp has been drained and converted to fertile farmland, but several acres are preserved with their flora and fauna intact.

Banyas, one of the sources of the Jordan River, is another nearby beauty spot, where spring water gushes from a rock to form a natural pool. A pagan shrine to the god Pan was built here, and its ruins can still be seen. Tel Hai, another of the Jordan's sources, is where Joseph Trumpeldor and his seven companions fell in 1920—the first Jewish soldiers fighting for Eretz Israel since the time of Bar Kochba. There is a museum there to their memory.

Biriya is a park just outside Safed, which has recently built a pony-trekking center. And down the mountain toward Tiberias are Rosh Pina, one of modern Israel's first settlements—recently restored and with guided tours available—and Vered Hagalil, Israel's American-style dude ranch, with horses for hire and riding tours of the Galilee.

Safed is one of the few places in Israel where you can get such a sense of the past. In place of the car you need in Tel Aviv, in the valley below Safed you need a good horse, and in the city's lanes you need a sturdy pair of shoes — not terribly different from the residents who built a commercial and mystical capital more than four centuries ago.

—Wendy Elliman

St. Louis

St. Louis has the distinction of having the only Jewish community in the United States led by a chief rabbi. At the same time, the city claims the largest Reform Jewish population per capita in the world.

From the beginning, there was a shift away from tradition by those who chose to express their heritage through philanthropy rather than worship. St. Louis was the gateway to the West, a frontier town where religion was not a priority and tradition not a value. This was a place for pioneers interested in opportunities and change. It nurtured firsts—the first synagogue, cathedral, and university west of the Mississippi; first walk-through aviary in the world; first ice-cream cone and first hot dog on a bun. It was the perfect setting for Reform Judaism to take hold so fiercely. While there was always a substantial force to maintain the tradition, the Reformers dedicated themselves to creating a powerful secular structure and welfare organizations whose influence on Jewish and non-Jewish life in the city was substantial.

History: Jews may have ventured into St. Louis shortly after Pierre Laclede founded it as a fur-trading post in 1764. Under the *Code Noir* (Black Code) of the French who ruled it, however, everyone was barred from the area except for Roman Catholics.

When Thomas Jefferson purchased the Louisiana Territory for the United States in 1803, restrictions on settlement were lifted. Within three years, the village's first Jew, Joseph Philipson, arrived from Philadelphia and established St. Louis's first permanent store. Originally from Poland, Philipson parlayed the ten thousand dollars in merchandise he brought with him from the East into a successful dry goods business; a sawmill; holdings in a bank, a distillery and a brewery—probably the first west of the Mississippi and a precursor to Anheuser Busch, the beer manufacturer for which St. Louis is famous.

In addition to helping build St. Louis's economy, Philipson was deeply involved in civic affairs. But he was so little involved as a Jew that his obituary cited his "constant practice of the precepts of Christianity" and noted that he was a member of no religious denomination. To his credit, however, he made it possible for more Jews to settle in St. Louis. It took three decades after Philipson's arrival for the first *minyan* to be formed, when 10 men rented a room above a grocery at the corner of Second Street and Spruce Avenue for Rosh Hashanah services in 1837. Four years later, United Hebrew Congregation was formed, and thus began Jewish communal life for the population of 100.

It didn't take long for differences to arise between those who followed the Ashkenazic services of Poland and those who didn't want to be fettered by tradition. The newcomers, more liberal Germans and Bohemians, founded Emanu El in 1847 and B'nai B'rith in 1849. They later merged and in 1855 began construction on the first synagogue west of the Mississippi, the octagonally-shaped B'nai El, which housed a congregation of Orthodox and Reform elements whose members had the freedom to practice and worship as they wished.

In the mid-nineteenth century the Jewish population of 5,000 was largely German and the Jews were generally merchants. (German Jews later developed the city's two major department store chains, Stix, Baer and Fuller and May Department Stores, represented in St. Louis as Famous-Barr and in other cities as Famous-Barr or

443

Hecht's.) Like the rest of the community, they began to move west, a few blocks at a time. Most settled in South St. Louis, with non-Jewish Germans, where they remained until well after World War I. Religiously, they moved progressively away from tradition. Shaare Emeth, the first congregation to be organized from its inception as a Reform temple by the more Reform members of B'nai El, was not Reform enough for the dissidents who sided with Rabbi Solomon Sonnenschein. They formed Temple Israel, which prohibited the wearing of *kippot* and *tallitot*, and did not perform *bar mitzvahs*. (It is less classically Reform today.)

When Russian and Eastern European Jews arrived beginning in the 1880s, they settled further north. The animosity between the well-established Germans and the traditional newcomers led to separation of more than their neighborhoods; they founded their own synagogues, which have developed into some of the city's Conservative congregations.

Rivalries were laid aside in 1923 (by which time the Jewish population had reached 50,000), when the Vaad Hoeir (literally, City Council), the United Orthodox Community, was established. Representatives of Orthodox congregations of St. Louis felt that all the synagogues should be organized to provide one standard of *kashrut* and to serve other communal needs. They elected a chief rabbi as the authority on these matters. Since only the Orthodox had an organized kashrut program, others—mainly Conservative Jews who observe dietary laws—trusted it and followed it. That the unified approach developed in St. Louis and not elsewhere may have been because the community's leadership was simply more amenable to cooperation.

The barriers between the different Jewish groups softened by the turn of the century, which also marked a breakthrough in relations with the non-Jewish community—the Jews becoming not merely supporters but partners in civic affairs. Five prominent Jews were selected to serve on the organizing committee of the 1904 World's Fair Exposition.

In fact, it was at the urging of Nathan Frank, the only Jew from Missouri ever elected to the United States Congress (1888–1890), that the fair was held in St. Louis. Frank, founder of the *St. Louis Star* (a major newspaper until the 1950s), had begun drumming up support for the idea while he was in Washington.

At the centenary celebration of the Louisiana Purchase—immortalized in cinema and song ("Meet Me in St. Louis")—the Jewish (now Israeli) flag flew with the flags of other nations. There were conflicts between traditionalists and secularists over how "Jewish" the Jerusalem Pavilion should be. The pavilion was one of the largest at the 1904 Exposition, covering thirteen acres. It presented a reproduction of the Holy City, including its most historic streets and sights, the Western Wall and the marketplace.

Following World War II, the Jews settled into University City, a pleasant area north of the Washington University campus. Those remaining when an exodus to the suburbs began in the 1960s worked to create a model of human rights, fighting the unfair housing practices that persisted in spite of antidiscrimination laws. Today, University City has a large black population, while many Jews can be found in Clayton, Ladue, Creve Coeur, Chesterfield, and Baldwin.

From the beginning, Jews were welcomed in St. Louis and had a lot to do with how the city looks, with its economy, and its cultural and educational life. Yet the Jewish Hospital was founded partly to provide a place for Jewish doctors to practice medicine, since they could not work elsewhere. Those who achieved top positions in industry did so only at firms founded or owned by Jews, and with few exceptions— like Louis P. Aloe, acting mayor during World War I, and Nathan Frank—Jews have not been elected to high political positions.

Substantial Jewish contributions helped pay for the microfilm reproductions of the Vatican's 600,000 manuscripts for the St. Louis University library. The city has the Mark C. Steinberg Memorial Skating Rink, the Moses Shoenberg School of Nursing, the Charles H. Yalem Children's Zoo, and numerous other facilities, including many buildings on university campuses, all made possible by Jewish philanthropists interested in a strong, viable city. Their own position of strength was demonstrated in the mid-1960s, when Mayor Alfonso Cervantes, of Spanish extraction, wanted to place a statue of Queen Isabella of Spain downtown. Loud protest from the Jewish community over honoring the instigator of the Inquisition and the Expulsion quashed his plans.

Community: What's remarkable about the St. Louis Jewish community is its stability—in geography, population, and character. Throughout its expansion it has remained in the central corridor of the city, gradually pushing west into the suburbs. University City remains home to the city's more traditional Jews (there's also a religious community in suburban Chesterfield), as well as a growing number of *baalei teshuvah.* A high proportion of the Jews, like St. Louisans in general, grew up in the city and stayed there or returned after college or other significant turning points in life. This creates familiarity, cohesiveness, and a sense of community that is much stronger than its numbers alone—53,500—would indicate.

Although all Jewish denominations are represented (there are nine Reform, nine Orthodox, one Reconstructionist, and three Conservative congregations), the liberal religious orientation of the community as a whole persists. However, the Reform congregations today have come back to some of the ritual they eschewed when they broke from the Orthodox tradition in the last century.

The central address and power base of the Jewish community is clearly the St. Louis Jewish Federation (12 Millstone Campus Drive; 314-432-0020), which honors the community's diversity but still expresses a Reform bent. Though St. Louis knows the sectarian differences common to all American Jewish communities, concerted efforts by communal leaders and Chief Rabbi and Rebbetzin Rivkin have maintained the cooperative spirit that has existed since the 1920s.

Sights: Virtually everything in St. Louis is within a twenty-minute drive of everything else. And to reach everything, you need a car. Nothing remains of pre-

World War I Jewish St. Louis, but it is possible to trace the movement west from where the community started, near the riverfront.

Arch without rival: Frame for a cathedral with an attention-grabbing inscription

St. Louis is probably most identified with the Gateway Arch, the engineering marvel with its legs set in a commanding stance right near the mighty Mississippi River. In the underground complex that houses the Museum of Westward Expansion, the Memorial Fountain commemorates the first Jewish worship service west of the river. Just across the Jefferson Memorial Expansion Grounds, the Old Cathedral frequently draws amazed looks for the gilded Hebrew letters above the entry inscribing what is supposed to be the name of God. The *heh*'s are actually *chet*'s, possibly the purposeful error of a Jewish craftsman who didn't want the holy designation on a non-Jewish house of worship.

Supreme Court Justice Louis D. Brandeis was admitted to the bar at the Old Court House (Broadway and Market Street), also the site of the Dred Scott inquest. A bronze bust of Brandeis was unveiled there on the fiftieth anniversary of his appointment as the first Jewish member of the Supreme Court. Around the corner,

445

the Brandeis Plaque set in the side of the building at 505 Chestnut Street marks the site where he began practicing law in 1878.

The home of the St. Louis Cardinals baseball team, supported with feverish intensity by their city, is Busch Memorial Stadium (Broadway and Seventh Street). Its Butch Yatkemann Clubhouse honors a man associated with the team for more than half a century as batboy and then equipment manager.

Aloe Plaza, facing Union Station at Market between Eighteenth and Twentieth, memorializes Louis P. Aloe, St. Louis's only Jewish mayor, who became nationally known for initiating a bond issue to provide for civic improvement on a scale unprecedented in the United States. Public subscription helped pay for Carl Milles's fountain, "The Meeting of the Waters," erected on the plaza in Aloe's honor.

Forest Park, site of the 1904 Exposition and a number of the city's most popular attractions, also holds several of Jewish interest: the Frank Bandstand in front of the Municipal Opera Theater (outdoor seating for 12,000), a gift of Nathan Frank to the city; the Bertha Guggenheim Memorial Fountain, erected by a son of the patroness of the park system and women's activist; and the American Jewish Tercentenary Marker, recognizing the three-hundredth anniversary of the first Jewish settlement in North America.

St. Louis has some of the grandest homes to be found in America, many of them facing the park along Lendell Boulevard, built there as foreign missions during the 1904 Exposition. Further north, and just west of Union Boulevard, architectural diversity and grandeur line the streets. While this was not a Jewish neighborhood as such, there was a time when a number of the homes were owned by prominent Jews. On Washington Terrace, introduced by a fairytale live-in terra-cotta gatehouse, were department store magnates David May (at number 5), Sydney Shoenberg (number 8), Julius Baer (number 11), and Morton J. May (number 18). Louis Aloe lived one block south, at 36 Kingsbury Place. On Union just across Delmar Boulevard is the first building expressly constructed as a Jewish community center (originally the YM-YWHA), now a police station.

A minister once jokingly asked if it is a Jewish law that a synagogue must be sold to a black church, since so many have been — at least one in every post–World War I Jewish neighborhood. Those worth a look are Temple Israel (a Corinthian palace at Kingshighway and Washington), Tpheris Israel (Klemm and Blaine), B'nai El (Delmar and Clara), and B'nai Amoona (Academy and Vernon). A later B'nai Amoona structure, on Trinity in University City, is now the Center of Contemporary Arts, and United Hebrew, the city synagogue most recently vacated for a new location closer to its suburban population, is now home to the Missouri Historical Society.

Among the most interesting synagogues currently in use is Temple Emanuel, built in 1962 (Conway and Ballas Roads). From the outside, it looks like a Star of David. Inside the sanctuary, a set of stained-glass windows, created by the English artist Margaret Trahane, pick up the sun as it moves across the building. The rosy round windows, one on each side of the worship space, are cloudlike in design, to depict God as spirit.

The new B'nai Amoona, at 324 South Mason Road in Creve Coeur, also uses a six-sided motif in a series of hexagons, the most dramatic of which is the three-tier capped crown of blue glass, specially created in Italy, which sits over the sanctuary. It creates the impression of the crown on each Torah scroll. The design theme is repeated in two other skylights and in the eternal light, an inverted model of the building. The buff-colored bricks are reminiscent of those made by Jewish slaves in Egypt. While contemporary, the building incorporates pieces of the congregation's history: The Moses, Aaron, Isaiah, and abstract stained-glass windows came from its 1918 home at Academy and Vernon Avenues, and the ark, tablets, and menorahs for the *bimah* from its building on Trinity.

Culture: The St. Louis Art Museum benefited from the bequest of Morton D. May (heir to the May Companies, established by his grandfather). He left to the museum one of the finest collections of German Expressionist paintings in the

United States, and the world's largest collection of Max Beckmann's paintings. May's bequest also contributed to the museum's collection of art of Africa, Oceania, and the Americas. Located in Forest Park, the first municipally sponsored art museum in the country originated as the Art Palace of the 1904 Exposition. Jewish artists represented are Chagall, Pisarro, Modigliani, James Rosenquist, and Jacques Lipchitz.

The Jewish Community Centers Association hosts an annual Jewish Folk Arts Festival in the fall or early winter, focusing on a different national group each year, and in November runs the Jewish Book Festival. It also presents ongoing lecture series. Recent speakers have included authors Ruth Gruber and Dennis Prager, Missouri Senator Kit Bond, and visiting scholars from the Melitz Center for Jewish-Zionist Education of Jerusalem. The JCCA is located at 2 Millstone Campus Drive in Creve Coeur. Call (314) 432-5700 for information on events.

Two galleries, both run out of private homes, specialize in Israeli artists. They are Galerie Rodin (314-994-9616) and Collectors Corner (314-727-0606). The two are among several art representatives who exhibit jointly at the annual Jewish Art Festival, held in the gallery of the JCCA. During the rest of the year, exhibits at the JCCA change every month or six weeks, and might at any time be focused on Judaica; Ethiopian Jewish crafts; individual Jewish or Israeli painters, sculptors, or weavers; or the work of local Jewish artisans.

Scholar-in-residence programs are occasionally held by synagogues, particularly Shaare Emeth (314-569-0100). Aish HaTorah, the local branch of a Jerusalem-based yeshiva responsible for a revival in Jewish learning through its educational outreach to Jews of all backgrounds, presents frequent lectures and occasional film programs (314-862-2474). The easiest way to find out what is going on in the St. Louis Jewish community is to consult the *St. Louis Jewish Light*, published every Wednesday.

One of the cultural stars of the city is the St. Louis Symphony Orchestra, brought to world acclaim under its Jewish musical director and conductor, Leonard Slatkin.

Eating: True to its name, the kosher No Bull Cafe serves only dairy lunches and dinners — very good ones at that — in a pleasant, modern setting near the JCCA (10477 Old Olive Street). The only other places in town to buy kosher meals are the modest corner of Simon Kohn's kosher butcher and grocery store across the street (10424 Old Olive), and the sit-down area at Sol's Meat Market (8627 Olive Street). Both serve standard delicatessen fare and a full range of entrées. At 8½ Euclid, the Sunshine Inn, a "sprouts place," serves a wide selection of vegetarian dishes.

Shabbat home hospitality can be arranged for anyone who needs *Shomer Shabbat* accommodation or kosher meals in University City within walking distance of three Orthodox *shuls*. (Call the Vaad Hoeir at 314-727-4662.)

Personalities: Isidor Bush, the editor of a leading intellectual journal in Vienna known nationally for bringing German ideas — and Jews — to the United States, helped organize the B'nai B'rith Congregation in St. Louis. One of his greatest contributions may have been his discovery of Joseph Pulitzer, who was employed at Bush's vineyards. When he recognized the young Jewish journalist's ability, Bush helped him land a position with the *Westliche Post,* from where he made his way to the *St. Louis Post-Dispatch* and a publishing empire.

St. Louis can claim to have nurtured native actress Shelley Winters (formerly Shirley Schrift), Broadway producer David Merrick (formerly David Margulies), writer Fanny Hurst, and film star Kevin Kline. Millions of people know about the city because of the efforts of two non-resident Jews, Irving Brecher and Fred F. Finkelhoffe, who wrote the screenplay for *Meet Me in St. Louis.*

Marc Saperstein, winner of a National Jewish Book Award, and the novelist Stanley Elkin are part of the intellectual community associated with Washington University. So, until their deaths, were the poet Howard Nemerov and Max Dimont, author of the classic *Jews, God, and History.* Whitney Harris, who is not Jewish, was United States prosecutor at the Nuremberg trials and is frequently seen at events sponsored by the Jewish community, which he supports financially as well. St. Louis natives include *New York Times* caricaturist Albert Hirschfeld; pitching great Ken Holtzman; Morris Fishbein, longtime head of the American Medical Association; and Gerald Swope, who was president of General Electric.

Many of St. Louis's Jewish personalities (including Winters, Pulitzer, Elkin, and Nemerov) are honored with brass stars and bronze plaques along the Walk of Fame in University City. Started in 1988 outside the Blueberry Hill Diner as a showcase for the city's cultural heritage, the Walk runs in the "Loop" area on Delmar from Kingsland on the west to just before Skinner on the east.

Reading: Harold Brodkey, sometimes called an American Proust, remembers the Jewish University City of his boyhood in stories like "The State of Grace." No other Jewish author has set works in St. Louis, but novels that provide a good orientation to the city include *Death Benefits* by Michael Kahn (Dutton), *White Palace* by Glenn Savin (Bantam) and *The Twenty-Seventh City* by Jonathan Franzen (Farrar, Straus & Giroux).

Day Trip: The home of one of the nineteenth century's great philo-Semites is an easy day trip from St. Louis. "The Jews constitute but one percent of the human race," observed Samuel Clemens, a.k.a. Mark Twain. "Properly, the Jew ought hardly to be heard of, but he is heard of and always has been heard of. His contributions to the world's list of great names in literature, science, art, music, finance, medicine, and abstruse learning are also way out of proportion to the weakness of his numbers."

Less than two hours northwest of St. Louis on The Great River Road, Hannibal has been commercialized since Clemens's youth, but in the Mark Twain Boyhood Home and Museum, Becky Thatcher House, and the Mark Twain Cave, the town offers a glimpse of what inspired his classics.

Recommendations: The hub of TWA, St. Louis is accessible by most major air carriers. The Hyatt Regency in the renovated Union Station is magnificent and well-located in the station's shopping/entertainment/dining complex. Almost a century after the fair, its a good place to meet in St. Louis.

—Lesli Koppelman Ross

St. Petersburg

When asked where the oldest complete Hebrew Bible in the world is located, it's a safe bet that few people would say St. Petersburg. It's even less likely that they'd make any connection between impressive city sights like the Winter Palace and the Peter and Paul Fortress and the Jewish history of Russia's prerevolutionary capital. That in itself is the challenge of visiting St. Petersburg—learning what to look for. Those who try will be rewarded for finding their way into the city's deep Jewish roots, which are a mirror image of the contradictions, peaks, and valleys of Jewish life in Russia.

Don't rush to find that Bible. Dating from 1009 or 1010, it spends most of the time in storage at the Saltykov-Schedrin State Public Library—although access is easing up. But armed with a keen eye and an appreciation for the triumphs and sufferings of St. Petersburg Jewry throughout the city's nearly 300-year existence, visitors can unlock a doorway to the past.

History: Russia's second largest city, St. Petersburg—known to the world for most of this century as Leningrad—was founded as in 1703 by Peter the Great, who made it his capital. Conversos and apostates were among the first to come to the city. Ironically, in a place where Jews would long have reason to fear the police, the first police minister in the new Russian capital was Anton Divier, of Portuguese-Jewish origin. Other Jews, many of them doctors or financiers (and at least one jester, Jan Dacosta, in the czar's court), arrived to serve the state or the army.

The small Jewish community suffered from the anti-Semitism that swept Russia during the eighteenth century. Two Jews were burned at the stake in St. Petersburg in 1738—one a Russian naval officer and nobleman who had secretly converted to Judaism, the other the Jewish farmer who had convinced him to do so. Neither status nor conversion helped much when it came to anti-Semitism; in 1748 one of the most outstanding foreign doctors and a member of the Russian Academy of Sciences was deprived of his pension when it was discovered that he was from a family of baptized Jews.

The partitions of Poland brought masses of Jews under Russian control, and by the end of the eighteenth century some made their way to St. Petersburg, as did Jews from Latvia and White Russia. The fortunes of Jews in the city and throughout the empire rose and fell according to the attitudes of the czars. Many left St. Petersburg during the reign of Czarina Elizabeth, but her successor, Catherine the Great (1762–96), attracted Jews. In the nineteenth and early twentieth centuries Jewish fortunes deteriorated under Nicholas I, improved under Alexander II, and declined again under Nicholas II.

Throughout the czarist era, however, permanent Jewish residence was highly restricted in St. Petersburg—except when it was totally forbidden. But from the handful who had permission and those who had temporary residence status, the Jewish community grew slowly, leasing a plot for a cemetery in 1802—the first Jewish communal act in the city's annals.

When Nicholas I came to power in 1825 there were about 200 Jews in the city. Despite his intolerance, during his reign Jewish army veterans were permitted to settle. They maintained a prayer house and also hosted Jews who came to the city on business. Despite the community's small size, its location in the Russian capital was pivotal. At the beginning of the nineteenth century, a group of local Jewish leaders began a tradition by approaching the authorities and seeking to speak on behalf of all Russian Jewry. This tradition, usually exercised by the head of the largest synagogue in the city, was inherited by Moscow's Jewish leaders when the Communists moved the country's capital.

The Russian public in St. Petersburg knew little about Jewish life, since most Jews were far away in the Pale of Settlement. One of the first St. Petersburg *maskilim*, Leiba Nevachovich, wrote *The Cry of the Jewish People* to defend the Jews against widespread libels and slanders. Ironically, he later converted to Christianity.

Substantial growth began when Alexander II, who came to power in 1855, gave both serfs and Jews more rights. Settlement privileges for educated and wealthy Jews and an influx of more Jewish craftsmen buoyed the Jewish community's numbers and talent.

By the 1850s St. Petersburg had its first major Jewish leader, Baron Horace Guenzburg; his family's Guenzburg Bank pioneered in the development of credit financing and helped build Russian railroads and open mines. Guenzburg, his father before him and his son after him headed the Jewish community. The Guenzburg mansion can still be seen at 17 Profsoyusov Boulevard. By 1881 the community numbered 17,000.

Shtetl people could not obtain residency permits, and religious practice had little place in St. Petersburg Jewish life. Instead the community excelled in political, social, and cultural areas, becoming a center for the Jewish Enlightenment. The government even encouraged this, while at the same time seeing to it that no religious center would spring up in the capital.

The Society for the Promotion of Culture Among the Jews of Russia was established in 1863 and united the Jewish intelligentsia throughout the Russian Empire. At the same time St. Petersburg became the center of the Russian Jewish press, with *Dawn* (1881–1906), one of the leading newspapers, featuring historian Simon Dubnow on its staff. The world's first Hebrew daily, *Ha-Yom*, began in 1886, prompting *Hamelitz*, a Hebrew paper that had started as a weekly, to switch to daily publication a few months later. Russia's first Yiddish daily, *Der Fraynd*, was launched in 1903.

The Choral Synagogue, completed in 1893 near the corner of Decembrist Street and Lermontovsky Prospekt, reflects the Reform approach of St. Petersburg Jewry at the time toward religious practice. The presence of the choir itself indicated its nontraditional stand, and the synagogue always had two rabbis, one for spiritual and one for official functions.

Exposure to the Enlightenment laid the foundations for St. Petersburg's emergence as a major center of Zionism. At the same time, pogroms throughout the country prompted Joseph Trumpeldor—a veteran of the Russo-Japanese War and later the hero of Tel Hai in northern Israel—to organize Jewish self-defense units in the city in 1917. That same year, the Conservatory in the city's Theatrical Square played host to the All-Russian Zionist Congress.

The suppression of the 1905 Revolution led to increased development of Jewish cultural life. Frustrated politically, the city's Jews turned to literature, history, music, and folklore. Countless societies were formed among the Jews, who numbered some 40,000 by the beginning of World War I. They were a dynamic, wealthy, educated, and modernized community, living in the city's better neighborhoods, praying at fifteen synagogues. While the city changed its name to Petrograd in 1914, the Jewish community continued to sustain itself through dozens of self-help organizations including ORT, founded in St. Petersburg in 1880.

Education thrived at all levels. Petrograd had the world's largest collection of Jewish books and manuscripts located in public and private libraries and in academic centers, a collection more prestigious than London's. But the community's face was changing. During World War I Jewish refugees, many of them more traditional shtetl people, began arriving from the front. When the revolutions of 1917 came, Leon Trotsky was by no means the only Jew to take part. On the fateful October evening when Lenin's followers captured the Winter

Palace, not only Bolsheviks but also other left-wing parties gathered at the Second Congress of Soviets, where all fourteen speakers were Jewish.

The last commander of the provisional government forces defending the Winter Palace against the Bolsheviks that night was also a Jew—Pinchas Ruttenberg, who was arrested and held in the Peter and Paul Fortress. He later became a Zionist and eventually laid the foundations for Israel's electric-power system.

Though the city was renamed Leningrad in honor of the Communist leader, the Revolution of 1917 marked the end of its dominance. The capital was moved to Moscow, a treaty moved the German border much closer, and the city's import-export trade foundered, its port ceasing to be a major connection to the West. The Bolsheviks stopped bringing food into the city, and in two years the population fell from 2.5 million to 700,000. People fled because they had nothing to eat, no electricity or running water. Many of the Jews who remained took jobs in the burgeoning Soviet bureaucracy, but leaders of the Jewish intelligentsia had either died of hunger, fled abroad, or been killed in the Red terror.

With economic life in the *shtetls* in ruins, many traditional Jews were drawn to the Soviet Union's industrial centers, Moscow and Leningrad. Though the city and its Jewish community had lost their preeminence to Moscow, Leningrad's Jewish population grew steadily, reaching 200,000 by the time Russia entered World War II in 1941. Jewish communal life, however, slowly disappeared. The Society for the Promotion of Culture Among the Jews of Russia was closed in 1929, the Jewish museum was shut down, and the Jewish Historical Society shuttered. The last Jewish school was closed in 1938 and its director arrested; other leading Jews suffered similar fates. Although the city's Jewish population was at its peak when the war began, it was also for the most part Jewishly illiterate.

Little is known about Jewish life in Leningrad during the war since few people kept records, fearing Stalin's secret police. The Jews certainly suffered as much as others during the first winter of the German siege, bringing their dead to the court of the Choral Synagogue. To unite the Soviet people in the war effort, more religious rights were granted in the middle of the war, and the Jewish community revived slightly after it ended. The synagogue was repaired, but most communal activities that Jews in the West take for granted were still forbidden.

Following the Six Day War many young Russian Jews were swept up in Jewish nationalist feelings and formed Zionist groups. The movement was stung by the 1970 Leningrad Hijacking Trial, in which several leading activists—including Mark Dymshitz, Hillel Butman, and Yosef Mendelevitch—were among those convicted. Widespread persecution followed, with people losing jobs and chances for higher education. But within two years of the trial the gates of the Soviet Union, long closed to emigrants, were opened and a large-scale movement to Israel began. Many Leningrad activists were among those who left.

Community: Russian Jewish life today is simultaneously exploding and imploding. All kinds of community activities and institutions are springing up, and many people long thought to be ethnic Russians are coming out of the closet as Jews. At the same time, masses of people for whom the burgeoning community structure is being built are leaving for Israel.

The best estimate is that St. Petersburg's Jews number some 140,000. It is still a largely assimilated, aged community with a high percentage of mixed marriages and singles. Jews are concentrated in engineering, computers, medicine, education, and as clerks. Despite the upheaval the Jewish communal structure looks increasingly like that of Jewish communities in the West. There are youth groups and Zionist organizations, a Hebrew teachers' union, research on Jewish history and anti-Semitism, restoration projects, and an open Jewish university. There are still apartment gatherings, but more and more of the city's Jewish life is coming out into the open.

St. Petersburg has two main Jewish cultural groups, both of which sponsor lectures and musical and theatrical events and can be of service to visitors. The Society for Jewish Culture, located in the Kirov Palace of Culture, is headed by Alexander Dobrusin; call 217-5311 for information on events. The St. Petersburg Jewish Association offers similar facilities but is less settled; for information on the association, or on Jewish St. Petersburg in general, contact Nate Geller at the National Conference on Soviet Jewry in New York (212-679-6122).

Though Moscow remains the largest Jewish community in the former Soviet Union, some recent visitors feel St. Petersburg has organized more quickly since Jewish communal life became legitimate. And St. Petersburg seems to be reestablishing a position of leadership in at least one respect. *Ami*, the city's Jewish newspaper, is the closest thing Russian Jewry has to a national voice.

Sights: Originally built on swamps, St. Petersburg is a city of canals and bridges along the Neva River, with endless embankments to walk along, especially during the "white nights" of summer, when there are almost twenty-four hours of daylight. The city's main central areas are the Admiralty Side, where most of the museums, statues, monuments, and historical buildings are located; Vasilyevsky Island; the Petrograd Side; and the Vyborg Side.

Visitors will naturally want to see the Winter and Summer palaces, the Hermitage, and the Vorontsov and Strogonov palaces. They will likewise enjoy touring the various outlying summer residences of the czars, which contain huge areas of parkland attracting local and foreign visitors. Sights related to Russian history will no doubt be pointed out by guides. For Jewish visitors, however, the trick is not in what you see, but in what you don't see.

When visiting the Peter and Paul Fortress, St. Petersburg's answer to the Bastille, which until 1921 was the jail for political prisoners, most guides will talk about the Decembrists and revolutionaries who were held there. Keep in mind one other famous inmate: Rabbi Schneur Zalman of Lyady, founder of Chabad hasidism, who was imprisoned in the fortress in 1799 and again in 1800.

A walk past the prestigious St. Petersburg Conservatory should remind you not only of the All-Russia Zionist Congress, but also of Anton Rubinstein, a baptized Jew who was its founder and the father of the Russian musical education system,

which has produced great talents over the years. The violinist Jascha Heifetz was a student there, and pianist Artur Rubinstein performed there.

The State Historical Archive is a grand building standing at Naberezhnaya Krasnogo Flota 4. It was also the home of Samuel Polyakov, a Jewish railroad builder and banker. The Aeroflot office at Nevsky Prospekt 7–9 was once the Jewish-run Bank of Vavelberg.

There are no purely Jewish neighborhoods in St. Petersburg, and the city never had a ghetto. Most Jews lived on the southern side, the left bank of the Big Neva River, and later concentrated near the Choral Synagogue in a neighborhood known as Kolomna behind the Kirov Opera and Ballet Theater.

The Choral Synagogue was so named because young boys sang there. A focal point of the Jewish community for years, the magnificent Moorish-style building also houses a small, somewhat older synagogue in the courtyard favored by local *hasidim*. The cream-colored building, with a domed central section and two lower projecting wings, was completed in 1893 when there were 20,000 Jews in St. Petersburg; its majesty is largely a reflection of their wealth and influence.

Many Jewish sights are unmarked but easily visited. At 18 Theatrical Square stands the former Jewish gymnasium, which provided education for students whose access to Russian schools was limited by a quota system. The building where *Dawn* was published is at 2 Theatrical Square.

Visitors to the bridge across the Moika River on Nevsky Prospekt (the city's main thoroughfare, lined with shops, cafés, and public buildings) should bear in mind that it was on that site in July 1903 that Pinchas Dashevsky attacked Pavolaki Krushevan—instigator of the Kishinev pogrom—with a knife. Dashevsky failed in his attempted assassination and spent several years in jail.

Perhaps nowhere else is the legacy of official anti-Semitism more palpable than when one visits St. Petersburg museums. More than anywhere else in the city, what informed museum visitors know will certainly transcend what they see. Not that St. Petersburg's museums don't rival the world's best. The State Russian Museum features a collection of the finest art works including those by Marc Chagall, who studied in St. Petersburg, and sculptor Marc Antokolsky.

It's next door at the Museum of Ethnography that what's not on display should stir your interest. In the 1920s and 1930s, the museum also housed an exhibit on Jews. Today none of it is on view, although the items from the exhibit are still in the museum's possession. It is believed that large parts of the collections of Judaica made their way here when Soviet authorities closed the city's Jewish Museum.

Many of the huge libraries throughout the city contain items of Jewish interest. The State Public Library has several collections, including the one assembled by the Karaite leader Abraham Firkovitch (1786–1874), said to number seventeen thousand items. A flour and corn merchant, Firkovitch collected items he found on his travels through the Middle East, including a fourteenth-century Karaite Torah from Damascus and the oldest complete Hebrew Bible in the world, signed by the scribe Samuel Ben Yakov in 1009 or 1010. Also in the library's collection is a burnt remnant of a Torah dated to the year 910. Scholars reportedly have better access to the library's collection than they did a few years ago. Hope is rising that these treasures will see the light of day. One possible source of help is Dr. Victor Lebedev, director of the Institute of Judaism and Jewish Culture, Box 341, St. Petersburg.

Preobrazhensky Cemetery dates from 1874. To reach it take the Metro to the Lomonosov Square station, then board a number 118 bus to the last stop opposite the cemetery on the left side of the Neva. Jews are no longer interred there, although it is possible to bury ashes in the grave of a relative. Visitors should be sure to see the cemetery's Memorial to Five War Dead, where Jews gather every year for Holocaust Remembrance Day ceremonies. With its striking *Magen David*, the memorial is inscribed with five names—Rosa Lurie-Gelb, Max Gelb, Yosef Lurie, Moisei Danishevski, and Yasha Aviosor. It contains no dates or epitaph, only places of death (Auschwitz, Stalingrad) indicating its connection to the death camps and battlefields of World War II; its metallic network of wire seems to symbolize barbed wire fences.

The cemetery also houses the graves of leading St. Petersburg Jewish figures, including David Katzenellenbogen, an Orthodox Polish rabbi who was brought to St. Petersburg to lead the Jewish community. A religious man in a secular town, he fought bravely for the rights of religious Jews and convinced Russian rulers to permit Jewish soldiers to be given leave on Passover so they would not have to eat bread.

Another face of St. Petersburg Jewish life comes to mind when visiting the grave of Vera Klimentievna Slutskaya, a member of the Communist party and "Professional Revolutionary, active participant in the Great October Socialist Revolution," as her gravestone reads. Born in Minsk, she was killed in November 1917 while transporting medical supplies to Red Guard detachments during the suppression of the Kerensky-Krasnov rebellion.

Side Trips: For starters, try taking a boat trip up and down the city's canals if the weather is warm. St. Petersburg faces water everywhere, and the main palaces all face the water. For a longer excursion that affords a fine view of the scenery surrounding the city, take a boat trip to Valaam (named after Balaam, the prophet who tried and failed to curse the Israelites), a monastery on an island on Lake Ladoga (St. Petersburg lies on the Gulf of Finland, and the Neva flows to it from this huge lake). Trips leave in the evening, with sleeping berths on the boat. The entire next day is spent on the island, and you return to St. Petersburg in the evening. There are no accommodations on the island itself.

Reading: Don't leave without reading *Crime and Punishment* and as many other Dostoyevski works as you can digest. The author's descriptions are extremely accurate and include various local sights down to the distances between them. Simon Dubnow's *The Book of Life* and any of his volumes on the Jews of Russia are recommended, as are works by Aleksander Pushkin, including his poem "The Bronze Horseman," which refers to a statue of Peter the Great in Decembrist Square. *The Jews of St. Petersburg* by Mikhail Beizer (Jewish Publication Society) includes details on the city's Jewish history and sights. *From St. Petersburg to Jerusalem* by Hillel Butman (Benmir Books) tells the story of the hijack trial activists and their fate after years in Soviet prisons.

Personalities: Those native to, or who lived in, St. Petersburg include Zalman Shazar, former president of Israel; S. An-ski, author of *The Dybbuk*; Nobel Prize–winning author Joseph Brodsky; and ballet stars Galina and Valery Panov. Because of its centrality in Russia, many prominent Jews visited and passed through, including Moses Montefiore, who came in 1846 to appeal for better treatment of the Jews, and Theodor Herzl, who came in 1903 in an effort to enlist Russian government support for Jewish settlement in Palestine.

If you are planning to pass through and need help on booking flights, finding a guide or putting together a Jewish itinerary, you can profit by contacting Alexander Smuckler at All Ways International, 5 Penn Plaza, Suite 102, New York, NY 10001 (212-947-0505).

More of Jewish St. Petersburg is opening up, but on the surface it still appears to offer little to offer a Jewish traveler. As its history and personalities testify, the rich Jewish heritage is just a little bit deeper.
—*Arieh Dean Cohen and Mikhail Beizer*

Samarkand

In an oasis midway between the cities of China and the West, astride the ancient caravan route known as the Silk Road, lies Samarkand. Alexander the Great conquered it, Genghis Khan razed it, Tamerlane rebuilt it as an architectural masterpiece of the Muslim world. Today, as part of the newly independent Republic of Uzbekistan, Samarkand is emerging from a century and a quarter of rule by czars and Soviets to an uncertain future. Dozens of nationalities, including Uzbeks, Tajiks, Russians and Jews, must redefine their relations. With the constraints of communism gone, the place of Islam has become a major question.

For Samarkand's 11,000 Jews, whose roots in the region go back two millennia, the new era presents a tough choice: to rebuild their community or to leave. In the Soviet Union, the Jews of Central Asia stood out for their tenacious maintenance of tradition. The Communists seized synagogues and arrested rabbis. But behind closed gates, in the courtyards of old Jewish quarter, Jews kept circumcising their sons, teaching their children prayers, and baking *matzah*. Since 1990, Jewish life has returned to the open—and has flourished. Samarkand's Jews have established schools, a culture center, a newspaper, even a *yeshivah*. The renaissance, though, may be short-lived. For many Jews, the most important opportunity of the post-Communist age is the chance to leave. To assist *aliyah* from the region, the Jewish Agency runs direct flights from Tashkent, Uzbekistan's capital, to Tel Aviv. Some Jewish activists predict that within a generation, only a tiny remnant of the ancient community will be left.

History: Known to the Greeks as Marakanda, Samarkand was well established on the Zerafshan River when Alexander the Great conquered it in 329 B.C.E. According to one chronicler, he proclaimed that "everything I have ever heard about Marakanda is true, except that it is more beautiful than I imagined."

No record exists of when Jews arrived in the region, but it was apparently before the Common Era. The *Book of Esther*, likely written in the first or second century B.C.E., says Jews lived in "all the provinces" of the Persian empire, an area that included Samarkand. The Talmud records a rabbi's visit to the Jewish community in Marv, another Silk Road city in the region, in the fourth century.

Central Asia fell to Muslim conquerors in the first half of the eighth century, about a hundred years after Muhammad's death. In the early years of the Muslim era, a group of Jewish merchants called the Radanites (probably Persian for "those who know the way") played a key role in trade between China and Europe, and one of their routes led through Central Asia. There are records that local Jews participated in the trade; those from further afield almost certainly hitched their camels along the road to spend Sabbath with a local community.

Benjamin of Tudela, the twelfth-century Jewish traveler, never got as far east as Samarkand, but he quoted reports of 50,000 Jews in the city. The number is almost surely a wild exaggeration but indicates a well-established community nevertheless. Muslim legends of the time describe Jews as bearers of technology and manners from beyond the region. One speaks of a Jew who taught Samarkand's people how to tile walls and how to build an aqueduct out of lead.

In 1220, Genghis Khan's hordes overran Samarkand, and the Mongol nomads leveled the city. But a century and a half later, a new empire builder, Tamerlane, made Samarkand capital of a kingdom that stretched west to modern-day Syria, and brought craftsmen from throughout the realm to build his mosques and mausoleums. Local Jewish traditions say he also brought Jewish dyers and weavers from the Middle East. Those trades became the major Jewish occupations in the area. Until the Russian conquest, says historian Michael Zand of Hebrew University, a Jew could be identified by his blue hands, marked with indigo dye.

In the 1500s, the Shaybanid dynasty of Uzbeks—tribesmen from the north, speaking a Turkic tongue—made their capital in Bukhara, 170 miles to the west. Samarkand became a backwater of the new emirate. Jewish life also centered in the city of Bukhara—so much so that European visitors would later refer to all of the region's Jews as "Bukharans." But conditions were tough. The Bukharan emirs strictly enforced Islamic laws that required Jews to pay a special tax, and to wear rope belts as a sign of shame.

The nineteenth century brought big changes. In 1843 Bukharan Jews acquired rights to build their own quarter, or *mahalla,* in Samarkand. Jews who had been forced to convert to Islam in the Persian city of Mashhad also arrived in Samarkand and returned to their original faith. Meanwhile, the emirate's Jews began trading with the Russian Empire. Ironically, the notoriously anti-Semitic Russians granted special privileges to Bukharan Jewish merchants. The move paid off; in 1868, Jews sided with Russian troops in a battle for Samarkand; the Russian victors, in turn, spared the Jewish quarter as they looted the city. Bukhara itself was reduced to a Russian vassal state, and its Jews began to pour into cities like Samarkand that were directly ruled by the czar. Some became millionaires—selling cotton to the Russians, buying manufactured cloth, expanding into mining and railroads. But Russian cloth put Jewish dyers out of business; many became peddlers, cobblers, and barbers.

During the last years of Russian rule, *aliyah* became common. Wealthy Bukharans built their own quarter in Jerusalem— then the city's most elegant—and used He-

brew printing presses to publish books in their Jewish dialect of Tajik, itself a form of Persian, for the folks back home.

Then came the Communist Revolution. The last emir of Bukhara fled to Afghanistan; Samarkand served briefly as capital of the new Uzbek Soviet Socialist Republic, before that role was shifted to Tashkent in 1930. Jewish life changed beyond recognition. Many of the great merchants were arrested; others emigrated. The government expropriated their mansions. In 1917, Samarkand had more than thirty synagogues; by the late 1930s, only one was still in use. Craftsmen were forced to become factory workers. Before the border was finally sealed in 1935, an estimated 4,000 Bukharan Jews fled to Iran and Afghanistan, then traveled on to Palestine. The Soviets settled hundreds of Bukharan Jewish families on collective farms in the 1920s; the Jews returned to the cities only in the 1950s.

At first, the Communists established Jewish schools, where classes were taught in Judeo-Tajik. There was a Judeo-Tajik newspaper—albeit printed in Latin characters—and a Jewish State Theater in Samarkand. But Sovietized Jewish culture didn't last long; the theater and paper were shut in 1938, the schools soon after. The Communists did make one lasting change: opening higher education to Jews, at least to some extent.

During the Russian and Soviet periods, Ashkenazi Jews also settled in Central Asia. The biggest influx came during World War II, when the Soviets evacuated thousands of Jews from the war zone. Most left after the war, but a sizable remnant stayed on.

Community: Samarkand's Jewish community of 11,000 includes an estimated 9,000 Bukharans and 2,000 Ashkenazis—among the city's 600,000 people. Before emigration began in the 1970s the Jewish total was 15,000. An estimated 7,000 of the city's Bukharan Jews still live in the Jewish *mahalla* of the Old City, a closely bound community that provides a striking contrast to the assimilation of most Soviet Jews. Other Bukharans live near each other on the wide, shaded streets built during czarist times. Marrying a non-Jew is still an aberration. "We can point to each spot on a map of the *mahalla* and tell you who lives there," says one young Bukharan, adding: "Until recently, we didn't know the Ashkenazis and they didn't know each other."

The Bukharan community is remarkably traditional, after seven decades of holding on to religion, Converso-like, despite Communist decrees. Under the Soviets, circumcision had to be performed secretly, but "even the Communists circumcised their sons," says Bakhor Kuinov, one of the community's two rabbis. At Passover, *matzah* was baked locally. Most families keep kosher in their homes, and five ritual slaughterers supply the community with meat. But few Jews have stayed fully observant, since any public observance of religious law — like not working on the Sabbath — invited the Communists' notice.

Throughout the Soviet era, many Bukharan children received religious education in secret, at least learning to read the Hebrew alphabet and recite basic prayers. A few learned much more. Immanuel Shimonov, the city's other rabbi, received his training almost entirely in Samarkand, and in secret. "Even my parents didn't know where I went to study," he says.

Now the secrecy is gone. A second synagogue opened in 1984, without the authorities' permission, in the New City. In 1990, two Jewish schools — one in the Old City, one in the new — began providing afternoon and Sunday classes. By 1992, enrollment reached 350, and several dozen older students were studying at Shimonov's Chabad-supported *yeshivah*.

The main communal organizations, though, are the cultural centers, a model common to Soviet minority groups seeking to revive their identity. The Bukharan Jewish Cultural Center opened in 1989; in 1991, the La'or Ashkenazi Jewish Cultural Center was set up. College-age Jews didn't see a reason to split; their Ma'ayan club serves both communities. In 1992, Marek Fazilov — an international grand master who heads the Uzbekistan Chess Association — began publishing *Shofar*, a Russian-language Jewish monthly.

Language is a major issue in Uzbekistan. Almost all Bukharan Jews speak both Tajik and Russian. The older ones prefer Tajik; the young use more Russian, the key to advancement in the Soviet Union. In 1989, though, as the Union began to crumble, Uzbekistan made Uzbek its official language and adopted a timetable for switching to that tongue in most workplaces, government offices, and law courts. If they have to become proficient in a new language, many Jews figure, it might as well be Hebrew or English, so the language policy has spurred emigration.

Finding an English-speaker in Samarkand isn't easy, though. The best bet is the Ma'ayan club; the contact person is Igor Sezanaev (telephone 35-26-59), who speaks some English and is likely to know university students or graduates who can act as translators.

Samarkand's Jewish history is closely linked to the "rag trade" — from Silk Route merchants to dyers of cotton — but there's no trace of such occupations today. Two Jewish trades that developed more recently — photography and cutting hair — remain popular. Until the 1970s, it's said, nearly every barber in town was a Jew. But like other Soviet Jews, Bukharans leaped at the chance for higher education; today many are teachers, doctors, and engineers.

If there is a Jewish line of work, it's music. Jewish performers are known both for their role in Uzbek folk music and the classic Central Asian music known as *shash makom*, or "six cycles." Until the 1960s, the local music scene was reputedly as Jewish as stand-up comedy in America. Jews danced, sang the ancient Persian lyrics of *shash makom*, and played the long, slender stringed instruments and the drums that give the music its flavor. Many Jews are still musicians, but they've gone academic; children of the great performers are often musicologists, or teach instruments — like the stringed *dutar* or the *doyra*, a wide drum played with two hands — in local conservatories.

Sights: Russian colonists laid out wide avenues, shaded by spreading trees; Soviet rulers added their standardized, faceless housing projects and statues of socialist saints — the city's monument to Lenin lasted until May 1992. But the real Samarkand is the core: blue-domed mosques, an immense bazaar, and narrow Old City alleyways.

Much of that core dates back to Tamerlane and his grandson Ulugh Beg in the fourteenth and fifteenth centuries. Both are buried in a mausoleum known as Gur-Emir, graced with an azure dome that seems to float upward from a tiled drum. If the tomb arouses associations with the Taj Mahal, it's not surprising. The Indian masterpiece was built by one of Tamerlane's descendants.

Across the Old City is Shakhi-Zinda, a set of mausoleums decorated in majolica, or glazed brick, which shimmers in the desert sun. The key tomb is said to be that of Kussam Ibn Abbas, a cousin of the prophet Muhammad who brought Islam to Central Asia. Before Ibn Abbas, the region's religions included Buddhism, Christianity, Zoroastrianism, and Judaism; only the Jews were able to maintain their faith under Muslim rule. No one really knows if the body of Ibn Abbas is in the tomb, but the tradition was enough to draw Muslim pilgrims and helped Samarkand become known as the "Second Mecca." Today there is again a steady flow of pilgrims, and a white-turbaned mullah often sits outside the tomb reciting prayers for visitors.

The rhythmic repetition of archways and minarets, of glazed bricks and sea-blue domes, reaches its greatest harmony at the Rigestan, a wide plaza faced by three medieval *madrassas*—Muslim religious academies. No one studies there today, but the Soviets maintained and restored the buildings as works of art.

Nearby Mulakondov Street, a thoroughfare of the Jewish quarter, provides a very different picture of Central Asian architecture. The narrow street runs between brick and whitewashed mud walls broken only by metal or wooden gates. Don't be deceived; this is no slum. Peek through a gate, and you'll probably see a spacious courtyard, paved in brick, shaded by trees or grape arbors, and surrounded by the windows and porches of one house or several. Inside the homes, thick carpets cover floors and some walls, creating the feeling of a royal tent. An entire extended family, with uncles, grandparents, and children, may live around one court.

The *mahalla* once stretched nearly to the Rigestan but has shrunk in recent years due to emigration, and the first houses now belong to Muslim Tajiks. On a brick house along Mulakondov Street you can spot a typical Soviet icon—a painting of a man in a suit, wearing a row of medals. That's Gavriel Mulakondov, a Bukharan Jewish musician who was awarded the title of "People's Artist" in the 1930s. The street was named for him in 1982, a decade after he died. Another main street in the quarter is named after Mikhail Tolmosov, also a Jewish musician and "People's Artist."

On an alleyway off Elizarov Street is the quarter's one active synagogue, built in the 1880s by a merchant named Rafael Kalantarov. Carved wooden gates lead into a courtyard; to its left is the main synagogue hall. From outside, the building seems plain; from within, it's stunning. The forty-foot-high dome is painted white and deep blue, a stylized cloudy night sky. Pointed arches support the dome. The *bimah*, placed in the center in Sephardi style, is wood, carved with Stars of David and floral designs. In the summer, weekday morning services are held in the courtyard—matching the local Muslim custom of having an open-air summer mosque together with a roofed hall for winter prayers.

There are many other synagogues in the quarter—or at least the ghosts of synagogues. Off Mulakondov Street, for instance, is government school number 26. Enter the courtyard, climb the crumbling steps of the building on the right, and look inside. On the back wall, above a primitive fresco of the Temple Mount, are the Hebrew words "Mount Zion, the Temple, the Western Wall." Peer up at the ceiling, with its heavy rafters ornately painted in green and red, a mark of prerevolutionary wealth.

A former synagogue at 54 Tolmosov takes local history a step further. After the Soviet authorities expropriated it, they made it a hospital, then a government culture club. In 1990, the political winds shifted. Now the Bukharan Jewish Cultural Center is located in part of the facility. In 1992, the local government gave the Jewish community use of the 27-room Leviov mansion down the block. Seized in the 1930s, it also served as a hospital. Community leaders now hope to turn part of it into a Jewish kindergarten.

But there is a better-preserved monument

to Jewish wealth in Samarkand: the Regional Museum at 54 Sovietskaya Street, outside the Old City. This was once the palatial home of Avraham Kalantarov, nephew of the man who built the synagogue. Avraham got little pleasure from the building—he built just before the Revolution and was forced to "give it to the Uzbek people." The mansion became the local headquarters of the Communist party; it was made a museum after the capital moved to Tashkent. Bring a translator, and a museum guide will show you through exhibits covering everything from the region's prehistory to the Soviet period—everything but the building's own history. The hall farthest from the entrance is most ornate, the ceiling dazzlingly ornamented in geometric and floral patterns. This was Kalantarov's private synagogue. One guide told a recent visitor that the room was "a hall for guests." A visitor pointed to the balcony at the back, hidden by latticework, and explained that women sit separately in Orthodox synagogues. The guide to the museum of nonhistory insisted: "It can't be a synagogue. It's too richly ornamented."

Side Trips: Samarkand lies midway between the cities of Bukhara and Tashkent—not only physically but in character. Head west through desert and the vast cotton fields of the collective farms to Bukhara, and you'll find a provincial town saturated with history. Tashkent, to the east, is a metropolis of 2 million people with few reminders of the past.

Bukhara is a treasure trove of mosques, *madrassas*, and other monuments. Genghis Khan actually left a few structures standing when he conquered the city, and the Bukharan emirs kept building right up to the Revolution, so the architectural record stretches over one thousand years. One of the oldest buildings is the twelfth-century Kalyan minaret, a 155-foot tower of intricate brickwork. In the last century, the emirs used the minaret for executions; among those thrown from the top, it's said, were Jews who refused royal orders to convert to Islam.

The Jewish quarter, with alleys even narrower than those in Samarkand, is home to almost all of the city's estimated 3,000 Bukharan Jews. About 2,500 Ashkenazis

live scattered around the city and maintain almost no contact with the organized community. To find the main synagogue, go to the Taq-i-Sarrafan, one of the domed bazaar buildings at the center of town, and turn south on Sovietskaya Street. The synagogue is several buildings down on your right.

Tashkent, the largest city in central Asia, is an endless array of concrete housing projects, with little to attract the visitor. A powerful earthquake in 1966 leveled much of the city and helped erase its history. Several museums make up for the lack of antiquities, especially the Museum of Applied Art with its fine collection of jewelry, carpets, musical instruments, and local crafts.

Tashkent's Jewish community of over 40,000 is mainly Ashkenazi and has been emigrating rapidly. The best bet for Jewish information is to call the Jewish Agency office at 223-314 or 223-315. The Israeli emissary speaks some English and can provide names and numbers of current activists in the Samarkand community, where emigration causes considerable turnover.

Personalities: Before the Communists came, Bukharan Jews were best known as merchants and musicians. One of the most successful entrepreneurs was Natan Davidoff, who built an empire including factories, land, a coal mine, and a railroad by the time of the Revolution, when he was thirty-seven. Davidoff continued to do business under the new regime until 1923, when he escaped to France.

The greatest of the prerevolutionary musicians was Levicha Babakhanov, court singer to the last two emirs of Bukhara. Babakhanov's grandson, who still lives in Bukhara, recounts that Levicha was discovered by another court musician who walked by his house, heard him singing, and told the ruler about him. The emir, Abd-al Ahad, was pleased with the voice, but not with it coming from a Jew's throat, and demanded that the singer convert and marry a Muslim. He relented only when he heard that Levicha already had a Jewish wife and three children. Years later, when the Red Army took Bukhara, the last emir wanted Levicha to flee with him. The singer refused again.

The Communists put the merchants out of business but didn't silence the musicians. Stars of the next generation included not only Gavriel Mulakondov and Mikhail Tolmosov but also their brothers. Mikhail Kalantarov—scion of the wealthy Samarkand family—was reportedly the first Central Asian composer to study Western music. Today one of the best-known Jewish performers is Tofa Pinkhasov of Bukhara, a star of Uzbek folk music.

In Israel, many Bukharans have quietly built fortunes in the gem trade. One such clan is the Ben-Davids, who have diversified into jewelry, construction, and real estate; some reports suggest they are the richest family in Jerusalem.

Reading and Listening: Guidebooks on the former Soviet Union go out of date quickly, as prices, travel regulations, and even the names of cities keep changing. For maps, lists of sights, and practical tips, the best is *USSR: A Travel Survival Kit*, by John Noble and John King, from the Lonely Planet series.

Samarkand is mentioned in three medieval classics—the Jewish *Travels of Rabbi Benjamin of Tudela*, the Christian *Marco Polo's Travels*, and the Muslim *Book of the Thousand Nights and One Night*, in which it is part of the setting for the opening story.

For a taste of modern Central Asia, hearing is better than reading. A cassette put out in 1991, *Bukhara: Musical Cross-roads of Asia*, includes pieces by non-Jewish and Jewish performers, including Tofa Pinkhasov. (It is issued by Smithsonian/Folkway Recordings and distributed by Rounder Records, One Camp Street, Cambridge, MA 02140.)

Recommendations: Most travelers reach Uzbekistan on Aeroflot from Moscow; there are flights to Tashkent, Samarkand, and Bukhara. Uzbekistan is trying to expand its direct air links with other countries, including Israel, and an El Al route from Tel Aviv to Tashkent may soon be a reality. Between cities in the republic, there are buses, trains, and planes, but locals warn that increasing crime makes it unsafe for foreigners to take the trains alone. You can also hire a driver to take you from one city to another.

There are no kosher or vegetarian restaurants in Samarkand. But unlike much of the former Soviet Union, Uzbekistan isn't suffering from food shortages. The bazaars are well stocked with fruits and vegetables of every variety, and with the flat, circular local bread. If you keep kosher, though, you'll need to pack your own protein.

The local custom is to leave your shoes at the door of a house, so bring footwear you can take off and put on easily. The main hotel in Samarkand is Intourist's Hotel Samarkand, but no one has much good to say about it. If you want luxury, stay home; this is a journey for the adventurous.

—*Gershom Gorenberg*

San Francisco

What kind of place sends two Jewish women to the United States Senate? A place of beauty and openness, a place that's good at building bridges. It is perhaps no accident that Dianne Feinstein of San Francisco and Barbara Boxer of Marin County live at opposite ends of the Golden Gate Bridge.

Whether it is warmed by sunlight or enveloped in fog, San Francisco is a city of unsurpassed beauty. Breathtaking views greet the visitor in every direction. It's a compact metropolis where just a few blocks can transport you from the cafés of Europe to the markets of Asia. It's the city where Humphrey Bogart stalked in *The Maltese Falcon* and Steve McQueen raced in *Bullitt*. It's the place that Mikhail Gorbachev, after his first visit, declared that if he were President Bush, he would charge a tax for the privilege of living. And it's a city where Jews never had to fight for acceptance because they were here from the very beginning.

History: Fewer than 900 people lived in San Francisco in 1848 when the cry of "Gold! Gold from the American River!" rang through the muddy, slumbering streets. In the ensuing year, 40,000 fortune hunters poured through the Golden Gate. Among them were adventurous Jews. Their journeys started with an arduous trek from Europe—mainly from Germany, although there were many from England and France, Polish Jews from the Prussian province of Posen, and a handful of Sephardim. Once in the New World, they faced the hazardous trip overland, the equally dangerous route around Cape Horn, or the malaria-infested Isthmus of Panama. When they arrived in California, most of the Jews stopped short of scrambling into the hills

with a pickax digging for gold. There were surer fortunes to be made outfitting those who gambled on getting rich in one leap. Mining towns were soon dotted with shacks whose proprietors were selling clothing, cigars, tobacco, food, and other necessities. A French Jewish intellectual, Daniel Levy, wrote to the editor of the Archives Israelites in France, "This preference for dealing in soft goods has reached the point that, in some mining areas where there are convenient terms for everything, these types of stores are called 'Jewshops,' even when run by Christians."

Their feet firmly planted on the path to riches, the immigrants left their "Jewshops" in the care of relatives from the old country and moved the base of their operations to San Francisco. Among those whose family fortunes started in this manner were Levi Strauss (clothing), Anthony Zellerbach (paper supplies), Joseph Brandenstein (MJB Coffee), Aaron Fleishhacker (banking) and William Haas (wholesale groceries).

The San Francisco in which they settled was a sprawling jumble of tents and shacks ablaze at night with the light of its many saloons. Inside, the activity centered around prostitution and gambling as well as drinking and brawling. The Jews, used to a far different lifestyle, brought with them a stabilizing influence. An article in the *San Francisco Herald* in 1851 demonstrates the regard that they enjoyed: "The Israelites constitute a numerous and intelligent class of our citizens and conduct themselves with great propriety and decorum. They are industrious and enterprising and make worthy members of our community."

The first Jewish services on the West Coast were held on Rosh Hashanah in 1849—a year before California became a

461

state—when 30 Jews responded to a notice in the local newspaper. The services were held in a tent near the waterfront. By Yom Kippur the number of worshipers had grown to nearly 50. A year later, 182 Jews, more than half the Jewish households in San Francisco, contributed money for a synagogue. But division arose in the ranks over which ritual, Polish or German, would be used. This dispute led to the formation of two congregations. To this day, you can get an argument about which congregation was organized first. What is certain is that one, comprised of the Germans mostly from Bavaria and three native-born Sephardim, organized Congregation Emanu-El meaning, "God is with us." The other congregation, Congregation Sherith Israel ("Loyal remnant of Israel"), was composed mostly of Polish Jews from Posen and English Jews. Both began life as Orthodox and today are the city's two leading Reform congregations.

The massive earthquake that hit San Francisco on April 12, 1906, and the subsequent fires that swept the city were, like the city itself, nondiscriminating. Among the institutions destroyed were three synagogues, the B'nai B'rith library, the headquarters of the Eureka Society (forerunner of the Jewish Family Service), the school and clinic of the Temple Emanu-El Sisterhood, and the offices of three Jewish newspapers.

Community: From the beginning Jews set a pattern for developing a sense of community, setting up the first two welfare organizations in San Francisco. In 1850 the Eureka Benevolent Society was founded to help the needy. A Jewish hospital, Mount Zion, which recently affiliated with the University of California's San Francisco Medical Center, dates back more than a century. Jews initiated innovative trends in social welfare. The Pacific Hebrew Orphan Asylum, sponsored by B'nai B'rith, which opened its doors in 1877, was the predecessor of Homewood Terrace, where small groups of orphans lived in a familylike setting in cottages with a team of social workers acting as mother and father in each home. In the 1930s, when young Jewish girls from outside the city came to San Francisco to work, the Emanu-El Residence Club, sponsored by the Women's Guild of Congregation Emanu-El, offered a proper place for the girls to live with everything from parlors to entertain male visitors to courses in etiquette to show them how. They were housed in a beautiful Julia Morgan–designed residence on Laguna and Page Streets, which is now a Zen Buddhist center. More recently, ten years of Jewish community effort resulted in the opening of Menorah Park, a 150-unit facility for senior citizens, a subsidized housing project adjacent to the San Francisco Jewish Community Center at 3200 California Street. Menorah Park, geared for individuals who are able to live independently in a community setting, has a waiting list so long that applications have not been accepted since 1990. Forty percent of the residents are recent Russian immigrants.

The Russians are just the latest wave of newcomers to San Francisco's Jewish community. In addition to thousands of American-born Jews who discovered the California dream in the decades since World War II, the community has been fed by Eastern European Jews at the beginning of the century and refugees from Germany in the 1930s and 1940s. Today, approximately 223,000 people live in the Bay Area's 90,000 Jewish households, comprising the sixth-largest Jewish community in the country.

In San Francisco there is no one Jewish section. The nearest thing the city ever had to a ghetto was the Fillmore Street area from the 1920s to the 1940s, where kosher restaurants, wonderful bakeries like the "Ukraine," and kosher markets flourished. Two Orthodox synagogues were located there, including one whose Hebrew teacher was the father of Yehudi Menuhin. The imposing Congregation Beth Israel at Fillmore and Geary had a huge stained-glass window that bathed the neighborhood in kaleidoscopic color on sunny days. When the congregation moved to the southern part of the city, the synagogue became the home of the ill-fated People's Church of Jim Jones, who led his followers to mass suicide in Guyana.

Only their pocketbooks determine where Jews live in San Francisco. They are scattered from Pacific Heights, Nob Hill, and

Sea Cliff to the Richmond and Sunset districts. The high price of real estate in the city and the desire for a more countrified lifestyle have sent many Jews into the suburbs, from the peninsula all the way down to San Jose, in Marin County across the Golden Gate Bridge, and across the bay in Alameda and Contra Costa Counties. Down the peninsula wealthy Jews built country estates in Hillsborough, Atherton, Los Altos, and Los Gatos. Young couples with children soon followed as developments like Millbrae and Foster City were built. Equally lovely Jewish homes can be found in Marin in communities like Belvedere, Tiburon, and Sausalito. Jews on their way up tend to settle in Larkspur, Mill Valley, and San Rafael. Soldiers from the east who saw the glories of the area during World War II and came back to raise families here settled in East Bay communities like Concord, Pleasant Hill, Lafayette, and Walnut Creek. Berkeley, with the University of California as its anchor, attracted — and still does — the individualists and the experimenters.

Everywhere Jews have gone, Jewish institutions have followed. The huge Marin Jewish Community Center (200 North San Pedro Road) that opened recently adjacent to Temple Rodof Sholom in San Rafael forms a focal point of Jewish activity for the Marin area. On the peninsula, there is the Albert L. Schultz JCC (655 Arastradero Road) in Palo Alto; Contra Costa's JCC is located in Walnut Creek (1355 Creekside Drive), the hub of Contra Costa; Berkeley has its community center (1414 Walnut Street) and there is one for the Oakland-Piedmont area (3245 Sheffield Avenue). Synagogues have likewise proliferated in the suburbs, and Jewish book and gift shops as well as innumerable bagel shops all calling themselves "the best this side of New York." There is still no strong Jewish fulcrum of kosher butchers or kosher restaurants, but with Chabad houses now moving out into the suburbs (there is one in Marin as well as in Berkeley adjacent to the UC campus), that may soon change, too.

Sights: What better place to start than at the Swig Tourist and Convention Center (a gift from the children of Jewish philanthropist Ben Swig to honor their father's seventy-fifth birthday) at the foot of Powell and Market near the cable car and adjacent to the BART (Bay Area Rapid Transit) station? Here you can pick up pamphlets, directions to all the area's major attractions and have patient volunteers answer all your questions

It has been said that San Francisco wears its past like a string around the finger. Reminders are everywhere — in the rusted fortifications in the Presidio which once guarded the entrance to the Golden Gate; in the four-foot-thick adobe walls of the Mission Dolores, the city's oldest structure; in the hitching-post at California and Leidesdorff Streets, and in the bronze plaque marking the original shoreline at Market and First streets.

And if the metaphor fits, it is also true that San Francisco wears its Jewish past like the fringes on a *tallit* draped around the shoulders of the city. Jewish "first family" names are everywhere. In Golden Gate park with the De Young Museum (after the founders of the *San Francisco Chronicle*) and the Steinhart Aquarium; out by the beach with Fleishhacker Zoo; in the Lakeside area with Sigmund Stern Grove (Stern was a nephew of Levi Strauss); in the financial district, with the wall decoration on the side of the Union Bank Building at 350 California Street where a marker designates that "These walrus heads carved from Sierra granite are from the Alaska Commercial Building which occupied this site until 1975," the giant company founded by brothers-in-law Louis Sloss and Lewis Gerstle, who had a virtual monopoly on the sale of its seals and salmon. The signs are also on Valencia Street in the Mission district, with the yellow-and-white clapboard Levi Strauss factory where the first Levis were made; on Post Street off Union Square in the newly enlarged Gump's, San Francisco's first Oriental and fine arts establishment, founded by Abe Gump more than a century ago; and on Geary Street, in one of the city's finest women's department stores, founded by the Dutch-born Jewess Mary Ann Magnin but called I. Magnin's in deference to her husband.

In addition to the older institutions

bearing the names of Jewish founders or benefactors, a new place worth a visit is the Cyril and Anna Magnin jade room in the Asian Art Museum, a wing of the De Young Museum in Golden Gate Park.

San Francisco also has its share of more explicitly Jewish sights. One of the city's newer museums is the Jewish Museum of San Francisco, in the Jewish Community Federation building at 121 Steuart Street. It features changing exhibitions of Jewish art, culture, history, and contemporary issues. Holiday celebrations and workshops encourage multigenerational activities. Museum and shop hours are: Sunday through Friday, 10 A.M. to 4 P.M. Tours are available, led by college docents.

The city's two largest synagogues are must-see attractions, a far cry from the tents in which they were first housed. Congregation Emanu-El, at Arguello and Lake Streets, recently underwent a multimillion dollar renovation of its present home, originally dedicated in April 1926. Designed by architect Arthur Brown, Jr., who built San Francisco's city hall following the 1906 earthquake and fire, the magnificently domed temple combines Byzantine features such as its great red cupola suggestive of the Hagia Sophia in Istanbul, and antique black marble columns with such California touches as open patios. The centerpiece of the sanctuary is the freestanding ark with thick bronze doors and jewel-encrusted walls covered with the symbols of the twelve tribes of Israel. Stained-glass windows, donated by the Haas family, feature abstract designs of fire and water.

Emanu-El often hosts exhibits of works by Bay Area Jewish artists, and it also has periodic exhibits from its permanent collection of Jewish ritual objects. The synagogue is a site of sporting, as well as religious, interest; if a World Series match between the New York Yankees and the Brooklyn Dodgers was a "Subway Series," then the 1989 match between the San Francisco Giants and the Oakland Athletics was the Emanu-El Series, since the team's owners, Walter Haas (A's) and Bob Lurie (who sold the Giants in 1992) are both members.

Sherith Israel's present home (2266 California Street) was consecrated in 1905. Designed in Romanesque style with Eastern overtones, it is a square building with a

Bay Byzantine: A masterpiece that hosts the tribes of Israel and the World Series

large central dome; the architect was Albert Pissis, a graduate of L'Ecole des Beaux Arts in Paris. The interior, with its decorated walls and ceiling, shows the Sephardic influence. The intricately carved woodwork is of Honduras mahogany; the Italian stained glass features biblical themes in dominant reds. The ark, built in 1854, has been used in every temple built by the congregation.

Sherith Israel's imposing structure was one of the few public buildings in the city to come through the earthquake and fire unscathed. Equally important, the temple's extensive library and collection of pioneer records were saved. The synagogue's survival, however, did no good for one of San Francisco's more notorious Jewish figures, the political boss Abe Ruef. After the earthquake the building's sanctuary, auditorium, and schoolrooms were turned over to the city for use as an interim Hall of Justice, and it was here that the graft trials of Ruef, Mayor Eugene Schmitz, and the board of supervisors were held.

If you want to know more about the gold rush era, visit the Wells Fargo History Museum at 420 Montgomery (near California Street). Here you will see an original stagecoach, learn all about the Pony Express riders, and see the portrait of I. W. Hellman, president from 1905 — when his Nevada Bank of San Francisco merged with Wells Fargo — to 1920.

You can watch the sewing of the famed Levi's "501s," the original jeans with the copper rivets, manufactured in the historic building at 250 Valencia Street. Tours are given on Wednesdays at 10:30 A.M. and 1 P.M.; they are designed for schools and organizations, but if you call ahead (415-565-9153), you can join in. A nice contrast to the little clapboard plant is the beautiful red brick Levi Plaza, world headquarters of the company, at 1155 Battery Street.

One of the most beautiful vantage points in the city also stands as a grim reminder of the Holocaust. George Segal's sculpture, installed in Lincoln Park in 1984, overlooks a sweeping view of the Golden Gate. *The Holocaust*, a bronze work coated stark white, depicts ten bodies heaped on the ground with a figure standing nearby in prison clothes peering through a barbed-wire fence. It has become both a work of public art and a community rallying spot. Though vandals occasionally try to desecrate the spot, visitors will often find fresh flowers left by anonymous donors.

The Haas-Lilienthal House, a Victorian located in Pacific Heights at 2007 Franklin Street, was given to the city by two of San Francisco's original Jewish families, who lived in it between 1886 and 1972. It offers visitors a look at genteel living in that bygone era. For tours, phone (415) 441-3000. While you're there, you might want to pick up a delightful book by a descendent, Frances Rothmann, titled *The Haas Sisters: A Look Back with Love*, detailing the social life of the time.

The oldest Jewish museum in the area, and one of the premier Jewish sights, is across the bay in Berkeley. The Judah Magnes Museum, at 2911 Russell Street, is housed in the lovely Burke mansion, once the residence of a 19th-century railroad official. Inside, you'll discover art (from Moritz Oppenheim to Maurice Sendak), artifacts, rare manuscripts, ceremonial objects, and important resource materials. Among the remarkable items in the collection are Torah binders, ceremonial silver, *Ner Tamids* from around the world, and ark decorations from India. Among the exhibits mounted at the Magnes in recent years have been those on underground Jewish art from the former Soviet Union and the history of Jewish posters.

The museum's collection also includes Holocaust artifacts and an extensive array of coins and medals. In addition, it houses the Western Jewish History Center and the Reutlinger Gallery, the scene of ever-changing exhibits of Jewish artists. Docent tours are available; the museum is open Sunday through Thursday, 10 A.M. to 4 P.M.

Day trips around the Bay Area include tours of the wine country in Napa and Sonoma. A new way to see the area is from a deluxe train, enjoying en route a gourmet meal with, of course, wine. Among the wineries to be visited are three kosher ones: Gan Eden, in Sebastopol (707-829-5686); Hagafen Cellars, in Napa (707-252-0781); and Weinstock Cellars, in Healdsburg (707-433-5607).

If boat rides are more to your liking, try the Angel Island Ferry, at Fisherman's Wharf, Pier 43. For $8.00 a round trip you not only get a wonderful view of the city and the bay, but a chance to visit (and picnic, if you wish) on Angel Island, the Ellis Island of the west. Here you will see the barracks where Chinese immigrants were held for processing (and deported back to China in many cases). Poignant poetry and graffiti still line the walls.

Culture: From the high-profile Jewish Film Festival to Jewish theaters and its Jewish museums, there is no question that the Bay area boasts of a rich environment for Jewish arts and culture. The area is a fertile ground for Jewish artists who experiment with a wide variety of media and modes. JACOB (Jewish Arts Community of the Bay) is the brainchild of Jacob Omanim, an organization that attempts to encourage and support the many independent creative endeavors and mounts periodic exhibits of Jewish crafts.

The award-winning Jewish Film Festival is run by Deborah Kaufman and Janis Plotkin, codirectors. The operation, which began here screening movies in theaters in San Francisco and Berkeley, is now international. Recent Jewish film festivals have been screened in Moscow and in Madrid (marking the five hundredth anniversary of the expulsion of Jews from Spain in 1492). Locally, the festival is held the last two weeks in July (one week in San Francisco, one week in Berkeley). For information on where to find it in the Bay Area or closer to where you live, call (415) 548-0556.

Three Jewish theaters thrive in the area.

One, the Traveling Jewish Theater, gives contemporary form to the streams of visionary experience that run through Jewish history, culture and imagination. They use a variety of themes, forms, and language including English, Yiddish, Hebrew, and Ladino to create original theater (telephone 415-861-4880). The New Jewish Theater is dedicated to exploring the Jewish experience by presenting English-language plays by well-known playwrights who interpret Jewish concerns. The Berkeley Jewish Theater is a repertory company that works out of the Jewish Community Center of Berkeley-Richmond.

Berkeley is also the home of the Klezmorim, a six-person brass and percussion ensemble that has been reviving the Jewish folk music of Eastern Europe. They have received national attention since a Carnegie Hall performance in 1983 and a Grammy nomination for their album, "Metropolis."

Intellectual life, like artistic creativity, is fertile and freestyle in the Bay Area. The Hillel Foundation of the University of California at Berkeley (2736 Bancroft Way) runs a Lehrhaus Judaica program with a wide range of courses. A very successful educational experiment under the direction of Fred Rosenbaum, the Lehrhaus has been "exported" to Stanford, San Francisco State, and other temple and center sites.

Congregation Beth Shalom in San Francisco, at Fourteenth Avenue and Clement Street, has a stimulating endowed lecture series which brings international as well as local personalities to speak. Temple Emanu-El offers a popular adult education program, and the Swig-endowed Department of Jewish Studies at the Jesuit University of San Francisco also brings noted national and international personalities to lecture. The American Jewish Committee sponsors "Inquiry Forum" programs on current events, which are open to the public. Call (415) 777-3820 for information.

The best way to find out about cultural programs or speakers is to pick up a copy of the *Northern California Jewish Community Bulletin*, published weekly and sold at one hundred newsstands throughout the Bay Area as well as in front of all Jewish centers. Once a year the paper also prints *Resource: A Guide to Jewish Life in Northern California*. You can get a copy for $5.00 by phoning the paper at (415) 957-9340.

It may not be great theater, and Fugazi Hall isn't Carnegie Hall, but a show that captures the fun and the zaniness of San Francisco is Beach Blanket Babylon, a musical satire on current events and personalities that has been running since 1972. Produced by Steve Silver, it depends for its laughs on the skyscraper hats worn by the cast that require special body harnesses to anchor them. When Queen Elizabeth and Prince Philip visited a few years ago, they marveled at the huge Big Ben that topped one hat, and remained goggle-eyed as the hat opened to reveal Parliament on one side, Buckingham Palace on another and pictures of the couple's children in the center. You'll need reservations well in advance (415-421-4222).

Personalities: Long before Dianne Feinstein and Barbara Boxer were elected to the Senate in 1992, Jews of the Bay Area were conspicuous in civic participation. In politics they have had leading roles from the beginning. Elkah and Isaac Cardozo were elected to the first state legislature; Washington Bartlett was an early mayor of San Francisco and later governor of California; Adolph Sutro, the engineer and bibliophile, was another mayor; Julius Kahn was elected to Congress and when he died before his term was over, his wife, Florence, was elected to his place, becoming the first Jewish congresswoman. Similarly, Sala Burton in recent times was elected to complete the term of her late husband, Congressman Philip Burton. Cyril Magnin, grandson of Mary Ann and I. Magnin, was San Francisco's chief of protocol, a volunteer job he created for himself, adding much to the luster of his beloved city. Feinstein herself was the first Jewish woman to be president of the city's board of supervisors and went on to become its first woman mayor; Boxer stepped up to the Senate after five terms in the House of Representatives.

A man who combined both the sense of community and the tradition of participating in politics was the real estate investor Benjamin Harrison Swig. Arriving from Boston in 1944 (at the age of fifty-one), Swig decided to make San Francisco his permanent residence when he bought the Fairmont Hotel. The son of an immigrant from Lithuania, he brought with him a rich tradition of *tzedakah*. He also became a Democratic kingmaker, taking an active part in presidential campaigns beginning with Adlai Stevenson, in the gubernatorial campaigns of Edmund (Pat) Brown, and in the mayoralty campaigns of Joseph Alioto. Like the scions of the Haas family, Ben's sons, Melvin and Richard, continue to carry on in the openhanded tradition of their father.

Other landmarks with Jewish origins or angles include the Bay Area's rail system, BART, which owes much to Adrian Falk, who served on the BART board for twelve years, eight of them as president; a plaque acknowledging his contribution stands at the Embarcadero station. Joseph Baerman Strauss was the builder of the Golden Gate Bridge. Other Jewish personalities past and present include Alice B. Toklas and Gertrude Stein, the cartoonist Rube Goldberg, violinists Isaac Stern and Yehudi Menuhin, author Irving Stone, and Herb Caen, whose column in the *San Francisco Chronicle* is perhaps the most widely read in the Bay Area. Oakland's Judah Magnes, for whom the museum is named, was not only the first rabbi born west of the Mississippi, but also a leading Zionist and a founder of Hebrew University in Jerusalem.

Eating: Strictly kosher restaurants include the Lotus Garden in Chinatown at 532 Grant Avenue (Asian vegetarian cuisine, under rabbinical supervision); the Mount Zion Hospital cafeteria, 1600 Divisadero Street (packaged, take-out, or on the premises), and Natan's Grill and Restaurant at 420 Geary (Israeli and Middle Eastern). In the East Bay, the Holy Land Kosher Restaurant, 677 Grand Avenue, Oakland, features homemade Ashkenazic and Sephardic dishes, and the Pita King at 1607 Palos Verde Mall in Walnut Creek is a kosher vegetarian deli.

If you have a sweet tooth, a unique candy store is Joseph Schmidt Confections, at 3489 Sixteenth Street, near the Castro district. Schmidt, an Israeli of Austrian descent, learned candy making from his grandfather. You've seen his truffles at stores like Neiman-Marcus and Macy's, but here you can buy the prize-winning designs from his kitchens, including all-chocolate long-stemmed roses, bouquets of tulips (dark chocolate with white chocolate flowers) in chocolate vases, and the white chocolate swans so popular with brides.

For lunch or dinner when you want a delicious meal as well as the good feeling from helping a worthy cause, try dining at Delancey Street, in its new multimillion dollar home on the Embarcadero at Brannan Street. The complex is run by psychologist Mimi Silbert, director of the Delancey Street Foundation, a self-help program for ex-convicts and recovering drug abusers; the dining room is one of the many training facilities on the beautiful complex. Don't expect anything amateurish. According to a restaurant critic from the *San Francisco Examiner*, "It is thoroughly professional and thoroughly enjoyable." You'll also enjoy the great waterfront view from either the indoor or outdoor areas.

Reading: A look back to the past is provided by Harriet Lane Levy, a friend of Gertrude Stein and Alice B. Toklas, in an autobiographical novel, *920 O'Farrell Street* (Arno Press), about the Polish Jews ("us") and German Jews ("them") in early San Francisco. Life in the Fillmore district during the Depression is remembered by journalist Jerry Flamm in *Good Life in the Hard Times* (Chronicle Books). Howard Fast's trilogy—*The Immigrants, The Second Generation,* and *The Establishment* (Houghton Mifflin)—portrays the sweep of San Francisco Jewish history in fiction. A glimpse of Jewish San Francisco's social life can be found in *Our City: The Jews of San Francisco* by Irena Narell (Howell-North) and *House of Harmony: Concordia-Argonaut's First 130 Years* by Bernice Scharlach (Western Jewish History Center of the Judah Magnes Museum), about the elite Jewish men's club founded in 1854. Fred Rosenbaum has delineated the history of Oakland Jewry in *Free to Choose: The Making of a Jewish Community in the American West* and the development of Congregation Emanu-El in *Architects of Reform,* both published by the Western Jewish History Center of the Magnes Museum.

Miscellany: Three *mikvehs* ring the Bay Area: Mikvah Israel B'nai David in San Francisco (415-921-4070), Beth Jacob Community Mikvah (510-482-1147) and Mikvah Taharas Israel, sponsored by Chabad, in Berkeley (510-848-7221).

In the grand tradition of "two Jews, three opinions," San Francisco now has three gay congregations. There is the Reform Congregation Sha'ar Zahov, and two Independents: Ahavat Shalom and Shir Nashim. The latter was formed for Jewish lesbians and bisexual women.

Recommendations: In a city where tourism is the number one industry, there is a plethora of good hotels no matter what your price range. In the luxury class is the Fairmont Hotel on Nob Hill, which, because it is also the locale of most Jewish organizational affairs, is like a family gathering place. Under the presidency of Richard Swig, Ben's son, the Fairmont is a bastion of tradition, encompassing both the original seven-story structure damaged by the earthquake and fire and reopened in 1907 and the twenty-one-story "Fairmont Tower," added in the 1960s. The hotel has kosher catering facilities.

In the middle price range, there's the Sheraton-at-Fisherman's-Wharf, 2500 Mason Street, across the street from Pier 39, four blocks from Ghirardelli Square, and two blocks from both cable car turnarounds. If you enjoy strolling, you can take a delightful twenty-five-minute walk from the elegantly appointed hotel, stopping for a cappuccino in a North Beach (the Italian quarter) café, browsing in the markets of Chinatown, and ending up in Union Square.

If cheery, immaculate pension-type accommodations are more your style, the best bargain in town is Hotel David, 480 Geary Street, a block from Union Square. This is a bed-and-breakfast hotel that also includes free dinner. Owner David Apfelbaum, whose David's Deli/Restaurant/Patisserie next door has been a favorite of locals and visiting celebrities since 1952, invites you to select from the breakfast menu cheese blintzes, potato pancakes, onions and eggs, and so on. The dinner menu includes such goodies as baked brisket of beef, kosher Chicago knockwurst, and Hungarian-style chicken paprika.

Warmed by sun or enveloped in fog, you can find Jewish sights and tastes in the city by the bay. And if a Jewish traveler stays long enough, the odds on being elected to the Senate are greater than anywhere else.

—Bernice Scharlach

Santiago

Cafecito (a little coffee) . . . *momentito* (a little moment) . . . *piedricito* (a little stone). . . . The diminutive comes easily to Chileans, and its frequent use tells much about the people and their country.

Some say this linguistic idiosyncracy reflects a national humbleness, a self-effacing humility derived from having been for so long a backwater. With desert in the north, Cape Horn and the Antarctic in the south, the Andes in the east, and twenty-seven hundred miles of west-coast Pacific, Chile was until recently as isolated as an island. An afterthought for both the Spaniards who first claimed it and the immigrants who chose it, its evolution has differed from other Latin American states.

Because its riches were not instantly evident—gold and silver did not flood its byways—most early arrivals came to settle, not plunder. Because the conquistadors wiped out most local Indians, Chile's citizenry has from early times been Western based. Because the country drew from lands beyond the Latin, including England, Germany, and Yugoslavia, its populace has long been polyethnic. The father of the country was Bernardo O'Higgins.

And notwithstanding two decades of unrest, Chile claims one of Latin America's more democratic histories. In a nation of pleasant, mild people (even their *empanadas* are reputedly less hot than other countries'), Chileans-in-the-street say they were deeply shaken by the turmoil and conflict created by three years of Salvador Allende's leftist rule (1970–73) and the subsequent seventeen years of General Augusto Pinochet's military government.

Though they now flood the sidewalks of Santiago with happy bustle and hope the worst is behind them, Chileans also recognize they are in a time of transition. On the verge of becoming a truly developed country, with their current efficiency and prosperity they admit confusion over the past, present, and most of all the future. And in this conundrum, the Jews share as much in the puzzle and puzzlement as anyone.

History: Jews have been woven into the Chilean fabric from its earliest days. When Diego de Almagro traveled south from Peru questing for gold and silver and discovered Chile in 1535, one of his officers was Rodrigo de Orgonos, a reputed Converso. Accompanying the conquistador Pedro de Valdivia, who founded Santiago at the foot of Santa Lucia Hill in 1541, was Diego García de Caceres, another reputed Converso. When a genealogical pamphlet was printed in Lima in 1619 naming de Caceres as a Jew, it caused a scandal, further heightened because other prominent families were cited as well.

Shortly thereafter the local inquisitional tribunal—based in Lima, from which Chile was then administered—created one of its leading martyrs by arresting Francisco Maldonado de Silva, a prominent surgeon. De Silva, credited with bringing the first medical texts to Chile, was the director of Santiago's leading hospital, San Juan de Diós, then located in the vicinity of today's Holiday Inn Crowne Plaza. He told his sister that he continued to live according to their Jewish heritage and she confessed to her priest. During twelve years in prison he circumcised himself with a pocket knife, fortified other Conversos in their faith, and even converted some Catholics to Judaism. He was burned at the stake on January 23, 1639, in the largest auto-da-fé yet held in the New World.

Despite continued inquisitional persecution of varying degrees, however, Converso settlement in Chile persisted throughout the seventeenth century. In London in 1656, ex-Converso Simón de Caceres tried to persuade Oliver Cromwell to let him lead a military contingent of Jews to conquer the "Wilde Custe" of Chile. Secret Judaizing so persisted that in 1699, the Inquisition in Lima was informed of twenty-eight area Conversos.

Though Jewish blood probably runs in many older Chilean families, Converso traces — and inquisitional activity against them — disappeared during the eighteenth century, when Chile closed its doors to foreigners. The Inquisition itself, however, was abolished only in the early nineteenth century as Chile began its struggle for independence. In this it was aided and abetted by descendants of Conversos.

In 1811, General José Miguel Carrera, who traced his heritage back to Diego García de Caceres, was nominated the first president of an independent Chile. Juan Albano Peyreyra, in whose home O'Higgins spent his childhood, may have had Jewish ancestry. And Diego Portales, the statesman whose concepts produced Chile's 1833 constitution, which provided the basis for Chilean government until 1925, also claimed lineage from Caceres. (His ideas calling for a strong impersonal executive were often noted by Pinochet.)

Though Roman Catholicism became the state religion of independent Chile and the open practice of other religions was forbidden, individual Jews throughout the nineteenth century made their way to — and in — the country. Among those arriving through the port of Valparaíso to settle there or move on to Santiago and beyond were Julio Bernstein, founder of Chile's first sugar refinery in Vina del Mar, bordering Valparaíso; Pedro Herzl, Chile's first Jewish doctor of the period; and the Danish-born Martin Levison Bloch, who in 1862 became the first Jew in the country's diplomatic service.

Though by 1865 Chilean law allowed non-Catholics to practice their religion at home and establish private schools, with succeeding laws permitting civil marriage and more religious tolerance, most of these Jews converted, married Spanish Catholics, and assimilated. Only toward the end of the nineteenth century, when Chile was re-ceiving other immigrant groups as well, did the roots of today's Jewish community take hold.

The first significant wave of Jews were Russians, initially those escaping pogroms and coming via Moisesville in Argentina. Shortly thereafter came those avoiding the effects of World War I and the Russian Revolution. As early as 1874, the Elias Braun family led the way to Chilean Patagonia.

Saloman Sack, a steel magnate, financed the University of Chile's School of Architecture. Also of Sack's generation were the radical senator Angel Faivovich and such confidants of Chilean president Arturo Alessandri as Naum Trumper and Daniel Schweitzer Speisky, who later represented Chile at the United Nations as both ambassador and president of the Security Council. Among Schweitzer's contemporaries were his brother, Miguel, a minister of justice, and Benjamin Cohen, a journalist with Chile's leading newspaper, El Mercurio, who became a UN undersecretary-general.

Succeeding the Russian influx by only a few years were those Jews who laid the basis for Chile's Sephardic community — newcomers from areas of the Balkan peninsula now held by Greece, Turkey, and Yugoslavia. These Ladino and Spanish speakers initially settled around Temuco, south of Santiago. With this group came the subsequently prominent Testa, Rueste, and Albala families. With the advent of Hitler a later immigrant wave arrived from Germany, followed by a Hungarian one after the 1956 uprising.

Other Chileans calling themselves Jews but not so recognized are some sects of Indians in the southern regions around Curacautín, Cunco and Gorbea. These groups, discovered in this century and using the name Iglesia Israelita, claim to have descended from Conversos and observe certain Jewish commandments and customs such as the Saturday Sabbath, a pork-free diet, and the Magen David on buildings and documents. They were represented in 1919 at the first Zionist-oriented Congress of Chilean Jewry, and a handful even made aliyah. But though alert to the appeal of stories about secret candelabras and the like, contemporary scholarship leans toward the conclusion that the Indians picked up their beliefs much more recently from Christian missionaries.

Chile has explicitly separated church and state since the 1920s. In this tolerant situation—marred only by some anti-Semitic agitation in the 1920s and 1930s—Jews have felt secure enough to participate in all aspects of life, including politics. Those willing to hazard an opinion say that prior to 1970 Jews were politically more or less balanced between right and left. Allende's ascendance changed the equation. During his regime some Jews were prominent, including Jacques Chonchol, minister of agriculture; Jacobo Shaulson, a Radical party Parliament member on the constitutional tribunal; Enrique Testa, professor of commercial law at the University of Chile; Jaime Faivovich, mayor of Santiago in 1972 (later held morally responsible for a couple of murders); and Volodia Teitelbaum, a senator and leader of the Communist party (who recently returned from exile). Yet under Allende about 10,000 of Chile's estimated 35,000 Jews left the country and veered right. In fact, the Air Force's second-in-command, Brigadier General José Berdichevsky Scher, was among those responsible for the bombing of La Moneda, the presidential palace in which Allende died. While individual Jews, particularly artists, did speak out against human rights abuses—and some, like Rabbi Angel Kreiman, did work with the church-supported La Vicaría de La Solidaridad—when democracy returned much of the Jewish community, like much of the Chilean society as a whole, confronted its rather passive stance.

One thing Jews appreciated about Pinochet was his positive attitude toward Israel—a matter of particular concern in Chile, where the Arab population of 350,000 is mostly Palestinian. Though primarily Christian descendants of immigrants who first arrived at the century's start along with Jews—with whom many do business—they now claim membership in the largest Palestinian diaspora community outside the Middle East. Their pressure led a basically pro-Israel Chile to abstain during the 1947 UN Partition vote.

Community: Possibly because of its pattern of immigration, possibly because of an unthreatening social climate, the Jewish community of Chile today is not coalesced. The church is a liberalizing force (a Jew, Santiago Benadava, has been Chile's ambassador to the Vatican); Jewish students prefer the private Catholic University to the University of Chile. Though an umbrella organization represents its interests to the general public, the community—about 95 percent of which resides in Santiago—is internally fragmented.

Though most of Chile's 30,000 Jews (including returnees under Pinochet) are well entrenched in the middle and upper-middle classes, and sometimes intermingle socially as well as religiously, various ethnic groups maintain their own synagogues.

The best known and most inclusive congregation is primarily of Eastern European Ashkenazim who organized their first *minyan* in 1906, and the first government-recognized Jewish institution, the Unión Israelita, in 1909. As more traditional Russian immigrants arrived they bought the first building used as a synagogue in 1916. Four years later these congregations merged into Círculo Israelita. In 1987, this merged for certain activities with the Orthodox Communidad Ashkenazi Israelita and became the Communidad Israelita de Santiago. More than half of Santiago's affiliated Jews are involved in this joint venture.

In 1934 the 5,000 or so Sephardim formed the Communidad Israelita Sefaradi, now at Ricardo Lyon 837. But because it was headed until recently by the outspoken Angel Kreiman, it was also well attended by worshipers from other congregations. The 8,000 to 10,000 German-speaking Jews who fled Hitler built their own synagogue, Sociedad Cultural Israelita B'ne Jisroel, at Portugal 810. And when the Hungarians came, they established M.A.Zs.E. at General Bustamante 86.

Denominational labels notwithstanding, most congregants of Santiago's half-dozen synagogues are Conservative or even more liberal. Under 1 percent are believed to maintain *kashrut*—most being adherents of the small Chabad and *Kolel* (advanced Torah study) movements.

Unlike Jews in other Latin American countries, Chile's are held in high regard by the community at large. Top government emissaries have regularly sat on the *bimah* for a half hour or so during Yom Kippur services at Círculo Israelita. One rabbi, having come from a different scene in Argentina, reports that in his first three years in Chile he converted nealy 30 non-Jews – apart from those involved in intermarriages. He cites the Jews' perceived prestige as one factor.

Sights: Santiago enjoys a spectacular setting – when it can be seen. Sprawling at the foot of the Andes, the city has the mountains for a cycloramic backdrop. But smog often obscures the peaks, making them like a set designer's vision. They break through the haze in early morning only to disappear again within minutes. Nevertheless, Santiago is a pleasant place with lots of green splashed among its Spanish colonial and beaux arts buildings and monuments; a number of grand plazas, squares, and pop-up hills edged with tropical foliage; and even taxi drivers who sometimes refuse tips. Add one of the liveliest street scenes this side of Marrakesh – with the snake charmers, tarantula salesmen, and trance dancers of the Plaza de Armas for starters and the Bohemian Bellavista neighborhood for dessert – and Santiago surely must rank these days as one of the world's fun cities.

Originally the Jews lived in downtown Santiago, particularly around Avenida Serrano, an area of textile manufacturers and tailors. Eventually, though, they spread eastward to more residential districts such as Providencia and Nunoa and thence to the mountain-bordering Las Condes. And in addition to the dozen or so city streets named for Jews, all these sections bear witness to the Jewish presence.

The downtown area is rife with the results of Jewish commerce. Dotting the walkways off Constitution Plaza – presided over by a statue of the Converso-descended statesman Portales facing La Moneda – are branches of such chain stores as Ripley's, Hite's, Johnson Clothes, Village stationery stores (the Chilean Hallmark), and Corona, which, with its outlets running from Arica in the north to Punto Arenas in the south of this string-bean-like country, may well be literally the world's longest chain of stores. Its and other windows display merchandise manufactured in Chile by Jews, primarily jeans such as Calvin Klein and Lee; the Pierre Cardin franchise is also Jewish-owned. On the corner of Moneda and San Antonio stands the International Bank, which, from its founding in 1944 until its expropriation by Allende, was the Jewish-owned Banco Israelita, formerly one of Chile's leading credit institutions. The current president of Chile's Republic National Bank of New York (owned by the Brazilian Safras) is Jewish, as is the management of the large Banco De A. Edwards chain run by the Ergas family (owners as well of the Pepsi Cola franchise and the Kempinski Hotel).

Also downtown is the sanctuary of the city's foremost congregation, Círculo Israelita. On a plot at Serrano and Tarapaca, well shielded from the street and also containing office buildings and a community center, this structure built around 1950 is now known as the Great Synagogue. It features a parquet floor, straight-backed pews, an overhanging horseshoe balcony, and as its most striking feature a stained-glass window that curves around behind the *bimah*. With the daylight shining through, the window casts light of blue and lavender with shades of yellow spreading out as a ribbon of flame under the Ten Commandments. Services are held daily; sightseers can gain entrance 9 A.M. to 6 P.M. through Tarapaca 870 by calling 383-020 or 331-436.

Heading toward Providencia – and into a prime red-light district – stands the beige structure that until recently housed Santiago's Sephardic congregation. At the intersection of Santa Isabél and a street still named Maimonides, the building is noteworthy because though it is now a church whose facade reads Iglesia de Diós, the parishioners have kept the menorah at the building's apex and the *Magen Davids* that decorate its windows.

In the nearby Nunoa area stands an unusual secular contribution to Santiago by the Jewish community. A two-story beige building at Avenida Grecia 2483 houses the two fire engines of the volunteer fire department, Bomba Israel. Founded because it is customary in Chile for fire fighting to be done on a volunteer basis, with various companies sponsored by different ethnic communities, Bomba Israel, whose upper-right facade boasts a gold-hued *Magen David*, possesses two fire engines. Both fly Israeli flags, probably the only fire engines outside Israel to do so. Though many company volunteers today are not Jewish, the firehouse contains a roster of Jewish names, including those of rabbis. The Firemen's International has also had a Chilean Jewish president, Octavia Hinzpeter.

Farther out of town in a leafy residential neighborhood stands another surprising sight. Where Avenida Manquehue crosses Avenida Colón, the Ten Commandments rises on ten-foot-high stone tablets. The inscription on this Spanish version says that it was copied exactly from the Jerusalem Bible and presented on the occasion of the first National Congress of Young Adventists in 1981.

Las Condes is home to Santiago's major Jewish sports and social club, the Estadio Israelita, whose membership includes all factions of the community. In addition to tennis courts, swimming pool, and soccer field, Estadio Israelita is an unusual Jewish community center for also having its own synagogue, Talmud Torah, and permanent rabbi. One of the leading events presented by the Estadio is its public Yom Haatzma'ut festival featuring an air show. For this the Chilean Air Force (whose main hospital is next door to the club) drops paratroopers with Israeli flags onto the playing field, and with puffs of smoke the planes paint the Israeli flag in the sky. Also in Las Condes is the Hebrew School, Colegio Hebreo, a spankingly modern plant with one thousand pupils and a bordering street named Ben Gurion.

Culture: Most Jewish-related cultural activities — such as the National Dance Festival, theatrical presentations and lectures in Spanish or Hebrew — take place under the supervision of the Departamento de Cultura of the Estadio Israelita, which will also know which synagogues are offering similar programs (telephone 220-1615 or 220-9607). Sundays during the Chilean lunchtime, 2:30–3:30 P.M., a Zionist-oriented radio program presents music, stories, and discussion. A weekly newspaper, *La Palabra*, is circulated by the Ashkenazic community to all the country's Jews. The Sephardic community publishes a monthly, *El Vocero*. In 1968 the University of Chile opened a Department of Jewish Studies, directed by Gunther Bohm at Miguel Claro 182 (telephone 427-720).

Personalities: The most famous Chilean Jew today is probably television personality Don Francisco, born Mario Kreutzberger. In addition to his regular variety show and fundraising telethon, his program is also heard in Miami. Among other leading Jews in the arts are actors Alejandro Cohen and Nissim Sharim; actresses Virginia Fischer, Jael Unger, and Anita Klesky; violinist Victor Tevah, once conductor of the National Symphony Orchestra and 1980 winner of the National Art Prize; and jazz musician Andy Pollack.

Works by Samy Benmayor are frequently exhibited in the National Museum and elsewhere. Among Chile's leading Jewish writers are leftists Sender Pilowsky and poet-publisher David Turkeltaub, not to mention United States–based Ariel Dorfman.

Leaders in science, medicine, and education include endocrinologist and anthropologist Alejandro Lipschuetz, whose studies of Southern Hemisphere Indians won him the National Science Prize in 1969; Dr. Abraham Horowitz, director of the Pan American Health Service for eighteen years; Dr. Grete Mostny, anthropologist, archeologist, and formerly curator of the Museum of Natural History; Efrain Friedmann, director of the Chilean Atomic Research Committee; Jaime Wisnaik, director of the department of engineering of the Catholic University of Santiago; and David Stichkin, twice rector of the University of Concepción.

Reading: For a general novelistic look at Chile immediately before and after the military coup, there is *Sweet Country* (Simon & Schuster) by Caroline Richards, who lived through the period. Other novels evocative of the country include *After Shocks, Near Escapes* by Stephen Dobyns (Viking), *The House of the Spirits* by Isabel Allende (Viking) and *Curfew* by José Donoso (Weidenfeld and Nicolson).

Recommendations: LanChile, an airline whose gracious service and efficient performance are a throwback to the days when air travel was a pleasure, flies to Santiago from New York, Miami, and Los Angeles. With its grand entrance staircase, high ceilings, and courtly personnel, the Hotel Carrera, in the heart of Santiago opposite Constitution Plaza and the Presidential Palace, combines convenience with Old World charm. Also in a classy and comfortable but more contemporary mode is the Holiday Inn Crowne Plaza on the edge of the Providencia district. While there are no public kosher restaurants in Santiago, kosher meals are served to the poor in Sukat David, a dining room in a complex of Jewish community buildings between Avenidas Miguel Claro and Manuel Montt, and visitors may partake by calling 274-5389. Two vegetarian restaurants are Naturista in downtown Santiago and El Huerto in Providencia.

Be sure to finish your meal with a Chilean *cafecito*.

—Phyllis Ellen Funke

São Paulo

At the entrance to Ibirapuera Park, São Paulo's great patch of urban greenery, stands a mammoth stone statue depicting a boat being transported over land. Before the bow prance some jaunty riders on horseback; at the stern are men pushing with all their might. The statue honors the *bandeirantes,* the pioneers who created a nation in Brazil's uncharted vastness; the boat represents the ship of state. And, in the eyes of Paulistas—as São Paulo's residents are called—those traveling on horseback are the fun-loving citizens of Rio de Janeiro, while those doing the heavy work are the Paulistas.

Indeed, intercity rivalries notwithstanding, São Paulo *is* the dynamo of Brazil. The largest and richest metropolis in South America, it is the commercial and industrial center of Brazil, not to mention the heart of its cultural life. This sprawling city, with skyscrapers sprouting everywhere, manufactures cars, textiles, steel, rubber, cement, paper, and a host of other products. It also offers Paulistas myriad nightclubs, restaurants, theaters, and museums when they play.

São Paulo, in existence since 1554, owes its drive today largely to the immigration of the last 150 years. It sought industrial rather than agricultural workers, and it got them—more Italians than in Venice, more Lebanese than in Beirut, and the most Japanese in a community outside Japan. Not for nothing is one of the main highways leading to São Paulo named for these immigrants and, not surprisingly, among the city's staunchest boosters are Paulista Jews.

History: The first Jew in Brazil arrived with its Portuguese discoverer, Pedro Alvares Cabral, in 1500. He was Gaspar da Gama, a Cristão Novo (New Christian), or Converso, and he led the way for the large number of Conversos who followed. According to Anita Novinsky, a specialist on New Christians at the University of São Paulo, "Brazil was made by Jews." She notes that colonial Brazil was agricultural and that 60 percent of the sugar plantations were owned by Conversos, who brought the sugar cane from Madeira. They were also engaged in the slave trade. Bento Texeira (Pinta), a New Christian, wrote "Prosopopeia," the first poem composed in Brazil.

Some Conversos moved to São Paulo, in southern Brazil, to get far away from the Inquisition's headquarters in the north. Scholars claim that they assimilated quickly and thoroughly, thus erasing Jewishness from the Brazilian scene until the nineteenth century. But evidence of jungle tribes who light Friday-night candles and don't eat pork and the appearance at one São Paulo synagogue of at least one Catholic a month searching for Jewish roots seem to belie this.

Novinsky notes that despite claims that Brazil is the largest Catholic country on earth, its Catholicism is weak, in part because of its Converso heritage. "This was a country of heretics," she says. "Because of the Jewish involvement, it is a peculiar civilization. Brazilians have a different approach to life and religion. They are not Orthodox; they are very liberal—because Judaism left its roots in the mentality."

This, then, was the climate that Jews from Alsace-Lorraine found when they began immigrating to São Paulo in the mid-nineteenth century. At first, only individuals came, but after the Franco-Prussian War of 1870–71, groups started arriving. It wasn't until the century's end, however, that they started organizing as Jews. Waves of immigrants came to São Paulo in the new century, and Jews joined this flood — not only from Eastern Europe, but also from Syria, Lebanon, and North Africa.

By the 1920s, both the Ashkenazim and Sephardim had established communal organizations. After the Nazis took power in 1933, many Jews came from Germany, Austria, Czechoslovakia, and Italy and, in 1936, a group of mostly German Jews founded what was to become São Paulo's most important synagogue, Congregação Israelita Paulista (CIP), in the liberal tradition. Other substantial immigrations followed World War II — Hungarians after the abortive 1956 revolution and, the same year, Egyptian Jews fleeing after the Sinai campaign. Jews from Argentina, Chile, and Uruguay arrived in the 1970s, and most recently there has been a Russian influx.

Because of the diversity of Brazilian society and its liberal background, there has been little anti-Semitism in the country. Some developed during the dictatorship of Getúlio Vargas, 1930–45, and restrictions were placed on Jewish immigration. But despite Josef Mengele and other Nazis having been hidden in the environs of São Paulo, the Jews of the city did not feel affected by it and were dumbfounded that their haven could have harbored such evil. Even during the years of military rule, the Jewish community fared well.

Community: Of Greater São Paulo's eighteen million people, 75,000 are Jewish — more than half of all those in Brazil. Vibrant, outgoing, proud of being Jews and Paulistas, these generally affluent Brazilians can be found in virtually all fields of endeavor. About half are in trade; a quarter are in industry; the rest are in communications, construction, education and health services, politics, and the arts.

Jewish families own Brazil's two biggest publishing companies, the Safra Bank, Brazil's sixth largest, and its two largest jewelry concerns, H. Stern and Amsterdam Sauer. Leon Feffer, one of Brazil's ten wealthiest men, who is responsible for 50 percent of the country's paper production, is a Paulista. So are Jacobo Lerner, the principal owner of the São Paulo Hilton; Marcos Lazaro, a top impresario; Etty Frazer, Bra-

zil's Julia Child; Mario Adler, Latin America's premier toymaker; and Déborah Bloch, a sex symbol in Brazil's films. Even Brazilian argot has been affected by Jews, since Petitstyl, the name of a Jewish-owned chain of children's clothing stores, has entered the language as a word of teasing.

Melting pot: Built by German Jews, Congregação Israelita Paulista has moved beyond its original ethnic base

São Paulo boasts about twenty synagogues, but only a handful are active. They range from Reform to Lubavitch — which runs young people's programs that attract from all corners of the community, including, on occasion, those who are habitués of Régine's, the Gallery, and other "in" nightspots in São Paulo. About 60 percent of Jewish Paulistas are Ashkenazim. CIP, with a 2,000-family membership, is the largest congregation on the continent (located at Rua Antonio Carlos 653; telephone 256-7811). The other leading Ashkenazic synagogues are Templo Beth-El (Rua Avanhandava 137-Esquina Rua Martinho Prado 128; telephone 256-8671) and Sinagoga Centro Israelita (Rua Newton Prado 76; telephone 220-0185).

The primary Sephardic synagogues are Ohel Yaakov and Beit Yaakov (Rua Bela Cintra 801; telephone 256-3115). The Sephardi and Ashkenazi groups experience their tensions but mix socially and professionally. Under the leadership of Rabbi Henry I. Sobel, they also mix religiously at CIP. Despite its predominantly German founders, CIP is the first major congregation to escape its ethnic base and attract native-born Brazilian Jews of all origins. And despite its Liberal orientation, in its attempt to serve the community at large it has an Orthodox minyan and takes public stands on such issues as human rights and interfaith action.

São Paulo's Jews support the Hospital Israelita Albert Einstein, considered the best in the country, if not on the continent. Jewish Paulistas send their children to four Orthodox and four secular Jewish schools. (There are three thousand students in the Instituto de Educação Hebraico Brasileiro Renascença, Rua Prates 790.) The social club, A Hebraica, with a membership of over 20,000, is one of the largest in the world.

Jewish publications include the Portuguese-language national bimonthly *Resenha Judaica* and monthly *O Hebreu, Menurah, Shalom,* and *Sefaradi Magazine.*

Sights: Jewish Paulistas give the impression that they are far too busy *doing* things to spend time contemplating them. Ask for sightseeing suggestions for the Jewish traveler and the response is a quizzical, "What could you possibly mean?"

One Jewish institution worth visiting is the club, A Hebraica. Except for the absence of sleeping quarters, it resembles a self-contained resort community, complete with swimming pools, tennis courts, indoor gyms, drama and movie theaters, dance studio, lecture hall, ballroom, library, synagogue, art gallery, several snack bars and restaurants (including a kosher one), bank, barber shop, and multilevel park areas with tree-lined walkways — all within the confines of the city. Jewish tourists may enter by showing their passports at the entrance; members of other Jewish organizations may, for a fee, use certain facilities. The club is located at Rua Hungria 1000 (telephone 211-9722).

On the northern fringe of central São Paulo is Bom Retiro — which means "Good Retreat" — the old Jewish neighborhood. It was in this well-worn but well-kept area of low buildings and little shops that the Jews began, as more than one community member would put it, "in the *shmatah* business." And still today, with Koreans moving in, there is a concentration of clothing and textile stores bearing names like Naomi, Rachel, and Apelbaum.

Here, too, are the offices of *O Hebreu,* at Rua Mamore 570, across the street from a tiny hasidic synagogue, whose *rebbetzin* appears on the balcony to chase away trespassers. Nearby, at the "V" formed by Rua Correa dos Santos and Rua Da Graça, is a larger, more modern synagogue, Sinagoga Israelita do Bom Retiro (Rua Da Graça 160), its two main walls coming nearly together, like the Allied Chemical Building's on Times Square in New York, to present a panel covered with Jewish motifs. The grillwork on its windows also forms *Magen Davids.*

At Rua Ribeiro de Lima 604 is Weltman's Papeis e Livros Ltda. (stationery and bookstore), with Hebrew–Portuguese dictionaries and titles like *Presença e Integração (Presence and Integration: The Contribution of the Jews to the Life and Progress of Brazil)* and *Judeus de Bombachas e Chimarrão (Riding Chaps and Brazilian Tea),* about Brazil's Jewish cowboys.

Most of Bom Retiro's Jews have moved on to neighborhoods like Brás, in the northnortheast, and Jardims, in the southsouthwest, and many have places at Guarujá, a fashionable coastal resort an hour away, whose buildings were constructed almost entirely by Jews.

The Jews of São Paulo are particularly proud of Albert Einstein Hospital — to the point that it is the hospital, more than neighborhoods, synagogues, or clubs, that many in the community consider its biggest "tourist" sight. Opened in 1971, Einstein Hospital symbolizes for them their integration into the São Paulo community. The hospital is south of the city's business center in the Morumbi area, known for glorious, though well-hidden, private estates. The street on which it is located, Albert Einstein, intersects another street named Fighters of the Ghetto (Rua Combatentes do Gueto). (Other streets in the city are named for the State of Israel, Habad, and

Horacio Lafer, a former Jewish finance minister of Brazil.) To visit the hospital, call 240-3322.

Culture and Eating: While most Jewish cultural activities—such as theater and Israeli dance programs—take place at the clubs and synagogues, there is a Casa da Cultura Judaica (Jewish cultural house), which sponsors debates, folk dancing classes, and other activities. Every Sunday, at 11 A.M. on São Paulo's channel 11, there is "Programa Mosaico," featuring community news and interviews with outstanding Jews.

Kosher restaurants include Buffet Mosaico, located in Club Hebraica, Buffetwegh at Rua Correa de Mello 172, and Kineret Lunches, down the street at Rua Correa de Mello 162.

General Sights: With its bustle, São Paulo offers more atmosphere than specific sights. Some of its special flavor can be enjoyed browsing in those ethnic neighborhoods that retain their traditional character. One is Barrio Oriental, with its colonies of Japanese, Chinese, and Koreans, in the streets adjacent to Rua Galvão Bueno in the Liberdade district; another is Barrio do Bixiga, with its Italian colony, in the streets adjacent to Rua 13 de Maio.

Another good pastime is to window-shop in one of the city's vast, architecturally intriguing shopping centers. Among those worth a look are Shopping Center Eldorado (Avenue Reboucas 3970, Pinheiros), and Shopping Center Ibirapuera (Avenue Ibirapuera 3103, Moema).

Check out the flea market in Praça da República on Sundays from 8 A.M. to 1 P.M.

or take a stroll in Ibirapuera Park. While there, stop in at the cavernous building that, every other year, houses the city's huge art show, the Bienal; the Museum of Contemporary Art is located in the park as well. The Lasar Segall Museum has a fine art collection, although, despite its name, it has nothing particularly Jewish.

Reading: If you want to do your homework and read up on Brazil and its Jews before getting there, try *The Jews in Colonial Brazil* by Arnold Wiznitzer (Columbia University Press) and *Masters and the Slaves: The History of Brazil* by Gilberto Freyre (Knopf). To get the flavor of South American myth and fantasy in a novel on Jewish experience, read *Centaur in the Garden* by Moacyr Scliar (Ballantine). *The Strange Nation of Rafael Mendes* (Harmony), also by Scliar, is the dreamlike story of a man whose newfound knowledge of Converso roots gives him the confidence to face a wide range of crises in his life.

Recommendation: The São Paulo Hilton, in the heart of town, is a fine hotel, and will be happy to make arrangements for kosher meals. What is more, its public relations director, Roberto da Veiga, is knowledgeable about the Jewish community and will answer all your questions. The elegant Maksoud Plaza and the Sheraton Mofarrej also cater to *kashrut*-observing groups. South American Tours U.S.A. puts together Jewish itineraries to Brazil. When it comes to seeing that Jewish travelers have a good time, there is no shortage of Paulistas doing the heavy work.

—Phyllis Ellen Funke

Savannah

Lovely Savannah, in the heart of the deep South, is the oldest and most historic city in Georgia. Ancient oaks festooned with Spanish moss, swaying palm trees, and elegantly restored mansions evoke images of times past, of the generations that shaped the "Port City" from a colonial village into a modern industrial, maritime, and tourist center.

You can almost feel the tradition as you stroll through the city's historic squares, visit its venerable places of worship, and see homes of prominent citizens of yesteryear. The Jewish presence in Savannah, which contributed greatly to the city's growth, also reflects pride and continuity. In fact, Georgia, which was founded in Savannah, was the only one of the original colonies in which Jews were present within months of its creation.

History: When the *Ann* sailed up the Savannah River in February 1733, there were about 120 settlers on board, downtrodden former English prisoners led by James Edward Oglethorpe, a member of the British Parliament. They founded Georgia, the last of the thirteen colonies, named for King George. The British hoped to gain a foothold in the area and extend their influence toward the Gulf of Mexico where the French and Spanish were already established. They also hoped to develop exports such as wine and silk, and convert the local Indians to the Anglican faith.

The next ship to drop anchor in Savannah was the *William and Sarah*, which had sailed from London with forty-two impoverished Jews—thirty-three Sephardim and nine Ashkenazim. The Sephardim had fled to England from the Portuguese Inquisition, and London's prosperous Bevis

Marks Synagogue sponsored their voyage to America. While in London the trustees of the new colony were debating the admission of Jews to Georgia, a yellow fever epidemic was raging in Savannah. When it was learned that a physician, Dr. Samuel Nuñes Ribeiro, was among the Jewish passengers, Oglethorpe admitted the entire group. The epidemic was stemmed thanks to Dr. Nuñes (who had been chief physician to the grand inquisitor in Lisbon), and the colony was saved.

So it was that on July 11, 1733, the largest settlement of Jews until then to arrive in the New World on one vessel stepped ashore, carrying with them a *Sefer Torah* with two mantles and a circumcision box given by a London merchant. It is believed a *minyan* was held that same day, inaugurating the third-oldest Jewish community in North America.

A remarkable chronicle kept by one of the new arrivals, Benjamin Sheftall, and continued by his son, Levi, left a valuable record of the Jewish settlement's history from 1733 to 1809. The "Sheftall Papers" recorded that by December 1733 Jews were granted land like other settlers, were able to bear arms, worship freely, hold office, and were treated with equality. Most Jewish-owned town lots were near today's Ellis Square. A number of Jews acquired farms, and farming and small trades became the main Jewish occupations.

Savannah Jews worshiped in various Jewish homes until 1735, when they formed their first congregation, naming it Kahal Kadoth Mickva Israel (later changed to Mickve Israel). Services were held in a tiny hut. A second Torah received in 1737 makes it probable that two congregations—one Sephardic, one Ashkenazic—func-

479

tioned briefly. Both Torahs can still be found at Mickve Israel; they are the oldest in continuous use on American soil.

The ground for a cemetery located at the south boundary of the settlement was given to the Jews by Oglethorpe in 1735 and was used until around 1770. In addition, Mordecai Sheftall had deeded part of his farm on Cohen Street to Mickve Israel to be used as a cemetery, and it served the community until the 1850s. Savannah's first *mikveh* was opened in 1738.

Memories of the Inquisition were evoked in 1740 when military encounters with the Spanish took place near today's Florida border. Most of Savannah's Sephardim fled northward to Charleston, South Carolina, for safety and better economic opportunity. Only two Nuñes family members and the Ashkenazic Sheftall and Minis families remained, leaving less than a *minyan*. The flight of Savannah Jews to Charleston was emblematic of a closeness between the two communities that exists to this day; after Hurricane Hugo in September 1989, the Jews of Savannah sent aid to their brethren in South Carolina.

After the Spanish threat was removed, many of the Sephardim returned to Savannah. Some of the men brought wives from other colonies and other American-born Jews moved there as well. Jews prospered as ranchers, merchants, exporters, importers, and factors (commission agents) at the busy Savannah wharf. Jewish men served in the Home Guard in peace and war. Jews mingled freely with non-Jews through organizations such as the Union Society (a charitable group), the Freemasons, and the Jockey Club.

During the American Revolution, Savannah was in chaos, with refugees flowing in and out. Several Jews, including Cushman Polock, Philip Minis, and the Sheftalls, distinguished themselves in the struggle for independence. The town was taken by the British on December 28, 1778, with almost five hundred revolutionaries slain or captured. Mordecai Sheftall, commissary for the Southern Department, and his teenage son, Sheftall, were imprisoned. Released after several months, they fled toward Charleston by boat but were recaptured and imprisoned on the island of Antigua. They were released again in 1779.

Sheftall Sheftall proudly wore his three-cornered soldier's cap the rest of his life and was dubbed "Cocked-Hat Sheftall."

During the unsuccessful siege of October 8–9, 1779, by French and American forces to recapture Savannah, the "Jew's burying ground," established by Mordecai Sheftall, was used as a rallying place and four cannons were placed there.

Jews who had fled during the Revolution gradually returned to Savannah; there were 100 Jews in the city by 1790—the year Mickve Israel was granted a perpetual charter. The congregation built its first synagogue in 1820 at Liberty and Whitaker Streets—a small wooden structure that was also the first Jewish house of worship built in Georgia. The building was destroyed by fire in December 1829, but the Torahs, ark, Eternal Light, books, and robes were rescued from the flames and used again in the brick building consecrated on the same site in 1841.

During the antebellum period, Savannah Jews prospered in Georgia's thriving commercial and industrial center. But prosperity, built on exports of cotton, rice, corn, and lumber, evaporated quickly when the Civil War led to the blockade of Southern ports. Savannah escaped the scorched-earth policy of General William Tecumseh Sherman, but the city fell to Union forces in December 1864.

Savannah's Jews suffered wartime shortages much as other citizens, with the additional shortage of kosher meat. But there were things to be thankful for. For Passover 1865, Northern Jews sent thousands of pounds of *matzah* to Savannah. Perhaps because they were so much a part of the city's history and culture, Savannah's Jews had been spared anti-Semitism and accusations of profiteering that occurred in other parts of Georgia, such as Thomasville, where Jews were prohibited from living or visiting. Savannah Jewry responded by issuing a proclamation denouncing the slander.

A number of Savannah Jews died for the Southern cause. The spirited Eugenia Levy Phillips was a Confederate spy, and her sister, Phoebe Levy Pember, was matron of the Confederacy's largest hospital in Richmond.

During the post–Civil War depression,

Savannah suffered a disastrous yellow fever outbreak (1875–76) in which one-sixth of the population died, including many Jews. Some Jews went into the hinterland as peddlers, or to settle in rural areas that had trading centers. But newcomers arrived in Savannah from Central and Eastern Europe, expanding the community.

Mickve Israel needed larger quarters and built its present, beautiful sanctuary at 20 East Gordon Street, facing Monterey Square, in 1878. The Gothic-style synagogue, the only one of its kind in the Western Hemisphere, was designed by the English architect Henry G. Harrison. At first, Mickve Israel used the Portuguese ritual, but changed gradually. An organ was installed, a choir of men and women sang some hymns in English, and eventually second days of festivals were no longer observed. By the early 1900s, Mickve Israel officially joined the Reform movement.

Community: Today, 2,800 Jews live in the metropolitan Savannah area, in a general population of 240,000. And the community is one of almost perfect balance, with an Orthodox and a Conservative synagogue having joined Reform Mickve Israel.

B'nai B'rith Jacob, the South's oldest congregation continuously affiliated with Orthodox Judaism, had two synagogues in the historic area, both at Montgomery and State streets. Its present spacious and modern building, dedicated in 1961, is on the South Side at Abercorn and Seventy-fourth streets.

Agudath Achim, established in 1903 as an Orthodox congregation, also had two synagogues in the historic district. Its second sanctuary, at Drayton and Waldburg streets, a Georgian-style building, is now a Masonic Lodge. Agudath Achim joined the Conservative movement in 1945, and its handsome new home at 9 Lee Boulevard was dedicated during the High Holy Days of 1971.

Sights: You'll find a wealth of information on Savannah's many parks, museums, and historic landmarks at the new Visitors Center and Savannah History Museum, 303 Martin Luther King Boulevard, located on the site of a Revolutionary War battle. A variety of bus, carriage, and walking tours originate there.

One of Savannah's nicknames is "The Walking City," and many Jewish sights are within walking distance of historic Bay Street, by the waterfront. Near the river, where the first Jews landed in Savannah, is an excellent place to begin a Jewish heritage tour. On July 11, 1983—the 250th anniversary of the arrival of the *William and Sarah*—Mickve Israel placed a plaque at Rousakis Plaza down a short stairway from the popular Riverfront Walk, near Cap'n Sam's Cruises. (The easiest way to reach Riverfront Walk is by elevator from the rear lobby of the Hyatt Regency Hotel, 2 West Bay Street. The alternative is a precarious flight of stairs or a street paved with ballast stones.)

Another plaque near the Hyatt Regency driveway marks the spot where Oglethorpe, who became a friend of the Jews, founded Georgia.

A dignified granite memorial erected by the Mordecai Sheftall Cemetery Trust to memorialize the first Jewish burial ground in Savannah can be reached by going about seven blocks from Bay Street along Bull Street to the intersection of Bull and Oglethorpe Streets. On the monument (located on the median strip, or commons) are a bronze menorah and plaques that list the names of the 16 people known to be buried there, including members of the Minis, Nuñes and Sheftall families.

Continue south on Bull Street a few blocks to Liberty Street, and go right one block to Whitaker Street. Embedded in the sidewalk is a plaque denoting the location of Mickve Israel's first synagogue; its story is told on a historic marker.

Continuing south on Bull Street for about eight blocks to Monterey Square, you can easily recognize the magnificent Gothic Mickve Israel by the large six-pointed star above the entrance at 20 East Gordon Street. A few feet from the synagogue's door is another landmark: a bronze statue of the Polish hero General Casimir Pulaski, who died in the unsuccessful American attempt to recapture Savannah from the British.

Inside Mickve Israel's exquisite sanctuary, a first-time visitor is often struck by the unusual juxtaposition of style and symbol. In the midst of a building design more often associated with cathedrals are Jewish symbols (the Decalogue, menorahs, the burning bush) in the pastel-colored stained-glass windows, the sound of the choir singing in Hebrew, and a traditional carved-wood ark. The simple wooden pews have velvet cushions. One of the marble wall plaques is a memorial to Judah Touro of New Orleans, who was a benefactor of the congregation.

Mickve Israel's museum is next door in the Mordecai Sheftall Memorial Building and exhibits many priceless objects, documents, portraits, and photographs that represent the congregation's history. The 1733 Torah that the Jewish colonists brought from London is prominently on view, tied with a 1794 wimple. One of the oldest organs used by the congregation is on display. Seven presidential letters received by the congregation—from Washington and Jefferson, among others—are exhibited also. There are guided tours of the sanctuary and museum on Monday through Friday, 10 A.M. to noon and 2:00 to 4:00 P.M. The museum can also be visited after services on Friday, 8:15 P.M. (except in midsummer) and Saturday, 11 A.M. (all year). For information on services and the museum, call (912) 233-1547.

A house once belonging to the Sheftall family, and since moved to a different location, can be seen on the way back toward Bay Street. Go about four blocks east on Gordon Street to Habersham Street, make a left on Habersham, and walk to the corner of York Street (facing Columbia Square). This historic house is now a Unitarian church.

You'll need transportation to reach the South Side Jewish institutions. If you don't have a car, you can go by taxi or bus (No. 13 or 14) down Abercorn Street.

Savannah's Jewish cultural heart is the Jewish Educational Alliance at 5111 Abercorn Street. The institution, equivalent to a Jewish community center, is in a spacious, tree-shaded building. Its lobby is decorated with paintings by artist Jack Levine portraying Hillel, King David, King Saul, Maimonides, and other scholars and kings.

Several blocks to the south is the white brick Orthodox Congregation B'nai B'rith Jacob, at 5444 Abercorn. The building's gilded window grilles lend a Middle Eastern flavor; its entrance hall is graced by the lintel, cornerstone, plaques, and pews from the congregation's first synagogue at Montgomery and State Streets. The main sanctuary, which seats twelve hundred, is divided into three sections; the two side sections are elevated for women. The entire wall where the ark stands is decorated with four huge murals painted over wooden panels that represent the granite stones of the Western Wall. These are filled with symbols from the Jewish calendar and Jewish history, such as the *shofar*, Seder plate, *lulav*, and *etrog*. The ark is a large walk-in room symbolic of the ancient Holy of Holies, with two tiers for the Torahs and a large Star of David in stained glass. Twelve large stained-glass windows in rich primary colors bear the emblems of the twelve tribes. For information about daily and *Shabbat* services, call (912) 354-7721.

A few blocks farther south, at 9 Lee Boulevard, is the Conservative congregation, Agudath Achim. The modern brown brick synagogue has a high-pitched roof and a sanctuary with walls of rich wood paneling representing Noah's ark. Two stained-glass windows flanking the ark vault skyward, representing the ladder in Jacob's dream. These brilliantly colored windows were created by the artist Jean-Jacques Duval. The objects displayed in the lobby include a silver *megillah* case handcrafted by Bernard Solomon, and a seven-branched brass candelabra. For information call (912) 352-4737.

Culture and Eating: The JEA welcomes visitors to its many activities, which include lectures, exhibits, and musical programs, especially by Israeli entertainers. Check the listings of the monthly Savannah *Jewish Times,* or call (912) 355-8111 for information on events.

Alan Gottlieb's Deli, operated under rabbinical supervision, is in Twelve Oaks Shopping Center, near B'nai B'rith Jacob Synagogue. Gottlieb's Bakery, 1601 Bull Street, sells kosher sandwiches.

General Sights: While taking your Jewish tour, you will see many of Savannah's twenty-two historic squares, bordered by elegant homes and churches of diverse periods and gardens of exquisite camellias, azaleas, and other lovely flowers. Three of the most popular "house museums" are the William Scarborough House, 41 Martin Luther King Boulevard; Owen-Thomas House, 124 Abercorn Street; and the Juliette Gordon Low Girl Scout National Center, at 142 Bull Street, named for the Girl Scouts' founder.

The Telfair Academy of Arts in the Telfair Mansion, 121 Barnard Street, has Regency-period rooms with eighteenth-, nineteenth- and twentieth-century American and European prints, paintings, drawings, porcelains, and costumes.

Back at the waterfront, the Ships of the Sea Museum, 504 East Bay Street, is a fascinating maritime center that celebrates great ships and sea captains, with excellent displays of models and memorabilia. Toward the harbor entrance (beyond the historical plaque marking the Jews' arrival) is a large bronze statue of a young girl waving a scarf. According to legend, the "Waving Girl," Florence Martius, greeted every ship that passed the little island in the river where she lived. Harbor cruises embark from Riverfront Plaza.

Personalities: S. Yates Levy was a major in the Confederate ranks, the highest military position held by any Southern Jew. He was also editor of Savannah's *Daily Advertiser*; his controversial editorials after the war led to his forced resignation. Herman Myers was Savannah's one and only Jewish mayor (1895–97 and 1899–1907). The screenwriter Hal Kanter, best known for *Pocketful of Miracles,* is a Savannah native.

Reading: *Third to None* by Rabbi Saul Jacob Rubin, rabbi emeritus of Congregation Mickve Israel, is a comprehensive history of the South's first Jewish community. (Order it from Congregation Mickve Israel, 20 East Gordon Street, Savannah, Georgia 31401 for $37.50, including postage.) Samuel Rezneck's *Unrecognized Patriots: The Jews in the American Revolution* (Greenwood Press) explores the role of Jews in the military, economic, and financial aspects of the American Revolution, including the heroic stories of Savannah's Jews. Richard Kluger's *Members of the Tribe* (Doubleday) is a fictional account of the Leo Frank case, which the author curiously moved to Savannah from its actual setting in Atlanta. Eugenia Price's *Savannah* (Doubleday) is an exciting historical romance of nineteenth-century Savannah.

Recommendations: To complete the atmosphere of Southern ambiance, spend a night in one of Savannah's charming inns, once lavish mansions, such as Mulberry Inn, 601 East Bay Street, or Planters Inn on Reynolds Square. For lodging overlooking the Savannah River, there are the Hyatt Regency Savannah, 2 West Bay, the Best Western Savannah Riverfront, and the Radisson Plaza, all adjacent to the river front. The Olde Pink House, next to Planters Inn, serves delicious Southern specialties in an elegant colonial decor. And unlike the first Jews who came to Savannah, you don't have to have a doctor with you to get in.

—*Helen Silver*

Seattle

It's easy to understand the appeal of the Sunbelt, but what would make a city with a reputation for fog and rain attract masses looking for a better life? Seattle is a new generation's San Francisco, a place where you can literally stick your head in the clouds (or where the clouds stick their feet in your head). Somewhat ironically, it is reputed that Seattleites buy more sunglasses per capita than residents of any other city. Some say it's wishful thinking. Others say the rapid weather changes cause people to whip out their sunglasses several times a day and forget them on a table or seat when the clouds return—as they always do.

Seattle boasts distinctions above and beyond the clouds. Its citizens read more books per capita than the people of any other city, it has more live theater performances than any other city west of the Hudson, and it is rapidly becoming a rock-music mecca.

If all this sounds like Seattle is creeping up on New York, it's not far from the plan—or impossible dream—of its founders. In the 1850s the settlers' motto was "New York Alki" (from a local Indian term meaning "some day"). They soon realized that something more related to their locale was in order, so they adopted the name of a noted Indian chief.

Today, metropolitan Seattle has some 2 million residents and is a magnet for people throughout the Northwest, western Canada, and the Far East. Seattle's fortunes seem inextricably tied to those of the giant Boeing Company, in nearby Everett. Thousands of Seattleites commute to jobs at the aerospace manufacturer. More and more, however, Boeing is sharing the local limelight with computer companies, including Microsoft and Nintendo.

The People of the Book have never constituted more than 2 percent of the population in this book-reader's haven, but Seattle stands out among North American Jewish communities in two ways. First, the local Jews share their city's pioneering history. Second, Seattle's Sephardim have had significant impact on the entire Jewish community since the first immigrants arrived from the Isle of Rhodes.

History: The first Jews came to the Pacific Northwest in the 1850s, and by the following decade a handful had settled permanently in Seattle. But as late as 1880 the city had only 86 Jews, who were little more than a satellite of the larger Jewish community across the Strait of Juan de Fuca in Victoria, British Columbia.

Things changed rapidly after the discovery of gold in Alaska. Seattle became the port of embarkation for the Yukon and the Klondike, and German and Polish Jews were attracted to the city to supply prospectors with the gear they needed. The Cooper-Levy General Store was the leading gold-rush outfitter. The Gatzert-Schwabacher clan put up the city's first brick building and sold everything from groceries to building materials. A fire destroyed much of Seattle in 1889, and the Schwabachers' wharf was the only one to survive; it served as Seattle's main point of entry for years thereafter.

When gold fever died down, many Jews who had been in Alaska as prospectors or peddlers settled in Seattle and became merchants. Polish and Russian Jews fleeing czarist pogroms swelled Seattle's Jewish population, which reached 4,500 by 1910; by then Seattle had also become a magnet for small-town Jews from the surrounding Northwest and Canada.

The first Sephardim arrived from Rhodes

and Turkey in 1902, enticed by Greek fishermen friends who were working off the Washington coast. Word spread rapidly among the Jewish communities around the Aegean, and by 1910 there were 600 Sephardim in Seattle; their number doubled after World War I. Today, they comprise about 15 percent of the community and are the third-largest Sephardic concentration in the United States, after New York and Los Angeles. On a proportional basis, they are the largest. The last big migration from Eastern Europe came during World War I, when thousands of Jews reached the United States via China and Japan. Seattle was their port of entry, and many decided to stay.

Seattle's first synagogue, Ohaveth Sholum, was established in 1889, and most of the city's prominent Jews belonged. The synagogue proved too Reform-minded for some of the newer arrivals, however, and disputes over religious observance and other issues led to its demise in 1896. The later waves of immigrants were less interested in integrating into the general community, at least in part because the boom spirit of the gold rush and western expansion had passed. They built their own community in the downtown area around Yesler Way and Cherry Street, where Jewish-owned shops catered primarily to Jews.

Congregation Bikur Cholim was founded in 1891 as an Orthodox synagogue, and it continues to follow religious tradition closely. In 1899, some of the leading pioneer Jews helped establish Temple De Hirsch, a Reform synagogue that is the city's largest congregation, and (aside from a branch *minyan* of Bikur Cholim) the last to remain in the central area.

Although the Jews were a tiny minority within the growing city, the people who congregated around Yesler Way in the early 1900s found their own internal divisions. The Ashkenazic majority spoke Yiddish, while the Sephardic minority maintained their use of Ladino. Ashkenazim and Sephardim often looked down at each other and ridiculed different customs. Ashkenazim called Sephardim "mazolas," because of the Sephardi tradition of cooking with oil. The Sephardim returned the compliment, referring to their East European brethren as "schmaltz." While Ashkenazi

and Sefardi children grew up together in the Yesler Way neighborhood, their families frowned on "intermarriage" between the groups.

Even within the Sephardic community, there were divisions. The traditions observed by the Jews of Rhodes differed from those observed in Turkish communities. Efforts to conduct joint High Holiday services in 1907 satisfied nobody. Soon thereafter, two Sephardic congregations were established: Sephardic Bikur Holim, for Turkish Jews, and Congregation Ezra Bessaroth, for Jews from Rhodes. Both began and remain Orthodox in orientation.

In the early years, the spiritual leadership was drawn largely from the ranks of lay membership. At Ezra Bessaroth, a tailor named David Behar was prevailed upon to become acting cantor until a permanent one could be hired. "Temporary" is a relative term; Reverend Behar — who is remembered today more for his talmudic knowledge and his piety than for his skill with a needle — was cantor of the congregation for nearly sixty years. Reflecting the community's occupational evolution, his successor, Isaac Azose, is an engineer at Boeing.

Community: Since World War II, Seattle has resumed its boom-town growth. In the last generation, spurred by an influx of Jews from California, the community has tripled in size to 29,000, including 4,000 Sephardim. (In contrast to the anti-intermarriage sentiments of a few generations ago, many Sephardim marry Ashkenazim today. Indeed, while the membership roster at Ezra Bessaroth still contains many distinctly Sephardic names such as Israel, Alhadeff and Behar, it also boasts a fair share of typically Ashkenazic names, including that of William H. Greenberg, the synagogue's rabbi emeritus.)

The three Orthodox synagogues were the first to move out of central Seattle; they relocated to Seward Park, in the southern part of town. Other synagogues and concentrations of Jews can be found in North Seattle, on Mercer Island and in Bellevue.

The nerve center of the community is still centrally located at 2031 Third Avenue, home not only of the Jewish Federation of Seattle (206-443-0303) but also of such diverse institutions as the Washington State

Jewish Historical Society and the weekly *Jewish Transcript*.

The University of Washington is at the heart of North Seattle, where a relatively new, young, and vibrant Jewish community is developing. Conservative Congregation Beth Shalom was founded in 1968 and attracts many intellectuals, including university faculty and others. UW's interdisciplinary Jewish Studies program offers courses on history, Hebrew, and religion, leading to B.A. and M.A. degrees. The lectures and other community activities sponsored by the program attract many people beyond the university community. Local Jews are prominent in academic circles; many others work as engineers and merchandisers.

Sights: Seattle is beautiful. Located on the Puget Sound, near Mount Rainier and in some of the most lush, green territory in the world, the natural charm merges with a bustling city that has been carefully designed not to destroy the environment. Few other cities can boast an equivalent of the Movement for Lesser Seattle, a semi-serious, semi-tongue-in-cheek organization dedicated to keeping newcomers from settling in the Northwest and to maintaining what is left of the city's small-town feeling.

Many old synagogue and school buildings still stand in the vicinity of Yesler Way and Cherry Street. A walk along these bygone centers of Jewish life reveals several imposing buildings adorned with Jewish stars, and impressive sanctuaries that have been converted to churches and community centers. The neighborhood has gone the way of old Jewish sections in many large American cities: in activity rooms that once housed after-school Hebrew classes, young black students now gather to study art; the platform that once served as a synagogue *bimah* now squeaks under the weight of modern dance exercises. But Yesler and Cherry have retained much of their old charm, with homeowners maintaining yards and children playing on the sidewalks.

Yesler and Cherry converge near First Avenue, and it's there that you can get a colorful Seattle orientation—with at least a hint of the city's Jewish ingredient—by taking Bill Speidel's Seattle Underground tour. More archeological than commercial (in other words, more like Jerusalem than like Underground Atlanta), it takes visitors under Pioneer Square and through, among others, one of the old Schwabacher buildings. The tours leave from 610 First Avenue; call (206) 682-1511 for information and (206) 682-4646 for reservations.

Many of Seattle's first Sephardim went into the fish trade. Some cooperated with the Greeks who had brought them to the new country by selling what the fishermen caught. Pike Place Market, a waterfront concentration of peddlers of fish, produce, and other goods, had many Jewish merchants. Today the sprawling open-air market, located near the downtown shopping district, features produce, fish, and local crafts. Once Seattle's prime shopping center, it is now one of its most popular tourist attractions.

Pike Street is also the home of Seattle's central synagogue (and the Northwest's largest), Temple De Hirsch Sinai. The original sanctuary, renowned for its beauty and acoustics, fell under the wrecking ball a few years ago, but the "new" sanctuary, completed in 1961 and adjacent to the garden that graces the site of the old building, boasts a circular sanctuary dominated by large stained-glass windows and a white marble *bimah*. In addition to its facility at 1511 E. Pike Street (telephone 206-323-8486), the temple also has a building in suburban Bellevue.

Seward Park, in the city's South End, is home to the three Orthodox synagogues, all of which have daily as well as *Shabbat* services. Sephardic Bikur Holim (6500 Second Avenue South; 206-723-3028) was completed in 1965 and is recognized by its wrought-iron gates and its wooden interior. Though the congregation is still predominantly of Turkish origin, the membership also includes smaller representations of Moroccan, Egyptian, and Ashkenazic Jews.

Congregation Ezra Bessaroth (5217 S. Brandon; 206-722-5500) is home to those whose families came from Rhodes. It has an imposing modern sanctuary with stained-glass windows and interior design in dominant purples and reds.

Bikur Cholim–Machzikay Hadath (5145 S. Morgan; 206-721-0970), whose founders were of Russian and Polish origin, is Seward Park's Ashkenazic outpost. Its mostly wood interior features stained-glass windows that meet at right angles above a corner, white-tiled *bimah*.

Pastoral Mercer Island sits in Lake Washington opposite Seward Park, but to get from the mainland concentration of Jews to the island community you have to take the long way around to get to the bridge. Herzl-Ner Tamid Conservative Congregation (3700 E. Mercer Way; 206-232-8555), the largest congregation on the island, boasts many Boeing engineers in its membership. They were instrumental in designing the sanctuary, which is nothing less than a work of aerodynamic art. The building's designers had to work around a steep slope on the plot of land. They met the synagogue's needs by building a *bimah* and ark that glide on an air cushion to the far end of the adjacent social hall to create an enlarged hall of worship for High Holidays. The synagogue has daily as well as Shabbat services, a Judaica shop, and a host of congregational activities.

Mercer Island is home to one of the city's two Jewish Community Centers; the other is in the North End near the university. Check the *Jewish Transcript* for Jewish cultural events at the centers or at the various synagogues.

Back in the center of town, the Washington State Jewish Historical Society (206-443-1903) has mountains of information about Seattle's Jewish pioneer history. The society offers guided tours, and its active members will provide information to anybody interested in undertaking self-guided tours.

Seattle Center is a quick monorail ride from downtown. Built for the 1962 World's Fair, it houses the Seattle Science Center, a sprawling, hands-on museum of technology that entertains the entire family. Also in Seattle Center are the Pacific Arts Center and several theaters and auditoriums that host concerts year-round.

Personalities: Bailey Gatzert was one of Seattle's early Jewish pioneers. He arrived in 1869 and became a successful businessman. In 1876, he was elected mayor of Seattle. A local elementary school bears his name.

Washington's late Senator Henry "Scoop" Jackson was a leading friend of Israel and Soviet Jews in Congress. He sponsored legislation that penalized the Soviet Union for its treatment of Jews who wanted to emigrate.

Seattle's leading Jewish philanthropists, Samuel and Althea Stroum, back many charities. Noted personalities from Seattle's Sephardic community include Marc Angel, author, head of the Rabbinical Council of America and spiritual leader of Shearith Israel, America's oldest Jewish congregation, in New York; and Victor Alhadeff, founder of the popular Egghead Software chain. Jazz saxophonist Kenny G (né Gorelick) learned to blow the *shofar* at Congregation Herzl-Ner Tamid, and has been known to give return performances in recent years. Steven Hill left his native Seattle to act in Hollywood. Mark Helperin left New York to live and write in Seattle. Dyan Cannon (née Samille Diane Friesen) was born in Tacoma and went to school in Seattle. Sol Lesser, the producer of the first Tarzan movies, was born in Spokane.

Eating: Once a kosher backwater, the Northwest is becoming kashrut friendly. Most centrally located of Seattle's kosher establishments (near the Pike Place Market) is the Kosher Delight Deli, 1509 First Avenue. The Bagel Deli, at 340 15th Avenue East, has light kosher meals, and diners sit on old wooden pews from the original Ashkenazic Bikur Cholim sanctuary; it also has a branch at 1309 NE 43rd Street. Seward Park has Two G's (dairy, 5300 Wilson Avenue South) and Park Deli (meat, 5011 South Dawson Street). For updates on *kashrut*, contact the Seattle Kashrut Board at (206) 723-0970.

Given its location and its mood, Seattle has a good selection of fish and vegetarian restaurants as well. Bamboo Garden, at 364 Roy Street, features vegetarian Chinese food. The Space Needle, which dominates Seattle's skyline, features a revolving restaurant with many fish entrees and a stunning view of the city and surrounding landscape; reservations are mandatory (206-443-2100).

Reading: There is no Jewish novel of Seattle, but there are books on the local scene with Jewish angles. The city figures in Saul Bellow's *More Die of Heartbreak* (Morrow). Edna Ferber's *Great Son* (Doubleday) provides good Pike Place color.

Many Seattleites carry a good paperback in their pockets, and not only in case they have to duck out of the rain. Seattle, in fact, gets a bum rap on the weather front. True, the winter months are foggy and gray, but the city gets just thirty-five inches of rain per year—less than New York. In fact, if you want to go native, be sure to pack two pairs of sunglasses.

—*Carl Schrag*

Sofia

Like a stage set behind a scrim—the gauzy curtain that, when backlit, creates a hazy effect—Bulgaria, at least to many Western eyes, seems veiled and a trifle unreal. Somewhere in the Balkans on the Black Sea and, until throughout the Cold War, steadfastly in the Soviet bloc, this country appears a bit removed from spotlit Europe. Yet here in the Continent's wings, a number of singular episodes in Jewish history have been played out—including the triumphant cliffhanging drama of World War II. In fact, though Bulgaria was an Axis member, with Hitler's emissaries regularly making their presence felt, not one person from Bulgaria proper lost his life because he was a Jew.

History: Given certain unusual aspects of Jewish history in Bulgaria—a country whose own story features Jews significantly—this climax of grace was not entirely astonishing. Well before the advent of the Bulgars themselves, Jews were living in this region of the Roman Empire. At least as early as Herod's time they coexisted, north of Greco-Turkish boundaries, alongside the Thracians. Jews who had sided with Cleopatra are believed to have fled here when her fortunes failed; a Jewish settlement in Macedonia was recorded in Caligula's day (37–41 C.E.); and a Latin inscription from the late second century was found at the village of Gigen on the Danube; it mentions an *archisynagogos* (community leader) named Joseph, and bears a menorah. Within the last couple of years, as the city of Plovdiv excavated for a new communications system, the mosaic floor of a second- or third-century synagogue was unearthed.

By the sixth century, Slavs from the north had migrated to the Balkans, followed by the Bulgars, a Turco-Tartar people from the steppes of southern Russia. From the Jewish standpoint this proved significant. Since they had been pushed out of their former lands by the Khazars, who established a kingdom from the Caspian to the Black Sea and eventually embraced Judaism, the Bulgars, who would fuse with the Slavs to become today's Bulgarians, were acquainted with the Jewish concepts they found in their new home. (Judah Halevi's philosophical work *Kuzari* is based on the legendary disputation conducted before the king of the Khazars, which ended in the monarch's adoption of Judaism.)

Consequently, en route to Christianity the Bulgarians flirted seriously with Judaism. Possibly because of this, they had princes named David, Moses, Aaron, and Samuel. And in the early days their faith emerged as a mixture of the Jewish, Christian, and pagan.

The role of the Jews in this is unclear. They may have proselytized or they may have been engaged by the Byzantines to make contact with the pagans. In any case, their presence was pervasive enough to create a haven for Jews persecuted in Byzantium as well as to influence Bulgarian representation to the papacy. Not only was the church questioned concerning how Bulgarians should relate to the Jews, but also, guidance was requested on other apparently Jewish-influenced matters, such as the offering of first fruits; the proper day of rest; the type of meat that could be eaten; burial rituals for suicides; and the period of sexual abstinence after pregnancy.

Jewish influence is also noted in the creation, in this Balkan region, of the Cyrillic alphabet, which based written Slavonic on a Bulgarian dialect. The alphabet is generally credited to the monks Cyril and Methodius, who in the ninth century worked at Ohrid in Macedonia, then part of Bulgaria. As natives of Salonika, they had studied with Jews. So when they needed symbols for sounds that didn't exist in the Greek alphabet, which was their primary source, they turned to Hebrew for letters for the sounds *ts, sh* and *kh,* among others.

Jews there fared well during the centuries prior to the final Ottoman conquest of Bulgaria in 1396. Jewish merchants immigrating from Italy and Ragusa (Dubrovnik) received royal privileges. Leo Mung, a talmudist, converted and became archbishop of the Ohrid diocese and primate of Bulgaria. The regional sect known as the Bogomils acknowledged Judaism's contribution to Christian doctrine. And in the mid-fourteenth century, the Bulgarian Czar Ivan Alexander married a Jewish woman named Sarah. Converted and baptized Theodora, she strongly influenced affairs of state.

Before the advent of the Ottomans, Bulgaria was so salubrious a Jewish destination that many arrived to escape persecution during the Crusades. Others came when Hungary expelled them in 1376. Even after the beginning of Turkish rule, Bavarian Jews banished in 1470 headed toward Bulgaria. And 30,000 more flooded into the area after their expulsion from Spain in 1492. (Among these was Joseph Caro, author of the *Shulchan Arukh,* who spent thirteen years in Nikopol before moving on to *Eretz Yisrael.*) Bulgaria thus experienced various Jewish crosswinds and, until 1640, Sofia had three separate Jewish communities — the Romaniote (who followed a Byzantine ritual), the Ashkenazim, and the Sephardim.

Just how they ultimately fared under Turkish rule is subject to debate. Initially, at least, they appeared to have been well off, particularly as privileged traders and businessmen, and sometimes as confidants to the sultans. However, with time their lot apparently fell.

Not surprisingly, the Jews were active in the Bulgarian nationalist revival. And when the time came in 1878 to join with the Russians in expelling the Turks, many Jews were in the forefront. One Jew, Leon Krudov, was noted for heroism in the decisive battle for the Shipka Pass. With the estab-lishment of an independent Bulgaria there were occasional outbreaks of anti-Semitism, but until the period just before World War II the Jews generally lived in tranquility.

However, in the period leading up to and during Bulgaria's alliance with Nazi Germany, the Jews' fate hung in the balance. There was pressure for deportation, and even while they clung to the tightrope they were subjected to a host of disabilities — specialized restrictions; confiscation of property; forced labor camps; even the dreaded yellow star. And those Jews in Thrace and Macedonia — which Bulgaria had reclaimed at the war's start — were indeed surrendered to the Nazis. Whether this as well as the hardships in Bulgaria proper resulted from malice or political maneuverings is unclear. However, when word leaked out of a plan to deport the Jews in Bulgaria proper, there was sufficient outcry from the Bulgarian populace — politicians, professionals, artists, and the clergy — that they were spared the fate of so many others.

Community: At war's end there were, as before, 50,000 Jews in Bulgaria with the majority residing in Sofia, the capital. For nearly a century, however, Zionism had been a potent elixir for many; others apparently feared the postwar socialist regime. Consequently 90 percent of Bulgaria's Jews swarmed to Israel, leaving 5,000 in Bulgaria today — of these, 3,000 are in Sofia, 450 in Plovdiv, and the remainder in eight other cities and towns including Varna, Bourges, and Plevin. According to some community members, most of the Jews who remained were idealists who believed in socialism. Jews work in all fields, with a disproportionate percentage in the arts and higher education.

Two government-sponsored operations minister to the Jews. The primary one is the Social, Cultural, and Educational Organization of Bulgarian Jews, with headquarters in Sofia and branches in the towns where Jews still reside. The second is the Central Jewish Religious Council, which deals with religious matters. Though the Jews had religious freedom even under orthodox Communist rule, few attend synagogue regularly (although services are held daily in Sofia and weekly in Plovdiv). But they come in greater numbers on the High Holy Days and Passover. Bulgaria does not have a rabbi, but Sofia has a *chazan* who adheres to the Sephardic ritual. While there are no facilities for observing *kashrut*, *matzah* is produced for Passover every year — in a candy factory.

Sights: Since much is still developing in Bulgaria, including tourism, it is not always easy to ferret out sights of particular Jewish interest. If one accepts hearsay — and in this case there appears no reason not to — Bulgaria, and particularly Sofia, harbors much uncatalogued Judaica. Beyond the synagogues and community centers, a lack of awareness of certain matters pervades even the Jewish community, and these days much time can be spent in wild goose chases.

Eclectic wonder: Sofia's synagogue combines Byzantine, Islamic, and European influences

Sofia's central synagogue, at Ekzarh Josif Street 16, was dedicated in 1909. The Bulgarian Jews welcomed the king to the dedication ceremonies on September 23, when he gave money for the relief of the Jewish poor. Among the largest Sephardic synagogues in Europe, it boasts a sixty-foot-high dome, vaults, and the scalloped and pillared archways of the East. Its cavernous main sanctuary, undergoing a long-term restoration, has elaborately decorated interior arches. Though much is in disarray, the massive two-ton, star-encrusted chandelier, the largest in the Balkans, still hangs over all, suggesting glory that was and will be. Elaborate in detail, the structure's plan is

probably derived from the Byzantine rather than indigenous European or Islamic sources. The synagogue has cusped and stilted arches and little turrets based on Islamic models; striped and rusticated surfaces and long thin windows of the sort seen in other contemporary Bulgarian buildings; and a squashed dome that may trace its ancestry to the Paris Opera House.

Further hints of Jewish life are visible in the small, brightly lit prayer room to the right of the entrance, where services are conducted today. The walls are adorned with pulpit covers and the like, ranging from elaborate silks and brocades to more naive motifs. The cabinets and walls of the synagogue's office to the left of the entrance contain additional Judaica — a Torah covered with square bits of silver stands out. The synagogue is open 9 A.M.–5:30 P.M. Monday through Friday, until noon Saturday, and is closed on Sunday. Call 831-273 — though you may find only Bulgarian and Spanish spoken.

The synagogue is in the heart of the former Jewish neighborhood (Jews now are scattered throughout the city). The tree-lined area more or less delineated by the major thoroughfares — Alexander Stambolski Street and Vitosha Boulevard, plus Iskar Street — was once the center of town..

The current focus of Jewish activity in Sofia is the headquarters of the Evreiski Dom, or Hebrew House, the Social, Cultural, and Educational Organization of the Jews, at Stambolski 50. A solid, yellowish, turn-of-the-century, multistory building, its corner premises once housed the Jewish-owned Gyula Bank, said to have been primarily for dowry loans (it is now a branch of the National Bank of Bulgaria). Its interior is noteworthy since the railings edging its staircase are decorated with Stars of David. Essentially a community center, Evreiski Dom houses administrative offices; the newspaper (*Evreiski Vesti*); card-playing and other meeting rooms; exhibition space (where local Jewish artists are sometimes featured; the Bulgarian and Israeli-inspired works of Suzi Aronova are typical of recent displays); and a museum documenting Bulgarian Jewish history from the time of independence through World War II.

Sofia celebrates its Jews in other ways as

well. Among its streets are Ephraim Ben Zion, Joseph Strossmeyer, Liza Kalo, Matti Rubenova and Makko Pappo (born Menachem Leon). The National Art Gallery includes works by Boris Schatz, Mattityahu HaCohen, David Peretz, Eliezer Alcheh, Mareo Behar, Sultana Suroshon, and Anna Crammer. The ancient stone mentioning the *archisynagogos* Joseph is in the collection of the Archaeological Museum. And there is a monument in the Jewish cemetery on the outskirts of town to those who died in the anti-Fascist resistance. A Greek synagogue allegedly once stood opposite the Sheraton.

Among Sofia's general sights, one not to be missed is the monumental Alexander Nevsky Memorial Church, whose choir sings at Sunday morning services in an unsurpassable acoustical setting. The low-lying excavations near the Sheraton are reminders that the Roman Empire reached to this corner of Europe. And to get away from it all, Bulgarian style, the best Sunday-in-the-park scene is in Vitosha National Park, in the cuckoo-laden mountains edging the city.

Side Trips: Plovdiv, Bulgaria's second city, can be visited in one long day trip from Sofia. Its rather neglected synagogue stands at Tsar Kalojan Street 13A, in the area known as the New Town. It is bordered by an empty lot in a yard next to apartment houses. With its marbleized columns, large dome, blue-toned Star-of-David-decorated frescoes and its faded gold fabric, it suggests an illustrious past. (Indeed, until the war's end, there were 7,000 Jews in Plovdiv, four synagogues, and a Jewish school. Today most of the city's Jews are retired professionals and educators.) A smaller chapel on the grounds hosts weekly services Fridays at 6 P.M. Since only Bulgarian, Spanish, and a smattering of Hebrew is spoken, a local guide's help is probably warranted; contact Menahem Keshales (224-597) or Avram Behar (262-654).

The synagogue's surroundings were once the city's Jewish neighborhood. A small park behind what's called the Thursday Market (though it operates every day) was known as Jewish Park and contained the *mikveh*. One main street in the area is

named Ulica Menahem Menachemov for a noted Jewish partisan. And all around the district are wall plaques commemorating other Jewish resistance fighters—among them Sabbitai Garti, shot in 1943 on the spot at the corner of Russaki Boulevard and Sixth of September Street; Albert Benvenisti, remembered on Tsar Kalojan Street; and Leon David Anabu, whose plaque on Kableushkov Street indicates that he died in 1936 while serving in the Bulgarian Brigade that fought in the Spanish Civil War. Plovdiv's Jewish Library and its House of Culture are located at Zaiemov Street 20.

Also from Sofia, an even shorter trip—one hour by car—may be made to Samakov, where the synagogue built by the Arieh family—a structure mixing various styles with that of national Bulgarian—has been restored. In Vidin, on Bulgaria's northern border, the Danube, the synagogue is being reconstructed but will be used as a concert hall and museum.

Culture and Reading: Entwined as they have been with the overall development of Bulgarian culture the Jews, not surprisingly, have contributed to it in various noteworthy ways. For example, the Bulgarian language has assimilated words from the Jews. In the southern part of the country the word for "friend" is *aver*, a cousin of the Hebrew *chaver*; in idiomatic speech, there's *tanto za tanto*—literally, "this for that," or "tit for tat"—from the Spanish Jews' *tanto por tanto*. The Spanish Jews also brought a yellow cheese called *cache vallo* which, in time, became the Bulgarian favorite, *kashkaval*. Strains used in Israeli melodies resound in local folk tunes; a circle dance here is called a *hora*—though the word possibly derives from Turkish.

The first book printed in Bulgaria was produced courtesy of Spanish Jews, who brought the type with them. During the nineteenth-century national revival came works by Bulgarians featuring Jews, usually positively, as fellow victims of oppression and fighters for social justice. Only after World War I, though, did the Jews themselves trade Ladino for Bulgarian; the pioneer in this movement was Dora Gabe, a poet who was later elected president of the Bulgarian PEN club. The Jews' subsequent literary contributions are considered a factor in the outcry raised on their behalf by fellow writers during World War II.

Today, the state printing house brings out books in English, often on the wartime Jewish scene. Among these are *Saving of the Jews in Bulgaria, 1941–1944* and *We, the Saved.* On occasion the Jewish community organizes concerts and discussions on topics of Jewish interest. Rather than noting religious holidays, which are considered within the synagogue's purview, it celebrates days connected with outstanding Jewish figures, such as Einstein.

There are no Jewish novels set in Bulgaria, although the first volume of Elias Canetti's memoirs, *The Tongue Set Free: Remembrance of a European Childhood* (Seabury Press), touches on the Nobel laureate's Bulgarian birth. Two general fictional pictures of the country are Dorothy Gilman's spy novel *The Elusive Mrs. Pollifax* (Doubleday) and Robert Littel's *The October Circle* (Houghton Mifflin), about a group of Bulgarian performers who decide to resist the Warsaw Pact invasion of Czechoslovakia. For an overview of the Jewish position in this Balkan land, see *Bulgaria and Her Jews* by Vicki Tamir (Yeshiva University Press).

Personalities: In addition to Elias Canetti, who left as a child, noted contemporary Bulgarian Jews include the musician and conductor Peter Stupel, who is president of the Sofia Music Festival; his son, Yuri, a composer; Leah Cohen, vice president of the Sofia Music Festival; pianist Maty Pinkas, a professor in Sofia's Academy of Music; actors Joseif Surchadjiev, Itak Finzi and Eva Volitcher; artists Andre Daniel of Varna and Johan Leviev of Plovdiv. Noted Bulgarian-born Israelis include Shulamit Shamir, wife of the former prime minister, and artists Nahum Gilboa and the late Avraham Ofek. Other celebrated Bulgarian-born Jews are pianist Alexis Weissenberg and artist Jules Pascin.

Recommendations: The centrally located Sheraton Sofia–Balkan Hotel operates according to modern tastes and standards. You can stay there in Western comfort and still feel you're behind the screen that obscures Bulgaria from the rest of the world.

—Phyllis Ellen Funke

Stockholm

When the Swedish actress Mai Britt married Sammy Davis, Jr., an American reporter asked if her parents objected to the match. "Of course not," Britt replied. "There is no anti-Semitism in Sweden."

The anecdote illustrates two facets of Swedish life. Though there are exceptions to every rule, Sweden has historically been highly receptive to Jews, especially once they were on the inside. And the popularity of books like John Louis Anderson's *Scandinavian Humor and Other Myths* (Perennial Library) notwithstanding, Swedes are not always as serious as they seem in the films of Ingmar Bergman.

Stockholm, with 1.5 million people, has the friendly ambiance and cleanliness of its ethnic cousin, Minneapolis, but geographically it is more like a mirror image. Midcontinental Minneapolis is on a land mass studded with lakes. The Stockholm area is mostly sea studded with islands, fourteen of which make up the city. There are twenty-four thousand in the surrounding archipelago.

Though Jews have never been numerous in Sweden, they loom larger in Swedish life than numbers alone indicate. And if one adds to the Jewish landscape three non-Jewish Swedes who figure in Jewish history, it is difficult to find a place in Stockholm that doesn't have a Jewish connection.

King Gustav III (1771–92) was not the first monarch to invite Jews to take up residence in Sweden, but he was the first to drop conversion as a condition for admission. He is also a large figure in Sweden's royal pantheon, because many of the nation's cultural institutions (theaters, museums, literary societies) owe their origins to him. It is perhaps no accident that, after two hundred years of participating in Swedish society, culture is the area in which Jews have had the most visible impact.

Alfred Nobel didn't *intend* for the prizes he endowed to honor Jews in particular, but the awards, inaugurated in 1901, constituted the first international institution that decidedly did not discriminate. The results have been obvious; though Jews are less than one percent of the world's population, 18 percent of the Nobel Prizes have been awarded to Jews. From the various bodies that choose the winners to the places the laureates visit each December, Stockholm is filled with Nobel "sights."

Stockholm was the home of Raoul Wallenberg, the diplomat who saved thousands of Hungarian Jews during World War II by issuing Swedish papers and setting up safe houses in Budapest under the Swedish flag. Swedes also know the Wallenbergs because the family is one of the nation's most prominent. Wallenbergs owned the Gota Canal and founded the Enskilda Bank (where Raoul worked briefly as a young man), which in turn helped build Sweden's railroads, paper industry, and merchant fleet. Today the bank is part of the Skandinaviska Enskilda Banken. One Wallenberg was ambassador to the United States; another was foreign minister.

History: There may have been trade links between the Vikings and the Jewish kingdom of the Khazars toward the end of the first millennium, but the first Jew known to set foot on Swedish soil was Benedict de Castro, a doctor consulted by Queen Christina in 1645. Jews visited the country over the next century and a half but could not settle unless they accepted baptism.

The community began in 1774, when Gustav III permitted Aaron Isaac, an engraver from Mecklenburg in northern Germany, to settle in Stockholm. A year later Isaac was allowed to bring over his brother, his partners, and their families. In 1779 with the king's support, the Swedish Parliament granted Jews a measure of religious freedom and settlement rights in Stockholm, Göteborg, and Norrköping.

Though there were ups and downs in the nineteenth century, Jewish rights were expanded considerably in 1838 and full emancipation was achieved in 1870.

Like the Vikings before them, both Sweden and its Jewish community owe much of their makeup to the sea. For most of history, water was the main highway (which explains why Sweden fought more battles in Poland than in Norway), and most of the Jews who have come to Sweden in various waves and wavelets since the eighteenth century have come from places that face Sweden from across the water — the original immigrants from northern Germany, early twentieth-century migrants from Russia and the Baltic states, wartime refugees from Denmark, refugees from the anti-Semitic purges in Poland in the 1960s, and today another handful of Russians. In addition to receiving Jews from the countries across the sea, since the late 1980s Stockholm's Jewish community has become a kind of mentor for the Jewish communities reemerging in the Baltic states.

Its liberal reputation notwithstanding, Sweden was traditionally a homogeneous society with restrictive immigration policies; in 1933 its Jewish population stood at 7,000. Swedish neutrality in the 1930s was accompanied by a pro-German sentiment at the top level of society. Admissions policy was further tightened with respect to people suspected of wanting to stay in the country permanently.

The basis of the policy was never anti-Semitism per se, and between 1933 and 1939, despite the restrictions, several thousand Jews, mainly from Germany, Austria, and Czechoslovakia, managed to reach Sweden. The decisive change in attitude came in 1942, when the Nazis began persecuting Jews whom Swedes saw as belonging to their extended family. The nation reacted strongly to the persecution of Norway's 1,800 Jews and admitted any who could reach Sweden (about half the com-

munity). Less than a year later Sweden offered asylum to the entire Danish Jewish community of 7,000. The following year the government sent Wallenberg to Budapest.

Wallenberg was not the only Swede to rescue Jews, nor the only one to pay dearly for his efforts. Count Folke Bernadotte, also a diplomat, was instrumental in getting 3,500 Jews released from concentration camps toward the end of the war; in 1948, while trying to mediate the Arab-Israeli dispute, he was assassinated in Jerusalem.

Jews made an enormous contribution to Sweden, and it was partly recognition of its experience with Jews that led Sweden to a more liberal postwar immigration policy, with an emphasis on the admission of refugees. The presence of Italians and Yugoslavs, Africans and Asians indicates that the days of a homogeneous Sweden are past.

Community: Sweden is one of the few countries where the Jewish population has more than doubled since the beginning of World War II. There are about 18,000 Jews in the country today, with about half in the Stockholm area and most of the remainder in Göteborg and Malmö (mainly Polish or Polish-descended Jews). Though most refugees have been from third-world countries, the Jewish community was augmented by infusions of Hungarians in 1956 and Czechs in 1968, in addition to the Poles. More recently a handful of Jews from the former Soviet Union have arrived.

Postwar immigration has had a dramatic impact on Jewish life. "Things have never been more active," observes Morton H. Narrowe, chief rabbi of Sweden. The community's buildings are no longer adequate for the level of activity. "It's a fantastic problem to have," Narrowe adds.

Before the war, intermarriage and assimilation were rampant. Partly because the postwar newcomers tended to be more traditional, and partly because the community has reached a critical mass of Jewish energy, it now seems capable of regenerating itself. Even some of the secularized Polish Jews who married gentiles in the 1960s, Narrowe says, are sending their children to Jewish schools.

But postwar refugee policy has a flip side that has caused the Jewish community some consternation. Sweden is nothing if not a champion of the underdog, a status that in the eyes of many was transferred from Israel to the Palestinians in 1967. The current government, much to the relief of the Jewish community, has found a middle ground between the pre-1967 embrace of Israel and the post-1967 embrace of the PLO.

In recent years the Jewish community has been embroiled in the case of a Moroccan-born radio figure convicted of inciting anti-Semitism and a related case of academic freedom versus hatemongering aroused by a university professor (eventually dismissed) who libeled Judaism and questioned the Holocaust. Aside from these cases, the biggest community-wide issue in recent years has been *kashrut*. *Shechitah* is illegal in Sweden (because of the halakhic objection to the requirement that animals must be stunned before slaughter), a relic of a time when Jews had little influence over legislation that affected them. Kosher meat must be imported from Denmark. (Ironically, Laplanders, whose slaughtering methods are similar to *shechitah*, are exempt from the ban.) Animal-rights advocates attempted to extend the law to fowl, but the Jewish community's opposition ultimately prevailed.

Sights: A good place to begin a Jewish tour of Stockholm is at the waterside square called Raoul Wallenbergs Torg, adjacent to the centrally located Berzelii Park. Just south of the square, at Wahrendorffsgatan 3, is the Great Synagogue of Stockholm. Few synagogues in Europe can boast as ideal a location. One of the gems of Jewish architecture, it is a living symbol of emancipation, built in the center of Stockholm in 1870, the year full Jewish equality was achieved. With its side to the narrow, curved street, the rectilinear, plastered brick building evokes the Second Temple. Imposing from the outside, the building is magnificent on the inside. Though the dominant interior design influences are Moorish and Baroque, the angled wooden brackets that support the ceiling are reminiscent of the many Viking-inspired ceilings that look like the inverted hull of a boat.

The cloth decorations on the *bimah* are believed to date from the eighteenth-

century founders of the Stockholm community. There is more certainty with respect to the Chanukkah menorah which stands on the *bimah*. Its legs are in the shape of the royal "G" in honor of King Gustav. It was donated in 1792, the year Gustav was assassinated.

The biggest crowd in the thousand-seat sanctuary gathers on the *Shabbat* before the awarding of the Nobel Prizes in early December. Jewish laureates (including winners of the Peace Prize, which is given in Oslo) are invited to the service and, Narrowe says, virtually all of them accept. Also in the synagogue is a library dedicated to Wallenberg.

The administrative building attached to the synagogue is also worth a visit. The wood-paneled boardroom is decorated with a portrait of King Gustav and scenes of Scandinavian Jewish life by the painter Geskel Salomon.

The Great Synagogue is just a few steps from Raoul Wallenbergs Torg (Wallenberg Square). Facing the north side of the square is the Royal Dramatic Theatre where Ingmar Bergman, Ingrid Bergman, and Greta Garbo made their first marks on Sweden. The theater is also one of the places where Jews have made a lasting imprint. Ludwig and Ragnar Josephson were both directors of the Royal Theatre, and Erland Josephson is today one of its leading actors. He has also been in many of Bergman's movies. Bergman himself pays a Jewish debt of sorts in his films. The physician in most of his stories is Dr. Furstenberg, named for the Jewish family doctor of his childhood.

Nybrogatan runs along the west side of the theater, and up the street at number 19 is Judaica House, the community's activity center. The ocher building with blue and white awnings houses a day school, a nursery school, a *mikveh*, a gift and book shop, and a kosher cafeteria. It is also a center of Jewish cultural activities such as dance, *klezmer,* a Yiddish society, and lectures. Not surprisingly, the lecturers include many Nobel laureates. Call Judaica House (679-51-60) for information on community events, synagogue prayer times, and *kashrut.*

The ritual of the Great Synagogue is Conservative. Orthodox congregation Adas

Jeshurun is located at Riddargatan 5 but entered through Judaica House on Nybrogatan. Many of Adas Jeshurun's furnishings came from a small synagogue in Hamburg and survived *Kristallnacht,* the night in November 1938 when Nazi gangs attacked synagogues all over Germany. (Another Orthodox synagogue, Adas Jisroel, is at St. Paulsgatan 13, in the southern part of the city.)

There were more than Jewish reasons for the 1987 naming of Raoul Wallenbergs Torg. This is the neighborhood in which Wallenberg grew up. His childhood home was a flat on Strandvägen, the waterfront drive of stately turn-of-the-century buildings. The trading company where he was working in 1943 when his Hungarian partner recommended him for the Budapest assignment was located at Strandvägen 7a.

Less than a ten-minute walk from the cluster of sights around Wallenberg Square is the historic center of Stockholm, the Gamla Stan. Situated on three little islands, it is a wonderful maze of medieval lanes and buildings.

At Själagårdsgatan 19 is a yellow-orange stone building that was Stockholm's first synagogue from 1795 to 1870. Now an architect's office, its second floor retains the columns that surrounded the central *bimah* and a balcony that was part of the women's gallery. Although the office is not open to the public, these details can be seen from the outside through large windows. The building was a police station for many years, and when the police moved out in the 1970s it was offered to the Jewish community for a museum. Community officials were sorely tempted, but it came down to a choice between the cost of renovating a building for a museum and upgrading its summer camp. "We chose the future over the past," Rabbi Narrowe says.

In the center of the Gamla Stan is the Storkyrkan. Perhaps the smallest cathedral in the world, it is both a parish church and the seat of the Lutheran diocese of Stockholm—and the place where monarchs are married and crowned. One of the prominent fixtures in the church is an eleven-foot, seven-branched bronze candelabrum. A menorah in all but name, it has been in the church since 1470. Guides routinely point out its similarity to a Jewish symbol, but its origins are obscure. The church also has the name of God written in Hebrew over the inner doorway and above the pulpit of the *pastor primarius.* In 1986 Elie Wiesel lectured from the pulpit, as does each year's Nobel Peace Prize winner.

Behind the Storkyrkan is Slottsbacken, a short hill of a street that runs along the royal palace down to the water. At the foot of the street is a statue of King Gustav facing across the water to one of the institutions he founded, the National Art Museum. To get from the statue to the museum, though, you need to walk about five minutes out of the way, over the Strömbron to the city's mainland, and turn right. You'll pass the Grand Hotel, where all the Nobel laureates stay in Stockholm, and the dock from which many boats leave for tours of the archipelago, before reaching the museum. The museum features paintings and drawings from the Renaissance to the present. Among the works exhibited are those of Ernst Josephson, a Jewish artist who was one of Sweden's most prominent cultural figures in the late nineteenth century.

A few minutes walk farther (but across Skeppsholmbron on the island of Skeppsholmen) is the Museum of Modern Art, which includes in its collection works by Chagall (*The Old Man and the Goat, The Circus*) and Modigliani.

Though the opportunity for a Jewish museum in the Gamla Stan was lost, Stockholm does have a new Jewish Museum at Halsingegatan 2 (telephone 310-143). Open to the public on Wednesdays and Sundays (with plans to expand its hours), it features artifacts from early Jewish life in Sweden and photographs of prominent Swedish Jews. Items in the museum include the first prayer composed for King Gustav, Aaron Isaac's Bible and a scale model of the Malmö synagogue. The photos capture the many facets of Swedish society, from journalism to theaters to department stores, in which Jews have been influential.

The two sites in central Stockholm most associated with the Nobel Prizes are the Concert Hall, where the award ceremony takes place, and the City Hall, where the postceremony banquet is held.

The Concert Hall (Konserthuset) at Kungsgatan and Hötorget is a blue stone building with gray columns facing a square with a produce market. (Stockholm's oldest high school, where Wallenberg studied in the early 1930s, was located around the corner from the site; the school, Nya Elementars Gymnasium, since moved to a new site, hosted an exhibit on Wallenberg's life in 1990.)

The City Hall (Stadshuset) is a red-brick waterfront building that mixes Viking, Oriental, and Italian Renaissance styles. The Nobel banquets are held in the blue room, a huge enclosed piazza that seats twelve hundred for the occasion. The City Hall is a tribute to Swedish democracy; the busts above its entrance are not of kings and politicians but of the carpenters, masons, and other workers who built the structure between 1911 and 1923. Inside are busts of the elite, including one of K. A. Wallenberg, one of the prime benefactors of the construction fund.

Personalities: Sweden's leading department store, NK, was founded by Jews. The Bonnier family was responsible for one of the country's leading publishing houses (Albert Bonnier was a patron of August Strindberg) and also for the founding of *Dagens Nyheter,* Stockholm's leading liberal daily. Most of Bonnier's descendants are Lutherans, but some still feel Jewish ties. Ake Bonnier, who is a priest, recently arranged for the family-founded publishing enterprise to ship newsprint to Estonia so a Jewish newspaper could publish.

Jacob Josephson, a protégé of Jenny Lind, was a leading composer and conductor. Sophie Elkan was known for her novels on the Swedish royal family; she was also the best friend of Selma Lagerlof, the Nobel laureate who wrote the Swedish classic, *The Gosta Berling Tales.* Lagerlof's work was brought to the screen by Mauritz Stiller, a Finnish-born Jewish producer who is even better known as the man who discovered Greta Garbo.

Nelly Sachs, the Nobel Prize–winning poet, lived the last thirty years of her life in Stockholm. Oscar Levertin was a poet and literary critic for *Svenska Dagbladet,* Stockholm's leading conservative daily. Lars Gustafsson (who now lives in Texas) is one of the leading contemporary Swedish

novelists. Hjalmar Mehr served as mayor of Stockholm in the 1960s.

Eating: The cafeteria at Judaica House is the only kosher restaurant in Stockholm. In addition to sit-down meals there, you can also get some kosher supplies at its shop. Frozen kosher meat is available at the Konsum Market on Sibyllegatan, opposite the Östermalmtorg subway station. There are also several vegetarian restaurants favored by local Jews. One, Örtagården, is just up the street from the Jewish community center, at Nybrogatan 31. Two others are Gröne Linjen, at Master Samuelsgatan 10 and Annorlunda, at Malmskillnadsgatan 50.

Reading: Cynthia Ozick's *The Messiah of Stockholm* (Knopf) deals with larger themes than local Jewish life, but it is certainly a story of a Jewish condition in a Swedish setting. A bit further afield, but beginning with a rabbi in Stockholm, is *Bernard Foy's Third Castling* (New Directions) by Lars Gustafsson. *The Prize* (Simon & Schuster), Irving Wallace's novel about the Nobel Prizes, stands up well even though it was written almost thirty years ago; its cast of laureates includes an obligatory Jewish scientist. August Strindberg's novel *The Red Room* captures the flavor of Stockholm's bohemian life in the late 19th century and includes a Jewish artist and a Jewish publisher in its cast of characters.

There have been several books about Raoul Wallenberg, including *Righteous Gentile* (Viking) by John Bierman, *Wallenberg: The Man in the Iron Web* (Prentice-Hall) by Elenore Lester; and *With Raoul Wallenberg in Budapest* (Holocaust Library) by Per Anger.

Recommendations: Summer is the high period for tourism in Sweden, but as Nobel season and Scandinavian ingenuity indicate, a winter visit can be both eventful and comfortable. Don't believe the story about Swedes settling in Minnesota because the climate was similar to what they had left behind. Minneapolis is much colder in winter than Stockholm.

SAS serves Stockholm from American gateways, and one of the best antidotes to jet lag is its EuroClass service, in which the reclining seats are the closest airborne equivalent to your bed at home. Two hotels stand out among the many in Stockholm. The Grand Hotel lives up to its name and offers the chance to rub shoulders with, or at least breathe the same air as, the Nobel greats. A unique and less expensive experience is the Mälardrottningen, located on a yacht moored at the Gamla Stan. The Mälardrottningen is adjacent to an open plaza that faces the City Hall across the water. It was on this plaza that Wallenberg designed his first project after returning from architecture studies at the University of Michigan in 1934. Though the project —

a swimming pool — was never built, the drawings he made while standing on the spot still exist, and it is a good place to contemplate the story of the Jews and their friends in a beautiful city.

Most of the sights of Jewish or general interest are within walking distance of the city center, and the subway is a good alternative to the expensive taxis. Swedes are friendly to a fault (anyone who thinks he is more than six months younger than you will offer you his seat on the bus), and when it comes to visitors from different cultures, the dominant attitude is that of Mai Britt.

—Alan M. Tigay

Strasbourg

What is the Jewish traveler to Strasbourg, a major city in the eastern French province of Alsace, to make of the twin statues of *Ecclesia,* the church, and of *Synagoga,* the synagogue, which frame the south portal of the city's cathedral? In what context are we to read the allegory of that text made of stone?

On the left as you face the portal stands the figure of an elegantly draped woman holding a chalice in one hand and a staff topped with a cross in the other. Her head bears a crown and on her lips is an arrogant smile of triumph. Compare the figure on the right, of a forlorn woman whose legs and breasts are erotically discernible through the thin cloth of her robe. Her head is inclined to the side in a gesture of submission, her lance is bent and broken, the Tablets of the Law in her left hand are about to fall heavily to the ground. Most devastatingly, she is blindfolded, so that she can see neither light nor truth.

One would think, on reading this "text," that neither Judaism nor Jewish life would have a chance of thriving on this soil. And yet, for 15,000 Jews in a population of 420,000 Strasbourgeois, Judaism flourishes. To understand how this is the case, if not precisely why it is so, a visit to Strasbourg is in order.

History: Although there were probably some Jews in Strasbourg during the reign of Charlemagne (eighth to ninth centuries), the earliest documentation of Jews in Strasbourg was made by Benjamin of Tudela toward the end of the twelfth century. From the existence of a Jewish cemetery in the city at that time, one can infer that there was a Jewish community flourishing in Strasbourg during the early thirteenth century.

The principal occupation of the Jews during the Middle Ages was moneylending, which, however useful to the local population, leads almost inexorably to resentment. Feelings turned even uglier when the Black Death ravaged Europe between 1348 and 1350, killing between a quarter and a half of the population. The Jews of many towns were accused of causing the plague by poisoning the wells, and thousands of Jews were massacred. Despite a bull issued by Pope Clement VI declaring the allegations against the Jews to be false, and despite a vehement defense of the city's Jews by the patricians of Strasbourg, hundreds of Strasbourg Jews were burned to death on a wooden scaffold in the city's Jewish cemetery.

From 1349, when Jews were banished from Strasbourg, to 1791, when full citizenship was given to the Jews of France, Strasbourg was officially *judenrein,* with most Jews living in outlying towns and villages. This state of affairs prevailed when Strasbourg was under German sovereignty, and when it was ruled by the French after 1681. During the modern period, Alsace has changed hands between France and Germany: in 1870 (to Germany); in 1918 (to France); in 1940 (Germany); in 1945 (France). Because of this history, the Strasbourgeois are passionate about French patriotism. Bending accuracy somewhat, residents are quick to point out that the Alsatian dialect still heard in the region is not German.

Jewish life in Strasbourg came to a virtual standstill during the Holocaust, when the Jews were evacuated to the south of France with the rest of the city's population in 1939. During the five-year Jewish absence from the region, the Nazis took pains to demolish the city's Great Synagogue on the quai Kléber. Several of Strasbourg's rabbis and community leaders were active in the Resistance, among them the martyred Chief Rabbi René Hirschler, for whom a street near the rebuilt Great Synagogue is named.

Community:

Strasbourg's Jewish community numbers 15,000 today. Though few in number in comparison with Paris and New York, Strasbourg's Jews make up in quality what they lack in quantity.

As Candide, the hero of Voltaire's satire of naive optimism in the face of disaster, counseled, "We must cultivate our own garden." Since the time when Napoleon organized the various Jewish communities of France into *Consistoires,* the Jews of Strasbourg have set out meticulously, elegantly, and effectively to cultivate a garden of autonomous social structures that today are the envy of many Jewish communities around the world.

In addition to Napoleon's initiative, Jewish communal life in Strasbourg also derives some benefit from the era of German control between 1870 and 1918. When France decreed the separation of church and state in 1905, Alsace and Lorraine were unaffected by the decree. When the two provinces were reintegrated into France after World War I, they came back with strong religious ties to the state, which they were permitted to keep. The chief rabbi of Strasbourg, for example, unlike the chief rabbi of Paris or of France, is a functionary of the state, his salary paid by the state. In the secular schools, the one hour of religious instruction required weekly by law is paid for by the state. In the religious day schools, the secular part of the curriculum is, again, underwritten by the state.

According to banker Robert Levy, president of the Strasbourg Jewish community, this has an obvious economic benefit. Fundraising campaigns are used mainly to supplement funds that come to the community from the state. Asked whether there is a price to pay in interference from the government for this munificence, Levy responds that the city is happy *not* to interfere in the affairs of the religious denominations it aids so generously. Thanks to this governmental support, says Levy, the community of Strasbourg is able to spend 40 percent of its budget on Jewish education.

Though Strasbourg's Jewish community, like all those of France, has been enriched by the influx of North African Jews, it is the only French city where Ashkenazim still outnumber Sephardim (by about three to one). Most of the city's Jews, Sephardic and Ashkenazic, live either near the Grand Synagogue or in the area of the Esplanade.

Sights:

The first stop on the itinerary of the Jewish traveler is the imposing Synagogue de la Paix, beautifully nestled into a corner of the Parc des Contades on la rue du Grand Rabbin René Hirschler. Built in 1958, the synagogue is not as architecturally distinguished as the one destroyed by the Germans, but is beautiful for its park setting and for the statement its massiveness makes to the outside world. Like the Jewish community, the Synagogue de la Paix is a presence on the Strasbourg landscape.

The synagogue's interior is more impressive than its facade. You will enjoy the circular sanctuary in the middle of a wide stage surmounted, as if by a protective cloud, by a large Shield of David. In addition to the main Shabbat service, there are two other minyanim in the Synagogue de la Paix—the Mercaz, for younger participants, and the beehivelike Sephardic minyan.

The Great Synagogue is also a community center, housing administrative offices, a nursery school and a kosher restaurant. There are, by the way, 10 other minyanim in Strasbourg. If you are interested in visiting any of the minyanim, day schools or Jewish residences, request more information from the Communauté Israélite de Strasbourg (8835-6135) or the Consistoire Israélite du Bas-Rhin (8832-7657).

An important visit of your tour will be to the Musée Alsacien (23 quai Saint Nicolas), which is housed in four contiguous Renaissance-style houses, with balustrades and balconies containing hundreds of fascinating artifacts of Alsatian folklore, including an impressive Judaica collection. The Jewish section of the museum has Torah pointers and *tefillin* bags, flowered Torah crowns and wooden Elijah's chairs,

Seder plates and *Haggadot, shofarot* and *chanukkiyot,* knives for ritual slaughter and *brit milah,* and even, upstairs, a reconstructed Alsatian *shteibel.* The museum also has an impressive *mizrach* collection. Look especially for the one depicting, in four panels, King David, King Solomon, Moses, and Aaron. Above the word *mizrach,* which the plaque explains is an abbreviation of the Hebrew phrase "On this side is the spirit of life," you will notice two Lions of Judah holding a tricolor coat-of-arms in their paws. On the tricolor background is a representation of the *coq gaulois,* the Gallic rooster, the popular secular symbol for France. According to Malou Schneider, curator of the Musée Alsacien, much of the Jewish folk art of Alsace bears witness to a curious crossing over from secular Alsatian artistic inspiration to popular Jewish religious art.

To see an example of cultural cross-fertilization in the other direction, one need only look at the cast-iron plaques displayed on the left wall as you enter the museum. There you see a series of reliefs depicting, among other scenes, Solomon's judgment and Absalom's death. The museum is filled with objects illustrating Torah motifs, such as Noah's ark and a portrayal of the two spies returning from Canaan bearing a cluster of grapes—an ideal image for tourism that chauffeured limousines in Israel have adopted. Don't be fooled by the proliferation of "Jewish" stars you'll see in the museum, warns Schneider. The six-pointed star is the ancient insignia of the brewers' guild. If you see one, you'll know you're not necessarily in the vicinity of Jews, but certainly near Alsatian beer.

It is only a short walk across the River Ill (pronounced "eel") to the magnificent Cathedral of Strasbourg. You'll want to stop at the south portal of the cathedral to take in the two statues of *Ecclesia* and *Synagoga* that flank the doors. A creatively Jewish way of reading this "text" is inspired by the figure of Solomon seated between the two female figures. Is the wise Hebrew king making one of his famous judgments between the two contending women? Certainly the graceful *Synagoga* cannot be deemed in error in the eyes of Solomon.

If you arrive at the cathedral around noon, you might consider purchasing

Text in stone: Emissions of light and hope through Synagoga's *blindfold*

tickets to see the playful clock perform a mechanical medieval morality play. From here, you might want to consider a seventy-five-minute boat ride along the river bordered by lush willow trees, or a visit to the nearby museum of the Château de Rohan. The Rohan museum also contains several works depicting Torah scenes, including paintings of Samson and Delilah, *Rebecca Receiving Presents from Abraham*, and *Lot's Daughters*. On Sundays at 11 A.M., you can see free Alsatian folk-dancing performances in the courtyard.

A must in Strasbourg is a visit to La Petit France, the city's charming old quarter of tanners' houses, an easy walk from the cathedral. This area is marvelous for leisurely strolling, for café sitting, or for souvenir shopping—for items like the painted ceramic molds for *Kougelhopf*, Alsace's regional cake.

Another highly recommended visit, especially for those traveling with children, is to the Parc de l'Orangerie across from the European Parliament. The park is noted for its manicured lawns, its storks' nests, and its lake. Take time to rent a rowboat for a half hour of seated exercise.

Side Trips: It is difficult to get an accurate picture of Jewish life in Strasbourg without taking several trips into the surrounding countryside. In Bischeim, a half-day drive north, is a beautiful sixteenth-century *mikveh* in the ancient Cour des Boecklin. Doubling back toward Strasbourg, continue west on RN 6 for 20 miles to the village of Marmoutier. There you will see how *sukkot* were built indoors under a movable roof, and the remnants of an ancient *mikveh*. The town's synagogue, which the Germans turned into a stable in 1940, has not been rehabilitated, since today there are only three Jews left in the town.

A full day's trip could begin with the eighteen-mile drive southwest to the picturesque village of Obernai where the synagogue on rue de Sélestat — still in use — dates from 1848. Forty miles west of Strasbourg, high in the Vosges mountains, is the site of the Natzweiler-Struthof concentration camp. The site was chosen by the Germans to inflict maximum suffering on its inhabitants; it is so cold in the mountains that a sweater is needed even in July. Guided tours are given in French or German; Americans can borrow an English-language pamphlet from the guide and tour the site on their own. After coming down from the camp, the next stop on the tour should be the village of Ville, where Dr. Francis Dreyfus has single-handedly restored the synagogue which the Germans turned into a dairy during the war.

For travelers who like to vary their mode of transportation, a day trip on the French National Railroad, a model of comfort, speed, and efficiency, is a good idea. The lovely city of Colmar is only forty minutes by train from Strasbourg. According to Jack Dreyfus, the congenial chief rabbi of the Upper Rhine, Jews have been living in Colmar and its environs since the Middle Ages. The area was in the past so Jewish, says Dreyfus, that "there were localities where there was a synagogue and no church."

Today, about 300 Jewish families — "a thousand souls," as they say locally — live in Colmar. Activities are carried out in a complex of buildings belonging to the Consistoire, including a magnificent old synagogue (located at 3 rue de la Cigogne), recently restored, complete with Gobelins tapestry, high ceilings, ornate columns, a rose window, several Elijah's chairs, a raised pulpit in the center off to the side, like in a cathedral, a *memorbuch* containing a prayer for Napoleon III and, tucked away in the *Aron Kodesh* (the holy ark), a silver Torah crown from Sighet, the Transylvanian birthplace of Elie Wiesel. The synagogue is also distinguished by its bell tower. Apparently, the non-Jewish architect felt that all houses of worship should have a belfry, so he put one in.

Also worth seeing in Colmar is the Bartholdi Museum, dedicated to the Colmar sculptor who designed the Statue of Liberty. A permanent exhibition of Jewish arts and crafts will open at the Musée Bartholdi within the year. Before heading for the station for your return trip to Strasbourg, you will want to spend a half hour meandering through Colmar's winding streets, taking in the local architecture.

Recommendations: If you travel to Strasbourg from Paris by car, you will want to stop off at Reims to see the Chagall windows in the cathedral there. War-history buffs will also want to visit the Maginot Line and the battlefields of Verdun, both easily accessible from the Autoroute. You can also get a seven-day French Rail and Drive Pass, available only from the French Rail office in New York (212-582-2110).

The only kosher restaurant in Strasbourg is Chalom, located in the community center of the Synagogue de la Paix, which serves traditional Ashkenazic fare.

Personalities: The Marx Brothers and French mime Marcel Marceau (born Markovitch) trace their origins to the Jewish communities of Alsace. Likewise some of the most important Jewish figures in French political history, such as Alfred Dreyfus, prewar premier Léon Blum, and the writer André Maurois. Other important Alsatian Jewish celebrities include Cerf Beer the eighteenth-century *Hofjude* most responsible for the emancipation of the Jews, Rabbi David Sinzheim, the chief rabbi of Strasbourg who served as the first president of the Sanhedrin convened by Napoleon in 1807; Rabbi Jacob Meyer, chief rabbi of Strasbourg for sixty years, who was the first Jew to be decorated with the French Legion of Honor; and the nineteenth-century artist Alphonse Levy, whose prints of family scenes in Alsace are in the collection of the Jewish Theological Seminary in New York.

The most important Jewish cultural figure to come out of Strasbourg and its environs is the late André Neher, whose Judaic scholarship and teaching left their stamp not only on the Jewish community of Strasbourg but on studious Jews worldwide. Today, the three most oft-repeated names in the world of Jewish learning in Strasbourg are Roland Goetschel, who inherited Neher's chair at the University of Strasbourg; sociologist Freddy Raphael; and especially Armand Abescassis, who is making a name for himself in the field of Jewish mysticism.

Reading: In his massive *Book of Abraham*, (Henry Holt), French novelist Marek Halter devotes four chapters to life in Strasbourg during the Middle Ages. Using a telegraphic style, he paints a vivid picture of both the oppression of Jewish life at the time of the Black Death, and the resiliency of Strasbourg's Jews.

A charming story about Jewish life in Alsace in the nineteenth century is told in *Friend Fritz,* a novel by Emile Erckmann and Alexandre Chatrian, two non-Jewish writers. The book is about Fritz Kobus, a non-Jew from the village of Hunebourg, a thirty-five-year-old propertied bachelor who sees no reason to change his status, and his best friend, the aged and sagacious Rabbi David Sichel, who believes that all men are better off married, and that society requires traditional families. Much of the novel focuses on the debates of the two friends, on the twenty-four matches proposed (and rejected) to Fritz by his *"rebbe,"* and on the quotation and creative misquotation of biblical texts by both characters. If you live in a community with a good university library, you should be able to find the book in English. If you can read French, the book is available in a garden-variety *Livre de Poche* edition. The ending of *Friend Fritz* is somewhat ambiguous for Jewish readers. Like the depictions of *Ecclesia* and *Synagoga,* it lends itself to musing about not only Jewish life in Strasbourg, but also the Jewish conditions in the Diaspora.

—Joseph Lowin

Sydney

"We live in a WASP fairyland," wrote one of Australia's best-known columnists. "[Australia is] the most multicultural country on earth, after Israel — but we don't admit to it." The best-kept secret about Australia is, in fact, that one out of every five Australians was born overseas — giving the country an exuberant plethora of nationalities, including about 90,000 Jews. In fact, when the Australian Jewish community marked its bicentennial in 1988 — the same year the nation celebrated its two hundredth birthday — it proved that the monocultural image of Australia was never a reality.

History: When Britain lost the United States as a colony, it turned to the far-off continent of Australia as a destination for its prisoners. In 1788, the First Fleet — 1,500 convicts including 16 Jews, and their guards — landed in Sydney to start a new colony. And while some Australians used to be ashamed of their ancestors, now it's become fashionable to claim that one's forebears stole a sheep or a loaf of bread and then helped build the country. Australia is one country where Jews were literally "present at the creation."

The first free Jewish settler was Esther Isaacs, who arrived after her husband, a deported convict, in 1816. Sydney's first congregation was organized in 1832 and its first president was Joseph Barrow Montefiore, a cousin of Sir Moses Montefiore. Initially services were held in private homes or Jewish-owned hotels, and in 1837 the community bought a house and converted it to a synagogue. Finally in 1844, when there were 900 Jews in the city, the first synagogue building was constructed.

During the gold rush of the 1850s, more Jews moved to Australia — mainly from England but some from Germany as well. Many who disembarked at Sydney initially set up stores in the smaller towns of New South Wales; eventually they or their children made their way back to the big city.

Most of Sydney's Jewish population is the result of two waves of immigration following the world wars, and subsequent smaller waves reflecting the crises that have affected Jews around the world. Though few countries represented at the 1938 Evian Conference opened their doors to Jews trying to flee Europe, Australia allotted 15,000 entry permits; 7,000 had been used by the time the war began in 1939 and brought immigration to a virtual halt.

The recent growth of the Sydney community is reflected in the proliferation of synagogues — from four as recently as 1933 to nineteen by the 1970s. The 1956 Hungarian Revolution doubled the city's Hungarian Jewish population; Polish anti-Semitism after the Six Day War brought new Polish immigrants. Although Australia's "white policy" in the 1940s and early 1950s limited immigration to the country, more recently its leaders have let in a flood of immigrants. Now the government turns to — where else? — Israel for programs to help arrivals adapt to their new land.

Community: While the majority of Melbourne's 42,000 Jews are of Eastern European, particularly Polish, origin, Sydney's 37,000-member community is predominantly Hungarian with a mixture of German, British, and Australian-born Jews. Big changes in the community took place in the 1980s as a result of the influx of immigrants from Russia and South Africa. (Even more affected than Sydney or Melbourne was Perth, on the Indian Ocean, where the South African wave doubled the Jewish community from 3,000 to 6,000 between 1986 and 1989). The Russians and South Africans present a study in contrasts. Those coming from the former Soviet Union arrived speaking a foreign language and with little Jewish background. Not only do the South Africans speak English, but most come from a more pervasive Jewish atmosphere than Australia's and have been able to move quickly not only into society but also into leadership roles in the Jewish community.

The traditional stereotype is that Melbourne's Jews are more observant than those in Sydney, but in reality the Jews of Sydney are far from assimilated. Over half of Sydney's Jewish children attend Jewish day schools and, as Susan Bures, editor of the *Australian Jewish Times,* points out, "Sydney is completely Zionist. Since 1967, there has been an increased identification of Jews as Jews and connected to Israel." Indeed, Sydney's Jewish leaders are proud of the high rate of *aliyah* among their young people, and they're optimistic that Australia's relatively low intermarriage rate—about 10 percent—will not increase. "With few exceptions," Rabbi Raymond Apple of Sydney's Great Synagogue says, "most Australian Jews who achieved high offices retained their Jewish observances." Other Australian authorities agree that there is less pressure for Jews to assimilate in Australia than in other Diaspora countries. With their history dating back to the nation's founding, Australian Jews find that there is virtually no social penalty for remaining who they are.

Anti-Semitism, although not widespread, is still felt by the Jewish community. One observer explains that it consists of traditional anti-Semitic feeling among those of British origin and of other new immigrants. The debate in recent years over the prosecution of war criminals who may have entered Australia has strained relations between Jews and Eastern European émigré associations, particularly the Ukrainians, although the conflict does not seem to have affected the low level of anti-Semitic attitudes that come out in public opinion surveys. And it has not impeded the success of Jews in professions such as medicine and law, nor the proliferation of shops in downtown Sydney with names like Cohen's Stamps.

Neighborhoods and Sights: The first Jewish convict settlers were illiterate in both English and Hebrew, and there was no kind of Jewish organization until a *chevrah kadisha* was formed in 1817. By 1878, the Great Synagogue, the first permanent synagogue in Sydney, was established, and services are still conducted there every day. The synagogue is in an imposing building in Sydney's bustling center, adjacent to Hyde Park (166 Castlereagh Street, telephone 267-2477). Two four-story towers flank the central portion of the building, which features a double-arched entry topped by a rosette window and a pointed arch. The spectacular sanctuary, in the best tradition of Victorian style, features a high arch over the *bimah*, a sweeping, multiarched balcony punctuated by brass chandeliers and, above the balcony, stained-glass windows set in arches that act as skylights. The building also houses a Jewish museum and library and sponsors educational and cultural activities

Most of Sydney's Jews, however, have settled outside the city in two suburban areas: Bondi and the North Shore. Bondi has the weathered look of an old-time seaside resort. Its stores, with their faded awnings, are on streets with manicured lawns and are perched on a cliff overlooking the ocean. At the Hakoah Club, 61–67 Hall Street, there are legal poker and slot machines, a dining room with a kosher section, and other game facilities, making Bondi seem like a Jewish miniature version of Atlantic City. Also in the area are the Lubavitch Yeshiva College, at 32 Flood Street, the Central Synagogue on Bon Accord Avenue, Jewish bookstores, and kosher butchers and bakeries.

The North Shore suburbs, about a half hour from downtown Sydney and the same distance from Bondi, also boast a coastline of lovely beaches. The suburbs, though, are spread out, and since there is no Jewish shopping area, most North Shore Jewish residents shop in Bondi. The North Shore is the section that has seen the largest influx of South Africans in the Sydney area.

The largest institution, the North Shore Synagogue (15 Treatts Road, Lindfield), which also sponsors two Jewish day schools, is set on several lush and tropical acres. One Sydney Jew observes that their *Shabbat Kiddush*, which is held outdoors, is like a "garden party." Rabbi David Kogut, spiritual leader of the synagogue, says that his facilities in Lindfield, and that of North Shore Temple Emanuel in Chatswood (28 Chatswood Avenue), cater to a growing community of young professional families.

Sydney's Jewish cultural scene has grown since the community observed its bicentennial in 1988. There is a Jewish theater and a folk center that sponsors Yiddish and other Jewish cultural activities. Check the listings in the weekly *Australian Jewish Times*. The best place to get general information about Jewish activities, prayer times, or kashrut is the New South Wales Jewish Board of Deputies, located at 3200 Darlinghust Road (telephone 360-1600).

A new addition to Sydney's cultural treasury, also on Darlinghurst Road, is the Museum of Australian Jewish History and the Holocaust. The section devoted to Australian Jewry has fascinating material on the convicts who founded Sydney's Jewish community and a reconstructed portion of George Street, where many Jews made their home in the midnineteenth century. The Holocaust section includes a recreation of a street in the Warsaw Ghetto; many of the artifacts in the exhibit were donated by survivors who live in Australia.

Personalities: John Harris, one of the Jewish convicts on the first ship to Sydney, must have been rehabilitated; he became Australia's first policeman. Also among the convict settlers was Isaac Solomon, said to be the model for Fagin in *Oliver Twist*. Barnett Levy founded Australia's first theater. Isaac Nathan, who arrived in Sydney from London in 1841, was the first resident composer and considered the father of Australian music; his works ranged from operas to melodies for Hebrew prayers to adaptations of Aborigine music. A matter of ongoing dispute is whether his grandson, the composer Harry Alfred Nathan, was the author of "Waltzing Matilda."

The first Australian governor-general — the highest ceremonial officer, who is appointed by the queen — was Sir Isaac Isaacs, a Melbourne Jew; Sydney got its turn with Zelman Cowan, who held the same post until 1982. Sir Saul Samuel was the first Jew elected to the Australian Parliament (in 1859) and was also a president of Sydney's Great Synagogue. Sir Daniel Levy was speaker of the New South Wales Legislative Assembly and also editor of the *Australian Hebrew*. Rising stars on the arts scene today include new Jewish immigrants such as Moscow-born Alexander Semetsky, a concert pianist who performs throughout Australia.

Eating: The B'nai B'rith center, near the Great Synagogue but on the opposite side of Hyde Park, has a formal restaurant with unusual kosher dishes, such as honey chicken and beef curry. It's at 22–38 Yurong Street. Another restaurant with atypical kosher cuisine is Bondi's Wei-Song Vegetarian Chinese Restaurant, at 96 Bronte Road. There is also a kosher dining room in the Hakoah Club. Traditional fare can be found at Shalom College, University of New South Wales (telephone 663-1366), and Lewis's Continental Kitchen at 2 Curlewis Street in Bondi and on Victoria Avenue in Chatswood.

General Sights: Historic Sydney has been restored at the Rocks, the rocky area near Sydney's harbor where the convicts first settled. Sydney's oldest surviving house as well as the Argyle Center — built with convict labor and now a mall filled with boutiques selling antiques and gems — are found there. Also in the area are restaurants that feature fresh fish, and where jazz bands often play.

For a panorama of both old and new Sydney, visitors can ride up to the observation deck of the Centre Point Tower in Sydney or ride around the city in ferries that cruise through Sydney harbor. Both afford excellent views of Sydney's landmark opera house, which was designed to look like sails billowing in the wind. One of the opera house's founders was Sir Asher Joel.

There are lovely parks and gardens in the city, particularly the Royal Botanic Gardens, which feature a palm grove and Australian rainforest trees. Spectacular scenery can also be found two hours from Sydney in the Blue Mountains, where visitors, if they're lucky, might spot a koala bear.

Reading: Sydney's Jewish literature is not as rich as Melbourne's, but Judah Waten's book *Alien Son* (Angus and Robertson), about his growing up in Melbourne, sheds some light on the Australian Jewish community. Another Australian Jewish author is Morris Lurie, whose comic short-story collections, such as *Inside the Wardrobe* (Outback Press), are available in the United States. For an introduction to a WASP fairyland with a multicultural layer just beneath the surface, Waten and Lurie are good places to start.

—Diana Katcher Bletter

Tel Aviv

Tel Aviv is a city "with no past and nothing but a future," wrote Max Nordau, physician, sociologist, and one of Theodor Herzl's first supporters. The quintessential twentieth-century city, Tel Aviv grew too fast to care about style or appearance. Often criticized for its impersonal streets lined with unexceptional buildings, Tel Aviv is a brash, polyglot microcosm of Israel, the nerve-center of the country's greatest surge forward. It is Israel's commercial showcase and shopping center — home of its industrial and agricultural organizations, its trade institutions, and its army. It is also home to its banks and newspapers — and this is one place where Jews really do control both. The largest completely Jewish city in the world (97 percent), it is also the hub of Israel's secular cultural life, providing entertainment and services for tens of thousands of nonresidents who converge on Tel Aviv daily.

The comparisons with Jerusalem are inevitable, and the rivalry between the two cities is as fierce as competition between New York and Los Angeles, or between Michigan and Michigan State. Each city has partisans who boast about how long it has been since they have made the fifty-minute drive to the other town. The differences between Israel's two principal centers are stark. In somewhat simplified terms, Jerusalem is quiet, Tel Aviv loud; Jerusalem is historic, Tel Aviv is an upstart; Jerusalem is spiritual, Tel Aviv down to earth and, to some, downright depraved. Perhaps more fundamental, Jerusalem is Jewish, Tel Aviv Israeli.

Once in a while, each city gets to live in the other's shoes. In a small country, Tel Aviv — a full half-hour from Arab territory — has always seemed removed from the tensions felt in Jerusalem, with its large Arab minority, its proximity to the West Bank, and its place in the international spotlight. For six weeks in 1991, however, Saddam Hussein reversed their roles. Fearful of hitting Arabs or Muslim holy sites in Jerusalem, he targeted his Scud missiles on Tel Aviv, making Israel's largest metropolitan area a front-line post for the first time since 1948. The city showed its pluck by weathering the missile storm, and before the war was over cars were sporting "I stayed in Tel Aviv" bumper stickers.

History: This city without a history rose out of the sands north of Jaffa in 1909, but its ultimate absorption of the older city made it heir to Jaffa's past.

Jaffa is one of the oldest ports in the world. Jonah set sail from there for his immortal encounter with the whale. There is documentation of Israelite settlement from the thirteenth century B.C.E., but for most of the biblical period it was under Egyptian or Philistine control. The city came under Jewish sovereignty when the Hasmoneans captured it; it was originally attacked by Judah Maccabbee in retaliation for the drowning of 200 Jaffa Jews. Pompey captured Jaffa in 66 B.C.E. but Julius Caesar returned it to Judea nineteen years later.

A Jewish presence in Jaffa was constant until the Crusades, when the city was repeatedly conquered and destroyed and its inhabitants dispersed or slaughtered. The period of modern development and growth is usually dated from its conquest by Napoleon's army, when the city's population was about 2,500.

Tel Aviv's emergence was prefigured when Rabbi Yeshaya Adjiman, from Istanbul, bought a house in Jaffa — the first in the city under Jewish ownership. Arab neighbors referred to it as Dar al-Yahud ("the Jewish house"), and it became both a hostel for incoming Jewish immigrants, mostly from North Africa, and the beginning of a nucleus of a Jewish neighborhood. Though many of the Jews coming into Palestine in the late nineteenth century bypassed Jaffa, the establishment of Jewish agricultural settlements in the area contributed to the city's progress and attracted Arab immigrants, particularly from Egypt, as well as Jews. After the city's wall was torn down in 1888, Jewish neighborhoods began to develop outside the old center. Neve Tzedek, which underwent some gentrification in the 1980s, was Jaffa's first Jewish quarter, started in 1887; it was followed four years later by Neve Shalom.

By the turn of the century, Jaffa was a crowded town, still predominantly Arab. Some 60 Jewish families decided to break away and build a modern, European-style garden city. They formed a home-building society, called it Ahuzat Bayit, elected Meir Dizengoff their chairman, and chose a waterless site north of Jaffa, where the landscape was sandy and jackals howled at night. There in 1909 they put up 60 single-story houses with gardens and linked them with paved streets. They named the township Tel Aviv, "hill of spring." The name was taken from a Babylonian city mentioned in the Book of Ezekiel and had been chosen as the title of the Hebrew translation of Theodor Herzl's novel *Altneuland*.

Zionists, poets, thinkers, and labor idealists were the first Tel Avivians. Poet Shaul Tchernichowsky (1875-1943) spoke for them all when he wrote: "It is . . . impossible not to love crowded Tel Aviv because this is, after all, the only spot on earth where a Jew can be simply a human being called a Jew—without any feeling that he is a Jew, and without even being aware of it." The city's development was arrested by World War I, when Turkish authorities expelled most of the Jews from Jaffa and Tel Aviv. But the Third *Aliyah*, which began after the war, and the 1922 annexation of the adjacent Jewish neighborhoods of Jaffa brought the new city's population to 15,000.

Tel Aviv's growth was prompted more by history than geography. It grew into Israel's leading city within three decades of its founding even though its shore was unsuitable for a port and the offshore sandstone ridges bar the sea breezes that make other parts of Israel's coast more comfortable during the summer. None of this mattered much to the immigrants of the Fourth *Aliyah*, which in the 1920s brought middle-class Polish and Rumanian Jews, changing Tel Aviv forever. Shunning life in the wilderness, these new immigrants opened shops and built factories, transforming the city from a quiet Jewish suburb of Jaffa into a lively, horn-honking, café-happy town. Women in high fashion strolled the potholed streets. Waiters in bow ties served vintage wines in fine restaurants. Real-estate speculators sold stucco seaside homes, which their owners furnished with expensive imports.

The foundations of the future state's culture were laid in the city in the 1920s as well, with the arrival of Habima—today Israel's premier theater company—from Moscow, the establishment of the *Eretz Yisrael* opera, the growth of the Histadrut labor federation, and the development of the Hebrew daily press. The 1930s brought the founding of the Philharmonic Orchestra and a new wave of immigrants from prewar Europe, bringing the population to 160,000 by 1939.

It was the Arabs of Jaffa, uneasily watching the Jewish township develop to the north, who inadvertently set it on the road to becoming the metropolis of today. In 1921, Arab mobs, enraged by international support for the Balfour Declaration, rampaged through the infant settlement. The British Mandatory authorities responded by granting Tel Aviv municipal autonomy. The coup de grace came fifteen years later when the Arab revolt (1936-1939) shut down the Jaffa docks; Tel Aviv responded by building its own docks.

Tel Aviv was bombed by Italian and French Vichy planes during World War II and it was a front-line city during Israel's War of Independence. The Defense Ministry to come grew on the Hagana, Irgun, and Lehi, all of which were headquartered in the city. In 1948 the residents of Tel Aviv fell under shelling from Arab forces based in Jaffa; the Jewish conquest of Jaffa saw the departure not only of Arab soldiers from as far away as Iraq but also of most of the city's Arab civilians.

Even before the founding of the state in 1948, Tel Aviv had become the center of Jewish life in Israel. It was a city of museums, concert halls, and theaters. It was in Tel Aviv that the State was declared and the first Knesset met. From its beginnings just outside Jaffa, the city gradually grew northward, with wealthier residents moving into the new neighborhoods where services were more expensive. In 1949, the supremacy of adolescent Tel Aviv over ancient Jaffa was formally enshrined with the amalgamation of the city into Tel Aviv-Yafo.

Community: In 1937, when Tel Aviv's first mayor, Meir Dizengoff, died, his friend Arthur Ruppin wrote in his diary: "Four years ago, Dizengoff told me he'd like to live until Tel Aviv had 100,000 inhabitants. Today it has 150,000. Who among us, when he dies, finds his wishes surpassed by 50 percent?"

Half a century later, the numbers are still growing. Some 320,000 people live in Tel Aviv itself, with another million in its surrounding suburbs. Like Israelis everywhere, Tel Aviv's citizens come from all the lands of dispersion, but compared with those in many other parts of the country—and especially in Jerusalem—they are the most Israeli of Israelis. True, there are cafés on Dizengoff Street where more Bulgarian or Polish is spoken than Hebrew, but it is in Tel Aviv that the melting pot has best taken hold. It is here in the first modern Jewish city that the secular, urban Israeli was forged—the Israeli who, hand in hand with the kibbutznik, indelibly imprinted his image on the newborn nation.

There are still ethnic pockets. North African and Yemenite Jews predominate in Neve Tzedek, Neve Shalom, and the Hatikva quarter. Many Iraqi Jews had so well blended into Ramat Gan that their presence was hardly noted until Saddam Hussein started sending the suburb messages from home in the form of Scud missiles. Even in more integrated neighborhoods individual apartment buildings may have clusters of Turkish, Russian, Argentine, or American Jews.

Sights: If Jerusalem is where Jewish visitors find their religious roots, Tel Aviv is where they see their lives in the Diaspora reflected back at them through an Israeli prism. The freeways and the shopping malls could look American suburban if it weren't for the signs in Hebrew. It is a city of stock and diamond exchanges, of fashion and traffic, of night life and gossip.

Tel Aviv's main street and the center of most of the local action is Dizengoff. It boasts the busiest sidewalk cafés, the fanciest stores, the most chic boutiques and the most stylish women. On Dizengoff Street, artists, film stars, housewives, and tourists congregate, to stroll, shop, or gorge themselves on pastries, blintzes, and ice cream. During the week, the city's cafés (on and off Dizengoff) are distinguished by their clientele, which may be characterized by age range, national origin, profession, or political affiliation. The clientele can change, and the cafés may come and go, but in recent years painters and writers could be found most mornings at the Frak (Dizengoff and Gordon). Stern (Dizengoff south of Arlosoroff) has been popular among elderly German Jews and among writers and editors of literary journals. The Oslo, at 192 Ibn Gvirol, was known as the spot for members of the National Religious Party in the morning and assignations in the afternoon.

Though the section of Dizengoff with most of the cafés and restaurants runs north and south, the street begins to curve at Dizengoff Square (actually a circle), a plaza which has been lifted onto a concrete dome to accommodate Tel Aviv's endless traffic. Atop the dome is Yaacov Agam's *Fire And Water*, a sculpture that combines color, music, jets of water, and flames in a compelling concert of movement and sound. Just up the street is Dizengoff Centre, the city's first indoor shopping mall, whose success inspired a larger and more impressive complex, Gan Ha'ir, on Ibn Gvirol near the Tel Aviv city hall. A miniature version of Chicago's Water Tower, Gan Ha'ir has elegant stores and restaurants surrounding an open-air plaza.

Most visitors to Tel Aviv stay in the beachfront hotels that dominate the city's skyline. The beach, which in the 1930s housed tent-camps of squatters, is now the center of Israeli luxury. International chains, from Hilton to Carlton to Sheraton, are well represented on the west side of Hayarkon Street. Less expensive hotels line the inland side of the street.

Tel Aviv is a beach city, and tourists are always outnumbered on the sand. The serious swimmers and exercisers, many of them over sixty, go between 4:30 A.M. (when the beach opens) and 8:00 A.M. Young people go later. On most days the scene is lively, with picnics, games of cards, and *sheshbesh* (backgammon) and the ubiquitous *kadimah* players.

The hotels are only part of the energetic development of Tel Aviv's seashore. There is also the promenade along most of the waterfront, which has come to rival the café and restaurant scene of Dizengoff, and Namir Square, a plaza of cafés and restaurants between the Hilton and Plaza Hotels, which comes alive as darkness falls. At the Tel Aviv marina—where sailboats can be rented by the hour, with or without a skipper—small craft from all over the world moor, and people come to fish, sail, dive, and wind surf.

Israel may have more art galleries per capita than any other country, and the map of Tel Aviv is loaded with places selling fine art and kitsch. The center of galleries, however, is along Gordon Street between the beach and Dizengoff. (The next largest concentration of galleries is in Old Jaffa.)

Also near the beach is Israel's modest answer to Mount Vernon, Ben Gurion House at 17 Ben Gurion Boulevard. This is the home the father of Israeli independence bought in 1927 in a then-isolated part of town; he had to trudge through sand dunes to reach it, and he read by kerosene lamp until the house was hooked up to the electric grid. The house now houses his library and many artifacts from his eventful life.

Tel Aviv's quick development can be seen in the city's center, where old houses on side streets sit in the shadow of modern office buildings a few feet away. In one little corner of the city, off Allenby Road, a good part of the nation's history can be found. At 22 Bialik Street is the house—

Israeli skyline: Modern architecture in the city "with no past and nothing but a future"

now a museum and library—where Haim Nahman Bialik, poet of Israel's national cultural renaissance, presided with his wife over Tel Aviv's literary and intellectual circles. Down the street at number 14 is the former home—also a museum—of artist Reuven Rubin, whose career was closely interwoven with the development of the country; his studio is preserved as he left it. At 27 Bialik is the Museum of the History of Tel Aviv–Jaffa, with artifacts, photos, and documents on the city's life and a good introductory video, "24 Hours in the Life of a City."

Unlike the row of high-rise hotels on the beach, the thirty-four-story Shalom Tower, tallest building in the Middle East, stands alone, dominating the lower office buildings at the southern end of central Tel Aviv. The building has an observation deck with spectacular views of the city, the Mediterranean, and the surrounding countryside.

Some of the city's most interesting residential architecture is in the center of town, along Rothschild Boulevard. Prime examples of the International Style, promoted by the Bauhaus school in the 1930s, line the street, featuring balconies with rounded corners and porthole windows aligned over the entrance and up through the stairwell.

Habima Square, at the north end of Rothschild Boulevard, is Israel's cultural heart. It is the site of the Mann Auditorium, home of the Israel Philharmonic Orchestra, under the direction of Zubin Mehta; and the Helena Rubinstein Pavilion, a branch of the Tel Aviv Museum. The main building of the Tel Aviv Museum is at 27 Shaul Hamelekh Boulevard. Though its permanent collection is less explicitly Jewish than that of the Israel Museum in Jerusalem, the Tel Aviv Museum showcases modern art, some by Israeli artists, and has had major exhibits of Jewish artists (such as Mauricy Gottlieb, whose best known work, *Jews at Prayer on Yom Kippur,* is in the permanent collection) and Israeli themes.

South Tel Aviv is more picturesque than north, with old houses and winding streets. The narrow lanes of Neve Tzedek look in many ways like they did when the future Nobel Laureate Shmuel Yosef Agnon lived and wrote there, in one of a group of houses that Jaffa Arabs dubbed "Parisian," because of their elegance. Amid the houses, some of them renovated, are restaurants and galleries.

The area of Ahuzat Bayit's first sixty homes is next to Neve Tzedek, tucked away behind the traffic and trade of Allenby Road, where the new city had overflowed by the 1920s. With its colonnades and archways, curved balconies and decorated facades, it is a successful, unabashed pastiche of a dozen different styles of architecture, its embrace extending from the European to the Oriental. The city's Middle Eastern belt stretches from the Carmel Market — a sensory floodgate of smells, sounds and every kind of merchandise — to the predominantly Yemenite Hatikva Quarter with its narrow, twisting streets and restaurants that draw people from all over the city.

Looking south from Tel Aviv's plush hotel strip, you can see the promontory of old Jaffa jutting into the sea. The old city's crumbling alleys and courtyards have been restored and this renovation, together with the thriving additions of an artists' quarter, a flea market selling everything but food, studios, antique shops, restaurants, and nightclubs, has turned the ancient port into a popular center of tourism and nightlife.

The "Israeli Experience," an hour-long fifty-one-projector multimedia celebration of Israeli life, is screened at the arabesque-shaped entrance to the old Jaffa mall. There is still a small Arab community in Jaffa, and there is continuity in the old atmosphere since most of the Jews who moved in after 1948 came from the Middle East and North Africa.

As Tel Aviv itself has spread across a wider expanse, its night life has also reached beyond the city's core. North of the hotels, where Hayarkon converges with Dizengoff and Ben Yehuda, is Little Tel Aviv, a flourishing area of restaurants and nightclubs. And if the nightclubs of Little Tel Aviv close too early for your taste, try Karlebach Street, which forks off the southern end of Ibn Gvirol. Because the area around Karlebach has no residential buildings, it has been declared a twenty-four-hour zone; a magnet for the city's young people, its cafés and cinemas come to life around 11:00 P.M. and don't slow down till 5:00 or 6:00 A.M.

North Tel Aviv houses the city's showpieces: its Exhibition Grounds, Stock Exchange and Diamond Exchange, Yarkon Park, Tel Aviv University, and the city hall.

Unlike many Diaspora cities, Tel Aviv is not noted for its synagogue architecture, which tends toward the utilitarian. Two places that rise to the top of the collection in aesthetics are the Great Synagogue (110 Allenby), noted for its dome with painted windows depicting Diaspora synagogues; and the Recanati Synagogue, built by Jews from Salonika at Jabotinsky and Ibn Gvirol.

Culture: Tel Aviv prides itself on its urbanity. Its cultural offerings range from open-air rock concerts in the park to performances by the world-class Israel Philharmonic Orchestra in the three thousand-seat Mann Auditorium. In addition to Israel's National Habima Theater there is the municipal Cameri Theater and the National Ballet. Tel Aviv has room for the avant-garde, as well: Beit Lessin (Medina Square at Weizmann Street) and the Tzavta Theater (downstairs in the arcade at 30 Ibn Gvirol Street) offer chamber music, fringe theater, and poetry readings and often showcase new works by Israeli composers, poets and playwrights. The best place to look for English-language listings of movies, plays, and concerts is *The Jerusalem Post*.

The city also abounds in museums. Perhaps the most visited, and most fun, is Beit Hatefutzot, the Nahum Goldmann Museum of the Jewish Diaspora, on the campus of Tel Aviv University in Ramat Aviv. Through dioramas, photos, and audiovisual displays it documents the wanderings of the Jewish people from the destruction of the First Temple twenty-five hundred years ago to the establishment of modern Israel. It has a computerized genealogical center (where long-lost relatives have been known to meet each other by coincidence). Among its displays one of the most striking is the set of models of synagogues, from America to China, from Poland to India.

Also in Ramat Aviv is the Eretz Israel Museum, with indoor and outdoor exhibits. It is best known for its collection of coins from ancient Israel and its ethnography section with examples of Jewish costumes from many countries. There is an archeological excavation on the grounds, and children especially like the British Mandate–period train in the garden.

At 16 Rothschild Boulevard is Independence Hall, the former home of Meir Dizengoff, where Israel's Declaration of Independence was signed. The former home of Haganah commander Eliahu Golomb, at 23 Rothschild Street, is the site of the Haganah Museum, which focuses on the War of Independence; it is balanced by the Etzel Museum, devoted to the Irgun Zvai Leumi, on the Herbert Samuel Promenade. Mementos of Israeli theater are on display at the Theater Museum at 3 Melchett Street.

Personalities: How do you single out Jewish personalities in a city that is 97 percent Jewish? Much of Israel's political and cultural leadership has called Tel Aviv home, from the poets Natan Alterman and Haim Nahman Bialik to President Ezer Weizman and Prime Minister Yitzhak Rabin. Other locals include the sculptor Menashe Kadishman, the satirist Ephraim Kishon, and Naomi Shemer, the composer and lyricist best known for *Jerusalem of Gold*. Tel Aviv has produced great violinists, from Pinchas Zukerman, who still lives there, to Yitzhak Perlman, who now lives in New York.

Reading: For the scents, color, and excitement of Tel Aviv's early years, try Natan Alterman's series of essays published as *Little Tel Aviv* (HaKibbutz HaMeuchad). Yigal Lossin's *Pillar of Fire* (B'nai B'rith Anti-Defamation League) is based on an excellent Israeli television series of the same name. It tells the story of modern Israel and is, of course, an excellent source about Tel Aviv. Barbara Rogan's novel, *Café Nevo* (Atheneum), offers a taste of a Tel Aviv café society teeming with local color and characters. Yaakov Shabtai's rich but moody novels *Past Continuous* (Jewish Publication Society) and *Past Perfect* (Viking) are set largely in Tel Aviv.

Recommendations: El Al Israel Airlines connects Tel Aviv with the world, and gives travelers the atmosphere of Israel as soon as they set foot on the plane. Tel Aviv is still slighted in some of the guide books, but the Israel Government Tourist Office (350 Fifth Avenue, New York, NY 10001; 212-560-0650) is a good place to call for information on sightseeing and cultural events.

There are many ways to experience Tel Aviv beyond traditional sightseeing. Two recommendations, from many possibilities, are to shop in a local department store, like Hamashbir on Allenby Road, or in one of the shopping malls, like those in central Tel Aviv or the Kanion in Ramat Gan. To get a notion of Israeli-style sports, go to a soccer game. The noisy fans at a typical game exhibit the depth of insult and the height of faith; when an opponent scores a goal, the crowd routinely chants, in Hebrew, "Son of a prostitute!" When the home team scores, the cheer is "There *is* a God!" A good place to stroll or watch Israelis at leisure is in Gan Hayarkon (Yarkon Park), which has outdoor concerts during the summer. An alternative to the choppier Mediterranean is renting a boat for a ride on the Yarkon River, which runs through the park. In the quintessential twentieth-century city there are still places to relax.

—Wendy Elliman

Thessaloniki

Once—because this is, after all, a once-upon-a-time story—Thessaloniki, or Salonika as it was called then, was virtually a Jewish city. On occasion the Jews comprised nearly half of an otherwise heterogeneous population, as they did at the turn of the 20th century when they numbered 70,000 of 150,000. Their real estate was privileged: they dwelled in the heart of the town and along a waterfront that encompassed one of the region's most important ports. Commerce, culture, and trade were in their hands; Jews were policemen, garbagemen, water sellers, and sailors. Because almost all longshoremen were Jewish, on *Shabbat* the harbor shut down completely.

A city born Macedonian and subsequently Byzantine, Venetian, Turkish and now Greek, Thessaloniki boasted during Ottoman rule one of the largest Jewish settlements in Europe and possibly the world's preeminent Sephardic community. A vision, however idealized, sees Jews as having lived for centuries unto millennia in Thessaloniki, free from expulsion or segregation, free, in fact, from most forms of persecution. The scene was perceived with such rosiness that in 1537 a poet called Thessaloniki the "Metropolis of Israel, city of Justice, mother of Israel, like Jerusalem."

But by the eve of World War II the idyll had begun to corrode. And the Holocaust eradicated all but minimal tokens of earlier glories. Thessaloniki's Jews were among the most decimated—only 4 percent survived—and the contemporary community is scarcely a shadow of its former self. Numbering a scant 1,300 in a population of a million, the Jews of Thessaloniki today are a presence barely felt.

History: Alef, bet, gimmel, dalet—alpha, beta, gamma, delta. Merely to glance at the Hebrew and Greek alphabets is to understand how early the two peoples made contact, how closely their histories were entwined. Greek Jewry likes to see itself as a major surviving link between today and antiquity, when the whole known Western world was Greek speaking. At whatever point the Jews started moving westward, they are mentioned as having been on Greek islands in 586 B.C.E., after the First Temple's destruction, and may have been with Darius during his campaign against the Scythians of East Macedonia in 513.

According to Jewish legend, Alexander the Great was so interested in Jewish thought that during the conquet of Israel in 322 B.C.E., he met the High Priest on Mount Scopus. How much Alexander actually did know of Judaism is debatable, but Jews probably did accompany his armies as mercenaries and providers and settled in various conquered lands.

When Cassandros, Alexander's brother-in-law, founded Thessaloniki in 315 B.C.E., he purportedly asked the Egyptian Ptolemy of the time to send Jewish artisans to help populate the new city. By the second century B.C.E., with more Hellenized Jews leaving homefront strife—this was the time of Antiochus and the Maccabees—they established communities along the Mediterranean coast and on the Greek mainland. When the Romans conquered Thessaloniki in 168 B.C.E., Jews were already there.

The apostle Paul—born Saul into a devout Jewish family in Tarsus—preached on three consecutive Sabbaths in Thessaloniki's Etz Haim Synagogue to its Romaniote, or Greek-speaking, Jews. Only when this and other congregations turned against him did he start addressing pagans.

The Jews of Thessaloniki lived pleasantly under Roman rule before Christianity had taken deep root. Thanks to the autonomy granted them, they began establishing extensive foreign trade ties. With the solidification of the Byzantine Empire and the zealous Christianizing practiced by Constantine the Great (306–337) and his successors, the Jews began suffering cyclically through anti-Jewish legislation.

However, since they were still protected by Roman law, by their perceived status as people of God, and by the occasional friendly emperor, they continued their trading operations even during the Crusaders' onslaughts. When Benjamin of Tudela visited in 1169 the community numbered 500. In the next century, as Byzantium recovered from instability and decline, it became a magnet for European Jewry — with Germans and Hungarians arriving in 1376 and the first Sephardim, after troubles in Spain, in 1391.

In 1430 the Turks occupied Thessaloniki, following this with the conquest of Byzantium's capital, Constantinople, in 1453. And since Thessaloniki's population had been greatly reduced during the fighting, the sultan, willing to grant minorities religious freedom, sought new subjects — preferably ones versed in trade.

When Spain ordered the expulsion of its Jews in 1492, the sultan happily invited them to his realm. Between then and the mid-sixteenth century they came — not only from Spain, but from Italy, Sicily, France, North Africa, and Portugal as well. Of these, 20,000 headed for this port. Given their contacts with coreligionists elsewhere, plus their education and sophistication, they gained control of the city's manufacturing, transportation, and finance.

They also quickly overwhelmed the resident Romaniotes. As settlers rather than refugees, they had a status the Romaniotes, who were seen as conquered Greeks, couldn't match. Nor could the Romaniotes compete with their culture, enterprise or numbers. The Romaniotes rapidly learned Spanish and Sephardic customs, and Thessaloniki took on a Spanish-Jewish character.

The Jews of Thessaloniki wove and dyed silk and wool; milled for gold and silver; made jewelry, clothing, leather, maps, and navigational instruments. They also introduced gunpowder, cannons, and printing to the Turks. The Sephardim founded about thirty congregations and their cultural inclinations turned the city into a center for religious and secular scholarship.

During the sixteenth century the city attracted such religious thinkers as Solomon Alkabez, author of *Lekhah Dodi*; Isaac Adarbi, who wrote of *Divrei Rivot* and *Divrei Shalom*; and Samuel di Medina (Rashdam) who left over a thousand responsa, many still respected by halakhic authorities. While also becoming a renowned center for Kabbalah study, the city established a school for such subjects as astronomy, natural sciences, and medicine. During this time the Ottoman Empire knew its heyday and its Jews a golden age.

Life grew rockier in the next century. Though the empire's decline affected the Jews, they managed to hold their own, at least in the secular world. Numbering 30,000 including newcomers, they now comprised half the city's population, and their trading ventures flourished with the export of grain, cotton, wool, silk, textiles, and tobacco.

But with worldly security came spiritual confusion; many began to speculate on the deeper meaning of their exile and were ripe for the advent of Shabbetai Tzvi, the false messiah who arrived in Thessaloniki in the mid-1650s. So influential was he that after his conversion to Islam and his death in 1683, about 300 Jewish families in the city converted as well. Thus Thessaloniki became the religious center for the Donmeh sect of "Jewish Muslims," who remained in the city until 1927. But the threat Shabbetai Tzvi represented prompted the Jewish community to reorganize in 1680, uniting its thirty congregations. The rabbinical courts resulting from this merger gained such a positive reputation that many Muslims and Greeks turned to them rather than Turkish ones for justice.

The nineteenth century's Industrial Revolution came to Thessaloniki, with the Jews — especially Conversos from Italy such as the Fernández, Modianos and Mizrahis — contributing much of the capital. In 1858 the Allatini flour mills were founded; in 1865 the first newspaper; in 1871, thanks to Baron Maurice de Hirsch, the railroad to Skopje was completed. In 1878 the Shaias textile industry was established; in 1888, the Allatini brothers formed the Bank of Salonika.

The twentieth century brought turmoil. Not only did the Young Turks rise against the Ottoman sultan, the entire Balkan region was a tinderbox, which eventually ignited World War I. After consolidating lands farther south in their kingdom, the Greeks finally made it back to Thessaloniki in 1912.

Initially they granted all minorities equal rights, and the Jews continued to flourish as merchants, lawyers, teachers, and physicians, not to mention stevedores. But the Jews of Thessaloniki posed a unique problem. The Greeks intended to Hellenize all their subjects, but unlike Jews elsewhere in the country, those of Thessaloniki constituted a self-contained society closed to and so resented by other Jews that among Ioannina Jews there was a saying, "God save me from the Greeks of Arta, the Turks of Ioannina, and the Jews of Salonika." Not only were many wealthy, cultured and possessed of their own language (which until today they insist is Judeo-Spanish, not Ladino), but they were also seen as pro-Turkish. A major fire in 1917, which destroyed most of the Jewish quarter and left 50,000 homeless, provided the prologue to the beginning of the end.

Though the Greeks were ready to compensate the Jews, they would not let them return to certain areas. In 1922 a law was passed prohibiting work on Sunday. Following the Treaty of Lausanne later in the decade, a major population exchange was undertaken between Greece and Turkey, and 100,000 Greeks from Anatolia and the Balkans were resettled in Thessaloniki. Such occurrences prompted further spurts of emigration. During the 1924–1935 political strife in Greece, anti-Semitism flared. And when during rioting in the early 1930s an entire Jewish neighborhood in Thessaloniki was burned, most of its residents left. On the eve of World War II, 55,000 Jews — still with good status but now only 20 percent of Thessaloniki's citizenry — remained.

When the war broke out Greece was neutral, but Italy attacked in October 1940. Though with British aid the Italians were forced back into Albania, the German invasion broke the resistance. While the Italians initially occupied most of Greece, the Bulgarians got western Thrace and the Germans got Macedonia and eastern Thrace. This division, plus the differences among themselves, provided Greek Jews of the various areas with widely diverse fates.

In February 1943 Dieter Wisliceny, Adolph Eichmann's deputy, arrived to initiate deportation plans. Because the Jews were scattered it was difficult to ghettoize them. But in successive waves they were herded into a de Hirsch housing development near the railroad station. The first transport left for Auschwitz on March 15, 1943, and by mid-May virtually all were gone.

Many wonder why Thessaloniki's Jews fared so badly. Some claim their centuries of safe living left them heedless and defenseless. Others claim they thought — since they had witnessed real population exchanges — they were going to new homes in Krakow. The community's isolation and the inability of many to speak accentless, if any, Greek, didn't aid their cause. But when they got to Auschwitz they worked in the underground. In *Survival in Auschwitz* Primo Levi wrote, "Next to us there is a group of Greeks, those admirable and terrible Jews of Thessaloniki, tenacious, thieving, wise, ferocious and united, so determined to live, such pitiless opponents in the struggle for life; those Greeks whom even the Germans respect. . . . "

After the war about a quarter of Thessaloniki's survivors emigrated, many joining compatriots in Israel. The community made a decided contribution to seamanship in the Jewish state. Initially spurred by early visits from David Ben Gurion and Yitzchak Ben Zvi, numbers of fishermen emigrated first to Akko, then to Haifa and Tel Aviv. After a 1933 visit by Haifa's mayor, Abba Khoushi, 300 dockworkers and their families went on *aliyah*, spearheading the drive of Jewish labor into the port. Some who left following anti-Semitic strife in the 1930s laid the foundations for Tel Aviv's port. And Greek settlers, mostly from Thessaloniki, established Moshav Zur Moshe, named for a prominent Ioannina Jew, in 1937.

Community:

Despite the fact that television in northern Greece recently broadcast a gung-ho Israeli movie about the taking of Sharm el-Sheikh in 1967 and an American one against anti-Semitism in the same week, the Jewish community of Thessaloniki today is perhaps one of the world's most skittish. Haunted and daunted by the Holocaust and wary of Greece's international politics—which have only recently turned in Israel s favor—its members make special efforts to maintain a low profile.

The community of 1,300 is believed to be a wealthy one and is said to own significant blocks of real estate in the downtown area. Thessaloniki's Jews—with Sephardim and Romaniote now united—prefer, though, to emphasize how their religious life has risen from the ashes, proud that they maintain a daily minyan, a rabbi, a kosher butcher, a school, a community center, various organizations, and an old-age home. In addition, they periodically organize lectures, art exhibitions, and concerts. Most these days are academics or professionals; few are religious. Though their numbers have been augmented by newcomers from Larissa and Kavala, there are some who maintain the community is stagnant and could benefit from strong leadership.

Sights:

Thessaloniki claims to be a living museum of Byzantium, since tucked into pockets all about town are churches and other edifices in a variety of Byzantine styles. Until this century, there were also synagogues making that claim. But the 1917 fire which destroyed the city's commercial center wiped out more than thirty synagogues plus *batei midrash*. Nevertheless, Thessaloniki still has reminders of erstwhile Jewish glory.

A good first destination is the promenade along the waterfront. Dominated by the circular White Tower, now a museum, the walkway follows the curve of the coast from the port along the seaside that edged the Jewish quarter.

Not far from the White Tower begins Vassilisis Olgas Street, paralleling the waterfront and running toward the airport. Along this street can be found excellent traces of the golden past—several turn-of-the-century villas and mansions or the ruins thereof, once owned by Jews.

At the junction of Olgas and 28 Oktovriou streets stands the Villa Modiano. This tree-encircled orange brick gingerbread building now housing the Folk Museum is dominated by arches and porticoes on its second story. The Villa Mordoh, with a facade of double-storied porticoes and balconies plus an onion-dome tower, stands at the junction of Olgas and 25 Martiou streets. It is now the municipal art gallery, the Pinakothiki.

At 198 Olgas is the Villa Allatini. This well-landscaped mansion, set back from the road and adorned with intricate brickwork and a steep central staircase, now houses the offices of the prefectural government. Back toward town and closer to the water is the Allatini factory, which still produces biscuits and other flour products bearing the well-known name.

Also in this general area is Saadi Levi Street, named for the publisher of one of Thessaloniki's earliest newspapers; a bit west of it, in the vicinity of Zaimi and Delfon Streets, is the building the Donmehs used for worship.

A little to the north where Papanastassiou, Karakassi, and Priamou streets intersect lies the Square of the Jewish Martyrs, a small tiered park with flagstone layers and little green rosebush-trimmed slopes topped by a playground. But the cheerful scene is marred: on the sign giving the place name, "Plateia Evreon Martiron," "Evreon" has been blocked out on both the Greek and English portions.

In the center of town are other reminders of previous Jewish preeminence. An L-shaped arcade, entered either at 32 Venizelou Street or 18 Ermou Street and filled with stalls selling buttons, lace, and other bric-a-brac is the Karasso Passage, named for the family that established it. About a block east, on Vassileos Irakliou Street on the left coming from Venizelou is a large, dirty, gray-stone, hangarlike building topped with a skylight and filled with fruit and vegetable stands. This is the popular Modiano Market.

Directly across the street in the building at 24 Irakliou is the Yad L'zichron Synagogue, used for daily services. On its walls is a listing of all the synagogues established in Thessaloniki from 1378 on. Upstairs is the Center for Historical Studies of the Jews of Salonika. On display are photos of people in traditional dress; rabbis in turbans; Jewish fishermen and parliamentarians and old synagogues; plus some caftans and a brocade Torah cover from Veria saved during the Holocaust by a Greek church official. The center is open Monday and Wednesday afternoons, or by appointment through the Israelite Community of Thessaloniki at 24 Tsikimi Street (telephone 275-701 or 272-840).

The main synagogue of the Monastiriotes is a short walk away at 35–37 Syngrou Street. Founded by families from Monastir (Bitola) in Yugoslavia, it was inaugurated in 1937. The ghetto's center during the war, unlike others it was preserved because the Red Cross used it as a warehouse. Shaded by tall trees, it is a whitish building of sectioned stucco with a marble pulpit and stained-glass windows featuring a menorah within a sunlike symbol. Though damaged in the 1978 earthquake, it has been restored. Ring the bell for the caretaker, who speaks Judeo-Spanish.

Near the railroad station was the site of the housing development, built by Baron de Hirsch in the 1880s, which was used as a holding pen during the war. A section of Thessaloniki University now stands there. A must-see general sight is the collection of artifacts in the Archaeological Museum from the excavations of the royal tomb of Philip of Macedon, Alexander's father, found in Vergina, a few minutes from Veria.

Side Trips: Just two hours from Thessaloniki by bus, less by car, lies Veria, where a Jewish community existed for two millennia. In fact, this was one place to which Paul fled when the Jews of Thessaloniki ran him out. His preaching here is memorialized by a plaza not far from the ancient Jewish quarter and its synagogue, possibly built on the site of the synagogue in which Paul talked. Today there are 3 Jewish families — amounting to 10 people — in Veria.

The old Jewish quarter lies off the main square, through a tunnel in the bordering wall, and is most easily found by asking for *Ta Evraica*. The area is a jumble of old wooden houses lining twisting dirt paths and hilly streets edged with wild vines and fig trees. On some houses, under the overhang of the roof can be seen inscriptions in Hebrew. Sometimes they were the owner's name; in one still-clear instance, the words cut into the wall read, "If I forget Thee, O Jerusalem. . . . "

The now idle three hundred-year-old synagogue lies down a rutted and stony path to the right of the quarter's entrance. It features a crumbling red-and-yellow tile roof and two pillars in front holding up the protruding red brick entranceway cover. Inside, the wooden floor is decayed and the ceiling seems about to collapse, but the Ten Commandments, carved in marble, remain clear and a *Magen David* motif is faintly discernible on the lectern cover. Through the windows can be heard the rushing of a creek whose waters were used as a *mikveh*. A network of tunnels enabling Jews to reach the synagogue secretly is said to run under the quarter. Mr. Cohen, at Verrois 1, (telephone 24774), speaks some French and will open the synagogue.

A longer trip from Thessaloniki — but one that prospective Jewish bridegrooms are said to have once made by foot — is the way to Ioannina, capital of the mountainous Epirus region and the indigenous Romaniotes who claim direct lineage to those who came from *Eretz Ysrael* after the fall of the Second Temple. From this religious and intellectual center, established in the eighth or ninth century, the Hellenized Jews with their special rites and rituals reigned over such communities as Arta, Preveza, Parga, and Agrinion. Their influence was sufficiently strong that here the Sephardim were assimilated by the Romaniotes, not the usual vice versa. The Romaniote service continues to be followed today by the remaining community of about sixty-five.

Traditionally the Jews of Ioannina lived both just outside and within the walls of the city, a compound of narrow streets, tiny squares, and vine-dripping balconies. They comprised three-quarters of the town's inhabitants. Some larger houses on Koundourioti Street, near the wall's outer circumference, still bear Hebrew inscriptions and *Magen Davids*. As to the latter, note the yellowish corner house at 11 Koundourioti, where two can be seen beneath upper windows.

Today almost all the town's Jews live nearby in a low apartment building next door to community headquarters at 18 Eliya Street, named for Joseph Eliya, a Jewish poet from Ioannina. The residence stands on the site of the New Synagogue, destroyed during the war. However, the large street with which Eliya intersects runs to the main passage through the old city walls. And a left turn just inside leads quickly to 16 Ioustinianou Street and the Old Synagogue. Just inside the gate a pleasant courtyard serves as a prologue to the freshly whitewashed building. Eight white pillars punctuate its interior, dominated by a multiarched ceiling. The ark is at one end of the room, the pulpit at the other, and banks of wooden pews run perpendicularly between them. For entry, contact the community office between 9 A.M. and 1 P.M. at 25-195; the secretary speaks only Greek. Another Mr. Cohen, who speaks some Hebrew, can usually be found at 25-541 between 1 and 6 P.M.

Also of interest in Ioannina are the bust of Joseph Eliya in Alsos Park; a municipal memorial to Holocaust victims on a triangular spit of land near the city walls; and the city's sprawling lake. Apart from figuring in certain local Jewish rituals, the lake is known for having received the victims of the tyrant Ali Pasha's vengeance, as well as providing the setting for the climax of Sidney Sheldon's *The Other Side of Midnight.*

Personalities: Among those Jewish families who emigrated to Palestine after World War I and made names there were the Recanatis — of whom Leon founded the Israel Discount Bank — and the Florentins, for which the Florentin quarter of Tel Aviv was named. *Triumph of the Spirit,* a feature film, is the story of Salamo Arouch, a Jewish stevedore from Thessaloniki. According to the movie, Arouch was middleweight champion of the Balkans in 1939 and fought more than two hundred opponents in Auschwitz for the entertainment of SS officers — and to save his life. Though the film captured the spirit of the time, some questioned whether it captured the true story, asserting that it was based more on the story of Jacko Razon. Both Razon and Arouch now live in Israel. Their dispute, though sad, is also a sign that life continues — albeit in Israel — for many of Thessaloniki's Jews.

—Phyllis Ellen Funke

Tokyo, Kobe, and Kyoto

When Prince Mikasa, younger brother of the late Emperor Hirohito, showed up for a Seder at Tokyo's Jewish Community Center a few years ago, it was more than a gesture. Asked by the rabbi if he wanted simply to observe or to participate actively, he chose the latter. Asked if he would like to be assigned a passage from the *Haggadah* in advance, he said no, he'd like to be called on like anyone else. When the Prince's turn came, he peered into the book that recounts the Israelites' Exodus from Egypt and read—in perfect Hebrew.

In the vast physical and human panorama of Japan—a California-sized country with 120 million people —there are little more than 1,000 Jews. The Japanese and Jewish peoples are as different from each other as any two modern cultures on earth. But as the prince's academic interest in Judaism and the ancient Near East indicate, there are points of intersection. Places of Jewish interest in Japan are few—no one should travel there to see Jewish sights alone—but in the process of traveling from one Jewish sight to another, the voyager can, in fact, see much of the country as well. The Jewish sights and connections can, moreover, be deceptive; if you do enough looking, you can become convinced that the Jews and Japanese are very important to each other.

History: There may have been Jews among the Portuguese and Dutch who traded with Japan in the sixteenth and seventeenth centuries, but they left no lasting mark on the country. Commodore Matthew Perry's opening of Japan in 1853 paved the way for a permanent Jewish community. Alexander Marks, who arrived in Yokohama in 1861, was the first Jewish resident of modern Japan; by the end of the

1860s, the city had 50 Jewish families from Poland, the United States, and England. Toward the close of the nineteenth century, two more communities emerged: a predominantly Sephardic one in Kobe and a mainly Russian one in Nagasaki.

The first Jewish–Japanese encounter to have a lasting impact on Japan came in 1904. Japan was at war with Russia and the governor of the Bank of Japan was sent to London to arrange for loans to finance the war effort. He got nowhere with the British banking elite, but while in London he had a chance meeting with the American investment banker Jacob Schiff, whose hatred for the Russians was fanned by the pogroms of the time. Schiff arranged for more than $200 million in loans, Japan won the war, and an American Jewish financier became a hero in Tokyo and was invited to lunch by Emperor Meiji. But his help also set the stage for a stereotype that would resurface periodically in Japan with both positive and negative facets—the belief in the worldwide influence of Jewish wealth.

Major historic events in Europe, from the Russian revolutions of 1905 and 1917 to Hitler's rise to power, produced minor waves of Jewish migration to Japan. By World War II the Nagasaki community had all but disappeared, leaving Kobe and the Tokyo-Yokohama area as the Jewish centers of Japan. In addition, there were larger communities in the portions of China occupied by Japan in the 1930s, particularly in Shanghai and Harbin.

World War II produced some of the most fascinating interactions between Jews and Japanese. Though allied with Nazi Germany, Japan resisted German urgings to institute anti-Jewish measures. There was a good deal of respect for the Jews among some Japanese officials—based, in part, on the belief in Jewish power—and there was even talk of setting up a Jewish state in Manchuria to exploit Jewish skills and gain support from powerful Jews in the West.

The Fugu Plan, as it became known, was never instituted, but Jews came nevertheless, partly through the efforts of Senpo Sugihara, Japan's consul general in Kovno, Lithuania. In 1941, against orders from the foreign ministry, he issued more than 5,000 Japanese transit visas to Jews who had fled to Lithuania a few steps ahead of the Germans. Among those who arrived in Japan with Sugihara visas was the entire Mir Yeshiva, the only Eastern European *yeshivah* to survive the war intact. For his efforts, Sugihara was fired. (Asked many years later why he had disobeyed orders, Sugihara quoted a samurai maxim from the Bushido code of ethics: "Even a hunter is not allowed to kill a bird who flies to him for refuge.") There is a tree in Sugihara's name at Yad Vashem, the Holocaust Memorial in Jerusalem.

In 1942, Mitsugi Shibata, the Japanese consul in Shanghai, became privy to a plan by the local Gestapo representative to kill the 25,000 Jews who lived there. He warned the Jewish community, whose leaders used contacts in the foreign ministry to have the plan quashed. Like Sugihara, Shibata lost his job.

There are areas in which Jews have left their mark on Japan, although not always in ways that are visible to the Japanese. Raphael Schoyer was mayor of Yokohama's foreign colony in the 1860s. He was also the founder of one of Japan's first foreign-language newspapers; Jews subsequently played a prominent role in English language journalism. *The Japan Times,* largest of the country's four English-language dailies, traces its roots to the prewar *Japan Advertiser,* which was owned by the Fleisher family.

The Jewish impact is more noticeable in music. Although Japan was first exposed to Western classical music in the late nineteenth century, it saw few practitioners until the influx of German Jewish refugees in the 1930s. When Joseph Rosenstock left Berlin in 1936, he headed for Tokyo to become the conductor of the Nippon Philharmonic. (He ultimately became conductor of New York's Metropolitan Op-

era.) One of the ironies of the war was that German officials in Tokyo often sat in the front row to hear classical music by an orchestra filled with Jewish musicians. Until the 1950s the Musashino Academy of Music—Japan's Juilliard—had a preponderance of Jewish instructors.

Community: Today's Jewish centers of Japan are Tokyo and Kobe. While there are some 1,000 Jews in the Tokyo area, only about 400 are affiliated with the community. About half are American, one-third are Israeli, and the remainder come from a variety of countries. There are roughly 500 Jews in the Kansai area—which includes Kyoto, Osaka, and Kobe—of whom fewer than 100 are affiliated with the Kobe synagogue.

As recently as twenty-five years ago, about 80 percent of Japan's Jews were permanent residents, working in the jewelry, toy, or garment businesses. Today, probably no more than 20 percent are long-term residents (including perhaps a dozen native Japanese converts to Judaism). The rest are mainly business consultants, corporate people on assignment, diplomats, journalists, and students. Many of the Jews in Tokyo live near the synagogue in Hiroo, or in the neighboring sections of Nishiazabu and Minamiazabu, an area with many foreign residents, embassies, expensive homes, and luxury apartment buildings.

Japan's Jewish presence embraces more than resident Jews. It also involves the twin issues of philo-Semitism and anti-Semitism. The country is home to not one but two Christian Zionist movements, both of which include love of the Jewish people and Israel among their religious tenets. The Tokyo-based Makuya uses Jewish symbols, particularly the menorah, has a *bar mitzvah* rite for thirteen-year-olds and sends many members to Israel to study Bible and Hebrew. The Kyoto-based Beit Shalom is a bit closer to mainstream evangelical Christianity and uses a Christian cross (sometimes within a Star of David), but embraces Jews and Israel with equal fervor. The two groups have congregations throughout Japan and, combined, have a membership of about 100,000.

No issue has caused more discussion among Japan's Jews in the past few years than the publication and popularity of several anti-Semitic books, notably those of Masami Uno, who borrows from the infamous *Protocols of the Elders of Zion* and posits various Jewish conspiracies to control the Japanese and world economies. While the books are a genuine cause for concern, Rabbi Michael Schudrich, who was the leader of the Tokyo community during the peak of the books' popularity in the mid-1980's, feels that Jews in the West make a mistake in trying to understand an Asian manifestation of anti-Semitism in terms of the European experience.

"The people who write these books are anti-Semitic," Schudrich says, "but not necessarily the people who buy them. People buy the books not to learn about Jews but because they think they might learn something about the Japanese economy." For every Japanese who reads one of the books and develops a negative opinion of Jews, it seems, there is another who, based on the same propaganda, concludes that Jews are admirable and worthy of emulation. During his tenure, Schudrich had at least one prospective Japanese convert who wanted to be Jewish so he could become rich. Even during World War II, when there was a lot more anti-Semitic literature in Japan, there was no anti-Jewish activity. In the year that anti-Semitic books on the economy were selling best (sales declined greatly with the economic upswing and then inched up when the economy sagged again), the Jewish center in Tokyo received "one nasty phone call," according to Schudrich.

Japan's relations with Israel have improved greatly since the late 1980s. Of all the industrialized nations, Japan is by far the most dependent on Arab oil and, as a consequence, was historically more deferential than the United States or Europe to the Arab boycott. But after years of an arm's-length trade relationship, Japanese business with Israel is growing steadily. Japanese trade delegations now routinely visit Israel, and every make of Japanese car can be found on Israel's roads — unlike the old days, when Subaru had the Israeli market and all the other manufacturers sold exclusively to the Arabs.

Sights: Tokyo is where tours of Japan begin. The center of the world's largest metropolitan area (27 million people, including eight million in Tokyo proper), it rivals New York for vibrancy, culture, wheeling and dealing, and manages to do so with virtually no crime or dirt. It is not, however, the locus of most of Japan's Jewish sights. In the midst of the Imperial Palace, Kabuki, cherry blossoms, geisha houses, myriad museums and choking traffic, Tokyo has only one place of purely Jewish interest, the building of the Jewish Community of Japan (8-8 Hiroo 3-chome, Shibuya-ku, Tokyo 150; telephone 3400-2559).

The old center (on the same site) was a Japanese-style mansion with a beautiful garden, but it was torn down in 1980. Half the land was sold to endow a more utilitarian building, with no garden. Nevertheless, the red-brick building, with windows that form the branches of a menorah on the facade, makes up a great deal in activity what it lost in aesthetics (and it does include, on the second floor, two rooms elegantly recreated from the original building). On the third floor is the synagogue, a small, European-style sanctuary with high-backed oak pews and a *bimah* in the center. Like many synagogues in remote communities, it must be all things to all Jews; it has one section for men, one for women, and one for mixed seating. It does not count women in the *minyan*. Though independent and Orthodox-leaning, its rabbis have traditionally come from the Conservative movement. The crowd at a typical service will be perhaps one-third tourists or short-term visitors. It will also include, on the average, three or four Japanese — students, members of one of the Christian Zionist movements, people with an academic interest in Judaism, or the merely curious.

Though the congregation is small, it has a school and a full range of activities, from a Passover cherry blossom tour to chamber music concerts, from movies to adult classes as diverse as Jewish folk dancing and Japanese flower arrangement. The center also has regular lectures on subjects of Jewish and Japanese interest; lecturers in recent years have included Elie Wiesel, Ed Koch, and Yitzchak Shamir.

On one wall in the community center building is a photograph-on-silk-screen piece of the old Tokyo synagogue by Tetsuya Noda, one of Japan's leading graphic artists. When Noda married the daughter of the Israeli ambassador, he converted to Judaism, and one of his best known works is an illustration of his conversion ceremony. He has done a variety of works on personal and Jewish themes, and his art can be found in the Tel Aviv Museum, the Israel Museum in Jerusalem, and the Tikotin Museum of Japanese Art in Haifa; one Tokyo gallery that carries his work is the Fuji TV Gallery at Yotsuya 3-chome, Kawada-cho.

A Christian Japanese artist who dealt with themes from the Hebrew Bible was Sadao Watanabe. His lithograph of *Canaan's Grapes* is reminiscent of the logo for Israel's Carmel Wine Company. His technique features biblical figures with Japanese faces. His work can be found in abundance at the Yoseido Gallery in the Ginza.

Though Makuya is based in Tokyo, and it appreciates visitors, it does not have a formal visitors' arrangement there as it has in Jerusalem. If you happen to be in the city's Denenchofu section, you can drive by the Makuya seminary, with the large menorah on the outside. It is possible to attend a Makuya religious service at one of the group's meeting places in central Tokyo, although aside from a few Hebrew songs, the service is entirely in Japanese. Those who want information should call 3705-1211.

If Tokyo marks the beginning of a trip to Japan, Kyoto (two hours and forty minutes west on the "bullet" train) is the heart of any journey. The ancient capital is filled with cultural treasures and temples. Since it was not bombed during the war, it also has an ingredient lacking in most other big Japanese cities — history. Among the essentials are Nijo Castle (residence of the shoguns) and the Buddhist temples of Kiyomizu and Daitokuji. What is perhaps most surprising, however, is that Kyoto has the largest number of Jewish sights.

The Beit Shalom movement, originally the Japan Christian Friends of Israel, takes its name from the guest house on its campus on the city's western outskirts (9 Utano Nagao-cho, Ukyo-ku, Kyoto; telephone 075-461-4603). Any Jewish visitor to Kyoto is invited to stay for three days at Beit Shalom, free of charge. The building is a blend of the Jewish and the Oriental. The house is Japanese; shoes are removed before entering and guests sleep on *futon* — mattresses placed on the floor. The Western-style living room has a display case that holds a small collection of menorahs and a Seder plate. On the walls are a copy of Israel's Declaration of Independence, and a photograph of former Ashkenazic chief rabbi of Israel Shlomo Goren, a one-time visitor.

Also on the grounds are Beit Shalom's headquarters church and seminary. If you're there on a Sunday, you may be lucky enough to hear the Shinonome Chorus, Beit Shalom's Hebrew-singing choir, which has performed in Israel and the United States. In front of the church is a statue of Anne Frank, a figure of near-worship for the church's members. (The Beit Shalom movement has a church in Nishinomiya, between Osaka and Kobe, dedicated to Anne Frank and including a memorial hall with items donated by Otto Frank, Anne's father.)

Though Beit Shalom does not officially embrace the theory of Japanese descent from the lost tribes, some of the evidence cited to support a connection is just a few miles away. Koryuji is a temple worth seeing for its Buddhist merit alone — the setting is beautiful and it is home to a remarkable eighth-century carved wooden Buddha, known as the Miroku Bosatsu, officially designated as a national treasure. Adherents of the lost-tribe theory believe that the statue's physical features and the position of its fingers are evidence of central Asian, and therefore Jewish, origin.

The statue and temple are lovely, if less than convincing as Jewish sights, but in a small residential section adjacent to the temple grounds things get a bit more spooky. Facing the road is a well that bears the inscription "Isara well." The word *Isara* is written in katakana, the Japanese phonetic characters used for words of foreign origin. It could mean "Israel's well." Of course, from a well built by a Jewish sojourner to evidence of "lost tribes" is still a quantum leap, but the well, at the very least, casts an aura of mystery over the origins of the Japanese–Jewish relationship.

If there is one Japanese who has a claim

to a Jewish pedigree it is Kampo Harada, probably Japan's best known calligrapher. He traces his ancestry to thirteenth-century China—a time and place where Jewish settlement is documented—and says the story that they were of Jewish origin has been handed down in his family. Though he has no halakhic stamp of approval, Kampo has always felt close to the Jewish people and to Israel and in the 1970s started what is now the largest collection of Judaica in the Far East. He has more than 4,000 books—from seventeenth-century Poland to twentieth-century America—on Jewish subjects, as well as a Torah and ark in a room of his calligraphy museum just a block from Kyoto's Heian Shrine, an important center of the Shintoism Kampo practices. The books are in Hebrew and English, neither of which Kampo knows, but the library/synagogue is part of his museum tour. The museum, Kampo Kaikan, is at 35 Minamigosho-machi, Okazaki, Sakyo-ku, Kyoto; telephone 771-6111.

Though the synagogue in Tokyo is lively, you'll have to go to Kobe, the port city forty-five minutes west of Kyoto, to see a synagogue that is truly beautiful. The modern building of the Jewish Community of Kansai (13-3 Kitano-cho 4-chome, Ikuta-ku, Kobe; telephone 221-7236) is located on a quiet street of traditional Japanese architecture about halfway up the mountain that Kobe is literally carved out of. The synagogue's interior features a marble-framed ark flanked by Japanese and Israeli flags. In addition to Shabbat and holiday services, at which about half the regulars are Sephardic, community activities include lectures, Israeli dancing, and an annual Seder at which tourists and casual visitors often outnumber Kobe Jews about four to one.

Beyond Tokyo and the Kansai, Jewish sights are fewer, but there are surprises. The city of Yaozu, near Nagoya, has a park called "The Hill of Humanity," dedicated to its native son Senpo Sugihara. The mayor of Kurose, a small town in Hiroshima Prefecture, wants to raise money for a Holocaust memorial; a sign for the Auschwitz Memorial Pavilion is standing in a field, waiting for construction financing to be raised. Isaac Stern gave a benefit concert in Hiroshima for the project a few

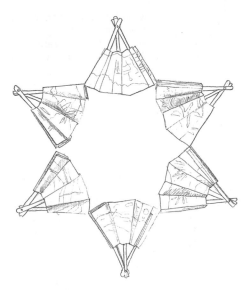

Mutual fan club: Jews and Japanese have produced some surprising stories together

years ago. Though the Jewish community of Nagasaki no longer exists, its cemetery, at Sakamoto Gaijin Bochi, has fascinating tombstones in many languages.

Japan can be a land of doubletakes for Jews. The swastika and the six-pointed star are often visible as insignia and design motifs at Buddhist and Shinto buildings. Neither has any connection with their usage by Jews or by Nazis. Symbols aside, you can also find the trail of Jews almost anywhere. One example among many is the town of Takayama, high in the Japanese Alps, remote from the major cities. At Minshuku Sosuke, a traditional inn whose interior belongs in a Kurosawa movie, visitors sit around an open pit, with a fire that keeps them and their tea warm. On the wall behind the patrons are testimonials written by satisfied guests—about one-third of which are in Hebrew.

Personalities: The personalities associated with Jewish Japan are not all Jewish, and some, like Jacob Schiff, never lived in Japan. Jewish residence would have started sooner if Commodore Perry had thought to bring along his son-in-law, August Belmont, the New York banker, politician, diplomat, and racing enthusiast for whom Belmont Raceway is named. Arthur Waley, an English Jew, was the foremost translator of Japanese and Chinese literature into English. Shaul Eisenberg, a German-Jewish refugee who grew up in Japan, is one of Israel's wealthiest businessmen. Setsuzo Kotsuji, a foreign ministry consultant who was helpful to Jews during the war, might have been designated a Righteous Gentile had he not converted to Judaism and changed his name to Abraham; he is buried in Jerusalem. David Sassoon was reputed to be the largest real estate owner in Kobe. There have not yet been any Jewish sumo wrestlers, but Iwatora, a sumotori (top division) competitor married a Jewish woman in 1980; they had two children before an amicable divorce, and there are reports that he has encouraged his Jewish sons (who still live in Japan) to follow in his heavy footsteps.

Books: Among the books that shed light on the Japanese-Japanese connection are *The Jews and the Japanese* (Tuttle) by Ben-Ami Shillony, who teaches Japanese history at the Hebrew University in Jerusalem; and *The Fugu Plan* (Paddington) by Marvin Tokayer and Mary Swartz, which details the World War II encounters. *The Japanese and the Jews,* by a Japanese with the pseudonym Isaiah Ben Dasan (Weatherhill), is a fascinating cross-cultural analysis. One of the themes of Chaim Potok's *Book of Lights* (Knopf, Random House) concerns a United States Army chaplain who feels guilt over the role his scientist father played in developing the atomic bomb. The best romantic encounter between the two cultures (albeit in an American setting) is Allan Appel's novel *The Rabbi of Casino Boulevard* (St. Martins).

Eating: Since fish is the main source of protein in the Japanese diet, it is relatively easy to observe *kashrut* in Japan. The Tokyo Jewish center has a restaurant and kosher kitchen, and can provide kosher take-out meals—although it asks for a

week's notice. Some Zen temples have vegetarian restaurants that are open to the public; ask at your hotel or call the Jewish Community for suggestions. One vegetarian restaurant near the Tokyo synagogue and recommended by the rabbi is Bodaiju, 1-1-1, Nishiazabu, Minato-ku. If you want traditional Jewish fare, there is Fox Bagels (6-15-19, Roppongi, Minato-ku), which is not kosher.

Recommendations: Japan Air Lines richly deserves its reputation for good service. Not only does it serve kosher food, but flight attendants treat passengers who order kosher meals as if they were holy — perhaps because the only people in Japan who follow religiously prescribed diets are priests.

Accommodation within walking distance of the Tokyo Jewish center include the Hotel Mentels (1-11-4, Nishiazabu, Minato-ku), and the Shimane Inn (7-1-5, Minami Aoyama, Minato-ku), both of which are within fifteen minutes. The better known luxury hotels like the ANA, Okura, New Otani, and Roppongi are farther, but still walkable. The best place to stay in a traditional Japanese inn is Kyoto; one *ryokan* where you won't spend your entire budget in one night is Rikiya.

One mistake often made by visitors to Japan is confusing modernization with Westernization. Try to do things there that help bridge the gap between East and West. See sumo by all means, but if you're a baseball fan see a Japanese game, with all its similarities and differences. One way to have a Japanese theater experience with no language barrier is to see a local production of a Broadway show you are already familiar with (*Les Miserables* and *Big River* are recent Tokyo hits). Unlike the mixed audience you will see at Kabuki shows, you probably won't see another foreigner. You may even sit next to a prince. The most popular Western musical ever to tour Japan was *Fiddler on the Roof.*

—*Alan M. Tigay*

Toronto

It was traditionally called "Toronto the Good," and in the last generation its good reputation has attracted immigrants from around the world. If Canada itself has become one of the world's premier cultural mosaics, Toronto is its multi-ethnic centerpiece. A solid part of the immigration has been Jewish, from far (Russia, South Africa) and near (Montreal). Though Jews have been part of the growth, however, their solid Canadian base is such that Toronto is hard pressed to consider them "ethnics" anymore.

With the growth have come some of the urban problems Toronto was famous for avoiding, but by any standard it is still a civilized place. Compared with much smaller cities south of the border, its streets are safe. Its subways are clean. Its people are pleasant. In fact, it has been hailed as the continent's newest metropolitan superstar, a place that urbanologist Jane Jacobs has called "the most hopeful and healthy city in North America."

Toronto has tall, modern buildings, but has also kept its neighborhoods. It has its commerce, but it also has culture. It abounds with good shopping and dining and, in its urban malls, often meshes the two. In short, it exudes the good life.

History: Though Canada's first Jewish settlement was in Montreal, by 1849 there were enough Jews in Toronto for Abraham Nordheimer—of a musical family relocated from Montreal—to obtain burial land for a Toronto Hebrew Congregation. In 1856 the Sons of Israel held Rosh Hashanah services, and shortly thereafter the two groups merged into the Holy Blossom Synagogue (so called because a member's father gave the congregation a silver Torah pointer on which were engraved—probably to en-

courage the flourishing of this then untamed section of Canada—the words *Pirchei Kodesh*, or "Holy Blossoms"). The congregation, which has since grown into Canada's largest, was originally made up of English, German, American, and Eastern European Jews; Orthodox at its inception, it joined the Reform movement in 1920.

In 1871, however, there were only 157 Jews in Toronto; Russia's pogroms helped boost the figure to 3,000 in 1901 and 18,000 in 1911. By 1931, there were 45,000. Most were Poles; many had come to Canada after the United States clamped down on immigration in 1924.

Not that Toronto was prejudice free. While the Jews themselves, despite the prevalence of spiritual leaders for each national segment, began mingling across their own ethnic lines—with affluence, not ancestry, becoming the chief social criterion—Toronto's once straight-laced, Anglo-Saxon society closed many social and economic avenues to Jews. Before World War I, Christian missionaries proselytized so much that the rabbi of Holy Blossom, in 1911, delivered a powerful sermon criticizing the Presbyterian church for supporting such activities.

Since the missions offered medical and social services, however, and since there were restrictions against Jews in certain areas—including the opportunity for doctors to admit patients to hospitals—the Jews established their own self-help institutions, among them Mount Sinai Hospital and what has become the Baycrest Center for Geriatric Care.

In addition, Toronto's Jews fostered strong ideologists, including radicals and communists who remained loyal to their causes until recent times. (Little wonder that the American anarchist Emma Goldman, after her deportation to Russia, lived in Toronto until her death above Switzer's Delicatessen on Spadina Avenue.)

Despite Canada's own immigration restrictions preceding and during World War II, German and Austrian Jews made their way to Toronto; later, the Canadian Jewish Congress worked with various needle-trade groups to bring over displaced persons.

After the war Canada began establishing antidiscrimination codes and relaxing its immigration laws. The 1956 Hungarian uprising propelled a new wave of Jews to Toronto—including many *chasidim*. In the 1960s, Sephardic Jews began arriving for the first time, from Morocco. Recent years have brought Jews from South Africa, the Soviet Union, the United States, Israel (an estimated 10,000) and, during times of uncertainty over separatism, Quebec. While the number from Montreal was relatively small, it was part of a historic change in the position of the two cities. When the Parti Québécois won control of the provincial government in 1976, Montreal was Canada's largest city and had the largest Jewish community. By the time the Liberal party returned to power in Quebec in 1985, Toronto ranked first in both categories.

Still, with Toronto's ethnic explosion, today's Jewish community of 150,000 seems no more visible than when it was half that size. They are just one minority among many in a metropolitan area of 3.5 million.

In recent years the equilibrium of Toronto Jewry has been disturbed by two court cases—one against James Keegstra, a teacher in Alberta accused of inculcating his students with Nazi doctrine; the other against Ernst Zundel, in Toronto, for calling the Holocaust a fraud. By and large, though, Toronto Jews today live free of anti-Semitism. And for having, early on, kept their religious and cultural identity, they are sometimes credited with pointing the way to multiculturalism.

Community: Despite the (relative) depth of Jewish roots in Toronto, many Jewish Torontonians are only one or, at most, two generations removed from their immigrant background. Perhaps this explains in part why Toronto's Jews tend to be somewhat more traditional than their American counterparts.

About half of Toronto's Jews are affiliated, in some way, with the community and, of these, 20 percent are Orthodox (including some who are ultra-Orthodox); 40 percent are Conservative (often in a stricter manner than Americans); 25 percent are Reform, and the remainder affiliated through nondenominational Jewish groups or activities. Of the fifty-odd synagogues in the city, there are five Reform (of which Holy Blossom is the leader); a dozen Conservative (Beth Tzedec is the largest in Canada); three North African Sephardic; one each Reconstructionist and European Liberal; and the rest Orthodox in various forms, led by Shaarei Shomayim. Toronto's Jews have established an extensive day school network that, be the education ultra-Orthodox, secular, or socialist, contributes considerably to promoting Jewish identity.

Originally, Toronto's English and German Jews lived in the once-fashionable downtown area east of Yonge Street, while the earliest Eastern European Jews were concentrated in St. John's Ward. Around the time of World War I, they began moving to the Spadina Avenue–Kensington Market area. In the early fifties, they started pushing north, and today about 25 percent of Greater Toronto's Jews live in Thornhill and Richmond Hill, with other concentrations in Don Mills, Unionville, Markham, and Vaughn, not to mention such towns to the west as Mississauga and Brampton.

Despite the spread, however, the community still has a heart. Beginning roughly where St. Clair Avenue intersects Bathurst Street, with pockets flaring out on either side all along the artery, there are, one after the other, Jewish-inhabited apartment buildings; Jewish-owned houses (including those in the wealthy Forest Hill section); synagogues from the *shtiebel*—or storefront—variety to the grand and grandiose; Jewish schools; Jewish service organizations; and Jewish businesses, shops, and restaurants.

The Jews of Toronto have good relations with other ethnic communities, many of whose causes they defend. Blacks and Jews, Italians and Jews, Chinese and Jews have traditionally worked well together. But when it comes to living quarters, according to Stephen A. Speisman, director of the Ontario Jewish Archives, "In Toronto, Jews like to live together."

Sights and Culture: Call it multiculturalism at its best. Or good-neighborliness. Or hacking par excellence. The fact is that the black taxi driver—a ninth-generation Canadian—immediately recognized the 4588 Bathurst Street address as the Jewish Community Center. "And while you're out there," he said, "there's a building a little farther on that has a lot of old photos of the Toronto Jewish community you should see."

How right he was. He failed only to mention that there were other sights in this vicinity as well, in both buildings that occupy the same tract of land. The Jewish Community Center, or "Y," is at 4588 Bathurst—virtually, but not quite, adjoining 4600, the Jewish Community Services Building officially named for Lipa Green.

To be sure, on the walls of the Lipa Green Building hang photos of the champion Toronto Jewish Softball League Team of the 1920s, the rhythm band of the Farband Shule, a Jewish farmer from rural Ontario, and the *zaftig* Ladies Auxiliary of Mount Sinai Hospital. Such are mere samples, however, from a six-thousand-photo collection housed in the building. Under Speisman's direction, the archives also include diaries and cemetery records, oral histories, and artifacts such as *Magen Davids* from demolished synagogues and a weatherbeaten sign that reads, unequivocally, "Gentiles Only."

Also on the walls is a series of original contemporary paintings, "Jewish Life in Canada," by William Kurelek, a leading Canadian artist from a Ukrainian Catholic background. The paintings belong to the province of Ontario but are on permanent loan to the Jewish Federation of Greater Toronto. Among the subjects covered are a Jewish wedding in Calgary, a Jewish baker, Passover, Yom Kippur, Jewish home life, and Jews in the clothing industry.

The Lipa Green building houses not one but two museums. The Holocaust Education and Memorial Centre has exhibits on European Jewish life before World War II as well as on the Holocaust itself; items on display range from Torahs to prison uniforms and ghetto currency. Designed as a learning center as well as a museum, the center features a slide presentation called "Images of the Past," a half-hour documentary narrated by Lorne Greene and a Hall of Memories, with names inscribed on ceramic tiles. The Oskar Asher Schmidt Jewish Museum—from which the photos in the building's lobby come—is the premier collection of Ontario Judaica, with photos, posters, and ritual objects relating to the province's Jewish history. In addition to the collections, the Lipa Green building houses a fifty-thousand-volume Jewish library. For information on events and exhibits in the Lipa Green building, call (416) 635-2882.

The Jewish Community Center, too, boasts outstanding attractions. One particularly fine facet is its four hundred forty-four-seat Leah Posluns Theater. Under the artistic direction of Reva Stern, the theater specializes in works that deal with issues and concerns of Jewish interest—"plays of Jewish sensibility and significance," Stern explains. Five productions are mounted each season in what is arguably the best Jewish theater facility in North America. Offerings in recent years have included *Golda, Raisins and Almonds, Are You Now or Have You Ever Been . . .* , and *Fiddler on the Roof.*

In the Jewish Community Centre building, too, is the Koffler Gallery, devoted to collecting and exhibiting contemporary Canadian art, with a special (though not exclusive) emphasis on Jewish artists. The gallery mounts its own shows and hosts traveling exhibits. In addition to its art and theater, the center hosts a Jewish Book Fair each fall. For information on programs and events at the center, call the box office at (416) 636-6752.

The Canadian Jewish News, published weekly in Toronto, is the best place to check for Jewish cultural happenings. There are programs of Jewish interest on CHIN, Toronto's multicultural radio station, and channel 47, its multicultural television station. A Jewish Information Service (416-635-5600) offers information on synagogues, kosher restaurants, and Jewish cultural events; advice for newcomers to Toronto; and directs callers to counseling or to programs for singles, children, or seniors.

Beth Tzedec Synagogue, flagship of the Conservative movement in Toronto, is at 1700 Bathurst. Built in 1964, the building is a light-masonry brick structure. The high-ceilinged twenty-five hundred-seat sanctuary features a marble *bimah* flanked by two fifty-foot-high bronze bas-relief panels by the sculptor Ernest Raab; the panels depict in words and symbols the Creation, the birth of the Jewish people, the Exodus, the history of persecution, and the healing power of faith and good works. In the synagogue's Mezzanine Banquet Hall is a set of the Chagall lithographs of the twelve tribes (along the lines of the Chagall windows in the Hadassah–Hebrew University Medical Center in Jerusalem). In its Fellowship Court is a floor mosaic of the zodiac that replicates the floor of the sixth-century synagogue excavated at Beit Alfa.

But what Beth Tzedec is perhaps best known for its is the Canadian branch of the Jewish Museum, under the auspices of the Jewish Theological Seminary of America. The museum includes the Cecil Roth Collection, one of the world's leading aggregations of Judaica, as well as numerous other exceptional items. The collection includes a wide variety of menorahs and *ketubot* as well as Jewish costumes and anti-Semitic caricatures. Among the works displayed are an eighteenth-century gold-illuminated Chinese *Megillah* from Kaifeng; a 1645 illuminated Venetian marriage contract, decorated with miniatures; a 1767 velvet-covered circumcision chair from Berlin; copies of the Song of Songs and the Book of Ruth inscribed on eggshells; and two century-old Persian rugs from Kashan, portraying the symbols of Judaism and ordered by a Persian shah to commemorate the exposure of an assassination plot against his Jewish court physician. For information about synagogue services, museum hours, and exhibits or other events at Beth Tzedec, call (416) 781-3511.

A block from Beth Tzedec is Holy Blossom Temple (1950 Bathurst), Toronto's most imposing synagogue and the city's leading Reform congregation. The cathedral-like facade is dominated by a sweeping arch encompassing three sets of wooden doors and a huge rose window with a Star of David in the center. Inside, the rose window, with its dominant reds and blues, is at the back of the sanctuary, which also features a carved wooden ceiling with a pointed arch and a lacework sculpture in plaster and stone that surrounds the ark. For information on services or events at Holy Blossom, call (416) 789-3291.

Apart from its specific sights, the visitor can easily become engulfed in the experience of Jewish Bathurst where, on a Sunday, there is a stream of people going into the Negev Importing Company asking for *Ma'ariv* the way they would ask for *The Times* in New York; and where, if you aren't careful, you can land in the middle of a talmudic discussion on the relative merits of Gryfe's Bagels (3421 Bathurst) versus Fairmount Bagels in Montreal. Toronto's bagels, in fact, can stand up to New York's best – and so can its pickles.

Along a three-block section in the vicinity of the Baycrest Center for Geriatric Care there exist such establishments as The Maven, a kosher MacDonald's-style burger joint; Chocolate Charm, purveying handmade chocolates; Dairy Treats Café/Bakery; Isaac's Bakery, specializing in Sephardi and French pastries; a storefront synagogue; two Jewish bookstores; Kosher King for snacks; and Chopstix, a kosher Chinese restaurant.

For a glimpse of the old neighborhood (on one of the few Toronto outings that should probably be confined to daylight hours), walk around the Spadina-Kensington area bounded by Dundas Street West, McCaul Street, College Street, and Bellevue Avenue. Along Spadina Avenue, which is now the heart of Chinatown, stands the Golden Harvest Theater, formerly Toronto's Yiddish Theater. At 58 Cecil Street there is a beige brick building with turquoise windowsill trim, which is now a community center but was once a synagogue. At the corner of Cecil and Henry streets is a red brick building topped with the crosses of the Russian Orthodox Church; this, too, was once a synagogue.

At 12–14 St. Andrews Street stands the Russian and Romanesque Minsker Synagogue (Anshei Minsk). And at Denison Square and Bellevue Avenue stands the Kiever Synagogue, officially called Rodfei Sholom Anshei Kiev, built in 1926 by

Ukrainian Jews. This synagogue is still operating and has been painstakingly restored. Among its exceptional features are its elaborately carved oak, chestnut, and walnut ark; its extensive brasswork; and its wall paintings of the signs of the zodiac, which were executed by an eleven-year-old girl and remain as examples of Canadian primitive art. Stephen Speisman, at (416) 635-2883, can tell visitors how they can visit the synagogue when it is not holding services, as well as how to take a walking tour through the neighborhood—which includes the Kensington Market, now a collection of Portuguese and West Indian outdoor food stalls, but formerly called the Jewish Market.

The Royal Ontario Museum is one of the few general museums in North America with a Judaica gallery. Focusing on holidays and life-cycle events, the collection includes pieces from the tenth century to the twentieth. Though the items come from all over Europe, some of the most striking pieces are from Italy, such as an eighteenth-century Venetian menorah and a nineteenth century Torah crown. Also in the museum collection are Jewish artifacts from Kaifeng. Located at 100 Queen's Park, the ROM is open every day except Monday, 10:00 A.M. to 6:00 P.M., and until 8:00 P.M. Tuesdays and Thursdays.

General Sights: Toronto boasts a number of institutions that belong to everyone, but which are, in one way or another, the creations of its Jews. Among the most touted are the properties of "Honest Ed" Mirvish. Mirvish is a flamboyant retailer who made his fortune with a garishly decorated, loudly hyped discount store at the corner of Bloor and Bathurst Streets—where customers still line up outside to be the first in for the day's specials. Bordering the store, however, is "Mirvish Village," a block of restored, pastel-colored Victorian houses, with antique shops, bookstores, and restaurants on the street level and artists' quarters upstairs. Bitten by the restoration bug, Mirvish went on to acquire the Royal Alexandra Theater, Toronto's flagship playhouse, which he redid in grand style (before he acquired London's Old Vic). The theater itself is worth visiting; on the same street stand a cluster of Mirvish restaurants, decorated with antiques, serving everything from steak and ribs to Chinese food.

Among Toronto's most illustrious builders—through struggling under the weight of recessionary real estate values—are the Reichman brothers, Ralph, Paul, and Albert. (Paul was named 1985's "Businessman of the Year" by Canada's *Financial Post*.) In addition to developing Toronto's waterfront, their company, Olympia and York, put up the seventy-two-story First Canadian Place, otherwise known as the Bank of Montreal building. Designed by Edward Durrell Stone, the bank is Toronto's tallest office building and embraces extensive office and shopping space as well as a kosher restaurant. (Indeed, the Reichmans hold *Minchah-maariv* services in their inner sanctum.) The brothers also have substantial real estate holdings and ongoing projects in Manhattan.

And at the base of the CN Tower, advertised as the world's tallest free-standing structure, is the "Tour of the Universe," a kiddie ride simulating a space trip, which is the brainchild of Moses Znaimer—who also founded Toronto's popular independent television station, City TV, and a cable music network.

Also to be seen are the Toronto Islands, offshore in Lake Ontario; the Casa Loma, a ninety-eight-room, twentieth-century Victorian castle in the center of the city; Eaton Centre, a vast indoor shopping mall; and Harbourfront, along Toronto's waterfront. From Toronto, Niagara Falls is an easy day trip.

Reading: Toronto's Jews haven't produced the wealth of urban literature that has come out of Montreal, although there is a body of work about Jewish life in smaller Ontario towns. *A Good Place to Come From, St. Farb's Day* (St. Martin's), and other works by Morley Torgov deal with experiences common to Canadian Jews. Howard Engel is the creator of Benny Cooperman, a Jewish detective who operates in and around Niagara Falls. A general fictional picture of Toronto life, with some Jewish characters, can be found in Marian

Engel's *The Year of the Child* (St. Martin's). Also worth a look are *The Jews of Toronto—A History to 1937* by Stephen A. Speisman (McClelland and Stewart) and *Spadina Avenue,* a history of the area with photos by Rosemary Donegan (Douglas and McIntyre).

Personalities: Among the best-known faces—past and present—to come out of Toronto's Jewish community are performers Lou Jacobi, Lloyd Bochner, Marilyn Lightstone, comedians Johnny Wayne and Frank Shuster, and CBS newsman Morley Safer. John Hirsch was director of the Shakespeare Festival in Stratford, Ontario. Lorne Greene, a native of Ottawa, moved to Toronto to start his professional career, while Bora Laskin left Toronto for Ottawa when he was appointed chief justice of Canada's Supreme Court. Toronto's Jews have been involved in politics since the nineteenth century, and the city has had two Jewish mayors, Nathan Phillips (1955–62)—for whom the plaza in front of the beautiful city hall is named—and Philip G. Givens (1963–66).

Jewish personalities who have emerged from Toronto in recent years include the children's singers Sharon (Lilienstein), Lois (Hampton) and Bram (Morrison), comedian and actor Howie Mandel, and "Saturday Night Live" producer Lorne Michaels. The most famous character to have been produced, or at least half-produced, by Toronto's Jews is the cocreation of Joe Shuster (a cousin of Frank Shuster). In his earliest days, Clark Kent, a.k.a. Superman, worked not for *The Daily Planet* but *The Daily Star*—which was based on the *Toronto Star*. Shuster's collaborator was Jerry Siegel, of Cleveland. Toronto may not be the salvation of civilization like Superman, but many of its personalities reflect the civilized place from which they come.

—Phyllis Ellen Funke

Vancouver

With its breathtaking seaside setting, Vancouver often is compared with Rio de Janeiro, San Francisco, Hong Kong, and Cape Town. Canada's third-largest city and gateway to the Pacific fares exceedingly well in such comparisons. Thoroughly modern, with dramatic glass-skinned skyscrapers, Vancouver is blessed with a deep natural harbor nestled between two evergreen-covered peninsulas and set at the base of the mile-high, snow-capped Coast Mountains.

Considering its age—barely one hundred—Vancouver is a cosmopolitan place. European and Oriental migrations have enriched it with a diverse and sophisticated population. Jewish settlers were some of the first and most influential immigrants to Canada's southwest corner.

History: The Spanish explorer José María Narvaez discovered Vancouver's outer harbor in 1791, and within a year George Vancouver's British party had sailed into the city's protected inner harbor. But Europeans didn't settle in the country of the Squamish, or "canoe Indians," until the 1850s. Discovery of gold on the Fraser and Thompson Rivers in 1857, and later in the Caribou and Yukon, spurred thousands of prospectors to swarm into the region.

Since there was no overland rail or road access to the mainland, the first settlers to the crown colony of British Columbia arrived by steamship from San Francisco at the port city of Victoria on Vancouver Island, off the mainland's west coast. The colony's first Jews came with this population rush to the new gold country. By the fall of 1858, there were enough Jews in Victoria to hold High Holy Day services in a house. In 1863 a synagogue was consecrated for the estimated 242 Jews in Victoria.

Most of these Jews, of German, Swiss, or Polish origin, came from California (including the first rabbi, who came from Sacramento) with experience of the earlier gold rush there. Some came from England, New Zealand, and Australia seeking their fortunes in the new territories. Although a few started out as miners and seal hunters, most were traders, merchants, and wholesalers who used Victoria as a base to supply the gold-rush towns.

Some pioneers settled on the mainland to prospect or to log fir and cedar. However, the major impetus for settlement was the selection of Vancouver as the western terminus of the Canadian Pacific Railroad. A handful of Jews, recognizing the potential business prospects, settled in Vancouver during its first days.

The most famous of these early Jewish settlers was Bavarian-born David Oppenheimer. Oppenheimer's unofficial title—"the Father of Vancouver"—came from his many contributions: He organized the water supply, built bridges, promoted tramlines, donated land for parks and schools, and founded an orphanage, as well as the city's YMCA. He became the city's mayor in 1888, holding the post for four years. (Though Oppenheimer was not the first Jewish mayor in North America, of all the million-plus metropolises on the continent today Vancouver was the first to have a Jew at the municipal helm.)

Until the 1880s, most Jewish immigrants to British Columbia already knew English and were easily assimilated into the Anglo-Canadian way of life. That began to change slowly with the beginning of the Russian pogroms, the relaxation of immigration restrictions, the completion of the transcontinental railroad, and a government policy of westward expansion. Eastern European Jews began moving to Canada. Compared with Montreal and Toronto, however, only a handful of these newcomers reached Vancouver by the late 1800s, and at the turn of the century the community numbered only 200.

While the first public High Holy Day services were held in 1892, Vancouver's first small synagogue, B'nai Yehudah, wasn't built until 1912. By 1921 the city's Jewish community numbered 1,300, more than half of whom lived in the working-class East End of town (now part of Vancouver's Chinatown). Though the English-speaking Reform-oriented Jews wanted a congregation separate from the Orthodox, Yiddish-speaking Eastern European immigrants, their numbers were insufficient and, as immigrants continued to arrive, the community turned increasingly toward Orthodoxy.

By 1921, the Reform group had suspended plans to build its own synagogue; instead, a new building large enough to accommodate the entire community was constructed. This new synagogue, renamed Schara Tzedeck, was the first substantial Jewish public building in Vancouver. Rabbi Nathan Mayer Pastinsky served as spiritual leader of the congregation for thirty years and was regarded by the community as the personification of Vancouver Jewry.

By 1931, the population of the community had reached 2,500, and most of the Jewish organizations existing today had been established. Several other congregations (Conservative, Reform, and Sephardic) were organized, the Jewish Community Centre was built, and a weekly Jewish newspaper started publication. Although instances of overt anti-Semitism in Vancouver were rare before World War II, a pervasive, insidious form of discrimination existed in social, business, and athletic organizations and in employment.

Today, Jews are as well integrated and accepted in Vancouver as in any North American city, but that didn't stop someone from throwing a Molotov cocktail at Temple Sholom in January 1985. The Reform synagogue was destroyed in what was the worst anti-Jewish incident in the city's history. The attack brought an outpouring of support. Other synagogues offered help, and space, non-Jews as well as Jews contributed to the rebuilding fund, and Mayor Michael Harcourt attended services in a show of solidarity. Three years later the new Temple Sholom opened on the same Oak Street site.

Community: Since World War II, Jews have come to Vancouver from Europe, the United States (especially during the Vietnam War), South America, South Africa, and the Middle East. But second- and third-generation Canadians have been the most numerous group of newcomers. In the 1950s and 1960s, sons and daughters of Jewish merchants, farmers, garment workers, and wholesalers, primarily from the prairie provinces, discovered professional and economic opportunities in British Columbia.

There are about 25,000 Jews living in metropolitan Vancouver, which has a population of more than 1.5 million. By the mid-1940s, the Jewish community had, by and large, left the East End, moving south of False Creek. In recent years there has been a Jewish migration to the bedroom communities of Richmond, Surrey, North Vancouver, West Vancouver, and even to the farther reaches of the metropolitan area.

Oak Street between Fifteenth and Fifty-seventh Avenues has become the center of the Jewish community with its concentration of synagogues, delicatessens, bakeries, the Jewish Community Centre, bookstore, day school, and senior citizens' home. Many Jewish organizations have their headquarters in the Jewish Community Centre building at 950 West Forty-first Avenue (telephone 604-266-9111).

There is also a sizable Jewish presence in the suburban areas of Richmond-Delta, the North Shore, and Burquest. About 1,000 Jews live in Richmond, where Conservative and Orthodox congregations and a Jewish country club are located.

The umbrella organization for community educational, cultural, and historical associations is the Jewish Federation of Greater Vancouver (950 West Forty-first Avenue; 604-266-8371). The Canadian Jewish Congress (with its Vancouver office in the same building as the federation) initiates anti-discrimination actions and human rights coalitions and is the voice of the community on all issues affecting the quality of Jewish life. Also in the same building is Shalom Vancouver: The Jewish Information and Welcome Service (605-266-9111), where visitors and newcomers can get information on everything from synagogues and special events to kosher and vegetarian food and hotels convenient to Jewish neighborhoods; the center is open Monday through Friday, 10:00 A.M. to 2:00 P.M.

Personalities: Dave Marks, a tailor and synagogue president, invited a visiting performer playing the local Orpheum vaudeville theater to a family Passover Seder. His daughter Sadie fell in love and married Benny Kubelsky of Chicago. The couple were better known by their stage names, Jack Benny and Mary Livingstone.

Leonard Frank immigrated to North America hoping to find his fortune in the Yukon gold mines. Instead, he won a camera in a mining-camp raffle and embarked on a long career photographing the rich and famous as well as nature and the outdoors. He was the first Vancouver resident to become an Associate of the Royal Photographic Society of Great Britain.

Several British Columbia Jews have gained recognition as public servants. In 1866—twenty years before Vancouver had its first Jewish mayor—Lumley Franklin was elected mayor of Victoria. In 1871, Henry Nathan of Victoria was the first Jew elected to the Canadian Parliament. Nearly a century later, Vancouver's David Barrett became the leader of Canada's New Democratic party and the first Jewish premier of British Columbia. Samuel Schultz became Canada's first Jewish judge when he was appointed to the Vancouver county court in 1914; Nathan T. Nemetz became the first Jewish chief justice of British Columbia as well as the first Jew in British Columbia named a university chancellor.

Sights: Tree-lined Oak Street, Vancouver's "Jewish Main Street," is a four-lane road running through Oakridge, an upper-middle-class neighborhood. In addition to the many Jewish buildings in this area, busy Oak Street is the site of Vancouver's largest

high school, three hospitals, and the Red Cross building.

Conservative Congregation Beth Israel, built in 1949, is Vancouver's largest synagogue, with 850 members. Located at 4350 Oak Street (telephone 604-731-4161), it has an elegant oak-walled sanctuary with a projecting *bimah* surrounded by seats on three sides. The ark has a face of Florentine marble and its bronze doors depict the Ten Commandments in the form of the Tree of Life. Beth Israel also has a small museum with about eighty items, including ritual objects acquired through family donations and antiquities purchased in Israel. A set of circumcision instruments donated by a *mohel's* son is accompanied by a booklet listing all the *brisses* the man performed; the son's name is the first on the list. Another intriguing item is a string of turquoise-and-brown Egyptian paste beads discovered at Jericho and dating to the Semitic shepherd kings of the Hyksos tribe (2000–1600 B.C.E.). Before visiting, call Beth Israel to make sure the museum is open.

The new Temple Sholom, opened in 1988, is at 7190 Oak Street. After its former building on the site was firebombed it held services in the Jewish Community Centre and weddings at Beth Israel. The synagogue has a Jerusalem-stone-like facade and a domed sanctuary whose white walls and many windows infuse it with light. Behind the synagogue is a biblical garden designed by the landscape architect Cornelia Oberlander. In the center of the garden, surrounded by Jerusalem pines, is a striking Holocaust monument depicting two distorted-figured parents and a baby.

One place worth seeing outside the center of Jewish activity is Congregation Beth Hamidrash, the Sephardic synagogue at 3231 Heather Street. Among its features are a decorative window by the Egyptian Jewish artist Albert Sion and an ancient Jewish scroll from Bombay.

David Oppenheimer's most visible contribution to Vancouver was the establishment of Stanley Park, an oasis of one thousand acres of park land in the city. A statue funded by public subscription and erected in 1911 at the entrance to the park is a tribute to Oppenheimer's preeminent position in early Vancouver history.

The Jewish Festival of the Arts Society,

located in the JCC, was organized to promote and develop Jewish arts in Vancouver and to expose the general community to Jewish culture. Among its ventures is a walking tour, "In the Footsteps of Jewish Vancouver 1886–1986," which emphasizes the people and heritage of the community. One of the high points of the tour is the original Schara Tzedek Synagogue at 700 East Pender Street. Though the congregation has moved (along with the original ark and *bimah*), the first building is marked with a commemorative plaque. Other important East End landmarks include Rabbi Pastinsky's home (641 East Georgia Street); the Council of Jewish Women-Neighborhood House, forerunner of the first Jewish Community Centre (800 Jackson Avenue); Ferrera Court, the apartment building where Jack Benny met his future wife (504 East Hastings Street); Zionist Hall, meeting place for many community organizations (456½ East Hastings Street); and the Oppenheimer brothers' warehouse, temporary site for the City Hall (100 Powell Street).

The tour also points out retail establishments founded by Vancouver's early Jews. One of these, Zebulon Frank's hardware store at 42 Water Street, is believed to be the location of the first Jewish religious services.

In addition to its tour, the society works with local institutions — like the Vancouver Symphony, the Vancouver Museum, and the Museum of Anthropology at the University of British Columbia — in bringing concerts, exhibits, and other cultural events of Jewish interest to the city. It mounts its own exhibits as well at the JCC and at local synagogues. It also sponsors the annual Jewish Film Festival in May and June. Visitors should call the society at (604) 266-0245 for the latest information regarding cultural events.

The Jewish Community Centre has an art gallery that features a small permanent collection and periodic exhibits, mostly of local Jewish artists. It also has a theater — recent productions have included *Yentl* and tales from Sholom Aleichem — and a lecture series.

The University of British Columbia has a chair of Judaic Studies and a Judaica library. The Vancouver Peretz School focuses on Yiddish language and literature. Continuing-education courses are offered through the Institute of Adult Jewish Studies.

The Jewish Western Bulletin is the weekly publication for Jews in British Columbia and the voice of the Jewish community to the outside world. It has listings of all community activities. A more recent media addition is the weekly television talk show *L'Chaim,* aired on the cable television network three times a week.

General Sights: Vancouverites delight in their city's spectacular natural setting. The city has five miles of beaches and more than fifty marinas. For magnificent city views, visit Grouse Mountain in North Vancouver, a short trip by car, bus, or seabus from downtown.

One of Vancouver's most unusual attractions is the University of British Columbia's Museum of Anthropology. Its collection of Northwest Coast Indian art features huge totem poles, feast bowls, ceremonial masks, and intricately carved works in silver, gold, stone, and wood.

Eating: The Rabbinical Council of Vancouver and Victoria certifies institutions and food stores. Up-to-date information on kashrut can be obtained from Shalom Vancouver (604-266-9111). Café Mercaz, the only kosher restaurant in the city, is located in the JCC. Leon's Kosher Corner and Butcher, a combination delicatessen and meat market, is at 3710 Oak Street. Kosher products can also be purchased at the Angler Smoke House at 8030 Granville Street.

Side Trip: Victoria is accessible by ferry, hydrofoil, or airplane from Vancouver. Much of the provincial capital's inner harbor area has been preserved in turn-of-the-century elegance. Considered by some to be more "British" than London, Victoria is home to Conservative Temple Emanu-El, Canada's oldest synagogue in continuous use, at 1461 Blanshard Street.

Designated a national historic site, Temple Emanu-El has been restored to its original beauty. In 1948, the synagogue was "modernized"; the original brick structure and nearly all the windows were covered with stucco. The massive wooden doors were removed and disappeared. A seven-foot skylight at the center of the vaulted ceiling was removed and covered with boards, and a false ceiling was installed, destroying the traditional gallery.

Today the building stands as it did in 1863. To commemorate the four-year restoration project, city and provincial dignitaries celebrated a reenactment of the original dedication of the synagogue, in which the entire community of Victoria participated.

Reading: The Jewish novel of Vancouver has yet to be written, but you can get a more general fictional taste of the city in L. R. Wright's *Love in the Temperate Zone* (Viking). The Jewish Historical Society of British Columbia (950 West 41 Avenue; 604-266-3529) does have a variety of publications, many written by Cyril Edel Leonoff, the society's founder and archivist. Two fascinating works are *Pioneers, Peddlers and Prayer Shawls: The Jewish Communities in British Columbia and the Yukon* and *Pioneer Jewish Merchants of Vancouver Island and British Columbia.* Such books will give you an idea of why the first Jews came. For an idea of what made them stay, all you have to do is look around.

—Ann C. Penn

Venice

"The most beautiful and magical of cities," writes John Julius Norwich in *A History of Venice,* and only partisans of Jerusalem will dispute his claim. The Italian masterpiece, its towers rising in subdued purples from the sea mists, expresses a people's determination to contrive shelter against the implacable forces of storm and wave.

The miracle of Venice is survival. Despite the fragility imposed by its unending struggle against slow submersion into the Adriatic, La Serenissima ("The Most Serene"), as the city is known, has remained virtually unchanged for over a thousand years, since its first settlers, fleeing the barbarians ravaging the Italian mainland, established themselves on the marshy islets of the coast to build their sanctuary.

Compare an eighteenth-century Canaletto engraving of the Rialto with a contemporary photograph of the storied bridge. Except for the difference in the dress of the pedestrians making the crossing, the scene is unchanged. During the week of Carnevale, when every second Venetian, it would seem, is parading the streets in the periwigs and pantaloons of remote ancestors, time seems to have made a complete stop. Nowhere is this stasis more apparent than in the ancient Venice Ghetto. Established on April 10, 1516—the second day of Passover—it was the first officially mandated ghetto in Europe.

History: Jews settled in Venice as early as the tenth century and became an important factor in the economic life of the city whose well-being depended on its commerce with the rest of the Mediterranean and, particularly, with the prosperous cities of the Middle East, where Jewish merchants were already well connected.

In 1516, however, their contributions to the economy of Venice were conveniently overlooked. The city was overcrowded with refugees as Venice was recovering from a disastrous war with the mainland. The Council of Ten, Venice's ruling body, yielded to priestly clamor to "get the Jews out of the way."

Geto is the Italian word for "foundry," and it was to the site of the Ghetto Nuovo, or new foundry—a swampy, malaria-ridden district far removed from the central Piazza San Marco—that the reigning doge consigned Venice's entire Jewish population. There were at the time more than a thousand men, women, and children involved in the move, and the Ghetto community would ultimately grow as large as 4,000.

The Ghetto Nuovo district was cut off from the rest of Venice by a network of canals and enclosed by a high wall of fortresslike dimensions. The existing walls were further strengthened and made higher, as one can see today, and all windows facing outward were bricked over, to circumvent unauthorized entrance or exit. Only two gates breached the walls, one leading west toward the Cannaregio Canal and the other, at the extreme east, facing the Church of San Girolamo. These passageways were guarded by shifts of Christian watchmen—paid for by the Jewish community within.

During their ghettoization, Venice's Jews were forced to wear distinguishing red hats, and they were barred from every livelihood except trading, moneylending, and selling secondhand clothing. They were capriciously and excessively taxed whenever the city ran short of money, and their holy books were incinerated in the Piazza San Marco. As Mary McCarthy writes in *Venice Observed,* "They bled the Jewish community in every conceivable way. Since the law forbade Jews to own land, the Republic forced them to rent the Ghetto in its entirety on a long lease; the day the Jews moved in, rentals were raised one-third."

Nevertheless, the Ghetto community flourished as one of Europe's great centers of Jewish culture. Jewish merchants from every city in Italy, from Germany, Salonika, and Constantinople came to do business in the Ghetto. Conversos from Spain and Portugal poured in, finding sanctuary from the Inquisition and expressing their long-buried Jewish identity. Paradoxically, the Venetian government that segregated its Jews also protected them. It needed their commercial skills, their enterprise, and their willingness to lend to the Christian poor at low rates—a risk no others would undertake. While the Ghetto is a stain on Venetian history, its inhabitants escaped the mob violence and pogroms that decimated Jewish communities across Western Europe, from Toledo to Frankfurt, from the Middle Ages to the French Revolution.

The stimulating effects of the Renaissance could not but infiltrate Venice Jewry, even after they moved into the Ghetto. By 1475, just two decades after Johannes Gutenberg invented movable type, Venetian Jewish artisans had set up the first Hebrew press and were carving out of wooden blocks as many as six different fonts of Hebrew characters. A generation later Daniel Bomberg, a Christian from Antwerp, earned from the Venetian Senate the "privilege" of printing Hebrew books. Employing Jews to fashion the letters and run the crude press, he produced his first work, the Torah, in November 1516, seven months after the Ghetto's institution. For the next thirty years, Bomberg and his staff of Jewish craftsmen, editors, and scholars pioneered in turning out such works as the first Bible with commentaries (the *Mikraot Gedolot*) and the first printed Talmud—an edition whose organization and page arrangement are followed to this day.

In 1553, thirty years after Bomberg's Talmud appeared, Pope Julius III declared the work blasphemous. On the first day of Rosh Hashanah that year, the Talmud was publicly burned in Rome. The Venetian Council of Ten followed suit and the Talmud, along with other Hebrew books, was burned in Venice a month later. Nevertheless, Hebrew printing survived in Venice, setting standards of book production and scholarship for the next two hundred fifty years.

The Jews of the Ghetto maintained their own free school, the only one in the city, and illiteracy was unknown. They were no less eager to acquire, or to create, works of art. The five synagogues that remain in the Ghetto today are an expression of this aesthetic refinement. The early seventeenth century was a golden age for the Ghetto. The risky but lucrative trade with the Middle East had become a virtual Jewish monopoly. The Ghetto's shops displayed spices, jewels, bolts of silk. The narrow streets were alive with well-dressed merchants speaking the languages of their travels or Judeo-Venetian—the special, almost secret, dialect Ghetto inhabitants used to discuss confidential matters. Simone Luzzatto was the community's rabbi for fifty years, during which he wrote the first major statement advocating official toleration of the Jews. Among the many responsa he prepared was one sanctioning travel by gondola on the Sabbath.

Another figure of the period was Sara Coppio Sullam, a patron of the arts whose Ghetto salon was a meeting place for both Jewish and Christian writers and scholars. She composed sonnets, some of them enunciating her pride in Judaism.

Sullam was a benefactor of one of the most engaging figures in the annals of Venetian Jewry. Leone Modena—rabbi, scholar, poet, playwright, composer, alchemist, marriage arranger, and incurable gambler—was the wunderkind of the Ghetto. At age 2½, he was on the *bimah* reading the *haftarah* of the week. At three he was translating Torah passages from Hebrew into Italian, and at thirteen he was translating Italian poetry into Hebrew. As a young rabbi in the Italian Synagogue, his sermons became so famous throughout the city that Christians joined Jews in the pews on *Shabbat* to hear him. Modena was as profound in his scholarship as he was brilliant in his speaking. His critique of the kabbalistic movement still serves modern scholars, and his refutation of Christian dogma is a classic of Hebrew literature.

The early seventeenth century was a

unique period for the Ghetto, never to be repeated. It was followed by new indignities. As the fortunes of the Venetian Republic declined through the eighteenth century, the government demanded ever greater tributes from the Jews. When French troops opened the Ghetto in 1797, some of the quarter's young men volunteered to join Napoleon's army in its sweep of Italy, afterward enduring the long march to Moscow and the bitter retreat in the frigid Russian winter. There are stories of Hebrew songs being chanted around the French campfires during the disastrous campaign.

The spirit of freedom was renewed forty years later when Jews played a leading role in the revived but short-lived Venetian Republic of 1848–49. Daniele Manin, who was of Jewish descent, was president of the provisional republican government, and two members of his cabinet were Jewish. A monument to the republican leader stands at Venice's Campo Manin, in front of the house where he lived.

The democratic revolution of 1848 had forced even the most reactionary governments of Europe to make concessions to their Jewish populations. In Rome, Pope Pius IX ordered that the walls of the ghettos in the Papal States be destroyed. When Venice was incorporated into the new kingdom of Italy, Jews were given full equality.

The generation of Venetian Jews that grew to maturity after the establishment of a united Italy is best represented by figures like Luigi Luzzatti, Italy's first Jewish prime minister (and a cousin of New York's Mayor Fiorello La Guardia). He had started his political career by organizing a mutual aid society for the gondoliers of Venice, an ill-paid group whose profession had been passed on from father to son since the invention of the gondola in the 13th century. Luzzatti went on to serve in the Italian Parliament for fifty years, and was elected prime minister in 1910. Until his death in 1927, he was also an active supporter of the Zionist agricultural settlements in Palestine.

Since the unification of Italy, the Jews of Venice have experienced only one interruption in more than a century of freedom. Mussolini treated Jews much as did the

Council of Ten—a combination of restriction and protection. That changed when German troops occupied Venice. On November 9, 1943, the Nazis began rounding up Venice's Jews. By the following August, 205 had been caught (another 500 had fled or were hidden by Christian friends). Assembled in the Campo di Ghetto Nuovo, Jews were marched down the Ghetto Vecchio, over the bridge spanning the Cannaregio Canal to the railroad station two hundred yards away and thence, by freight car, to their deaths at Auschwitz. Among them was Chief Rabbi Adolfo Ottolenghi, who chose to stay with his flock rather than escape.

Community: Government and church pronouncements notwithstanding, the relations of the people of the Ghetto with their fellow Venetians were "constant and intimate," as the historian Cecil Roth put it. "Jews and Christians worked together, played together, and quarreled together." Rabbi Luzzatto described the Venetian people as "more pleasing and kindly with the Jews than any other in the world." If you're lucky enough to be in Venice for the annual Carnevale, you'll delight in the spectacle of thousands of Venetians filling the vast Piazza San Marco, dressed in costumes of the sixteenth and seventeenth centuries—when all the city flocked to the Ghetto to observe the elaborate and imaginative Purim balls. The Council of Ten passed ordinances forbidding Christians to attend them, to no avail.

The Jews of Venice today—no more than 500 in a city of 350,000—are completely assimilated into the life of the city and live all over. Most Venetian Jews trace their roots in Italy back many centuries. No more than twenty reside within the confines of the Ghetto, where the community offices are still based.

The Jews are largely in business and the professions—doctors, lawyers, engineers, and civil servants. S. Lattes and Company, publisher of scientific literature, continues a tradition that has been in the family since 1839. The Levi Foundation, on the Grand Canal, supports a variety of artistic enterprises in the tradition of Joshua Ben David Levi, an eighteenth-century Venetian poet who composed his works in Hebrew. The Luzzattos, who came to Venice in the fifteenth century, have produced a line of poets, scholars, rabbis, and public figures who have been outstanding in every generation. Danielle Luzzatto Gardner, the Venetian-born wife of President Carter's ambassador to Italy, has been active on the Save Venice Committee. With the help of that organization, her generation of Luzzattos fulfilled the restoration of the Luzzatto Chapel, in which their ancestors had worshipped four centuries ago, as one of the architectural ornaments of the Ghetto.

Sights: The Jews of Venice are dispersed throughout the city, but their roots are still in the Ghetto. The area now teems, as it did before 1516, with working-class Christian families. Their bright-colored and freshly laundered shirts and skirts are strung out on rope lines suspended between the top floors of the buildings facing one another across the narrow waterways. The Fondamenta di Cannaregio (the embankment along one side of the Ghetto) bustles with neighborhood trattorie, fishermen display their catch from boats tied up along the canal; men and women hawk fresh fruits and vegetables barged in from nearby islands. Only a few yards distant is the entrance to the Ghetto, a living museum of Jewish culture and history.

The modern visitor approaches the Ghetto by motor-driven vaporetto instead of the traditional gondola, and no longer passes through the heavy gates that once sealed Jews in the Ghetto from sundown to sunrise. Holes in the worn brick indicate the position of the hinges of the gates. Though the gates have vanished, the Ghetto itself remains as it has been for nearly five centuries. Beyond its entrance on the embankment of the Cannaregio Canal is the long, narrow, tunnel-like alley that leads into its center. The passage is barely ten feet wide and, like a canyon, threads its way between the rows of "skyscrapers"—the drab seven- and eight-story tenements which were raised to that elevation, of necessity, to house the thousands who were herded into the meager quarter's confines.

To get there, take the number 5 vaporetto. Disembark at the Ferrovia (railroad station) landing, walk to the right along the

Lista di Spagna, cross the bridge over the Cannaregio Canal, and immediately turn left on the Fondamenta di Cannaregio for about seventy-five yards. Then turn into the narrow alley called Ghetto Vecchio, which leads into the heart of the old Jewish quarter.

The Ghetto's five surviving synagogues are the highlight of any tour, but visitors must seek them out behind the shabby facades and on the upper floors of the crowded tenements in which they were housed, and hidden. Four of the synagogues represent the "nations" that made up the Jewish community: the Levantine, immigrants from the Near East; the Spanish, exiles from Spain and Portugal; the German, composed of Ashkenazim from Central Europe; and the Italian, descendants of Jews who had migrated to Venice from cities on the Italian mainland.

The synagogues were designed by the foremost Venetian architects of the sixteenth century. Master craftsmen—sculptors, really—carved the mahogany *bimah* and the oak benches. The curtains before the ark and the mantles covering the Torah scrolls were embroidered by the most expert needlewomen, from the finest silk imported from China. The city's leading silversmiths were employed to impart a richness and an intricacy of detail to Torah ornaments, candelabras, chandeliers, spice boxes, and Seder plates.

The museum near the German Synagogue (Scuola Tedesca) has a comprehensive display of these artifacts. Guides, mostly students from the University of Venice who are fluent in English, conduct tours of all five synagogues. You'll get a hint of the past magnificence of the community and its synagogues, along with the message that financial aid is sorely needed so that the small Jewish community can continue with the periodic restorations that are required to maintain its aging masterpieces.

The tour begins at the Ghetto Vecchio, which, despite its name (meaning "old foundry"), was established after the Ghetto Nuovo. Follow the alley as it widens into the Campiello delle Scuole (the Little Square of the Synagogues). To the left is the carved wooden door that opens into the Spanish Synagogue (Scuola Spagnola). It is the largest of the five and has functioned with only one interruption—the years of the Nazi occupation—since the sixteenth century. Services are held under the guidance of Rabbi Roberto Della Rocca. Among the outstanding feature's of the sanctuary are the oval gallery, the multi-branched chandeliers and the straight center aisle, flanked by wooden pews, which runs from *bimah* to organ pipes.

On the opposite side of the square from the Spanish Synagogue is the ornate building that contains both the Levantine Synagogue (Scuola Levantina) and the Luzzatto Chapel. Unique among the five synagogues, the Levantine was not placed inconspicuously in a preexisting structure but built as an edifice unto itself. It was dedicated in the second half of the sixteenth century.

Beyond the Campiello delle Scuole, the Ghetto Vecchio continues over a bridge and into the much greater expanse of the Campo Ghetto Nuovo, the central plaza and heart of the Jewish quarter, where the other synagogues are located. The oldest is the German, built in 1528 for the German community, some of whose ancestors had come to Venice as merchants as early as the thirteenth century. In the Ghetto's discreet style, the facade blends into those of adjoining buildings; only the motif of five high windows (three walled up) with arches in white stone distinguishes the synagogue from the dwellings around it. Like the Spanish Synagogue, the German has an oval gallery, though here it is lower. The ark is at the top of four pink marble steps and, at the opposite end of the sanctuary, stands the wooden, canopied *bimah*.

To the right of the German is the Canton Synagogue (Scuola Canton), erected in 1531 and the second oldest in the Ghetto. It probably takes its name from the Canton family, German bankers who had it built as a private chapel. Another theory is that the name derives from its location: *Canton* is the Venetian word for "corner" and the synagogue stands at the corner of the great plaza. Often confused with buildings around it, the Canton Synagogue is identifiable by its high wooden dome, in the shape of an umbrella, mounted on what appears to be an octagonal drum.

Next to the Canton, on the south side of the plaza, is the Italian Synagogue (Scuola Italiana). It dates from 1575 and is the newest and least elaborate of the five, a reflection of the status of the Italian "nation," the poorest and smallest segment of the community. The Italian Synagogue is also scarcely distinguishable from its neighbors, except for the five high, arched windows (like the German Synagogue's) and a crest above the center window with an inscription, in Italian: "Holy Italian Community in the year 1575."

Sabbath and holiday services are conducted at the Spanish Synagogue during the summer and the Levantine in winter, when crowds are smaller. Details on Sabbath and weekday services are available from the Jewish community office at Ghetto Nuovo 2899 (telephone 715-012), which is also a social and cultural center of the community.

In addition to the synagogues and community center, visitors to the Ghetto should see the grim, artistic reminder of more recent history—a sculpture by the Lithuanian-born artist Arbit Blatas. Along the western side of the Campo Ghetto Nuovo is a brick wall, its surface chipped and faded after the passage of centuries. Atop the wall there are still strands of barbed wire installed by the Nazis when they used the Ghetto as a gathering place for Jews. It was on this Ghetto wall that Blatas and his wife, opera star Regina Resnik, proposed to mount the seven bronzed tablets of the completed sculpture. The preservation-minded city fathers, who deliberate on the replacement of a single paving block in the Piazza San Marco, were quick and enthusiastic in granting approval.

Beyond the Ghetto there are many places in Venice with Jewish connections. Among the mosaics in St. Mark's are those on *The Judgment of Solomon* and the lives of Abraham, Joseph, and Moses. Titian's ceiling paintings in the Basilica of Santa Maria della Salute depict *Abraham's Sacrifice, Cain and Abel,* and *David Killing Goliath.* The School of St. Rocco has many Hebrew Bible themes inside, including Tintoretto's ceiling paintings of *The Rain of Manna* and *Moses Causing the Water to Run from the Rocks,* and Tiepolo's altar paintings, *Abraham and the Angels* and *Hagar Abandoned*.

In the Palace of the Doges, *The Judgment of Solomon* is one of the images that appears in the series of thirty-eight carved capitals. Bassano's *The Return of Jacob* is in the palace's Hall of the Anti-Collegium. Left of the building's facade, in the Piazetta, is a statue of Solomon.

The Ca d'Oro, a fifteenth-century palace on the Grand Canal, was given to the Italian government by Baron Giorgio Franchetti, a prominent Venetian Jew, in 1916. He donated his personal art collection for display in the palace, but the building's chief attraction is its presentation of fifteenth-century Venetian patrician life.

Recommendations: Once you reach Marco Polo Airport outside Venice, be sure to take the motor launch across the lagoon to the city rather than the motor bus. The boat affords the classic — and breathtaking — approach by water, and you land in the center of everything, at the foot of the Piazza San Marco. A good place to stay is the Londra Palace, a former palazzo with the intimacy and charm one looks for in Europe. All the rooms face the lagoon, and the walk to San Marco is only five minutes along the lagoon's broad embankment.

Venice is a walker's city and simply by virtue of this there is eye contact and communication with other pedestrians on tiny bridges, in the narrow twisting alleys and the unexpected plazas. Mass transport, aboard the various lines of the vaporetti, is among best in the world. The fare is cheap and there are reduced fares for getting on and off, as one should, to explore.

Eating: There are no kosher restaurants in Venice, but kosher lunches and a warm welcome are available at the Casa di Riposo (the home for the aged) at Ghetto Nuovo 2874, which serves traditional Venetian Jewish dishes. Travelers, and especially groups, are advised to make reservations in

Foundry and boundary: Jews on the run from the Inquisition and local Christians who appreciated Purim customs traveled the canals that led to Venice's ghetto

advance at 716-002. Among the restaurants favored by Venetians themselves are Paradiso Perduto, Cannaregio 2540, a few hundred yards from the Ghetto, and Montin on the Fondamenta di Borgo. More expensive is the Corte Sconta, near the Arsenal, at Calle del Pestrin 3886. The pasta and fish dishes are superb and the meal is concluded with amaretti, the almond-flavored cookies that originated in the bakeries of the Ghetto.

Shopping: The Ghetto Vecchio and the Campo (the Ghetto's central plaza) offer good craft shops selling the products of local artisans in brass, silver, and glass. There is a lot of kitsch but also much of good quality. Judaica is available from Mordehai Fusetti at Ghetto Vecchio 1219. Elsewhere in the city, try Vogini for leather goods, Paul & Co. or Salviti for glass, Jesurum for laces and linens, and Roberta di Camerino for high fashion. Mrs. di Camerino is from an old Venetian Jewish family.

Reading: One can hardly discuss the Venetian Ghetto without reference to Shake-speare's *Merchant of Venice* and all the alleys of discussion into which it can lead. One of the most intriguing critiques is in Heinrich Heine's *Jewish Stories and Hebrew Melodies* (Markus Wiener), in which the German Jewish poet argues that Shylock is the most respectable character in the play. An engrossing, and erotic, spinoff of Shakespeare, featuring a twentieth-century actress playing Jessica transported back to the sixteenth-century ghetto is Erica Jong's *Serenissima* (Houghton Mifflin).

Venice's chroniclers range from Niccolò Machiavelli to Jan Morris. The definitive guidebook is Lorenzetti's *Venice and Its Lagoon* (Edizioni Lint). Two invaluable paperbacks are *History of the Jews in Venice* by Cecil Roth (Schocken) and *Venice: A Portable Reader* by Toby Cole (Lawrence Hill). A more recent history is *The Ghetto of Venice* by Riccardo Calimani (Dutton). Another useful work is *The Ghetto of Venice, Its Synagogues and Museum* (Carucci Editore) by Giovannina Reinisch Sullam, a descendant of Sara Sullam. It is well worth the trouble of finding — which is something you might say of Venice itself.

—*Gabriel Levenson*

Vienna

In November 1918, with the end of World War I and the collapse of the thousand-year Austro-Hungarian Empire, Sigmund Freud told Ernst Lothar, a young disciple who was interviewing him: "Like you, I feel an unrestrained affection for Vienna—although, perhaps unlike you, I know her abysses."

Freud would always have this love–hate relationship with the city in which he spent seventy-nine of his eighty-three years, sharing such feelings with the other great Jews of his time—Herzl, Schnitzler, Buber, Schönberg, Mahler, and scores more—who made Vienna, for half a century, one of the major intellectual centers of the world.

A like dualism must affect sensitive visitors to the Austrian capital today. They will find—more readily than its abysses—the apexes: Schönbrunn and the Prater, the Ringstrasse and the Kunsthistorisches Museum, the elegant shops on the Kärntnerstrasse and the *gemütlich* wine cellars of Grinzing. At the same time, beyond the whipped cream and the waltzes, they can uncover the evidence of a rich, often tragic history that cannot but enhance their travel experience.

In the years since Freud spoke with Lothar, Vienna has gone through the great social programs of the 1920s, the crushing attacks on the progressive (and mainly Jewish-led) Social Democratic party during the early 1930s, the Anschluss with Nazi Germany in 1938, the destruction of a Jewish community of almost 200,000 between 1939 and 1945, the postwar reconstruction of Austria, and the painful echoes of the Nazi era dredged up by Kurt Waldheim's presidency. The Austrian government belatedly and reluctantly accepted its obligation to reeducate a population whose families have been steeped in anti-Semitism

for generations and who themselves still admit—85 percent of them according to a recent survey—to lingering prejudices against their Jewish fellow citizens. Waldheim's Nazi past seemed to win him more votes in the 1986 presidential election than it cost him. Perhaps Freud would not have been surprised.

History: Jewish history in Vienna follows the same pattern as in almost every other city of Western Europe: early settlement in Roman times; persecution when the indigenous tribes adopted Christianity; intermittent toleration and expulsion during the Middle Ages; capricious cycles of reform and repression in the sixteenth century to the eighteenth; and the beginnings of the genuine acceptance after the French Revolution. Perhaps the most important exception from the European rule came during the Black Death epidemic that wiped out a third of the continent's population in 1348–49; Vienna was one of the few cities where Jews were *not* accused of causing the scourge, and the city became a refuge for Jews fleeing other stricken areas.

A turning point came in 1683 when financial support from Imperial Court agents Samson Wertheimer and Samuel Oppenheimer helped the Austrian Army to repel Turkish invaders, driving them out of Central Europe for good. Since then, Jews have been active in every sphere of Viennese life.

There were still restrictions, however, and as late as 1777 there were only 520 Jews in the city. By 1782, following the "Toleranzpatent" of Emperor Joseph II (which paved the way for full civil rights in 1867), there was already such growth that the community could set up a Hebrew printing press that soon became the center for Hebrew publishing in Central Europe.

Opportunities expanded for bankers and merchants, for clerks and civil servants, scholars and journalists. Vienna became a center of the *Haskalah* movement, which opened the hitherto closed world of traditional Jewish thought to the influences of secularism.

Vienna's Jewish golden age really began after the Revolution of 1848, in which Jews played a leading role. During the succeeding ninety years the Jews would dominate Vienna's cultural and intellectual life. Even before the official emancipation, however, the liberalized atmosphere reached out to previously sheltered Jewish womanhood, and there emerged such figures as Fanny Arnstein, daughter and wife of prominent bankers, whose salon was a meeting place for the personalities of the time, including the emperor himself, and Mozart, who was for some time in her employ.

There was hardly a field in which Jews did not make remarkable contributions to the city and empire. Jews prominent in medicine in Vienna were Sigmund Freud,

Headmaster: A doctor's understanding for a patient's troubles and a city's abysses

Alfred Adler, Wilhelm Reich, and Theodor Reik; in Zionist politics, Theodor Herzl and Max Nordau; in theology, Martin Buber; in music, Gustav Mahler and Arnold Schönberg, Oscar Straus, and Emmerich Kálmán; in theater, Max Reinhardt, Fritz Kortner, Lily Darvas, and Elisabeth Bergner; in letters, Arthur Schnitzler, Franz Kafka, Stefan Zweig, and Felix Salten.

Three of the four Austrians who won the Nobel Prize in medicine were Jews, and by the late nineteenth century more than half Vienna's physicians and dentists, 60 percent of its lawyers, and substantial numbers of university teachers and others in the liberal professions were Jewish. Most of the leaders of the Social Democratic party also were Jews—men like Viktor Adler, one of its founders, Max Adler, and Otto Bauer.

It was a brilliant period, from the 1880's—when Herzl was writing his feuilletons in the *Neue Freie Presse* and Freud beginning his medical practice—until 1938, when Austria's Anschluss with Germany brought the era to a tragic end. In the polyglot, multinational Austro-Hungarian Empire, with its heady mixture of races and cultures, there was a kind of aesthetic democracy, in which the Jews were the first among equals. For all of that, Vienna was steeped in anti-Semitism. The traditional animus against the Jews had been essentially religious. The prejudice acquired a new rationale—racism—with the writings of Wilhelm Marr, a German demagogue of the mid-nineteenth century who in 1879 coined the term "anti-Semitism" to describe the mission of the organization he founded that year, the League of Anti-Semites. Marr's spiritual heir was Vienna-born Georg von Schönerer, who elevated anti-Semitism into a major disruptive force in Austrian political life.

Schönerer's career ended when he was jailed for wrecking the offices of the Jewish-owned *Neues Wiener Tageblatt* and beating up members of what he had described as a "Jewish rag." But he was soon followed by another anti-Semite, whose influence has persisted to this day. Karl Lueger, who started as a liberal, lacked the fanatic conviction of Schönerer but utilized anti-Semitic slogans with much greater success. A handsome, blond, archetypal Aryan—

known as *Der schöne Karl* (the beautiful Charles)—he was idolized by the lower middle class and the artisans of Vienna, to whom he cynically appealed as the "victims" of Jewish bankers and businessmen. Though he actually had some Jewish friends, he was repeatedly elected mayor of Vienna on a platform of anti-Semitism. As mayor, he implemented a municipal socialism of sorts—a city-owned gasworks, electric street lighting and electrified trams, improved waterworks. To this day, Lueger is revered as one of the greatest mayors of Vienna. A street and a square are named for him. The consequences of his ideology and the National Socialism it inspired are insufficiently recognized.

Lueger died in 1910, and his funeral evoked one of the greatest outpourings of humanity, up until then, in Vienna's history. Among the mourners was Adolf Hitler, then a struggling young artist who lived in a men's hostel in the working-class Sixteenth District of the city. Hitler had just been rejected from the Academy of Fine Arts and was earning a few *groschen* by selling his sentimental Vienna cityscapes to Jewish frame dealers. The paintings had little intrinsic value, but they served as fillers for the picture frames which were being promoted.

Both von Schönerer and Lueger figure in *Mein Kampf*: Lueger's techniques—rallying the alienated mobs—and the slogans of anti-Semitism would reach their apocalypse in Hitler's hands. Just as the mayor's funeral brought out the people of Vienna in 1910, the Anschluss in March 1938 would bring many, many more into the streets. By then, any opposition to union with Germany had been stifled. The Social Democratic party had been crushed; the thousands of Austrians opposed to Nazi rule would be thrown into concentration camps, most to be executed.

World War I had reduced the vast, multinational empire to an insignificant monolingual country. Its language was German, and the dream of fusion with another nation speaking the same tongue had been shared by almost every element in Austrian society—from the Social Democrats to the most extreme monarchists, from Cardinal Innitzer who welcomed Hitler to the Viennese poor who could suddenly find jobs in the German arms industry. Austria's anti-Semitic tradition didn't hurt its enthusiasm for union with Germany. *Kristallnacht*, the night of November 9–10, 1938, when Germany's synagogues were burned, was celebrated as much in Vienna as in Berlin.

The dream of many Austrians, however, was an immediate nightmare for the country's 200,000 Jews, 180,000 of whom lived in Vienna. In the first, frenzied days of Anschluss thousands cheered and jeered at the spectacle of the leading Jewish citizens parading the square with "I am Jew" placards around their necks. They were forced to scrub the pavement, on which opponents of the plebiscite had futilely painted election slogans. Among the street cleaners was Rabbi David Israel Taglicht, who declared, "I am cleaning God's earth."

The Austrian Nazis had been assiduous students of the tactics of their German comrades, and they moved much more rapidly to rob, expel, and eventually murder their Jewish fellow citizens. One hundred thousand escaped before war broke out; 70,000 died; fewer than 1,000, who had somehow hidden in Vienna until it was liberated by the Red Army, survived to form the nucleus of a new postwar community.

Austrian Nazism had made its own contribution to the extermination of Austrian, and all European, Jewry. Such native sons as Hitler and Eichmann had set an example. The undoing of their deeds is a major and difficult undertaking to which all Austria's postwar governments have addressed themselves, with varying degrees of energy and success.

Community: Leon Zelman, director of Jewish Welcome Service, likes to describe Vienna's present-day Jewish community (virtually the entire Jewish population of Austria) as a phoenix risen from the ashes. Indeed, from the ashes it rose, but it is a modest phoenix. The 800 who emerged from the ruins of the city were joined by displaced persons from the concentration camps, by refugees from the Hungarian counterrevolution of 1956, and from the Czech and Polish expulsions of 1968–69, by Soviet Jews in the 1970s, and by natives who felt impelled to return "home" from Israel and the United States. There are now about 7,000 members of the community, and they enjoy the facilities of a wide range of institutions.

The Polish-born Zelman was liberated from Mauthausen, Austria's "own" concentration camp, at seventeen. The Welcome Service he organized in 1980 serves as a resource center to provide local people and visitors with information about Jewish life and history. It is under the city's auspices, with a former Vienna mayor as its honorary president and the World Jewish Congress as its "support system."

Once the center of an empire, postwar Vienna was a center of neutrality, and the result is often the same. The meeting place for both confrontation and conciliation between Russians and Americans, it served as the point of entry for more than 2 million refugees from other lands since 1945, including more than 200,000 Jews. Austria's expected entry into the European Community could restore the sense of a vast hinterland, or at least the feeling that it is part of something larger, that it lost with its empire.

With a constant movement of peoples through Vienna and beyond, to Israel, the United States, and Western Europe, the Jewish community has managed, miraculously, to sustain its structure. An older generation of natives, who returned to reclaim stolen assets or to spend final days in a beloved home town, is dying out. A middle generation has taken root — children of the returnees and, on a larger scale, Jews from the former Soviet Union (many from the Central Asian republics) who now constitute a majority — and who account for the overwhelming majority of the community's children.

Many newcomers from the former Soviet Union came without a sense of Jewish roots and initially avoided registering with the community. Mainly through the efforts of Chabad, the Lubavitch movement, Georgian and Bokharan Jews have joined in increasing numbers and attend services, at their own synagogue. Their connection with religious life has helped them make what would otherwise have been a difficult adaptation. Many of the immigrants run grocery stalls or shoe repair shops on Mexicoplatz — in contrast to the established

European Jews who work in medicine, law, engineering, the government, and business.

Perhaps 10 percent of the community is actively Orthodox, although all ten of the synagogues and *batei midrash* are fully observant. There are no Reform, Conservative, or Reconstructionist congregations in Vienna, but the Stadttempel, the one hundred fifty-year-old synagogue, ecumenically embraces worshippers along a wide range of commitment — from atheists to adherents of Agudat Israel.

The Gemeinde (community), with offices next to the Stadttempel on Seitenstettengasse, is the official body of Viennese Jewry, recognized as such by law. Those who register with it pay it a percentage of their annual income tax. The government partially subsidizes the agency with an annual allocation besides covering the salaries of the sixteen top executives (out of a total staff of 150).

Gemeinde funds help support an old-age home, the maintenance of cemeteries (including one dating from 1571), and Zvi Perez Chajes, a day school with 200 students. The Gemeinde also supports a half dozen Talmud Torahs and kindergartens, a Jewish student organization, and several Zionist youth groups.

There is a growing trend among young Jews in Vienna to identify with Judaism — if not religiously, certainly culturally and socially. They are conscious of the importance of a Jewish presence in the city and the country which Hitler had pledged to make *judenrein*. Until recently, this growing consciousness was, by and large, a quiet phenomenon. The Waldheim campaign and election, which uncovered a layer of Austrian anti-Semitism, also prompted Viennese Jewry to be more outspoken than at any time since the war.

The pantheon of Jewish greats may never reappear in Vienna. Today's community doesn't have the critical mass to generate a specifically Jewish culture, with writers like Schnitzler or Zweig who gave voice to the Jewish condition of their times, let alone infuse the general culture with Jewish elements. There are no longer Jewish neighborhoods, as in pre-Anschluss days, when there were forty-two synagogues in the city. Most of Vienna's prewar Jewish population lived either in the First District (the heart of the Old City) or in the Second and Twentieth Districts, on the island opposite the First, separated from it by the Danube Canal. But there is a Jewish presence, nonetheless, and a Jewish past that is an ineradicable part of the Viennese experience.

Personalities: There are a few exceptions. Former Chancellor Bruno Kreisky, though ambivalent about his Jewishness, was instrumental in the campaign to educate Austria about Nazism. Two Viennese Jews who have played major roles in dealing with the Holocaust are Simon Wiesenthal, whose Documentation Center has been a prime clearing house in the worldwide search for war criminals, and Peter Sichrovsky, of the postwar generation, whose book *Strangers in Their Own Land* (Basic Books) addresses the perennial question of how Jews can live in Germany and Austria today. Topsy Kuppers, a Dutch-born Jewish actress, is known for her one-woman shows at the Freie Bühne Theater; one recent performance was *Lola Blau,* a traditional Viennese cabaret production about a Jewish actress before, during, and after Hitler.

Though Vienna's decline began with the breakup of the Austro-Hungarian Empire in 1918, its Jewish intelligentsia helped create an afterglow of greatness until 1938. And to this day, Vienna's Jewish sons and daughters enrich the parts of the world in which they are settled. A highly selective list of the Viennese Jews who have made their marks after emigrating includes the composer Frederick Loewe, Charles Bludhorn of Gulf + Western, Supreme Court Justice Felix Frankfurter, film directors Billy Wilder and Otto Preminger, singer and film star Theodore Bikel, and the mayor of Jerusalem, Teddy Kollek.

Sights: There is much to see in and around Jewish Vienna, and the office of the Welcome Service, in the heart of the city, is the place to pick up brochures, information, and knowledgeable guides. It is at Stephansplatz 10, First District, in the very center of the Old City, where the Romans built their encampment almost two thousand years ago. The Welcome Center (telephone 63-88-91) can arrange tours of Jewish Vienna and of Jewish sights outside the city as well. Be sure to get a copy of the booklet distributed by the Welcome Service entitled *Heritage and Mission: Jewish Vienna.*

For almost a thousand years the broad, cobblestoned expanse of Stephansplatz has been the heart of the city. Dominating the square is Stephansdom, the magnificent twelfth-century cathedral that was gutted by Allied bombers during World War II and has been meticulously restored to its former grandeur, including the replacement of the original medieval stained-glass windows depicting the Vienna Jews of the period. Building stones from the nearby Rothschild mansion, which had been razed, were used in the repairs. The forty synagogues destroyed by the German and Austrian Nazis were not rebuilt; there was no need to, since there were no longer worshippers to use them.

A short walk from the cathedral is the one synagogue that survived—perhaps because it is inconspicuously blended into a continuous facade with adjoining buildings. The oldest existing Jewish structure in the city, the Stadttempel (City Temple), at Seitenstettengasse 4, conceals an elaborate, elliptical interior. Thanks to the insistence of the government, in 1826, that it not be erected as a separate structure, it escaped notice when the other synagogues were attacked in 1938. Guided tours can be arranged through the secretary, at 53-1-04. The Jewish community offices are next door.

A few blocks distant is Judenplatz, the main square of the Jewish community for five hundred years. The Mizrachi organization maintains a small *beit midrash* and school at Judenplatz 8 (telephone 535-4153) and does a fine job of educating young Iranian Jews in the principles of Judaism. At any given time in recent years, there have been 200 to 300 Iranian children sheltered in Vienna, transients who remain in the city only long enough to obtain visas to the United States. The modest school is well worth seeing. Its head is Josef Meir, a Vienna native who emigrated to Israel and has returned for an extended tour of duty. He is delighted to show visitors about—and to take them down five flights of cellar stairs, illuminated only by candlelight, to a subterranean *mikveh* dating from the fifteenth century.

In the square outside the five-story Mizrachi walk-up is a statue of Gotthold Ephraim Lessing, the philo-Semitic author of *Nathan the Wise.* The bronze sculpture was moved from its spot in an obscure part of the city to this site of greater relevance. The monument has helped establish the tone and direction of Vienna's Jews in affirming their enduring presence and of the city's authorities in attempting to secure it.

There are many other locations of special interest in the First District of the city, all within easy walking distance of the Welcome Service on Stephansplatz. Most significant is the Austrian Resistance Museum at Wipplingerstrasse 8. It offers schoolchildren and the public a permanent collection of documents and oral history, a library, traveling exhibits, and other materials relating to the Austrian struggle against Nazism.

There is a statute of Karl Lueger, the mayor who inspired Hitler, but as a counterbalance there are now dozens of statues and plaques throughout the city in honor of those who died in the underground fight against Nazism. The monuments and street signs named for prominent Viennese Jews, systematically removed after Anschluss, have been returned to their appropriate places, along with newer memorials. A brochure published by the Social Democratic Party and available at the Welcome Service, lists all these memorials, with a brief description of each. Among the streets and monuments in the brochure are Theodor Herzlhof, a municipal housing project in Leopoldstadt, the heart of the old Jewish quarter; Desider Friedmanhof at Ferdinandstrasse 23, an apartment house named for the last president of the Jewish community before the Holocaust; Arnsteingasse, a street in the 15th District named for the Baron Nathan von Arnstein and his wife, Fanny; and Viktor Adlerplatz, a square in the 10th District named for the founder of the Social Democratic Party. The many streets named for Jews include Rosa Luxembourggasse, Mahler-strasse, Spinozagasse, Stefan Zweigplatz, Kafkastrasse, and Werfelstrasse.

Also among the listings in the brochure is the Zvi Perez Chajes day school, named for Vienna's chief rabbi between the World Wars. The handsome reconstructed building is on the site of the prewar school. It became the deportation point at which the city's Jews were gathered by the SS — under the direction of Adolf Eichmann — and shipped to Auschwitz. At the time of the rededication of the school in 1984, Rudolf Kirchschlager, then president of the Austrian Republic, delivered the keynote speech. Visits to the school, at Castellez-gasse 35 in the Second District, can be arranged by calling 333-196.

At Salztorgasse 6 is the Simon Wiesenthal Documentation Center (officially the Documentation Center of the Union of Jewish Victims of the Nazis), where the famed Nazi hunter maintains an ongoing file on the history and present whereabouts of his "clients." For permission to visit the center, call 63-91-31.

A ten-minute metro-plus-tram ride from Stephansplatz is the Sigmund Freud House at Berggasse 19. The second-floor apartment where Freud lived and worked from 1891 to 1938 (the year of his flight to London, where he died in 1939) has been preserved as it was during that period of his life. The hundreds of items on display were assembled by Freud's daughter, Anna, and by the family housekeeper, Paula Fichtl. The memorabilia include pipe and walking stick, cigar boxes and books, letters and photographs, writing desk and psychoanalytic couch.

It is all laid out in affectionate detail, as if the great man had just walked out of the apartment for coffee and conversation at his favorite café. It was (and is) Café Landtmann, at the corner of Dr. Karl Lueger Ring and Löwelstrasse. Freud would relax over tarok, a four-handed card game he loved passionately — as did that bane of his being, none other than Lueger himself.

Eating: Around the corner from the Stadttempel and part of the same, large community-owned building is the kosher Noah's Ark Restaurant (telephone

533-1374). Also community-owned, it is now run by two experienced restaurateurs from Warsaw. The food is first class; the ambiance, elegant and discreet; the cost, very reasonable. At Hollandstrasse 3 in Leopoldstadt (in the Second District) is a kosher restaurant operated by Lubavitch (33-46-74 or 33-35-65). Vegetarian food is available in the First District at Siddhartha, Fleischmarkt 16. Such restaurants are rare in a city of carnivores. This one is expensive, but very good.

Side Trips: Mauthausen, the former concentration camp two hours west of Vienna, attracts hundreds of thousands of Austrians annually, and is regularly visited by schoolchildren. In recent years, recruits into the Austrian Army have taken an oath of allegiance there. The preserved camp has been the focal point of the government's efforts to educate the nation about the fate of the country's Jews, Austrian collaboration with Hitler, and, not least of all, the Austrian Resistance.

The Jewish museum of Eisenstadt, thirty-two miles south of Vienna, is located in the mansion of what was once the home of the Wolf family, the most prominent Jews of the area—the province of Burgenland. Financed by the government, the museum collection memorializes the Eisenstadt Jewish community of 446, which was never reconstituted after the war, and presents a detailed picture of Jewish life in the twelve countries that were, at one time, part of the Austro-Hungarian Empire. The museum is on Museumgasse, adjacent to the Unterberggasse, in the city's old Jewish quarter. On the Unterberggasse itself is Samson Wertheimer's Synagogue, built in 1750 and recently restored.

Reading: The flavor of Vienna at its Jewish height is captured in many novels set in the era. Noteworthy are Frederic Morton's *The Forever Street* (Doubleday), which takes the Spiegelglass family from their arrival in the city in the 19th century to the Nazi period, and Irving Stone's *The Passions of the Mind*, which focuses on Sigmund Freud. The father of psychoanalysis meets Sherlock Holmes (and rids him of his cocaine addiction) in *The Seven Percent Solution* by Nicholas Meyer (Dutton); if you have a chance, see the movie with Alan Arkin as Freud. A less whimsical Sigmund is Montgomery Clift in the 1962 film *Freud*. The beginning of Theodor Herzl's novel *Old New Land* (Herzl Press) is also set in Vienna.

Two important general studies of Austria, and Vienna, are Carl E. Schorske's *Fin-de-Siècle Vienn*a (Vintage Press) and William M. Johnston's *The Austrian Mind* (University of California). Evocative portraits of the city include Frederic Morton's *A Nervous Splendor* (Little, Brown), Heimito von Doderer's *The Demons* (Knopf), Robert Musil's *The Man Without Qualities* (Coward-McCann), and the works of Arthur Schnitzler—like *Viennese Novelettes, The Little Comedy,* or *My Youth in Vienna.* The best guidebook for an insider's view of the city is *Viennnawalks* by J. Sydney Jones (Holt, Rinehart & Winston). Marsha L. Rozenblit has written *The Jews of Vienna, 1867-1914: Assimilation and Identity* (SUNY Press), a detailed study of the community during its golden age.

If you have trouble finding books on Vienna at home, try Shakespeare & Co., an English-language bookstore at Sterngasse 2, just around the corner from the Noah's Ark Restaurant. The combination of good kosher food and good literature is unbeatable. If Vienna had its abysses even as the capital of an empire, it has its apexes even as the capital of a small country.

—*Gabriel Levenson*

Vilnius (Vilna)

The first and perhaps most lasting impression that strikes a Jewish visitor to Vilnius, the capital of newly independent Lithuania—even beyond the ever-present signs of Soviet-style economic hardship—is its apparent homogeneity. In the streets and shops, at the theater and sports arena, the people of Vilnius look and act like members of a family at ease in their home.

This impression is striking because right before Vilnius went into the tunnel of Soviet history from which it recently emerged, it was a polymorphous city whose 60,000 Jews formed more than 40 percent of the population. Today there is nary a trace of that once pervasive presence. Not only are the people gone, so is the place where they lived. Vilna—as it was known to its Yiddish-speaking citizens—is no more. There are Jews in the Lithuanian capital today, and like everyone else they have new hope, but there is no doubt in their minds that the place where they live is called Vilnius.

History: Vilnius was founded in 1323 by Duke Gedeminas, a Lithuanian empire builder who called for workers, merchants, and craftsmen to come and build the state. Among the Russians, Germans, and other non-Lithuanians who answered was at least a handful of Jews. Toward the end of the century Jews were granted a royal privilege to live in Vilnius. According to disputed sources, by 1440 there grew up around the *alte kloyz,* a Jewish house of prayer and study, the city's first Jewish community. Expelled in 1495, the Jews were permitted to return during the reign of Sigismund I (1506–1548), who despite his liberalism permitted a *De non tolerandis judaeis* edict to be issued. The first indication of an organized community is in 1568, when the Jews of Vilna were required to pay a poll tax.

The period also saw the beginning of the celebrated Shulhoyf, a courtyard that would house thirty *shuls* and more than one hundred *minyanim.*

The sixteenth century saw the beginning of the Great Synagogue, distinguished by its modest exterior and a five thousand-square-foot sanctuary. Its builders adapted creatively to the rule that no synagogue be higher than a church by placing the entrance below street level. The first Vilna Ghetto, on many counts a benign though poverty-stricken one, was established in 1663.

The peculiar character of Vilna Jewry, a successful blend of religious and secular learning, dates to the eighteenth century when Rabbi Elijah ben Solomon Zalman, the Vilna Gaon (1720–1797), made his presence felt as a pious and enlightened leader. The teachings of the reclusive Gaon, a fierce opponent of the hasidic movement, influenced the *mitnaged* circles that played such a prominent role in Lithuanian Jewish thought into the twentieth century. Though he feared the *Haskalah* (enlightenment) threatened Jewish faith and tradition, he was in favor of some if its principles, especially the study of natural sciences, and his stance against hasidism probably helped in Vilna's development as a *Haskalah* center.

In the nineteenth century Napoleon, impressed by the extent of Jewish culture, dubbed Vilna "the Jerusalem of Lithuania." Romm Press, publisher of the famous *Vilna Shas* (Talmud), had by the end of the century grown into the most important Jewish publishing house in Europe.

By the turn of the century, Jewish cultural life in Vilna was in its prime and the community was bursting with activity that continues to have an impact on Jews around the world. Among the Jewish institutions either founded or headquartered in Vilna in the early twentieth century were the Bund, Hovevei Zion, Mizrachi, Po'alei Zion, Agudat Yisrael, and the YIVO Institute for Jewish Research. The Vilna Truppe, the preeminent Yiddish theater company, was emblematic of the flowering of Yiddish poetry and prose; its production of *The Dybbuk*, which toured Europe and the United States in 1921, was perhaps the greatest triumph in the history of the Yiddish stage.

While all this was going on at the surface, the ground underneath Jewish Vilna was being subjected to geopolitical tremors. As of old, Lithuania was alternately being conquered and reconquered by Germany, Poland, and Russia. Vilnius itself in 1920 was taken from Lithuania and made part of Poland, later to be returned by Stalin, who unceremoniously proceeded to gobble up the whole country in 1940. This signaled the beginning of the end for Vilna's Jews.

Even before the Germans entered the city on June 15, 1941, the Soviets had closed all of Vilna's Jewish cultural institutions and exiled its "capitalist" Jews to Siberia. Lithuanian nationalists, on the other hand, eager to believe Nazi claims that all Jews were Communists, not only welcomed the German invasion with open arms but also did a considerable amount of shooting of Jews both before and during the occupation. During the war two ghettos were built and liquidated by the Germans and their local helpers in Vilna. Seventy thousand Jews were shot to death in the forest of Ponary about six miles outside Vilna and lie buried there in mass graves they were made to dig themselves. Vilna—Jewish Vilna— had vanished from the face of the earth.

Community: Vilna's desolation was evident to the survivors who returned in 1946 only to see the *Shulhoyf* reduced to a ruin. About the only Jewish building left intact was the more modern Choral Synagogue, a Romanesque and Moorish edifice that had been built outside the cramped confines of the Jewish quarter in 1904. Stalin quashed the first Jewish effort to rebuild, but even he did not succeed in destroying the synagogue, which today attracts a *Shabbat minyan* of aged locals and

a scattering of visitors. Until the late 1980s the synagogue, the Cultural Society of Lithuanian Jews and a handful of survivors groups and benevolent societies were the only signs of Jewish life in the capital of Soviet Lithuania.

Two factors combined to turn things around, to create a true Jewish revival in Vilnius: *perestroika* and the Lithuanian People's Front (Sajudis), the independence movement. When the Soviets eased restrictions on the study of Hebrew and on *aliyah,* Jewish activists in Vilnius like Emmanuelis Zingeris, currently a member of the Parliament, seized the opportunity. Taking at their word the assertions of the leaders of the national movement, in particular President Vytautas Landsbergis, that they were neither neo-Fascist nor anti-Semitic, Zingeris worked closely with them to create and strengthen Jewish communal institutions.

Jews in Lithuania and abroad had their doubts about such assurances shortly after independence was achieved in September 1991, when the government began granting pardons to Lithuanians who had been convicted of anti-Soviet activity; among those pardoned were some identified as killers of Jews during World War II. But the government responded with sensitivity to Jewish concerns. About President Landsbergis, whose own family hid Jews during the war, there are no doubts.

Synagogue row: The disappearance of the Shulhoyf *and a Vilna that is no more*

Today Vilnius has a Jewish Museum in a building at Pamenkalnio 8e newly renovated under state auspices. A recent exhibit, Fifty Years After the Holocaust, featuring stark black-and-white photographs by David Davidovich, depicting the effects of genocide on the urban landscape, is indicative of the institution's plans to address Jewish life and history. There is also a Jewish National School where Hebrew is taught to adults, teenagers and, lately, elementary-school students; a Jewish kindergarten; and a sleepaway camp for sixty children who sing Zionist and Yiddish songs and dance Israeli and hasidic dances among the pine trees of the Nemincinya Forest on the outskirts of the city. Plans for the future include a Jewish community center, a publishing house, and a video on Jewish Vilnius.

B'nai B'rith has invested heavily in promoting the building of a Vilnius Jewish community. Vilnius has also been adopted by the United Jewish Federation of MetroWest, New Jersey, which underwrites the travel of visiting scholars. Sofia Zibutsiene, director of the Zalman Reisen Foundation for Jewish Culture (located at Vesulskio 14, telephone 651-178), works closely with both organizations and her office also serves as the Israel information center of Vilnius, where a steady stream of the city's Jews finalize their plans for *aliyah.*

Estimates vary but the consensus is that there are about five thousand Jews in Vilnius today. Most are not of Lithuanian origin but Russian Jews who came after the war, and many are leaving for Israel. For those who choose to remain permanently there is a new variety of cultural resources—there is a Jewish newspaper, *Yerushalayim d'Lita,* published in Yiddish, Russian, and Lithuanian; a Yiddish culture society which organizes evenings of poetry and music; a Jewish amateur theater group and a radio program, *"Pa'amon Vilna"* (The Bell of Vilna).

Other signs of Jewish vitality include a department of Judaic Studies at Vilnius University, a Jewish department at the Lithuanian Book Palace which classifies books and manuscripts saved from the Holocaust, and a government project to restore Jewish religious artifacts stored in what was until recently called the Museum of Atheism. More than two-thirds of those studying Yiddish and Jewish history at the university, however, are non-Jews—Lithuanians whose interest in Yiddish culture does not differ substantially from the scholarly pursuit of dead cultures, however fascinating. At the Book Palace, the problem is different but similar: To whom do these remnants of Lithuanian Jewish culture belong—to the state, for whom they represent the past of one of many ethnic groups, or to the Jewish people, for whom these documents are necessary for the self-understanding of a living people? This question is currently being addressed by YIVO in New York, which considers reclaiming these documents a top priority.

Sights: The *Shulhoyf*, heart of Vilna Jewry for three centuries, exists no longer, although a magnificent replica can be found in the exhibit of European synagogues at Israel's Museum of the Jewish Diaspora in Tel Aviv. A good description comes from *Synagogues of Europe* (MIT Press) by Carol Herselle Krinsky. "The courtyard was a small open space entered through metal gates at each end, tucked between streets inhabited almost entirely by Jews," she writes. "Around the courtyard stood 14 synagogues—in the 1880s there may have been 30—the ritual bath, the neighborhood well and fountain, the kosher slaughterhouse and community offices. The renowned Strashun Library stood at the entrance to the main synagogue complex, and booksellers sold their volumes in its courtyard."

A tour of the old Jewish quarter, where now one can see only street signs for Gaono Street and Jews' Street, is futile unless you engage the services of a knowledgeable guide. Two of the best are Roza Beliauskiene, a curator at the Jewish Museum (779-787), and Ilye Lempert (650-577), a young expert in Jewish history. On your right as you enter the old quarter on Zydu (Jews') Street is a kindergarten building where the Great Synagogue once stood. On your left is a green expanse crossed by paved walks. This open space, uncharacteristic of neighborhoods dating back to the Middle Ages, represents blocks of buildings where Jews lived before the war. The crisscrossing pavements are remnants of the narrow lanes of the old quarter. Underground there is a network of medieval cellars — *malines* — where the Jews lived for extended periods during times of persecution.

There were two ghettos in Vilna during the war, the larger for the bulk of the Jewish population, the smaller for children and old people. Among the buildings still standing are the former Jewish gymnasium where the Judenrat met, the publishing house that was used as a prison, the ghetto theater and library.

Located at Pylimo 39, the Choral Synagogue, the only one in Vilnius today, is a galleried basilica of mixed Romanesque and Moorish style. The Tablets of the Law atop the entrance and the oriental ark in the sanctuary are remnants of its former magnificence.

A visit to the Book Palace, at Rasytoju 4, where you can view *seforim* rescued from the famous Lithuanian Yeshiva of Telz and letters of such Jewish luminaries as Albert Einstein and historian Simon Dubnow, is in order. Call director Fera Bramson, 222-536 (office) or 731-354 (home) for an appointment.

The most important Jewish site lies about six miles outside the city in the Ponary Forest. There where the massacres took place are three monuments. One, built by the Soviets, commemorates the 100,000 "Soviet citizens" murdered there by the Nazis; no mention of the Jews is made, nor until recently were Jews mentioned on a monument built by the Lithuanians. In 1991, thanks to a donation by an Israeli and underwritten by the new Lithuanian government, a monument to the Jews shot at Ponary was dedicated in the presence of more than fifty luminaries from Israel including Jerusalem's Mayor Teddy Kollek.

Side Trips: Take an eighteen-mile taxi ride to Trakai, the castle of Duke Gedeminas before he founded Vilnius. The restored red-stone edifice sits on a lake dotted with sailboats; and if you can't actually see the Karaite community that settled here centuries ago, you can muse about it at one of the outdoor cafés.

About sixty miles northwest of Vilnius is Kaunas (Kovno). There engineer Chaim Bargman (telephone 779-948), who also teaches Hebrew at the Kovno branch of the Jewish School, will show you the building — at the corner of Paneriu and Jesiboto (Yeshivah) Streets — that was supposed to serve as part of the Slobodka Yeshiva before the Germans took it over. He can also show you the street where Ludwig Zamenhof, the Jew who developed Esperanto, lived; and the infamous IX Fortas (Fort Nine) prison adjoining the Field of Death where on October 28, 1941, 9,000 Jews were killed by the Nazis and their local collaborators. He will also explain how the 64 Jews used by the Germans to burn the corpses engineered a daring and successful escape. The prison houses three torture chambers, and etched on the prison's walls one can see the names of some of the 900 French Jews who died there on May 18, 1944. Kovno was where the Japanese consul Senpo Sugihara issued visas to Jewish refugees in violation of his orders from the Foreign Ministry; expelled by Soviet authorities shortly before the German invasion, he walked to the central railway station taking his visa stamp with him, and was still stamping passports as he leaned out the window from his departing train.

One hundred and twenty miles farther northwest is Shauliai (Shavli), where one can see the efforts of a community of 500 to keep up Jewish life. Shauliai's Jewish Center, housed in a former Communist Party hotel at Visinskio Gatve 24, has a library, reading room, social and recreation hall, and an exposition on the Jewish ghetto that demonstrates the parallels between Nazism and Communism. The exhibition was mounted by Label Lipshitz, head of Shauliai's Jewish Cultural Center, who has documented which Lithuanians collaborated with the Nazis and can point out almost a dozen spots in the forests where Jews were massacred by locals.

Personalities: The dominant figure in Vilna's Jewish history is the Vilna Gaon, but there are many other outstanding talmudists in Vilna's past, including Rabbi Hayyim ben Isaac Volozhiner and Rabbi Isaac Elhanan Spektor, after whom Yeshiva University's Rabbinical Seminary in New York is named. Violinist Jascha Heifetz was born in Vilna, as was sculptor Mark Antokolski, who sought to create a Jewish art of the spirit. Poet Czeslaw

Milosz, a non-Jew born in Vilnius, writes feelingly on the Jewish condition. The Holocaust produced many Jewish heroes, among them Israeli poet Abba Kovner and Yitzhak Wittenberg, who sacrificed his life to save the inhabitants of the Vilna Ghetto. The famous partisans' anthem, *Mir Zehnen Doh* ("We Are Here"), was composed in the Vilna Ghetto by Hirsch Glick. The city has produced many great writers, including Yiddish poet Abraham Sutzkever and novelist Chaim Grade, whose writings are permeated with Jewish values.

The best known Jew in Vilnius today is Grigory Kanovich, whose novels depict *shtetl* life; his most popular work is *Candles in the Wind,* ripe for translation. An outspoken critic of official anti-Semitism while serving as a Supreme Soviet deputy, he became chairman of the Jewish Community of Lithuania after independence.

Reading and Viewing: Two recent books of reminiscences are Yiddish actor Joseph Buloff's *From the Old Market Place* (Harvard University Press) and Esther Hautzig's *Remember Who You Are* (Crown). Hautzig left Vilna as a teenager before the war never to return, but her descriptions are all the more vivid because of that. She says her mother urged her not to go back: *"Makh nisht keyn churbn fun dayne sheyne zikhroynes"* ("Don't destroy your beautiful memories").

To get an idea of just how Jewish Jewish Vilna was, read Chaim Grade's novel *The Agunah* (Twayne) or his memoir *My Mother's Sabbath Days* (Schocken), in which he brings to life the courtyard culture of the Jews. Jean-François Steiner told the story of Yitzhak Wittenberg and the resistance in the Vilna Ghetto in the opening chapters of *Treblinka* (Simon & Schuster). Lucy Dawidowicz's *From That Place and Time* (W. W. Norton) is an account of her research internship at YIVO before the war and of her narrow escape from the Nazis. Israel Cohen's 1943 classic *History of the Jews of Vilna* has been reissued by the Jewish Publication Society.

A fascinating collection of documents and photographs was assembled by Leizer Ran for his 1974 two-volume *Jerusalem of Lithuania* (Vilna Album Committee). Mira Van Doren, a Vilna native, produced the ninety-minute public television documentary *Vilna: The Vanished City,* available to groups by writing to The Vilna Project, 130 West 57 Street, New York, NY 10019. *Ghetto,* a play by Israeli Yehoshua Sobol, is the last of a trilogy about the theatrical troupe that flourished there.

Those who don't have these memories but would like a share in them would do well to compare these artistically wrought reminiscences of Jewish Vilna with the reality of what is now merely—and for the Jews, sadly—Vilnius.

—Joseph Lowin

Warsaw

The meeting had been arranged on an hour's notice. The host, a Polish-Jewish journalist, had been anxious to meet a friend of a friend. The visitor, a foreign Jewish reporter, wondered what it would be like to spend an evening in a Warsaw Jewish apartment.

"Please forgive me," said the host, pointing to the television set as his guest entered. "I've been waiting all week to see this performance of Vivaldi's *Four Seasons.* It's being played by four of Poland's top violinists."

As the visitor listened to the music, the inevitable thought occurred. There must have been a time when virtually all the violinists in Poland were Jews.

"By the way," the host said, indicating the first artist, "She's Jewish."

One out of four isn't bad.

When the second violinist came on, the host interjected, "Her father is Jewish."

Among other things, the evening confirmed the experience of many Jewish visitors to Poland. Officially there are very few Jews, but there are a lot of unexplained blips on the Jewish radar screen.

For four decades, Warsaw was locked firmly behind the Iron Curtain, off limits to all but the most intrepid Jewish travelers. The Communists took power after the Nazis had reduced Polish Jewry by 90 percent, and over the succeeding 40 years, emigration, purges, and age took care of most of the remainder.

Now in the mad rush after the 1989 revolution, Warsaw has emerged as one of Central Europe's most accessible cities. It ranks among the richest in Jewish connections, albeit mostly in the past tense. Poland is often referred to as a giant Jewish graveyard, but as the experience with Vi-

valdi indicates, the cycle of Jewish life in Warsaw still turns. On the fringes of the graves are some flowers of Jewish life.

History: In its time Warsaw was the greatest center of European Jewry. Jews came to Poland a thousand years ago, but for much of the past millennium they lived mainly in villages. The first record of Jewish settlement in Warsaw is from 1414, and the first Jewish quarter there was in the area of Waski Dunaj and Piekarska in the Old Town.

While Jews in other parts of Poland enjoyed official protection and quickly assumed important roles in commerce, Warsaw's population refused to accept a Jewish presence and the Jews were banished in 1483. Late in the sixteenth century, they began to return, and by 1765 they numbered 2,500. Thirty years later they had increased to 6,700, of whom 30 percent were either merchants or craftsmen. The eighteenth century brought periodic expulsions and readmissions, but the overall trend was one of growth.

While Warsaw's Jews were struggling for acceptance among their Catholic neighbors, important developments were unfolding elsewhere in Poland. In the second half of the eighteenth century, hasidism reached the city, and after Warsaw came under Prussian rule German Jews arrived and spurred the growth of a community of *maskilim.* In 1802 they established the German Synagogue where prayers were recited in German. By 1804, Jews constituted 17 percent of Warsaw's 67,000 residents.

By the 1860s (when the city was under Russian rule), all restrictions on where Jews could live or what trades they could practice were revoked. But legal equality didn't mean acceptance. The 1881 Warsaw pogrom revealed continued anti-Jewish sentiments.

In 1882 Warsaw had 300 synagogues, 200 of which were hasidic. The number of *mitnaged* synagogues grew as many Jews fled Lithuania and took up residence in Warsaw. At the same time, the early seeds of Zionism began to flourish in Warsaw. It was young Polish Zionist emigrants who founded Rehovot and, later, Tel Aviv. Opponents of the Zionist dream established the socialist Bund. Assimilation was a major problem in the city; many young Jews did not affiliate with any of the disparate groups.

There were 130,000 Jews in Warsaw in 1882, one-third of the city's population. Assimilationist trends notwithstanding, this was the beginning of the peak of Jewish activity in the city, which would end with the German invasion in 1939. The Jewish community bulged and Yiddish culture — with daily newspapers, theaters, schools — flourished. By 1917, on the eve of Polish independence, Warsaw's Jews numbered 343,000, or 41 percent of the population, and constituted the largest Jewish center on the European continent.

Between the world wars, Jewish culture and anti-Semitism lived in tandem, with the Catholic majority taking steps to limit Jewish influence in commerce and finance. On the eve of World War II the Jewish community of Warsaw numbered 395,000. Eliminating such a major center of Jewish life was a high German priority from the start.

After the German occupation, the Jews were forced to live in specific parts of the city, and the boundaries of the ghetto were reduced regularly. Conditions inside the walls were terrible, and made worse by the constant influx of Jews deported from surrounding towns and villages. Some 500,000 Jews were crowded into the ghetto by the beginning of 1941, but by the time of the Warsaw Ghetto Uprising, only 60,000 were left in the ghetto. The rest had been sent to Treblinka or other death camps, or succumbed to starvation or disease.

The Ghetto Uprising was one of the proudest moments of the Holocaust. Led by Mordecai Anielewicz, the ragged remnants of the community began a battle to the death against the German military machine on April 19, 1943. Armed only with a few outdated weapons, they proved no match for the German forces, but they inflicted heavy losses and kept the battle going until June. A handful of Jewish fighters escaped to the forests surrounding Warsaw and continued to fight.

Community: Depending on how one defines community, and who is asked, estimates of Poland's Jewish population vary between 5,000 and more than 20,000 — the vast majority of both numbers living in Warsaw. The city has no distinguishably Jewish neighborhood.

Not a neighborhood perhaps, but a block. In one compound on Grzybowski Place can be found the Jewish community's offices, the State Jewish Theater, and the city's only functioning synagogue. Together with a few other offices on the block, these buildings form the core of what remains of Warsaw's Jewish life.

Until the late 1980s conventional wisdom was that Warsaw's Jewish community consisted of the mostly frail elderly who had resisted leaving Poland in the waves of emigration that followed government-sponsored anti-Semitic campaigns in 1956 and 1968. Indeed, most of the official members of the Jewish community, and most worshipers in the Nozyk Synagogue each *Shabbat*, are over seventy. But in recent years a new phenomenon has emerged — young people exploring long-dormant Jewish roots.

Many of Warsaw's young Jews had only one Jewish parent or grandparent, and few even knew they were Jewish before they reached their teens. In many cases becoming Jewish was the way they rebelled against Communist parents. Today their numbers have grown and they have their own social club, summer camp, and active social-educational schedule. They meet in members' homes to celebrate holidays, add to their minimal knowledge of Jewish history and tradition, and simply enjoy the company of other Jews.

Relations between the elderly Jews and their young counterparts are chilly. The children of most of the elderly Jews emigrated. For the most part, the parents of the young Jews want nothing to do with their Jewish heritage. Thus, a visitor can talk to the elderly at the Nozyk Synagogue and hear the story that nobody will perpetuate Jewish tradition in Warsaw in a few years. Upon leaving the synagogue, he can walk a few steps to the Jewish community building and engage in a lively discussion with the under-thirty set that hangs out in the Jewish Information and Tourist Bureau. Clearly, Warsaw has some young Jews; they just aren't the children of the old Jews.

Even among the small corps of young Jewish activists most are married to Catholics. Only time will tell how this community will fare, but past predictions that Jewish life would disappear from Warsaw have always proven to be premature.

In addition to the old Jews and the young Jews, there are many in Warsaw who know of Jewish parents or grandparents who do not affiliate with either group. And every few weeks, it seems a new story circulates about an adult Pole who has just discovered that he or she is Jewish.

Sights: Warsaw was virtually destroyed in World War II and the city today consists of a charming Old Town (Rynek Starego Miasta) rebuilt according to eighteenth-century paintings alongside large areas of Stalinist monoliths and graceful areas of prewar style. Its wide boulevards are lined with trees and flowers, and overall it is far more attractive than the gray image most Westerners have of the city.

The difficult transition to democracy and a free market has produced alternating periods of great hope and near-despair and an unpredictable economy. You can buy absolutely anything imaginable in the shops along the main streets (including Jerusalem Boulevard, which takes its name from an eighteenth century Jewish neighborhood) — for a price. A few years ago, Warsaw had low prices and very few options; today, prices have come in line with those in the West, and market forces ensure that everything is available.

The Nozyk Synagogue is located in the compound behind the Jewish community building at 12–16 Grzybowski Place. Built with private funds at the turn of the twentieth century, it operated until the war, when the Germans converted it into a sta-

ble. The sandstone building stood in disrepair for decades, but the Polish government restored it in the early 1980s. The six hundred-seat neo-Romanesque sanctuary is dominated by two rows of thick pillars which support balconies that serve as the women's section. It is open to visitors on Thursdays between 10:00 A.M. and 3:00 P.M. Groups can make arrangements to gain admittance at other times. Services are held on Friday evening and Shabbat morning.

On a typical Saturday morning anywhere from a dozen to 100 people gather to pray — depending on how many tourists and business people from around the world are in attendance. The majority of local worshippers are at least seventy, although a few young people can be found. The rabbi, Menahem Joskowicz, came from Israel in 1989 and has focused his efforts on working with the elderly community. Since he arrived he has injected a new sense of hope into the lives of the old Jews who want to identify with religious Judaism.

The Jewish community building in front of the synagogue courtyard houses the State Jewish Theater, where Yiddish-language productions play to audiences of mainly Catholic Poles and Jewish tourists. Established in 1950, its prime purpose was to serve as a public-relations tool for the Communist regime. Most theatergoers understand the Yiddish plays only with the assistance of earphones that provide simultaneous translation into Polish. (The prewar Jewish theater, founded by Rachel Kaminska (Ida's mother) in 1888, was located where the Victoria Intercontinental Hotel now stands on Krolewska Street.)

If Grzybowski Place is the center of Warsaw's Jewish life, the area around Zamenhofa and Anielewicza is the center of the Jewish past. This was the heart of the Warsaw Ghetto and the scene of the revolt. The ghetto was leveled during the uprising and rebuilt after the war. Today it is a quiet area of low-rise apartment buildings which looks a bit surprisingly like a typical section of Tel Aviv, perhaps a testament to the training of some of Israel's early architects.

The bronze-and-granite Ghetto Fighters' Monument on Zamenhofa Street stands on the site of the central Jewish command post where the first fusillade was fired at the Germans. The monument by Natan Rapaport, an exact copy of which stands at Yad Vashem in Jerusalem, depicts seven figures — from a baby to a grandfather — amid the flames of the ghetto. The thirty-five-foot monument was erected by the Polish government in 1948, on the fifth anniversary of the Warsaw Ghetto Uprising.

A few feet from the monument is the manhole cover through which the Jewish fighters entered and exited the city's sewer during the uprising. Another memorial, with the Hebrew letter *bet* (for *Bereishit*, the first word of the Torah) adorning the manhole cover, was erected on the site to mark the third anniversary of the uprising.

A fascinating comparison can be made between the monument to the Ghetto Uprising and the memorial to the general Warsaw uprising a few blocks away at the corner of Midowa and Dluga. The latter, which commemorates the city-wide revolt against the Germans which took place a year after the Ghetto Uprising, depicts armed Poles emerging from a sewer. The Polish Catholic rebels look grim and determined to save their homeland. The Jewish fighters, who knew all was lost but dignity, look inflamed.

A block up from the Ghetto Fighters' monument, at Mila 18 (opposite a building that is now Mila 1) the main bunker of the Jewish fighters, stands a mound of earth with a memorial garden at the top.

The Umschlagplatz on Stawki Street is where the Germans assembled Jews for deportation to Treblinka. The first selections took place in 1942, and by the time the ghetto was eliminated, 300,000 Warsaw Jews had met their fate there. A marble memorial stands on the site enclosing a wall of remembrance. (Until the mid-1980s a gas station occupied the lot next to the Umschlagplatz. When Tel Aviv Mayor Shlomo Lahat visited Warsaw, he complained to the authorities, who promptly had the gas station closed.)

Along the streets between the Ghetto Memorial and the Umschlagplatz are twelve stone markers with the names and brief biographies of Jews who perished in, or were deported from, the ghetto. Erected in 1988, to mark the forty-fifth anniversary of the uprising, the markers are frequently sprayed with anti-Semitic graffiti in Polish and German, a sad testimony to the racism that continues to plague Poland, despite the decimation of its huge Jewish community. Among others, they memorialize Anielewicz, his best friend and top lieutenant Arie Wilner, Janusz Korczak, and historian Emanuel Ringelblum. But however much the area is dominated by the Holocaust, it has Jewish connections that predate World War II.

Zamenhofa Street is named for Ludwig Zamenhof, a Jewish idealist who tried to pave the way to world peace. His tool was Esperanto, a language he invented in the hope that it would become the world's lingua franca. Zamenhofa 5, where Zamenhof lived from 1898 to 1917, is marked with a memorial plaque in Polish and Esperanto. The first monument, erected on the site in 1928, was destroyed by the Nazis; the new sign was put up by the International Congress of Esperantists in 1959.

Along with the ghetto itself, the ghetto wall was destroyed, but one small section remains — far from the other monuments. It is located in the courtyard of Zlota 60, across the road from the new Holiday Inn. On the right side as you enter, toward the back of the playground, the twenty-seven-foot section of the wall shows a map of the original ghetto.

The Jewish cemetery on Okopowa Street was established in 1806 and has more than 250,000 graves. It is one of Poland's last functioning Jewish burial grounds and is the final resting place for many prominent Jews, including Zamenhof, Rachel Kaminska, and I. L. Peretz. Many people who died in death camps are memorialized with plaques in the cemetery, including Janusz Korczak.

The cemetery escaped World War II largely unscathed, unlike many other Jewish cemeteries throughout Poland, where the Nazis used tombstones to pave roads. Apparently there was no shortage of building materials in the Warsaw area during the war. Today it is overgrown, but some local organizations do minimal maintenance work. Readers of Hebrew or Yiddish will be fascinated by the poetry and heartfelt inscriptions that adorn many of the elaborate markers. The cemetery is open to the public Sunday through Thursday between 9:00 A.M. and 3:00 P.M., and Friday from 9:00 A.M. until noon.

A bit off the beaten track, at Krochmalna 92, is an orphanage founded by Janusz Korczak, one of the heroes of the Warsaw Ghetto. When the children of his orphanage were deported to Trebelinka, Korczak, who had been a prominent personality in prewar Poland, turned down offers for his freedom and accompanied his children to the death camp. The yellow stone building on Krochmalna, which he was forced to vacate when the ghetto was formed, is filled with busts and portraits of Korczak.

The Jewish Historical Institute, located opposite Warsaw City Hall at 3–5 Tlomackie Street, was established after the war and is affiliated with the Polish Academy of Sciences. Standing at the edge of the site of Warsaw's Great Synagogue, blown up by the Nazis in "celebration" over the liquidation of the ghetto, it houses a museum of art and artifacts of the destroyed community and a multilingual library that has the largest collection in Poland of books on Jewish topics. The Institute recently received additional space in a just-completed office tower built on the site of the synagogue. Although it is strapped for cash, plans call for mounting special exhibitions in the new space. The institute is open Monday through Friday from 9:00 A.M. until 3:00 P.M. (Call 271-843 for information.)

The National Museum on Jerusalem Boulevard has several paintings depicting Jewish or Hebrew Bible themes. Among them are Jan Victors's *Blessing of Jacob*, Pieter Lastman's *Esther and Ahasueros*, and Mauricy Gottlieb's *Portrait of a Young Jew*.

For modern Jewish culture, the best place to be is Café Ejlat, a Jewish club at Allée Ujadowskie 47. Run by the Polish-Israeli Friendship Society, the café offers Jewish camaraderie and occasional entertainment such as Yiddish songs. Call 285-472 for information.

Personalities: Several leaders of the new Poland have Jewish roots (with which they identify in varying degrees), although it seems that the number of people fingered as Jewish exceeds all estimates of the local Jewish population. Konstanty Gebert, a psychologist and writer for the daily newspaper *Gazeta Wyborcza,* openly identifies as a Jew. The paper's editor, Adam Michnik, acknowledges Jewish origin but identifies as a Pole. Bronislaw Geremek, who was one of the senior figures in Solidarity with Lech Walesa and went on to become leader of Parliament's Solidarity bloc, is of Jewish origin. There are several Jews at the weekly *Polityka*, the only newspaper that protested the 1968 anti-Semitic purge (and survived).

The list of Jews who lived in Warsaw and made good is endless. It includes the Yiddish writers I. L. Peretz and Isaac Bashevis Singer, the actress Ida Kaminska, who fled to New York after the 1968 purges, and movie mogul Samuel Goldwyn, who left as a child. Jewish political figures who lived or studied in Warsaw include David Ben Gurion, Menachem Begin, and Rosa Luxemburg.

Side Trips: The devastation of Warsaw's Jewish community is apparent all over the city, but a pilgrimage to Treblinka raises it to starkly devastating proportions. Hundreds of thousands of Jews were deported from the Umschlagplatz to Treblinka, two hours from Warsaw. In all, 800,000 Jews died at Treblinka.

Unlike Auschwitz, which included work camps, and where non-Jews as well as Jews were sent, Treblinka was exclusively a death camp and exclusively for Jews. As the Germans retreated in defeat, they blew up every structure at the camp, leaving only clues of the horrors that had transpired there. Today in place of the factory of death stands an impressive memorial composed of seventeen thousand boulders, rocks and pebbles, each representing a different community whose residents perished at Treblinka.

Yizkor memorial candles lie scattered around the expanse of rocks, providing what might be the most telling evidence of the Jewish people's determination to cherish and respect the memories of the dead. At the center of the field of stones is a towering stone memorial shaped like a mausoleum, topped with a menorah.

A trip to Treblinka can be combined with a visit to a less depressing Jewish sight in the village of Tikoczin, near Bialystock. Though there are no Jews in the village today, the cobbled streets and wooden houses look much as they did when Tikoczin was predominantly Jewish. In the center of town stands a baroque synagogue, now the local museum. Restored to its prewar beauty, the building's most striking feature after the architecture is the collection of prayers and psalms written in huge script on the interior walls.

Less than three hours from Warsaw by express train, Cracow offers a wealth of Jewish history. In contrast to Warsaw, which was utterly destroyed in World War II, Cracow escaped the Nazis physically intact. The beautiful city has been designated one of a limited number of historical cities around the world by UNESCO.

Most sites of Jewish interest are located in the Kazimierz quarter of town, which was originally established as a separate city just beyond Cracow city limits, but is now a poorer neighborhood of town. In the early seventeenth century, a royal edict forced the city's Jews to move to Kazimierz. Although the order was soon reversed, most of the city's Jews remained in the quarter.

During the two decades before World War II, Jews made up about 25 percent of Cracow's population, and although most lived in Kazimierz they could be found on almost every street in the city. During the war, the Nazis forced Jews to live in a ghetto that was in an industrial part of town.

Most synagogues and Jewish sites are open only for groups by prior arrangement. If you travel to Cracow alone, ask for help in your hotel. The Ramu Synagogue, built of wood in 1553 and rebuilt with stone four years later, is at 49 Szeroka Street. It holds Friday night and *Shabbat* morning services; attendance is low, but tour groups boost it occasionally.

The Communists renovated the fourteenth-century Old Synagogue at Szeroka 2, turning it into a Museum of Jewish Culture in Poland. The Romanesque building, partly below street level, is open Wednesday and Thursday from 9:00 A.M. to 3:30 P.M., Friday between 11:00 A.M. and 6:00 P.M., and Saturday and Sunday from 9:00 A.M. until 3:30 P.M.

The most exciting Jewish happening in Cracow is the annual Jewish Culture Festival, held in May or June. Started by two non-Jews who have an interest in Jewish culture, the festival includes a variety of movies, musical performances, plays and exhibitions brought from throughout the world.

There is an annual spring festival of Jewish music in Kazimierz, with traditional Jewish music performed by local and foreign ensembles. The highlight is a major outdoor concert in front of the Old Synagogue, where huge crowds—mostly non-Jews—gather. For information on the festivals, call 337-814 or fax 221-455.

Reading: Two good fictional accounts of the Warsaw Ghetto Uprising are *Mila 18* by Leon Uris (Doubleday) and *The Wall* by John Hersey (Knopf). Three of Singer's books that capture prewar Jewish Warsaw are *The Manor, The Family Moskat,* and *In My Father's Court* (Farrar, Straus & Giroux). A recent novel about Jews living as gentiles during wartime Warsaw is Louis Begley's *Wartime Lies* (Knopf). For a documentary look at Polish Jewry at its peak, there are the film and book versions of *Image Before My Eyes* (Schocken). *Kiddush Hashem* by Rabbi Simon Huberband (Yeshiva University Press), a close associate of Warsaw Ghetto historian Emanuel Ringelblum in his clandestine Oneg Shabbat group, is the definitive account of social and religious life in Poland during the war years. Other outstanding scholarly works are *The War Against the Jews* (Bantam) by Lucy Dawidowicz and *The Holocaust Kingdom* (Holocaust Publications) by Alexander Donat.

Singer's books were off-limits during most of the Communist era, but now they are very popular among educated Poles. A local publishing house is in the process of putting together a library of the works of Polish and Eastern European Jewish writers, including Sholom Aleichem.

Recommendations: Anyone visiting Warsaw without the benefit of an organized tour that focuses on Jewish sights can profit by contacting one of the offices that caters to the needs of Jewish visitors. The Jewish Information and Tourist Bureau (telephone 200-793, fax 200-556), has guidebooks and maps of Jewish points of interest and can plan a complete itinerary.

The Jewish Tours Department of Orbis, the country's giant travel company, which has made the transition from Communism to a competitive market, can arrange guides who have undergone special training in Jewish history and have good knowledge of sights of Jewish interest (telephone 261-795 or 273-360).

Warsaw has seen a construction boom in recent years as the city gears up for increased tourism. The Holiday Inn and Marriott both opened in 1989, and the luxurious Sobieski made a splash in 1992 with its exterior painted in a rainbow of bright colors. Several older hotels have been renovated.

Lot Polish Airlines, which has undergone a major turnaround that includes increasing use of American aircraft and a new emphasis on service, is the only carrier that serves Warsaw from both the United States and Israel (kosher meals are available on request). Delta offers connections from many American cities via Frankfurt, and El Al shares the Warsaw–Tel Aviv route with Lot.

Although some packaged kosher food can be purchased in Pewex shops in major Warsaw hotels, and increasing amounts of Israeli produce and foods can be found on supermarket shelves, groups that want to observe kashrut bring prepared kosher foods from Western Europe. The Menora kosher restaurant, located alongside the Jewish community building, is open daily and offers a selection of traditional Jewish and Polish food.

Many tourist services are offered only during the summer, but like the experience in the Warsaw apartment, when it comes to finding Jewish flowers in the desert of Poland's Jewish history, you may find surprises in any one of the four seasons.

—Carl Schrag

Washington

With the bedrock of equality in the American political system, Washington has long been a place Jews turned to when something needed fixing. From the one-man lobbying efforts of Cesar Kaskel and Arnold Fischel during the Civil War to the 250,000 people who gathered to demand freedom for Soviet Jews on the eve of the Reagan–Gorbachev summit in 1987, the role of American Jews in the nation's political life has always been apparent. Arms locked with African-American leaders demonstrating for civil rights, Star of David banners amid signs calling for more pressure for Soviet emigration, in a *Sukkat Shalom* across the street from the White House to demonstrate for a nuclear freeze, Jews have been a ubiquitous part of the political scene.

A large, permanent Jewish presence, however, is a relatively recent thing. Though their numbers — 165,000 — and location suggest the historic communities of the East Coast, the actual profile of Washington Jewry more resembles the upstart communities of the Sunbelt. Whatever the origins, however, the diverse collection of government officials and workers, professionals, merchants, homemakers, and students is part of the pulse of the national capital, helping to shape the country's laws, culture, and development. Jewish visibility is strengthened by the presence of the national offices of many Jewish organizations that monitor congressional legislation, from aid to Israel to school prayer.

History: Isaac Polock, the first Jew to settle in Washington, in 1795, built six townhouses between the White House and nearby Georgetown, the last of which was torn down in 1983. Polock, who arrived five years before the federal government was moved to the District of Columbia, later returned to his native Savannah, Georgia; but a member of his household, Raphael Jones, a teacher and possibly a *shochet*, lived in Washington until his death.

In 1840, Washington's Jewish population numbered only 25 in a total population of 23,340. It grew rapidly, however, with a large influx of Jews, many of whom settled in Georgetown, where they worked as artisans and shop owners. During the Civil War, Jews came to Washington as civil servants or soldiers, afterward making it their home.

Abraham Lincoln was the first president to become involved directly in questions of Jewish rights, and in the two major issues put before him during his presidency he proved to be a friend indeed. When Congress in 1861 passed a law requiring that all military chaplains be "regularly ordained ministers of some Christian denomination," Arnold Fischel, a New York rabbi representing the Board of Delegates of American Israelites, visited Lincoln to protest. On the president's initiative, a new chaplaincy law permitting rabbis to serve was passed in 1862.

When General Ulysses S. Grant expelled all Jews from the areas of Kentucky and Tennessee under his military command in 1862, Cesar Kaskel, a Jewish businessman from Paducah, Kentucky, headed for Washington. Ushered in to see the president with the help of a Cincinnati congressman he had met when his boat stopped there, Kaskel not only got the help he requested but also engaged in one of the great truth-and-power conversations of Jewish history. As retold by Bertram W. Korn in his classic work *American Jewry and the Civil War,* Lincoln said, "And so the children of Israel were driven from the happy land of Canaan?" Kaskel responded, "Yes, and that is why we have come unto Father Abraham's bosom, asking protection." Lincoln's answer: "And this protection they shall have at once," with which he sat down and wrote an order revoking Grant's action. Grant, incidentally, never explained or apologized for the expulsion order, but it is the only known anti-Semitic act committed by a man who, when he became president, made numerous Jewish appointments and was widely regarded as a friend of the Jewish community.

Though the majority of American Jews before the Civil War lived in the North, the first Jews to serve in the Senate — Judah P. Benjamin of Louisiana and David Levy Yulee of Florida, later served the Confederacy. After the war, poverty-stricken Jews who left the South also put down roots in the growing city. Between 1860 and 1910, flourishing jewelry, shoe, furniture, and department stores were established by the Lansburgh, Hecht, Rich, Harris, Hahn, Kann, and Schwartz families.

Between the two world wars, especially during the New Deal, many young Jewish college graduates joined Washington's official ranks. As the Jewish population grew, many moved from "D.C." to the fast-expanding suburbs of northern Virginia and southern Maryland. Beautiful synagogues, community centers, kosher markets, and day schools were built, making these communities vital and self-sustaining.

Community: The Washington Jewish community gained cohesiveness with the founding of its first synagogue, Washington Hebrew Congregation, in 1852, under the leadership of Navy Captain Jonas Philips Levy and twenty-one other members. When this congregation joined the Reform movement and installed an organ two decades later, some of its more traditional members built their own synagogue, Adas Israel, at Sixth and G Streets, N.W.; President Ulysses S. Grant and his cabinet attended the synagogue's dedication in 1876.

With the community's growth, other Orthodox congregations were soon formed — Ohev Shalom, Talmud Torah, Beth Shalom, and Kesher Israel in Georgetown.

Kesher Israel still graces N Street in Georgetown. Most of the other old synagogues are now churches, their Jewish symbols still visible.

Social support organizations were gradually organized, and Washington's first Jewish Community Center was founded in 1925; its first day school in the 1940s. The first Embassy of Israel was established in 1948 in an elegant old townhouse on Twenty-second Street, just off Embassy Row. Among the major Jewish organizations that maintain their national headquarters in Washington are B'nai B'rith, the Jewish War Veterans, and the American Israel Public Affairs Committee, the Jewish community's foreign-policy lobby.

But if the structure of the community is old, until World War II Washington was still a Jewish backwater, with fewer Jews than Rochester, New York, or Passaic, New Jersey. Between 1943 and the present — while its numbers were escalating from 13,000 to 165,000 — the Jewish community's expansion into the suburbs was diffuse rather than concentrated in one neighborhood. In the Silver Spring, Maryland, area, a community of Orthodox Jews centers its activities around the Silver Spring Jewish Community Center on Arcola Avenue and the Hebrew Day School of Montgomery County and Yeshiva of Greater Washington on University Boulevard. Numerous synagogues and schools serve Jews in the Rockville area and the Greater Washington Jewish Community Center in Rockville is centrally located to serve Jews of Rockville, Bethesda, Potomac, Silver Spring, and upper Montgomery County.

A variety of religious and cultural activities has also developed in the northern Virginia suburbs of Fairfax, Falls Church, Alexandria, Arlington, and Reston.

Perhaps because Washington itself is a city with a large transient population, the Jewish community, too, lacks deep roots, in contrast to other large Jewish communities in the East, where families and businesses go back many generations. Curiously, many Washington-born Jews, mostly highly trained professionals, have not remained in the city to carry on family businesses, but have settled all over the United States and overseas, making the native-born Washingtonian hard to find. Some notable exceptions are the late Hyman Goldman, whose son, Aaron, followed in his business and philanthropic footsteps; and the Smith, Rodman, and Kay families all in the construction business — also known as philanthropists and community leaders.

Sights: There's no need to go off the beaten track to see Washington's meaningful Jewish sights. Most can be seen on walking tours around or in the national shrines and museums. What better way to begin a tour of Washington than with a visit to Capitol Hill, its panoramic vista stretching across the Mall to the Lincoln Memorial, where guided tours begin at the main rotunda?

Statues by American Jewish sculptor Jo Davidson of the late Senator Robert La Follette and humorist Will Rogers can be seen on the House side of the Capitol. Davidson's bust of Henry Wallace is in the corridor east of the Senate chamber. While on "The Hill," a visit to your congressman or senator can be arranged by calling the Capitol exchange at (202) 224-3121.

Across the street from the Capitol is the majestic Supreme Court building, First and East Capitol Streets, N.E. Among the portraits of deceased Supreme Court justices exhibited are those of Louis Brandeis, Benjamin Cardozo, Felix Frankfurter, and Abe Fortas.

Down the street from the Supreme Court, also facing the Capitol, is the exquisite Italian Renaissance Library of Congress (First and Pennsylvania Avenue, S.E.), which has the largest collection of rare Hebrew and Yiddish texts in any governmental collection.

Washington's historic first synagogue, the original Adas Israel, built in 1876, is a short walk from Capitol Hill at Third and G streets, N.W. Today it houses the Lillian and Albert Small Jewish Museum of Washington and the Jewish Historical Society of Greater Washington. The small, two-story building with elongated arched windows on the second floor, was built in a late colonial style reminiscent of the simplicity of a Quaker meeting house. It is surrounded by a wrought-iron fence with Star of David motif said to be inspired by a similar fence at the old synagogue on the isle of Rhodes. The ark is in a bay that protrudes from the back wall, a design feature once popular in Bavarian synagogues. When it was built at the corner of Sixth and G Streets, N.W. (it was moved to its current site in 1969) it was in the center of the closest thing Washington ever had to a Jewish neighborhood.

The restored sanctuary is on the building's second floor. The all-wood interior looks the way it did when President Grant and members of his cabinet attended its dedication. The women's gallery is held up by spindle columns; a low-hanging brass chandelier is suspended from a small cupola. Exhibits on Washington Jewish life and history are found on the building's main floor. The Historical Society also has an oral history library, publishes books and pamphlets, arranges Jewish tours, and makes the sanctuary available for cultural events. The museum is open 11:00 A.M. to 3:00 P.M., Sunday through Thursday (telephone 202-789-0900). Incidentally, the current Congregation Adas Israel stands at 2850 Quebec Avenue, N.W.

Portraits of Americans who have made great contributions in a variety of fields are exhibited at the Smithsonian's National Portrait Gallery, Eighth and F Streets, N.W. Among the dozens of American Jews whose images grace the gallery's walls in painting, photograph or poster form are George Gershwin and Albert Einstein, Edna Ferber and Sandy Koufax, Helena Rubinstein and Elie Wiesel, Marilyn Monroe and Arthur Miller, Jackson Pollock and Louise Nevelson, Lillian Wald and Leonard Bernstein. Not all the portraits are in the public parts of the gallery, but it is usually possible to see the portraits in the gallery's offices by just asking. Hadassah founder Henrietta Szold is in room 302 (the Office of the Registrar), sharing space with Carl Sandburg, among others. Golda Meir can be found in room 195 (the Office of Education); she and Winston Churchill are the only non-Americans in the collection. In the same building as the gallery, the National Museum of American Art has large collections of works by Jewish artists, including Chaim Gross, Ben Shahn, Mark Rothko, and Raphael Soyer.

Probably the most traversed tourist path in America is the Mall, the long grassy stretch, flanked by the buildings of the Smithsonian, between the Capitol and the Washington Monument. About midway between these landmarks is the intriguing, circular-shaped Hirshhorn Museum and Sculpture Garden, named for the late art collector Joseph Hirshhorn, who donated his multimillion-dollar collection to the government. Hirshhorn arrived in the United States a poor Latvian Jewish immigrant and grew up in New York's Williamsburg section. While quite young he made a fortune in the stock market and later in uranium. Works by many leading Jewish artists are shown in the museum's permanent and changing exhibits and in its magnificent sunken sculpture garden.

Just across the Mall from the Hirshhorn, the National Museum of Natural History (Twelfth Street and Constitution, N.W.), has a collection of seventeenth-to-nineteenth-century Judaica. It was contributed by Cyrus Adler in 1893 and is displayed in the Hall of Asiatic Cultures.

The newest addition to the Mall (though it actually lies about fifty yards off the Mall proper, on Fifteenth Street, N.W.) is the United States Holocaust Memorial Museum, dedicated in 1993. Many years in planning and construction, the museum was designed to describe in art, poetry, photographs, film and video accounts the searing details of the Final Solution. The building encompasses the Hall of Knowledge, an interactive, computer-based environment for self-learning; and the Holocaust Research Institute, which includes archives, a library, movie theater, and education center.

After visitors view the permanent and special exhibitions, they enter the majestic six-sided Hall of Remembrance with its lofty skylight. This shrine for individual contemplation and formal ceremonies serves as the national memorial to the Holocaust victims. The 1.5 million children who perished are memorialized by a Children's Wall covered with thousands of tiles hand-painted by American schoolchildren. In addition to Jews, the museum also describes the fate of other victims of Nazi Germany—the handicapped and infirm, homosexuals, Jehovah's Witnesses, political and religious dissidents, Gypsies, Poles, and Russian prisoners of war. The

section of Fifteenth Street where the memorial is located has been renamed Raoul Wallenberg Place. Like all the museums on the Mall, the Holocaust Memorial is open daily, 10:00 A.M. to 5:00 P.M.

There is a loose cluster of Jewish sights north and west of the Mall. The headquarters of B'nai B'rith International, 1649 Rhode Island Avenue, N.W., houses the Klutznick Museum, one of the nation's outstanding Judaica collections. Permanent exhibits portray twenty centuries of Jewish life, ranging from ancient coins to modern ceremonial objects and contemporary art. Special exhibits depict milestones in the Jewish experience. Among the more intriguing objects on display are a three-foot-tall, onion-domed spice box and a World War I Krupp shell casing decorated with Jewish motifs at the Bezalel Academy in Jerusalem. The museum is open 10:00 A.M. to 5:30 P.M., Sunday through Friday.

The "sleeper" among Jewish collections in Washington—and perhaps in America—belongs to the Jewish War Veterans, which dedicated its national headquarters at 1811 R Street, N.W., in 1984. Its National Memorial and Museum, honoring American Jews who served and died in America's wars, has a small permanent exhibit and mounts fascinating periodic shows on every aspect of the American Jewish military experience. Objects and documents in the museum's collection date back to the War of 1812 and include displays on Jewish Medal of Honor winners from the Civil War and Jewish services held in Saudi Arabia during the Gulf War. A recent photo exhibit included scenes, mostly from World War II, including GIs making *matzah* balls in New Guinea and conducting a Seder on a hospital ship. To coincide with the opening of the Holocaust Memorial and Museum in 1993, the JWV mounted an exhibit on death camp liberators. The museum is open 10:00 A.M. to 4:00 P.M., Monday through Friday, and Sundays by appointment for groups of ten or more.

Many foreign nations contributed exquisite furnishings to the John F. Kennedy Center for the Performing Arts, 2700 F Street, N.W., in Washington's Foggy Bottom area. One of the loveliest is the Israeli lounge, a reception room near the concert hall, decorated by artists commissioned by the State of Israel. One wall of carved African walnut by Nehemia Azaz portrays biblical musical instruments. On the other walls, line drawings by kibbutz artist Yehezkel Kimchi depict the vitality of modern Israel. Forty ceiling panels by Shraga Weil, in vibrant blues, reds, and golds, re-create musical scenes from the Bible. The lounge is open only during tours of the Kennedy Center and during special performances.

Kesher Israel sits at 2801 N Street, N.W., in Georgetown, not far from where Washington's first Jewish resident, Isaac Polock, made his home in 1795. Though built in 1911, the three-story corner structure of light orange brick blends gracefully with the older town houses on the block, the arched windows adding a bit of Mediterranean flavor to the otherwise colonial street. A simple arch over the entry is supported by two columns; a Star of David adorns the pointed arch at the top of the facade. Kesher Israel is Orthodox, and has daily services—probably the most convenient for visitors staying downtown, in the Dupont Circle area or Georgetown. Call (202) 333-2337 for information on services.

East meets Middle East: The Israeli Embassy adds a Mediterranean touch to Washington

There are more sweeping Mediterranean arches at the impressive chancery of the Embassy of Israel, 3514 International Drive, N.W. (off Connecticut Avenue). In addition to its Middle Eastern design motifs, the building is decorated with Israeli art and sculpture. While private visits are permitted only by invitation or on official business, special briefings for groups may be arranged by writing to the embassy's speakers bureau several weeks in advance.

Culture: Visitors are always welcome to join in the many activities at the Greater

Washington Jewish Community Center at 6125 Montrose Road in Rockville (telephone 301-881-0100). Its Goldman Fine Arts Gallery mounts excellent exhibits by Jewish and Israeli artists and craftsmen. A typical weekend features a concert by the JCC symphony or choral group, or a show by a world-class performer. Films, book fairs, and Yiddish plays and programs are frequently presented. Visitors are also welcome at the Jewish Community Center of Northern Virginia, 8900 Little River Turnpike, Fairfax, Virginia (telephone 703-437-7264) The revitalized District of Columbia Jewish Community Center at 1836 Jefferson Street, N.W., has speakers, films, children's activities, and study groups (telephone 202-775-1765).

Popular Sunday morning lectures held at many area synagogues and centers are open to the public. The outstanding Sunday Scholar Series, offered free of charge, October through March, at the Washington Hebrew Congregation, McComb Street, N.W., at Massachusetts Avenue, features world-famous writers, theologians, and rabbis. For listings of Sunday breakfast lectures and other cultural activities check the *Washington Jewish Week,* available on newsstands, or call "Just Ask," the Jewish Information and Referral Service, at (301) 770-4848.

Eating: The Washington area has many restaurants serving vegetarian and organic food. One kosher spot in the city is Hunan Deli, 2300 H Street, N.W. on the George Washington University campus. There are more kosher restaurants in the Maryland suburbs, including The Jaffa Gate at 2420 Blueridge Avenue and the Nut House, 11419 Georgia Avenue, both dairy establishments in Wheaton. For information on *kashrut* contact the Rabbinical Council of Greater Washington at (202) 291-6052.

Personalities: A Washington cantor's son, Asa Yoelson, gained fame as singer, vaudevillian, and actor Al Jolson, and starred in the first full-length talkie, *The Jazz Singer.* Contemporary Washingtonians making a name for themselves in the arts are Zelda Fischandler, founding director of the Arena Stage repertory theater; Martin Feinstein, general director of the Washington Opera, and the actress Goldie Hawn. Daniel Boorstin, the Pulitzer Prize-winning historian, was for many years the Librarian of Congress. Many Jews work in the news media including *Washington Post* publisher Donald Graham, Watergate reporter Carl Bernstein, CNN's Wolf Blitzer and ABC's Ted Koppel. There are also thirty-four Jewish members of the House of Representatives and ten Jewish senators; after the 1992 elections two states — California and Wisconsin — had "all Jewish" delegations in the Senate.

General Sights: The Smithsonian's superb museums facing the Mall offer as much education and entertainment as one's time — and feet — allow. America's most revered documents, the Declaration of Independence, the Constitution, and the Bill of Rights are displayed at the stately National Archives, Pennsylvania Avenue at Eighth Street, N.W. The National Archives is a good place to go for genealogical research; among other things, it has some immigration passenger lists of ships arriving at many Atlantic, Pacific, and Gulf Coast ports from 1820 to the early twentieth century. The National Archives frequently mounts exhibits of documents of Jewish interest in its holdings, such as the recent poster exhibit, *Holocaust: Documentary Evidence.*

Since its opening on July 4, 1976, the National Air and Space Museum has become the city's most popular museum. Its fantastic exhibits illustrate every facet of man's exploration of space. In its Spacearium, named for Albert Einstein, you can gaze into the wonders of the solar system.

The National Museum of American History, at Constitution and Fourteenth Street, N.W., frequently exhibits articles from its eight hundred fifty-piece Judaica collection as part of current exhibits on American history.

General Culture: Works by top artists are exhibited at the National Gallery of Art, Corcoran Art Gallery, Phillips Collection, and the Freer Gallery. The Kennedy Center presents concerts, operas, and plays with leading performers. From June to September, Wolf Trap Farm in Virginia presents varied musical performances — from bluegrass to Vienna waltzes to the 1812 Overture with live cannon — in a lovely outdoor setting. The National Theater, Arena Stage, and Folger Shakespeare Theater present the classics, new works, and Broadway hits. Washington newspapers carry current listings.

Reading: The Jewish Historical Society of Greater Washington has published two condensed oral histories of Washingtonians, available from the Society, 701 Third Street, N.W., Washington, DC 20001; call (202) 729-0900 for current prices. *Jews in Greater Washington, A Panoramic History of Washington Jewry for the Years 1795-1960* by Hillel Marans is out of print but may be obtained through the library. *Jews and American Politics* by Stephen D. Isaacs (Doubleday) is available, however. For a general fictional look at Washington life and politics, read *Advise and Consent* by Allen Drury (Doubleday). *Good as Gold* (Simon & Schuster) by Joseph Heller is the story of a Jewish secretary of state. For an idea of what it might be like to have a Jewish president, look for Michael Halberstam's novel *The Wanting of Levine* (Lippincott). Gold and Levine may be fictional characters, but they are emblematic of the very real participation of Jews in every facet of life in Washington.

—Helen Silver

Zurich

Israel, according to the dream, was supposed to be the Switzerland of the Middle East — a refuge, an oasis of peace and neutrality, a bastion of stability that would attract investment. It hasn't exactly worked out that way, but it doesn't take many days in Switzerland to realize that there are some striking parallels with the Jewish state. Both are small countries surrounded by large neighbors. Both are democracies that embrace great cultural diversity. In Zurich, Switzerland's largest city as well as its financial and cultural capital, the parallels are particularly visual. The city's symbol, like Jerusalem's, is a lion (the main synagogue is on Löwenstrasse, or "Lion Street"), and the streetcars are all painted the color of the canton's crest — blue and white.

But perhaps the strongest parallel is military. Like Israel, Switzerland has universal military service, and Swiss men do several weeks of reserve duty every year until they are in their fifties. This similarity is not lost on the Swiss people, who, despite their country's official neutrality, have always been kindly disposed toward Israel. Army connections play a major role in advancement at Switzerland's banks, and the admiration of Switzerland's military leaders for Israel's army has, according to one Jewish community leader in Zurich, had a positive impact on trade between the two countries.

Where do Switzerland's 20,000 Jews fit into this picture? They are Israel oriented but fundamentally Swiss, participating in every facet of the country's life, including those for which it is best known. Zurich's major banks include Julius Baer and Co., founded by a Jew whose descendants are Jewish and Christian; one of the main financial institutions in Basel is the Dreyfuss Bank. One of the country's leading chocolate makers is Camille Bloch who, after leading the Jewish community of Berne, became president of the Federation of Swiss Jewish Communities. There are Jewish watchmakers in the French-speaking part of the country. While there are no prominent Jewish cheese makers, there have been Jewish cattle farmers in the canton of Aargau for more than three hundred years. The country has yet to produce a Jewish Olympic champion, but Zurich does have a Jewish ski club.

History: Jews may be a minuscule part of the Swiss banking elite today, but they were the prime moneylenders of Zurich after their arrival in 1273. From their base in the Judengasse (Jews' Street) they loaned money to the city, the aristocracy, and borrowers as far away as Frankfurt and Venice. They were allowed to own property and to practice their faith. Though small, the community did produce one talmudic scholar of note, Moses of Zurich, who wrote the *Semak Zurich*.

It was not all comfort and prosperity, however. Jews were heavily taxed and required to wear distinguishing hats. When the Black Death swept Switzerland in 1348 — and with it the rumor that Jews had caused it by poisoning the wells — the municipal council in Zurich initially tried to protect the Jews. Public pressure ultimately forced the council to yield, and Jews were burned at the stake on February 22, 1349. Over the next century the Jews were repeatedly expelled and allowed to return to Zurich. The cycle of expulsion and readmission went on throughout Switzerland until the seventeenth century, when Jews were permanently expelled from the entire country.

But not exactly. Jews continued to live in

Aargau — a canton that did not join the Swiss Confederation until 1803 — mainly in the towns of Endingen and Lengnau. When the French Revolution and developing industrial economy opened the door for Jews in the larger cities of Switzerland in the 19th century, village Jews from Aargau formed the core of the new communities. They were joined by migrants from Alsace, in France, and Germany. Pressure from France, which complained about discrimination against French Jews in Switzerland, and from the United States Senate, which once refused to ratify a commercial treaty with Switzerland because of the absence of civil rights for Jews, was instrumental in achieving emancipation for Swiss Jewry. Equality came in 1866, when a new Swiss constitution granted Jews freedom of residence throughout the country and guaranteed them the same civic status as Christians; Switzerland was the last country in Europe to make such guarantees. The only exception to Jewish religious freedom is a law that, in effect, bans kosher slaughtering. After a campaign by animal rights activists, an 1893 plebiscite outlawed slaughtering in which the animal is not stunned first. To this day, Swiss Jews must import kosher meat from France and the Netherlands.

Switzerland was the primary venue for the congresses of the World Zionist Organization. While most were held in Basel, two of particular importance met in Zurich. It was at the 16th Zionist Congress, in 1929, that the expanded Jewish Agency was set up as an independent authority to represent the *yishuv* in Palestine in dealings with world Jewry, the British Mandatory Government, and other countries. The 20th Zionist Congress, held in Zurich in 1937, was the first in which the official record was kept solely in Hebrew.

Despite the hospitality to Zionist Congresses, during World War II official Swiss policy was inhospitable toward Jewish refugees. It was a Swiss suggestion that led to Germany stamping the passports of Jews with the letter *J*, so that authorities would be able to identify potential refugees at their borders. Swiss Jews, and some non-Jews, bitterly fought this policy. There are many stories of Swiss harboring Jews who managed to enter the country illegally, and

toward the end of the war more refugees were admitted. Even those who criticized official policy, however, noted that on a proportional basis, Switzerland's record on admitting refugees was no worse than that of any other neutral nation (it admitted 25,000 during the war). Criticism of the wartime policy played a role in the government's decision to admit Jewish refugees from Hungary and Egypt in 1956 and from Czechoslovakia in 1968.

Community: Zurich's Jewish population is about 7,000, one percent of the 700,000 people who live in Zurich and its environs. It is the largest Jewish community in Switzerland and was — until the post–Cold War surge of immigration to Berlin — the largest in the German-speaking world. Many of Zurich's Jews still trace their roots to Endingen and Lengnau, others to France and Germany. Because of the complications of becoming a citizen of Switzerland — where national citizenship is granted only after cantonal citizenship — only about 60 percent of Zurich's Jews have Swiss nationality.

The city actually has four separate "communities." By far the largest is the Israelitische Cultusgemeinde, nominally Orthodox but embracing people whose personal practice varies widely. The Israelitische Religionsgesellschaft and Agudas Achim are Orthodox in name and practice and include larger proportions of Eastern European Jews. Or Chadash is a liberal congregation, with a ritual akin to Conservative Judaism in the United States; because of opposition from the more Orthodox communities, it has not joined the Federation of Swiss Jewish Communities.

Altogether Zurich has four synagogues and an additional sixteen *minyans*. While Jews can be found all over the city, they tend to cluster near the synagogues, particularly in the Enge section. Enge is also home to the closest thing the community has to a nerve center. The building at Lavaterstrasse 33 houses the headquarters of the Israelitische Cultusgemeinde (telephone 201-1659), a cultural center which hosts lectures and symposiums, a theater, a discotheque, a kosher restaurant, a library and a day school (one of two in the city). The Federation of Swiss Jewish Communities is located nearby at Gotthardstrasse 65 (telephone 201-5583).

Switzerland's cultural mix, in which everyone is a member of one minority or another, makes it an essentially tolerant place. It is 65 percent German-speaking, 18 percent French, and 11 percent Italian; a good number of the German Swiss are Catholic and a majority of the French Swiss are Protestant. Nevertheless, there is some social anti-Semitism, not to mention the sizable portion of the population that is virtually unaware of a Jewish presence. Two things have helped change the picture in recent years. Since 1982, an exhibition on the Jews of Switzerland, mounted by the Federation, has traveled to the main exposition halls of Switzerland, attracting many non-Jews. *The Boat Is Full,* a dramatic film about Swiss refugee policy during the war, has also prompted much discussion. The movie, made by Markus Imhoof, who is not Jewish, was the Swiss entry for an Academy Award as best foreign film in 1981.

Sights: It would be difficult to find a city in which the Jewish sights are better integrated into the landscape than Zurich. Virtually all the places of Jewish interest are near the center of town and easily reached by streetcar or on foot.

The oldest Jewish site in the city is the Judengasse. Although it no longer exists, it was more or less on the site of today's Froschaugasse, a narrow alley, less than a hundred yards long, in the heart of the old quarter on the eastern bank of the Limmat River. A medieval street of pink, yellow, and gray buildings, it has antique dealers, bookstores, and boutiques. There are no traces of its Jewish past, although Pinkus Genossenschaft, one of the bookstores, still bears the name of its Jewish former owner, and people on the street are generally aware of the area's Jewish past. In one of the buildings opposite Pinkus's, the remains of a *mikveh* were found. Period maps of the street indicate that the synagogue stood about at the corner of Froschaugasse and Rindermarkt.

Today, most of Zurich's Jews live on the western bank. The largest congregation (Israelitische Cultusgemeinde) has its synagogue near the heart of the city, at Löwenstrasse 10. The brown-and-white Moorish-style building, with its twin domes, was built in 1883. A bit weatherbeaten on the outside, it is sparse on the inside. Its high-backed wooden pews, traditional in Europe, look impermanent and its stained-glass windows are of modest design. Next door to the synagogue is Adass, a kosher grocery.

In America, synagogue architecture and upkeep tend to be more utilitarian among the more observant. In Switzerland it is the opposite. Zurich's most attractive and best-kept synagogue is that of the more rigorously Orthodox Religionsgesellschaft, at Freigutstrasse 37 (telephone, 201-8057). The salmon-and-gray building, perched on a small hill, features menorahs and Stars of David around its crown. Inside it has a central *bimah*, in the Sephardic style, and well-polished, high-backed pews. The stained-glass windows lean toward Art Deco and the ceiling is a series of small arches decorated with Middle Eastern motifs in sand colors.

The most centrally located synagogue, however, is the modest home of Or Chadash, the liberal congregation, at Fortunagasse 13, just steps from the Bahnhofstrasse, Zurich's main shopping street (telephone 211-1152) .

Bear in mind that most synagogues in Switzerland are open only while services are in progress, although tours can sometimes be arranged by phoning ahead. Daily and *Shabbat* prayer times for most synagogues are printed in the weekly *Israelitisches Wochenblatt*, published in Zurich, and the *Jüdische Rundschau*, published in Basel with an extensive Zurich edition.

One of the most important sights of Jewish interest in Zurich is a church—the Gothic and Romanesque Fraumünster (located at Münsterhof square). In the church's fifteenth-century chancel is a set of five stained-glass windows by Marc Chagall. It was a Chagall exhibit at the Zurich Kunsthaus, the city's fine-arts museum, in 1967, that prompted the Fraumünster's fathers to commission him to do their windows. After they saw his work, Chagall was deemed "better qualified than almost any other contemporary artist to create a cycle of windows with a religious message." What is striking is that the windows are so Jewish. Four of the five are on themes from the Hebrew Bible.

The red window, on the north side of the chancel, depicts the Prophets, most prominently Elisha, Elijah, and Jeremiah. The blue window on the south side represents the Law, with Moses sitting on a throne (at the top) and Isaiah receiving the message of peace (at the bottom). On the east wall of the chancel are the blue "Jacob" window, the only one devoted to a single figure, and the yellow "Zion" window, with its images of biblical and contemporary Jerusalem. They flank the green "Christ" window. Even in the one window devoted to the New Testament, there are signs of the Jewish creator of the images. Joseph, the father of Jesus, appears at the bottom of the window close to the figure of King David in the Zion window, as if to show the link between the Christian messiah and the house of David. The figure of Jesus on the cross is not unusual for Chagall; one of the recurrent themes in his work, from biblical subjects to the Holocaust, is the crucifixion of Jews. In addition to the series in the chancel, Chagall also did the circular "Creation of the World" window on the south transept, a section of the church that dates to the twelfth century. As striking as the Chagall windows is the way they are regarded. There are other stained-glass windows in the church—beautiful, more classical in design, including one by Augusto Giacometti—that are barely mentioned by tour guides. On the tours, Chagall is always identified as a Jew.

This same emphasis can be found at the Kunsthaus (situated on the Heimplatz). Though the museum has equally large collections of work by Picasso, Miró, and Munch, among others, it is Chagall whose work is housed in its own room, the Saal Marc Chagall. There are only thirteen paintings in the room, but they represent a remarkable cross-section of Chagall's career from 1910 to 1968. Among them are *Passage Through the Red Sea, Above Vitebsk,* and *Lights of Marriage.* Two of the works, *The War* and *The Martyr,* show crucifixions of Jewish figures.

Personalities: Zurich has been the birthplace or the adopted home of many prominent Jews. David Farbstein, a native of Warsaw, was the first Jew to serve in the Swiss Parliament, where he spoke Yiddish

(and was understood). The Swiss Government's reaction to the Arab oil shock of 1973 was to appoint Michael Kohn, a prominent engineer, president of the nation's energy commission. More recently, Ursula Koch, a Socialist environmentalist, was elected to the Zurich municipal government. Zurich natives include Felix Bloch, an American who won the Nobel Prize for physics in 1952, and Paul Guggenheim, a judge in the International Court of Justice. Perhaps the most prominent Jew ever to make Zurich his home was Albert Einstein. Einstein earned his degree at Zurich's Federal Institute of Technology in 1900; during his studies there he also became a Swiss citizen. Denied a teaching post on graduation—for reasons that may have included anti-Semitism—he took a job at the patent office in Berne. After the publication of his Special Theory of Relativity in 1905, the University of Zurich began to pursue him. He finally accepted a teaching post in Zurich in 1912. Zurich was also the birthplace of one of the best known fictional Jews, Leopold Bloom. James Joyce's hero may have been a Dubliner, but he was created during Joyce's Swiss exile.

Eating: The kosher restaurant Schalom, located in the community center building at Lavaterstrasse 33, must have one of the most extensive menus in the world. Its fare ranges from the Swiss (fondue and wienerschnitzel) to the Eastern European (gefilte fish and potato latkes) to the Middle Eastern (*hummus* and lamb kabob). For dairy meals there is Fein and Schein at Schöntalstrasse 14.

Some of the dishes for which Switzerland is best known, like fondue and rösti (fried potatoes), can be enjoyed even by those who observe *kashrut.* While there are many excellent restaurants in Zurich, one particularly good one is Le Dezaley, at Römergasse 7-9.

General Sights and Side Trips: Zurich is a walker's city, from the elegant shops on the Bahnhofstrasse to the quays and gardens that line the banks of the Limmat and Lake Zurich (the Zürichsee). Two things that should not be missed are a boat trip on the Zürichsee and a visit to the Swiss National Museum, with its striking exhibits of every aspect of Swiss life and culture.

No one, however, comes to Switzerland just to see Zurich. There is virtually no area of the country that can't be reached in a day from Zurich. Berne, the Swiss capital, is seventy minutes away by train. The old town, surrounded on three sides by a bend in the Aare River, is a fantasy world of colonnaded seventeenth- and eighteenth-century buildings. Just a few minutes' walk from the old town, at Kapellenstrasse 2, is Berne's synagogue. A small gem, the yellow-and-white stone building is the center for Berne's 600 Jews. The interior features floral-patterned stained-glass windows and the polished-wood pews and floors characteristic of Central European synagogue design. In addition to being an attraction in its own right, Berne is also a good starting point for tours of the Bernese Alps. Aside from ski centers, two of the most popular, and spectacular, lookouts are the Schilthorn and Jungfraujoch.

Fifty minutes south of Zurich is Lucerne, a medieval city and contemporary resort. Closer to the mountains, the city and the excursions on Lake Lucerne offer more spectacular scenery than Zurich. Lucerne's synagogue is at Bruchstrasse 51. In addition to its views and its ambiance, Lucerne is noted for the Swiss Transport Museum.

If you want to see the cradle of contemporary Swiss Jewish life, Endingen and Lengnau are less than an hour from Zurich, to the northwest. (Take the train to Baden and, from there, a bus to the two towns, which are seven minutes apart. Don't be confused by Swiss maps. The country has several towns called Lengnau; the one with Jewish connections is the one closest to Zurich, in Aargau Canton.) In Lengnau, ancestral home of the Guggenheim mining family, the oldest synagogue in Switzerland, built in 1847, stands on the town square. In Endingen, once a veritable *shtetl*, the synagogue, with its belfry, is still the tallest building in town, and the only house of worship. There is still one Jewish family in Endingen, the Blochs, at Buckstrasse 2.

Reading: There is a fair amount of literature on the Jews of Zurich and Switzerland, but little of it has been translated into English. Kurt Guggenheim based some of his novels on his Zurich childhood, but they are available only in German. Two informative books available from the Federation of Swiss Jewish Communities are *Juden in Zürich* and *Juden in der Schweiz*.

Jewish characters do appear, usually somewhat marginally, in the books of Switzerland's two leading novelists, Friedrich Dürrenmatt and Max Frisch. Their works are available in English. Look particularly for Dürrenmatt's *The Quarry*.

Recommendations: There are plenty of good hotels in Zurich, though they tend to be expensive. One hostelry noted for both price and location is the Florhof, at Florhofgasse 4, located in what was once a private mansion. It is a three-minute walk from the Kunsthaus and a five-minute walk from both the Froschaugasse and the university.

There are no kosher hotels in Zurich, but there are many in the resort areas. Arosa, Engelberg, Grindelwald, Lugano, Montreux, and St. Moritz all have kosher hotels. The Swiss National Tourist Office has information on them all, as well as pamphlets on sights of Jewish interest. You can write to the SNTO at 608 Fifth Avenue, New York, NY 10020 (telephone 212-757-5944); it also has offices in San Francisco (415-362-2260) and Toronto (416-971-9734). Swissair publishes a comprehensive guide to kosher restaurants in Europe and updates it at regular intervals.

Switzerland is an easy country to travel in. The rail system is superb, the people are helpful, and the scenery unbeatable. Though some Swiss may be barely cognizant of Jews, the tourist authorities are sensitive to Jewish needs and concerns. The main synagogue in Zurich is pointed out on the tours arranged by the municipal travel office and the Jewish community is described. There is a Jewish chapel in Terminal B of the Zurich airport, which serves not only visitors to the city but also the many transit passengers who go through the O'Hare of Europe. While the differences between Switzerland and Israel are still more numerous than the similarities, it has a familiar feel nevertheless.

—Alan M. Tigay

About the Editor

Alan M. Tigay is the executive editor of *Hadassah Magazine*. He has contributed articles to *The People's Almanac* and *The Book of Lists*, and to many periodicals, including *The Chicago Sun-Times*, *Newsday*, the *San Francisco Examiner*, and *The New York Times*. A graduate of the University of Michigan and the Columbia University Graduate School of Journalism, he lives with his wife and son in Montclair, New Jersey.